THE UK'S BEST-SELLING COUNTY ATLASES*

PHILIP'S

STREET A

North Yorkshire

www.philips-maps.co.uk
First published in 2002 by Philip's,
a division of Octopus Publishing Group Ltd
www.octopusbooks.co.uk
Carmelite House
50 Victoria Embankment
London EC4Y 0DZ
An Hachette UK Company
www.hachette.co.uk

Fourth edition with interim revision 2015
Second impression 2016
NYODA

ISBN 978-1-84907-368-4 (spiral)

*Sales figures from the 2014 Travel Publishing Year Book, data from Nielsen BookScan, for UK street atlases covering county destinations.

**All streets named in the source Ordnance Survey dataset at the time of going to press are included in this Philip's Street Atlas.

Printed in China

Contents

III **Key to map symbols**

IV **Key to map pages**

VI **Route planning**

X Administrative and Postcode boundaries

1 **Street maps** at 1¾ inches to 1 mile

208 **Street maps** at 3½ inches to 1 mile

233 **Street map** of York at 7 inches to 1 mile

234 **Index** of towns, villages, streets, hospitals, industrial estates, railway stations, schools, shopping centres, universities and places of interest

Key to map symbols

- **Motorway with junction number**
- **Primary route** – dual/single carriageway
- **A road** – dual/single carriageway
- **B road** – dual/single carriageway
- **Minor road** – dual/single carriageway
- **Other minor road** – dual/single carriageway
- **Road under construction**
- **Tunnel, covered road**
- **Rural track, private road or narrow road in urban area**
- **Gate or obstruction to traffic** – restrictions may not apply at all times or to all vehicles
- **Path, bridleway, byway open to all traffic, restricted byway**
- **Pedestrianised area**
- BS22 **Postcode boundaries**
- **County or unitary authority boundaries**
- **Railway with station**
- **Tunnel**
- **Railway under construction**
- **Metro station**
- **Private railway station**
- **Miniature railway**
- **Tramway, tramway under construction**
- **Tram stop, tram stop under construction**
- **Bus, coach station**
- **Ambulance station**
- **Coastguard station**
- **Fire station**
- **Police station**
- **Accident and Emergency entrance to hospital**
- **Hospital**
- **Place of worship**
- **Information centre** – open all year
- **Shopping centre, parking**
- **Park and Ride, Post Office**
- **Camping site, caravan site**
- **Golf course, picnic site**
- ROMAN FORT **Non-Roman antiquity, Roman antiquity**
- Univ **Important buildings, schools, colleges, universities and hospitals**
- **Woods, built-up area**
- River Medway **Water name**
- **River, weir**
- **Stream**
- **Canal, lock, tunnel**
- **Water**
- **Tidal water**
- 58 87 246 **Adjoining page indicators and overlap bands** – the colour of the arrow and band indicates the scale of the adjoining or overlapping page (see scales below)

The dark grey border on the inside edge of some pages indicates that the mapping does not continue onto the adjacent page

The small numbers around the edges of the maps identify the 1-kilometre National Grid lines

Abbreviations

Acad	**Academy**	Meml	**Memorial**
Allot Gdns	**Allotments**	Mon	**Monument**
Cemy	**Cemetery**	Mus	**Museum**
C Ctr	**Civic centre**	Obsy	**Observatory**
CH	**Club house**	Pal	**Royal palace**
Coll	**College**	PH	**Public house**
Crem	**Crematorium**	Recn Gd	**Recreation ground**
Ent	**Enterprise**	Resr	**Reservoir**
Ex H	**Exhibition hall**	Ret Pk	**Retail park**
Ind Est	**Industrial Estate**	Sch	**School**
IRB Sta	**Inshore rescue boat station**	Sh Ctr	**Shopping centre**
Inst	**Institute**	TH	**Town hall / house**
Ct	**Law court**	Trad Est	**Trading estate**
L Ctr	**Leisure centre**	Univ	**University**
LC	**Level crossing**	W Twr	**Water tower**
Liby	**Library**	Wks	**Works**
Mkt	**Market**	YH	**Youth hostel**

Enlarged maps only

- **Railway or bus station building**
- **Place of interest**
- **Parkland**

The map scale on the pages numbered in green is 1¾ inches to 1 mile
2.76 cm to 1 km • 1:36206

0 ½ mile 1 mile 1½ miles **2 miles**
0 500m 1 km 1½ km **2km**

The map scale on the pages numbered in blue is 3½ inches to 1 mile
5.52 cm to 1 km • 1:18103

0 ¼ mile ½ mile ¾ mile **1 mile**
0 250m 500m 750m **1km**

The map scale on the pages numbered in red is 7 inches to 1 mile
11.04 cm to 1 km • 1:9051

0 220yds 440yds 660yds **½ mile**
0 125m 250m 375m **500m**

Key to map pages

113	Map pages at 1¾ inches to 1 mile
221	Map pages at 3½ inches to 1 mile
233	Map pages at 7 inches to 1 mile

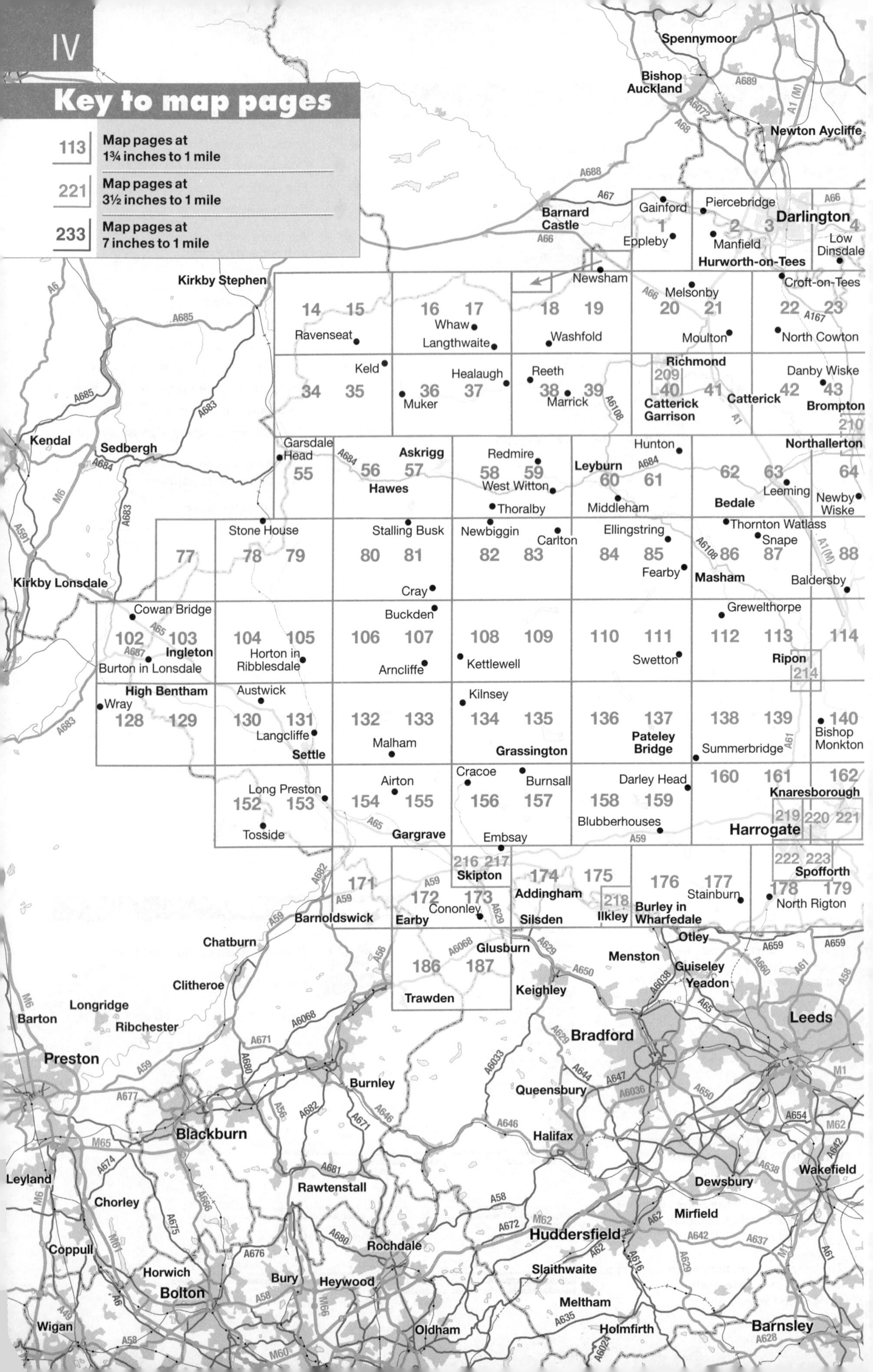
Spennymoor
Bishop Auckland
A689
A1(M)
A6072
A68
Newton Aycliffe
A688
A67
Barnard Castle
A66
Gainford
1
Eppleby
Piercebridge
2
Manfield
3
Darlington
4
Low Dinsdale
Hurworth-on-Tees
Kirkby Stephen
A6
A685
Newsham
Melsonby
Croft-on-Tees
14 15
Ravenseat
16 17
Whaw
Langthwaite
18 19
Washfold
20 21
Moulton
22 23
A167
North Cowton
Keld
34 35
Muker
36 37
Healaugh
Reeth
38 39
Marrick
A6108
Richmond
209
40 41
Catterick Garrison
Catterick
A1
Danby Wiske
42 43
Brompton
210
Northallerton
Kendal
Sedbergh
A684
M6
A683
A591
Garsdale Head
55
56 57
Askrigg
Hawes
Redmire
58 59
West Witton
Thoralby
Leyburn
60 61
Hunton
Middleham
62 63
Bedale
Leeming
64
Newby Wiske
Stone House
77
78 79
Stalling Busk
80 81
Cray
Newbiggin
82 83
Carlton
Ellingstring
84 85
Fearby
Thornton Watlass
Snape
86 87
Masham
88
Baldersby
Kirkby Lonsdale
Cowan Bridge
102 103
A65
A687
Ingleton
Burton in Lonsdale
104 105
Horton in Ribblesdale
Buckden
106 107
Arncliffe
108 109
Kettlewell
110 111
Swetton
Grewelthorpe
112 113
Ripon
214
114
High Bentham
Wray
128 129
Austwick
130 131
Langcliffe
Settle
132 133
Malham
Kilnsey
134 135
Grassington
136 137
Pateley Bridge
138 139
Summerbridge
A61
140
Bishop Monkton
Long Preston
152 153
Tosside
Airton
154 155
Gargrave
Cracoe
Burnsall
156 157
Embsay
Darley Head
158 159
Blubberhouses
A59
160 161
Knaresborough
162
219 220 221
Harrogate
A682
171
216 217
Skipton
174 175
Addingham
176 177
Stainburn
178 179
222 223
Spofforth
North Rigton
172 173
Cononley
A629
Barnoldswick
Earby
Silsden
218
Ilkley
Burley in Wharfedale
Chatburn
A56
A6068
Glusburn
186 187
Trawden
Otley
Menston
Guiseley
Yeadon
A659
A660
A658
A650
A6038
Clitheroe
Keighley
Longridge
Barton
Ribchester
Leeds
Bradford
Preston
A671
A680
A6033
A644
A647
A6036
M1
Burnley
Queensbury
A677
A646
A654
M62
Blackburn
Halifax
M65
A674
A681
A638
Wakefield
Leyland
Rawtenstall
Dewsbury
Chorley
A666
A675
A58
A672
Mirfield
Huddersfield
A62
A642
A637
Coppull
M61
A676
A680
Rochdale
A616
Horwich
Slaithwaite
Bury
Heywood
Bolton
A6
M66
Meltham
Wigan
A49
A635
Oldham
Holmfirth
Barnsley
A628
M60
A6024

Key to map symbols

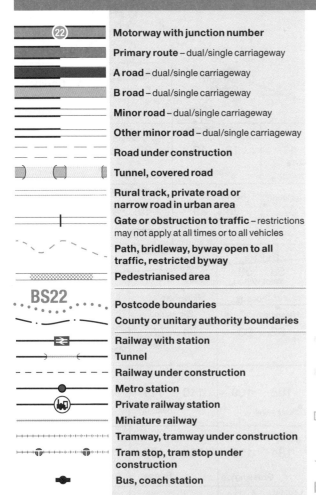

- Motorway with junction number
- Primary route – dual/single carriageway
- A road – dual/single carriageway
- B road – dual/single carriageway
- Minor road – dual/single carriageway
- Other minor road – dual/single carriageway
- Road under construction
- Tunnel, covered road
- Rural track, private road or narrow road in urban area
- Gate or obstruction to traffic – restrictions may not apply at all times or to all vehicles
- Path, bridleway, byway open to all traffic, restricted byway
- Pedestrianised area

- BS22 Postcode boundaries
- County or unitary authority boundaries

- Railway with station
- Tunnel
- Railway under construction
- Metro station
- Private railway station
- Miniature railway
- Tramway, tramway under construction
- Tram stop, tram stop under construction
- Bus, coach station

- Ambulance station
- Coastguard station
- Fire station
- Police station

- Accident and Emergency entrance to hospital
- Hospital

- Place of worship
- Information centre – open all year
- Shopping centre, parking
- P&R PO Park and Ride, Post Office
- Camping site, caravan site
- Golf course, picnic site
- ROMAN FORT Non-Roman antiquity, Roman antiquity

- Univ Important buildings, schools, colleges, universities and hospitals
- Woods, built-up area

- River Medway Water name
- River, weir
- Stream
- Canal, lock, tunnel
- Water
- Tidal water

- 58 87 246 **Adjoining page indicators and overlap bands** – the colour of the arrow and band indicates the scale of the adjoining or overlapping page (see scales below)

The dark grey border on the inside edge of some pages indicates that the mapping does not continue onto the adjacent page

The small numbers around the edges of the maps identify the 1-kilometre National Grid lines

Enlarged maps only

- Railway or bus station building
- Place of interest
- Parkland

Abbreviations

Acad	**Academy**	Meml	**Memorial**
Allot Gdns	**Allotments**	Mon	**Monument**
Cemy	**Cemetery**	Mus	**Museum**
C Ctr	**Civic centre**	Obsy	**Observatory**
CH	**Club house**	Pal	**Royal palace**
Coll	**College**	PH	**Public house**
Crem	**Crematorium**	Recn Gd	**Recreation ground**
Ent	**Enterprise**	Resr	**Reservoir**
Ex H	**Exhibition hall**	Ret Pk	**Retail park**
Ind Est	**Industrial Estate**	Sch	**School**
IRB Sta	**Inshore rescue boat station**	Sh Ctr	**Shopping centre**
Inst	**Institute**	TH	**Town hall / house**
Ct	**Law court**	Trad Est	**Trading estate**
L Ctr	**Leisure centre**	Univ	**University**
LC	**Level crossing**	W Twr	**Water tower**
Liby	**Library**	Wks	**Works**
Mkt	**Market**	YH	**Youth hostel**

The map scale on the pages numbered in green is 1¾ inches to 1 mile
2.76 cm to 1 km • 1:36 206

0 – ½ mile – 1 mile – 1½ miles – **2 miles**
0 – 500m – 1 km – 1½ km – **2km**

The map scale on the pages numbered in blue is 3½ inches to 1 mile
5.52 cm to 1 km • 1:18 103

0 – ¼ mile – ½ mile – ¾ mile – **1 mile**
0 – 250m – 500m – 750m – **1km**

The map scale on the pages numbered in red is 7 inches to 1 mile
11.04 cm to 1 km • 1:9 051

0 – 220yds – 440yds – 660yds – **½ mile**
0 – 125m – 250m – 375m – **500m**

Key to map pages

113	Map pages at 1¾ inches to 1 mile
221	Map pages at 3½ inches to 1 mile
233	Map pages at 7 inches to 1 mile

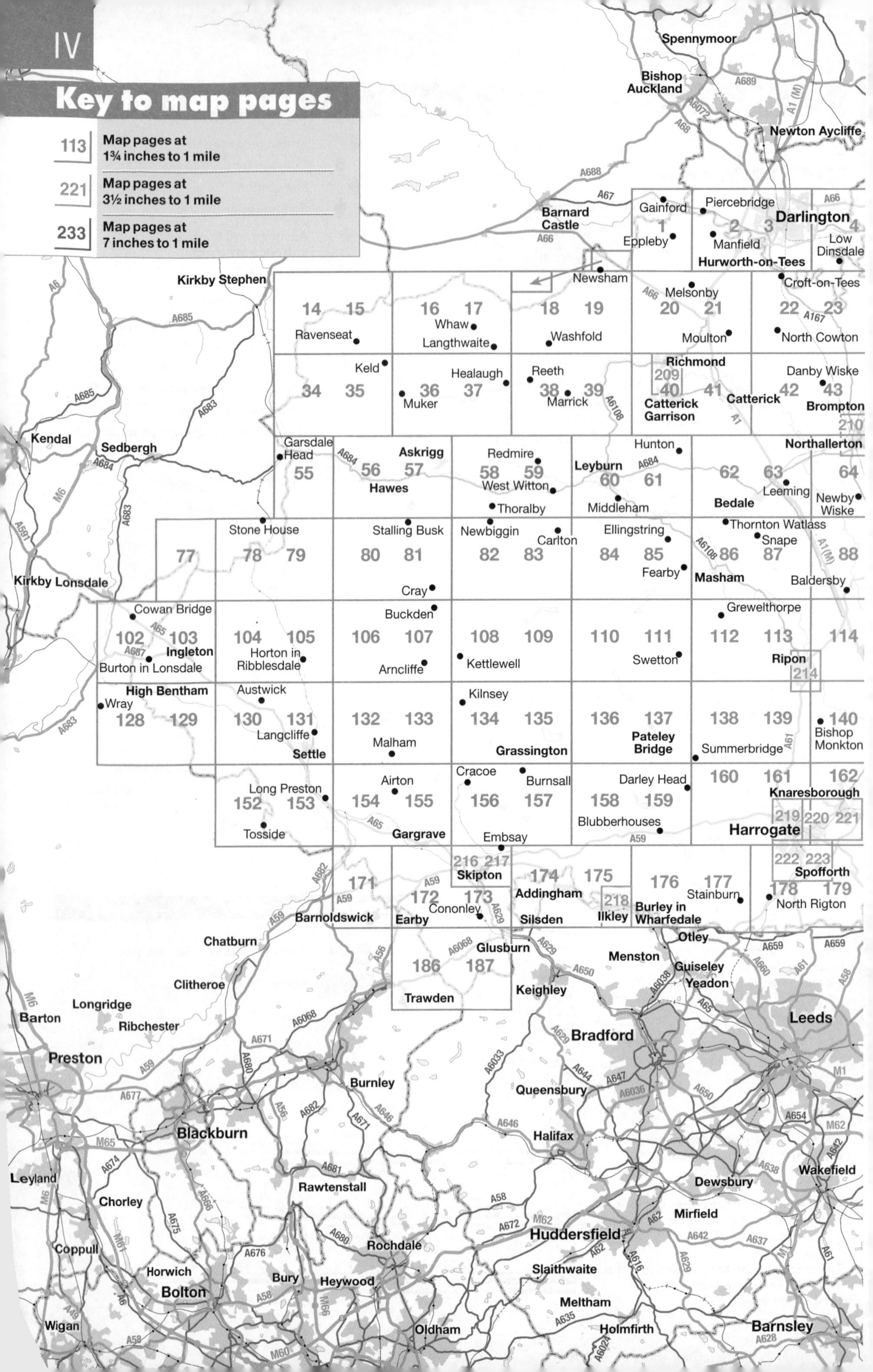

Spennymoor
Bishop Auckland
A689
A1(M)
A6072
A68
Newton Aycliffe
A688
A67
Barnard Castle
A66
Gainford
1
Eppleby
Piercebridge
2
3
Manfield
Darlington
4
A66
Low Dinsdale
Hurworth-on-Tees
Kirkby Stephen
Newsham
Croft-on-Tees
A6
A685
14 15
Ravenseat
16 17
Whaw
Langthwaite
18 19
Washfold
A66
Melsonby
20 21
Moulton
22 23
A167
North Cowton
Keld
34 35
36 37
Muker
Healaugh
Reeth
38 39
Marrick
A6108
Richmond
209
40
Catterick Garrison
41
Catterick
A1
Danby Wiske
42 43
Brompton
210
A685
A683
Kendal
Sedbergh
A684
M6
Garsdale Head
55
A684
56 57
Askrigg
Hawes
Redmire
58 59
West Witton
Thoralby
Leyburn
A684
60 61
Middleham
Hunton
62 63
Leeming
Bedale
Northallerton
64
Newby Wiske
A591
A683
Kirkby Lonsdale
77
Stone House
78 79
Stalling Busk
80 81
Cray
Newbiggin
82 83
Carlton
Ellingstring
84 85
Fearby
A6108
86 87
Masham
Thornton Watlass
Snape
A1(M)
88
Baldersby
Cowan Bridge
102 103
A65
A687
Ingleton
Burton in Lonsdale
104 105
Horton in Ribblesdale
Buckden
106 107
Arncliffe
108 109
Kettlewell
110 111
Swetton
Grewelthorpe
112 113
Ripon
214
114
High Bentham
Wray
128 129
A683
Austwick
130 131
Langcliffe
Settle
132 133
Malham
Kilnsey
134 135
Grassington
136 137
Pateley Bridge
138 139
Summerbridge
A61
140
Bishop Monkton
Long Preston
152 153
Tosside
Airton
154 155
A65
Gargrave
Cracoe
Burnsall
156 157
Embsay
Darley Head
158 159
Blubberhouses
A59
160 161
162
Knaresborough
219 220 221
Harrogate
A682
171
A59
Barnoldswick
A59
172 173
216 217
Skipton
Cononley
A629
Earby
174 175
Addingham
Silsden
218
Ilkley
176 177
Stainburn
Burley in Wharfedale
222 223
Spofforth
178 179
North Rigton
Chatburn
A56
A6068
Glusburn
186 187
Trawden
A629
Keighley
A650
Menston
Otley
A6038
Guiseley
Yeadon
A65
A659
A660
A61
A659
A58
Clitheroe
M6
Barton
Longridge
Ribchester
Preston
A59
A671
A6068
A680
Burnley
A6033
A629
Bradford
A644
A647
A6036
Queensbury
A650
Leeds
M1
A677
Blackburn
A56
A682
A671
A646
A646
Halifax
A654
M62
M65
A674
Leyland
Chorley
A666
A681
Rawtenstall
A58
A672
M62
Huddersfield
A62
A638
Dewsbury
Mirfield
A642
Wakefield
A642
A637
M6
M61
A675
Coppull
Horwich
A676
A680
Rochdale
A62
A616
A629
Slaithwaite
M1
A61
Bolton
A6
Bury
Heywood
A58
M66
Wigan
A49
A58
M60
Oldham
Meltham
A635
Holmfirth
A6024
Barnsley
A628

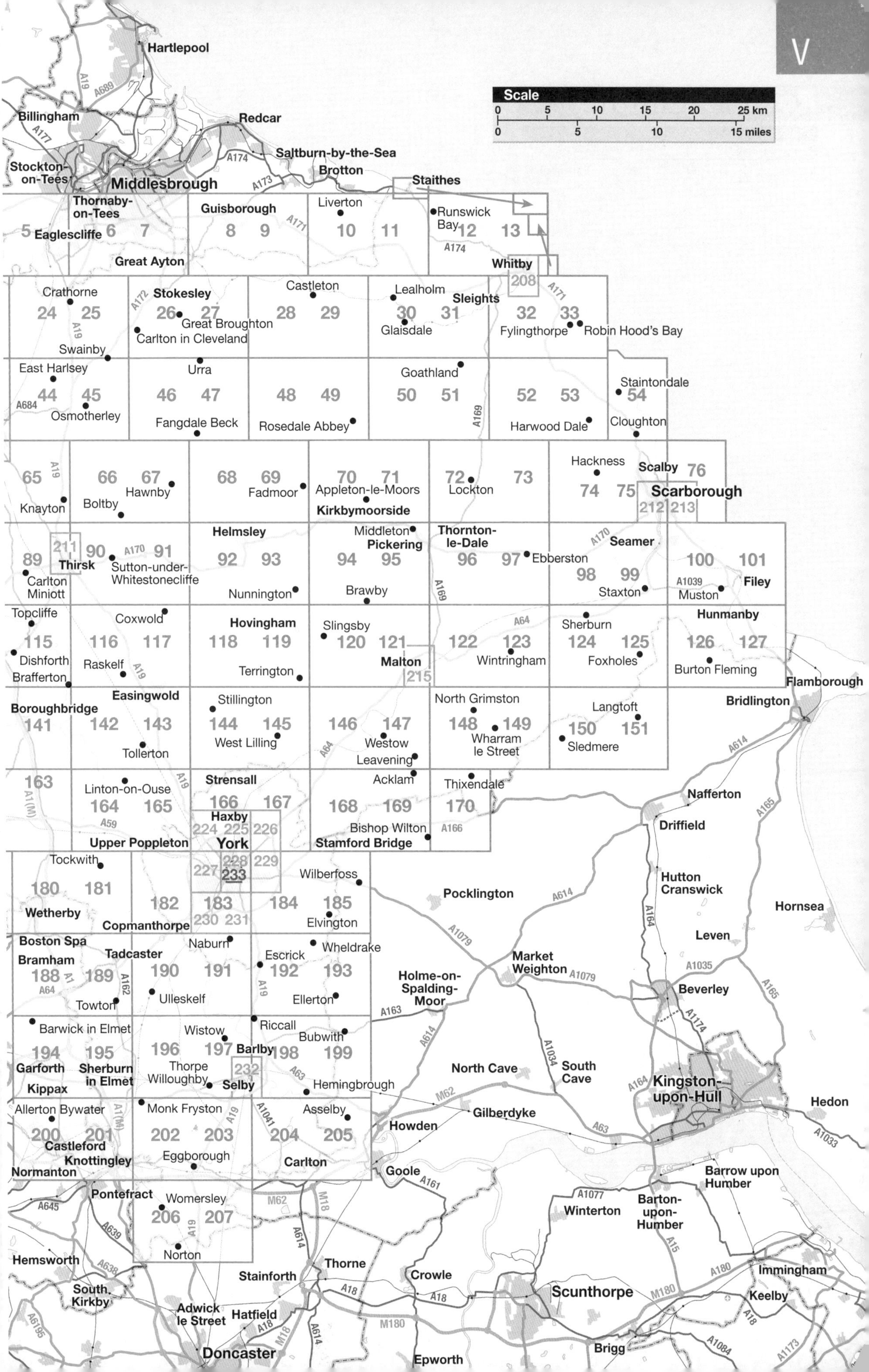
Scale
0 5 10 15 20 25 km
0 5 10 15 miles
Hartlepool
Billingham
Redcar
Saltburn-by-the-Sea
Brotton
Staithes
Stockton-on-Tees
Middlesbrough
Thornaby-on-Tees
Guisborough
Liverton
Runswick Bay
5 Eaglescliffe 6 7
8 9
10 11
12 13
Great Ayton
Whitby
208
Crathorne
24 25
Stokesley
26 27
Great Broughton
Carlton in Cleveland
Castleton
28 29
Lealholm
30 31
Sleights
Glaisdale
32 33
Fylingthorpe
Robin Hood's Bay
Swainby
East Harlsey
44 45
Osmotherley
Urra
46 47
Fangdale Beck
48 49
Rosedale Abbey
Goathland
50 51
52 53
Harwood Dale
Staintondale
54
Cloughton
65
Knayton
66 67
Hawnby
Boltby
68 69
Fadmoor
70 71
Appleton-le-Moors
Kirkbymoorside
72 73
Lockton
Hackness
74 75
Scalby 76
Scarborough
212 213
89
211
Thirsk
Carlton Miniott
90 91
Sutton-under-Whitestonecliffe
Helmsley
92 93
Nunnington
Middleton
Pickering
94 95
Brawby
Thornton-le-Dale
96 97
Ebberston
Seamer
98 99
Staxton
100 101
Filey
Muston
Topcliffe
115
Dishforth
Brafferton
Coxwold
116 117
Raskelf
Hovingham
118 119
Terrington
Slingsby
120 121
Malton
215
122 123
Wintringham
Sherburn
124 125
Foxholes
Hunmanby
126 127
Burton Fleming
Flamborough
Bridlington
Boroughbridge
141
Easingwold
142 143
Tollerton
Stillington
144 145
West Lilling
146 147
Westow
Leavening
North Grimston
148 149
Wharram le Street
Langtoft
150 151
Sledmere
163
Linton-on-Ouse
164 165
Strensall
166 167
Haxby
224 225 226
York
Upper Poppleton
Acklam
168 169
Bishop Wilton
Stamford Bridge
Thixendale
170
Nafferton
Driffield
Tockwith
180 181
Wetherby
227 228 229
233
Wilberfoss
182
183
230 231
184 185
Elvington
Copmanthorpe
Pocklington
Hutton Cranswick
Hornsea
Boston Spa
Bramham
188 189
Tadcaster
Towton
Naburn
190 191
Ulleskelf
Escrick
192 193
Wheldrake
Ellerton
Holme-on-Spalding-Moor
Market Weighton
Leven
Beverley
Barwick in Elmet
194 195
Garforth
Kippax
Sherburn in Elmet
Wistow
196 197
Thorpe Willoughby
Barlby
232
Selby
Riccall
198 199
Bubwith
Hemingbrough
North Cave
South Cave
Kingston-upon-Hull
Hedon
Allerton Bywater
200 201
Castleford
Knottingley
Normanton
Monk Fryston
202 203
Eggborough
204 205
Asselby
Carlton
Howden
Gilberdyke
Goole
Barrow upon Humber
Winterton
Barton-upon-Humber
Pontefract
Womersley
206 207
Norton
Hemsworth
South Kirkby
Stainforth
Thorne
Crowle
Scunthorpe
Immingham
Keelby
Adwick le Street
Hatfield
Doncaster
Epworth
Brigg
A19
A689
A177
A174
A173
A171
A172
A684
A169
A170
A1039
A64
A1(M)
A59
A166
A614
A1079
A164
A1035
A165
A1174
A162
A163
A1034
A63
A1041
A1033
A1077
A161
M62
M18
A645
A639
A638
A6195
A18
M180
A15
A180
A1084
A1173

Route Planning

Scale

0 5 10 15 km

0 5 10 miles

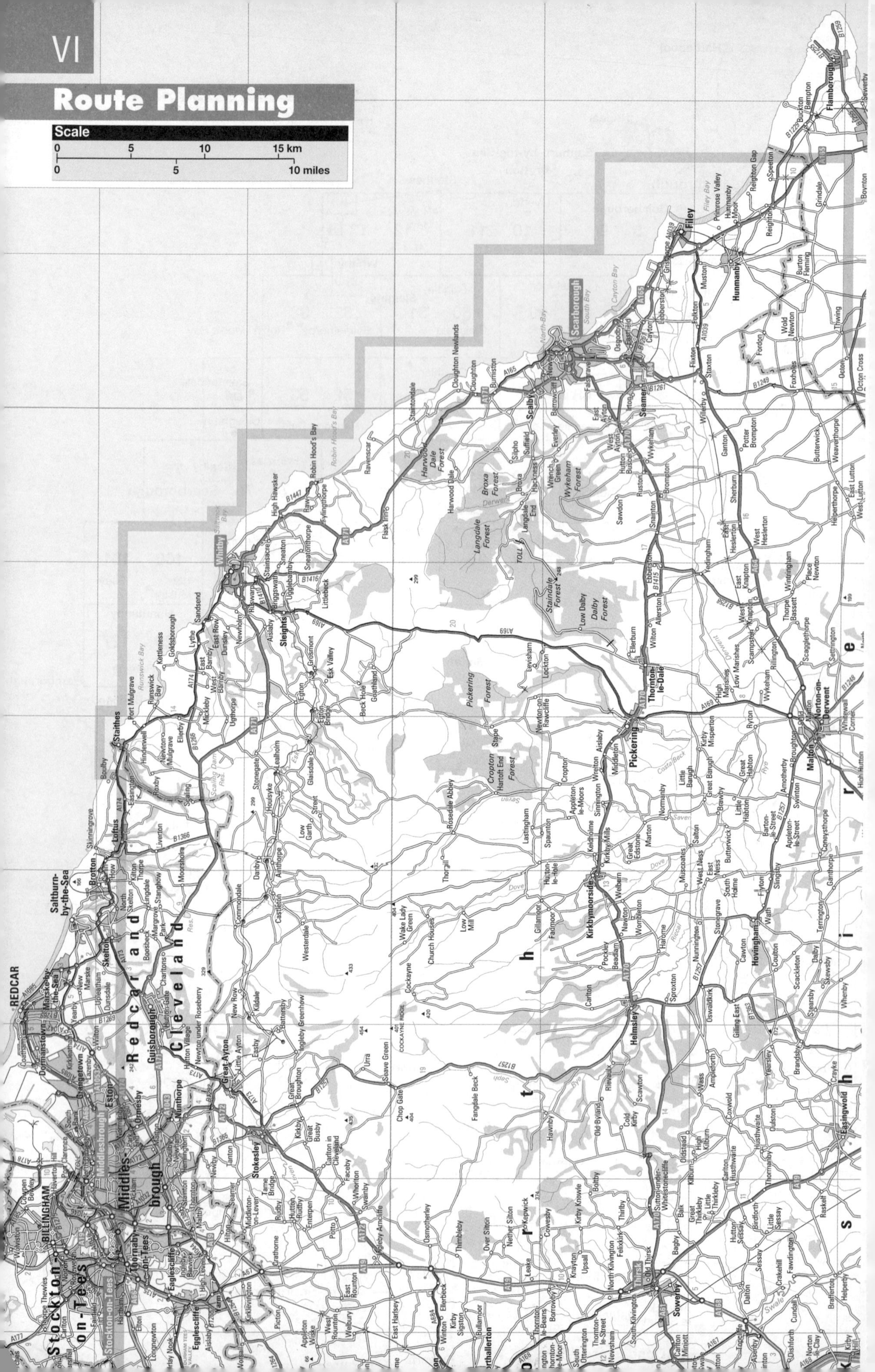

BRIDLINGTON BAY
Bridlington
Hornsea
Aldbrough
Driffield
Nafferton
Hutton Cranswick
Beverley
Leven
Hedon
Kingston-upon-Hull
KINGSTON UPON HULL
HUMBER
Humber Bridge
Barton-upon-Humber
Barrow upon Humber
Immingham
Cottingham
Kirk Ella
Anlaby
Hessle
North Ferriby
South Cave
North Cave
Market Weighton
Pocklington
Holme-on-Spalding-Moor
Gilberdyke
Howden
Goole
Winterton
Thorne
Crowle
Stainforth
Snaith
Carlton
Selby
Barlby
Stamford Bridge
Strensall
Haxby
York
Bishopthorpe
Copmanthorpe
Upper Poppleton
Tadcaster
Sherburn in Elmet
Knottingley
Castleford
Featherstone
Hemsworth
Kippax
Garforth
Boston Spa
Bramham
Boroughbridge
East Riding of Yorkshire
City of York
North Lincolnshire

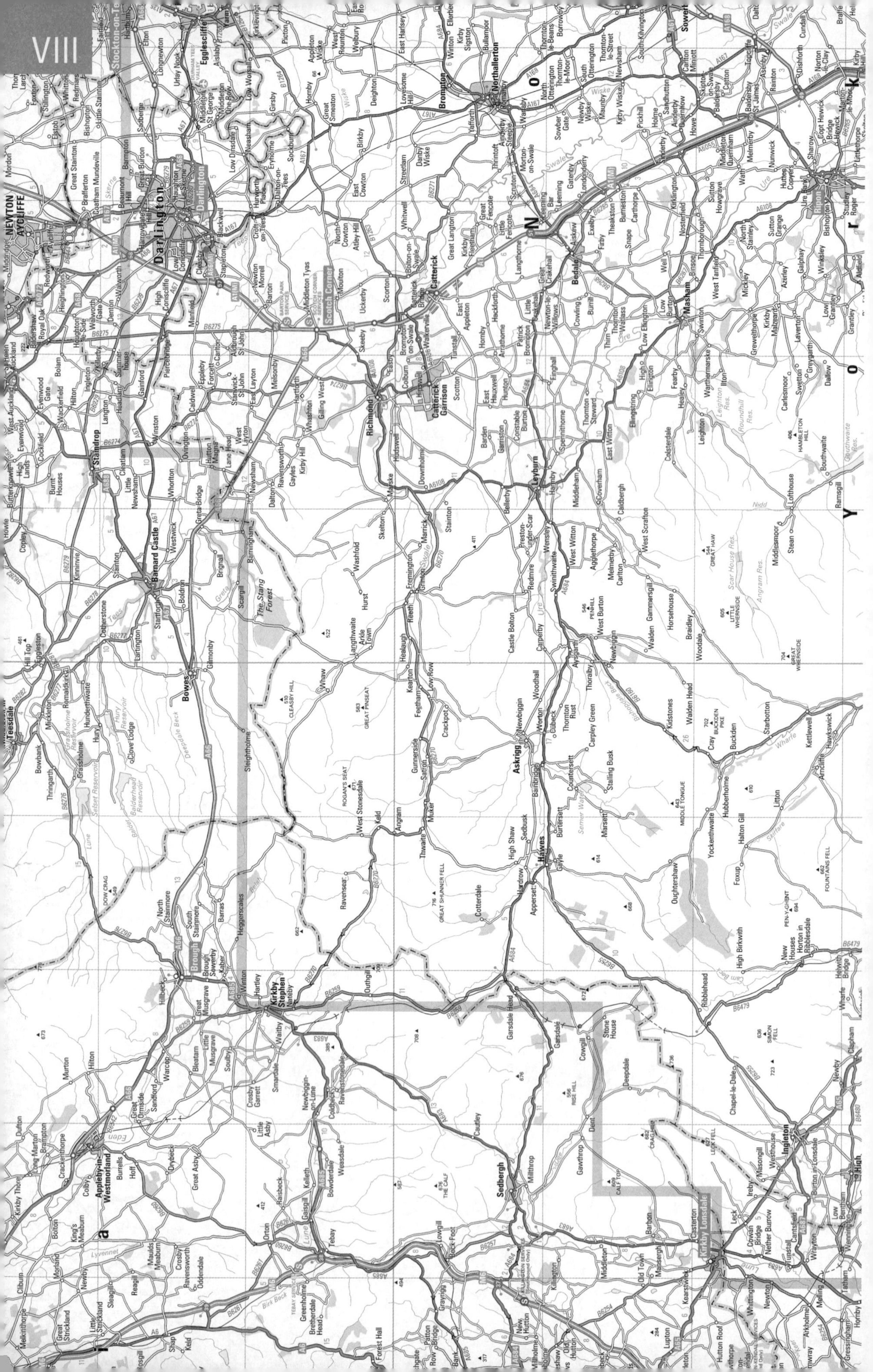
VIII
NEWTON AYCLIFFE
Darlington
Stockton-on-Tees
Northallerton
Richmond
Catterick Garrison
Catterick
Scotch Corner
Barnard Castle
Staindrop
Teesdale
Bowes
Brough
Kirkby Stephen
Appleby-in-Westmorland
Sedbergh
Hawes
Askrigg
Leyburn
Bedale
Masham
Ripon
Ingleton
Kirkby Lonsdale
Tebay
Shap
The Stang Forest
Wensley
Middleham
Thirsk
Y o r k
N o r

LEEDS
Harrogate
Knaresborough
Wetherby
Boston Spa
Otley
Ilkley
Skipton
Keighley
Bingley
Shipley
Bradford
Halifax
Huddersfield
Dewsbury
Wakefield
Brighouse
Todmorden
Burnley
Nelson
Colne
Clitheroe
Accrington
Blackburn
Darwen
Rochdale
Bury
Horwich
Chorley
Longridge
Settle
Grassington
Pateley Bridge
Bentham
Gisburn Forest
Blackburn with Darwen
West Yorkshire

Major administrative and Postcode boundaries

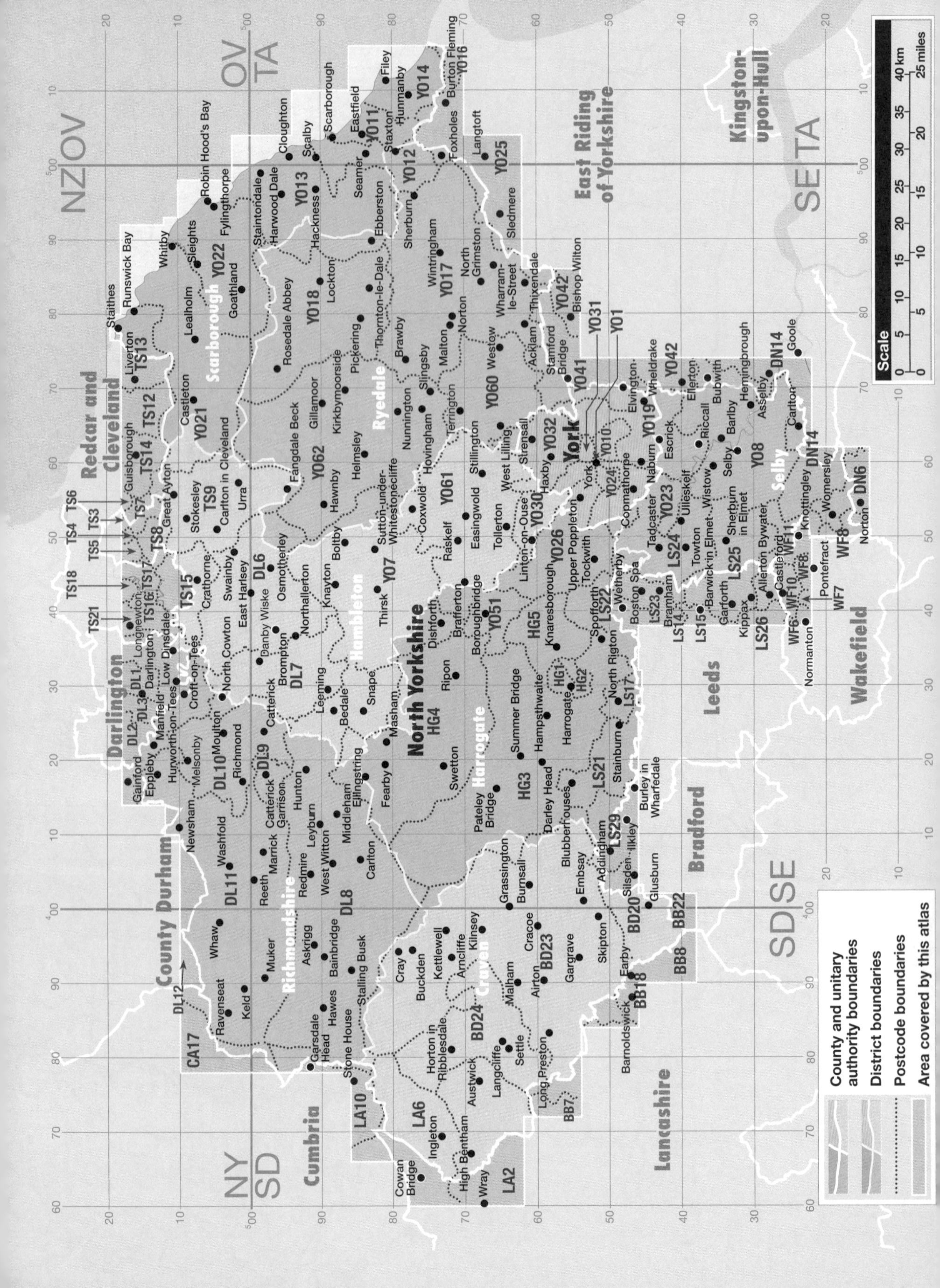

Scale: 1¾ inches to 1 mile
0 ¼ ½ mile
0 250m 500m 750m 1 km

2

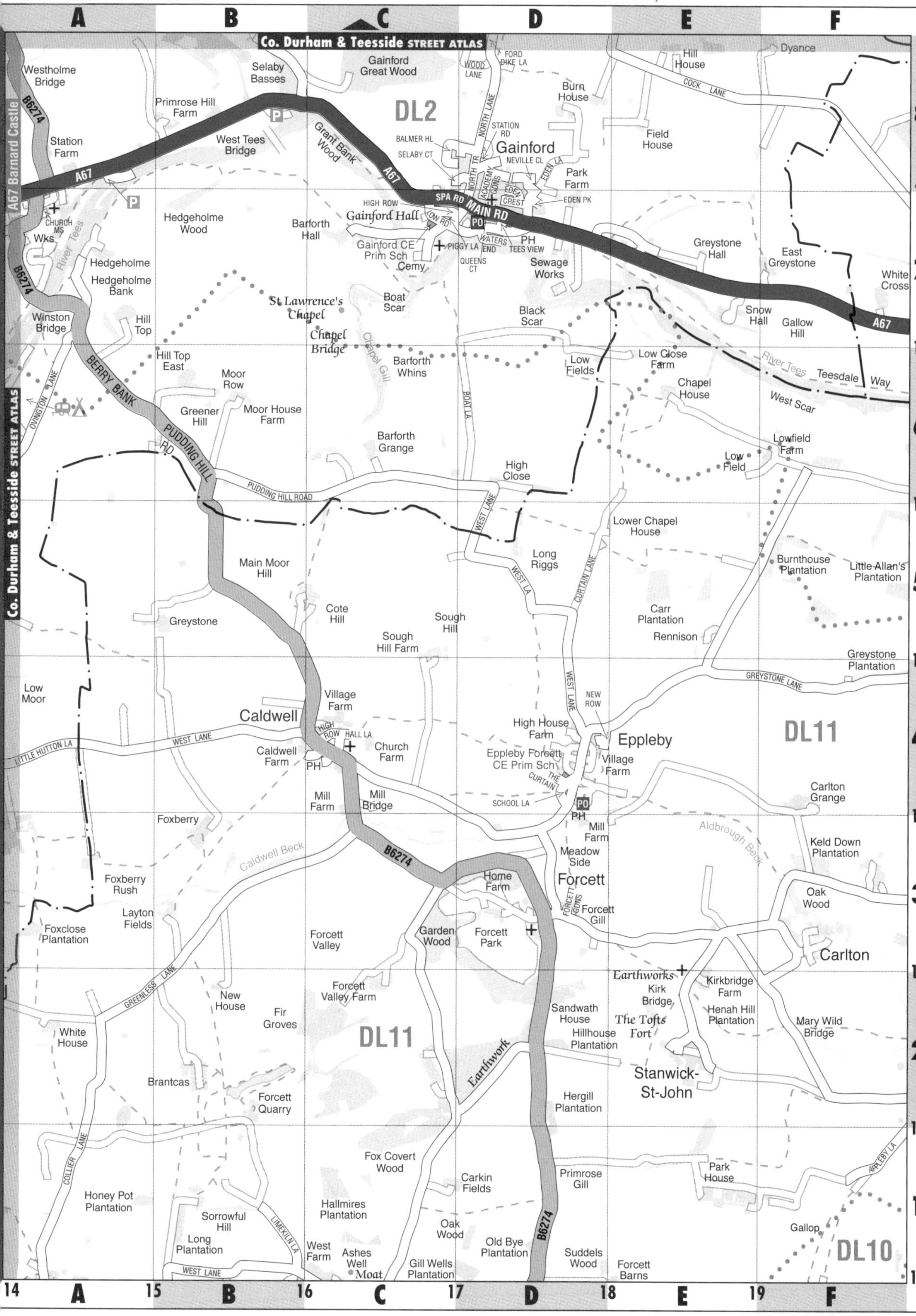

A
B
C
D
E
F
Co. Durham & Teesside STREET ATLAS
Westholme Bridge
Selaby Basses
Gainford Great Wood
WOOD LANE
FORD DIKE LA
Hill House
Dyance
COCK LANE
Primrose Hill Farm
DL2
Burn House
Field House
B6274
Station Farm
West Tees Bridge
Grant Bank Wood
NORTH LANE
STATION RD
BALMER HL
SELABY CT
Gainford
NEVILLE CL
EDEN LA
Park Farm
A67 Barnard Castle
A67
CHURCH MS
Wks
River Tees
Hedgeholme Wood
Barforth Hall
HIGH ROW
Gainford Hall
SPA RD
MAIN RD
PO
EDEN PK
EDEN CREST
ACADEMY GDNS
NORTH TR
LOW RD
WATERS END
PIGGY LA
PH
TEES VIEW
QUEENS CT
Gainford CE Prim Sch
Cemy
Sewage Works
Greystone Hall
East Greystone
White Cross
Hedgeholme
Hedgeholme Bank
St Lawrence's Chapel
Boat Scar
Black Scar
Snow Hall
Gallow Hill
Winston Bridge
Hill Top
Chapel Bridge
Chapel Gill
Hill Top East
Barforth Whins
Low Fields
Low Close Farm
River Tees
Teesdale Way
OVINGTON LANE
BERRY BANK
Moor Row
Chapel House
West Scar
Greener Hill
Moor House Farm
BOAT LA
PUDDING HILL RD
Barforth Grange
Lowfield Farm
Low Field
High Close
PUDDING HILL ROAD
WEST LANE
Lower Chapel House
Main Moor Hill
Long Riggs
WEST LA
CURTAIN LANE
Burnthouse Plantation
Little Allan's Plantation
Cote Hill
Sough Hill
Carr Plantation
Greystone
Sough Hill Farm
Rennison
Greystone Plantation
GREYSTONE LANE
Low Moor
Village Farm
WEST LANE
NEW ROW
Caldwell
High House Farm
Eppleby
DL11
LITTLE HUTTON LA
WEST LANE
HIGH ROW
HALL LA
Church Farm
Caldwell Farm
PH
Eppleby Forcett CE Prim Sch
THE CURTAIN
Village Farm
Carlton Grange
Mill Farm
Mill Bridge
SCHOOL LA
PO
PH
Foxberry
Mill Farm
Aldbrough Beck
Keld Down Plantation
Caldwell Beck
Meadow Side
B6274
Home Farm
Foxberry Rush
Forcett
Oak Wood
FORCETT GDNS
Forcett Gill
Layton Fields
Foxclose Plantation
Forcett Valley
Garden Wood
Forcett Park
Carlton
Earthworks
Kirk Bridge
Kirkbridge Farm
GREENLESS LANE
Forcett Valley Farm
New House
Sandwath House
Henah Hill Plantation
The Tofts Fort
Mary Wild Bridge
Fir Groves
Hillhouse Plantation
White House
DL11
Earthwork
Stanwick-St-John
Brantcas
Hergill Plantation
Forcett Quarry
COLLIER LANE
Fox Covert Wood
Primrose Gill
Park House
APPLEBY LA
Carkin Fields
Honey Pot Plantation
Hallmires Plantation
Sorrowful Hill
LIMEKILN LA
Oak Wood
Gallop
Long Plantation
Old Bye Plantation
B6274
DL10
West Farm
Ashes Well
Moat
Gill Wells Plantation
Suddels Wood
Forcett Barns
WEST LANE
8
17
7
16
6
15
5
14
4
13
3
12
2
11
1
10
14
15
16
17
18
19

20
2

1

Scale: 1¾ inches to 1 mile
0 ¼ ½ mile
0 250m 500m 750m 1 km

A
B
C
D
E
F
Co. Durham & Teesside STREET ATLAS
8
17
7
16
6
15
5
14
4
13
3
12
2
11
1
10
20
21
22
23
24
25
B6275
B6279
Fulbeck Bridge
Willowbeds Plantation
Flatts Plantation
NEWTON LANE
Hopewell
Moat
High Carlbury Farm
Ulnaby Village
Low Walworth Farm
Town End Farm
Fanny Barks (Fox Covert)
Ulnaby Hall
Garthorne Farm
Thornton Hall
Cocker Beck
Archdeacon Newton
Piercebridge Grange
COCK LANE
ULNABY LANE
Works
Thornton Plantation
Cabin House
Carlbury
Mill Hill
Beck Side Farm
JEDBURGH
MALVERN CR
A1(M)
A67
Tumulus
Low Carlbury Farm
Morley Hill
Branksome
Piercebridge
PH
Piercebridge Farm
Fort
High Coniscliffe CE Prim Sch
High Coniscliffe
Hall Moor Farm
River Tees
Bridge End
Cliffe
Ulnaby Beck
B6279
Coniscliffe Grange
Cliffe Hall
West Wood
Betty Watson's Hill
LAWSON'S CT
ST EDWIN'S CL
MILL LA
Brookside Farm
Glebe Farm
Lark House
THE GREEN
Tumuli
Holme House
Crow Wood
DL2
Prospect Farm
DL3
Merrybent
Baydale Beck
ARNCLIFFE GR
BEDBURN DRIVE
HALNABY AV
BURNESTON CT
CRAIG MILLER PK
Cliffe Bank
Allan's Grange
Crabby Plantation
NURSERY LA
MERRYBENT DR
Great Allan's Plantation
Swine Lairs Farm
Broken Scar Pumping and Filtration Works
Glebe Farm
Greystones
Coronation Plantation
Nine Acre Plantation
BACK LANE
GATE LANE
Low Coniscliffe
GREYSTONE LANE
Manfield CE Prim Sch
Sewage Works
WOOD LANE
WELL BANK
The Holmes
Lane Ends Farm
GLEBE
GLEBE CL
Manfield Scar
Tees Cottage Pumping Station
BOWLING GREEN LA
Abbey Farm
Howden Hill Wood
Street House
Manfield
GRUNTON LANE
Manor Farm
BOATHOUSE LA
THE GREEN
Cleasby
Namen's Leases Farm
BRICKKILN LANE
Howden Hill
Thornbush Bush
Hollymoor Hall
MOOR LANE
Pinkney Carr Farm
Manfield Fox Covert
DERE STREET ROMAN ROAD
High House
Cold Knuckles
A66(M)
COTTAGERS LANE
New Wood
Manor Farm
Lucy Cross Wood
57
Aldbrough St John
DL11
Long Leases
Grunton
SPENCELEY PL
1 HARTHORN CT
2 KILTON CT
3 OLD BOROUGH STEADINGS
Old Wood
PO
APPLEBY LA
ST JOHN'S PARK
Sewage Works
Brettanby Covert
Brettanby Plantation
DL10
CLEASBY LANE
Cleasby Grange
Cowclose House
Aldbrough Beck
Crossbury Bank Wood
Brettanby Farm
Beck House
Wath Urn Bridge
Middle Belt
Clowbeck Farm
Jolby Grange
Clow Beck
Micklow Hill
Millpasture Plantation
Jolby Manor
Micklow Farm
Watherne
Bow Bridge
JOLBY LANE
Willow Bridge
JOLBY LA

1
21

Scale: 1¾ inches to 1 mile
0 ¼ ½ mile
0 250m 500m 750m 1 km

A7
1 SHORTHORN LA
2 WILDAIR CL
3 RED ROSE CL
4 COLLINGSWAY
5 HUBBACK SQ
6 BAKEWELL MEWS
7 HOLDERNESS DR
8 OLD FAVOURITES WALK
9 SKERNINGHAM AVE
10 COALPITS LA
11 COMETS GARTH
12 TEESWATER DR
13 ALDERMAN LEACH DR
14 JOHN FOWLER WY

B7
1 BRINKBURN DR
2 AUCKLAND OVAL
3 WESTGATE RD
4 HOLDERNESS DR
5 RAINHILL WY
6 PARADISE WY
7 LOCOMOTION LA
8 HONEYPOT LA

4

F6
1 AYRESOME WY
2 WIMBLEDON CL
3 HEADINGLEY CRES
4 WHITE HART CRES
5 MURRAYFIELD WY
6 BRAMALL LA
7 DEEPDALE WY
8 ANFIELD CT
9 AINTREE CT
10 AVIEMORE CT
11 EPSOM CT
12 ELLAND CT
13 BISLEY CT
14 CHEPSTOW CT
15 KEMPTON CT
16 HICKSTEAD CT
17 MALLORY CT
18 BADMINTON CT
19 TRAFFORD CT
20 HARRINGAY CRES
21 ROKER CL

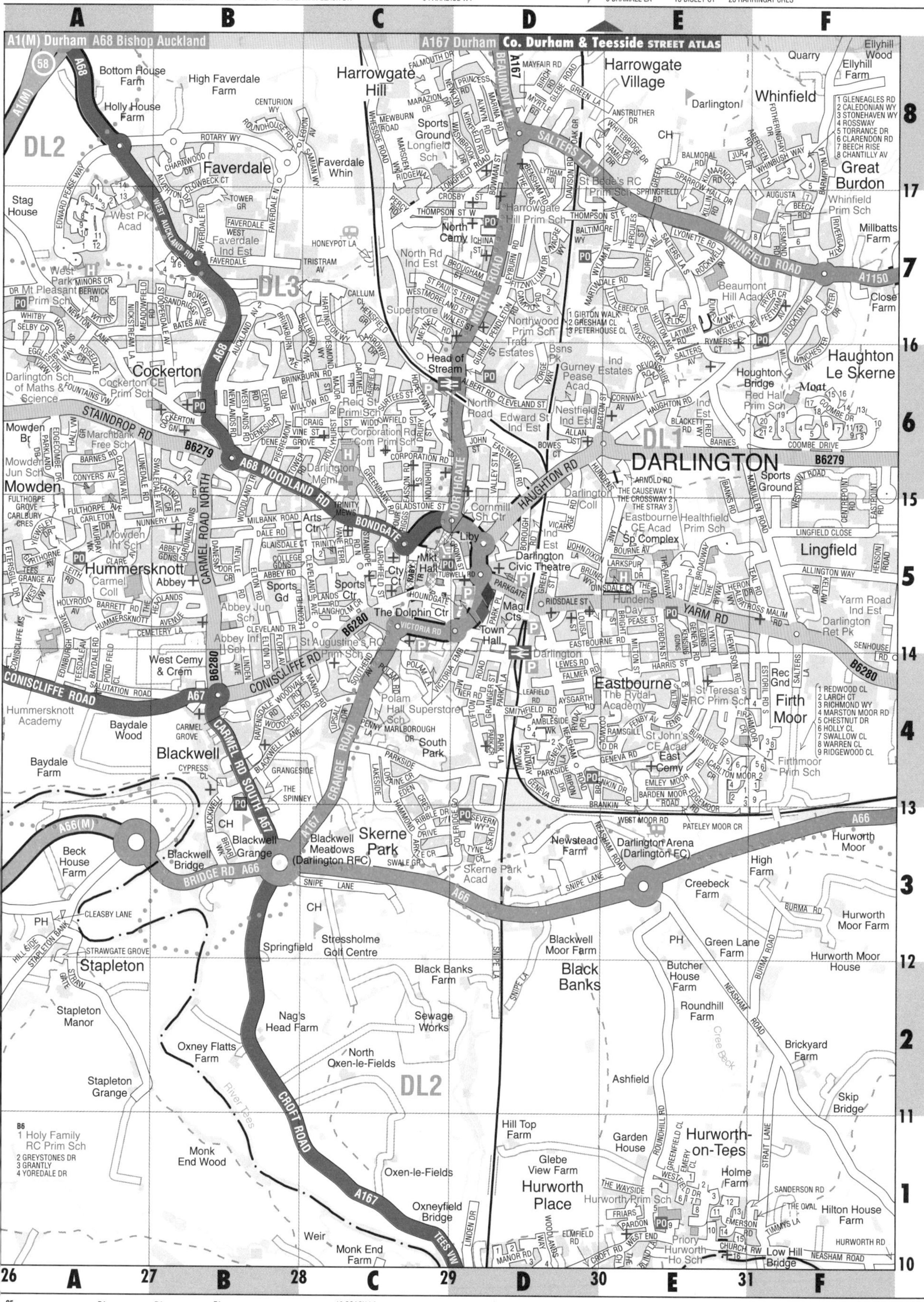

B6
1 Holy Family RC Prim Sch
2 GREYSTONES DR
3 GRANTLY
4 YOREDALE DR

C5
1 Queen Elizabeth 6th Form Coll
2 SCHOLARS PK

D1
1 HAWKSWOOD
2 EDEN CL
3 GRANGE AVE
4 HUNTERS CL

D4
1 TA Centre
2 TEBAY CL
3 PUDSEY WK
4 KESWICK GR
5 ULLSWATER AVE

E1
1 HORNBY CL
2 CROSSFIELD CL
3 SYCAMORE CL
4 MOWBRAY DR
5 ROUNDHILL CL
6 SOUTHFIELD CL
7 DALE CL
8 MALVERN CL
9 GREENSIDE CT
10 COACH LA
11 MANORFIELDS
12 MINSTER WK
13 BRYAN CL
14 LYCH GT
15 THE GABLES
16 CHURCH VW

22

4

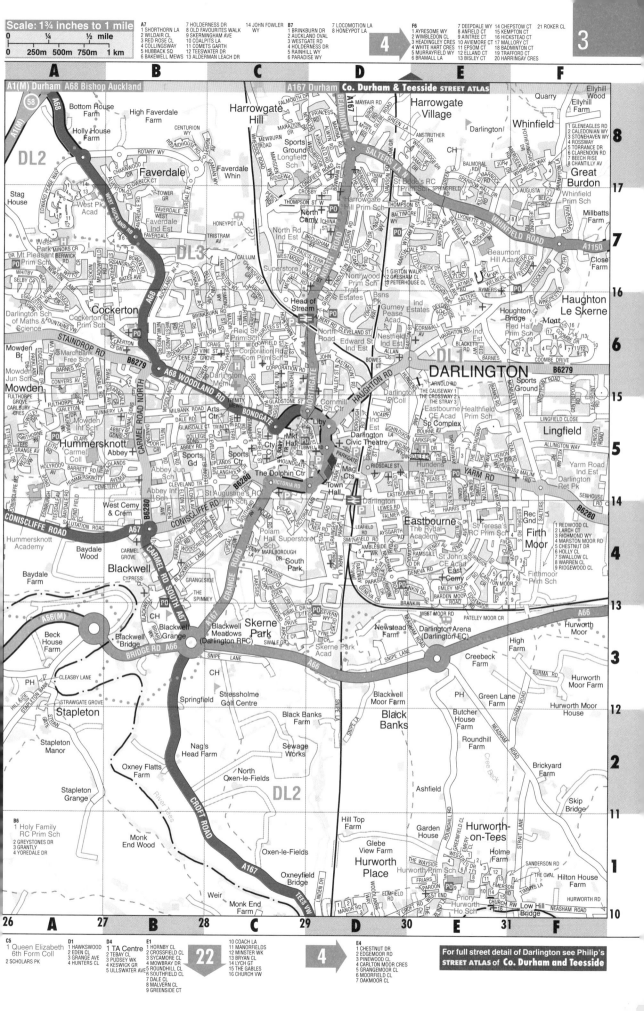

E4
1 CHESTNUT DR
2 EDGEMOOR RD
3 PINEWOOD CL
4 CARLTON MOOR CRES
5 GRANGEMOOR CL
6 MOORFIELD CL
7 OAKMOOR CL

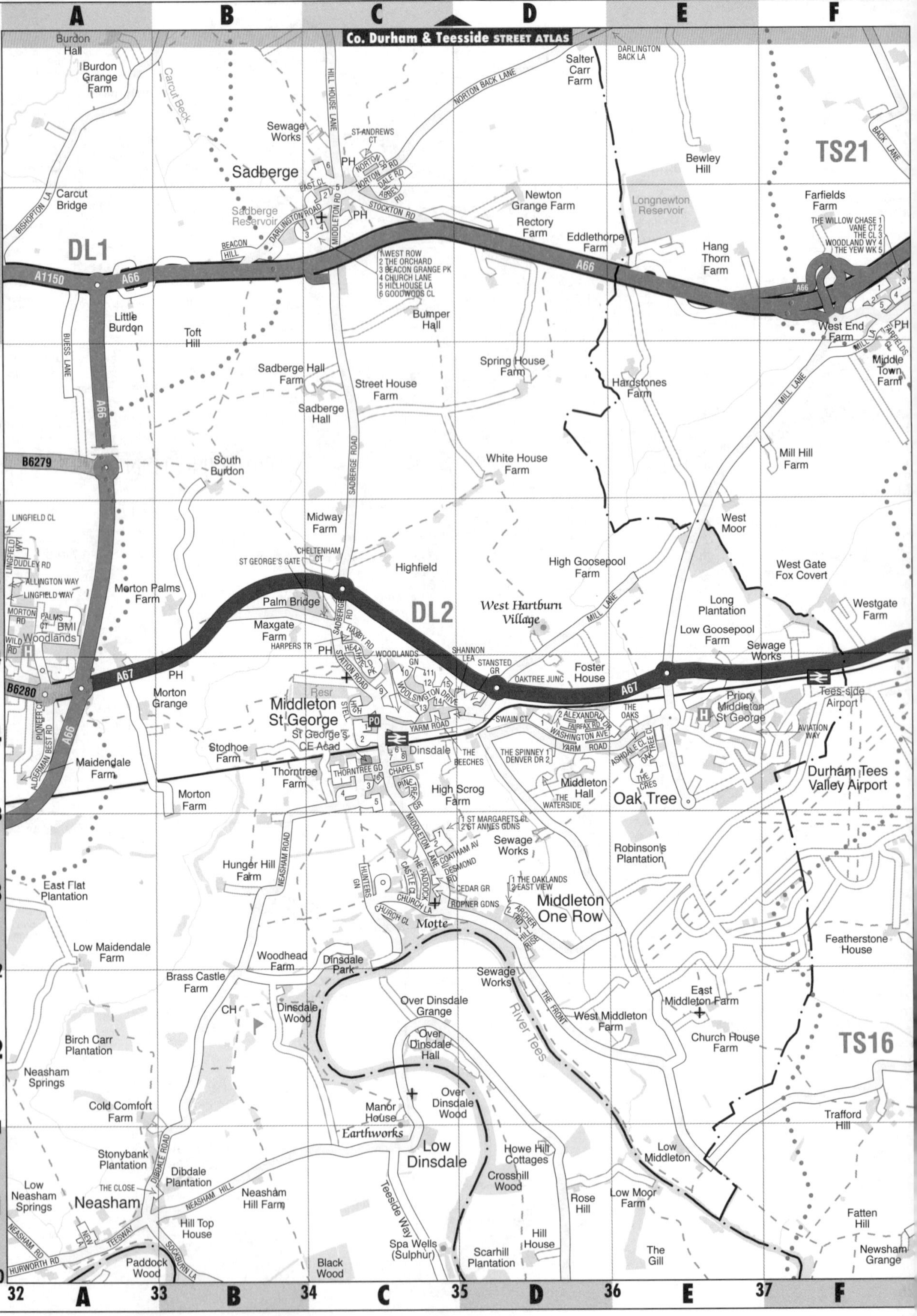
A
B
C
D
E
F
Co. Durham & Teesside STREET ATLAS
Burdon Hall
Burdon Grange Farm
Carcut Beck
Sewage Works
Sadberge
Sadberge Reservoir
Carcut Bridge
BISHOPTON LA
DL1
A1150
A66
Little Burdon
Toft Hill
BUESS LANE
HILL HOUSE LANE
ST ANDREWS CT
NORTON BACK LANE
NORTON RD
DALE RD
ABBEY RD
STOCKTON RD
EAST CL
DARLINGTON ROAD
MIDDLETON ROAD
BEACON HILL
1 WEST ROW
2 THE ORCHARD
3 BEACON GRANGE PK
4 CHURCH LANE
5 HILLHOUSE LA
6 GOODWOODS CL
Salter Carr Farm
DARLINGTON BACK LA
Newton Grange Farm
Rectory Farm
Eddlethorpe Farm
Longnewton Reservoir
Bewley Hill
Hang Thorn Farm
TS21
BACK LANE
Farfields Farm
THE WILLOW CHASE 1
VANE CT 2
THE CL 3
WOODLAND WY 4
THE YEW WK 5
West End Farm
MILL LA
FARFIELDS CL
PH
Middle Town Farm
Bumper Hall
Sadberge Hall Farm
Street House Farm
Sadberge Hall
Spring House Farm
Hardstones Farm
MILL LANE
Mill Hill Farm
B6279
South Burdon
White House Farm
SADBERGE ROAD
LINGFIELD CL
LINGFIELD WY
DUDLEY RD
ALLINGTON WAY
LINGFIELD WAY
MORTON RD
PALMS CT
BMI Woodlands
WILD RD
Midway Farm
CHELTENHAM CT
ST GEORGE'S GATE
Highfield
High Goosepool Farm
West Moor
West Gate Fox Covert
Morton Palms Farm
Palm Bridge
DL2
West Hartburn Village
Long Plantation
Westgate Farm
Maxgate Farm
HARPERS TR
HAXBY RD
HEATHFIELD PK
STATION ROAD
WOODLANDS GN
SHANNON LEA
STANSTED GR
OAKTREE JUNC
Foster House
Low Goosepool Farm
Sewage Works
B6280
A67
Morton Grange
Middleton St George
Resr
WOOLSINGTON DRIVE
YARM ROAD
SWAIN CT
ALEXANDRIA DR
FAIRFAX RD
WASHINGTON AVE
YARM ROAD
THE OAKS
Priory Middleton St George
Tees-side Airport
AVIATION WAY
Durham Tees Valley Airport
PIONEER CL
ALDERMAN BEST RD
Maidendale Farm
St George's CE Acad
Stodhoe Farm
Dinsdale
THE BEECHES
THE SPINNEY 1
DENVER DR 2
ASHDALE CL
OAK TREE CL
THE CRES
Oak Tree
Middleton Hall
THE WATERSIDE
Thorntree Farm
THORNTREE GD
CHAPEL ST
PINE TREE GR
High Scrog Farm
Morton Farm
1 ST MARGARETS CL
2 ST ANNES GDNS
Sewage Works
Robinson's Plantation
NEASHAM ROAD
Hunger Hill Farm
MIDDLETON LANE
THE PADDOCK
COATHAM AV
DESMOND RD
East Flat Plantation
HUNTERS GN
CASTLE CL
CHURCH LA
CHURCH CL
CEDAR GR
ROPNER GDNS
1 THE OAKLANDS
2 EAST VIEW
ARCHER RD
HILL RISE
Middleton One Row
Motte
Low Maidendale Farm
Woodhead Farm
Dinsdale Park
Brass Castle Farm
Sewage Works
Featherstone House
CH
Dinsdale Wood
Over Dinsdale Grange
THE FRONT
River Tees
West Middleton Farm
East Middleton Farm
Birch Carr Plantation
Over Dinsdale Hall
Church House Farm
TS16
Neasham Springs
Cold Comfort Farm
Manor House
Over Dinsdale Wood
Earthworks
Trafford Hill
Stonybank Plantation
Low Dinsdale
Howe Hill Cottages
Low Middleton
Dibdale Plantation
DIBDALE ROAD
Crosshill Wood
Low Neasham Springs
THE CLOSE
Neasham
NEASHAM HILL
Neasham Hill Farm
Teesside Way
Rose Hill
Low Moor Farm
Fatten Hill
NEASHAM RD
NEW LA
TEESWAY
Hill Top House
Hill House
Spa Wells (Sulphur)
Scarhill Plantation
The Gill
Newsham Grange
HURWORTH RD
Paddock Wood
SOCKBURN LA
Black Wood
8
17
7
16
6
15
5
14
4
13
3
12
2
11
1
10
32
33
34
35
36
37

C4
1 GRENDON GDNS
2 THE GREENWAY
3 CEDARWOOD
4 POUNTEYS CL
5 WESTACRES
6 DINSDALE CT
7 DINSDALE CL
8 THE MEADOWS
9 MT PLEASANT CL
10 FARNBOROUGH CT
11 RINGWAY GR
12 YEADON WALK
13 HEATHROW CL
14 MANSTON CT
15 PRESTWICK CT
16 THORNTREE VILLAS

Scale: 1¾ inches to 1 mile

0 ¼ ½ mile

0 250m 500m 750m 1 km

D8
1 LEYBURN GR
2 HACKFORTH RD
3 SKEEBY CL
4 WOODHALL GR
5 OAKTREE GR
6 LEIGHTON RD
7 FEARBY RD
8 BOLDRON CL
9 BIRKDALE RD
10 ARRATHORNE RD

E8
1 BRANKSOME GR
2 REETH RD
3 WOODSIDE GR
4 KENTON CL
5 JESMOND GR
6 PARKWOOD DR
7 HARPER TERR
8 FRASER RD

6

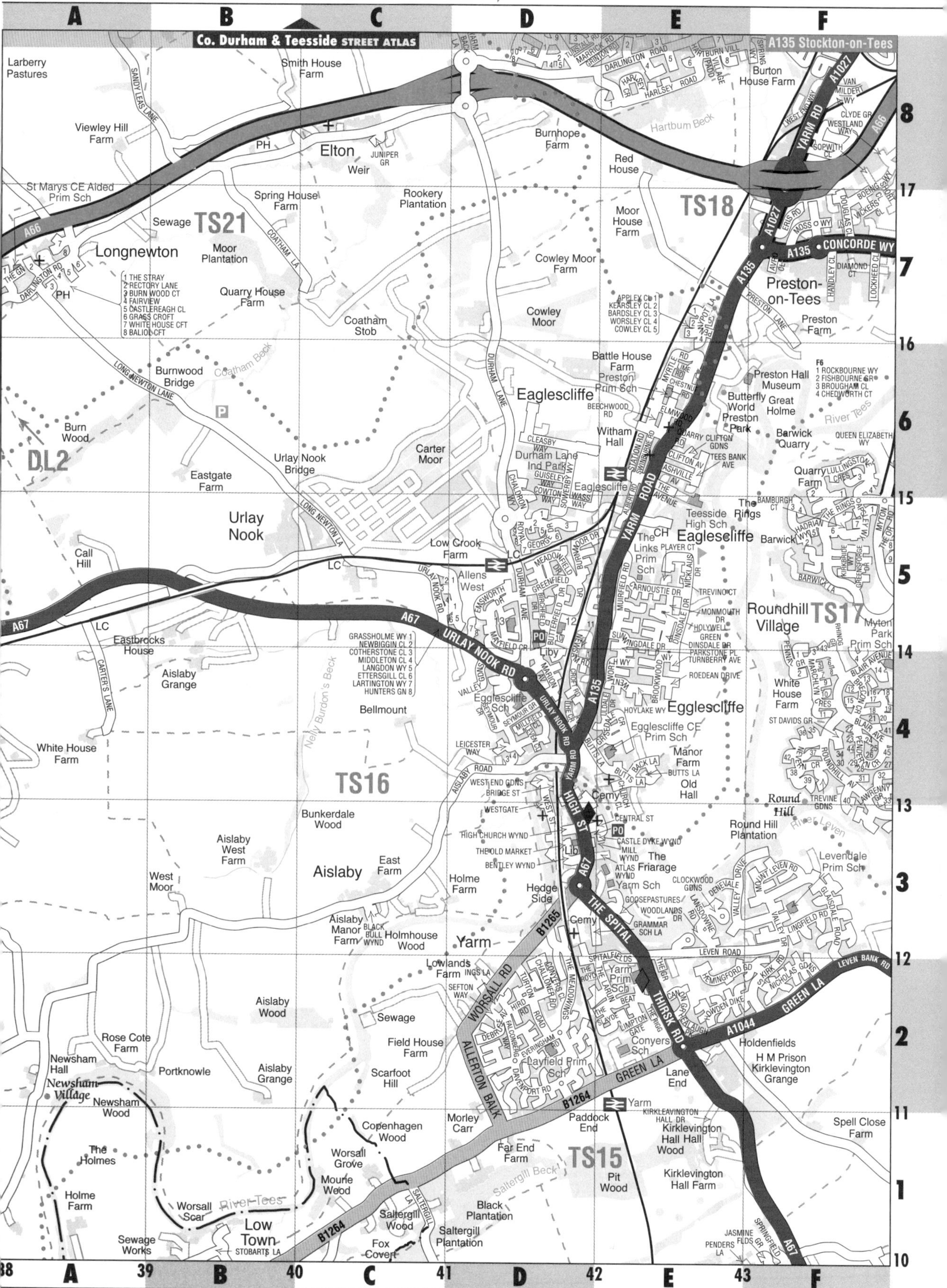

D4
1 CLEVELAND GD
2 SOUTH VW
3 BURDON WY
4 CARR BRIDGE CL

D5
1 PEASE CT
2 DILIGENCE WY
3 BLACK DIAMOND WY
4 CARRIAGE WK
5 LOCOMOTION CT
6 GRAINGER CL
7 TREVITHICK CL
8 BURDALE CL
9 TALISMAN CL
10 ABBEYFIELD DR
11 WEST VW TERR
12 Junction Farm Prim Sch
13 Durham Lane Prim Sch

F4
1 BRONABER CL
2 BALA CL
3 RHOBELL VW
4 SNOWDON GR
5 MERIONETH CL
6 GLYDER CT
7 DOVEY CT
8 CONWY GR
9 GARMON CL
10 CAMBRIAN CT
11 HARLECH CT
12 DINAS CT
13 SUGAR LOAF CL
14 CRADOC GR
15 CENNON GR
16 LIBANUS CT
17 VAYNOR DR
18 BEACONS LA
19 TALYBONT GR
20 CRIBYN CL
21 USK CT
22 BLORENGE CT
23 GILWERN CT
24 CLYDACH GR
25 TRECASTELL
26 HENRHYD CL
27 LT AYTON LA
28 MORLAIS CT
29 HONDDU CT
30 ST BRIDES CT
31 PRESELI GR
32 TALBENNY GR
33 PENBERRY GDNS
34 ST DAVIDS GR
35 NOLTON CT
36 NEWGALE CL
37 HASGUARD WY
38 RAMSEY GDNS
39 CALDEY GDNS
40 CROSSWELL PK
41 ABERBRAN CT
42 NEWPORT CL
43 ARENNIG CT
44 HATTERALL CT
45 TARELL CT

24

6

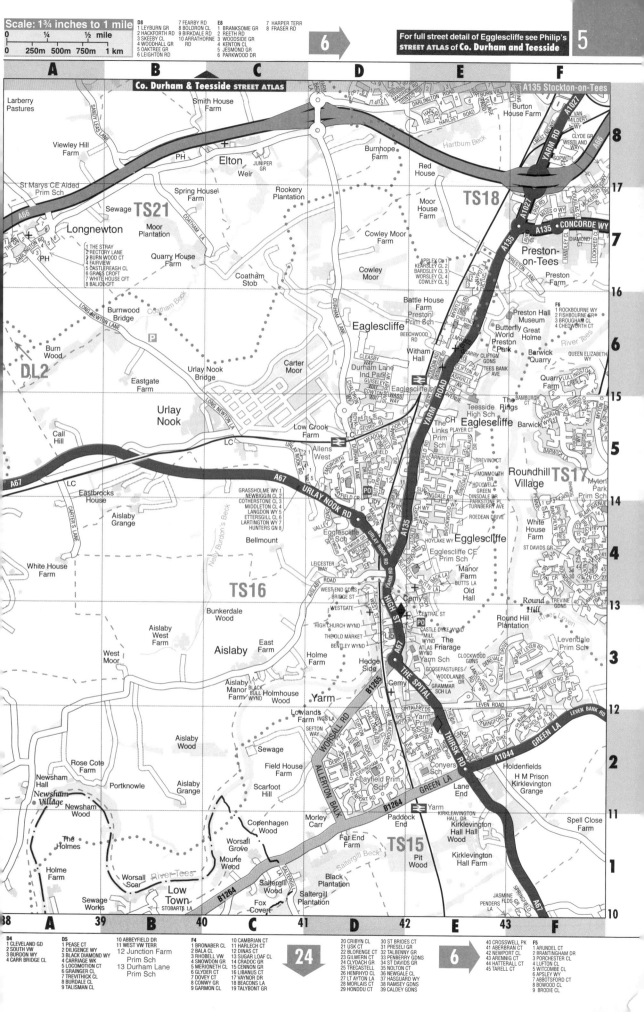

F5
1 ARUNDEL CT
2 BRANTINGHAM DR
3 PORCHESTER CL
4 LUFTON CL
5 WITCOMBE CL
6 APSLEY WY
7 ABBOTSFORD CT
8 BOWOOD CL
9 BRODIE CL

A5
1 BURGHLEY DR
2 BROADLANDS
3 LITTLE PASTURE
4 THE PASTURE
5 THE ORCHARD
6 CHURCH FIELD WY
7 HILLWAY
8 BARWICK FIELDS
9 BARWICK CL
10 BARWICK VW
11 WARBLER CL
12 THE ORCHARD
13 BURDON GARTH

5

A6
1 HOMESTEAD GARTH
2 STONEBRIDGE CRES
3 HOUGHTON BANKS
4 BROUGH FIELD CL
5 LEAZON HL
6 BRAMFIELD WY
7 TRENHOLME CL
8 LAMBFIELD WY

B8
1 LINCOLN PL
2 MALTBY PL
3 HENRIETTA CL
4 LINDISFARNE AVE
5 NORTHALLERTON RD
6 GUISBOROUGH RD

D8
1 ROCKINGHAM CT
2 CRANAGE CL
3 THORNFIELD RD

F8
1 HOLLYHURST AVE
2 EVERGREEN WK
3 SALTERSGILL CL
4 ALMOND CT

Scale: 1¾ inches to 1 mile
0 ¼ ½ mile
0 250m 500m 750m 1 km

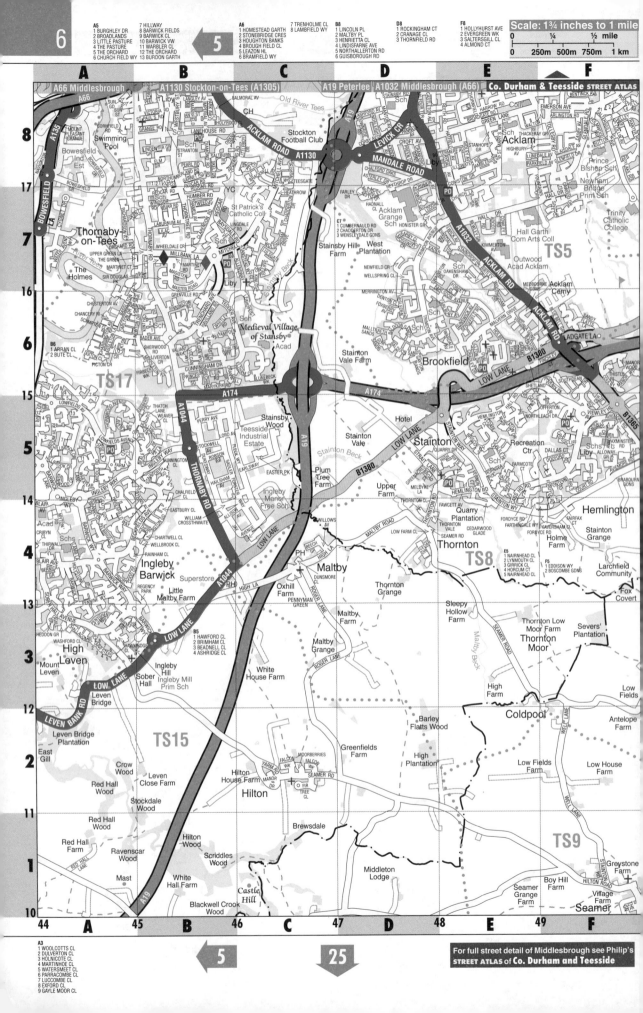

A3
1 WOOLCOTTS CL
2 DULVERTON CL
3 HOLNICOTE CL
4 MARTINHOE CL
5 WATERSMEET CL
6 PARRACOMBE CL
7 LUCCOMBE CL
8 EXFORD CL
9 GAYLE MOOR CL

Scale: 1¾ inches to 1 mile
0 ¼ ½ mile
0 250m 500m 750m 1 km

B6
1 THE WICKETS
2 MEMORIAL DR
3 CLEVELAND DR

B8
1 CHANTRY CL
2 CHADWELL AVE
3 HIGHMEAD WK

C8
1 MARTON GR
2 BOURNEMOUTH AVE

D8
1 DUNHOLM AVE
2 APPLETREE GDNS

8

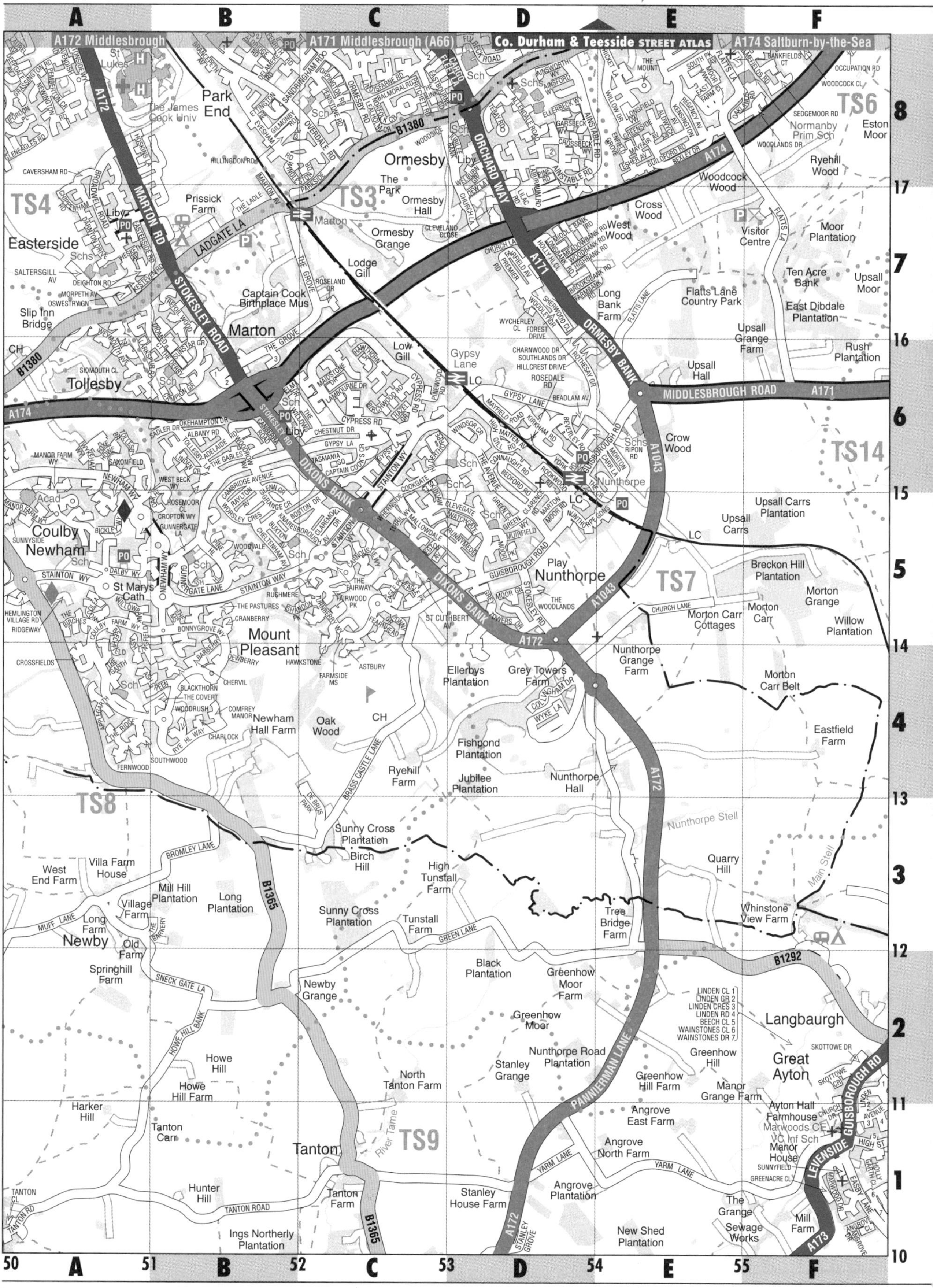

For full street detail of Middlesbrough see Philip's STREET ATLAS of Co. Durham and Teesside

26

8

D6
1 REDWING RISING
2 PEREGRINE CT
3 Galley Hill Prim Sch

F7
1 WHELDRAKE CL
2 HESLINGTON GDNS
3 HUBY CT
4 BROMPTON AVE
5 ALLERSTON WY
6 HOVINGHAM DR
7 MONKTON RISE
8 THIRLBY WY
9 EDSTON DR
10 SKELTON CT
11 CARLTON CL
12 MINISKIP CL
13 APPLETON CL
14 WOODALE CL
15 SLEIGHTS CT
16 Prior Pursglove Coll
17 Askham Bryan Coll
18 Chaloner Prim Sch

Scale: 1¾ inches to 1 mile
0 ¼ ½ mile
0 250m 500m 750m 1 km

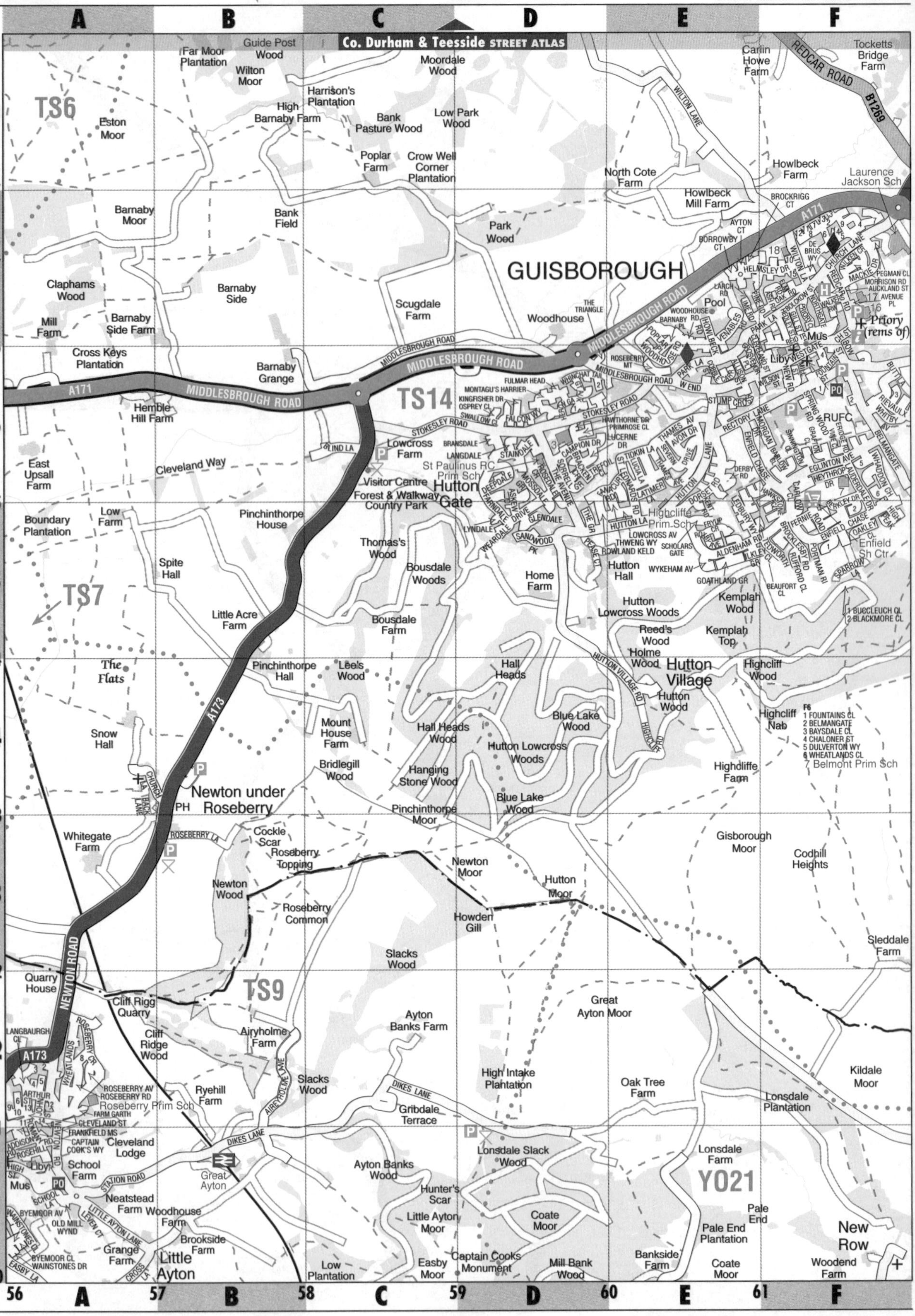

A2
1 ORCHARD CL
2 BRADLEYS TERR
3 CHURCHILL CL
4 SPENCE CT
5 ROWAN DR
6 CENTRAL WY
7 CALIFORNIA GR
8 ROSEBERRY DR
9 OAKLANDS
10 THE HAWTHORNS
11 ROMANY RD
12 WOODBINE CL
13 WHINSTONE VW
14 EDWARD KITCHING TERR

For full street detail of Guisborough see Philip's STREET ATLAS of Co. Durham and Teesside

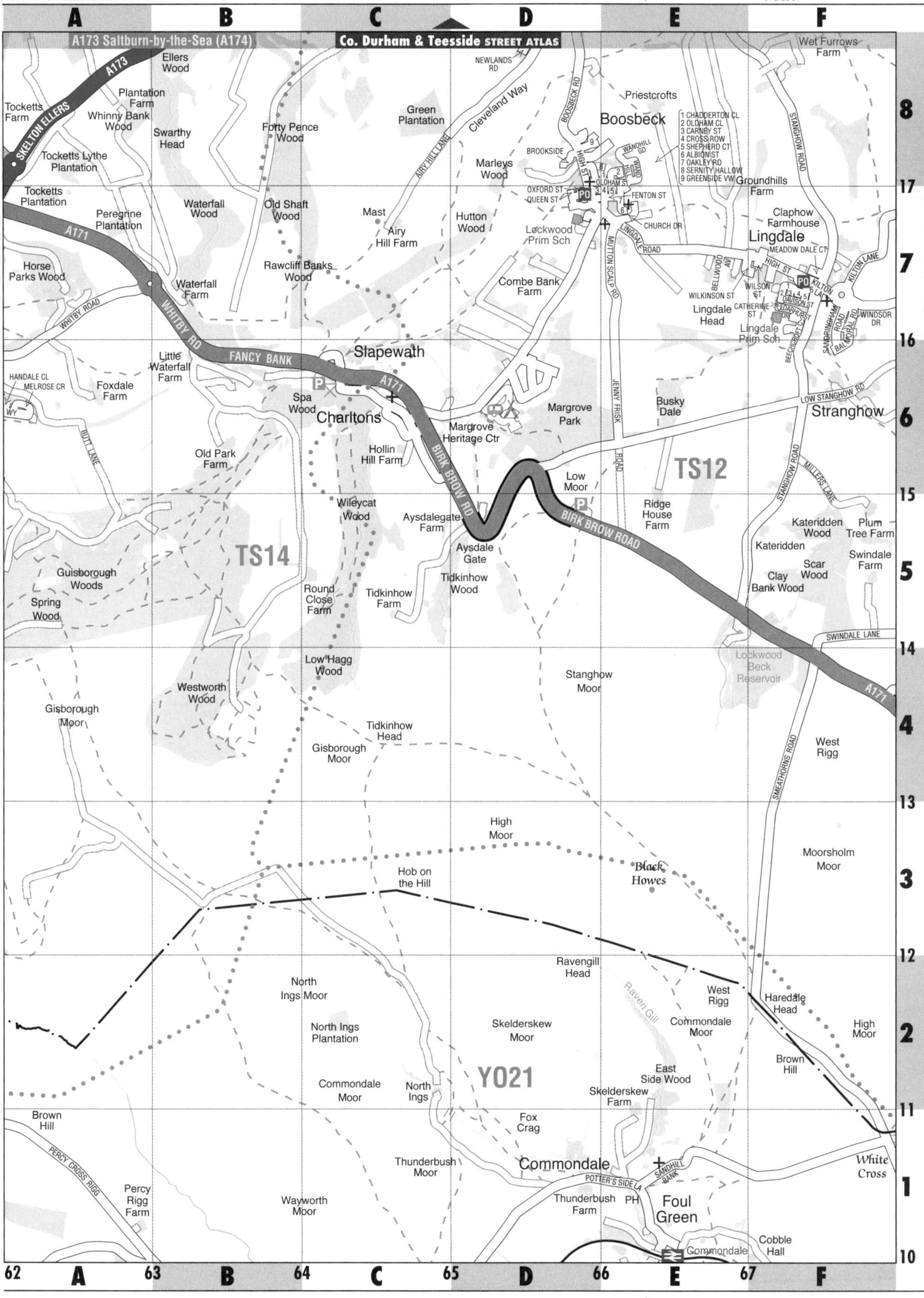
A B C D E F
A173 Saltburn-by-the-Sea (A174)
Co. Durham & Teesside STREET ATLAS
8
17
7
16
6
15
5
14
4
13
3
12
2
11
1
10
62 63 64 65 66 67
Ellers Wood
Plantation Farm
Whinny Bank Wood
Swarthy Head
Tocketts Farm
SKELTON ELLERS
A173
Tocketts Lythe Plantation
Tocketts Plantation
Peregrine Plantation
Waterfall Wood
Forty Pence Wood
Old Shaft Wood
Green Plantation
Cleveland Way
NEWLANDS RD
AIRY HILL LANE
Marleys Wood
Mast
Airy Hill Farm
Hutton Wood
Rawcliff Banks Wood
Horse Parks Wood
A171
WHITBY ROAD
Waterfall Farm
WHITBY RD
FANCY BANK
Little Waterfall Farm
Slapewath
Spa Wood
Charltons
HANDALE CL
MELROSE CR
Foxdale Farm
BUTT LANE
Old Park Farm
Hollin Hill Farm
BIRK BROW RD
Margrove Heritage Ctr
Margrove Park
Combe Bank Farm
Lockwood Prim Sch
Priestcrofts
Boosbeck
BOOSBECK RD
BROOKSIDE
HIGH ST
OXFORD ST
QUEEN ST
OLDHAM ST
FENTON ST
WANDHILL GD
CHURCH DR
LINGDALE ROAD
MUTTON SCALP RD
JENNY FRISK ROAD
1 CHADDERTON CL
2 OLDHAM CL
3 CARNBY ST
4 CROSS ROW
5 SHEPHERD CT
6 ALBION ST
7 OAKLEY RD
8 SERNITY HALLOW
9 GREENSIDE VW
Groundhills Farm
Claphow Farmhouse
Lingdale
MEADOW DALE CT
HIGH ST
BELLWOOD AV
WILKINSON ST
WILSON ST
CATHERINE ST
DAVISON ST
CEDARHURST DR
Lingdale Head
Lingdale Prim Sch
BEECHCROFT CL
KILTON LA
KILTON LANE
SANDRINGHAM ROAD
BALMORAL RD
WINDSOR DR
Wet Furrows Farm
STANGHOW ROAD
LOW STANGHOW RD
Stanghow
Busky Dale
TS12
Low Moor
Ridge House Farm
MILLERS LANE
Kateridden Wood
Plum Tree Farm
Kateridden
Swindale Farm
Scar Wood
Clay Bank Wood
BIRK BROW ROAD
Wileycat Wood
Aysdalegate Farm
Aysdale Gate
Tidkinhow Wood
TS14
Guisborough Woods
Spring Wood
Round Close Farm
Tidkinhow Farm
SWINDALE LANE
Lockwood Beck Reservoir
Low Hagg Wood
Westworth Wood
Stanghow Moor
Gisborough Moor
Tidkinhow Head
West Rigg
SMEATHORNS ROAD
High Moor
Moorsholm Moor
Black Howes
Hob on the Hill
Ravengill Head
Raven Gill
West Rigg
Haredale Head
North Ings Moor
North Ings Plantation
Skelderskew Moor
Commondale Moor
High Moor
Brown Hill
YO21
East Side Wood
Commondale Moor
North Ings
Skelderskew Farm
Brown Hill
Fox Crag
PERCY CROSS RIGG
Thunderbush Moor
Commondale
SANDHILL BANK
White Cross
POTTER'S SIDE LA
Percy Rigg Farm
Wayworth Moor
Thunderbush Farm
PH
Foul Green
Commondale
Cobble Hall

Scale: 1¾ inches to 1 mile
0 ¼ ½ mile
0 250m 500m 750m 1 km

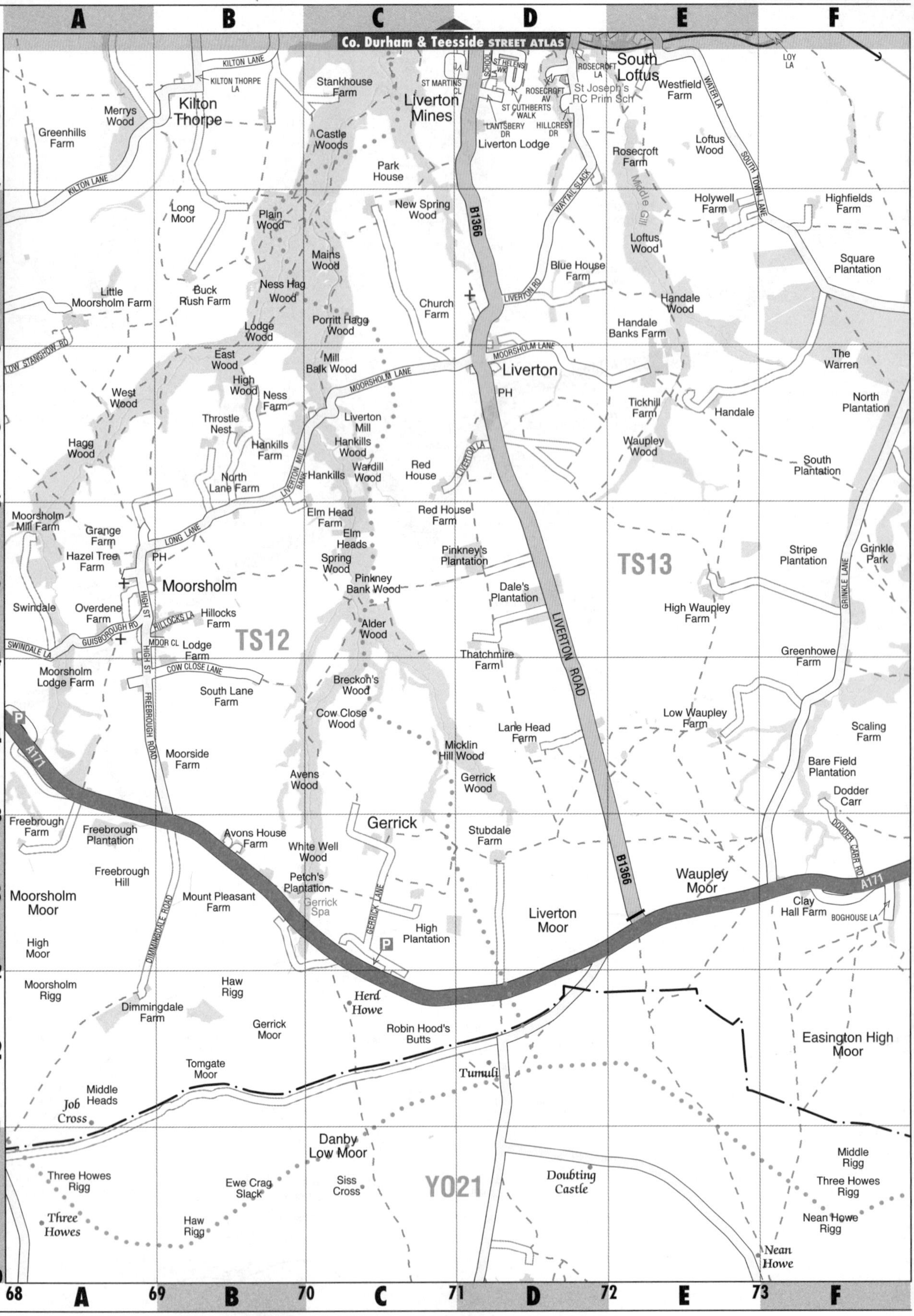
A B C D E F
Co. Durham & Teesside STREET ATLAS
8 17 7 16 6 15 5 14 4 13 3 12 2 11 1 10
68 69 70 71 72 73
KILTON LANE
KILTON THORPE LA
Merrys Wood
Kilton Thorpe
Greenhills Farm
Stankhouse Farm
Castle Woods
ST MARTINS CL
Liverton Mines
SCHOOL WK
ST HELENS WK
ROSECROFT LA
ROSECROFT AV
ST CUTHBERTS WALK
LANTSBERY DR
HILLCREST DR
Liverton Lodge
South Loftus
St Joseph's RC Prim Sch
Westfield Farm
WATER LA
LOY LA
Loftus Wood
Rosecroft Farm
SOUTH TOWN LANE
Park House
KILTON LANE
Long Moor
Plain Wood
New Spring Wood
B1366
WAYTAIL SLACK
Middle Gill
Holywell Farm
Highfields Farm
Loftus Wood
Mains Wood
Blue House Farm
Square Plantation
Little Moorsholm Farm
Buck Rush Farm
Ness Hag Wood
Church Farm
LIVERTON RD
Handale Wood
Porritt Hagg Wood
Lodge Wood
Handale Banks Farm
LOW STANGHOW RD
East Wood
Mill Balk Wood
MOORSHOLM LANE
MOORSHOLM LANE
Liverton
The Warren
West Wood
High Wood
Ness Farm
PH
Tickhill Farm
North Plantation
Throstle Nest
Liverton Mill
Handale
Hagg Wood
Hankills Farm
Hankills Wood
Waupley Wood
Wardill Wood
Red House
LIVERTON LA
South Plantation
North Lane Farm
LIVERTON MILL BANK
Hankills
Moorsholm Mill Farm
Elm Head Farm
Red House Farm
Grange Farm
Elm Heads
LONG LANE
Hazel Tree Farm
PH
Spring Wood
Pinkney's Plantation
TS13
Stripe Plantation
Grinkle Park
Moorsholm
Pinkney Bank Wood
Dale's Plantation
GRINKLE LANE
Swindale
Overdene Farm
HIGH ST
Hillocks Farm
HILLOCKS LA
High Waupley Farm
GUISBOROUGH RD
TS12
Alder Wood
SWINDALE LA
MOOR CL
Lodge Farm
Thatchmire Farm
LIVERTON ROAD
Greenhowe Farm
Moorsholm Lodge Farm
HIGH ST
COW CLOSE LANE
South Lane Farm
Breckon's Wood
Cow Close Wood
Low Waupley Farm
P
FREEBROUGH ROAD
Lane Head Farm
Scaling Farm
A171
Moorside Farm
Micklin Hill Wood
Bare Field Plantation
Avens Wood
Gerrick Wood
Dodder Carr
Freebrough Farm
Freebrough Plantation
Avons House Farm
Gerrick
Stubdale Farm
DODDER CARR RD
White Well Wood
B1366
Waupley Moor
Freebrough Hill
Petch's Plantation
A171
Moorsholm Moor
DIMMINGDALE ROAD
Mount Pleasant Farm
Gerrick Spa
GERRICK LANE
Liverton Moor
Clay Hall Farm
BOGHOUSE LA
High Moor
P
High Plantation
Moorsholm Rigg
Haw Rigg
Herd Howe
Dimmingdale Farm
Gerrick Moor
Robin Hood's Butts
Easington High Moor
Tomgate Moor
Tumuli
Middle Heads
Job Cross
Danby Low Moor
Middle Rigg
Three Howes Rigg
Ewe Crag Slack
Siss Cross
YO21
Doubting Castle
Three Howes Rigg
Three Howes
Haw Rigg
Nean Howe Rigg
Nean Howe

Scale: 1¾ inches to 1 mile
0 ¼ ½ mile
0 250m 500m 750m 1 km

A8
1 RYELANDS PARK
2 MEADOWLANDS CL
3 OATLANDS GR
4 WHEATLANDS DR
5 PARK LA
6 TWIZZIE GILL VW

12 13

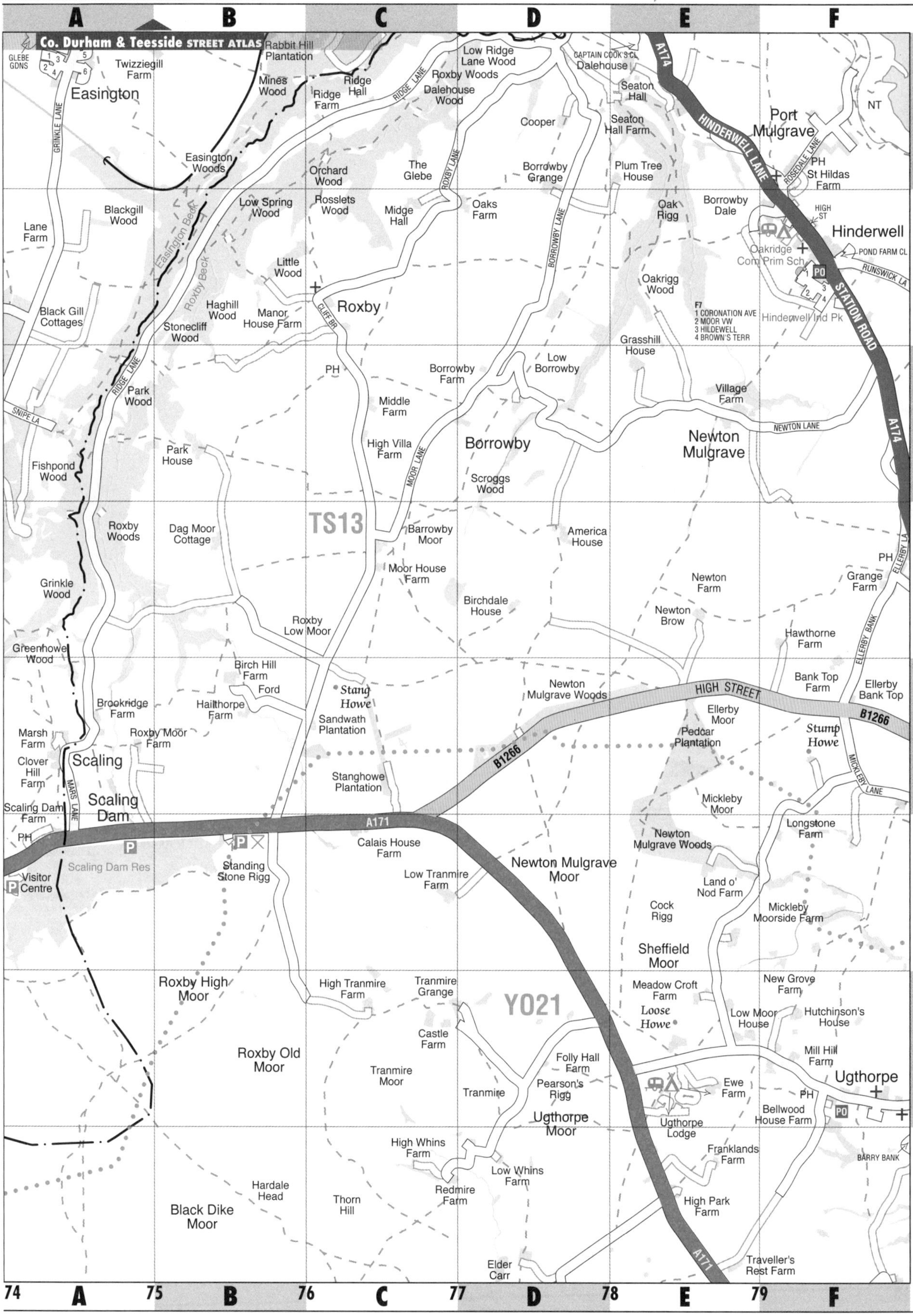

30 12

11

Scale: 1¾ inches to 1 mile
0 ¼ ½ mile
0 250m 500m 750m 1 km

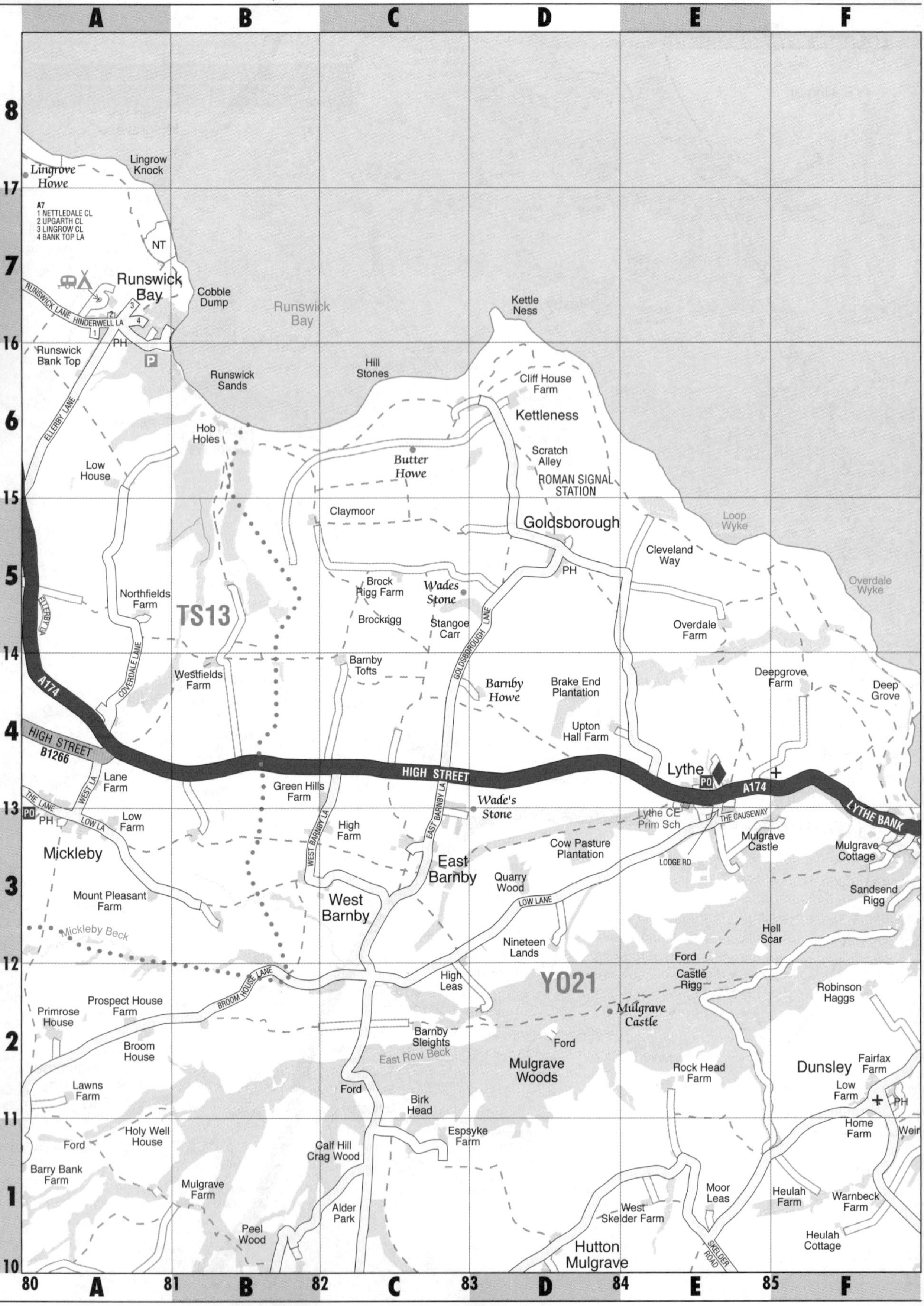

A B C D E F
8
17
7
16
6
15
5
14
4
13
3
12
2
11
1
10
80 81 82 83 84 85
Lingrove Howe
Lingrow Knock
A7
1 NETTLEDALE CL
2 UPGARTH CL
3 LINGROW CL
4 BANK TOP LA
NT
Runswick Bay
Cobble Dump
Runswick Bay
Kettle Ness
RUNSWICK LANE
HINDERWELL LA
PH
P
Runswick Bank Top
Runswick Sands
Hill Stones
Cliff House Farm
Kettleness
ELLERBY LANE
Hob Holes
Butter Howe
Scratch Alley
ROMAN SIGNAL STATION
Low House
Claymoor
Goldsborough
Loop Wyke
Cleveland Way
PH
Brock Rigg Farm
Wades Stone
Overdale Wyke
Northfields Farm
TS13
Brockrigg
Stangoe Carr
Overdale Farm
ELLERBY LA
COVERDALE LANE
GOLDSBOROUGH LANE
Westfields Farm
Barnby Tofts
Barnby Howe
Brake End Plantation
Deepgrove Farm
Deep Grove
A174
Upton Hall Farm
HIGH STREET
B1266
HIGH STREET
Lythe
PO
A174
LYTHE BANK
Lane Farm
WEST LA
Green Hills Farm
Wade's Stone
THE LANE
PO
PH
LOW LA
Low Farm
High Farm
WEST BARNBY LA
EAST BARNBY LA
Lythe CE Prim Sch
THE CAUSEWAY
Mulgrave Castle
Mulgrave Cottage
Mickleby
Cow Pasture Plantation
LODGE RD
East Barnby
Quarry Wood
Mount Pleasant Farm
West Barnby
LOW LANE
Sandsend Rigg
Mickleby Beck
Nineteen Lands
Hell Scar
Ford
Castle Rigg
BROOM HOUSE LANE
High Leas
YO21
Robinson Haggs
Primrose House
Prospect House Farm
Mulgrave Castle
Broom House
Barnby Sleights
Ford
East Row Beck
Mulgrave Woods
Rock Head Farm
Dunsley
Fairfax Farm
Low Farm
PH
Lawns Farm
Ford
Birk Head
Home Farm
Weir
Holy Well House
Ford
Espsyke Farm
Calf Hill Crag Wood
Barry Bank Farm
Mulgrave Farm
Alder Park
Moor Leas
Heulah Farm
Warnbeck Farm
West Skelder Farm
Peel Wood
SKELDER ROAD
Heulah Cottage
Hutton Mulgrave

11

31

Scale: 1¾ inches to 1 mile
0 ¼ ½ mile
0 250m 500m 750m 1 km

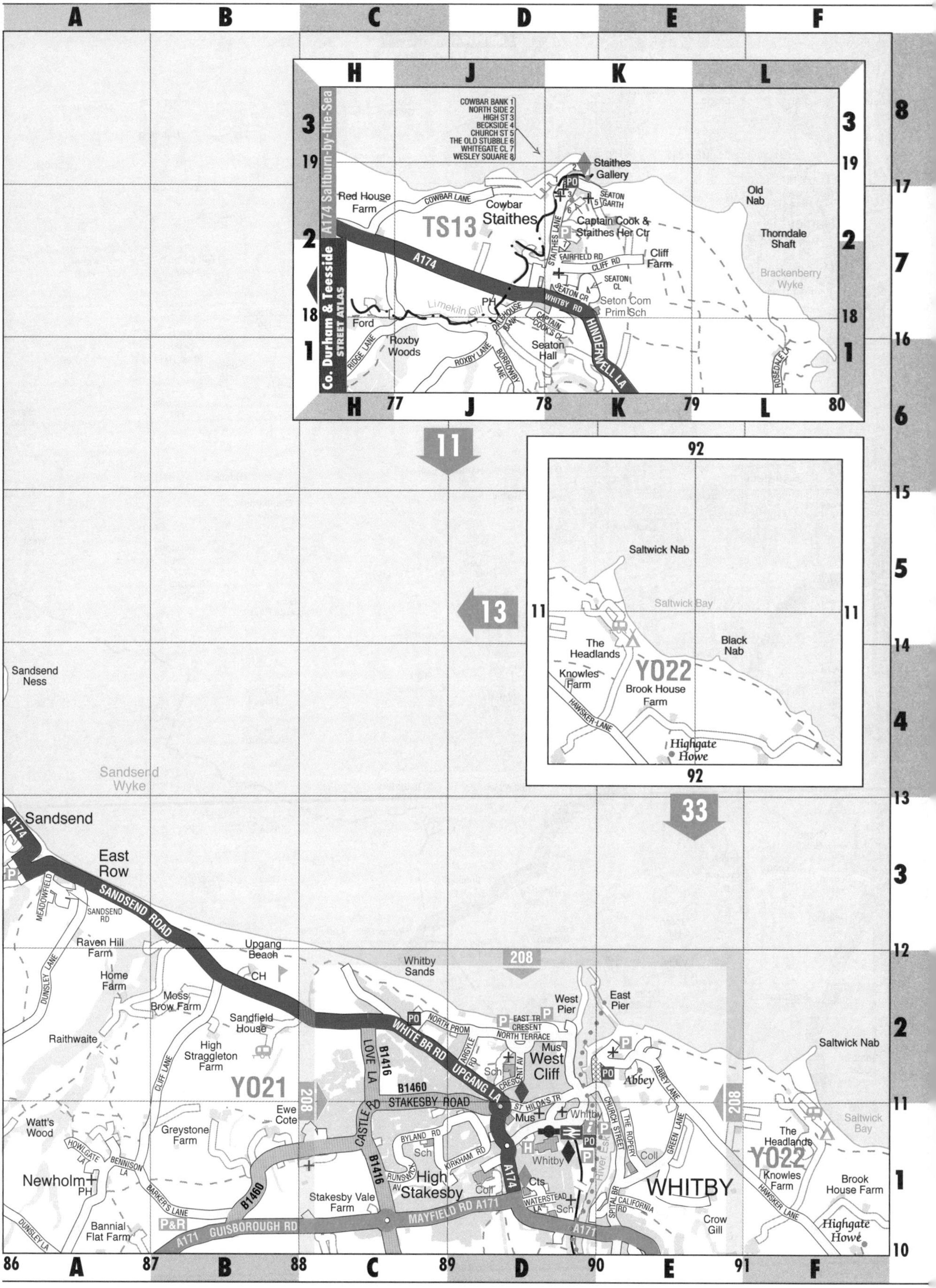

Co. Durham & Teesside STREET ATLAS
A174 Saltburn-by-the-Sea
COWBAR BANK 1
NORTH SIDE 2
HIGH ST 3
BECKSIDE 4
CHURCH ST 5
THE OLD STUBBLE 6
WHITEGATE CL 7
WESLEY SQUARE 8
Staithes Gallery
Red House Farm
Cowbar
Staithes
TS13
Captain Cook & Staithes Her Ctr
Old Nab
Thorndale Shaft
Brackenberry Wyke
Cliff Farm
Seton Com Prim Sch
Roxby Woods
Seaton Hall
Ford
Limekiln Gill
HINDERWELL LA
Saltwick Nab
Saltwick Bay
The Headlands
Black Nab
Knowles Farm
YO22
Brook House Farm
Highgate Howe
HAWSKER LANE
Sandsend Ness
Sandsend Wyke
Sandsend
East Row
SANDSEND ROAD
Raven Hill Farm
Home Farm
Upgang Beach
Moss Brow Farm
Whitby Sands
Sandfield House
High Straggleton Farm
Raithwaite
YO21
Watt's Wood
Greystone Farm
Ewe Cote
Newholm
Bannial Flat Farm
Stakesby Vale Farm
High Stakesby
West Cliff
West Pier
East Pier
Abbey
WHITBY
Crow Gill
River Esk
A171 GUISBOROUGH RD
MAYFIELD RD A171
STAKESBY ROAD
WHITE BR RD
UPGANG LA

11
13
33
32

For full street detail of the highlighted area see page 208.

Scale: 1¾ inches to 1 mile
0 ¼ ½ mile
0 250m 500m 750m 1 km

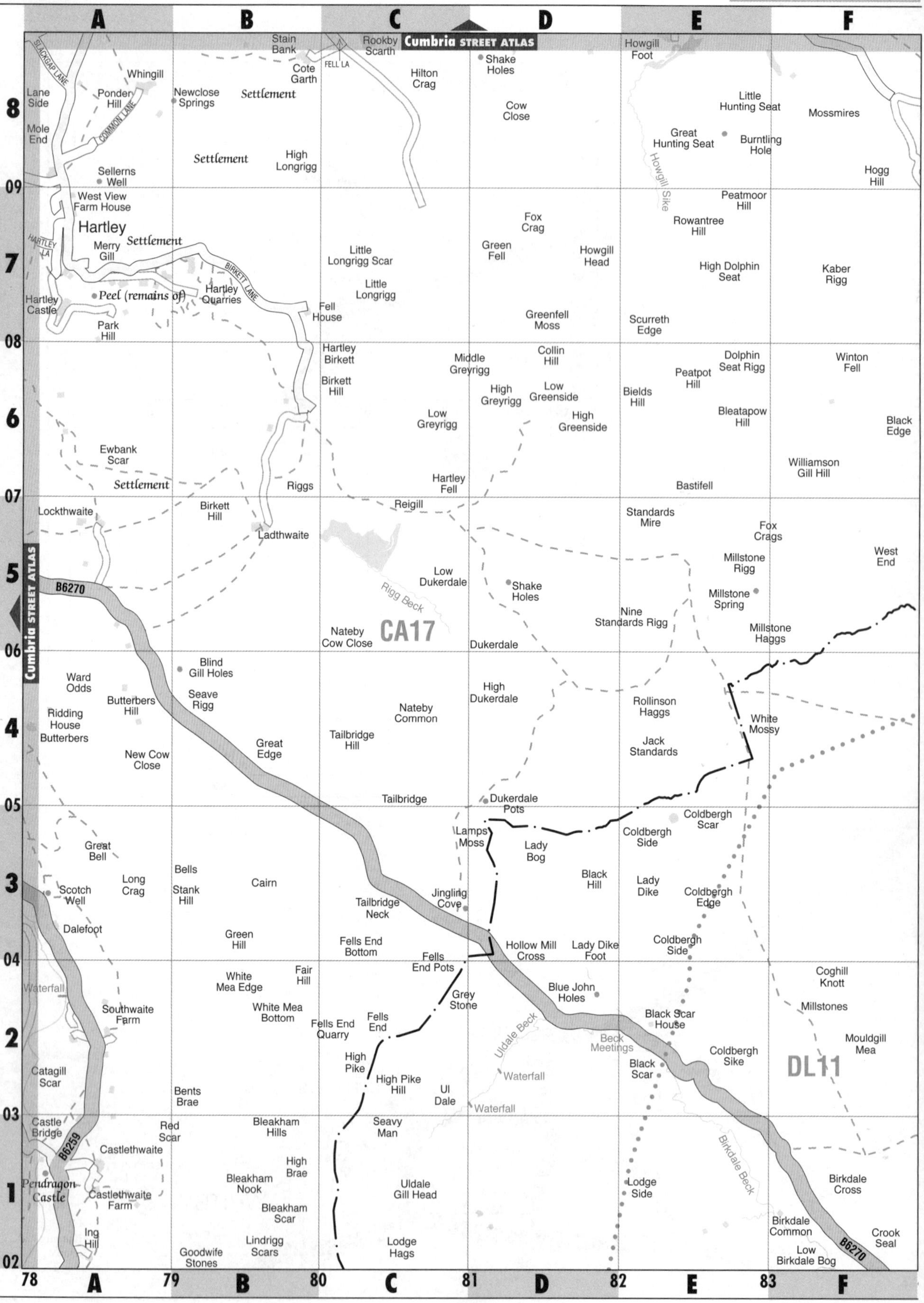

34

Scale: 1¾ inches to 1 mile
0 ¼ ½ mile
0 250m 500m 750m 1 km

16

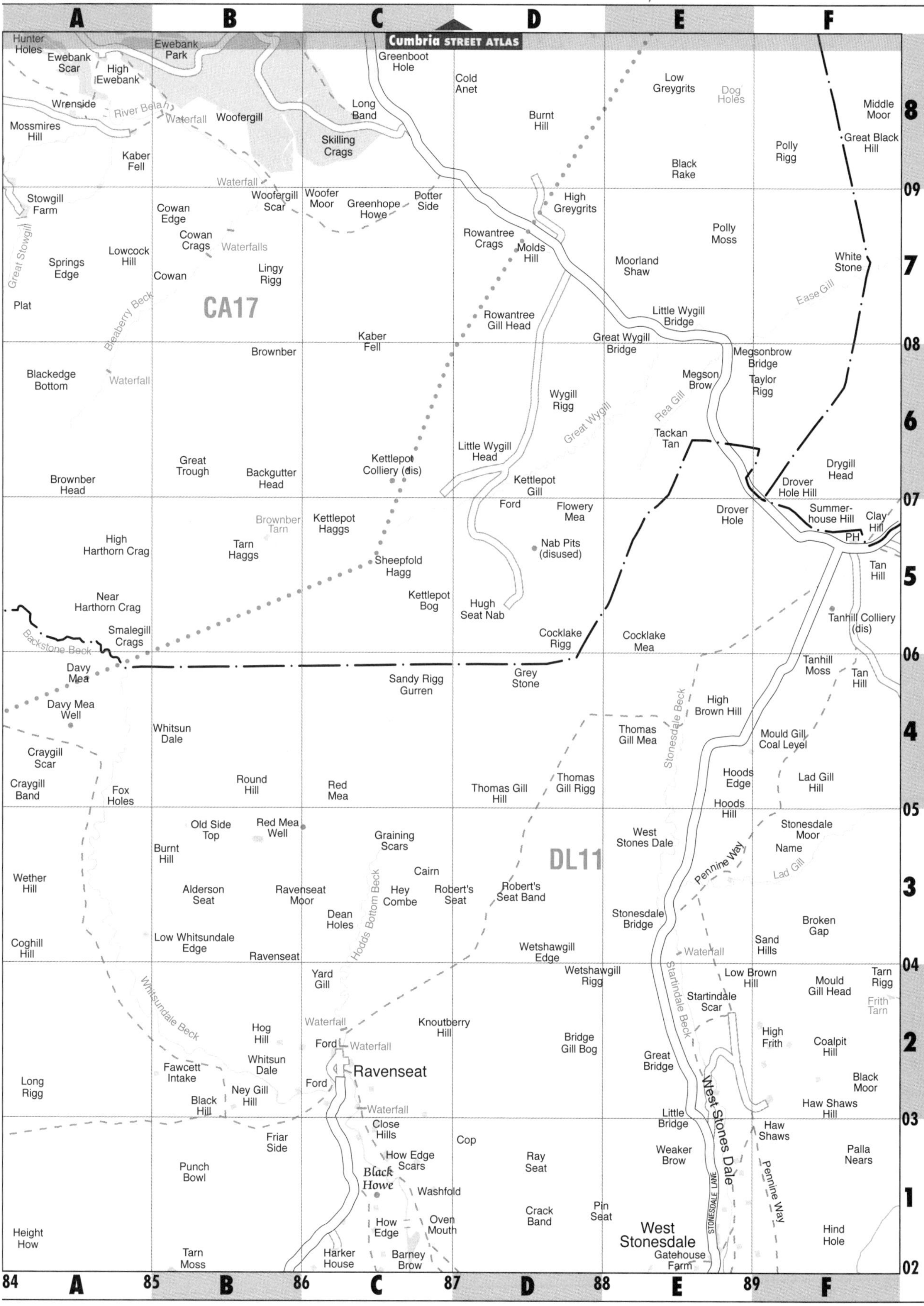
A
B
C
D
E
F
Cumbria STREET ATLAS
Hunter Holes
Ewebank Scar
High Ewebank
Ewebank Park
Greenboot Hole
Cold Anet
Low Greygrits
Dog Holes
Wrenside
River Belah
Waterfall
Woofergill
Long Band
Burnt Hill
Middle Moor
Mossmires Hill
Skilling Crags
Great Black Hill
Polly Rigg
Kaber Fell
Black Rake
Waterfall
Stowgill Farm
Cowan Edge
Woofergill Scar
Woofer Moor
Greenhope Howe
Potter Side
High Greygrits
Polly Moss
Great Stowgill
Cowan Crags
Waterfalls
Rowantree Crags
Molds Hill
Springs Edge
Lowcock Hill
Cowan
Lingy Rigg
Moorland Shaw
White Stone
Plat
Breaberry Beck
CA17
Rowantree Gill Head
Ease Gill
Little Wygill Bridge
Kaber Fell
Great Wygill Bridge
Brownber
Megsonbrow Bridge
Blackedge Bottom
Waterfall
Megson Brow
Taylor Rigg
Wygill Rigg
Great Wygill
Rea Gill
Tackan Tan
Little Wygill Head
Great Trough
Kettlepot Colliery (dis)
Drygill Head
Brownber Head
Backgutter Head
Kettlepot Gill
Drover Hole Hill
Ford
Flowery Mea
Drover Hole
Summer-house Hill
Clay Hill
High Harthorn Crag
Brownber Tarn
Kettlepot Haggs
Tarn Haggs
Nab Pits (disused)
PH
Sheepfold Hagg
Tan Hill
Near Harthorn Crag
Kettlepot Bog
Hugh Seat Nab
Tanhill Colliery (dis)
Smalegill Crags
Backstone Beck
Cocklake Rigg
Cocklake Mea
Davy Mea
Sandy Rigg Gurren
Grey Stone
Tanhill Moss
Tan Hill
Davy Mea Well
High Brown Hill
Whitsun Dale
Thomas Gill Mea
Stonesdale Beck
Mould Gill Coal Level
Craygill Scar
Craygill Band
Fox Holes
Round Hill
Red Mea
Thomas Gill Hill
Thomas Gill Rigg
Hoods Edge
Lad Gill Hill
Hoods Hill
Old Side Top
Red Mea Well
Graining Scars
West Stones Dale
Stonesdale Moor
Burnt Hill
Name
Pennine Way
DL11
Wether Hill
Cairn
Lad Gill
Alderson Seat
Ravenseat Moor
Hey Combe
Robert's Seat
Robert's Seat Band
Dean Holes
Hodds Bottom Beck
Stonesdale Bridge
Broken Gap
Coghill Hill
Low Whitsundale Edge
Ravenseat
Wetshawgill Edge
Waterfall
Sand Hills
Yard Gill
Wetshawgill Rigg
Low Brown Hill
Tarn Rigg
Whitsundale Beck
Startindale Beck
Startindale Scar
Mould Gill Head
Waterfall
Knoutberry Hill
Frith Tarn
Hog Hill
Ford
Waterfall
High Frith
Bridge Gill Bog
Coalpit Hill
Whitsun Dale
Great Bridge
Fawcett Intake
Ravenseat
Long Rigg
Ney Gill Hill
Ford
West Stones Dale
Black Moor
Black Hill
Waterfall
Haw Shaws Hill
Little Bridge
Close Hills
Haw Shaws
Friar Side
Cop
Weaker Brow
Palla Nears
How Edge Scars
Ray Seat
Punch Bowl
Black Howe
Pennine Way
Washfold
STONESDALE LANE
Crack Band
Pin Seat
How Edge
Oven Mouth
Hind Hole
Height How
West Stonesdale
Tarn Moss
Harker House
Barney Brow
Gatehouse Farm
8
09
7
08
6
07
5
06
4
05
3
04
2
03
1
02
84
85
86
87
88
89

35

16

15

Scale: 1¾ inches to 1 mile
0 ¼ ½ mile
0 250m 500m 750m 1 km

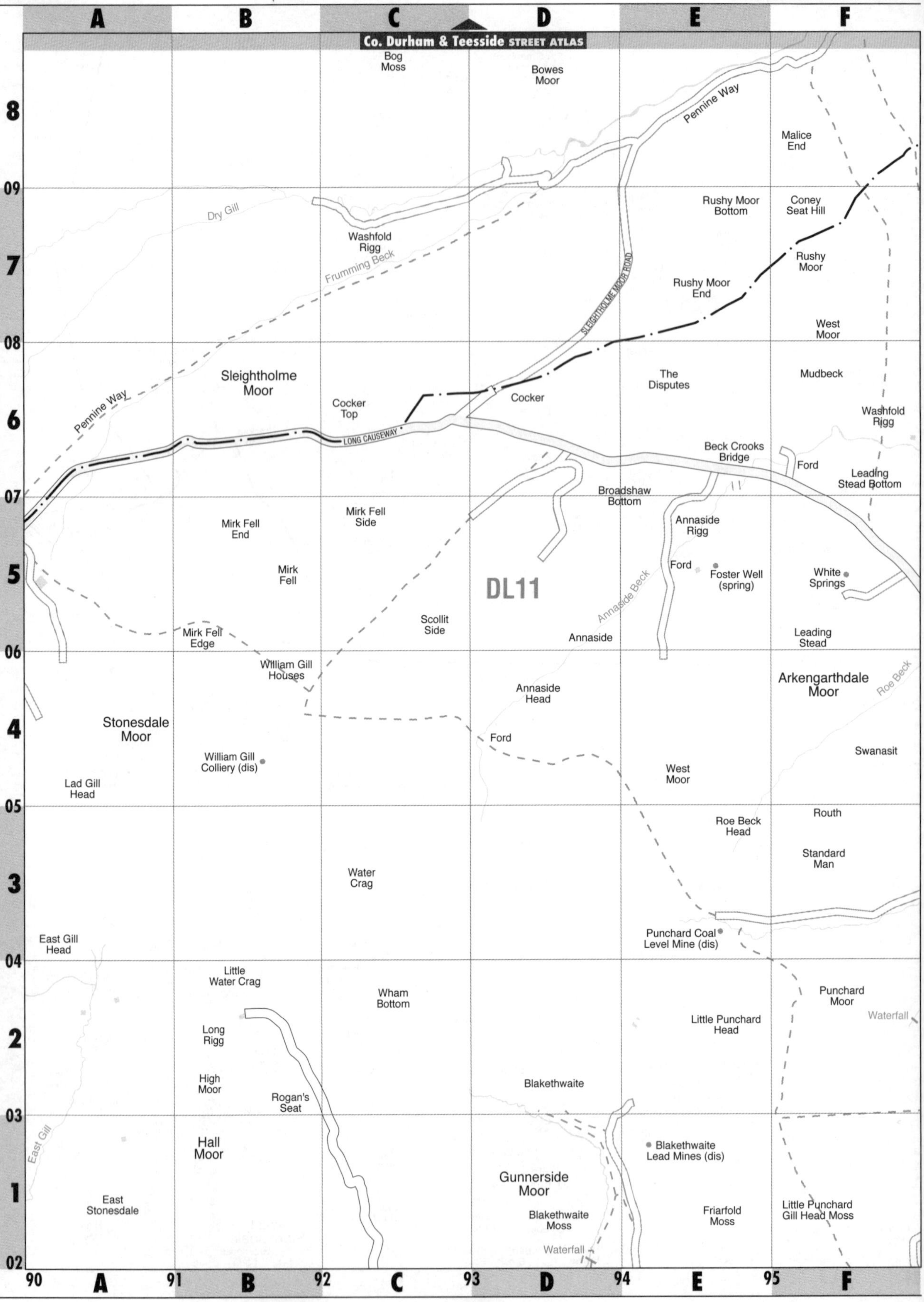
A
B
C
D
E
F
Co. Durham & Teesside STREET ATLAS
Bog Moss
Bowes Moor
Pennine Way
Malice End
Dry Gill
Rushy Moor Bottom
Coney Seat Hill
Washfold Rigg
Frumming Beck
Rushy Moor
Rushy Moor End
SLEIGHTHOLME MOOR ROAD
West Moor
Sleightholme Moor
The Disputes
Mudbeck
Pennine Way
Cocker Top
Cocker
Washfold Rigg
LONG CAUSEWAY
Beck Crooks Bridge
Ford
Leading Stead Bottom
Broadshaw Bottom
Mirk Fell End
Mirk Fell Side
Annaside Rigg
Mirk Fell
Ford
Foster Well (spring)
White Springs
DL11
Annaside Beck
Scollit Side
Mirk Fell Edge
Annaside
Leading Stead
William Gill Houses
Annaside Head
Arkengarthdale Moor
Roe Beck
Stonesdale Moor
Ford
William Gill Colliery (dis)
Swanasit
West Moor
Lad Gill Head
Roe Beck Head
Routh
Standard Man
Water Crag
Punchard Coal Level Mine (dis)
East Gill Head
Little Water Crag
Wham Bottom
Punchard Moor
Waterfall
Little Punchard Head
Long Rigg
High Moor
Blakethwaite
Rogan's Seat
East Gill
Hall Moor
Blakethwaite Lead Mines (dis)
Gunnerside Moor
East Stonesdale
Blakethwaite Moss
Friarfold Moss
Little Punchard Gill Head Moss
Waterfall
8
09
7
08
6
07
5
06
4
05
3
04
2
03
1
02
90
91
92
93
94
95

15

36

Scale: 1¾ inches to 1 mile
0 ¼ ½ mile
0 250m 500m 750m 1 km

18

A B C D E F
Co. Durham & Teesside STREET ATLAS
Bow Hills Head
Bow Hills
Bow Hills Moss
Tom Bog Rigg
Bleakhow Moss
High Seavy Rigg
Middle Bent
Waterfall
Scargill High Moor
Spanham Scar
Scargill Mine (dis)
Tarnhow Hill
White Crag Moss
White Crag
White Crag
Jinglepot Hole
Robin Dub (spring)
Long Rigg
White Crag End
Faggergill Moss
Mud Beck
West Moor
Dale Head Common
Faggergill Scar
Elsey Crag
Doorgill Head
Hoove Tarn
Cleasby Hill
Peat Moor
Shivery Scar
Hurrgill Head
Stang
Faggergill Moor
Hurrgill Rigg
Faggergill Lead Mine (dis)
Hoove
Ravens Park
DL11
New Bridge
Dale Head
Peat Moor Rigg
Hart Holes
Arndale Head
Hill Top Farm
Smithson Holes Green
Gale Head Moor
Shaw Side
STANG TOP
High Faggergill
The Rigg
Park Head
Stang Side
Roe Beck Bridge
Shepherd's Lodge
Punchard Gate House
Seal Houses Moor
Routh Top
Low Faggergill
Kitley Hill House
Shaw Farm
Dry Gill Bottom
Punchard House
Punchard Gill Bridge
Seal Houses
Dry Gill Edge
Alcock Hush Mine (dis)
Low Moor
Peat Moor Hill
Routh Level Mine (dis)
Tongue End
Whaw Bridge
Whaw
Float Lead Shafts (dis)
Ford
Whaw Gill Bridge
Little Punchard Gill
Stone's Lead Level Mine (dis)
Whaw Gill
Arkengarthdale
Wood House
High Eskeleth Farm
STANG LANE
Windegg Ings
Waterfall
Hill Side
Windegg Scar
Whaw Moor
Danby Lead Level Mine (dis)
Eskeleth Bridge
Stang Bridge
Low Moor
Whaw Edge
Scar House
Crag End
Rowantree Head
Low Rake
Peat Moor Green
North Rake Hush
Hotel
West House
Arkengarthdale CE Prim Sch
Flincher Bottom Moss
Moulds Top
Langthwaite Scar
Great Pinseat
BOULDERSHAW LANE
Langthwaite
Booze Moor
High Green
Forefield Rake
Wetshaw Head
P
Surrender Ground
Ford
Booze
Sewage Works
Whetshaw Bottom
Turf Moor Hush
8 09 7 08 6 07 5 06 4 05 3 04 2 03 1 02
96 97 98 99 00 01

37
18

17

Scale: 1¾ inches to 1 mile
0 ¼ ½ mile
0 250m 500m 750m 1 km

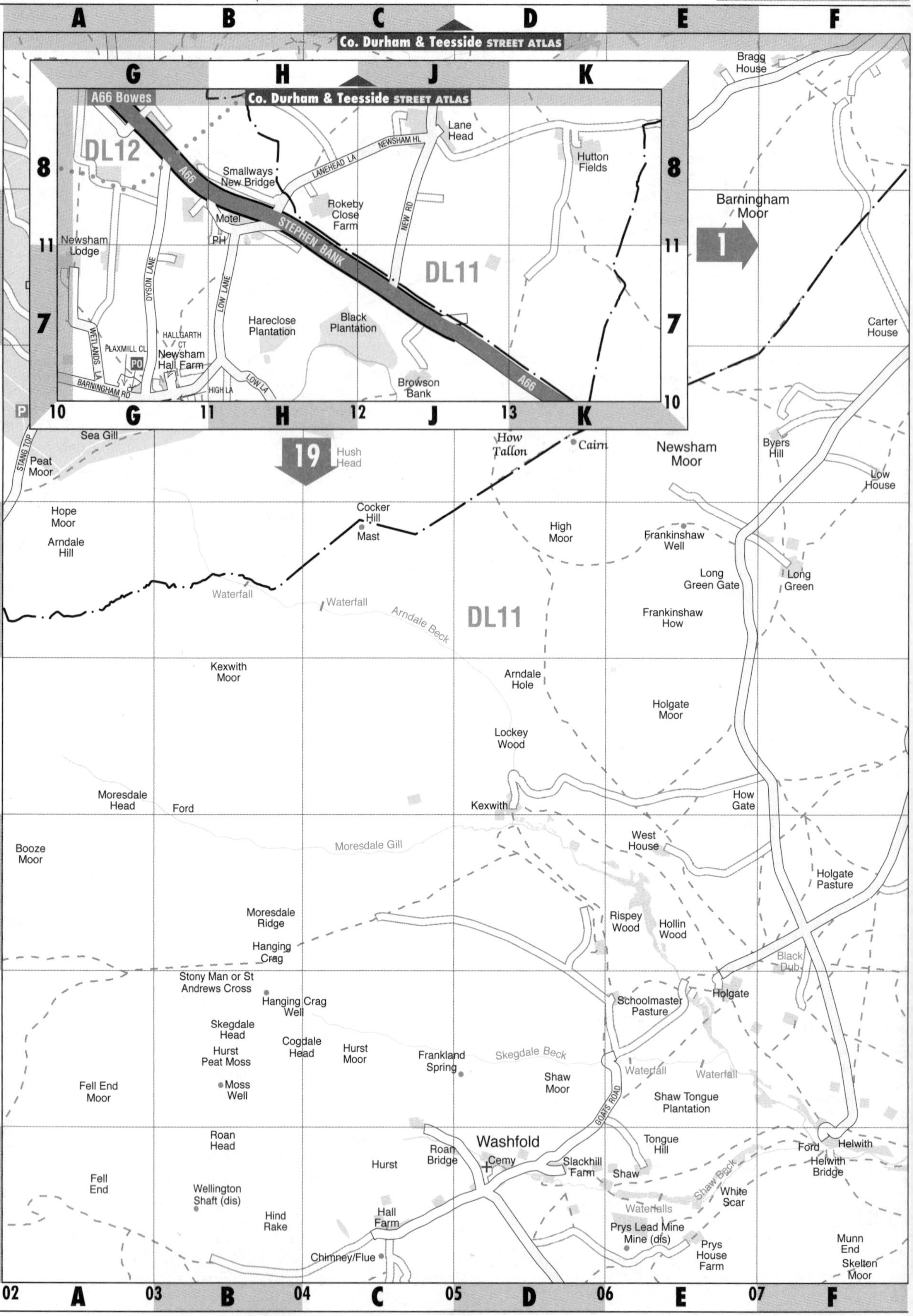

Co. Durham & Teesside STREET ATLAS
A66 Bowes
DL12
DL11
Smallways New Bridge
Lane Head
Hutton Fields
Rokeby Close Farm
Motel
PH
STEPHEN BANK
A66
NEWSHAM HL
LANEHEAD LA
NEW RD
Newsham Lodge
DYSON LANE
LOW LANE
Hareclose Plantation
Black Plantation
Browson Bank
WETLANDS LA
FLAXMILL CL
HALLGARTH CT
Newsham Hall Farm
BARNINGHAM RD
HIGH LA
LOW LA
Bragg House
Barningham Moor
1
Carter House
Sea Gill
STANG TOP
Peat Moor
19
Hush Head
How Tallon
Cairn
Newsham Moor
Byers Hill
Low House
Hope Moor
Arndale Hill
Cocker Hill
Mast
High Moor
Frankinshaw Well
Long Green Gate
Long Green
Waterfall
Waterfall
Arndale Beck
Frankinshaw How
Kexwith Moor
Arndale Hole
Holgate Moor
Lockey Wood
Moresdale Head
Ford
Kexwith
How Gate
Booze Moor
Moresdale Gill
West House
Holgate Pasture
Moresdale Ridge
Rispey Wood
Hollin Wood
Hanging Crag
Black Dub
Stony Man or St Andrews Cross
Hanging Crag Well
Schoolmaster Pasture
Holgate
Skegdale Head
Hurst Peat Moss
Cogdale Head
Hurst Moor
Frankland Spring
Skegdale Beck
Waterfall
Waterfall
Fell End Moor
Moss Well
Shaw Moor
Shaw Tongue Plantation
GOATS ROAD
Roan Head
Washfold
Roan Bridge
Cemy
Slackhill Farm
Tongue Hill
Ford
Helwith
Helwith Bridge
Hurst
Shaw
Shaw Beck
Fell End
Wellington Shaft (dis)
White Scar
Waterfalls
Hind Rake
Hall Farm
Prys Lead Mine Mine (dis)
Prys House Farm
Munn End
Chimney/Flue
Skelton Moor

17

38

Scale: 1¾ inches to 1 mile
0 ¼ ½ mile
0 250m 500m 750m 1 km

18
20

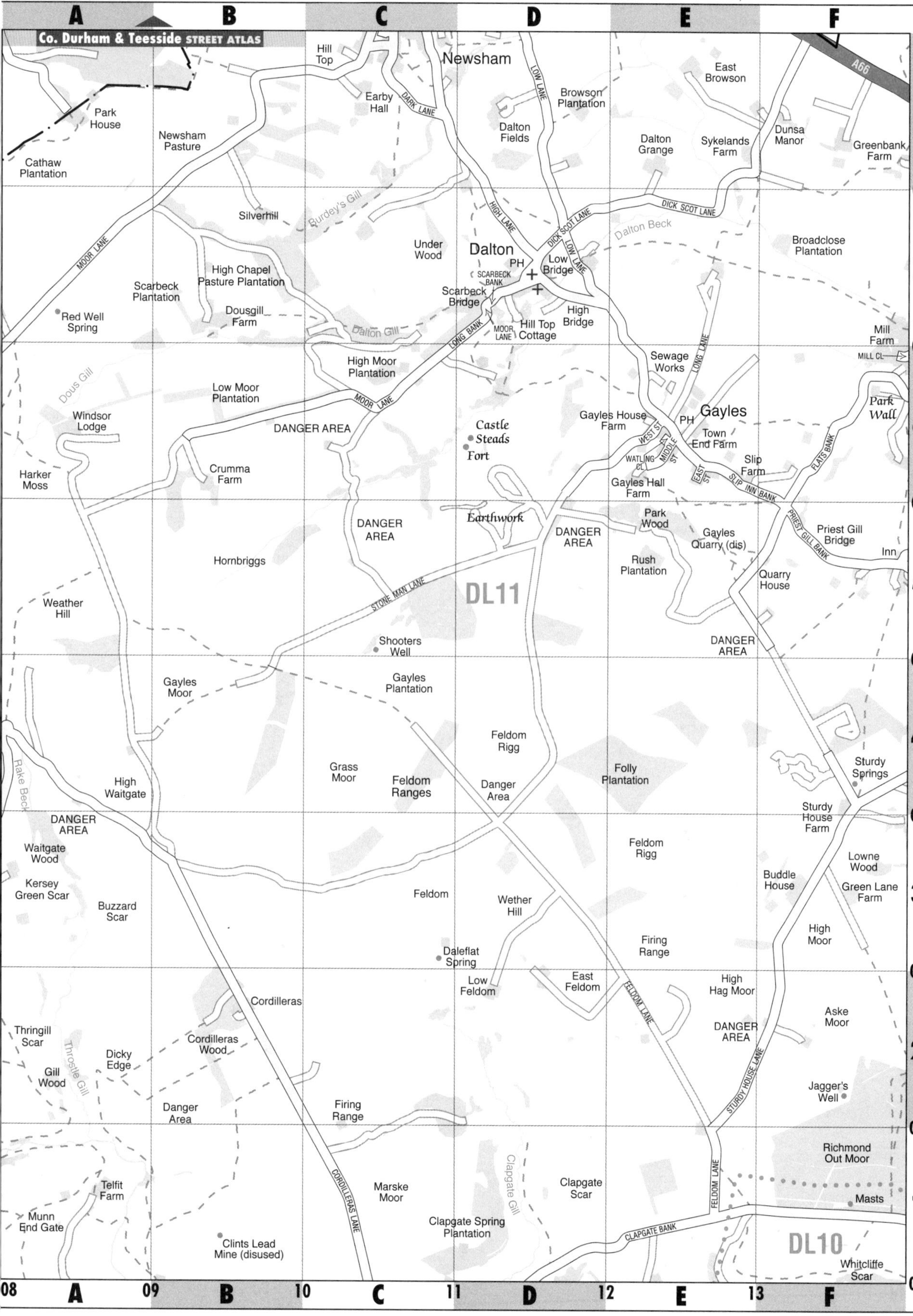

39
20

Scale: 1¾ inches to 1 mile
0 ¼ ½ mile
0 250m 500m 750m 1 km

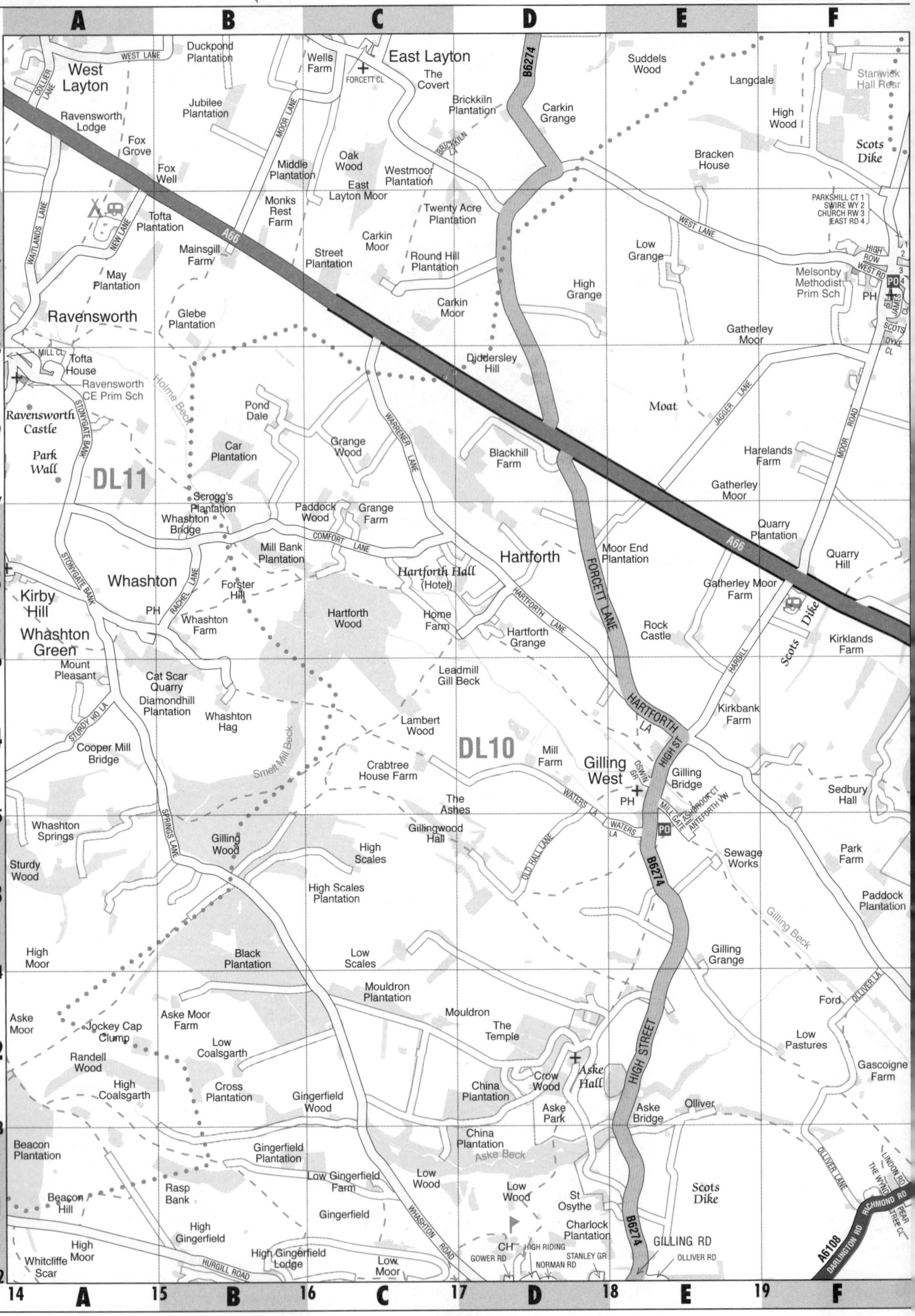
A
B
C
D
E
F
8
09
7
08
6
07
5
06
4
05
3
04
2
03
1
02
14
15
16
17
18
19
West Layton
WEST LANE
Duckpond Plantation
Wells Farm
East Layton
FORCETT CL
The Covert
B6274
Suddels Wood
Langdale
Stanwick Hall Resr
COLLIER LANE
Jubilee Plantation
MOOR LANE
Brickkiln Plantation
Carkin Grange
High Wood
Ravensworth Lodge
Fox Grove
Oak Wood
BRICKKILN LA
Bracken House
Scots Dike
Fox Well
Middle Plantation
Westmoor Plantation
East Layton Moor
Monks Rest Farm
Twenty Acre Plantation
PARKSHILL CT 1
SWIRE WY 2
CHURCH RW 3
EAST RD 4
WAITLANDS LANE
Tofta Plantation
A66
WEST LANE
NEW LANE
Carkin Moor
Low Grange
HIGH ROW
Mainsgill Farm
Street Plantation
Round Hill Plantation
WEST RD
May Plantation
Melsonby Methodist Prim Sch
PO
PH
High Grange
ST JAMES CL
Ravensworth
Glebe Plantation
Carkin Moor
SCOTS DYKE CL
Gatherley Moor
MILL CL
Tofta House
Diddersley Hill
Ravensworth CE Prim Sch
Holme Beck
Pond Dale
Moat
JAGGER LANE
Ravensworth Castle
STONYGATE BANK
Grange Wood
MOOR ROAD
WARRENER LANE
Car Plantation
Blackhill Farm
Harelands Farm
Park Wall
DL11
Gatherley Moor
Scrogg's Plantation
Paddock Wood
Grange Farm
Whashton Bridge
COMFORT LANE
Quarry Plantation
Mill Bank Plantation
Moor End Plantation
Hartforth
Quarry Hill
Whashton
STONYGATE BANK
RACHEL LANE
Forster Hill
Hartforth Hall (Hotel)
FORCETT LANE
Gatherley Moor Farm
Kirby Hill
PH
Whashton Farm
Hartforth Wood
HARTFORTH LANE
Whashton Green
Home Farm
Hartforth Grange
Rock Castle
Scots Dike
Kirklands Farm
Mount Pleasant
Cat Scar Quarry
Leadmill Gill Beck
HARGILL
Diamondhill Plantation
HARTFORTH LA
Kirkbank Farm
SPRINGS LANE
Whashton Hag
Lambert Wood
STURDY HO LA
Smelt Mill Beck
DL10
Mill Farm
HIGH ST
Cooper Mill Bridge
Crabtree House Farm
Gilling West
OSWIN GR
Gilling Bridge
Sedbury Hall
PH
ASHBROOK CT
ANTEFORTH VW
The Ashes
WATERS LA
MILL GATE
Whashton Springs
Gilling Wood
Gillingwood Hall
WATERS LA
PO
Sewage Works
Park Farm
OLD HALL LANE
Sturdy Wood
High Scales
B6274
High Scales Plantation
Paddock Plantation
Gilling Beck
High Moor
Black Plantation
Low Scales
Gilling Grange
Mouldron Plantation
OLLIVER LA
Aske Moor
Aske Moor Farm
Mouldron
The Temple
Ford
Jockey Cap Clump
Low Pastures
Low Coalsgarth
HIGH STREET
Randell Wood
Crow Wood
Aske Hall
Gascoigne Farm
High Coalsgarth
Cross Plantation
Gingerfield Wood
China Plantation
Aske Park
Aske Bridge
Olliver
Beacon Plantation
Gingerfield Plantation
China Plantation
Aske Beck
OLLIVER LANE
LINDON RD
THE WYND
Beacon Hill
Rasp Bank
Low Gingerfield Farm
Low Wood
Low Wood
St Osythe
Scots Dike
RICHMOND RD
PEAR TREE CL
Gingerfield
Charlock Plantation
B6274
A6108
DARLINGTON RD
High Gingerfield
CH
HIGH RIDING
GILLING RD
WHASHTON ROAD
High Moor
GOWER RD
NORMAN RD
STANLEY GR
OLLIVER RD
Whitcliffe Scar
HURGILL ROAD
High Gingerfield Lodge
Low Moor

Scale: 1¾ inches to 1 mile
0 ¼ ½ mile
0 250m 500m 750m 1 km

2
22

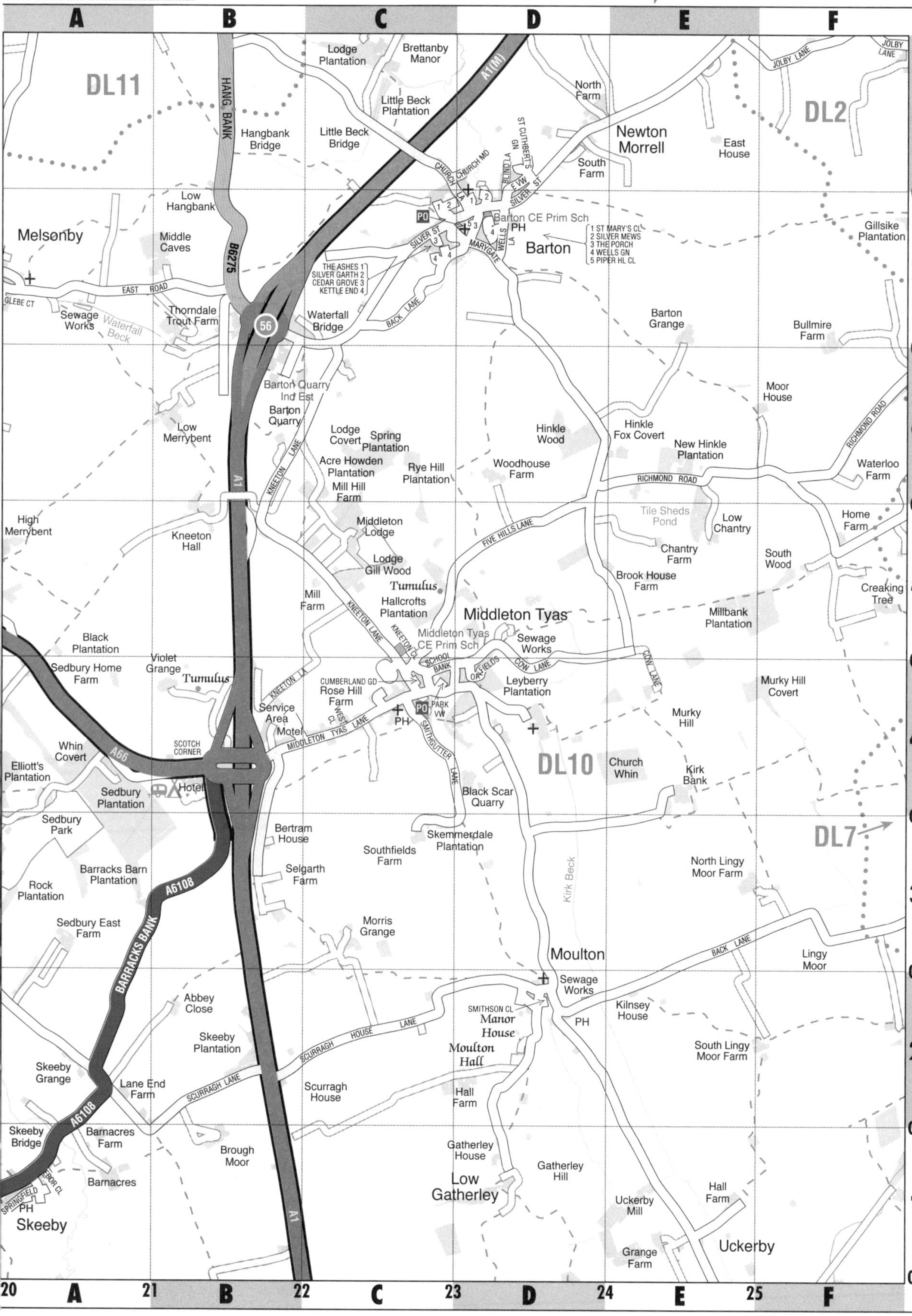

41
22

21
3

C8
1 LEWIS CL
2 CARROLL PL
3 RECTORY LA
4 THE MILL RACE

D8
1 LINDEN DRIVE
2 BAXBY TERRACE
3 BELGRAVE TERR
4 CEDAR MEWS
5 GRANGE AVE
6 FOX CL
7 WOODLANDS WAY
8 AVON ROAD
9 ASHVILLE DRIVE

Scale: 1¾ inches to 1 mile
0 ¼ ½ mile
0 250m 500m 750m 1 km

A B C D E F
8 09 7 08 6 07 5 06 4 05 3 04 2 03 1 02
26 27 28 29 30 31
Jolby Farm
Croft Grange
Monk End
SOUTH PD
Croft CE Prim Sch
TEES VIEW
HURWORTH TERR
RAILWAY TERR
HURWORTH ROAD
ELMFIELD RD
Hurworth Sch
JOLBY LANE
RICHMOND ROAD
Crow Wood
Cemy
A167
Croft-on-Tees
PILMORE MEWS
BLIND LA
Low Hail Farm
Sewage Works
Newbus Grange
Crow Wood
Castle Wood
Clervaux Castle
Sweet Well Wood
Old Spa Farm
New Spa
Tees Bridge
High Rockliffe
Eryholme Wood
Dobbs Hall Farm
West Wood
Pheasant Covert
Canny Well Wood
Low Rockliffe
Rockcliffe Scar
Eryholme Scar
Brickyard Farm
ERYHOLME LANE
Paradise Farm
Little Stranbrough Plantation
Stand Alone
River Tees
Bay Horse Farm
Black Wood
Bullmire Whin
Willow Garth
Stranbrough Plantation
DL2
RUSKIN CL
BYRON CT
ORCHARD CL
Moat
Dalton Wood
PH
Holmes Plantation
Dalton-on-Tees
Burn Sike
Pepperfield Farm
Westfields
Lodge Farm
Wilson Hill Plantation
Walmire Plantations
West Vince Moor
Vince Moor
Dalton Bridge
Burn Sike Bridge
Tewit Castle
NORTHALLERTON ROAD
Rear Wood
WEST LANE
Halnaby Hall
Croft Motor Racing Circuit
White House
Thorntree House
Steadfield House Farm
Birch Carr
Moorhouse Farm
Cowper House Farm
A167
DL10
Portobello
Birch Springs
Forty Acre Wood
Bagley Farm
B1263
Haswell Grange
Barf House
Cowton Moor
Cowton Fields Farm
Halnaby Grange
Dalton Gates Farm
Paddock Farm Water Gardens
Dalton Gates
Markstone House
MOULTON LANE
Cowton Grange
BACK LANE
HOLYWELL LANE
Cockleberry Farm
RABY LANE
Bowlturner House
DL6
Tender Heads Plantations
Cramble Cross
North Cowton
Corn Hill
West View Farm
North & South Cowton Com Prim Sch
HILL TOP CT
LANCASTER RD
SILVER HL
HOLYWELL LA
Springfield Farm
Raby Cottages
Cemy
Station Farm
ST LUKES CL
BLACKSMITH CT
PH
ANVIL WAY
GREEN LANE
Redmire Hall Farm
Uckerby Fox Covert
Sewage Works
Black Wood
DL7
Temple House Farm
East Cowton
White Head Farm
CONYERS RD
ST MARY'S CL
PO
PH
Cross Rein Farm
DAKYN CL
BOYNTON RD
WYCLIFFE RD
GOLDEN ACRES
Manor House
Howl Beck
East Cowton CE Prim Sch
High Greenbury
Atley Fields
Church Farm
Bungalow Farm
Green Lane Farm
DL10
Westfield House
Manor House
Sewage Works
PH
Castle Farm
Atley Hill
Greenbury Grange
Scorton Road Farm
B1263
Cowton Castle
Thistle Wood
Old Hall Farm

21
42

Scale: 1¾ inches to 1 mile
0 ¼ ½ mile
0 250m 500m 750m 1 km

4
24

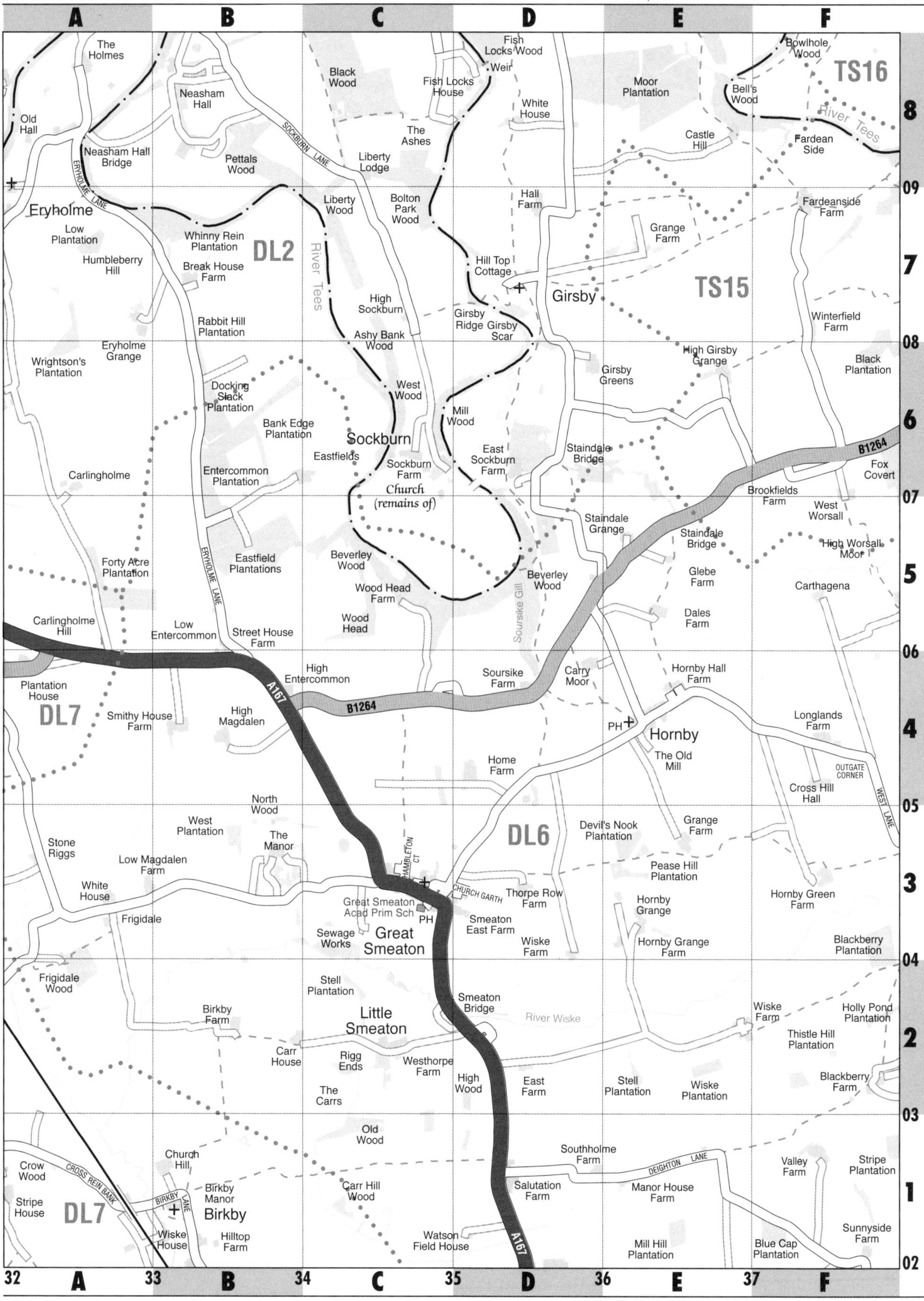

43
24

23
5

E8
1 ASH GR
2 BIRCH CL
3 BRAESIDE
4 GROVE BANK
5 KNOWLES CL
6 WESTLANDS
7 HALL MOOR CL
8 THE GREEN
9 STRATHMORE DR
10 MOOR CL
11 ST MARTINS WY
12 MANOR GARTH

F8
1 JASMINE FIELDS
2 TOWN END CL
3 LEVINGTON CT
4 LEVINGTON MS
5 PENDERS LA

Scale: 1¾ inches to 1 mile
0 ¼ ½ mile
0 250m 500m 750m 1 km

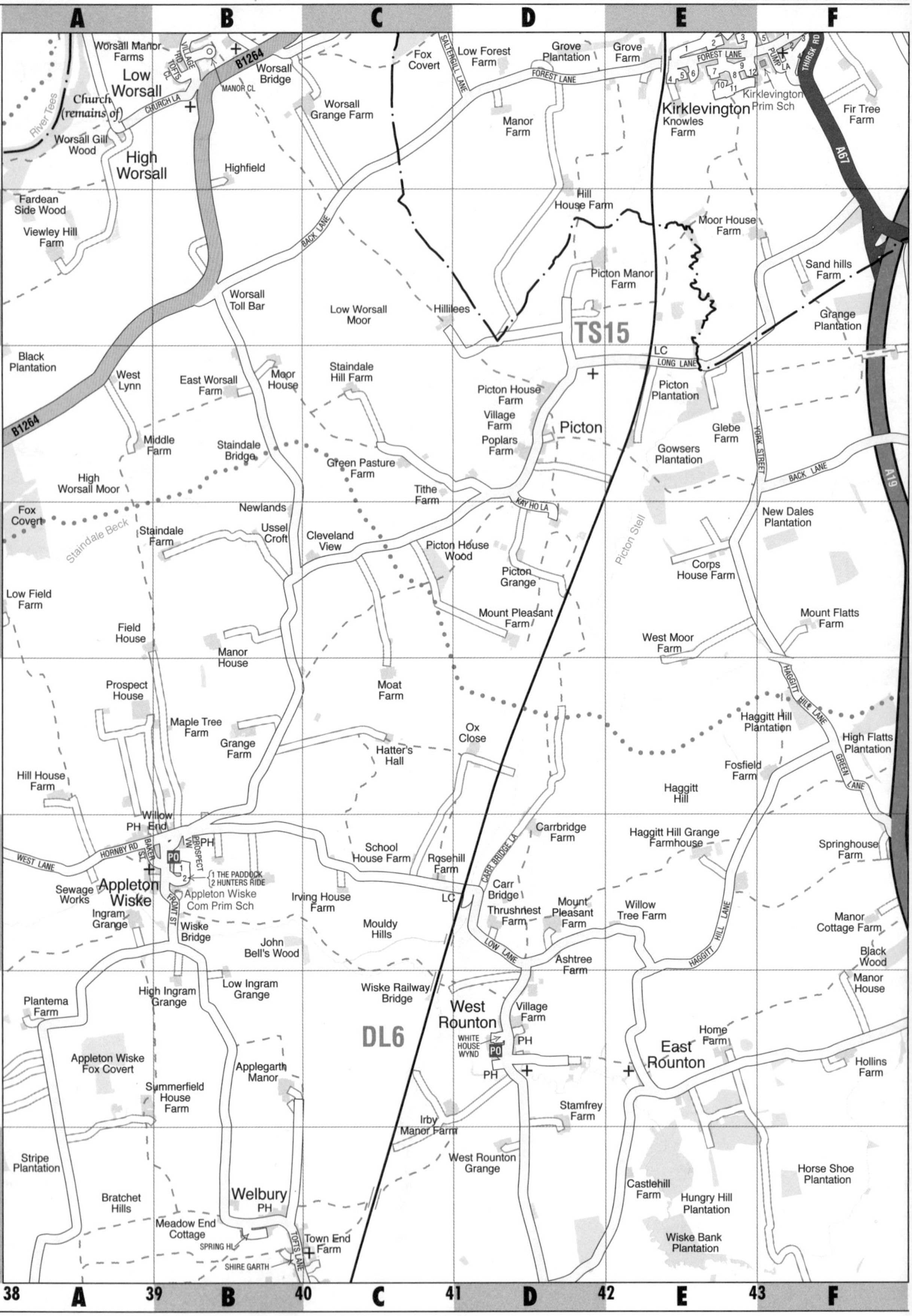

23
44

Scale: 1¾ inches to 1 mile
0 ¼ ½ mile
0 250m 500m 750m 1 km

C5
1 CODLIN RD
2 NORTH END
3 NORTHCLIFFE CRES
4 NORTHFIELDS
5 HUNDALE RD
6 LEVENDALE
7 DEEPDALE
8 THE WICKETS
9 GLENDALE
10 WESTHOLME
11 COLDIE HL
12 WYND CL
13 WILLINS CL
14 THE OLD ORCHARD

D5
1 THE GROVE
2 SOUTH VIEW
3 HUTTON BANK
4 LEVENSIDE
5 EAST SIDE
6 POPLAR AVE

6
26

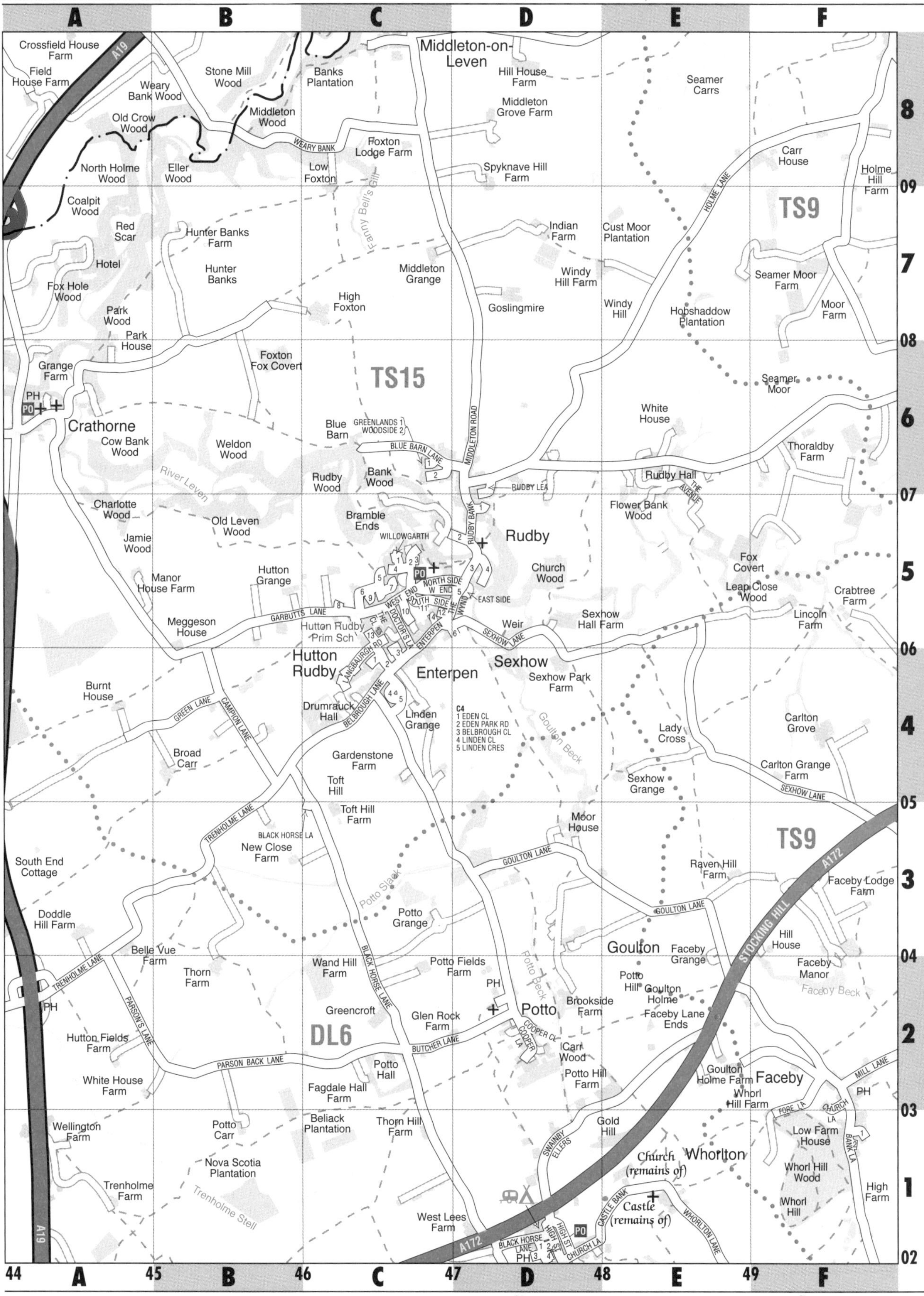

D1
1 GARBUTT LA
2 EMERSON CL
3 HEATHER CL
4 GARBUTT LA

F1
1 CLEVELAND VW
2 BIRCH DR

45
26

25

C8
1 CEDARWOOD AVE
2 BEECHWOOD AVE
3 DALEWOOD WK
4 CHERRYWOOD AVE
5 COPSEWOOD WK
6 ELMWOOD CL
7 PINEWOOD WK
8 MEADOWFIELD
9 QUEENS DR

7

C7
1 SPRINGFIELD GDNS
2 WESTFIELD RD
3 WEAVERS CT
4 THE GARTH
5 MANOR CL
6 THE STRIPE
7 THREE TUNS WYND
8 ANGEL CT
9 LEVEN WYND
10 BRIDGE RD
11 THE BEECHES
12 LADY HULLOCKS CT
13 ROSE HL DR
14 ST MARYS CL
15 WEST GN

Scale: 1¾ inches to 1 mile
0 ¼ ½ mile
0 250m 500m 750m 1 km

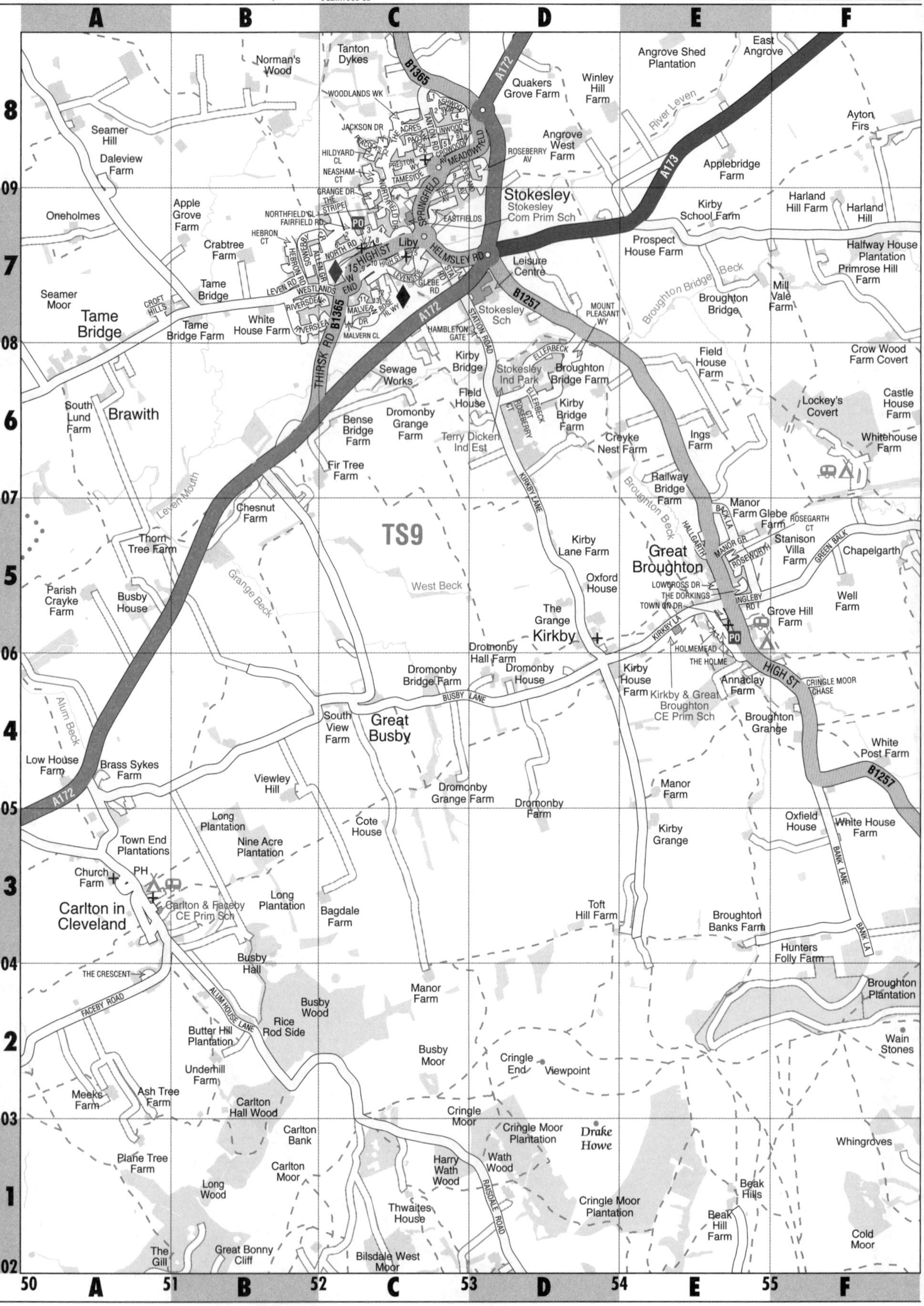

Scale: 1¾ inches to 1 mile
0 ¼ ½ mile
0 250m 500m 750m 1 km

8
28

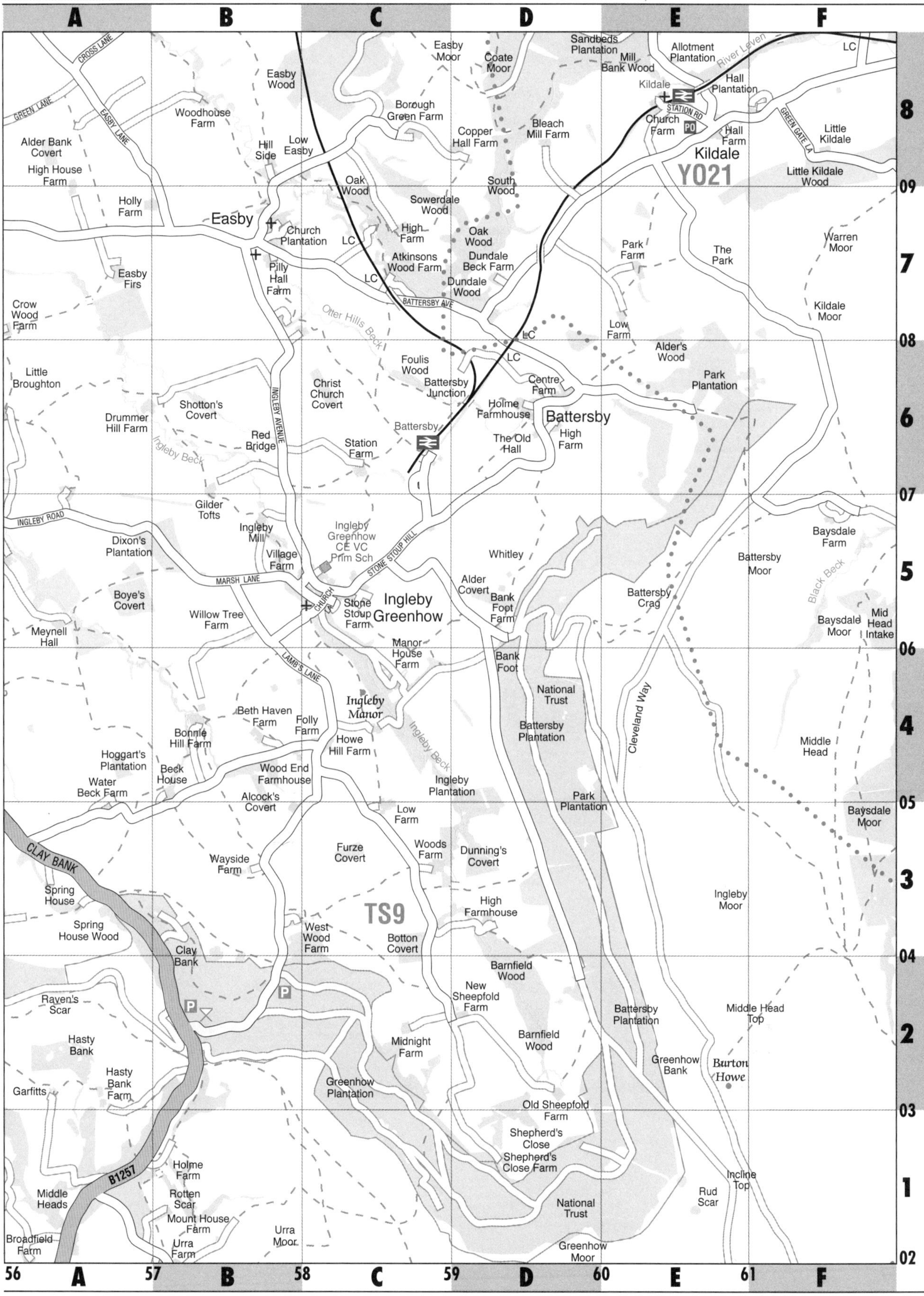

47
28

27
9

Scale: 1¾ inches to 1 mile
0 ¼ ½ mile
0 250m 500m 750m 1 km

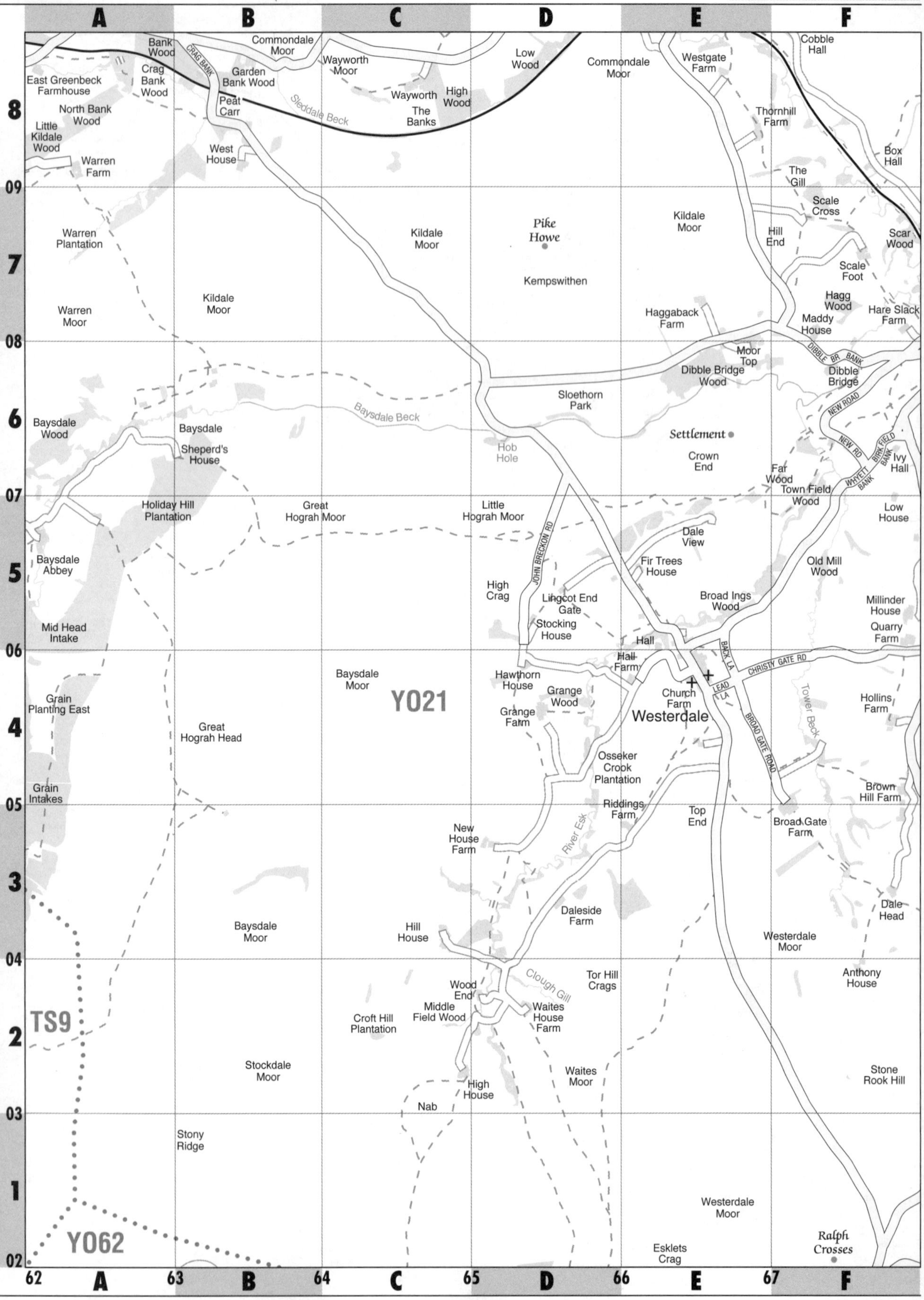

Scale: 1¾ inches to 1 mile
0 ¼ ½ mile
0 250m 500m 750m 1 km

10
30

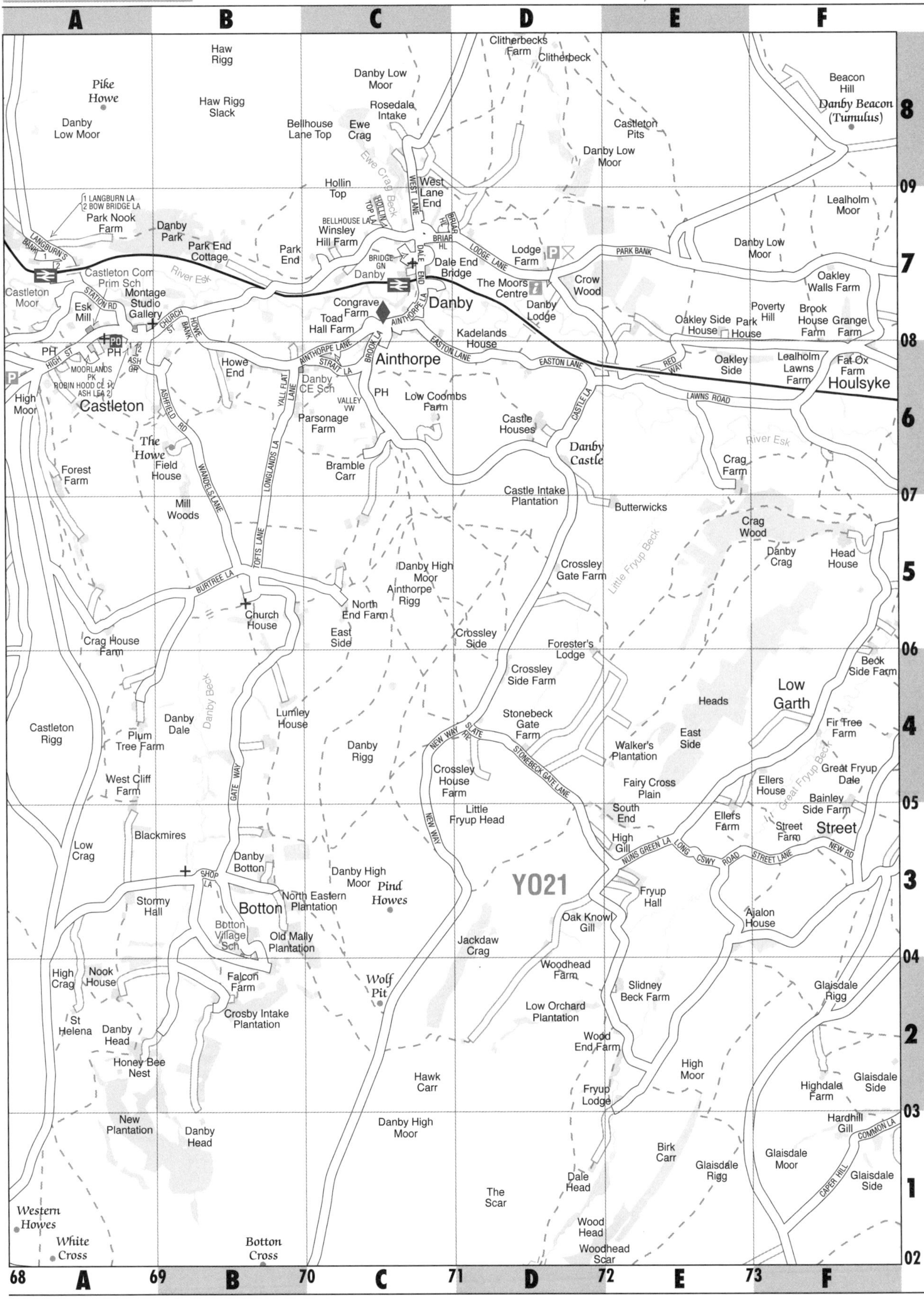

49
30

29
11

Scale: 1¾ inches to 1 mile
0 ¼ ½ mile
0 250m 500m 750m 1 km

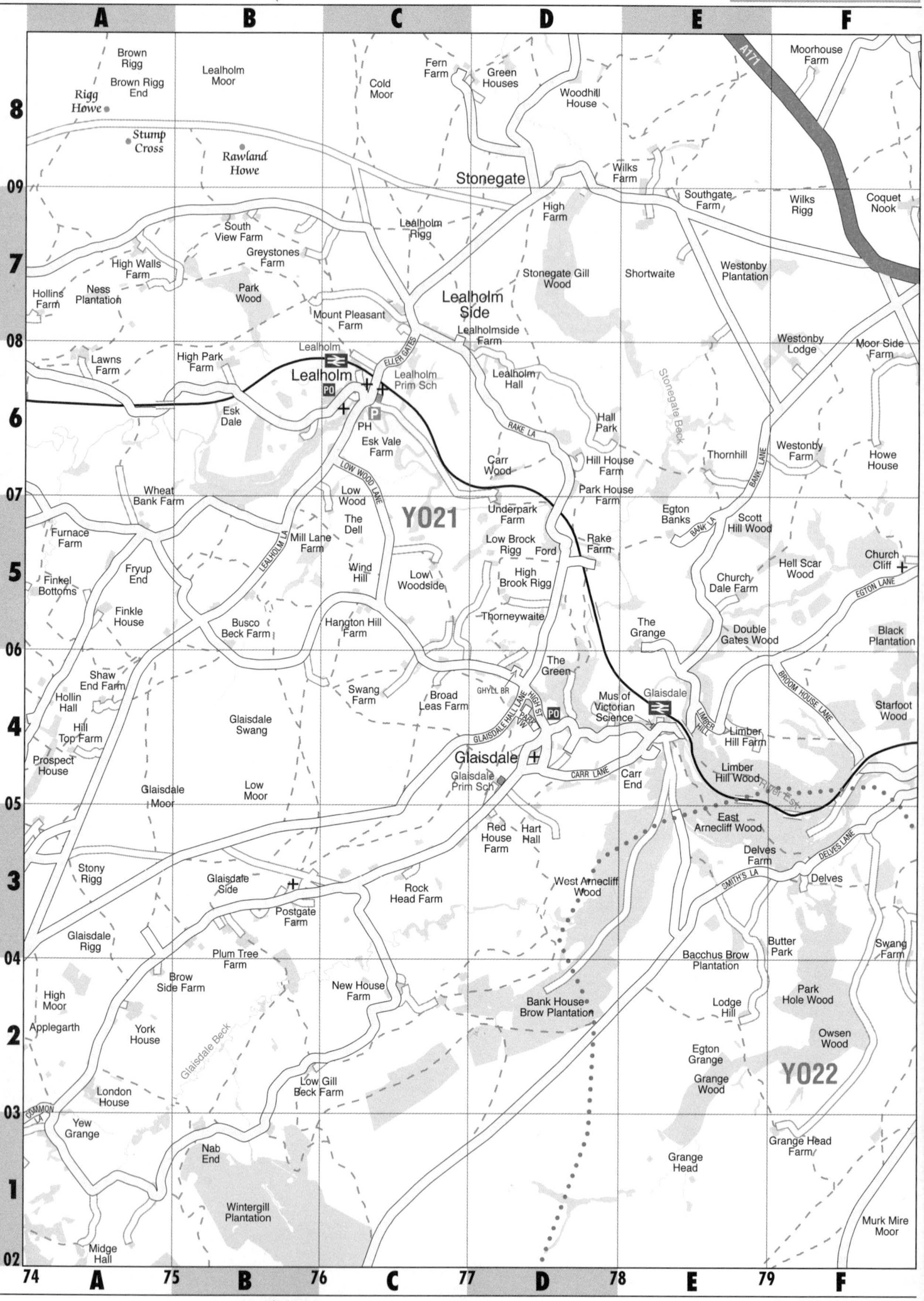

29
50

Scale: 1¾ inches to 1 mile
0 ¼ ½ mile
0 250m 500m 750m 1 km

12
32

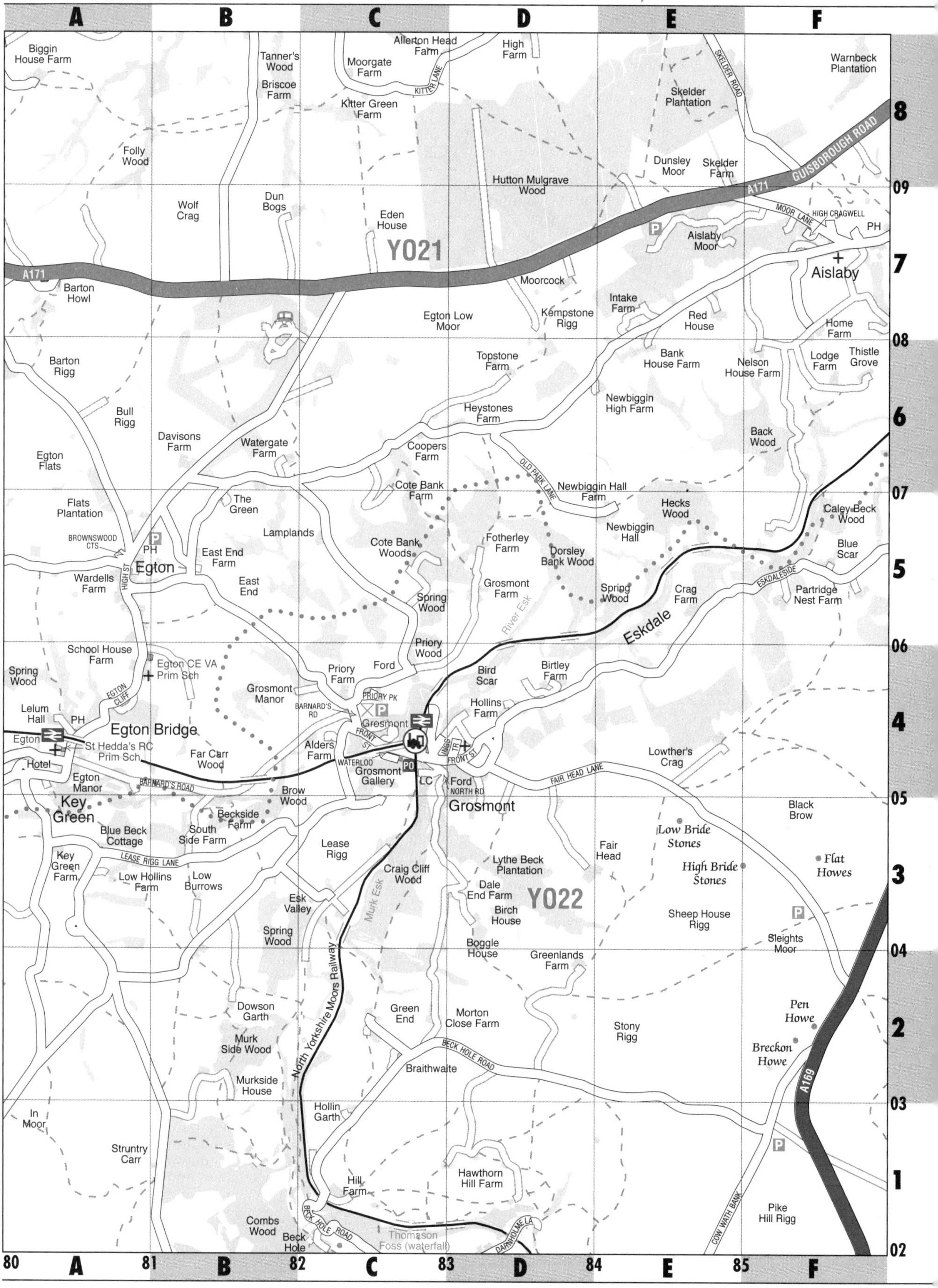

51
32

A6
1 THE AVENUE
2 BANK CL
3 ORCHARD RD
4 LOWDALE CT
5 SMIDDYFIELDS
6 NETHERBY CL
7 SELSTONE CR
8 NARROWFIELD
9 HALL PASTURE
10 BIRCH CRES
11 FOURACRE DR
12 SPRING CL
13 YEWTREE CL

31
13

Scale: 1¾ inches to 1 mile
0 ¼ ½ mile
0 250m 500m 750m 1 km

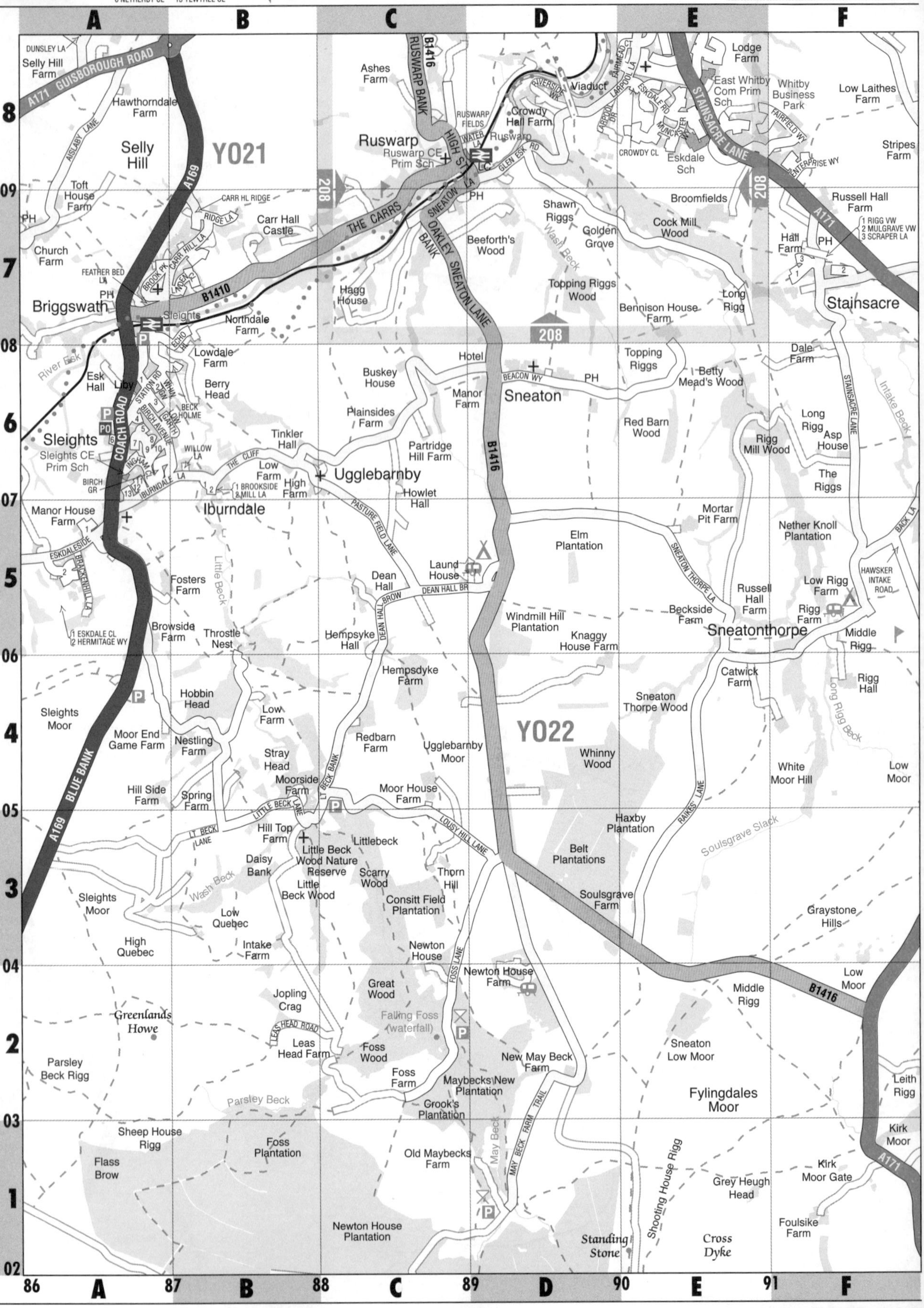

31
52
For full street detail of the highlighted area see page 208.

Scale: 1¾ inches to 1 mile
0 ¼ ½ mile
0 250m 500m 750m 1 km

C3
1 THORPE GN BANK
2 KINGSTON GARTH
3 MIDDLEWOOD CL
4 MIDDLEWOOD GARTH
5 MIDDLEWOOD CRES
6 THORPE BANK

D4
1 MOUNT PLEASANT N
2 MOUNT PLEASANT E
3 MOUNT PLEASANT S
4 THE CLOSE
5 PROSPECT FIELD

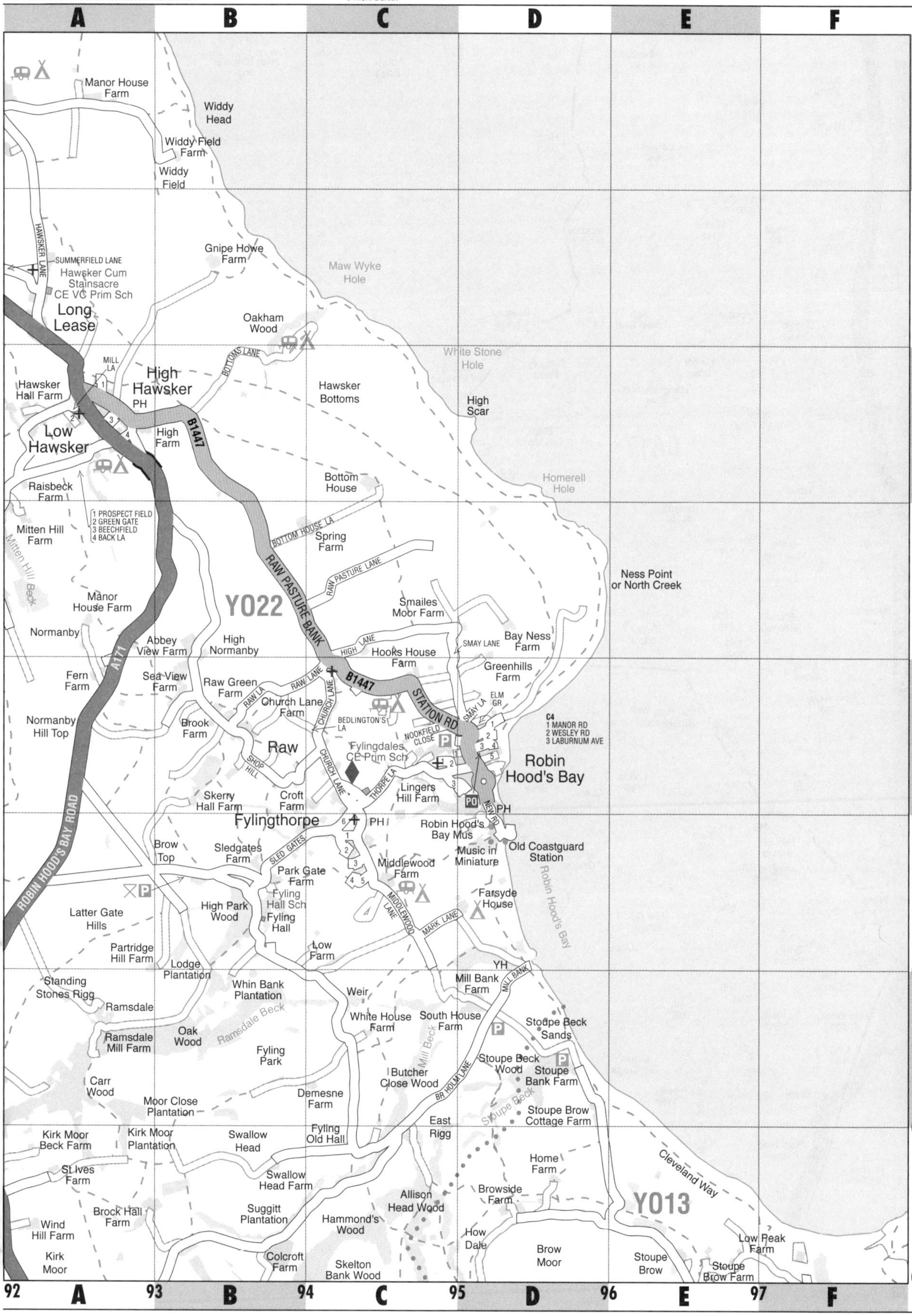

A
B
C
D
E
F
8
09
7
08
6
07
5
06
4
05
3
04
2
03
1
02
92
93
94
95
96
97
Manor House Farm
Widdy Head
Widdy Field Farm
Widdy Field
HAWSKER LANE
SUMMERFIELD LANE
Hawsker Cum Stainsacre CE VC Prim Sch
Long Lease
Gnipe Howe Farm
Maw Wyke Hole
Oakham Wood
BOTTOMS LANE
MILL LA
Hawsker Hall Farm
High Hawsker
PH
Low Hawsker
High Farm
B1447
Hawsker Bottoms
White Stone Hole
High Scar
Raisbeck Farm
Bottom House
Homerell Hole
1 PROSPECT FIELD
2 GREEN GATE
3 BEECHFIELD
4 BACK LA
Mitten Hill Farm
Mitten Hill Beck
BOTTOM HOUSE LA
Spring Farm
RAW PASTURE BANK
RAW PASTURE LANE
Ness Point or North Creek
Manor House Farm
YO22
Smailes Moor Farm
Normanby
Abbey View Farm
High Normanby
HIGH LANE
Hooks House Farm
SMAY LANE
Bay Ness Farm
A171
Fern Farm
Sea View Farm
Raw Green Farm
RAW LA
RAW LANE
CHURCH LANE
Greenhills Farm
ELM GR
SMAY LA
Church Lane Farm
BEDLINGTON'S LA
STATION RD
C4
1 MANOR RD
2 WESLEY RD
3 LABURNUM AVE
Normanby Hill Top
Brook Farm
Raw
NOOKFIELD CLOSE
Fylingdales CE Prim Sch
Robin Hood's Bay
SHOP HILL
CHURCH LANE
THORPE LA
Lingers Hill Farm
PO
NEW RD
PH
ROBIN HOOD'S BAY ROAD
Skerry Hall Farm
Croft Farm
Fylingthorpe
PH
Robin Hood's Bay Mus
Brow Top
Sledgates Farm
SLED GATES
Music in Miniature
Old Coastguard Station
Park Gate Farm
Middlewood Farm
Robin Hood's Bay
Fyling Hall Sch
MIDDLEWOOD LANE
Farsyde House
Latter Gate Hills
High Park Wood
Fyling Hall
MARK LANE
Partridge Hill Farm
Low Farm
Lodge Plantation
YH
Standing Stones Rigg
Whin Bank Plantation
Weir
Mill Bank Farm
MILL BANK
Ramsdale
Ramsdale Beck
Ramsdale Mill Farm
Oak Wood
White House Farm
South House Farm
Stoupe Beck Sands
Mill Beck
Fyling Park
Stoupe Beck Wood
Stoupe Bank Farm
Carr Wood
Butcher Close Wood
BR HOLM LANE
Moor Close Plantation
Demesne Farm
Stoupe Beck
Stoupe Brow Cottage Farm
Kirk Moor Beck Farm
Kirk Moor Plantation
Swallow Head
Fyling Old Hall
East Rigg
Cleveland Way
St Ives Farm
Swallow Head Farm
Home Farm
Allison Head Wood
Browside Farm
YO13
Brock Hall Farm
Suggitt Plantation
Wind Hill Farm
Hammond's Wood
How Dale
Brow Moor
Low Peak Farm
Kirk Moor
Colcroft Farm
Skelton Bank Wood
Stoupe Brow
Stoupe Brow Farm

14

Scale: 1¾ inches to 1 mile

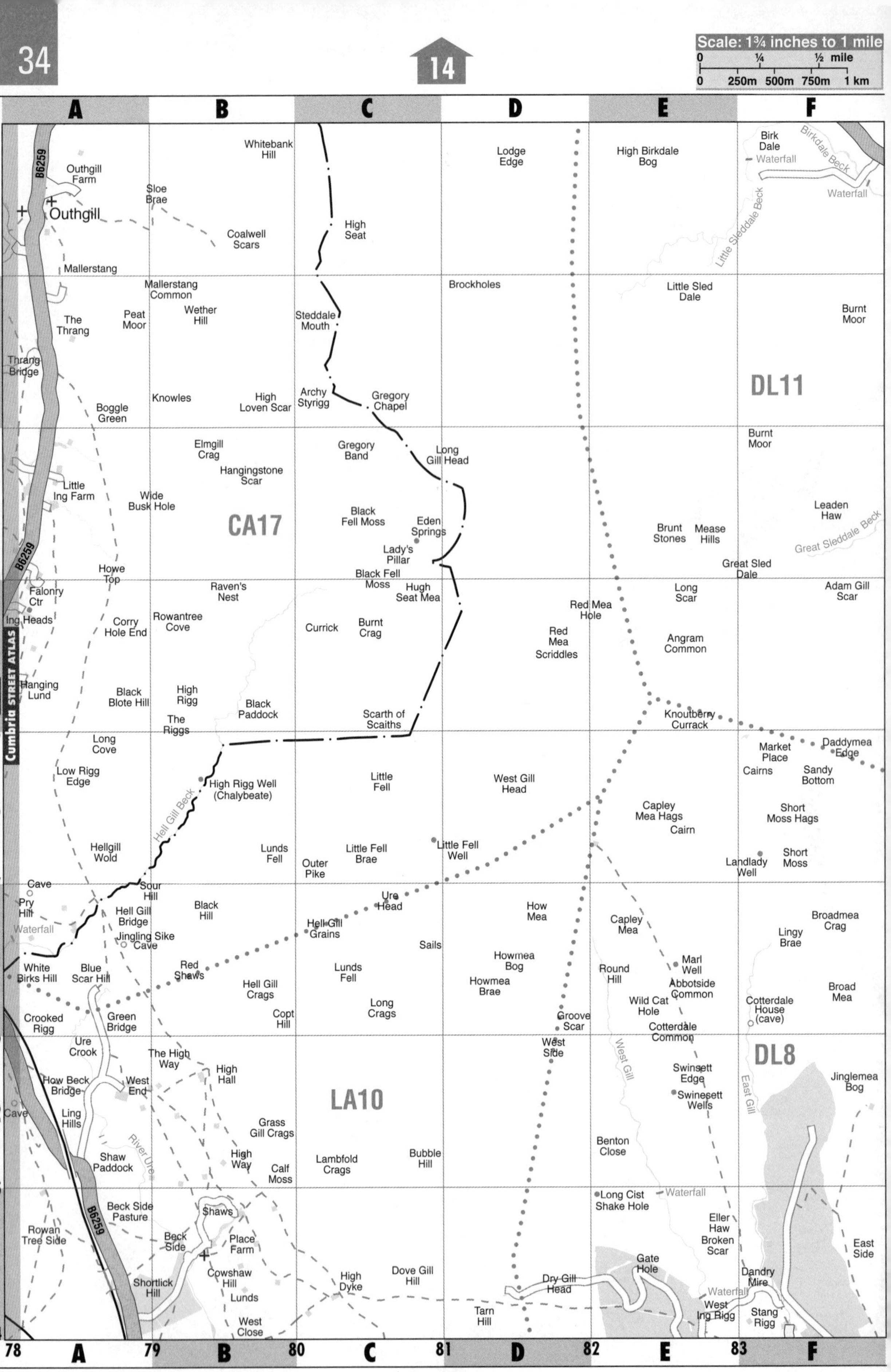
A B C D E F
8
01
7
00
6
99
5
98
4
97
3
96
2
95
1
94
78 79 80 81 82 83
Outhgill Farm
Outhgill
Sloe Brae
Whitebank Hill
Coalwell Scars
High Seat
Mallerstang
Lodge Edge
High Birkdale Bog
Birk Dale
Waterfall
Birkdale Beck
Little Sleddale Beck
Mallerstang Common
Brockholes
Little Sled Dale
The Thrang
Peat Moor
Wether Hill
Steddale Mouth
Burnt Moor
Thrang Bridge
DL11
Boggle Green
Knowles
High Loven Scar
Archy Styrigg
Gregory Chapel
Elmgill Crag
Gregory Band
Long Gill Head
Hangingstone Scar
Little Ing Farm
Wide Busk Hole
CA17
Black Fell Moss
Eden Springs
Leaden Haw
Brunt Stones
Mease Hills
Great Sleddale Beck
Lady's Pillar
Great Sled Dale
Howe Top
Black Fell Moss
Hugh Seat Mea
Long Scar
Adam Gill Scar
Raven's Nest
Falonry Ctr
Ing Heads
Corry Hole End
Rowantree Cove
Curick
Burnt Crag
Red Mea Hole
Red Mea Scriddles
Angram Common
Hanging Lund
Black Blote Hill
High Rigg
Black Paddock
Scarth of Scaiths
Knoutberry Currack
The Riggs
Long Cove
Market Place
Daddymea Edge
Cairns
Sandy Bottom
Low Rigg Edge
High Rigg Well (Chalybeate)
Little Fell
West Gill Head
Capley Mea Hags
Cairn
Short Moss Hags
Hell Gill Beck
Hellgill Wold
Lunds Fell
Outer Pike
Little Fell Brae
Little Fell Well
Landlady Well
Short Moss
Cave
Pry Hill
Sour Hill
Hell Gill Bridge
Black Hill
Ure Head
How Mea
Capley Mea
Broadmea Crag
Lingy Brae
Waterfall
Jingling Sike Cave
Hell Gill Grains
Sails
Howmea Bog
Marl Well
White Birks Hill
Blue Scar Hill
Red Shaws
Hell Gill Crags
Lunds Fell
Howmea Brae
Round Hill
Abbotside Common
Broad Mea
Crooked Rigg
Green Bridge
Copt Hill
Long Crags
Groove Scar
Wild Cat Hole
Cotterdale House (cave)
Cotterdale Common
Ure Crook
The High Way
West Side
West Gill
DL8
High Hall
How Beck Bridge
West End
Swinsett Edge
Swinesett Wells
Jinglemea Bog
East Gill
Cave
Ling Hills
LA10
Grass Gill Crags
River Ure
Shaw Paddock
High Way
Calf Moss
Lambfold Crags
Bubble Hill
Benton Close
Long Cist Shake Hole
Waterfall
Beck Side Pasture
Shaws
Rowan Tree Side
Beck Side
Place Farm
Eller Haw Broken Scar
East Side
Gate Hole
Cowshaw Hill
High Dyke
Dove Gill Hill
Dry Gill Head
Dandry Mire
Shortlick Hill
Lunds
Waterfall
West Ing Rigg
Stang Rigg
Tarn Hill
West Close
B6259
Cumbria STREET ATLAS

55

Scale: 1¾ inches to 1 mile
0 ¼ ½ mile
0 250m 500m 750m 1 km

15
36

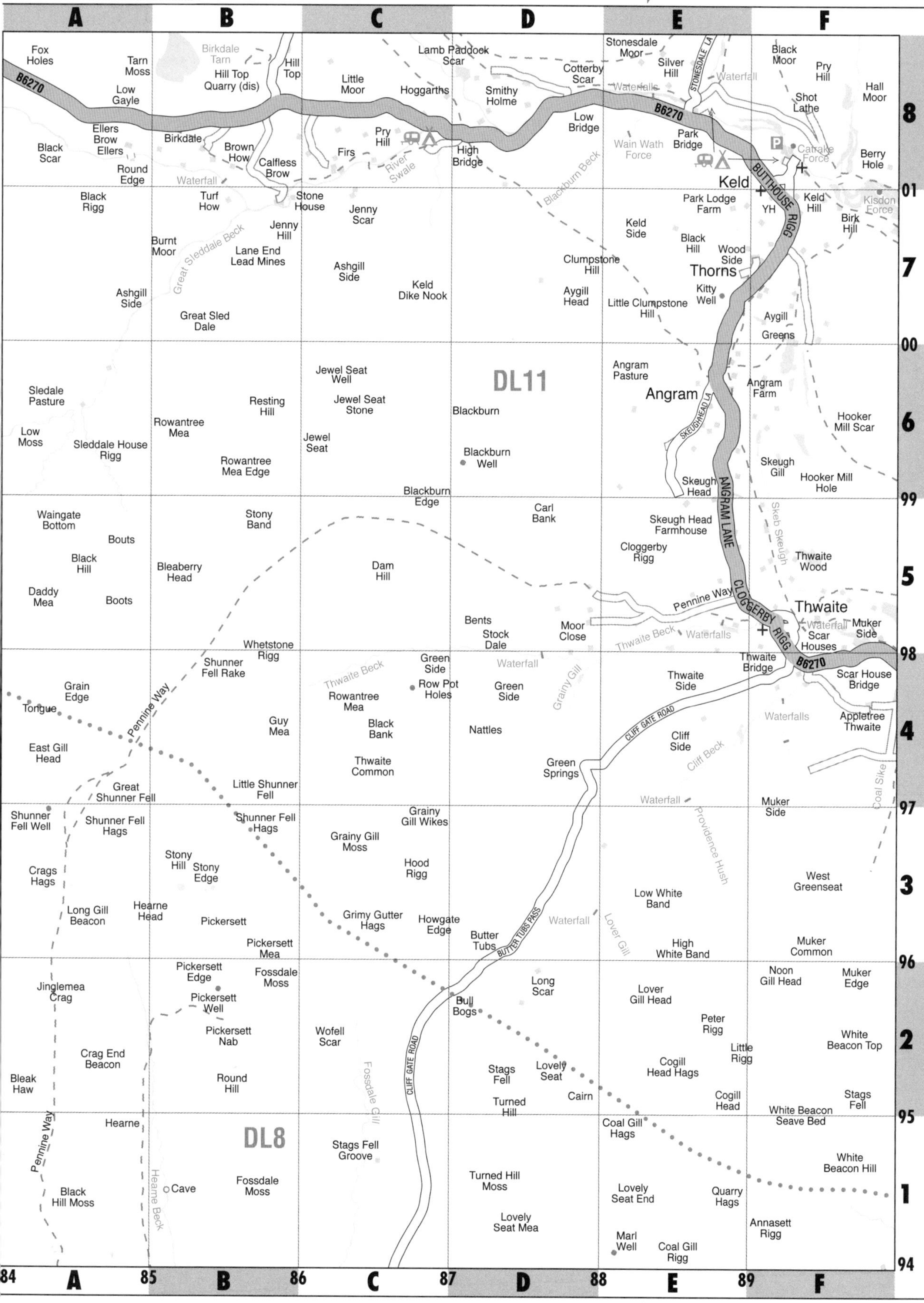

56
36

35
16

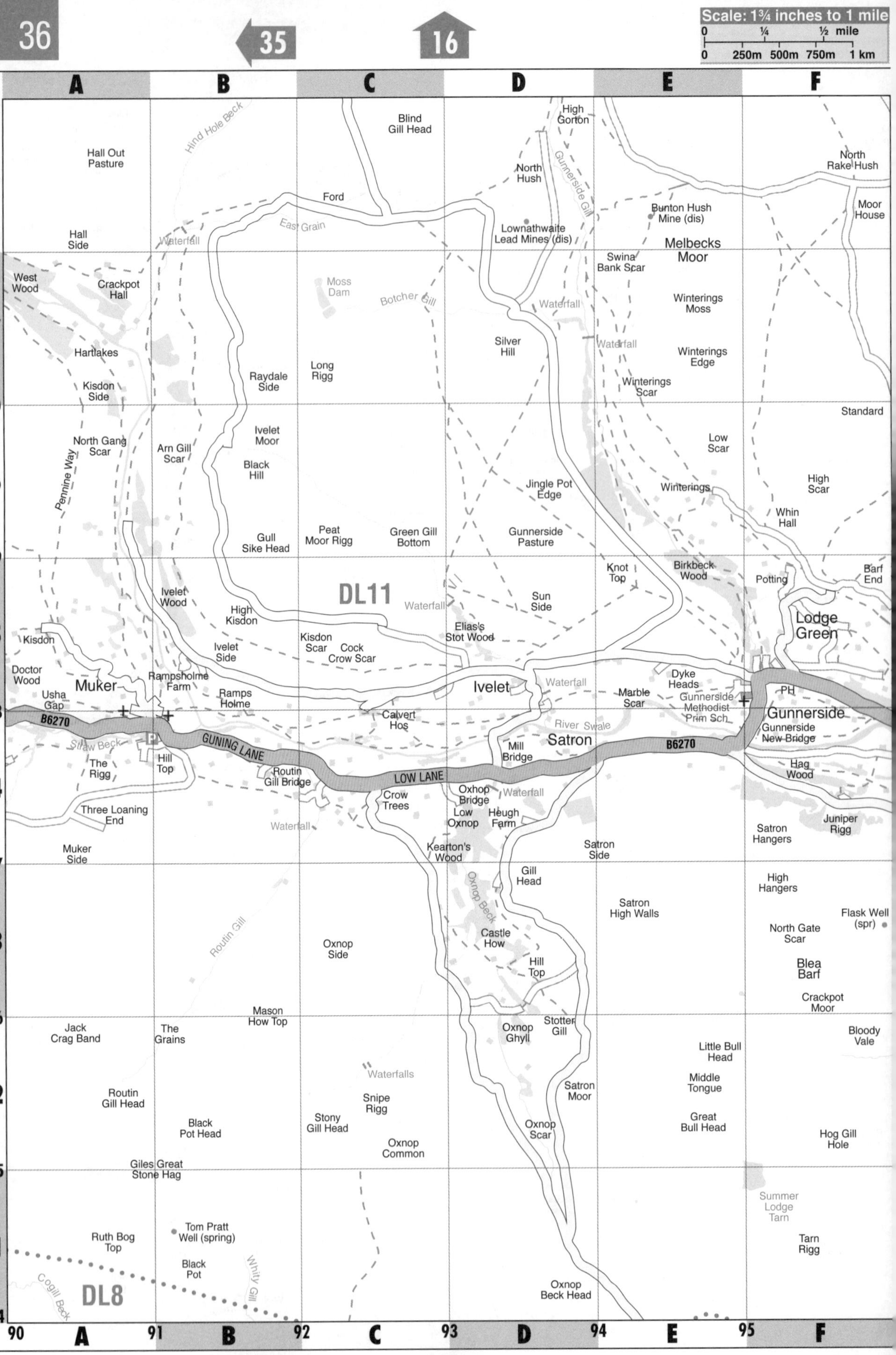
Scale: 1¾ inches to 1 mile
0 ¼ ½ mile
0 250m 500m 750m 1 km
A
B
C
D
E
F
8
01
7
00
6
99
5
98
4
97
3
96
2
95
1
94
90
91
92
93
94
95
Hind Hole Beck
Hall Out Pasture
Blind Gill Head
High Gorton
North Hush
Gunnerside Gill
North Rake Hush
Ford
Moor House
Bunton Hush Mine (dis)
Hall Side
East Grain
Waterfall
Lownathwaite Lead Mines (dis)
Melbecks Moor
Swina Bank Scar
West Wood
Crackpot Hall
Moss Dam
Botcher Gill
Waterfall
Winterings Moss
Waterfall
Hartlakes
Silver Hill
Winterings Edge
Long Rigg
Raydale Side
Kisdon Side
Winterings Scar
Standard
Ivelet Moor
North Gang Scar
Arn Gill Scar
Low Scar
Black Hill
Pennine Way
Jingle Pot Edge
Winterings
High Scar
Whin Hall
Gull Sike Head
Peat Moor Rigg
Green Gill Bottom
Gunnerside Pasture
Knot Top
Birkbeck Wood
Barf End
Potting
DL11
Ivelet Wood
Waterfall
Sun Side
High Kisdon
Lodge Green
Elias's Stot Wood
Kisdon
Kisdon Scar
Cock Crow Scar
Ivelet Side
Doctor Wood
Rampsholme Farm
Dyke Heads
Muker
Ivelet
Waterfall
PH
Usha Gap
Ramps Holme
Marble Scar
Gunnerside Methodist Prim Sch
Gunnerside
B6270
Calvert Hos
River Swale
Straw Beck
P
Satron
B6270
Gunnerside New Bridge
Mill Bridge
GUNING LANE
The Rigg
Hill Top
Routin Gill Bridge
LOW LANE
Hag Wood
Crow Trees
Oxnop Bridge
Waterfall
Three Loaning End
Low Oxnop
Heugh Farm
Juniper Rigg
Satron Hangers
Waterfall
Satron Side
Muker Side
Kearton's Wood
Gill Head
High Hangers
Oxnop Beck
Satron High Walls
Flask Well (spr)
North Gate Scar
Routin Gill
Castle How
Oxnop Side
Blea Barf
Hill Top
Crackpot Moor
Mason How Top
Stotter Gill
Jack Crag Band
The Grains
Oxnop Ghyll
Bloody Vale
Little Bull Head
Waterfalls
Satron Moor
Middle Tongue
Routin Gill Head
Snipe Rigg
Stony Gill Head
Black Pot Head
Oxnop Scar
Great Bull Head
Hog Gill Hole
Oxnop Common
Giles Great Stone Hag
Summer Lodge Tarn
Tom Pratt Well (spring)
Tarn Rigg
Ruth Bog Top
Black Pot
Whity Gill
Cogill Beck
DL8
Oxnop Beck Head

35
57

Scale: 1¾ inches to 1 mile
0 ¼ ½ mile
0 250m 500m 750m 1 km

17
38

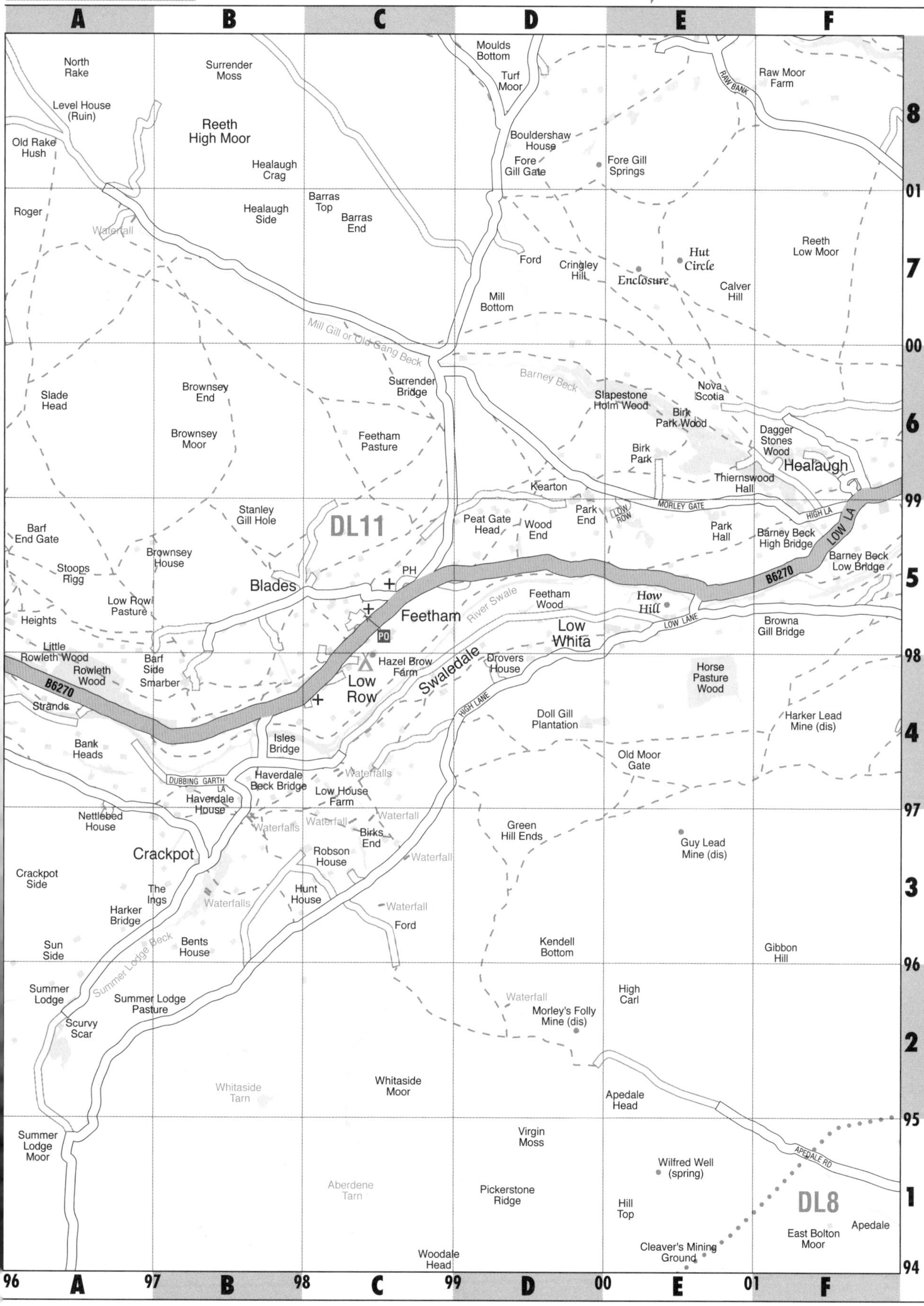

58
38

B6
1 QUAKER CL
2 LANGHORNE DR
3 ANVIL SQ

37
18

Scale: 1¾ inches to 1 mile
0 ¼ ½ mile
0 250m 500m 750m 1 km

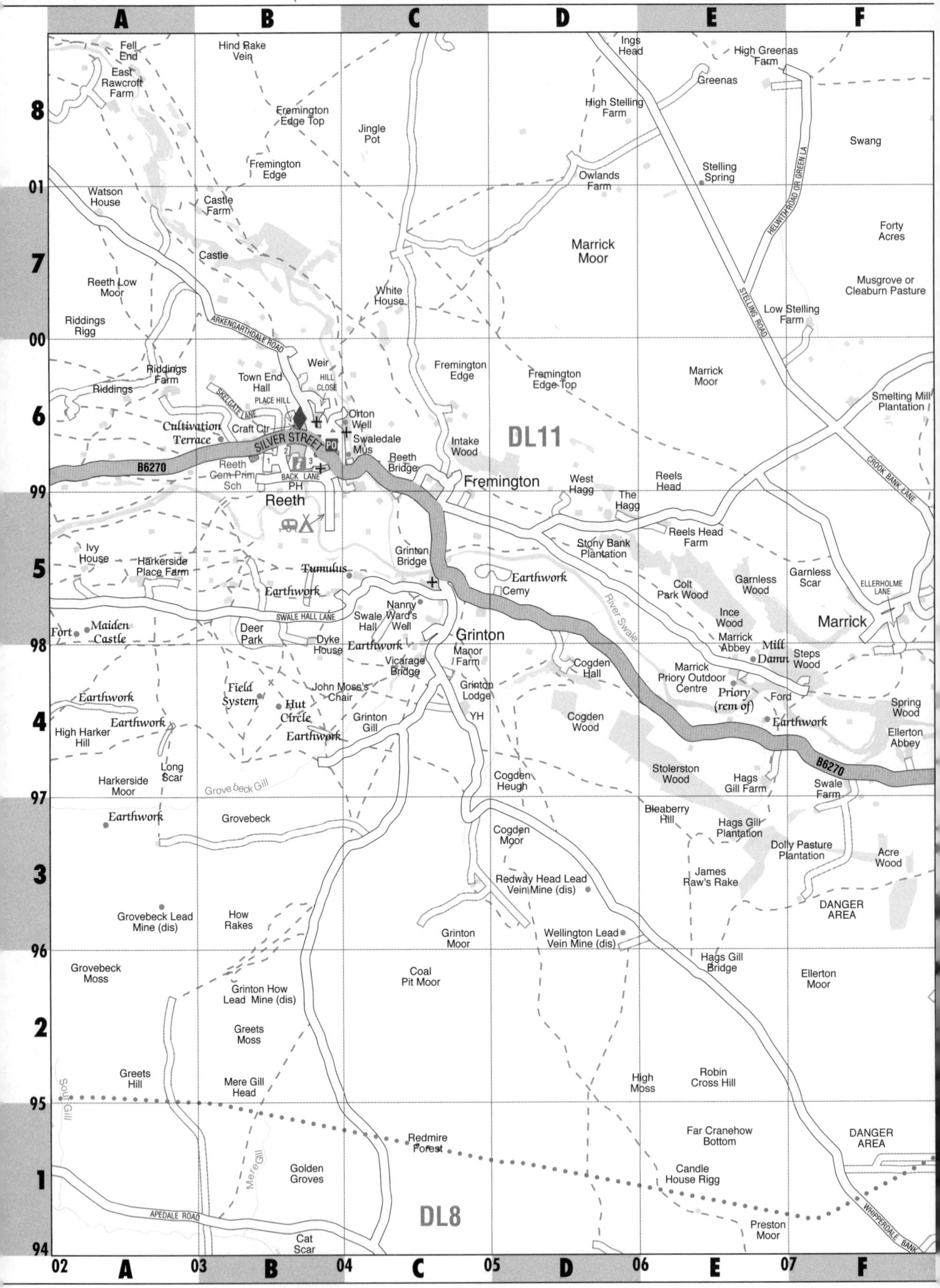

37
59

Scale: 1¾ inches to 1 mile
0 ¼ ½ mile
0 250m 500m 750m 1 km

19
40

60
40

39

F5
1 WESTRIDGE CRES
2 FALKLAND RD
3 ALBERMARLE DR
4 CRAVENDALE RD
5 MAPLE CL
6 CHESTNUT CL
7 GRANGE RD
8 MANOR GR

20

For full street detail of the highlighted area see page 209.

Scale: 1¾ inches to 1 mile
0 ¼ ½ mile
0 250m 500m 750m 1 km

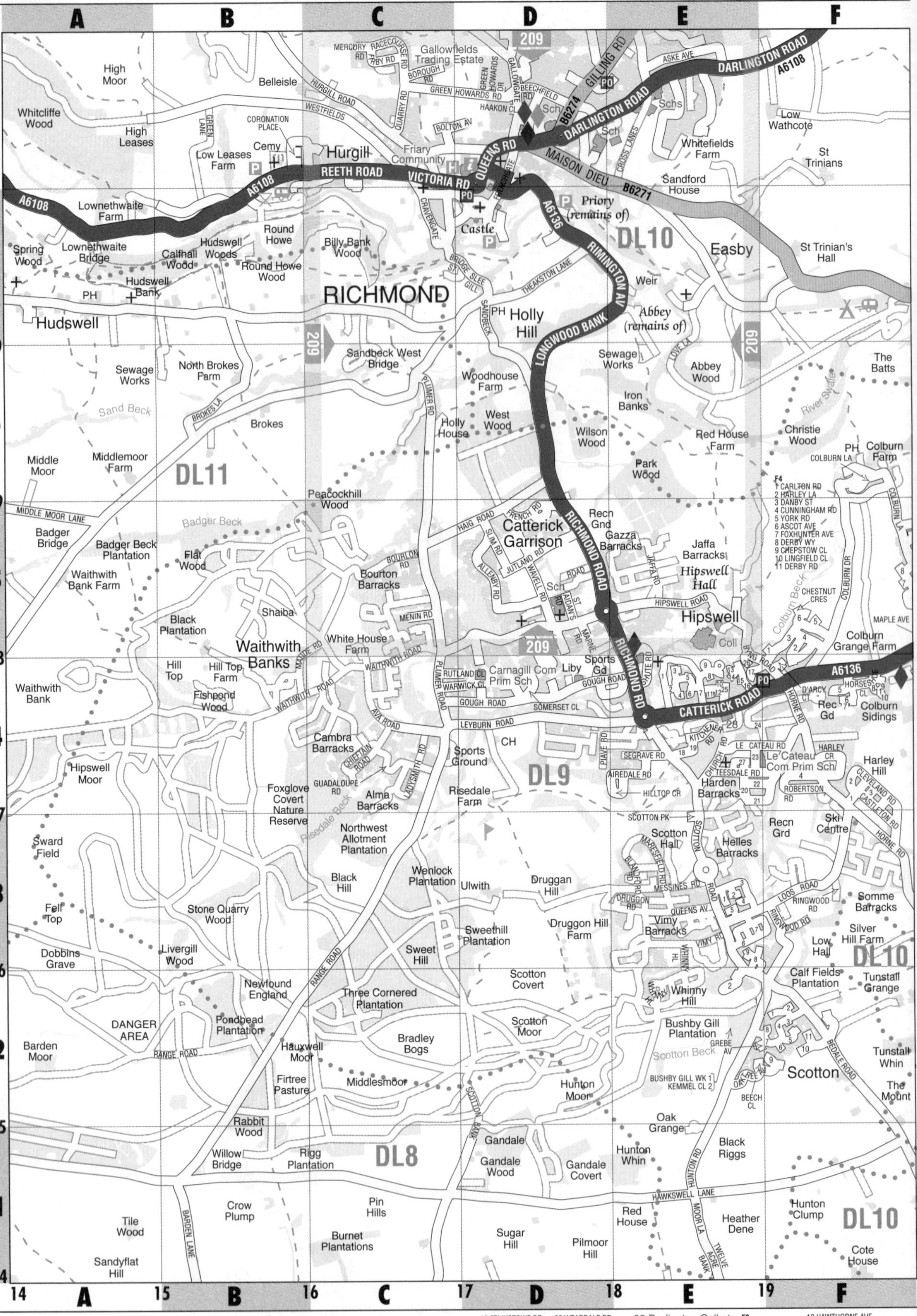
A B C D E F
8
01
7
00
6
99
5
98
4
97
3
96
2
95
1
94
14 15 16 17 18 19
209
High Moor
Belleisle
Whitcliffe Wood
High Leases
Low Leases Farm
CORONATION PLACE
Cemy
Hurgill
HURGILL ROAD
WESTFIELDS
QUARRY RD
MERCURY RD
RACECOURSE RD
FRBY RD
BOROUGH RD
Gallowfields Trading Estate
GREEN HOWARDS RD
GALLOWGATE
BEECHFIELD RD
HAAKON CL
BOLTON AV
Friary Community
QUEENS RD
REETH ROAD
VICTORIA RD
A6108
CRAVENGATE
FRENCHGATE
GILLING RD
B6274
DARLINGTON ROAD
ASKE AVE
A6108
Schs
Sch
CROSS LANES
Low Wathcote
Whitefields Farm
St Trinians
MAISON DIEU
B6271
Sandford House
Priory (remains of)
Castle
A6136
RIMMINGTON AV
DL10
Easby
St Trinian's Hall
Lownethwaite Farm
Round Howe
Billy Bank Wood
Spring Wood
Lownethwaite Bridge
Calfhall Wood
Hudswell Woods
Round Howe Wood
Hudswell Bank
PH
RICHMOND
BRIDGE ST
SLEE GILL
THEAKSTON LANE
SANDBECK
Holly Hill
Weir
Abbey (remains of)
Hudswell
LONGWOOD BANK
Sewage Works
LOVE LA
Abbey Wood
The Batts
Sandbeck West Bridge
Sewage Works
North Brokes Farm
PLUMER RD
Woodhouse Farm
Iron Banks
River Swale
Sand Beck
BROKES LA
Brokes
Holly House
West Wood
Wilson Wood
Red House Farm
Christie Wood
PH
Colburn Farm
COLBURN LA
Middle Moor
Middlemoor Farm
DL11
Park Wood
F4
1 CARLTON RD
2 HARLEY LA
3 DANBY ST
4 CUNNINGHAM RD
5 YORK RD
6 ASCOT AVE
7 FOXHUNTER AVE
8 DERBY WY
9 CHEPSTOW CL
10 LINGFIELD CL
11 DERBY RD
MIDDLE MOOR LANE
Peacockhill Wood
HAIG ROAD
FRENCH RD
Catterick Garrison
RICHMOND ROAD
Recn Gnd
Gazza Barracks
Jaffa Barracks
Badger Beck
Badger Bridge
Badger Beck Plantation
Flat Wood
BOURLON RD
SLIM RD
JUTLAND RD
JAFFA RD
Hipswell Hall
COLBURN DR
COLBURN LA
Waithwith Bank Farm
Bourton Barracks
ALLENBY RD
WAVELL RD
Sch
ROAD
Colburn Beck
CHESTNUT CRES
Black Plantation
Shaiba
MENIN RD
ST AIDAN'S RD
HIPSWELL ROAD
Hipswell
Coll
MAPLE AVE
Colburn Grange Farm
Waithwith Banks
MAIDE RD
White House Farm
WAITHWITH ROAD
MARNE RD
Sports Gd
BYNG ROAD
Hill Top
Hill Top Farm
RUTLAND CL
WARWICK CL
Carnagill Com Prim Sch
Liby
GOUGH ROAD
A6136
Waithwith Bank
Fishpond Wood
GOUGH ROAD
SOMERSET CL
CATTERICK ROAD
HORNE RD
D'ARCY CT
HORSES CL
Rec Gd
Colburn Sidings
AVA ROAD
LEYBURN ROAD
CH
KITCHENER RD
LE CATEAU RD
Cambra Barracks
CHIEFTAIN ROAD
LADYSMITH RD
Sports Ground
PIAVE RD
SEGRAVE RD
CHURCH RD
Le Cateau Com Prim Sch
HARLEY CR
Harley Hill
Hipswell Moor
GUADALOUPE RD
Foxglove Covert Nature Reserve
Alma Barracks
Risedale Farm
DL9
AIREDALE RD
HILLTOP CR
TEESDALE RD
Harden Barracks
ROBERTSON RD
CLEVELAND RD
CASTLETON RD
Risedale Beck
Northwest Allotment Plantation
SCOTTON PK
SCOTTON RD
Scotton Hall
Helles Barracks
Recn Grd
Ski Centre
HORNE RD
Sward Field
MARESFIELD RD
BLANDFORD RD
Black Hill
Wenlock Plantation
Ulwith
Druggan Hill
MESSINES RD
LOOS ROAD
RINGWOOD RD
Somme Barracks
Fell Top
Stone Quarry Wood
DRUGGON RD
QUEENS AV
Vimy Barracks
RINGWOOD RD
Sweethill Plantation
Druggon Hill Farm
VIMY RD
Low Hall
Silver Hill Farm
Dobbins Grave
Livergill Wood
Sweet Hill
WHINNY HL
DL10
RANGE ROAD
Scotton Covert
Calf Fields Plantation
Tunstall Grange
Newfound England
Three Cornered Plantation
Whinny Hill
DANGER AREA
Pondhead Plantation
Scotton Moor
Bushby Gill Plantation
Barden Moor
RANGE ROAD
Hauxwell Moor
Bradley Bogs
Scotton Beck
GREBE AV
Tunstall Whin
BUSHBY GILL WK 1
KEMMEL CL 2
Scotton
BEDALE ROAD
Firtree Pasture
Middlesmoor
Hunton Moor
OAK TREE AV
BEECH CL
The Mount
SCOTTON BANK
Oak Grange
Rabbit Wood
Gandale
Hunton Whin
Black Riggs
Willow Bridge
Rigg Plantation
DL8
Gandale Wood
Gandale Covert
HUNTON RD
HAWKSWELL LANE
Crow Plump
Pin Hills
Red House
MOOR LA
Heather Dene
Hunton Clump
DL10
Tile Wood
BARDEN LANE
Burnet Plantations
Sugar Hill
Pilmoor Hill
TWELVE ACRE BANK
Cote House
Sandyflat Hill

39

E3
1 SAN CARLOS CL
2 GOOSE GN CL
3 GOODWOOD RD
4 STANLEY CL
5 TUMBLEDOWN CL
6 HAMBLETON RD
7 FIELD GR
8 SCOTTON GDNS
9 ORCHARD MS

E4
1 HEATHERDENE RD
2 VICKERS RD
3 BROWNING CL
4 ENFIELD CL
5 MAXIM CL
6 WESSON CL
7 BELTON PK DR
8 DUMFRIES SQ
9 SIDMOUTH SQ

61

10 FELIXSTOWE DR
11 WATCHET RD
12 FILEY CL
13 ST OSWALDS RD
14 ST OSWALDS CL
15 ST MARTINS CL
16 VICARAGE RD
17 LINTON RISE
18 BERWICK RD
19 QUENTIN RD

20 WEARDALE RD
21 WENSLEYDALE RD
22 SWALEDALE RD
23 BROUGH RD
24 WINDSOR RD
25 OLD HOSPITAL COMPOUND
26 KINGFISHER DR
27 TEESDALE TERR

28 Darlington Coll at Catterick Garrison

F2
1 FALCON CL
2 CURLEW CR
3 KINGFISHER CT
4 MALLARD RD
5 OSPREY CL
6 HERON CT
7 KESTREL DR
8 WOODCOCK DR
9 BIRCH CL

10 HAWTHORNE AVE
11 MEANEE RD

Scale: 1¾ inches to 1 mile
0 ¼ ½ mile
0 250m 500m 750m 1 km

A5
1 ST GILES' CL
2 ST PETER'S CL
3 BRIDGE CL
4 ST CUTHBERT'S AVE
5 BROUGH AVE
6 CORONATION AVE
7 SUTTON AVE
8 COLVILLE CRES
9 MEADOWFIELD RD
10 CONSTANTINE AVE
11 CONSTANTINE GR
12 COLVILLE RD
13 BRAMBLE CL
14 CHERRY TREE WY
15 PEPPERMINT DR
16 COTTEE WY
17 ORCHID CT
18 PRIMROSE CT
19 FOXGLOVE CT
20 CROCUS CT
21 LAVENDER CT
22 WALKERVILLE AVE
23 FIRST AVE
24 FIFTH AVE
25 BLUE NILE WY
26 FOURTH AVE
27 FRANCIS DR
28 BAILEY CT
29 EASTON WAY
30 FOSS WY
31 FRANCIS DR
32 DICKENS DR
33 BRONTE DR
34 COOKSON WY
35 KIPLING DR
36 HAWKINS DR
37 FROBISHER DR
38 DRAKES CL
39 BEECHER STOWE DR
40 DARWIN DR
41 CHURCHILL DR
42 FORBES CT
43 MITCHELL GR
44 COPPERBEECH WAY
45 WALNUT AVE
46 ELM TREE AVE
47 SAYERS WYND
48 MAGPIE WALK

21
42

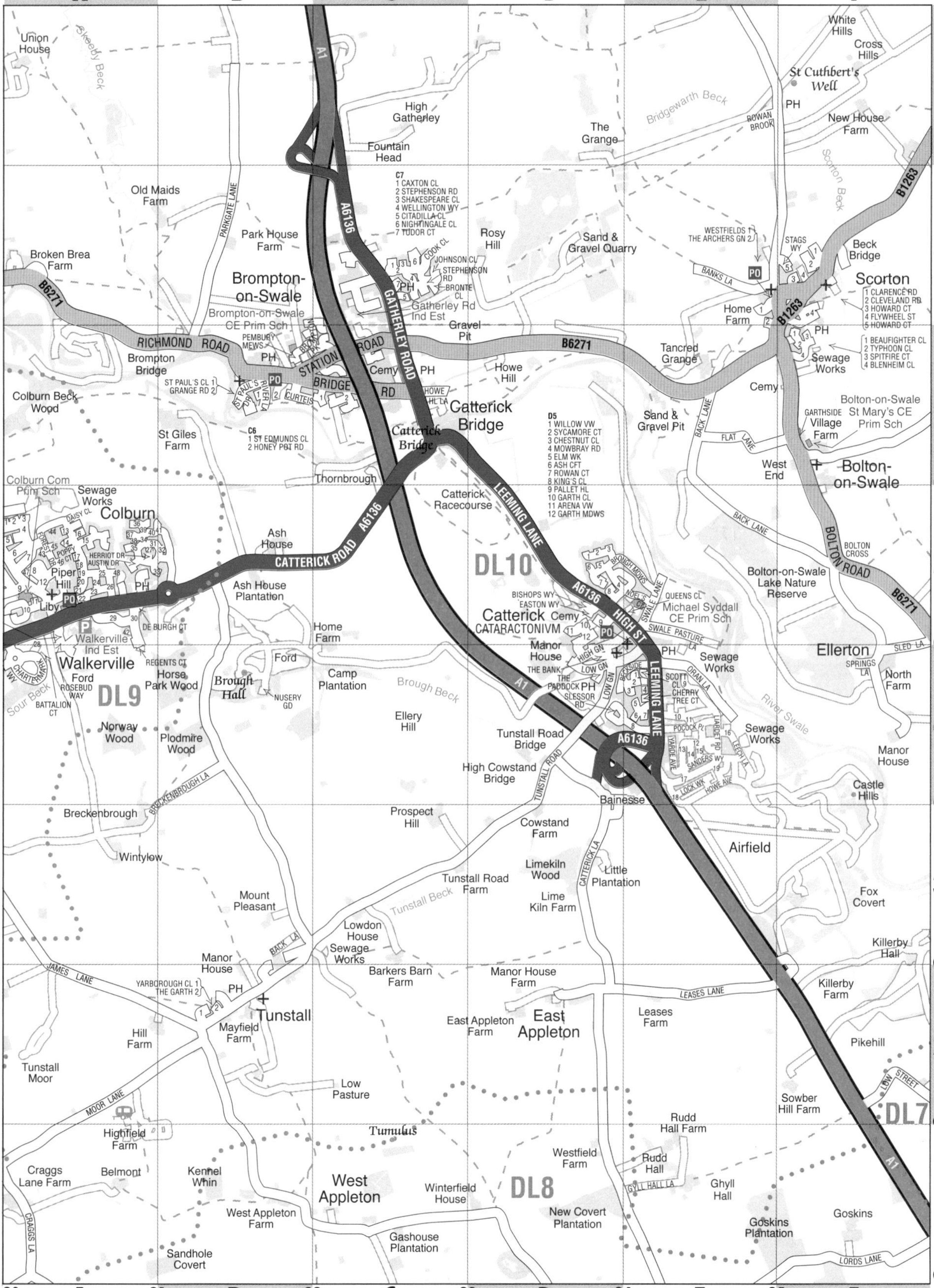

62
42

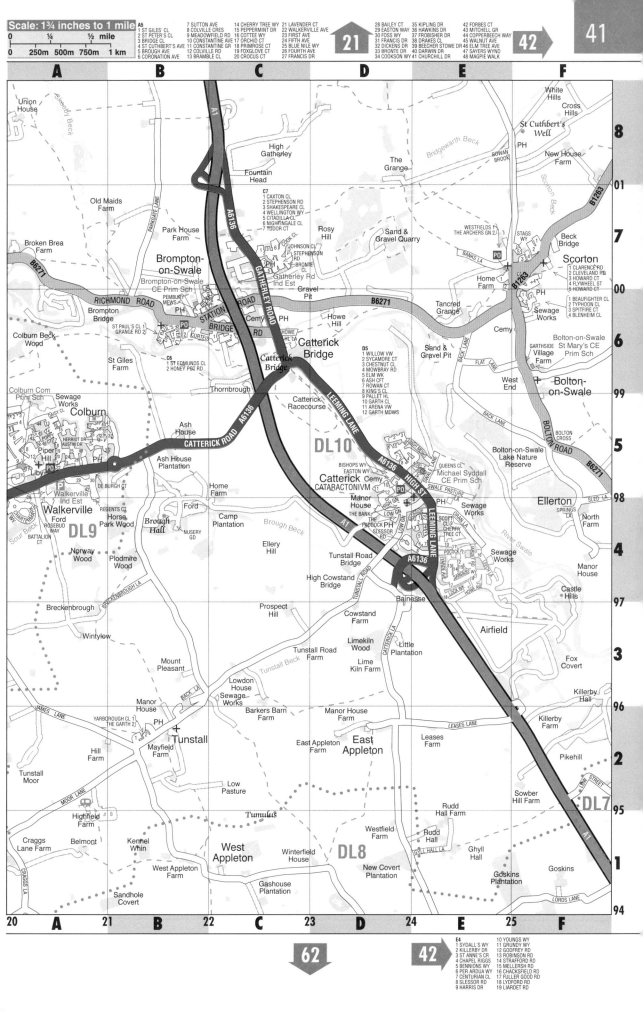

E4
1 SYDALL'S WY
2 KILLERBY DR
3 ST ANNE'S CR
4 CHAPEL RIGGS
5 BENNIONS WY
6 PER ARDUA WY
7 CENTURIAN CL
8 SLESSOR RD
9 HARRIS DR
10 YOUNGS WY
11 GRUNDY WY
12 GODFREY RD
13 ROBINSON RD
14 STRAFFORD RD
15 MELLERSH RD
16 CHACKSFIELD RD
17 FULLER GOOD RD
18 LYDFORD RD
19 LIARDET RD

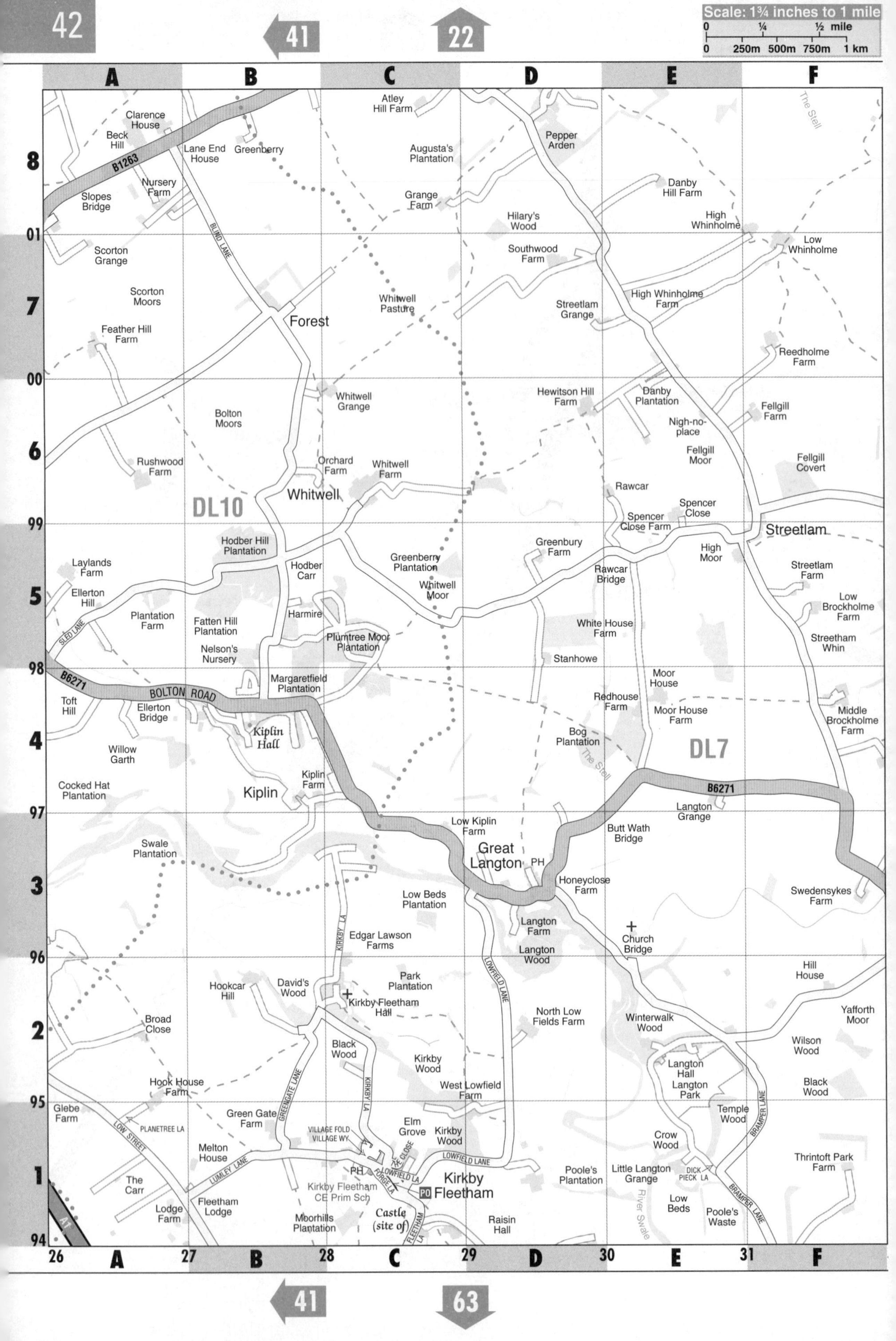
41
22
Scale: 1¾ inches to 1 mile
0 ¼ ½ mile
0 250m 500m 750m 1 km
A B C D E F
8 01 7 00 6 99 5 98 4 97 3 96 2 95 1 94
26 27 28 29 30 31
Clarence House
Beck Hill
B1263
Lane End House
Greenberry
Atley Hill Farm
Augusta's Plantation
Pepper Arden
The Stell
Nursery Farm
Slopes Bridge
Grange Farm
Danby Hill Farm
Hilary's Wood
High Whinholme
Low Whinholme
BLIND LANE
Scorton Grange
Southwood Farm
Scorton Moors
Whitwell Pasture
Streetlam Grange
High Whinholme Farm
Forest
Feather Hill Farm
Reedholme Farm
Whitwell Grange
Hewitson Hill Farm
Danby Plantation
Fellgill Farm
Bolton Moors
Nigh-no-place
Fellgill Moor
Fellgill Covert
Rushwood Farm
Orchard Farm
Whitwell Farm
Rawcar
DL10
Whitwell
Spencer Close
Spencer Close Farm
Streetlam
Hodber Hill Plantation
Greenbury Farm
High Moor
Laylands Farm
Hodber Carr
Greenberry Plantation
Rawcar Bridge
Streetlam Farm
Ellerton Hill
Whitwell Moor
Low Brockholme Farm
Plantation Farm
Fatten Hill Plantation
Harmire
White House Farm
SLED LANE
Nelson's Nursery
Plumtree Moor Plantation
Streetham Whin
Stanhowe
B6271
Margaretfield Plantation
Moor House
BOLTON ROAD
Toft Hill
Ellerton Bridge
Redhouse Farm
Moor House Farm
Middle Brockholme Farm
Kiplin Hall
Willow Garth
Bog Plantation
DL7
Kiplin Farm
Cocked Hat Plantation
Kiplin
Langton Grange
Low Kiplin Farm
Butt Wath Bridge
Swale Plantation
Great Langton
PH
Honeyclose Farm
Low Beds Plantation
Swedensykes Farm
Langton Farm
KIRKBY LA
Edgar Lawson Farms
Church Bridge
Langton Wood
Hill House
Park Plantation
Hookcar Hill
David's Wood
LOWFIELD LANE
Kirkby Fleetham Hall
North Low Fields Farm
Yafforth Moor
Broad Close
Winterwalk Wood
Wilson Wood
Black Wood
Kirkby Wood
Langton Hall
Hook House Farm
West Lowfield Farm
Langton Park
Black Wood
GREENGATE LANE
Glebe Farm
PLANETREE LA
LOW STREET
Green Gate Farm
Temple Wood
BRAMPER LANE
VILLAGE FOLD
VILLAGE WY
Elm Grove
Kirkby Wood
Crow Wood
Melton House
LUMLEY LANE
THE CLOSE
LOWFIELD LANE
Thrintoft Park Farm
PH
LOWFIELD LA
FORGE LA
Kirkby Fleetham
Poole's Plantation
Little Langton Grange
DICK PIECK LA
The Carr
Kirkby Fleetham CE Prim Sch
PO
River Swale
Low Beds
Lodge Farm
Fleetham Lodge
Moorhills Plantation
Castle (site of)
FLEETHAM LA
Raisin Hall
Poole's Waste
A1
41
63

Scale: 1¾ inches to 1 mile
0 ¼ ½ mile
0 250m 500m 750m 1 km

23
44

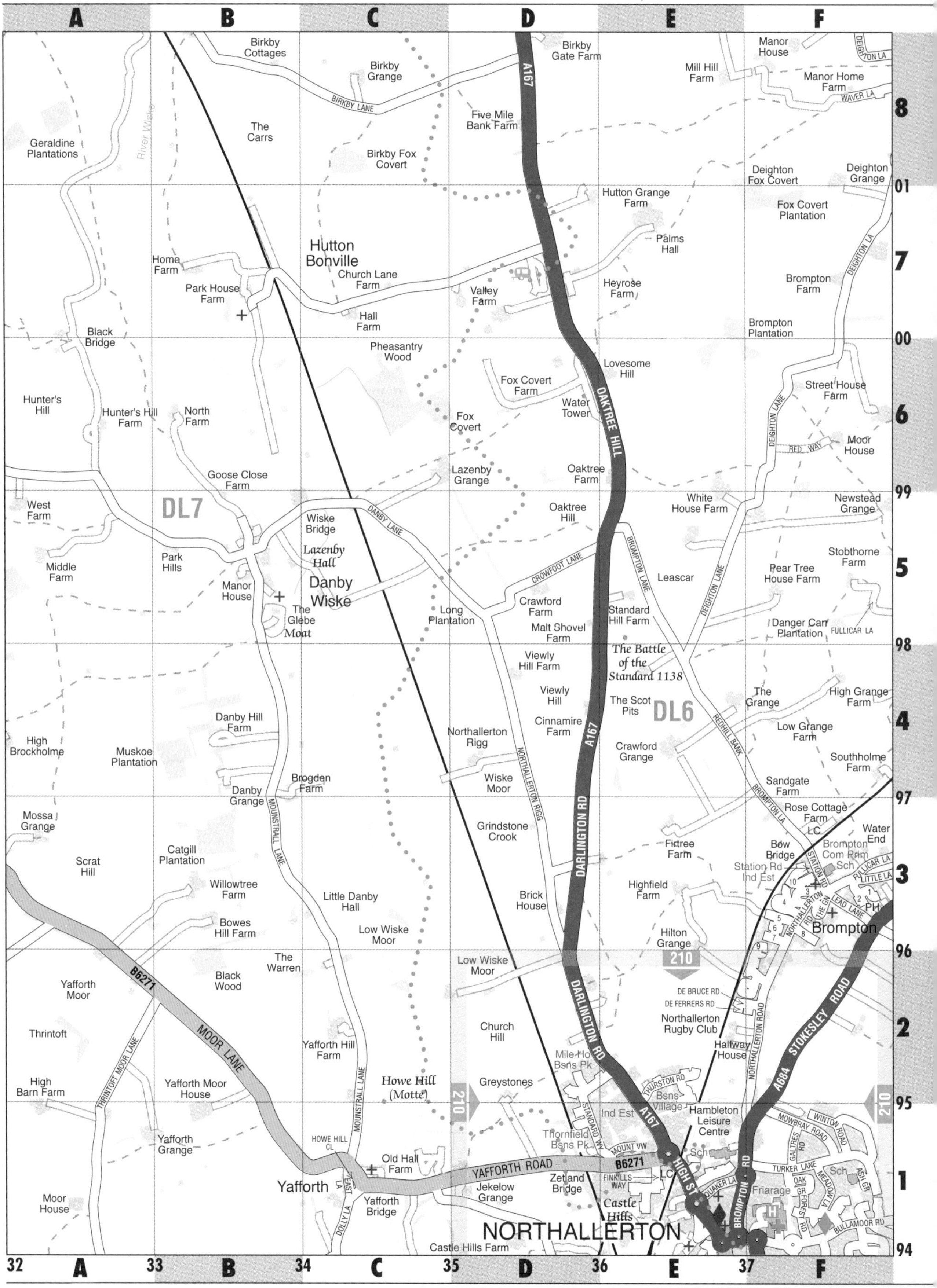

64
44

F3
1 DANELAW FIELDS
2 DANELAW
3 CHURCH VW
4 ORCHARD GR
5 LODGE LA
6 VIKINGS CT
7 CORBER HL
8 MILL HL CL
9 FERNWOOD CL
10 LINEN WY

43
24

Scale: 1¾ inches to 1 mile
0 ¼ ½ mile
0 250m 500m 750m 1 km

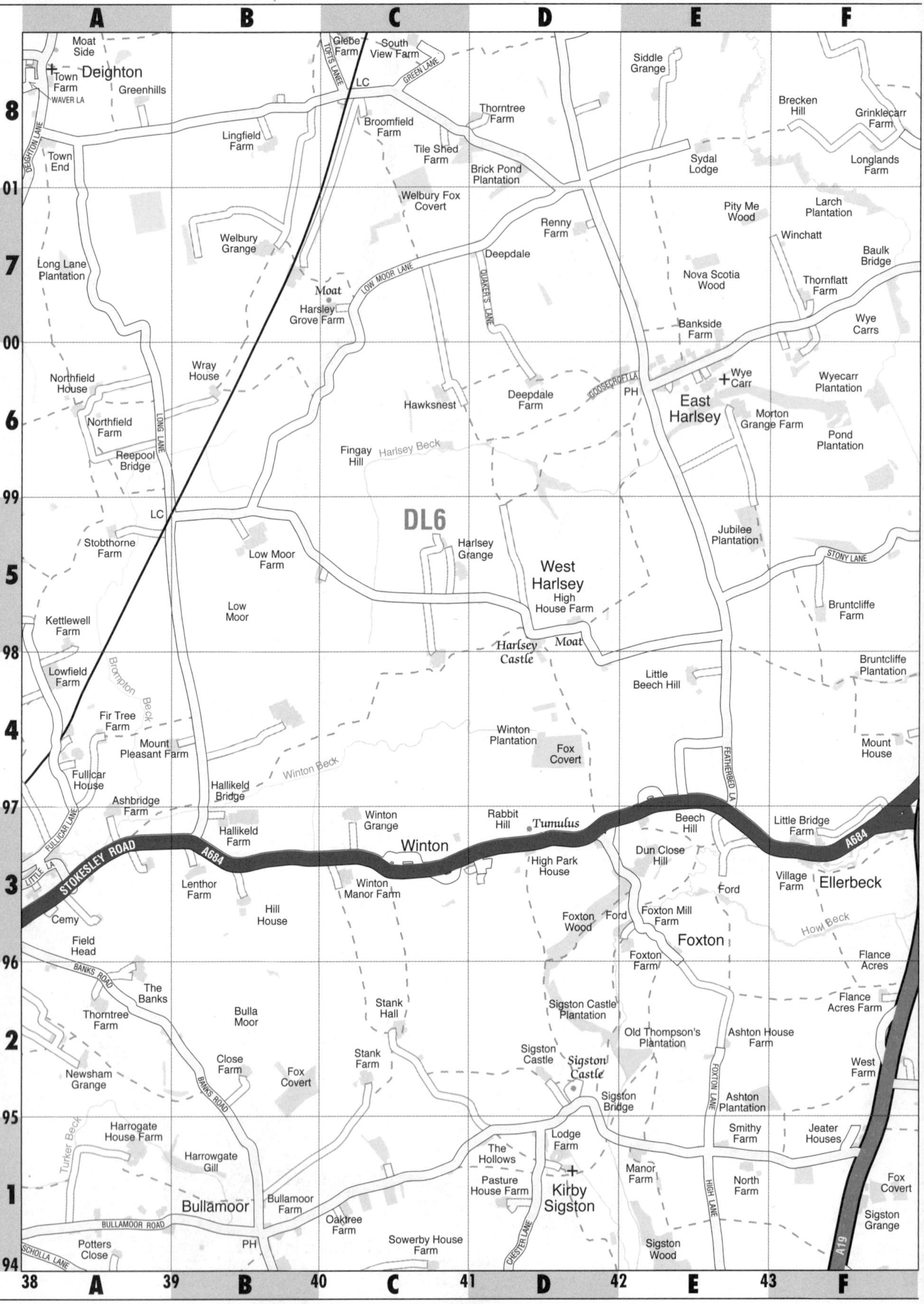
A B C D E F
8
01
7
00
6
99
5
98
4
97
3
96
2
95
1
94
38 39 40 41 42 43
Moat Side
Deighton
Town Farm
WAVER LA
Greenhills
Glebe Farm
TOFTS LANE
South View Farm
GREEN LANE
LC
DEIGHTON LANE
Town End
Lingfield Farm
Broomfield Farm
Thorntree Farm
Siddle Grange
Brecken Hill
Grinklecarr Farm
Tile Shed Farm
Brick Pond Plantation
Sydal Lodge
Longlands Farm
Welbury Fox Covert
Renny Farm
Pity Me Wood
Larch Plantation
Welbury Grange
Winchatt
Deepdale
Baulk Bridge
Long Lane Plantation
Moat
LOW MOOR LANE
QUAKER'S LANE
Nova Scotia Wood
Thornflatt Farm
Harsley Grove Farm
Bankside Farm
Wye Carrs
Wray House
Northfield House
GOOSECROFT LA
PH
Wye Carr
Wyecarr Plantation
Hawksnest
Deepdale Farm
East Harlsey
Morton Grange Farm
Northfield Farm
LONG LANE
Pond Plantation
Reepool Bridge
Fingay Hill
Harlsey Beck
DL6
Jubilee Plantation
Stobthorne Farm
Low Moor Farm
Harlsey Grange
STONY LANE
West Harlsey
High House Farm
Low Moor
Bruntcliffe Farm
Kettlewell Farm
Harlsey Castle
Moat
Bruntcliffe Plantation
Lowfield Farm
Brompton Beck
Little Beech Hill
Fir Tree Farm
Winton Plantation
Mount Pleasant Farm
Fox Covert
Mount House
Fullicar House
Winton Beck
FEATHERBED LA
Hallikeld Bridge
Ashbridge Farm
FULLICAR LANE
Winton Grange
Rabbit Hill
Tumulus
Beech Hill
Little Bridge Farm
Hallikeld Farm
STOKESLEY ROAD
A684
Winton
Dun Close Hill
A684
LITTLE LA
Lenthor Farm
High Park House
Winton Manor Farm
Village Farm
Ellerbeck
Ford
Cemy
Hill House
Foxton Wood
Ford
Foxton Mill Farm
Field Head
Foxton
How Beck
Foxton Farm
Flance Acres
BANKS ROAD
The Banks
Sigston Castle Plantation
Flance Acres Farm
Thorntree Farm
Bulla Moor
Stank Hall
Old Thompson's Plantation
Ashton House Farm
Newsham Grange
Close Farm
Fox Covert
Stank Farm
Sigston Castle
Sigston Castle
FOXTON LANE
West Farm
BANKS ROAD
Sigston Bridge
Ashton Plantation
Harrogate House Farm
Turker Beck
Lodge Farm
Smithy Farm
Jeater Houses
Harrowgate Gill
The Hollows
Manor Farm
North Farm
Fox Covert
Pasture House Farm
Kirby Sigston
HIGH LANE
Bullamoor
Bullamoor Farm
Sigston Grange
BULLAMOOR ROAD
Oaktree Farm
CHESTER LANE
Potters Close
PH
Sowerby House Farm
Sigston Wood
A19
SCHOLLA LANE

43
65

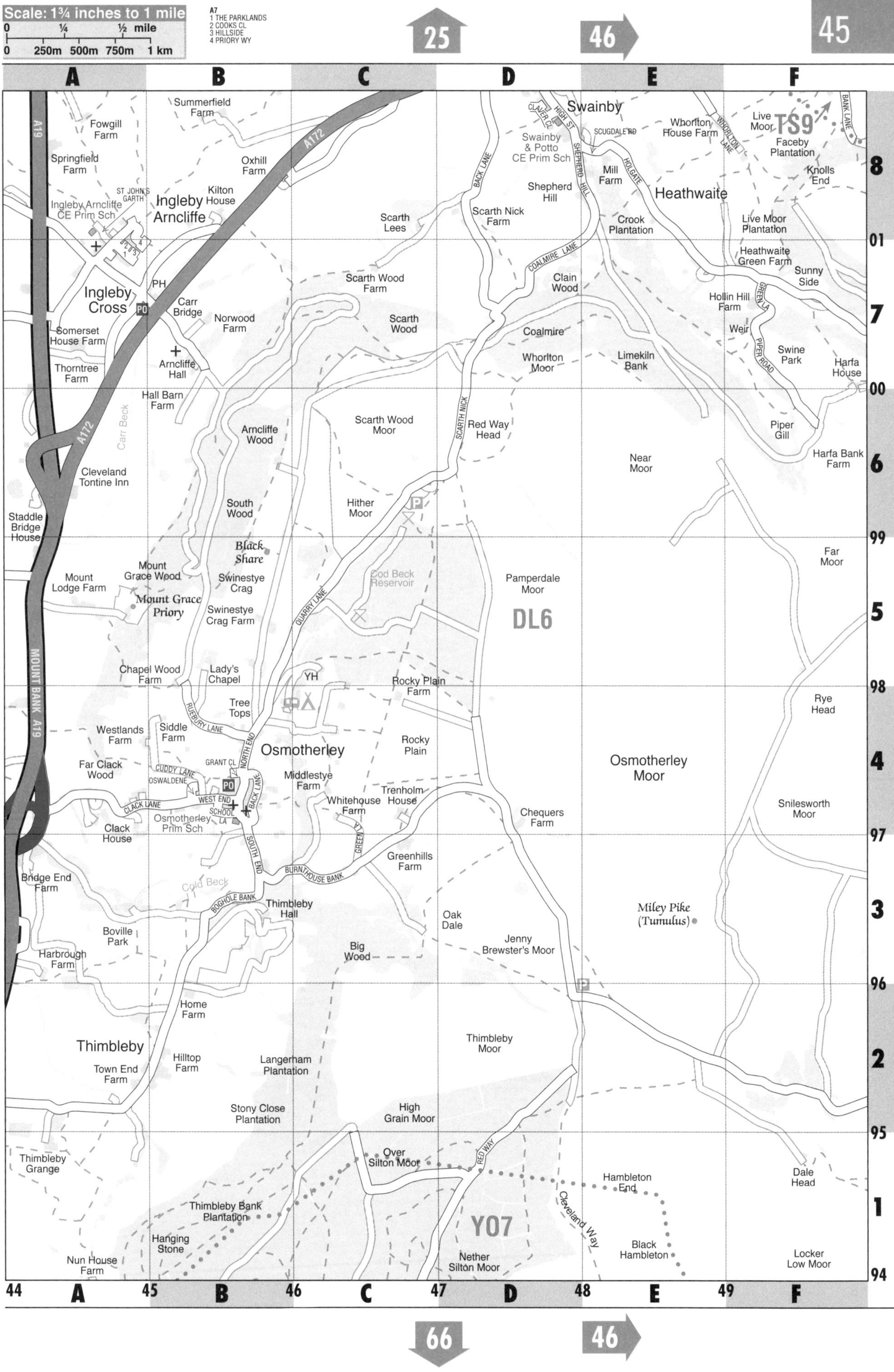

Scale: 1¾ inches to 1 mile
0 ¼ ½ mile
0 250m 500m 750m 1 km
A7
1 THE PARKLANDS
2 COOKS CL
3 HILLSIDE
4 PRIORY WY
25
46
A B C D E F
Summerfield Farm
Fowgill Farm
Springfield Farm
Oxhill Farm
A172
A19
Swainby
CLAVER CL
HIGH ST
SCUGDALE RD
Swainby & Potto CE Prim Sch
Whorlton House Farm
WHORLTON LANE
Live Moor
TS9
BANK LANE
Faceby Plantation
Knolls End
BACK LANE
SHEPHERD HILL
HOLGATE
Mill Farm
Shepherd Hill
Heathwaite
ST JOHN'S GARTH
Ingleby Arncliffe CE Prim Sch
Ingleby Arncliffe
Kilton House
Scarth Lees
Scarth Nick Farm
Crook Plantation
Live Moor Plantation
Heathwaite Green Farm
Sunny Side
COALMIRE LANE
Clain Wood
PH
Ingleby Cross
PO
Carr Bridge
Norwood Farm
Scarth Wood Farm
Scarth Wood
Hollin Hill Farm
GREEN LA
Weir
Coalmire
Somerset House Farm
Arncliffe Hall
Thorntree Farm
Whorlton Moor
Limekiln Bank
PIPER ROAD
Swine Park
Harfa House
Hall Barn Farm
Carr Beck
Arncliffe Wood
Scarth Wood Moor
SCARTH NICK
Red Way Head
Piper Gill
Harfa Bank Farm
Cleveland Tontine Inn
Near Moor
South Wood
Hither Moor
P
Staddle Bridge House
Black Share
Far Moor
Mount Grace Wood
Mount Lodge Farm
Swinestye Crag
Cod Beck Reservoir
Pamperdale Moor
Mount Grace Priory
QUARRY LANE
Swinestye Crag Farm
DL6
MOUNT BANK A19
Chapel Wood Farm
Lady's Chapel
YH
Rocky Plain Farm
Rye Head
Tree Tops
RUEBURY LANE
Westlands Farm
Siddle Farm
NORTH END
Osmotherley
Rocky Plain
Osmotherley Moor
Far Clack Wood
CUDDY LANE
GRANT CL
OSWALDENE
Middlestye Farm
Trenholm House
BACK LANE
WEST END
Whitehouse Farm
CLACK LANE
SCHOOL LA
Chequers Farm
Snilesworth Moor
Osmotherley Prim Sch
Clack House
GREEN LA
SOUTH END
Greenhills Farm
BURNTHOUSE BANK
Bridge End Farm
Cold Beck
BOGHOLE BANK
Thimbleby Hall
Miley Pike (Tumulus)
Oak Dale
Boville Park
Big Wood
Jenny Brewster's Moor
Harbrough Farm
Home Farm
Thimbleby
Hilltop Farm
Langerham Plantation
Thimbleby Moor
Town End Farm
Stony Close Plantation
High Grain Moor
Thimbleby Grange
Over Silton Moor
RED WAY
Hambleton End
Dale Head
Cleveland Way
Thimbleby Bank Plantation
YO7
Hanging Stone
Black Hambleton
Nun House Farm
Nether Silton Moor
Locker Low Moor
8 01 7 00 6 99 5 98 4 97 3 96 2 95 1 94
44 45 46 47 48 49
66
46

45
26

Scale: 1¾ inches to 1 mile
0 ¼ ½ mile
0 250m 500m 750m 1 km

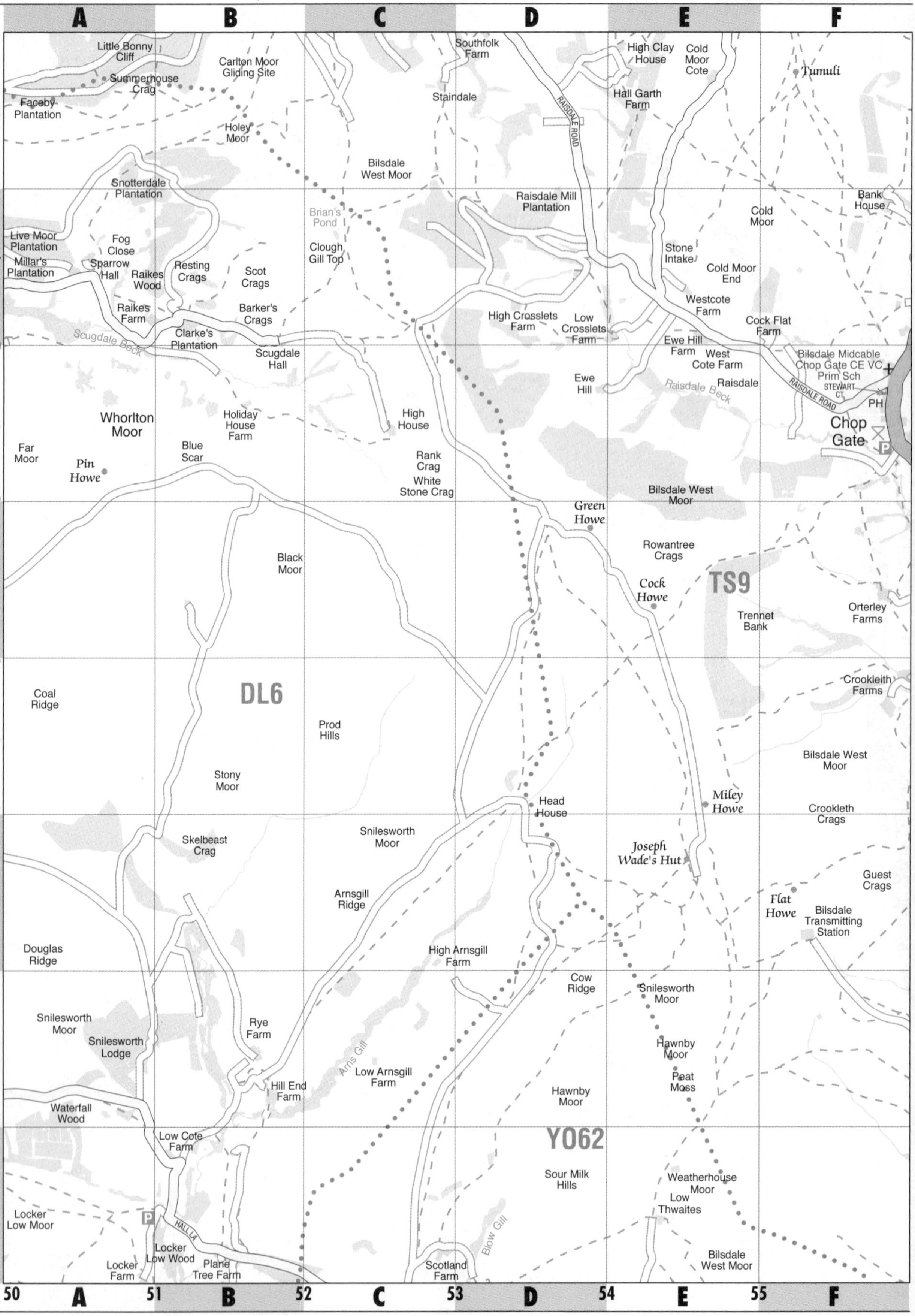

45
67

Scale: 1¾ inches to 1 mile
0 ¼ ½ mile
0 250m 500m 750m 1 km

27
48

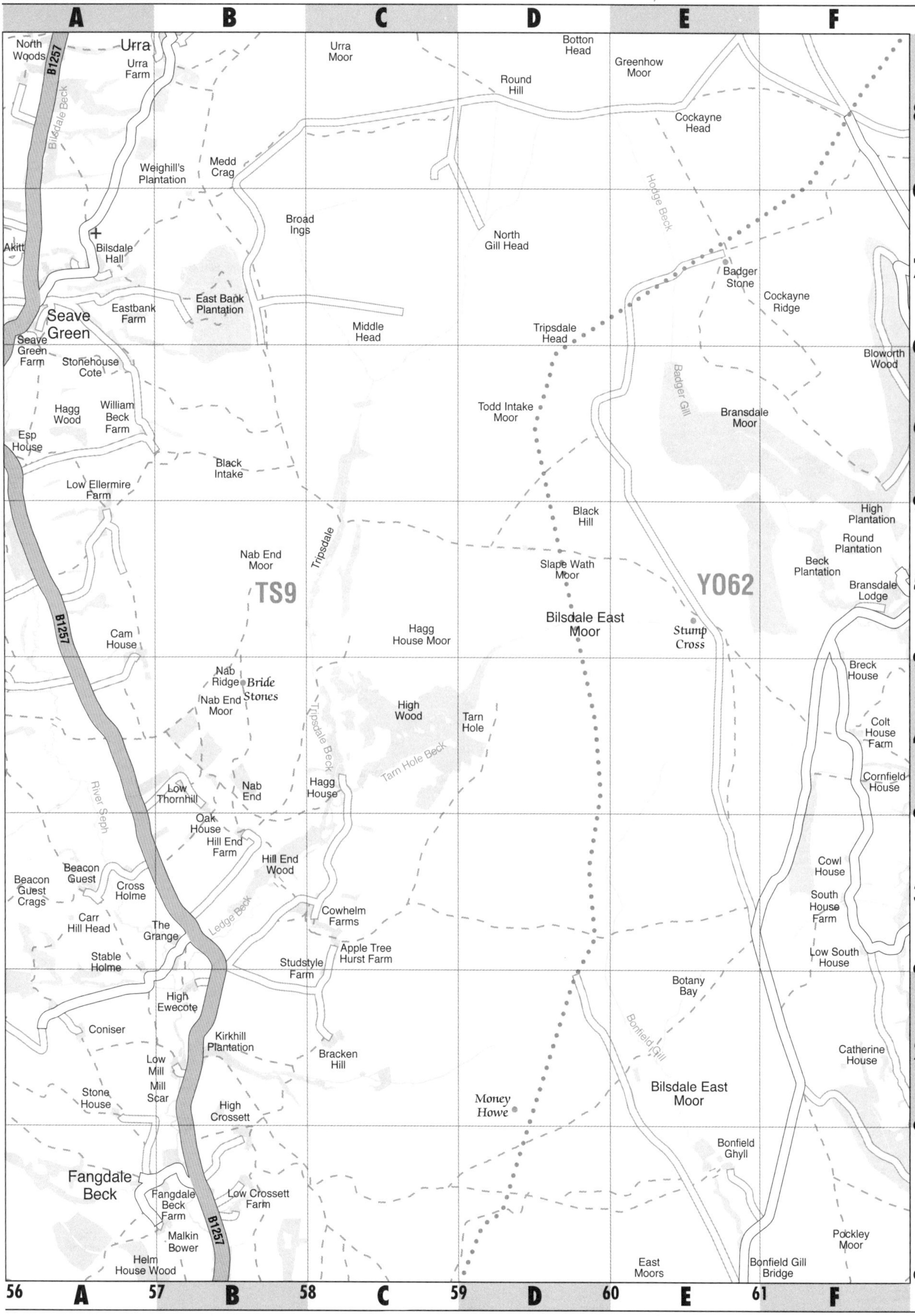

68
48

47
28
Scale: 1¾ inches to 1 mile
0 ¼ ½ mile
0 250m 500m 750m 1 km

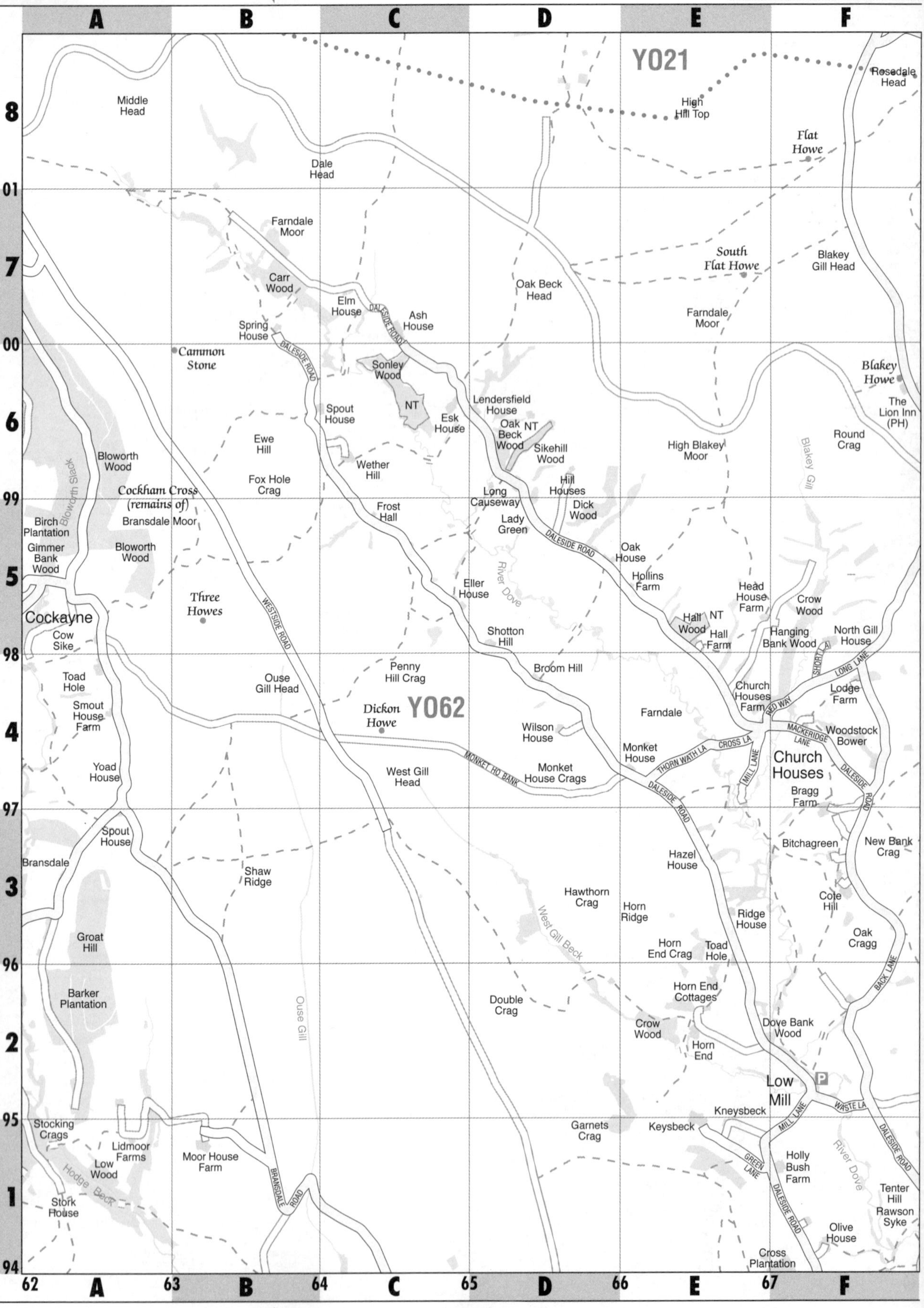

47
69

Scale: 1¾ inches to 1 mile

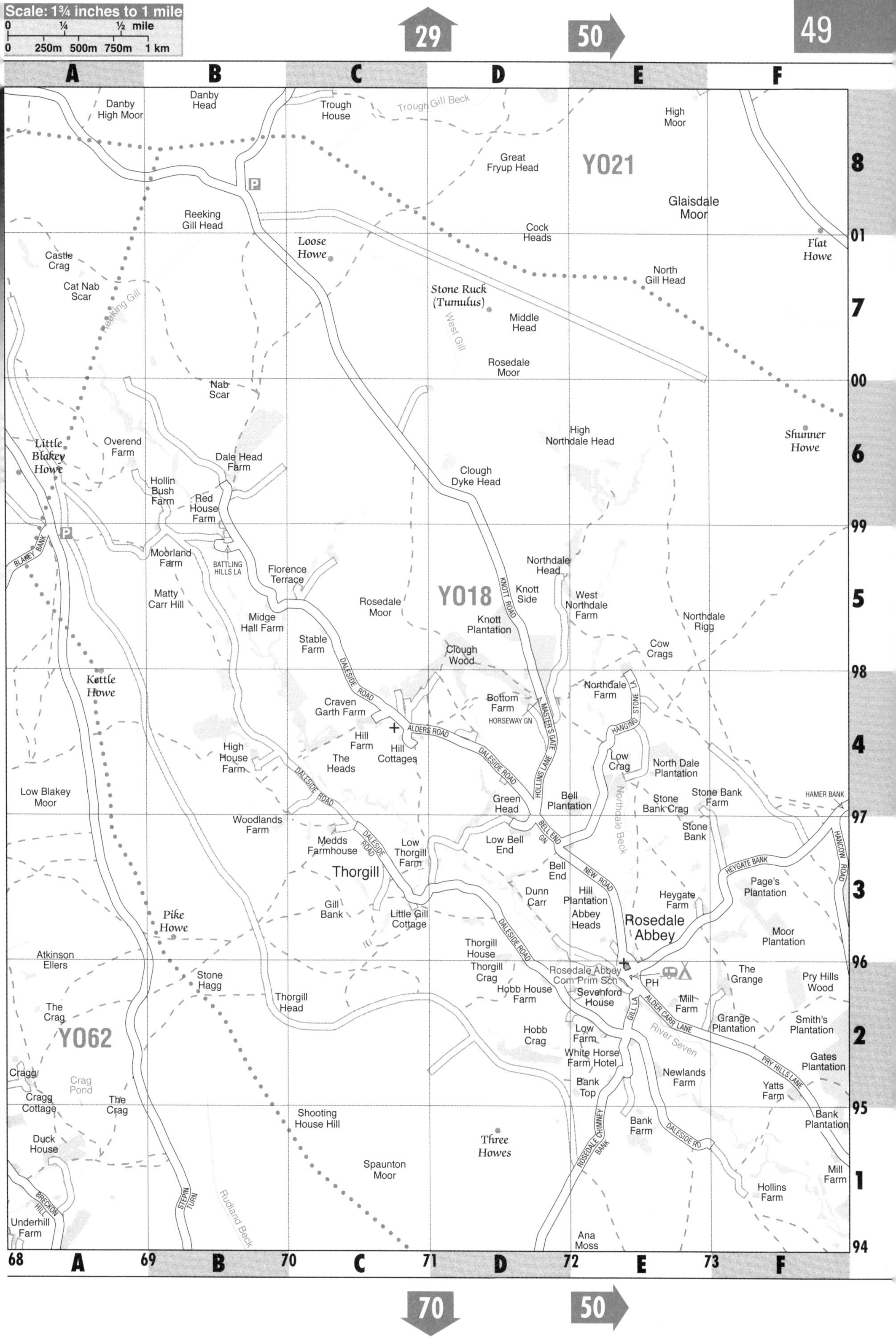

49
30

Scale: 1¾ inches to 1 mile
0 ¼ ½ mile
0 250m 500m 750m 1 km

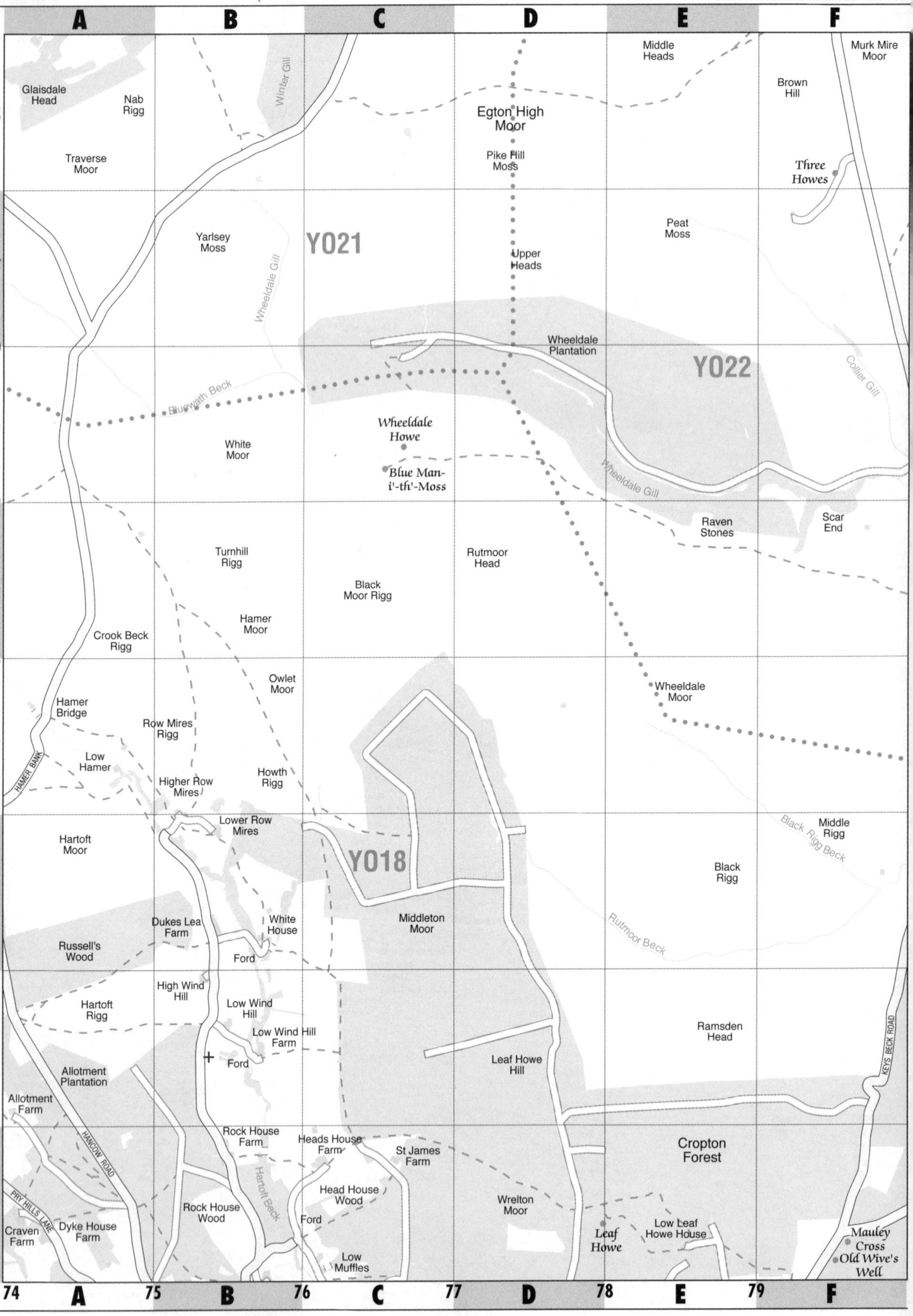

49
71

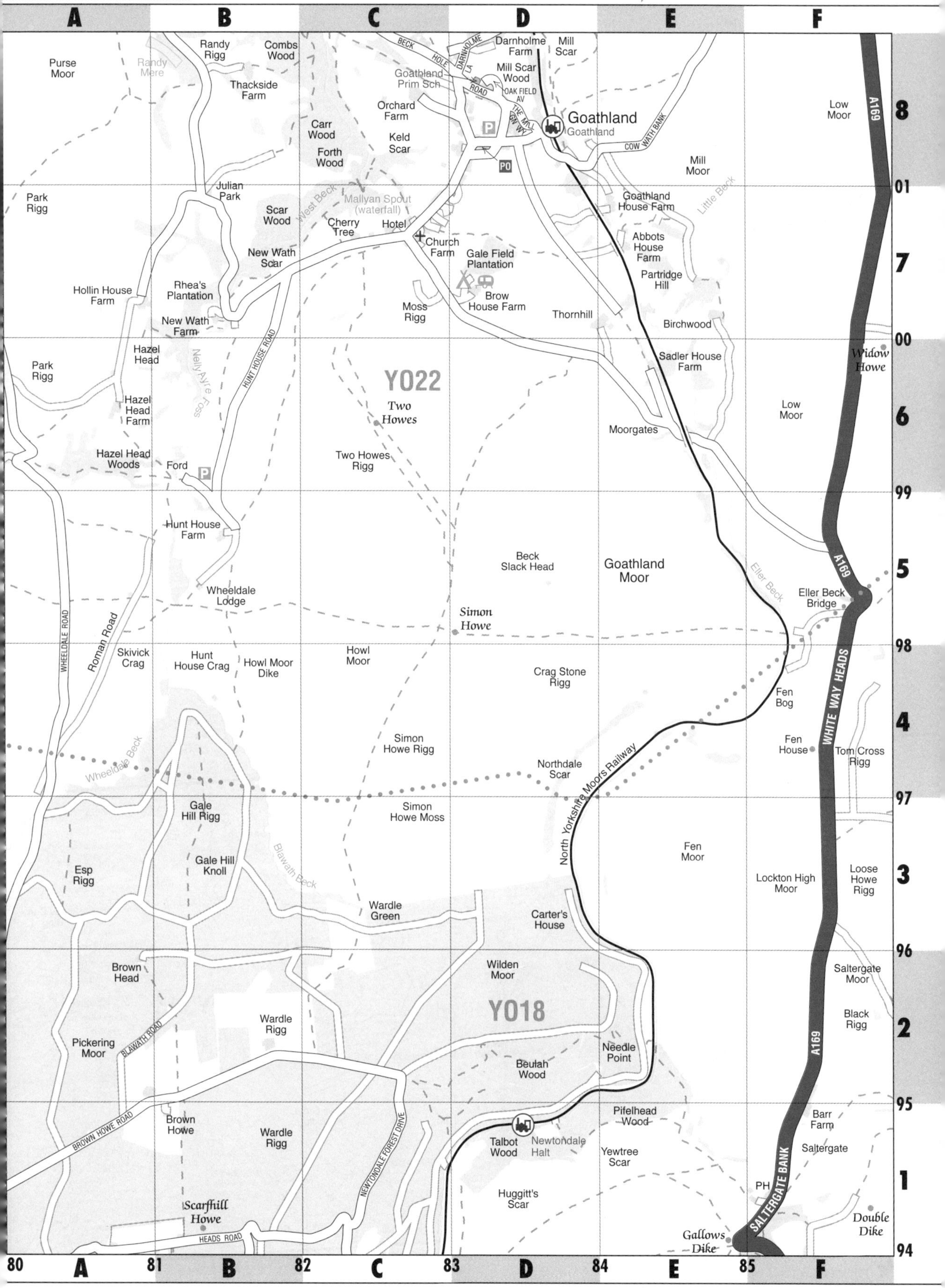
A B C D E F
Purse Moor
Randy Mere
Randy Rigg
Combs Wood
Thackside Farm
Darnholme Farm
Mill Scar
Mill Scar Wood
Goathland Prim Sch
Beck Hole Road
Darnholme La
Oak Field Av
The Mill Gn Wy
Orchard Farm
Carr Wood
Keld Scar
Forth Wood
Goathland
Goathland
Cow Wath Bank
Low Moor
A169
Mill Moor
Park Rigg
Julian Park
Scar Wood
West Beck
Mallyan Spout (waterfall)
Cherry Tree
Hotel
Church Farm
Goathland House Farm
Little Beck
Abbots House Farm
Partridge Hill
New Wath Scar
Gale Field Plantation
Hollin House Farm
Rhea's Plantation
Brow House Farm
Moss Rigg
Thornhill
Birchwood
New Wath Farm
Hazel Head
Park Rigg
Hunt House Road
Nelly Ayre Foss
YO22
Sadler House Farm
Widow Howe
Hazel Head Farm
Two Howes
Low Moor
Moorgates
Hazel Head Woods
Ford
Two Howes Rigg
Hunt House Farm
Beck Slack Head
Goathland Moor
Eller Beck
Wheeldale Lodge
Eller Beck Bridge
Simon Howe
Roman Road
Wheeldale Road
Skivick Crag
Hunt House Crag
Howl Moor Dike
Howl Moor
Crag Stone Rigg
Fen Bog
White Way Heads
Simon Howe Rigg
Fen House
Tom Cross Rigg
Wheeldale Beck
Northdale Scar
North Yorkshire Moors Railway
Gale Hill Rigg
Simon Howe Moss
Fen Moor
Esp Rigg
Gale Hill Knoll
Blawath Beck
Lockton High Moor
Loose Howe Rigg
Wardle Green
Carter's House
Brown Head
Wilden Moor
Saltergate Moor
YO18
Wardle Rigg
Black Rigg
Pickering Moor
Blawath Road
Needle Point
Beulah Wood
Brown Howe Road
Brown Howe
Wardle Rigg
Newtondale Forest Drive
Pifelhead Wood
Barr Farm
Talbot Wood
Newtondale Halt
Yewtree Scar
Saltergate
Saltergate Bank
PH
Huggitt's Scar
Scarfhill Howe
Heads Road
Gallows Dike
Double Dike
8 01 7 00 6 99 5 98 4 97 3 96 2 95 1 94
80 A 81 B 82 C 83 D 84 E 85 F

51
32

Scale: 1¾ inches to 1 mile
0 ¼ ½ mile
0 250m 500m 750m 1 km

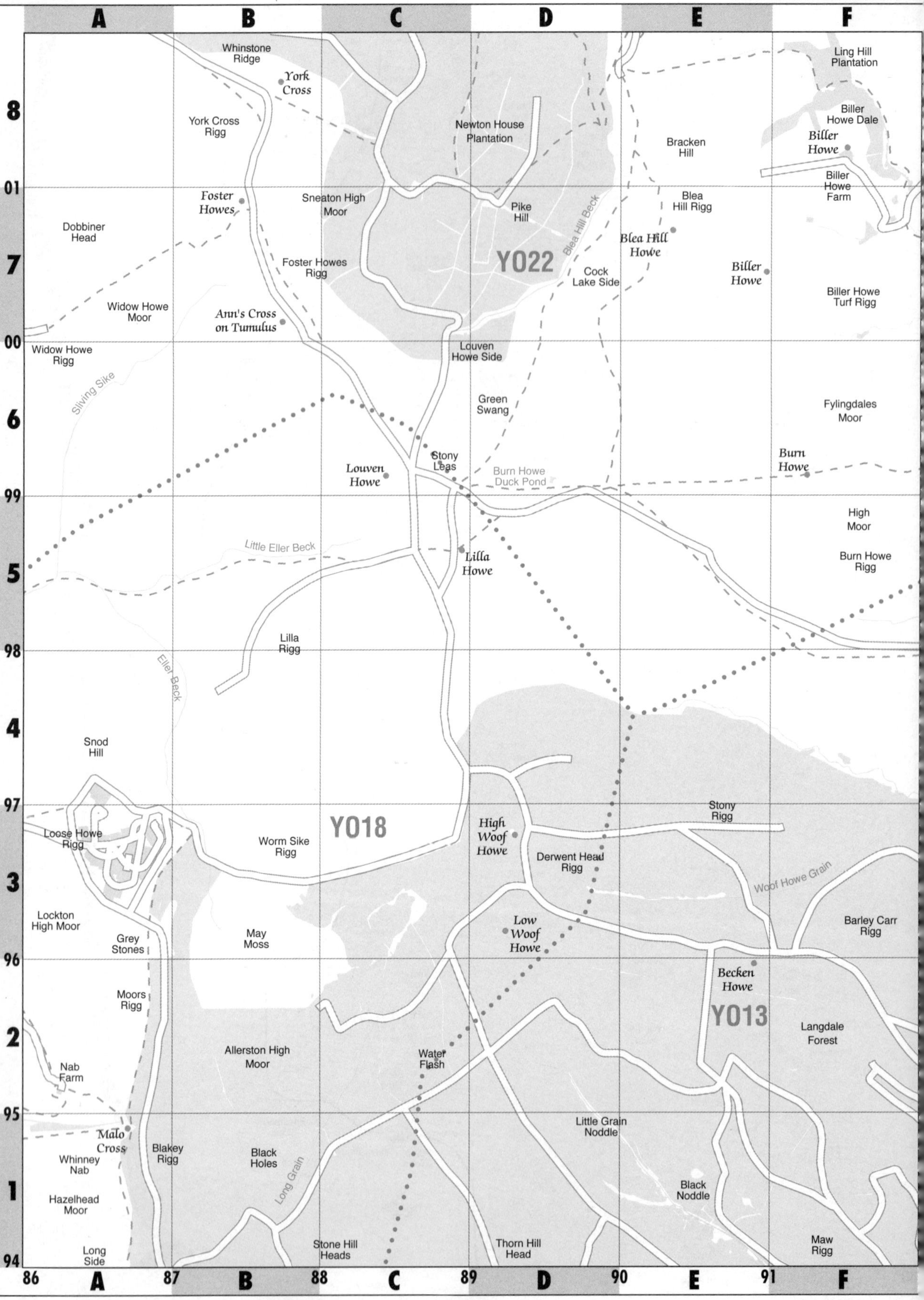
A
B
C
D
E
F
8
01
7
00
6
99
5
98
4
97
3
96
2
95
1
94
86
87
88
89
90
91
Whinstone Ridge
York Cross
York Cross Rigg
Newton House Plantation
Bracken Hill
Ling Hill Plantation
Biller Howe Dale
Biller Howe
Biller Howe Farm
Foster Howes
Sneaton High Moor
Pike Hill
Blea Hill Rigg
Blea Hill Beck
Dobbiner Head
Blea Hill Howe
YO22
Foster Howes Rigg
Cock Lake Side
Biller Howe
Biller Howe Turf Rigg
Widow Howe Moor
Ann's Cross on Tumulus
Widow Howe Rigg
Louven Howe Side
Sliving Sike
Green Swang
Fylingdales Moor
Stony Leas
Burn Howe
Louven Howe
Burn Howe Duck Pond
High Moor
Little Eller Beck
Lilla Howe
Burn Howe Rigg
Lilla Rigg
Eller Beck
Snod Hill
Stony Rigg
Loose Howe Rigg
YO18
Worm Sike Rigg
High Woof Howe
Derwent Head Rigg
Woof Howe Grain
Lockton High Moor
May Moss
Low Woof Howe
Barley Carr Rigg
Grey Stones
Becken Howe
Moors Rigg
YO13
Langdale Forest
Allerston High Moor
Water Flash
Nab Farm
Malo Cross
Little Grain Noddle
Whinney Nab
Blakey Rigg
Black Holes
Long Grain
Black Noddle
Hazelhead Moor
Long Side
Stone Hill Heads
Thorn Hill Head
Maw Rigg

51
73

Scale: 1¾ inches to 1 mile

33
54

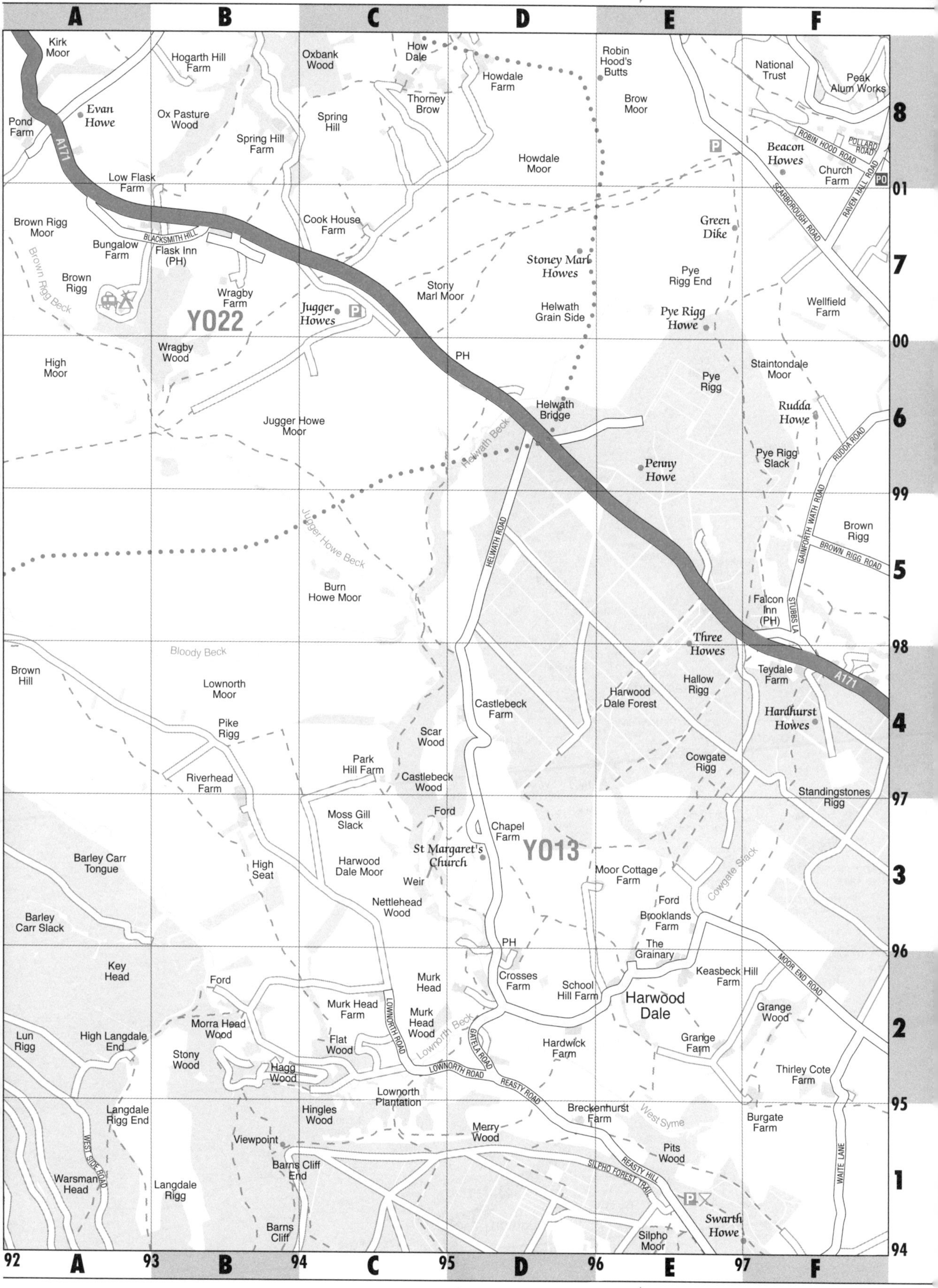

74
54

Scale: 1¾ inches to 1 mile
0 ¼ ½ mile
0 250m 500m 750m 1 km

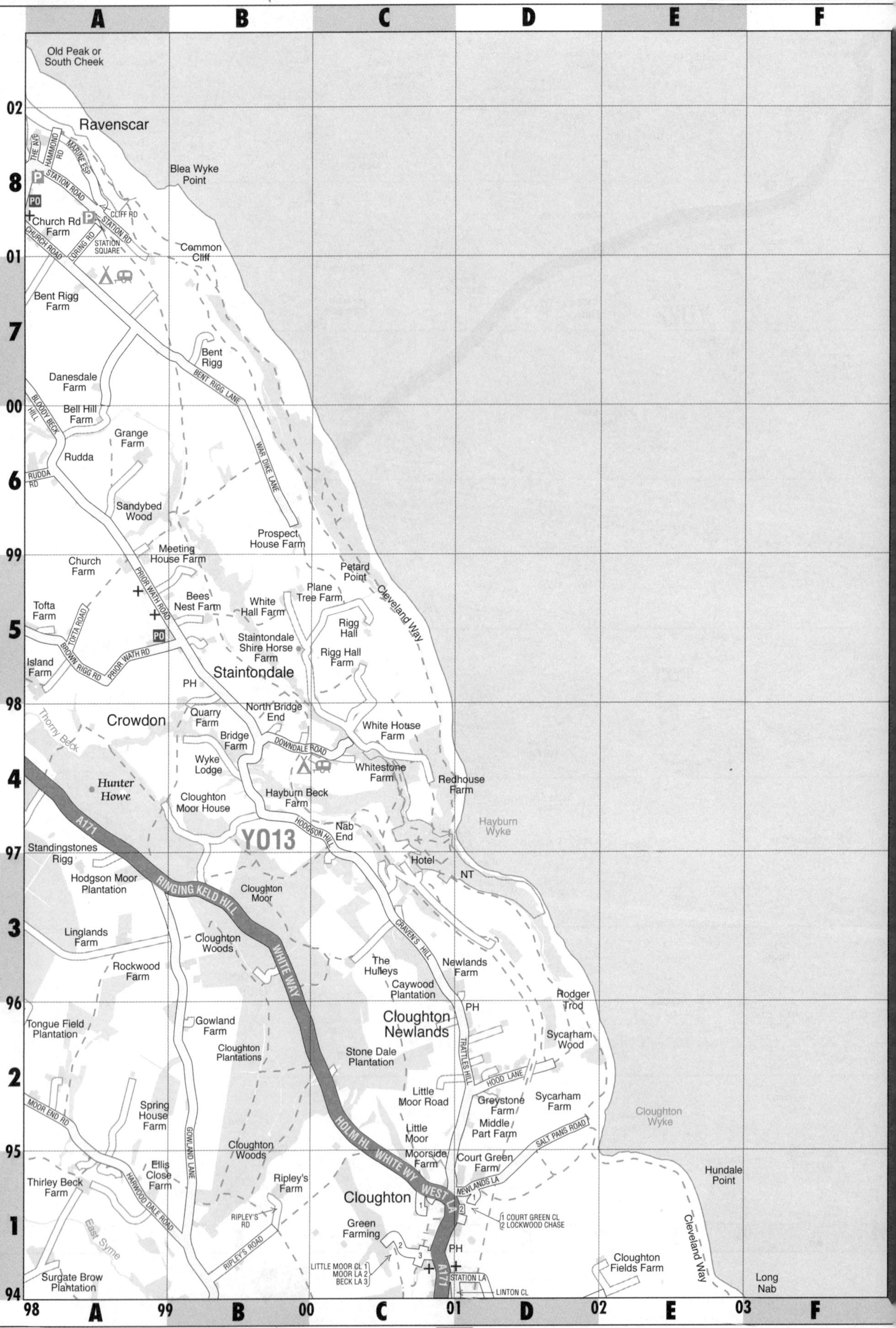
A
B
C
D
E
F
Old Peak or South Cheek
Ravenscar
THE AVE
HAMMOND RD
MARINE ESP
STATION ROAD
Blea Wyke Point
PO
Church Rd Farm
CLIFF RD
STATION RD
STATION SQUARE
LORING RD
CHURCH ROAD
Common Cliff
Bent Rigg Farm
Bent Rigg
BENT RIGG LANE
Danesdale Farm
Bell Hill Farm
BLOODY BECK HILL
Grange Farm
Rudda
RUDDA RD
WAR DIKE LANE
Sandybed Wood
Prospect House Farm
Meeting House Farm
Church Farm
Petard Point
Plane Tree Farm
Cleveland Way
White Hall Farm
Bees Nest Farm
PRIOR WATH ROAD
Tofta Farm
TOFTA ROAD
Rigg Hall
Staintondale Shire Horse Farm
Rigg Hall Farm
PRIOR WATH RD
BROWN RIGG RD
Island Farm
Staintondale
PH
North Bridge End
Crowdon
Quarry Farm
White House Farm
Thorny Beck
Bridge Farm
DOWNDALE ROAD
Wyke Lodge
Whitestone Farm
Redhouse Farm
Hunter Howe
Cloughton Moor House
Hayburn Beck Farm
A171
Hayburn Wyke
Nab End
HODGSON HILL
YO13
Standingstones Rigg
Hotel
NT
Hodgson Moor Plantation
RINGING KELD HILL
Cloughton Moor
CRAVEN'S HILL
Linglands Farm
Cloughton Woods
WHITE WAY
Rockwood Farm
The Hulleys
Newlands Farm
Caywood Plantation
Rodger Trod
PH
Tongue Field Plantation
Gowland Farm
Cloughton Newlands
Sycarham Wood
Cloughton Plantations
Stone Dale Plantation
TRATTLES HILL
HOOD LANE
Little Moor Road
Greystone Farm
Sycarham Farm
MOOR END RD
Spring House Farm
HOLM HL
Middle Part Farm
Cloughton Wyke
GOWLAND LANE
Little Moor
SALT PANS ROAD
Cloughton Woods
Moorside Farm
Court Green Farm
Ellis Close Farm
WHITE WY
Hundale Point
Thirley Beck Farm
Ripley's Farm
WEST LA
NEWLANDS LA
Cloughton
HARWOOD DALE ROAD
RIPLEY'S RD
1 COURT GREEN CL
2 LOCKWOOD CHASE
East Syme
Green Farming
Cleveland Way
RIPLEY'S ROAD
PH
Cloughton Fields Farm
LITTLE MOOR CL 1
MOOR LA 2
BECK LA 3
Surgate Brow Plantation
STATION LA
Long Nab
LINTON CL
02
8
01
7
00
6
99
5
98
4
97
3
96
2
95
1
94
98
99
00
01
02
03

Scale: 1¾ inches to 1 mile
0 ¼ ½ mile
0 250m 500m 750m 1 km

34
56

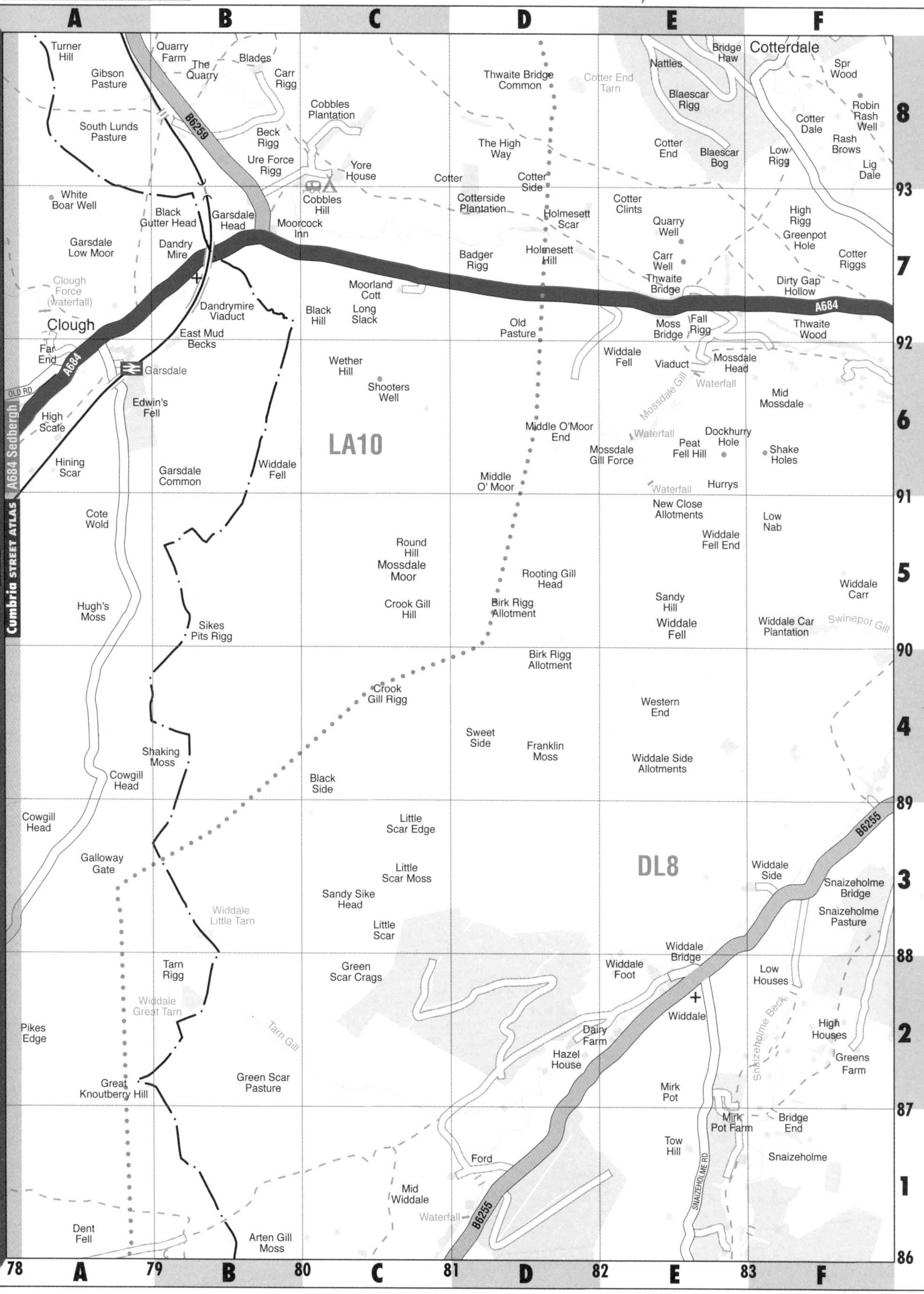
A
B
C
D
E
F
Turner Hill
Gibson Pasture
Quarry Farm
The Quarry
Blades
Carr Rigg
Cobbles Plantation
Thwaite Bridge Common
Cotter End Tarn
Nattles
Bridge Haw
Cotterdale
Spr Wood
Blaescar Rigg
Robin Rash Well
Cotter Dale
Rash Brows
South Lunds Pasture
B6259
Beck Rigg
Ure Force Rigg
Yore House
The High Way
Cotter End
Blaescar Bog
Low Rigg
Lig Dale
Cotter
Cotter Side
White Boar Well
Cobbles Hill
Cotterside Plantation
Cotter Clints
High Rigg
Black Gutter Head
Garsdale Head
Moorcock Inn
Holmesett Scar
Quarry Well
Greenpot Hole
Garsdale Low Moor
Dandry Mire
Badger Rigg
Holmesett Hill
Carr Well
Cotter Riggs
Clough Force (waterfall)
Moorland Cott
Thwaite Bridge
Dirty Gap Hollow
Dandrymire Viaduct
Black Hill
Long Slack
A684
Clough
Old Pasture
Moss Bridge
Fall Rigg
Thwaite Wood
Far End
East Mud Becks
Wether Hill
Widdale Fell
Viaduct
Mossdale Head
A684
Garsdale
OLD RD
Shooters Well
Mossdale Gill
Waterfall
Mid Mossdale
High Scale
Edwin's Fell
A684 Sedbergh
LA10
Middle O'Moor End
Waterfall
Dockhurry Hole
Peat Fell Hill
Mossdale Gill Force
Shake Holes
Hining Scar
Garsdale Common
Widdale Fell
Middle O' Moor
Waterfall
Hurrys
New Close Allotments
Cote Wold
Low Nab
Round Hill
Mossdale Moor
Widdale Fell End
Rooting Gill Head
Sandy Hill
Widdale Carr
Hugh's Moss
Crook Gill Hill
Birk Rigg Allotment
Widdale Fell
Widdale Car Plantation
Swinepot Gill
Sikes Pits Rigg
Birk Rigg Allotment
Crook Gill Rigg
Western End
Sweet Side
Franklin Moss
Widdale Side Allotments
Shaking Moss
Cowgill Head
Black Side
Cowgill Head
Little Scar Edge
B6255
Galloway Gate
Little Scar Moss
DL8
Widdale Side
Snaizeholme Bridge
Sandy Sike Head
Snaizeholme Pasture
Widdale Little Tarn
Little Scar
Widdale Bridge
Tarn Rigg
Green Scar Crags
Widdale Foot
Low Houses
Widdale Great Tarn
Widdale
Pikes Edge
Tarn Gill
Dairy Farm
Snaizeholme Beck
High Houses
Hazel House
Greens Farm
Great Knoutberry Hill
Green Scar Pasture
Mirk Pot
Mirk Pot Farm
Bridge End
Tow Hill
Snaizeholme
Ford
SNAIZEHOLME RD
Mid Widdale
Waterfall
B6255
Dent Fell
Arten Gill Moss
93
7
92
6
91
5
90
4
89
3
88
2
87
1
86
78
79
80
81
82
83

79
56

55
35

Scale: 1¾ inches to 1 mile
0 ¼ ½ mile
0 250m 500m 750m 1 km

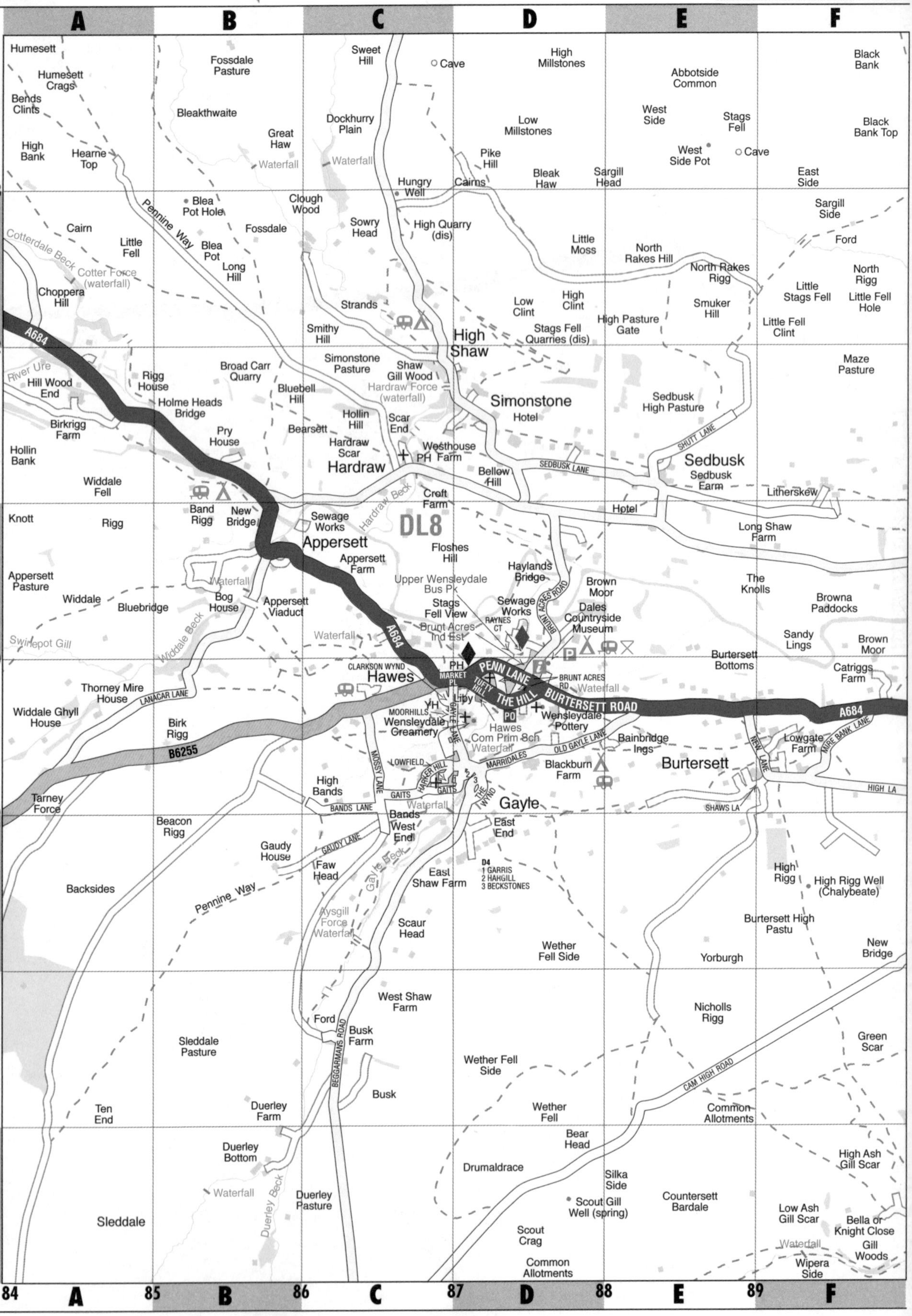
A B C D E F
8
93
7
92
6
91
5
90
4
89
3
88
2
87
1
86
84 85 86 87 88 89
Humesett
Humesett Crags
Bends Clints
High Bank
Hearne Top
Fossdale Pasture
Bleakthwaite
Great Haw
Waterfall
Sweet Hill
Dockhurry Plain
Cave
High Millstones
Low Millstones
Pike Hill
Hungry Well
Cairns
Bleak Haw
Sargill Head
Abbotside Common
West Side
West Side Pot
Stags Fell
Cave
Black Bank
Black Bank Top
East Side
Sargill Side
Ford
Blea Pot Hole
Pennine Way
Cairn
Cotterdale Beck
Cotter Force (waterfall)
Little Fell
Blea Pot
Long Hill
Fossdale
Clough Wood
Sowry Head
High Quarry (dis)
Little Moss
North Rakes Hill
North Rakes Rigg
North Rigg
Little Stags Fell
Little Fell Hole
Smuker Hill
Choppera Hill
Strands
Smithy Hill
High Shaw
Low Clint
High Clint
Stags Fell Quarries (dis)
High Pasture Gate
Little Fell Clint
A684
River Ure
Hill Wood End
Rigg House
Broad Carr Quarry
Simonstone Pasture
Shaw Gill Wood
Hardraw Force (waterfall)
Simonstone
Hotel
Sedbusk High Pasture
Maze Pasture
Holme Heads Bridge
Bluebell Hill
Birkrigg Farm
Hollin Bank
Pry House
Bearsett
Hollin Hill
Hardraw Scar
Scar End
Westhouse Farm
PH
Hardraw
Bellow Hill
SEDBUSK LANE
SHUTT LANE
Sedbusk
Sedbusk Farm
Litherskew
Widdale Fell
Band Rigg
New Bridge
Sewage Works
Hardraw Beck
Croft Farm
Hotel
Knott
Rigg
DL8
Appersett
Long Shaw Farm
Appersett Farm
Floshes Hill
Haylands Bridge
Appersett Pasture
Waterfall
Widdale
Bluebridge
Bog House
Appersett Viaduct
Upper Wensleydale Bus Pk
Brown Moor
The Knolls
Browna Paddocks
Stags Fell View
Sewage Works
Dales Countryside Museum
RAYNES CT
BRUNT ACRES ROAD
Swinepot Gill
Widdale Beck
Waterfall
Brunt Acres Ind Est
Sandy Lings
Brown Moor
Burtersett Bottoms
Catriggs Farm
CLARKSON WYND
PH
MARKET PL
PENN LANE
TUFTY HILL
THE HILL
BRUNT ACRES RD
Waterfall
Hawes
Thorney Mire House
LANACAR LANE
Widdale Ghyll House
Lby
YH
MOORHILLS
Wensleydale Creamery
GAYLE LANE
PO
Wensleydale Pottery
BURTERSETT ROAD
A684
Birk Rigg
Hawes Com Prim Sch
Waterfall
OLD GAYLE LANE
Bainbridge Ings
Lowgate Farm
MIRE BANK LANE
B6255
MOSSY LANE
LOWFIELD
HARKER HILL
MARRIDALES
Blackburn Farm
Burtersett
NEW LANE
High Bands
GAITS
GAITS
THE WYND
Gayle
HIGH LA
Tarney Force
BANDS LANE
Waterfall
Bands West End
SHAWS LA
Beacon Rigg
East End
Gaudy House
GAUDY LANE
D4
1 GARRIS
2 HAHGILL
3 BECKSTONES
Faw Head
Gayle Beck
East Shaw Farm
High Rigg
High Rigg Well (Chalybeate)
Backsides
Pennine Way
Aysgill Force Waterfall
Scaur Head
Burtersett High Pastu
Wether Fell Side
Yorburgh
New Bridge
West Shaw Farm
Nicholls Rigg
Ford
BEGGARMANS ROAD
Busk Farm
Sleddale Pasture
Green Scar
Wether Fell Side
CAM HIGH ROAD
Busk
Ten End
Duerley Farm
Wether Fell
Common Allotments
Bear Head
Duerley Bottom
Drumaldrace
High Ash Gill Scar
Silka Side
Waterfall
Duerley Beck
Duerley Pasture
Countersett Bardale
Scout Gill Well (spring)
Low Ash Gill Scar
Bella or Knight Close
Sleddale
Scout Crag
Waterfall
Gill Woods
Common Allotments
Wipera Side

55
80

35
58

Scale: 1¾ inches to 1 mile
0 ¼ ½ mile
0 250m 500m 750m 1 km

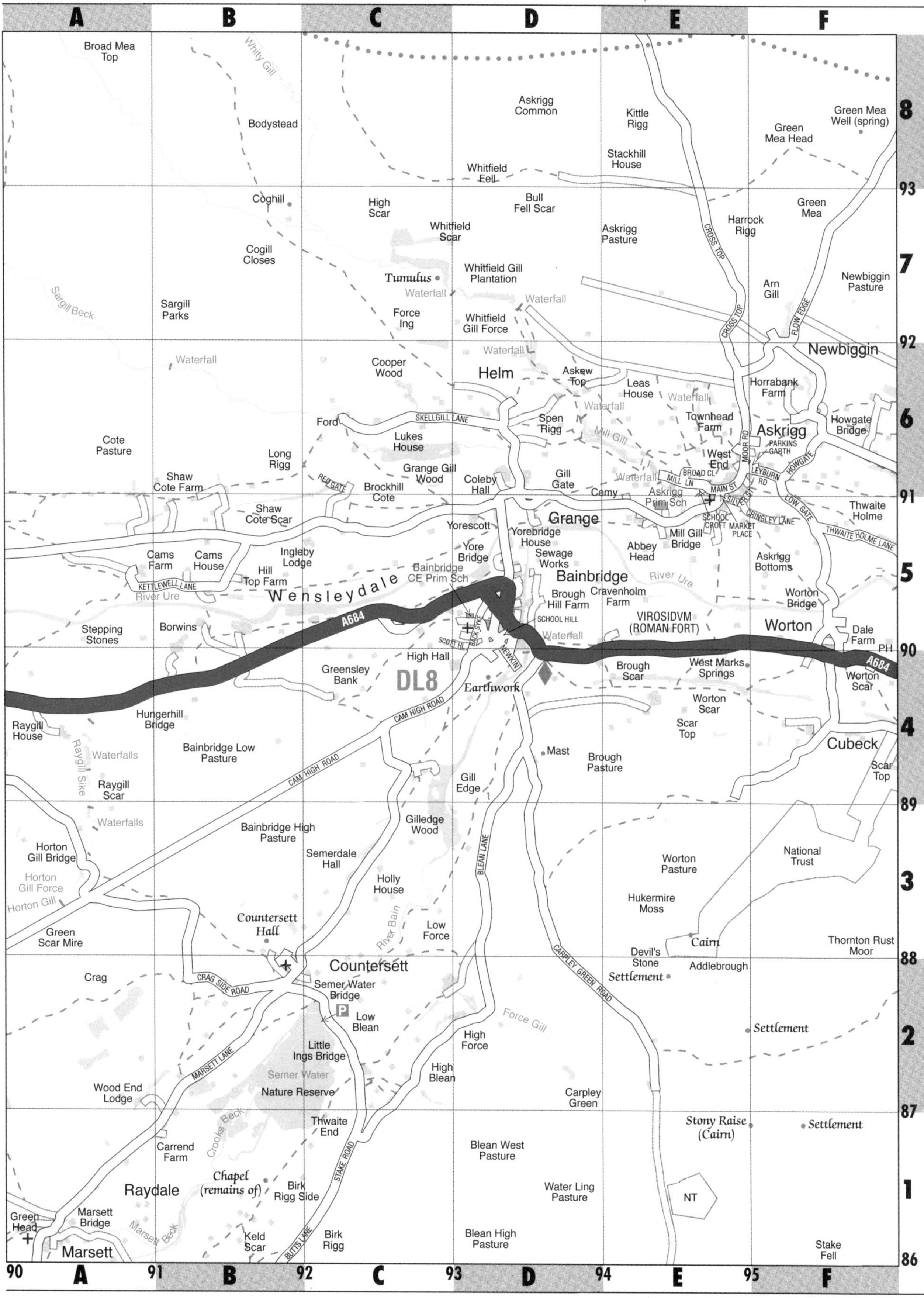

81
58

57
37

Scale: 1¾ inches to 1 mile
0 ¼ ½ mile
0 250m 500m 750m 1 km

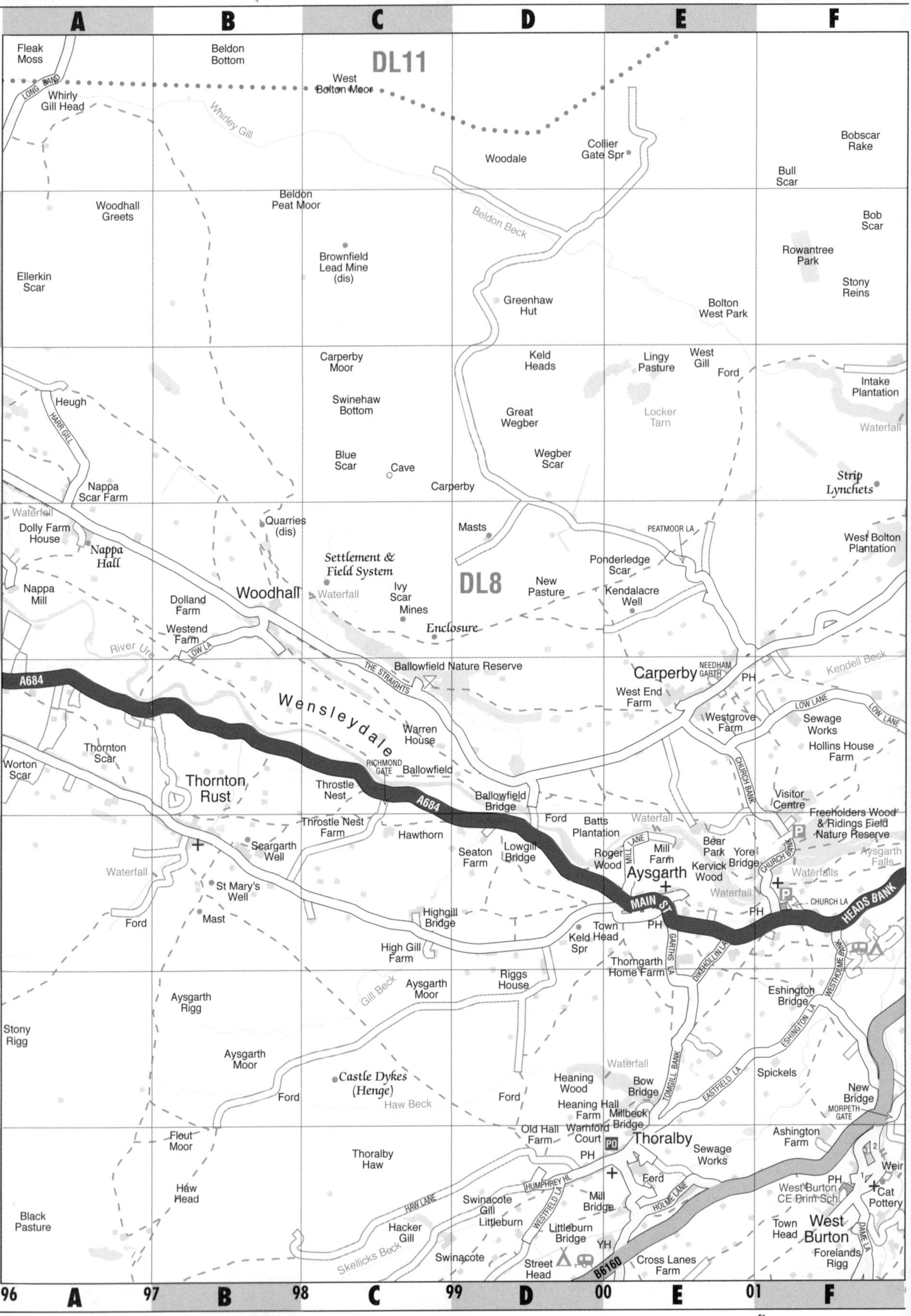

57
82

F1
1 BACK NOOK
2 FRONT NOOK
3 KING GARTH

Scale: 1¾ inches to 1 mile
0 ¼ ½ mile
0 250m 500m 750m 1 km

38
60

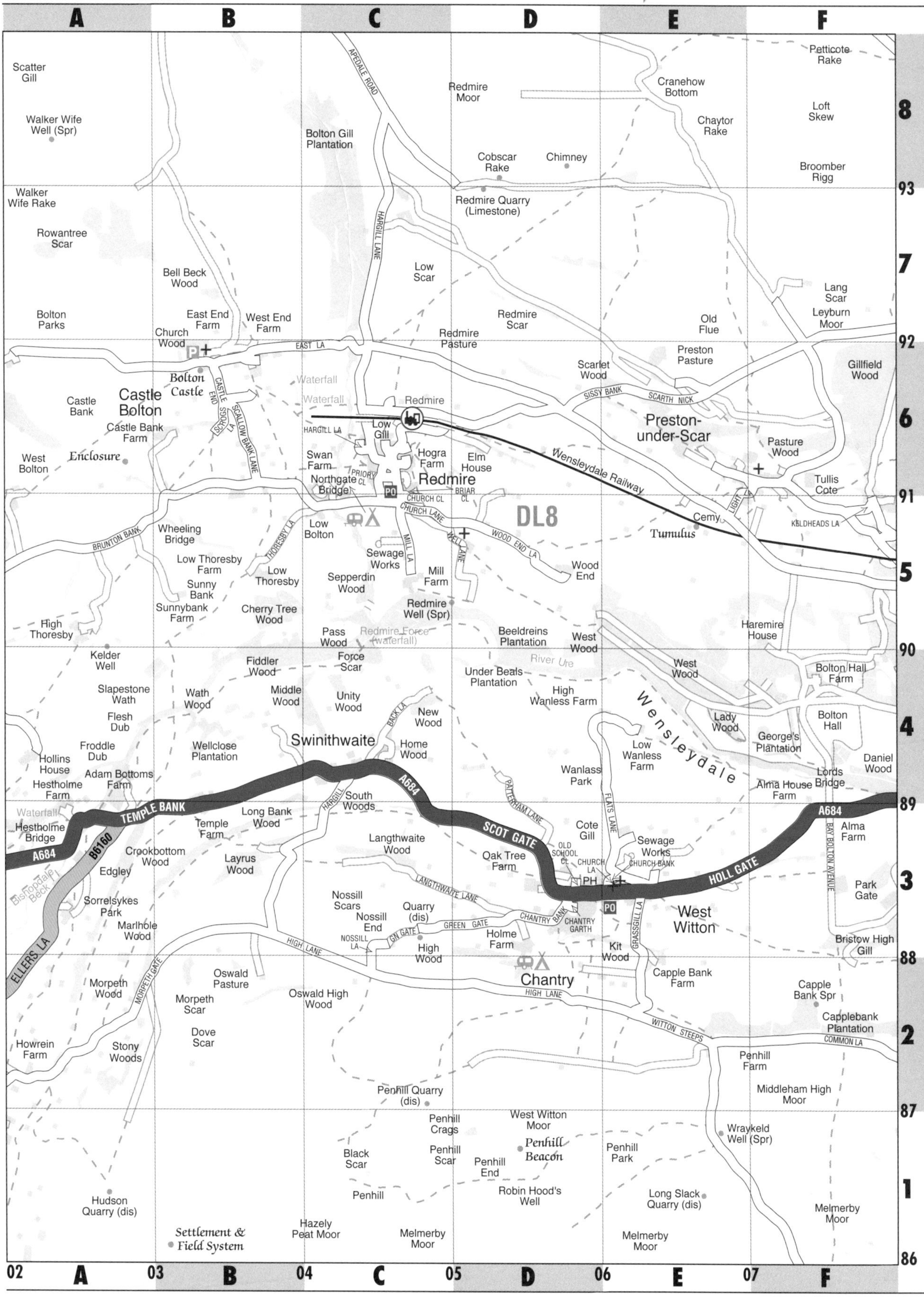

83
60

59

D5
1 SPRINGFIELD CL
2 DALE WY
3 WOODBURN DR
4 THORNBOROUGH CRES
5 WOODSIDE
6 MAYTHORNE
7 WENSLEYDALE AVE
8 HIGH ST
9 THE NURSERIES
10 SHAWL TERR
11 HARMBY RD
12 BOLTON WY
13 BOLTON CT
14 WENSLEY RD
15 RAILWAY ST
16 YOREDALE AVE
17 HETTON GARTH
18 SOUTH VW
19 ST MATTHEW'S CL
20 MIDDLEHAM RD
21 PARK VW
22 ELLERCLOSE RD
23 CLIFF DR
24 HAWTHORN CL
25 QUARRY HILLS LA

39

Scale: 1¾ inches to 1 mile
0 ¼ ½ mile
0 250m 500m 750m 1 km

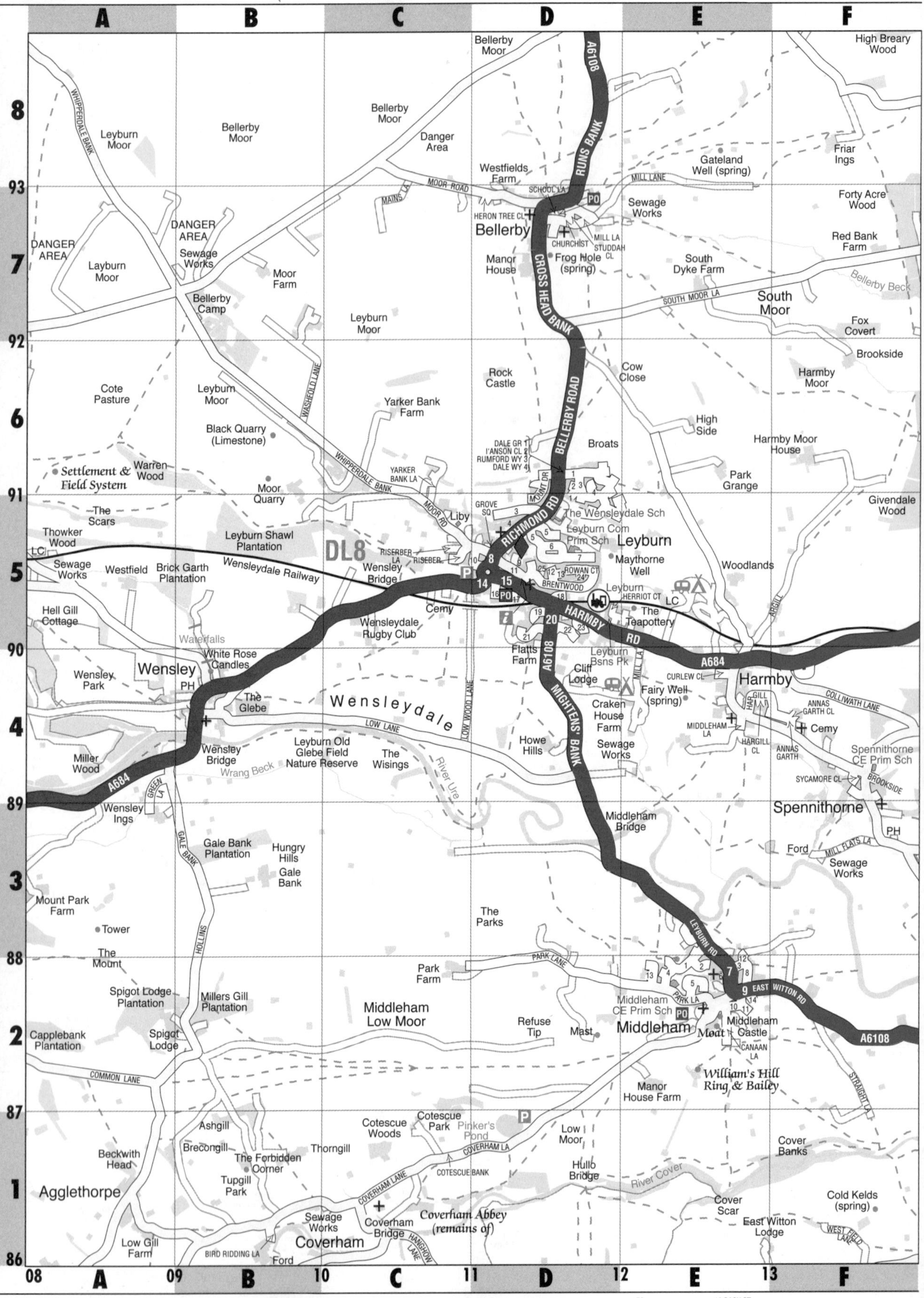

A B C D E F
8 93 7 92 6 91 5 90 4 89 3 88 2 87 1 86
08 09 10 11 12 13
Bellerby Moor
A6108
High Breary Wood
WHIPPERDALE BANK
Leyburn Moor
Bellerby Moor
Danger Area
RUNS BANK
Gateland Well (spring)
Friar Ings
Westfields Farm
MOOR ROAD
MILL LANE
MAINS LA
SCHOOL LA
PO
Sewage Works
Forty Acre Wood
HERON TREE CL
Bellerby
CHURCHIST
MILL LA
STUDDAH CL
Red Bank Farm
DANGER AREA
Sewage Works
Layburn Moor
Moor Farm
Manor House
Frog Hole (spring)
CROSS HEAD BANK
South Dyke Farm
Bellerby Beck
Bellerby Camp
SOUTH MOOR LA
South Moor
Leyburn Moor
Fox Covert
Brookside
Rock Castle
Cow Close
Harmby Moor
Cote Pasture
Leyburn Moor
WASHFOLD LANE
Yarker Bank Farm
BELLERBY ROAD
High Side
Black Quarry (Limestone)
DALE GR 1
I'ANSON CL 2
RUMFORD WY 3
DALE WY 4
Broats
Harmby Moor House
Settlement & Field System
Warren Wood
YARKER BANK LA
MOUNT DR
Park Grange
Moor Quarry
The Scars
GROVE SQ
Liby
RICHMOND RD
The Wensleydale Sch
Givendale Wood
Thowker Wood
Leyburn Shawl Plantation
DL8
Leyburn Com Prim Sch
Leyburn
LC
RISEBER LA
RISEBER
ROWAN CT
Maythorne Well
Woodlands
Sewage Works
Westfield
Brick Garth Plantation
Wensleydale Railway
Wensley Bridge
BRENTWOOD
Leyburn
HERRIOT CT
LC
Hell Gill Cottage
Cemy
Wensleydale Rugby Club
HARMBY RD
The Teapottery
ARGILL
Waterfalls
White Rose Candles
Flatts Farm
Leyburn Bsns Pk
A684
Wensley Park
Wensley
PH
Cliff Lodge
MILL LA
CURLEW CL
Harmby
COLLIWATH LANE
The Glebe
Wensleydale
MIGHTENS' BANK
Fairy Well (spring)
Craken House Farm
ANNAS GARTH CL
LOW LANE
LOW WOOD LANE
MIDDLEHAM LA
Cemy
Miller Wood
Wensley Bridge
Leyburn Old Glebe Field Nature Reserve
The Wisings
Howe Hills
Sewage Works
HARGILL CL
ANNAS GARTH
Spennithorne CE Prim Sch
Wrang Beck
River Ure
SYCAMORE CL
BROOKSIDE
A684
GREEN LA
Wensley Ings
Middleham Bridge
Spennithorne
PH
GALE BANK
Gale Bank Plantation
Hungry Hills
Gale Bank
Ford
MILL FLATS LA
Sewage Works
Mount Park Farm
Tower
HOLLINS
The Parks
LEYBURN RD
The Mount
PARK LANE
Park Farm
EAST WITTON RD
Spigot Lodge Plantation
Millers Gill Plantation
Middleham Low Moor
Middleham CE Prim Sch
PARK LA
Capplebank Plantation
Spigot Lodge
Refuse Tip
Mast
Middleham
Moat
Middleham Castle
CANAAN LA
A6108
COMMON LANE
William's Hill Ring & Bailey
Manor House Farm
STRAIGHT LA
Ashgill
Cotescue Woods
Cotescue Park
Pinker's Pond
P
Low Moor
Beckwith Head
Brecongill
The Forbidden Corner
Thorngill
COVERHAM LA
Cover Banks
COTESCUE BANK
Hullo Bridge
Tupgill Park
COVERHAM LANE
River Cover
Agglethorpe
Cold Kelds (spring)
Cover Scar
Sewage Works
Coverham Bridge
Coverham Abbey (remains of)
East Witton Lodge
WEST FIELD LANE
Low Gill Farm
Coverham
HANGHOW LANE
BIRD RIDDING LA
Ford

59

84

E2
1 ST ALKELDA'S RD
2 KINGSLEY DR
3 NORTH RD
4 THE SPRINGS
5 PARK LA
6 CHURCH ST
7 KIRKGATE
8 BACK LA
9 MARKET PL
10 BACK ST
11 GROVE TERR
12 DOG HILL
13 SHARP HL CL
14 BLACK BULL YARD

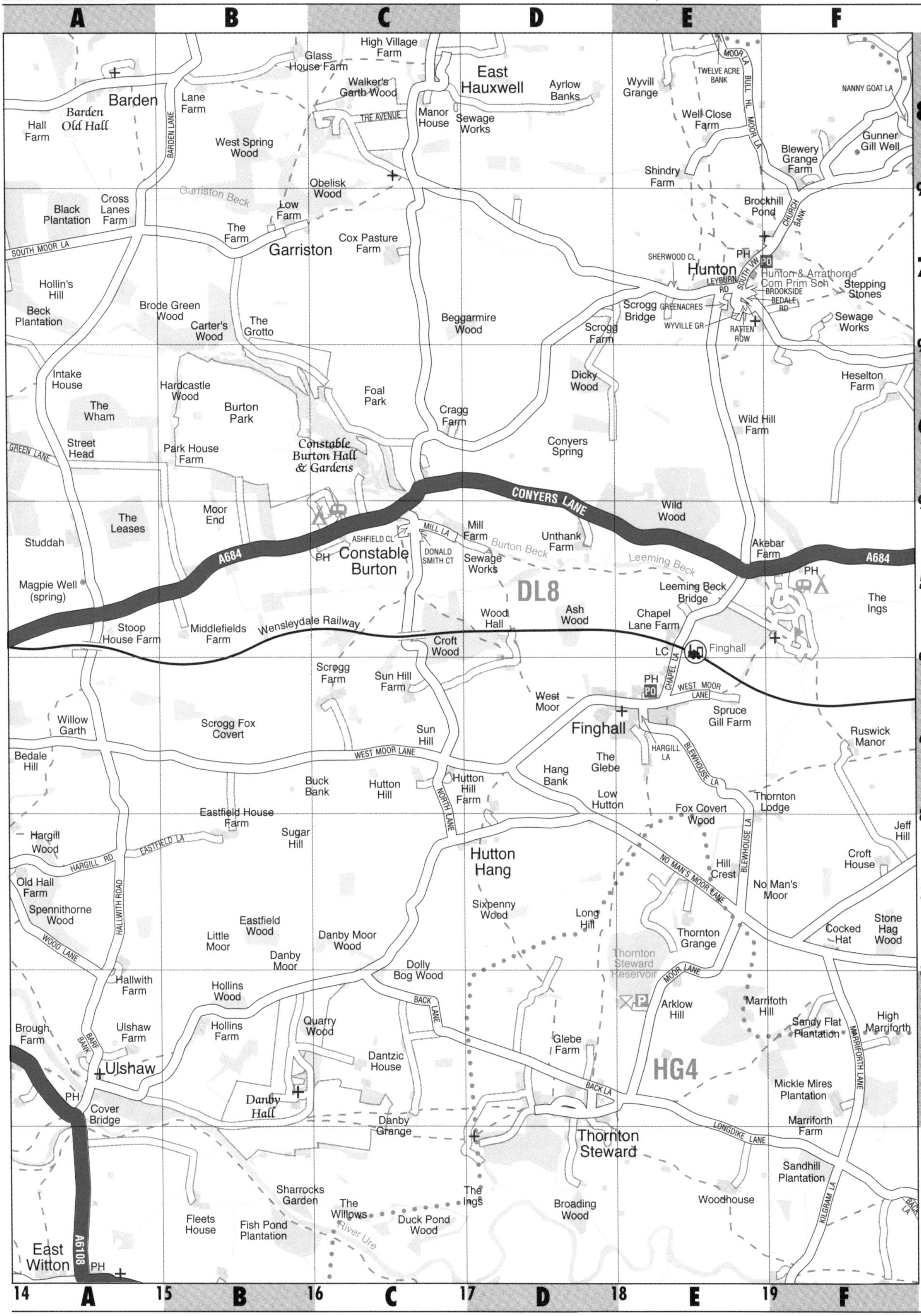
A
B
C
D
E
F
Glass House Farm
High Village Farm
East Hauxwell
Ayrlow Banks
Wyvill Grange
TWELVE ACRE BANK
MOOR LA
BULL HL
MOOR LA
NANNY GOAT LA
Barden
Barden Old Hall
Hall Farm
Lane Farm
BARDEN LANE
Walker's Garth Wood
THE AVENUE
Manor House
Sewage Works
Well Close Farm
Gunner Gill Well
Blewery Grange Farm
West Spring Wood
Shindry Farm
Obelisk Wood
Garriston Beck
Black Plantation
Cross Lanes Farm
Low Farm
The Farm
Garriston
Cox Pasture Farm
Brockhill Pond
CHURCH BANK
SOUTH MOOR LA
SHERWOOD CL
PH
PO
Hunton
LEYBURN RD
SOUTH VW
Hunton & Arrathorne Com Prim Sch
BROOKSIDE
BEDALE RD
Stepping Stones
Hollin's Hill
Beck Plantation
Brode Green Wood
Carter's Wood
The Grotto
Beggarmire Wood
Scrogg Bridge
GREENACRES
WYVILLE GR
Scrogg Farm
RATTEN ROW
Sewage Works
Intake House
Hardcastle Wood
Burton Park
Foal Park
Dicky Wood
Heselton Farm
The Wham
Cragg Farm
Wild Hill Farm
Street Head
GREEN LANE
Park House Farm
Constable Burton Hall & Gardens
Conyers Spring
CONYERS LANE
The Leases
Moor End
Mill Farm
MILL LA
ASHFIELD CL
Wild Wood
Studdah
A684
PH
Constable Burton
DONALD SMITH CT
Sewage Works
Burton Beck
Unthank Farm
Akebar Farm
Leeming Beck
A684
PH
Magpie Well (spring)
DL8
Leeming Beck Bridge
The Ings
Stoop House Farm
Middlefields Farm
Wensleydale Railway
Wood Hall
Ash Wood
Chapel Lane Farm
Croft Wood
LC
Finghall
CHAPEL LA
Scrogg Farm
Sun Hill Farm
PH
PO
WEST MOOR LANE
Willow Garth
Scrogg Fox Covert
West Moor
Spruce Gill Farm
Sun Hill
Finghall
Ruswick Manor
Bedale Hill
WEST MOOR LANE
HARGILL LA
BLEWHOUSE LA
The Glebe
Buck Bank
Hutton Hill
Hutton Hill Farm
Hang Bank
Low Hutton
Thornton Lodge
NORTH LANE
Eastfield House Farm
Fox Covert Wood
Hargill Wood
Sugar Hill
EASTFIELD LA
Jeff Hill
Hutton Hang
HARGILL RD
Hill Crest
BLEWHOUSE LA
Croft House
NO MAN'S MOOR LANE
Old Hall Farm
No Man's Moor
Spennithorne Wood
HALLWITH ROAD
Sixpenny Wood
Long Hill
Cocked Hat
Stone Hag Wood
Eastfield Wood
Thornton Grange
WOOD LANE
Little Moor
Danby Moor Wood
Thornton Steward Reservoir
Danby Moor
Dolly Bog Wood
MOOR LANE
Hallwith Farm
Hollins Wood
Arklow Hill
Marrifoth Hill
BACK LANE
High Marriforth
Sandy Flat Plantation
Brough Farm
Ulshaw Farm
Hollins Farm
Quarry Wood
Glebe Farm
MARRIFORTH LANE
BARF BANK
Ulshaw
Dantzic House
HG4
Mickle Mires Plantation
BACK LA
PH
Danby Hall
Cover Bridge
Marriforth Farm
Danby Grange
Thornton Steward
LONGDIKE LANE
Sandhill Plantation
Sharrocks Garden
The Ings
The Willows
Broading Wood
Woodhouse
BACK LA
KILGRAM LA
Fleets House
Fish Pond Plantation
Duck Pond Wood
River Ure
East Witton
A6108
PH
8
93
7
92
6
91
5
90
4
89
3
88
2
87
1
86
14
15
16
17
18
19
A
B
C
D
E
F

61 41

Scale: 1¾ inches to 1 mile
0 ¼ ½ mile
0 250m 500m 750m 1 km

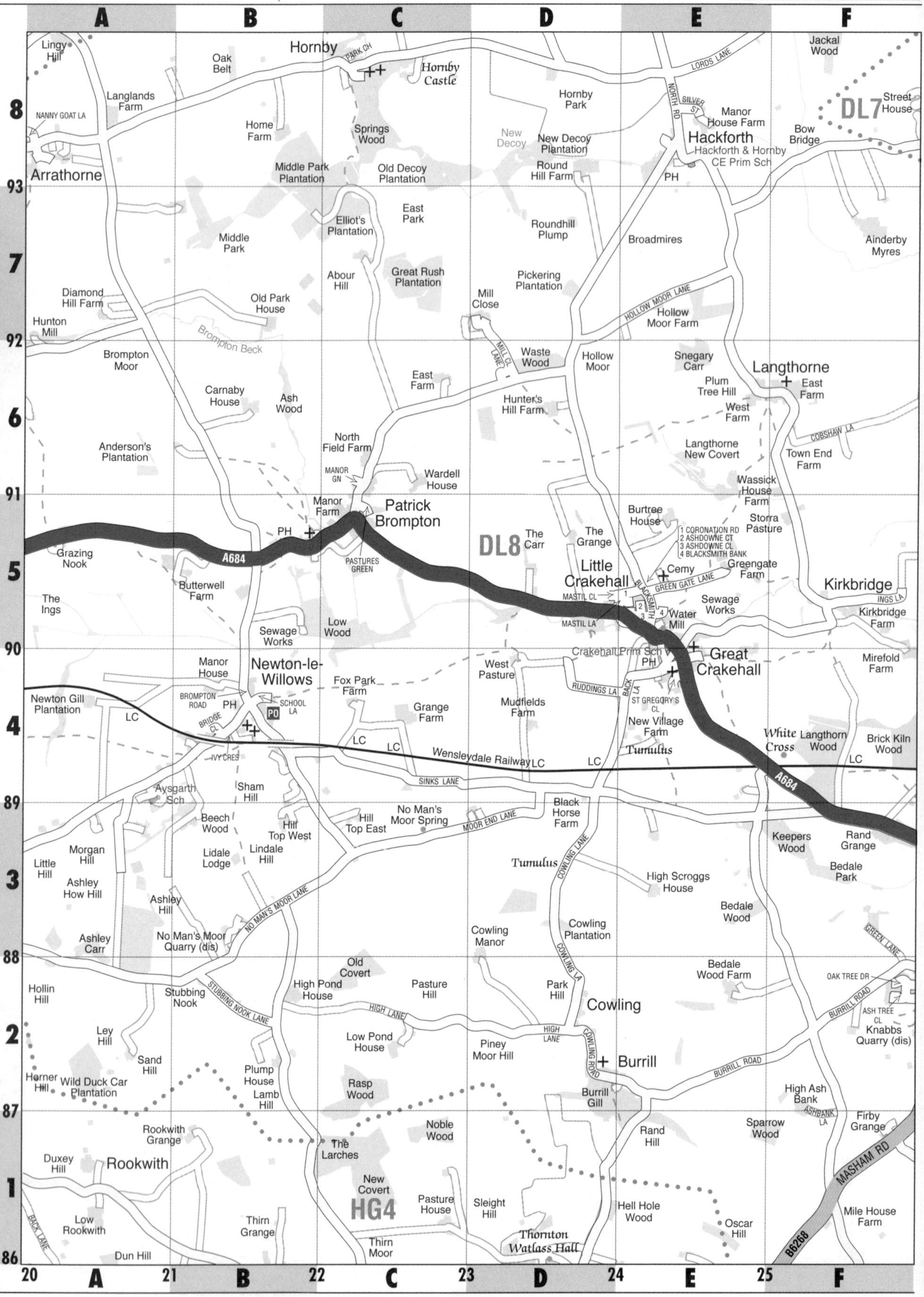

61 86

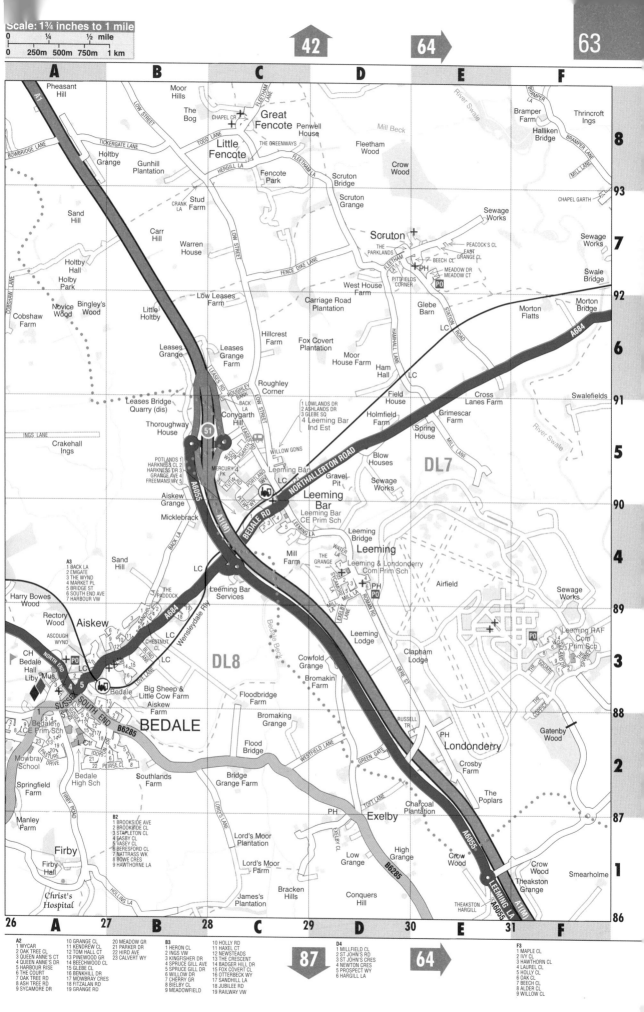

Scale: 1¾ inches to 1 mile
0 ¼ ½ mile
0 250m 500m 750m 1 km

42
64

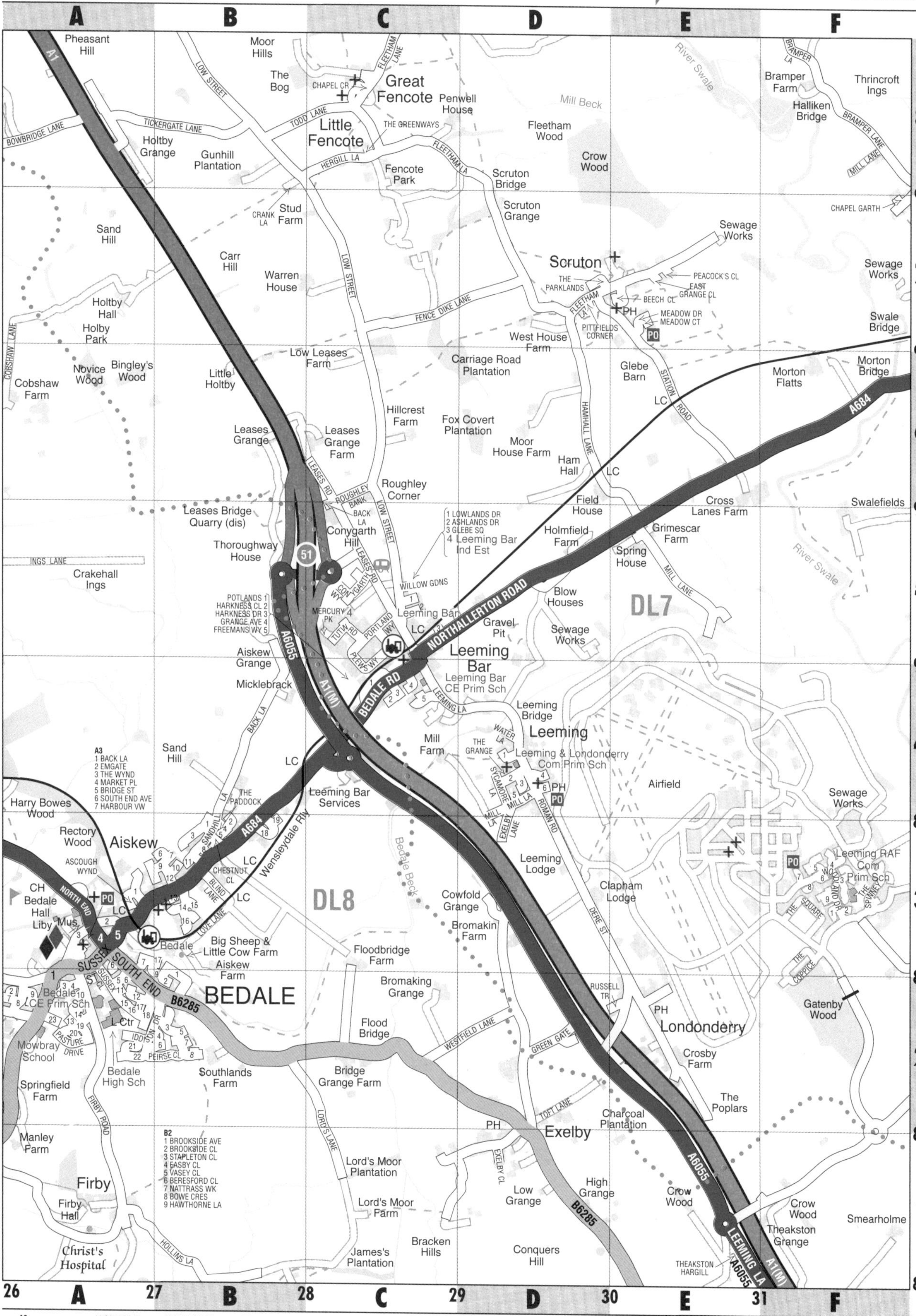

A2
1 WYCAR
2 OAK TREE CL
3 QUEEN ANNE'S CT
4 QUEEN ANNE'S DR
5 HARBOUR RISE
6 THE COURT
7 OAK TREE RD
8 ASH TREE RD
9 SYCAMORE DR
10 GRANGE CL
11 KENDREW CL
12 TOM HALL CT
13 PINEWOOD GR
14 BEECHWOOD CL
15 GLEBE CL
16 BENKHILL DR
17 MOWBRAY CRES
18 FITZALAN RD
19 GRANGE RD
20 MEADOW GR
21 PARKER DR
22 HIRD AVE
23 CALVERT WY

B3
1 HERON CL
2 INGS VW
3 KINGFISHER DR
4 SPRUCE GILL AVE
5 SPRUCE GILL DR
6 WILLOW DR
7 CHERRY GR
8 BIELBY CL
9 MEADOWFIELD
10 HOLLY RD
11 HAXEL CT
12 NEWSTEADS
13 THE CRESCENT
14 BADGER HILL DR
15 FOX COVERT CL
16 OTTERBECK WY
17 SANDHILL LA
18 JUBILEE RD
19 RAILWAY VW

87

D4
1 MILLFIELD CL
2 ST JOHN'S RD
3 ST JOHN'S CRES
4 NEWTON CRES
5 PROSPECT WY
6 HARGILL LA

64

F3
1 MAPLE CL
2 IVY CL
3 HAWTHORN CL
4 LAUREL CL
5 HOLLY CL
6 OAK CL
7 BEECH CL
8 ALDER CL
9 WILLOW CL

Scale: 1¾ inches to 1 mile
0 ¼ ½ mile
0 250m 500m 750m 1 km

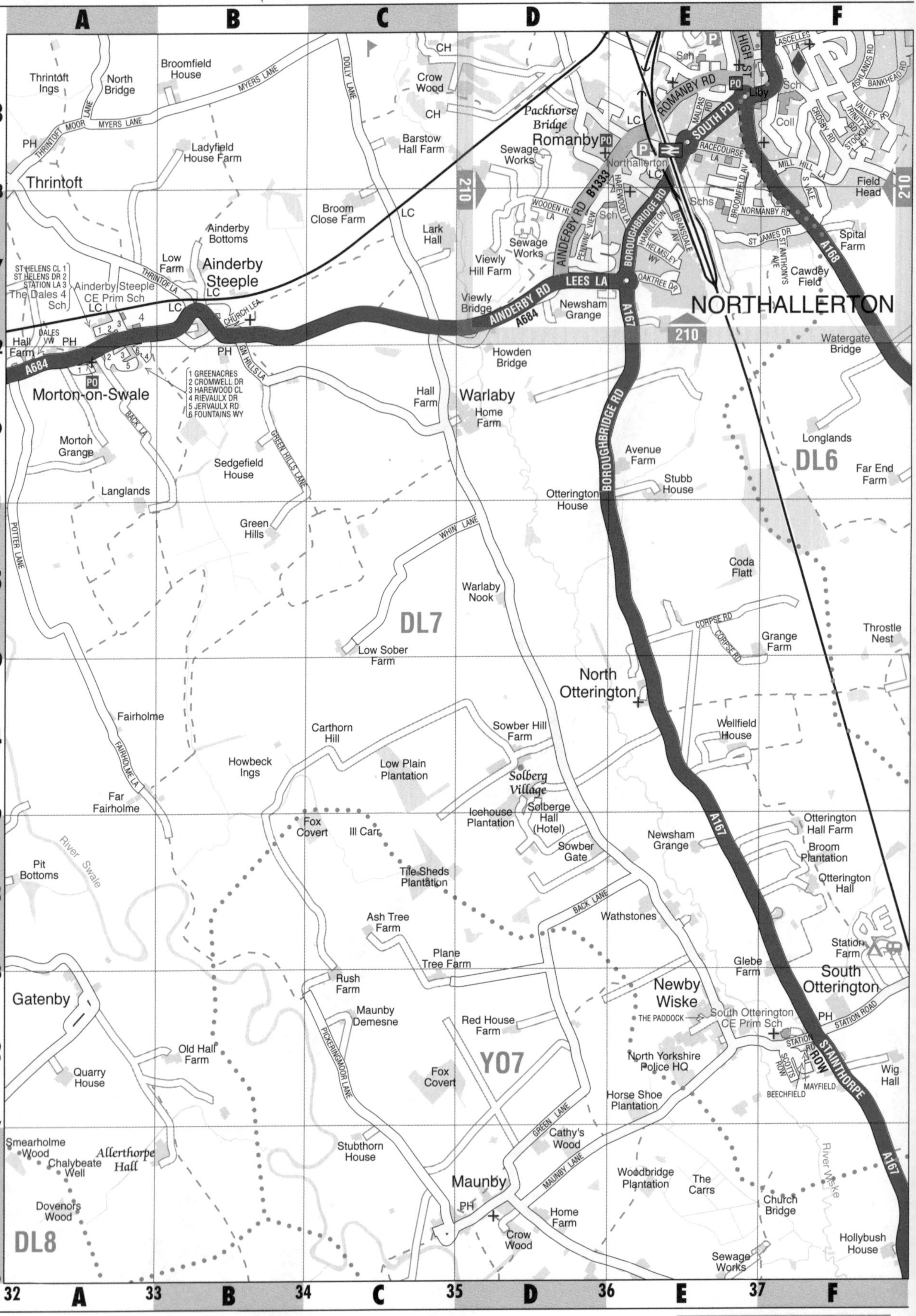
A B C D E F
8
93
7
92
6
91
5
90
4
89
3
88
2
87
1
86
32 33 34 35 36 37
Thrintoft Ings
North Bridge
Broomfield House
MYERS LANE
Crow Wood
CH
Packhorse Bridge
Romanby
Sch
ROMANBY RD
MALPAS RD
SOUTH PD
HIGH ST
LASCELLES LA
Lbry
Coll
CROSBY RD
TRINITY RD
STOCKDALE CT
VALLEY RD
ASHLANDS RD
BANKHEAD RD
MILL HILL LA
Field Head
THRINTOFT MOOR
PH
Thrintoft
Ladyfield House Farm
Barstow Hall Farm
Sewage Works
Northallerton
LC
RACECOURSE LA
BROOMFIELD AV
Schs
NORMANBY RD
S VALE
Broom Close Farm
Lark Hall
WOODEN HILL LA
AINDERBY RD
B1333
HAREWOOD LA
PENNINE VIEW
BOROUGHBRIDGE RD
HAMBLETON AV
HELMSLEY WY
BRANSDALE
ST JAMES DR
ST ANTHONYS AVE
Spital Farm
A168
Ainderby Bottoms
Low Farm
Ainderby Steeple
Viewly Hill Farm
OAKTREE DR
Cawdey Field
ST HELENS CL 1
ST HELENS DR 2
STATION LA 3
The Dales 4
Ainderby Steeple CE Prim Sch
THRINTOFT LA
Viewly Bridge
LEES LA
Newsham Grange
NORTHALLERTON
CHURCH LEA
A684
A167
210
Hall Farm
DALES VW
Watergate Bridge
GREEN HILLS LA
Howden Bridge
Morton-on-Swale
1 GREENACRES
2 CROMWELL DR
3 HAREWOOD CL
4 RIEVAULX DR
5 JERVAULX RD
6 FOUNTAINS WY
Hall Farm
Warlaby
Home Farm
BACK LA
Morton Grange
Avenue Farm
Longlands
DL6
Sedgefield House
Stubb House
Far End Farm
Langlands
Otterington House
GREEN HILLS LANE
POTTER LANE
Green Hills
WHIN LANE
Coda Flatt
Warlaby Nook
DL7
CORPSE RD
Grange Farm
Throstle Nest
Low Sober Farm
North Otterington
Fairholme
Carthorn Hill
Sowber Hill Farm
Wellfield House
FAIRHOLME LA
Howbeck Ings
Low Plain Plantation
Solberg Village
Far Fairholme
Icehouse Plantation
Solberge Hall (Hotel)
Fox Covert
Ill Carr
Otterington Hall Farm
Newsham Grange
Broom Plantation
River Swale
Sowber Gate
Pit Bottoms
Tile Sheds Plantation
Otterington Hall
BACK LANE
Wathstones
Ash Tree Farm
Station Farm
Plane Tree Farm
Glebe Farm
South Otterington
Gatenby
Rush Farm
Newby Wiske
Maunby Demesne
THE PADDOCK
South Otterington CE Prim Sch
Red House Farm
STATION RD
STATION ROAD
PICKERINGMOOR LANE
Old Hall Farm
YO7
North Yorkshire Police HQ
SCOTTS ROW
MAYFIELD
STAINTHORPE ROW
Quarry House
Fox Covert
Wig Hall
BEECHFIELD
Horse Shoe Plantation
GREEN LANE
Cathy's Wood
Smearholme Wood
Allerthorpe Hall
Chalybeate Well
Stubthorn House
MAUNBY LANE
Woodbridge Plantation
The Carrs
River Wiske
Maunby
Dovenors Wood
Church Bridge
Home Farm
DL8
Crow Wood
Hollybush House
Sewage Works

For full street detail of the highlighted area see page 210.

Scale: 1¾ inches to 1 mile
0 ¼ ½ mile
0 250m 500m 750m 1 km

44
66

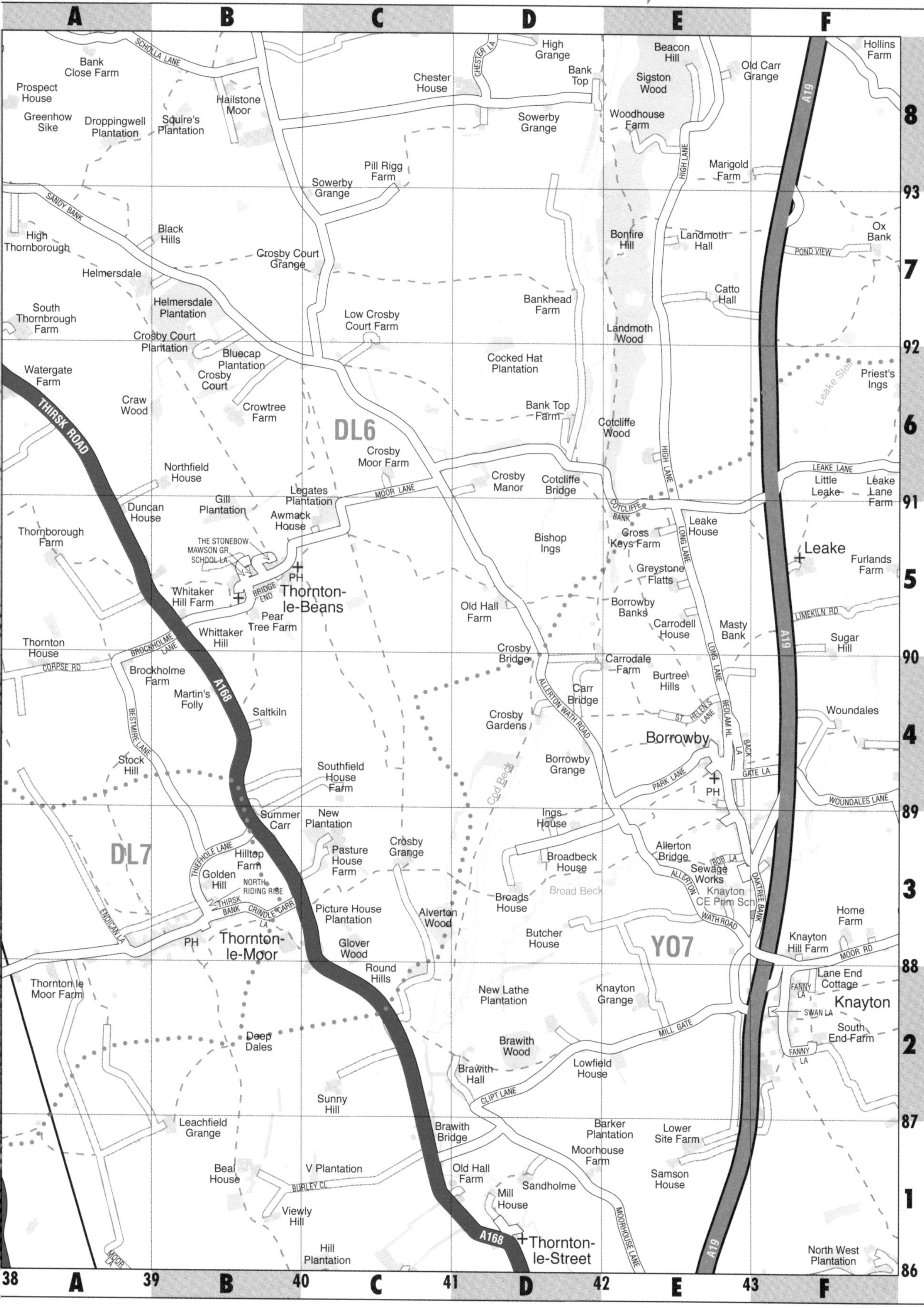

89
66

65
45

Scale: 1¾ inches to 1 mile
0 ¼ ½ mile
0 250m 500m 750m 1 km

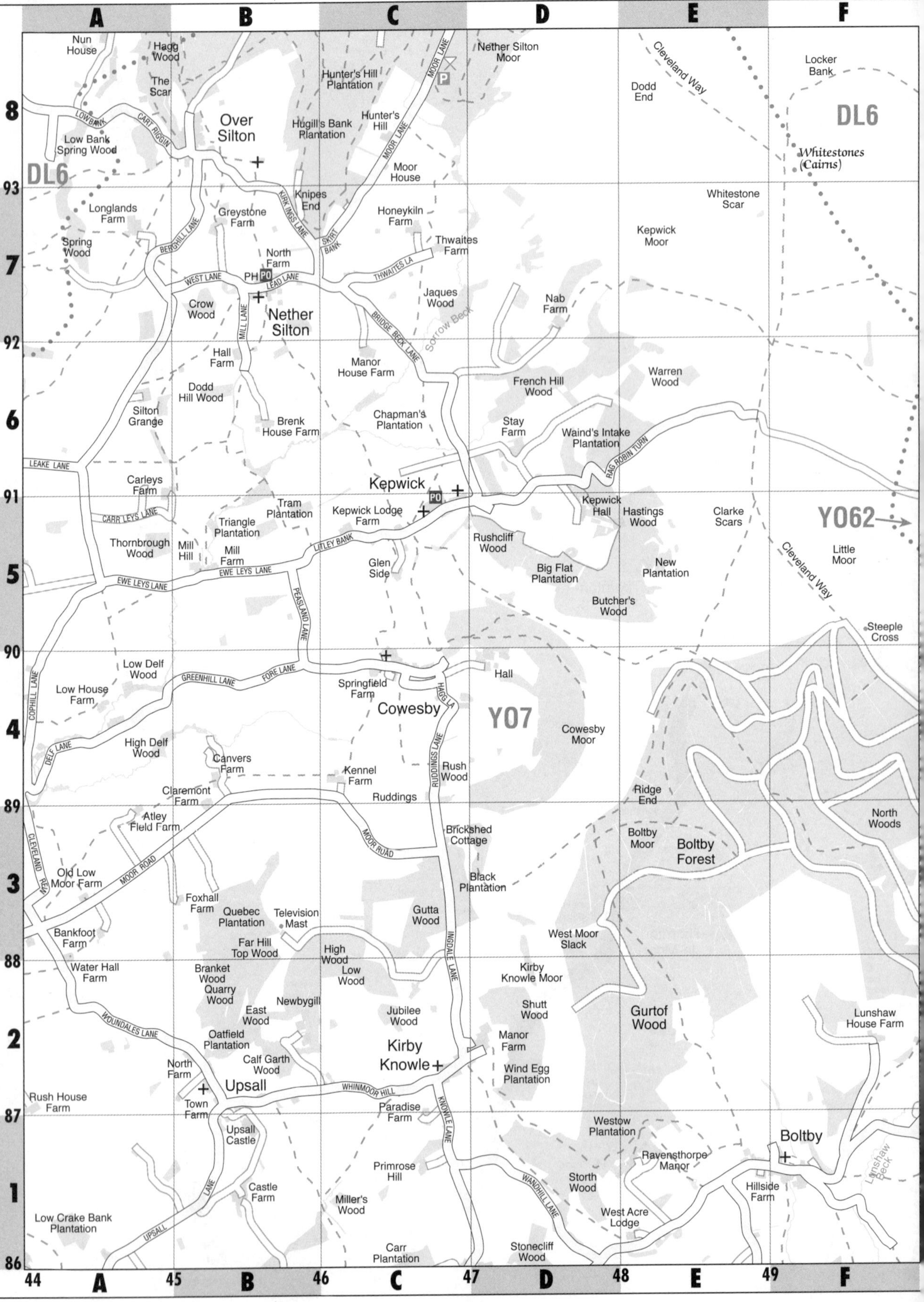

65
90

Scale: 1¾ inches to 1 mile

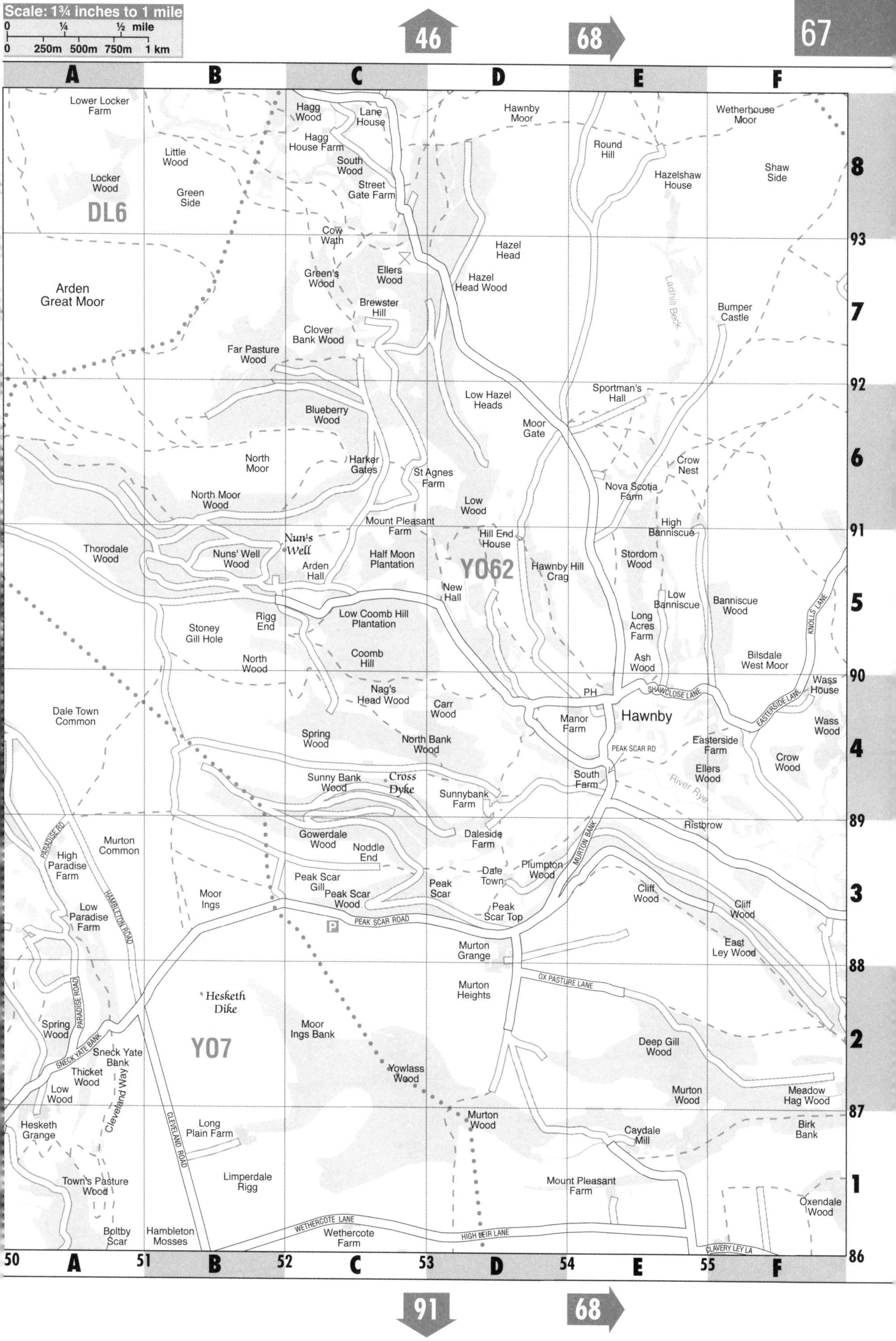

67
47

Scale: 1¾ inches to 1 mile
0 ¼ ½ mile
0 250m 500m 750m 1 km

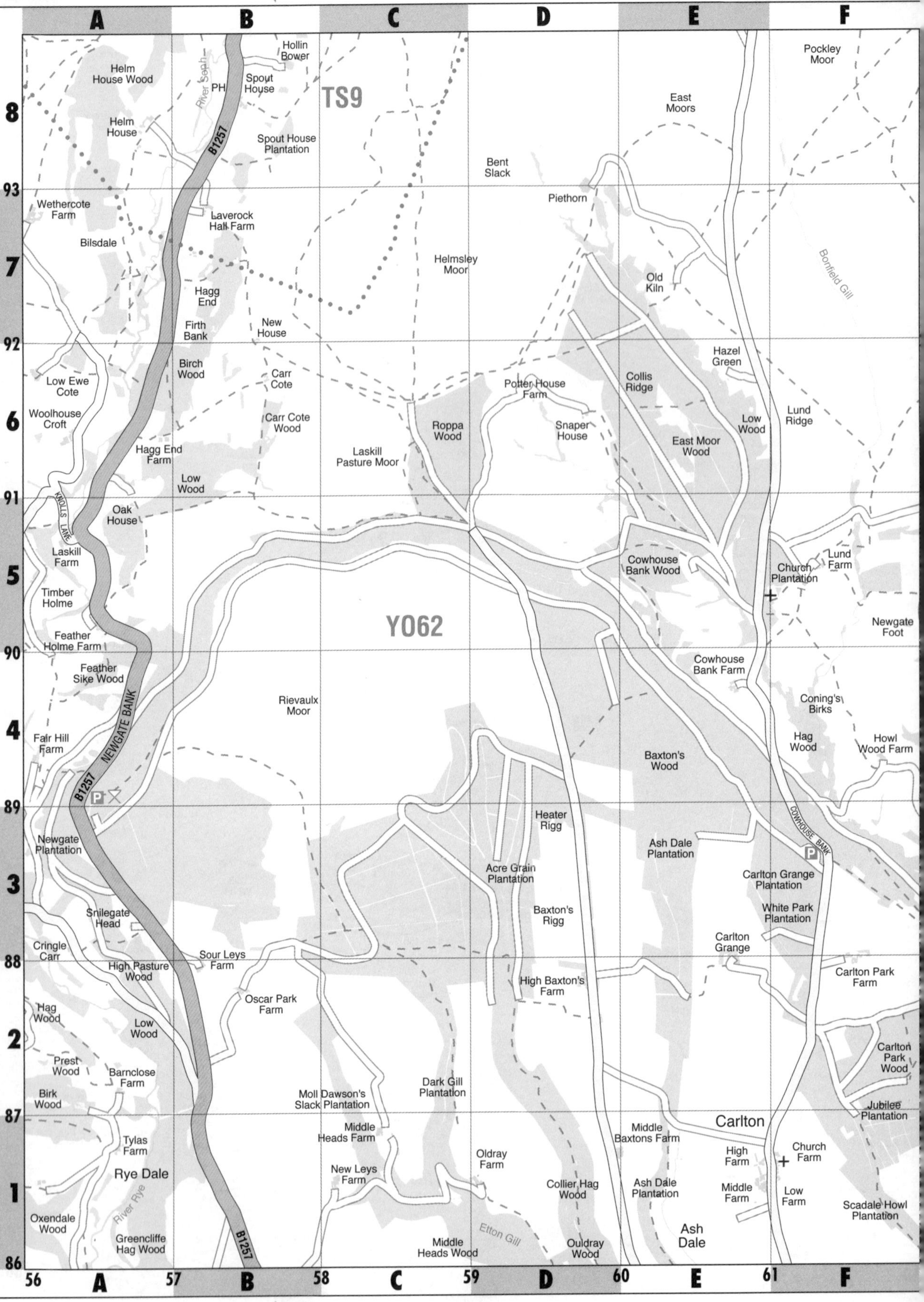
A B C D E F
56 57 58 59 60 61
86 1 87 2 88 3 89 4 90 5 91 6 92 7 93 8
TS9
YO62
Helm House Wood
Helm House
Hollin Bower
Spout House
PH
River Seph
B1257
Spout House Plantation
Pockley Moor
East Moors
Bent Slack
Piethorn
Wethercote Farm
Laverock Hall Farm
Bilsdale
Helmsley Moor
Old Kiln
Bonfield Gill
Hagg End
Firth Bank
New House
Hazel Green
Collis Ridge
Low Ewe Cote
Birch Wood
Carr Cote
Potter House Farm
Lund Ridge
Low Wood
Woolhouse Croft
Carr Cote Wood
Roppa Wood
Snaper House
East Moor Wood
Laskill Pasture Moor
Hagg End Farm
Low Wood
Knolls Lane
Oak House
Laskill Farm
Cowhouse Bank Wood
Church Plantation
Lund Farm
Timber Holme
Newgate Foot
Feather Holme Farm
Cowhouse Bank Farm
Feather Sike Wood
Newgate Bank
Rievaulx Moor
Coning's Birks
Fair Hill Farm
Baxton's Wood
Hag Wood
Howl Wood Farm
P
Heater Rigg
Cowhouse Bank
Newgate Plantation
Ash Dale Plantation
Acre Grain Plantation
Carlton Grange Plantation
Baxton's Rigg
White Park Plantation
Snilegate Head
Carlton Grange
Cringle Carr
Sour Leys Farm
High Pasture Wood
High Baxton's Farm
Carlton Park Farm
Oscar Park Farm
Hag Wood
Low Wood
Carlton Park Wood
Prest Wood
Barnclose Farm
Moll Dawson's Slack Plantation
Dark Gill Plantation
Birk Wood
Jubilee Plantation
Middle Heads Farm
Middle Baxtons Farm
Carlton
Tylas Farm
Oldray Farm
High Farm
Church Farm
Rye Dale
New Leys Farm
Collier Hag Wood
Ash Dale Plantation
Middle Farm
Low Farm
River Rye
Scadale Howl Plantation
Oxendale Wood
Etton Gill
Ash Dale
Greencliffe Hag Wood
Middle Heads Wood
Ouldray Wood

67
92

Scale: 1¾ inches to 1 mile
0 ¼ ½ mile
0 250m 500m 750m 1 km

48
70

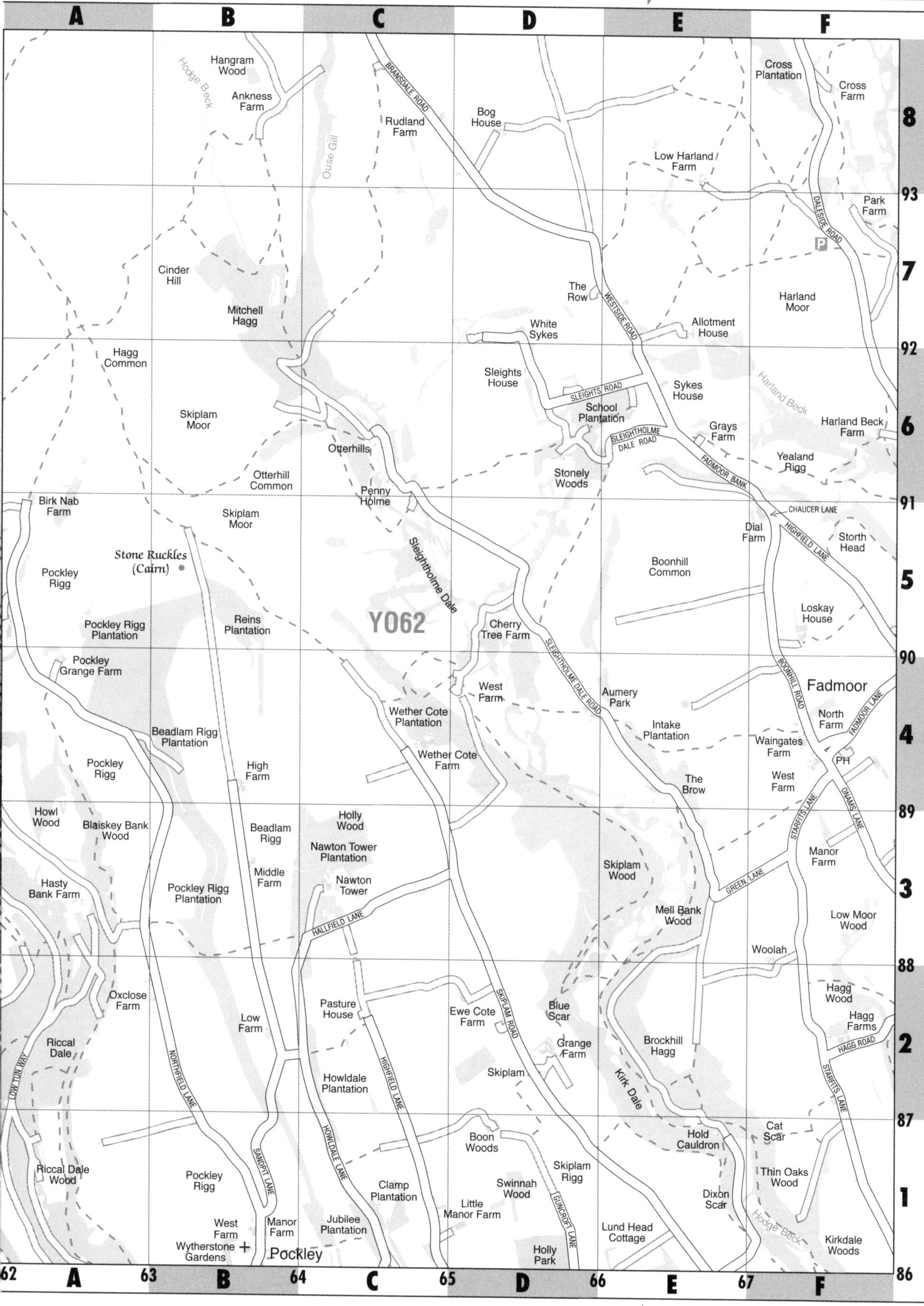

93
70

Scale: 1¾ inches to 1 mile
0 ¼ ½ mile
0 250m 500m 750m 1 km

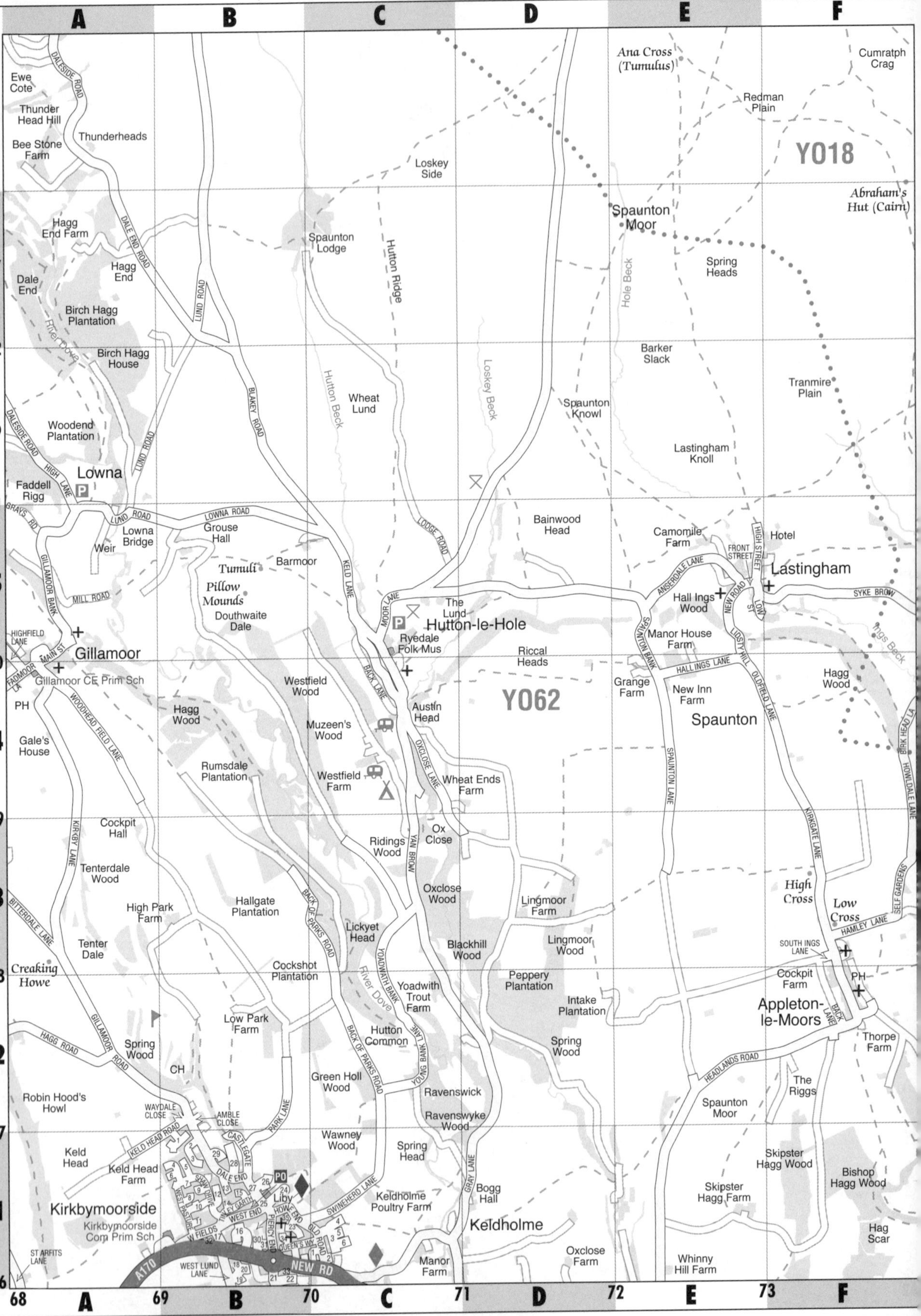

B1
1 KELD HEAD OR
2 RYEDALE VW
3 RYEDALE CRES
4 POPLAR AVE
5 WILLOW RISE
6 BEECH DR
7 ASH GR
8 CEDAR VALE
9 OAK CL
10 LIME CH
11 RIPLEY CL
12 BROOKE CL
13 MANOR CL
14 TINLEY GDNS
15 TOWN FARM CL
16 FEVERSHAM DR
17 WEST LUND
18 SHERBROOKE CL
19 SLINGSBY GARTH
20 PARKERS MNT
21 INGS LA
22 CARTER LA
23 OXCROFT
24 CHURCH ST
25 MARKET PL
26 CROWN SQ
27 HIGH MKT PL
28 MANOR VALE LA
29 MANOR GDNS
30 WAINDS FIELD
31 NEVILLE WK
32 WESTFIELD MS
33 WEIGHBRIDGE CL
34 PETCH GARTH
35 MARSH LA

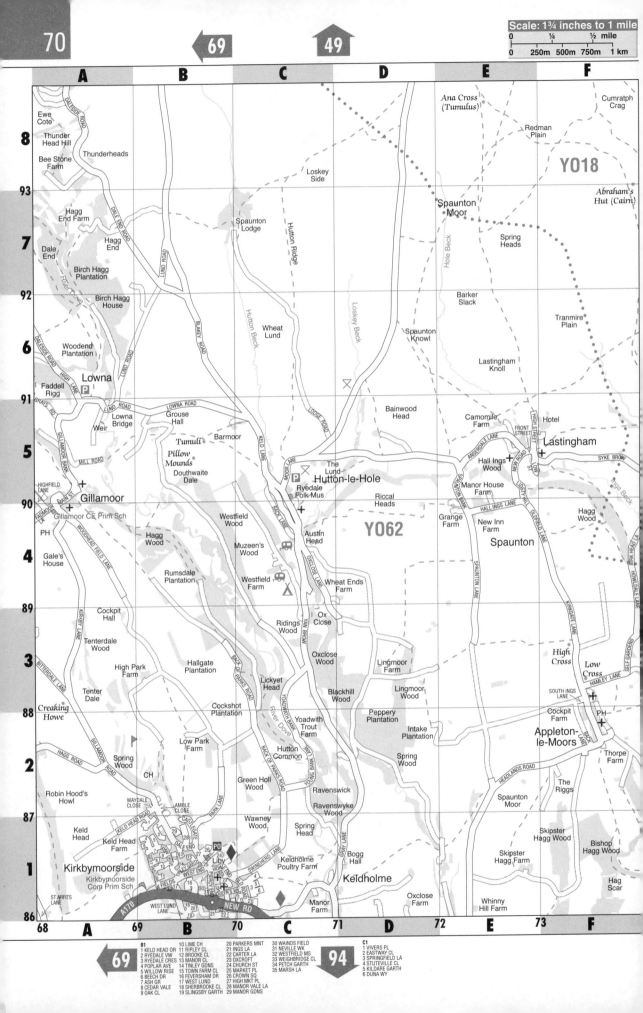

C1
1 VIVERS PL
2 EASTWAY CL
3 SPRINGFIELD LA
4 STUTEVILLE CL
5 KILDARE GARTH
6 DUNA WY

Scale: 1¾ inches to 1 mile
0 ¼ ½ mile
0 250m 500m 750m 1 km

50
72

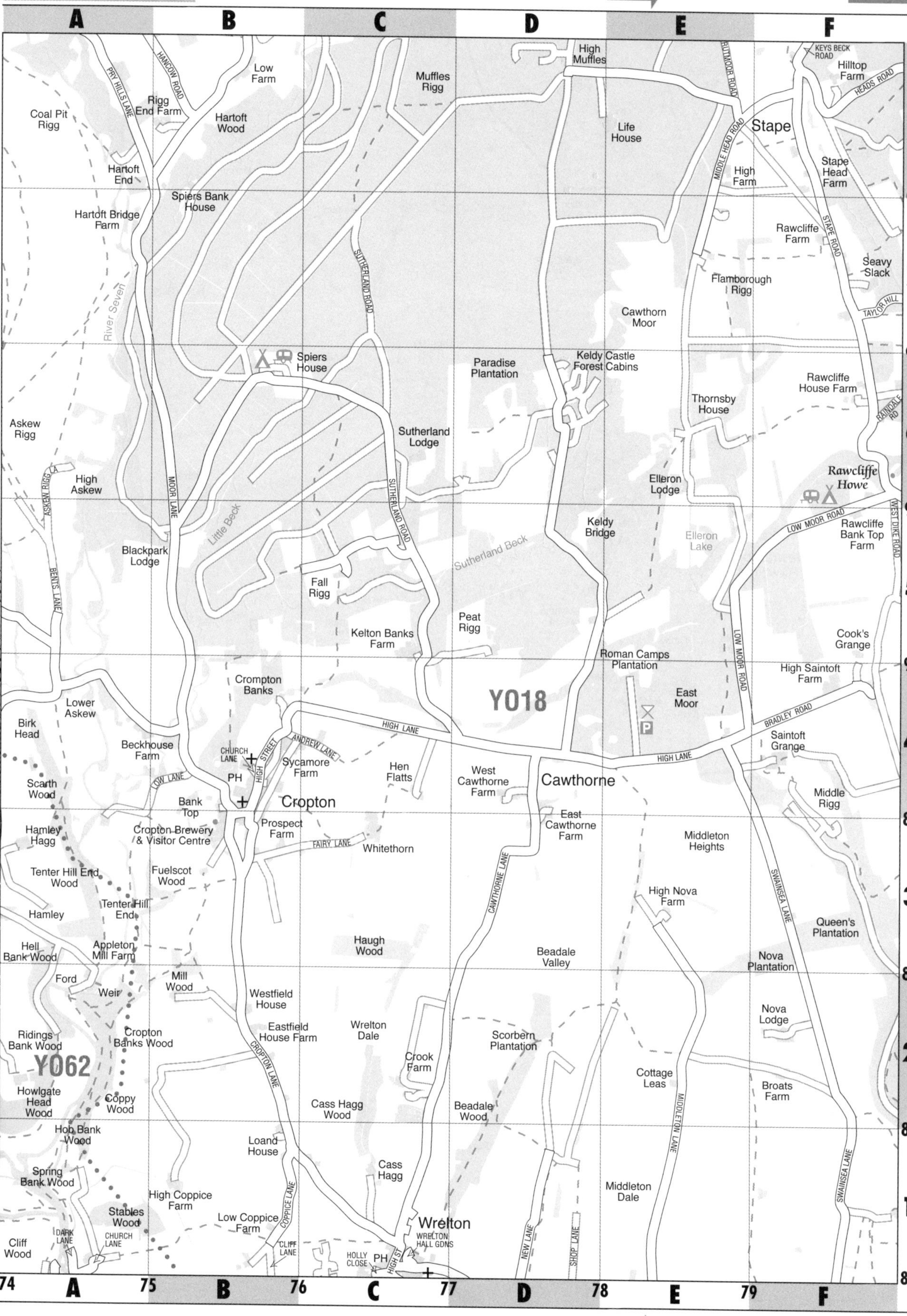

95
72

71
51

Scale: 1¾ inches to 1 mile
0 ¼ ½ mile
0 250m 500m 750m 1 km

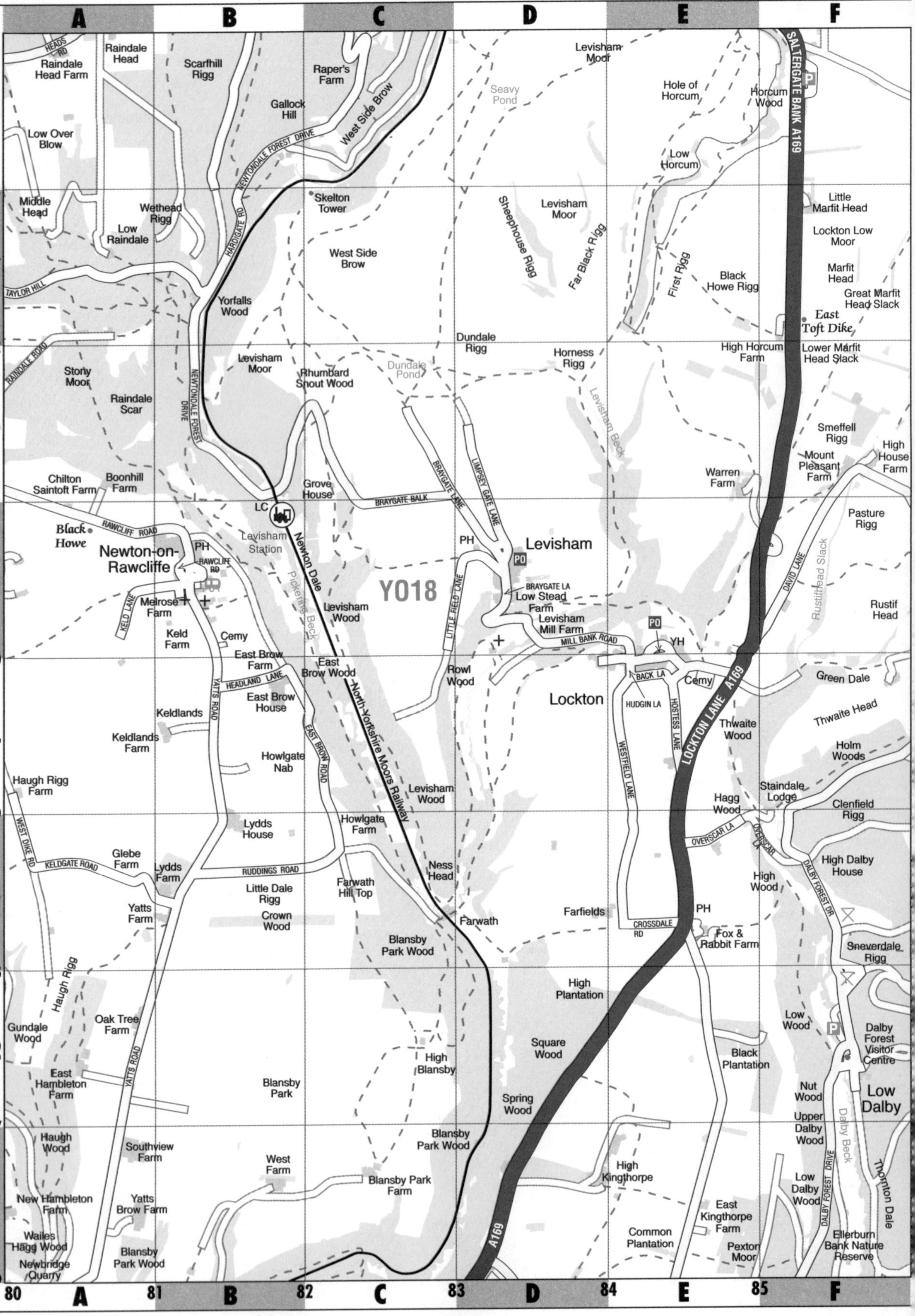

71
96

Scale: 1¾ inches to 1 mile
0 ¼ ½ mile
0 250m 500m 750m 1 km

52
74

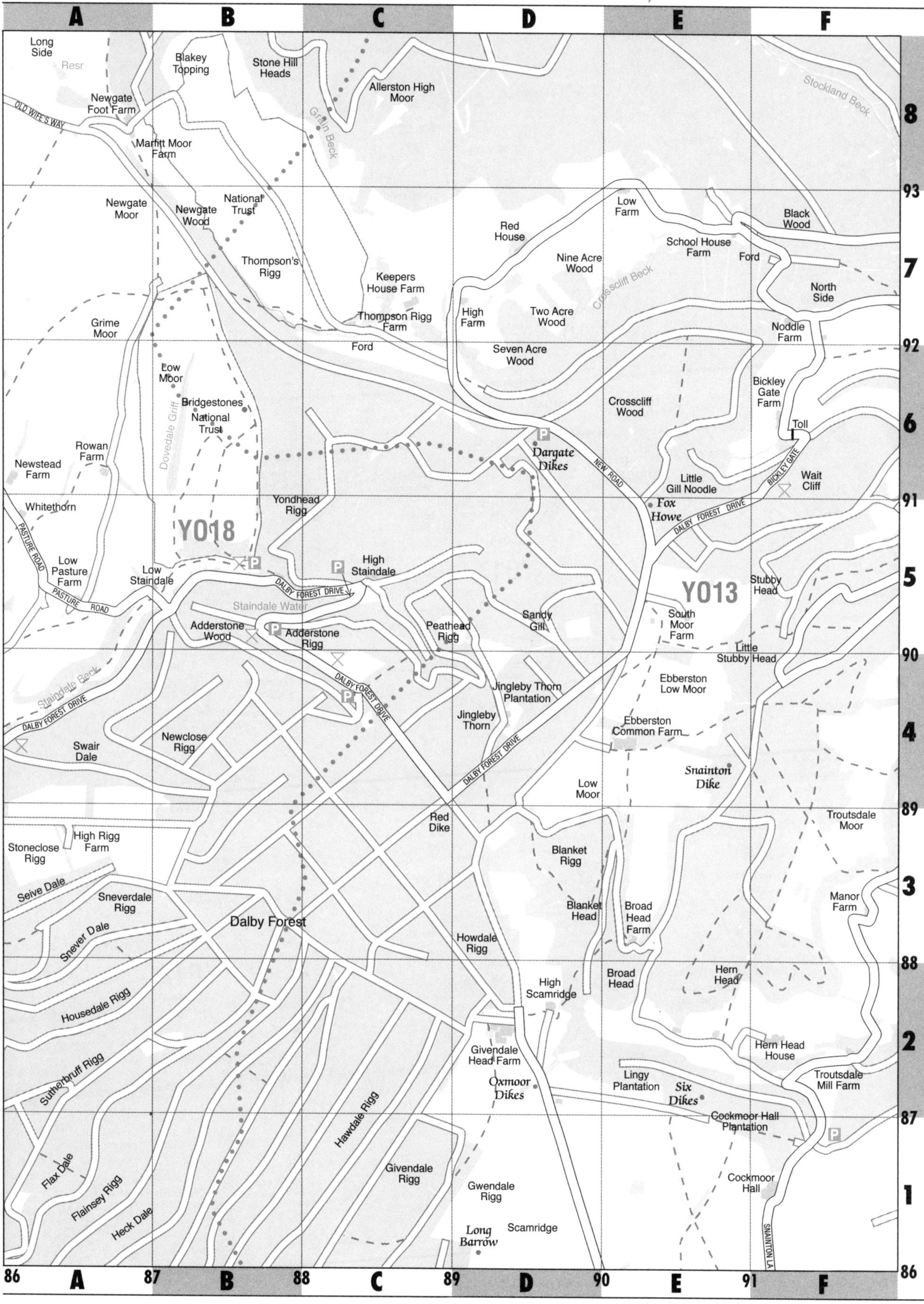

97
74

73
53

Scale: 1¾ inches to 1 mile
0 ¼ ½ mile
0 250m 500m 750m 1 km

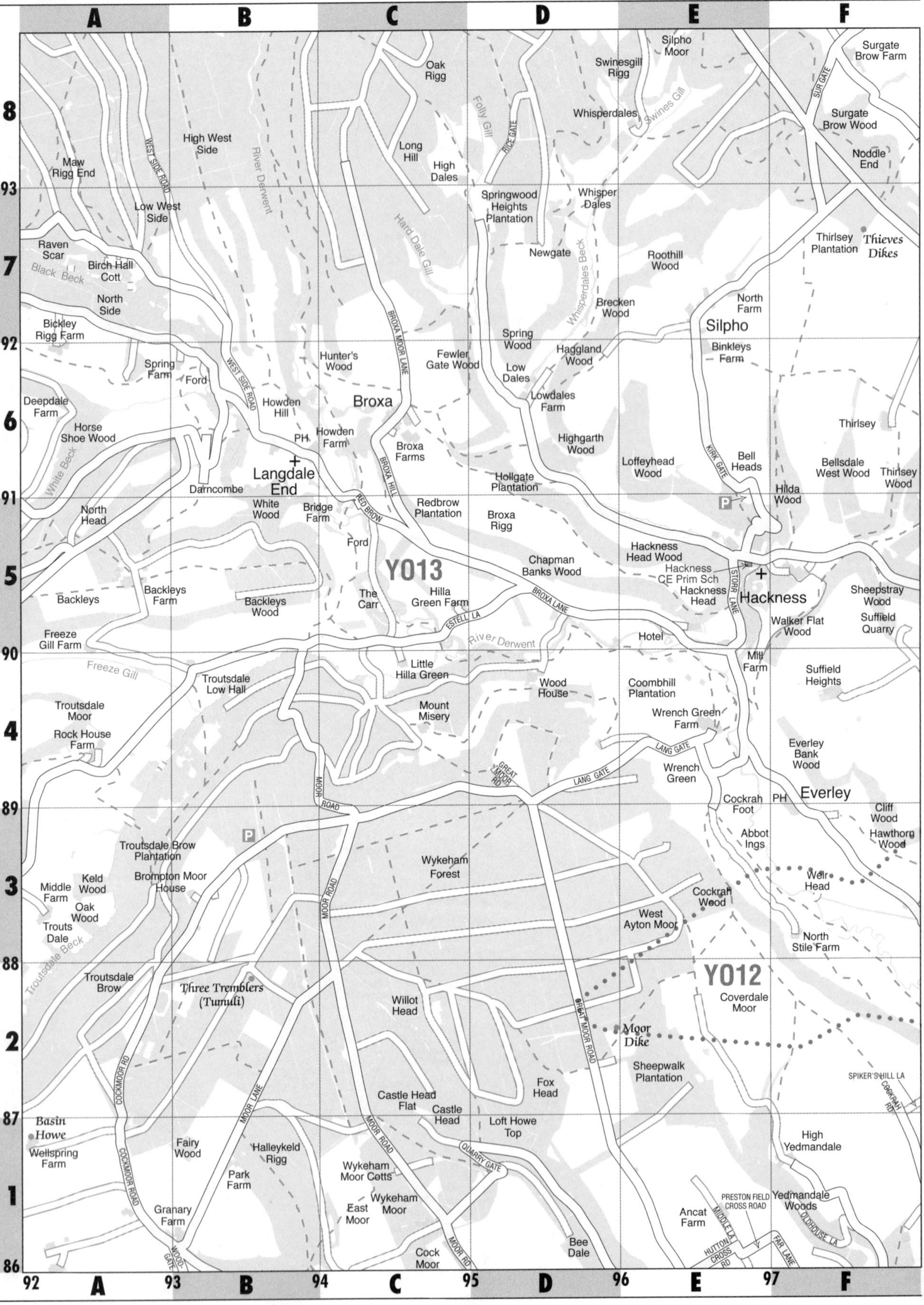

73
98

D5
1 ANNADALE GR
2 WREA HEAD CL
3 COOKS GDNS
4 IVY BANK CT
5 STONY CT
6 ELLIS GDNS
7 CASTLE VW
8 STONY LA
9 LANCASTER CL
10 QUEEN ELIZABETH DR
11 DUCHY AVE
12 BEECH DR
13 WEST PARK RD
14 THE PARK
15 EAST PARK RD
16 FIELD CL RD
17 LANCASTER WY
18 CHICHESTER CL
19 WEST AVE
20 SOUTH AVE
21 EAST AV
22 LOW ST
23 HALL PK CL
24 FLOCK LEYS
25 HALL PK GR
26 TIBBY BUTTS
27 SCALBY BECK RD
28 RIVERSIDE
29 THOMPSON CL
30 COW WATH CL
31 HAGUE AVE
32 ELLISON AVE
33 BIELBY CL
34 DANES DYKE
35 NEWBY FARM CL
36 NEWBY FARM CRES
37 PINFIELD CL

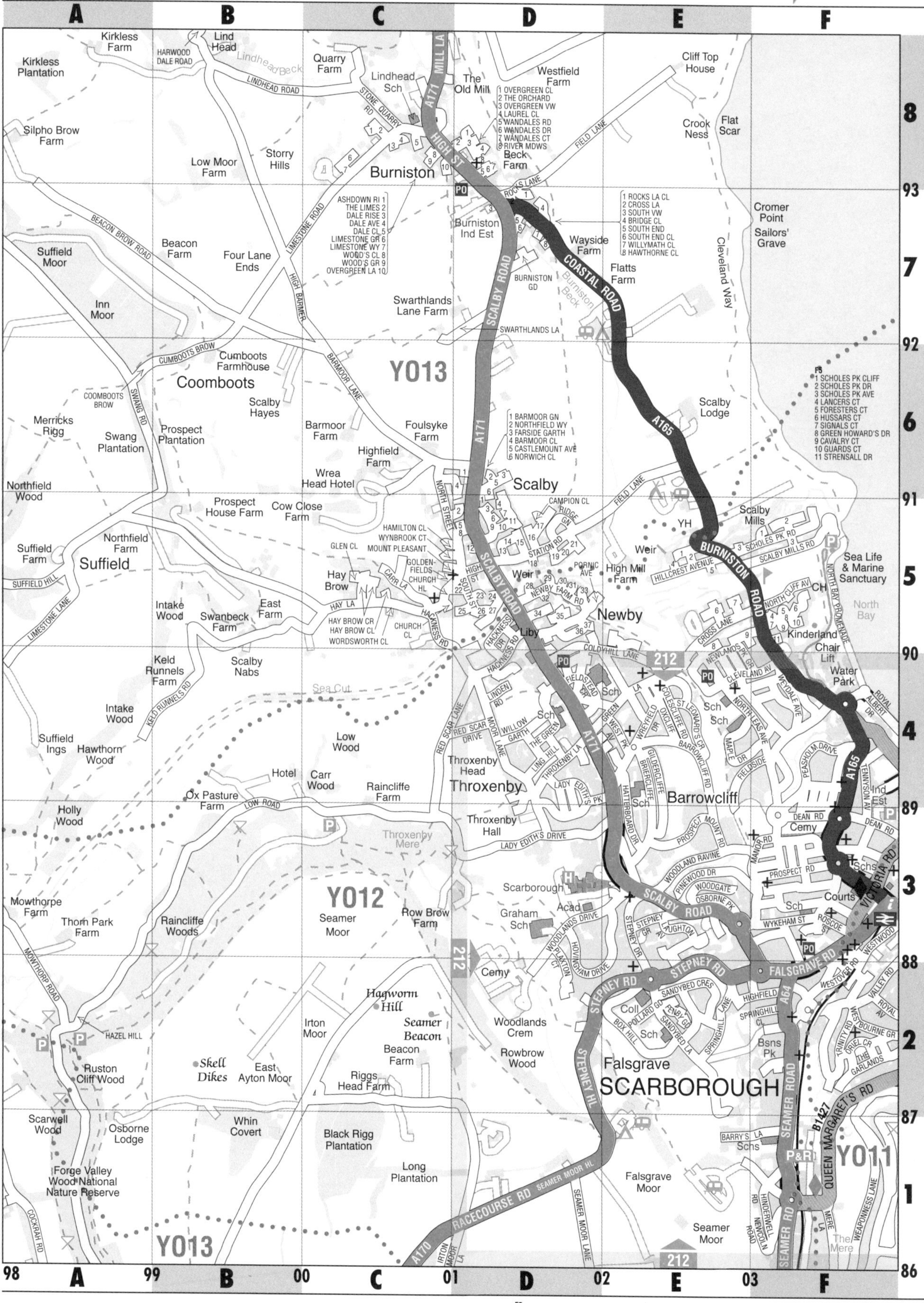

E5
1 HIGH MILL DR
2 HILLCREST GR
3 RYCROFT RD
4 FAIRWAY
5 SEAVIEW AVE
6 WESTFIELD AVE
7 MAYFIELD AVE
8 HAREWOOD AVE
9 BRIARDENE AVE

For full street detail of the highlighted area see page 212.

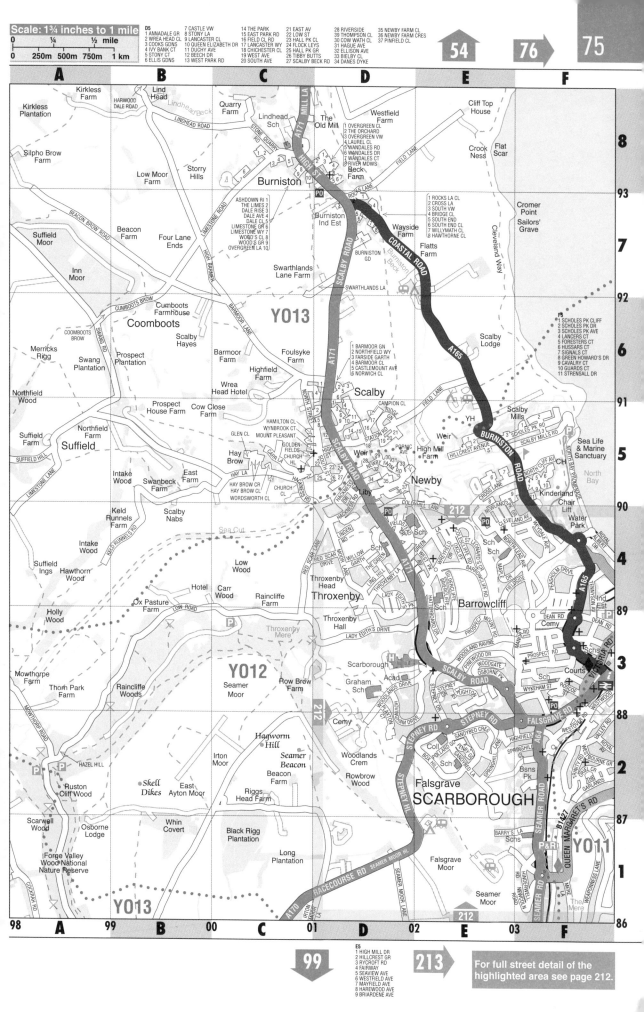

75

Scale: 1¾ inches to 1 mile

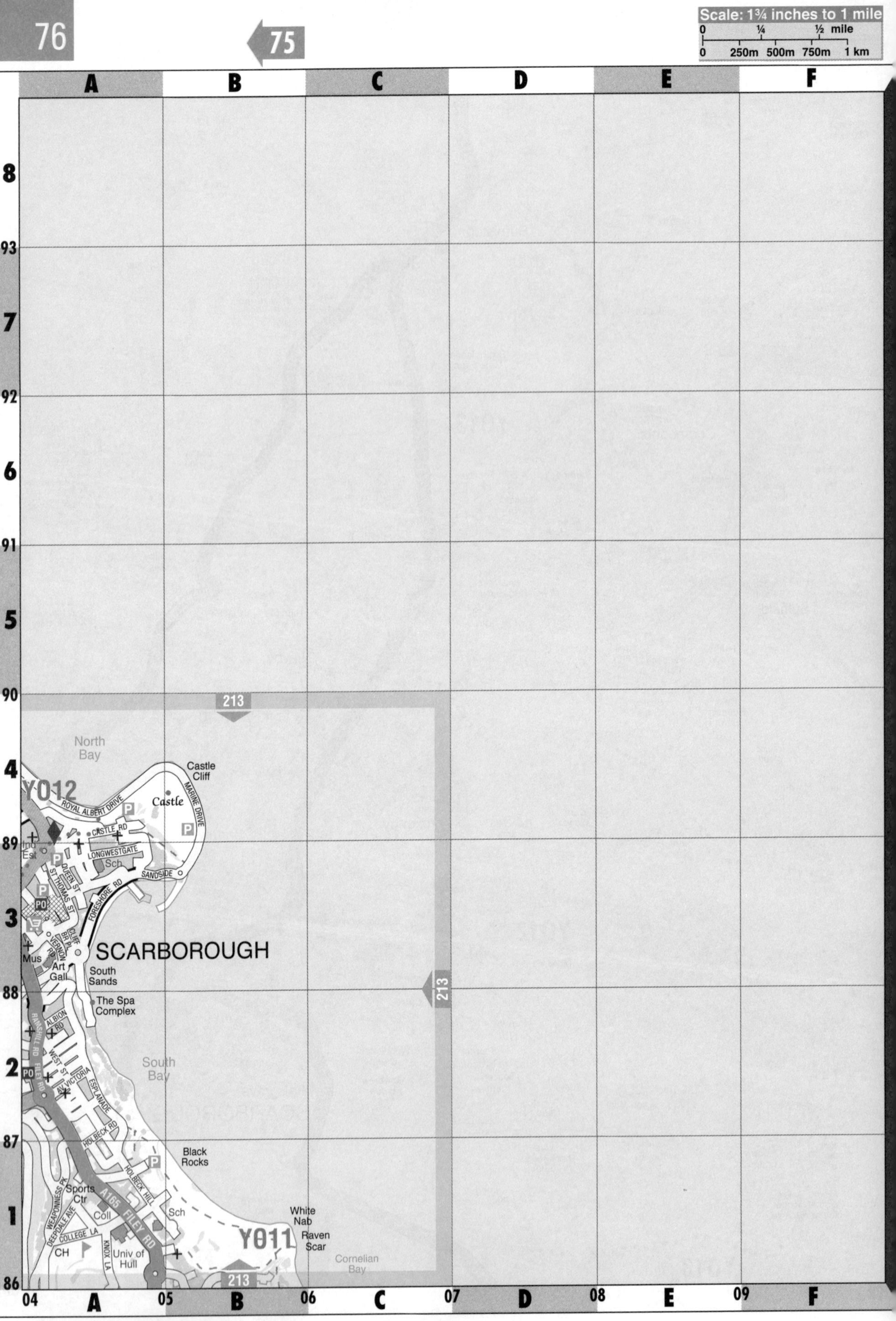

A B C D E F
8
93
7
92
6
91
5
90
213
North Bay
4
Castle Cliff
YO12
Castle
ROYAL ALBERT DRIVE
MARINE DRIVE
CASTLE RD
89
Ind Est
LONGWESTGATE
Sch
SANDSIDE
ST THOMAS ST
QUEEN ST
FORESHORE RD
PO
3
VERNON RD
CLIFF BR
SCARBOROUGH
Mus
Art Gall
South Sands
88
213
The Spa Complex
ALBION RD
RAMSHILL RD
WEST ST
2
South Bay
PO
FILEY RD
AV VICTORIA
ESPLANADE
87
HOLBECK RD
Black Rocks
HOLBECK HILL
1
Sports Ctr
WEAPONNESS PK
DEEPDALE AVE
A165 FILEY RD
Coll
Sch
White Nab
COLLEGE LA
YO11
Raven Scar
CH
KNOX LA
Univ of Hull
Cornelian Bay
213
86
04 05 06 07 08 09
A B C D E F

For full street detail of the highlighted area see page 213.

212

100

Scale: 1¾ inches to 1 mile
0 ¼ ½ mile
0 250m 500m 750m 1 km

78

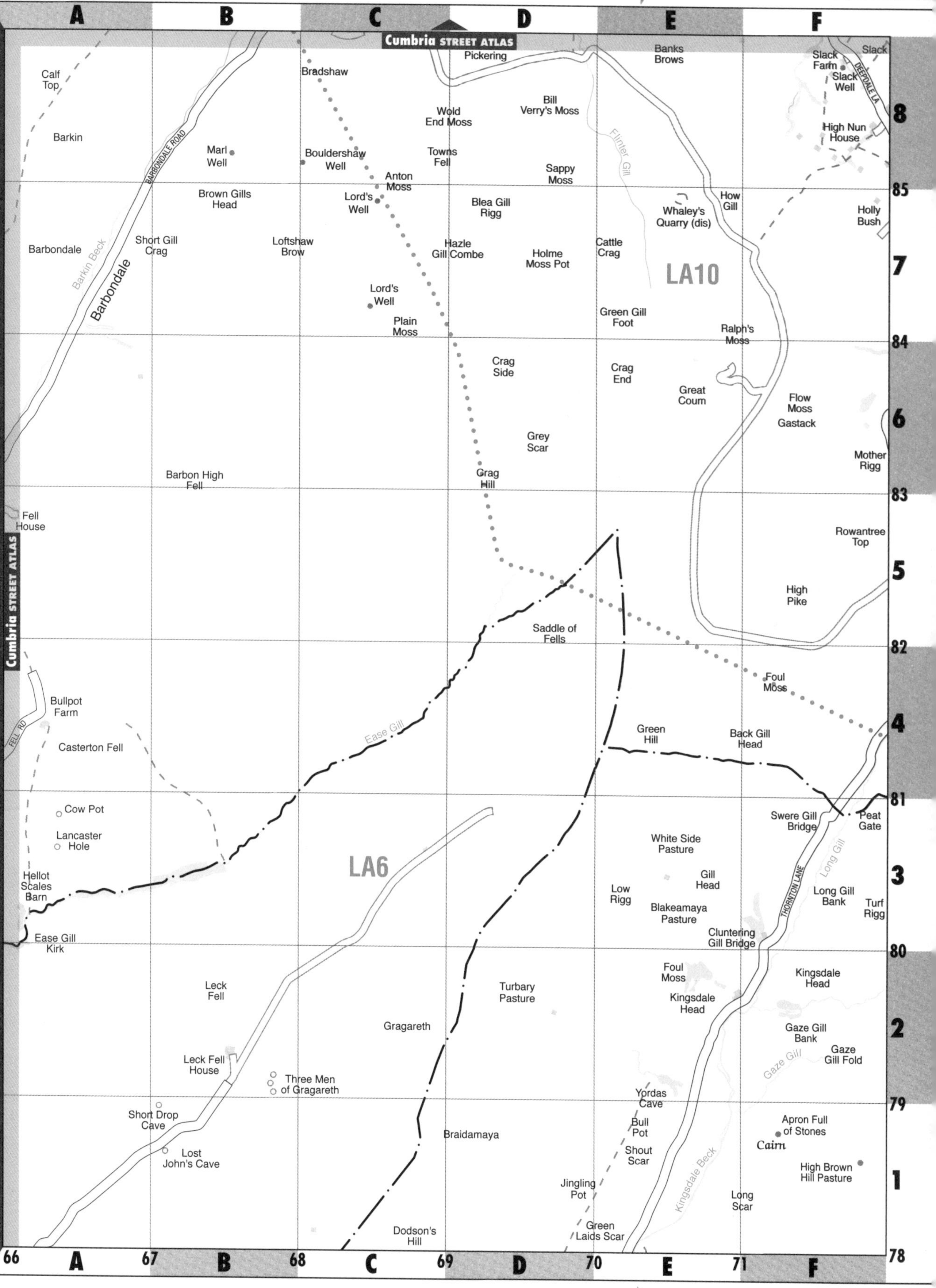
A
B
C
D
E
F
Cumbria STREET ATLAS
Calf Top
Barkin
Bradshaw
Pickering
Banks Brows
Slack Farm
Slack
Slack Well
DEEPDALE LA
Bill Verry's Moss
Wold End Moss
High Nun House
Marl Well
Bouldershaw Well
Towns Fell
BARBONDALE ROAD
Flinter Gill
Anton Moss
Sappy Moss
Brown Gills Head
Lord's Well
Blea Gill Rigg
How Gill
Whaley's Quarry (dis)
Holly Bush
Barbondale
Barkin Beck
Short Gill Crag
Loftshaw Brow
Hazle Gill Combe
Holme Moss Pot
Cattle Crag
LA10
Lord's Well
Plain Moss
Green Gill Foot
Ralph's Moss
Crag Side
Crag End
Great Coum
Flow Moss
Gastack
Grey Scar
Mother Rigg
Barbon High Fell
Crag Hill
Fell House
Rowantree Top
High Pike
Saddle of Fells
Foul Moss
Bullpot Farm
FELL RD
Ease Gill
Green Hill
Back Gill Head
Casterton Fell
Cow Pot
Lancaster Hole
Swere Gill Bridge
Peat Gate
White Side Pasture
LA6
Long Gill
Hellot Scales Barn
Gill Head
Low Rigg
Long Gill Bank
Turf Rigg
Blakeamaya Pasture
THORNTON LANE
Ease Gill Kirk
Cluntering Gill Bridge
Foul Moss
Kingsdale Head
Leck Fell
Turbary Pasture
Kingsdale Head
Gragareth
Gaze Gill Bank
Gaze Gill
Gaze Gill Fold
Leck Fell House
Three Men of Gragareth
Yordas Cave
Short Drop Cave
Bull Pot
Apron Full of Stones
Braidamaya
Cairn
Shout Scar
Lost John's Cave
Kingsdale Beck
High Brown Hill Pasture
Jingling Pot
Long Scar
Dodson's Hill
Green Laids Scar
8
85
7
84
6
83
5
82
4
81
3
80
2
79
1
78
66
67
68
69
70
71

103
78

77

Scale: 1¾ inches to 1 mile
0 ¼ ½ mile
0 250m 500m 750m 1 km

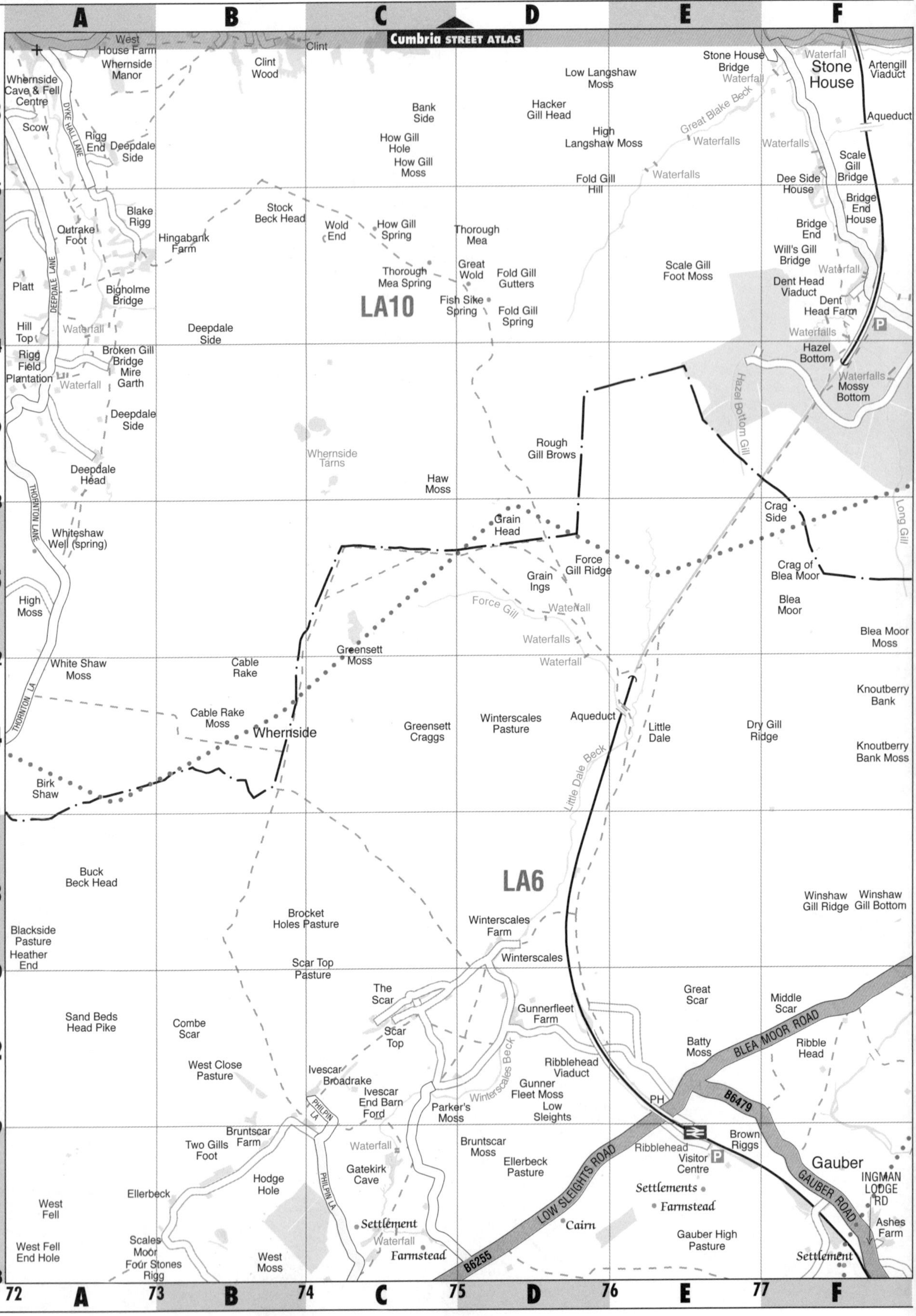

A B C D E F
Cumbria STREET ATLAS
8 85 7 84 6 83 5 82 4 81 3 80 2 79 1 78
72 73 74 75 76 77
West House Farm
Clint
Whernside Manor
Clint Wood
Whernside Cave & Fell Centre
DYKE HALL LANE
Scow
Rigg End
Deepdale Side
Bank Side
How Gill Hole
How Gill Moss
Low Langshaw Moss
Hacker Gill Head
High Langshaw Moss
Fold Gill Hill
Stone House Bridge
Waterfall
Great Blake Beck
Waterfalls
Stone House
Artengill Viaduct
Aqueduct
Scale Gill Bridge
Dee Side House
Bridge End House
Bridge End
Will's Gill Bridge
Dent Head Viaduct
Dent Head Farm
Hazel Bottom
Mossy Bottom
Hazel Bottom Gill
Blake Rigg
Outrake Foot
Hingabank Farm
Stock Beck Head
Wold End
How Gill Spring
Thorough Mea
Thorough Mea Spring
Great Wold
Fold Gill Gutters
Fish Sike Spring
Fold Gill Spring
LA10
Scale Gill Foot Moss
DEEPDALE LANE
Platt
Bigholme Bridge
Hill Top
Deepdale Side
Rigg Field Plantation
Broken Gill Bridge
Mire Garth
Deepdale Side
Deepdale Head
Whernside Tarns
Haw Moss
Rough Gill Brows
THORNTON LANE
Whiteshaw Well (spring)
Grain Head
Force Gill Ridge
Grain Ings
Crag Side
Long Gill
Crag of Blea Moor
Blea Moor
Blea Moor Moss
High Moss
Force Gill
Greensett Moss
White Shaw Moss
Cable Rake
Cable Rake Moss
Whernside
Greensett Craggs
Winterscales Pasture
Aqueduct
Little Dale
Dry Gill Ridge
Knoutberry Bank
Knoutberry Bank Moss
THORNTON LA
Little Dale Beck
Birk Shaw
Buck Beck Head
LA6
Winshaw Gill Ridge
Winshaw Gill Bottom
Blackside Pasture
Heather End
Brocket Holes Pasture
Winterscales Farm
Winterscales
Scar Top Pasture
The Scar
Sand Beds Head Pike
Combe Scar
Scar Top
Gunnerfleet Farm
Great Scar
Middle Scar
BLEA MOOR ROAD
Batty Moss
Ribble Head
West Close Pasture
Ivescar
Broadrake
Ivescar End Barn Ford
Winterscales Beck
Ribblehead Viaduct
Gunner Fleet Moss
Low Sleights
Parker's Moss
PH
B6479
PHILPIN LA
Bruntscar Farm
Two Gills Foot
Bruntscar Moss
Ellerbeck Pasture
Ribblehead
Visitor Centre
Brown Riggs
Gauber
Gatekirk Cave
Hodge Hole
Ellerbeck
LOW SLEIGHTS ROAD
Settlements
Farmstead
GAUBER ROAD
INGMAN LODGE RD
West Fell
Settlement
Cairn
Ashes Farm
West Fell End Hole
Scales Moor
Four Stones Rigg
West Moss
Farmstead
B6255
Gauber High Pasture

77

104

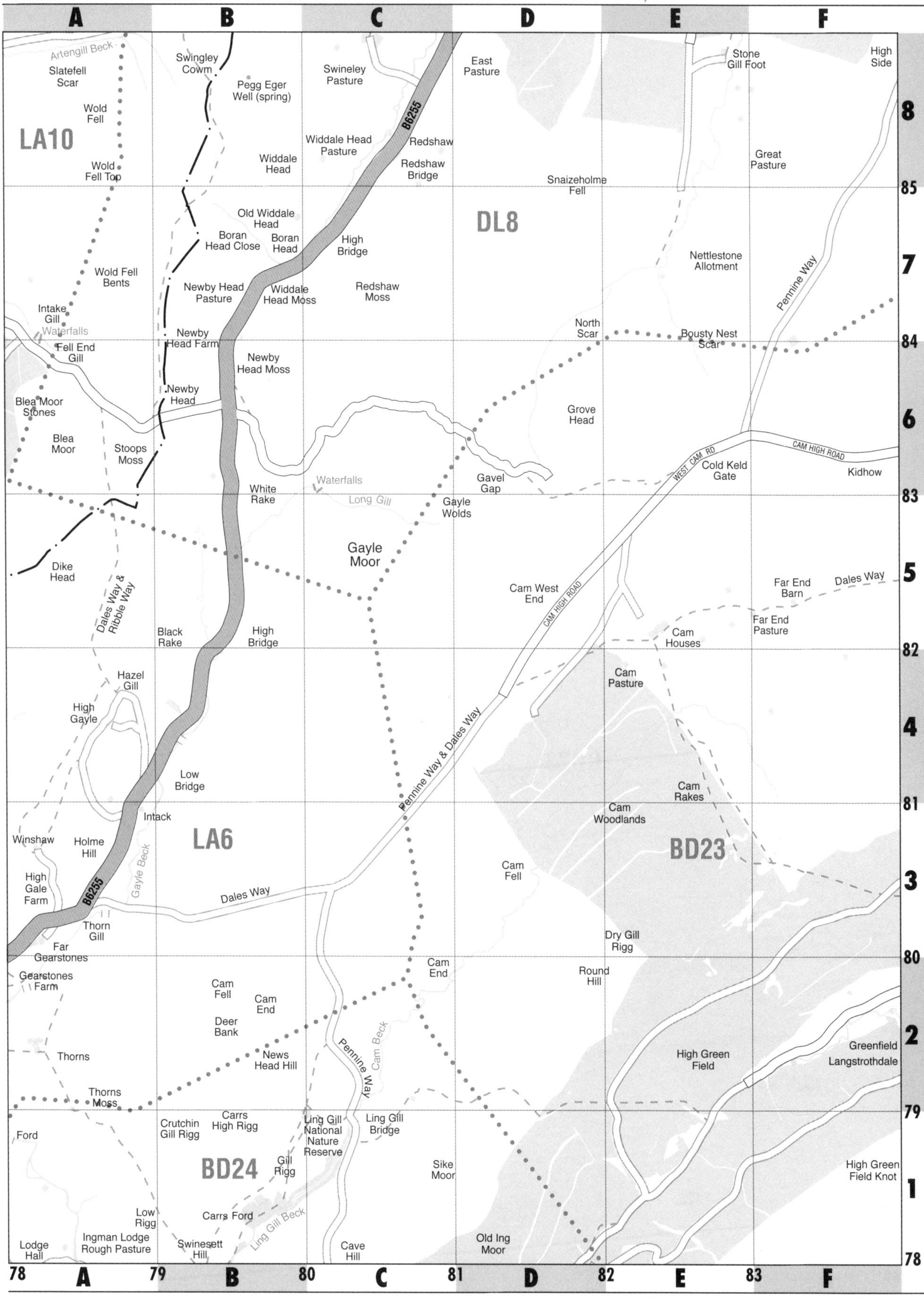
A
B
C
D
E
F
Artengill Beck
Slatefell Scar
Swingley Cowm
Pegg Eger Well (spring)
Swineley Pasture
East Pasture
Stone Gill Foot
High Side
Wold Fell
LA10
Wold Fell Top
B6255
Widdale Head
Widdale Head Pasture
Redshaw
Redshaw Bridge
Great Pasture
Snaizeholme Fell
Old Widdale Head
Boran Head Close
Boran Head
High Bridge
DL8
Nettlestone Allotment
Wold Fell Bents
Newby Head Pasture
Widdale Head Moss
Redshaw Moss
Pennine Way
Intake Gill
Waterfalls
Fell End Gill
Newby Head Farm
Newby Head Moss
North Scar
Bousty Nest Scar
Blea Moor Stones
Newby Head
Grove Head
Blea Moor
Stoops Moss
Waterfalls
White Rake
Long Gill
Gavel Gap
WEST CAM RD
Cold Keld Gate
CAM HIGH ROAD
Kidhow
Gayle Wolds
Gayle Moor
Dike Head
Dales Way & Ribble Way
Cam West End
CAM HIGH ROAD
Far End Barn
Dales Way
Far End Pasture
Black Rake
High Bridge
Cam Houses
Hazel Gill
Cam Pasture
High Gayle
Pennine Way & Dales Way
Low Bridge
Cam Rakes
Intack
Cam Woodlands
Winshaw
Holme Hill
LA6
BD23
High Gale Farm
Gayle Beck
Cam Fell
B6255
Dales Way
Thorn Gill
Far Gearstones
Dry Gill Rigg
Gearstones Farm
Cam End
Round Hill
Cam Fell
Cam End
Deer Bank
Thorns
News Head Hill
Pennine Way
Cam Beck
High Green Field
Greenfield
Langstrothdale
Thorns Moss
Crutchin Gill Rigg
Carrs High Rigg
Ling Gill National Nature Reserve
Ling Gill Bridge
Ford
BD24
Gill Rigg
Sike Moor
High Green Field Knot
Low Rigg
Carrs Ford
Ling Gill Beck
Lodge Hall
Ingman Lodge Rough Pasture
Swinesett Hill
Cave Hill
Old Ing Moor
8
85
7
84
6
83
5
82
4
81
3
80
2
79
1
78
78
79
80
81
82
83

79
56
Scale: 1¾ inches to 1 mile
0 ¼ ½ mile
0 250m 500m 750m 1 km

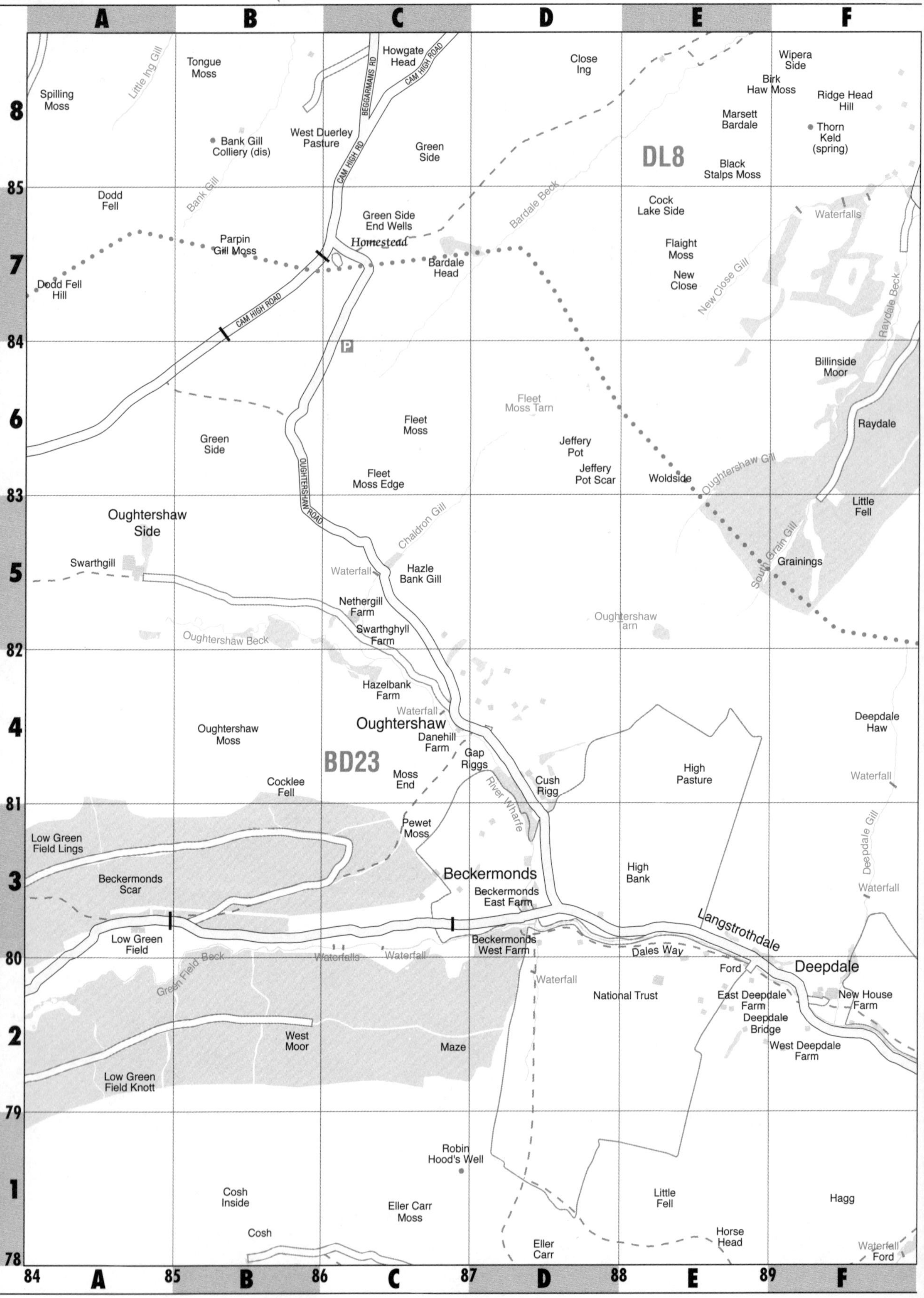

79
106

Scale: 1¾ inches to 1 mile
0 ¼ ½ mile
0 250m 500m 750m 1 km

57
82

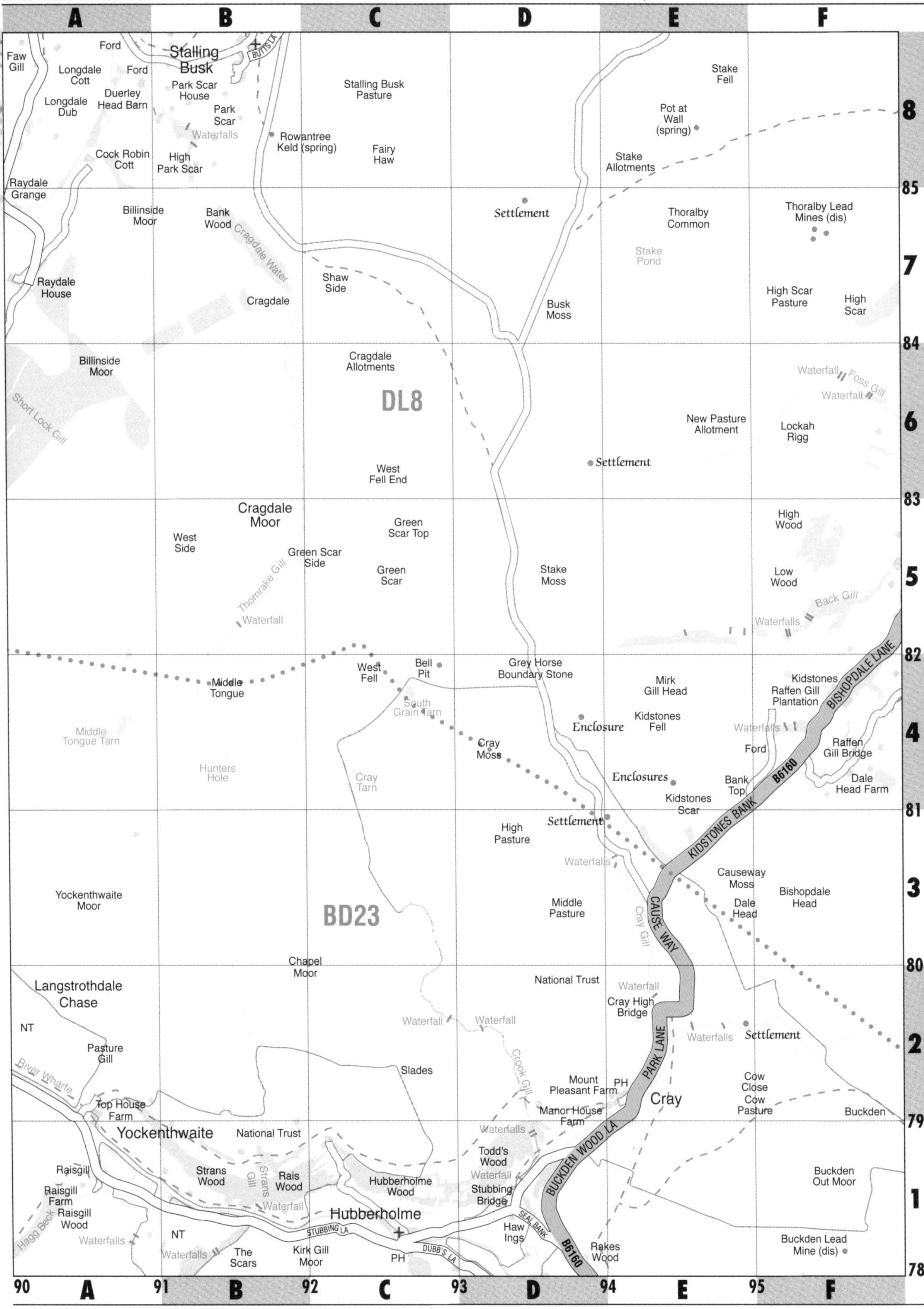
A
B
C
D
E
F
Faw Gill
Ford
Stalling Busk
BUTTS LA
Longdale Cott
Ford
Longdale Dub
Duerley Head Barn
Park Scar House
Park Scar
Stalling Busk Pasture
Stake Fell
Pot at Wall (spring)
Waterfalls
Rowantree Keld (spring)
Fairy Haw
Cock Robin Cott
High Park Scar
Stake Allotments
Raydale Grange
Billinside Moor
Bank Wood
Cragdale Water
Settlement
Thoralby Common
Thoralby Lead Mines (dis)
Stake Pond
Raydale House
Shaw Side
Cragdale
Busk Moss
High Scar Pasture
High Scar
Billinside Moor
Cragdale Allotments
DL8
Waterfall
Foss Gill
Waterfall
Short Lock Gill
New Pasture Allotment
Lockah Rigg
Settlement
West Fell End
Cragdale Moor
Green Scar Top
High Wood
West Side
Green Scar Side
Green Scar
Stake Moss
Low Wood
Thornrake Gill
Back Gill
Waterfall
Waterfalls
West Fell
Bell Pit
Grey Horse Boundary Stone
Middle Tongue
Mirk Gill Head
Kidstones Raffen Gill Plantation
BISHOPDALE LANE
South Grain Tarn
Kidstones Fell
Enclosure
Middle Tongue Tarn
Waterfalls
Cray Moss
Ford
Raffen Gill Bridge
Hunters Hole
Cray Tarn
Enclosures
Bank Top
B6160
Dale Head Farm
Kidstones Scar
KIDSTONES BANK
High Pasture
Settlement
Waterfalls
Causeway Moss
Yockenthwaite Moor
Bishopdale Head
Middle Pasture
Dale Head
CAUSE WAY
Cray Gill
BD23
Chapel Moor
Langstrothdale Chase
National Trust
Waterfall
Cray High Bridge
NT
Waterfall
Waterfall
Waterfalls
Settlement
PARK LANE
Pasture Gill
Crook Gill
River Wharfe
Slades
Mount Pleasant Farm
PH
Cray
Cow Close
Cow Pasture
Top House Farm
Manor House Farm
Buckden
Yockenthwaite
National Trust
Waterfalls
Todd's Wood
Raisgill
Strans Wood
Strans Gill
Rais Wood
Hubberholme Wood
Waterfall
BUCKDEN WOOD LA
Buckden Out Moor
Raisgill Farm
Stubbing Bridge
Raisgill Wood
Waterfall
Hubberholme
Hagg Beck
SEAL BANK
Haw Ings
Waterfalls
NT
STUBBING LA
Waterfalls
The Scars
Kirk Gill Moor
DUBB'S LA
PH
B6160
Rakes Wood
Buckden Lead Mine (dis)
8
85
7
84
6
83
5
82
4
81
3
80
2
79
1
78
90
91
92
93
94
95

107
82

81
58

Scale: 1¾ inches to 1 mile

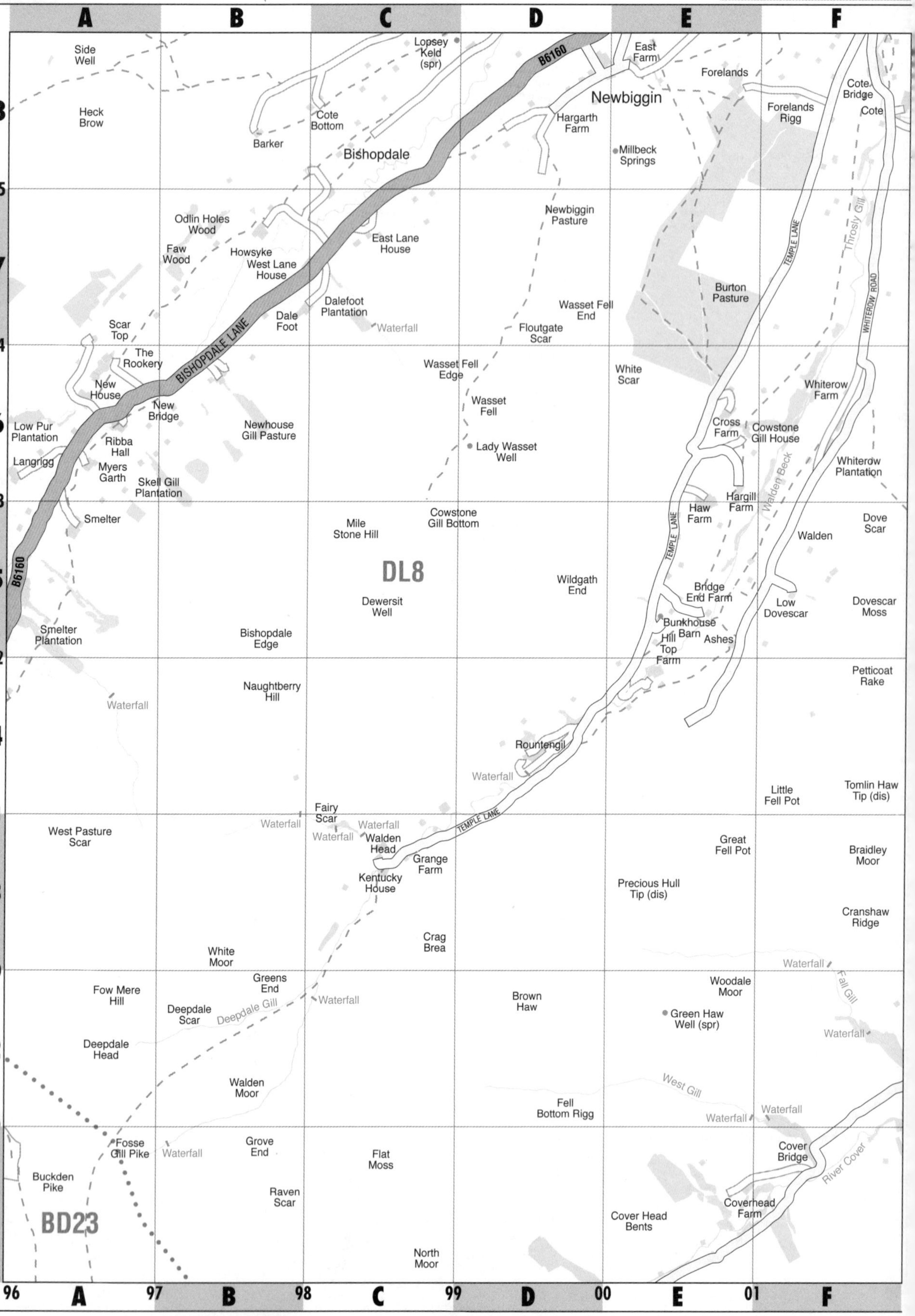

81
108

Scale: 1¾ inches to 1 mile

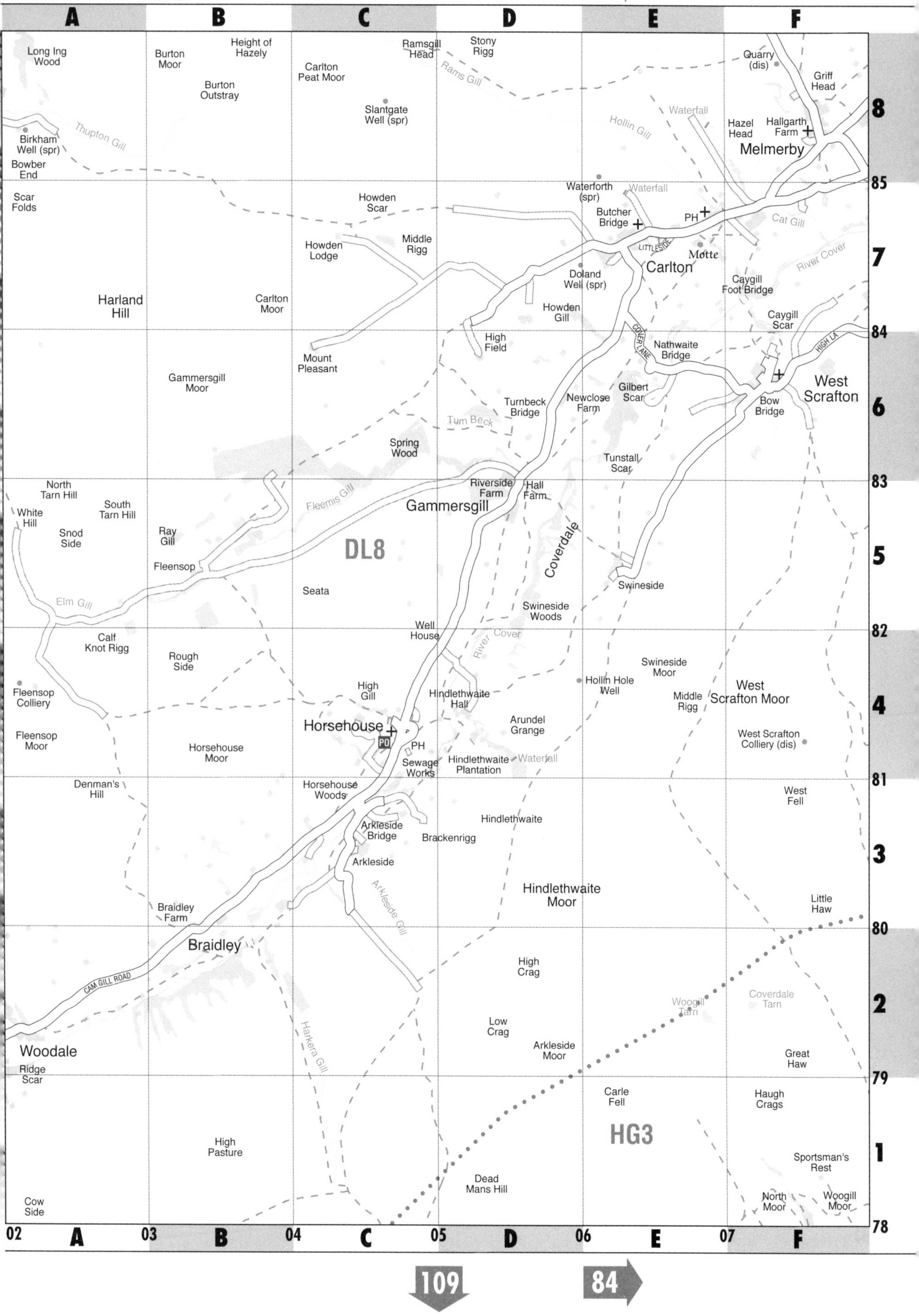

83
60

Scale: 1¾ inches to 1 mile
0 ¼ ½ mile
0 250m 500m 750m 1 km

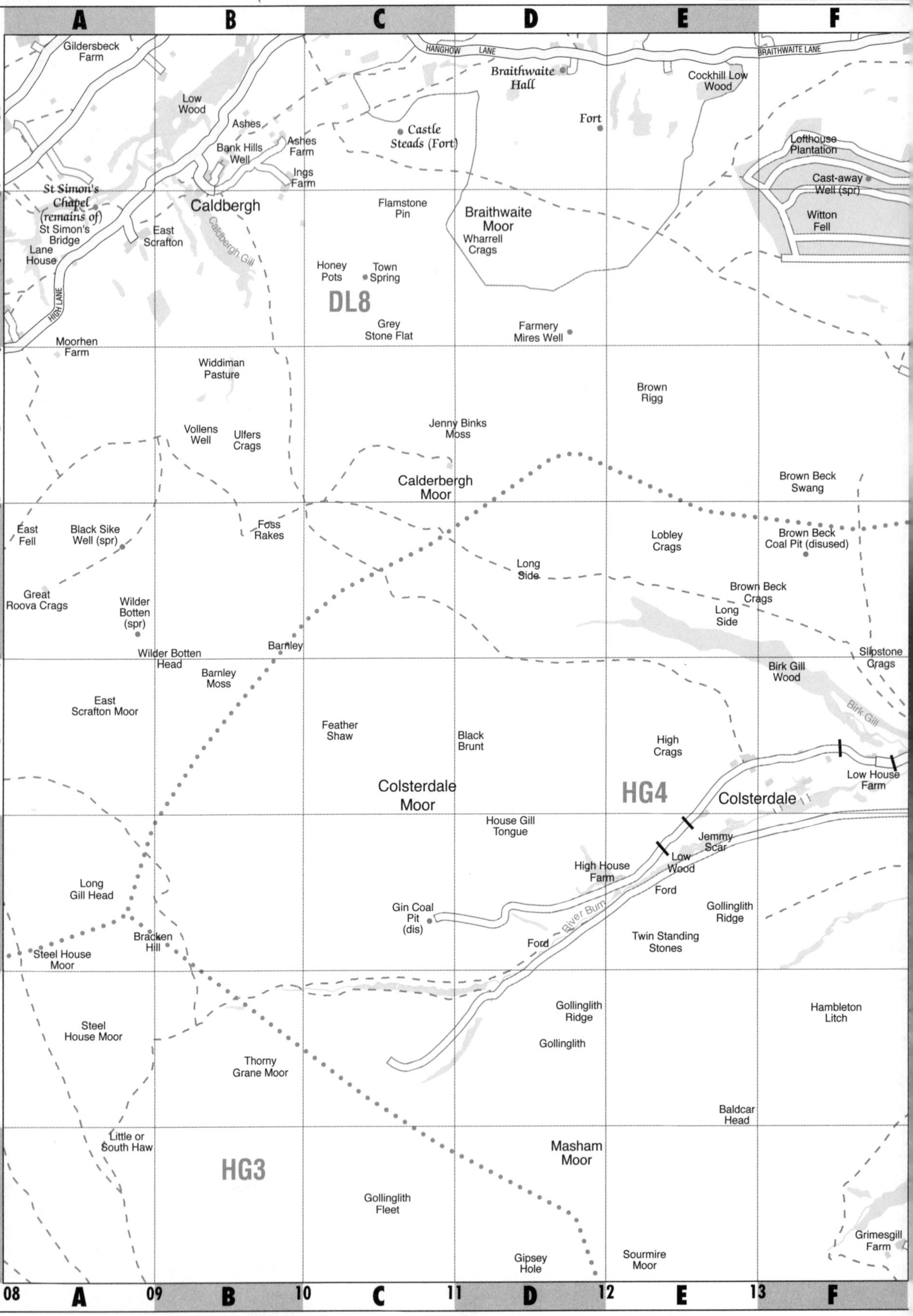

83
110

Scale: 1¾ inches to 1 mile
0 ¼ ½ mile
0 250m 500m 750m 1 km

61
86

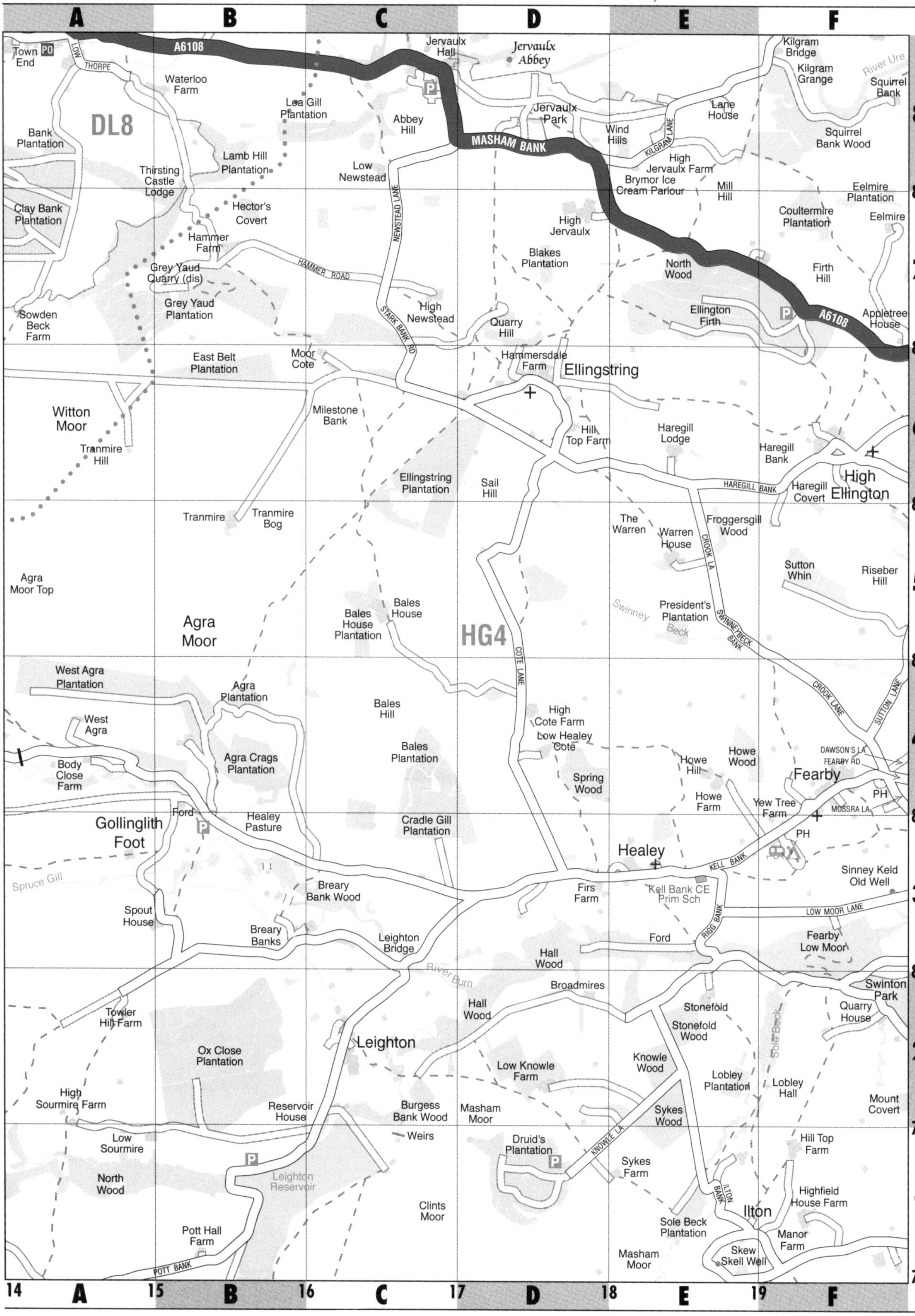
A B C D E F
8
85
7
84
6
83
5
82
4
81
3
80
2
79
1
78
14 15 16 17 18 19
A6108
Town End
PO
LOW THORPE
Waterloo Farm
Lea Gill Plantation
Jervaulx Hall
Jervaulx Abbey
Kilgram Bridge
Kilgram Grange
River Ure
Squirrel Bank
DL8
Bank Plantation
Abbey Hill
Jervaulx Park
Lane House
Wind Hills
KILGRAM LANE
Squirrel Bank Wood
MASHAM BANK
Lamb Hill Plantation
Thirsting Castle Lodge
Low Newstead
High Jervaulx Farm
Brymor Ice Cream Parlour
Mill Hill
Eelmire Plantation
Clay Bank Plantation
Hector's Covert
Coultermire Plantation
Eelmire
Hammer Farm
NEWSTEAD LANE
High Jervaulx
Blakes Plantation
Grey Yaud Quarry (dis)
HAMMER ROAD
North Wood
Firth Hill
Grey Yaud Plantation
High Newstead
STARK BANK RD
Quarry Hill
Ellington Firth
A6108
Appletree House
Sowden Beck Farm
East Belt Plantation
Moor Cote
Hammersdale Farm
Ellingstring
Witton Moor
Milestone Bank
Hill Top Farm
Haregill Lodge
Haregill Bank
Tranmire Hill
High Ellington
HAREGILL BANK
Haregill Covert
Ellingstring Plantation
Sail Hill
Tranmire
Tranmire Bog
The Warren
Warren House
Froggersgill Wood
CROOK LA
Agra Moor Top
Sutton Whin
Riseber Hill
Bales House
Bales House Plantation
Swinney Beck
President's Plantation
SWINNEY BECK BANK
Agra Moor
HG4
COTE LANE
West Agra Plantation
Agra Plantation
Bales Hill
CROOK LANE
SUTTON LANE
West Agra
High Cote Farm
Low Healey Cote
Bales Plantation
Howe Wood
DAWSON'S LA
FEARBY RD
Agra Crags Plantation
Body Close Farm
Spring Wood
Howe Hill
Fearby
Howe Farm
Yew Tree Farm
PH
MOSSRA LA
Ford
Gollinglith Foot
Healey Pasture
Cradle Gill Plantation
PH
Healey
KELL BANK
Spruce Gill
Breary Bank Wood
Firs Farm
Kell Bank CE Prim Sch
Sinney Keld Old Well
Spout House
LOW MOOR LANE
RIGG BANK
Breary Banks
Leighton Bridge
Ford
Fearby Low Moor
Hall Wood
River Burn
Broadmires
Swinton Park
Towler Hill Farm
Hall Wood
Stonefold
Stonefold Wood
Quarry House
Ox Close Plantation
Leighton
Sole Beck
Knowle Wood
Low Knowle Farm
Lobley Plantation
Lobley Hall
High Sourmire Farm
Reservoir House
Burgess Bank Wood
Masham Moor
Sykes Wood
Mount Covert
Low Sourmire
Weirs
Druid's Plantation
KNOWLE LA
Hill Top Farm
North Wood
Leighton Reservoir
Sykes Farm
Highfield House Farm
Clints Moor
ILTON BANK
Ilton
Sole Beck Plantation
Manor Farm
Pott Hall Farm
POTT BANK
Masham Moor
Skew Skell Well

111
86

85
62

Scale: 1¾ inches to 1 mile
0 ¼ ½ mile
0 250m 500m 750m 1 km

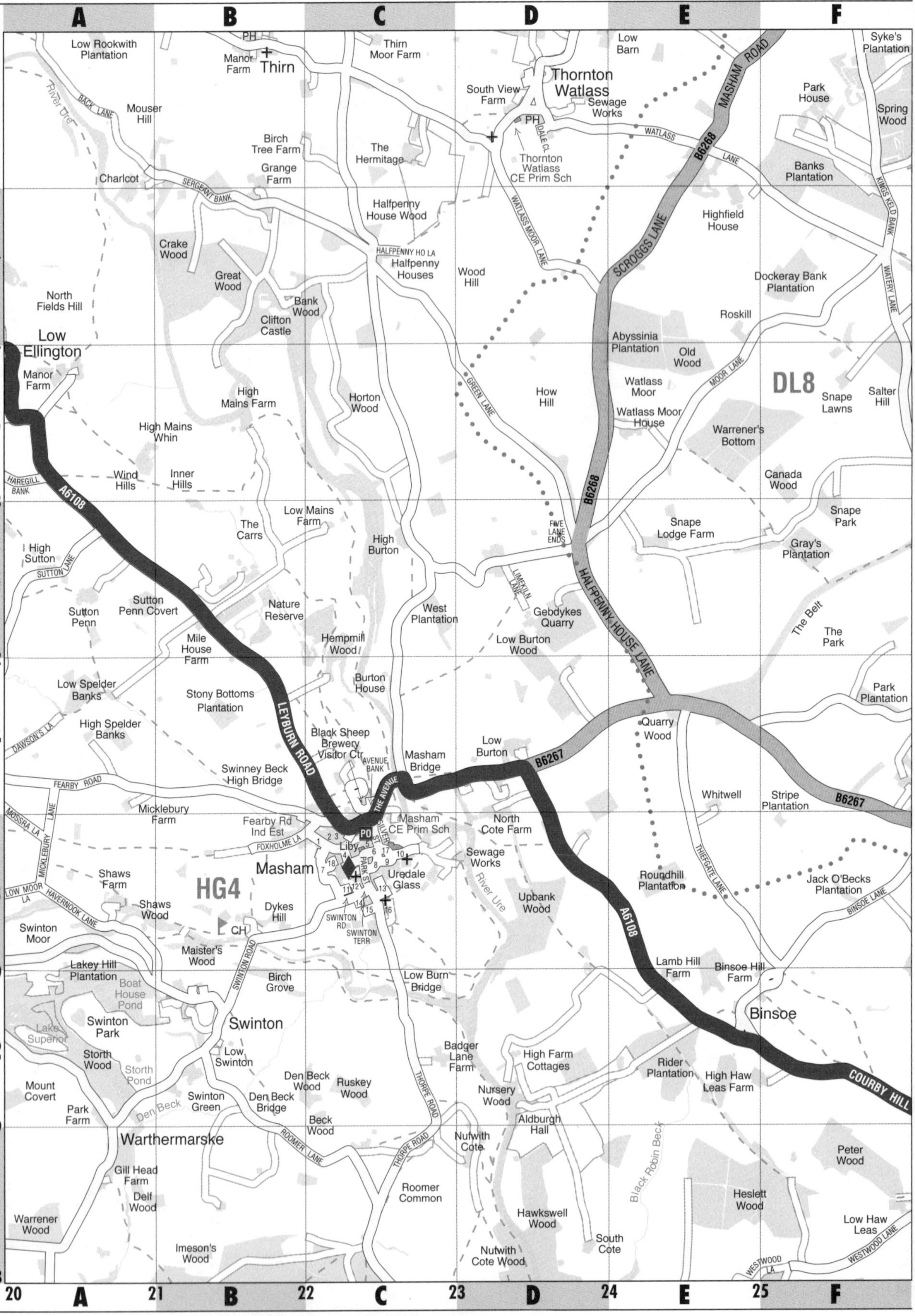

85
112

C3
1 WESTHOLME RD
2 WESTHOLME CRES
3 WESTHOLME CT
4 RED LA
5 COLLEGE LA
6 CHURCH ST
7 THE OAKS
8 CHAPMAN LA
9 MARKET PL
10 MILLGATE
11 SWINBURN RD
12 SWINBURN CT
13 PARK DR
14 FISHER ROW
15 RODNEY TERR
16 IBBETSON CL
17 LITTLE MKT PL
18 THE BEECHES

Scale: 1¾ inches to 1 mile
0 ¼ ½ mile
0 250m 500m 750m 1 km

63
88

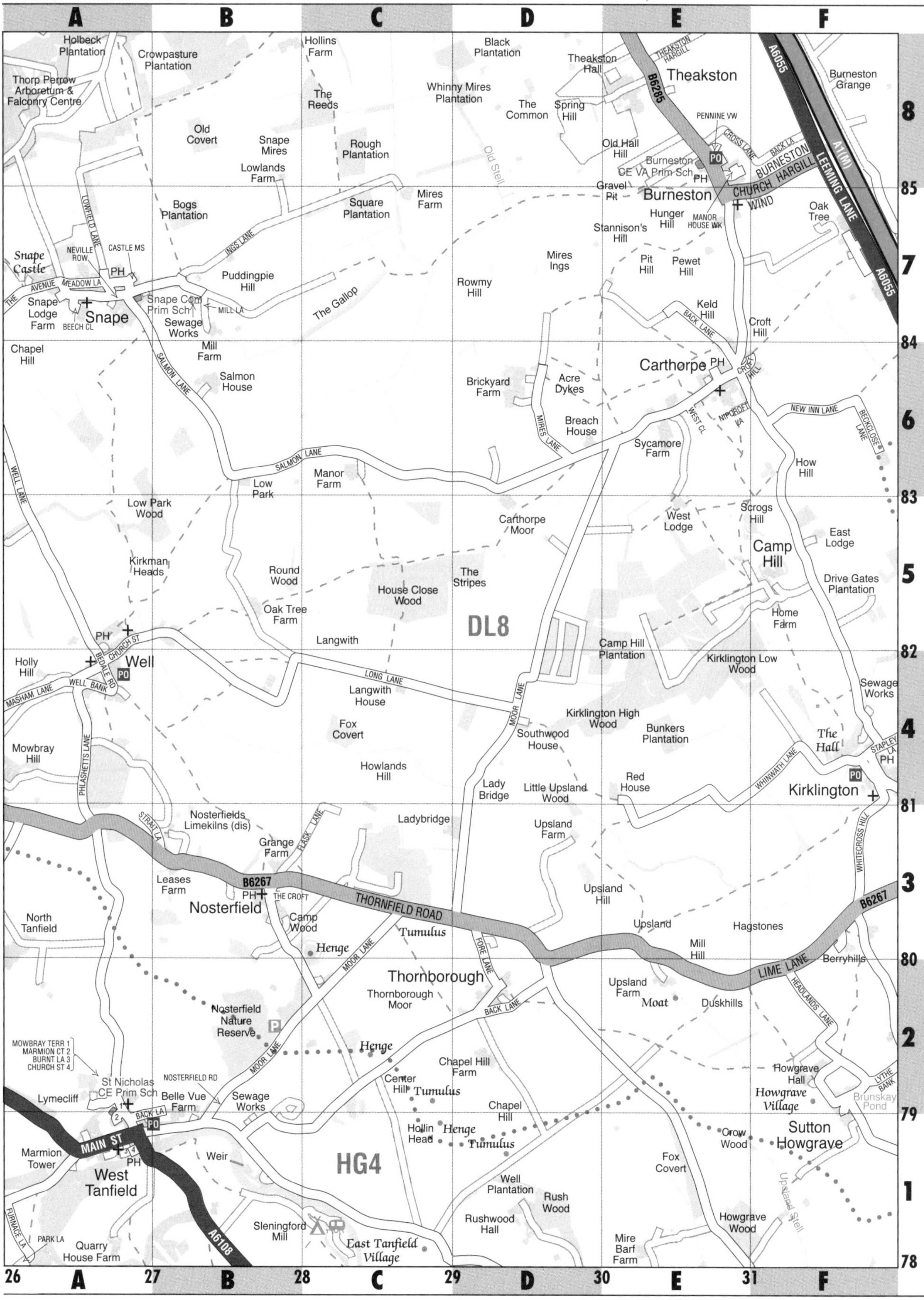

113
88

87
64

Scale: 1¾ inches to 1 mile
0 ¼ ½ mile
0 250m 500m 750m 1 km

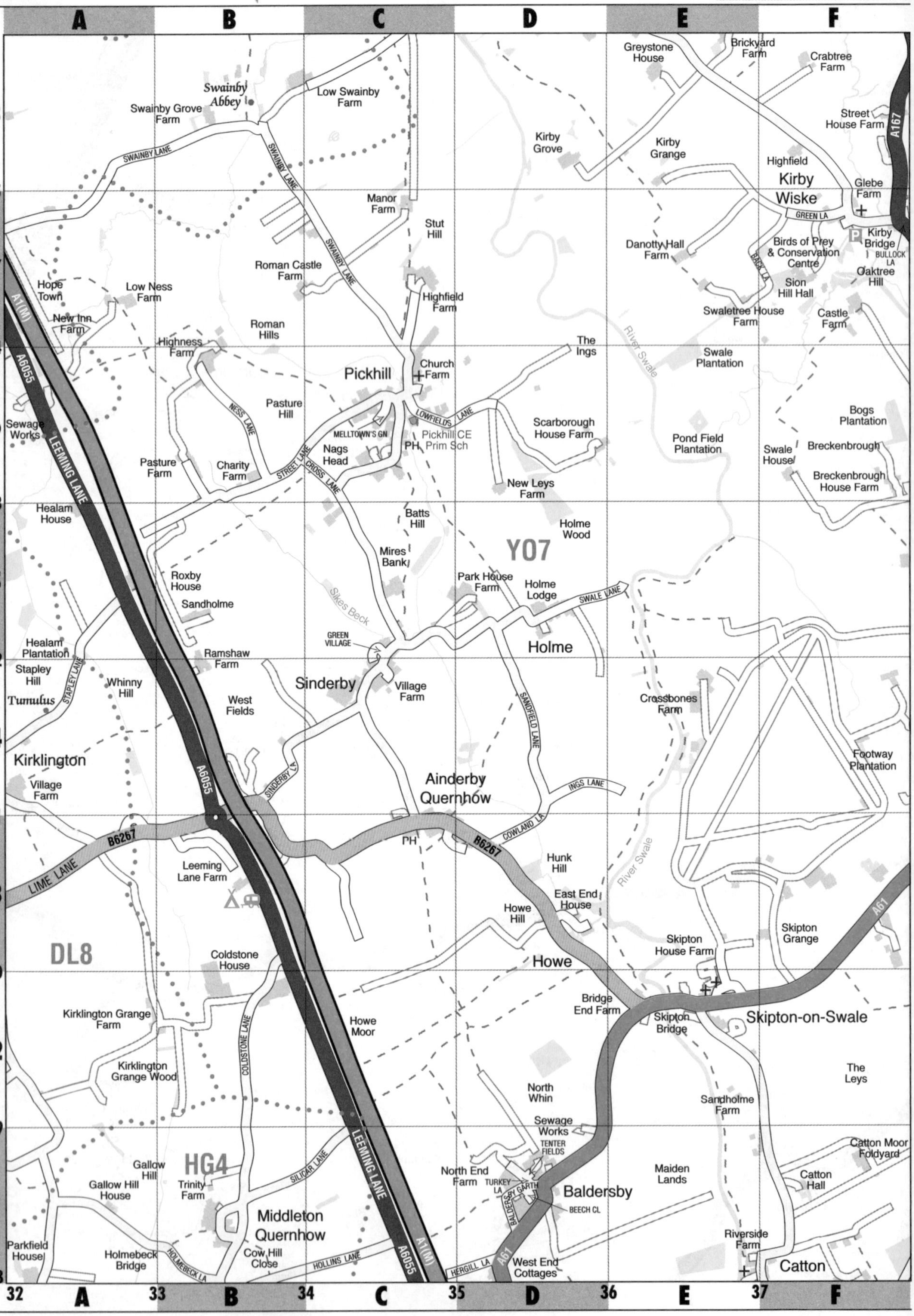

87
114

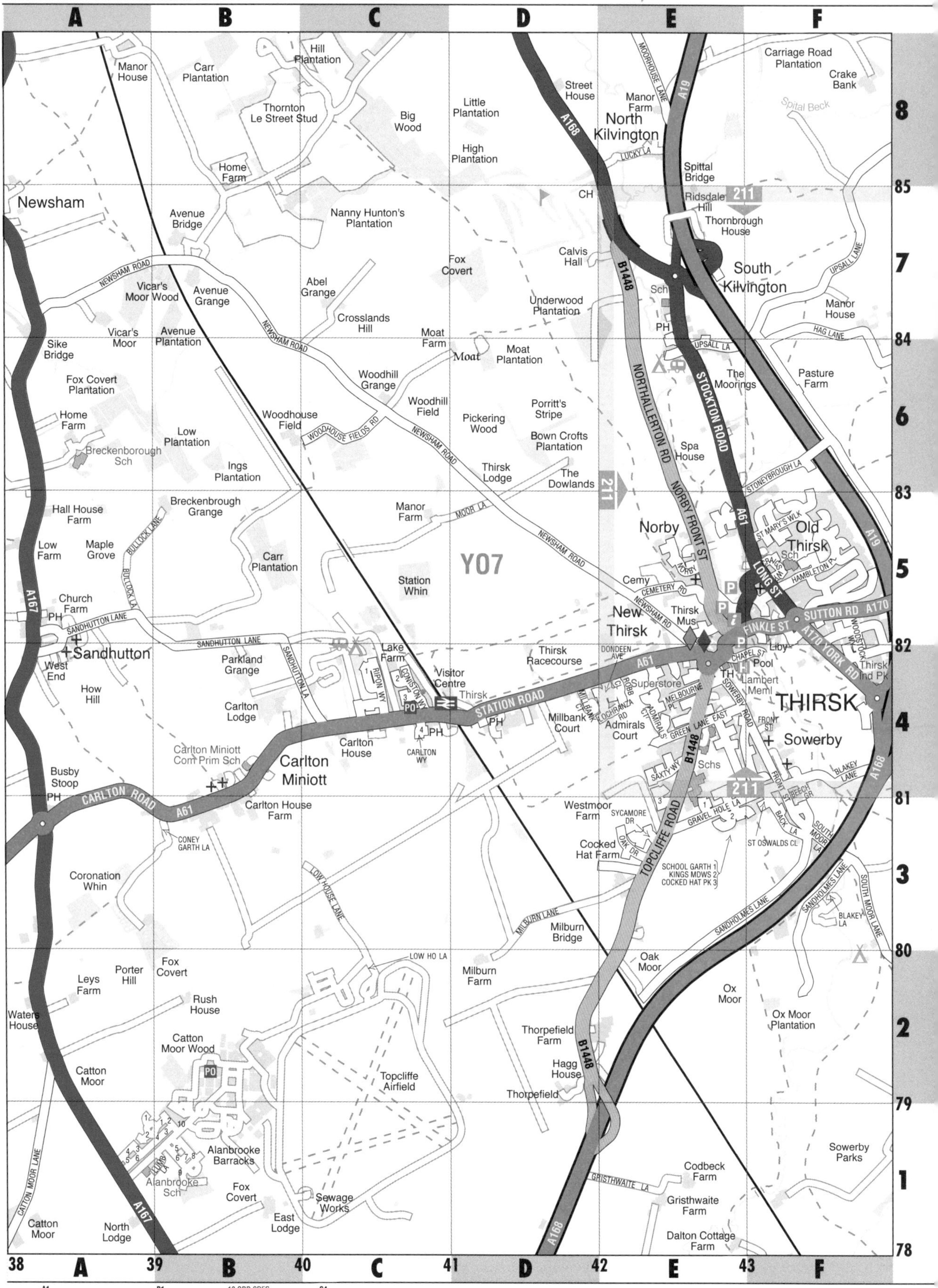

A1
1 CHESTNUT CRES
2 CHESTNUT AVE
3 OAK DR
4 SYCAMORE AVE
5 WOODLAND VW
6 LARCH RD

B1
1 CHESTNUT AVE
2 HAWTHORN DR
3 ELM RD
4 BEECH AVE
5 CHESHIRE SQ
6 WHITTLE ST
7 THE GREEN
8 TRENCHARD ST
9 THE COVERT
10 ORR CRES

C4
1 CLEVELAND WY
2 RYDAL CL
3 THIRLMERE CL
4 CARLTON CL

89
66
For full street detail of the highlighted area see page 211.

Scale: 1¾ inches to 1 mile
0 ¼ ½ mile
0 250m 500m 750m 1 km

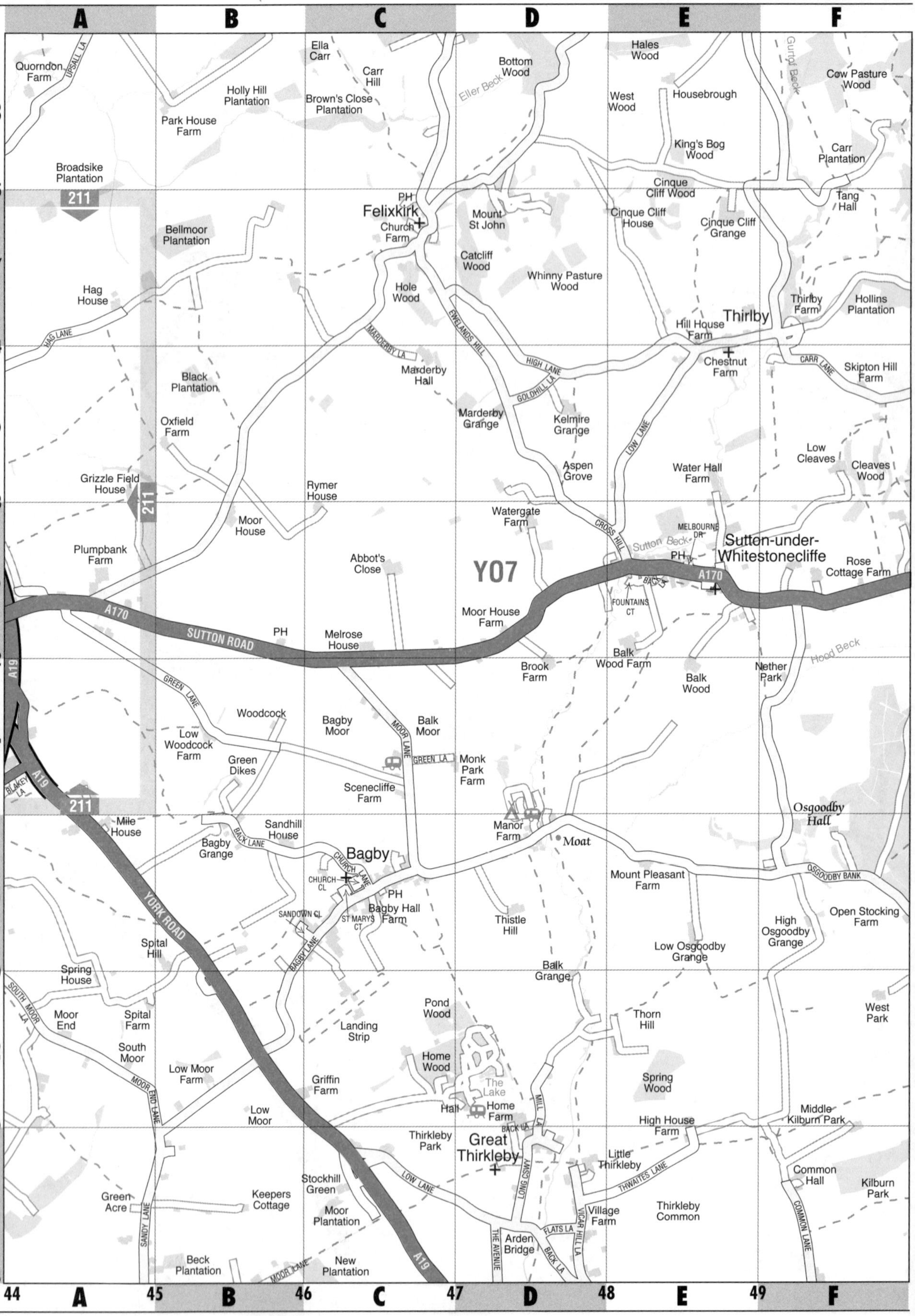

89
116

Scale: 1¾ inches to 1 mile
0 ¼ ½ mile
0 250m 500m 750m 1 km

67
92

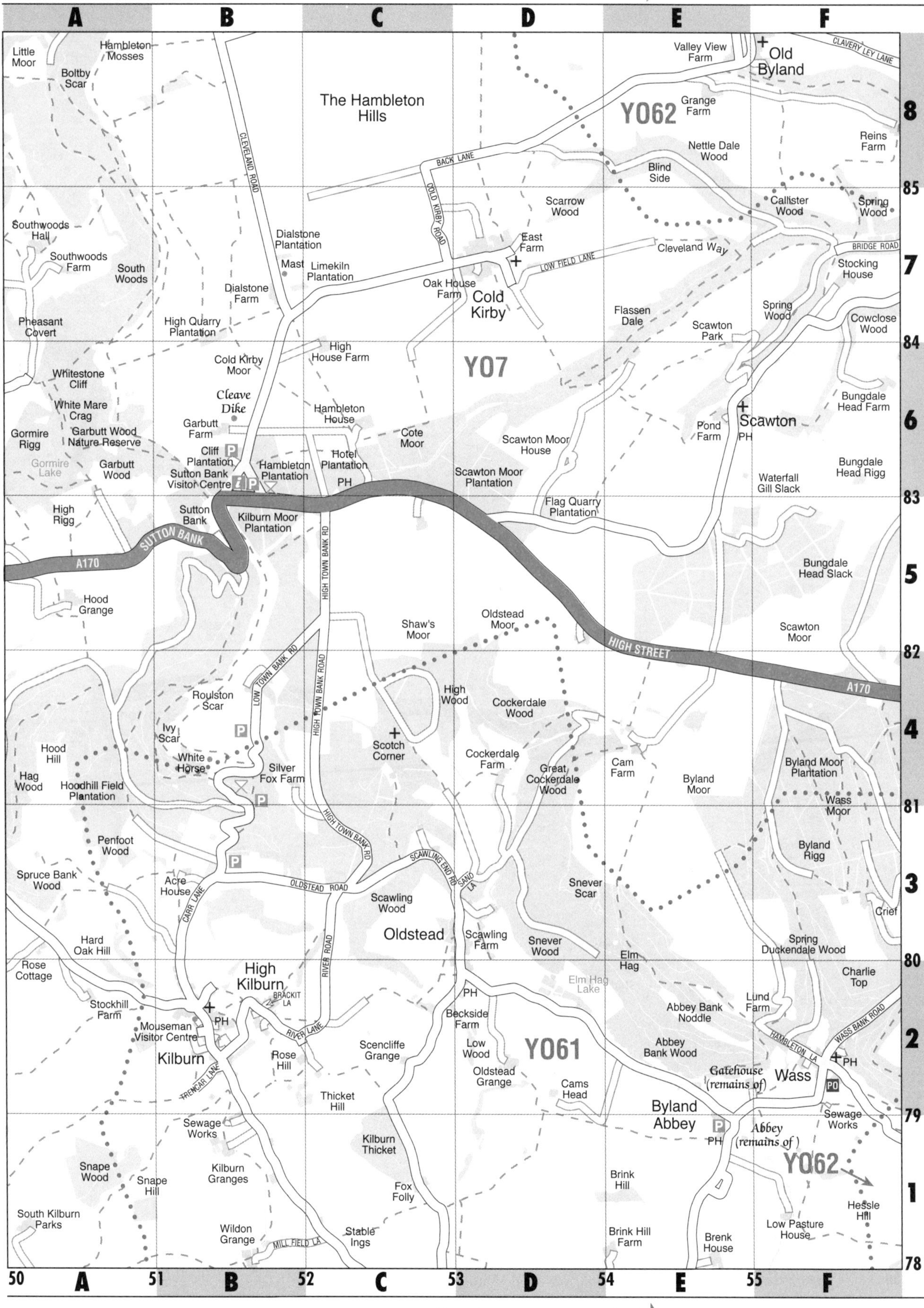

117
92

91
68

F6
1 ELMSLAC CL
2 CANONS GARTH LA
3 STONE GARTH
4 HIGH ST
5 CHURCH ST
6 CASTLEGATE
7 BUCKINGHAM SQ
8 BUCKINGHAM SQ
9 BOROGATE
10 MARKET PL
11 MARKET PL
12 BRIDGE ST
13 RYEGATE
14 POTTERGATE
15 BELL'S CT
16 EASTGATE
17 THE CRESCENT
18 SOUTH GATE
19 SOUTHLANDS
20 ALLENBY RD
21 CHAPEL CL
22 CROSLAND CL
23 CONOWL CL
24 ACRES CL
25 RICCAL DR
26 STOREY CL
27 BR FARM CL

Scale: 1¾ inches to 1 mile
0 ¼ ½ mile
0 250m 500m 750m 1 km

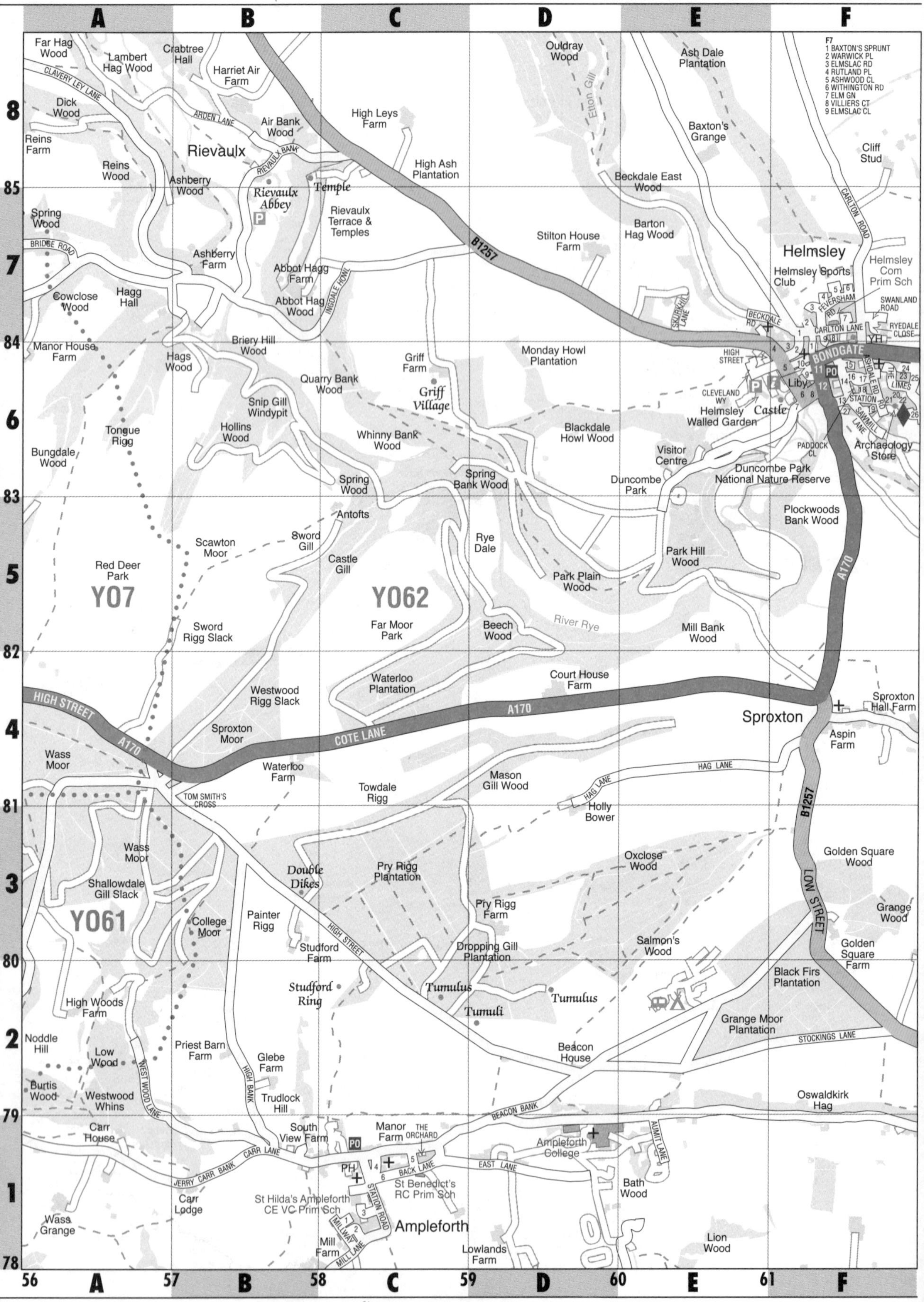

C1
1 BIRDFORTH WY
2 FAIRFAX CL
3 VALLEY VW
4 OLD STATION RD
5 THE ORCHARD
6 ST HILDA'S WK

91
118

Scale: 1¾ inches to 1 mile
0 ¼ ½ mile
0 250m 500m 750m 1 km

69
94

D7
1 BIRKLANDS
2 THE ORCHARDS
3 HOWLDALE LA
4 SCHOOL LA
5 BRIAR PK
6 CHAPEL ST
7 BELLABY PK
8 BECKETT CL
9 THE SIDINGS
10 ASHTON GN

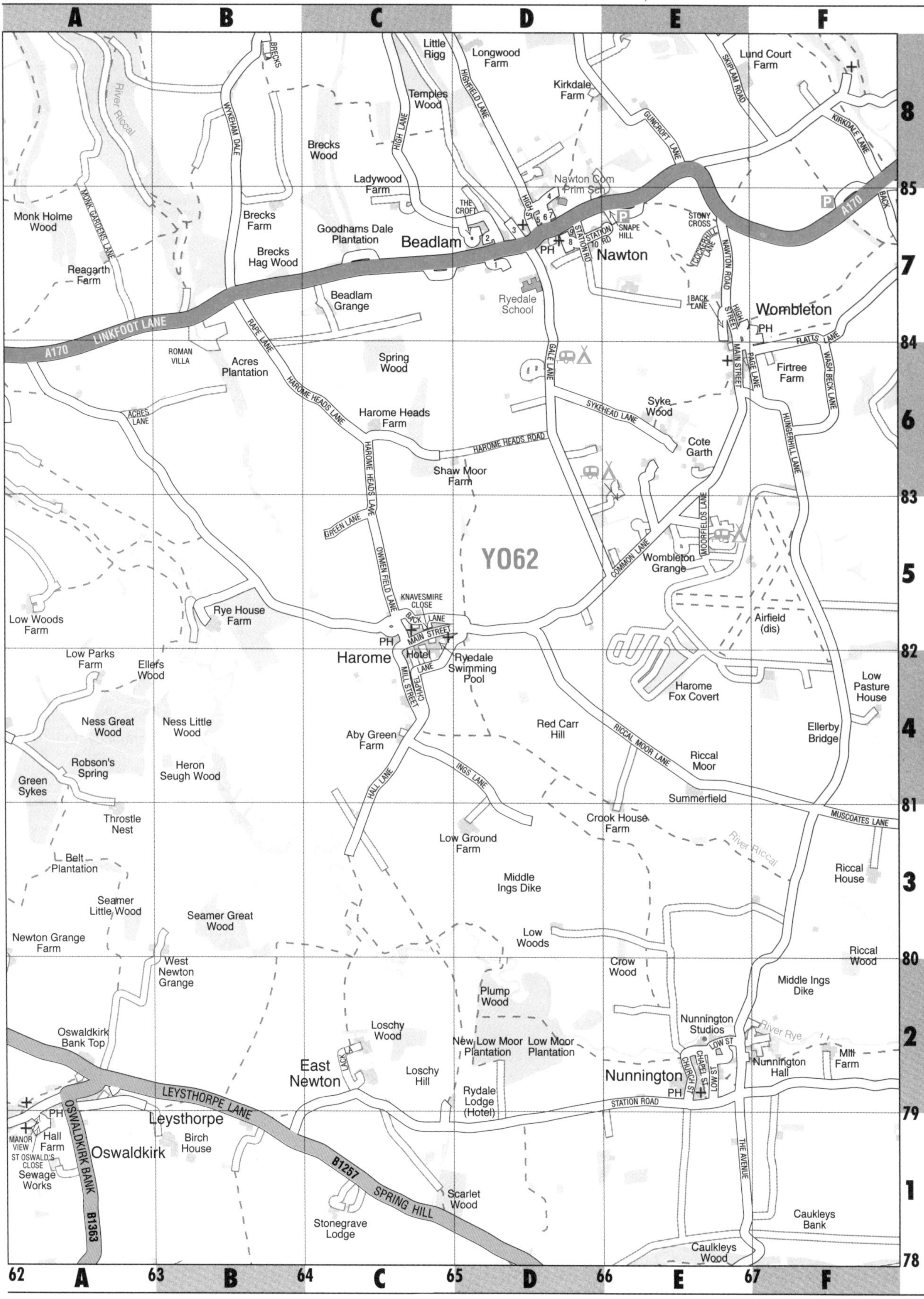

119
94

Scale: 1¾ inches to 1 mile
0 ¼ ½ mile
0 250m 500m 750m 1 km

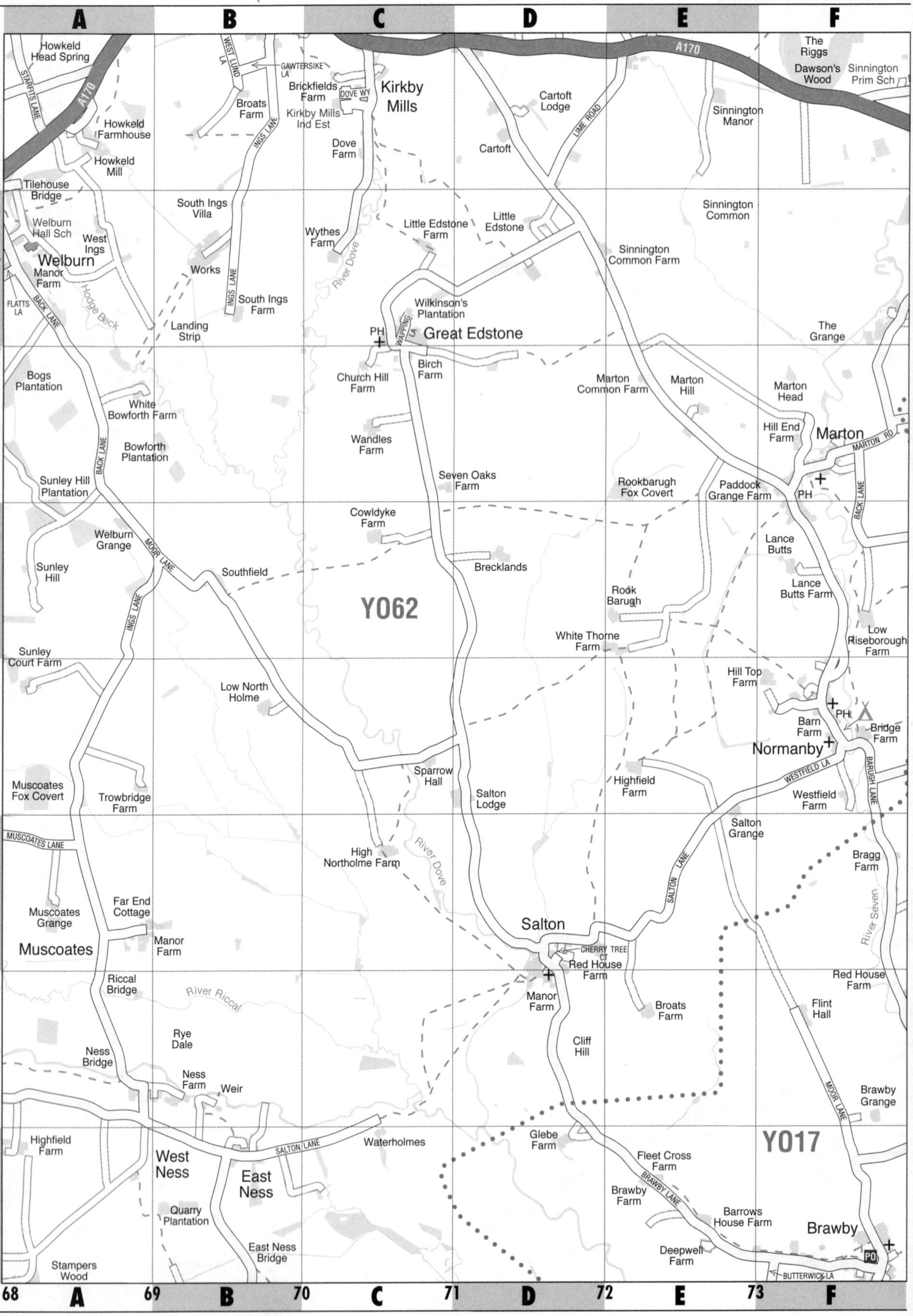

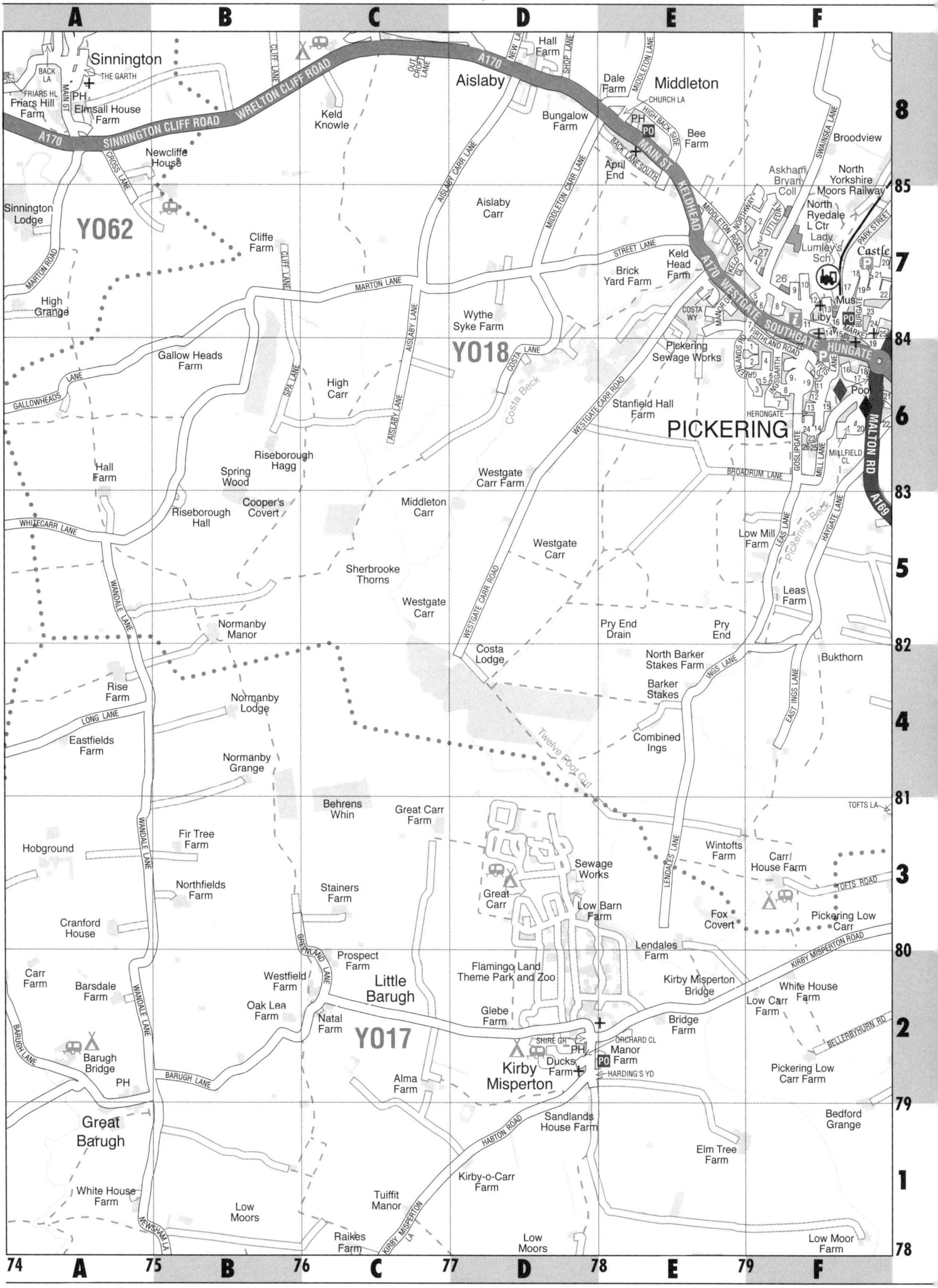
A
B
C
D
E
F
Sinnington
BACK LA
THE GARTH
FRIARS HL
Friars Hill Farm
MAIN ST
PH
Elmsall House Farm
A170
SINNINGTON CLIFF ROAD
WRELTON CLIFF ROAD
CROSS LANE
Newcliffe House
CLIFF LANE
Keld Knowle
OUT CROFT LANE
Aislaby
NEW LA
Hall Farm
SHOP LANE
Dale Farm
MIDDLETON LANE
Middleton
CHURCH LA
Bungalow Farm
PH
PO
HIGH BACK SIDE
BACK LANE SOUTH
MAIN ST
Bee Farm
April End
KELDHEAD
Askham Bryan Coll
SWAINSEA LANE
Broadview
North Yorkshire Moors Railway
North Ryedale L Ctr
Lady Lumley's Sch
Castle
Sinnington Lodge
YO62
AISLABY CARR LANE
Aislaby Carr
MIDDLETON CARR LANE
MIDDLETON ROAD
NORTHWAY
LITTLEDALE
PARK STREET
MARTON ROAD
Cliffe Farm
STREET LANE
Keld Head Farm
Brick Yard Farm
High Grange
MARTON LANE
A170
WESTGATE
SOUTHGATE
HUNGATE
Mus
Liby
BURGATE
MARKET
COSTA WY
MANOR DR
Wythe Syke Farm
Gallow Heads Farm
AISLABY LANE
YO18
COSTA LANE
FIRTHLAND ROAD
GREENLANDS RD
Pickering Sewage Works
GALLOWHEADS LANE
SPA LANE
High Carr
Costa Beck
WESTGATE CARR ROAD
Stanfield Hall Farm
HERONGATE
Pool
INGS GARTH
PICKERING
MALTON RD
GOSLIPGATE
MILL LANE
MILLFIELD CL
Hall Farm
Spring Wood
Riseborough Hagg
Westgate Carr Farm
BROADRUM LANE
Riseborough Hall
Cooper's Covert
Middleton Carr
A169
WHITECARR LANE
Westgate Carr
Low Mill Farm
LEAS LANE
Pickering Beck
HAYGATE LANE
Sherbrooke Thorns
WANDALE LANE
Westgate Carr
Leas Farm
Normanby Manor
Pry End Drain
Pry End
WESTGATE CARR ROAD
Costa Lodge
North Barker Stakes Farm
INGS LANE
Bukthorn
Rise Farm
Barker Stakes
EAST INGS LANE
LONG LANE
Normanby Lodge
Twelve Foot Cut
Eastfields Farm
Combined Ings
Normanby Grange
Behrens Whin
Great Carr Farm
TOFTS LA
Hobground
Fir Tree Farm
WANDALE LANE
Wintofts Farm
Carr House Farm
LENDALES LANE
Sewage Works
Northfields Farm
Stainers Farm
Great Carr
TOFTS ROAD
Low Barn Farm
Fox Covert
Pickering Low Carr
Cranford House
Lendales Farm
KIRBY MISPERTON ROAD
GREENLAND LANE
Prospect Farm
Flamingo Land Theme Park and Zoo
Carr Farm
Westfield Farm
Little Barugh
Kirby Misperton Bridge
White House Farm
Barsdale Farm
WANDALE LANE
Low Carr Farm
Oak Lea Farm
Natal Farm
Glebe Farm
Bridge Farm
BELLERBYHURN RD
BARUGH LANE
YO17
SHIRE GR
PH
ORCHARD CL
Manor Farm
PO
Barugh Bridge
Ducks Farm
HARDING'S YD
Kirby Misperton
Pickering Low Carr Farm
PH
BARUGH LANE
Alma Farm
Great Barugh
HABTON ROAD
Sandlands House Farm
Bedford Grange
Elm Tree Farm
Kirby-o-Carr Farm
White House Farm
Tuiffit Manor
Low Moors
NEWSHAM LA
KIRBY MISPERTON LA
Raikes Farm
Low Moors
Low Moor Farm
8
85
7
84
6
83
5
82
4
81
3
80
2
79
1
78
74
75
76
77
78
79

95
72

Scale: 1¾ inches to 1 mile
0 ¼ ½ mile
0 250m 500m 750m 1 km

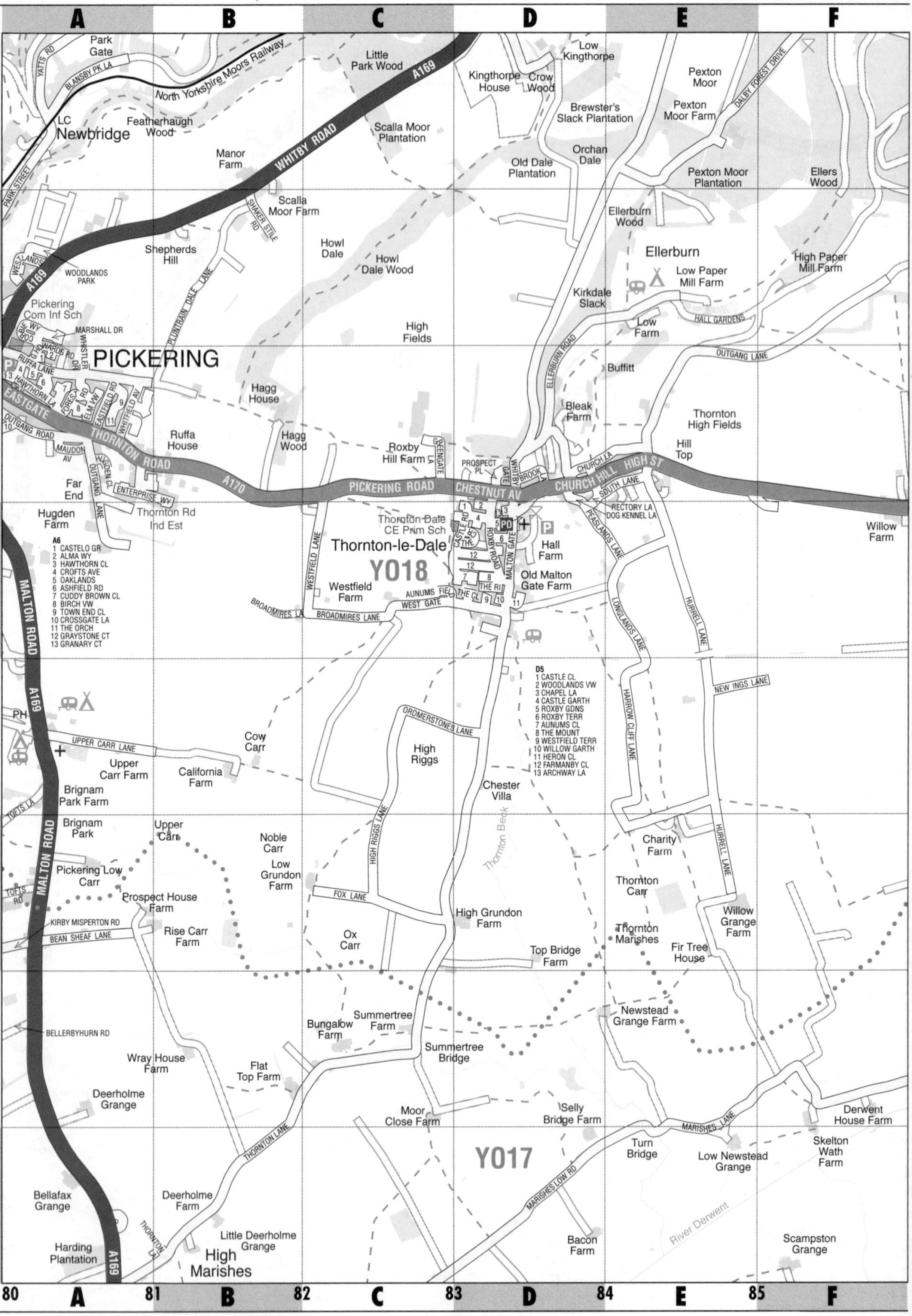

95
122

Scale: 1¾ inches to 1 mile
0 ¼ ½ mile
0 250m 500m 750m 1 km

73
98

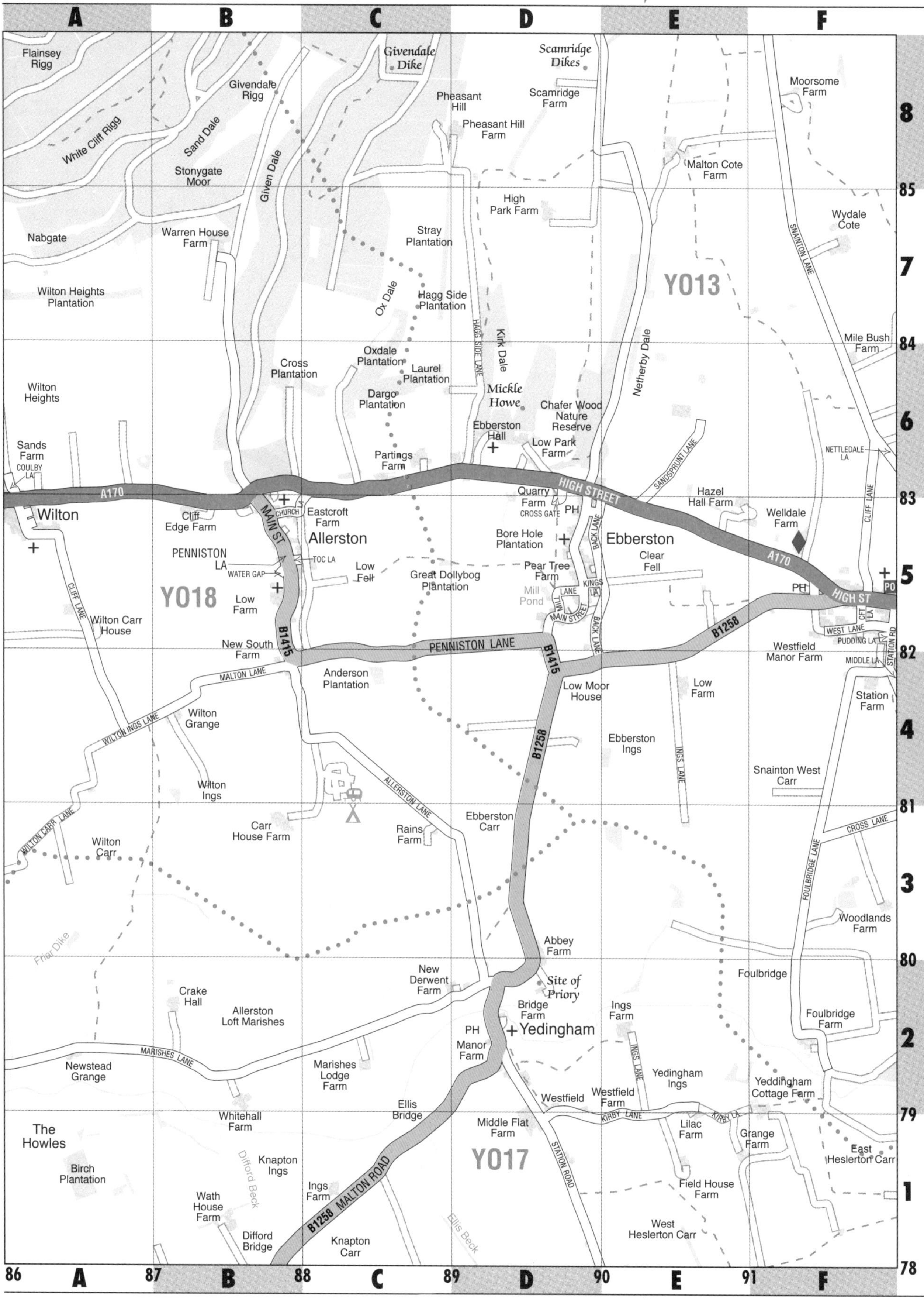

123
98

97
74

Scale: 1¾ inches to 1 mile
0 ¼ ½ mile
0 250m 500m 750m 1 km

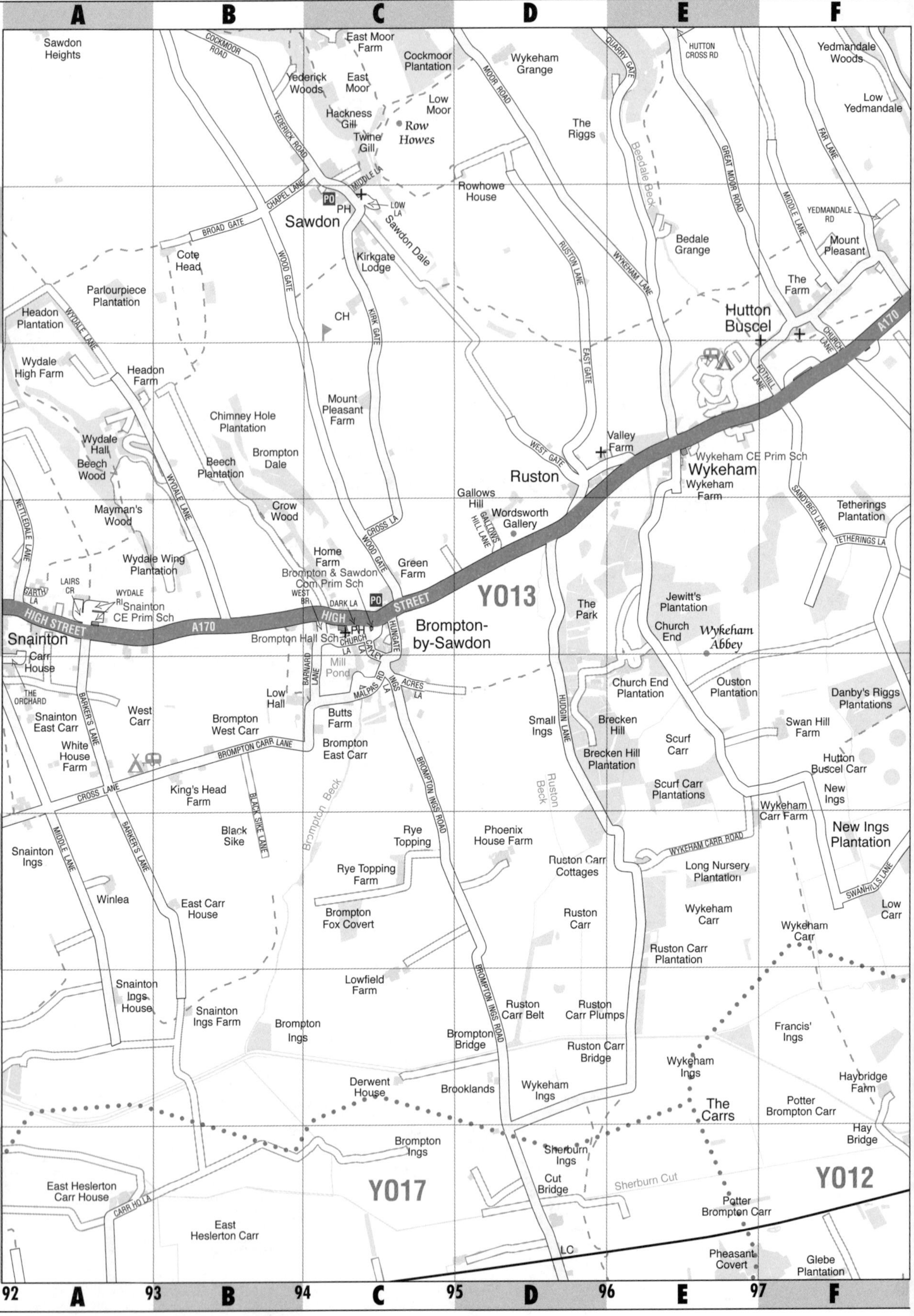

A7
1 CASTLE RISE
2 YEDMANDALE RD
3 MILL LA
4 DREAKEN FOLD
5 WILSON'S LA
6 STATION CL
7 WEST ACRES CL
8 BEECH LA
9 HEWLEY DR
10 MORLEY DR
11 BROUGHTON RD
12 CANDLER AVE
13 WILKINSONS CL

D6
1 THE GROVE
2 PASTURE LA
3 EASTGATE
4 MAYFIELD DR
5 BELL CL
6 THE GREEN

75

7 RAINFORD CL
8 DENISON AVE
9 WHITE HORSE LA
10 LONDESBOROUGH PK
11 STAPLETON CL
12 WELBOURN DR

212
100

F7
1 BURTONDALE RD
2 DUNCOMBE CL
3 CONISTON WY
4 ROXBY GDNS
5 DAWNAY CL
6 CONISTON GDNS
7 RYDALE CRES
8 THE LEAS
9 LINGHOLM CRES
10 RIDGEWAY
11 DALE EDGE
12 RYEFIELD CL

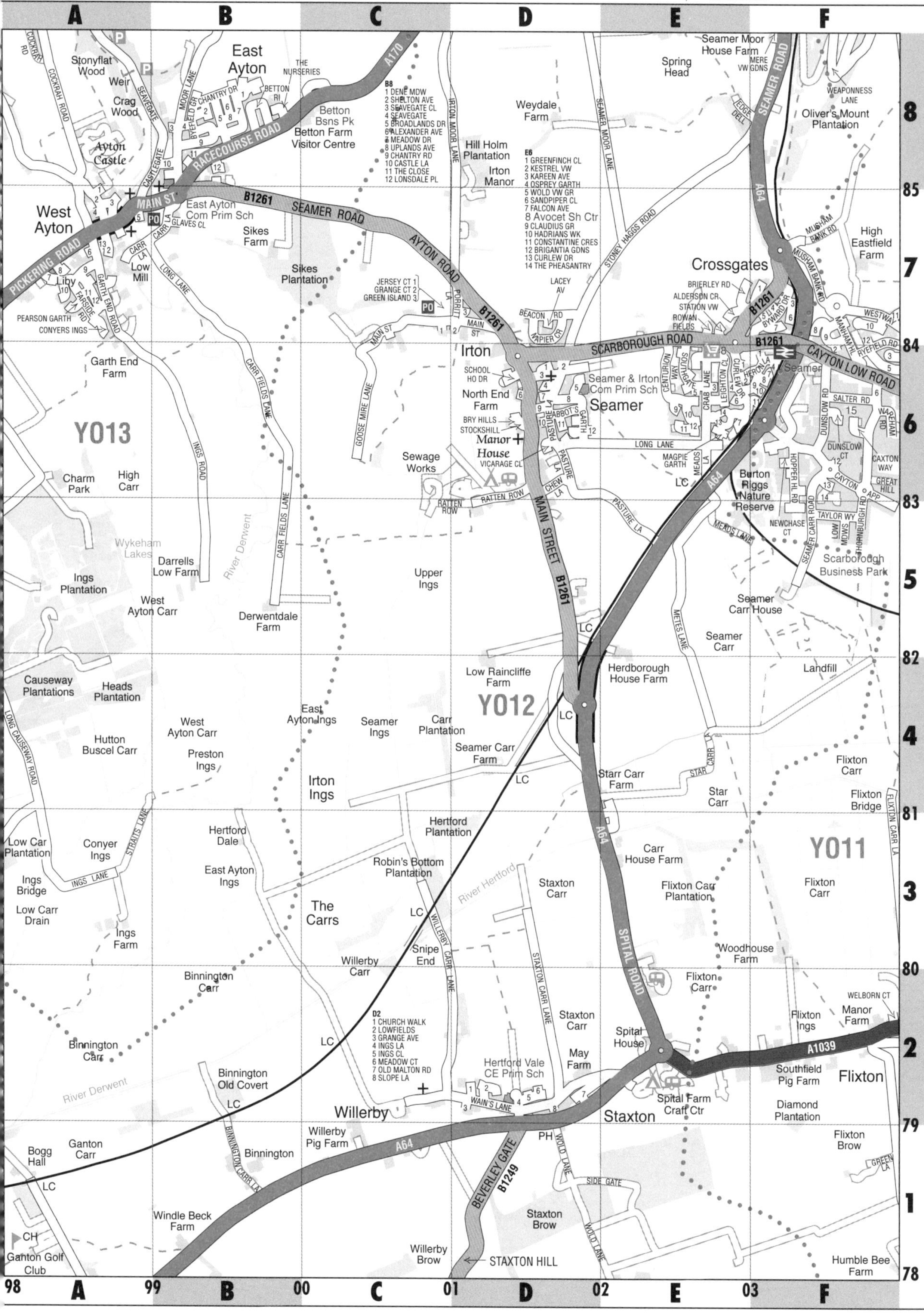

125
100

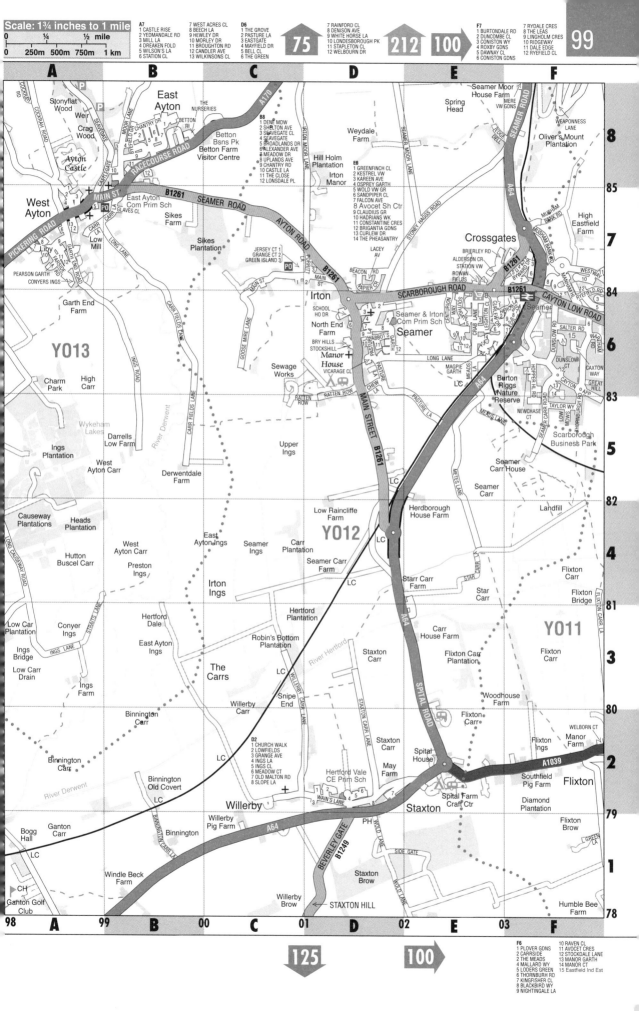

F6
1 PLOVER GDNS
2 CARRSIDE
3 THE MEADS
4 MALLARD WY
5 LODERS GREEN
6 THORNBURH RD
7 KINGFISHER CL
8 BLACKBIRD WY
9 NIGHTINGALE LA
10 RAVEN CL
11 AVOCET CRES
12 STOCKDALE LANE
13 MANOR GARTH
14 MANOR CT
15 Eastfield Ind Est

B6
1 FENWICK CL
2 ESTILL CL
3 MOUNT VW RD
4 WEST END VW
5 WEST END CT
6 IVY HOUSE CL
7 LODGE CL
8 LIMEKILN LA
9 BECK HOLE
10 SPRING GDNS
11 BEVERLEY RD
12 BEVERLEY CL
10 CHAPEL LA
14 GREEN PARK RD
15 GREEN PARK AVE
16 THE PASTURES
17 NESFIELD CL
18 EAST CARR
19 FLOWER CT
20 PENTON RD
21 EAST LEA VW
22 STANLEY CL
23 WEST GARTH GDNS
24 GREEN CROFT GDNS

99

213

B7
1 SEAVIEW AVE
2 BRADWORTH DR
3 BRADWORTH CL
4 STUART CL
5 SOUTHWOLD CL
6 SOUTHWOLD RI
7 SOUTHWOLD
8 SOUTHWOLD CRES
9 HAWSON CL
10 FENTON CL
11 KNOLLS CL
12 REDCLIFF CL
13 SHEPHERDS DR
14 PLOUGHMANS CT
15 WAIN CL
16 THE FURROWS
17 SHIRE CFT
18 SHIRE CL
19 MIDDLEFIELD CL

Scale: 1¾ inches to 1 mile
0 ¼ ½ mile
0 250m 500m 750m 1 km

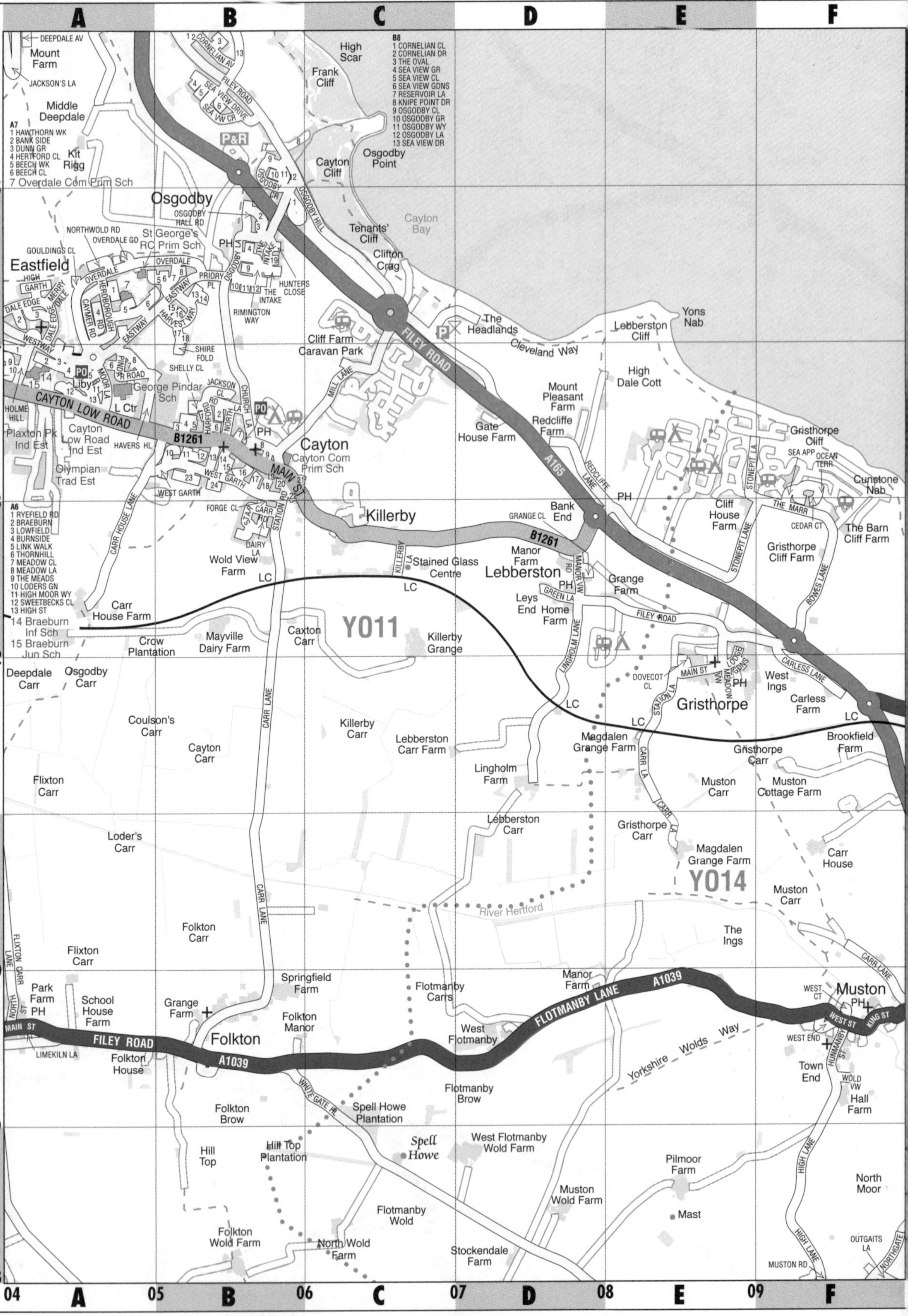

99

126

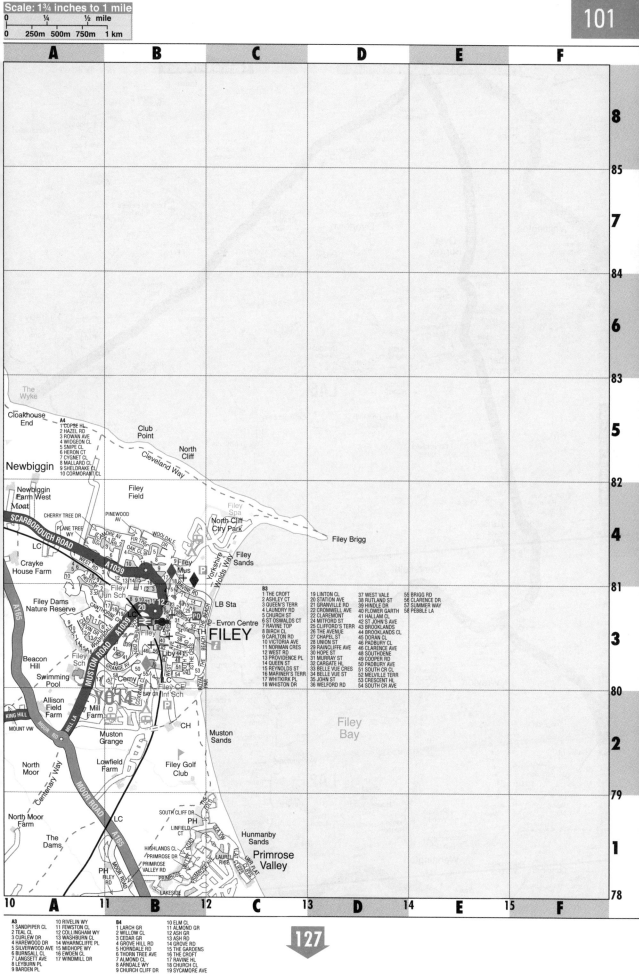

Scale: 1¾ inches to 1 mile
0 ¼ ½ mile
0 250m 500m 750m 1 km

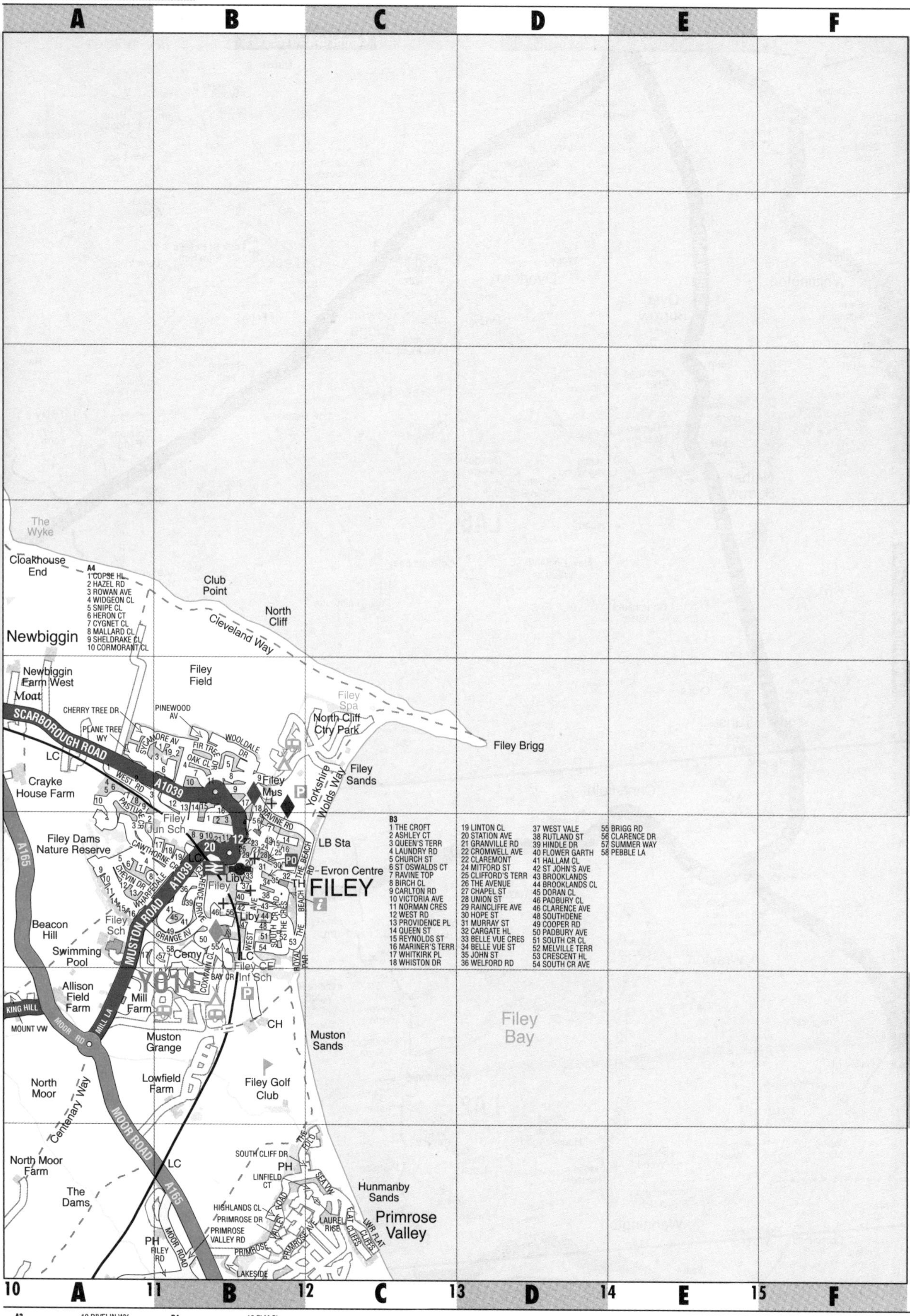

A3
1 SANDPIPER CL
2 TEAL CL
3 CURLEW DR
4 HAREWOOD DR
5 SILVERWOOD AVE
6 BURNSALL CL
7 LANGSETT AVE
8 LEYBURN PL
9 BARDEN PL
10 RIVELIN WY
11 FEWSTON CL
12 COLLINGHAM WY
13 WASHBURN CL
14 WHARNCLIFFE PL
15 MIDHOPE WY
16 EWDEN CL
17 WINDMILL DR

B4
1 LARCH GR
2 WILLOW CL
3 CEDAR GR
4 GROVE HILL RD
5 HORNDALE RD
6 THORN TREE AVE
7 ALMOND CL
8 ARNDALE WY
9 CHURCH CLIFF DR
10 ELM CL
11 ALMOND GR
12 ASH GR
13 ASH RD
14 GROVE RD
15 THE GARDENS
16 THE CROFT
17 RAVINE HL
18 CHURCH CL
19 SYCAMORE AVE

127

Scale: 1¾ inches to 1 mile

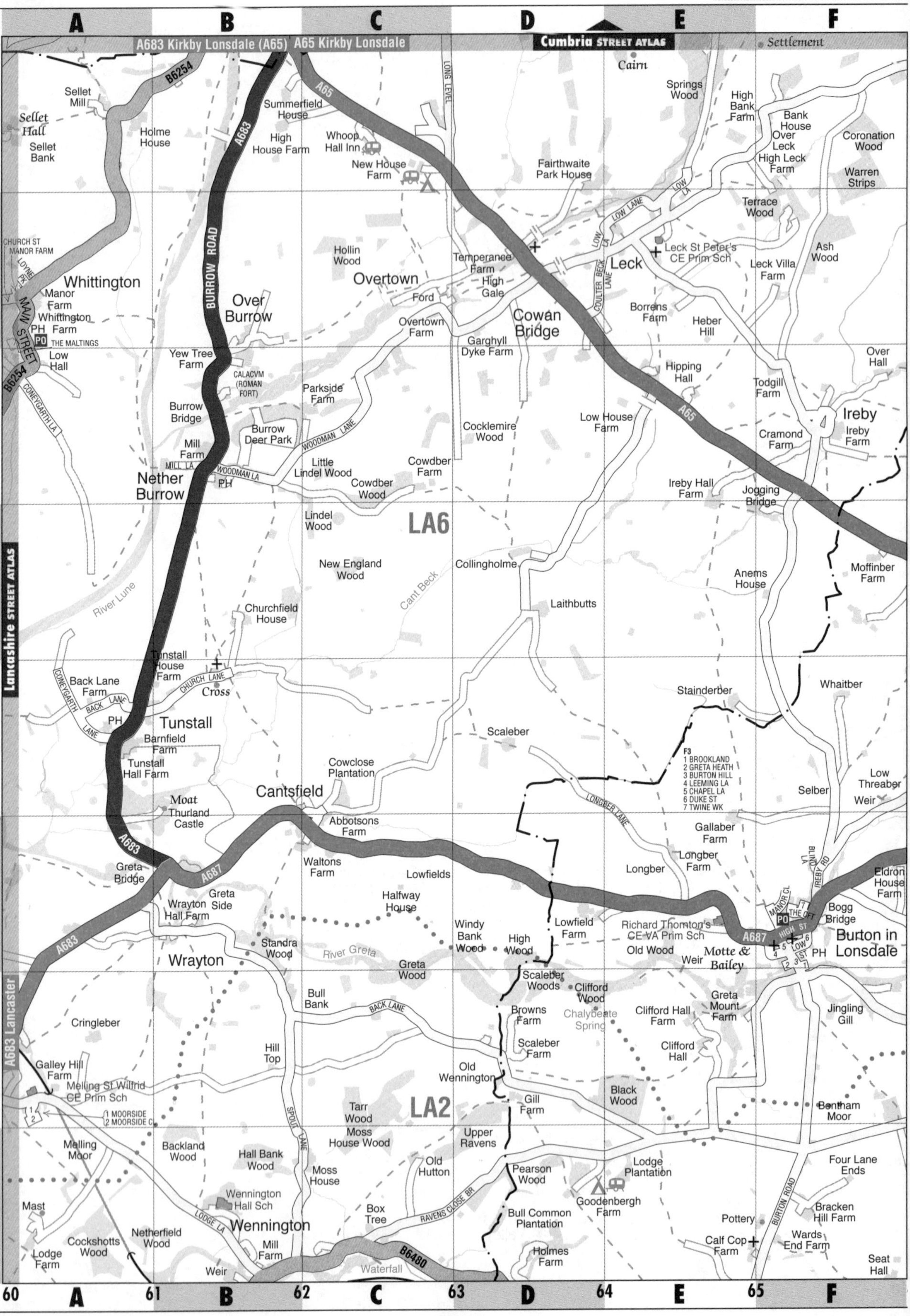

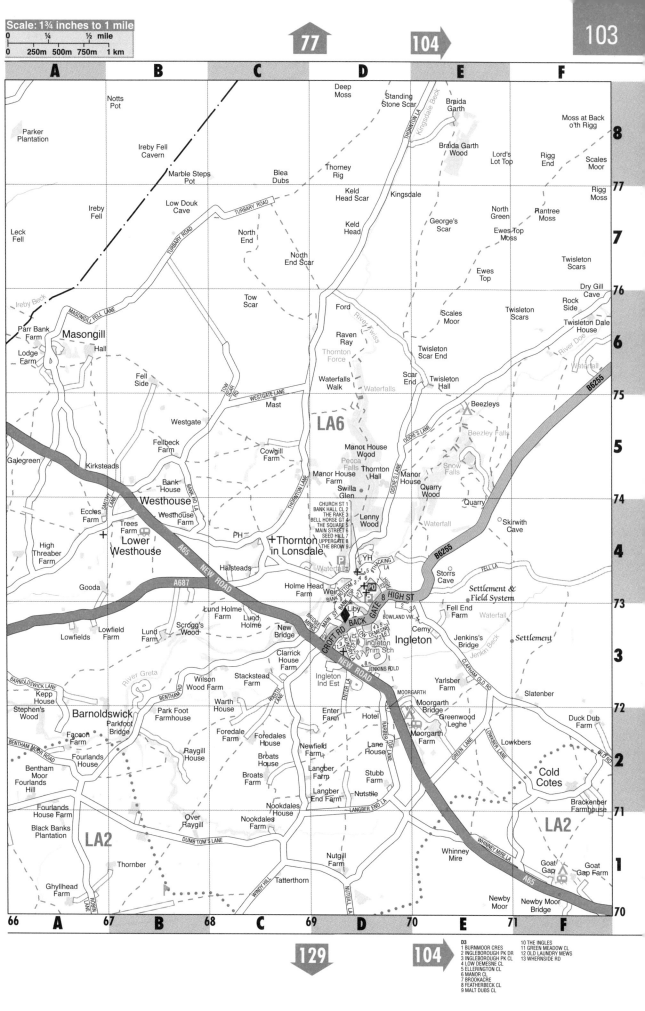

Scale: 1¾ inches to 1 mile
0 ¼ ½ mile
0 250m 500m 750m 1 km

77
104

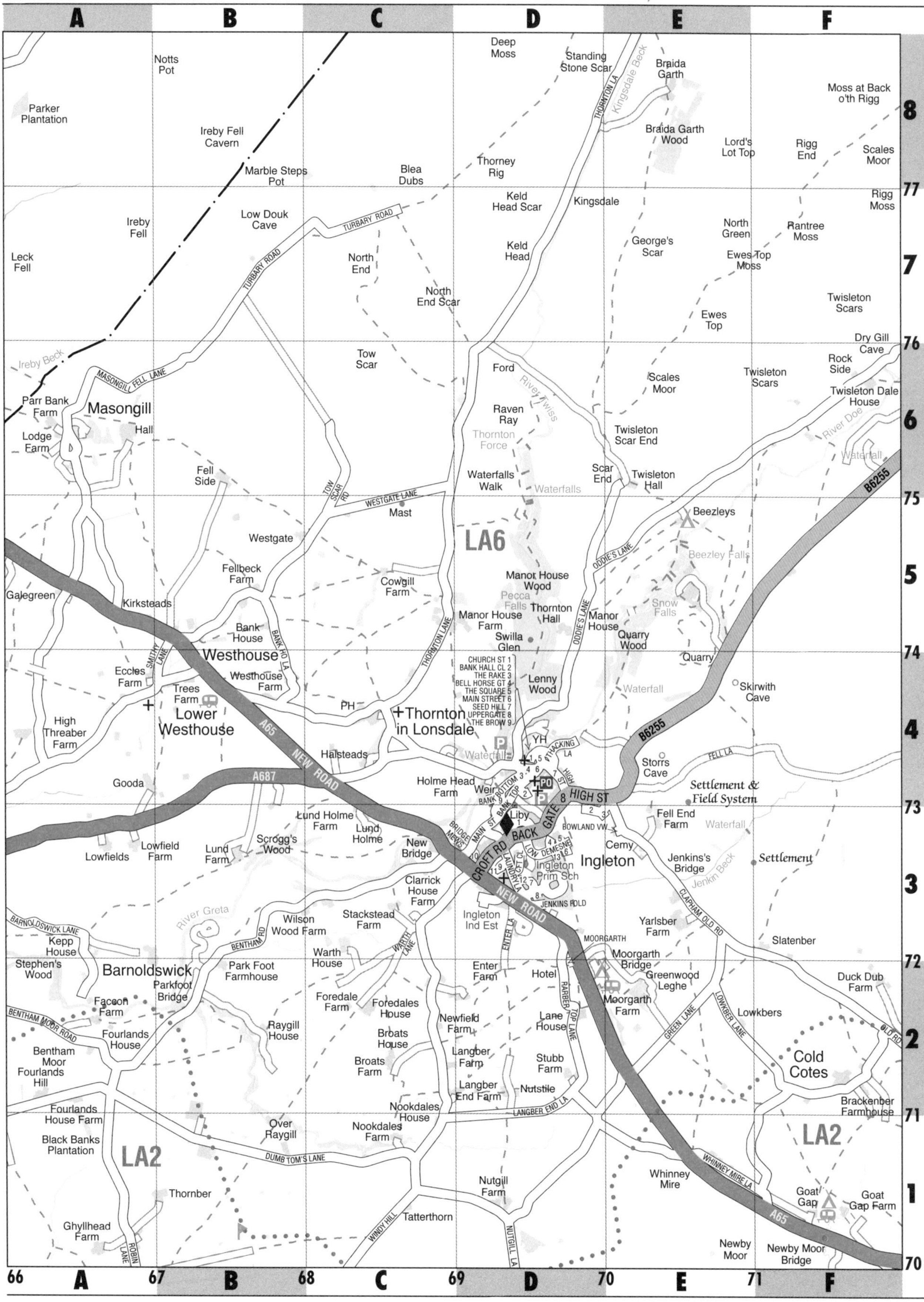

129
104

D3
1 BURNMOOR CRES
2 INGLEBOROUGH PK DR
3 INGLEBOROUGH PK CL
4 LOW DEMESNE CL
5 ELLERINGTON CL
6 MANOR CL
7 BROOKACRE
8 FEATHERBECK CL
9 MALT DUBS CL
10 THE INGLES
11 GREEN MEADOW CL
12 OLD LAUNDRY MEWS
13 WHERNSIDE RD

103
78

Scale: 1¾ inches to 1 mile

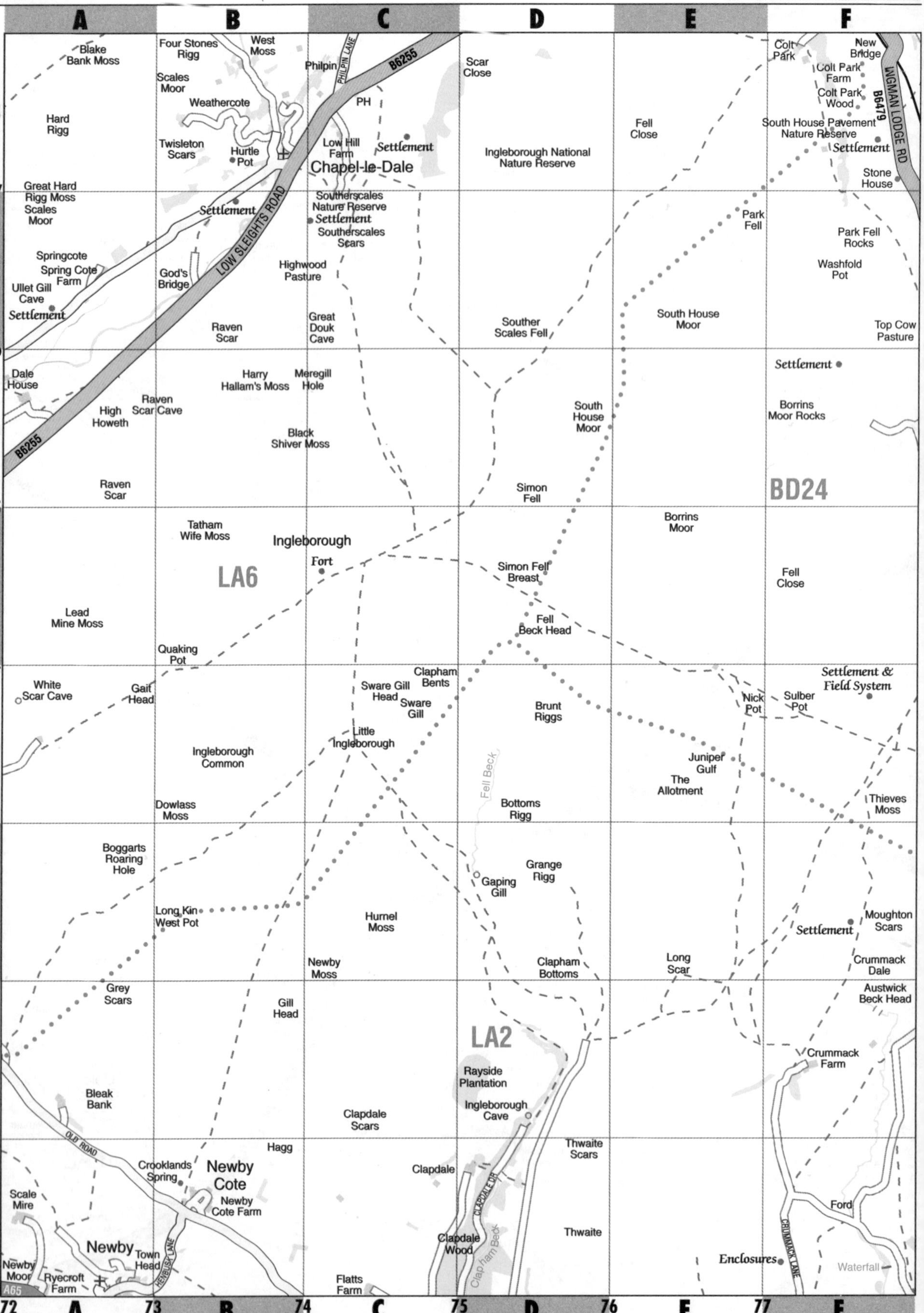

103
130

Scale: 1¾ inches to 1 mile
0 ¼ ½ mile
0 250m 500m 750m 1 km

79
106

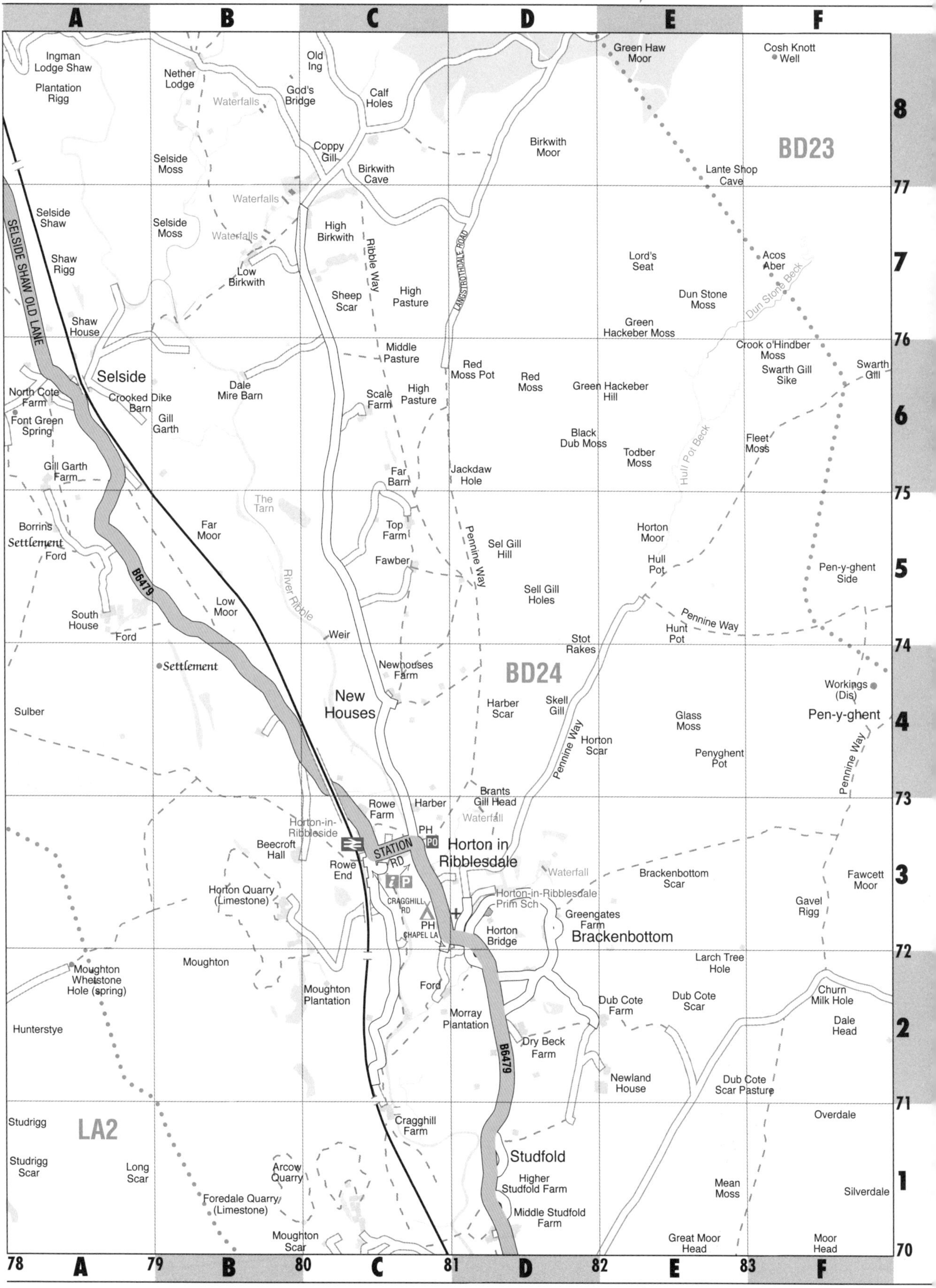
A
B
C
D
E
F
8
7
6
5
4
3
2
1
77
76
75
74
73
72
71
70
78
79
80
81
82
83
Ingman Lodge Shaw
Plantation Rigg
Nether Lodge
Waterfalls
God's Bridge
Old Ing
Calf Holes
Green Haw Moor
Cosh Knott Well
BD23
Coppy Gill
Birkwith Cave
Birkwith Moor
Lante Shop Cave
Selside Moss
Selside Shaw
Shaw Rigg
Selside Moss
Waterfalls
Waterfalls
SELSIDE SHAW OLD LANE
High Birkwith
Ribble Way
LANGSTROTHDALE ROAD
Lord's Seat
Acos Aber
Low Birkwith
Sheep Scar
High Pasture
Dun Stone Moss
Dun Stone Beck
Green Hackeber Moss
Shaw House
Selside
Middle Pasture
Red Moss Pot
Red Moss
Crook o'Hindber Moss
Swarth Gill Sike
Swarth Gill
North Cote Farm
Crooked Dike Barn
Dale Mire Barn
Scale Farm
High Pasture
Green Hackeber Hill
Font Green Spring
Gill Garth
Black Dub Moss
Todber Moss
Hull Pot Beck
Fleet Moss
Gill Garth Farm
Far Barn
Jackdaw Hole
The Tarn
Borrins
Settlement
Ford
Far Moor
Top Farm
Pennine Way
Sel Gill Hill
Horton Moor
Hull Pot
Pen-y-ghent Side
Fawber
B6479
River Ribble
Low Moor
Sell Gill Holes
South House
Ford
Weir
Pennine Way
Hunt Pot
Stot Rakes
Settlement
Newhouses Farm
BD24
Workings (Dis)
Sulber
New Houses
Harber Scar
Skell Gill
Glass Moss
Pen-y-ghent
Pennine Way
Horton Scar
Penyghent Pot
Pennine Way
Brants Gill Head
Rowe Farm
Harber
Horton-in-Ribbleside
Waterfall
PH
PO
Horton in Ribblesdale
Beecroft Hall
STATION RD
Rowe End
Waterfall
Brackenbottom Scar
Fawcett Moor
Horton Quarry (Limestone)
CRAGGHILL RD
Horton-in-Ribblesdale Prim Sch
Gavel Rigg
Greengates Farm
PH
CHAPEL LA
Horton Bridge
Brackenbottom
Moughton
Larch Tree Hole
Moughton Whetstone Hole (spring)
Moughton Plantation
Ford
Churn Milk Hole
Dub Cote Farm
Dub Cote Scar
Hunterstye
Morray Plantation
Dale Head
B6479
Dry Beck Farm
Newland House
Dub Cote Scar Pasture
Studrigg
LA2
Cragghill Farm
Overdale
Studfold
Studrigg Scar
Long Scar
Arcow Quarry
Higher Studfold Farm
Mean Moss
Silverdale
Foredale Quarry (Limestone)
Middle Studfold Farm
Moughton Scar
Great Moor Head
Moor Head

131
106

105
80

Scale: 1¾ inches to 1 mile
0 ¼ ½ mile
0 250m 500m 750m 1 km

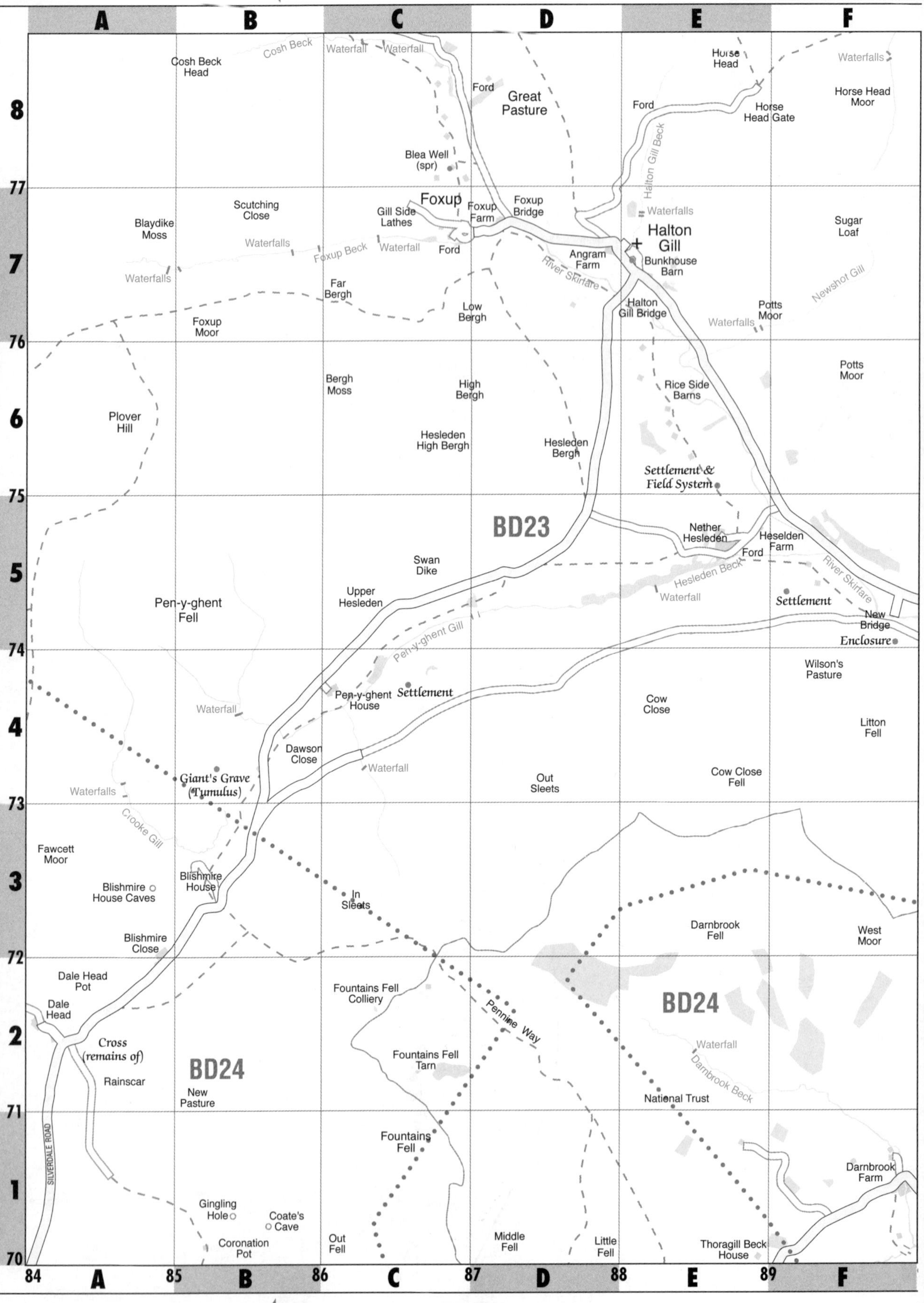
A
B
C
D
E
F
8
77
7
76
6
75
5
74
4
73
3
72
2
71
1
70
84
85
86
87
88
89
Cosh Beck Head
Cosh Beck
Waterfall
Waterfall
Ford
Great Pasture
Horse Head
Waterfalls
Ford
Horse Head Gate
Horse Head Moor
Halton Gill Beck
Blea Well (spr)
Scutching Close
Foxup
Gill Side Lathes
Foxup Farm
Foxup Bridge
Waterfalls
Halton Gill
Sugar Loaf
Blaydike Moss
Waterfalls
Foxup Beck
Waterfall
Ford
Angram Farm
Bunkhouse Barn
Waterfalls
River Skirfare
Far Bergh
Low Bergh
Halton Gill Bridge
Potts Moor
Newshot Gill
Waterfalls
Foxup Moor
Potts Moor
Bergh Moss
High Bergh
Rice Side Barns
Plover Hill
Hesleden High Bergh
Hesleden Bergh
Settlement & Field System
BD23
Nether Hesleden
Heselden Farm
Ford
Swan Dike
Hesleden Beck
River Skirfare
Upper Hesleden
Pen-y-ghent Fell
Waterfall
Settlement
New Bridge
Pen-y-ghent Gill
Enclosure
Wilson's Pasture
Pen-y-ghent House
Settlement
Cow Close
Waterfall
Litton Fell
Dawson Close
Waterfall
Giant's Grave (Tumulus)
Out Sleets
Cow Close Fell
Waterfalls
Crooke Gill
Fawcett Moor
Blishmire House
Blishmire House Caves
In Sleets
Darnbrook Fell
West Moor
Blishmire Close
Dale Head Pot
Fountains Fell Colliery
Dale Head
Pennine Way
BD24
Cross (remains of)
Fountains Fell Tarn
Waterfall
BD24
Rainscar
Dambrook Beck
New Pasture
National Trust
SILVERDALE ROAD
Fountains Fell
Darnbrook Farm
Gingling Hole
Coate's Cave
Coronation Pot
Out Fell
Middle Fell
Little Fell
Thoragill Beck House

105
132

Scale: 1¾ inches to 1 mile
0 ¼ ½ mile
0 250m 500m 750m 1 km

81
108

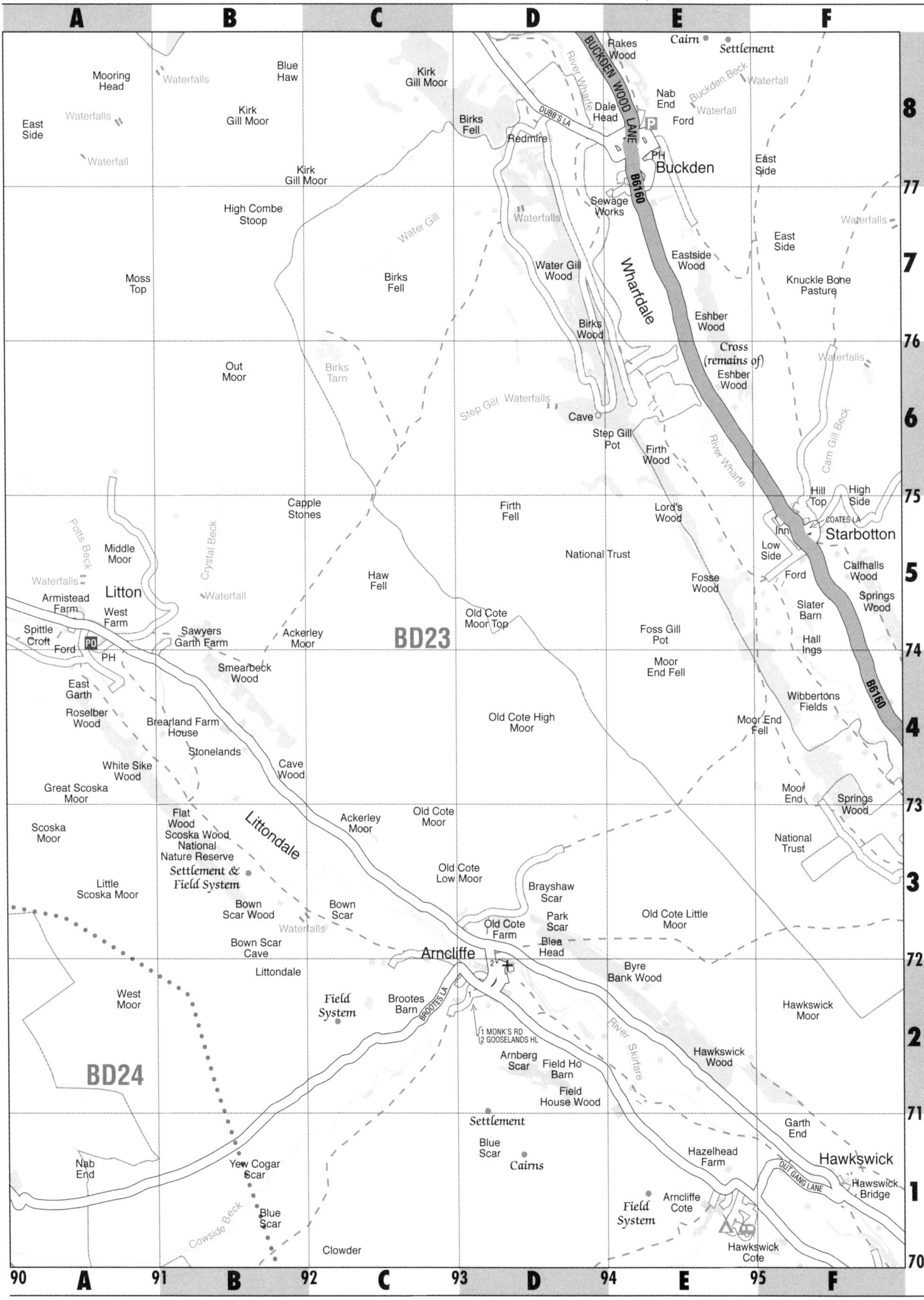

133
108

107
82

Scale: 1¾ inches to 1 mile
0 ¼ ½ mile
0 250m 500m 750m 1 km

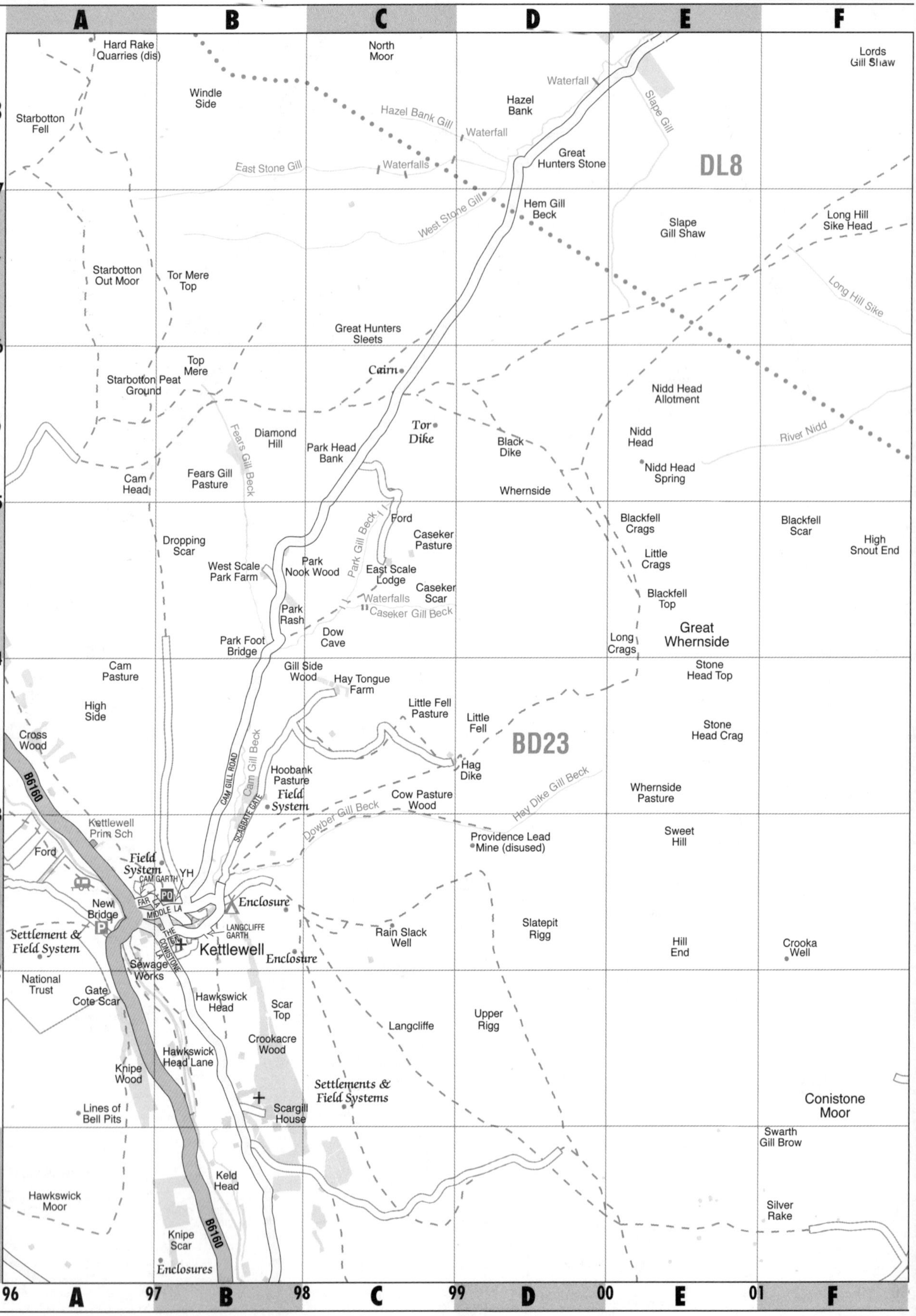
A B C D E F
8
77
7
76
6
75
5
74
4
73
3
72
2
71
1
70
96 97 98 99 00 01
Hard Rake Quarries (dis)
North Moor
Lords Gill Shaw
Waterfall
Slape Gill
Windle Side
Starbotton Fell
Hazel Bank Gill
Hazel Bank
Waterfall
Great Hunters Stone
DL8
East Stone Gill
Waterfalls
Hem Gill Beck
West Stone Gill
Slape Gill Shaw
Long Hill Sike Head
Starbotton Out Moor
Tor Mere Top
Long Hill Sike
Great Hunters Sleets
Top Mere
Cairn
Starbotton Peat Ground
Nidd Head Allotment
Fears Gill Beck
Diamond Hill
Tor Dike
Black Dike
Nidd Head
River Nidd
Park Head Bank
Nidd Head Spring
Cam Head
Fears Gill Pasture
Whernside
Ford
Blackfell Crags
Blackfell Scar
Dropping Scar
Park Gill Beck
Caseker Pasture
High Snout End
Little Crags
West Scale Park Farm
Park Nook Wood
East Scale Lodge
Caseker Scar
Blackfell Top
Waterfalls
Caseker Gill Beck
Park Rash
Great Whernside
Park Foot Bridge
Dow Cave
Long Crags
Cam Pasture
Gill Side Wood
Hay Tongue Farm
Stone Head Top
Little Fell Pasture
High Side
Little Fell
Cross Wood
BD23
Stone Head Crag
Hag Dike
Cam Gill Beck
Hoobank Pasture
B6160
CAM GILL ROAD
Hay Dike Gill Beck
Whernside Pasture
Field System
Cow Pasture Wood
SCABBATE GATE
Dowber Gill Beck
Kettlewell Prim Sch
Sweet Hill
Providence Lead Mine (disused)
Ford
Field System
YH
CAM GARTH
PO
FAR LA
MIDDLE LA
Enclosure
New Bridge
LANGCLIFFE GARTH
Slatepit Rigg
Rain Slack Well
Settlement & Field System
THE GREEN
CONISTONE LA
Kettlewell
Enclosure
Hill End
Crooka Well
Sewage Works
National Trust
Gate Cote Scar
Hawkswick Head
Scar Top
Langcliffe
Upper Rigg
Crookacre Wood
Hawkswick Head Lane
Knipe Wood
Settlements & Field Systems
Conistone Moor
Lines of Bell Pits
Scargill House
Swarth Gill Brow
Keld Head
Hawkswick Moor
Silver Rake
B6160
Knipe Scar
Enclosures

107
134

Scale: 1¾ inches to 1 mile
0 ¼ ½ mile
0 250m 500m 750m 1 km

83
110

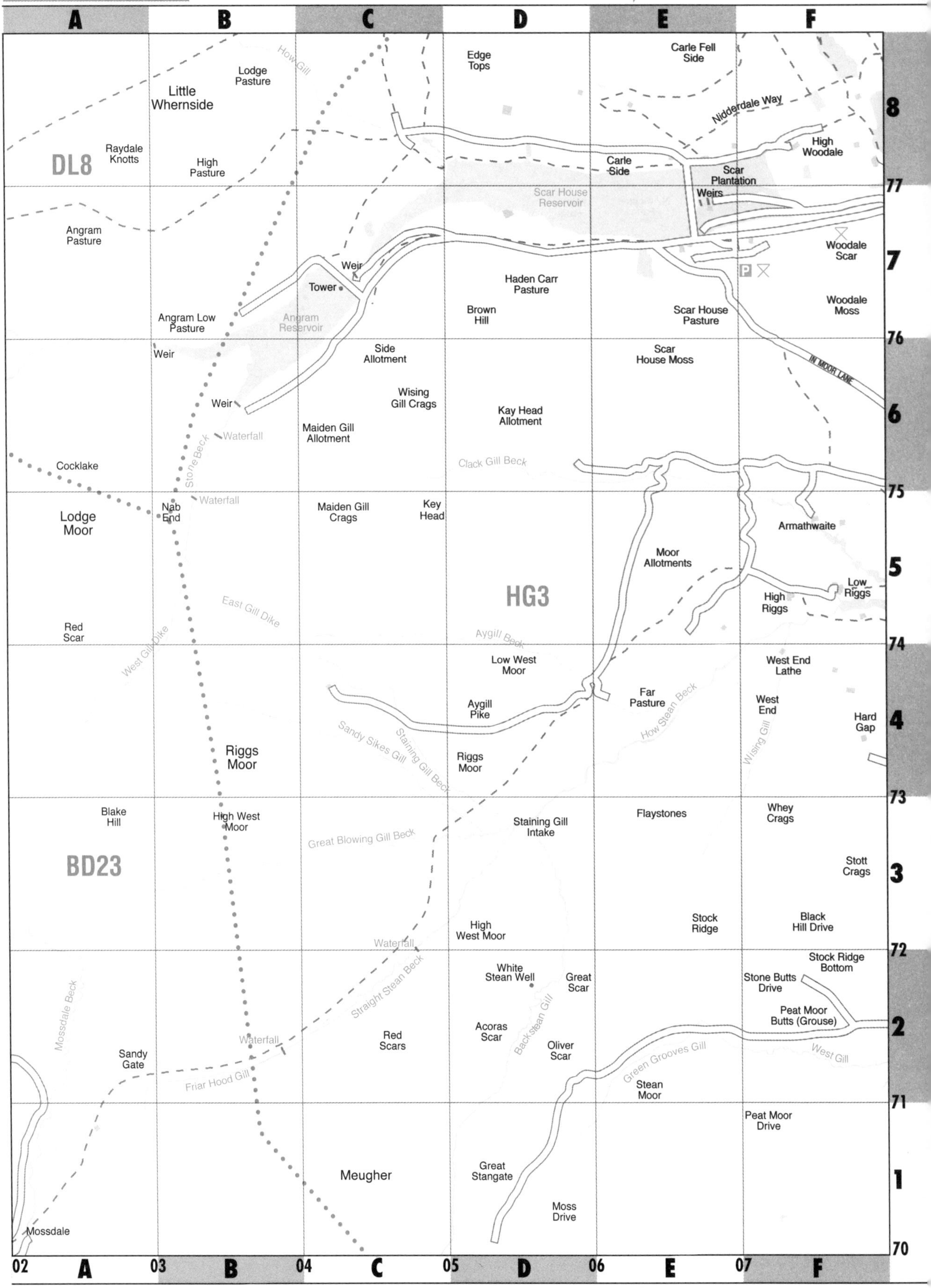

135
110

109
84

Scale: 1¾ inches to 1 mile
0 ¼ ½ mile
0 250m 500m 750m 1 km

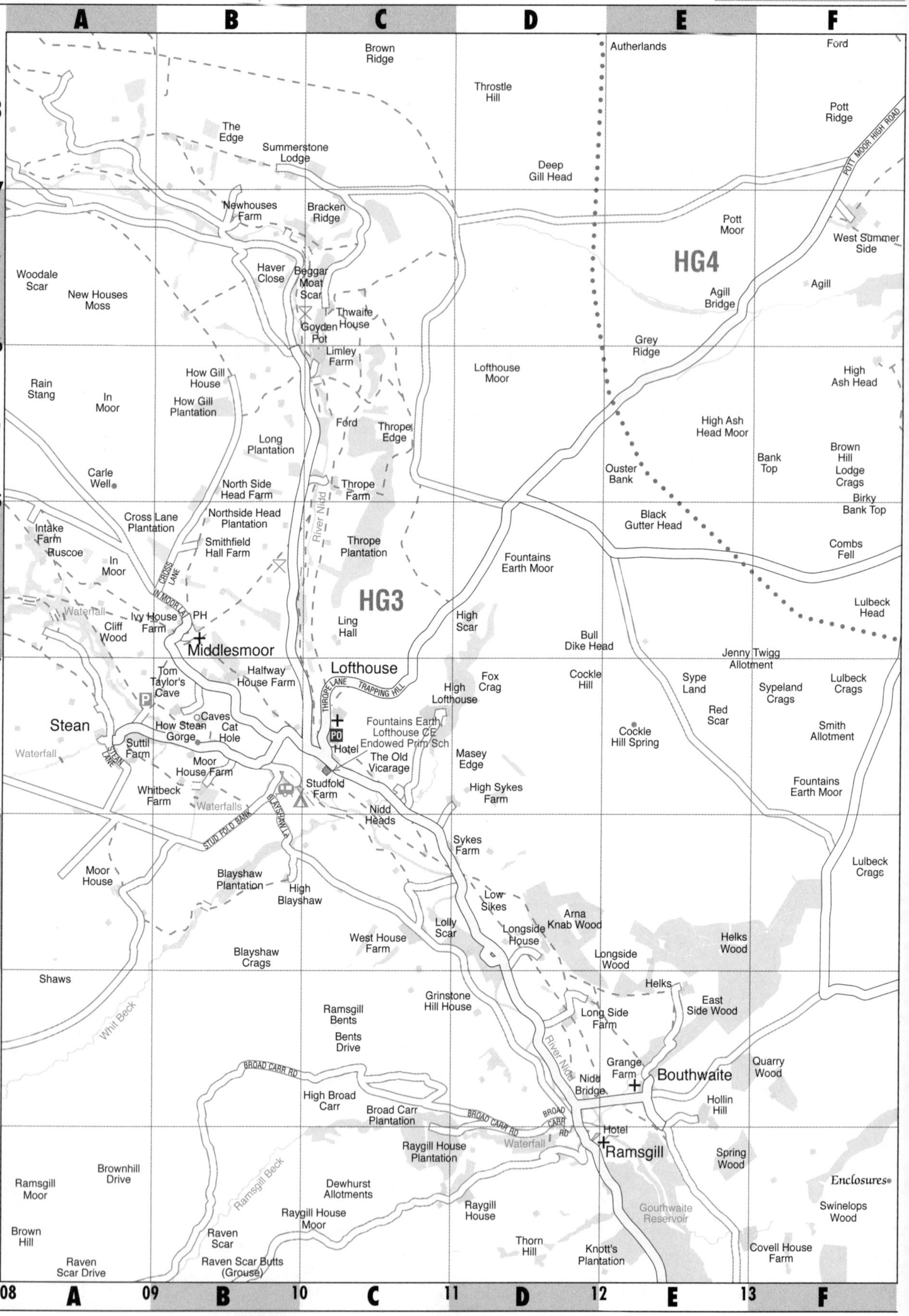

109
136

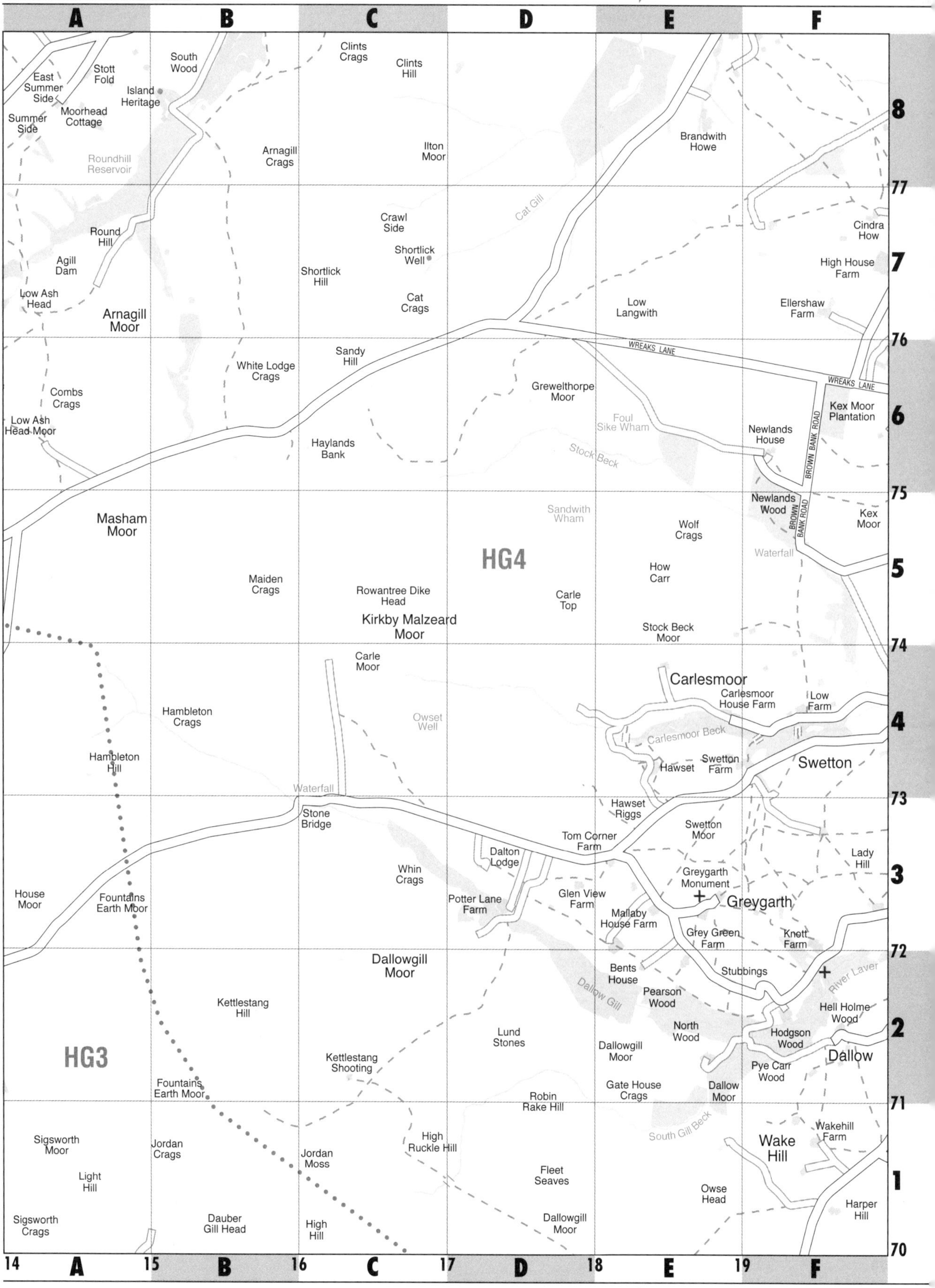
A B C D E F
Clints Crags
Clints Hill
South Wood
East Summer Side
Stott Fold
Island Heritage
Summer Side
Moorhead Cottage
Arnagill Crags
Ilton Moor
Brandwith Howe
Roundhill Reservoir
Cat Gill
Crawl Side
Round Hill
Shortlick Well
Cindra How
Agill Dam
Shortlick Hill
High House Farm
Low Ash Head
Cat Crags
Low Langwith
Ellershaw Farm
Arnagill Moor
Sandy Hill
WREAKS LANE
White Lodge Crags
Grewelthorpe Moor
Combs Crags
Kex Moor Plantation
Low Ash Head Moor
Foul Sike Wham
Newlands House
Haylands Bank
Stock Beck
BROWN BANK ROAD
Newlands Wood
Sandwith Wham
Kex Moor
Masham Moor
Wolf Crags
Waterfall
HG4
How Carr
Maiden Crags
Rowantree Dike Head
Carle Top
Kirkby Malzeard Moor
Stock Beck Moor
Carle Moor
Carlesmoor
Carlesmoor House Farm
Low Farm
Hambleton Crags
Owset Well
Carlesmoor Beck
Hambleton Hill
Hawset
Swetton Farm
Swetton
Stone Bridge
Hawset Riggs
Swetton Moor
Tom Corner Farm
Dalton Lodge
Lady Hill
Whin Crags
Greygarth Monument
House Moor
Fountains Earth Moor
Potter Lane Farm
Glen View Farm
Greygarth
Mallaby House Farm
Grey Green Farm
Knott Farm
Dallowgill Moor
Bents House
Stubbings
River Laver
Kettlestang Hill
Dallow Gill
Pearson Wood
Hell Holme Wood
North Wood
Lund Stones
Hodgson Wood
Dallowgill Moor
HG3
Kettlestang Shooting
Dallow
Pye Carr Wood
Fountains Earth Moor
Gate House Crags
Dallow Moor
Robin Rake Hill
South Gill Beck
Wakehill Farm
Sigsworth Moor
Jordan Crags
High Ruckle Hill
Wake Hill
Jordan Moss
Light Hill
Fleet Seaves
Owse Head
Harper Hill
Sigsworth Crags
Dauber Gill Head
High Hill
Dallowgill Moor
14 15 16 17 18 19
8 77 7 76 6 75 5 74 4 73 3 72 2 71 1 70

111
86

Scale: 1¾ inches to 1 mile
0 ¼ ½ mile
0 250m 500m 750m 1 km

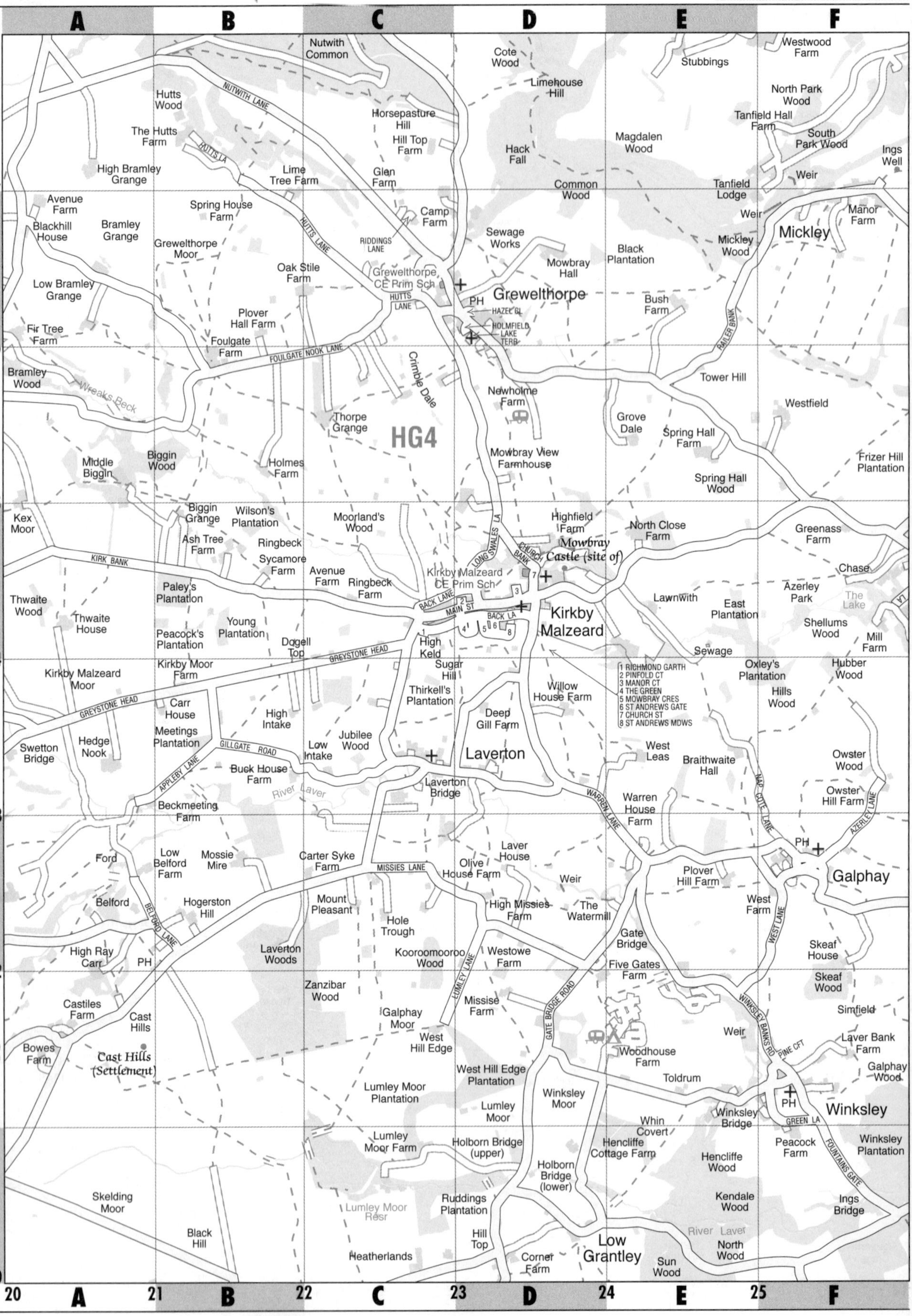

111
138

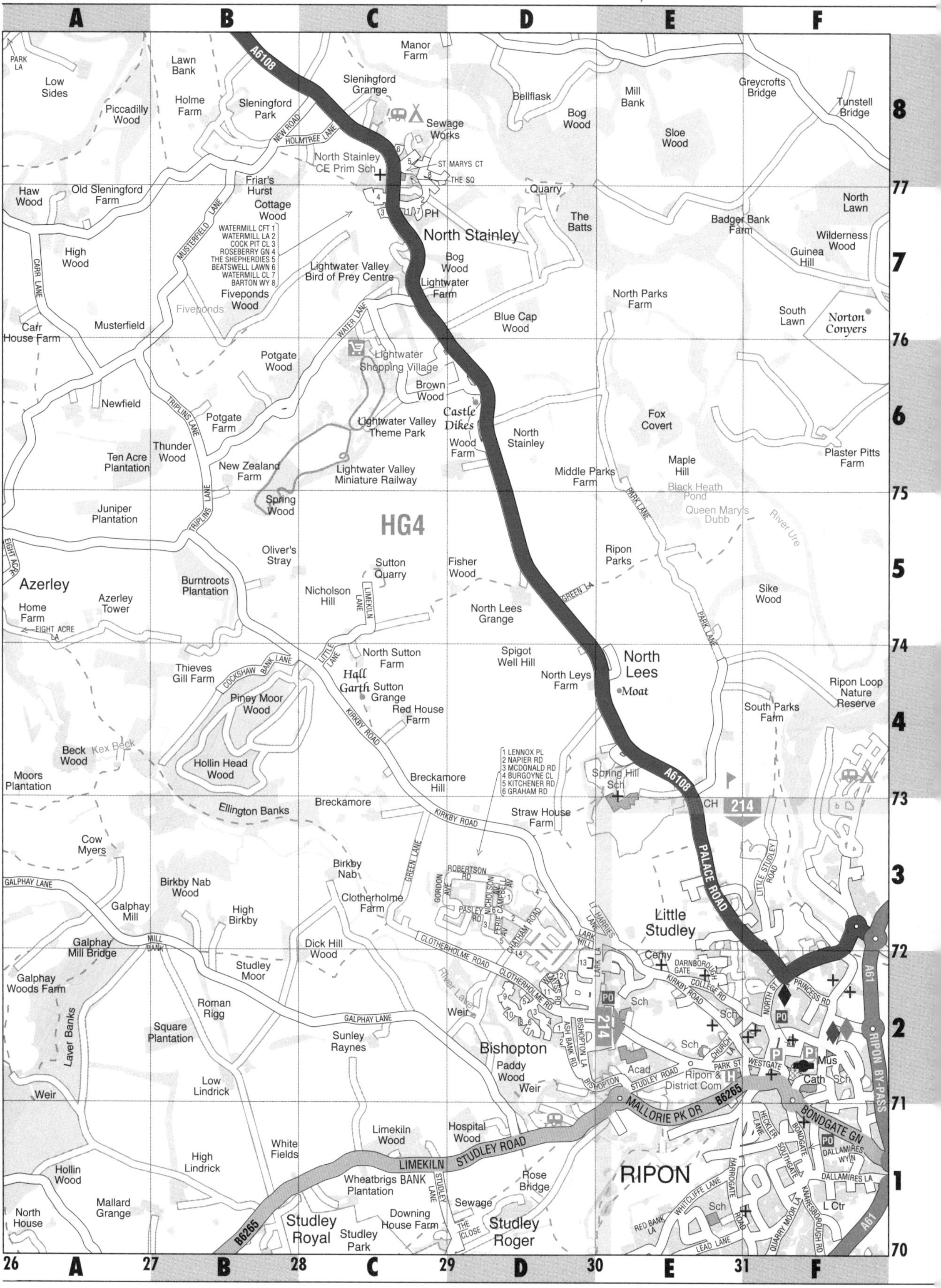

D2
1 ASH BANK CL
2 ASH BANK AVE
3 BELLMAN WK
4 CORNBELL GATE
5 HORNBLOWER CL
6 DOUBLEGATES AVE
7 DOUBLEGATES WK
8 DOUBLEGATES CL
9 DOUBLEGATES GN
10 DOUBLEGATES CT
11 WEMYSS RD
12 WAYNE TARBARD CL
13 LARK HILL CRES
14 TARBARD AVE

For full street detail of the highlighted area see page 214.

113
88

Scale: 1¾ inches to 1 mile
0 ¼ ½ mile
0 250m 500m 750m 1 km

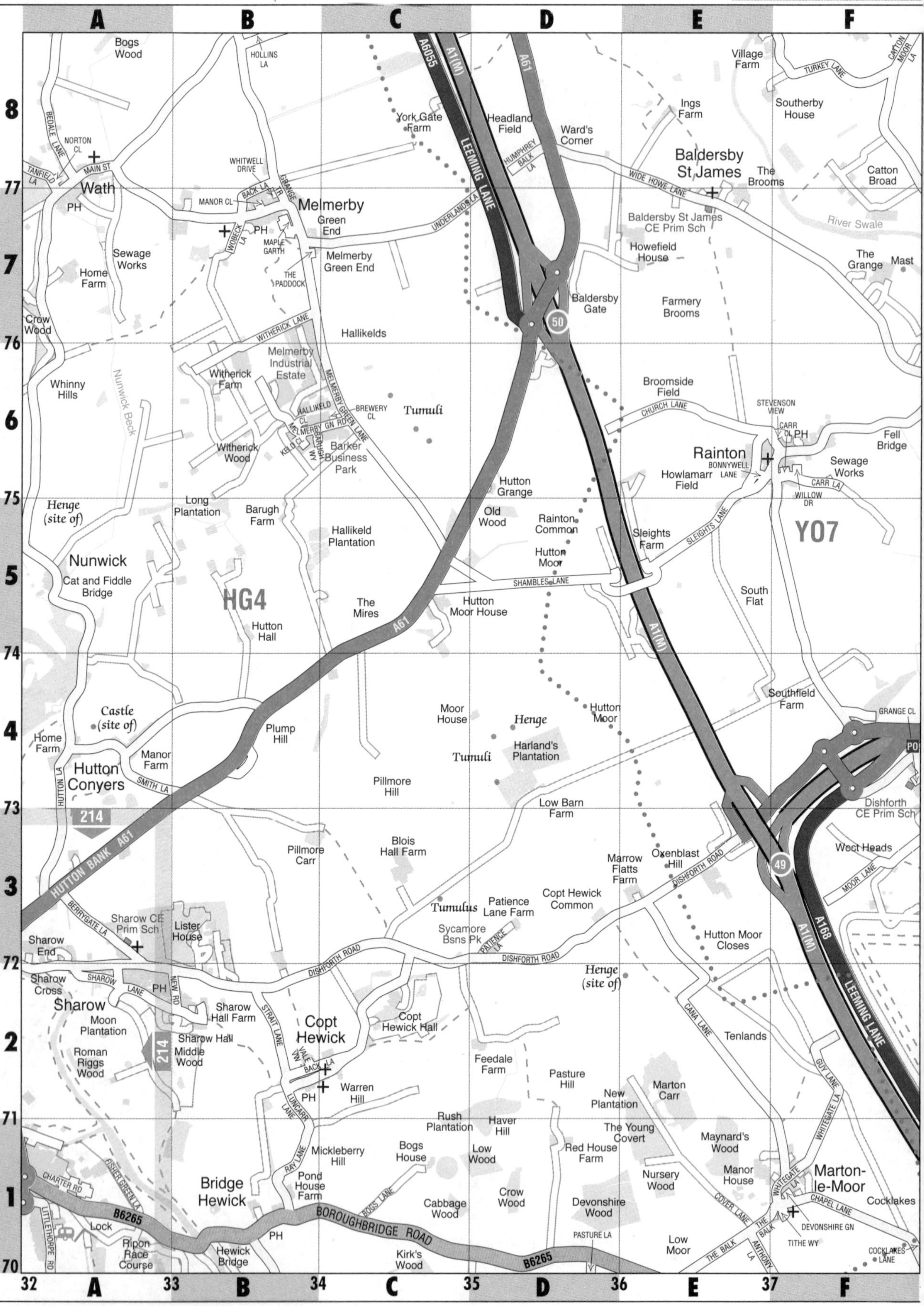

214
140
For full street detail of the highlighted area see page 214.

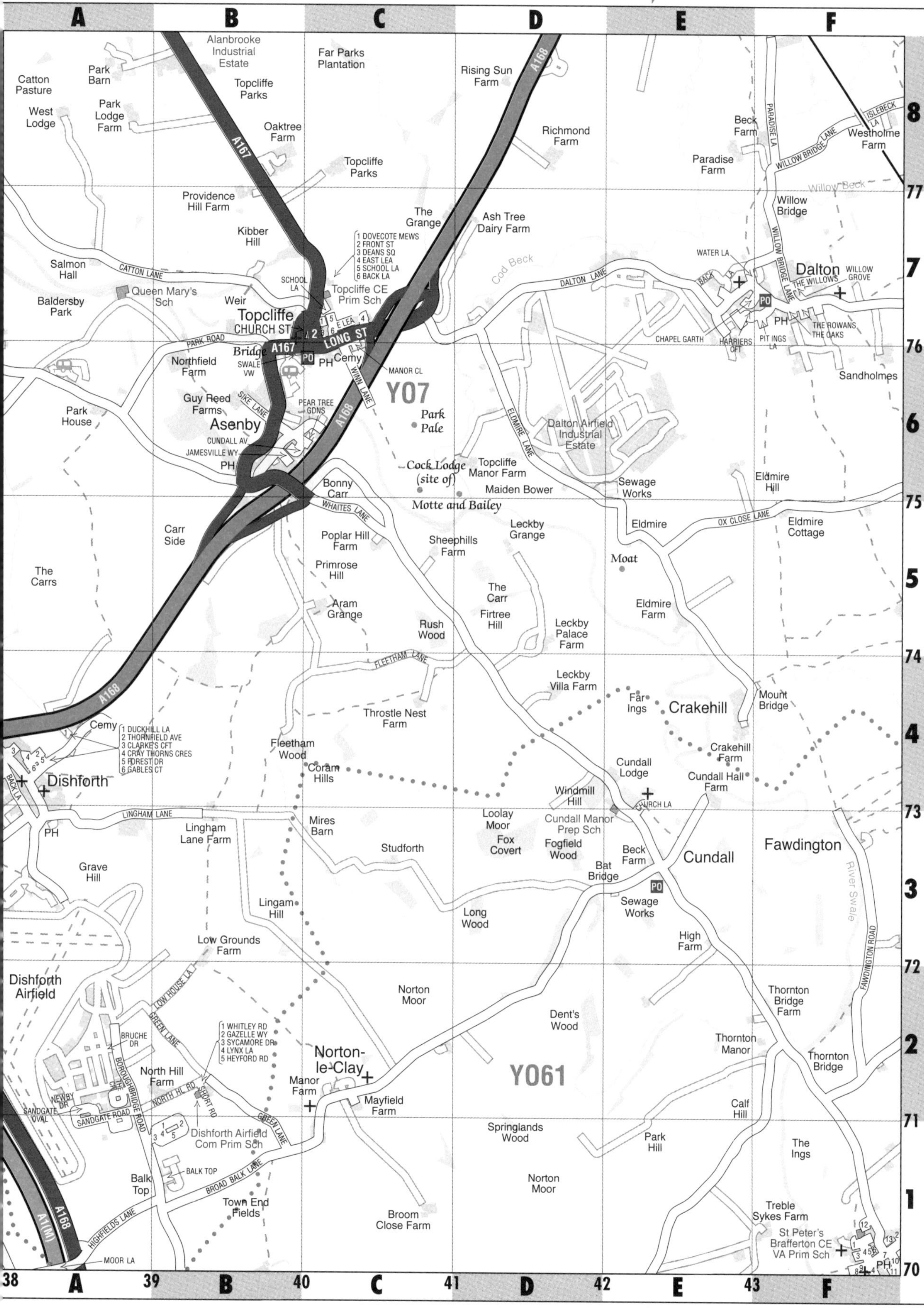

F1
1 HOLLY GARTH
2 MANOR DR
3 BAFFERTON HALL GDNS
4 HALL LANE
5 FOX GARTH
6 THE ORCHARDS
7 RASKELF RD
8 THE MALTINGS
9 BRIDGE ST
10 BACK LA
11 THE LEAS
12 ST PETERS CL
13 BIRCHWOOD GDNS

115
90

Scale: 1¾ inches to 1 mile
0 ¼ ½ mile
0 250m 500m 750m 1 km

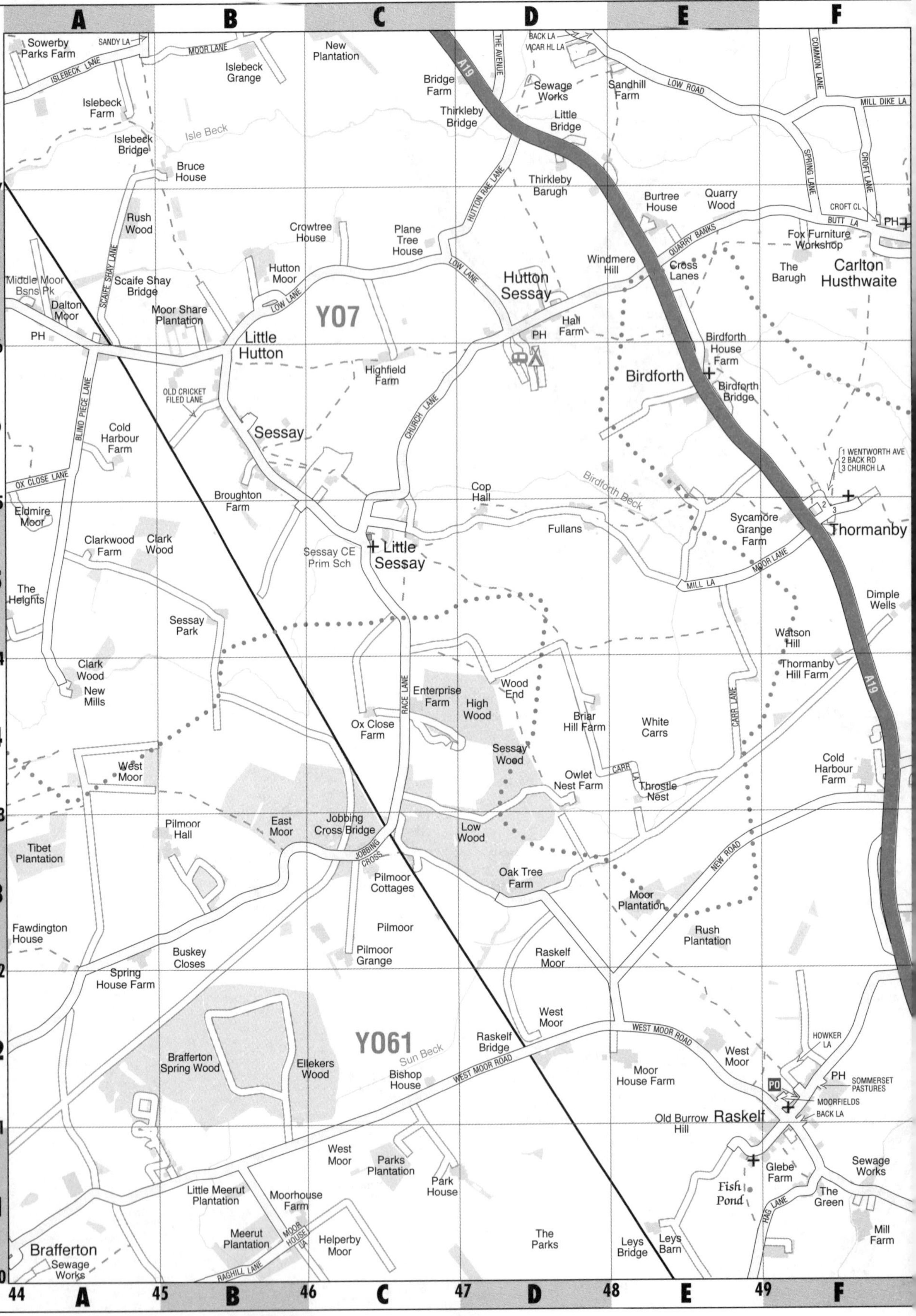

115
142

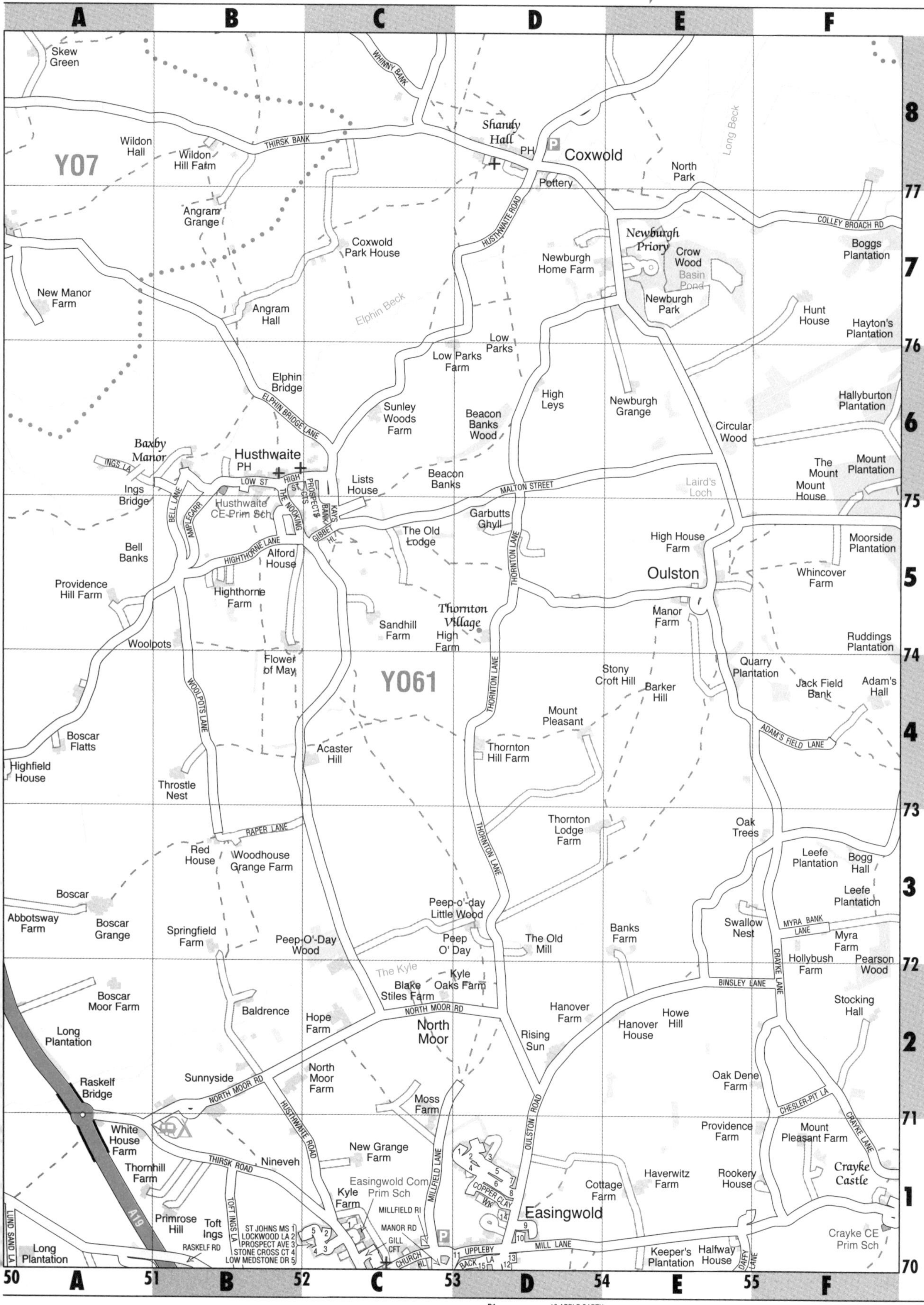

D1
1 PENNY LA
2 BARNS WRAY
3 WOODSIDE CL
4 LARCH RISE
5 MALLISON HL DR
6 ROWEN AVE
7 TOWER CFT
8 LIME TREE AVE
9 THORNLANDS
10 APPLE GARTH
11 SPRING ST
12 OXENBY PL
13 PADDOCK RI
14 CEDAR PL
15 ORCHARD CL

117
92

Scale: 1¾ inches to 1 mile
0 ¼ ½ mile
0 250m 500m 750m 1 km

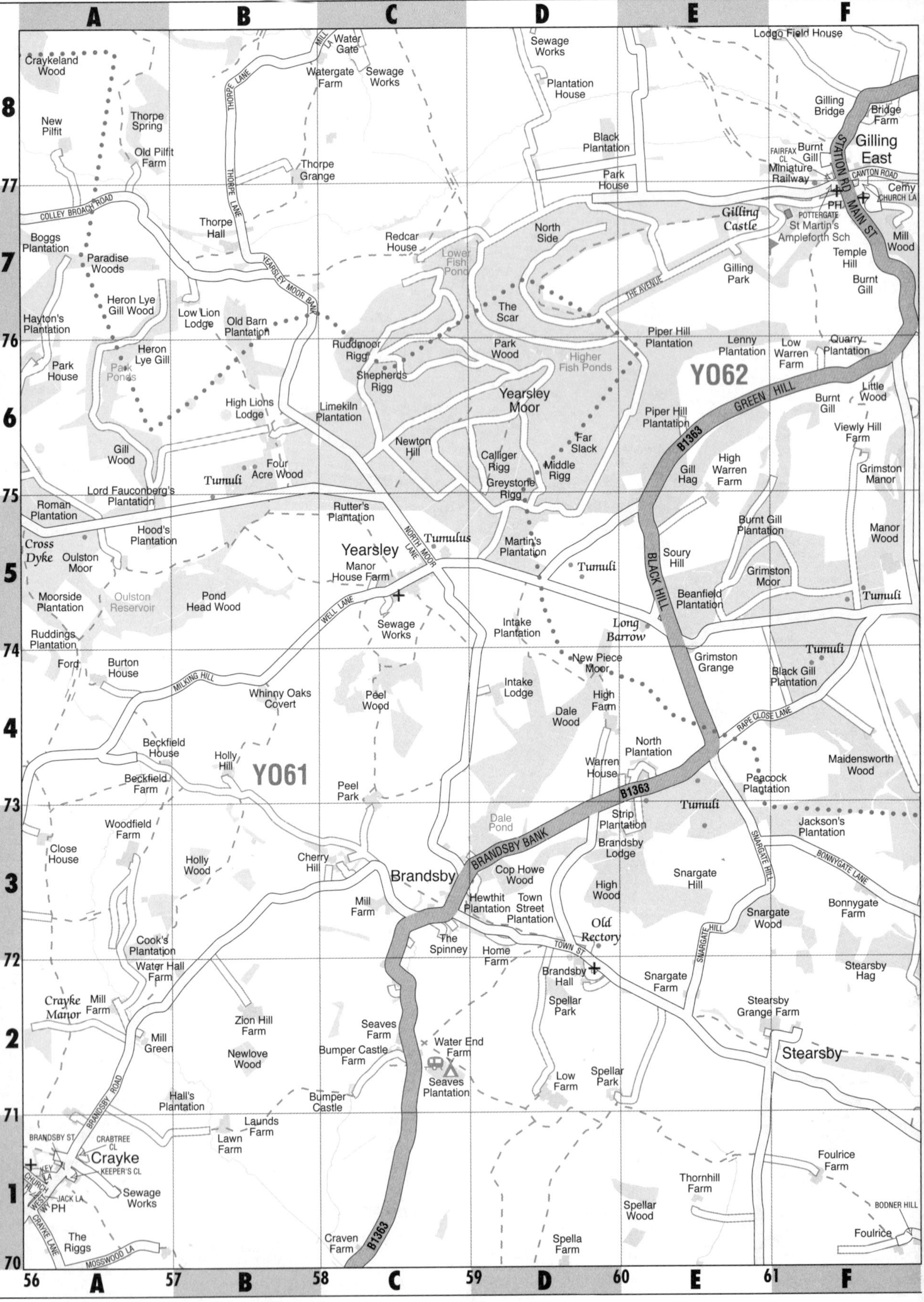
A
B
C
D
E
F
8
77
7
76
6
75
5
74
4
73
3
72
2
71
1
70
56
57
58
59
60
61
Craykeland Wood
New Pilfit
Thorpe Spring
Old Pilfit Farm
THORPE LANE
Water Gate
Watergate Farm
Sewage Works
Thorpe Grange
Sewage Works
Plantation House
Black Plantation
Park House
Lodge Field House
Gilling Bridge
Bridge Farm
Gilling East
FAIRFAX CL
Burnt Gill
Miniature Railway
STATION RD
MAIN ST
CAWTON ROAD
Cemy
CHURCH LA
PH
POTTERGATE
Gilling Castle
St Martin's Ampleforth Sch
Mill Wood
Temple Hill
Burnt Gill
Gilling Park
THE AVENUE
COLLEY BROACH ROAD
Boggs Plantation
Paradise Woods
Thorpe Hall
Redcar House
Lower Fish Pond
North Side
Heron Lye Gill Wood
Low Lion Lodge
Old Barn Plantation
YEARSLEY MOOR BANK
The Scar
Hayton's Plantation
Heron Lye Gill
Park House
Park Ponds
Ruddmoor Rigg
Shepherds Rigg
Park Wood
Higher Fish Ponds
Piper Hill Plantation
Lenny Plantation
Low Warren Farm
Quarry Plantation
YO62
Yearsley Moor
GREEN HILL
Little Wood
Burnt Gill
High Lions Lodge
Limekiln Plantation
Piper Hill Plantation
Viewly Hill Farm
Newton Hill
Far Slack
B1363
Gill Wood
Four Acre Wood
Tumuli
Calliger Rigg
Middle Rigg
Gill Hag
High Warren Farm
Grimston Manor
Greystone Rigg
Lord Fauconberg's Plantation
Roman Plantation
Rutter's Plantation
NORTH MOOR LANE
Tumulus
Burnt Gill Plantation
Manor Wood
Hood's Plantation
Cross Dyke
Oulston Moor
Yearsley
Martin's Plantation
Soury Hill
Manor House Farm
Tumuli
BLACK HILL
Grimston Moor
Moorside Plantation
Oulston Reservoir
Pond Head Wood
WELL LANE
Beanfield Plantation
Tumuli
Sewage Works
Intake Plantation
Long Barrow
Ruddings Plantation
Ford
Burton House
Grimston Grange
Tumuli
MILKING HILL
New Piece Moor
Black Gill Plantation
Whinny Oaks Covert
Peel Wood
Intake Lodge
High Farm
Dale Wood
RAPE CLOSE LANE
Beckfield House
North Plantation
Holly Hill
YO61
Maidensworth Wood
Beckfield Farm
Warren House
Peacock Plantation
Peel Park
B1363
Tumuli
Woodfield Farm
Dale Pond
Strip Plantation
Jackson's Plantation
Close House
Holly Wood
Cherry Hill
BRANDSBY BANK
Brandsby Lodge
SNARGATE HILL
BONNYGATE LANE
Brandsby
Cop Howe Wood
Snargate Hill
Mill Farm
Hewthit Plantation
Town Street Plantation
High Wood
Bonnygate Farm
Snargate Wood
Old Rectory
SNARGATE HILL
Cook's Plantation
The Spinney
Home Farm
TOWN ST
Water Hall Farm
Brandsby Hall
Snargate Farm
Stearsby Hag
Crayke Manor
Mill Farm
Spellar Park
Stearsby Grange Farm
Zion Hill Farm
Seaves Farm
Mill Green
Water End Farm
Stearsby
Newlove Wood
Bumper Castle Farm
Seaves Plantation
Low Farm
Spellar Park
BRANDSBY ROAD
Hall's Plantation
Bumper Castle
Launds Farm
BRANDSBY ST
CRABTREE CL
Crayke
Lawn Farm
Foulrice Farm
KEY LA
KEEPER'S CL
CHURCH HL
WEST WY
JACK LA
PH
Sewage Works
Thornhill Farm
Spellar Wood
BODNER HILL
CRAYKE LANE
The Riggs
MOSSWOOD LA
Craven Farm
B1363
Spella Farm
Foulrice

117
144

Scale: 1¾ inches to 1 mile
0 ¼ ½ mile
0 250m 500m 750m 1 km

93
120

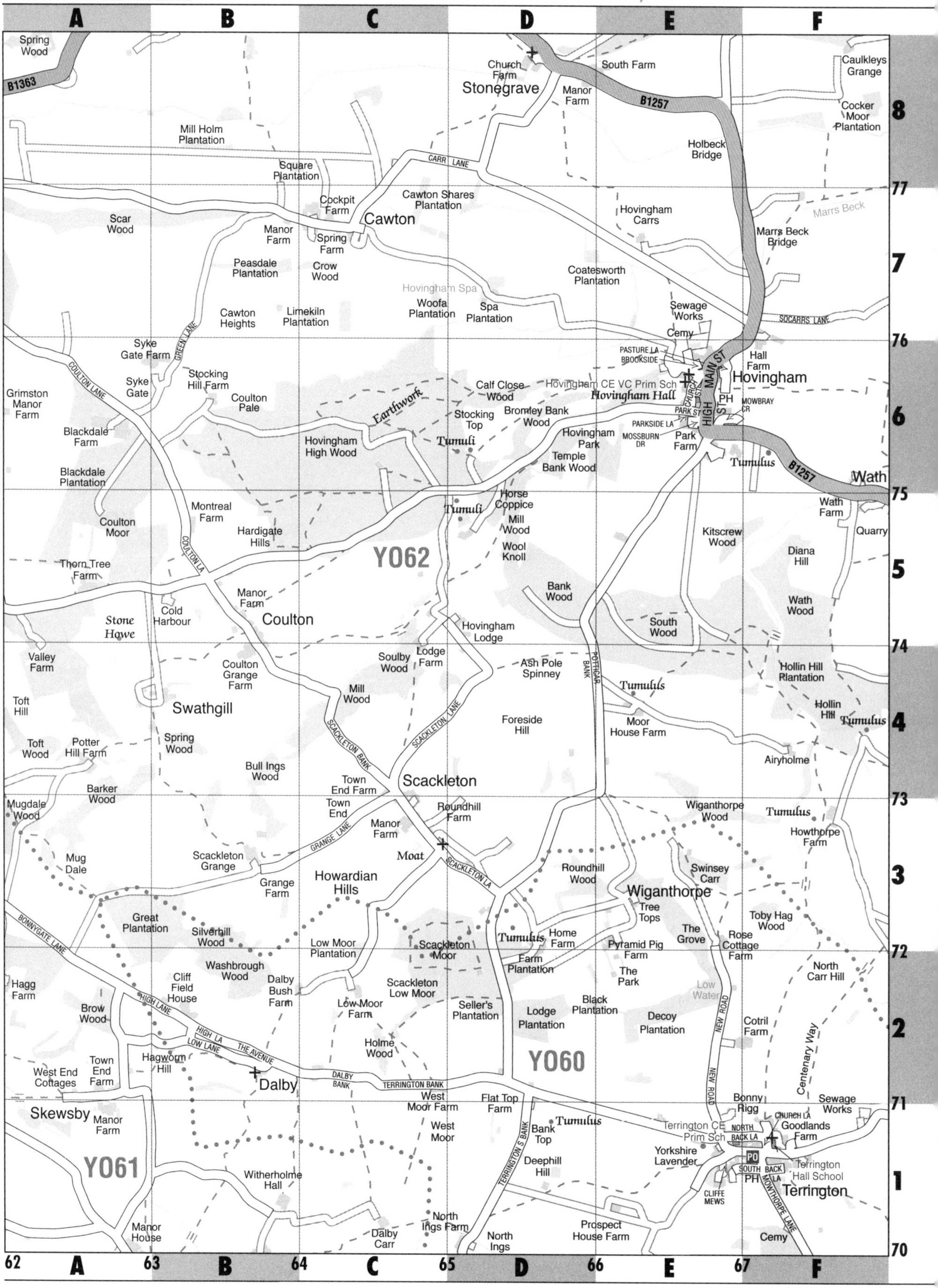

119
94

Scale: 1¾ inches to 1 mile
0 ¼ ½ mile
0 250m 500m 750m 1 km

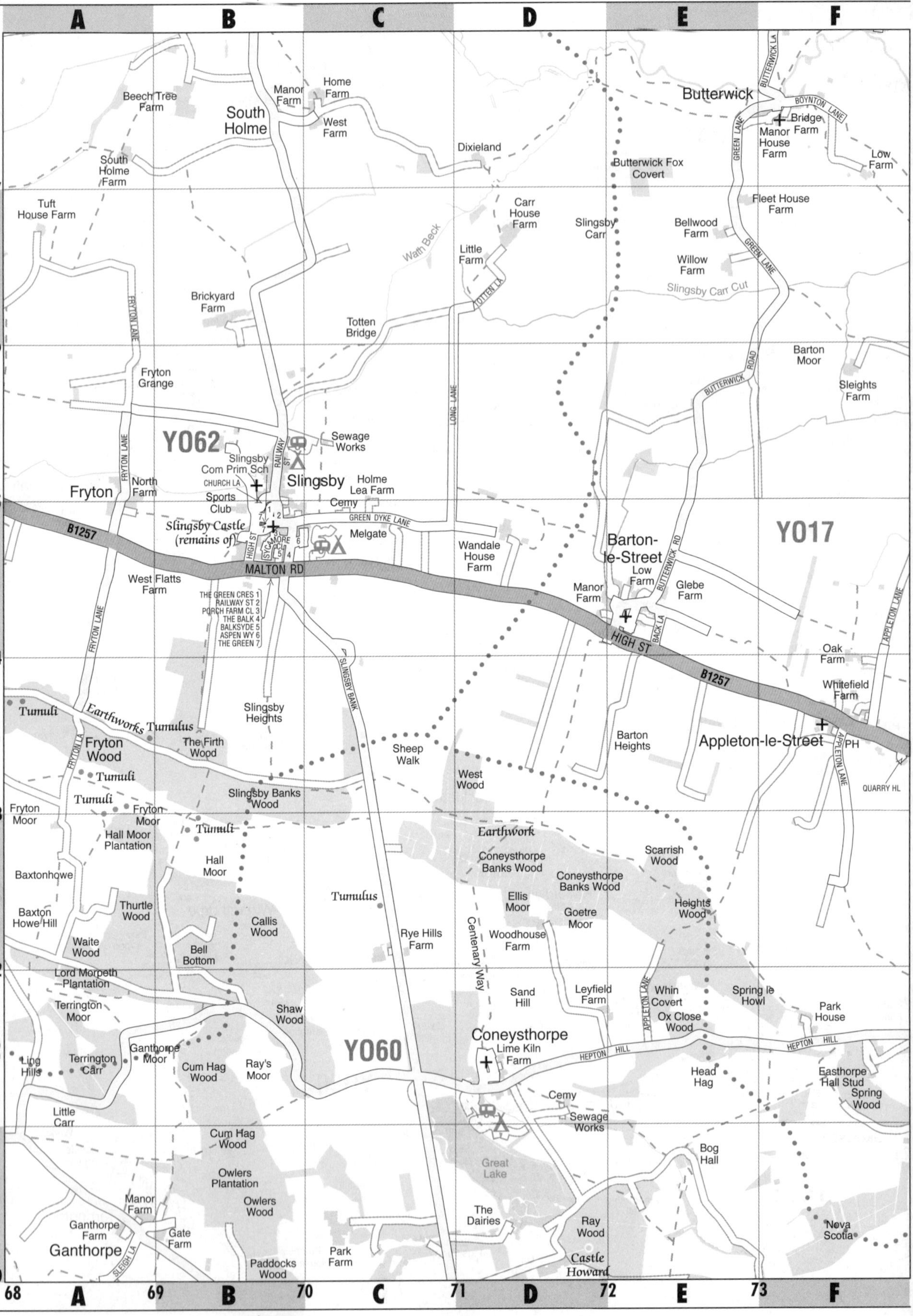
A B C D E F
Butterwick
South Holme
Beech Tree Farm
Manor Farm
Home Farm
West Farm
Dixieland
Bridge Farm
Manor House Farm
Low Farm
South Holme Farm
Butterwick Fox Covert
Tuft House Farm
Carr House Farm
Slingsby Carr
Bellwood Farm
Fleet House Farm
Willow Farm
Little Farm
Wath Beck
Slingsby Carr Cut
Brickyard Farm
Totten Bridge
Fryton Grange
Barton Moor
Sleights Farm
Y062
Sewage Works
Slingsby Com Prim Sch
Slingsby
Holme Lea Farm
Fryton
North Farm
Sports Club
Cemy
Slingsby Castle (remains of)
Melgate
Wandale House Farm
Barton-le-Street
Y017
B1257
MALTON RD
West Flatts Farm
Low Farm
Manor Farm
Glebe Farm
THE GREEN CRES 1
RAILWAY ST 2
PORCH FARM CL 3
THE BALK 4
BALKSYDE 5
ASPEN WY 6
THE GREEN 7
HIGH ST
Oak Farm
Whitefield Farm
Tumuli
Earthworks
Tumulus
Slingsby Heights
Fryton Wood
The Firth Wood
Sheep Walk
Barton Heights
Appleton-le-Street
PH
QUARRY HL
West Wood
Slingsby Banks Wood
Fryton Moor
Hall Moor Plantation
Earthwork
Coneysthorpe Banks Wood
Scarrish Wood
Hall Moor
Baxtonhowe
Tumulus
Ellis Moor
Goetre Moor
Heights Wood
Baxton Howe Hill
Thurtle Wood
Callis Wood
Rye Hills Farm
Woodhouse Farm
Centenary Way
Waite Wood
Bell Bottom
Lord Morpeth Plantation
Sand Hill
Leyfield Farm
Whin Covert
Spring le Howl
Terrington Moor
Shaw Wood
Ox Close Wood
Park House
Coneysthorpe
Y060
Ling Hills
Terrington Carr
Ganthorpe Moor
Cum Hag Wood
Ray's Moor
Lime Kiln Farm
HEPTON HILL
Head Hag
Easthorpe Hall Stud
Spring Wood
Cemy
Little Carr
Sewage Works
Cum Hag Wood
Bog Hall
Great Lake
Owlers Plantation
Manor Farm
Owlers Wood
The Dairies
Ray Wood
Nova Scotia
Ganthorpe Farm
Ganthorpe
Gate Farm
Park Farm
Paddocks Wood
Castle Howard
FRYTON LANE
FRYTON LA
LONG LANE
TOTTEN LA
GREEN DYKE LANE
RAILWAY ST
CHURCH LA
HIGH ST
SYCAMORE CL
SLINGSBY BANK
BUTTERWICK LA
BOYNTON LANE
GREEN LANE
BUTTERWICK ROAD
BUTTERWICK RD
BACK LA
APPLETON LANE
APPLETON LA
SLEIGH LA
68 69 70 71 72 73
8 77 7 76 6 75 5 74 4 73 3 72 2 71 1 70

119
146

Scale: 1¾ inches to 1 mile
0 ¼ ½ mile
0 250m 500m 750m 1 km

95
122

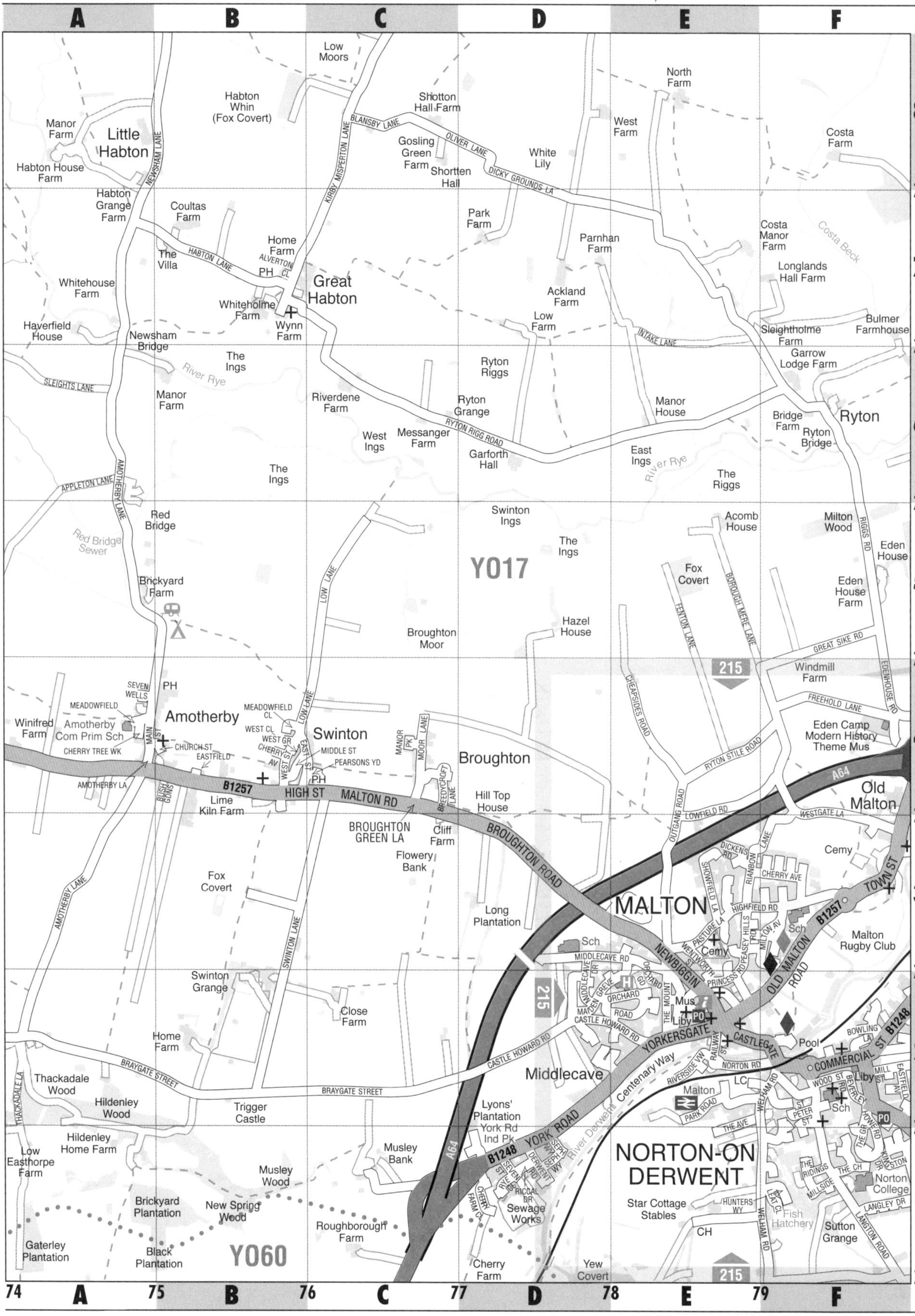
A
B
C
D
E
F
8
77
7
76
6
75
5
74
4
73
3
72
2
71
1
70
74
75
76
77
78
79
Low Moors
Habton Whin (Fox Covert)
Shotton Hall Farm
North Farm
West Farm
Manor Farm
Little Habton
NEWSHAM LANE
BLANSBY LANE
KIRBY MISPERTON LANE
Gosling Green Farm
OLIVER LANE
White Lily
Costa Farm
Habton House Farm
Shortten Hall
DICKY GROUNDS LA
Habton Grange Farm
Coultas Farm
Park Farm
Costa Manor Farm
Costa Beck
Home Farm
Parnhan Farm
The Villa
HABTON LANE
ALVERTON CL
PH
Great Habton
Whitehouse Farm
Longlands Hall Farm
Ackland Farm
Whiteholme Farm
Wynn Farm
Low Farm
Haverfield House
Sleightholme Farm
Bulmer Farmhouse
Newsham Bridge
INTAKE LANE
Garrow Lodge Farm
The Ings
Ryton Riggs
River Rye
SLEIGHTS LANE
Manor Farm
Riverdene Farm
Ryton Grange
Manor House
Bridge Farm
Ryton
Ryton Bridge
RYTON RIGG ROAD
West Ings
Messanger Farm
Garforth Hall
East Ings
River Rye
The Ings
The Riggs
APPLETON LANE
AMOTHERBY LANE
Swinton Ings
Acomb House
Milton Wood
Red Bridge
The Ings
RIGGS RD
Eden House
Red Bridge Sewer
YO17
Fox Covert
Eden House Farm
Brickyard Farm
LOW LANE
FENTON LANE
BOROUGH MERE LANE
Broughton Moor
Hazel House
GREAT SIKE RD
215
Windmill Farm
SEVEN WELLS
PH
MEADOWFIELD
MEADOWFIELD CL
LOW LANE
CHEAPSIDES ROAD
FREEHOLD LANE
EDENHOUSE RD
Winifred Farm
Amotherby Com Prim Sch
Amotherby
WEST CL
WEST GR
Swinton
MANOR PK
MOOR LANE
Eden Camp Modern History Theme Mus
CHERRY TREE WK
MAIN ST
CHURCH ST
EASTFIELD
CHERRY AV
WEST ST
EAST ST
MIDDLE ST
PEARSONS YD
Broughton
RYTON STILE ROAD
A64
AMOTHERBY LA
BUSH GDNS
B1257
PH
HIGH ST
MALTON RD
Hill Top House
Old Malton
Lime Kiln Farm
BREEDYCROFT LANE
OUTGANG ROAD
LOWFIELD RD
WESTGATE LA
BROUGHTON GREEN LA
Cliff Farm
BROUGHTON ROAD
Cemy
Flowery Bank
DICKENS RD
RIANBOW LANE
SHOWFIELD LA
CHERRY AVE
AMOTHERBY LANE
Fox Covert
MALTON
HIGHFIELD RD
TOWN ST
B1257
Long Plantation
PASTURE LA
PEASEY HILLS RD
MILTON AV
Sch
SWINTON LANE
Sch
WENTWORTH ST
Cemy
OLD MALTON ROAD
Malton Rugby Club
NEWBIGGIN
MIDDLECAVE RD
MIDDLECAVE DR
MAIDEN GREVE
ORCHARD RD
ORCHARD GD
Swinton Grange
215
H
ORCHARD ROAD
THE MOUNT
PRINCESS RD
Close Farm
Mus
Liby
PO
CASTLE HOWARD RD
Home Farm
YORKERSGATE
CASTLEGATE
RAILWAY ST
Pool
BOWLING LA
B1248
CASTLE HOWARD RD
COMMERCIAL ST
BRAYGATE STREET
NORTON RD
Middlecave
Centenary Way
RIVERSIDE VW
Thackadale Wood
MILL ST
EASTFIELD AV
THACKADALE LA
BRAYGATE STREET
LC
WOOD ST
Liby
BEVERLEY RD
Malton
PARK ROAD
Hildenley Wood
Trigger Castle
Lyons' Plantation
WELHAM RD
Sch
ST PETER ST
York Rd Ind Pk
THE AVE
PO
Hildenley Home Farm
Musley Bank
A64
B1248
YORK ROAD
SEPH WY
NORTON-ON DERWENT
THE GR
MONE RD
Low Easthorpe Farm
River Derwent
SEVEN ST
DERWENT RD
THE RIDINGS
THE CH
KINGSTON DR
Musley Wood
RYE CL
RICCAL DR
MILLSIDE
Norton College
Brickyard Plantation
New Spring Wood
Star Cottage Stables
HUNTERS WY
LEAT CL
LANGLEY DR
CHERRY FARM CL
Sewage Works
Fish Hatchery
Roughborough Farm
CH
Sutton Grange
LANGTON ROAD
Gaterley Plantation
Black Plantation
YO60
WELHAM RD
Cherry Farm
Yew Covert
215

147
122
For full street detail of the highlighted area see page 215.

Scale: 1¾ inches to 1 mile
0 ¼ ½ mile
0 250m 500m 750m 1 km

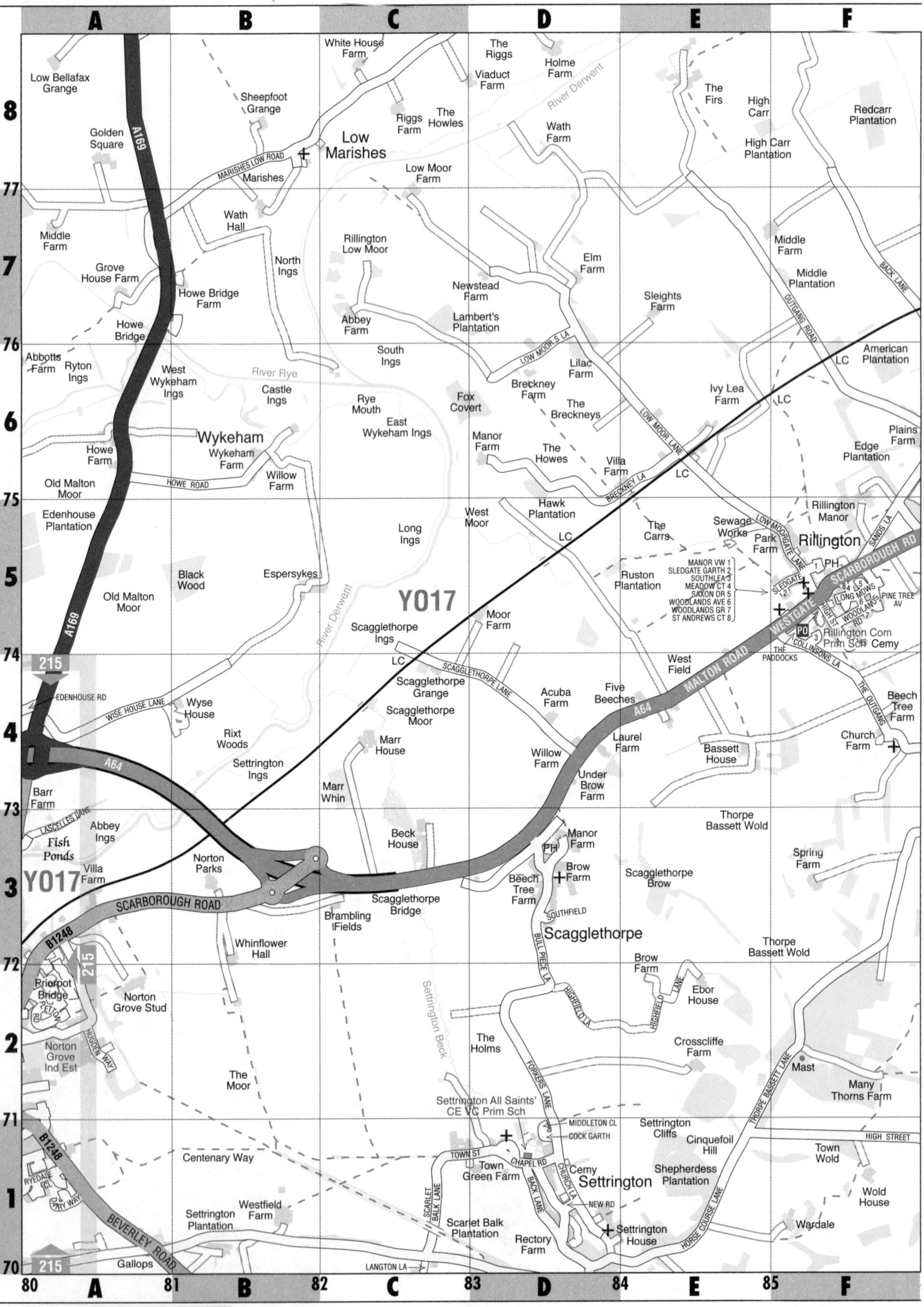
A
B
C
D
E
F
8
77
7
76
6
75
5
74
4
73
3
72
2
71
1
70
80
81
82
83
84
85
Low Bellafax Grange
White House Farm
The Riggs
Holme Farm
Viaduct Farm
River Derwent
The Firs
High Carr
Redcarr Plantation
Sheepfoot Grange
Riggs Farm
The Howles
Wath Farm
High Carr Plantation
Golden Square
A169
Low Marishes
MARISHES LOW ROAD
Marishes
Low Moor Farm
Middle Farm
Wath Hall
Rillington Low Moor
Elm Farm
Middle Farm
Grove House Farm
North Ings
Middle Plantation
BACK LANE
Howe Bridge Farm
Newstead Farm
Sleights Farm
OUTGANG ROAD
Howe Bridge
Abbey Farm
Lambert's Plantation
Abbotts Farm
Ryton Ings
West Wykeham Ings
South Ings
LOW MOOR'S LA
Lilac Farm
LC
American Plantation
River Rye
Castle Ings
Rye Mouth
Fox Covert
Breckney Farm
Ivy Lea Farm
The Breckneys
East Wykeham Ings
Wykeham
Wykeham Farm
Manor Farm
LOW MOOR LANE
Plains Farm
Howe Farm
The Howes
Edge Plantation
Villa Farm
Old Malton Moor
HOWE ROAD
Willow Farm
BRECKNEY LA
Rillington Manor
Edenhouse Plantation
West Moor
Hawk Plantation
The Carrs
Sewage Works
LOW MOORGATE LANE
SANDS LA
Long Ings
Park Farm
Rillington
SCARBOROUGH RD
PH
Black Wood
Espersykes
Ruston Plantation
MANOR VW 1
SLEDGATE GARTH 2
SOUTHLEA 3
MEADOW CT 4
SAXON DR 5
WOODLANDS AVE 6
WOODLANDS GR 7
ST ANDREWS CT 8
SLEDGATE
LONG MOWS
WOODLANDS
PINE TREE AV
Old Malton Moor
YO17
WESTGATE
HIGH ST
PO
Rillington Com Prim Sch
Cemy
Moor Farm
Scagglethorpe Ings
THE PADDOCKS
COLLINSONS LA
215
West Field
SCAGGLETHORPE LANE
Scagglethorpe Grange
MALTON ROAD
THE OUTGANG
EDENHOUSE RD
Acuba Farm
Five Beeches
Beech Tree Farm
WISE HOUSE LANE
Wyse House
Scagglethorpe Moor
A64
Rixt Woods
Marr House
Laurel Farm
Church Farm
Bassett House
Settrington Ings
Willow Farm
Under Brow Farm
Barr Farm
Marr Whin
Thorpe Bassett Wold
LASCELLES LANE
Abbey Ings
Fish Ponds
Beck House
Manor Farm
Spring Farm
Norton Parks
Brow Farm
Villa Farm
Beech Tree Farm
Scagglethorpe Brow
YO17
SCARBOROUGH ROAD
Scagglethorpe Bridge
Brambling Fields
SOUTHFIELD
B1248
Whinflower Hall
Scagglethorpe
BULL PIECE LA
Thorpe Bassett Wold
Brow Farm
Priorpot Bridge
Settrington Beck
HIGHFIELD LA
HIGHFIELD LANE
Ebor House
Norton Grove Stud
PETTON RD
HUGDEN WAY
Norton Grove Ind Est
The Holms
Crosscliffe Farm
FORKERS LANE
Mast
THORPE BASSETT LANE
The Moor
Many Thorns Farm
Settrington All Saints' CE VC Prim Sch
MIDDLETON CL
COCK GARTH
Settrington Cliffs
HIGH STREET
B1248
Cinquefoil Hill
Centenary Way
TOWN ST
Town Green Farm
CHAPEL RD
Cemy
Town Wold
Shepherdess Plantation
RYEDALE CL
DAIRY WAY
Settrington
CHURCH LA
Wold House
Westfield Farm
SCARLET BALK LANE
BACK LANE
NEW RD
HORSE COURSE LANE
Settrington Plantation
BEVERLEY ROAD
Scarlet Balk Plantation
Settrington House
Wardale
Rectory Farm
Gallops
LANGTON LA

Scale: 1¾ inches to 1 mile
0 ¼ ½ mile
0 250m 500m 750m 1 km

97
124

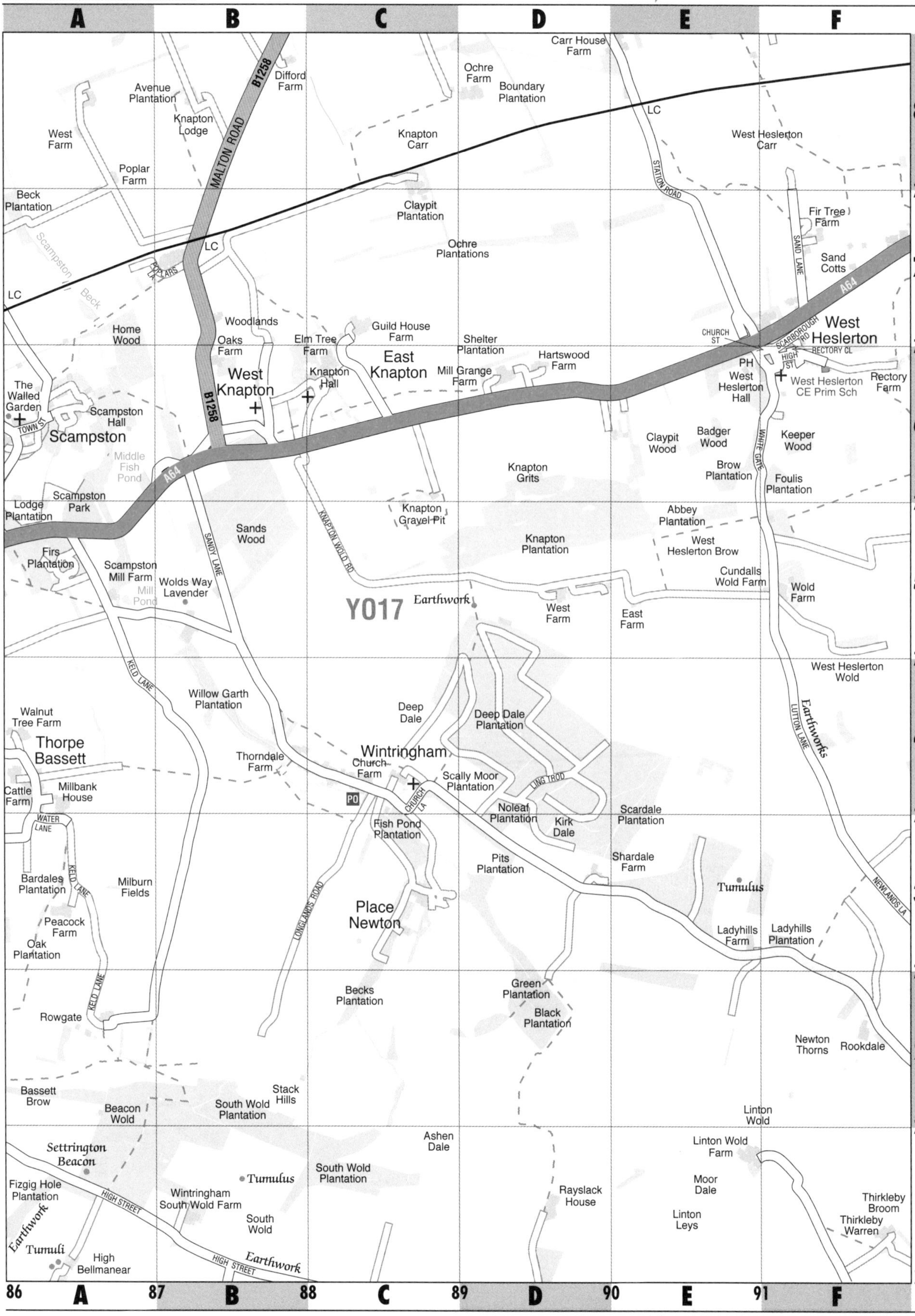

149
124

123
98

Scale: 1¾ inches to 1 mile
0 ¼ ½ mile
0 250m 500m 750m 1 km

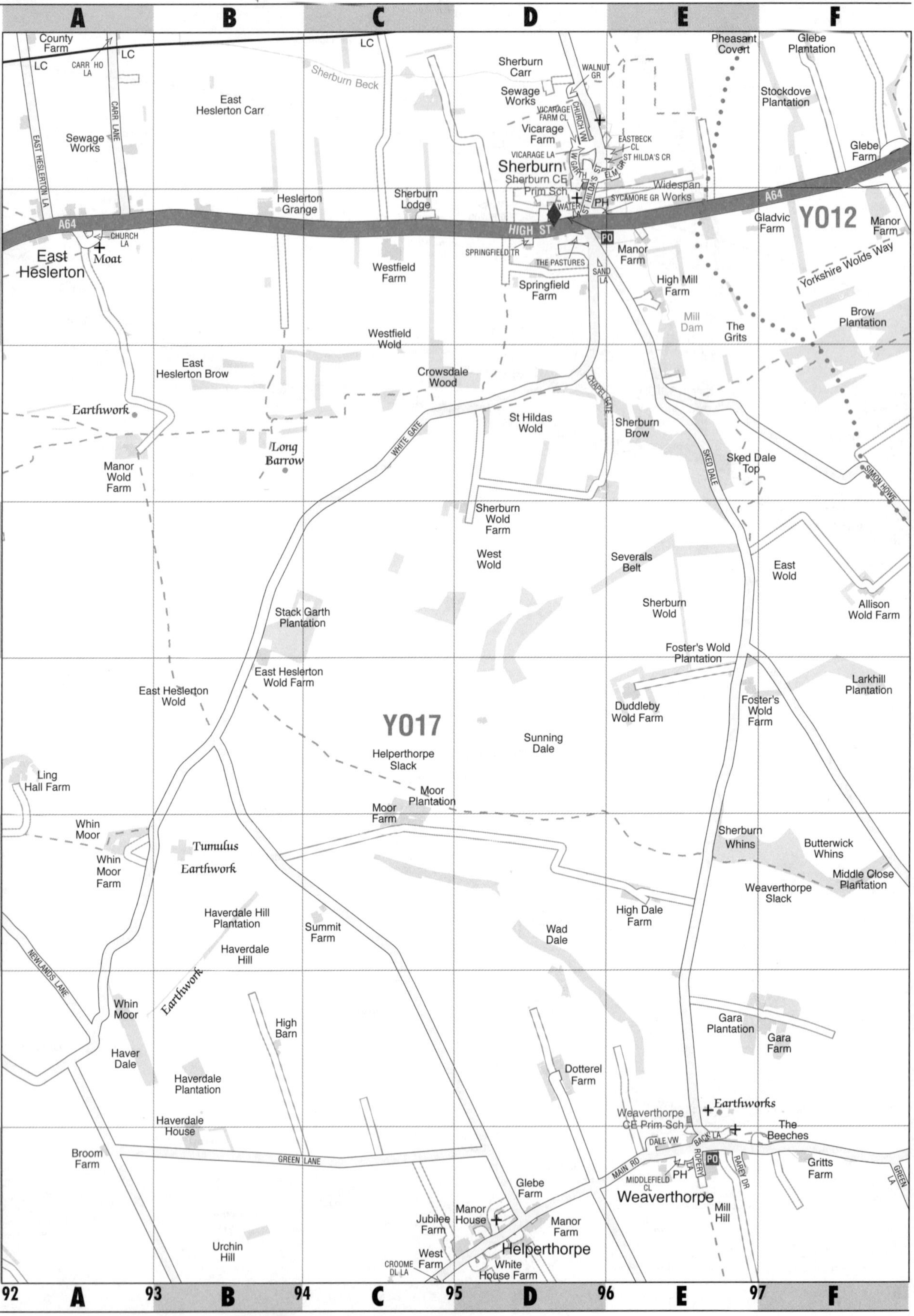

123
150

99
126

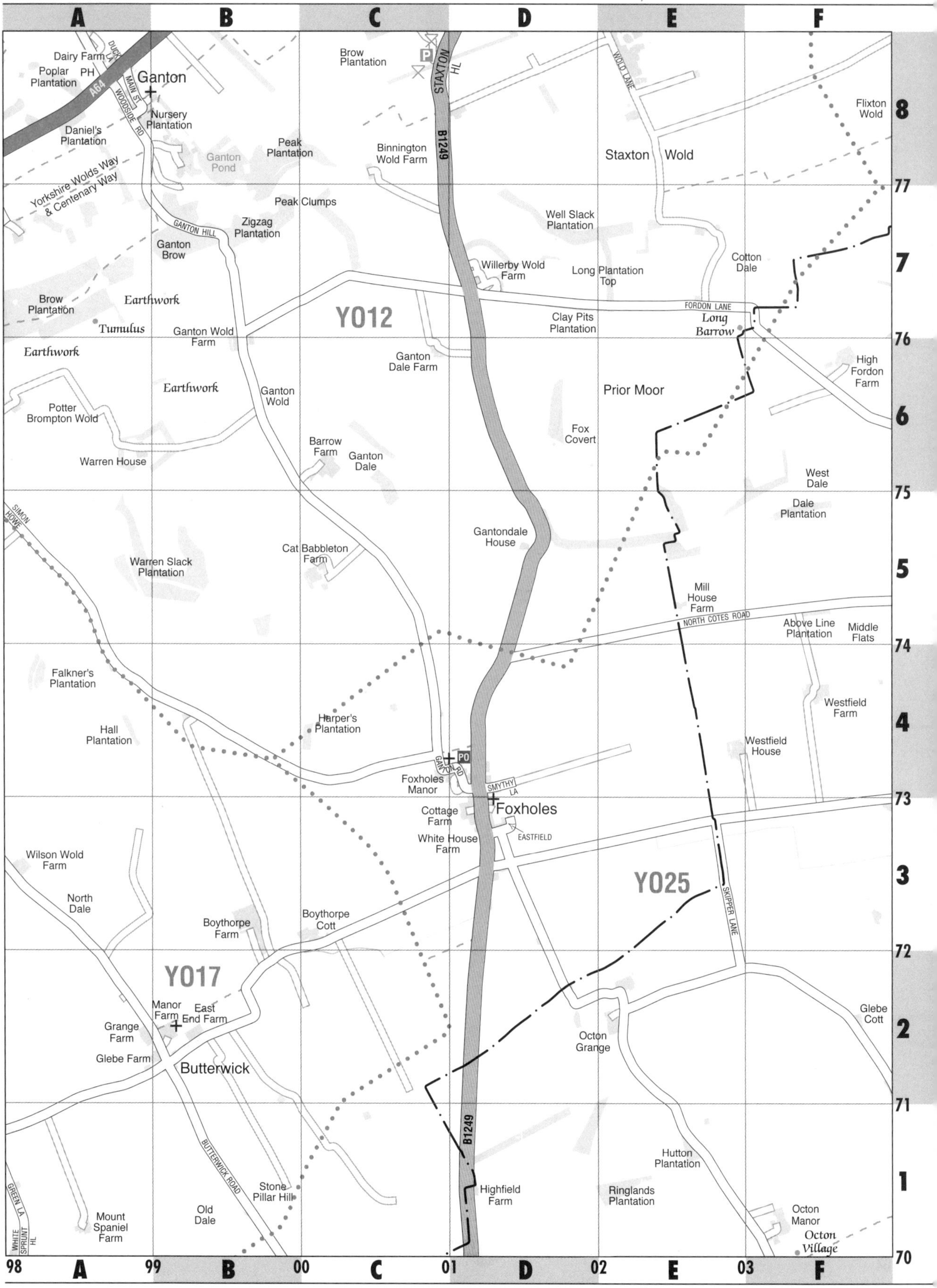

151
126

125
100

F8
1 OWSTON RD
2 MITFORD RD
3 MITFORD CL
4 OUTGAITS CL
5 WENTWORTH WY
6 SIMPSON AVE
7 HIGH CFT
8 CASTLE HL
9 BOWLING GN LA
10 CHURCH HL
11 HUNGATE CT
12 VICARAGE CL
13 FONTAYNE RD
14 BARDNEY RD
15 ROWEDALE CL
16 AMBREY CL
17 PARK RISE
18 OLIVER'S CL
19 ROSEMOOR CL
20 HARBOROUGH CL
21 EASTFIELD
22 GARTON LA
23 VICARAGE CL

Scale: 1¾ inches to 1 mile
0 ¼ ½ mile
0 250m 500m 750m 1 km

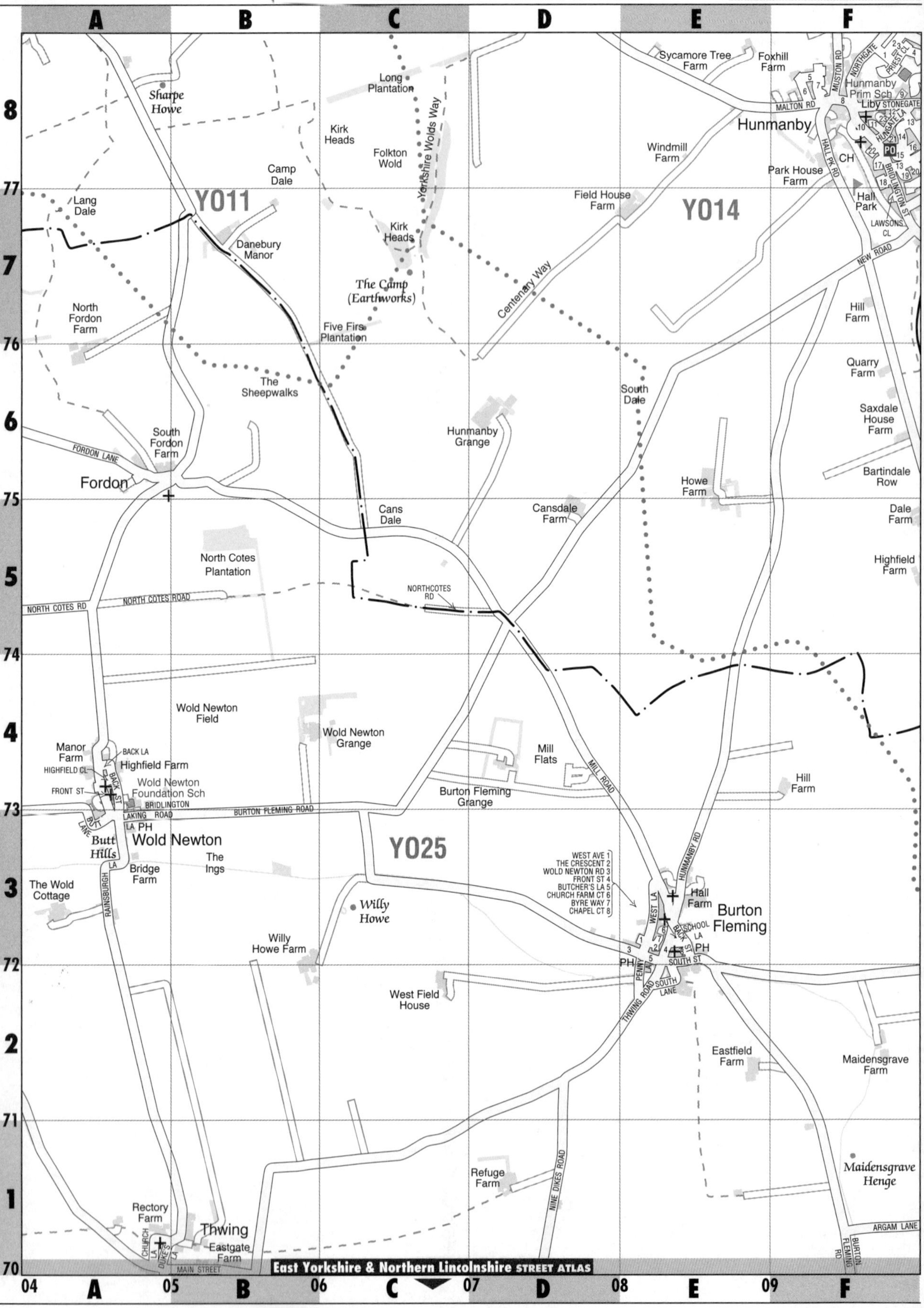
A
B
C
D
E
F
8
77
7
76
6
75
5
74
4
73
3
72
2
71
1
70
04
05
06
07
08
09
Sharpe Howe
Long Plantation
Yorkshire Wolds Way
Kirk Heads
Folkton Wold
Camp Dale
Lang Dale
YO11
Danebury Manor
The Camp (Earthworks)
North Fordon Farm
Five Firs Plantation
The Sheepwalks
South Fordon Farm
FORDON LANE
Fordon
Cans Dale
Hunmanby Grange
North Cotes Plantation
NORTH COTES RD
NORTH COTES ROAD
NORTHCOTES RD
Sycamore Tree Farm
Foxhill Farm
MALTON RD
MUSTON RD
NORTHGATE
PRIEST CL
Hunmanby Prim Sch
Liby
STONEGATE
HUNGATE LA
Hunmanby
Windmill Farm
HALL PK RD
CH
PO
BRIDLINGTON ST
Park House Farm
Hall Park
LAWSONS CL
Field House Farm
YO14
Centenary Way
NEW ROAD
Hill Farm
Quarry Farm
South Dale
Saxdale House Farm
Bartindale Row
Howe Farm
Cansdale Farm
Dale Farm
Highfield Farm
Wold Newton Field
Wold Newton Grange
Manor Farm
BACK LA
HIGHFIELD CL
Highfield Farm
FRONT ST
BACK ST
Wold Newton Foundation Sch
BRIDLINGTON
LAKING ROAD
LA
PH
BURTON FLEMING ROAD
BUTT LANE
Butt Hills
Wold Newton
The Ings
Bridge Farm
RAINSBURGH LA
The Wold Cottage
Mill Flats
MILL ROAD
Burton Fleming Grange
Hill Farm
YO25
WEST AVE 1
THE CRESCENT 2
WOLD NEWTON RD 3
FRONT ST 4
BUTCHER'S LA 5
CHURCH FARM CT 6
BYRE WAY 7
CHAPEL CT 8
HUNMANBY RD
WEST LA
Hall Farm
Burton Fleming
SCHOOL LA
PH
SOUTH ST
PENNY LA
SOUTH LANE
THWING ROAD
Willy Howe
Willy Howe Farm
West Field House
Eastfield Farm
Maidensgrave Farm
Maidensgrave Henge
Refuge Farm
NINE DIKES ROAD
ARGAM LANE
BURTON FLEMING RD
Rectory Farm
Thwing
CHURCH LA
DUKE'S LA
Eastgate Farm
MAIN STREET

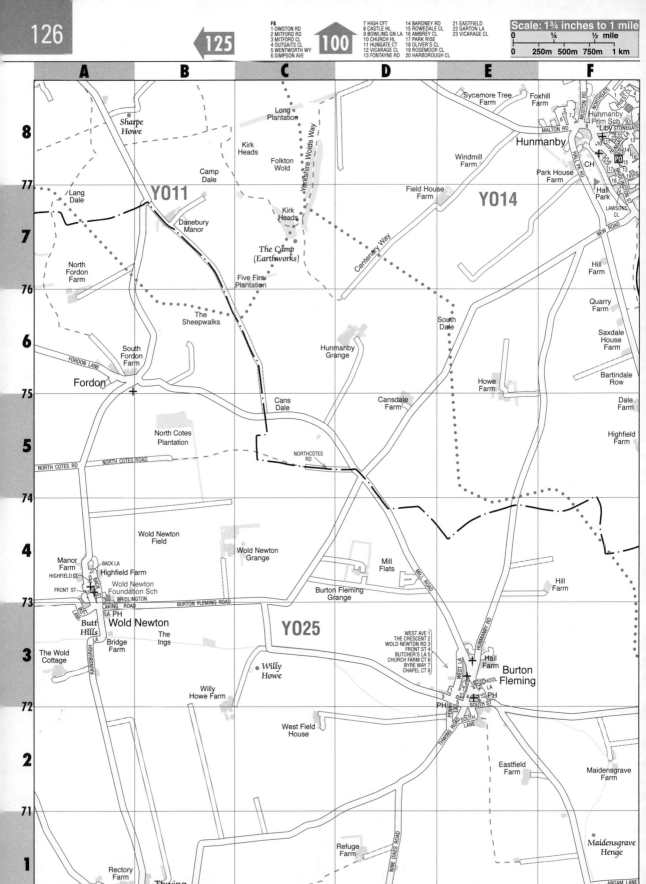

125

Scale: 1¾ inches to 1 mile
0 ¼ ½ mile
0 250m 500m 750m 1 km

A8
1 WRANGHAM DR
2 LENNOX CL
3 BURLYN RD
4 CHERRY RD
5 HAWKE GARTH
6 MANOR GDNS
7 CECIL RD
8 HOWES RD
9 WATSON CL
10 HAMERTON RD
11 HAMERTON CL
12 GRIMSTON RD
13 STRICKLAND RD
14 PERCY RD
15 HAVERCROFT RD
16 COWLINGS CL

101

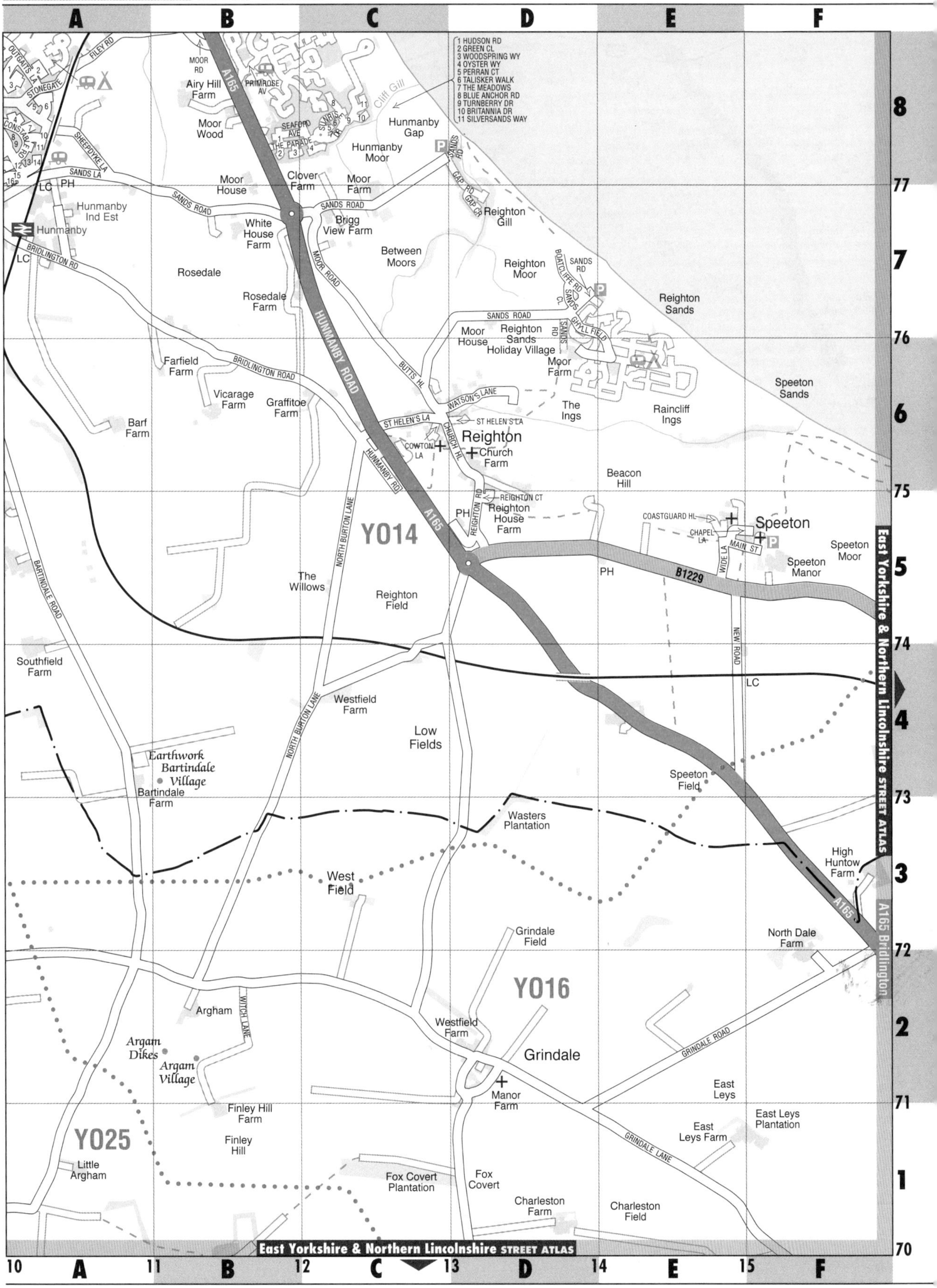

1 HUDSON RD
2 GREEN CL
3 WOODSPRING WY
4 OYSTER WY
5 PERRAN CT
6 TALISKER WALK
7 THE MEADOWS
8 BLUE ANCHOR RD
9 TURNBERRY DR
10 BRITANNIA DR
11 SILVERSANDS WAY
Airy Hill Farm
Moor Wood
Moor House
Hunmanby Ind Est
Hunmanby
Hunmanby Gap
Hunmanby Moor
Clover Farm
Moor Farm
Brigg View Farm
White House Farm
Reighton Gill
Between Moors
Reighton Moor
Rosedale
Rosedale Farm
Reighton Sands
Moor House
Reighton Sands Holiday Village
Moor Farm
Farfield Farm
Vicarage Farm
Graffitoe Farm
Barf Farm
The Ings
Raincliff Ings
Speeton Sands
Reighton
Church Farm
Beacon Hill
Reighton House Farm
Speeton
Speeton Moor
Speeton Manor
YO14
The Willows
Reighton Field
Southfield Farm
Westfield Farm
Low Fields
Earthwork Bartindale Village
Bartindale Farm
Speeton Field
Wasters Plantation
High Huntow Farm
West Field
Grindale Field
North Dale Farm
YO16
Argham
Argam Dikes
Argam Village
Westfield Farm
Grindale
Manor Farm
East Leys
East Leys Plantation
East Leys Farm
Finley Hill Farm
Finley Hill
YO25
Little Argham
Fox Covert Plantation
Fox Covert
Charleston Farm
Charleston Field
HUNMANBY ROAD
A165
B1229
SANDS ROAD
BRIDLINGTON ROAD
MOOR ROAD
NORTH BURTON LANE
BARTINDALE ROAD
GRINDALE ROAD
GRINDALE LANE
WITCH LANE
NEW ROAD
A165 Bridlington

102

E8
1 CROWTREES
2 DOCTOR'S HL
3 EAST VW
4 COLLINGWOOD DR

F8
1 YEWTREE DR
2 HILLSIDE RD
3 HARLEY CL
4 LOW BENTHAM RD
5 THE SIDINGS

Scale: 1¾ inches to 1 mile
0 ¼ ½ mile
0 250m 500m 750m 1 km

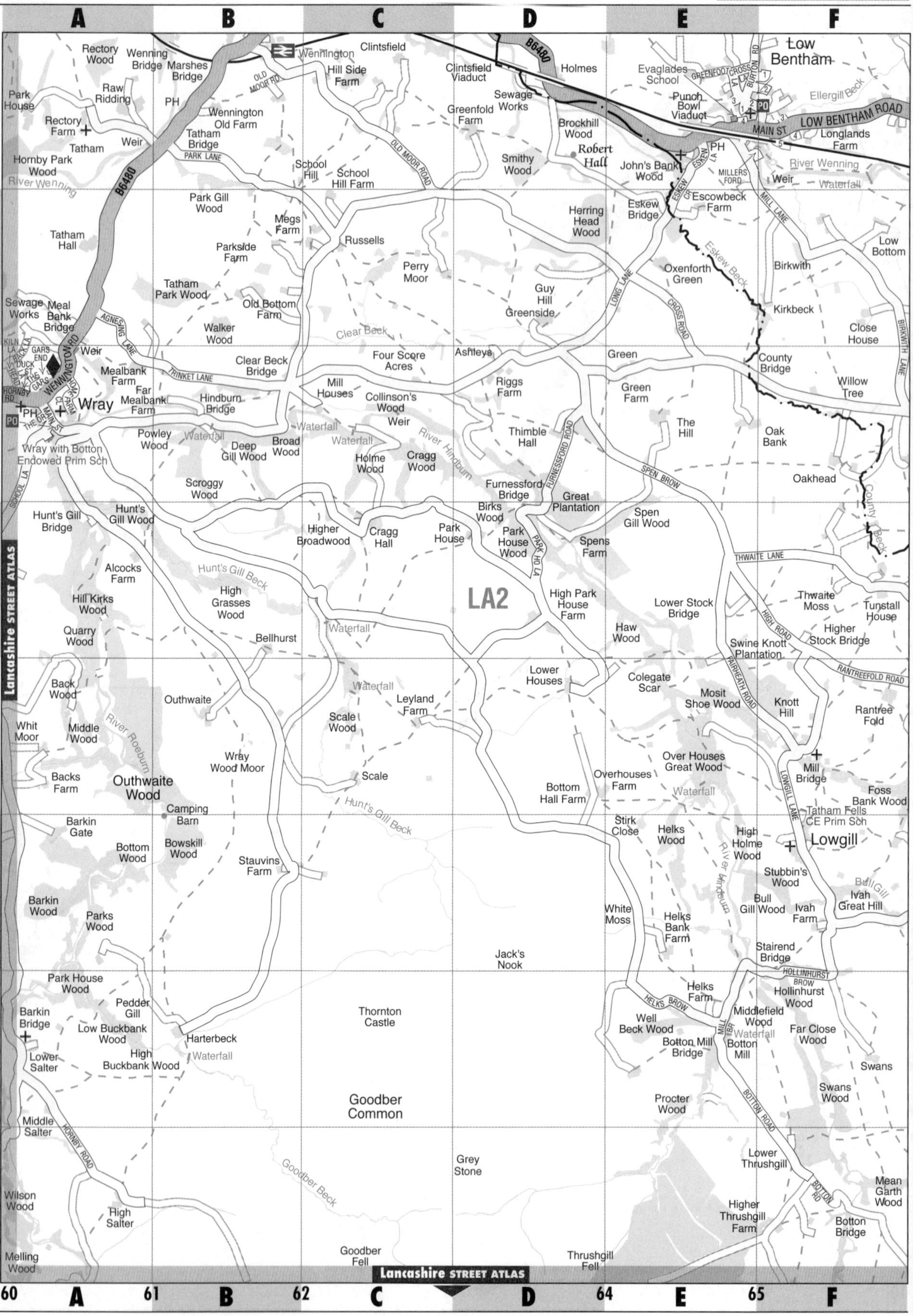

A B C D E F
8 69 7 68 6 67 5 66 4 65 3 64 2 63 1 62
60 61 62 63 64 65
Rectory Wood
Wenning Bridge
Marshes Bridge
Wennington
Clintsfield
Hill Side Farm
Clintsfield Viaduct
B6480
Holmes
Evaglades School
Low Bentham
Park House
Raw Ridding
PH
OLD MOOR RD
Wennington Old Farm
Sewage Works
Greenfold Farm
Punch Bowl Viaduct
Ellergill Beck
Rectory Farm
Tatham
Tatham Bridge
PARK LANE
Weir
Brockhill Wood
Robert Hall
LOW BENTHAM ROAD
MAIN ST
Longlands Farm
GREENFOOT
CROSS LA
BURTON RD
PO
Hornby Park Wood
River Wenning
School Hill
School Hill Farm
OLD MOOR ROAD
Smithy Wood
John's Bank Wood
ESKEW
MILLERS FORD
Waterfall
Park Gill Wood
Megs Farm
Herring Head Wood
Eskew Bridge
Escowbeck Farm
MILL LANE
Tatham Hall
Parkside Farm
Russells
Low Bottom
Perry Moor
Oxenforth Green
Eskew Beck
Birkwith
Tatham Park Wood
Guy Hill
LONG LANE
CROSS ROAD
Sewage Works
Meal Bank Bridge
Old Bottom Farm
Greenside
Kirkbeck
Close House
AGNES GHYLL LANE
Walker Wood
Clear Beck
BIRKWITH LANE
KILN LA
GARS END
DUCK ST
THE GARS
HEAD
WENNINGTON RD
Clear Beck Bridge
Four Score Acres
Ashleys
Green
County Bridge
TRINKET LANE
Mealbank Farm
HORNBY RD
Mill Houses
Riggs Farm
Green Farm
Willow Tree
Wray
Far Mealbank Farm
Hindburn Bridge
Collinson's Wood
PH
THE DR
MAIN ST
HOME FARM CL
Weir
River Hindburn
The Hill
Oak Bank
Powley Wood
Waterfall
Thimble Hall
FURNESSFORD ROAD
Deep Gill Wood
Broad Wood
Holme Wood
Cragg Wood
Wray with Botton Endowed Prim Sch
SPEN BROW
Oakhead
SCHOOL LA
Scroggy Wood
Furnessford Bridge
Great Plantation
County Beck
Hunt's Gill Bridge
Hunt's Gill Wood
Birks Wood
Spen Gill Wood
Higher Broadwood
Cragg Hall
Park House
Park House Wood
PARK HO LA
Spens Farm
Alcocks Farm
THWAITE LANE
Hunt's Gill Beck
LA2
High Park House Farm
Thwaite Moss
Tunstall House
Hill Kirks Wood
High Grasses Wood
Lower Stock Bridge
Quarry Wood
Waterfall
Haw Wood
Higher Stock Bridge
Bellhurst
HIGH ROAD
Swine Knott Plantation
RANTREEFOLD ROAD
Back Wood
Lower Houses
Colegate Scar
Waterfall
Outhwaite
Leyland Farm
Mosit Shoe Wood
FAIRHEATH ROAD
Knott Hill
Rantree Fold
Whit Moor
Middle Wood
River Roeburn
Scale Wood
Over Houses Great Wood
Mill Bridge
Wray Wood Moor
Backs Farm
Outhwaite Wood
Scale
Bottom Hall Farm
Overhouses Farm
Waterfall
LOWGILL LANE
Foss Bank Wood
Camping Barn
Hunt's Gill Beck
Tatham Fells CE Prim Sch
Barkin Gate
Stirk Close
Helks Wood
High Holme Wood
Lowgill
Bottom Wood
Bowskill Wood
River Hindburn
Stauvins Farm
Stubbin's Wood
Bull Gill
Barkin Wood
White Moss
Helks Bank Farm
Bull Gill Wood
Ivah Farm
Ivah Great Hill
Parks Wood
Stairend Bridge
Jack's Nook
HOLLINHURST BROW
Park House Wood
Helks Farm
Hollinhurst Wood
Pedder Gill
HELKS BROW
Thornton Castle
Middlefield Wood
Barkin Bridge
Low Buckbank Wood
Well Beck Wood
MILL BRI
Waterfall
Far Close Wood
Harterbeck
Botton Mill Bridge
Botton Mill
Lower Salter
High Buckbank Wood
Waterfall
Swans
Goodber Common
Procter Wood
Swans Wood
BOTTON ROAD
Middle Salter
HORNBY ROAD
Grey Stone
Lower Thrushgill
Goodber Beck
Mean Garth Wood
BOTTON RD
Wilson Wood
Higher Thrushgill Farm
Botton Bridge
High Salter
Melling Wood
Goodber Fell
Thrushgill Fell
Lancashire STREET ATLAS

Scale: 1¾ inches to 1 mile
0 ¼ ½ mile
0 250m 500m 750m 1 km

A7
1 MAYFIELD RD
2 MILLHOLME DR
3 HOLME PK
4 HILLCROFT

A8
1 WESLEY CL
2 GOODENBER CRES
3 BANKS WY
4 BANKS RI
5 TWEED ST
6 GRASMERE DR
7 KING ST
8 LAKEBER CL
9 GAS HO LA
10 WESLEY WY
11 BUTTERBERGH
12 HIGHCROFT

103
130

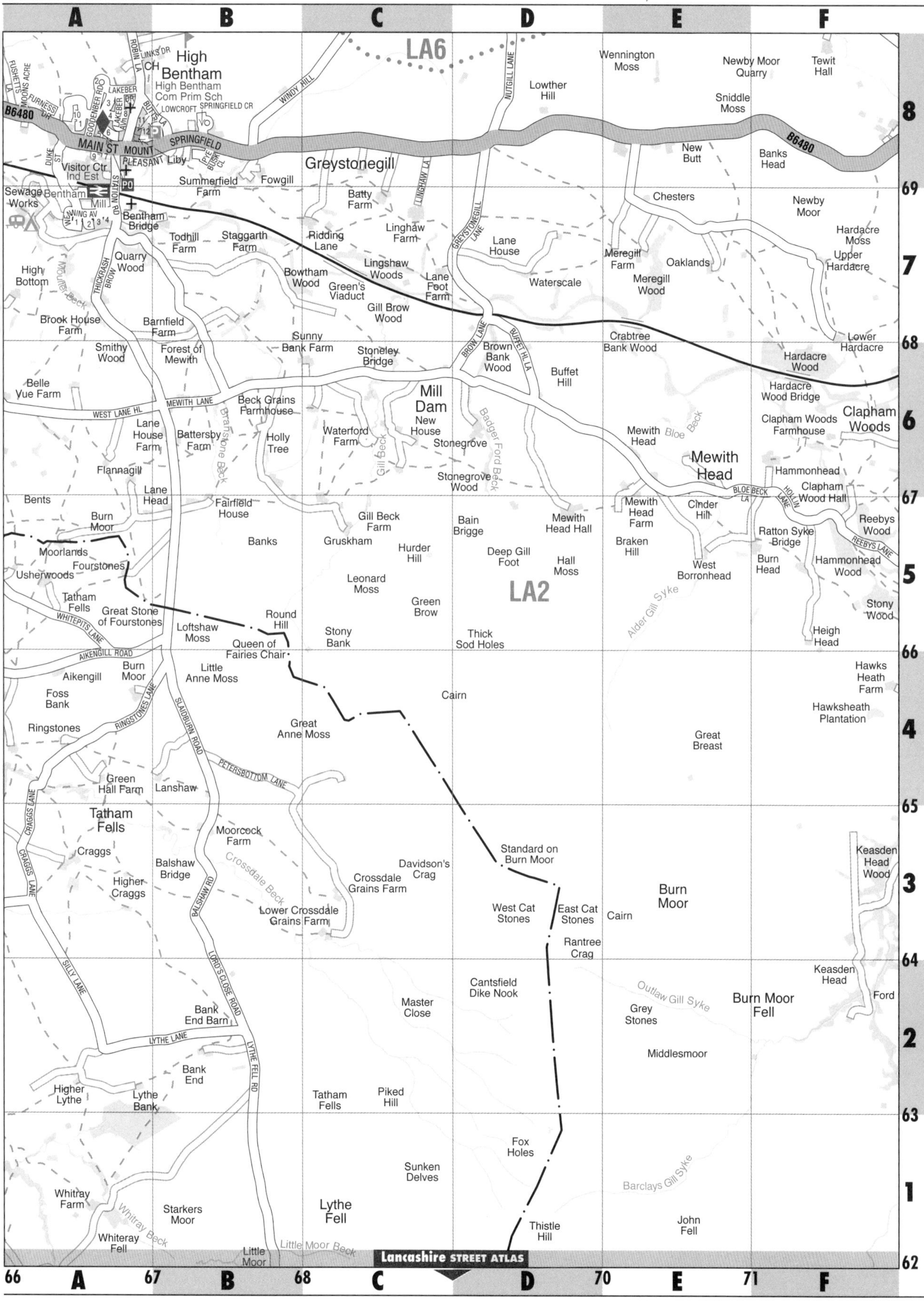

130

129

C8
1 THE GREEN
2 CLAPDALE WY
3 CROSS HAW LA

104

Scale: 1¾ inches to 1 mile
0 ¼ ½ mile
0 250m 500m 750m 1 km

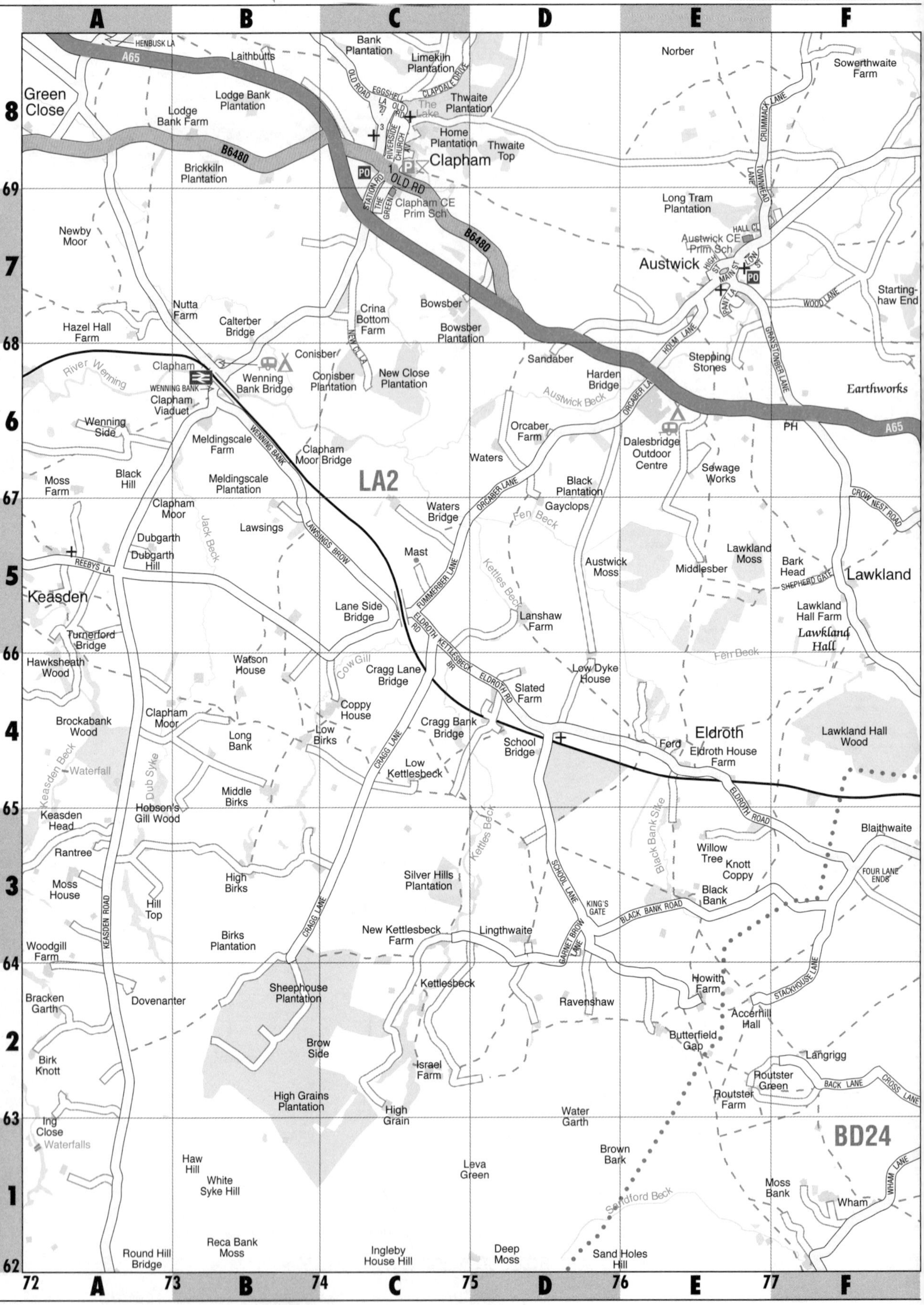
A
B
C
D
E
F
HENBUSK LA
A65
Laithbutts
Bank Plantation
Limekiln Plantation
Norber
Sowerthwaite Farm
Green Close
Lodge Bank Plantation
Lodge Bank Farm
OLD ROAD
EGGSHELL LA
CLAPDALE DRIVE
Thwaite Plantation
The Lake
CRUMMACK LANE
8
B6480
RIVERSIDE
CHURCH AV
Home Plantation
Thwaite Top
Clapham
Brickkiln Plantation
OLD RD
STATION RD
THE GREEN
PO
Clapham CE Prim Sch
69
Long Tram Plantation
LANE
TOWNHEAD
HALL CL
Austwick CE Prim Sch
Newby Moor
7
Austwick
HIGH ST
MAIN ST
PO
PANT LA
Starting-haw End
WOOD LANE
Crina Bottom Farm
Bowsber
Nutta Farm
Hazel Hall Farm
Calterber Bridge
Bowsber Plantation
NEW CL LA
GRAYSTONGER LANE
68
Conisber
Sandaber
HOLM LANE
Stepping Stones
River Wenning
Clapham
WENNING BANK
Clapham Viaduct
Wenning Bank Bridge
Conisber Plantation
New Close Plantation
Harden Bridge
Austwick Beck
Earthworks
6
Wenning Side
Meldingscale Farm
WENNING BANK
Orcaber Farm
ORCABER LA
Dalesbridge Outdoor Centre
PH
A65
Clapham Moor Bridge
Waters
Sewage Works
Moss Farm
Black Hill
Meldingscale Plantation
LA2
Black Plantation
67
Clapham Moor
ORCABER LANE
Waters Bridge
Gayclops
Fen Beck
CROW NEST ROAD
Jack Beck
Lawsings
Dubgarth
Dubgarth Hill
LAWSINGS BROW
Mast
Kettles Beck
Lawkland Moss
Austwick Moss
Middlesber
Bark Head
SHEPHERD GATE
Lawkland
5
REEBYS LA
Keasden
FUMMERBER LANE
Lane Side Bridge
ELDROTH RD
Lanshaw Farm
Lawkland Hall Farm
Turnerford Bridge
KETTLESBECK BR
Lawkland Hall
66
Hawksheath Wood
Watson House
Cow Gill
Cragg Lane Bridge
ELDROTH RD
Low Dyke House
Fen Beck
Slated Farm
Coppy House
Clapham Moor
Brockabank Wood
Cragg Bank Bridge
Lawkland Hall Wood
4
Long Bank
Low Birks
CRAGG LANE
School Bridge
Eldroth
Ford
Eldroth House Farm
Keasden Beck
Waterfall
Dub Syke
Low Kettlesbeck
Middle Birks
ELDROTH ROAD
65
Keasden Head
Hobson's Gill Wood
Kettles Beck
Black Bank Syke
Blaithwaite
Rantree
Willow Tree
Knott Coppy
FOUR LANE ENDS
3
Moss House
High Birks
Silver Hills Plantation
SCHOOL LANE
Black Bank
KING'S GATE
BLACK BANK ROAD
Hill Top
KEASDEN ROAD
CRAGG LANE
Lingthwaite
New Kettlesbeck Farm
Birks Plantation
GARNET BROW LANE
Woodgill Farm
64
Kettlesbeck
Howith Farm
STACKHOUSE LANE
Bracken Garth
Dovenanter
Sheephouse Plantation
Ravenshaw
Accerhill Hall
2
Butterfield Gap
Brow Side
Langrigg
Birk Knott
Israel Farm
Routster Green
BACK LANE
CROSS LANE
Routster Farm
High Grains Plantation
High Grain
Water Garth
63
Ing Close
Waterfalls
BD24
Brown Bark
Haw Hill
White Syke Hill
Leva Green
WHAM LANE
1
Moss Bank
Sandford Beck
Wham
Round Hill Bridge
Reca Bank Moss
Ingleby House Hill
Deep Moss
Sand Holes Hill
62
72
73
74
75
76
77

129

Scale: 1¾ inches to 1 mile
0 ¼ ½ mile
0 250m 500m 750m 1 km

105
132

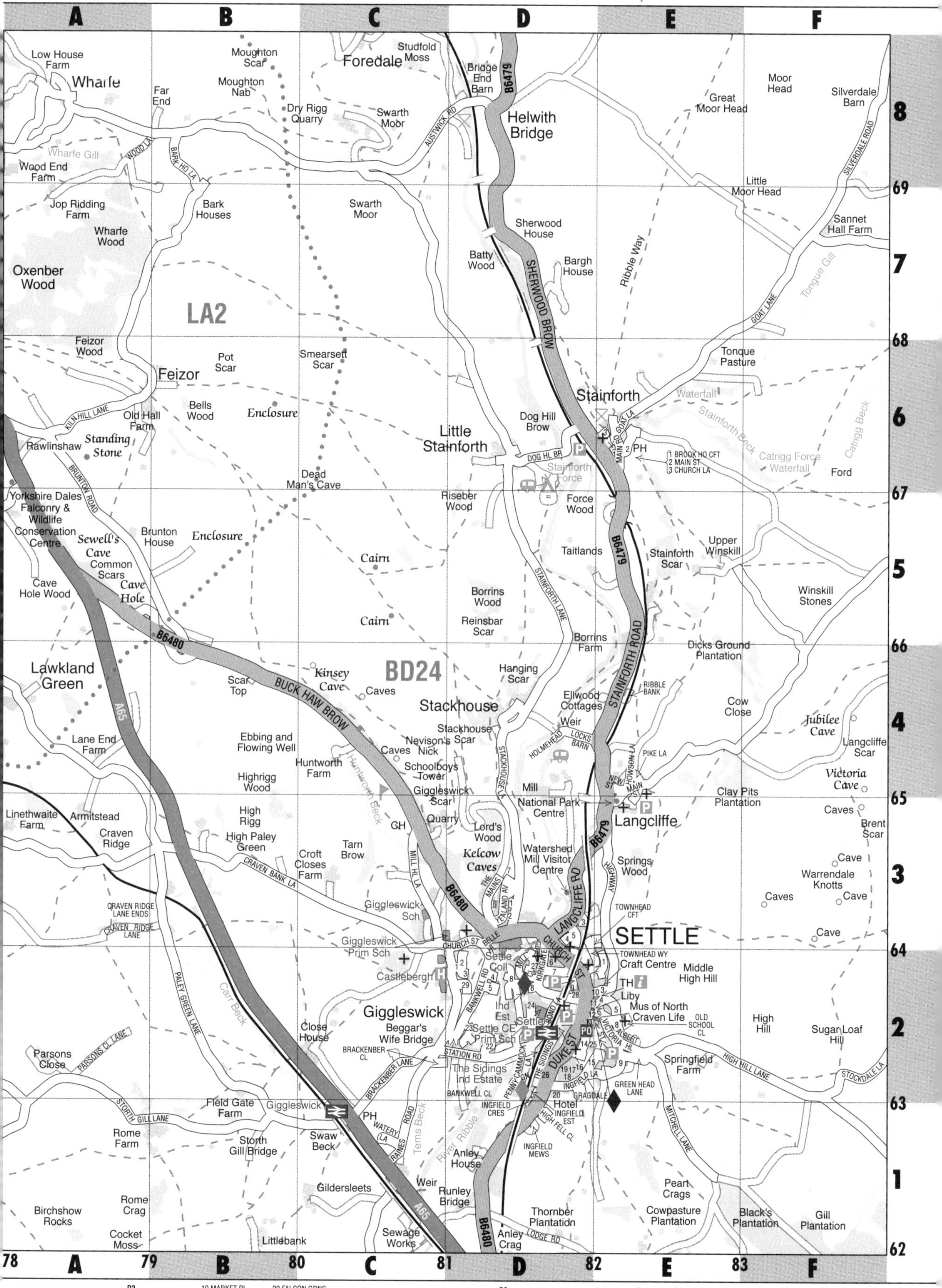

D2
1 BUCKS LA
2 TEMS ST
3 TEMS SIDE
4 KENDALMANS
5 RIVERSDALE
6 TILLMAN CL
7 MARSHFIELD RD
8 KINGS MILL LA
9 WHITEFRIARS CT
10 MARKET PL
11 CHEAPSIDE
12 CHAPEL ST
13 CRAGDALE
14 HIGH HL GR ST
15 LWR GREENFOOT
16 BIRCHWOOD CL
17 FALCON CL
18 LONGDALE AVE
19 DELANEY CL
20 FALCON GDNS
21 SOWARTH FIELD
22 SANDHOLME CL
23 LORD'S CL
24 NEW RD
25 GROVE PK GDNS
26 IVY DENE CL
27 MIDDLE CRAVEN RD
28 BISHOPDALE CT
29 RAINES GARTH

153

D3
1 MAINSFIELD CL
2 MAINSFIELD RISE
3 BARREL SYKES
4 NORTHFIELDS AVE
5 NORTHFIELDS CRES
6 BR END YD
7 MEADOW RI
8 ELMHURST GDNS

132

E2
1 TOWN HEAD AVE
2 TOWNHEAD
3 CONSTITUTION HL
4 CASTLE HL
5 CASTLEBERGH LA
6 HIGH ST
7 CHAPEL SQ
8 SCHOOL HL
9 COMMERCIAL ST

131
106

Scale: 1¾ inches to 1 mile
0 ¼ ½ mile
0 250m 500m 750m 1 km

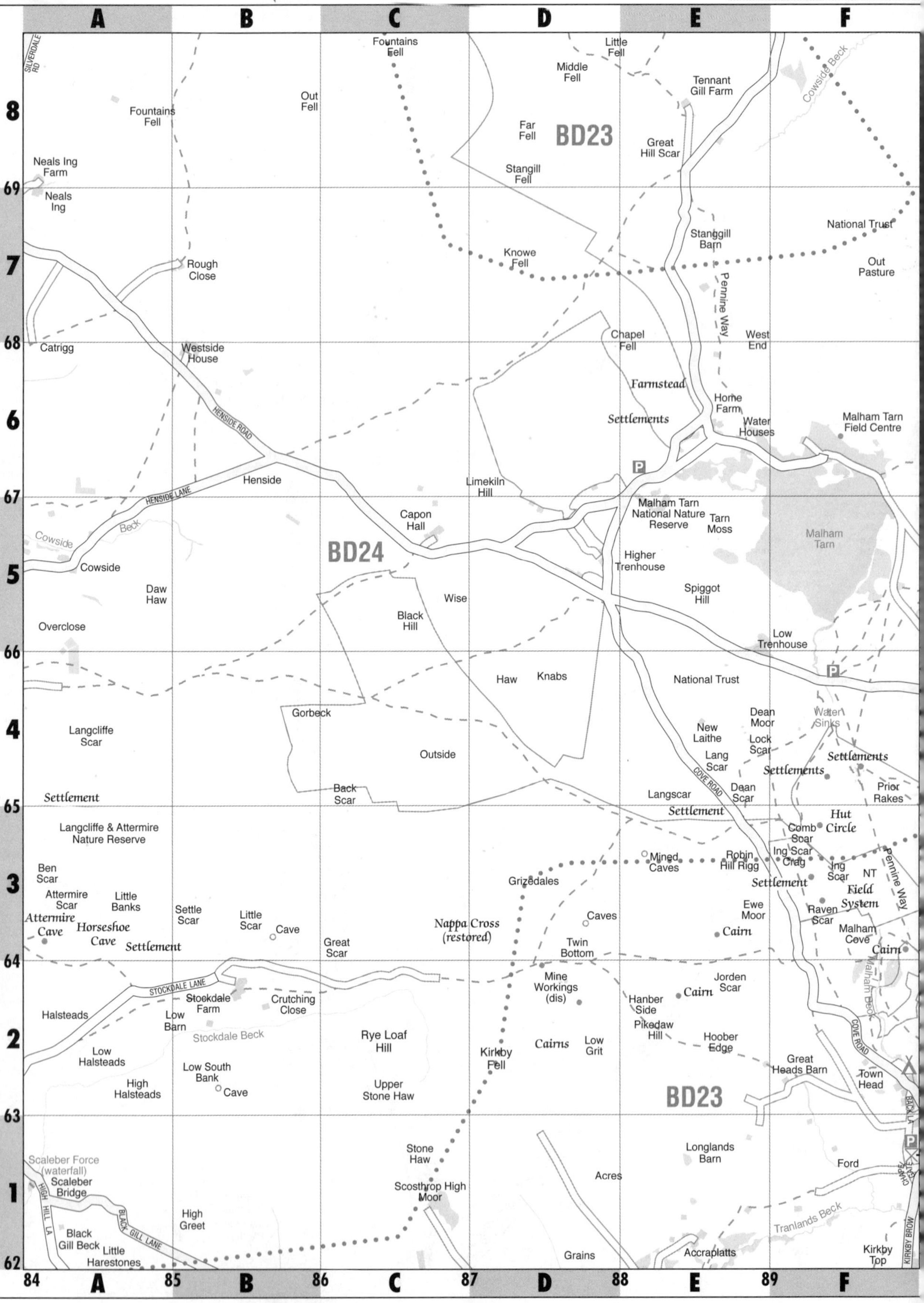
A
B
C
D
E
F
SILVERDALE RD
Fountains Fell
Little Fell
Middle Fell
Tennant Gill Farm
Cowside Beck
Out Fell
Fountains Fell
Far Fell
BD23
Great Hill Scar
Neals Ing Farm
Neals Ing
Stangill Fell
Stanggill Barn
National Trust
Rough Close
Knowe Fell
Out Pasture
Pennine Way
Catrigg
Westside House
Chapel Fell
West End
Farmstead
Home Farm
HENSIDE ROAD
Settlements
Water Houses
Malham Tarn Field Centre
Henside
Limekiln Hill
HENSIDE LANE
Malham Tarn National Nature Reserve
Tarn Moss
Capon Hall
Cowside
Beck
BD24
Malham Tarn
Cowside
Higher Trenhouse
Daw Haw
Wise
Spiggot Hill
Black Hill
Overclose
Low Trenhouse
Haw
Knabs
National Trust
Gorbeck
Dean Moor
Water Sinks
New Laithe
Langcliffe Scar
Lock Scar
Outside
Lang Scar
Settlements
COVE ROAD
Settlements
Back Scar
Dean Scar
Prior Rakes
Settlement
Langscar
Settlement
Hut Circle
Langcliffe & Attermire Nature Reserve
Comb Scar
Ing Scar Crag
Robin Hill Rigg
Mined Caves
Ben Scar
Grizedales
Ing Scar
NT
Settlement
Pennine Way
Attermire Scar
Little Banks
Field System
Ewe Moor
Settle Scar
Little Scar
Raven Scar
Attermire Cave
Horseshoe Cave
Caves
Nappa Cross (restored)
Cave
Cairn
Malham Cove
Settlement
Great Scar
Twin Bottom
Cairn
Malham Beck
STOCKDALE LANE
Mine Workings (dis)
Jorden Scar
Stockdale Farm
Crutching Close
Hanber Side
Cairn
Halsteads
Low Barn
Pikedaw Hill
Stockdale Beck
Rye Loaf Hill
COVE ROAD
Low Grit
Hoober Edge
Cairns
Kirkby Fell
Low Halsteads
Low South Bank
Great Heads Barn
Town Head
High Halsteads
Cave
Upper Stone Haw
BD23
BACK LA
Stone Haw
Longlands Barn
Scaleber Force (waterfall)
Ford
Scaleber Bridge
Acres
CHAPEL GATE
HIGH HILL LA
Scosthrop High Moor
Tranlands Beck
High Greet
BLACK GILL LANE
Black Gill Beck
Little Harestones
KIRKBY BROW
Kirkby Top
Grains
Accraplatts
8
69
7
68
6
67
5
66
4
65
3
64
2
63
1
62
84
85
86
87
88
89

131
154

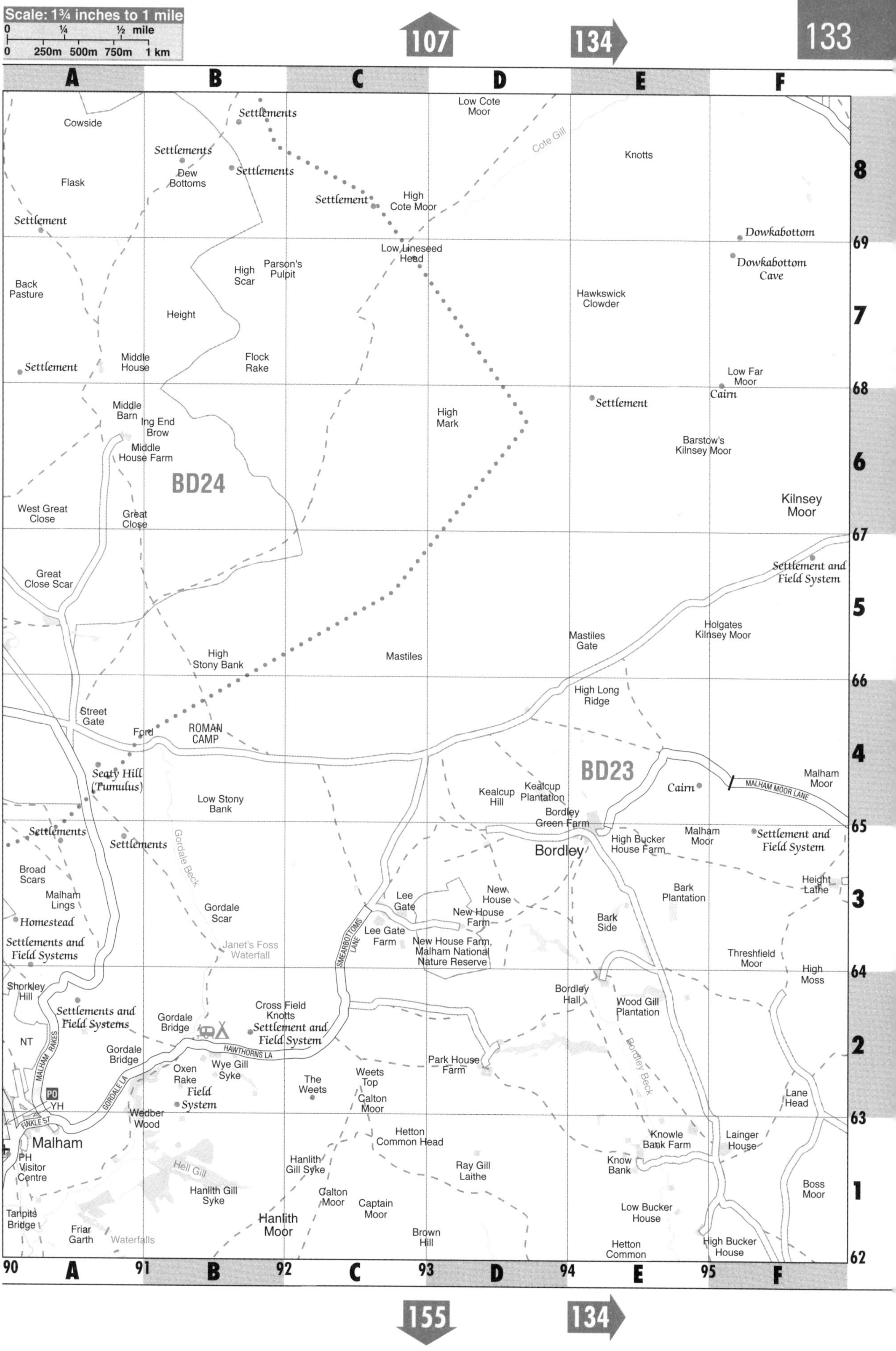
Scale: 1¾ inches to 1 mile
0 ¼ ½ mile
0 250m 500m 750m 1 km
107
134
A B C D E F
Low Cote Moor
Cowside
Settlements
Settlements
Dew Bottoms
Settlements
Cote Gill
Knotts
Flask
Settlement
High Cote Moor
Settlement
Dowkabottom
Dowkabottom Cave
Low Lineseed Head
Back Pasture
High Scar
Parson's Pulpit
Hawkswick Clowder
Height
Middle House
Flock Rake
Settlement
Low Far Moor
Cairn
Settlement
Middle Barn
Ing End Brow
High Mark
Barstow's Kilnsey Moor
Middle House Farm
BD24
Kilnsey Moor
West Great Close
Great Close
Great Close Scar
Settlement and Field System
Holgates Kilnsey Moor
Mastiles Gate
High Stony Bank
Mastiles
High Long Ridge
Street Gate
Ford
ROMAN CAMP
Seaty Hill (Tumulus)
BD23
Malham Moor
Kealcup Hill
Kealcup Plantation
Cairn
MALHAM MOOR LANE
Low Stony Bank
Bordley Green Farm
Settlements
Settlements
Gordale Beck
Bordley
High Bucker House Farm
Malham Moor
Settlement and Field System
Broad Scars
Height Lathe
Malham Lings
Gordale Scar
Lee Gate
New House
Bark Plantation
Homestead
New House Farm
Bark Side
Settlements and Field Systems
Janet's Foss Waterfall
SMEARBOTTOMS LANE
Lee Gate Farm
New House Farm, Malham National Nature Reserve
Threshfield Moor
High Moss
Shorkley Hill
Bordley Hall
Wood Gill Plantation
Settlements and Field Systems
Gordale Bridge
Cross Field Knotts
Settlement and Field System
NT
MALHAM RAKES
Gordale Bridge
HAWTHORNS LA
Park House Farm
Bordley Beck
Oxen Rake
Wye Gill Syke
The Weets
Weets Top
PO
YH
GORDALE LA
Field System
Calton Moor
Lane Head
FINKLE ST
Wedber Wood
Hetton Common Head
Knowle Bank Farm
Lainger House
Malham
PH
Visitor Centre
Hell Gill
Hanlith Gill Syke
Ray Gill Laithe
Know Bank
Hanlith Gill Syke
Calton Moor
Captain Moor
Boss Moor
Low Bucker House
Tarpits Bridge
Friar Garth
Waterfalls
Hanlith Moor
Brown Hill
Hetton Common
High Bucker House
8 69 7 68 6 67 5 66 4 65 3 64 2 63 1 62
90 91 92 93 94 95
155
134

133
108

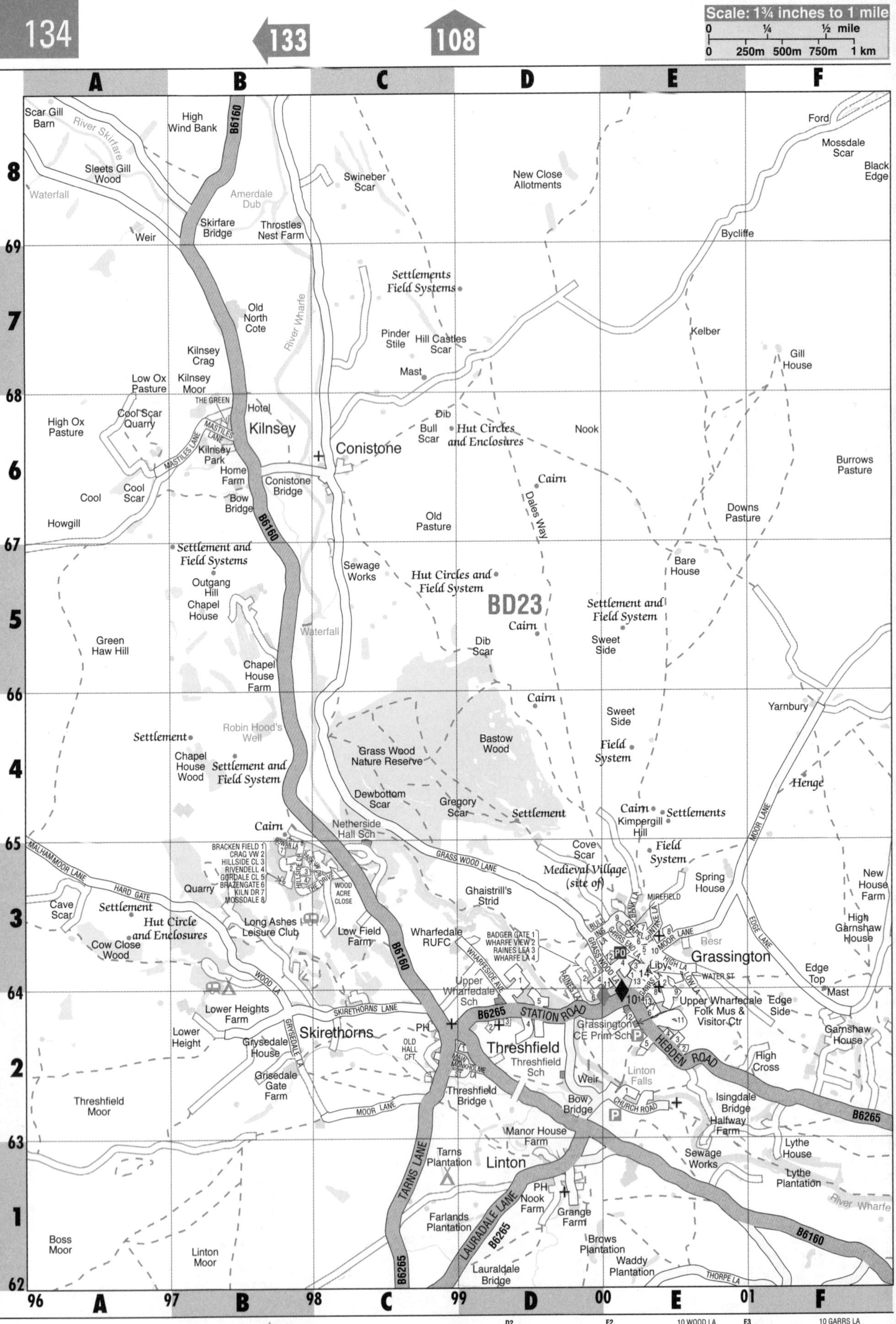
Scale: 1¾ inches to 1 mile
0 ¼ ½ mile
0 250m 500m 750m 1 km
A B C D E F
Scar Gill Barn
River Skirfare
High Wind Bank
B6160
Sleets Gill Wood
Waterfall
Amerdale Dub
Swineber Scar
New Close Allotments
Ford
Mossdale Scar
Black Edge
Skirfare Bridge
Throstles Nest Farm
Weir
Bycliffe
Settlements Field Systems
Old North Cote
River Wharfe
Pinder Stile
Hill Castles Scar
Kelber
Gill House
Kilnsey Crag
Mast
Low Ox Pasture
Kilnsey Moor
THE GREEN
Hotel
High Ox Pasture
Cool Scar Quarry
Kilnsey
MASTILES LANE
Dib
Bull Scar
Hut Circles and Enclosures
Nook
Conistone
Kilnsey Park
Home Farm
Conistone Bridge
Burrows Pasture
Cairn
Cool
Cool Scar
Bow Bridge
Downs Pasture
Howgill
Old Pasture
Dales Way
Settlement and Field Systems
Sewage Works
Hut Circles and Field System
Bare House
Outgang Hill
Chapel House
BD23
Settlement and Field System
Green Haw Hill
Waterfall
Dib Scar
Sweet Side
Chapel House Farm
Yarnbury
Settlement
Robin Hood's Well
Grass Wood Nature Reserve
Bastow Wood
Field System
Chapel House Wood
Henge
Dewbottom Scar
Gregory Scar
Kimpergill Hill
Settlements
Netherside Hall Sch
MOOR LANE
MALHAM MOOR LANE
BRACKEN FIELD 1
CRAG VW 2
HILLSIDE CL 3
RIVENDELL 4
GORDALE CL 5
BRAZENGATE 6
KILN DR 7
MOSSDALE 8
GRASS WOOD LANE
Cove Scar
Medieval Village (site of)
Spring House
New House Farm
HARD GATE
Quarry
WOOD ACRE CLOSE
Ghaistrill's Strid
MIREFIELD
Cave Scar
Hut Circle and Enclosures
Long Ashes Leisure Club
Low Field Farm
Wharfedale RUFC
BADGER GATE 1
WHARFE VIEW 2
RAINES LEA 3
WHARFE LA 4
Resr
High Garnshaw House
Cow Close Wood
Grassington
EDGE LANE
Edge Top
WOOD LA
WHARFESIDE AVE
WATER ST
Mast
Upper Wharfedale Sch
Upper Wharfedale Folk Mus & Visitor Ctr
Edge Side
Lower Heights Farm
SKIRETHORNS LANE
B6265
STATION ROAD
Grassington CE Prim Sch
Garnshaw House
Lower Height
Skirethorns
PH
Grysedale House
GRYSEDALE LA
OLD HALL CFT
Threshfield
HEBDEN ROAD
Threshfield Sch
High Cross
Grisedale Gate Farm
Linton Falls
Weir
Threshfield Bridge
Bow Bridge
Isingdale Bridge
Threshfield Moor
MOOR LANE
CHURCH ROAD
Halfway Farm
Manor House Farm
Lythe House
Tarns Plantation
Linton
Sewage Works
TARNS LANE
Lythe Plantation
Nook Farm
Grange Farm
River Wharfe
LAURADALE LANE
Farlands Plantation
Boss Moor
Linton Moor
Brows Plantation
Waddy Plantation
Lauraldale Bridge
THORPE LA
96 97 98 99 00 01
62 63 64 65 66 67 68 69

133
156

D2
1 HOME CROFT
2 PIECE CROFT
3 DOCTOR LAITHE
4 PIECE FIELDS
5 HIGH BANK
6 RAINES MEADOWS

E2
1 LINTON FALLS
2 AYNHAM CL
3 BARDEN FELL VIEW
4 FELL VIEW SQ
5 SEBDER LA
6 SPRINGFIELD RD
7 SPRINGFIELD CT
8 GILLS FOLD
9 SCAR FIELD
10 WOOD LA
11 HARDY MDWS
12 ACRE LANE
13 BROUGHTON
14 PLETTS FOLD

E3
1 SUMMERS FOLD
2 SCAR ST
3 BROWNS FOLD
4 MOODY STY LA
5 CHAMBER END FOLD
6 CHAPEL FOLD
7 CHAPEL CROFT
8 MOOR CROFT
9 HIGHCROFT
10 GARRS LA
11 SOUTH WOOD LA
12 WISP HILL
13 MAIN ST
14 Gemini Studios Art Gallery

109
136

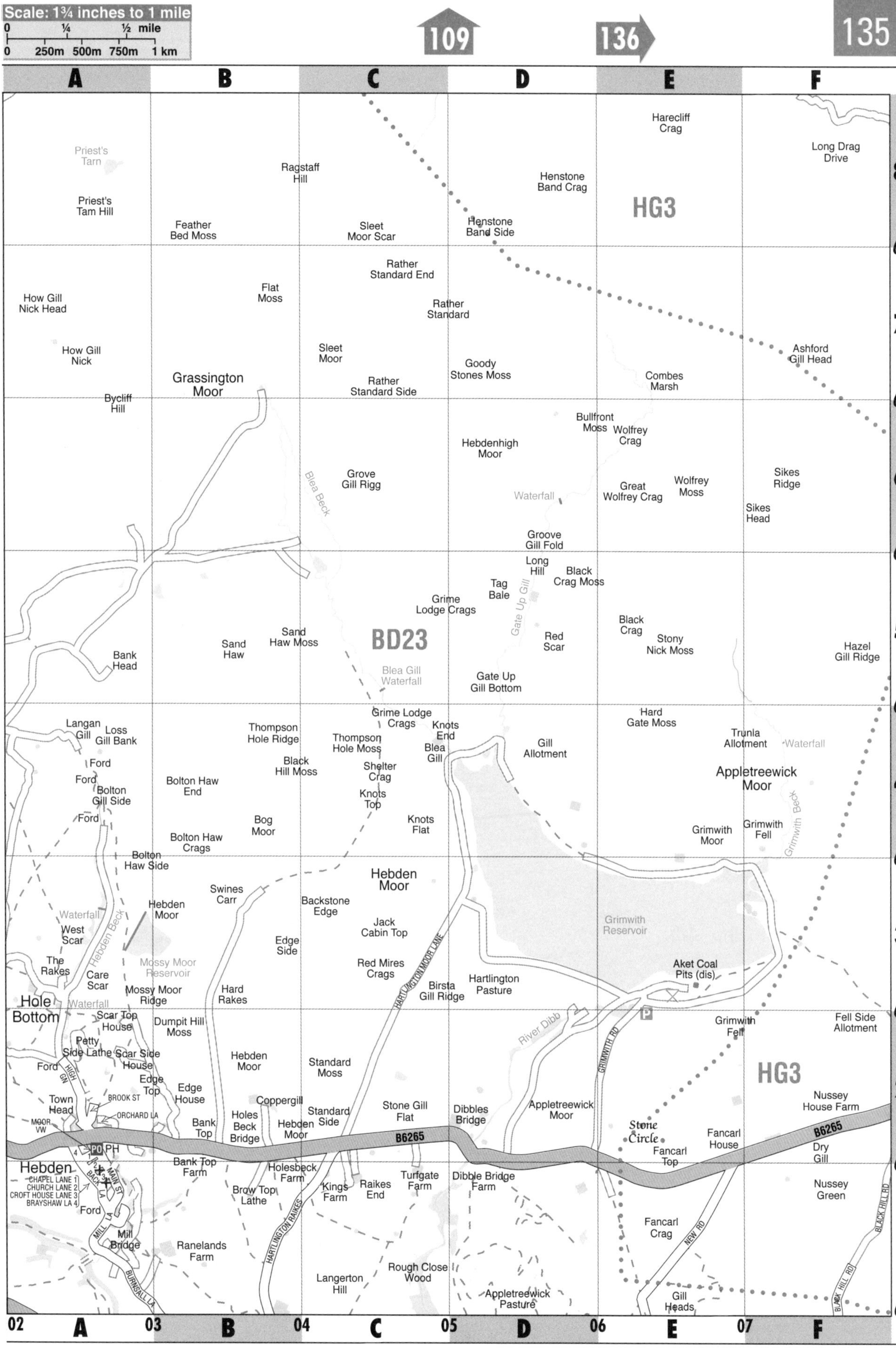

157
136

135
110

Scale: 1¾ inches to 1 mile
0 ¼ ½ mile
0 250m 500m 750m 1 km

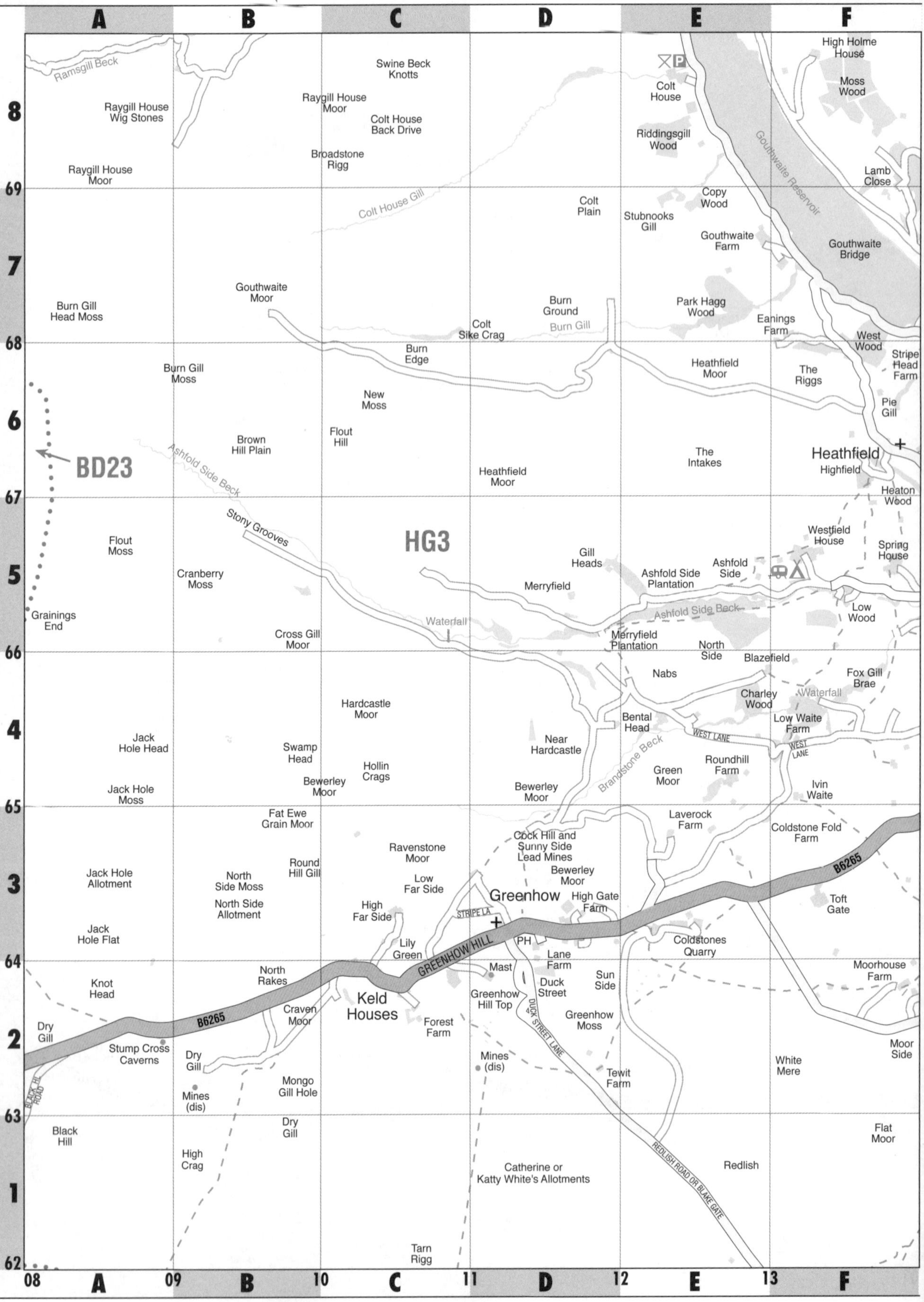

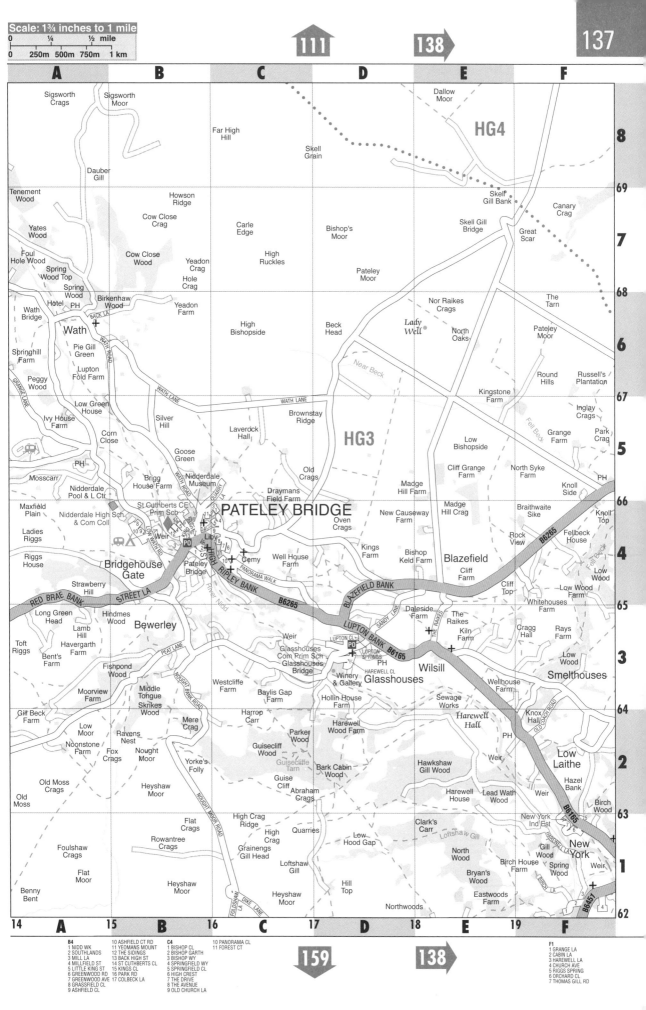

Scale: 1¾ inches to 1 mile
0 ¼ ½ mile
0 250m 500m 750m 1 km

111
138

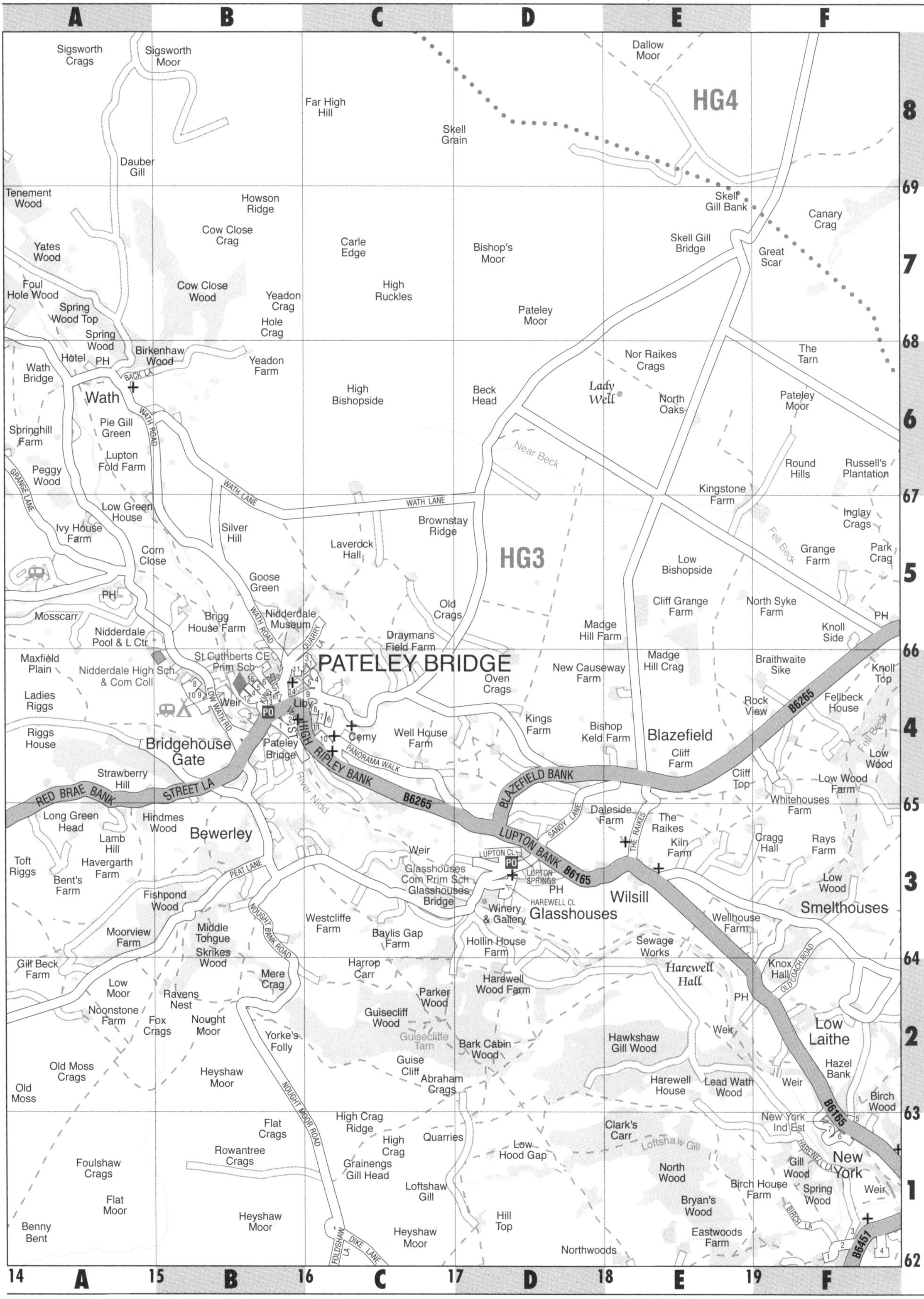
A
B
C
D
E
F
Sigsworth Crags
Sigsworth Moor
Far High Hill
Skell Grain
Dallow Moor
HG4
Dauber Gill
Tenement Wood
Howson Ridge
Cow Close Crag
Carle Edge
Bishop's Moor
Skell Gill Bank
Skell Gill Bridge
Canary Crag
Great Scar
Yates Wood
Foul Hole Wood
Spring Wood Top
Cow Close Wood
Yeadon Crag
Hole Crag
High Ruckles
Pateley Moor
Spring Wood
Hotel
PH
Birkenhaw Wood
BACK LA
Yeadon Farm
Wath Bridge
Wath
High Bishopside
Beck Head
Lady Well
Nor Raikes Crags
North Oaks
The Tarn
Pateley Moor
Pie Gill Green
WATH ROAD
Springhill Farm
Near Beck
Round Hills
Russell's Plantation
Lupton Fold Farm
Peggy Wood
GRANGE LANE
WATH LANE
Kingstone Farm
Low Green House
WATH LANE
Brownstay Ridge
Inglay Crags
Ivy House Farm
Silver Hill
Laverock Hall
HG3
Low Bishopside
Fell Beck
Grange Farm
Park Crag
Corn Close
Goose Green
PH
Old Crags
Cliff Grange Farm
North Syke Farm
Mosscarr
Brigg House Farm
Nidderdale Museum
WATH ROAD
QUARRY LA
Madge Hill Farm
Knoll Side
PH
Nidderdale Pool & L Ctr
Draymans Field Farm
Maxfield Plain
St Cuthberts CE Prim Sch
PATELEY BRIDGE
Madge Hill Crag
Braithwaite Sike
Knoll Top
Nidderdale High Sch & Com Coll
Oven Crags
New Causeway Farm
Ladies Riggs
LOW WATH RD
Weir
KING ST
Liby
Rock View
B6265
Fellbeck House
PO
WEST
HIGH
Cemy
Well House Farm
Kings Farm
Bishop Keld Farm
Blazefield
Fell Beck
Riggs House
Bridgehouse Gate
Pateley Bridge
PANORAMA WALK
Cliff Farm
Low Wood
Strawberry Hill
RIPLEY BANK
River Nidd
BLAZEFIELD BANK
Cliff Top
Low Wood Farm
RED BRAE BANK
STREET LA
B6265
Whitehouses Farm
Long Green Head
Hindmes Wood
Daleside Farm
THE RAIKES
The Raikes
Lamb Hill
Bewerley
LUPTON BANK
SANDY LANE
Cragg Hall
Rays Farm
Toft Riggs
Havergarth Farm
Weir
LUPTON CL
Kiln Farm
Bent's Farm
PEAT LANE
Glasshouses Com Prim Sch
PO
LUPTON SPRINGS
B6165
Low Wood
Glasshouses Bridge
PH
Wilsill
Fishpond Wood
HAREWELL CL
Smelthouses
Westcliffe Farm
Winery & Gallery
Glasshouses
Wellhouse Farm
Moorview Farm
Middle Tongue
NOUGHT BANK ROAD
Baylis Gap Farm
Hollin House Farm
Sewage Works
Skrikes Wood
OLD COACH ROAD
Gill Beck Farm
Harrop Carr
Harewell Hall
Knox Hall
Mere Crag
Harewell Wood Farm
Low Moor
Ravens Nest
Parker Wood
PH
Noonstone Farm
Fox Crags
Nought Moor
Guisecliff Wood
Low Laithe
Yorke's Folly
Guisecliffe Tarn
Bark Cabin Wood
Hawkshaw Gill Wood
Weir
Old Moss Crags
Heyshaw Moor
Guise Cliff
Hazel Bank
Old Moss
Abraham Crags
Harewell House
Lead Wath Wood
Weir
NOUGHT MOOR ROAD
Birch Wood
Flat Crags
High Crag Ridge
Clark's Carr
New York Ind Est
B6165
High Crag
Quarries
Low Hood Gap
Loftshaw Gill
Foulshaw Crags
Rowantree Crags
Grainengs Gill Head
North Wood
Gill Wood
HAREWELL LA
New York
Birch House Farm
Spring Wood
Weir
Flat Moor
Loftshaw Gill
Bryan's Wood
BIRCH LA
Heyshaw Moor
Hill Top
Heyshaw Moor
Eastwoods Farm
Benny Bent
FOLDSHAW LA
DIKE LANE
Northwoods
B6451
8
69
7
68
6
67
5
66
4
65
3
64
2
63
1
62
14
15
16
17
18
19

B4
1 NIDD WK
2 SOUTHLANDS
3 MILL LA
4 MILLFIELD ST
5 LITTLE KING ST
6 GREENWODD RD
7 GREENWOOD AVE
8 GRASSFIELD CL
9 ASHFIELD CL
10 ASHFIELD CT RD
11 YEOMANS MOUNT
12 THE SIDINGS
13 BACK HIGH ST
14 ST CUTHBERTS CL
15 KINGS CL
16 PARK RD
17 COLBECK LA

C4
1 BISHOP CL
2 BISHOP GARTH
3 BISHOP WY
4 SPRINGFIELD WY
5 SPRINGFIELD CL
6 HIGH CREST
7 THE DRIVE
8 THE AVENUE
9 OLD CHURCH LA
10 PANORAMA CL
11 FOREST CT

F1
1 GRANGE LA
2 CABIN LA
3 HAREWELL LA
4 CHURCH AVE
5 RIGGS SPRING
6 ORCHARD CL
7 THOMAS GILL RD

159
138

Scale: 1¾ inches to 1 mile
0 ¼ ½ mile
0 250m 500m 750m 1 km

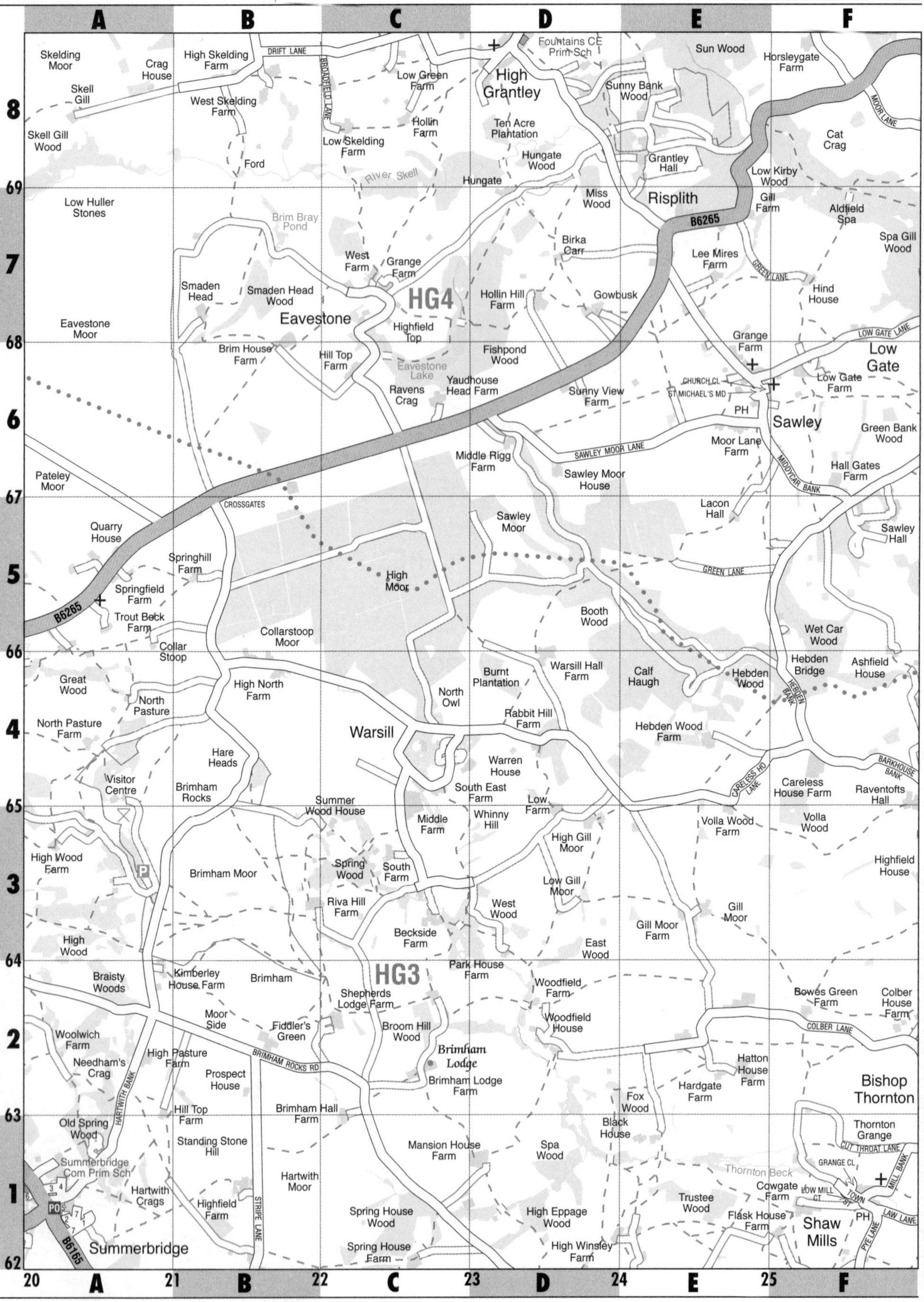
A B C D E F
8 69 7 68 6 67 5 66 4 65 3 64 2 63 1 62
20 21 22 23 24 25
Skelding Moor
Crag House
High Skelding Farm
DRIFT LANE
BROADFIELD LANE
Fountains CE Prim Sch
Sun Wood
Horsleygate Farm
Skell Gill
West Skelding Farm
Low Green Farm
High Grantley
Sunny Bank Wood
MOOR LANE
Skell Gill Wood
Hollin Farm
Ten Acre Plantation
Cat Crag
Low Skelding Farm
Hungate Wood
Grantley Hall
Ford
River Skell
Hungate
Low Kirby Wood
Low Huller Stones
Miss Wood
Risplith
Gill Farm
Aldfield Spa
Brim Bray Pond
B6265
Spa Gill Wood
Birka Carr
West Farm
Grange Farm
Lee Mires Farm
Smaden Head
Smaden Head Wood
HG4
Hollin Hill Farm
Gowbusk
GREEN LANE
Hind House
Eavestone
Eavestone Moor
Highfield Top
Grange Farm
LOW GATE LANE
Brim House Farm
Hill Top Farm
Fishpond Wood
Low Gate
Eavestone Lake
CHURCH CL
Low Gate Farm
Ravens Crag
Yaudhouse Head Farm
Sunny View Farm
ST MICHAEL'S MD
PH
Sawley
Green Bank Wood
Moor Lane Farm
SAWLEY MOOR LANE
Middle Rigg Farm
Sawley Moor House
MIDDYCAR BANK
Hall Gates Farm
Pateley Moor
CROSSGATES
Lacon Hall
Sawley Moor
Quarry House
Sawley Hall
Springhill Farm
GREEN LANE
High Moor
Springfield Farm
B6265
Trout Beck Farm
Booth Wood
Collarstoop Moor
Wet Car Wood
Collar Stoop
Great Wood
Burnt Plantation
Warsill Hall Farm
Calf Haugh
Hebden Bridge
Hebden Wood
Ashfield House
High North Farm
North Owl
HEBDEN BANK
North Pasture
North Pasture Farm
Rabbit Hill Farm
Hebden Wood Farm
Warsill
Hare Heads
Warren House
BARKHOUSE BANK
CARELESS HO LANE
Careless House Farm
Raventofts Hall
Visitor Centre
Brimham Rocks
Summer Wood House
South East Farm
Low Farm
Middle Farm
Whinny Hill
Volla Wood Farm
Volla Wood
High Wood Farm
High Gill Moor
Highfield House
P
Brimham Moor
Spring Wood
South Farm
Low Gill Moor
Riva Hill Farm
West Wood
Gill Moor
Beckside Farm
Gill Moor Farm
High Wood
East Wood
Braisty Woods
Kimberley House Farm
Brimham
HG3
Park House Farm
Woodfield Farm
Bowes Green Farm
Colber House Farm
Shepherds Lodge Farm
Moor Side
Fiddler's Green
Broom Hill Wood
Woodfield House
COLBER LANE
Woolwich Farm
Brimham Lodge
BRIMHAM ROCKS RD
High Pasture Farm
Needham's Crag
HARTWITH BANK
Prospect House
Brimham Lodge Farm
Hatton House Farm
Hardgate Farm
Bishop Thornton
Fox Wood
Hill Top Farm
Brimham Hall Farm
Black House
Thornton Grange
Old Spring Wood
Standing Stone Hill
Mansion House Farm
Spa Wood
CUT THROAT LANE
Summerbridge Com Prim Sch
GRANGE CL
MILL BANK
Thornton Beck
Hartwith Moor
Hartwith Crags
Cowgate Farm
LOW MILL CT
TOWN ST
Highfield Farm
STRIPE LANE
Trustee Wood
PO
High Eppage Wood
Spring House Wood
Flask House Farm
Shaw Mills
PH
LAW LANE
PYE LANE
Summerbridge
B6165
High Winsley Farm
Spring House Farm

A1
1 WHINBUSH LA
2 THE CRESCENT
3 HARTWITH AVE
4 HARTWITH GN
5 WHINFIELD BWS
6 FOUNDRY LA
7 THE WHINFIELDS

Scale: 1¾ inches to 1 mile
0 ¼ ½ mile
0 250m 500m 750m 1 km

For full street detail of the highlighted area see page 214.
113
140

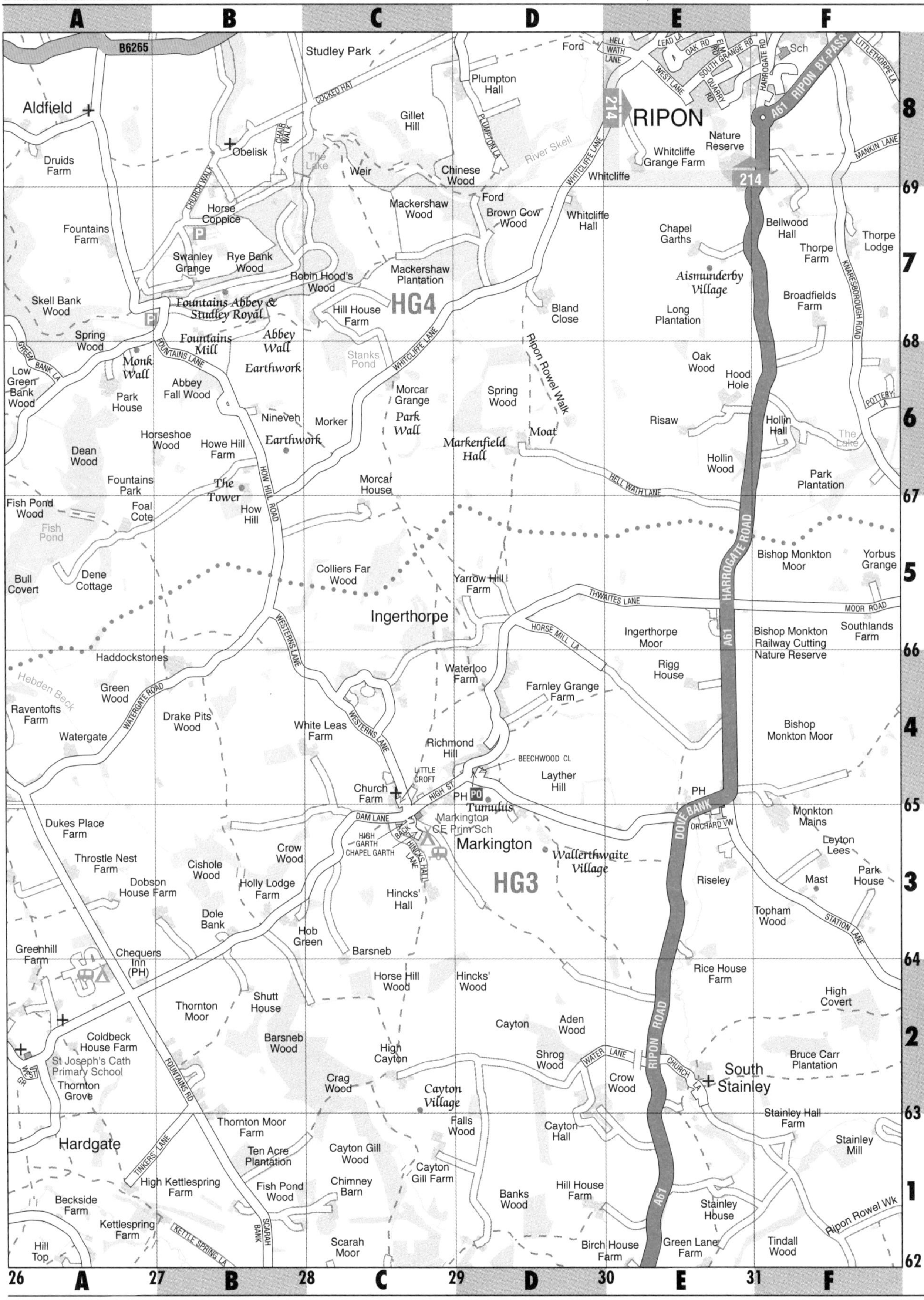

161
140

139
114

Scale: 1¾ inches to 1 mile
0 ¼ ½ mile
0 250m 500m 750m 1 km

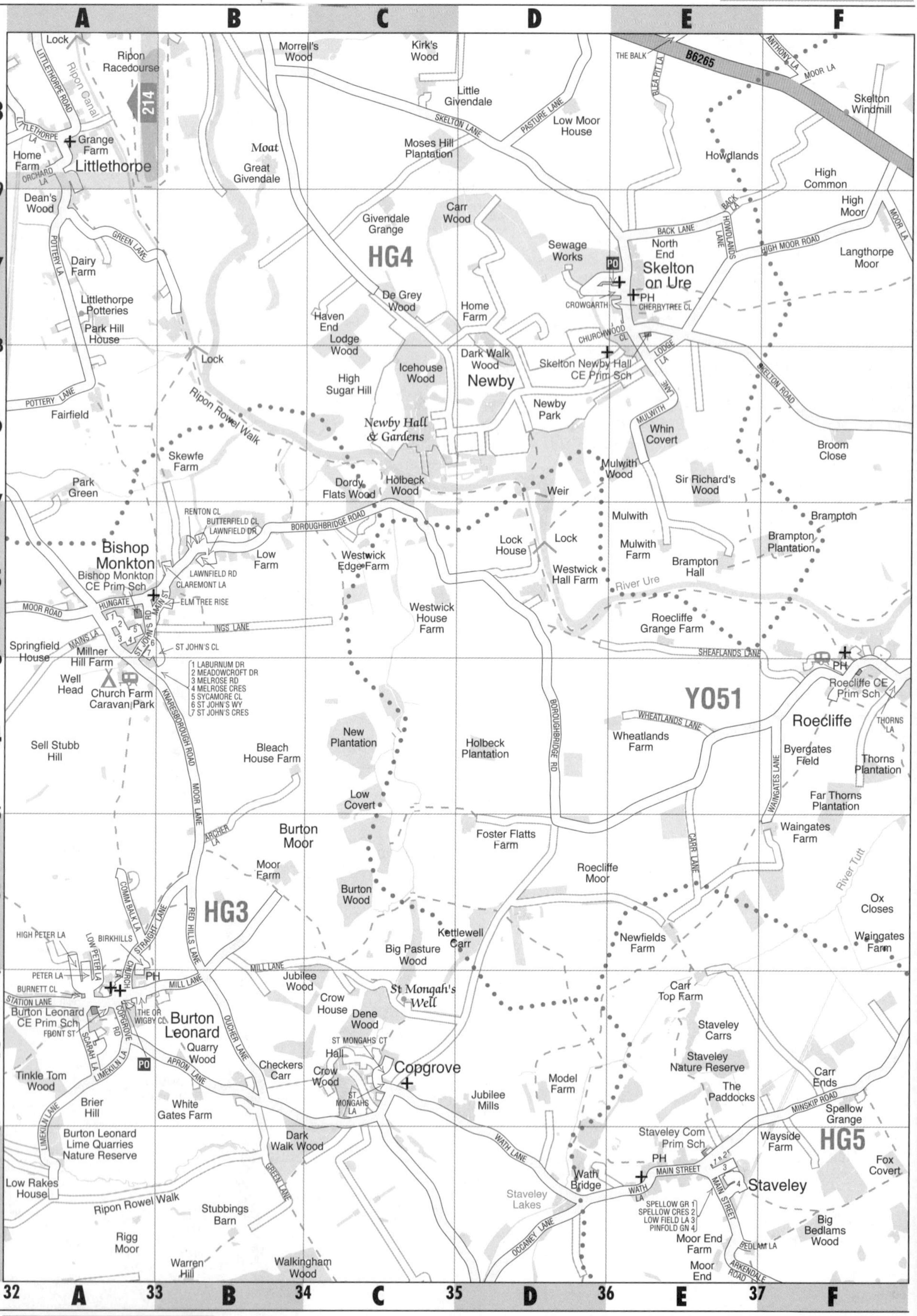
A
B
C
D
E
F
8
69
7
68
6
67
5
66
4
65
3
64
2
63
1
62
32
33
34
35
36
37
Lock
Ripon Racecourse
Ripon Canal
214
LITTLETHORPE ROAD
LITTLETHORPE LA
Grange Farm
Home Farm
Littlethorpe
ORCHARD LA
Dean's Wood
POTTERY LA
GREEN LANE
Dairy Farm
Littlethorpe Potteries
Park Hill House
POTTERY LANE
Fairfield
Park Green
Moat
Great Givendale
Morrell's Wood
Kirk's Wood
Little Givendale
SKELTON LANE
PASTURE LANE
Low Moor House
Moses Hill Plantation
Givendale Grange
Carr Wood
HG4
De Grey Wood
Haven End
Lodge Wood
High Sugar Hill
Icehouse Wood
Home Farm
Dark Walk Wood
Newby
Newby Park
Newby Hall & Gardens
Lock
Ripon Rowel Walk
Skewfe Farm
Dordy Flats Wood
Holbeck Wood
Sewage Works
PO
Skelton on Ure
PH
CROWGARTH
CHERRYTREE CL
CHURCHWOOD CL
Skelton Newby Hall CE Prim Sch
LODGE LA
MULWITH LANE
Whin Covert
Mulwith Wood
Weir
THE BALK
B6265
BLEA PIT LA
ANTHONY LA
MOOR LA
Skelton Windmill
Howdlands
High Common
High Moor
MOOR LA
BACK LA
BACK LANE
HOWDLANDS LANE
North End
HIGH MOOR ROAD
Langthorpe Moor
SKELTON ROAD
Broom Close
Sir Richard's Wood
Brampton
Brampton Plantation
Mulwith
Mulwith Farm
Brampton Hall
Lock House
Lock
Westwick Hall Farm
River Ure
Roecliffe Grange Farm
SHEAFLANDS LANE
PH
Roecliffe CE Prim Sch
YO51
Roecliffe
THORNS LA
WHEATLANDS LANE
Wheatlands Farm
Byergates Field
Thorns Plantation
Far Thorns Plantation
WAINGATES LANE
Waingates Farm
Bishop Monkton
Bishop Monkton CE Prim Sch
RENTON CL
BUTTERFIELD CL
LAWNFIELD DR
BOROUGHBRIDGE ROAD
LAWNFIELD RD
CLAREMONT LA
ELM TREE RISE
INGS LANE
ST JOHN'S CL
MAIN ST
ST JOHN'S RD
HUNGATE
MOOR ROAD
MAINS LA
Springfield House
Millner Hill Farm
Well Head
Church Farm Caravan Park
1 LABURNUM DR
2 MEADOWCROFT DR
3 MELROSE RD
4 MELROSE CRES
5 SYCAMORE CL
6 ST JOHN'S WY
7 ST JOHN'S CRES
KNARESBOROUGH ROAD
Low Farm
Westwick Edge Farm
Westwick House Farm
BOROUGHBRIDGE RD
Sell Stubb Hill
Bleach House Farm
New Plantation
Holbeck Plantation
Low Covert
MOOR LANE
ARCHER LA
Burton Moor
Foster Flatts Farm
CARR LANE
Roecliffe Moor
River Tutt
Ox Closes
Moor Farm
Burton Wood
HG3
COMM BALK LA
STRAIGHT LANE
RED HILLS LANE
Kettlewell Carr
Newfields Farm
Waingates Farm
HIGH PETER LA
BIRKHILLS
LOW PETER LA
PETER LA
BURNETT CL
STATION LANE
CHURCH LA
PH
MILL LANE
Big Pasture Wood
Jubilee Wood
St Mongah's Well
Carr Top Farm
Burton Leonard CE Prim Sch
FRONT ST
SCARAH LA
COPGROVE RD
THE OR WIGBY CL
Burton Leonard
Quarry Wood
OUCHER LANE
Crow House
Dene Wood
ST MONGAHS CT
Hall
Staveley Carrs
Staveley Nature Reserve
Tinkle Tom Wood
LIMEKILN LA
PO
APRON LANE
Checkers Carr
Crow Wood
ST MONGAHS LA
Copgrove
Model Farm
Jubilee Mills
The Paddocks
Carr Ends
Brier Hill
White Gates Farm
MINSKIP ROAD
Spellow Grange
LIMEKILN LANE
Burton Leonard Lime Quarries Nature Reserve
Dark Walk Wood
WATH LANE
Staveley Com Prim Sch
PH
Wayside Farm
HG5
Fox Covert
Low Rakes House
GREEN LANE
Wath Bridge
MAIN STREET
WATH LA
Staveley
Ripon Rowel Walk
Staveley Lakes
SPELLOW GR 1
SPELLOW CRES 2
LOW FIELD LA 3
PINFOLD GN 4
MAIN STREET
Stubbings Barn
OCCANEY LANE
Big Bedlams Wood
Rigg Moor
Moor End Farm
BEDLAM LA
Warren Hill
Walkingham Wood
Moor End
ARKENDALE ROAD

For full street detail of the highlighted area see page 214.
139
162

Scale: 1¾ inches to 1 mile
0 ¼ ½ mile
0 250m 500m 750m 1 km

B5
1 VALUATION LA
2 HORSEFAIR
3 FISHERGATE
4 CHATSWORTH GR
5 HALL SQ
6 HIGH ST
7 BACK LA
8 DRUIDS MEADOW
9 ARROWS TERR
10 ARROWS CRES
11 ST HELENA
12 FLORENCE CT
13 CHURCH MEWS
14 MALLARD WK
15 NEW ROW
16 ST JAMES' MDW
17 KINGFISHER REACH
18 SPRINGFIELD RD
19 SPRINGFIELD DR
20 SPRINGFIELD CL
21 SPRINGFIELD GR
22 SOUTHOLME CL
23 SOUTHOLME WK
24 LANCASTER CT
25 PYSBURY WK
26 SADLERS CT
27 BATTLE CL
28 HARCLAY GARTH
29 CYGNET MEWS

115 142

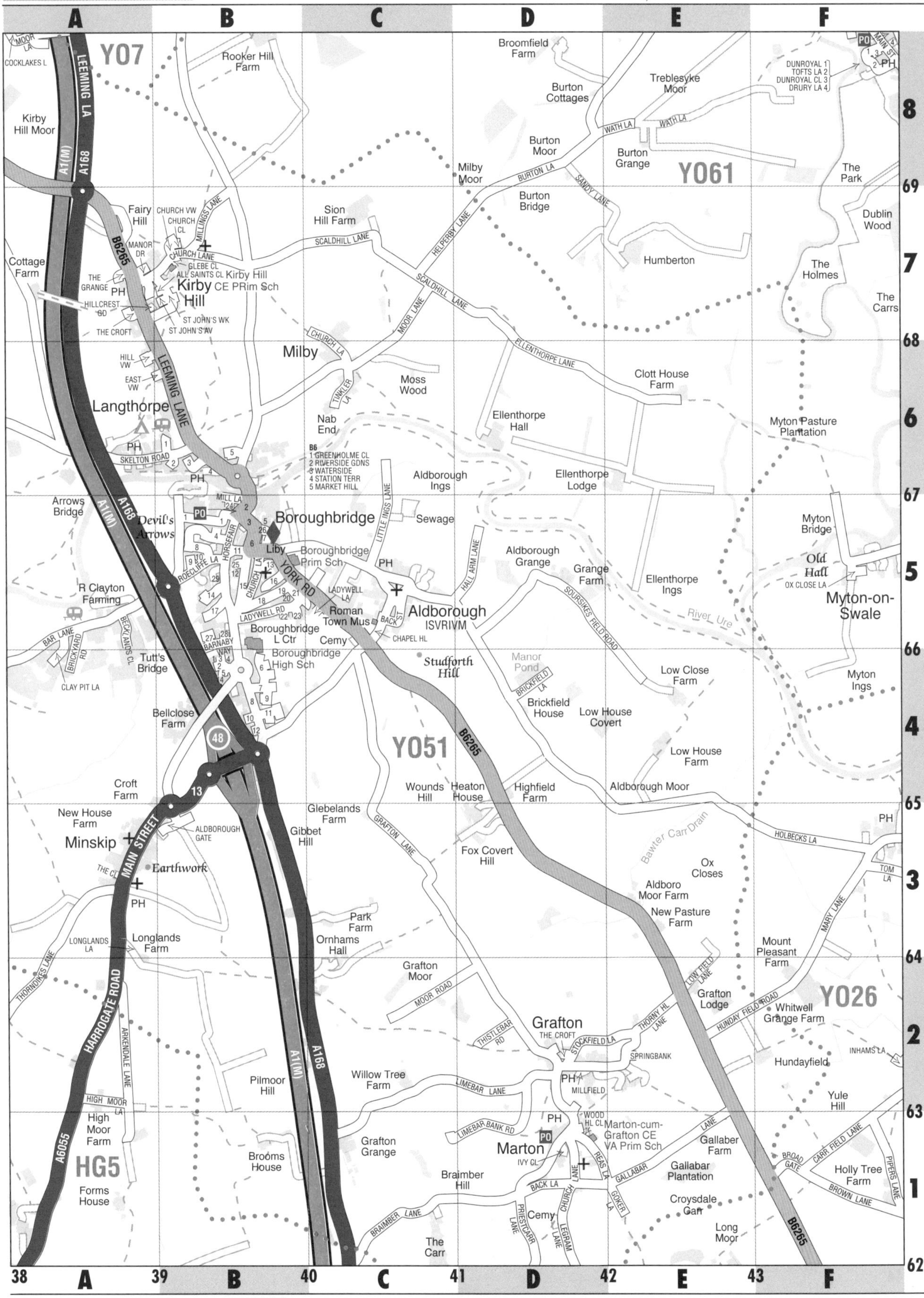

B4
1 LAWSON AVE
2 HAZEL RD
3 FOTHERGILL WY
4 SMITHSON GR
5 CRAVEN WY
6 HUNTERS ROW
7 THE RIDINGS
8 WETHERBY RD
9 HARNESS LA
10 ASHBOURNE RD
11 THE CHASE
12 ASHBOURNE CL
13 ALDBOROUGH GATE
14 ABEL CLOSE

163 142

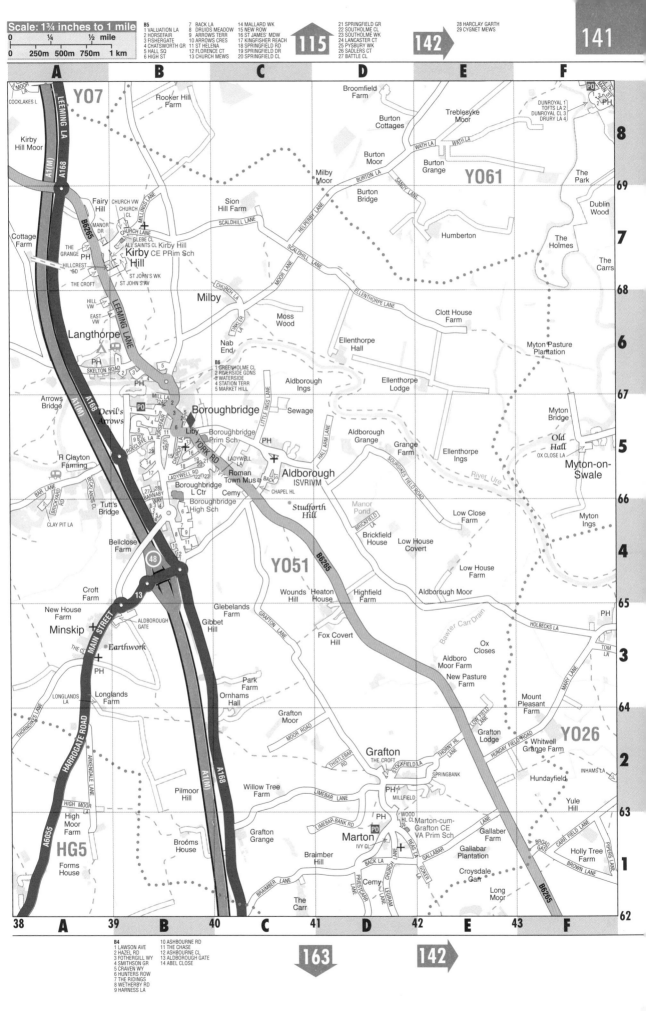

141
116

Scale: 1¾ inches to 1 mile
0 ¼ ½ mile
0 250m 500m 750m 1 km

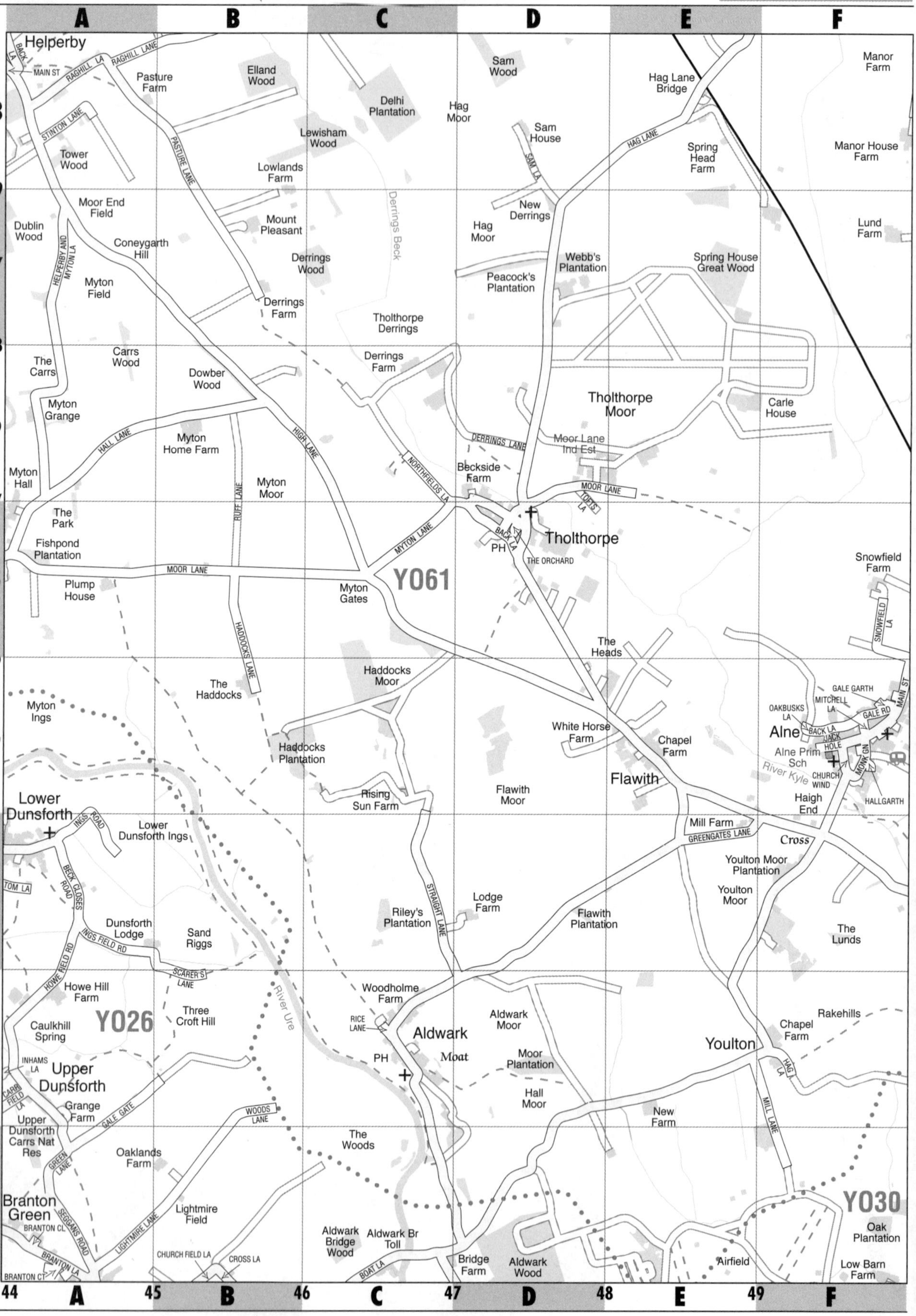

141
164

Scale: 1¾ inches to 1 mile
0 ¼ ½ mile
0 250m 500m 750m 1 km

C8
1 THE OLD ORCHARD
2 SPRING ST
3 THE NURSERIES
4 STONEFIELD LA
5 CHURCH ST
6 THE SPINNEY
7 MARKET PL
8 DROVERS CT
9 STONEFIELD GARTH
10 NEW INN LANE
11 WINDROSS SQ
12 LITTLE LA
13 CHAPEL LA
14 CROFT CL
15 CATHERINE LOVE DR
16 CHASE GARTH RD
17 SHOWFIELD DR
18 TIPLADY CL
19 HUNTERS CL
20 ROSEMARY CT
21 HAMBLETON GARTH
22 WILKINSONS CT
23 GATE GRAINS LA
24 POST OFFICE SLIP
25 BONNEY CFT LA
26 SUSKERS CL
27 DRIFFIELD AVE

117
144

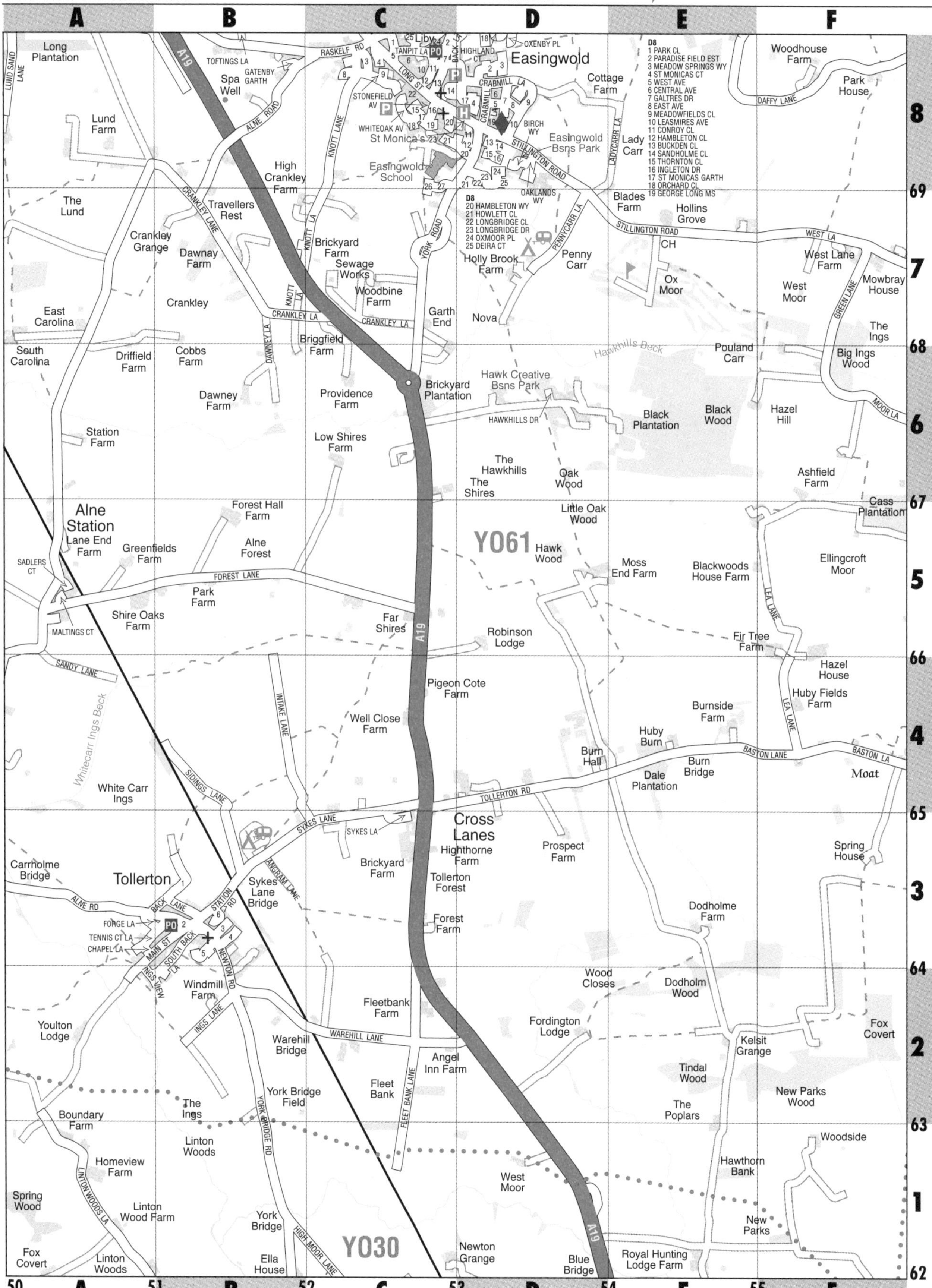

B3
1 MOORLANDS LA
2 THE GREEN
3 KYLE CL
4 HAMBLETON VW
5 CHURCH CL
6 JUBILEE CT
7 STATION CT

165
144

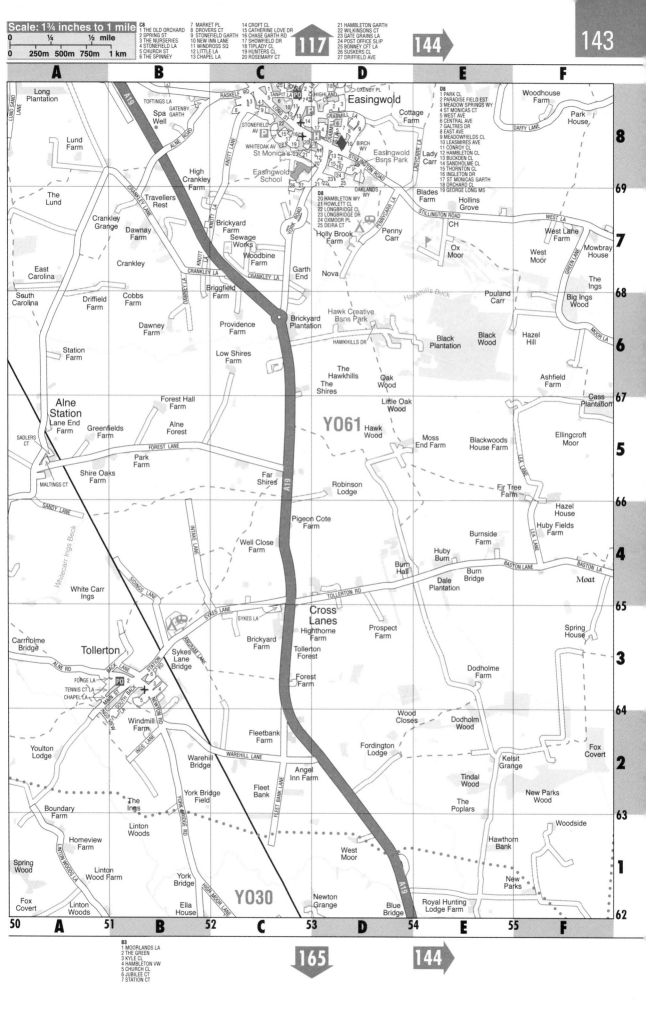

143
118

Scale: 1¾ inches to 1 mile
0 ¼ ½ mile
0 250m 500m 750m 1 km

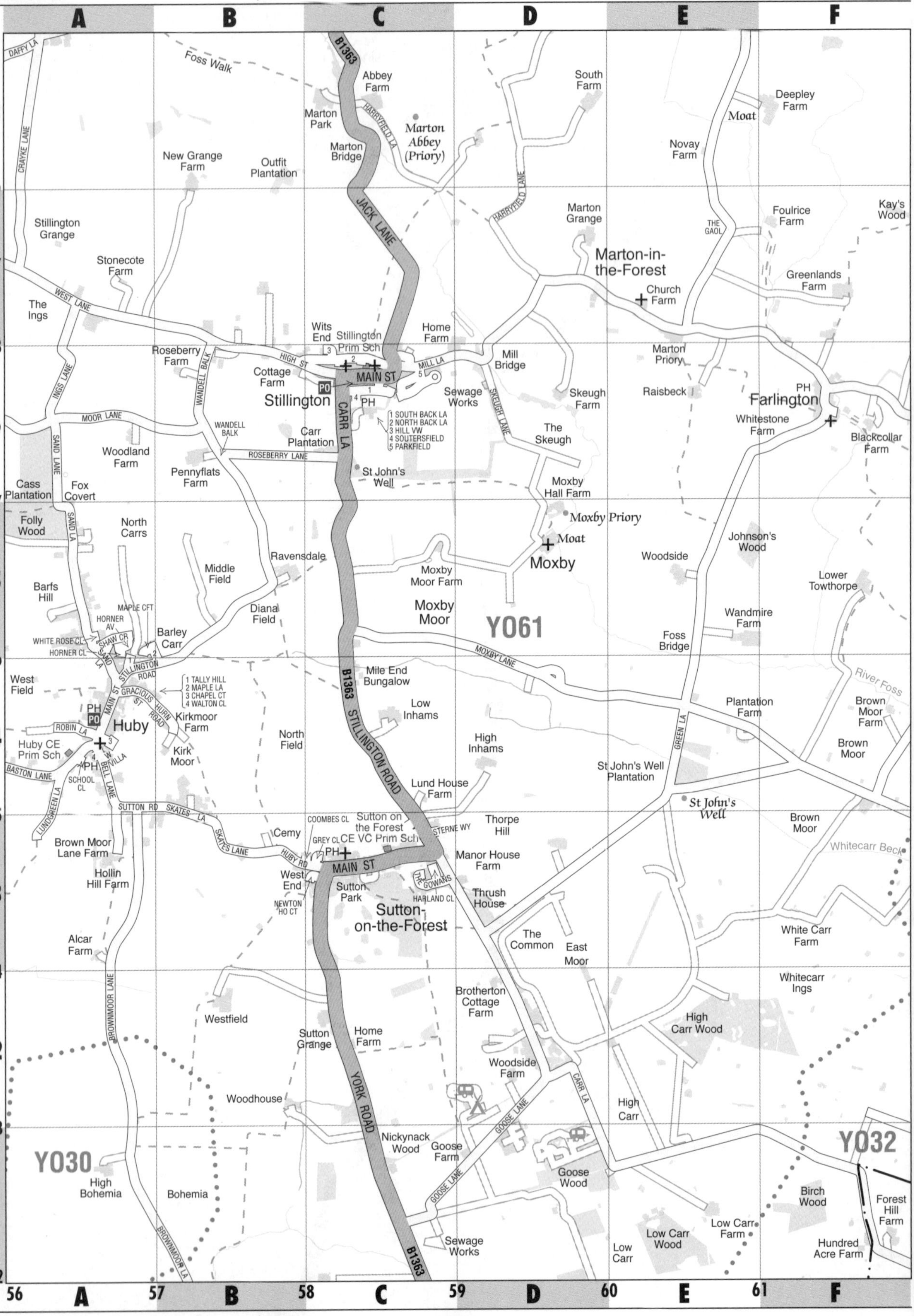

143
166

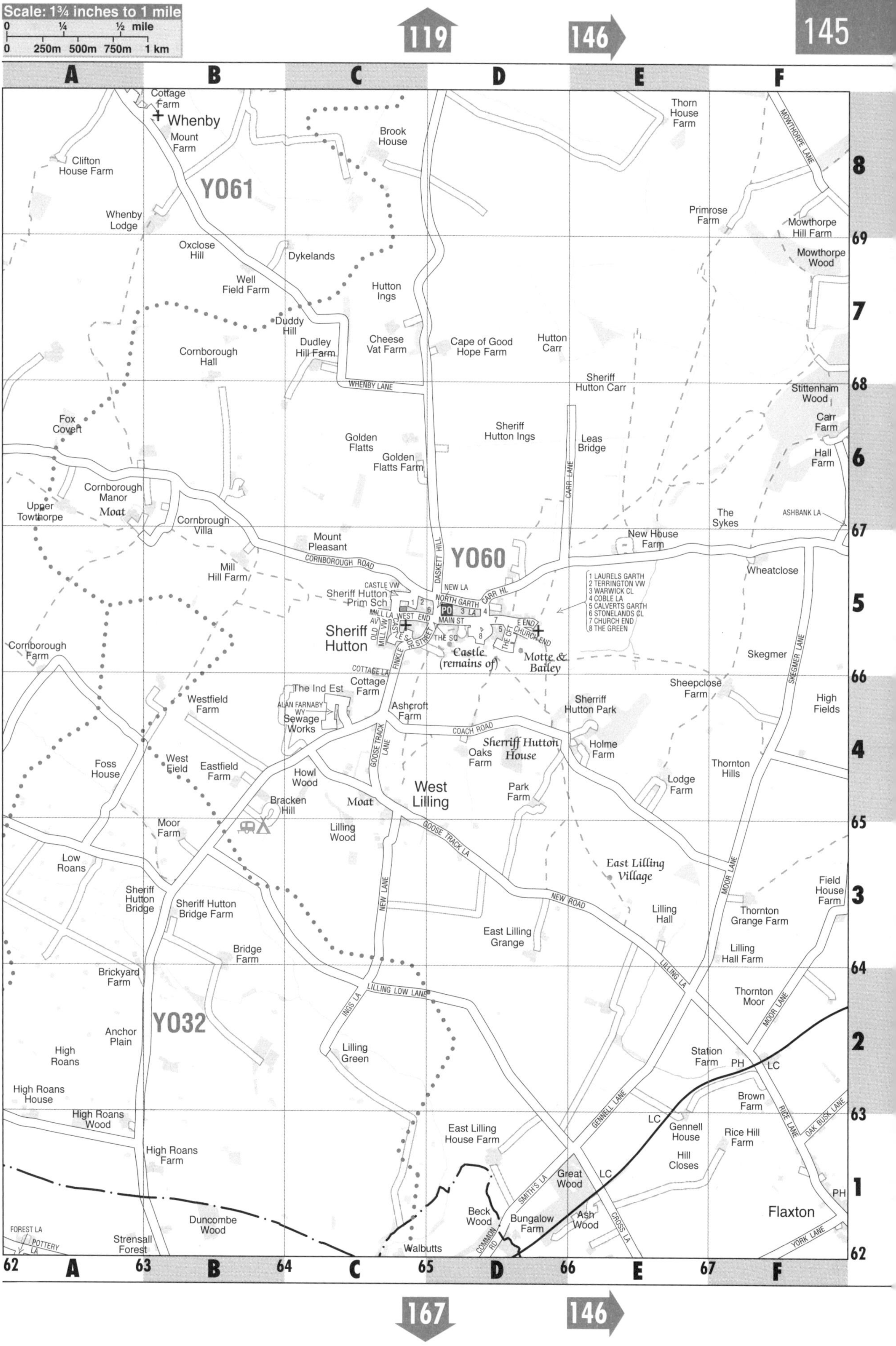
Scale: 1¾ inches to 1 mile
119
146
A
B
C
D
E
F
Whenby
Cottage Farm
Mount Farm
Clifton House Farm
YO61
Whenby Lodge
Brook House
Thorn House Farm
Primrose Farm
Mowthorpe Hill Farm
Mowthorpe Wood
MOWTHORPE LANE
Oxclose Hill
Dykelands
Well Field Farm
Hutton Ings
Duddy Hill
Dudley Hill Farm
Cheese Vat Farm
Cape of Good Hope Farm
Hutton Carr
Cornborough Hall
WHENBY LANE
Sheriff Hutton Carr
Stittenham Wood
Carr Farm
Hall Farm
Fox Covert
Golden Flatts
Golden Flatts Farm
Sheriff Hutton Ings
Leas Bridge
CARR LANE
Cornborough Manor
Moat
Upper Towthorpe
Cornbrough Villa
The Sykes
ASHBANK LA
Mount Pleasant
DASKETT HILL
YO60
New House Farm
CORNBOROUGH ROAD
Mill Hill Farm
Wheatclose
1 LAURELS GARTH
2 TERRINGTON VW
3 WARWICK CL
4 COBLE LA
5 CALVERTS GARTH
6 STONELANDS CL
7 CHURCH END
8 THE GREEN
Sheriff Hutton Prim Sch
CASTLE VW
NEW LA
NORTH GARTH
CARR HL
PO
MILL LA
WEST END
MAIN ST
E END
CHURCH END
Sheriff Hutton
MILL VW
OLD AV
EASTLE SIDE
STREET
THE SQ
THE CFT
FINKLE
Castle (remains of)
Motte & Bailey
Cornborough Farm
Skegmer
COTTAGE LA
Cottage Farm
The Ind Est
Sheepclose Farm
Westfield Farm
ALAN FARNABY WY
Sewage Works
Ashcroft Farm
Sherriff Hutton Park
High Fields
SKEGMER LANE
COACH ROAD
Sherriff Hutton House
Holme Farm
West Field
Foss House
Eastfield Farm
GOOSE TRACK LANE
Howl Wood
Oaks Farm
Thornton Hills
Lodge Farm
Bracken Hill
Moat
West Lilling
Park Farm
Moor Farm
Lilling Wood
GOOSE TRACK LA
Low Roans
East Lilling Village
MOOR LANE
Field House Farm
Sheriff Hutton Bridge
Sheriff Hutton Bridge Farm
NEW LANE
NEW ROAD
Lilling Hall
Thornton Grange Farm
East Lilling Grange
Bridge Farm
Lilling Hall Farm
Brickyard Farm
LILLING LOW LANE
LILLING LA
Thornton Moor
Anchor Plain
YO32
INGS LA
MOOR LANE
High Roans
Lilling Green
Station Farm
PH
LC
High Roans House
Brown Farm
High Roans Wood
East Lilling House Farm
GENNELL LANE
LC
Gennell House
RICE LANE
OAK BUSK LANE
Rice Hill Farm
High Roans Farm
Hill Closes
Great Wood
LC
SMITH'S LA
PH
Duncombe Wood
Beck Wood
Bungalow Farm
Ash Wood
CROSS LA
Flaxton
FOREST LA
POTTERY LA
Strensall Forest
COMMON RD
Walbutts
YORK LANE
62
63
64
65
66
67
68
69
1
2
3
4
5
6
7
8
167
146

145
120

Scale: 1¾ inches to 1 mile
0 ¼ ½ mile
0 250m 500m 750m 1 km

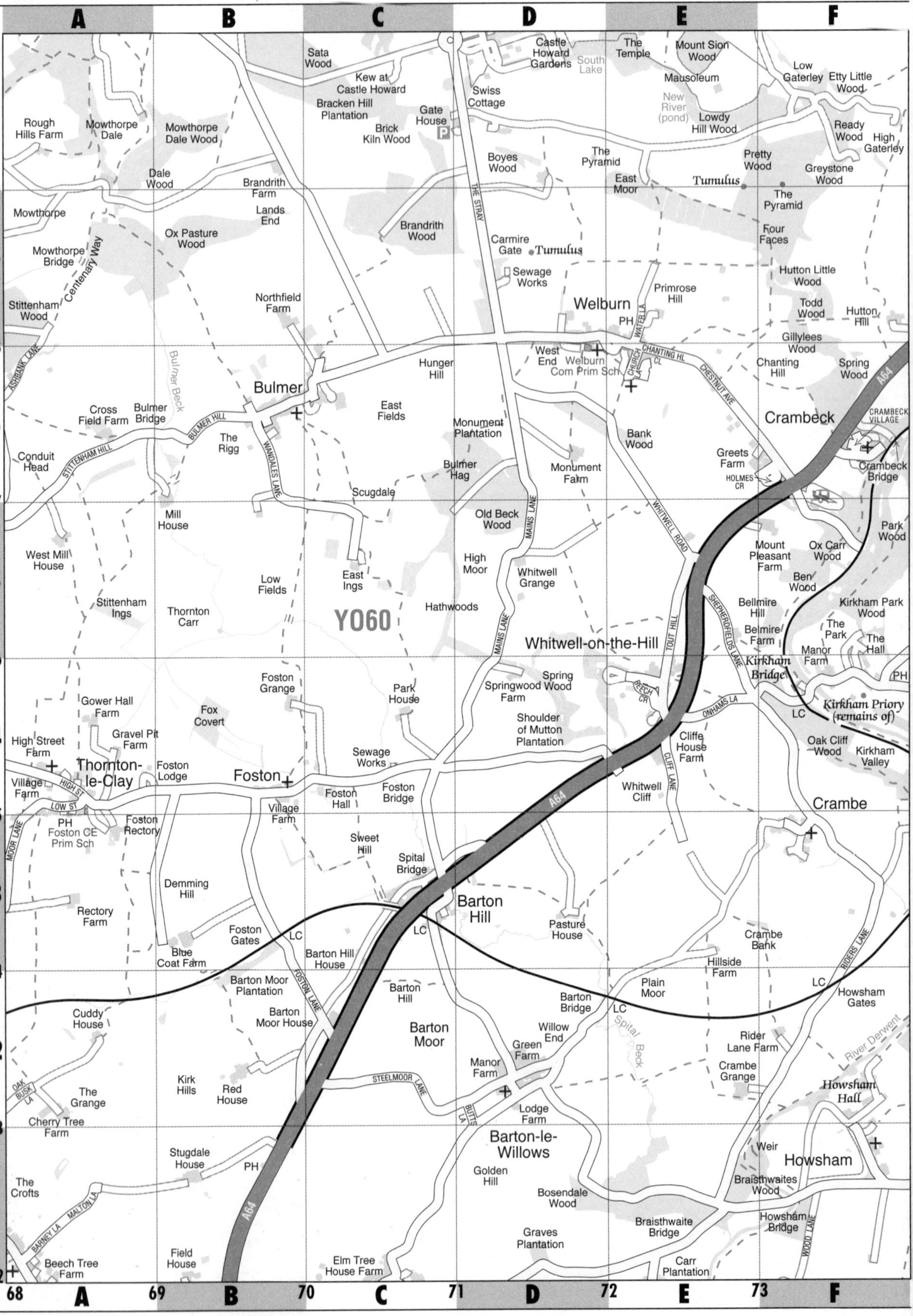

145
168

Scale: 1¾ inches to 1 mile
0 ¼ ½ mile
0 250m 500m 750m 1 km

121
148
215

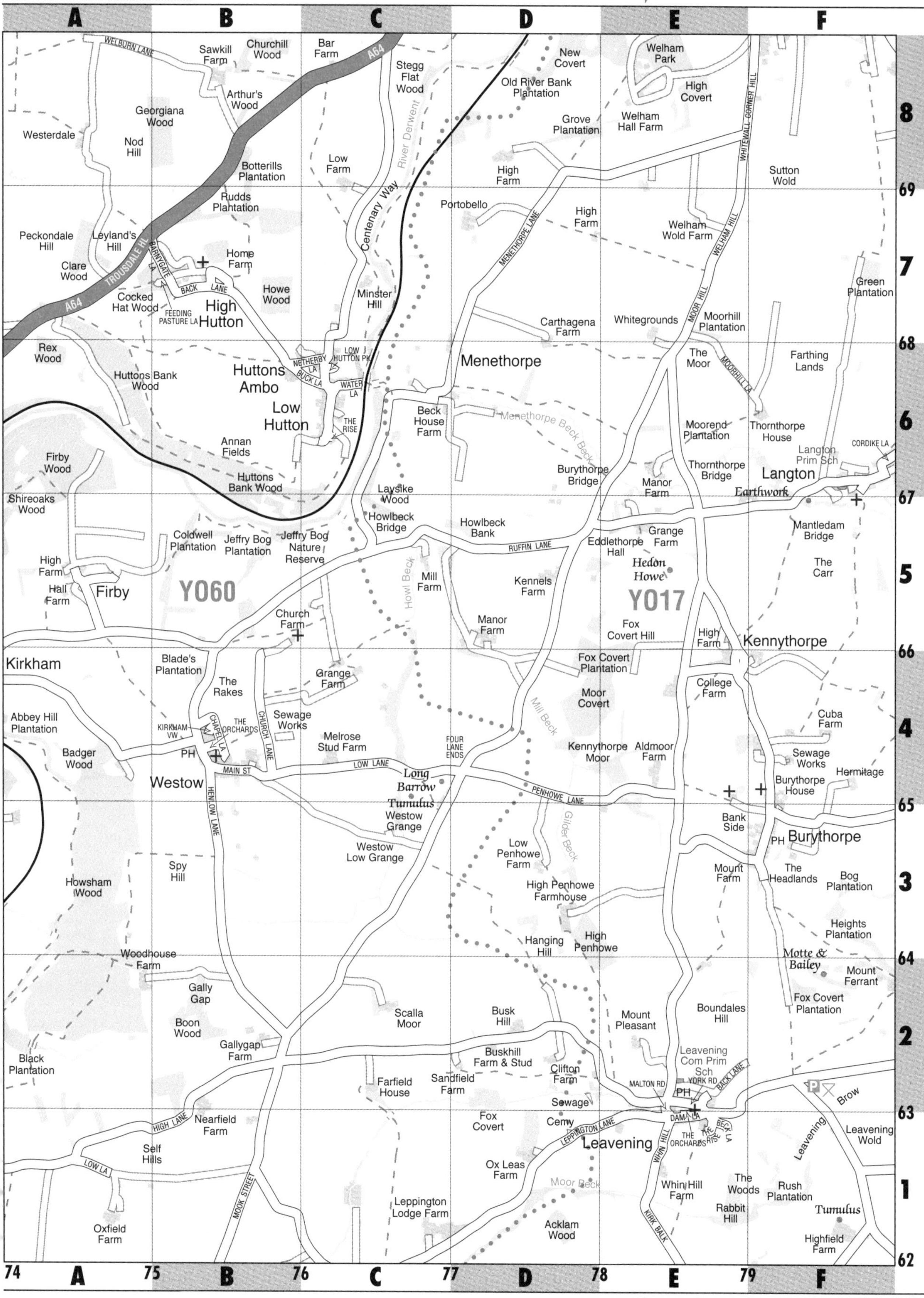

169
148

147
122

Scale: 1¾ inches to 1 mile
0 ¼ ½ mile
0 250m 500m 750m 1 km

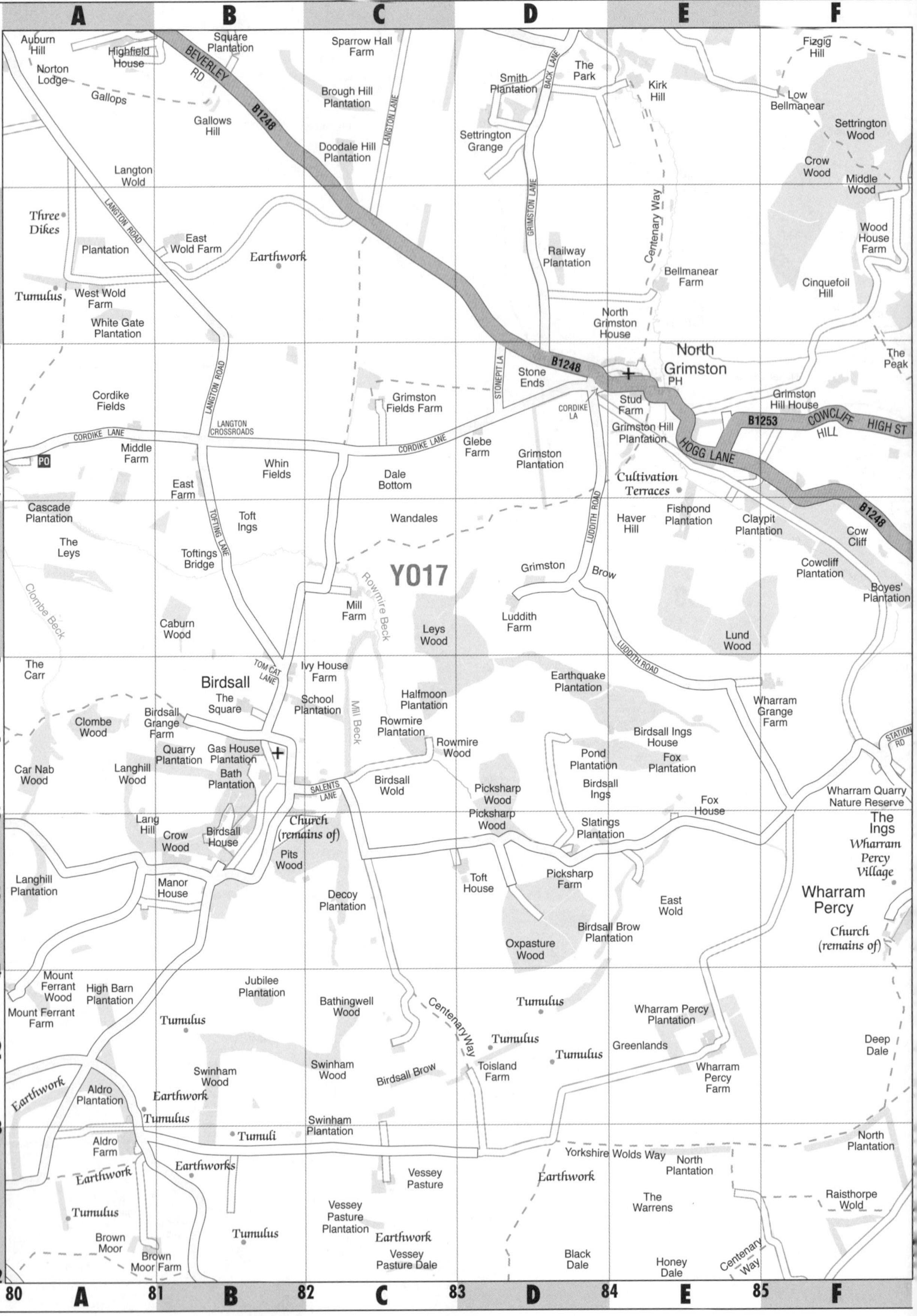
A B C D E F
8
69
7
68
6
67
5
66
4
65
3
64
2
63
1
62
80 81 82 83 84 85
Auburn Hill
Norton Lodge
Highfield House
Square Plantation
Gallops
Gallows Hill
BEVERLEY RD
B1248
Sparrow Hall Farm
Brough Hill Plantation
Doodale Hill Plantation
LANGTON LANE
Smith Plantation
BACK LANE
The Park
Kirk Hill
Settrington Grange
Fizgig Hill
Low Bellmanear
Settrington Wood
Crow Wood
Middle Wood
Langton Wold
Three Dikes
LANGTON ROAD
Plantation
East Wold Farm
Earthwork
GRIMSTON LANE
Railway Plantation
Centenary Way
Bellmanear Farm
Wood House Farm
Cinquefoil Hill
Tumulus
West Wold Farm
White Gate Plantation
North Grimston House
North Grimston
PH
The Peak
Cordike Fields
LANGTON ROAD
STONEPIT LA
Stone Ends
Grimston Fields Farm
Stud Farm
Grimston Hill House
B1253
COWCLIFF HILL
HIGH ST
CORDIKE LANE
LANGTON CROSSROADS
Middle Farm
PO
CORDIKE LANE
Glebe Farm
CORDIKE LA
Grimston Hill Plantation
HOGG LANE
Grimston Plantation
Whin Fields
Dale Bottom
Cultivation Terraces
East Farm
Cascade Plantation
TOFTING LANE
Toft Ings
Wandales
LUDDITH ROAD
Haver Hill
Fishpond Plantation
Claypit Plantation
Cow Cliff
The Leys
Toftings Bridge
YO17
Grimston
Brow
Cowcliff Plantation
Clombe Beck
Rowmire Beck
Mill Farm
Caburn Wood
Leys Wood
Luddith Farm
Boyes' Plantation
Lund Wood
The Carr
TOM CAT LANE
Ivy House Farm
LUDDITH ROAD
Birdsall
The Square
School Plantation
Halfmoon Plantation
Earthquake Plantation
Wharram Grange Farm
Clombe Wood
Birdsall Grange Farm
Mill Beck
Rowmire Plantation
Birdsall Ings House
Quarry Plantation
Gas House Plantation
Rowmire Wood
Pond Plantation
Fox Plantation
STATION RD
Car Nab Wood
Langhill Wood
Bath Plantation
SALENTS LANE
Birdsall Wold
Picksharp Wood
Birdsall Ings
Wharram Quarry Nature Reserve
Fox House
Lang Hill
Crow Wood
Birdsall House
Church (remains of)
Picksharp Wood
Slatings Plantation
The Ings
Wharram Percy Village
Pits Wood
Langhill Plantation
Manor House
Toft House
Picksharp Farm
Decoy Plantation
East Wold
Wharram Percy
Birdsall Brow Plantation
Church (remains of)
Oxpasture Wood
Mount Ferrant Wood
High Barn Plantation
Jubilee Plantation
Mount Ferrant Farm
Bathingwell Wood
Centenary Way
Tumulus
Wharram Percy Plantation
Tumulus
Tumulus
Tumulus
Greenlands
Deep Dale
Swinham Wood
Swinham Wood
Birdsall Brow
Toisland Farm
Wharram Percy Farm
Earthwork
Aldro Plantation
Earthwork
Tumulus
Tumuli
Swinham Plantation
North Plantation
Aldro Farm
Yorkshire Wolds Way
North Plantation
Earthwork
Earthworks
Vessey Pasture
Earthwork
Raisthorpe Wold
Tumulus
Vessey Pasture Plantation
The Warrens
Brown Moor
Tumulus
Earthwork
Brown Moor Farm
Vessey Pasture Dale
Black Dale
Honey Dale
Centenary Way

147
170

123
150

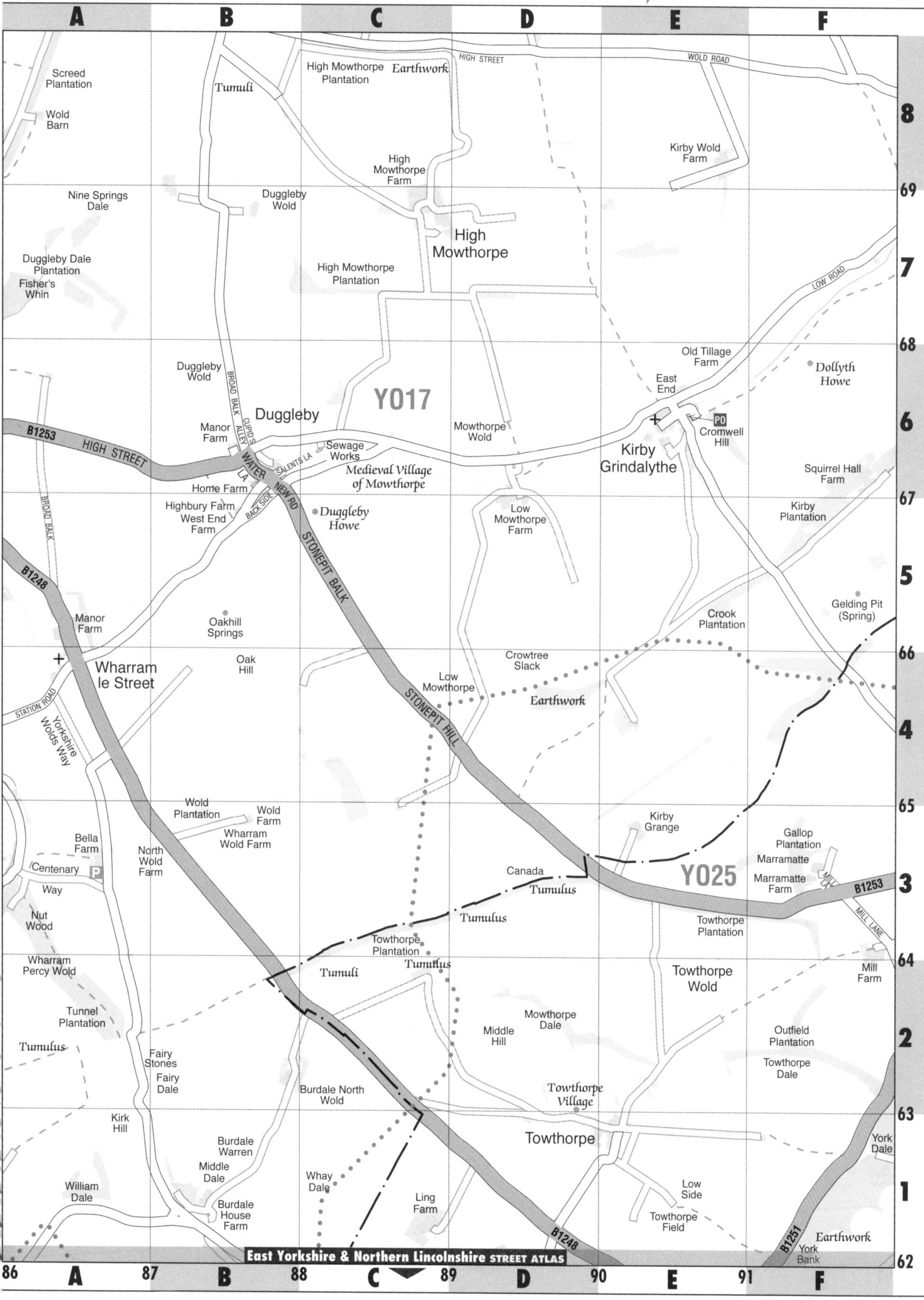
A
B
C
D
E
F
Screed Plantation
Wold Barn
Tumuli
High Mowthorpe Plantation
Earthwork
HIGH STREET
WOLD ROAD
8
High Mowthorpe Farm
Kirby Wold Farm
69
Nine Springs Dale
Duggleby Wold
High Mowthorpe
Duggleby Dale Plantation
Fisher's Whin
High Mowthorpe Plantation
7
LOW ROAD
68
Old Tillage Farm
Dollyth Howe
Duggleby Wold
BROAD BALK
YO17
East End
Duggleby
Manor Farm
CUPIDS ALLEY
B1253
HIGH STREET
Mowthorpe Wold
PO
Cromwell Hill
6
Sewage Works
Kirby Grindalythe
WATER LA
SALENTS LA
Medieval Village of Mowthorpe
Squirrel Hall Farm
Home Farm
NEW RD
67
Highbury Farm
West End Farm
BACK SIDE
Duggleby Howe
Low Mowthorpe Farm
Kirby Plantation
BROAD BALK
STONEPIT BALK
B1248
5
Manor Farm
Oakhill Springs
Crook Plantation
Gelding Pit (Spring)
66
Wharram le Street
Oak Hill
Crowtree Slack
Low Mowthorpe
Earthwork
STATION ROAD
Yorkshire Wolds Way
STONEPIT HILL
4
65
Wold Plantation
Wold Farm
Kirby Grange
Bella Farm
Wharram Wold Farm
Gallop Plantation
North Wold Farm
Marramatte
Centenary Way
P
Canada
YO25
Marramatte Farm
MILL LA
B1253
3
Tumulus
Nut Wood
Tumulus
MILL LANE
Towthorpe Plantation
Towthorpe Plantation
Tumulus
64
Wharram Percy Wold
Tumuli
Towthorpe Wold
Mill Farm
Tunnel Plantation
Mowthorpe Dale
Middle Hill
Outfield Plantation
2
Tumulus
Fairy Stones
Towthorpe Dale
Fairy Dale
Burdale North Wold
Towthorpe Village
63
Kirk Hill
Towthorpe
York Dale
Burdale Warren
Middle Dale
Whay Dale
William Dale
Low Side
1
Burdale House Farm
Ling Farm
Towthorpe Field
B1248
B1251
Earthwork
York Bank
62
86
87
88
89
90
91

150

149
124

Scale: 1¾ inches to 1 mile
0 ¼ ½ mile
0 250m 500m 750m 1 km

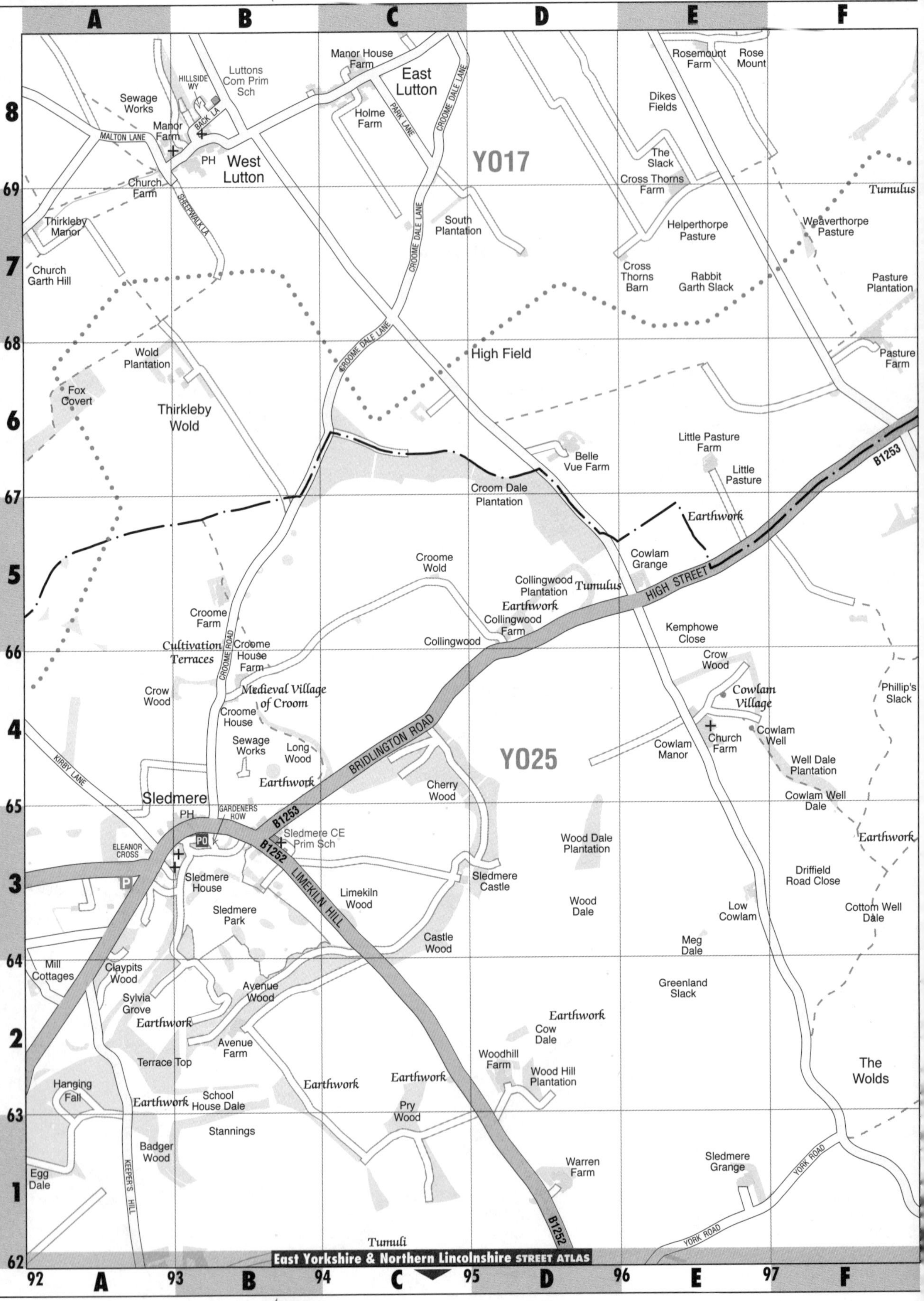
A
B
C
D
E
F
8
69
7
68
6
67
5
66
4
65
3
64
2
63
1
62
92
93
94
95
96
97
Rosemount Farm
Rose Mount
Manor House Farm
East Lutton
Luttons Com Prim Sch
HILLSIDE WY
BACK LA
Sewage Works
Manor Farm
MALTON LANE
PH
West Lutton
Holme Farm
PARK LANE
CROOME DALE LANE
YO17
Dikes Fields
The Slack
Cross Thorns Farm
Church Farm
SHEEPWALK LA
Thirkleby Manor
South Plantation
Helperthorpe Pasture
Weaverthorpe Pasture
Tumulus
Church Garth Hill
Cross Thorns Barn
Rabbit Garth Slack
Pasture Plantation
Wold Plantation
High Field
Pasture Farm
Fox Covert
Thirkleby Wold
Little Pasture Farm
Belle Vue Farm
Little Pasture
B1253
Croom Dale Plantation
Earthwork
Cowlam Grange
Croome Wold
Collingwood Plantation
Tumulus
HIGH STREET
Earthwork
Collingwood Farm
Croome Farm
Collingwood
Kemphowe Close
Cultivation Terraces
CROOME ROAD
Croome House Farm
Crow Wood
Crow Wood
Cowlam Village
Phillip's Slack
Medieval Village of Croom
Croome House
BRIDLINGTON ROAD
Church Farm
Cowlam Well
KIRBY LANE
Sewage Works
Long Wood
YO25
Cowlam Manor
Well Dale Plantation
Earthwork
Cherry Wood
Sledmere
PH
GARDENERS ROW
B1253
Cowlam Well Dale
ELEANOR CROSS
PO
Sledmere CE Prim Sch
B1252
Wood Dale Plantation
Earthwork
Sledmere House
LIMEKILN HILL
Sledmere Castle
Driffield Road Close
Limekiln Wood
Wood Dale
Cottom Well Dale
Sledmere Park
Low Cowlam
Castle Wood
Meg Dale
Mill Cottages
Claypits Wood
Avenue House
Avenue Wood
Greenland Slack
Sylvia Grove
Earthwork
Earthwork
Cow Dale
Avenue Farm
Woodhill Farm
Terrace Top
Wood Hill Plantation
The Wolds
Hanging Fall
Earthwork
Earthwork
School House Dale
Earthwork
Pry Wood
Stannings
Badger Wood
Warren Farm
Sledmere Grange
YORK ROAD
Egg Dale
KEEPER'S HILL
B1252
YORK ROAD
Tumuli

149

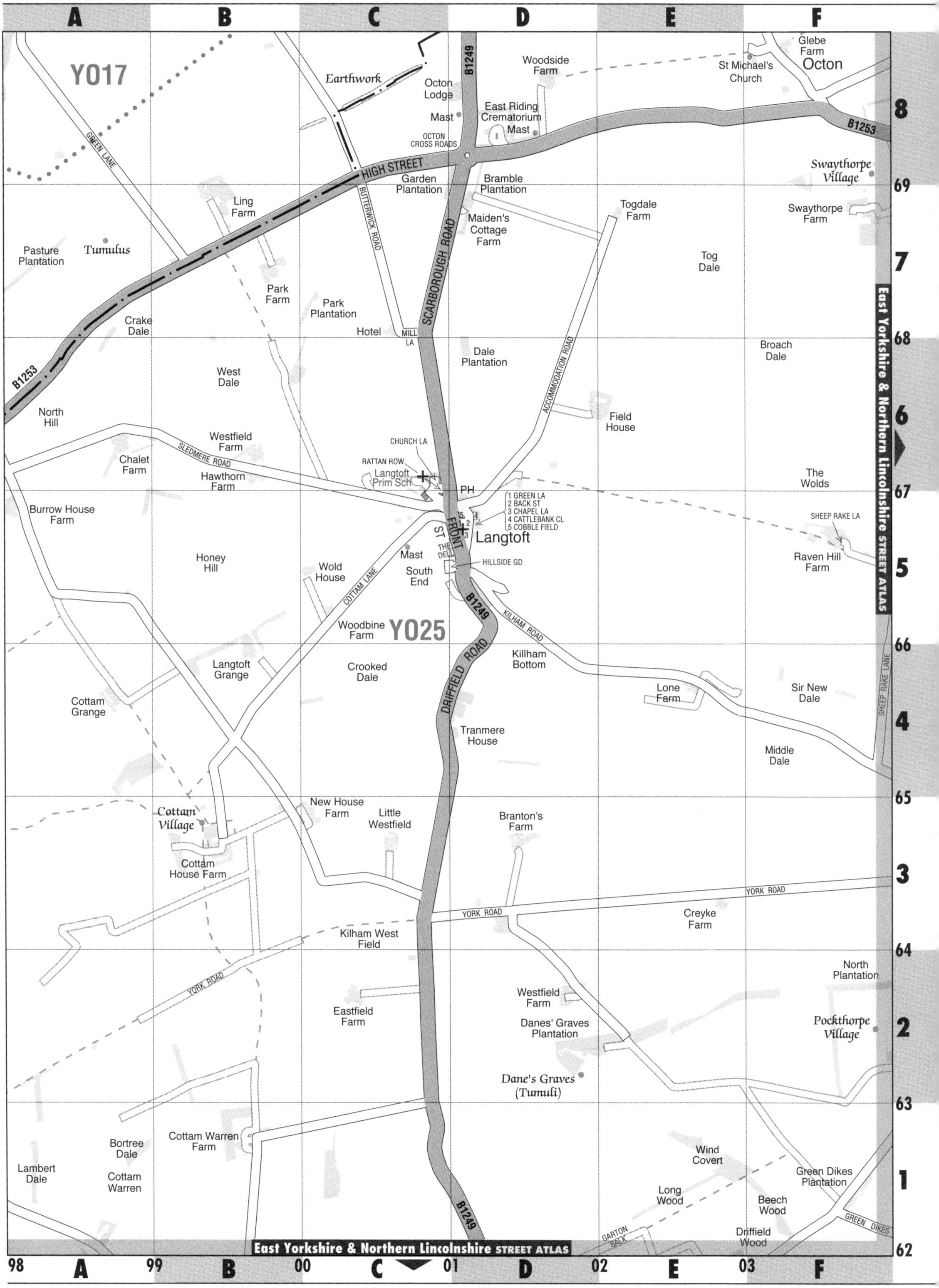
A
B
C
D
E
F
YO17
Earthwork
Octon Lodge
Woodside Farm
Glebe Farm
St Michael's Church
Octon
Mast
East Riding Crematorium
Mast
OCTON CROSS ROADS
B1249
B1253
GREEN LANE
HIGH STREET
Garden Plantation
Bramble Plantation
Swaythorpe Village
Swaythorpe Farm
Ling Farm
BUTTERWICK ROAD
Maiden's Cottage Farm
Togdale Farm
Pasture Plantation
Tumulus
Tog Dale
SCARBOROUGH ROAD
Park Farm
Park Plantation
Crake Dale
Hotel
MILL LA
Broach Dale
Dale Plantation
ACCOMMODATION ROAD
West Dale
North Hill
Field House
Westfield Farm
CHURCH LA
Chalet Farm
SLEDMERE ROAD
RATTAN ROW
Hawthorn Farm
Langtoft Prim Sch
PH
The Wolds
1 GREEN LA
2 BACK ST
3 CHAPEL LA
4 CATTLEBANK CL
5 COBBLE FIELD
Burrow House Farm
FRONT ST
Langtoft
SHEEP RAKE LA
THE DELL
Honey Hill
Mast
Wold House
HILLSIDE GD
Raven Hill Farm
South End
COTTAM LANE
KILHAM ROAD
Woodbine Farm
YO25
Langtoft Grange
Crooked Dale
DRIFFIELD ROAD
Killham Bottom
Lone Farm
Sir New Dale
SHEEP RAKE LANE
Cottam Grange
Tranmere House
Middle Dale
New House Farm
Little Westfield
Branton's Farm
Cottam Village
Cottam House Farm
YORK ROAD
YORK ROAD
Creyke Farm
Kilham West Field
North Plantation
YORK ROAD
Westfield Farm
Eastfield Farm
Danes' Graves Plantation
Pockthorpe Village
Dane's Graves (Tumuli)
Cottam Warren Farm
Bortree Dale
Wind Covert
Green Dikes Plantation
Lambert Dale
Cottam Warren
Long Wood
Beech Wood
GARTON BALK
Driffield Wood
GREEN DIKES
East Yorkshire & Northern Lincolnshire STREET ATLAS
8
69
7
68
6
67
5
66
4
65
3
64
2
63
1
62
98
99
00
01
02
03

130

Scale: 1¾ inches to 1 mile

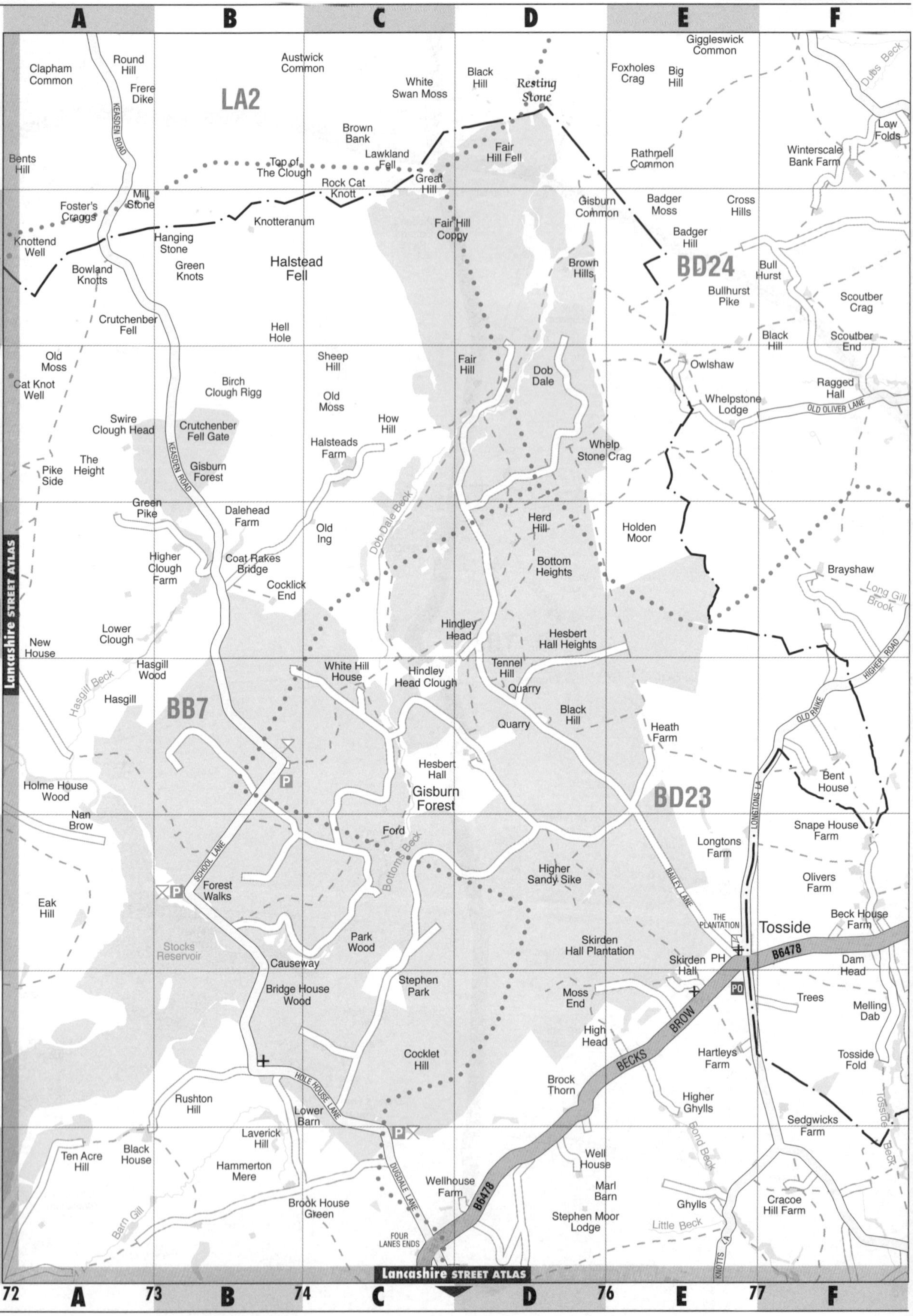

A
B
C
D
E
F
Clapham Common
Round Hill
Frere Dike
KEASDEN ROAD
LA2
Austwick Common
White Swan Moss
Black Hill
Resting Stone
Foxholes Crag
Big Hill
Giggleswick Common
Dubs Beck
Low Folds
Brown Bank
Lawkland Fell
Fair Hill Fell
Rathmell Common
Winterscale Bank Farm
Bents Hill
Top of The Clough
Rock Cat Knott
Great Hill
Mill Stone
Foster's Craggs
Knotteranum
Fair Hill Coppy
Gisburn Common
Badger Moss
Cross Hills
Badger Hill
Knottend Well
Hanging Stone
Green Knots
Halstead Fell
Brown Hills
BD24
Bull Hurst
Bullhurst Pike
Scoutber Crag
Bowland Knotts
Crutchenber Fell
Hell Hole
Black Hill
Scoutber End
Old Moss
Cat Knot Well
Sheep Hill
Fair Hill
Dob Dale
Owlshaw
Birch Clough Rigg
Old Moss
Ragged Hall
Whelpstone Lodge
OLD OLIVER LANE
Swire Clough Head
Crutchenber Fell Gate
How Hill
Halsteads Farm
Whelp Stone Crag
Pike Side
The Height
Gisburn Forest
Green Pike
Dalehead Farm
Old Ing
Dob Dale Beck
Herd Hill
Holden Moor
Higher Clough Farm
Coat Rakes Bridge
Bottom Heights
Brayshaw
Cocklick End
Long Gill Brook
Lower Clough
New House
Hindley Head
Hesbert Hall Heights
Hasgill Wood
White Hill House
Hindley Head Clough
Tennel Hill
Quarry
HIGHER ROAD
Hasgill Beck
Hasgill
BB7
Black Hill
Quarry
Heath Farm
OLD BAKE
P
Hesbert Hall
Bent House
Holme House Wood
Gisburn Forest
BD23
LONGTONS LA
Nan Brow
Ford
Snape House Farm
Longtons Farm
Bottoms Beck
Higher Sandy Sike
SCHOOL LANE
Forest Walks
Olivers Farm
Eak Hill
BAILEY LANE
THE PLANTATION
Tosside
Beck House Farm
Park Wood
Stocks Reservoir
Skirden Hall Plantation
Causeway
Skirden Hall
PH
B6478
Dam Head
Bridge House Wood
Stephen Park
PO
Moss End
Trees
Melling Dab
High Head
BROW
Cocklet Hill
BECKS
Hartleys Farm
Tosside Fold
HOLE HOUSE LANE
Brock Thorn
Rushton Hill
Higher Ghylls
Lower Barn
Sedgwicks Farm
Laverick Hill
Tosside Beck
Ten Acre Hill
Black House
Hammerton Mere
Well House
Bond Beck
DUGDALE LANE
Wellhouse Farm
Marl Barn
Ghylls
Cracoe Hill Farm
Barn Gill
Brook House Green
B6478
Stephen Moor Lodge
Little Beck
FOUR LANES ENDS
KNOTTS LA
Lancashire STREET ATLAS
8
61
7
60
6
59
5
58
4
57
3
56
2
55
1
54
72
73
74
76
77

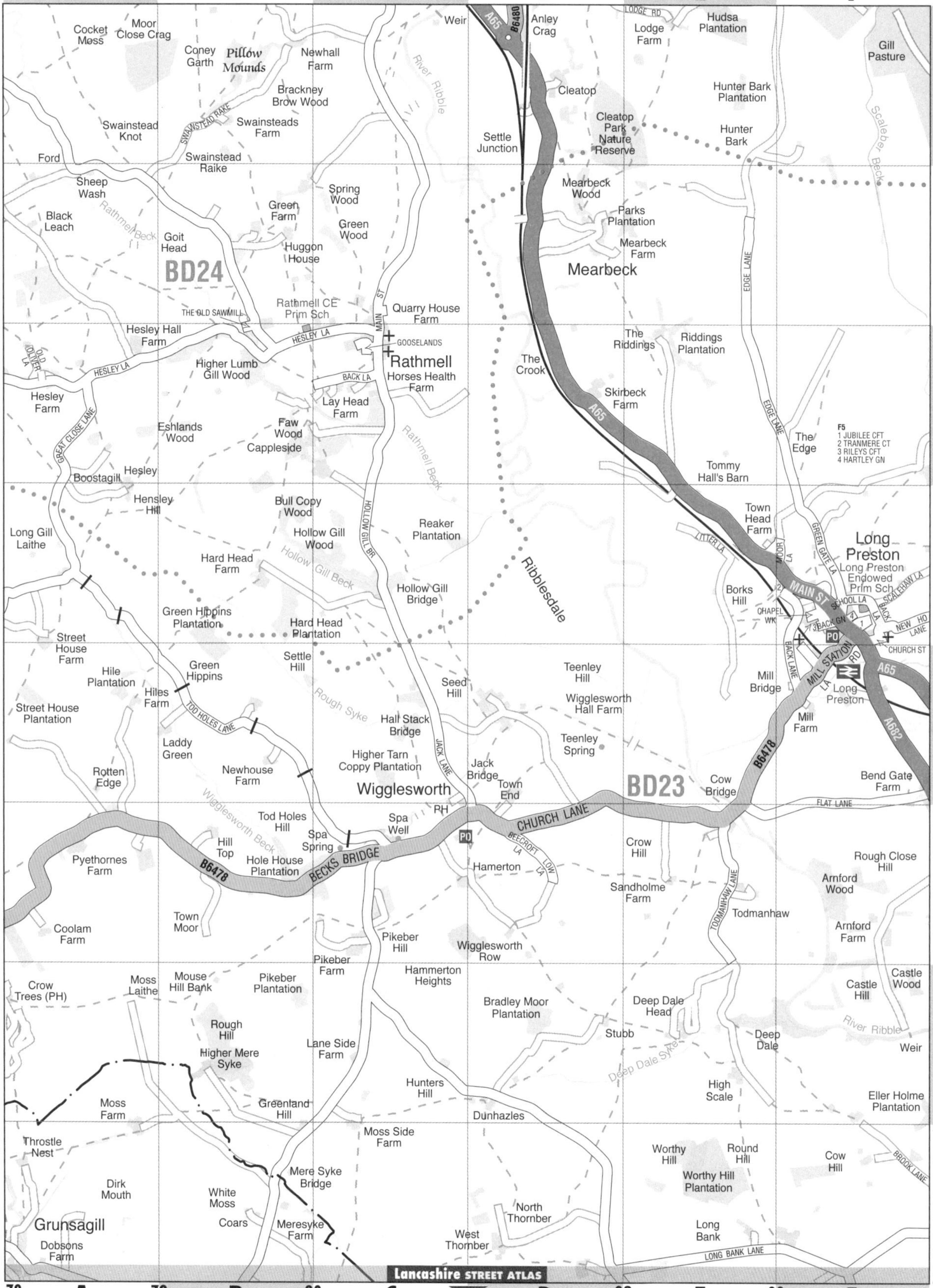
Scale: 1¾ inches to 1 mile
131
154
Rathmell
Wigglesworth
Mearbeck
Long Preston
Grunsagill
Ribblesdale
BD24
BD23
A65
A682
B6478
B6480
River Ribble
Settle Junction
Cleatop Park Nature Reserve
Hollow Gill Bridge
Becks Bridge
Church Lane
Hesley La
Great Close Lane
Tod Holes Lane
Hollow Gill Br
Jack Lane
Edge Lane
Todmanhaw Lane
Long Bank Lane
Brook Lane
Main St
Mill Station Rd
F5
1 JUBILEE CFT
2 TRANMERE CT
3 RILEYS CFT
4 HARTLEY GN
Lancashire STREET ATLAS

153
132

Scale: 1¾ inches to 1 mile
0 ¼ ½ mile
0 250m 500m 750m 1 km

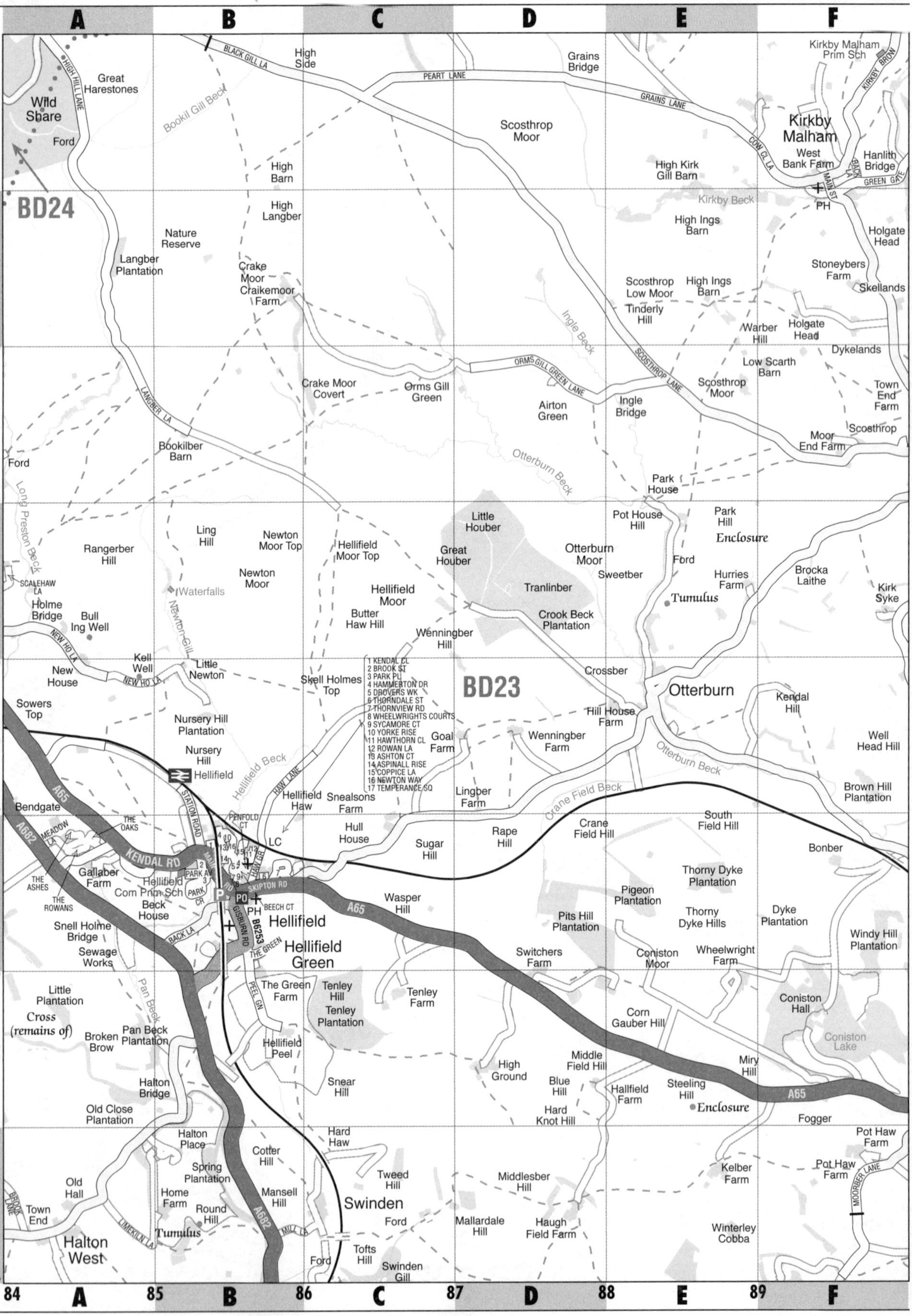
A
B
C
D
E
F
8
7
6
5
4
3
2
1
61
60
59
58
57
56
55
54
84
85
86
87
88
89
BD24
BD23
Wild Share
Ford
Great Harestones
HIGH HILL LANE
BLACK GILL LA
High Side
PEART LANE
Grains Bridge
GRAINS LANE
Kirkby Malham Prim Sch
KIRKBY BROW
Kirkby Malham
West Bank Farm
Hanlith Bridge
BACK LA
GREEN GATE
MAIN ST
PH
COW CL LA
Bookil Gill Beck
Scosthrop Moor
High Barn
High Kirk Gill Barn
Kirkby Beck
High Langber
High Ings Barn
Holgate Head
Nature Reserve
Langber Plantation
Crake Moor
Craikemoor Farm
Scosthrop Low Moor
High Ings Barn
Stoneybers Farm
Skellands
Tinderly Hill
Ingle Beck
Warber Hill
Holgate Head
Dykelands
Low Scarth Barn
ORMS GILL GREEN LANE
SCOSTHROP LANE
Crake Moor Covert
Orms Gill Green
Airton Green
Ingle Bridge
Scosthrop Moor
Town End Farm
LANGBER LA
Scosthrop
Moor End Farm
Bookilber Barn
Otterburn Beck
Ford
Long Preston Beck
Park House
Ling Hill
Newton Moor Top
Hellifield Moor Top
Little Houber
Pot House Hill
Park Hill
Enclosure
Rangerber Hill
Great Houber
Otterburn Moor
Ford
SCALEHAW LA
Waterfalls
Newton Moor
Hellifield Moor
Tranlinber
Sweetber
Hurries Farm
Brocka Laithe
Kirk Syke
Tumulus
Holme Bridge
Bull Ing Well
Butter Haw Hill
Crook Beck Plantation
Newton Gill
NEW HO LA
Wenningber Hill
Kell Well
Little Newton
New House
NEW HO LA
Skell Holmes Top
Crossber
Otterburn
Kendal Hill
1 KENDAL CL
2 BROOK ST
3 PARK PL
4 HAMMERTON DR
5 DROVERS WK
6 THORNDALE ST
7 THORNVIEW RD
8 WHEELWRIGHTS COURTS
9 SYCAMORE CT
10 YORKE RISE
11 HAWTHORN CL
12 ROWAN LA
13 ASHTON CT
14 ASPINALL RISE
15 COPPICE LA
16 NEWTON WAY
17 TEMPERANCE SQ
Sowers Top
Hill House Farm
Nursery Hill Plantation
Goal Farm
Wenningber Farm
Well Head Hill
Nursery Hill
Otterburn Beck
Hellifield
Hellifield Beck
HAW LANE
A65
Hellifield Haw
Snealsons Farm
Lingber Farm
Brown Hill Plantation
Bendgate
STATION ROAD
Crane Field Beck
PENFOLD CT
Hull House
Rape Hill
Crane Field Hill
South Field Hill
THE OAKS
MEADOW LA
LC
Sugar Hill
Bonber
A682
KENDAL RD
Gallaber Farm
PARK AV
HAW GR
THE ASHES
Hellifield Com Prim Sch
PARK CR
SKIPTON RD
Thorny Dyke Plantation
PO
Wasper Hill
Pigeon Plantation
THE ROWANS
Beck House
PH
BEECH CT
A65
Thorny Dyke Hills
Dyke Plantation
Snell Holme Bridge
Hellifield
Pits Hill Plantation
Windy Hill Plantation
BACK LA
GISBURN RD
B6253
THE GREEN
Sewage Works
Hellifield Green
Switchers Farm
Coniston Moor
Wheelwright Farm
Little Plantation
The Green Farm
Tenley Hill
Tenley Farm
PEEL GN
Coniston Hall
Cross (remains of)
Tenley Plantation
Corn Gauber Hill
Broken Brow
Pan Beck
Pan Beck Plantation
Coniston Lake
Hellifield Peel
Middle Field Hill
High Ground
Miry Hill
Halton Bridge
Snear Hill
Blue Hill
Hallfield Farm
Steeling Hill
A65
Enclosure
Old Close Plantation
Hard Knot Hill
Fogger
Halton Place
Hard Haw
Pot Haw Farm
Cotter Hill
Spring Plantation
Tweed Hill
Middlesber Hill
Kelber Farm
Pot Haw Farm
MOORBER LANE
Old Hall
Home Farm
Mansell Hill
BROOK LANE
Town End
Round Hill
Swinden
LIMEKILN LA
A682
Tumulus
Ford
Mallardale Hill
Haugh Field Farm
Winterley Cobba
MILL LA
Halton West
Tofts Hill
Ford
Swinden Gill

153
171

Scale: 1¾ inches to 1 mile
0 ¼ ½ mile
0 250m 500m 750m 1 km

133
156

A B C D E F

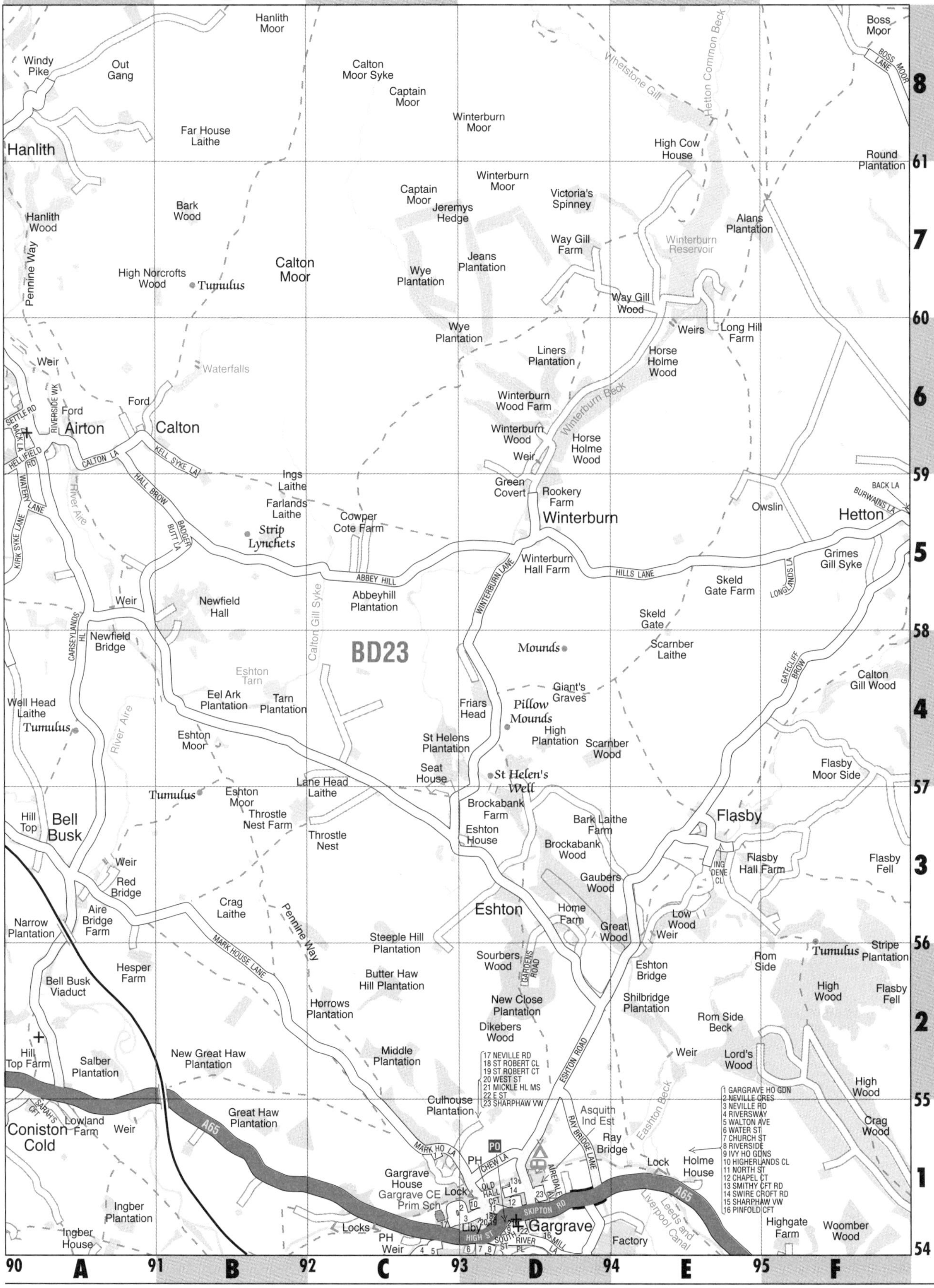

A B C D E F

172
156

155
134
Scale: 1¾ inches to 1 mile
0 ¼ ½ mile
0 250m 500m 750m 1 km

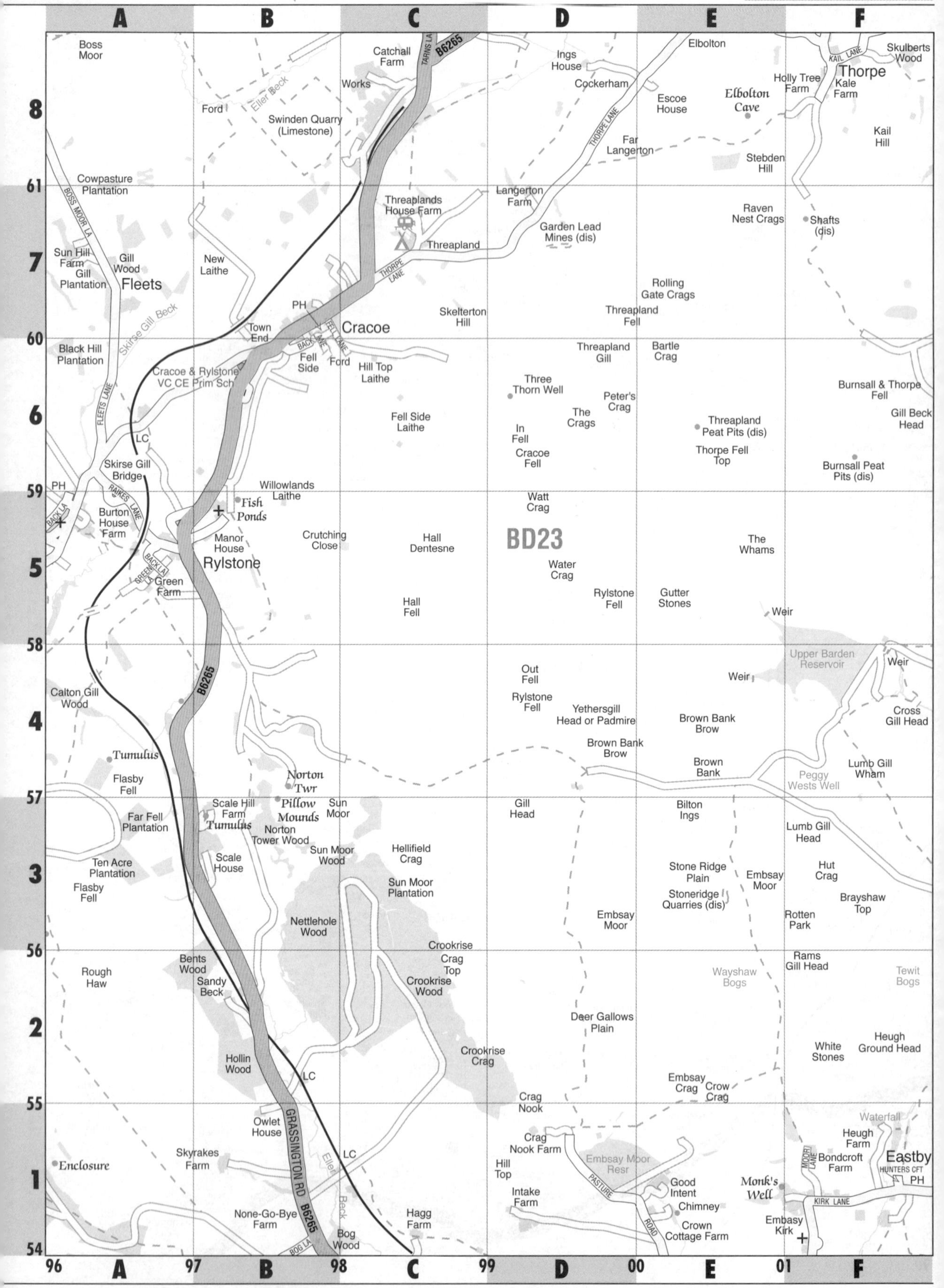

155
216
217

Scale: 1¾ inches to 1 mile
0 ¼ ½ mile
0 250m 500m 750m 1 km

135
158

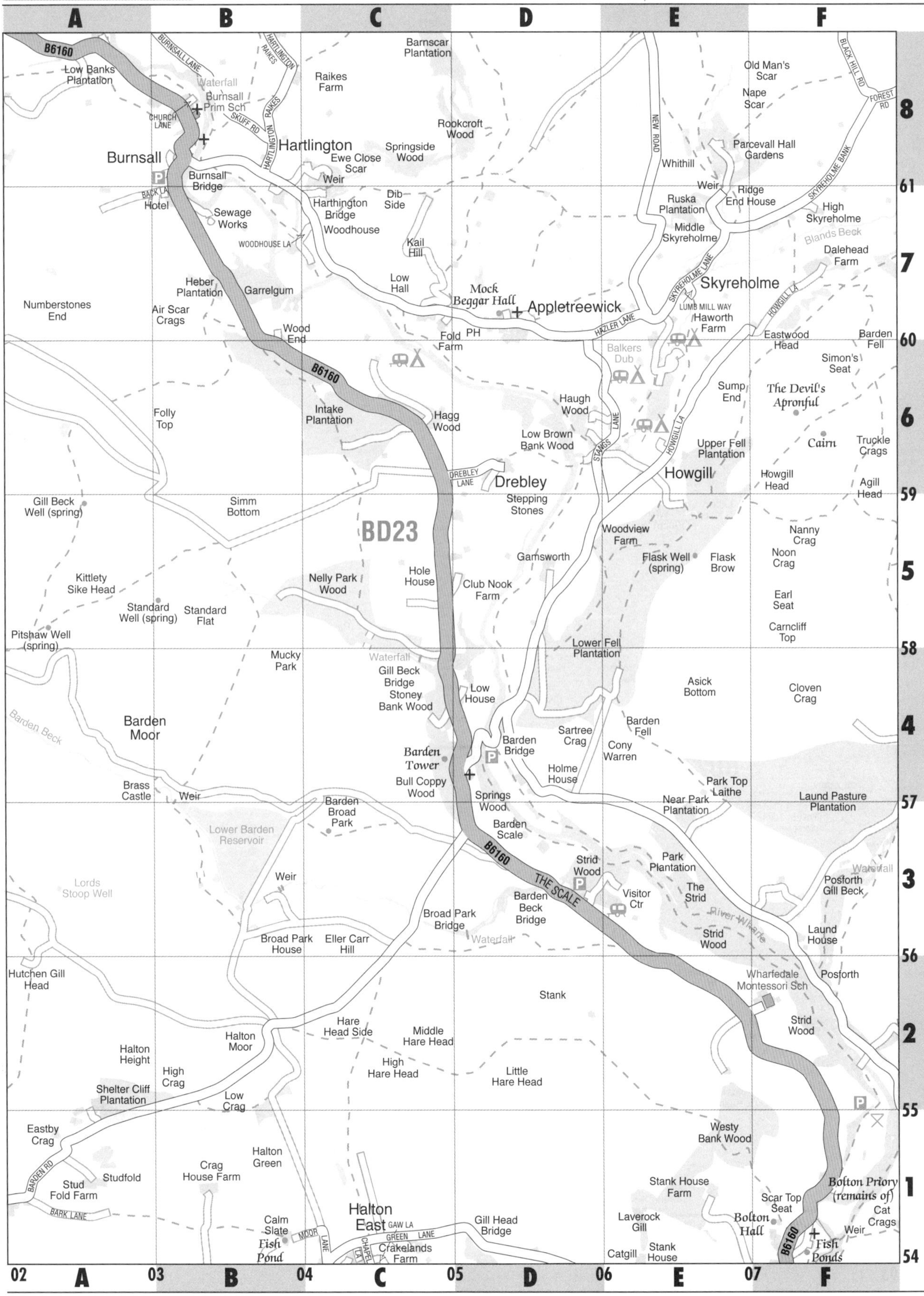

174
158

157
136

Scale: 1¾ inches to 1 mile
0 ¼ ½ mile
0 250m 500m 750m 1 km

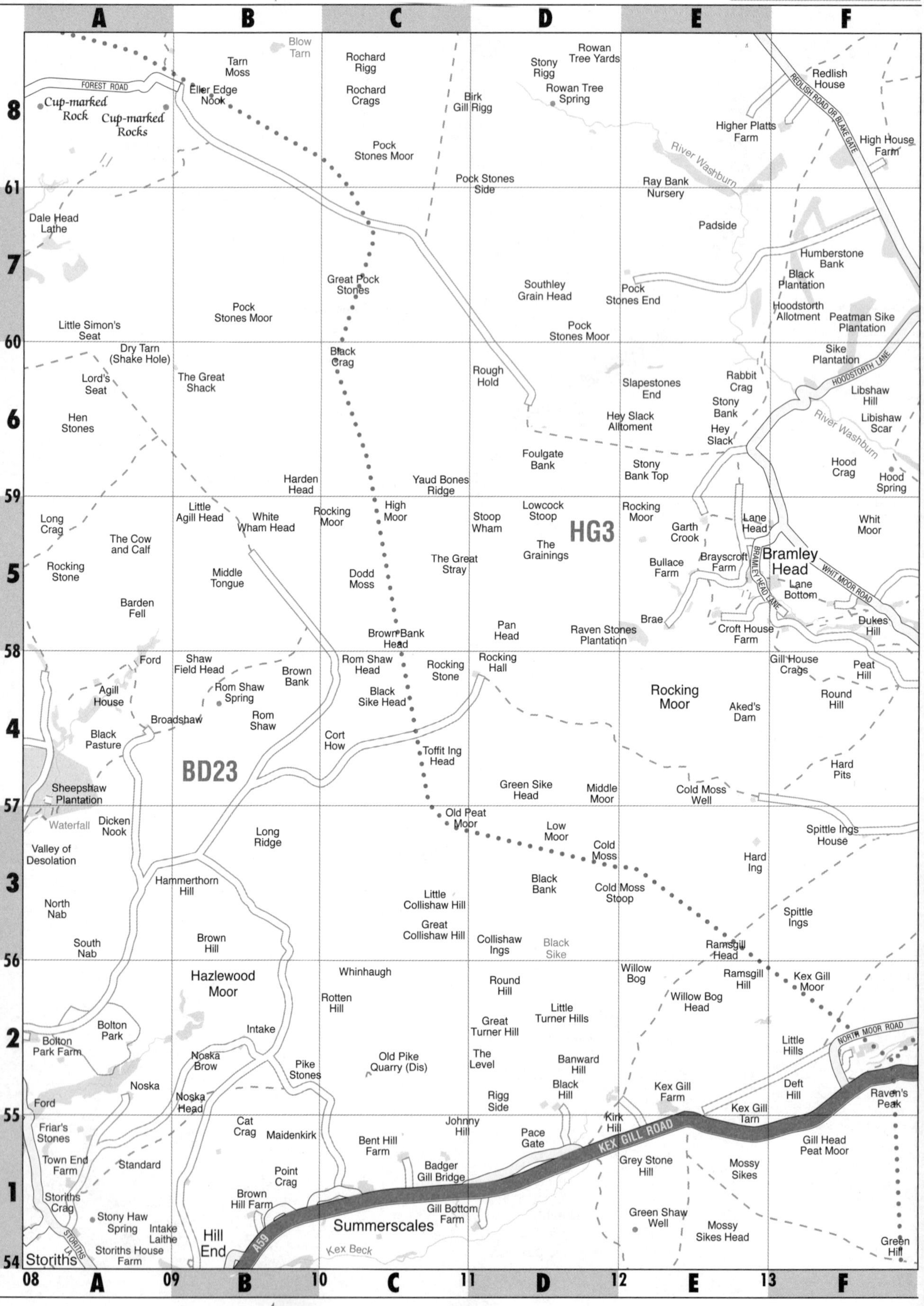
A B C D E F
8
61
7
60
6
59
5
58
4
57
3
56
2
55
1
54
08 09 10 11 12 13
Blow Tarn
Tarn Moss
Rochard Rigg
Rochard Crags
Rowan Tree Yards
Stony Rigg
Rowan Tree Spring
Birk Gill Rigg
FOREST ROAD
Cup-marked Rock
Cup-marked Rocks
Eller Edge Nook
Redlish House
REDLISH ROAD OR BLAKE GATE
Higher Platts Farm
High House Farm
Pock Stones Moor
River Washburn
Pock Stones Side
Ray Bank Nursery
Dale Head Lathe
Padside
Humberstone Bank
Black Plantation
Great Pock Stones
Southley Grain Head
Pock Stones End
Hoodstorth Allotment
Peatman Sike Plantation
Pock Stones Moor
Little Simon's Seat
Pock Stones Moor
Sike Plantation
Dry Tarn (Shake Hole)
Black Crag
HOODSTORTH LANE
Rough Hold
Lord's Seat
The Great Shack
Slapestones End
Rabbit Crag
Libshaw Hill
Stony Bank
Hen Stones
Hey Slack Allotment
Hey Slack
Libishaw Scar
Foulgate Bank
Hood Crag
Stony Bank Top
Hood Spring
Harden Head
Yaud Bones Ridge
Long Crag
Little Agill Head
White Wham Head
Rocking Moor
High Moor
Stoop Wham
Lowcock Stoop
HG3
Rocking Moor
Garth Crook
Lane Head
Whit Moor
The Cow and Calf
The Grainings
Rocking Stone
Middle Tongue
Dodd Moss
The Great Stray
Bullace Farm
Brayscroft Farm
Bramley Head
BRAMLEY HEAD LANE
WHIT MOOR ROAD
Lane Bottom
Barden Fell
Brae
Dukes Hill
Brown Bank Head
Pan Head
Raven Stones Plantation
Croft House Farm
Ford
Shaw Field Head
Rom Shaw Head
Rocking Stone
Rocking Hall
Gill House Crags
Peat Hill
Brown Bank
Agill House
Rom Shaw Spring
Black Sike Head
Rocking Moor
Round Hill
Aked's Dam
Broadshaw
Rom Shaw
Black Pasture
Cort How
Toffit Ing Head
BD23
Hard Pits
Sheepshaw Plantation
Green Sike Head
Middle Moor
Cold Moss Well
Waterfall
Dicken Nook
Old Peat Moor
Valley of Desolation
Long Ridge
Low Moor
Spittle Ings House
Cold Moss
Hard Ing
Hammerthorn Hill
Black Bank
Cold Moss Stoop
North Nab
Little Collishaw Hill
Spittle Ings
Great Collishaw Hill
Brown Hill
Collishaw Ings
Black Sike
South Nab
Ramsgill Head
Whinhaugh
Willow Bog
Hazlewood Moor
Ramsgill Hill
Kex Gill Moor
Round Hill
Rotten Hill
Willow Bog Head
Little Turner Hills
Bolton Park
Great Turner Hill
Intake
NORTH MOOR ROAD
Bolton Park Farm
Little Hills
Noska Brow
Old Pike Quarry (Dis)
The Level
Pike Stones
Banward Hill
Noska
Black Hill
Kex Gill Farm
Deft Hill
Ford
Noska Head
Rigg Side
Raven's Peak
Friar's Stones
Cat Crag
Maidenkirk
Johnny Hill
Kirk Hill
Kex Gill Tarn
Bent Hill Farm
Pace Gate
KEX GILL ROAD
Town End Farm
Standard
Badger Gill Bridge
Grey Stone Hill
Gill Head Peat Moor
Point Crag
Mossy Sikes
Storiths Crag
Brown Hill Farm
Gill Bottom Farm
Green Shaw Well
Stony Haw Spring
Intake Laithe
Hill End
Summerscales
Mossy Sikes Head
STORITHS LA
A59
Kex Beck
Green Hill
Storiths House Farm
Storiths

157
175

Scale: 1¾ inches to 1 mile

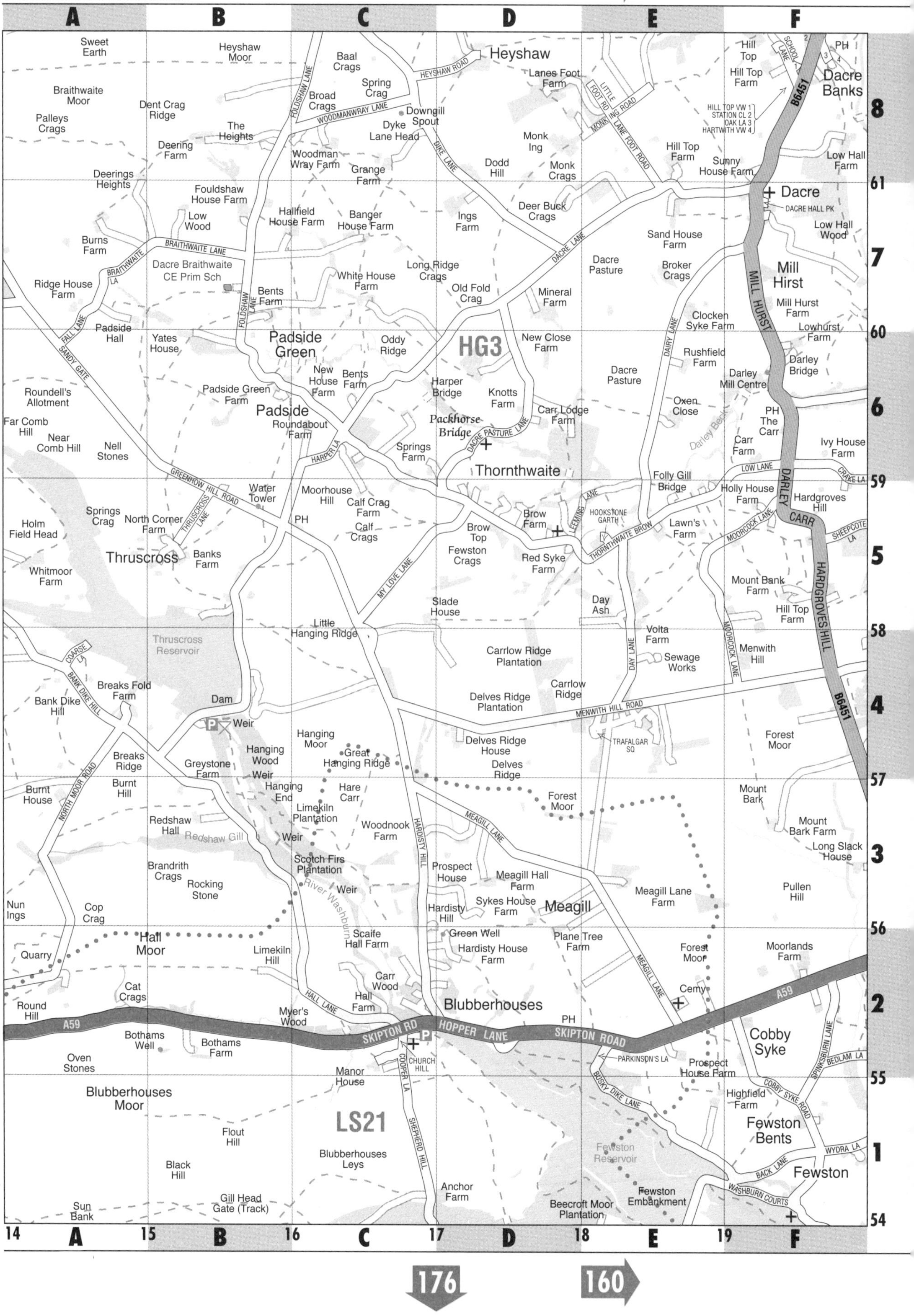

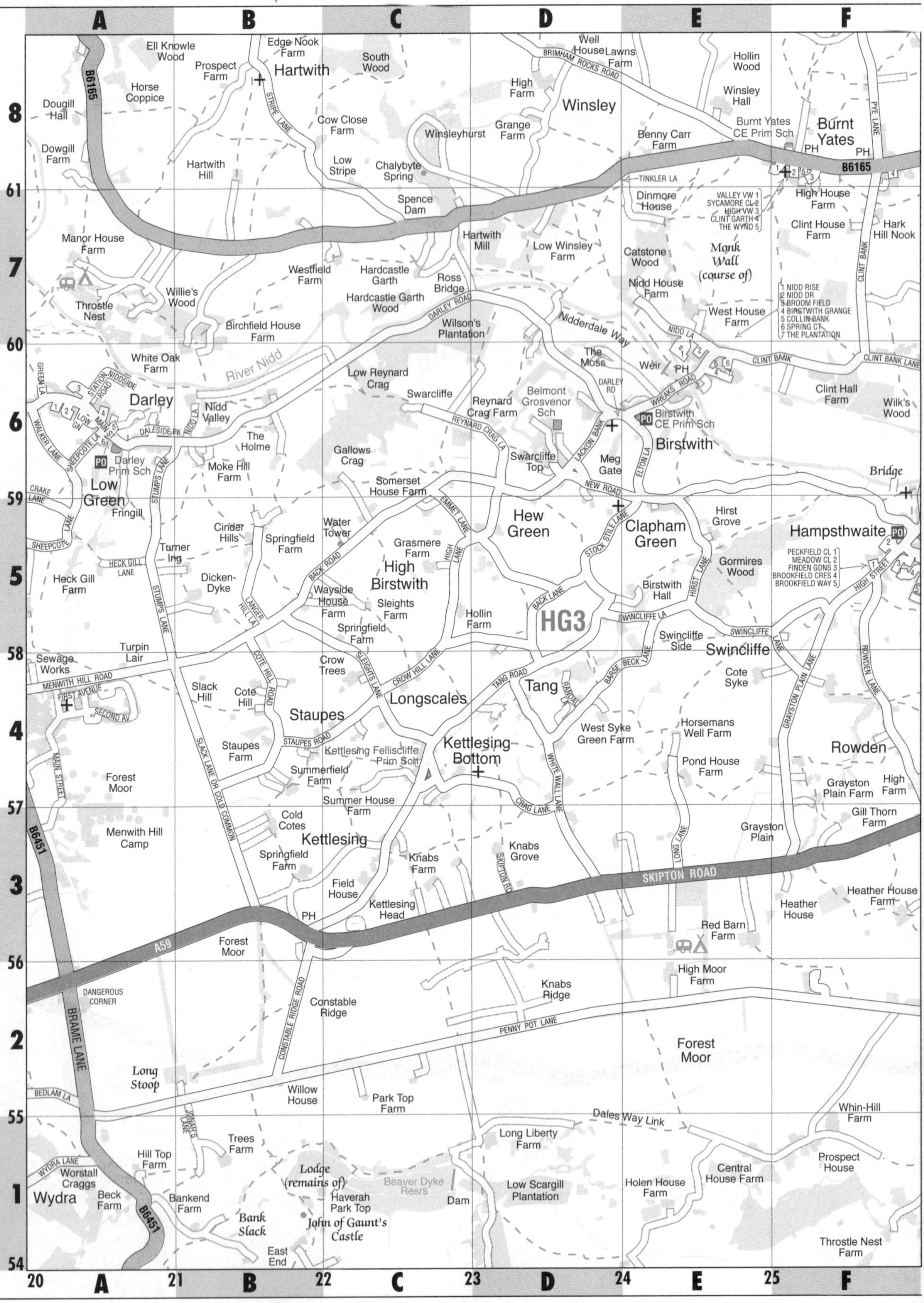
A B C D E F
8
61
7
60
6
59
5
58
4
57
3
56
2
55
1
54
20 A 21 B 22 C 23 D 24 E 25 F
Ell Knowle Wood
Edge Nook Farm
Hartwith
South Wood
Well House
Lawns Farm
BRIMHAM ROCKS ROAD
Hollin Wood
Prospect Farm
Horse Coppice
Dougill Hall
B6165
STRIPE LANE
High Farm
Winsley
Winsley Hall
Burnt Yates CE Prim Sch
Burnt Yates
PYE LANE
Cow Close Farm
Winsleyhurst
Grange Farm
Benny Carr Farm
PH
Dowgill Farm
Hartwith Hill
Low Stripe
Chalybyte Spring
TINKLER LA
B6165
Spence Dam
Dinmore House
VALLEY VW 1
SYCAMORE CL 2
HIGH VW 3
CLINT GARTH 4
THE WYND 5
High House Farm
Clint House Farm
Hark Hill Nook
Manor House Farm
Hartwith Mill
Low Winsley Farm
Catstone Wood
Monk Wall (course of)
CLINT BANK
Westfield Farm
Hardcastle Garth
Ross Bridge
Nidd House Farm
Throstle Nest
Willie's Wood
Hardcastle Garth Wood
DARLEY ROAD
1 NIDD RISE
2 NIDD DR
3 BROOM FIELD
4 BIRSTWITH GRANGE
5 COLLIN BANK
6 SPRING CT
7 THE PLANTATION
Birchfield House Farm
Wilson's Plantation
Nidderdale Way
West House Farm
NIDD LA
White Oak Farm
River Nidd
The Moss
Weir
PH
CLINT BANK
CLINT BANK LANE
GREEN LA
STATION ROAD
NIDDSIDE
Low Reynard Crag
DARLEY RD
WREAKS ROAD
Darley
Swarcliffe
Reynard Crag Farm
Belmont Grosvenor Sch
Clint Hall Farm
Wilk's Wood
Nidd Valley
REYNARD CRAG LA
LACKON BANK
Birstwith CE Prim Sch
Birstwith
WALKER LANE
LOW GN
MAIN ST
DALESIDE PK
MIDDLE LA
The Holme
Gallows Crag
Swarcliffe Top
Meg Gate
ELTON LA
SHEEPCOTE LA
Darley Prim Sch
Moke Hill Farm
Bridge
STUMPS LANE
Somerset House Farm
NEW ROAD
CRAKE LANE
Low Green
Fringill
Water Tower
EMMET LANE
Hew Green
Clapham Green
Hirst Grove
Hampsthwaite
SHEEPCOTE LANE
Cinder Hills
Springfield Farm
Grasmere Farm
STOCK STILE LANE
Turner Ing
HIGH LANE
Gormires Wood
PECKFIELD CL 1
MEADOW CL 2
FINDEN GDNS 3
BROOKFIELD CRES 4
BROOKFIELD WAY 5
HECK GILL LANE
BACK ROAD
High Birstwith
HIRST LANE
Heck Gill Farm
Dicken-Dyke
Wayside House Farm
BACK LANE
Birstwith Hall
HIGH STREET
Sleights Farm
LANGER HILL LA
Hollin Farm
HG3
SWINCLIFFE LA
Springfield Farm
Swincliffe Side
SWINCLIFFE
Turpin Lair
Swincliffe
Sewage Works
Crow Trees
CROW HILL LANE
TANG ROAD
Tang
BECK LANE
BARSE
Cote Syke
MENWITH HILL ROAD
FIRST AVENUE
SECOND AV
COTE HILL ROAD
SLEIGHTS LANE
Longscales
RANDAL
ROWDEN LANE
Slack Hill
Cote Hill
Staupes
GRAYSTON PLAIN LANE
West Syke Green Farm
Horsemans Well Farm
Staupes Farm
STAUPES ROAD
Kettlesing Bottom
Rowden
Kettlesing Felliscliffe Prim Sch
Pond House Farm
SLACK LANE OR COLD COMMON
MAIN STREET
Forest Moor
Summerfield Farm
Grayston Plain Farm
High Farm
WHITE WALL LANE
Summer House Farm
CRAG LANE
Gill Thorn Farm
Cold Cotes
B6451
Menwith Hill Camp
Kettlesing
Knabs Grove
Grayston Plain
Springfield Farm
Knabs Farm
SKIPTON RD
LONG LANE
SKIPTON ROAD
Field House
Kettlesing Head
Heather House
Heather House Farm
PH
Red Barn Farm
Forest Moor
A59
High Moor Farm
Constable Ridge
Knabs Ridge
DANGEROUS CORNER
CONSTABLE RIDGE ROAD
BRAME LANE
PENNY POT LANE
Forest Moor
Long Stoop
Willow House
BEDLAM LA
Park Top Farm
Dales Way Link
Whin-Hill Farm
Trees Farm
JONAH'S LANE
Long Liberty Farm
Hill Top Farm
Prospect House
Central House Farm
WYDRA LANE
Worstall Craggs
Lodge (remains of)
Beaver Dyke Resrs
Low Scargill Plantation
Holen House Farm
Wydra
Beck Farm
Bankend Farm
Haverah Park Top
Dam
B6451
Bank Slack
John of Gaunt's Castle
Throstle Nest Farm
East End

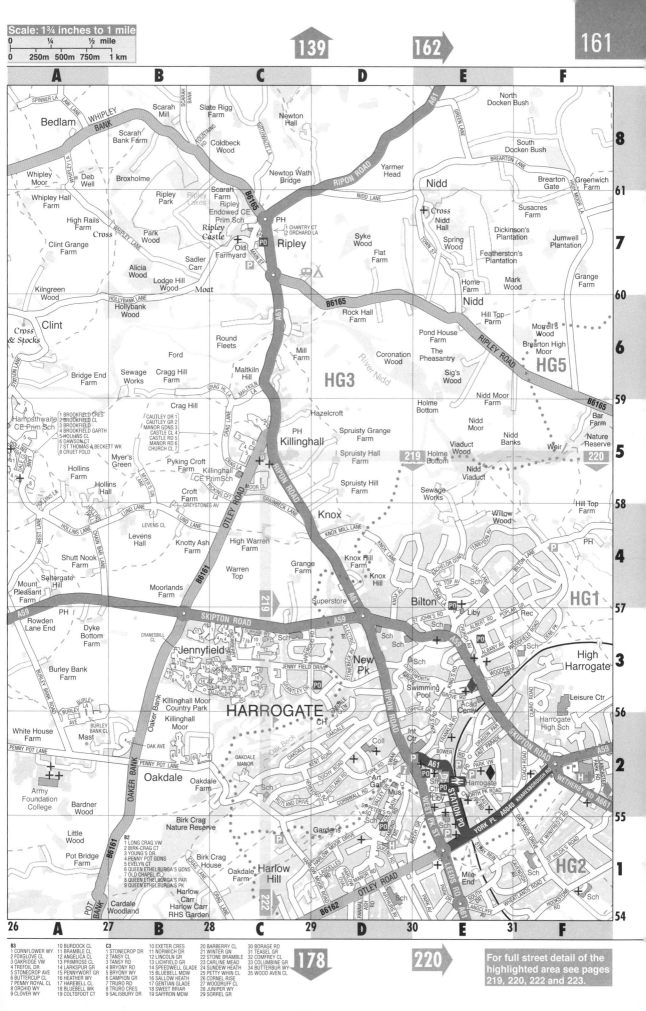

Scale: 1¾ inches to 1 mile
0 ¼ ½ mile
0 250m 500m 750m 1 km

139
162

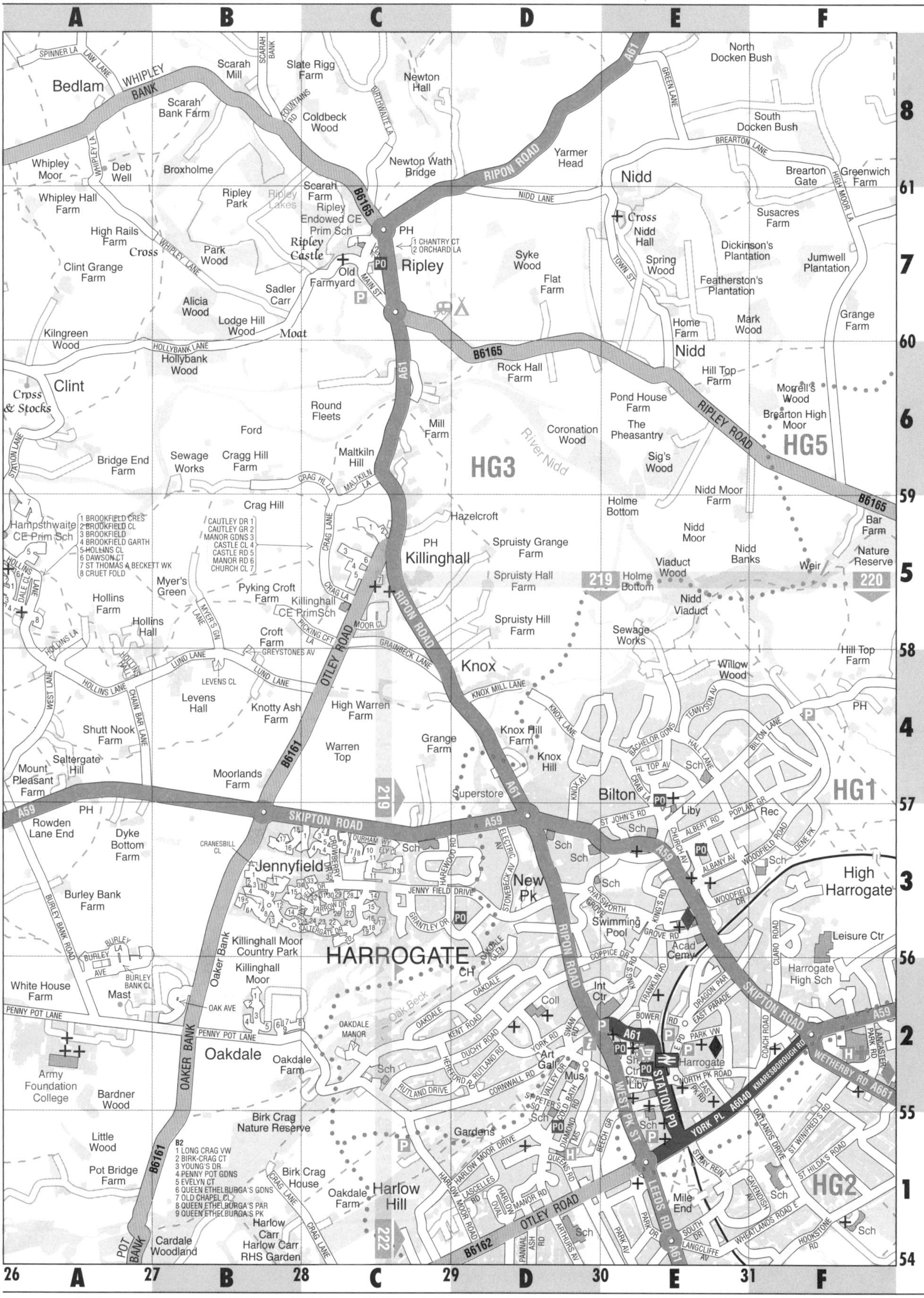

B3	10 BURDOCK CL	C3	10 EXETER CRES	20 BARBERRY CL	30 BORAGE RD
1 CORNFLOWER WY	11 BRAMBLE CL	1 STONECROP DR	11 NORWICH DR	21 WINTER GN	31 TEASEL GR
2 FOXGLOVE CL	12 ANGELICA CL	2 TANSY CL	12 LINCOLN GR	22 STONE BRAMBLE	32 COMFREY CL
3 OAKRIDGE VW	13 PRIMROSE CL	3 TANSY RD	13 LICHFIELD GR	23 CARLINE MEAD	33 COLUMBINE GR
4 TREFOIL DR	14 LARKSPUR GR	4 BRYONY RD	14 SPEEDWELL GLADE	24 SUNDEW HEATH	34 BUTTERBUR WY
5 STONECROP AVE	15 PENNYWORT GR	5 BRYONY WY	15 BLUEBELL MDW	25 PETTY WHIN CL	35 WOOD AVEN CL
6 BUTTERCUP CL	16 HEATHER WY	6 CAMPION GR	16 SALLOW HEATH	26 CORNEL RISE	
7 PENNY ROYAL CL	17 HAREBELL CL	7 TRURO RD	17 GENTIAN GLADE	27 WOODRUFF CL	
8 ORCHID WY	18 BLUEBELL WK	8 TRURO CRES	18 SWEET BRIAR	28 JUNIPER WY	
9 CLOVER WY	19 COLTSFOOT CT	9 SALISBURY DR	19 SAFFRON MDW	29 SORREL GR	

178
220

For full street detail of the highlighted area see pages 219, 220, 222 and 223.

161
140

Scale: 1¾ inches to 1 mile
0 ¼ ½ mile
0 250m 500m 750m 1 km

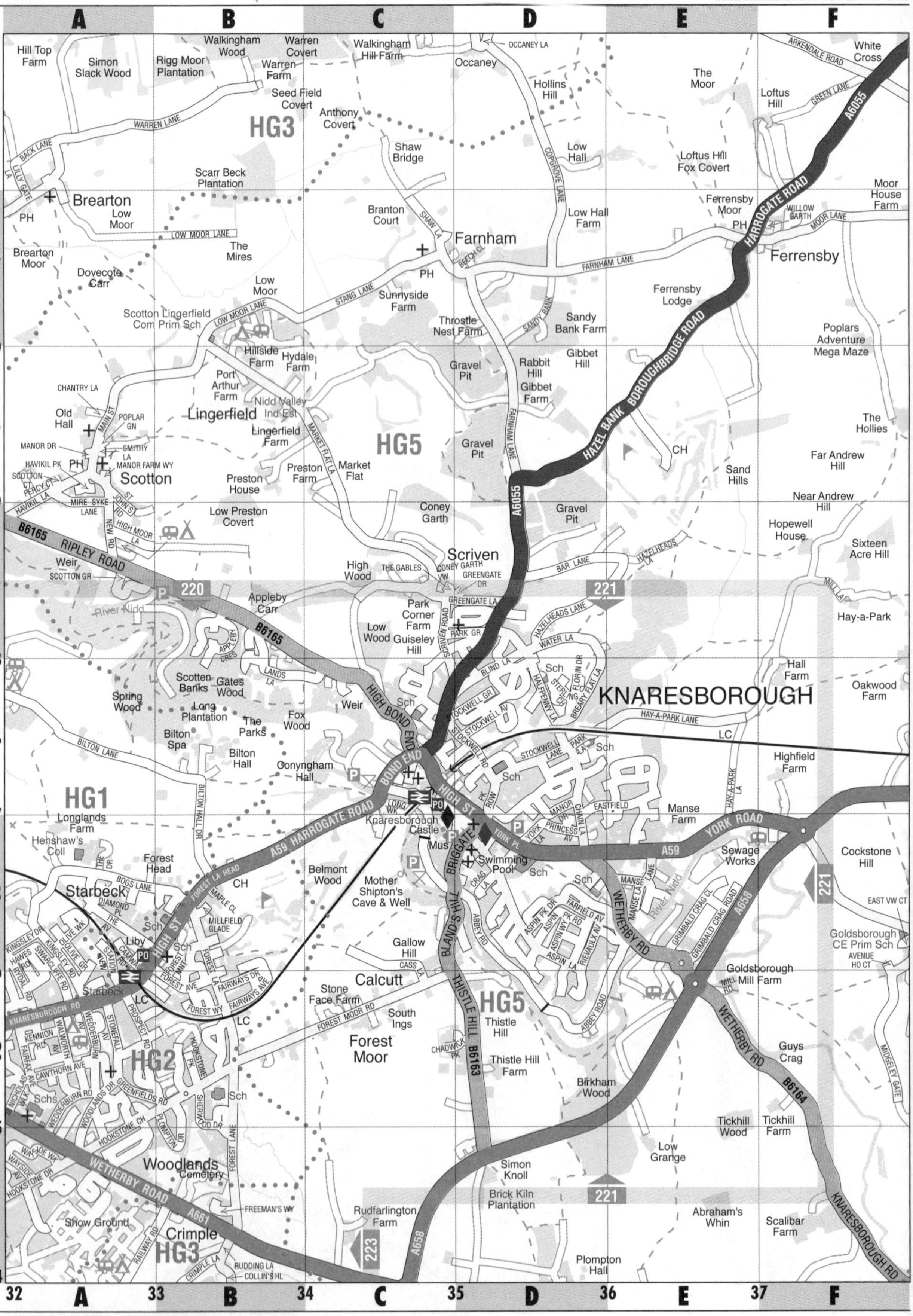
A B C D E F
8
61
7
60
6
59
5
58
4
57
3
56
2
55
1
54
32 33 34 35 36 37
Hill Top Farm
Simon Slack Wood
Rigg Moor Plantation
Walkingham Wood
Warren Covert
Warren Farm
Walkingham Hill Farm
OCCANEY LA
Occaney
Hollins Hill
The Moor
ARKENDALE ROAD
White Cross
Loftus Hill
GREEN LANE
A6055
Seed Field Covert
Anthony Covert
HG3
WARREN LANE
BACK LANE
LILLY GATE LA
Shaw Bridge
COPGROVE LANE
Low Hall
Loftus Hill Fox Covert
Moor House Farm
Scarr Beck Plantation
Brearton
PH
Low Moor
LOW MOOR LANE
Branton Court
SHAW LA
Low Hall Farm
Ferrensby Moor
HARROGATE ROAD
WILLOW GARTH
MOOR LANE
Brearton Moor
The Mires
Farnham
BEECH CL
FARNHAM LANE
Ferrensby
Dovecote Carr
Low Moor
STANG LANE
Sunnyside Farm
Ferrensby Lodge
Scotton Lingerfield Com Prim Sch
LOW MOOR LANE
Throstle Nest Farm
SANDY BANK
Sandy Bank Farm
BOROUGHBRIDGE ROAD
Poplars Adventure Mega Maze
Hillside Farm
Hydale Farm
Gravel Pit
Rabbit Hill
Gibbet Hill
Gibbet Farm
CHANTRY LA
Port Arthur Farm
Nidd Valley Ind Est
HAZEL BANK
Old Hall
MAIN ST
POPLAR GN
Lingerfield
Lingerfield Farm
MARKET FLAT LA
HG5
Gravel Pit
FARNHAM LANE
The Hollies
CH
MANOR DR
SMITHY LA
Far Andrew Hill
HAVIKIL PK
PH
MANOR FARM WY
Scotton
Preston Farm
Market Flat
Sand Hills
SCOTTON CT
PERCY CL
Preston House
HAVIKIL LA
MIRE SYKE LANE
ST JOHN'S RD
Near Andrew Hill
Low Preston Covert
Coney Garth
A6055
Gravel Pit
B6165
NEW RD
HIGH MOOR LA
Hopewell House
RIPLEY ROAD
Sixteen Acre Hill
Scriven
HAZELHEADS LA
Weir
SCOTTON GR
High Wood
THE GABLES
CONEY GARTH VW
GREENGATE DR
BAR LANE
220
221
MILL LA
River Nidd
Appleby Carr
GREENGATE LA
Park Corner Farm
HAZELHEADS LANE
Hay-a-Park
Low Wood
Guiseley Hill
SCRIVEN ROAD
PARK GR
WATER LA
58
APPLEBY CRES
B6165
Sch
FLORIN DR
LANDS LA
BLIND LA
HALFPENNY LA
STERLING
BREARY FLAT LA
Hall Farm
Scotten Banks
Gates Wood
Spring Wood
Weir
Sch
HIGH BOND END
STOCKWELL GR
KNARESBOROUGH
Oakwood Farm
Long Plantation
Fox Wood
STOCKWELL AV
HAY-A-PARK LANE
The Parks
STOCKWELL RD
Bilton Spa
BILTON LANE
Bilton Hall
Conyngham Hall
BOND END
STOCKWELL LANE
PARK LA
Sch
LC
Highfield Farm
HAY-A-PARK LA
BILTON HALL DR
HG1
Sch
PK ROW
A59 HARROGATE ROAD
LONG WK
HIGH ST
EASTFIELD
Manse Farm
Longlands Farm
Knaresborough Castle
PO
MANOR
CHAIN LA
YORK PL
YORK PRINCESS AV
YORK ROAD
Henshaw's Coll
Mus
A59
THE DR
Forest Head
Sewage Works
BRIGGATE
Swimming Pool
Cockstone Hill
FOREST LA HEAD
Sch
BOGS LANE
Belmont Wood
Mother Shipton's Cave & Well
CRAG LA
Sch
MANSE LA
Starbeck
CH
221
DIAMOND PL
MAPLE CL
WETHERBY RD
River Nidd
GRIMBALD CRAG CL
EAST VW CT
ASPIN PK DR
FARFIELD AV
ASPIN DR
HIGH ST
Sch
MILLFIELD GLADE
ABBEY RD
ASPIN PK RD
GRIMBALD CRAG ROAD
A658
Goldsborough CE Prim Sch
KINGSLEY DR
OLIVE WK
HAWES
KINGSLEY RD
Liby
BLAND'S HILL
RIEVAULX AV
AVENUE HO CT
OLIVE GR
SWARCLIFFE RD
PO
Sch
FOREST MT
Gallow Hill
CASS LA
ASPIN LA
Goldsborough Mill Farm
RYDAL RD
STATION AV
FOREST LA
FAIRWAYS DR
Calcutt
MILL RD
Starbeck
FOREST AV
FAIRWAYS AV
Stone Face Farm
THISTLE HILL
HG5
KNARESBOROUGH RD
LC
PROSPECT RD
FOREST WY
FOREST MOOR RD
South Ings
ABBEY ROAD
KENNION RD
WALWORTH AV
WEDDERBURN AV
STONEFALL AV
LC
Thistle Hill
WETHERBY RD
Guys Crag
FAIRFAX AV
HOOKSTONE PK
Forest Moor
HG2
CHADWICK PK
B6163
Thistle Hill Farm
CAWTHORN AVE
MIDGELEY GATE
Schs
WEDDERBURN RD
GREENFIELDS RD
Sch
Birkham Wood
B6164
WOODLANDS DR
SHERWOOD DR
ST NICHOLAS RD
HOOKSTONE CH
PLOMPTON DR
FOREST LANE
Tickhill Wood
Tickhill Farm
WAYSIDE DR
HOOKSTONE DR
Woodlands Cemetery
Low Grange
Simon Knoll
WETHERBY ROAD
Brick Kiln Plantation
221
A661
FREEMAN'S WY
Rudfarlington Farm
Abraham's Whin
Scalibar Farm
KNARESBOROUGH RD
Show Ground
Crimple
HG3
RAILWAY RD
CRIMPLE LA
223
A658
RUDDING LA
COLLIN'S HL
Plompton Hall

For full street detail of the highlighted area see pages 220, 221 and 223.

161
179

Scale: 1¾ inches to 1 mile
0 ¼ ½ mile
0 250m 500m 750m 1 km

141
164

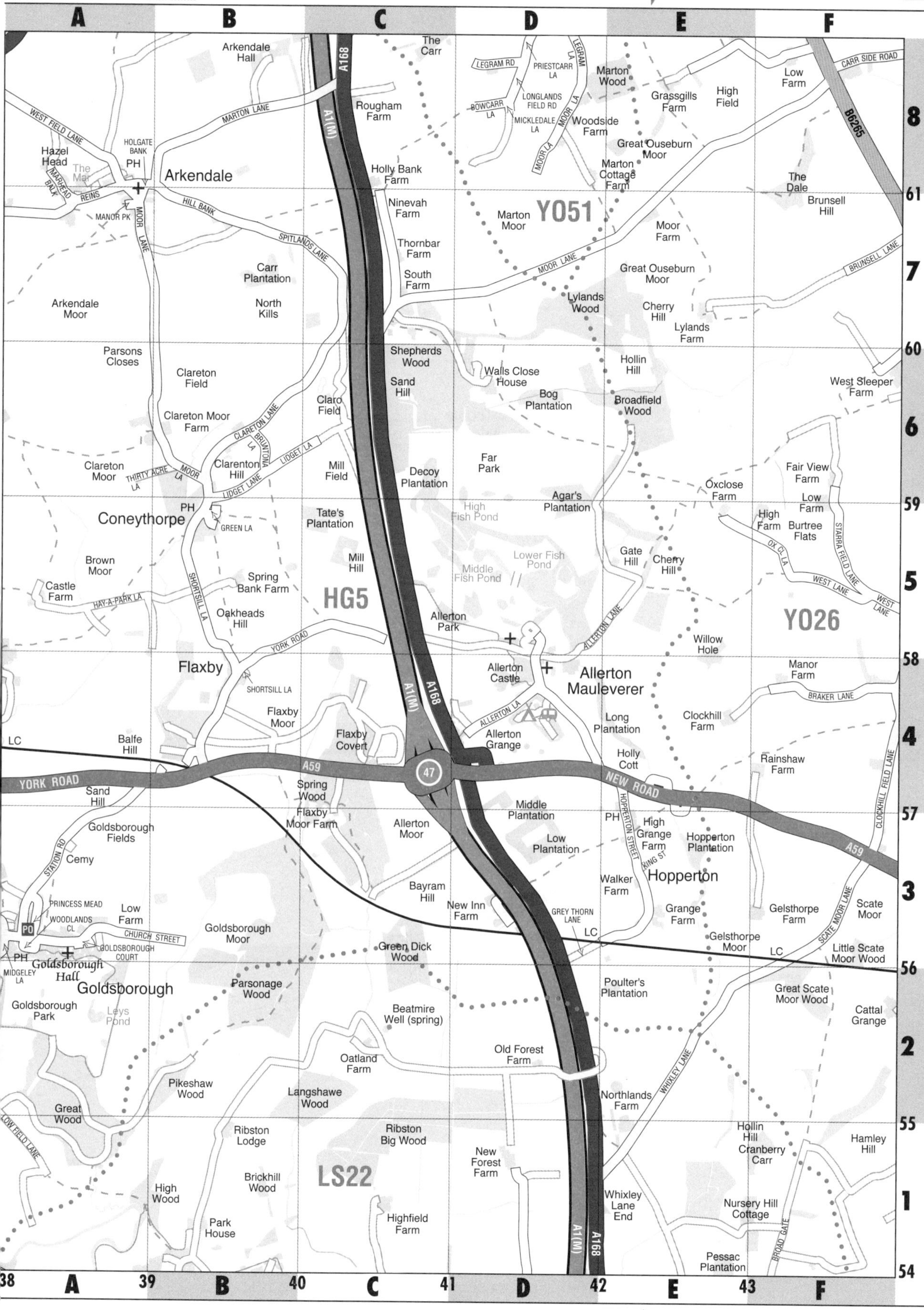

180
164

A8
1 SPRINGFIELD RISE
2 CHURCH FIELD LA
3 TOWNEND CT

163

142

F7
1 HALF MOON ST
2 BEECH TREE CT
3 GRANGE GARTH
4 LINTON PL
5 LINTON MDW
6 MILL LA
7 MAPLE GR
8 WHITE ROSE CL

F8
1 THE PADDOCK
2 GREEN CL
3 GROSVENOR SQ

Scale: 1¾ inches to 1 mile
0 ¼ ½ mile
0 250m 500m 750m 1 km

A B C D E F

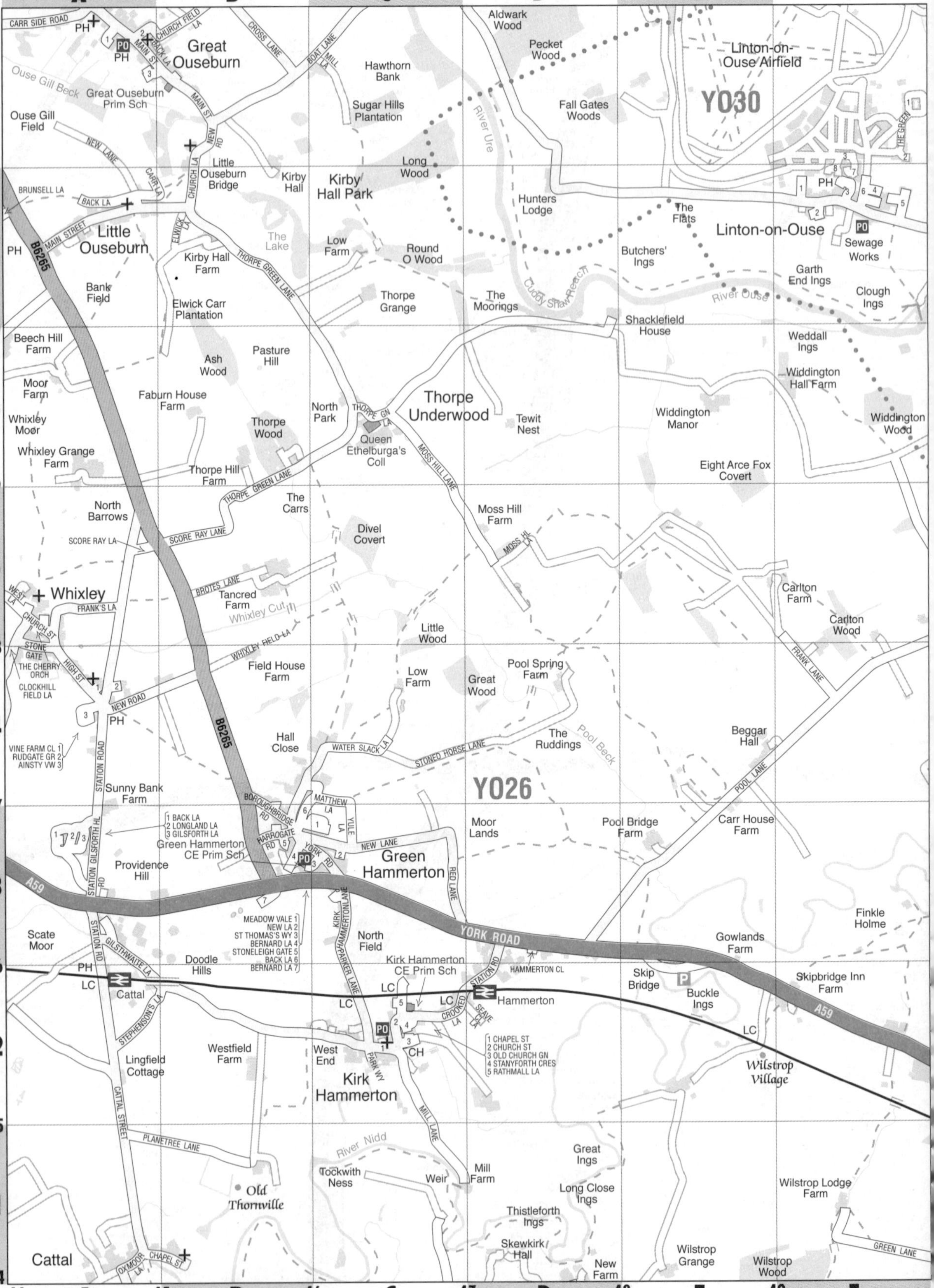

44 A 45 B 46 C 47 D 48 E 49 F

163

181

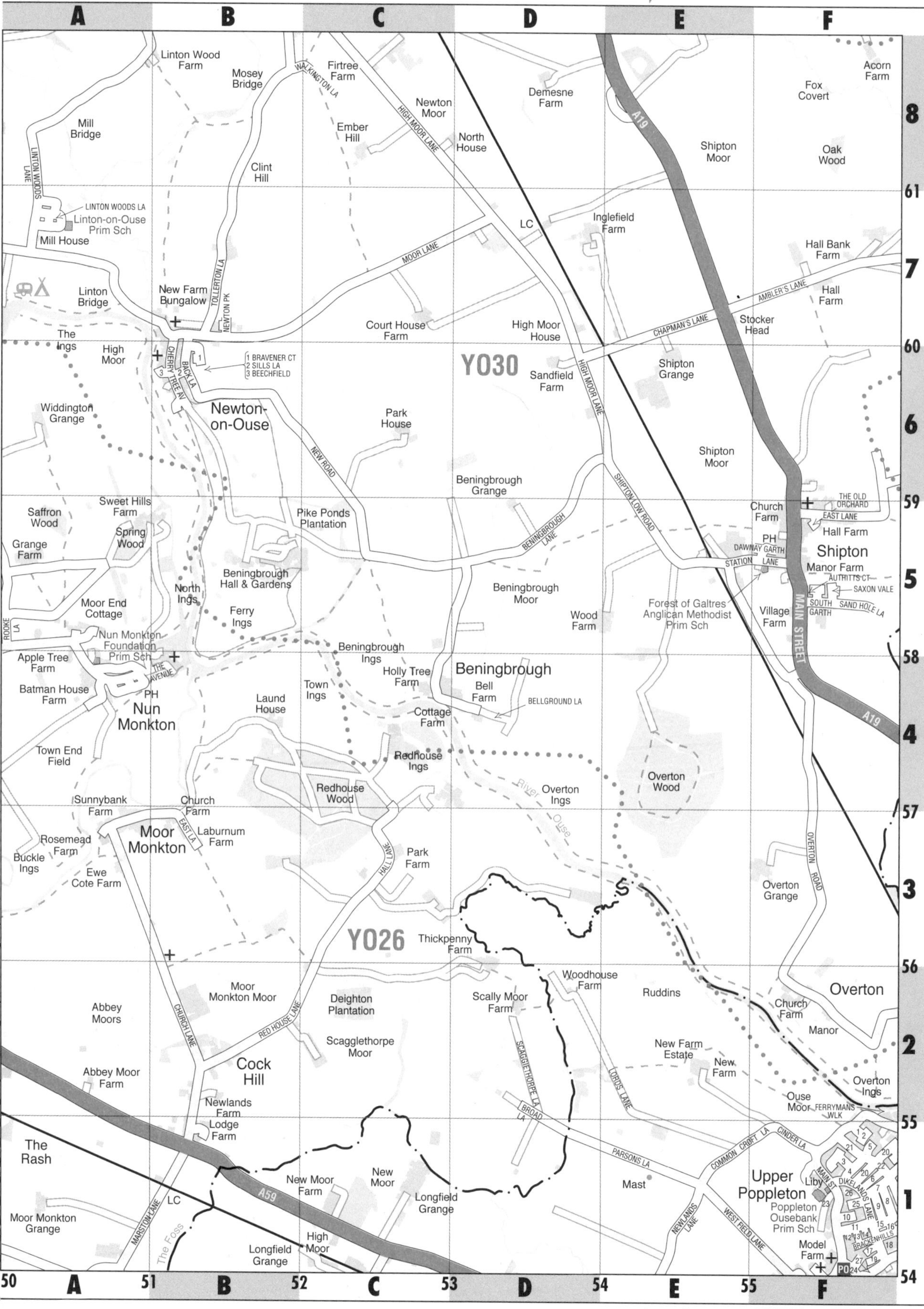

F1
1 RIVERSIDE WALK
2 RIVERSIDE GDNS
3 BANKSIDE CL
4 SPRINGFIELD RD
5 LITTLEFIELD CL
6 MONTAGUE WALK
7 EBOR WAY
8 PEAR TREE AVE
9 ELM TREE AVE
10 LIMEGARTH
11 CHANTRY GAP
12 GROVE GDNS
13 CHANTRY GR
14 CHANTRY AVE
15 APPLE GARTH
16 CHERRY GROVE
17 SYCAMORE VIEW
18 FAIRWAY DR
19 DIKELANDS CL
20 NETHER WY
21 RIVERSVALE DR
22 ALLERTON DR
23 SCHOOL LA
24 STATION RD
25 BEECH WY
26 THE BEECHES
27 LONGRIDGE GDNS

E5
1 VILLAGE GARTH
2 LONGCROFT
3 RIPLEY GR
4 SOUTHLANDS
5 THE AVENUE
6 REDWOOD DR
7 MULBERRY DR
8 ASH LA
9 ELM END
10 COPPICE CL
11 LITTLE LA
12 HAWTHORN AVE
13 BIRCH LA
14 FLETCHER CT
15 ST MARY'S CL
16 SANDY LA
17 CHURCH LA
18 BROAD OAK LA
19 WESTFIELD PL
20 WESTFIELD RD
21 WESTFIELD CL
22 ST NICHOLAS WY
23 PLANTATION WY
24 MIDDLE BANKS
25 HORNSEY GARTH
26 GLEBE WY
27 FOREST CL
28 CHURCHFIELD DR
29 SANDYLAND
30 HEADLAND CL
31 WANDHILL
32 KENNEDY DR
33 ABELTON GR
34 ORCHARD PADDOCK
35 LARCH WY
36 ACACIA GR
37 CYPRUS GR
38 ELDER GR
39 WALNUT CL
40 MINSTER CL

165
144

Scale: 1¾ inches to 1 mile
0 ¼ ½ mile
0 250m 500m 750m 1 km

A B C D E F
Low Bohemia Farm
Bull Lane Bridge
Laund House Farm
Grange Farm
Broad Oaks Farm
YO61
Broad Oak
Martin Hill Farm
Haxby Wood
Low Carr
White House Farm
High Grange
Haxby Moor
Haxby Lodge Farm
Golden Hill Farm
YO30
Rosecroft Farm
Greenthwaite Grange
Greenthwaite
Grange House
Newlands Farm
North Hall Moor
Plainville Farm
Haxby Moor
Yew Tree Farm
Thornville Farm
Pasture Farm
Jubilee Farm
Haxby Grange Farm
Wigginton Moor
Flat Top Farm
Chipchase Farm
Spur House Farm
Rose Cottage Farm
Moor Farm
Stud Farm
Moorlands Wood
Moorlands Nature Reserve
Moorlands
Moorlands Farm
Cemy
Ralph Butterfield Prim Sch
Sports Club
Home Farm
Hall Moor Farm (South)
Hall Moor
Wigginton Prim Sch
Wigginton
Haxby Landing
Skelton Moor
224
225
Lock House
Woodside Farm
Park Farm
Plantation Farm
YO32
Haxby
Wigginton Moor
Hurns Bridge
Glebe Farm
Villa Farm
New Farm
Haxby Gates
Skelton
St Catherines
Skelton Prim Sch
Brecks Farm
Skelton Plantation
Moor Plantation
Joseph Rowntree Sch
Rawcliffe Moor
Clifton Gate Farm
Hall Farm
Kettlestring Farm
Manor House
Skelton Pk Trad Est
YO30
Poplar Plantation
New Earswick
Folly Bridge
Clifton Moor
Skelton Bridge
Rawcliffe Farm
Coppins Farm
Huntington
Ind Est
Nether Poppleton
Poppleton Ings
Bootham Stray
Sewage Works
Rawcliffe
Trad Est
YO26
Works
YO31
York Road
Sutton Road
Wigginton Road
Shipton Road
A1237
A19
B1363
56 57 58 59 60 61
54 1 55 2 56 3 57 4 58 5 59 6 60 7 61 8

For full street detail of the highlighted area see pages 224 and 225.

165
227
228

D5
1 CASTLE CL
2 WINDSOR DR
3 TOWN END GDNS
4 STEEPLE CL
5 HAREWOOD CL
6 DELAMERE CL
7 ETON DR
8 SAXFORD WAY
9 CANTERBURY CL
10 HAMBLETON VIEW
11 BACK LA
12 WESTFIELD GR
13 BURRILL DR
14 TWIN PIKE WY
15 STABLER CL
16 HELMSLEY GR
17 CORNER CL
18 LANCAR CL
19 WATERINGS
20 BUTTERS CL
21 CORBAN WY
22 BUTT HILL
23 SUNNYSIDE

F5
1 FARNDALE CL
2 SANDHOLME
3 NEWDALE
4 KELDALE
5 NORTHCROFT
6 RUSHWOOD CL
7 LANSDOWN WY
8 SCRIVEN GR
9 WOODCOCK CL
10 FALCON CL
11 MALLARD WY
12 HALL RISE
13 FOLKS CL
14 OLD COPPICE
15 NEW FORGE CT
16 CHATSWORTH DR
17 RIVERSDALE
18 NETHERWINDINGS
19 THORNHILLS
20 GARTHS END
21 THE LANDINGS
22 LANDING LA
23 WINDMILL WY
24 LINLEY AVE
25 WEST NOOKS

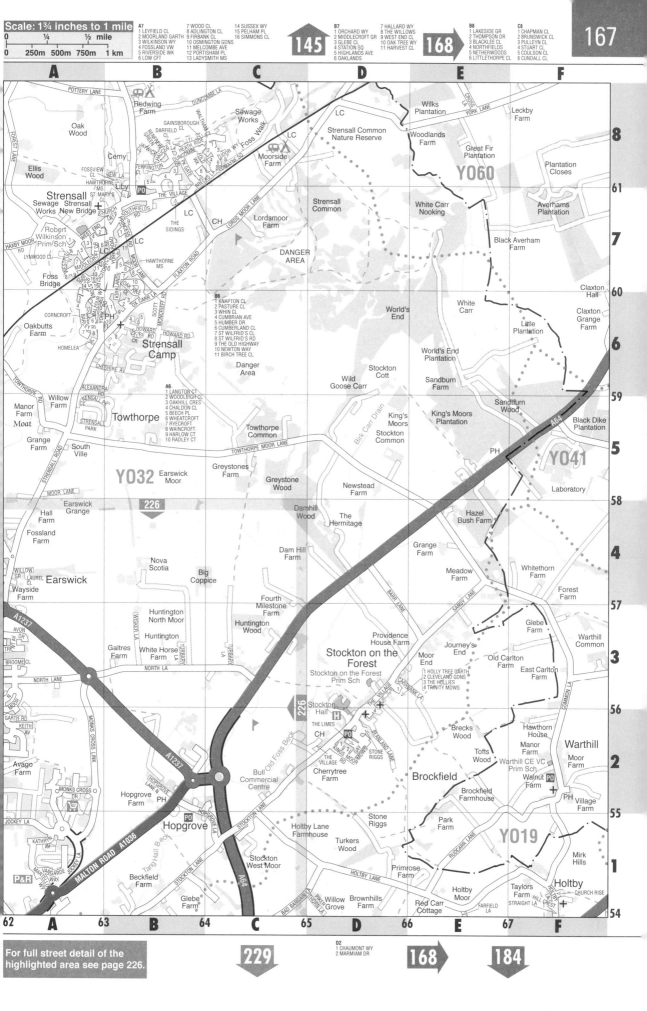

Scale: 1¾ inches to 1 mile
0 ¼ ½ mile
0 250m 500m 750m 1 km

A7
1 LEYFIELD CL
2 MOORLAND GARTH
3 WILKINSON WY
4 FOSSLAND VW
5 RIVERSIDE WK
6 LOW CFT
7 WOOD CL
8 ADLINGTON CL
9 FIRBANK CL
10 OSMINGTON GDNS
11 MELCOMBE AVE
12 PORTISHAM PL
13 LADYSMITH MS
14 SUSSEX WY
15 PELHAM PL
16 SIMMONS CL

145

B7
1 ORCHARD WY
2 MIDDLECROFT GR
3 GLEBE CL
4 STATION SQ
5 HIGHLANDS AVE
6 OAKLANDS
7 HALLARD WY
8 THE WILLOWS
9 WEST END CL
10 OAK TREE WY
11 HARVEST CL

168

B8
1 LAKESIDE GR
2 THOMPSON DR
3 BLACKLEE CL
4 NORTHFIELDS
5 NETHERWOODS
6 LITTLETHORPE CL

C8
1 CHAPMAN CL
2 BRUNSWICK CL
3 PULLEYN CL
4 STUART CL
5 COULSON CL
6 CUNDALL CL

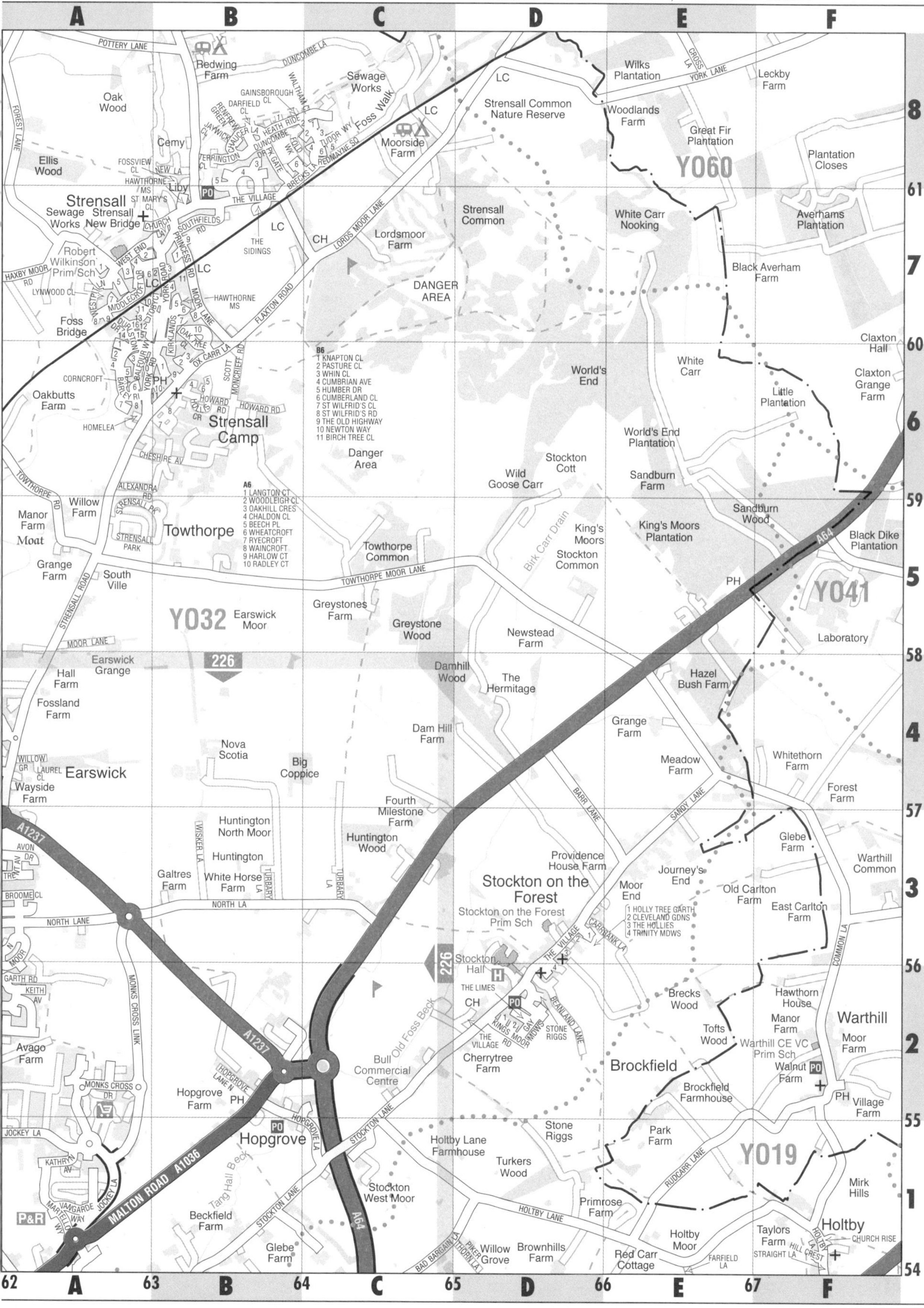

For full street detail of the highlighted area see page 226.

229

D2
1 CHAUMONT WY
2 MARMIAM DR

168

184

Scale: 1¾ inches to 1 mile
0 ¼ ½ mile
0 250m 500m 750m 1 km

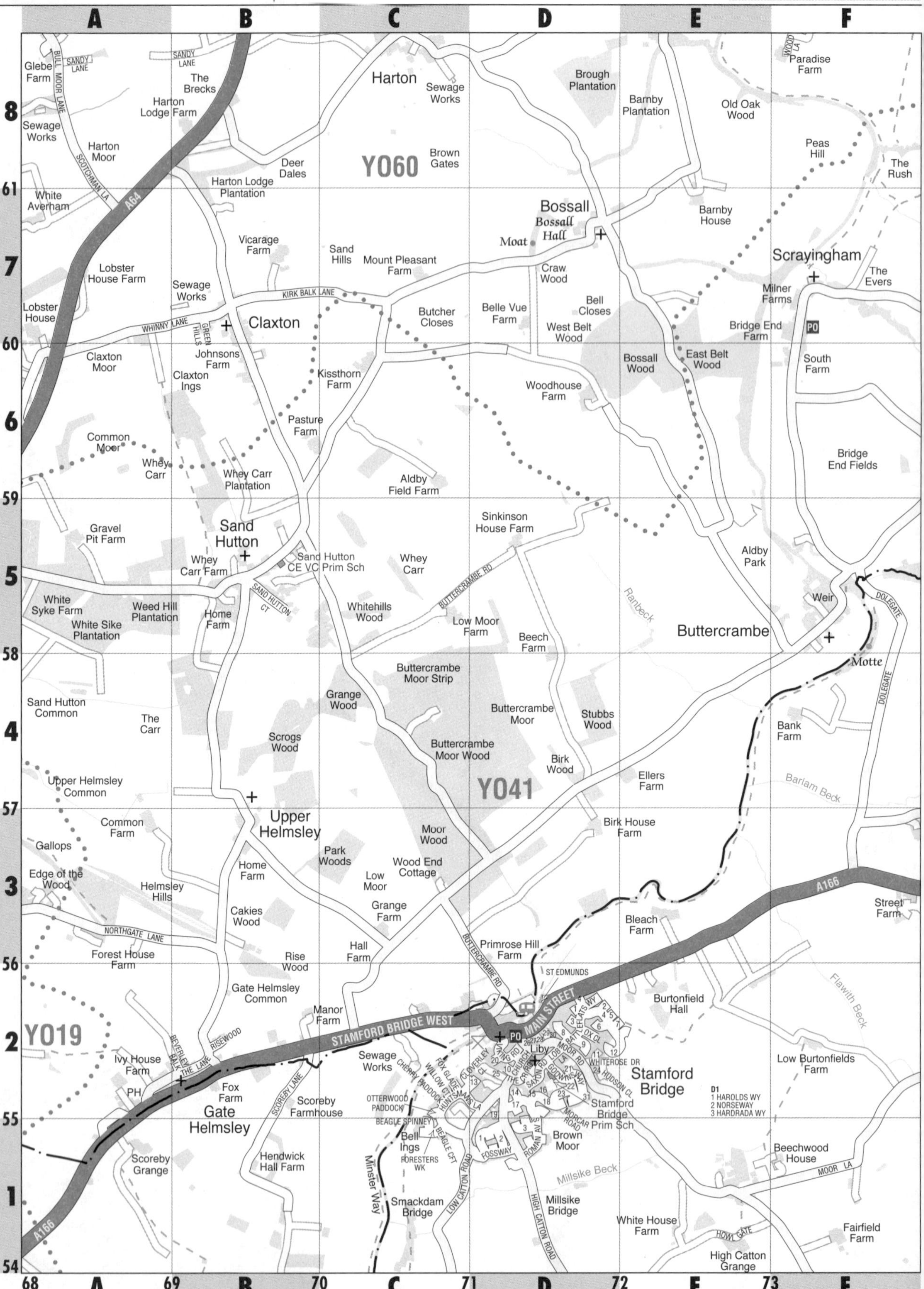
A
B
C
D
E
F
8
61
7
60
6
59
5
58
4
57
3
56
2
55
1
54
68
69
70
71
72
73
Glebe Farm
SANDY LANE
BULL MOOR LANE
The Brecks
Harton Lodge Farm
Harton
Sewage Works
Brough Plantation
Barnby Plantation
Old Oak Wood
Paradise Farm
WOOD LA
Sewage Works
Harton Moor
SCOTCHMAN LA
A64
Deer Dales
YO60
Brown Gates
Peas Hill
The Rush
White Averham
Harton Lodge Plantation
Bossall
Bossall Hall
Moat
Barnby House
Vicarage Farm
Sand Hills
Mount Pleasant Farm
Craw Wood
Scrayingham
The Evers
Lobster House Farm
Sewage Works
KIRK BALK LANE
Bell Closes
Milner Farms
Lobster House
WHINNY LANE
GREEN HILLS
Claxton
Butcher Closes
Belle Vue Farm
West Belt Wood
Bridge End Farm
PO
Claxton Moor
Johnsons Farm
Claxton Ings
Kissthorn Farm
Bossall Wood
East Belt Wood
South Farm
Woodhouse Farm
Pasture Farm
Common Moor
Whey Carr
Whey Carr Plantation
Aldby Field Farm
Bridge End Fields
Gravel Pit Farm
Sand Hutton
Sinkinson House Farm
Whey Carr Farm
Sand Hutton CE VC Prim Sch
Whey Carr
Aldby Park
SAND HUTTON CT
BUTTERCRAMBE RD
Ranbeck
Weir
DOLEGATE
White Syke Farm
Weed Hill Plantation
White Sike Plantation
Home Farm
Whitehills Wood
Low Moor Farm
Beech Farm
Buttercrambe
Motte
Buttercrambe Moor Strip
Sand Hutton Common
The Carr
Grange Wood
Buttercrambe Moor
Stubbs Wood
DOLEGATE
Bank Farm
Scrogs Wood
Buttercrambe Moor Wood
Birk Wood
Upper Helmsley Common
YO41
Ellers Farm
Barlam Beck
Upper Helmsley
Common Farm
Birk House Farm
Gallops
Moor Wood
Park Woods
Home Farm
Edge of the Wood
Wood End Cottage
Low Moor
Helmsley Hills
A166
Grange Farm
Cakies Wood
Street Farm
Bleach Farm
NORTHGATE LANE
BUTTERCRAMBE RD
Primrose Hill Farm
Hall Farm
Forest House Farm
Rise Wood
ST EDMUNDS
Flawith Beck
Gate Helmsley Common
MAIN STREET
Burtonfield Hall
Manor Farm
YO19
STAMFORD BRIDGE WEST
RISEWOOD
BEVERLEY BALK
PO
Liby
Sewage Works
Ivy House Farm
THE LANE
WHITEROSE DR
Low Burtonfields Farm
HUDSON CL
OX CL
FOX GLADE
CHERRY PADDOCK
WILLOW CL
MAINS LA
CLOVERLEY CL
THE CHURCH
SAXON RD
MOOR RD
GODWINSWAY
Stamford Bridge
PH
Fox Farm
Scoreby Farmhouse
SCOREBY LANE
OTTERWOOD PADDOCK
HUNTS
Stamford Bridge Prim Sch
D1
1 HAROLDS WY
2 NORSEWAY
3 HARDRADA WY
Gate Helmsley
BEAGLE SPINNEY
Bell Ings
BEAGLE CFT
MORCAR ROAD
Brown Moor
FORESTERS WK
FOSSWAY
ROMAN AV
Beechwood House
Scoreby Grange
Hendwick Hall Farm
Millsike Beck
MOOR LA
Minster Way
LOW CATTON ROAD
Smackdam Bridge
Millsike Bridge
HIGH CATTON ROAD
White House Farm
Fairfield Farm
HOWL GATE
A166
High Catton Grange

D2
1 BRIDLINGTON RD
2 DERWENT CL
3 DANESWELL CL
4 BURTON FIELDS RD
5 GARROWBY VW
6 KINGSWAY
7 DARLEY CL
8 WHARTON RD
9 ST JOHN'S RD
10 CHURCH LA
11 EGREMONT CL
12 BURTON FIELDS CL
13 HEATHER BANK
14 TOSTIG CL
15 FAIRFAX
16 SCHOOL CL
17 ROMAN AVE N
18 GODWINSWAY
19 BUTTS CL
20 VIKING CL
21 MIDGLEY CL
22 BROWN MOOR
23 FURLONG RD
24 ETTY CL
25 STONE WALL COTTAGE LA
26 THE OLD WOODYARD
27 GREEN BANK LA
28 FIRS GARTH LA
29 BLACKSMITHS LA
30 ROSEBERY WOOD
31 JOHN WARD CL

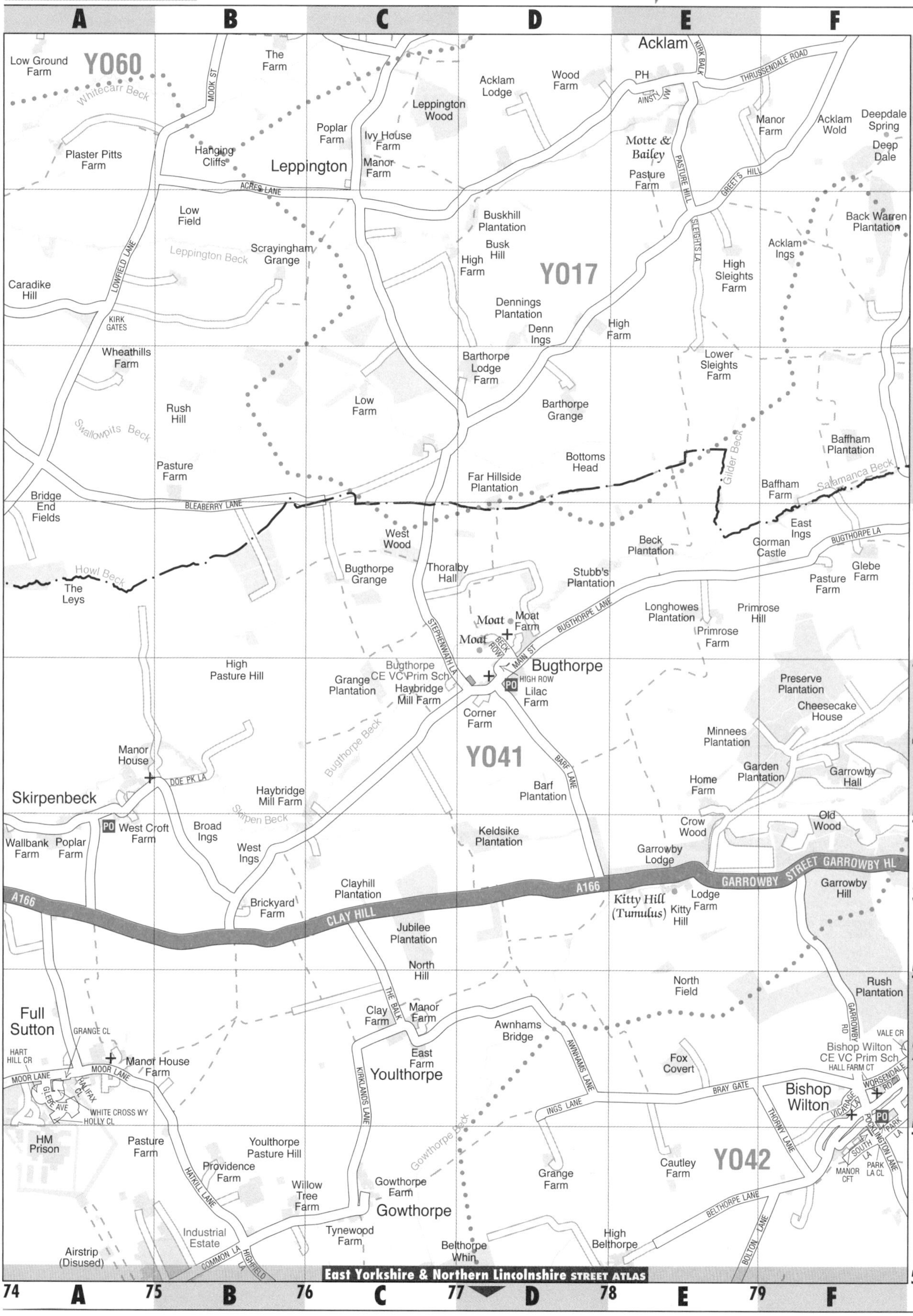
A
B
C
D
E
F
Low Ground Farm
YO60
Whitecarr Beck
The Farm
MOOK ST
Acklam Lodge
Wood Farm
Acklam
KIRK BALK
PH
THRUSSENDALE ROAD
Leppington Wood
Poplar Farm
Ivy House Farm
Manor Farm
Leppington
Hanging Cliffs
Plaster Pitts Farm
Motte & Bailey
Pasture Farm
PASTURE HILL
Manor Farm
Acklam Wold
Deepdale Spring
Deep Dale
GREET'S HILL
ACRES LANE
Low Field
Buskhill Plantation
Busk Hill
High Farm
YO17
Back Warren Plantation
Acklam Ings
High Sleights Farm
SLEIGHTS LA
Leppington Beck
Scrayingham Grange
LOWFIELD LANE
Caradike Hill
KIRK GATES
Dennings Plantation
Denn Ings
High Farm
Wheathills Farm
Barthorpe Lodge Farm
Lower Sleights Farm
Low Farm
Rush Hill
Swallowpits Beck
Barthorpe Grange
Baffham Plantation
Gilder Beck
Pasture Farm
Bottoms Head
Far Hillside Plantation
Baffham Farm
Salamanca Beck
Bridge End Fields
BLEABERRY LANE
West Wood
Beck Plantation
East Ings
Gorman Castle
BUGTHORPE LA
Howl Beck
The Leys
Bugthorpe Grange
Thoralby Hall
Stubb's Plantation
Pasture Farm
Glebe Farm
Moat
Moat Farm
Longhowes Plantation
Primrose Hill
Primrose Farm
BUGTHORPE LANE
STEPHENWATH LA
BECK ROW
MAIN ST
HIGH ROW
Bugthorpe
Bugthorpe CE VC Prim Sch
Grange Plantation
Haybridge Mill Farm
High Pasture Hill
Lilac Farm
Corner Farm
Preserve Plantation
Cheesecake House
Minnees Plantation
YO41
Bugthorpe Beck
BARF LANE
Manor House
Skirpenbeck
DOE PK LA
Haybridge Mill Farm
Barf Plantation
Home Farm
Garden Plantation
Garrowby Hall
Skirpen Beck
West Croft Farm
Broad Ings
Wallbank Farm
Poplar Farm
West Ings
Keldsike Plantation
Crow Wood
Old Wood
Garrowby Lodge
GARROWBY STREET GARROWBY HL
A166
CLAY HILL
Clayhill Plantation
Brickyard Farm
Kitty Hill (Tumulus)
Kitty Hill
Lodge Farm
Garrowby Hill
Jubilee Plantation
North Hill
North Field
Rush Plantation
Full Sutton
GRANGE CL
THE BALK
Clay Farm
Manor Farm
Awnhams Bridge
GARROWBY RD
VALE CR
Bishop Wilton CE VC Prim Sch
HALL FARM CT
HART HILL CR
Manor House Farm
MOOR LANE
East Farm
Youlthorpe
AWNHAMS LANE
Fox Covert
WORSENDALE RD
MOOR LANE
HALIFAX CL
GLEBE AVE
WHITE CROSS WY
HOLLY CL
KIRKLANDS LANE
BRAY GATE
Bishop Wilton
INGS LANE
THORNY LANE
VICARAGE LA
HM Prison
Pasture Farm
Youlthorpe Pasture Hill
Gowthorpe Beck
POCKLINGTON LANE
SOUTH LA
PARK LA
Providence Farm
HATKILL LANE
Willow Tree Farm
Gowthorpe Farm
Gowthorpe
Grange Farm
Cautley Farm
YO42
MANOR CFT
PARK LA CL
BELTHORPE LANE
Industrial Estate
Tynewood Farm
Belthorpe Whin
High Belthorpe
BOLTON LANE
Airstrip (Disused)
COMMON LA
HIGHFIELD LA
8
61
7
60
6
59
5
58
4
57
3
56
2
55
1
54
74
75
76
77
78
79

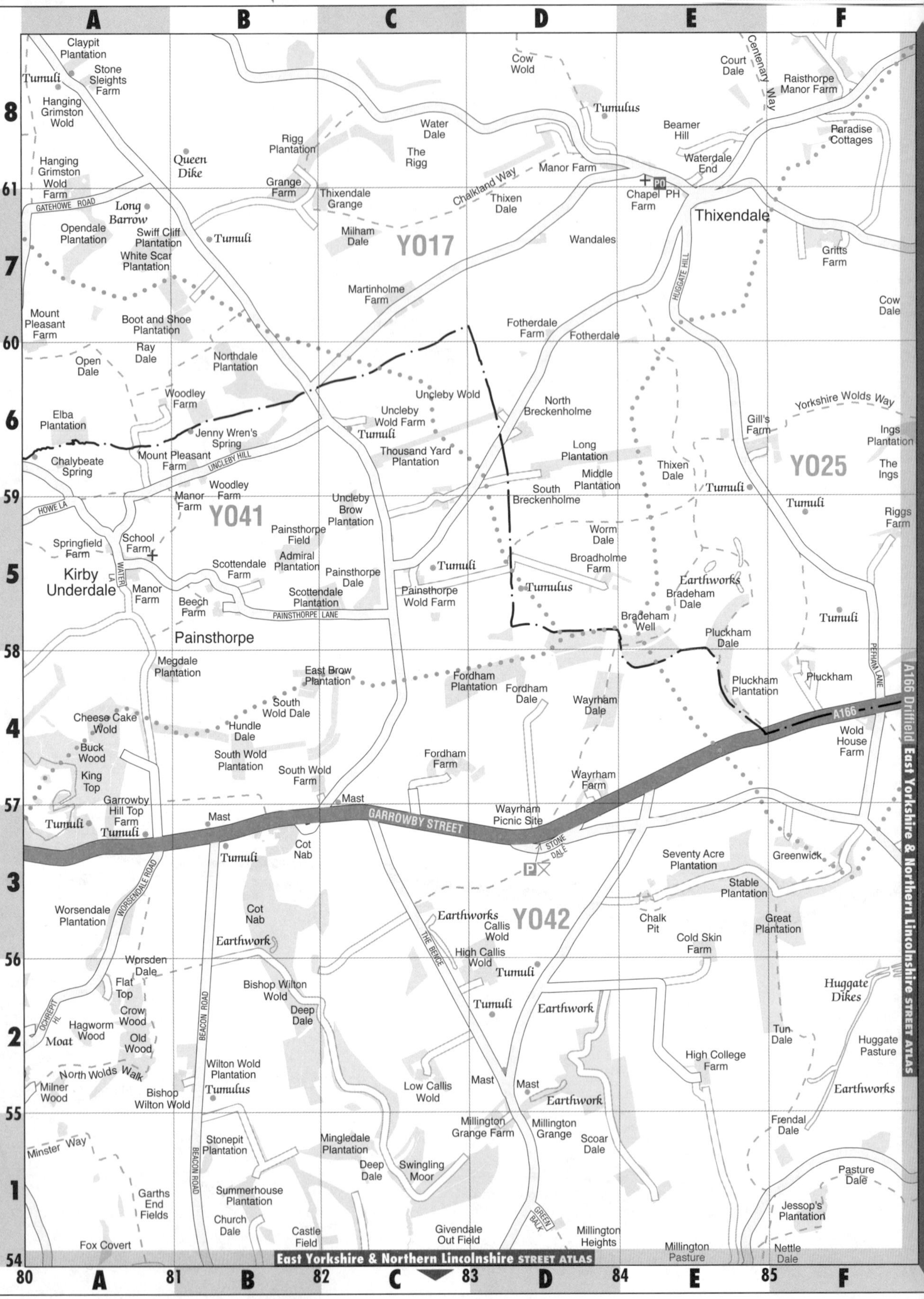
A
B
C
D
E
F
8
61
7
60
6
59
5
58
4
57
3
56
2
55
1
54
80
81
82
83
84
85
Claypit Plantation
Tumuli
Stone Sleights Farm
Hanging Grimston Wold
Hanging Grimston Wold Farm
Queen Dike
Rigg Plantation
Grange Farm
Thixendale Grange
Water Dale
The Rigg
Cow Wold
Tumulus
Court Dale
Centenary Way
Raisthorpe Manor Farm
Beamer Hill
Paradise Cottages
Waterdale End
Manor Farm
Chalkland Way
Thixen Dale
Chapel Farm
PH
PO
Thixendale
GATEHOWE ROAD
Long Barrow
Opendale Plantation
Swift Cliff Plantation
White Scar Plantation
Tumuli
Milham Dale
YO17
Wandales
HUGGATE HILL
Gritts Farm
Martinholme Farm
Mount Pleasant Farm
Boot and Shoe Plantation
Cow Dale
Fotherdale Farm
Fotherdale
Ray Dale
Open Dale
Northdale Plantation
Uncleby Wold
North Breckenholme
Yorkshire Wolds Way
Woodley Farm
Elba Plantation
Uncleby Wold Farm
Tumuli
Gill's Farm
Ings Plantation
Jenny Wren's Spring
Thousand Yard Plantation
Long Plantation
Chalybeate Spring
Mount Pleasant Farm
UNCLEBY HILL
YO25
Thixen Dale
The Ings
Middle Plantation
Woodley Farm
Manor Farm
Uncleby Brow Plantation
South Breckenholme
HOWE LA
YO41
Tumuli
Riggs Farm
Painsthorpe Field
Worm Dale
Springfield Farm
School Farm
Admiral Plantation
Broadholme Farm
Kirby Underdale
WATER LA
Scottendale Farm
Painsthorpe Dale
Tumuli
Earthworks
Manor Farm
Tumulus
Bradeham Dale
Beech Farm
Scottendale Plantation
Painsthorpe Wold Farm
PAINSTHORPE LANE
Bradeham Well
Tumuli
Painsthorpe
Pluckham Dale
PEFHAM LANE
Megdale Plantation
East Brow Plantation
Fordham Plantation
Fordham Dale
Pluckham Plantation
Pluckham
A166 Driffield
South Wold Dale
Wayrham Dale
A166
Cheese Cake Wold
Hundle Dale
Wold House Farm
Buck Wood
South Wold Plantation
Fordham Farm
King Top
South Wold Farm
Wayrham Farm
Mast
Garrowby Hill Top Farm
Mast
GARROWBY STREET
Wayrham Picnic Site
Tumuli
Tumuli
Cot Nab
STONE DALE
Tumuli
Seventy Acre Plantation
Greenwick
WORSENDALE ROAD
Stable Plantation
Worsendale Plantation
Cot Nab
Earthworks
Callis Wold
YO42
Chalk Pit
Great Plantation
Earthwork
THE BENCE
Cold Skin Farm
Worsden Dale
High Callis Wold
Tumuli
Huggate Dikes
Flat Top
Bishop Wilton Wold
Tumuli
Earthwork
Crow Wood
OCHREPIT HL
Hagworm Wood
Deep Dale
BEACON ROAD
Moat
Old Wood
Tun Dale
Huggate Pasture
High College Farm
North Wolds Walk
Wilton Wold Plantation
Milner Wood
Tumulus
Bishop Wilton Wold
Low Callis Wold
Mast
Mast
Earthwork
Earthworks
Millington Grange Farm
Millington Grange
Frendal Dale
Minster Way
Stonepit Plantation
Mingledale Plantation
Scoar Dale
Deep Dale
Swingling Moor
Pasture Dale
Garths End Fields
BEACON ROAD
Summerhouse Plantation
Jessop's Plantation
GREEN BALK
Church Dale
Castle Field
Givendale Out Field
Millington Heights
Fox Covert
Millington Pasture
Nettle Dale
East Yorkshire & Northern Lincolnshire STREET ATLAS

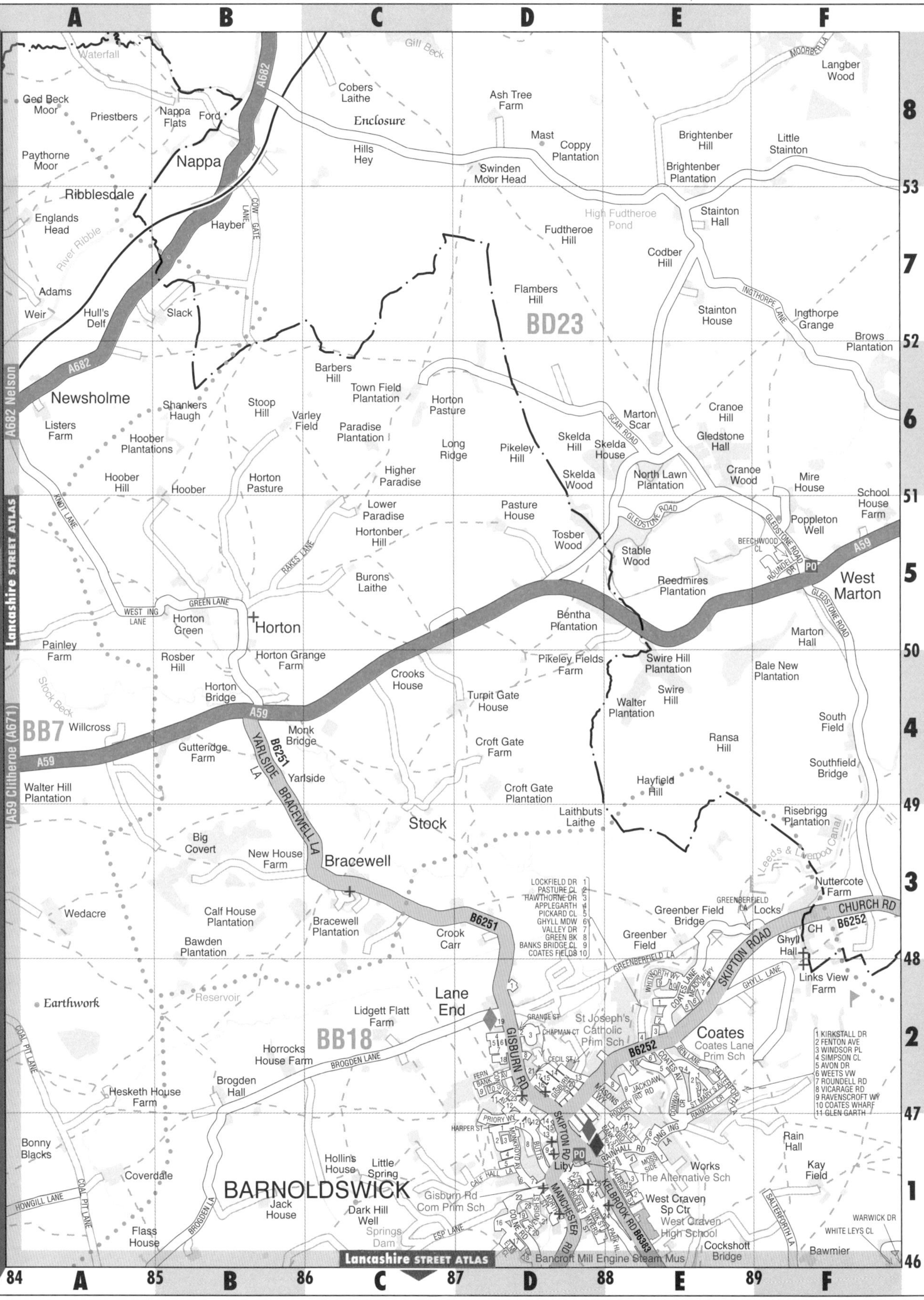

D1
1 RYLSTONE DR
2 DARNBROOK RD
3 GORDALE CL
4 INGLEBOROUGH DR
5 PEN-Y-GHENT WY
6 MILL ST
7 PARROCK ST
8 TAYLOR ST
9 COMMERCIAL ST
10 HOLLINS RD
11 PENNINE WY
12 FEDERATION ST
13 ASH GR
14 DAM HEAD RD
15 LEONARD ST
16 SYCAMORE WY
17 CHESTNUT DR
18 BANCROFT FOLD
19 SMITH ST
20 SACKVILLE ST
21 LONGFIELD CT
22 WESTGATE
23 BEECH ST
24 FRANK ST
25 ROOK ST
26 BACK CHAPEL ST
27 PHILIP ST
28 MALHAM VW CL

D2
1 BANKS HL
2 WEST FIELD RD
3 BLAKELEY CRES
4 FOSTER RD
5 LOUVAIN ST
6 ARTHUR ST
7 CARR RD
8 GLEDSTONE VW
9 GREAT CROFT CL
10 AMBLESIDE AVE
11 MILTON GROVE
12 RICHMOND RD
13 WEST CLO RD
14 COLIN ST
15 BRACEWELL ST
16 BOLLAND ST
17 EDMONDSON ST
18 ROBINSON FOLD
19 BROGDEN VW
20 CORNMILL PL
21 BRUCE ST
22 RICHMOND AVE
23 FREDERICK ST

E1
1 VICTORIA RD
2 CLARENCE ST
3 CLIFFORD ST
4 RIDING CL
5 WELLHOUSE ST
6 HILL ST
7 CLAYTON ST
8 CORONATION ST
9 FRANK ST
10 STUART ST
11 HAVRE PK
12 ETHEL ST
13 TURNER ST
14 UNITY ST
15 LOWER PARK ST

172

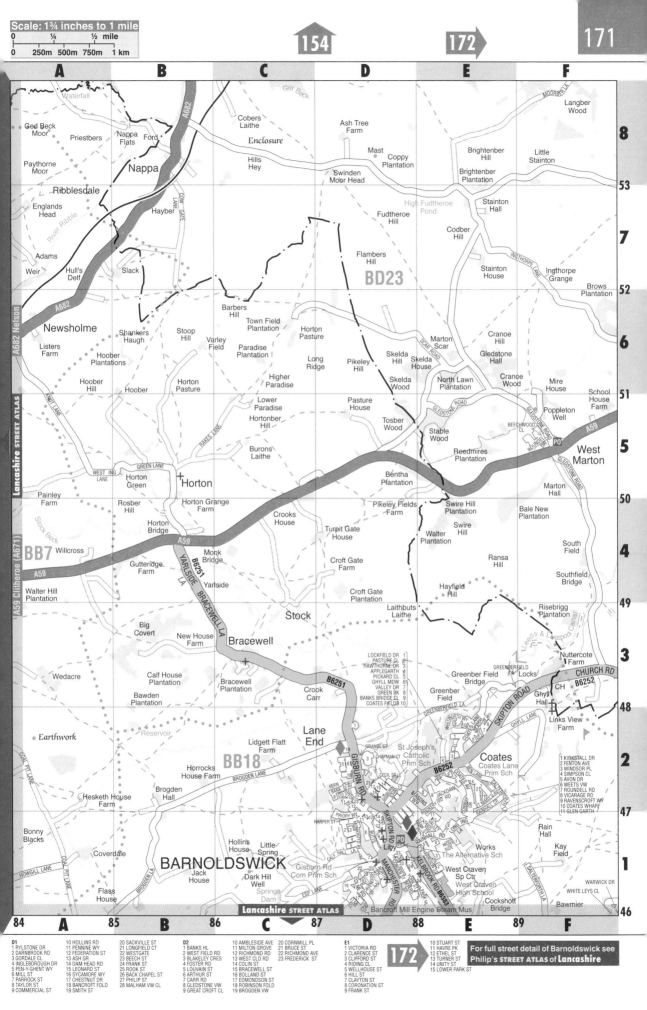

For full street detail of Barnoldswick see Philip's STREET ATLAS of Lancashire

171
155

Scale: 1¾ inches to 1 mile
0 ¼ ½ mile
0 250m 500m 750m 1 km

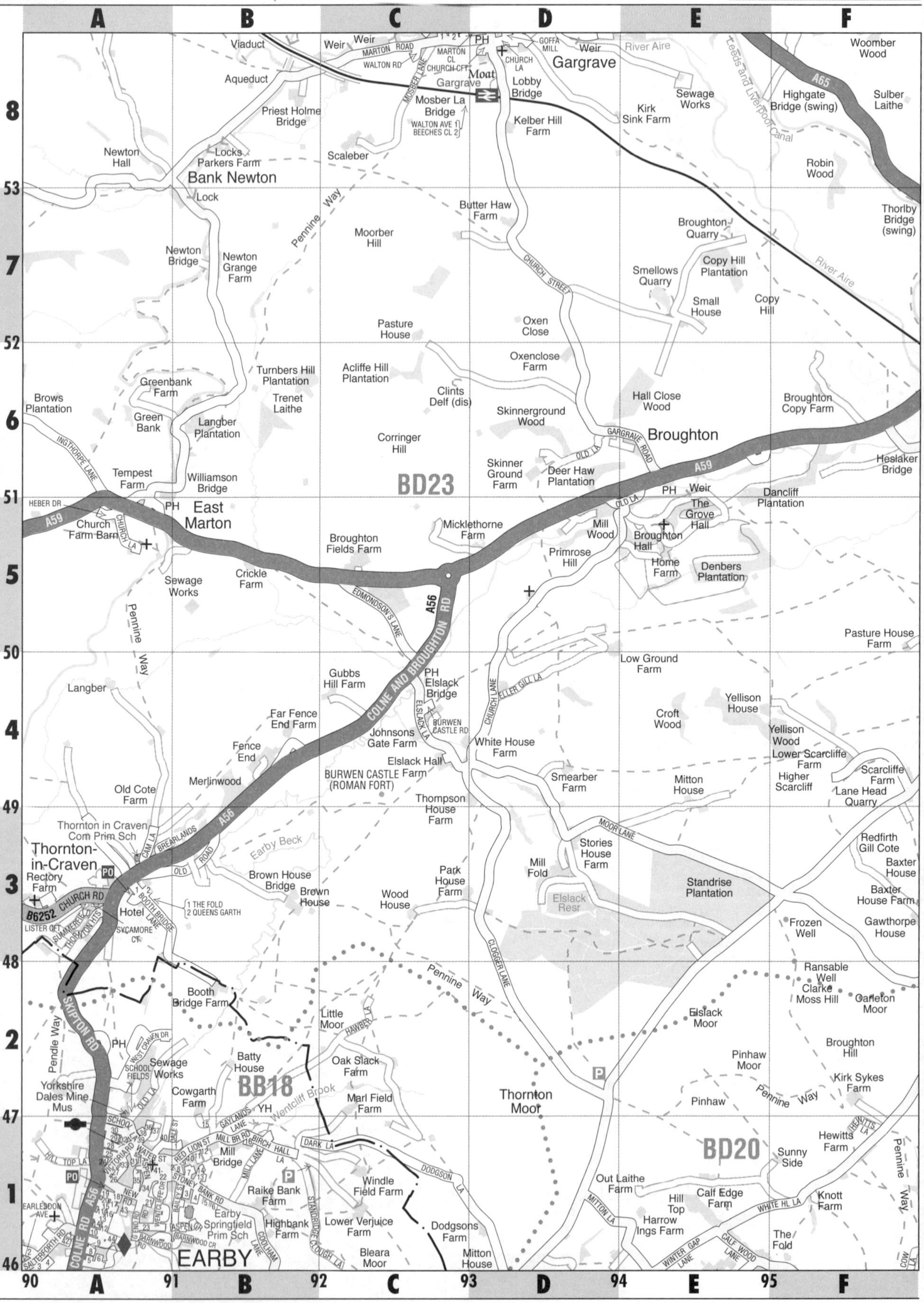

A1
1 BEECH AVE
2 WARWICK DR
3 KENILWORTH DR
4 TYSELEY GR
5 GREEN WLK
6 DALE VW
7 BROOKFIELD WY
8 JAGOE RD
9 LINDEN RD
10 ROSTLE TOP RD
11 JOHN ST
12 HARTLEY ST
13 BARRET ST
14 CROSS ST
15 APPLEGARTH ST
16 WILLIAM ST
17 COWGILL ST
18 BROOK ST
19 GEORGE ST
20 JAMES ST
21 RUSHTON AVE
22 CHAPEL ST
23 BAWHEAD RD
24 VICTORIA ST
25 ALBION RD
26 BOOT ST
27 EDWARD ST
28 ALBION ST
29 HIGHFIELD RD
30 LINCOLN RD
31 GOODALL CL
32 VALLEY RD
33 ALBERT ST
34 GREEN END RD
35 GREEN END AVE
36 SHUTTLEWORTH ST
37 WADDINGTON ST
38 GROVE ST
39 LOWER CROFT ST
40 CEMETERY RD
41 RILEY ST
42 THE SYCAMORES
43 MOSTYN AVE
44 ROSTLE TOP RD
45 VICTORIA MS

171
186

B1
1 ALDER HILL ST
2 WELBURY CL
3 SPRINGMOUNT
4 SPRINGFIELD AVE
5 PLEASANT VW
6 MOORLAND AVE
7 LONG GREEN
8 STOOPES HL
9 SELBOURNE TERR
10 EARLHAM ST
11 DUXBURY ST
12 NOOK CFT
13 REEVAL CL
14 BROWNROYD
15 COWGARTH LA
16 HEATHER BROW

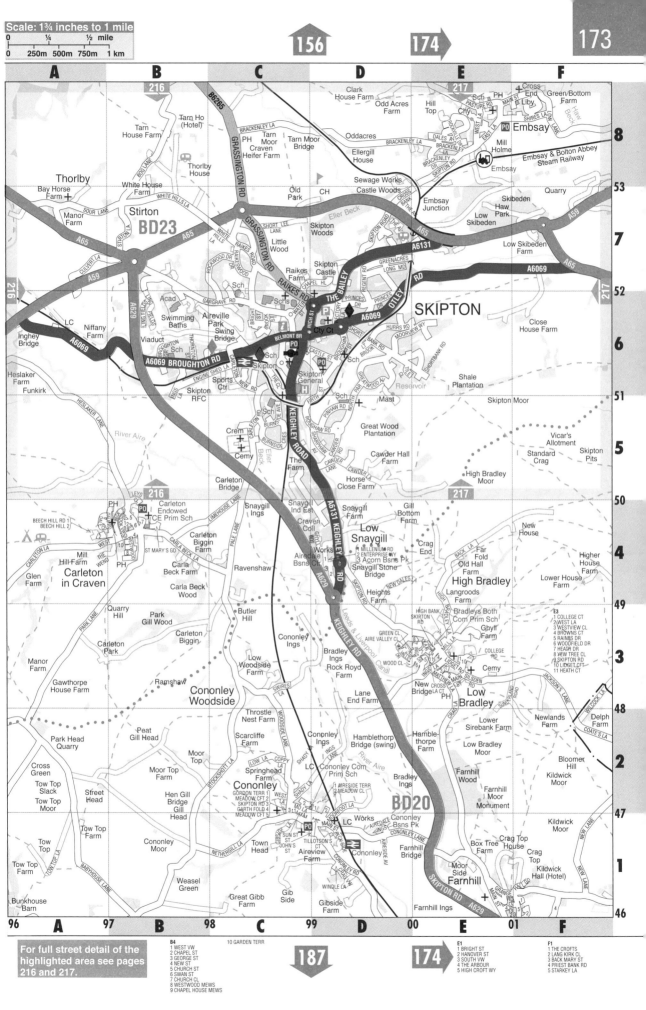

Scale: 1¾ inches to 1 mile
0 ¼ ½ mile
0 250m 500m 750m 1 km

156
174

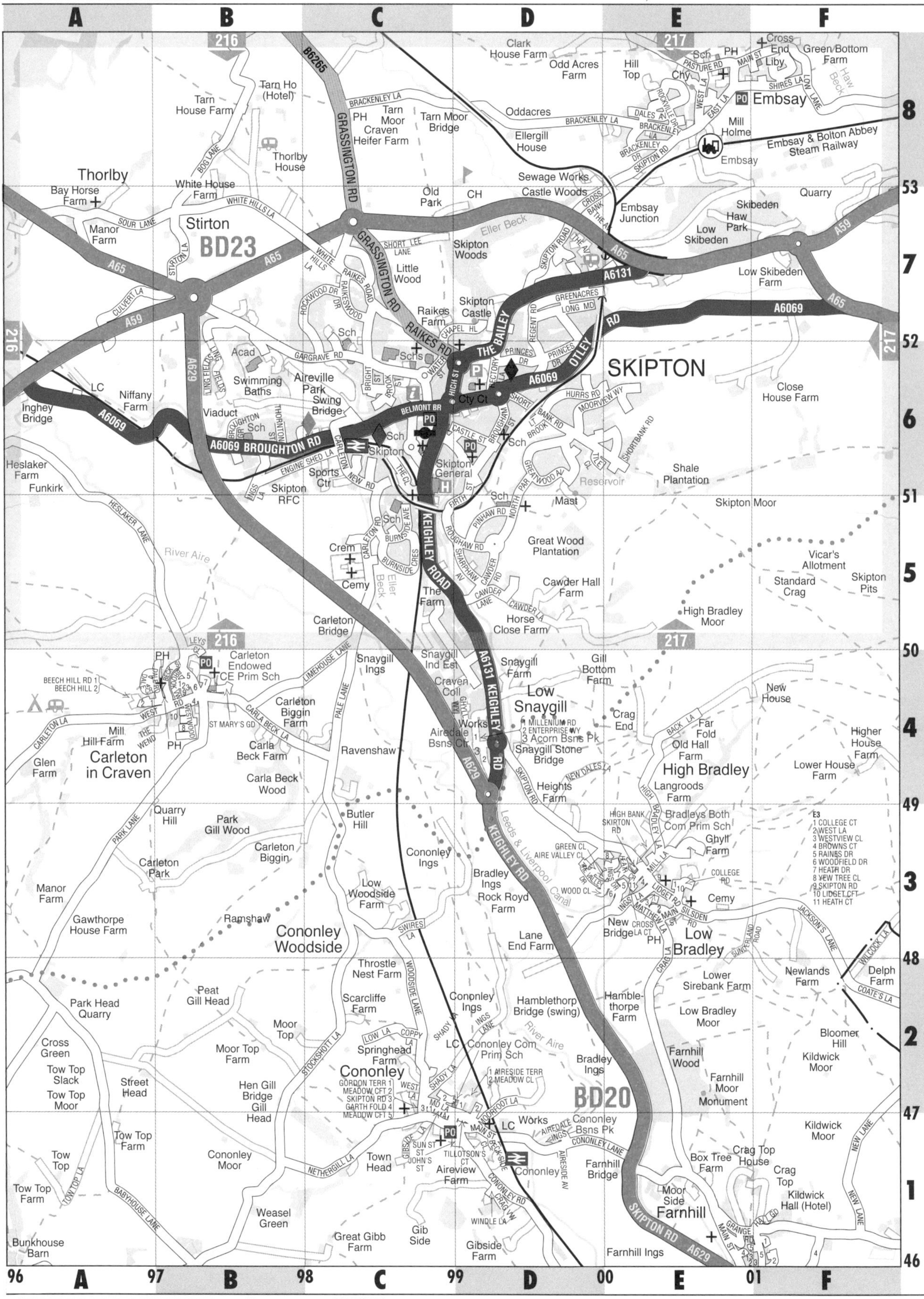
A
B
C
D
E
F
216
217
B6265
Clark House Farm
Odd Acres Farm
Hill Top
Sch
PH
Cross End
Green Bottom Farm
Chy
Liby
PASTURE RD
MAIN ST
SHIRES LA
LOW LANE
Haw Beck
Embsay
Mill Holme
Embsay & Bolton Abbey Steam Railway
Tarn Ho (Hotel)
Tarn House Farm
BRACKENLEY LA
PH
Tarn Moor
Craven Heifer Farm
Tarn Moor Bridge
Oddacres
Ellergill House
GRASSINGTON RD
Thorlby House
BOG LANE
Thorlby
Bay Horse Farm
White House Farm
WHITE HILLS LA
Old Park
CH
Sewage Works
Castle Woods
Embsay Junction
Skibeden
Haw Park
Quarry
Low Skibeden
SOUR LANE
Manor Farm
Stirton
BD23
STIRTON LA
A65
A59
Eller Beck
SHORT LEE LANE
Skipton Woods
Little Wood
Low Skibeden Farm
A6131
CULVERT LA
Raikes Farm
Skipton Castle
GREENACRES
LONG MD
A6069
RAIKES RD
CHAPEL HL
THE BAILEY
OTLEY RD
216
217
A629
Acad
Sch
GARGRAVE RD
Schs
SKIPTON
LC
Niffany Farm
Swimming Baths
Aireville Park
Swing Bridge
HIGH ST
Cty Ct
A6069
Inghey Bridge
Viaduct
BELMONT BR
PO
SHORT BANK RD
Close House Farm
A6069 BROUGHTON RD
Sch
Skipton
CASTLE ST
PO
Sch
Heslaker Farm
Funkirk
ENGINE SHED LA
Sports Ctr
Skipton RFC
Skipton General
Reservoir
Shale Plantation
Sch
Mast
Skipton Moor
HESLAKER LANE
River Aire
Sch
KEIGHLEY ROAD
Crem
Cemy
Great Wood Plantation
Vicar's Allotment
Standard Crag
Skipton Pits
Eller Beck
The Farm
Cawder Hall Farm
Carleton Bridge
Horse Close Farm
High Bradley Moor
50
PH
LEYS
216
217
PO
Carleton Endowed CE Prim Sch
BEECH HILL RD 1
BEECH HILL 2
Snaygill Ings
Snaygill Ind Est
Snaygill Farm
Gill Bottom Farm
LIMEHOUSE LANE
Craven Coll
Low Snaygill
New House
Carleton Biggin Farm
A6131 KEIGHLEY RD
Crag End
WEST
CARLA BECK LA
ST MARY'S GD
PALE LANE
Works
Airedale Bsns Ctr
1 MILLENNIUM RD
2 ENTERPRISE WY
3 Acorn Bsns Pk
Snaygill Stone Bridge
BACK LA
Far Fold
Old Hall Farm
Higher House Farm
CARLETON LA
Mill
Hill Farm
Carleton in Craven
Glen Farm
PH
Carla Beck Farm
Ravenshaw
High Bradley
Lower House Farm
Carla Beck Wood
NEW DALES LA
Heights Farm
Langroods Farm
SKIPTON RD
49
Quarry Hill
PARK LANE
Park Gill Wood
Butler Hill
HIGH BANK
SKIPTON RD
Bradleys Both Com Prim Sch
E3
1 COLLEGE CT
2 WEST LA
3 WESTVIEW CL
4 BROWNS CT
5 RAINES DR
6 WOODFIELD DR
7 HEATH DR
8 YEW TREE CL
9 SKIPTON RD
10 LIDGET CFT
11 HEATH CT
Carleton Biggin
Carleton Park
Cononley Ings
Leeds & Liverpool Canal
KEIGHLEY RD
GREEN CL
AIRE VALLEY CL
Ghyll Farm
MILL LA
COLLEGE RD
Manor Farm
Low Woodside Farm
Bradley Ings
Rock Royd Farm
WOOD CL
LIDGET RD
Cemy
SILSDEN RD
JACKSON'S LANE
Gawthorpe House Farm
Ramshaw
Cononley Woodside
SWIRES LA
Lane End Farm
New Bridge
CROSS LA
CT
MATTHEW LA
MAIN ST
PH
Low Bradley
SUNDERLAND ROAD
WILCOCK LA
Throstle Nest Farm
Lower Sirebank Farm
Newlands Farm
Delph Farm
48
CRAG LA
COATE'S LA
Park Head Quarry
Peat Gill Head
WOODSIDE LANE
Scarcliffe Farm
Cononley Ings
Hamblethorp Bridge (swing)
Hamble-thorpe Farm
Low Bradley Moor
Moor Top
LOW LA
COPPY LA
SHADY LA
INGS LANE
Bloomer Hill
Cross Green
Moor Top Farm
Springhead Farm
LC
Cononley Com Prim Sch
River Aire
Farnhill Wood
Kildwick Moor
Tow Top Slack
Street Head
STOCKSHOTT LA
Cononley
Bradley Ings
Tow Top Moor
Hen Gill Bridge
GORDON TERR 1
MEADOW CFT 2
SKIPTON RD 3
GARTH FOLD 4
MEADOW CFT 5
WEST LA
1 AIRESIDE TERR
2 MEADOW CL
Farnhill Moor
Monument
Gill Head
BD20
MOORFOOT LA
Works
LC
Cononley Bsns Pk
Kildwick Moor
Tow Top Farm
PO
AIREDALE INGS
CONONLEY LANE
NEW LANE
Tow Top
Cononley Moor
GIBSIDE LA
SUN ST
ST JOHN'S ST
Town Head
TILLOTSON'S CT
Cononley
Farnhill Bridge
Box Tree Farm
Crag Top House
Crag Top
NETHERGILL LA
Aireview Farm
AIRESIDE AV
CONONLEY RD
Tow Top Farm
TOW TOP LA
Moor Side
Farnhill
Kildwick Hall (Hotel)
NEW LANE
BABYHOUSE LANE
Weasel Green
CRAG VW
WINDLE LA
SKIPTON RD
A629
GRANGE RD
HALL GR
MAIN ST
Bunkhouse Barn
Great Gibb Farm
Gib Side
Gibside Farm
Farnhill Ings
8
53
7
52
6
51
5
50
4
49
3
48
2
47
1
46
96
97
98
99
00
01

For full street detail of the highlighted area see pages 216 and 217.

B4
1 WEST VW
2 CHAPEL ST
3 GEORGE ST
4 NEW ST
5 CHURCH ST
6 SWAN ST
7 CHURCH CL
8 WESTWOOD MEWS
9 CHAPEL HOUSE MEWS
10 GARDEN TERR

187
174

E1
1 BRIGHT ST
2 HANOVER ST
3 SOUTH VW
4 THE ARBOUR
5 HIGH CROFT WY

F1
1 THE CROFTS
2 LANG KIRK CL
3 BACK MARY ST
4 PRIEST BANK RD
5 STARKEY LA

173
157

E4
1 PARSON'S LA
2 MOOR PK CL
3 MOOR PK CRES
4 TURNER LA
5 BIG MD DR
6 GILL CL
7 STAMP HL CL
8 THE STREET
9 BROADFIELD WY
10 LIME CL
11 HAWTHORN CL

Scale: 1¾ inches to 1 mile
0 ¼ ½ mile
0 250m 500m 750m 1 km

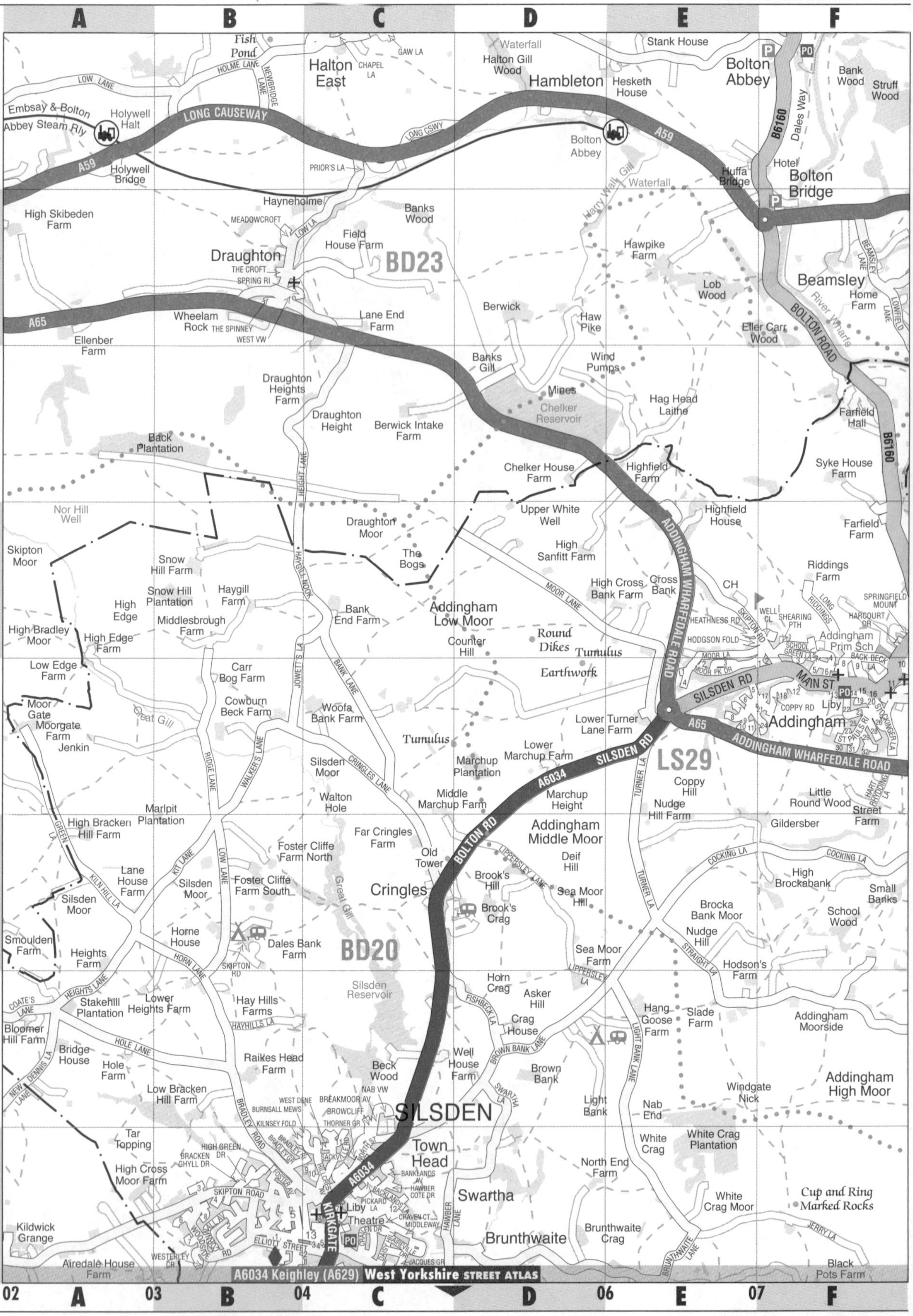

F4
1 MOOR PK WY
2 MOOR PK GR
3 CRAVEN CRES
4 BURNS HILL
5 COCKSHOTT PL
6 WHARFEDALE VW
7 HIGH BANK CL
8 CHAPEL ST
9 SUGAR HILL
10 AYNHOLME CL
11 KILNERS CFT
12 TOWN HEAD FOLD
13 BECKSIDE CL
14 RIDLEYS FOLD
15 GEORGE ST
16 DRUGGIST LA
17 JONATHAN GARTH
18 HILLSIDE CL
19 WEST CFT
20 OLD STATION WY
21 ACRE FOLD
22 SOUTHFIELD TERR
23 SOUTHFIELD LA
24 BROWNSFIELD RD
25 ST JOHNS AVE
26 MOUNT PLEASANT
27 ST CHRISTOPHERS DR
28 SOUTHFIELD RD
29 ST MICHAELS WY
30 ST LEONARDS CL
31 ST PETERS CFT
32 ST IANS CFT

173

B1
1 HAWTHORNE ST
2 GLOUCESTER AVE
3 SKIPTON RD
4 SILSDEN HO GDNS
5 Hothfield Jun Sch
6 HAWKCLIFFE VW
7 CROSSMOOR CL
8 LOWER PARK GN

C1
1 MONKMANS WHARF
2 MILLFIELDS
3 KING ST
4 QUEEN ST
5 MILL FIELD CT
6 BECKSIDE CT
7 WESLEY PL
8 NICOLSONS PL
9 LAITHE CL
10 HAYHILLS RD
11 EAST DENE
12 WAYSIDE MS
13 Aire View Inf Sch

For full street detail of Silsden see Philip's STREET ATLAS of West Yorkshire

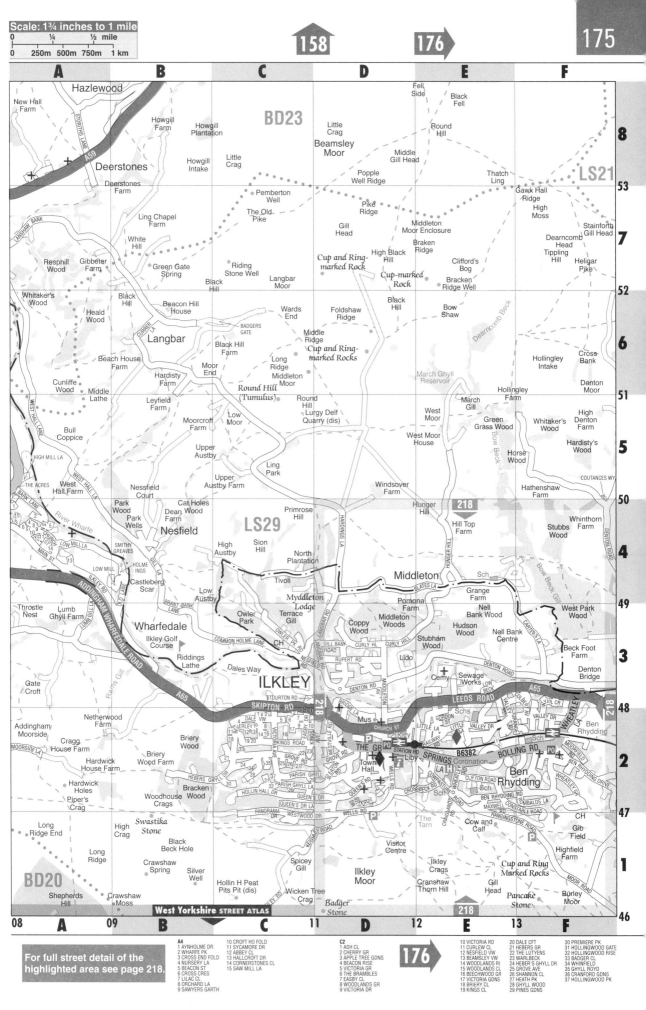

Scale: 1¾ inches to 1 mile
0 ¼ ½ mile
0 250m 500m 750m 1 km

158
176

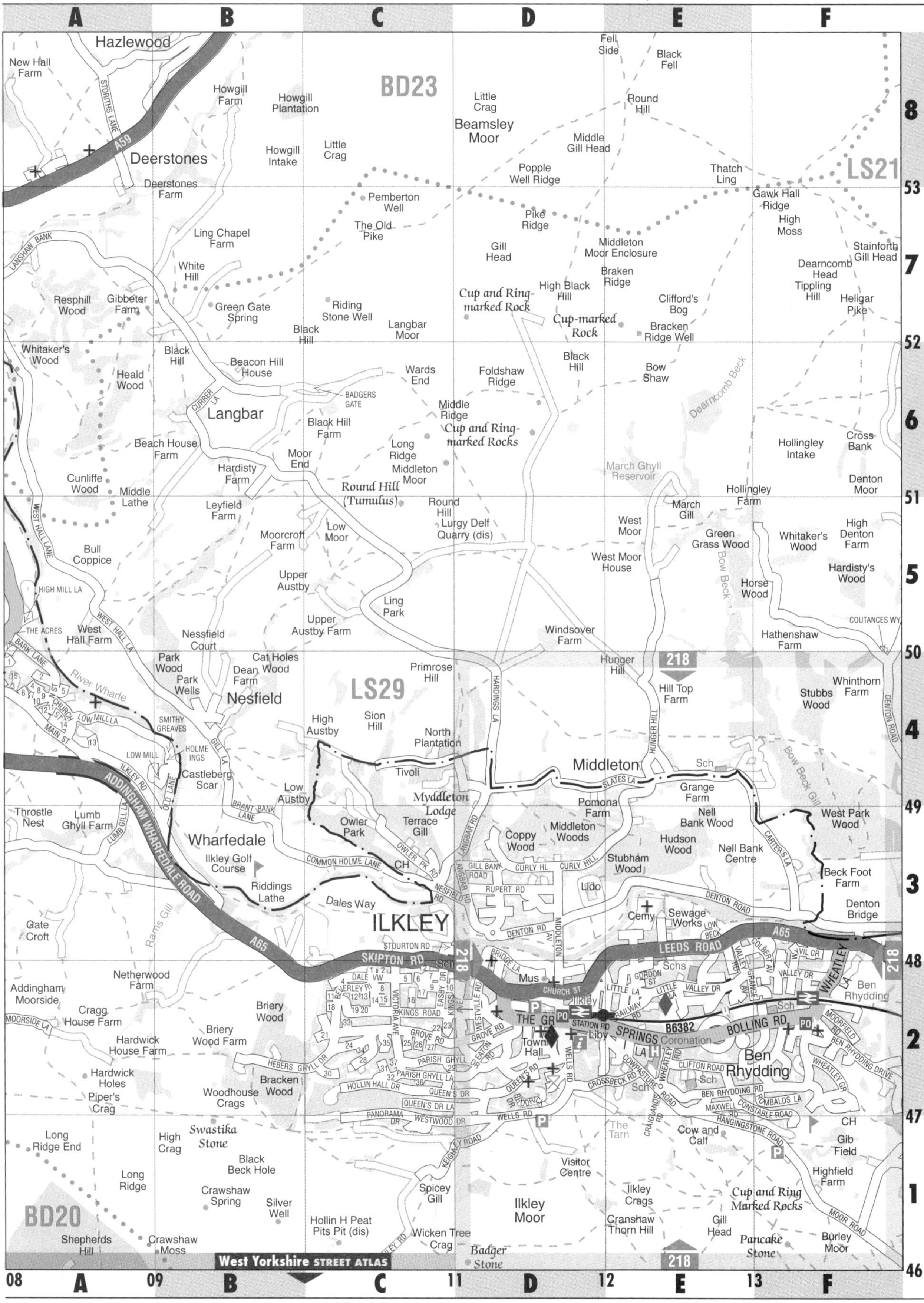

For full street detail of the highlighted area see page 218.

176

A4
1 AYNHOLME DR
2 WHARFE PK
3 CROSS END FOLD
4 NURSERY LA
5 BEACON ST
6 CROSS CRES
7 LILAC CL
8 ORCHARD LA
9 SAWYERS GARTH
10 CROFT HO FOLD
11 SYCAMORE DR
12 ABBEY CL
13 HALLCROFT DR
14 CORNERSTONES CL
15 SAW MILL LA

C2
1 ASH CL
2 CHERRY GR
3 APPLE TREE GDNS
4 BEACON RISE
5 VICTORIA GR
6 THE BRAMBLES
7 EASBY CL
8 WOODLANDS GR
9 VICTORIA DR
10 VICTORIA RD
11 CURLEW CL
12 NESFIELD VW
13 BEAMSLEY VW
14 WOODLANDS RI
15 WOODLANDS CL
16 BEECHWOOD GR
17 VICTORIA GDNS
18 BRIERY CL
19 KINGS CL
20 DALE CFT
21 HEBERS GR
22 THE LUTYENS
23 WARLBECK
24 HEBER'S GHYLL DR
25 GROVE AVE
26 SHANNON CL
27 HEATH PK
28 GHYLL WOOD
29 PINES GDNS
30 PREMIERE PK
31 HOLLINGWOOD GATE
32 HOLLINGWOOD RISE
33 BADGER CL
34 WHINFIELD
35 GHYLL ROYD
36 CRANFORD GDNS
37 HOLLINGWOOD PK

175
159

Scale: 1¾ inches to 1 mile
0 ¼ ½ mile
0 250m 500m 750m 1 km

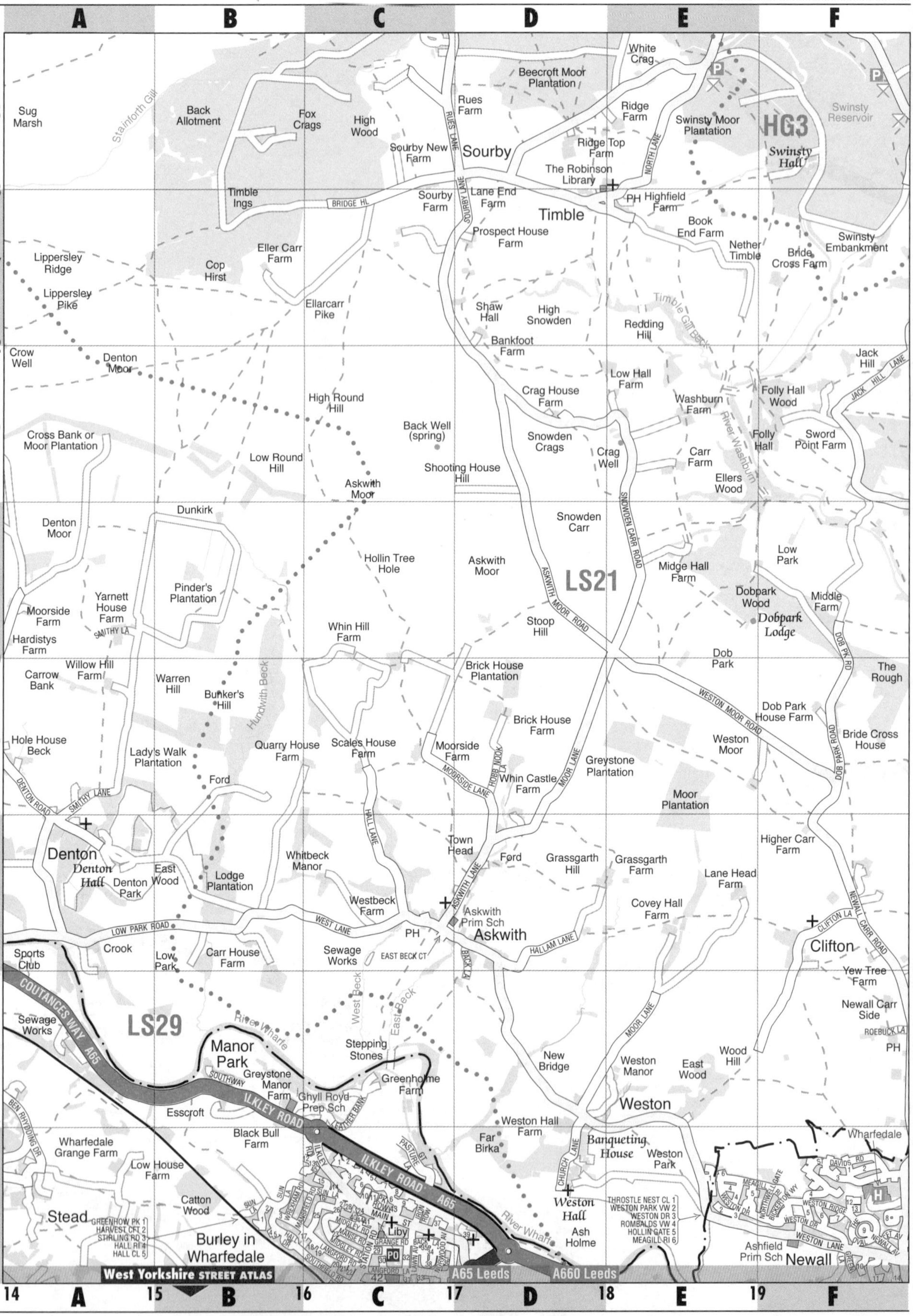
A B C D E F
8
7
6
5
4
3
2
1
53
52
51
50
49
48
47
46
14 15 16 17 18 19
Sug Marsh
Back Allotment
Stainforth Gill
Fox Crags
High Wood
Rues Farm
RUES LANE
Beecroft Moor Plantation
White Crag
Ridge Farm
Swinsty Moor Plantation
HG3
Swinsty Reservoir
Swinsty Hall
Sourby New Farm
Sourby
Ridge Top Farm
NORTH LANE
The Robinson Library
Timble Ings
BRIDGE HL
Sourby Farm
SOURBY LANE
Lane End Farm
PH
Highfield Farm
Timble
Book End Farm
Nether Timble
Bride Cross Farm
Swinsty Embankment
Prospect House Farm
Lippersley Ridge
Cop Hirst
Eller Carr Farm
Lippersley Pike
Ellarcarr Pike
Shaw Hall
High Snowden
Timble Gill Beck
Redding Hill
Bankfoot Farm
Crow Well
Denton Moor
Jack Hill
JACK HILL LANE
Low Hall Farm
Crag House Farm
Washburn Farm
Folly Hall Wood
High Round Hill
Back Well (spring)
Cross Bank or Moor Plantation
Snowden Crags
Crag Well
Folly Hall
Sword Point Farm
Carr Farm
River Washburn
Low Round Hill
Shooting House Hill
Askwith Moor
Ellers Wood
Dunkirk
Snowden Carr
SNOWDEN CARR ROAD
Denton Moor
Hollin Tree Hole
Askwith Moor
LS21
Midge Hall Farm
Low Park
Pinder's Plantation
Yarnett House Farm
Moorside Farm
SMITHY LA
Hardistys Farm
ASKWITH MOOR ROAD
Dobpark Wood
Middle Farm
Dobpark Lodge
Whin Hill Farm
Stoop Hill
Carrow Bank
Willow Hill Farm
Warren Hill
Brick House Plantation
Dob Park
DOB PK RD
The Rough
Bunker's Hill
Hundwith Beck
WESTON MOOR ROAD
Dob Park House Farm
Brick House Farm
Hole House Beck
Lady's Walk Plantation
Quarry House Farm
Scales House Farm
Moorside Farm
Weston Moor
Bride Cross House
DOB PARK ROAD
HOBB NOOK LA
MOORSIDE LANE
Whin Castle Farm
MOOR LANE
Greystone Plantation
DENTON ROAD
SMITHY LANE
Ford
HALL LANE
Moor Plantation
Denton
Denton Hall
Denton Park
East Wood
Lodge Plantation
Whitbeck Manor
Town Head
Ford
Grassgarth Hill
Grassgarth Farm
Higher Carr Farm
Lane Head Farm
ASKWITH LANE
Westbeck Farm
Askwith Prim Sch
Covey Hall Farm
LOW PARK ROAD
WEST LANE
Askwith
HALLAM LANE
CLIFTON LA
Clifton
NEWALL CARR ROAD
Sports Club
Crook
Low Park
Carr House Farm
Sewage Works
PH
EAST BECK CT
BACK LA
Yew Tree Farm
COUTANCES WAY
A65
Sewage Works
LS29
West Beck
East Beck
MOOR LANE
Newall Carr Side
River Wharfe
ROEBUCK LA
PH
Manor Park
SOUTHWAY
Greystone Manor Farm
Stepping Stones
Greenholme Farm
New Bridge
Weston Manor
East Wood
Wood Hill
Ghyll Royd Prep Sch
LEATHER BANK
Weston
Esscroft
ILKLEY ROAD
Weston Hall Farm
BEN RHYDDING DR
Black Bull Farm
Far Birka
Banqueting House
Wharfedale
Wharfedale Grange Farm
PASTURE
CHURCH LANE
Weston Park
ST DAVIDS RD
Low House Farm
ILKLEY ROAD
A65
MEAGILL RI
NORTHFIELD GATE
BICKERTON WY
Catton Wood
SUN LA
WREXHAM RD
MAIN ST
Weston Hall
THROSTLE NEST CL 1
WESTON PARK VW 2
WESTON DR 3
ROMBALDS VW 4
HOLLIN GATE 5
MEAGILL RI 6
WESTON DR
WESTON RIDGE
Stead
GREENHOW PK 1
HARVEST CFT 2
STIRLING RD 3
HALL RI 4
HALL CL 5
Burley in Wharfedale
MIDGLEY RD
GRANGE RD
Liby
River Wharfe
Ash Holme
WESTON LANE
Ashfield Prim Sch
Newall
NEWALL AV
PO
LANGFORD LA
SOUTHFIELD RD
STATION
LAWN AV
NORWOOD
A65 Leeds
A660 Leeds
West Yorkshire STREET ATLAS

218

C1
1 TANFIELD DR
2 GREYSTONE CL
3 FAR MEAD CFT
4 PASTURE FOLD
5 MILL VW
6 LONG MDWS
7 GREENHOLME CL
8 OLD MILL CL
9 WILLOW TREE GDNS
10 NORTH PAR
11 PEEL PL
12 WOODPECKER RD
13 WELLFIELD LA
14 THORNTON ST
15 MARIA ST
16 MELROSE DR
17 LANGFORD CT
18 MIDGE HALL CL
19 LANGFORD MEWS
20 WILLOW CL
21 LANGFORD CL
22 ASH TREE WK
23 MANSE CRES
24 HILL TOP
25 WEST VIEW AVE
26 WEST VIEW RD
27 BOOTH ST
28 VICTORIA RD
29 BECKSIDE CL
30 LANGFORD RIDE
31 FOSTER CL
32 GRANGEFIELD AVE
33 ST PHILIP'S WY
34 CROWN ST
35 LAWN RD
36 NORWOOD CL
37 YORK RD
38 FENTON ST
39 CORN MILL LA
40 AMY BUSFIELD GN
41 RICHARD GOSSOP CT
42 Burley Oaks Prim Sch
43 LION CT
44 ALBERT SIMMONS WY
45 GRITSTONE CL

F1
1 KELL BECK
2 ST MARTINS AVE
3 ST RICHARDS RD
4 RUMPLE CFT
5 RIDDING GATE
6 WILKINSON WY
7 WESTON CRES
8 CROFT HOUSE DR
9 THE GREEN
10 BELMONT AVE
11 GRANGE VW
12 ST MARTINS FIELD
13 MARRINER CL
14 NEWALL CL

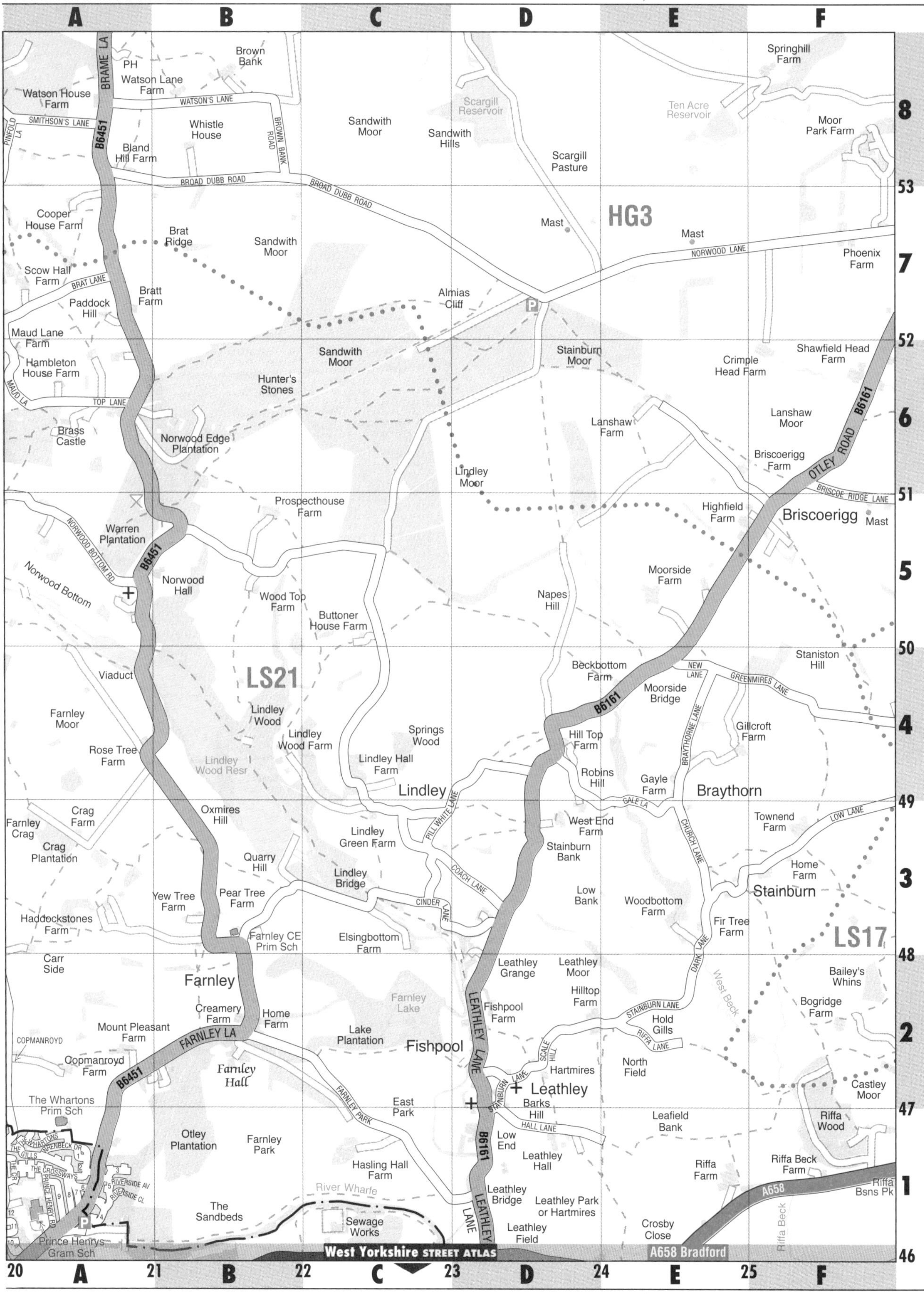
A
B
C
D
E
F
8
53
7
52
6
51
5
50
4
49
3
48
2
47
1
46
20
21
22
23
24
25
BRAME LA
PH
Watson Lane Farm
Brown Bank
Watson House Farm
WATSON'S LANE
SMITHSON'S LANE
PINFOLD LA
B6451
Whistle House
BROWN BANK ROAD
Bland Hill Farm
Sandwith Moor
Sandwith Hills
Scargill Reservoir
Scargill Pasture
Ten Acre Reservoir
Springhill Farm
Moor Park Farm
BROAD DUBB ROAD
Cooper House Farm
Brat Ridge
Sandwith Moor
Mast
HG3
Mast
NORWOOD LANE
Phoenix Farm
Scow Hall Farm
BRAT LANE
Paddock Hill
Bratt Farm
Almias Cliff
P
Maud Lane Farm
Hambleton House Farm
MAUD LA
TOP LANE
Sandwith Moor
Hunter's Stones
Stainburn Moor
Crimple Head Farm
Shawfield Head Farm
Brass Castle
Norwood Edge Plantation
Lanshaw Farm
Lanshaw Moor
B6161
OTLEY ROAD
Briscoerigg Farm
Lindley Moor
BRISCOE RIDGE LANE
NORWOOD BOTTOM RD
Warren Plantation
Prospecthouse Farm
Highfield Farm
Briscoerigg
Mast
Norwood Bottom
Norwood Hall
Wood Top Farm
Moorside Farm
Napes Hill
Buttoner House Farm
Staniston Hill
Viaduct
LS21
Beckbottom Farm
NEW LANE
GREENMIRES LANE
Moorside Bridge
Farnley Moor
Lindley Wood
Lindley Wood Farm
Springs Wood
Hill Top Farm
BRAYTHORNE LANE
Gillcroft Farm
Rose Tree Farm
Lindley Wood Resr
Lindley Hall Farm
Lindley
PILL WHITE LANE
Robins Hill
Gayle Farm
Braythorn
GALE LA
Farnley Crag
Crag Farm
Oxmires Hill
Lindley Green Farm
West End Farm
CHURCH LANE
Townend Farm
LOW LANE
Crag Plantation
Quarry Hill
Lindley Bridge
Stainburn Bank
COACH LANE
Home Farm
Stainburn
Yew Tree Farm
Pear Tree Farm
CINDER LANE
Low Bank
Woodbottom Farm
Fir Tree Farm
Haddockstones Farm
Farnley CE Prim Sch
Elsingbottom Farm
DARK LANE
LS17
Carr Side
Leathley Grange
Leathley Moor
West Beck
Bailey's Whins
Farnley
Farnley Lake
Hilltop Farm
Bogridge Farm
Creamery Farm
Home Farm
LEATHLEY LANE
Fishpool Farm
STAINBURN LANE
Hold Gills
Mount Pleasant Farm
FARNLEY LA
Lake Plantation
RIFFA LANE
COPMANROYD
Fishpool
SCALE HILL
Copmanroyd Farm
Farnley Hall
Hartmires
North Field
Leathley
Castley Moor
The Whartons Prim Sch
FARNLEY PARK
East Park
STAINBURN LANE
Barks Hill
Leafield Bank
Riffa Wood
HALL LANE
Otley Plantation
Farnley Park
Low End
Leathley Hall
Riffa Farm
Riffa Beck Farm
THE WHARTONS
WRENBECK DR
THE GILLS
THE CROSSWAYS
PRINCE HENRY RD
RIVERSIDE AV
RIVERSIDE CL
Hasling Hall Farm
River Wharfe
Leathley Bridge
Leathley Park or Hartmires
A658
Riffa Bsns Pk
The Sandbeds
Sewage Works
LEATHLEY LANE
Leathley Field
Crosby Close
Riffa Beck
Prince Henrys Gram Sch
West Yorkshire STREET ATLAS
A658 Bradford

A1
1 WRENBECK AVE
2 WRENBECK CL
3 RIVERSIDE DR
4 RIVERSIDE PK
5 RIVERSIDE CRES
6 TURNER CRES
7 ATHELSTAN LA
8 CHIPPENDALE RISE
9 HARECROFT RD
10 NEWALL HALL PK
11 OATLANDS DR
12 PRINCE HENRYS CT

177 161 219

Scale: 1¾ inches to 1 mile
0 ¼ ½ mile
0 250m 500m 750m 1 km

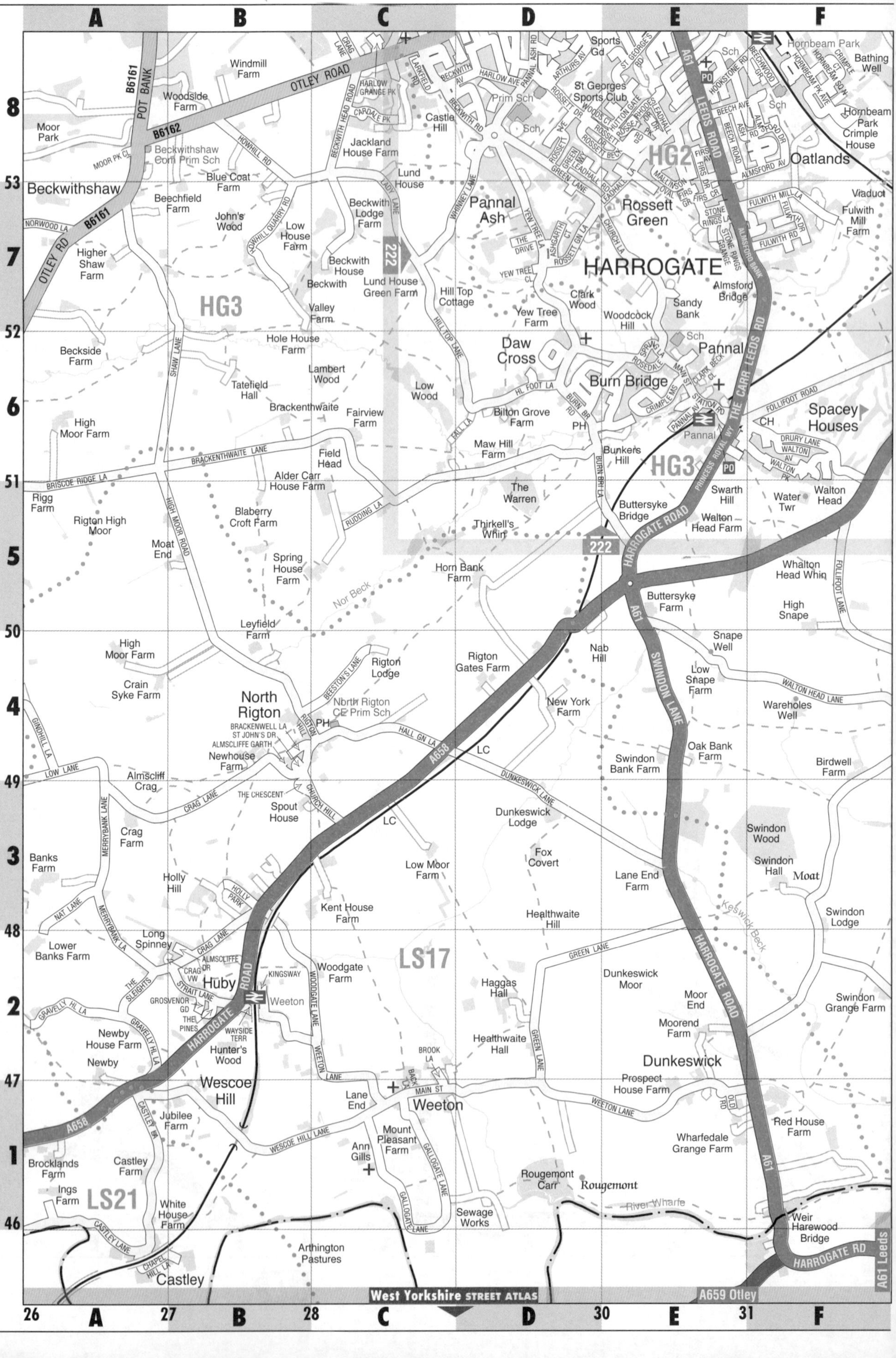

E6
1 CLIVE RD
2 CASTLE CL
3 BEECH LA
4 CANBY LA
5 CHURCH HL
6 MILL CL
7 MANOR GARTH
8 SCHOOL LA
9 CHURCH LA

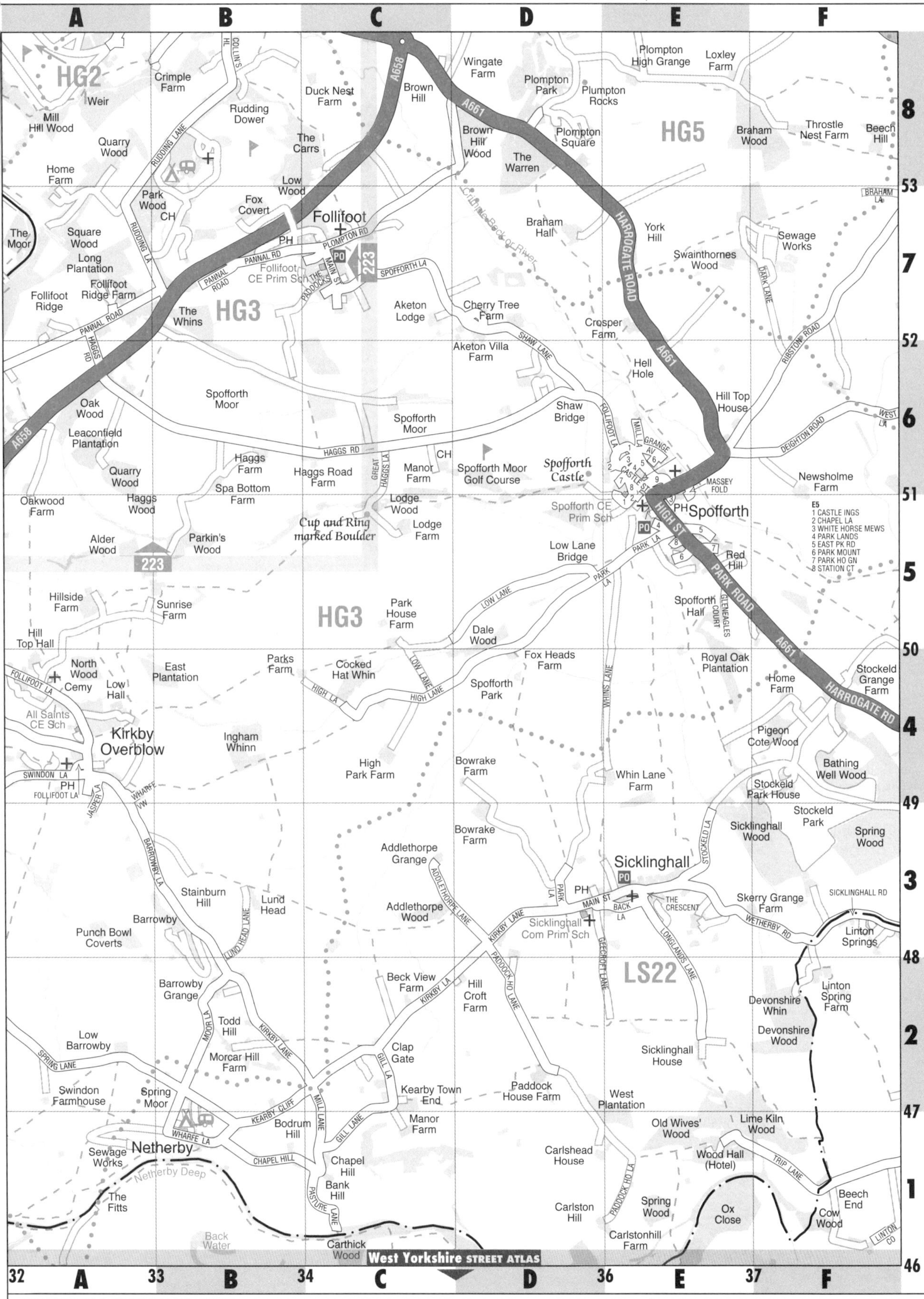

179
163

Scale: 1¾ inches to 1 mile
0 ¼ ½ mile
0 250m 500m 750m 1 km

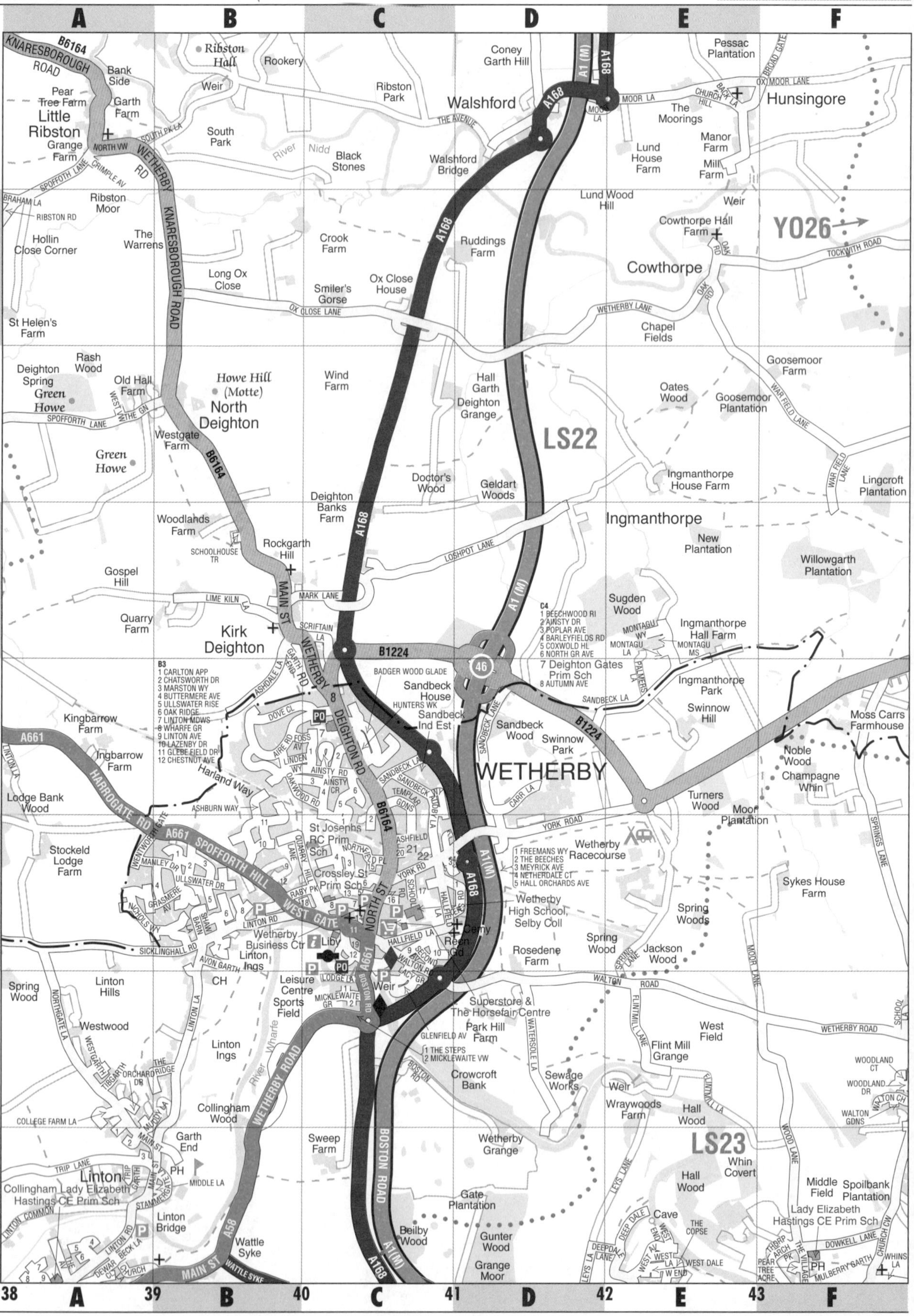
A B C D E F
8
53
7
52
6
51
5
50
4
49
3
48
2
47
1
46
38 39 40 41 42 43
B6164
KNARESBOROUGH ROAD
Ribston Hall
Rookery
Bank Side
Weir
Pear Tree Farm
Garth Farm
Little Ribston
Grange Farm
SOUTH PK LA
NORTH VW
South Park
River Nidd
Black Stones
Ribston Park
THE AVENUE
Walshford
Walshford Bridge
Coney Garth Hill
A1(M)
A168
MOOR LA
Pessac Plantation
OX MOOR LANE
BROAD GATE
CHURCH HILL
BACK LA
Hunsingore
The Moorings
Manor Farm
Mill Farm
Lund House Farm
Lund Wood Hill
Weir
Cowthorpe Hall Farm
OAK RD
YO26
TOCKWITH ROAD
Cowthorpe
WETHERBY LANE
Chapel Fields
SPOFFOTH LANE
CRIMPLE AV
BRAHAM LA
RIBSTON RD
Ribston Moor
Hollin Close Corner
The Warrens
WETHERBY RD
KNARESBOROUGH ROAD
Crook Farm
Ruddings Farm
Long Ox Close
Smiler's Gorse
Ox Close House
OX CLOSE LANE
St Helen's Farm
Deighton Spring
Rash Wood
Green Howe
Old Hall Farm
WEST VW
THE GN
SPOFFORTH LANE
Howe Hill (Motte)
North Deighton
Wind Farm
Hall Garth
Deighton Grange
Goosemoor Farm
Oates Wood
Goosemoor Plantation
WAR FIELD LANE
LS22
Westgate Farm
Green Howe
B6164
Doctor's Wood
Geldart Woods
Ingmanthorpe House Farm
Lingcroft Plantation
Deighton Banks Farm
Woodlands Farm
SCHOOLHOUSE TR
Rockgarth Hill
LOSHPOT LANE
Ingmanthorpe
New Plantation
Willowgarth Plantation
Gospel Hill
LIME KILN LA
MAIN ST
MARK LANE
Sugden Wood
Quarry Farm
Kirk Deighton
SCRIFTAIN LA
B1224
C4
1 BEECHWOOD RI
2 AINSTY DR
3 POPLAR AVE
4 BARLEYFIELDS RD
5 COXWOLD HL
6 NORTH GR AVE
7 Deighton Gates Prim Sch
8 AUTUMN AVE
MONTAGU WY
MONTAGU LA
MONTAGU MS
Ingmanthorpe Hall Farm
Ingmanthorpe Park
PALMERS LA
46
B3
1 CARLTON APP
2 CHATSWORTH DR
3 MARSTON WY
4 BUTTERMERE AVE
5 ULLSWATER RISE
6 OAK RIDGE
7 LINTON MDWS
8 WHARFE GR
9 LINTON AVE
10 LAZENBY DR
11 GLEBE FIELD DR
12 CHESTNUT AVE
ASHDALE LA
GARTH END
BADGER WOOD GLADE
Sandbeck House
HUNTERS WK
Sandbeck Ind Est
SANDBECK LA
Swinnow Hill
Moss Carrs Farmhouse
Kingbarrow Farm
DOVE CL
DEIGHTON RD
B1224
Sandbeck Wood
Swinnow Park
A661
LINTON LA
Ingbarrow Farm
Harland Way
AIRE RD
FOSS AV
LINDEN WY
AINSTY RD
AINSTY CR
OAKWOOD RD
SANDBECK LA
SANDBECK WY
TEMPLAR GDNS
KUDBY LA
WETHERBY
CARR LA
Noble Wood
Champagne Whin
Lodge Bank Wood
ASHBURN WAY
B6164
Turners Wood
Moor Plantation
HARROGATE RD
WENTWORTH GATE
A661 SPOFFORTH HILL
St Josephs RC Prim Sch
ASHFIELD
YORK ROAD
Wetherby Racecourse
SPRINGS LANE
Stockeld Lodge Farm
MANLEY DR
ULLSWATER DR
GRASMERE AV
QUARRY LANE
NORTHFIELD PL
YORK RD
1 FREEMANS WY
2 THE BEECHES
3 MEYRICK AVE
4 NETHERDALE CT
5 HALL ORCHARDS AVE
Crossley St Prim Sch
RABY PK
SCHOOL
HALLFIELD LA
Wetherby High School, Selby Coll
Sykes House Farm
NICHOLS WY
BARN
SHAW
WEST GATE
NORTH ST
LINTON RD
Wetherby Business Ctr
Liby
HALLFIELD LA
Cerny Recn Gd
Spring Woods
Spring Wood
Rosedene Farm
SPRING LA
Jackson Wood
SICKLINGHALL RD
AVON GARTH
Linton Ings
CH
Leisure Centre Sports Field
LODGE LA
MICKLEWAITE GR
BOSTON RD
SECOND
WALTON RD
LACY GR
Weir
Superstore & The Horsefair Centre
WALTON ROAD
FLINTMILL LANE
MOOR LANE
Spring Wood
Linton Hills
NORTHGATE LA
LINTON LA
Park Hill Farm
GLENFIELD AV
1 THE STEPS
2 MICKLEWAITE VW
WATERSOLE LA
West Field
WETHERBY ROAD
SCHOOL LA
Westwood
WESTGARTH
TIBGARTH
ORCHARD
THE RIDGE
Linton Ings
River Wharfe
WETHERBY ROAD
BOSTON RD
Crowcroft Bank
Sewage Works
Flint Mill Grange
WOODLAND CT
WOODLAND DR
WALTON CH
WALTON GDNS
COLLEGE FARM LA
MUDDY LA
Collingham Wood
Weir
Wraywoods Farm
Hall Wood
FLINTMILL LA
Garth End
MAIN ST
Sweep Farm
Wetherby Grange
LS23
WOOD LANE
Whin Covert
TRIP LANE
Linton
PH
MIDDLE LA
BOSTON ROAD
LEYS LANE
Collingham Lady Elizabeth Hastings CE Prim Sch
STAMMERGATE
LINTON COMMON
Gate Plantation
Hall Wood
Middle Field
Spoilbank Plantation
Lady Elizabeth Hastings CE Prim Sch
Linton Bridge
A58
Beilby Wood
Cave
DEEP DALE
WEST END
THE COPSE
DOWKELL LANE
CHURCH CW
Wattle Syke
Gunter Wood
DEEPDALE LANE
WEST AV
WEST LA
W END
WEST DALE
THORP ARCH
THE VILLAGE
PEAR TREE ACRE
MULBERRY GARTH
WHINS LA
PH
LINTON RD
BECK LA
DEWAR CL
CHURCH
MAIN ST
WATTLE SYKE
A168
A1(M)
Grange Moor
LEYS LA

A1
1 NORTHGATE LA
2 NORTHGATE RISE
3 NORTHCOTE FOLD
4 OSPREY CL
5 KINGFISHER REACH
6 TERN PK
7 BISHOPDALE DR
8 GARSDALE FOLD
9 COTTERDALE HOLT

179

C3
1 COXWOLD VW
2 NORTH GR
3 WOODHILL VW
4 BARLEYFIELDS RD
5 BARLEYFIELDS LA
6 SANDRINGHAM RD
7 ST JAMES'S ST
8 CROSSLEY ST
9 FIRST AVE
10 THIRD AVE
11 BANK ST
12 MARKET PL
13 HUDSON CL
14 CHURCH ST
15 NORTHFIELD MS
16 FARRIERS CT
17 THE CHASE
18 COOPER RD
19 THE SHAMBLES

188

20 DEIGHTON CL
21 York Road Est
22 Cromwell Office Park

For full street detail of Wetherby see Philip's STREET ATLAS of West Yorkshire

Scale: 1¾ inches to 1 mile
0 ¼ ½ mile
0 250m 500m 750m 1 km

164
182

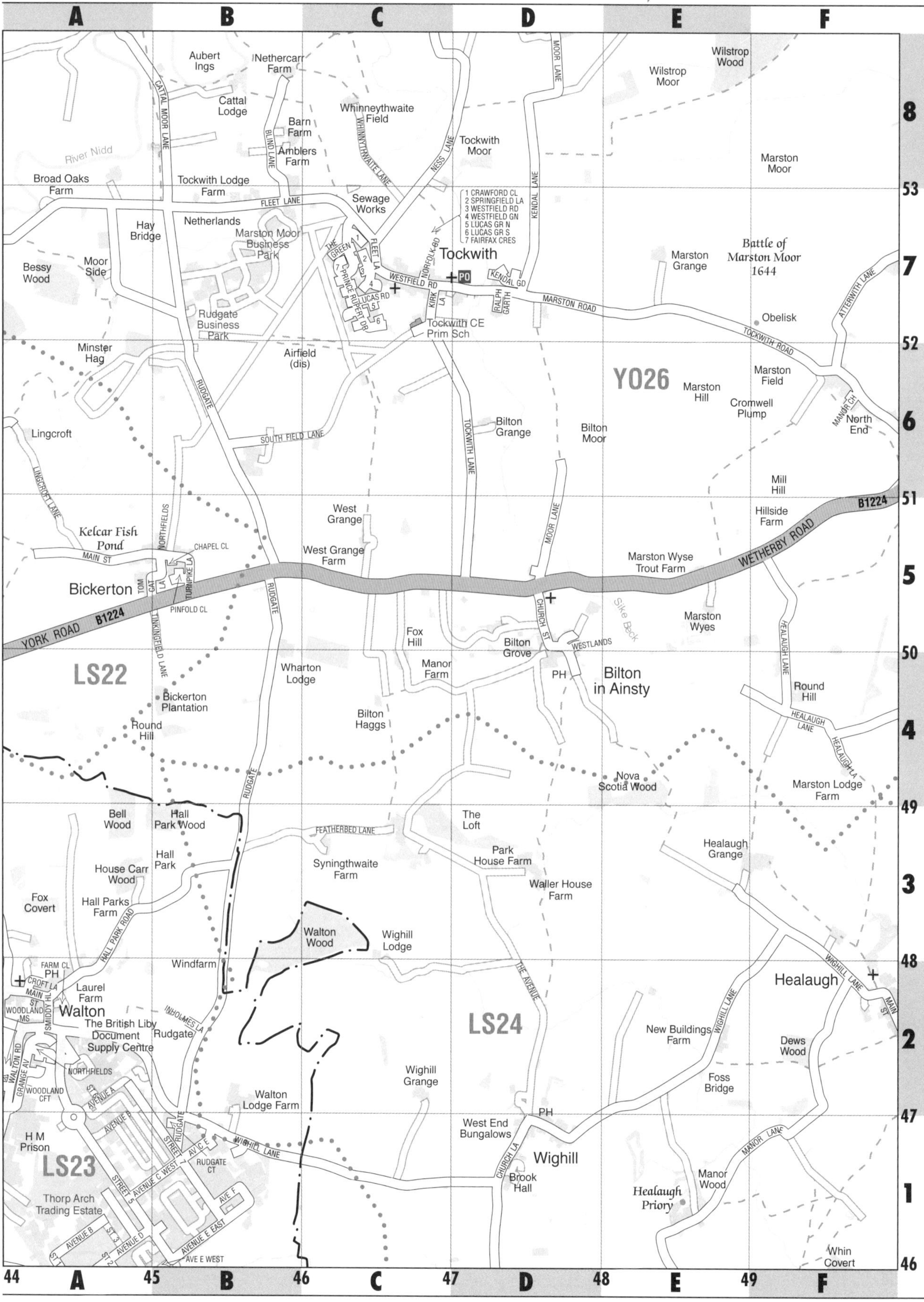

189
182

181
165

Scale: 1¾ inches to 1 mile
0 ¼ ½ mile
0 250m 500m 750m 1 km

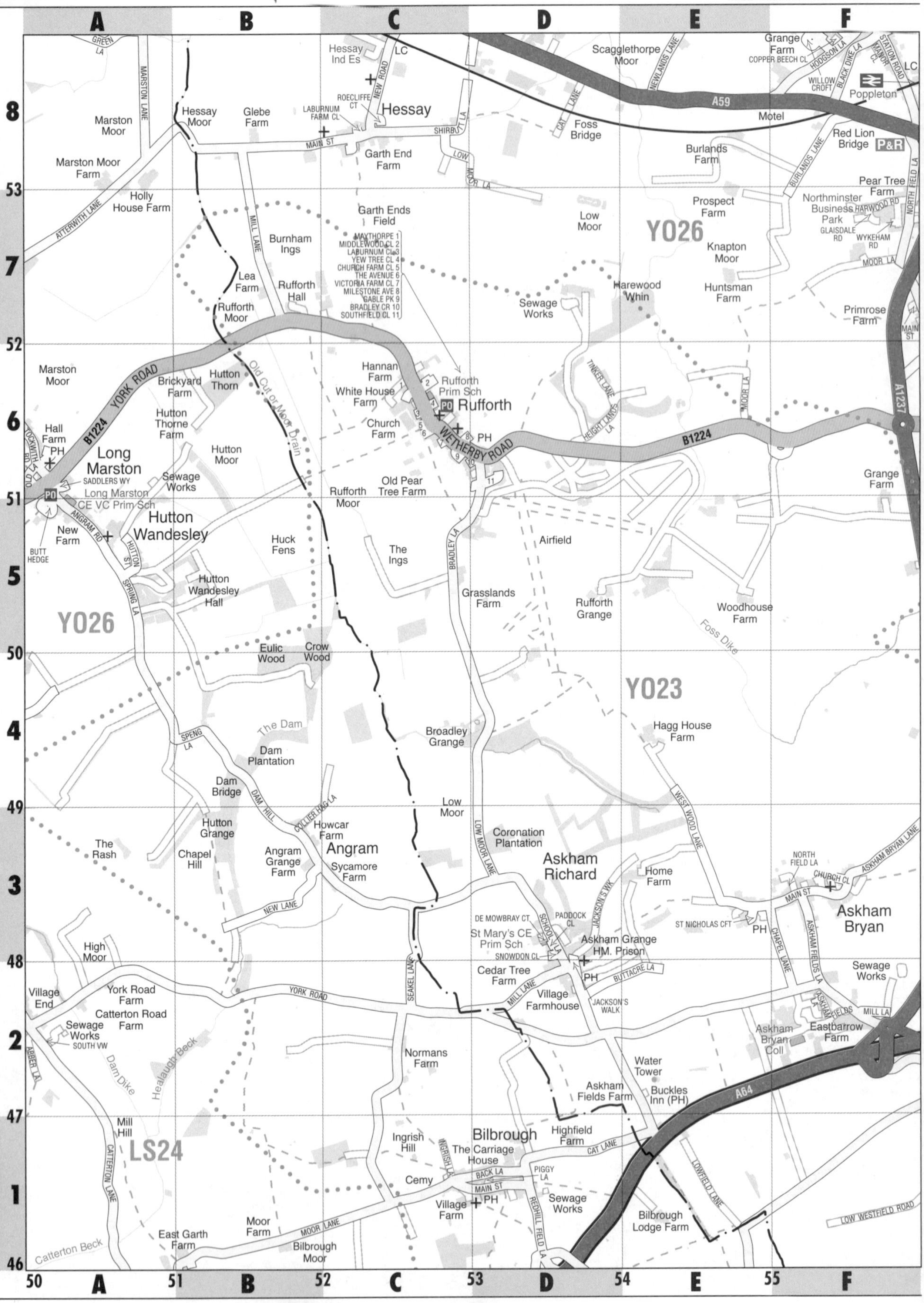

181
190

Scale: 1¾ inches to 1 mile
0 ¼ ½ mile
0 250m 500m 750m 1 km

224
225
229

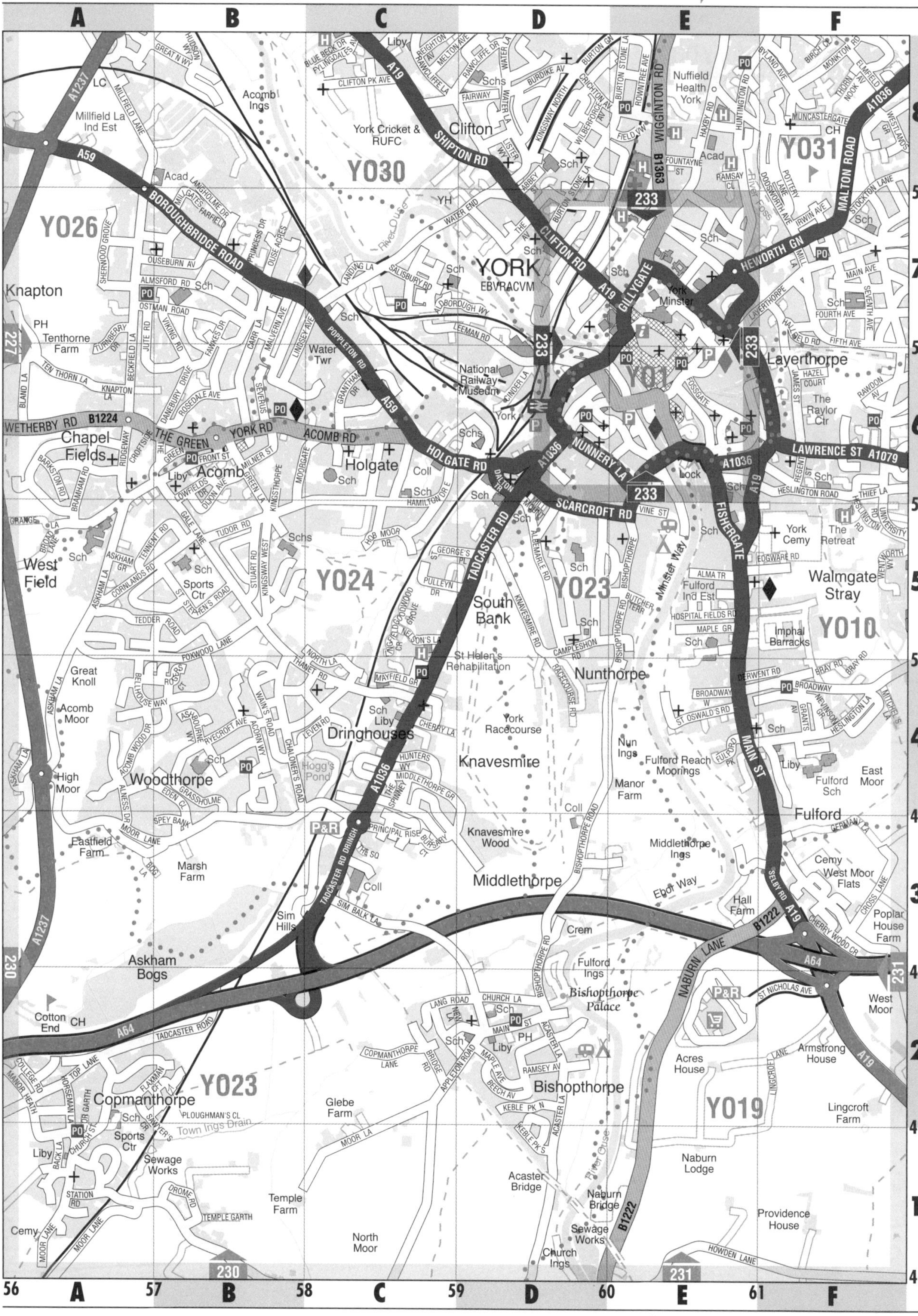

191
184

For full street detail of the highlighted area see pages 227, 228, 230 and 231.

For full street detail of the highlighted area see page 233.

228
226
167

F7
1 GORSE HL
2 HOLLY TREE CFT
3 ASPEN CL
4 ORCHARD CTS
5 PETERCROFT CL
6 KENDAL CL
7 UNDERCROFT
8 THORNCROFT
9 SAWYERS WK
10 CONEYCROFT
11 KEEPERS WY
12 WESTWOOD MEWS
13 SCAUDERCROFT
14 GREENCROFT CT
15 LIME TREE MEWS
16 OX CALDER CL
17 GREENCROFT LA
18 GREENSIDE
19 ASHDALE RD
20 THE GREEN
21 HUNTERS WOOD WY
22 DEERSTONE WY
23 GREENSIDE WLK
24 GREENSIDE CL

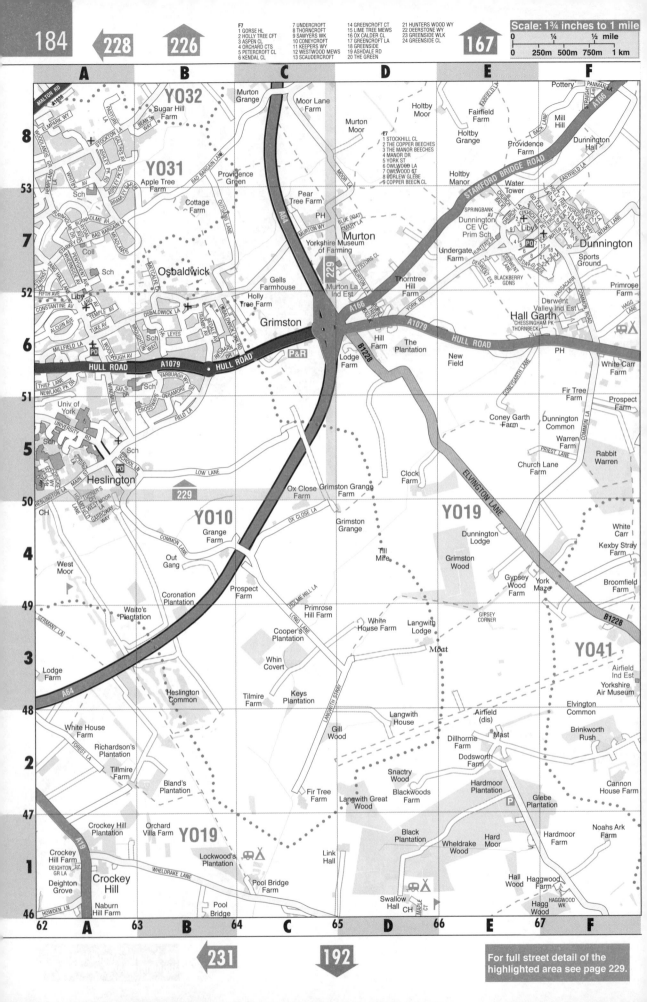

Scale: 1¾ inches to 1 mile
0 ¼ ½ mile
0 250m 500m 750m 1 km

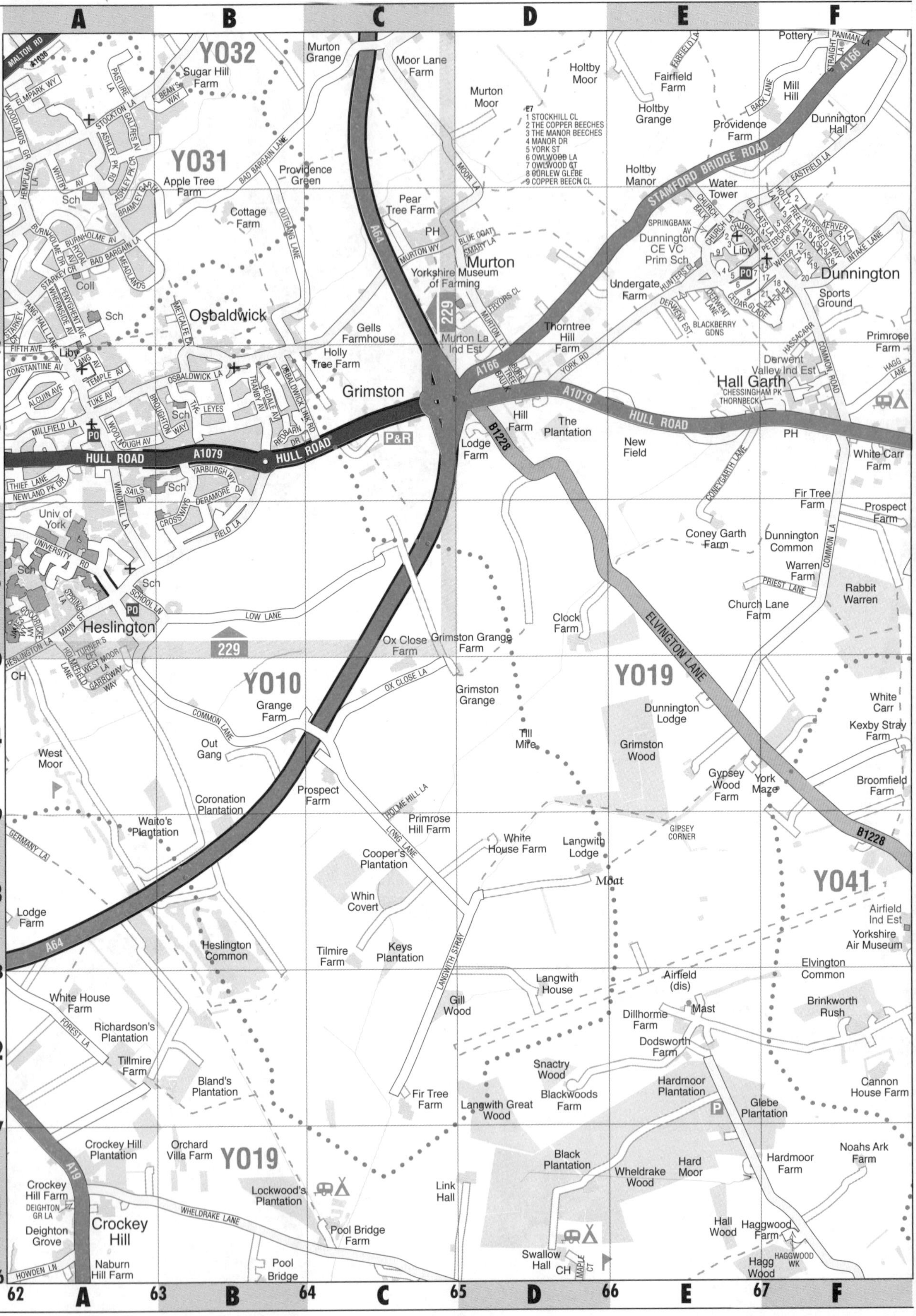

231
192

For full street detail of the highlighted area see page 229.

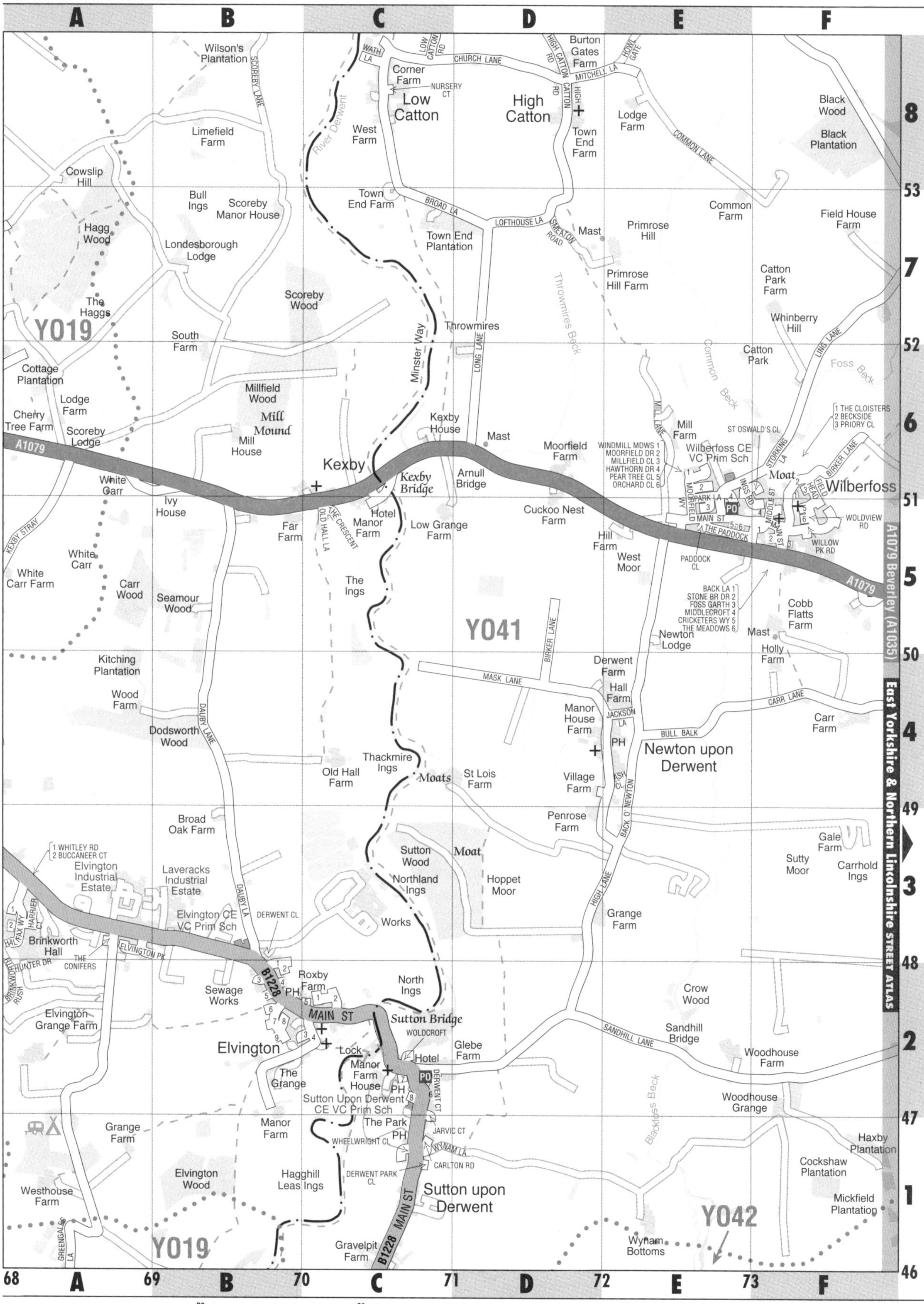

B2
1 WHITE HOUSE GR
2 BEECH CL
3 LORRAINE AVE
4 HILLGARTH CT
5 DOVECOTE GARTH
6 BECK CL
7 BECKSIDE
8 BELVOIR AVE
9 ALVIN WK

C2
1 RIVERSIDE CL
2 RIVERSIDE GDNS
3 CHURCH GN
4 CHURCH LA
5 BLACKSMITHS CL
6 JASMINE GARTH
7 SUTTON PK
8 ST VINCENT'S CL

A7
1 UNITY ST
2 SCHOOL ST
3 VICARAGE RD
4 LOW FD
5 FORT'S BG

172

Scale: 1¾ inches to 1 mile
0 ¼ ½ mile
0 250m 500m 750m 1 km

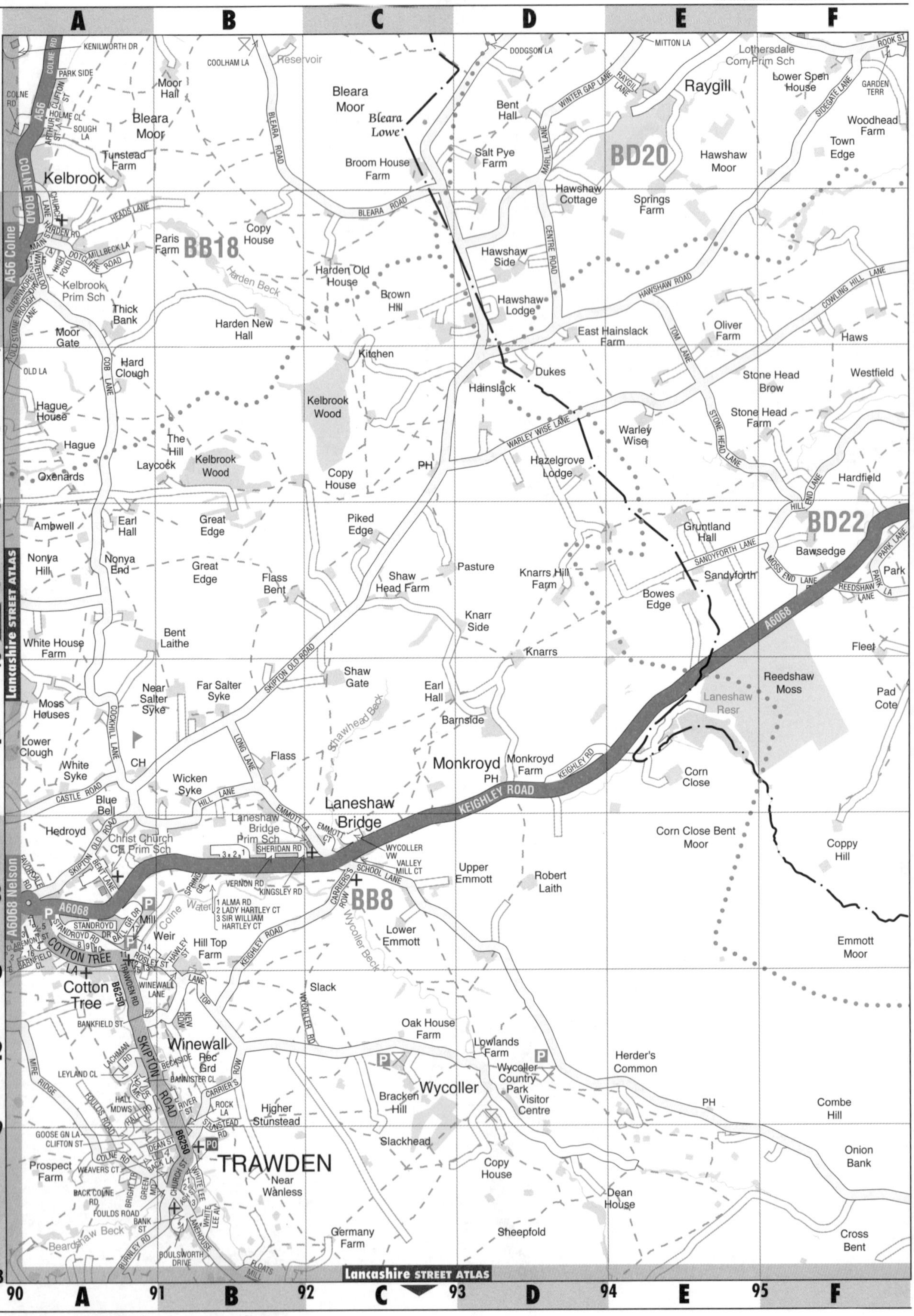

A B C D E F
8
45
7
44
6
43
5
42
4
41
3
40
2
39
1
38
90 91 92 93 94 95
KENILWORTH DR
COOLHAM LA
Reservoir
DODGSON LA
MITTON LA
Lothersdale Com Prim Sch
ROOK ST
Raygill
Lower Spen House
GARDEN TERR
PARK SIDE
COLNE RD
A56
Moor Hall
Bleara Moor
Bleara Lowe
Bent Hall
WINTER GAP LANE
RAYGILL LANE
SIDEGATE LANE
Woodhead Farm
HOLME CL
SOUGH LA
Bleara Moor
BLEARA ROAD
MARLHILL LANE
BD20
Town Edge
Tunstead Farm
Broom House Farm
Salt Pye Farm
Hawshaw Moor
Kelbrook
COLNE ROAD
Hawshaw Cottage
Springs Farm
HEADS LANE
BLEARA ROAD
CENTRE ROAD
A56 Colne
Paris Farm
BB18
Copy House
Hawshaw Side
MILLBECK LA
DOTCLIFFE ROAD
Harden Old House
Kelbrook Prim Sch
Harden Beck
Brown Hill
Hawshaw Lodge
HAWSHAW ROAD
COWLING HILL LANE
Thick Bank
Harden New Hall
East Hainslack Farm
TOM LANE
Oliver Farm
OLD STONE TROUGH LANE
Moor Gate
Haws
Kitchen
OLD LA
COB LANE
Hard Clough
Dukes
Hainslack
Stone Head Brow
Westfield
Kelbrook Wood
Hague House
Stone Head Farm
Warley Wise
WARLEY WISE LANE
STONE HEAD LANE
The Hill
Hague
PH
Hazelgrove Lodge
Laycock
Kelbrook Wood
Copy House
Hardfield
Oxenards
HILL END LANE
Ambwell
Earl Hall
Great Edge
Piked Edge
Gruntland Hall
BD22
SANDYFORTH LANE
Nonya Hill
Nonya End
Bawsedge
Great Edge
Flass Bent
Shaw Head Farm
Pasture
Knarrs Hill Farm
Sandyforth
MOSS END LANE
PARK LANE
Park
REEDSHAW LANE
Bowes Edge
A6068
Knarr Side
Lancashire STREET ATLAS
Bent Laithe
White House Farm
Fleet
Knarrs
SKIPTON OLD ROAD
Shaw Gate
Reedshaw Moss
Far Salter Syke
Earl Hall
Near Salter Syke
Pad Cote
Moss Houses
Laneshaw Resr
Shawhead Beck
Barnside
COCKHILL LANE
Lower Clough
LONG LANE
Flass
Monkroyd
Monkroyd Farm
KEIGHLEY RD
CH
White Syke
Corn Close
Wicken Syke
PH
HILL LANE
KEIGHLEY ROAD
CASTLE ROAD
Blue Bell
Laneshaw Bridge
EMMOTT LA
Laneshaw Bridge Prim Sch
EMMOTT CT
Corn Close Bent Moor
Hedroyd
Christ Church CE Prim Sch
SHERIDAN RD
WYCOLLER VW
VALLEY MILL CT
Coppy Hill
SKIPTON OLD ROAD
BENT LANE
SCHOOL LANE
Upper Emmott
Robert Laith
VERNON RD
KINGSLEY RD
CARRIER'S ROW
A6068 Nelson
A6068
Colne Water
Mill
1 ALMA RD
2 LADY HARTLEY CT
3 SIR WILLIAM HARTLEY CT
BB8
STANDROYD
STANDROYD RD
Weir
Wycoller Beck
Lower Emmott
Emmott Moor
COTTON TREE
Hill Top Farm
HAWLEY ST
ROSLEY ST
KEIGHLEY ROAD
Cotton Tree
B6250
WINEWALL LANE
LANE TOP
Slack
WYCOLLER RD
NEW ROW
BANKFIELD ST
Oak House Farm
Winewall
Rec Grd
Lowlands Farm
Herder's Common
SKIPTON ROAD
LEYLAND CL
BECKSIDE
BANNISTER CL
Wycoller Country Park Visitor Centre
Wycoller
MIRE RIDGE
CARRIER'S ROW
FOULDS ROAD
HALL MDWS
RIVER ST
ROCK LA
Higher Stunstead
Bracken Hill
PH
Combe Hill
STUNSTEAD RD
GOOSE GN LA
CLIFTON ST
DEAN ST
B6250
Slackhead
Onion Bank
COLNE RD
WEAVERS CT
Prospect Farm
TRAWDEN
Copy House
BACK COLNE RD
CHURCH ST
WHITE LEE
Near Wanless
Dean House
FOULDS ROAD
BANK ST
Beardshaw Beck
Germany Farm
Sheepfold
Cross Bent
BURNLEY RD
BOULSWORTH DRIVE
FLOATS MILL
LANEHOUSE

Lancashire STREET ATLAS

A3
1 KEIGHLEY RD
2 CLARENCE ST
3 CRAVEN ST
4 BOULSWORTH GR
5 MONMOUTH ST
6 ACRESFIELD
7 LONG MEADOW
8 LAMBETH ST
9 HOLLINGTON ST
10 CLARENDON ST
11 WINEWALL RD
12 HOLME ST
13 HARTINGTON ST
14 DUKE ST
15 BRIGHT ST
16 ING DENE AVE
17 MILLBROOK CT

B1
1 CLARENCE ST
2 LAMBERT ST
3 EAST VIEW
4 Trawden Forest Prim Sch

Scale: 1¾ inches to 1 mile
0 ¼ ½ mile
0 250m 500m 750m 1 km

173

B6
1 ACRE MEADOW
2 ACRE RD
3 WOODLAND ST
4 SUN ST
5 WALTON ST
6 CROSS ST
7 GREEN ST
8 SPRINGWELL CL
9 COLLINGE RD
10 QUEEN ST
11 LAYCOCK FIELDS
12 ROYD CT
13 GIBB ST

E8
1 BLACK ABBEY LA
2 RYECROFT WY
3 VALLEY VW
4 WASHBURN DR
5 BEANLANDS PL
6 HOPP'S RD
7 WHEATLANDS LA
8 WHEATLANDS AVE
9 RYELAND ST
10 JAMES ST
11 CAMPBELL ST
12 YORK ST
13 CHURCH ST
14 NORTH ST
15 PARKER ST
16 PARK ST
17 BACK STATION RD
18 ANDERTON ST
19 STATION GR
20 WHEATLANDS GARTH
21 THOMAS ST
22 IVY PL
23 NEWBY DR

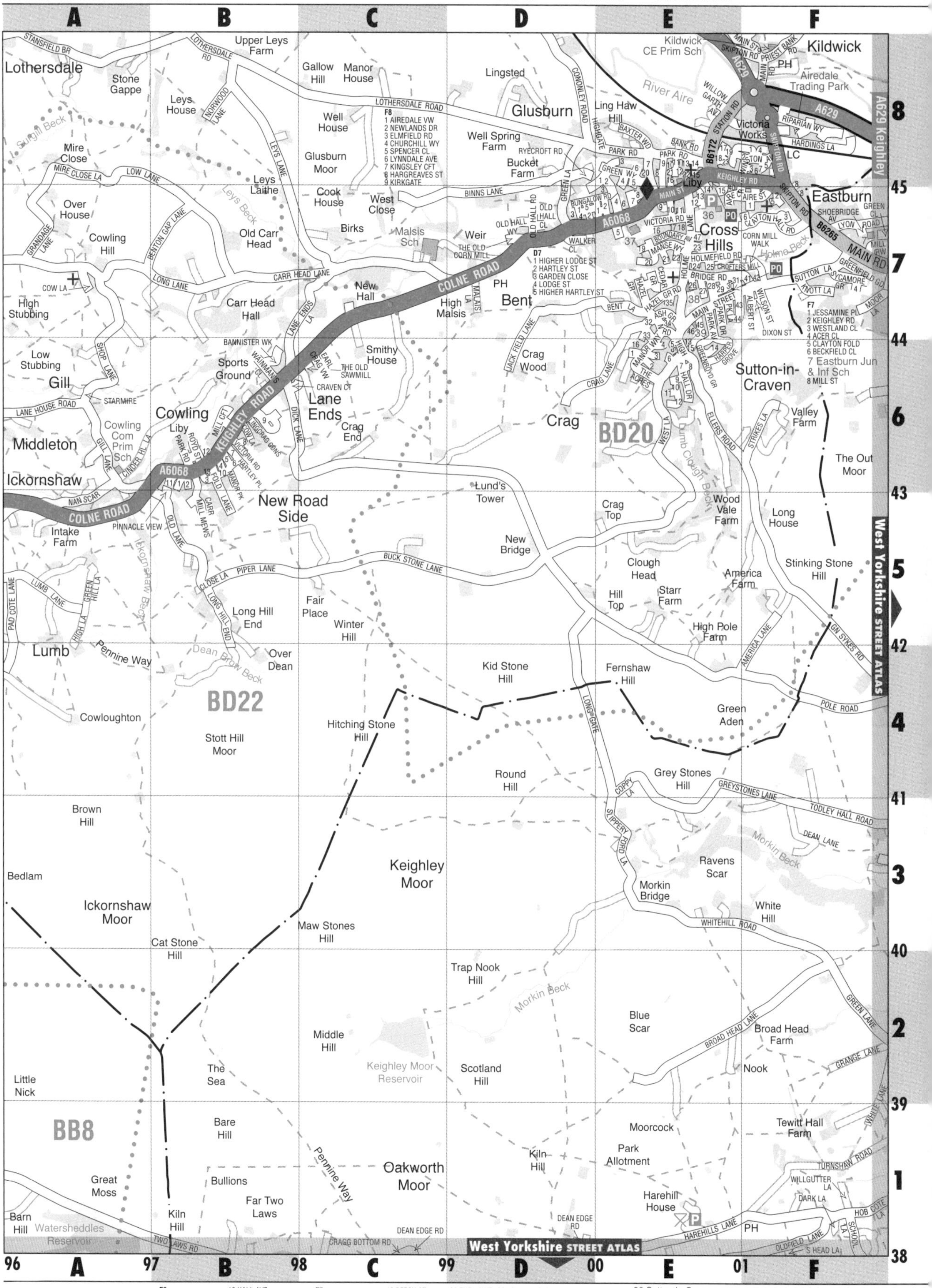

E6
1 THE CROFTS
2 THE POPLARS
3 EARLS VW
4 ROSEMOUNT CT
5 LISTER HILL
6 WEST CROFT
7 HARPERS SQ
8 OVERBURN RD
9 HALL WAY
10 HALL AVE
11 HALL CL
12 NORTH AVE
13 GREENROYD DR
14 DOVELANDS
15 WET INGS LA
16 WILLOW WY

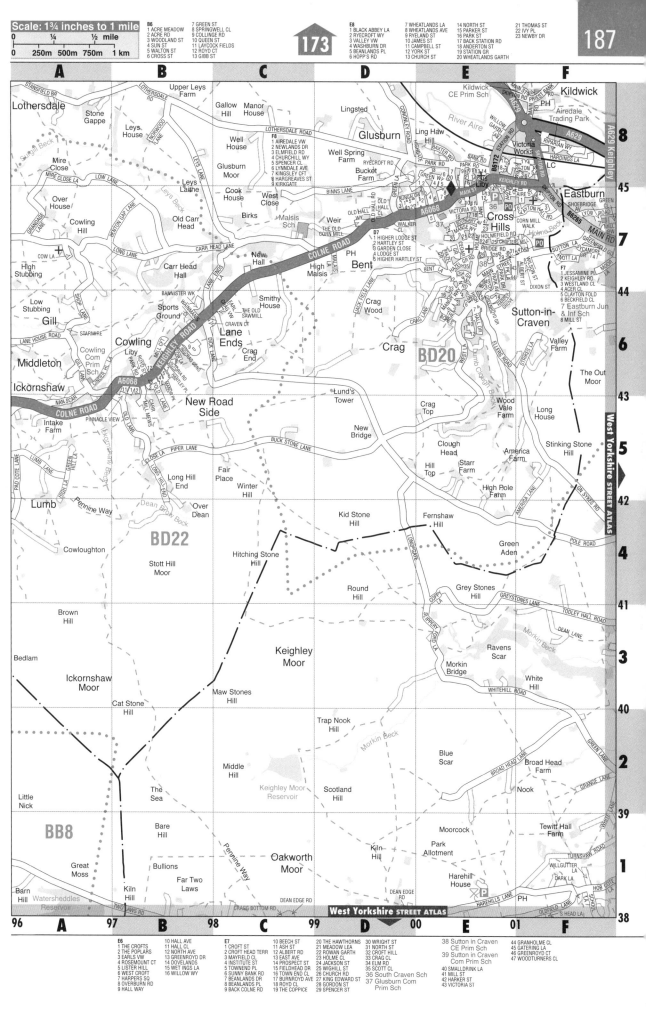

E7
1 CROFT ST
2 CROFT HEAD TERR
3 MAYFIELD CL
4 INSTITUTE ST
5 TOWNEND PL
6 SUNNY BANK RD
7 BEANLANDS DR
8 BEANLANDS PL
9 BACK COLNE RD
10 BEECH ST
11 ASH ST
12 ALBERT RD
13 EAST AVE
14 PROSPECT ST
15 FIELDHEAD DR
16 TOWN END CL
17 BURNROYD AVE
18 ROYD CL
19 THE COPPICE
20 THE HAWTHORNS
21 MEADOW LEA
22 ROWAN GARTH
23 HOLME CL
24 JACKSON ST
25 WIGHILL ST
26 CHURCH RD
27 KING EDWARD ST
28 GORDON ST
29 SPENCER ST
30 WRIGHT ST
31 NORTH ST
32 CROFT HILL
33 CRAG CL
34 ELM RD
35 SCOTT CL
36 South Craven Sch
37 Glusburn Com Prim Sch
38 Sutton in Craven CE Prim Sch
39 Sutton in Craven Com Prim Sch
40 SMALLDRINK LA
41 MILL ST
42 HARKER ST
43 VICTORIA ST
44 GRANHOLME CL
45 GATERING LA
46 GREENROYD CT
47 WOODTURNERS CL

A8
1 BISHOPDALE DR
2 COVERDALE GARTH
3 LANGWITH AVE
4 GREEN LA
5 THE CROFT
6 THE CLOSE
7 MILLGARTH CT
8 THE GARTH
9 LOWCROFT
10 THE VALE

E8
1 SPRINGFIELD
2 CHESTNUT AVE
3 St Edward's Catholic Prim Sch

180

4 West Oaks Sen Specialist Sch & Coll
5 Primrose Lane Prim Sch
6 St Marys CE Sch
7 St Johns RC Sch for the Deaf

Scale: 1¾ inches to 1 mile
0 ¼ ½ mile
0 250m 500m 750m 1 km

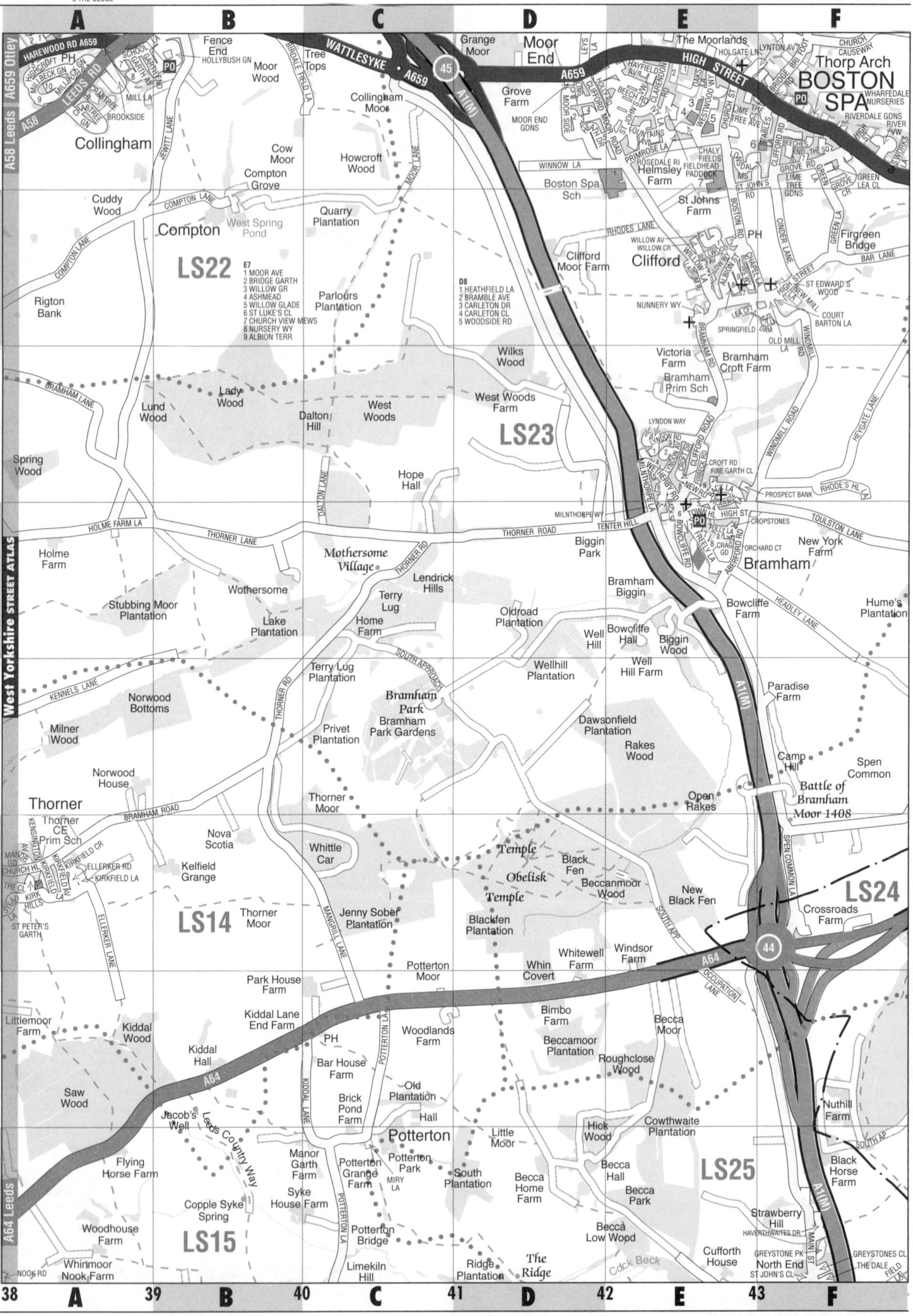

194

E5
1 ALMSHOUSE HL
2 FOLLY VW
3 THE CRAG
4 CHURCH HL
5 LOW WY
6 FRONT ST
7 FREELY FIELDS
8 FOSSARDS CL

E6
1 LYNDON CL
2 LYNDON SQ
3 THE KNOLL
4 LYNDON CRES
5 MILNTHORPE GDNS
6 MILNTHORPE CL
7 MILNTHORPE GARTH
8 BRADFORDS CL
9 CHURCH MDWS

For full street detail of Boston Spa see Philip's STREET ATLAS of West Yorkshire

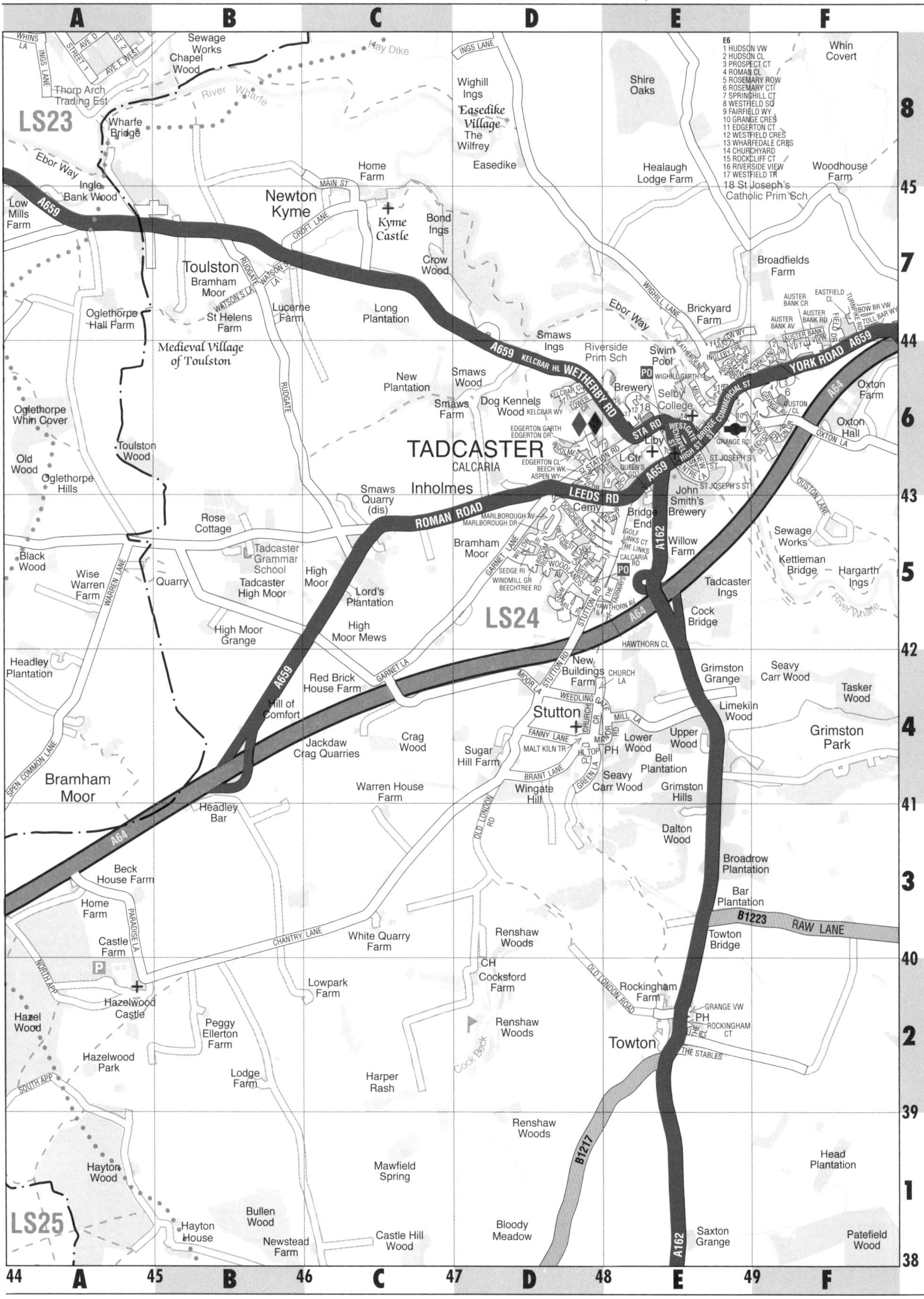
A B C D E F
E6
1 HUDSON VW
2 HUDSON CL
3 PROSPECT CT
4 ROMAN CL
5 ROSEMARY ROW
6 ROSEMARY CT
7 SPRINGHILL CT
8 WESTFIELD SQ
9 FAIRFIELD WY
10 GRANGE CRES
11 EDGERTON CT
12 WESTFIELD CRES
13 WHARFEDALE CRES
14 CHURCHYARD
15 ROCKCLIFF CT
16 RIVERSIDE VIEW
17 WESTFIELD TR
18 St Joseph's Catholic Prim Sch
LS23
LS24
LS25
TADCASTER
CALCARIA
Thorp Arch Trading Est
Sewage Works
Chapel Wood
Hay Dike
River Wharfe
Wharfe Bridge
Ebor Way
Ingle Bank Wood
Low Mills Farm
A659
Newton Kyme
Home Farm
Kyme Castle
Bond Ings
Crow Wood
Wighill Ings
Easedike Village
The Wilfrey
Easedike
Shire Oaks
Healaugh Lodge Farm
Whin Covert
Woodhouse Farm
Broadfields Farm
Toulston
Bramham Moor
St Helens Farm
Lucerne Farm
Long Plantation
Oglethorpe Hall Farm
Medieval Village of Toulston
New Plantation
Smaws Wood
Smaws Farm
Smaws Ings
Dog Kennels Wood
Riverside Prim Sch
Swim Pool
Brewery
Selby College
Brickyard Farm
Oxton Farm
Oxton Hall
WETHERBY RD
LEEDS RD
YORK ROAD
ROMAN ROAD
Oglethorpe Whin Cover
Old Wood
Oglethorpe Hills
Toulston Wood
Smaws Quarry (dis)
Inholmes
Cemy
Bridge End
John Smith's Brewery
Willow Farm
Sewage Works
Kettleman Bridge
Hargarth Ings
Rose Cottage
Tadcaster Grammar School
Tadcaster High Moor
Black Wood
Wise Warren Farm
Quarry
High Moor
Lord's Plantation
Bramham Moor
Tadcaster Ings
Cock Bridge
High Moor Grange
High Moor Mews
A64
A162
Headley Plantation
Red Brick House Farm
Hill of Comfort
New Buildings Farm
Stutton
Grimston Grange
Seavy Carr Wood
Tasker Wood
Limekiln Wood
Grimston Park
Jackdaw Crag Quarries
Crag Wood
Sugar Hill Farm
Lower Wood
Upper Wood
Bell Plantation
Seavy Carr Wood
Grimston Hills
Bramham Moor
Warren House Farm
Wingate Hill
Headley Bar
Dalton Wood
Beck House Farm
Broadrow Plantation
Home Farm
Bar Plantation
B1223
RAW LANE
Castle Farm
CHANTRY LANE
White Quarry Farm
Renshaw Woods
Towton Bridge
Hazelwood Castle
Lowpark Farm
Cocksford Farm
Rockingham Farm
Hazel Wood
Peggy Ellerton Farm
Renshaw Woods
Towton
Hazelwood Park
Lodge Farm
Harper Rash
Cock Beck
Renshaw Woods
B1217
Hayton Wood
Mawfield Spring
Head Plantation
Hayton House
Bullen Wood
Newstead Farm
Castle Hill Wood
Bloody Meadow
Saxton Grange
Patefield Wood
44 45 46 47 48 49
45 44 43 42 41 40 39 38
8 7 6 5 4 3 2 1

189
182

Scale: 1¾ inches to 1 mile
0 ¼ ½ mile
0 250m 500m 750m 1 km

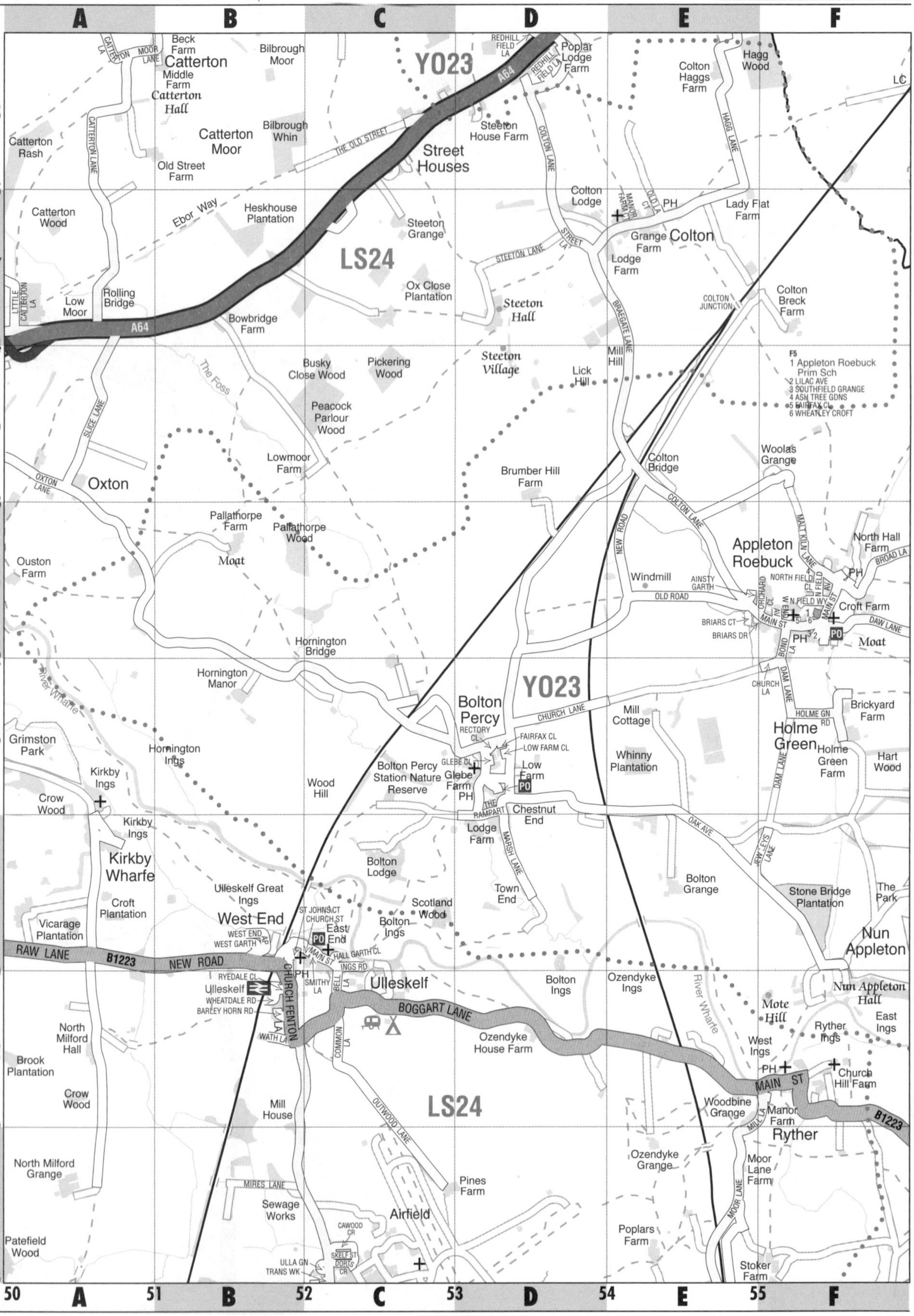

189
196

C7
1 THE CRESCENT
2 LILAC AVE
3 PLEASANT AVE
4 BEECH AVE
5 CHERRY TREE DR
6 CUNDALL DR
7 THE WILLOWS
8 OAK AVE
9 THE CLOSE
10 ELM AVE
11 THE VINES
12 PHEASANT WY
13 SWANLOW DR

D8
1 MAIN ST
2 FERRY FARM CL
3 MAYPOLE GR
4 ST MATTHEW'S CT

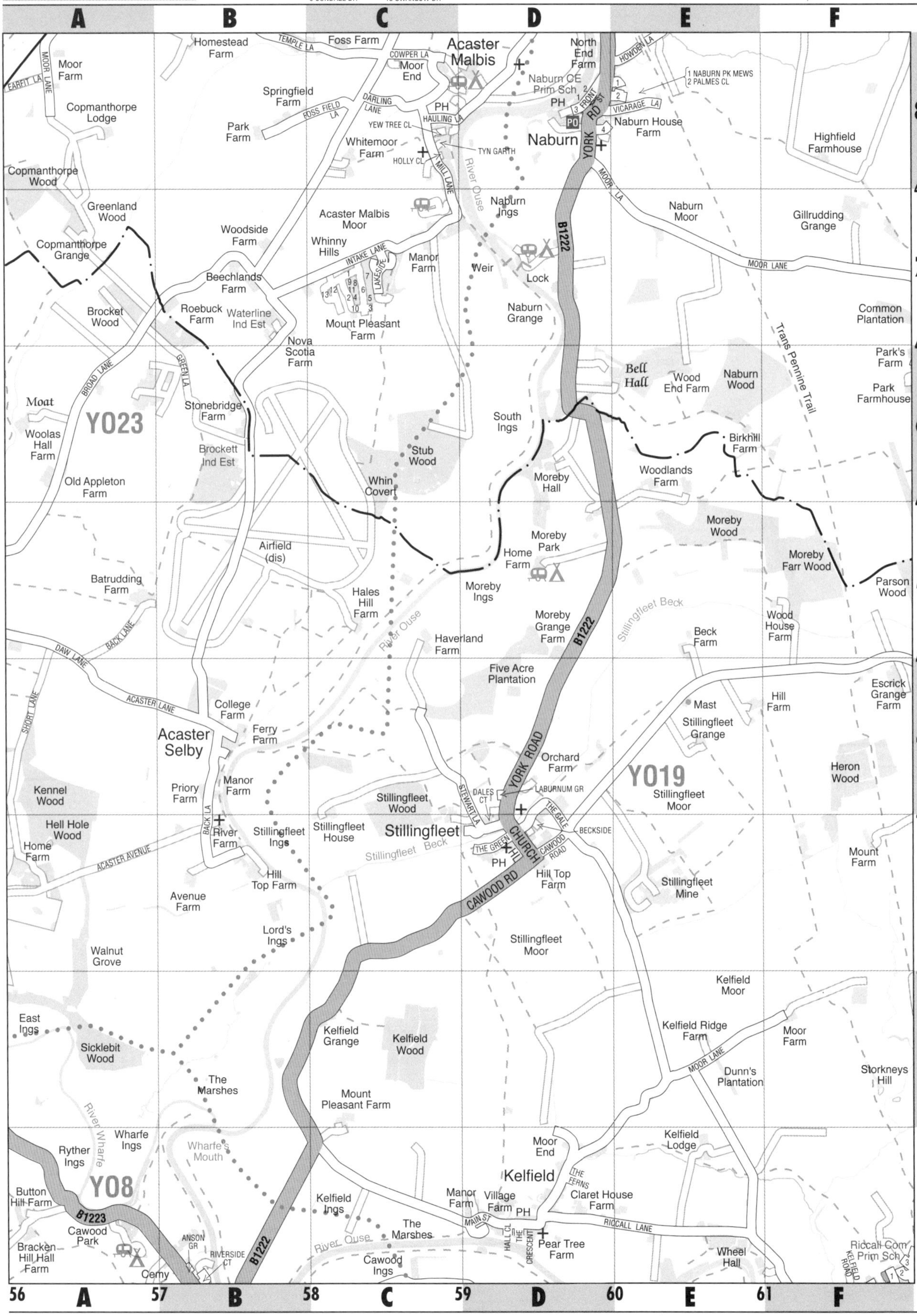

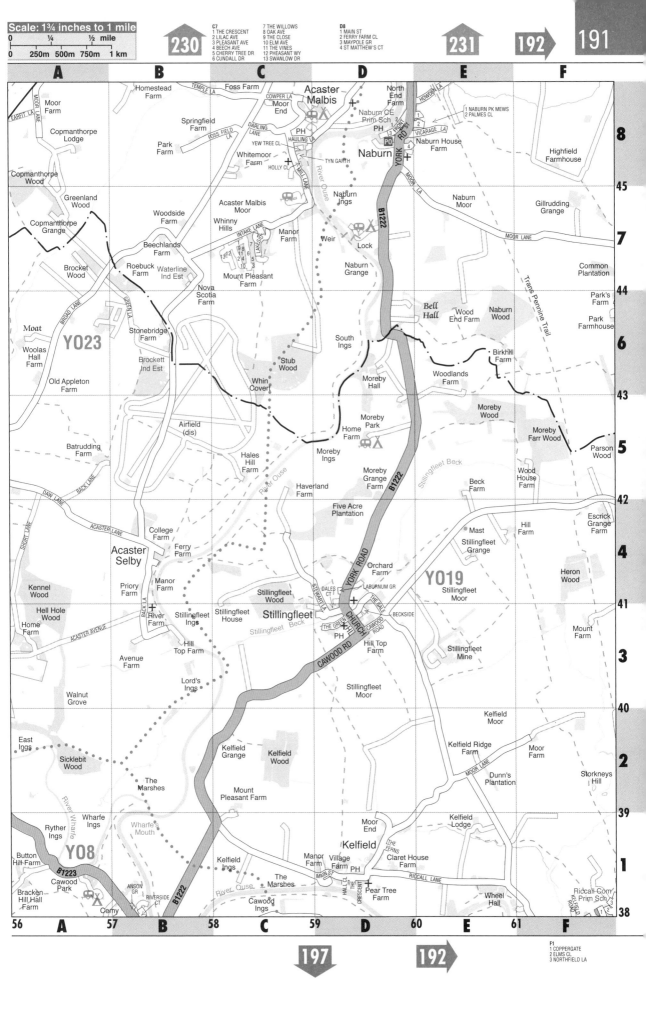

F1
1 COPPERGATE
2 ELMS CL
3 NORTHFIELD LA

Scale: 1¾ inches to 1 mile
0 ¼ ½ mile
0 250m 500m 750m 1 km

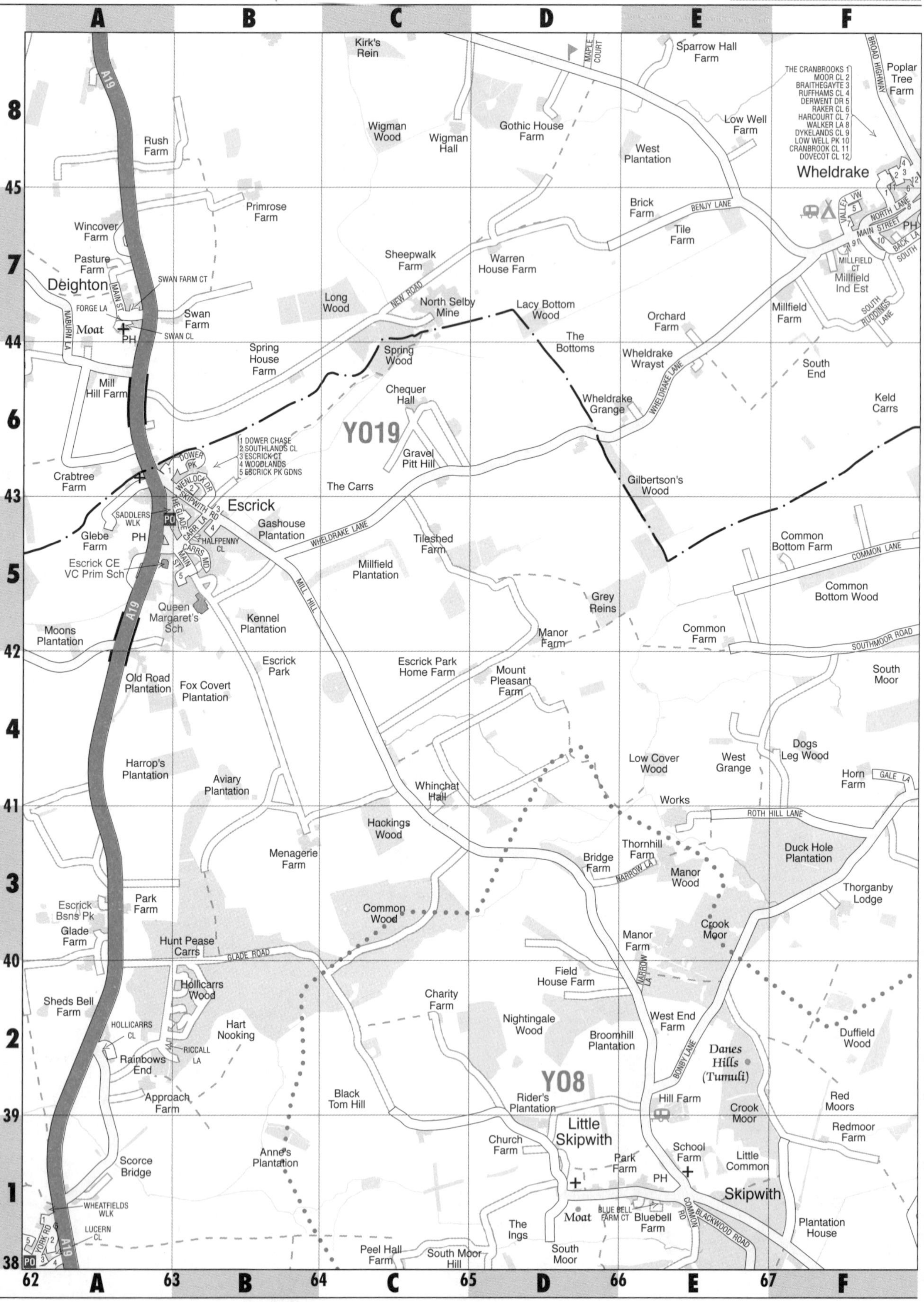
A
B
C
D
E
F
Kirk's Rein
Sparrow Hall Farm
MAPLE COURT
BROAD HIGHWAY
Poplar Tree Farm
THE CRANBROOKS 1
MOOR CL 2
BRAITHEGAYTE 3
RUFFHAMS CL 4
DERWENT DR 5
RAKER CL 6
HARCOURT CL 7
WALKER LA 8
DYKELANDS CL 9
LOW WELL PK 10
CRANBROOK CL 11
DOVECOT CL 12
A19
Rush Farm
Wigman Wood
Wigman Hall
Gothic House Farm
Low Well Farm
West Plantation
Wheldrake
Primrose Farm
Brick Farm
BENJY LANE
Tile Farm
VALLEY VW
NORTH LANE
MAIN STREET
BACK LA
SOUTH
PH
Wincover Farm
Pasture Farm
Deighton
MAIN ST
SWAN FARM CT
Sheepwalk Farm
Warren House Farm
MILLFIELD CT
Millfield Ind Est
NEW ROAD
Long Wood
North Selby Mine
Lacy Bottom Wood
Orchard Farm
Millfield Farm
SOUTH RUDDINGS LANE
FORGE LA
NABURN LA
Moat
Swan Farm
SWAN CL
PH
Spring House Farm
Spring Wood
The Bottoms
Wheldrake Wrayst
South End
Mill Hill Farm
Chequer Hall
Wheldrake Grange
WHELDRAKE LANE
Keld Carrs
YO19
1 DOWER CHASE
2 SOUTHLANDS CL
3 ESCRICK CT
4 WOODLANDS
5 ESCRICK PK GDNS
DOWER PK
WENLOCK DR
SKIPWITH RD
Gravel Pitt Hill
Crabtree Farm
The Carrs
Gilbertson's Wood
Escrick
SADDLERS WLK
THE GLADE
CARR LA
PO
Gashouse Plantation
WHELDRAKE LANE
Glebe Farm
PH
HALFPENNY CL
Tileshed Farm
Common Bottom Farm
COMMON LANE
Escrick CE VC Prim Sch
CARRS MDW
MAIN ST
Millfield Plantation
MILL HILL
Common Bottom Wood
Grey Reins
Queen Margaret's Sch
Kennel Plantation
Moons Plantation
A19
Manor Farm
Common Farm
SOUTHMOOR ROAD
Escrick Park
Escrick Park Home Farm
Mount Pleasant Farm
South Moor
Old Road Plantation
Fox Covert Plantation
Dogs Leg Wood
Harrop's Plantation
Low Cover Wood
West Grange
Horn Farm
GALE LA
Aviary Plantation
Whinchat Hall
Works
ROTH HILL LANE
Hackings Wood
Thornhill Farm
Duck Hole Plantation
Menagerie Farm
Bridge Farm
NARROW LA
Manor Wood
Thorganby Lodge
Escrick Bsns Pk
Park Farm
Common Wood
Crook Moor
Glade Farm
Hunt Pease Carrs
GLADE ROAD
Manor Farm
NARROW LA
Field House Farm
Hollicarrs Wood
Sheds Bell Farm
Charity Farm
HOLLICARRS CL
Hart Nooking
Nightingale Wood
West End Farm
Duffield Wood
Broomhill Plantation
RICCALL LA
Rainbows End
BONBY LANE
Danes Hills (Tumuli)
YO8
Approach Farm
Black Tom Hill
Rider's Plantation
Hill Farm
Red Moors
Crook Moor
Little Skipwith
Redmoor Farm
Church Farm
School Farm
Scorce Bridge
Anne's Plantation
Park Farm
Little Common
PH
Skipwith
WHEATFIELDS WLK
COMMON RD
BLACKWOOD ROAD
Moat
BLUE BELL FARM CT
Bluebell Farm
Plantation House
LUCERN CL
YORK RD
The Ings
Peel Hall Farm
South Moor Hill
South Moor
PO
62
63
64
65
66
67
8
45
7
44
6
43
5
42
4
41
3
40
2
39
1
38

A1
1 MILL LA
2 HOLMES DR
3 CHAPEL LA
4 CHAPEL WK
5 PINFOLD CL
6 FERN CT

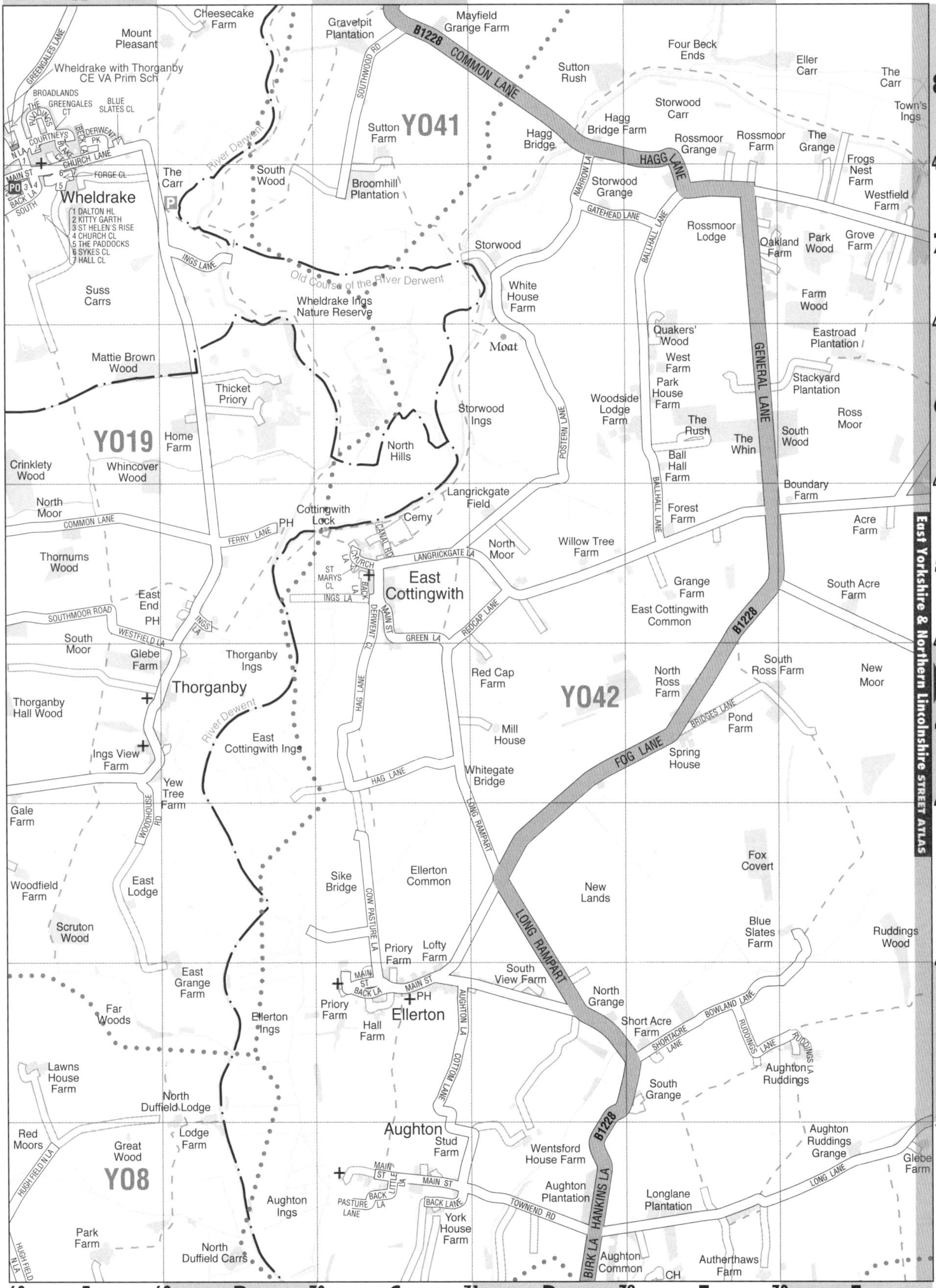
Scale: 1¾ inches to 1 mile
0 ¼ ½ mile
0 250m 500m 750m 1 km
185
A B C D E F
Cheesecake Farm
Mount Pleasant
Wheldrake with Thorganby CE VA Prim Sch
Gravelpit Plantation
Mayfield Grange Farm
B1228 COMMON LANE
Sutton Rush
Four Beck Ends
Eller Carr
The Carr
Town's Ings
Sutton Farm
YO41
Hagg Bridge
Hagg Bridge Farm
Storwood Carr
Rossmoor Grange
Rossmoor Farm
The Grange
Frogs Nest Farm
Westfield Farm
HAGG LANE
The Carr
South Wood
Broomhill Plantation
Wheldrake
Storwood Grange
Rossmoor Lodge
Oakland Farm
Park Wood
Grove Farm
River Derwent
Storwood
Old Course of the River Derwent
Wheldrake Ings Nature Reserve
White House Farm
Suss Carrs
Farm Wood
Eastroad Plantation
Quakers' Wood
Mattie Brown Wood
Moat
West Farm
Park House Farm
Stackyard Plantation
Thicket Priory
Storwood Ings
Woodside Lodge Farm
The Rush
GENERAL LANE
Ross Moor
YO19
Home Farm
North Hills
The Whin
South Wood
Crinklety Wood
Whincover Wood
Ball Hall Farm
Boundary Farm
North Moor
Cottingwith Lock
Langrickgate Field
Forest Farm
Acre Farm
Thornums Wood
Cemy
North Moor
Willow Tree Farm
East Cottingwith
Grange Farm
South Acre Farm
East End
East Cottingwith Common
South Moor
Glebe Farm
Thorganby Ings
Red Cap Farm
South Ross Farm
New Moor
Thorganby
North Ross Farm
YO42
Thorganby Hall Wood
Mill House
Pond Farm
East Cottingwith Ings
Ings View Farm
Yew Tree Farm
Spring House
FOG LANE
Whitegate Bridge
Gale Farm
Fox Covert
Sike Bridge
Ellerton Common
Woodfield Farm
East Lodge
New Lands
Scruton Wood
LONG RAMPART
Blue Slates Farm
Ruddings Wood
Priory Farm
Lofty Farm
East Grange Farm
South View Farm
North Grange
Far Woods
Ellerton Ings
Priory Farm
Ellerton
Hall Farm
Short Acre Farm
Lawns House Farm
South Grange
Aughton Ruddings
North Duffield Lodge
Red Moors
Great Wood
Lodge Farm
Aughton
Stud Farm
Wentsford House Farm
Aughton Ruddings Grange
Glebe Farm
YO8
Aughton Ings
Aughton Plantation
Longlane Plantation
York House Farm
Park Farm
North Duffield Carrs
Aughton Common
CH
Autherthaws Farm
BIRK LA
HANKINS LA
B1228
TOWNEND RD
LONG LANE
68 69 70 71 72 73
45 44 43 42 41 40 39 38
8 7 6 5 4 3 2 1
East Yorkshire & Northern Lincolnshire STREET ATLAS
1 DALTON HL
2 KITTY GARTH
3 ST HELEN'S RISE
4 CHURCH CL
5 THE PADDOCKS
6 SYKES CL
7 HALL CL

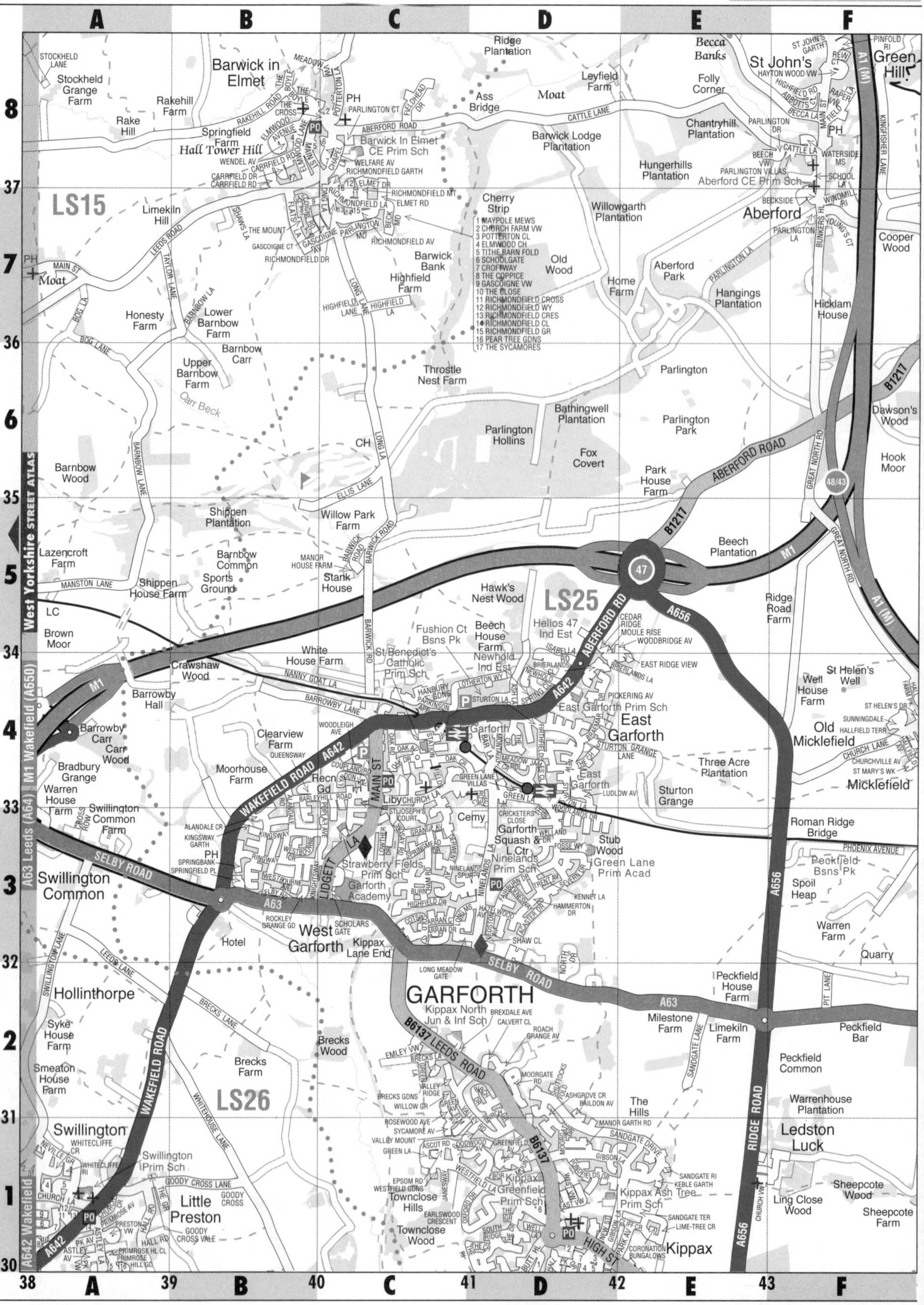

A1
1 WHITECLIFFE DR
2 LOWTHER DR
3 LOWTHER CRES
4 CHURCH CL
5 SMEATON GR
6 THE PLEASANCE
7 SPRINGWELL AVE
8 WOODLAND CRES
9 THE CREST
10 SPRINGWELL RD
11 SPRINGWELL AVE
12 THE DRIVE
13 SCOTT CL
14 ST MARY'S AVE
15 PRIMROSE HL DR
16 PRIMROSE HL GR

D1
1 TATEFIELD PL
2 HANOVER PL
3 THE INTAKE
4 APPLE TREE LA
5 APPLE TREE MS
6 CHURCHFIELD LA
7 APPLE TREE WALK

For full street detail of Garforth see Philip's STREET ATLAS of West Yorkshire

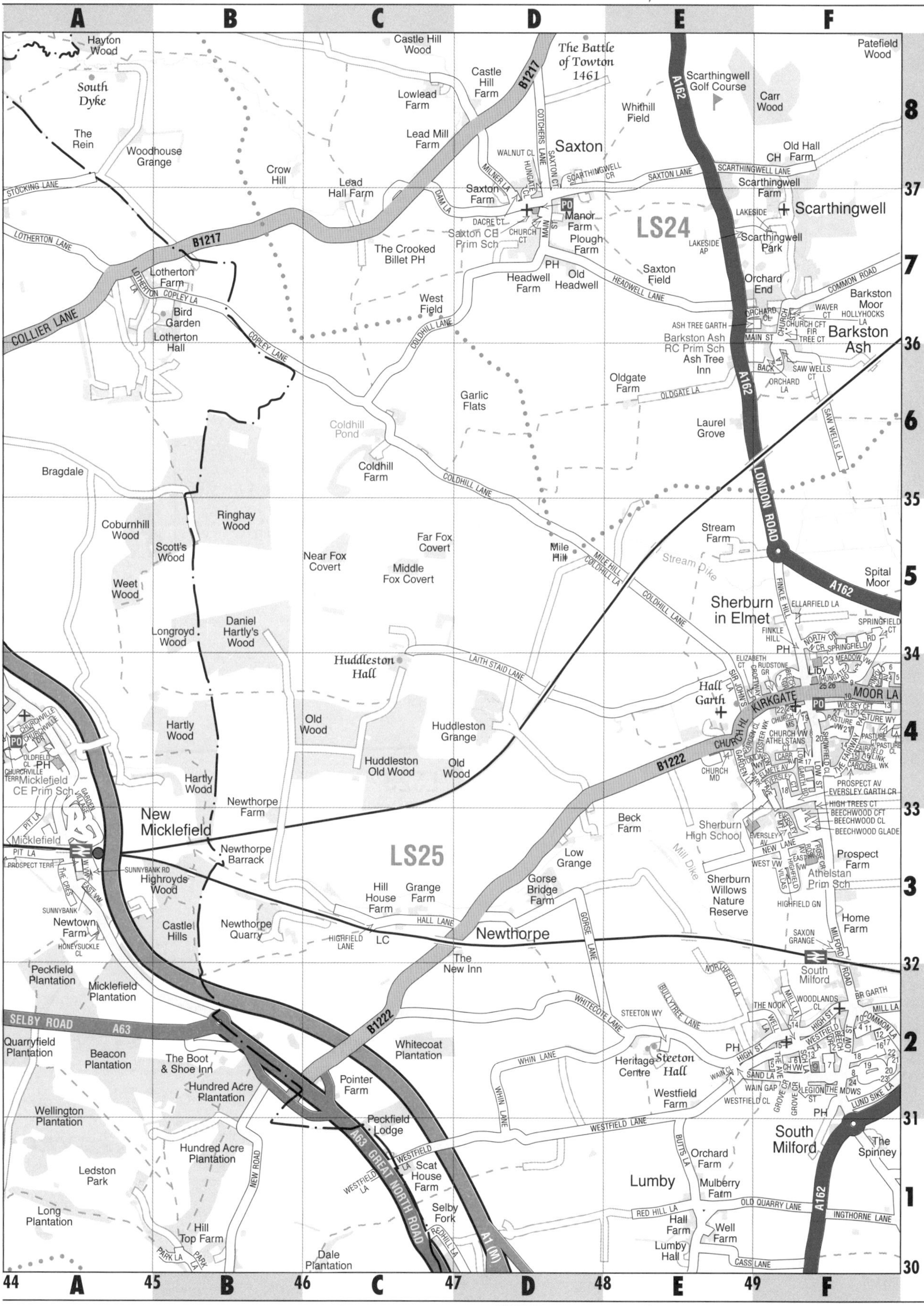

F2
1 WESTFIELD CT
2 MAPLE CL
3 BEECH CL
4 CAWDEL CL
5 THE HAVEN
6 ORCHARD CL
7 STEINCROFT RD
8 SOUTHLANDS CL
9 South Milford Prim Sch
10 MULBERRY CT
11 CAWDEL WY
12 BURLEY CL
13 THE LIMES
14 WOODLANDS LA
15 INGLENOOK CL
16 BARLEY WLK
17 THE HAYWAIN
18 HARVESTER WY
19 MILFORD WAY
20 SWAN ROAD
21 SOUTHLANDS CT
22 THATCH CL
23 NURSERY CL
24 FIELD VIEW

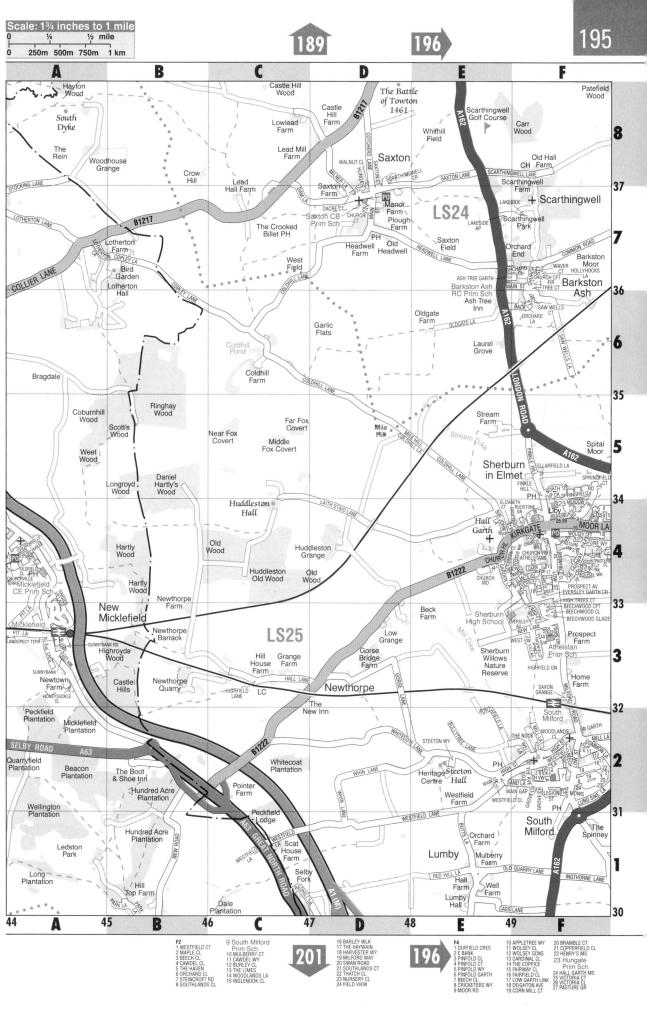

F4
1 DUFFIELD CRES
2 E BANK
3 PINFOLD CL
4 PINFOLD CT
5 PINFOLD WY
6 PINFOLD GARTH
7 BEECH CL
8 CRICKETERS WY
9 MOOR RD
10 APPLETREE WY
11 WOLSEY CL
12 WOLSEY GDNS
13 CARDINAL CL
14 THE COPPICE
15 FAIRWAY CL
16 FAIRFIELD CL
17 LOW GARTH LINK
18 DEIGHTON AVE
19 CORN MILL CT
20 BRAMBLE CT
21 COPPERFIELD CL
22 HENRY'S MS
23 Hungate Prim Sch
24 HALL GARTH MS
25 VICTORIA CT
26 VICTORIA CL
27 PASTURE GR

195 190

Scale: 1¾ inches to 1 mile
0 ¼ ½ mile
0 250m 500m 750m 1 km

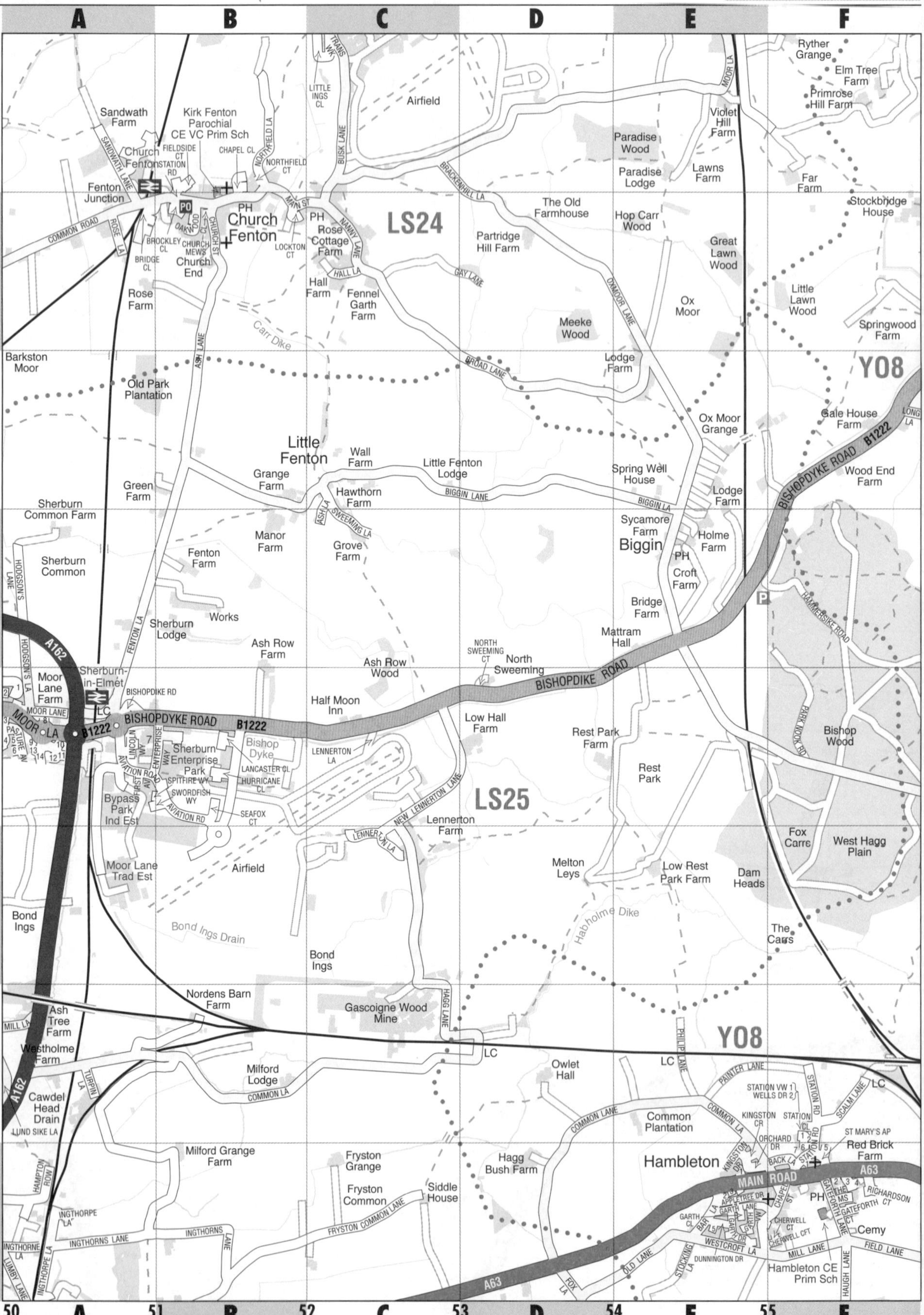

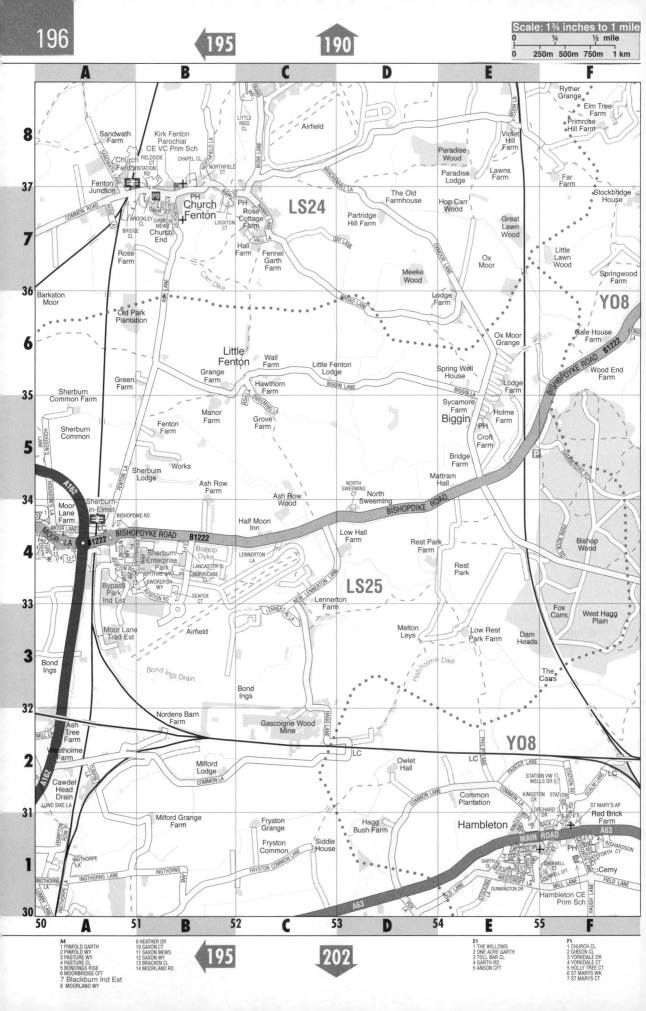

A4
1 PINFOLD GARTH
2 PINFOLD WY
3 PASTURE WY
4 PASTURE CL
5 BONDINGS RISE
6 MOORBRIDGE CFT
7 Blackburn Ind Est
8 MOORLAND WY
9 HEATHER DR
10 SAXON CT
11 SAXON MEWS
12 SAXON WY
13 BRACKEN CL
14 MOORLAND RD

E1
1 THE WILLOWS
2 ONE ACRE GARTH
3 TOLL BAR CL
4 GARTH RD
5 ANSON CFT

F1
1 CHURCH CL
2 GIBSON CL
3 YORKDALE DR
4 YORKDALE CT
5 HOLLY TREE CT
6 ST MARYS WK
7 ST MARYS CT

195 202

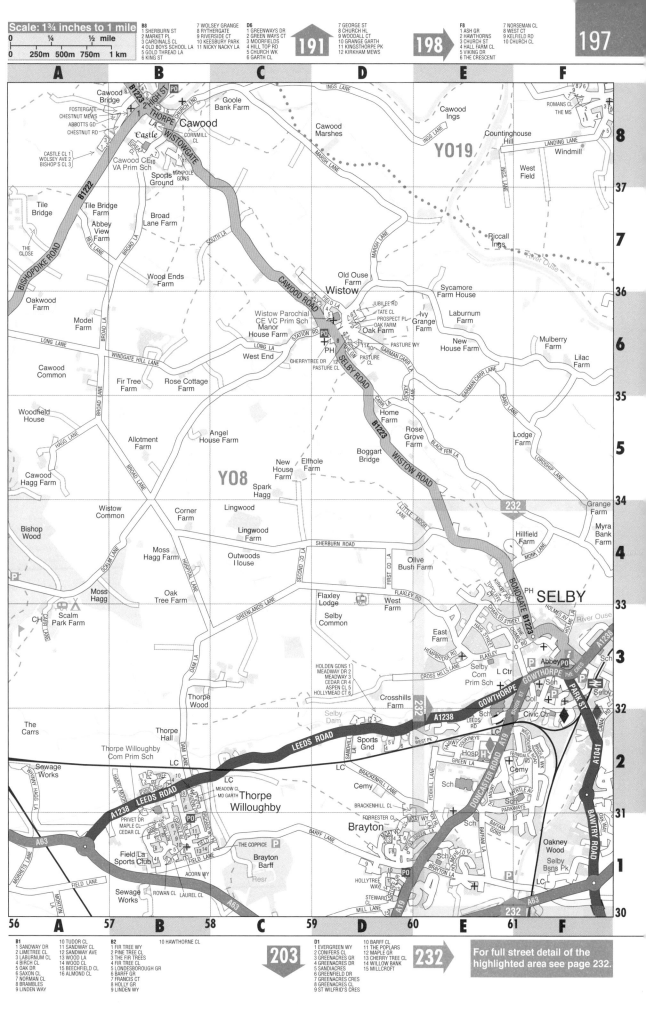

Scale: 1¾ inches to 1 mile
0 ¼ ½ mile
0 250m 500m 750m 1 km

B8
1 SHERBURN ST
2 MARKET PL
3 CARDINALS CL
4 OLD BOYS SCHOOL LA
5 GOLD THREAD LA
6 KING ST
7 WOLSEY GRANGE
8 RYTHERGATE
9 RIVERSIDE CT
10 KEESBURY PARK
11 NICKY NACKY LA

D6
1 GREENWAYS DR
2 GREEN WAYS CT
3 MOORFIELDS
4 HILL TOP RD
5 CHURCH WK
6 GARTH CL
7 GEORGE ST
8 CHURCH HL
9 WOODALL CT
10 GRANGE GARTH
11 KINGSTHORPE PK
12 KIRKHAM MEWS

191

198

F8
1 ASH GR
2 HAWTHORNS
3 CHURCH ST
4 HALL FARM CL
5 VIKING DR
6 THE CRESCENT
7 NORSEMAN CL
8 WEST CT
9 KELFIELD RD
10 CHURCH CL

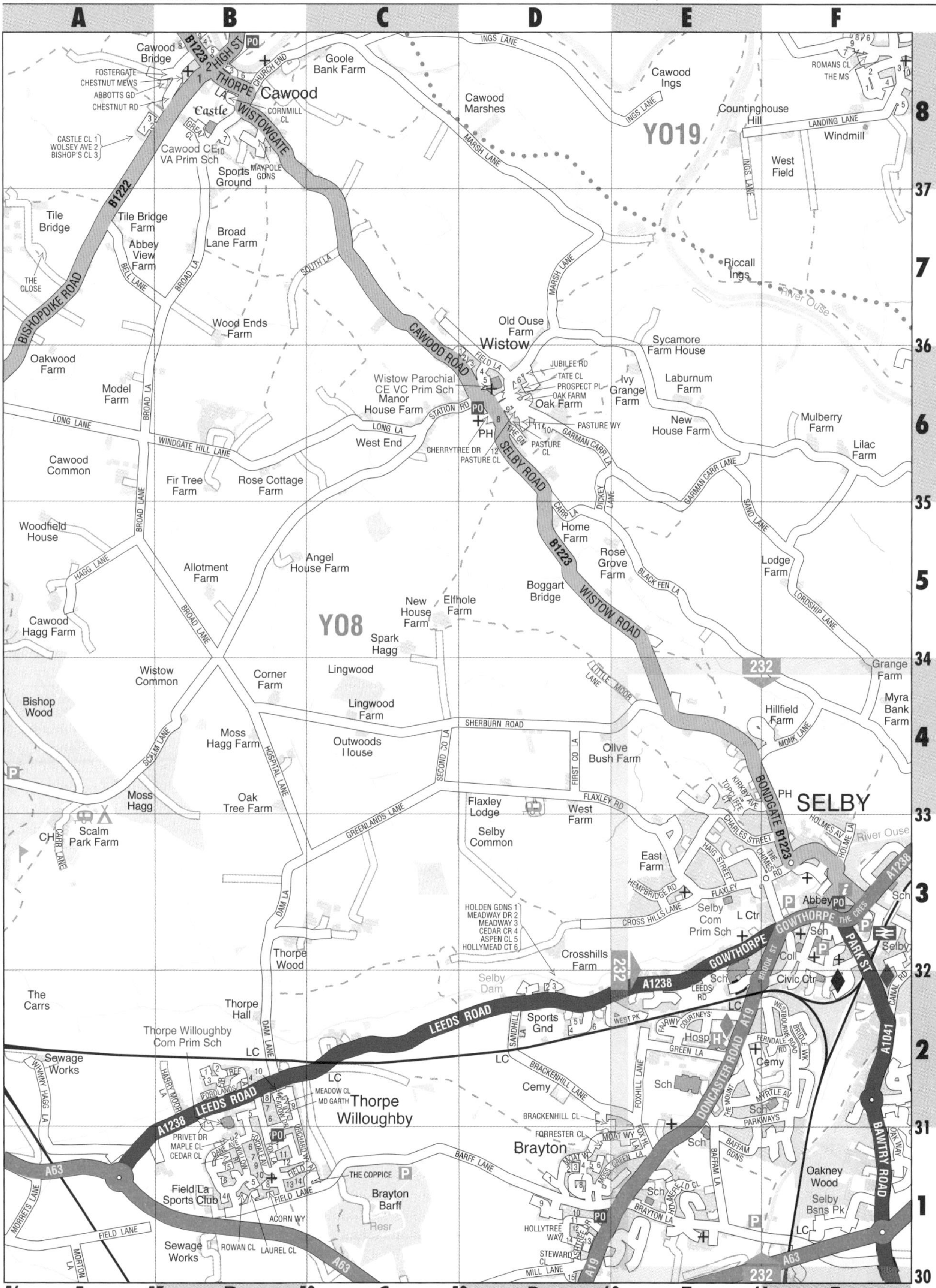

B1
1 SANDWAY DR
2 LIMETREE CL
3 LABURNUM CL
4 BIRCH CL
5 OAK DR
6 SAXON CL
7 NORMAN CL
8 BRAMBLES
9 LINDEN WAY
10 TUDOR CL
11 SANDWAY CL
12 SANDWAY AVE
13 WOOD LA
14 WOOD CL
15 BEECHFIELD CL
16 ALMOND CL

B2
1 FIR TREE WY
2 PINE TREE CL
3 THE FIR TREES
4 FIR TREE CL
5 LONDESBOROUGH GR
6 BARFF GR
7 FRANCIS CT
8 HOLLY GR
9 LINDEN WY
10 HAWTHORNE CL

203

D1
1 EVERGREEN WY
2 CONIFERS CL
3 GREENACRES GR
4 GREENACRES DR
5 SANDIACRES
6 GREENFIELD DR
7 GREENACRES CRES
8 GREENACRES CL
9 ST WILFRID'S CRES
10 BARFF CL
11 THE POPLARS
12 MAPLE GR
13 CHERRY TREE CL
14 WILLOW BANK
15 MILLCROFT

232

For full street detail of the highlighted area see page 232.

A8
1 MANOR GARTH
2 BACK LA
3 SILVER ST
4 NOVA SCOTIA WY
5 DANES CT
6 KING RUDDING CL
7 BECKWITH HALL DR
8 STATION RISE

197
192

Scale: 1¾ inches to 1 mile
0 ¼ ½ mile
0 250m 500m 750m 1 km

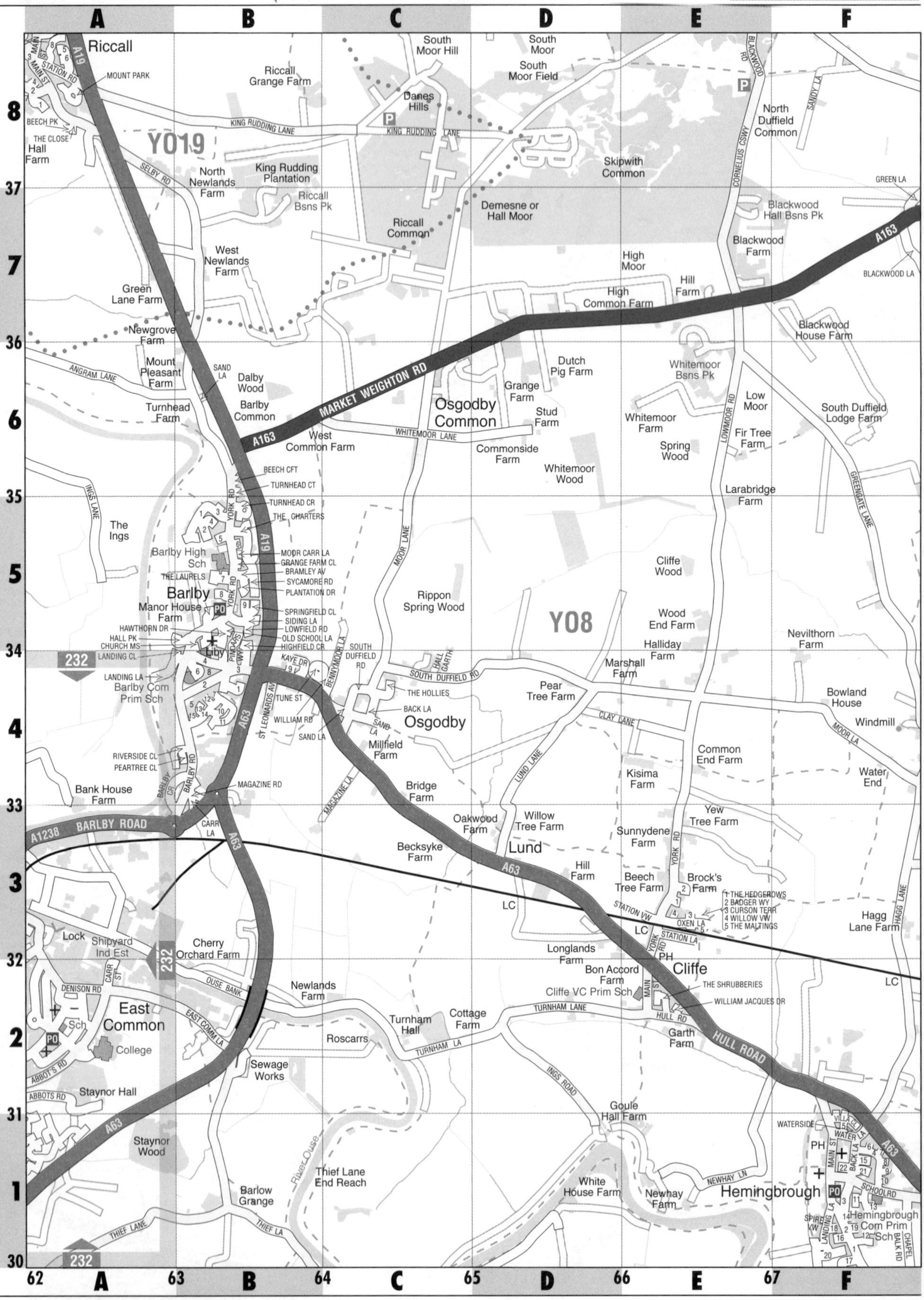

For full street detail of the highlighted area see page 232.
232
204

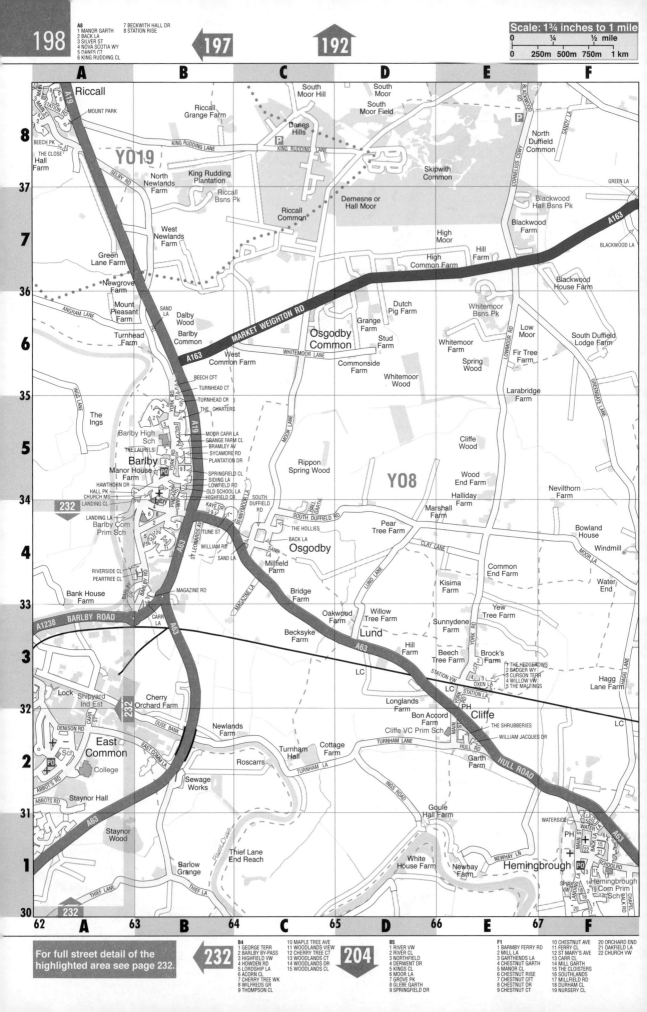

B4
1 GEORGE TERR
2 BARLBY BY-PASS
3 HIGHFIELD VW
4 HOWDEN RD
5 LORDSHIP LA
6 ACORN CL
7 CHERRY TREE WK
8 WILFREDS GR
9 THOMPSON CL
10 MAPLE TREE AVE
11 WOODLANDS VIEW
12 CHERRY TREE CT
13 WOODLANDS CT
14 WOODLANDS DR
15 WOODLANDS CL

B5
1 RIVER VW
2 RIVER CL
3 NORTHFIELD
4 DERWENT DR
5 KINGS CL
6 MOOR LA
7 GROVE PK
8 GLEBE GARTH
9 SPRINGFIELD DR

F1
1 BARMBY FERRY RD
2 MILL LA
3 GARTHENDS LA
4 CHESTNUT GARTH
5 MANOR CL
6 CHESTNUT RISE
7 CHESTNUT CFT
8 CHESTNUT DR
9 CHESTNUT CT
10 CHESTNUT AVE
11 FERRY CL
12 ST MARY'S AVE
13 CARR CL
14 MILL GARTH
15 THE CLOISTERS
16 SOUTHLANDS
17 MILLFIELD RD
18 DURHAM CL
19 NURSERY CL
20 ORCHARD END
21 OAKFIELD LA
22 CHURCH VW

Scale: 1¾ inches to 1 mile

0 ¼ ½ mile

0 250m 500m 750m 1 km

A7
1 WILLOW DR
2 OAK RD
3 WESTFIELD RD
4 GARTH AVE
5 MANOR DR
6 MANOR CL
7 CHESTNUT CL
8 LIME CL
9 ASH CL

D7
1 MEADOWFIELD
2 VICARAGE CL
3 STAITHE ST
4 CHURCH CL
5 HONEY POT
6 MANOR CT

193

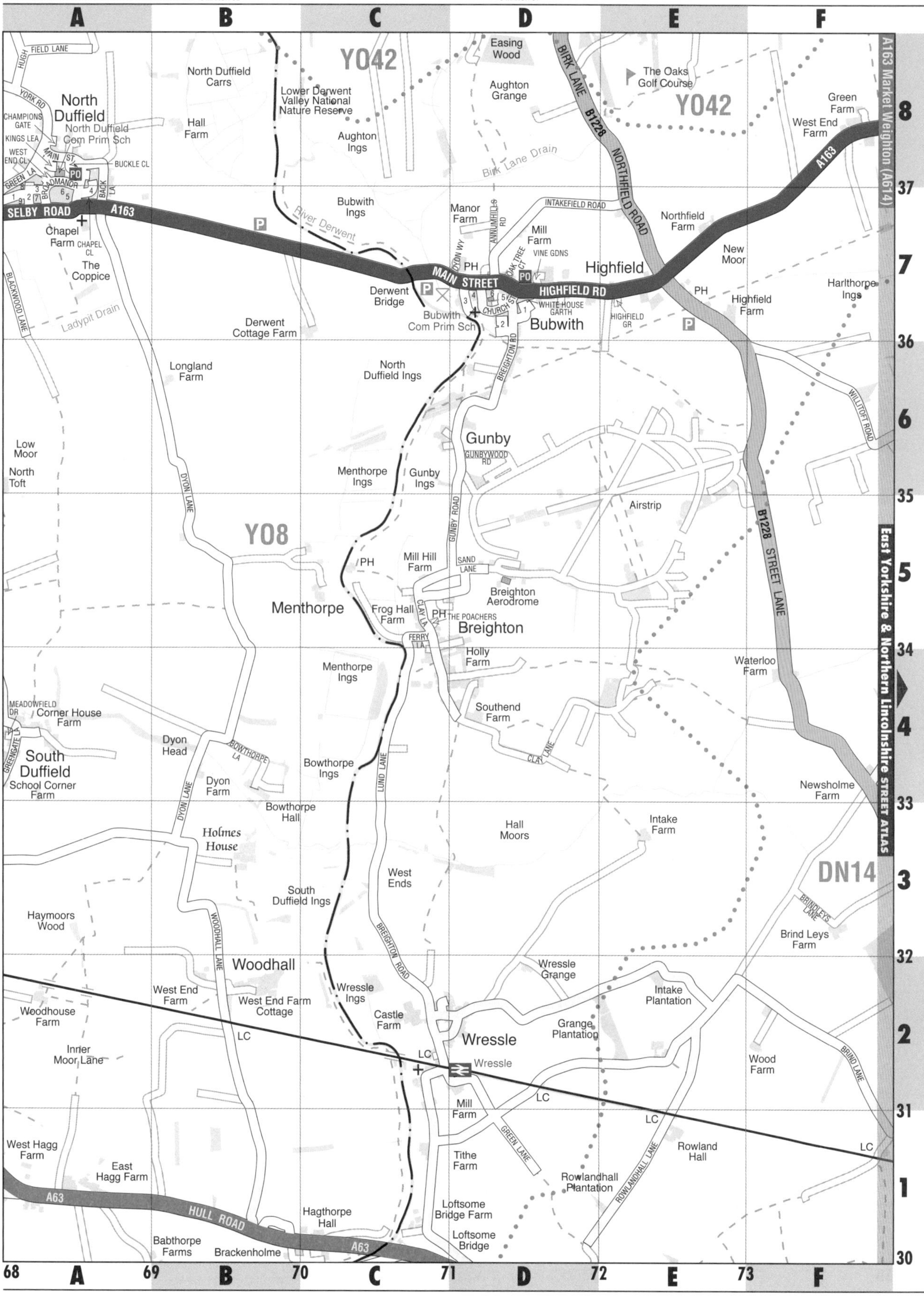

A B C D E F
North Duffield
North Duffield Carrs
Hall Farm
Lower Derwent Valley National Nature Reserve
YO42
Easing Wood
Aughton Grange
Aughton Ings
The Oaks Golf Course
Green Farm
West End Farm
BIRK LANE
B1228
NORTHFIELD ROAD
A163
Birk Lane Drain
Bubwith Ings
Manor Farm
Mill Farm
INTAKEFIELD ROAD
Northfield Farm
New Moor
SELBY ROAD
Chapel Farm
The Coppice
River Derwent
MAIN STREET
HIGHFIELD RD
Highfield
Harlthorpe Ings
Highfield Farm
Derwent Bridge
Bubwith Com Prim Sch
Bubwith
Derwent Cottage Farm
Ladypit Drain
BLACKWOOD LANE
Longland Farm
North Duffield Ings
BREIGHTON RD
WILLITOFT ROAD
Gunby
GUNBYWOOD RD
Low Moor
North Toft
Menthorpe Ings
Gunby Ings
GUNBY ROAD
Airstrip
YO8
DYON LANE
Mill Hill Farm
SAND LANE
Breighton Aerodrome
Menthorpe
Frog Hall Farm
THE POACHERS
Breighton
FERRY LA
Holly Farm
Menthorpe Ings
Waterloo Farm
STREET LANE
Corner House Farm
South Duffield
School Corner Farm
Dyon Head
BOWTHORPE LA
Dyon Farm
Bowthorpe Ings
Southend Farm
CLAY LANE
Newsholme Farm
Bowthorpe Hall
Holmes House
Hall Moors
Intake Farm
LUND LANE
West Ends
DN14
Haymoors Wood
South Duffield Ings
WOODHALL LANE
BRINDLEYS LANE
Brind Leys Farm
Woodhall
Wressle Grange
Woodhouse Farm
West End Farm
West End Farm Cottage
Wressle Ings
Castle Farm
Intake Plantation
Wressle
Grange Plantation
Inner Moor Lane
Wood Farm
BRIND LANE
Mill Farm
GREEN LANE
West Hagg Farm
East Hagg Farm
Tithe Farm
ROWLANDHALL LANE
Rowland Hall
Rowlandhall Plantation
A63
HULL ROAD
Hagthorpe Hall
Loftsome Bridge Farm
Loftsome Bridge
Babthorpe Farms
Brackenholme
A163 Market Weighton (A614)
East Yorkshire & Northern Lincolnshire STREET ATLAS
68 69 70 71 72 73
30 31 32 33 34 35 36 37

205

A2
1 STUART GR
2 LANGDALE DR
3 LANGDALE AVE
4 LANGDALE MEWS
5 ESKDALE CL
6 BRANSDALE CL
7 ARMSTRONG CL
8 CLAYTON MEWS
9 CLAYTON PL
10 BRANSDALE MEWS
11 BRANSDALE AVE
12 ESKDALE CT
13 STABLERS WK
14 BROOME CL
15 SALISBURY CL
16 FREESTON CT
17 PIPPIN'S APP
18 FREESTON DR
19 TRURO DR
20 FALMOUTH CRES
21 POLPERRO CL
22 REDRUTH DR
23 TRURO WK

E4
1 VICKERS ST
2 MARSHALL MS
3 CAMBRIDGE ST
4 Castleford Half Acres Prim Sch

194

F4
1 Castleford Acad
2 Castleford Wheldon Inf Sch
3 St Joseph's Catholic Prim Sch

Scale: 1¾ inches to 1 mile
0 ¼ ½ mile
0 250m 500m 750m 1 km

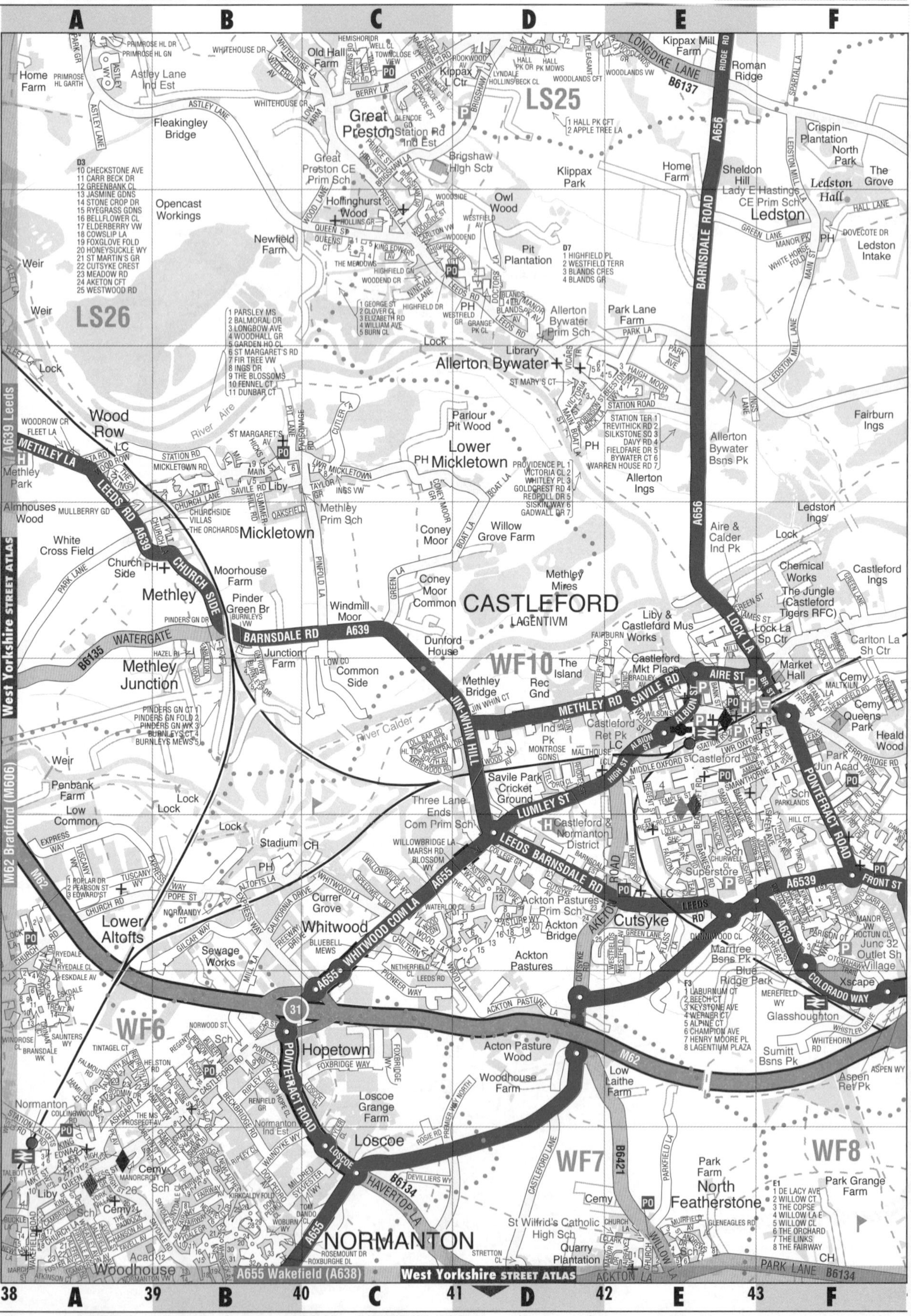
A B C D E F
LS25
LS26
WF10
WF6
WF7
WF8
Great Preston
Kippax
Ledston
Allerton Bywater
Lower Mickletown
Mickletown
Methley
Methley Junction
CASTLEFORD
LAGENTIVM
Whitwood
Lower Altofts
Hopetown
Loscoe
NORMANTON
North Featherstone
Cutsyke
Glasshoughton
Woodhouse
BARNSDALE ROAD
PONTEFRACT ROAD
M62
A639 Leeds
M62 Bradford (M606)
A655 Wakefield (A638)
West Yorkshire STREET ATLAS

38 39 40 41 42 43

A1
1 WEBSTER PL
2 SOVEREIGN GDNS
3 STANLEY CTS
4 WATSON ST
5 RAILWAY TERR
6 MARKET PL
7 ASSEMBLY ST
8 EXCHANGE ST
9 CROSS QUEEN ST
10 WAKEFIELD RD
11 CHURCH LA
12 CHEAPSIDE
13 GARDEN ST
14 SMIRTHWAITE VW
15 ST MICHAELS GN
16 MILL HL
17 CHURCH FIELDS
18 CHURCH CT
19 CARLTON CL
20 GRANVILLE ST
21 KESTREL MEWS
22 KINGFISHER CT
23 AMBLER CT
24 HANSON CT
25 THE MOUNT
26 Normanton All Saints CE Inf Sch

B1
1 CARLTON GDNS
2 BECKBRIDGE LA
3 NEWFIELD CT
4 FAIRWAY GDNS
5 BROOKFIELD CT
6 NEWFIELD AVE
7 NEWFIELD CL
8 FAIRWAY CL
9 FAIRWAY MDWS
10 SNYDALE CT
11 PRINCESS CT
12 CLARKSON CT
13 THORNE CL
14 LYNDALE GR
15 QUEENSBURY CT
16 KINGSTON DR
17 WINDSOR CL
18 ADDISON AVE
19 M BROOK CH
20 CARNOUSTIE GDNS
21 OAKMONT CL
22 MORRIS FIELDS
23 OAKLAND HILLS
24 KINGSTON DR
25 SWALE APP
26 LAKESIDE CT
27 SUNNINGDALES
28 GLENEAGLES CT
29 GLENEAGLES DR
30 BELFRY WY
31 GOSSIDE GR
32 LINDRICK CL
33 WESTERN GALES WY

B2
1 MACKINNON AVE
2 CROSSMAN DR
3 MOORHOUSE CL
4 CROFT AVE
5 HAREWOOD AVE
6 OXFORD ST
7 NELSON ST
8 BRIDGE ST
9 CORONATION ST

D3
1 ORCHARD GR
2 CARR BECK RD
3 DUNNIWOOD DR
4 DUNNIWOOD CL
5 CARR BECK VW
6 THE BRAMBLINGS
7 BIRCHEN CL
8 WILLOWBRIDGE CL
9 CHERRY TREE CL

For full street detail of Castleford see Philip's STREET ATLAS of West Yorkshire

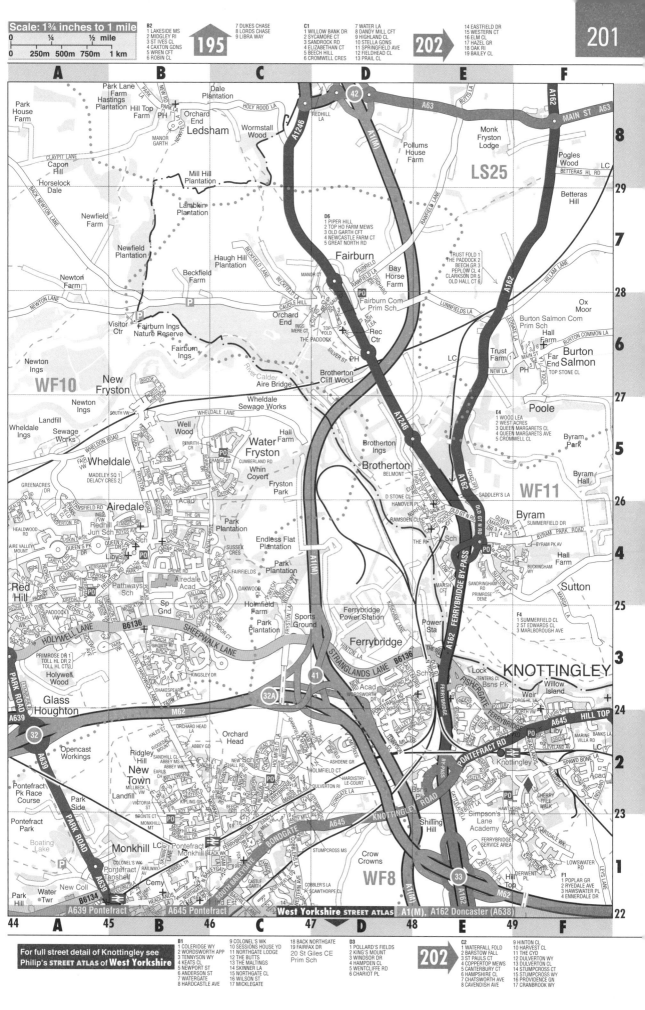

Scale: 1¾ inches to 1 mile
0 ¼ ½ mile
0 250m 500m 750m 1 km

195
202

B2
1 LAKESIDE MS
2 MIDGLEY RI
3 ST IVES CL
4 CAXTON GDNS
5 WREN CFT
6 ROBIN CL
7 DUKES CHASE
8 LORDS CHASE
9 LIBRA WAY

C1
1 WILLOW BANK DR
2 SYCAMORE CT
3 SANDROCK RD
4 ELIZABETHAN CT
5 BEECH HILL
6 CROMWELL CRES
7 WATER LA
8 DANDY MILL CFT
9 HIGHLAND CL
10 STELLA GDNS
11 SPRINGFIELD AVE
12 FIELDHEAD CL
13 PRAIL CL
14 EASTFIELD DR
15 WESTERN CT
16 ELM CL
17 HAZEL GR
18 OAK RI
19 BAILEY CL

A B C D E F

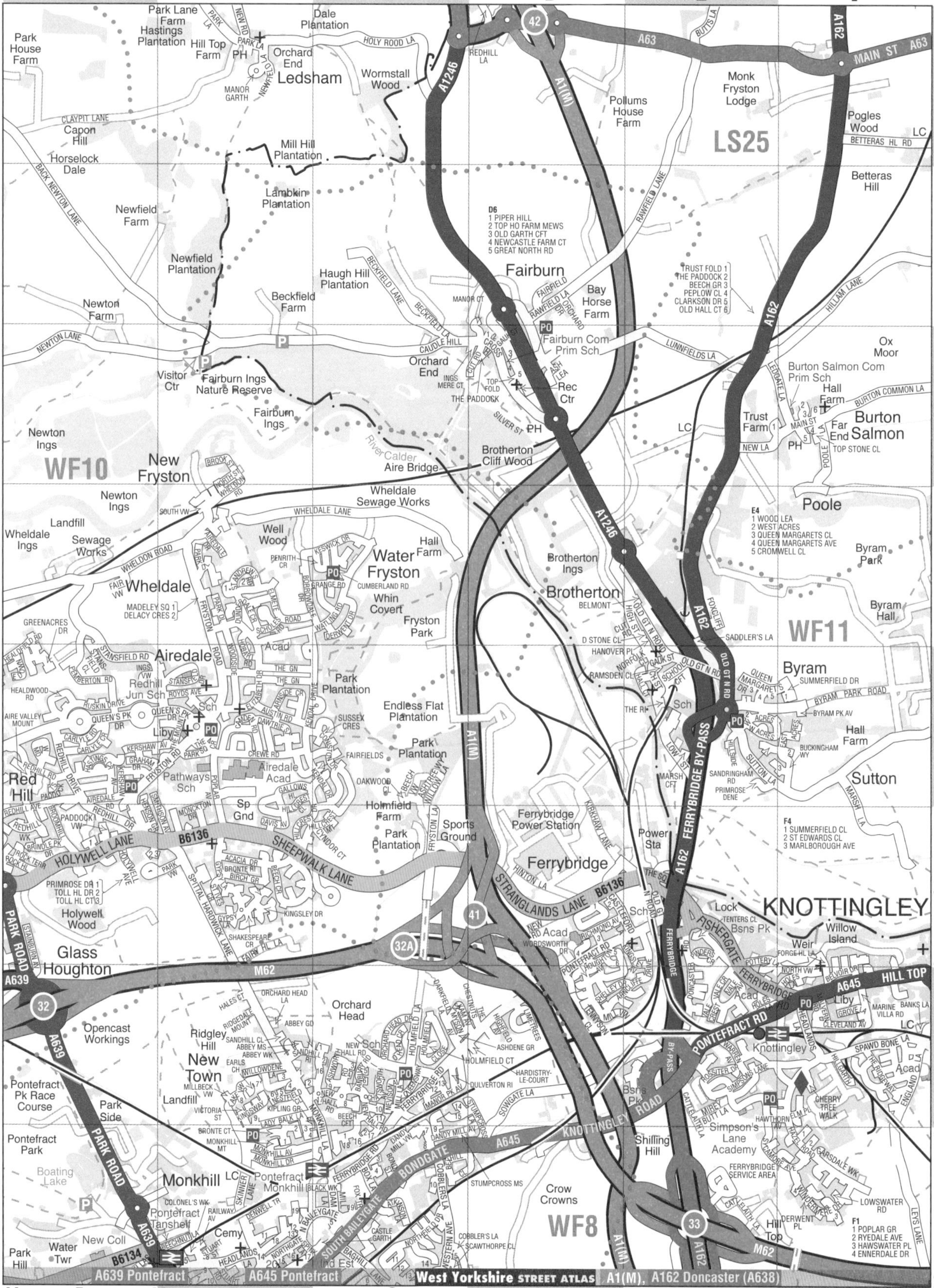

8 29 7 28 6 27 5 26 4 25 3 24 2 23 1 22

44 45 46 47 48 49
A B C D E F

For full street detail of Knottingley see Philip's STREET ATLAS of West Yorkshire

B1
1 COLERIDGE WY
2 WORDSWORTH APP
3 TENNYSON WY
4 KEATS CL
5 NEWPORT ST
6 ANDERSON ST
7 WATERGATE
8 HARDCASTLE AVE
9 COLONEL'S WK
10 SESSIONS HOUSE YD
11 NORTHGATE LODGE
12 THE BUTTS
13 THE MALTINGS
14 SKINNER LA
15 NORTHGATE CL
16 WILSON ST
17 MICKLEGATE
18 BACK NORTHGATE
19 FAIRFAX DR
20 St Giles CE Prim Sch

D3
1 POLLARD'S FIELDS
2 KING'S MOUNT
3 WINDSOR DR
4 HAMPDEN CL
5 WENTCLIFFE RD
6 CHARIOT PL

202

C2
1 WATERFALL FOLD
2 BARSTOW FALL
3 ST PAULS CT
4 COPPERTOP MEWS
5 CANTERBURY CT
6 HAMPSHIRE CL
7 CHATSWORTH AVE
8 CAVENDISH AVE
9 HINTON CL
10 HARVEST CL
11 THE CYD
12 DULVERTON WY
13 DULVERTON CL
14 STUMPCROSS CT
15 STUMPCROSS WY
16 PROVIDENCE GN
17 CRANBROOK WY

A8
1 DEER PK CT
2 PRIORY PARK GR
3 PRIORY PARK CL
4 CHURCH LA
5 OLD VICARAGE LA
6 ORCHARD CL
7 THE MEADOWS
8 HILLCREST
9 HILLSIDE CL
10 CHESTNUT GREEN
11 PREBENDAL CL
12 ABBEYSTONE WY

201

A7
1 PINE TREE LA
2 ROSE LEA CL
3 HILLAM HALL VW
4 HILLAM HALL LA
5 HILLAM HALL CL
6 BEDFORDS FOLD

196

Scale: 1¾ inches to 1 mile
0 ¼ ½ mile
0 250m 500m 750m 1 km

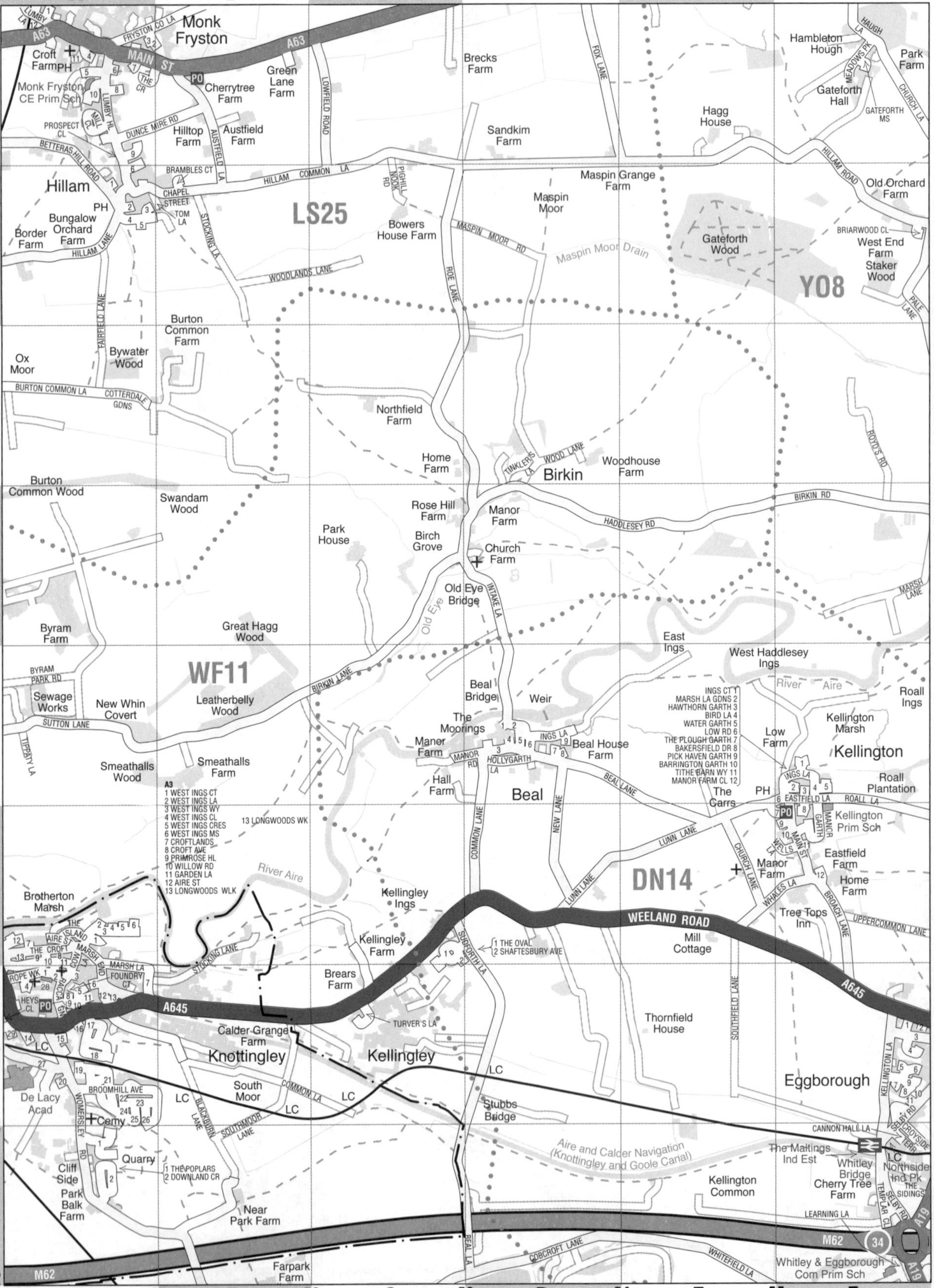

28 Knottingley St Botolphs CE Acad
29 MORLEY AVE

A2
1 PRIMROSE VALE
2 TITHE BARN RD
3 SUNNY BANK
4 ST BOLTOPHS CL
5 FOUNDRY LA
6 FERNLEY GREEN CL
7 TRUNDLES LA
8 GRENLEY ST
9 LAMB INN RD
10 EAST VW
11 RACCA AVE
12 HARKER ST
13 LOW GN
14 MIDDLE LA
15 GILLANN ST
16 WEELAND CT
17 SPRINGFIELDS AVE
18 SPRINGFIELDS
19 BROOMHILL GR
20 QUARRY AVE
21 BROOMHILL WK
22 BROOMHILL PL
23 BROOMHILL CL
24 BROOMHILL SQ
25 BROOMHILL CR
26 BROOMHILL DR
27 SPAWD BONE LA

201

206

D4
1 GARTH MILL
2 MARSH LA
3 MAIN ST
4 RIVERDALE
5 CRAVEN GARTH
6 BROAD LA
7 VILLAGE FARM CT
8 GABLES CL
9 VILLAGE FARM CL

F2
1 WESTFIELD RD
2 WESTFIELD CL
3 WESTFIELD AVE
4 WESTFIELD GR
5 TABARD HAMLET
6 TABARD RD
7 THE TABARDS
8 THE HAMLET
9 KELLINGTON CT
10 MILLERS DR
11 CARLTON CL

197 232 204

Scale: 1¾ inches to 1 mile
0 ¼ ½ mile
0 250m 500m 750m 1 km

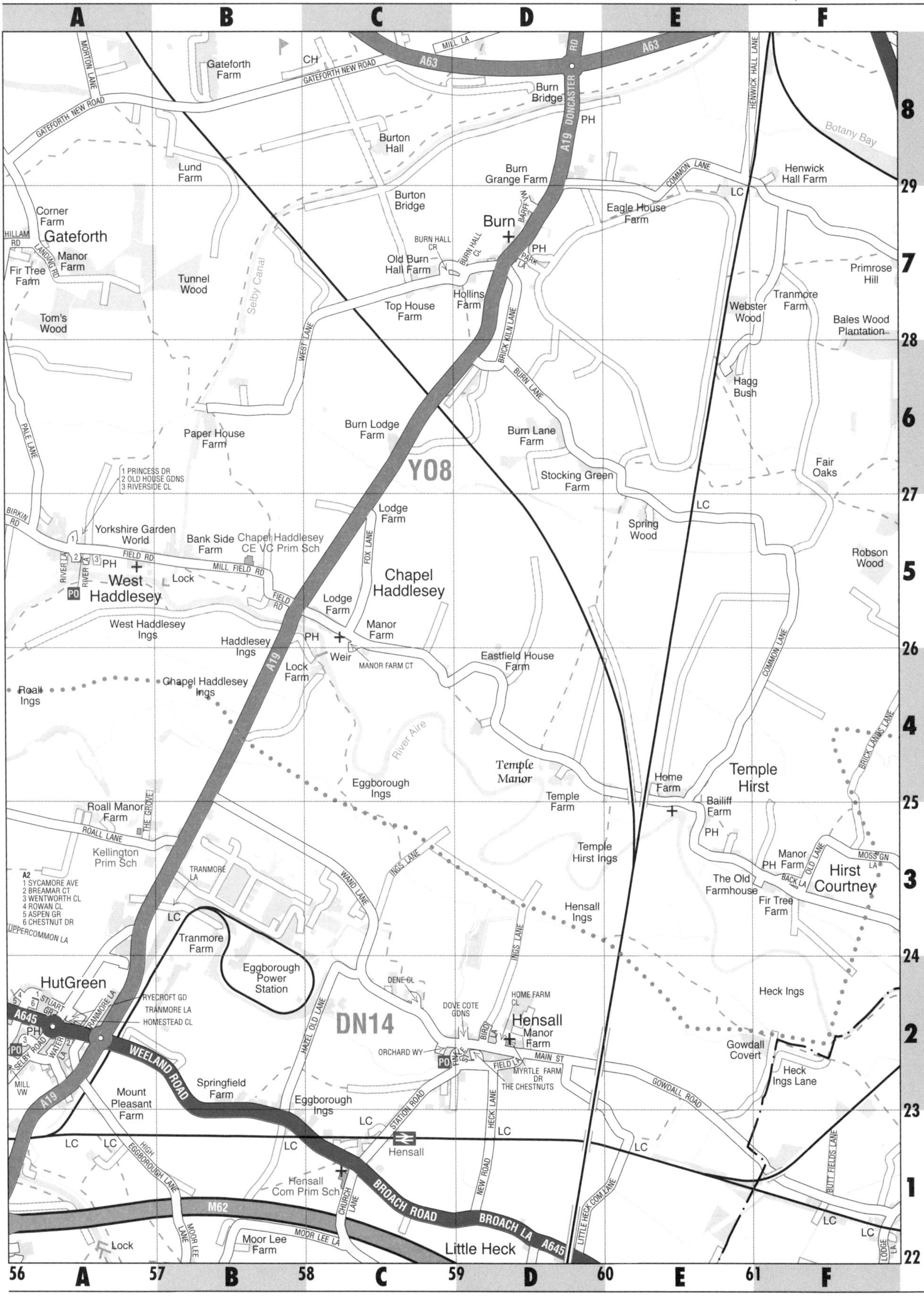

207 204

A B C D E F

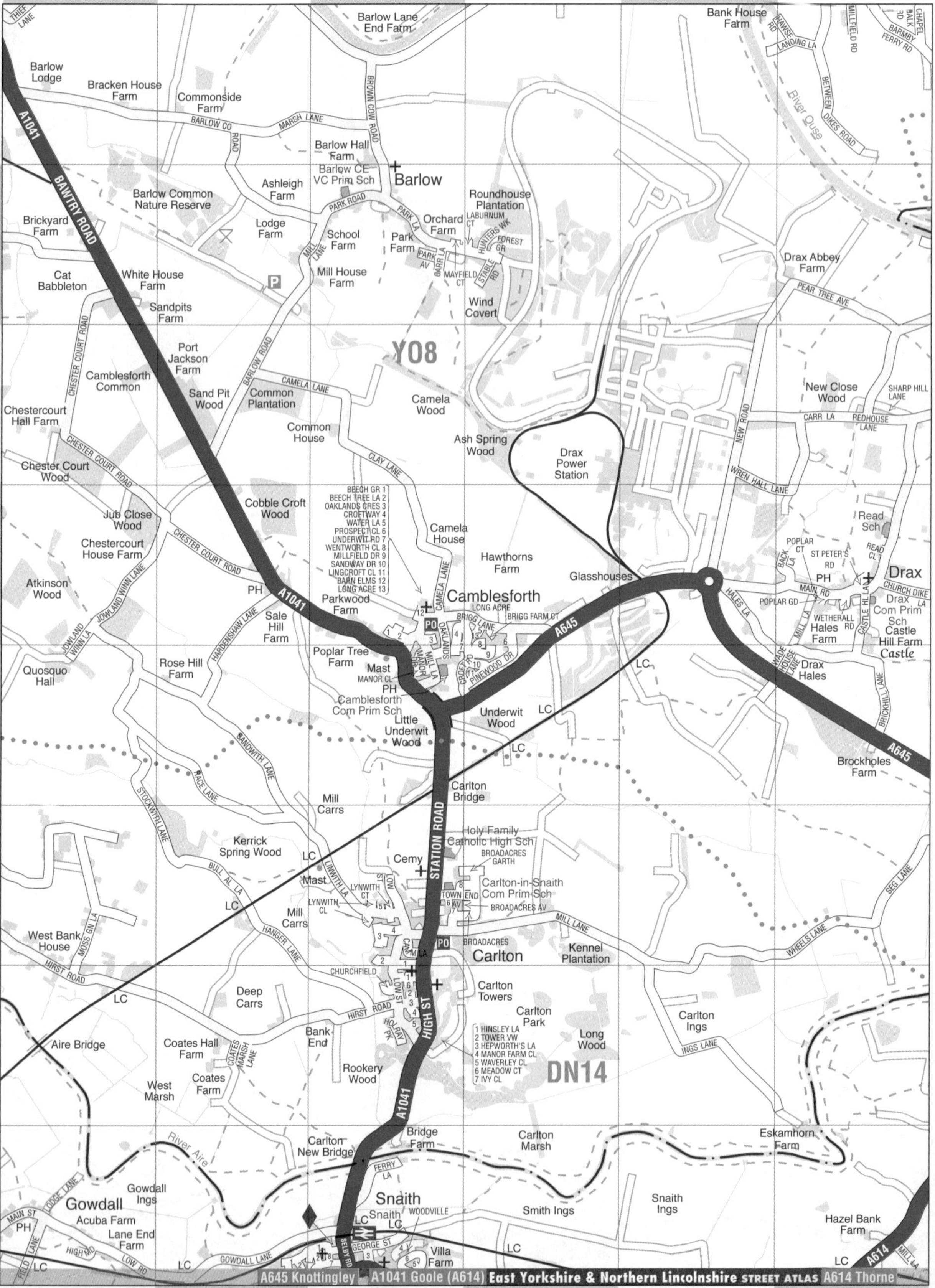
Barlow Lane End Farm
Bank House Farm
Barlow Lodge
Bracken House Farm
Commonside Farm
BARLOW CO ROAD
MARSH LANE
BROWN COW ROAD
A1041
BAWTRY ROAD
Barlow Hall Farm
Barlow CE VC Prim Sch
Barlow
Ashleigh Farm
Barlow Common Nature Reserve
Roundhouse Plantation
Brickyard Farm
Lodge Farm
PARK ROAD
PARK LA
School Farm
Park Farm
Orchard Farm
LABURNUM CT
HUNTERS WK
FOREST GR
STABLE RD
MAYFIELD CT
Mill House Farm
MILL LANE
Cat Babbleton
White House Farm
Sandpits Farm
Wind Covert
Drax Abbey Farm
PEAR TREE AVE
River Ouse
BETWEEN DIKES ROAD
MILLFIELD RD
BARMBY FERRY RD
LANDING LA
YO8
Port Jackson Farm
CHESTER COURT ROAD
Camblesforth Common
Sand Pit Wood
Common Plantation
CAMELA LANE
BARLOW ROAD
Camela Wood
Chestercourt Hall Farm
Common House
Ash Spring Wood
Drax Power Station
New Close Wood
SHARP HILL LANE
CARR LA
REDHOUSE LANE
NEW ROAD
WREN HALL LANE
Chester Court Wood
CLAY LANE
Cobble Croft Wood
Jub Close Wood
Camela House
Read Sch
READ CL
POPLAR CT
ST PETER'S RD
Chestercourt House Farm
Hawthorns Farm
Glasshouses
Drax
CHURCH DIKE LA
Atkinson Wood
PH
Parkwood Farm
Camblesforth
LONG ACRE
BRIGG FARM CT
BRIGG LANE
OAKLANDS
PINEWOOD DR
CROFT RD
Drax Com Prim Sch
WETHERALL RD
Hales Farm
Castle Hill Farm
Castle
JOWLAND WINN LANE
HARDENSHAW LANE
Sale Hill Farm
Poplar Tree Farm
Mast
MANOR CL
A645
Quosquo Hall
Rose Hill Farm
Camblesforth Com Prim Sch
Underwit Wood
Little Underwit Wood
LC
Drax Hales
BRICKHILL LANE
Brockholes Farm
SANDWITH LANE
RACE LANE
STOCKWITH LANE
Mill Carrs
Carlton Bridge
STATION ROAD
Kerrick Spring Wood
Holy Family Catholic High Sch
BROADACRES GARTH
Cemy
Carlton-in-Snaith Com Prim Sch
TOWN END AV
BROADACRES AV
LYNWITH CT
LYNWITH CL
LINWITH LA
BULL AL LA
West Bank House
MOSS GN LA
HANGER LANE
MILL LANE
SEG LANE
WHEELS LANE
Kennel Plantation
BROADACRES
Carlton
CHURCHFIELD
HIRST ROAD
Carlton Towers
Deep Carrs
Carlton Park
Carlton Ings
INGS LANE
Bank End
HIGH ST
1 HINSLEY LA
2 TOWER VW
3 HEPWORTH'S LA
4 MANOR FARM CL
5 WAVERLEY CL
6 MEADOW CT
7 IVY CL
Long Wood
Aire Bridge
Coates Hall Farm
COATES MARSH LANE
Rookery Wood
DN14
West Marsh
Coates Farm
Bridge Farm
Carlton Marsh
Eskamhorn Farm
River Aire
Carlton New Bridge
FERRY LA
Gowdall Ings
Snaith
Snaith Ings
Gowdall
Smith Ings
Acuba Farm
Lane End Farm
Hazel Bank Farm
MAIN ST
LODGE LANE
HIGH RD
LOW RD
GOWDALL LANE
FIELD LANE
GEORGE ST
SELBY RD
WOODVILLE
Villa Farm
A614
A645 Knottingley
A1041 Goole (A614)
East Yorkshire & Northern Lincolnshire STREET ATLAS
A614 Thorne

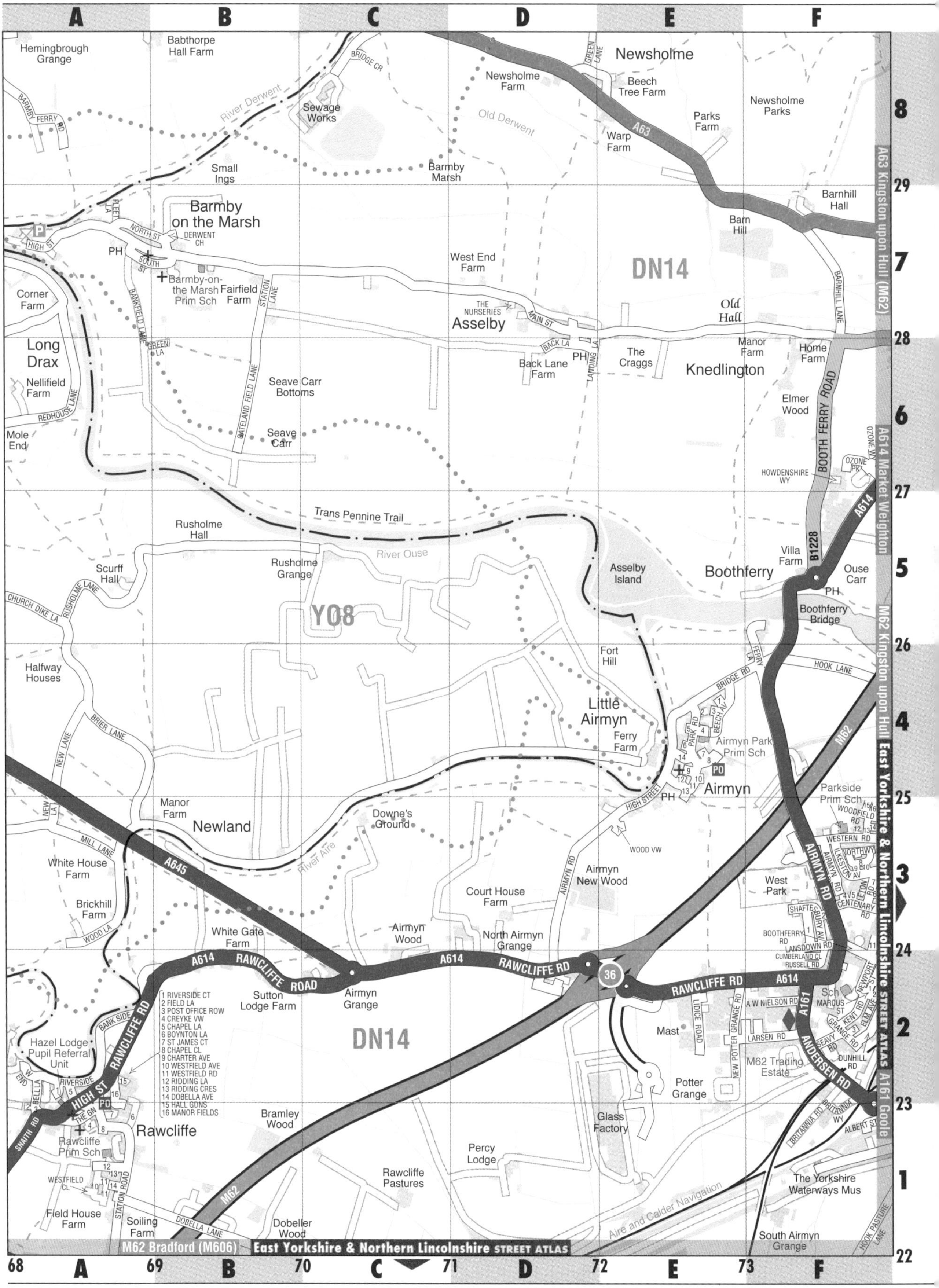
A B C D E F
8 29 7 28 6 27 5 26 4 25 3 24 2 23 1 22
68 69 70 71 72 73
Hemingbrough Grange
Babthorpe Hall Farm
Newsholme
Newsholme Farm
Beech Tree Farm
Newsholme Parks
Parks Farm
Warp Farm
Sewage Works
River Derwent
Old Derwent
A63
Small Ings
Barmby Marsh
Barnhill Hall
Barn Hill
Barmby on the Marsh
DERWENT CH
PH
Barmby-on-the Marsh Prim Sch
Fairfield Farm
West End Farm
DN14
Corner Farm
THE NURSERIES
Asselby
Old Hall
Long Drax
Nellifield Farm
Back Lane Farm
The Craggs
Manor Farm
Home Farm
Knedlington
Seave Carr Bottoms
Elmer Wood
BOOTH FERRY ROAD
Mole End
Seave Carr
HOWDENSHIRE WY
OZONE PK
Trans Pennine Trail
Rusholme Hall
River Ouse
Rusholme Grange
Asselby Island
Villa Farm
Boothferry
Ouse Carr
B1228
A614
Scurff Hall
YO8
Boothferry Bridge
Halfway Houses
Fort Hill
HOOK LANE
Little Airmyn
Ferry Farm
Airmyn Park Prim Sch
Airmyn
PO
Manor Farm
Newland
Downe's Ground
Parkside Prim Sch
M62
A645
River Aire
White House Farm
Brickhill Farm
WOOD VW
Airmyn New Wood
West Park
Court House Farm
AIRMYN RD
White Gate Farm
Airmyn Wood
North Airmyn Grange
A614 RAWCLIFFE ROAD
A614 RAWCLIFFE RD
36
RAWCLIFFE RD
Airmyn Grange
Sutton Lodge Farm
Mast
1 RIVERSIDE CT
2 FIELD LA
3 POST OFFICE ROW
4 CREYKE VW
5 CHAPEL LA
6 BOYNTON LA
7 ST JAMES CT
8 CHAPEL CL
9 CHARTER AVE
10 WESTFIELD AVE
11 WESTFIELD RD
12 RIDDING LA
13 RIDDING CRES
14 DOBELLA AVE
15 HALL GDNS
16 MANOR FIELDS
Hazel Lodge Pupil Referral Unit
HIGH ST
Rawcliffe
Rawcliffe Prim Sch
Bramley Wood
Glass Factory
Potter Grange
M62 Trading Estate
ANDERSEN RD
A161
Percy Lodge
Rawcliffe Pastures
The Yorkshire Waterways Mus
Field House Farm
Soiling Farm
Dobeller Wood
Aire and Calder Navigation
South Airmyn Grange
M62 Bradford (M606)
East Yorkshire & Northern Lincolnshire STREET ATLAS
A63 Kingston upon Hull (M62)
A614 Market Weighton
M62 Kingston upon Hull
A161 Goole

E4
1 BEECH GR
2 CHESTNUT AVE
3 BEECH AVE
4 PERCY DR
5 HALL CL
6 PARK CL
7 COURTS CL
8 WOODLAND WY
9 ST DAVID'S VW
10 PARSONS CL
11 PARSON'S WK
12 CHURCH VW
13 THE CROSSINGS
14 THE PADDOCK

F2
1 MANUEL ST
2 HENRY ST
3 CHESTNUT AVE

F3
1 GROSVENOR AVE
2 PARK AVE
3 PARKLANDS
4 CAMBRIDGE AVE
5 AIRMYN AVE
6 DEVONSHIRE DR
7 WINDSOR DR
8 BELVEDERE CRES
9 CHATSWORTH DR
10 SANDRINGHAM DR
11 BARTHOLOMEW AVE
12 BEAUMONT CT
13 COBBLER HILL
14 CHARLES DR
15 HOOD GR
16 BIRT GROVE

202

Scale: 1¾ inches to 1 mile
0 ¼ ½ mile
0 250m 500m 750m 1 km

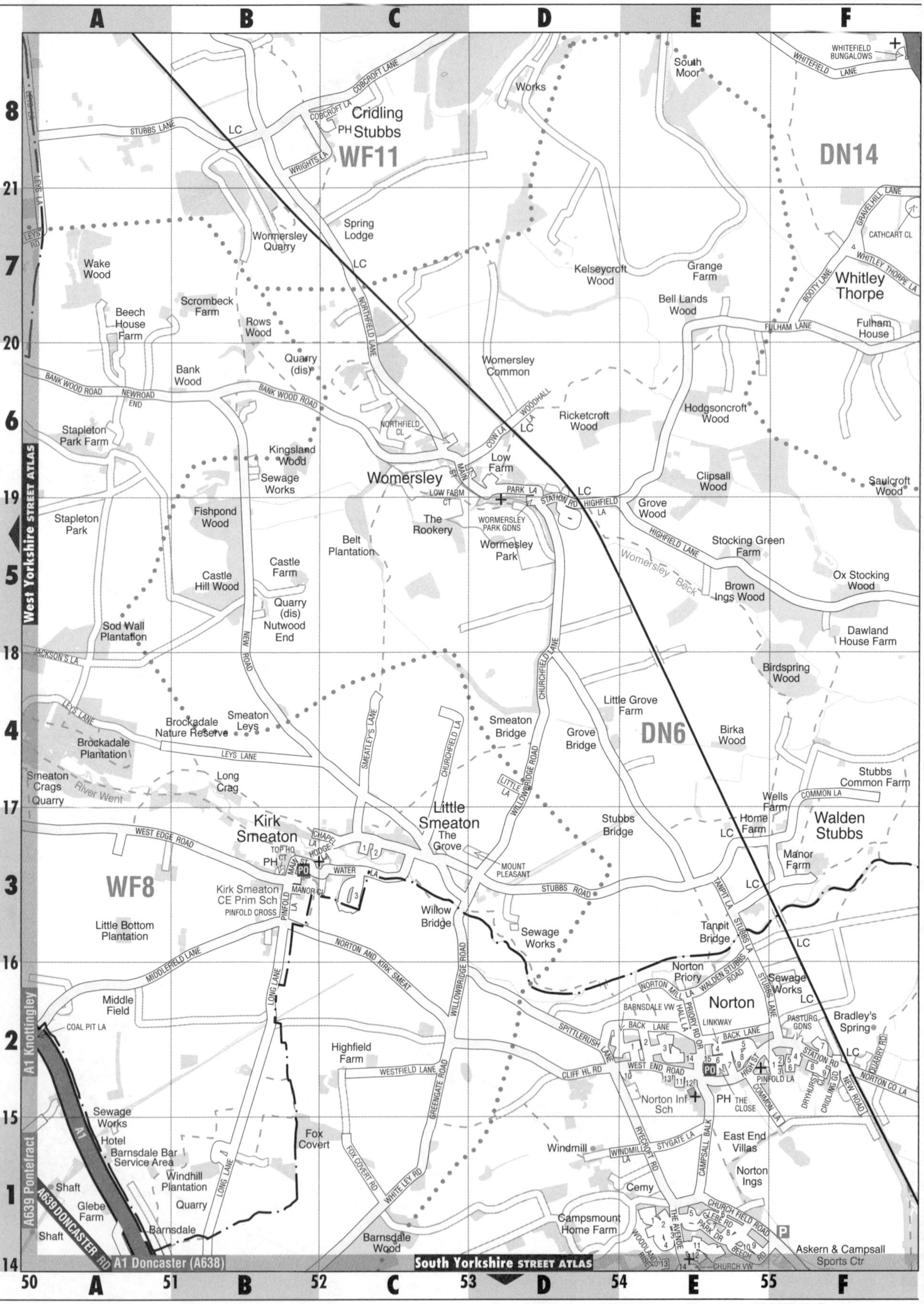

C3
1 WENTDALE
2 STAN VALLEY
3 SPRINGFIELD CRES

E1
1 TENNYSON AVE
2 SHAKESPEARE AVE
3 BYRON AVE
4 WORDSWORTH AVE
5 WELLINGTONIA DR
6 LANGLEYS RD
7 EAST VW
8 GRANGE RD
9 WILLOW RD
10 VAUGHAN RD
11 CAMPSALL PK RD
12 CAMPSALL HALL RD
13 SHERWOOD CL
14 HIGH ST

E2
1 BROC-O-BANK
2 NEWTHORPE RD
3 FORRESTER'S CL
4 TRAFFORD RD
5 ARUNDEL RD
6 ADELAIDE RD
7 HEADINGLEY RD
8 ORCHARD DR
9 ORCHARD CL
10 RYECROFT AVE
11 FIR TREE DR
12 MANOR CL
13 WINDMILL MD
14 KIPLIN DR
15 LANGOLD DR

F2
1 LYNDHURST DR
2 LYNDHURST CL
3 LYNDHURST RISE
4 ASHBURNHAM CL
5 ASHBURNHAM WK
6 DENVER RD
7 MANOR GARTH
8 SWAN SYKE DR
9 DRYHURST CL

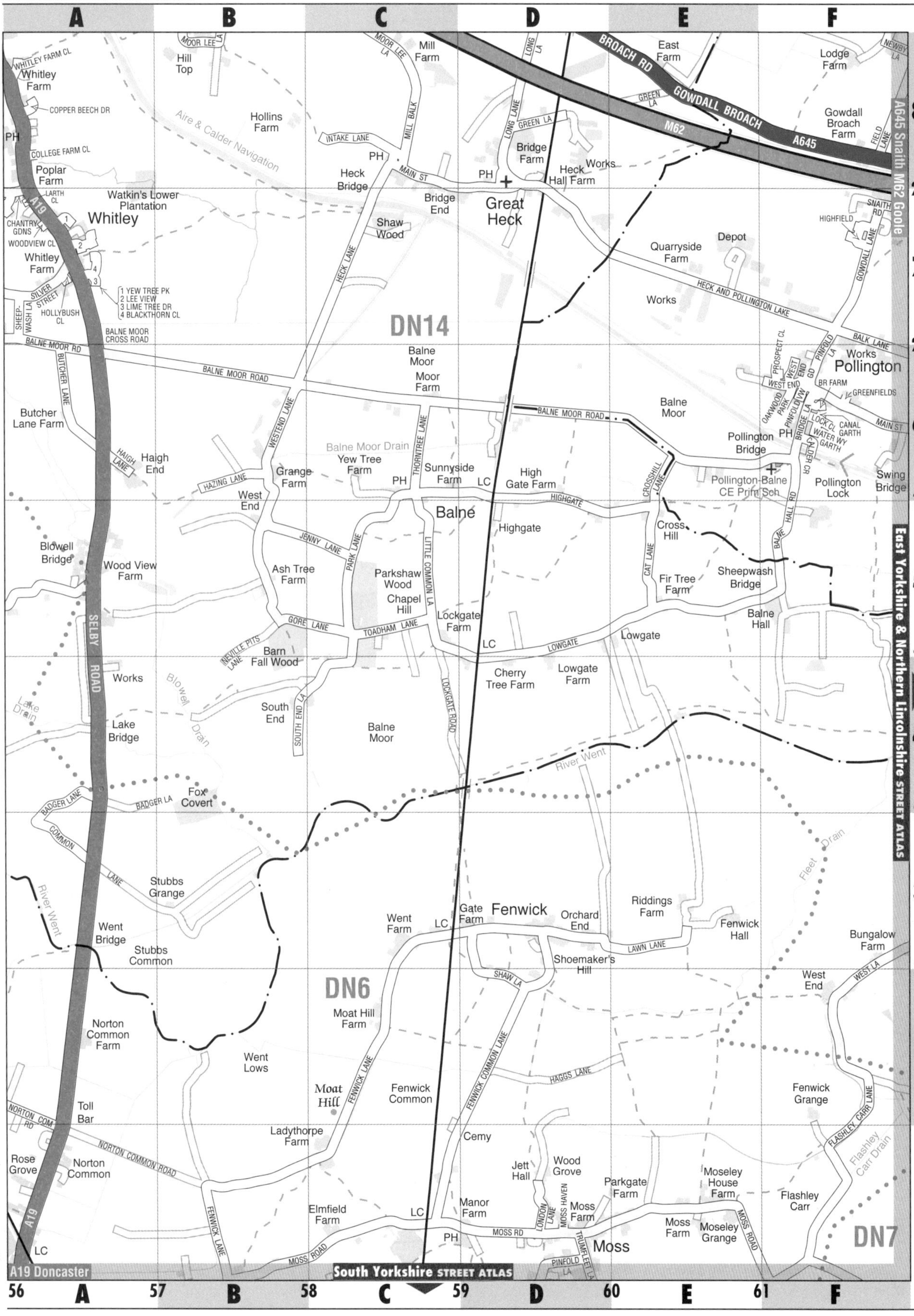

South Yorkshire STREET ATLAS
East Yorkshire & Northern Lincolnshire STREET ATLAS

B7
1 WHITE POINT AVE
2 CHARLTON AVE
3 MARLBOROUGH AVE
4 BLENHEIM AVE
5 WEST CLIFF AVE
6 NORTHWAY

C7
1 WESTLANDS AVE
2 FIELD HOUSE RD
3 NEWLANDS AV
4 ST HILDA'S GDNS
5 SOUTHLANDS AVE

13

C6
1 FOUNTAINS CL
2 HARROWING DR
3 ROSEDALE CL
4 LIME GR
5 PINEWOOD CL
6 KIRKHAM CL
7 AUCKLAND WY
8 SOUTHEND GDNS
9 ARUNDEL PL
10 CAYGILL ST

13

D6
1 ANGEL YD
2 WELLINGTON RD
3 VICTORIA PL
4 STATION SQ
5 PRINCESS PL
6 ENDEAVOUR WHARF
7 WINDSOR CRES
8 PANNETT WY
9 LYNDHURST CL
10 SPRING HL TERR
11 FALCON TERR
12 GEORGE ST
13 GRAY ST
14 ALBION PL
15 GROVE ST
16 ELGIN ST
17 MEADOWFIELDS CT
18 BROOMFIELD TERR
19 LANGBORNE RD
20 ROSE & CROWN YD
21 VICTORIA SQ
22 LANGBORNE RD
23 ALBION TERR
24 UNION RD
25 Whitby Archives & Heritage Ctr

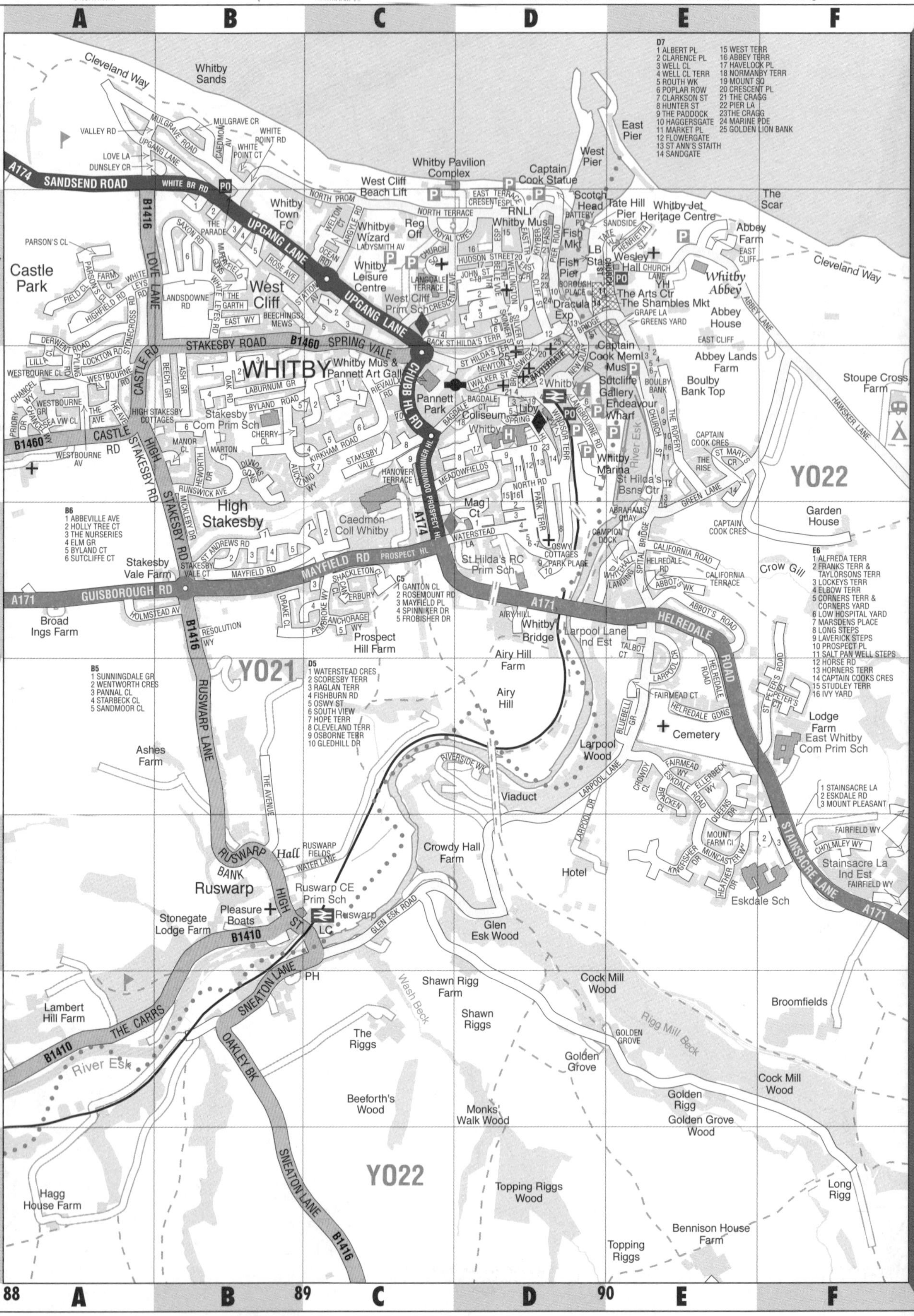

32
32
32

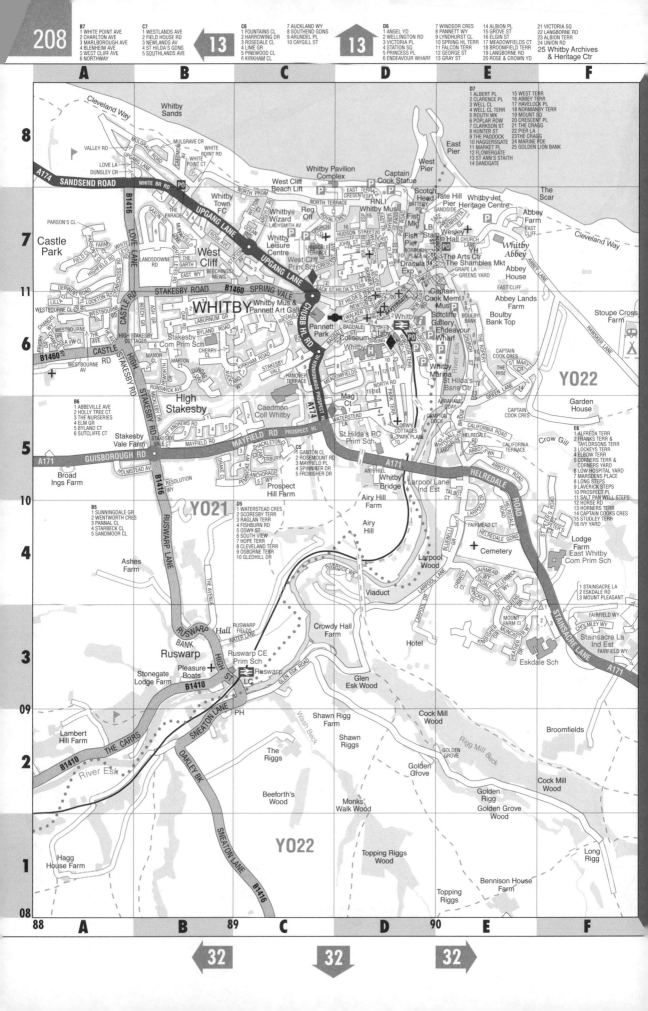

C6
1 ROSEMARY LA
2 WATERLOO ST
3 RYDER'S WYND
4 TOWER ST CASTLE WK
5 PARKINSON'S YD
6 THE BAR
7 CHANTRY WYND
8 FINKLE ST
9 TRINITY CHURCH SQ
10 TOWER ST
11 CASTLE WYND
12 WATERLOO
13 MARKET SQ
14 THORNHILL

40 20 40

E8
1 WHITEFIELDS GATE
2 WHITEFIELDS WK
3 WHITE CANONS WK
4 WHITE CANONS CT
5 WHITE FRIARS WK
6 WHITE FRIARS GDNS

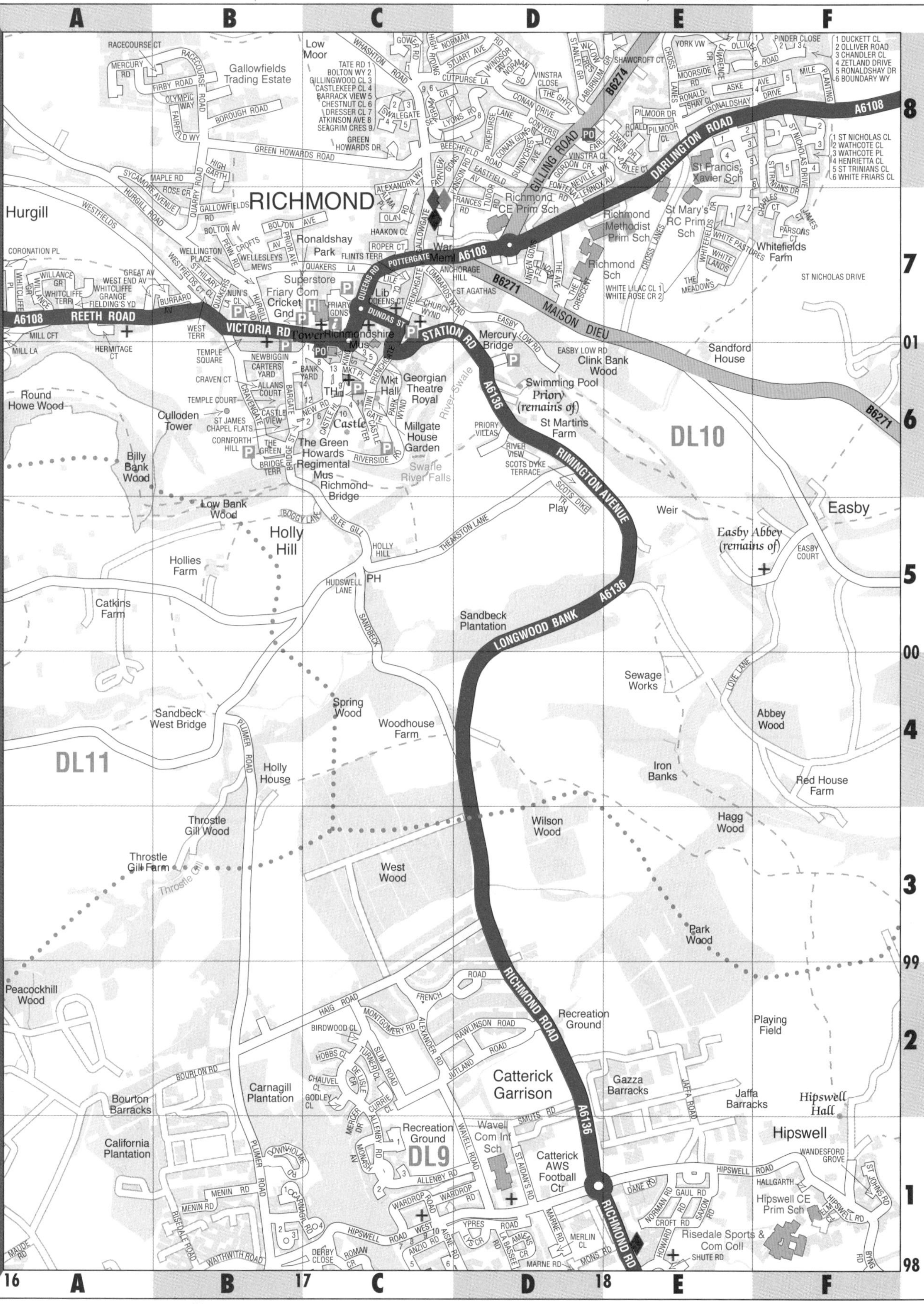

B1
1 MARNE CL
2 BADGERBECK RD
3 MONS CL

C1
1 MACDONELL CL
2 BURSTALL DR
3 GLASGOW DR
4 MEUSE CL
5 EL ALAMEIN RD
6 SALERNO CL
7 KENT CT
8 DEVON CT
9 DORSET CT
10 SUSSEX CT

40 40

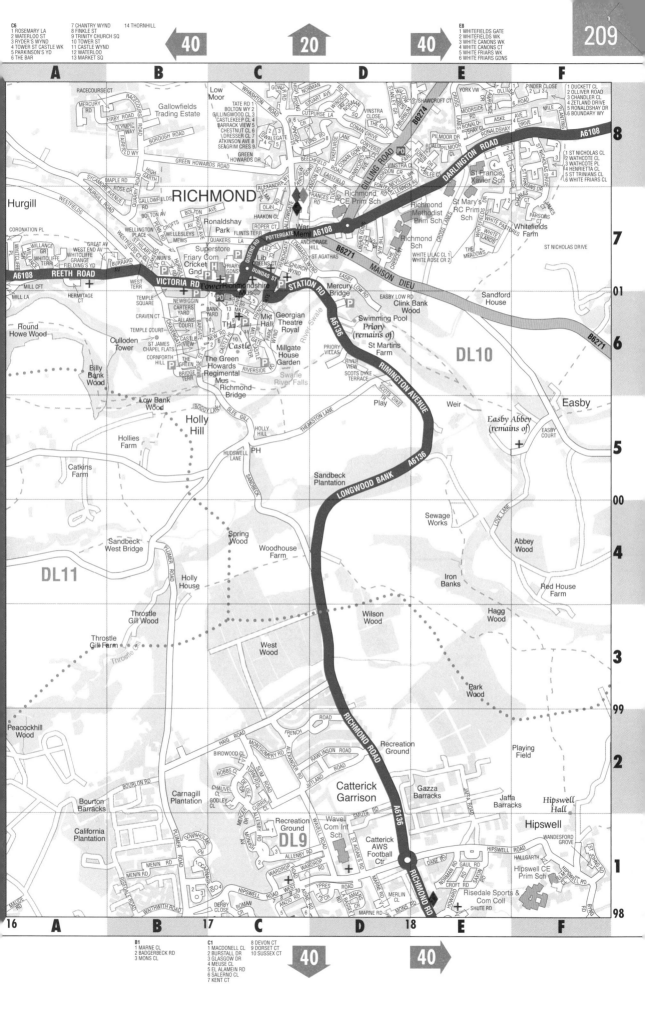

D4
1 SPRINGWELL TERR EAST
2 SPRINGWELL TERR WEST
3 SPRINGWELL GDNS

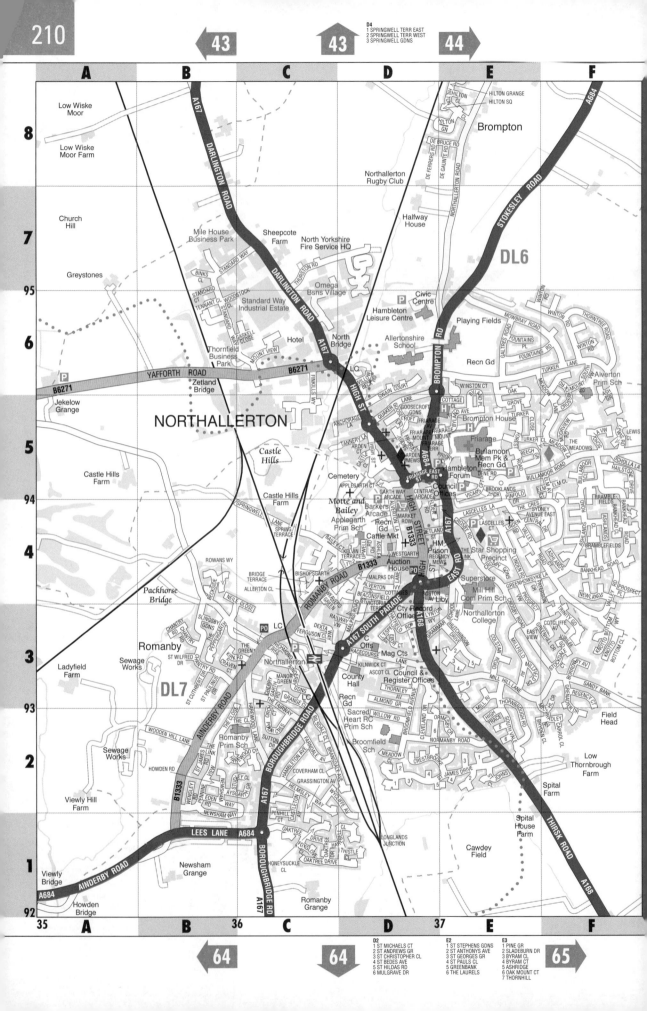

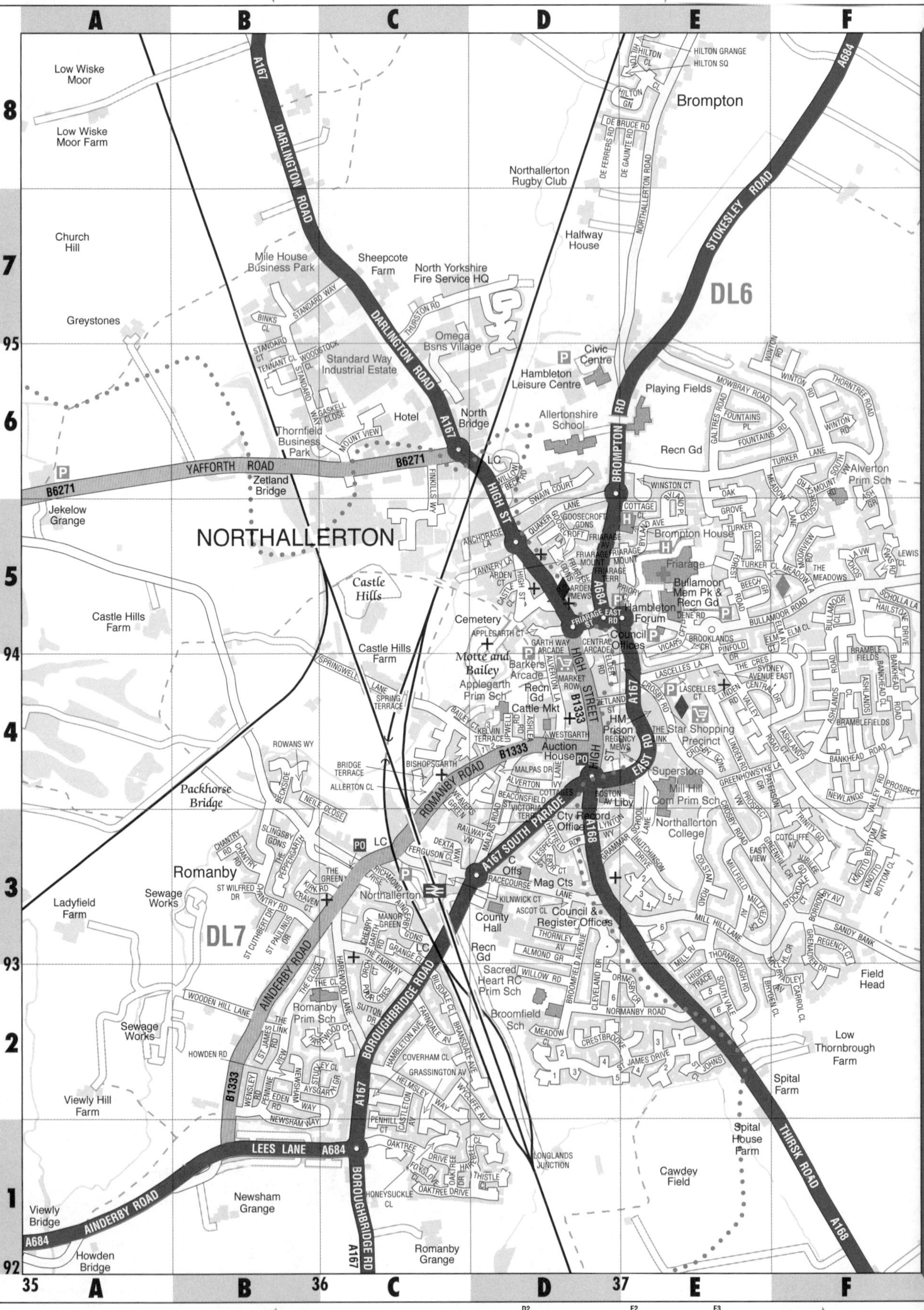

D2
1 ST MICHAELS CT
2 ST ANDREWS GR
3 ST CHRISTOPHER CL
4 ST BEDES AVE
5 ST HILDAS RD
6 MULGRAVE DR

E2
1 ST STEPHENS GDNS
2 ST ANTHONYS AVE
3 ST GEORGES GR
4 ST PAULS CL
5 GREENBANK
6 THE LAURELS

E3
1 PINE GR
2 SLADEBURN DR
3 BYRAM CL
4 BYRAM CT
5 ASHRIDGE
6 OAK MOUNT CT
7 THORNHILL

89 89 90 90

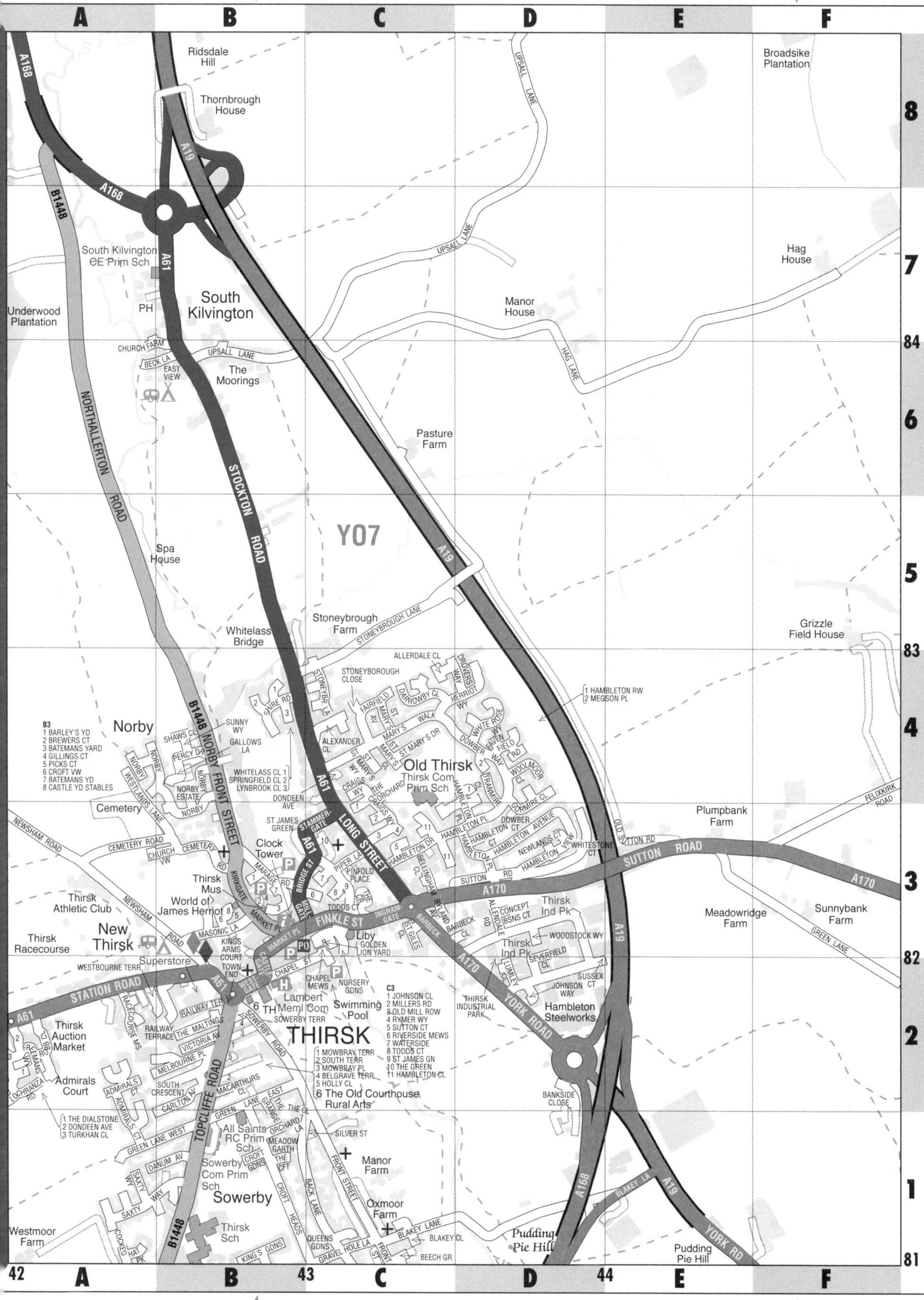

89 89 90 90

C8
1 ST MARK'S CL
2 ST JOSEPHS CL
3 GREYLANDS PK GR
4 GREYLANDS PK RD
5 HEATHCLIFF GDNS

75

D8
1 HAREWOOD AVE
2 NEWLANDS PK GR
3 WOODVILLE AVE
4 VERNON GR
5 HIGHDALE AVE

75

E5
1 FAIRFAX ST
2 BRITANNIA ST
3 IRETON ST
4 BRINKBURN RD
5 HARLEY ST
6 FALSGRAVE MEWS

F6
1 WREA LA
2 LOWER CLARK ST
3 LOWER WILLIAM ST
4 MELROSE ST
5 CLIFTON ST
6 VINE ST
7 FRANKLIN ST
8 MURCHISON PL
9 PROSPECT RD
10 ALBEMARLE BK RD
11 NORTHWAY
12 BROOK ST

F7
1 VICTORIA PARK
2 VICTORIA PARK AVE
3 LANGDALE RD
4 SANDRINGHAM ST
5 SYDNEY ST
6 DURHAM ST

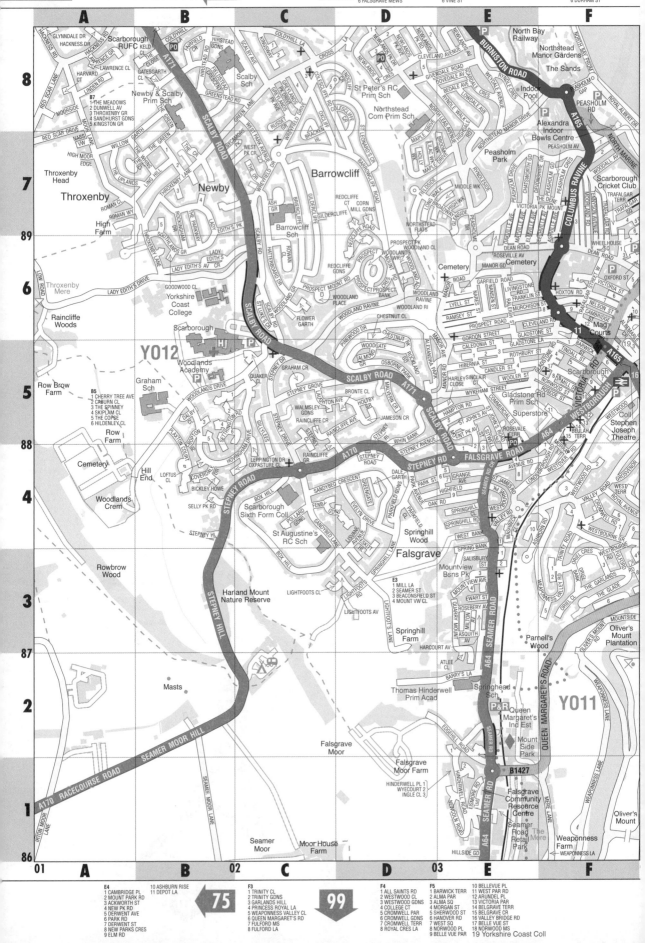

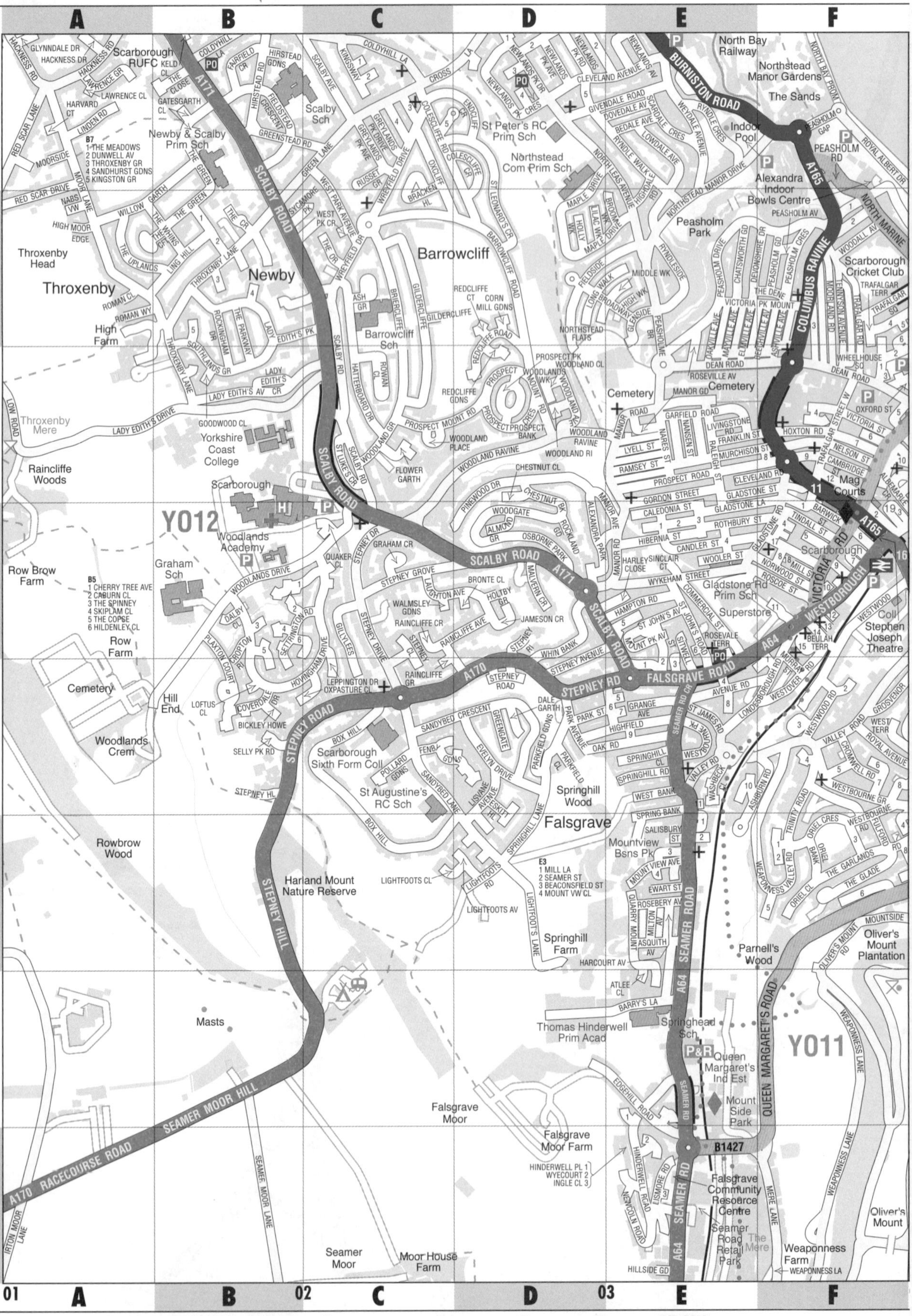

E4
1 CAMBRIDGE PL
2 MOUNT PARK RD
3 ACKWORTH ST
4 NEW PK RD
5 DERWENT AVE
6 PARK RD
7 DERWENT ST
8 NEW PARKS CRES
9 ELM RD
10 ASHBURN RISE
11 DEPOT LA

75

F3
1 TRINITY CL
2 TRINITY GDNS
3 GARLANDS HILL
4 PRINCESS ROYAL LA
5 WEAPONNESS VALLEY CL
6 QUEEN MARGARET'S RD
7 FULFORD MS
8 FULFORD LA

99

F4
1 ALL SAINTS RD
2 WESTWOOD CL
3 WESTWOOD GDNS
4 COLLEGE CT
5 CROMWELL PAR
6 CROMWELL GDNS
7 CROMWELL TERR
8 ROYAL CRES LA

F5
1 BARWICK TERR
2 ALMA PAR
3 ALMA SQ
4 MORGAN ST
5 SHERWOOD ST
6 HANOVER RD
7 WEST SQ
8 NORWOOD PL
9 BELLE VUE PAR
10 BELLEVUE PL
11 WEST PAR RD
12 ARUNDEL PL
13 VICTORIA PAR
14 BELGRAVE TERR
15 BELGRAVE CR
16 VALLEY BRIDGE RD
17 BELLE VUE ST
18 NORWOOD MS
19 Yorkshire Coast Coll

A6
1 REGENT ST
2 JAMES PL
3 GEORGE ST
4 NORTH TERR
5 AUBOROUGH ST
6 LANCASTER ST
7 CLARENCE PL
8 SILVER ST
9 MARIAS CT
10 FRIAR'S GDNS
11 FRIARS WY
12 UNION ST
13 BEDFORD ST
14 SUSSEX ST
15 PROVIDENCE PL
16 ABERDEEN WK
17 ABERDEEN ST
18 ALBERMARLE CRES
19 ABERDEEN LA
20 ABERDEEN PL
21 ABERDEEN TERR
22 NORTH ST LA
23 CHAPEL RD
24 MARKET ST
25 MARKET WY
26 ST HELEN'S SQ
27 BLAND'S CLIFF
28 PROSPECT PL
29 WATERHOUSE LA
30 Balmoral Sh Ctr

76
76

A B C D E F
8
7
89
6
5
88
4
3
87
2
1
86
04 05 06
North Bay
A7
1 ALBERT RD
2 CLARENCE RD
3 HOWARD ST
4 STANLEY ST
5 DURHAM PL
6 DURHAM ST
7 CLARK ST
8 ALBERT ST
9 VINCENT ST
10 NEW QUEEN ST
11 MARLBOROUGH ST
12 BLENHEIM ST
13 LOWER CLARK ST
14 Lower Clark St Ind Est
Clarence Gardens
Castle Cliff
Castle
YMCA & Leisure Centre
YO12
YO11
St Mary's Chapel
Castle Hill
Hall
MARINE DRIVE
MULGRAVE PL
SPREIGHT LANE STEPS
CHURCH LA
GRAHAM CL
CASTLE CRESCENT
CASTLE GDS
PARADISE
LONGWESTGATE
PRINCESS ST
OVERTON TERR
QUAY ST
SANDSIDE
HM Coastguard
Friarage Com Prim Sch
Council Offices
Terror Tower
LB Sta
Visitor Ctr
Old Harbour
Vincent's Pier
Luna Park
WEST PIER
Fish Market
Outer Harbour
Lighthouse
Futurist Theatre
Market Hall
Blands Cliff Gall
Opera House Casino
Council Offices
Tram - Cliff Lift
McBean Steps
Cliff Lift
THE SPA FOOTBRIDGE
FORESHORE ROAD
Brunswick Sh Ctr
Liby
TH
PO
B6
1 GARIBALDI ST
2 CHURCH ST
3 CHURCH STAIRS ST
4 SPRINGFIELD
5 COOK'S ROW
6 ST MARY'S ST
7 ST SEPULCHRE ST
8 LEADING POST ST
9 GLOBE ST
10 MERCHANT'S ROW
11 PRINCESS SQ
12 PRINCESS LA
13 TUTHILL
14 EAST SANDGATE
15 BURR BANK
16 CASTLE TERR
17 PRINCESS TERR
18 WHITEHEAD HILL
19 WEST SANDGATE TERR
20 FRIARAGE
A5
1 WESTBOROUGH
2 VERNON RD
3 VERNON PL
4 HARCOURT PL
5 ST NICHOLAS CLIFF
6 CLIFF BR PL
7 CLIFF BR TERR
8 CRESCENT BACK RD
9 BELVOIR TERR
10 FALCONERS SQ
11 PAVILION SQ
12 PAVILION TERR
13 Woodend Creative Centre
Rotunda Mus
Scarborough Art Gallery & Crescent Art Studio
VALLEY BR PAR
South Sands
SCARBOROUGH
Spa Complex
A4
1 CAMBRIDGE TERR
2 GROSVENOR CRES
3 ALBION CRES
4 OLIVER ST
5 ST MARTIN'S SQ
6 CARLTON TERR
7 SOUTH ST
8 GREENFIELD RD
9 ST MARTIN'S RD
10 ST MARTIN'S PL
11 WESTBOURNE GR
12 ROYAL CRES
13 ST MARTIN'S SQ
14 CROWN BACK CL
South Bay
RAMSHILL RD
Tram - Cliff Lift
ESPLANADE
A3
1 PRINCESS ROYAL PK
2 BACK AVENUE VICTORIA
3 GRANVILLE SQ
BELVEDERE TERR
FILEY RD
B1427
A165
B1364
Black Rocks
YO11
Cleveland Way
ABRAM'S VW
FILEY ROAD
SEA CLIFF ROAD
Scarborough Sports Centre
Oliver's Mount Plantation
Scarborough Coll
CHANDLERS CT
WHEATCROFT AVENUE
HOLBECK HILL
WEAPONNESS DRIVE
COLLEGE LANE
Univ of Hull at Scarborough
St Martin's CE VA Prim Sch
ST MICHAEL'S LA
White Nab
Raven Scar
CH
South Cliff Golf Club
KNOX LANE
DEEPDALE AVE
JACKSON'S LA
MICHAEL MOUNT RD
CORNELIAN DRIVE
CORNELIAN CL
Cornelian Bay

100
76

C4
1 REDSHAW CL
2 REDSHAW GR
3 HECKLER CL
4 WATERSIDE
5 BREWERY LA
6 BONDGATE GREEN CL
7 SOUTHGATE CL
8 CAVENDISH TERR
9 PARK SQ
10 GLADSTONE TERR
11 WELLINGTON GDNS

113
113

C5
1 ST WILFRID'S RD
2 ST WILFRID'S PL
3 WESTBOURNE GR
4 FINKLE CL
5 FINKLE ST
6 OLD MARKET PL
7 HIGH SKELLGATE
8 WILLIAMSON DR
9 WELLINGTON MEWS
10 WELLINGTON ST
11 KIRKGATE
12 BEDERN BANK
13 MINSTER CL
14 WILLIAMSON CL
15 MALLARD CL
16 BEDERN CT
17 FISHERGATE
18 QUEEN ST
19 MARKET PLACE EAST
20 MARKET PLACE SOUTH
21 MARKET PLACE WEST
22 MINSTER CL
23 MARKET PLACE NORTH

114

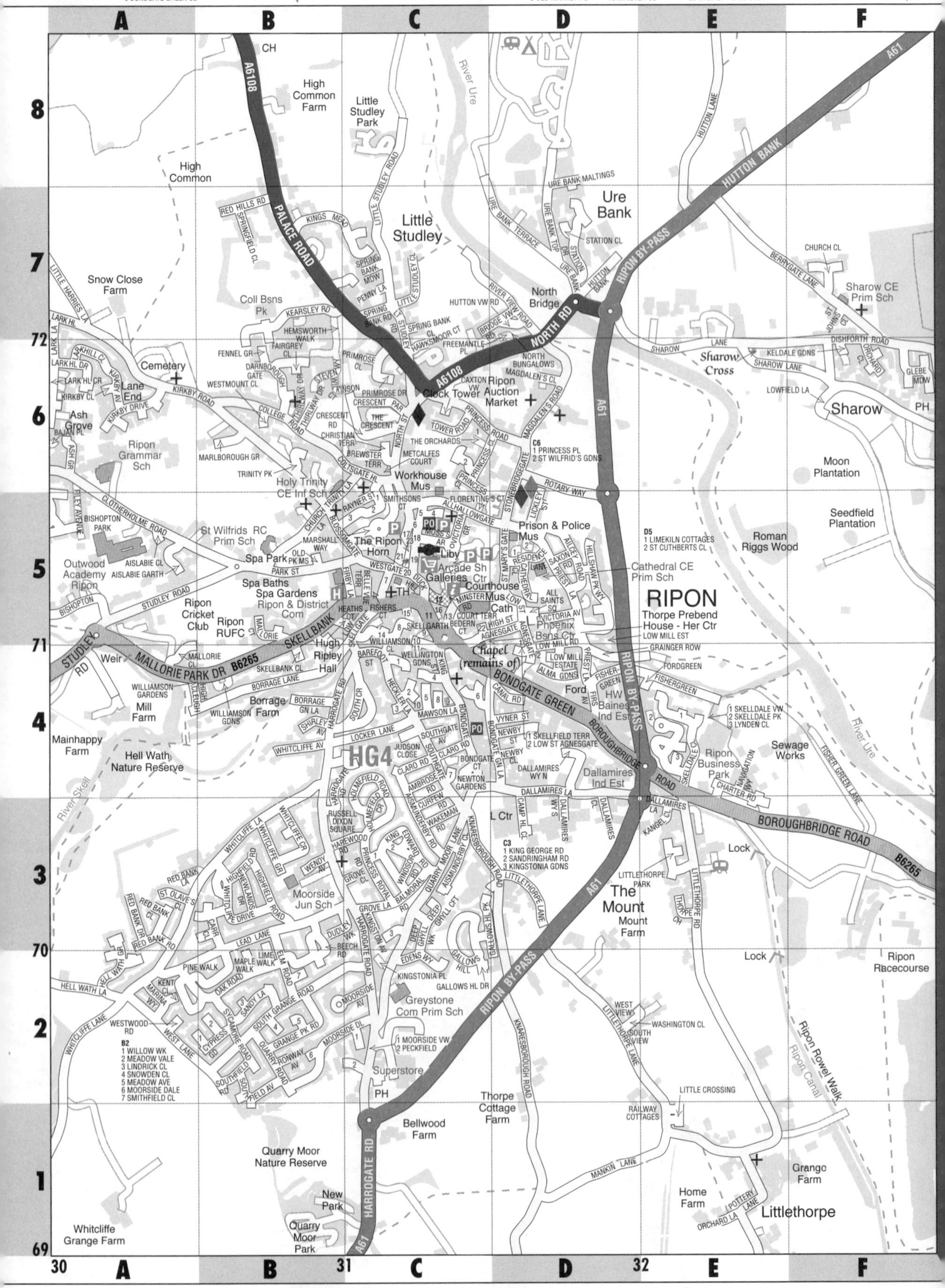

139
139
140

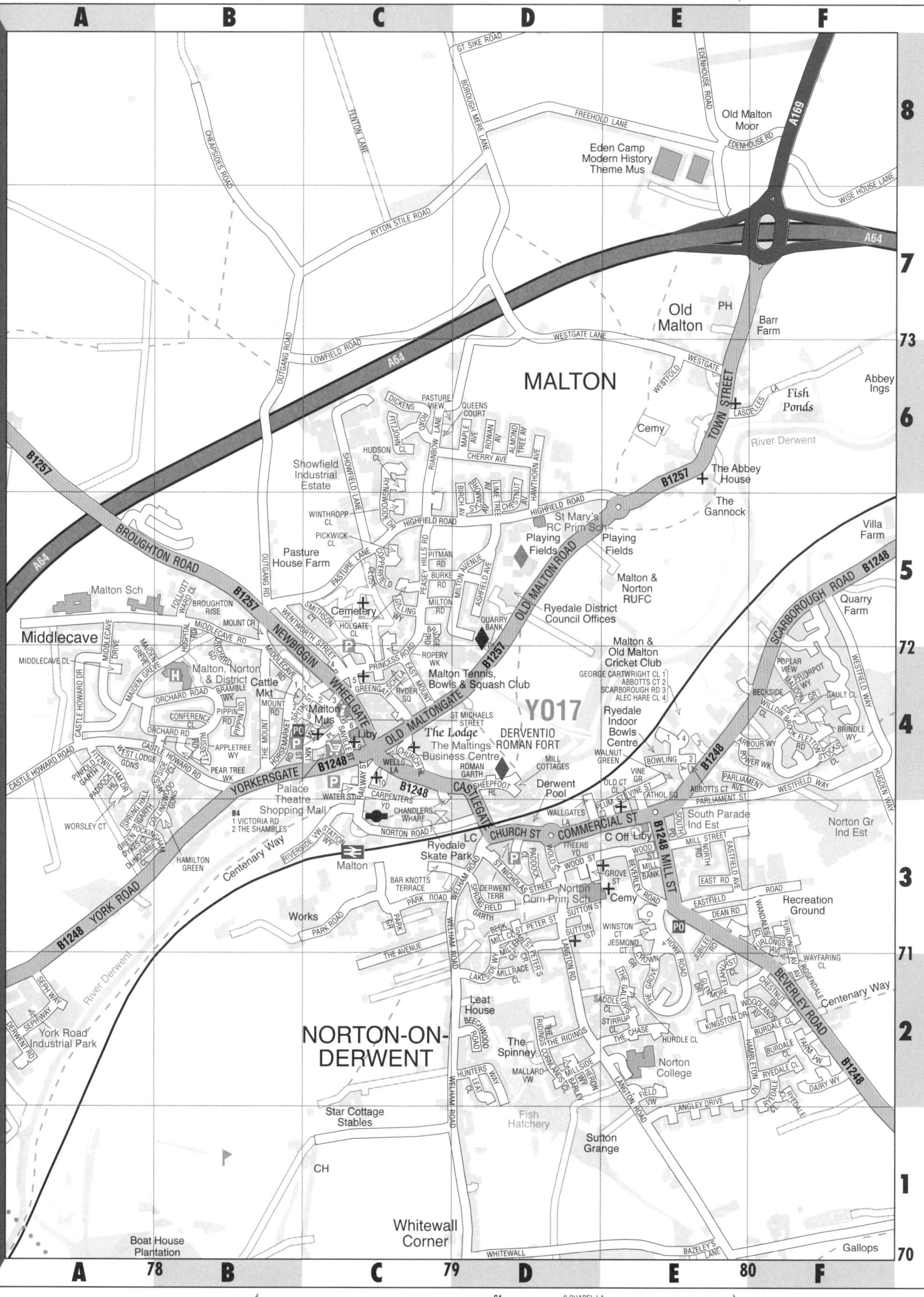

C4
1 SPITAL FIELD CT
2 NEWGATE
3 FINKLE ST
4 PUMP LA
5 PRINCESS TERR
6 ST MICHAEL ST
7 ST LEONARD'S CL
8 THE SHAMBLES
9 CHAPEL LA
10 CARPENTERS YD

172
156

F4
1 PARK ST
2 PRIMROSE HL
3 VICTORIA TERR
4 HALLAM'S YD
5 THE PINFOLD
6 BACK O THE BECK
7 WATSON'S HO
8 CANAL YD
9 BAY HORSE YD
10 VICTORIA ST
11 SHEEP ST
12 DEVONSHIRE PL
13 COACH ST YD
14 GLADSTONE ST
15 BIRTWHISTLE'S YD
16 Water St Com Prim Sch
17 St Stephen's Cath Prim Sch

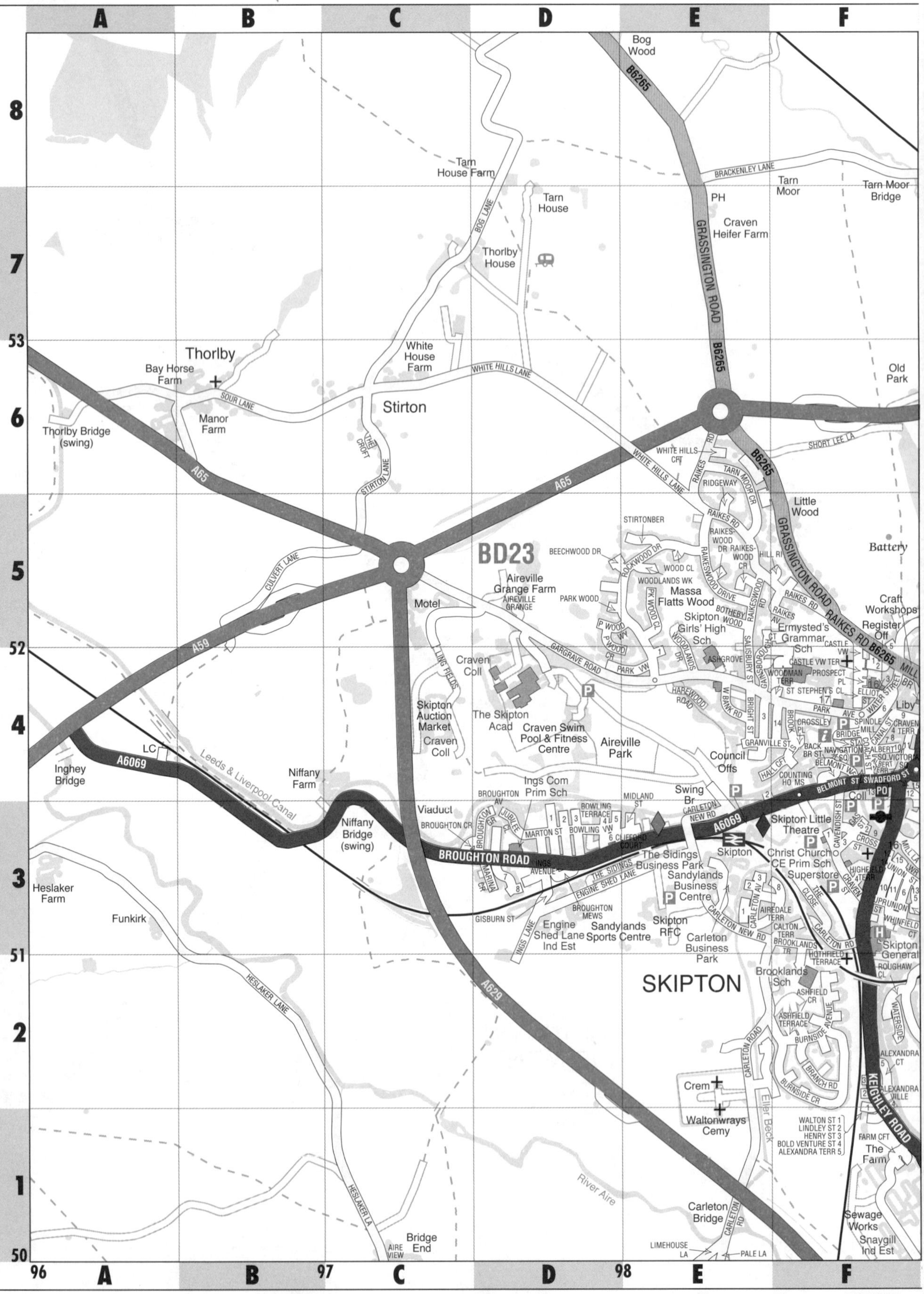

D3
1 SAWLEY ST
2 CLITHEROE ST
3 THORNTON ST
4 PENDLE ST
5 GREENFIELD ST
6 RUSKIN AVE
7 NIFFANY GDNS
8 STATION VW

E3
1 AIREDALE MEWS
2 GLYNWED CT
3 ELLER MEWS

E4
1 ROCKWOOD CL
2 BELLEVUE TERR
3 BELGRAVE ST

F3
1 CLIFFORD ST
2 HIRDS YD
3 CARLETON ST
4 CHURCH ST
5 UNION TERR
6 CUMBERLAND ST
7 SOUTHFIELD TERR
8 LINTON CT
9 THANET'S CT
10 PEMBROKE ST
11 BENNETT ST
12 TUFTON PL
13 SPINNERS CT
14 BRINDLEY MILL
15 BRINDLEY CT
16 Bowers Wharf

172
173

A4
1 BUNKERS HL
2 JERRY CFT
3 ALMA TERR
4 ERMYSTED ST
5 PROVIDENCE PL
6 VICTORIA SQ
7 CRAVEN TERR

B5
1 FALLOW FIELD
2 MEADOW RISE
3 OVERDALE GRA
4 SKIBEDEN CT
5 NEW LAITHE CL

C7
1 BRACKENLEY GR
2 BRACKENLEY AVE
3 BRACKENLEY CL
4 MIDGLEY CL
5 SANDY LA

156

174

E8
1 HAW PK
2 PRIORY VW
3 BEACON VW
4 LOW BANK
5 MOORLAND CL

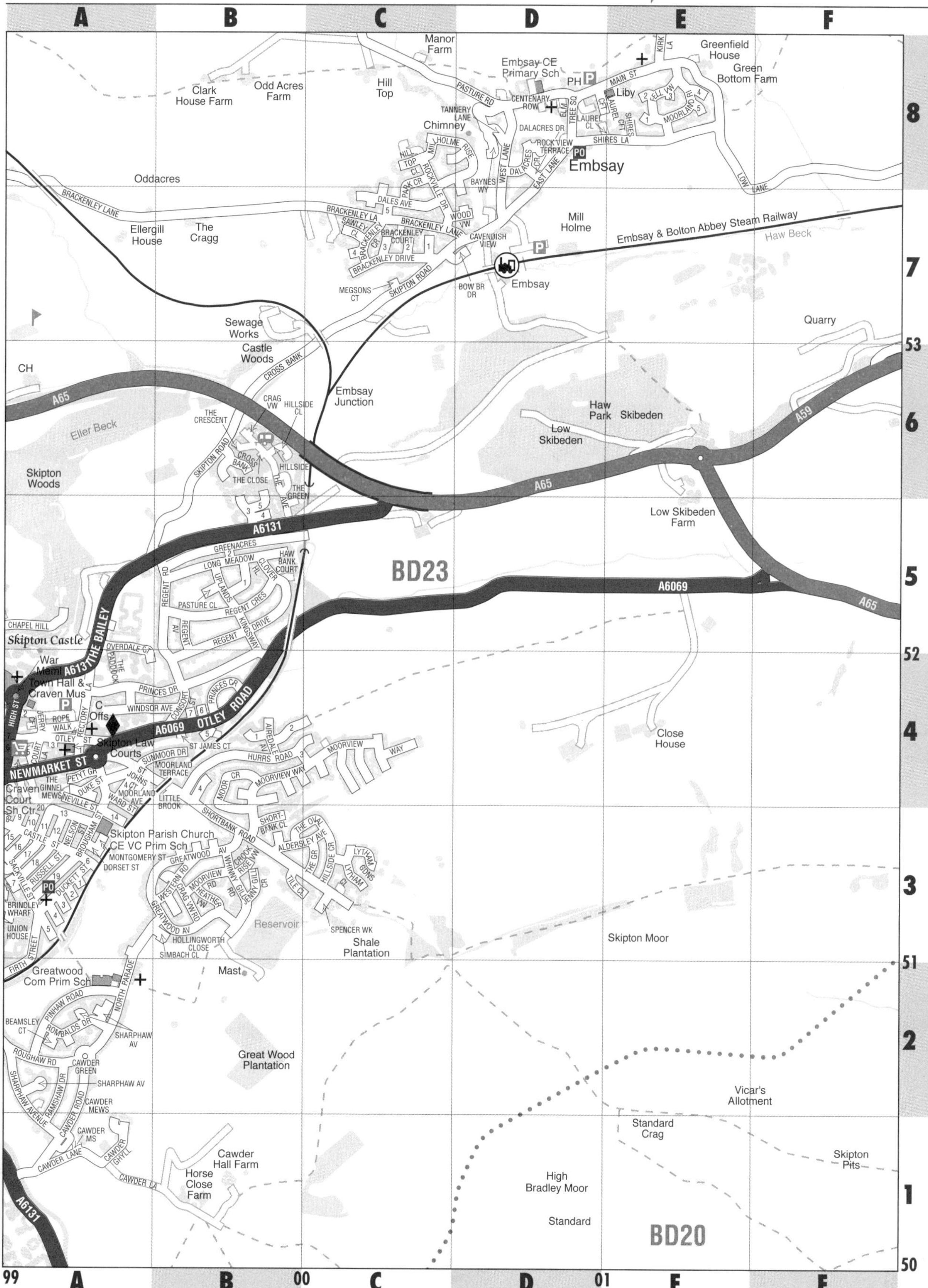

A3
1 SOUTHEY ST
2 BYRON ST
3 COWPER ST
4 MILTON ST
5 UPPER SACKVILLE ST
6 EAST CASTLE ST
7 SIDGWICK CT
8 GOSCHEN ST
9 CROMWELL ST
10 FAIRFAX ST
11 LAMBERT ST
12 WELLINGTON ST
13 DEVONSHIRE ST
14 EAST NEVILLE ST
15 ROMILLE ST
16 DAWSON ST
17 GEORGE ST
18 ROWLAND ST
19 WESTMORELAND ST
20 BROOKSIDE

B4
1 WHARFEDALE CL
2 WENSLEYDALE AVE
3 HURRS RD
4 RANKIN'S WELL RD
5 SPRINGFIELDS
6 QUEEN ST
7 KING ST

173

174

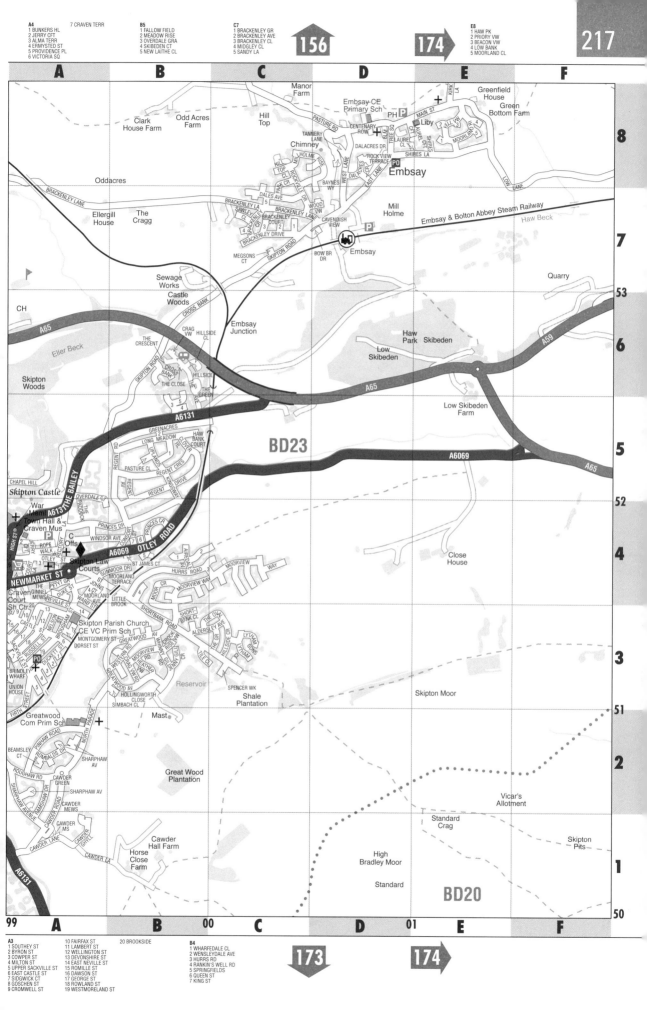

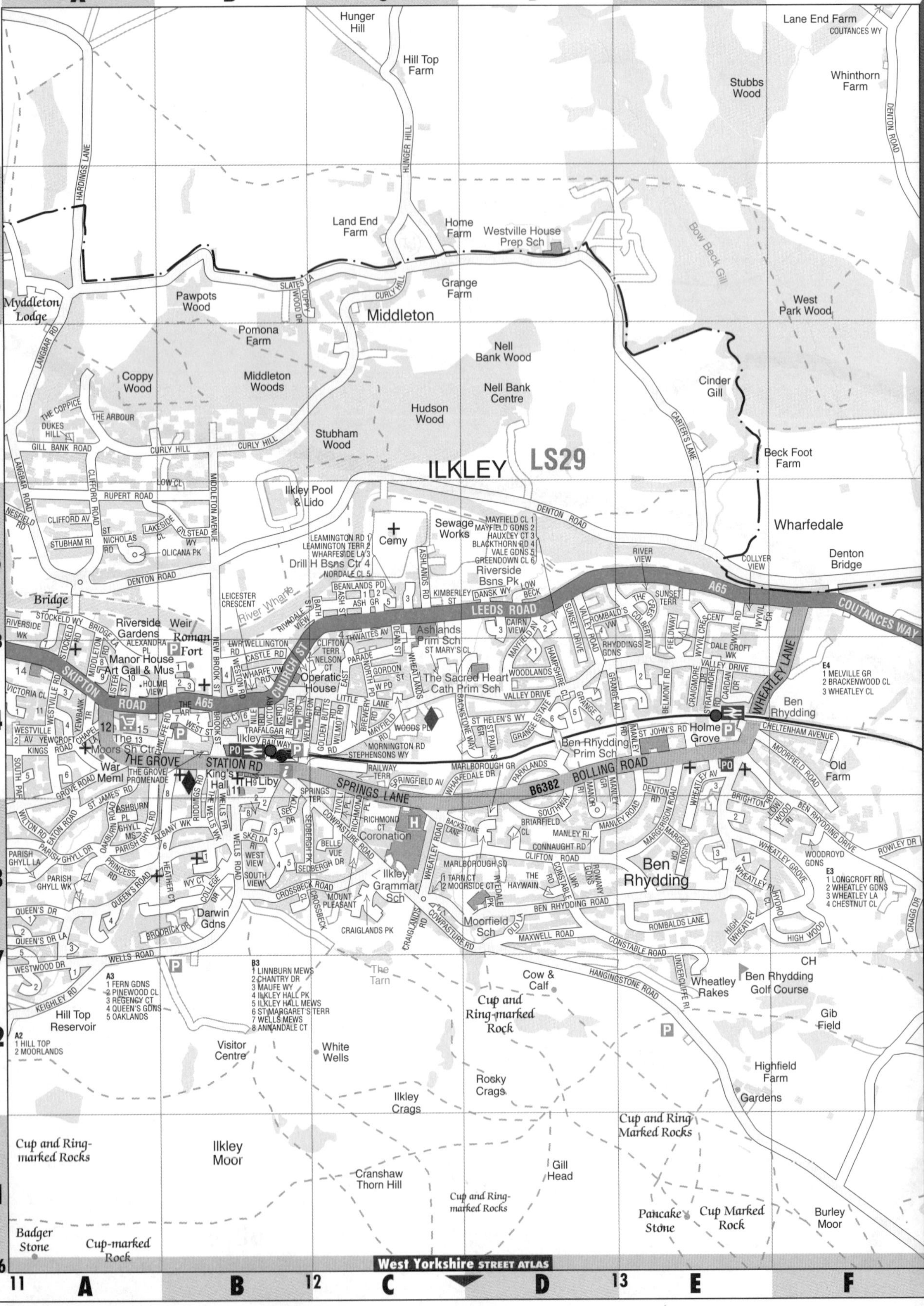
A B C D E F
8 7 6 5 4 3 2 1
49 48 47 46
11 12 13
Hunger Hill
Hill Top Farm
Lane End Farm
COUTANCES WY
Whinthorn Farm
Stubbs Wood
DENTON ROAD
HUNGER HILL
HARDINGS LANE
Land End Farm
Home Farm
Westville House Prep Sch
Bow Beck Gill
Grange Farm
Myddleton Lodge
Pawpots Wood
SLATES LA
COPPY WOOD DR
CURLY HILL
Middleton
West Park Wood
Pomona Farm
Nell Bank Wood
LANGBAR RD
Coppy Wood
Middleton Woods
Nell Bank Centre
Cinder Gill
Hudson Wood
THE COPPICE
THE ARBOUR
DUKES HILL
Stubham Wood
CARTER'S LANE
Beck Foot Farm
GILL BANK ROAD
CURLY HILL
ILKLEY
LS29
LANGBAR ROAD
CLIFFORD ROAD
LOW CL
MIDDLETON AVENUE
Ilkley Pool & Lido
RUPERT ROAD
DENTON ROAD
Wharfedale
NESFIELD RD
CLIFFORD AV
LAKESIDE CL
GILSTEAD WY
Sewage Works
MAYFIELD CL 1
MAYFIELD GDNS 2
HAUXLEY CT 3
BLACKTHORN RD 4
VALE GDNS 5
GREENDOWN CL 6
Cemy
LEAMINGTON RD 1
LEAMINGTON TERR 2
WHARFESIDE LA 3
Drill H Bsns Ctr 4
NORDALE CL 5
STUBHAM RI
ST NICHOLAS RD
OLICANA PK
ASHLANDS RD
Riverside Bsns Pk
RIVER VIEW
Denton Bridge
COLLYER VIEW
DENTON ROAD
KIMBERLEY ST
DANSK WY
LOW BECK
BEANLANDS PD
Bridge
LEICESTER CRESCENT
River Wharfe
SUNSET TERR
A65
COUTANCES WAY
LEEDS ROAD
RIVERSIDE WK
STOCKELD WY
BRIDGE LA
Riverside Gardens
Weir
Roman Fort
ALEXANDRA PL
CAIRN VIEW
Ashlands Prim Sch
ST MARY'S CL
THWAITES AV
Manor House Art Gall & Mus
WELLINGTON
CASTLE RD
CLIFTON TERR
NELSON CT
PARADE
GORDON ST
The Sacred Heart Cath Prim Sch
WOODLANDS
VALLEY DRIVE
VALLEY DRIVE
DALE CROFT WK
E4
1 MELVILLE GR
2 BRACKENWOOD CL
3 WHEATLEY CL
SKIPTON ROAD
HOLME VIEW
CHURCH ST
Operatic House
WHEATLEY LANE
Ben Rhydding
VICTORIA CL
WESTVILLE RD
WESTVILLE
YEWCROFT
KINGS ROAD
CHAPEL
The Moors Sh Ctr
War Meml
THE GROVE
STATION RD
Ilkley
RAILWAY
WOODS PL
ST HELEN'S WY
ST JOHN'S RD
Holme Grove
CHELTENHAM AVENUE
MOORFIELD ROAD
Old Farm
Ben Rhydding Prim Sch
MORNINGTON RD
STEPHENSONS WY
MARLBOROUGH GR
PARKLANDS
BOLLING ROAD
B6382
SPRINGS LANE
SPRINGFIELD AV
WHARFEDALE DR
PO
King's Hall
The Liby
THE GROVE PROMENADE
GROVE ROAD
ST JAMES' RD
ASHBURN PL
GHYLL MS
PARISH GHYLL RD
ALBANY WK
THE WELLS WK
WELLS ROAD
RICHMOND CT
Coronation
H
SOUTHWAY
BRIARFIELD CL
MANLEY RI
MANLEY ROAD
MARGERISON ROAD
WHEATLEY AV
BRIGHTON RD
BEN RHYDDING DRIVE
ROWLEY DR
WHEATLEY GROVE
WOODROYD GDNS
PARISH GHYLL LA
PARISH GHYLL DR
PARISH GHYLL WK
PRINCESS RD
QUEEN'S ROAD
HEATHER CT
IVY CT
COLLEGE RD
SKELDA RI
WEST VIEW
SOUTH VIEW
BELLE VUE
SEDBERGH DR
COWPASTURE ROAD
WHEATLEY ROAD
Ilkley Grammar Sch
MARLBOROUGH SQ
CONNAUGHT RD
CLIFTON ROAD
1 TARN CT
2 MOORSIDE CT
THE HAYWAIN
Ben Rhydding
E3
1 LONGCROFT RD
2 WHEATLEY GDNS
3 WHEATLEY LA
4 CHESTNUT CL
CROSSBECK ROAD
MOUNT PLEASANT
Moorfield Sch
BEN RHYDDING ROAD
ROMBALDS LANE
HIGH WOOD
CRAGG DR
QUEEN'S DR
Darwin Gdns
BRODRICK DR
CRAIGLANDS PK
CRAIGLANDS RD
MAXWELL ROAD
CONSTABLE ROAD
QUEEN'S DR LA
WESTWOOD DR
WELLS ROAD
KEIGHLEY RD
B3
1 LINNBURN MEWS
2 CHANTRY DR
3 MAUFE WY
4 ILKLEY HALL PK
5 ILKLEY HALL MEWS
6 ST MARGARET'S TERR
7 WELLS MEWS
8 ANNANDALE CT
The Tarn
Cow & Calf
HANGINGSTONE ROAD
UNDERCLIFFE RI
Wheatley Rakes
Ben Rhydding Golf Course
CH
A3
1 FERN GDNS
2 PINEWOOD CL
3 REGENCY CT
4 QUEEN'S GDNS
5 OAKLANDS
Hill Top Reservoir
Cup and Ring-marked Rock
Gib Field
A2
1 HILL TOP
2 MOORLANDS
Visitor Centre
White Wells
Rocky Crags
Highfield Farm
Ilkley Crags
Gardens
Cup and Ring Marked Rocks
Cup and Ring-marked Rocks
Ilkley Moor
Gill Head
Cranshaw Thorn Hill
Cup and Ring-marked Rocks
Pancake Stone
Cup Marked Rock
Burley Moor
Badger Stone
Cup-marked Rock

A4
1 NORTH CFT GR RD
2 KINGS AV
3 YEWBANK CL
4 KINGSWAY DR
5 BIRCHWOOD CT
6 WESTVILLE CL
7 OLD BRIDGE RISE
8 SADDLERS CFT
9 BACK MIDDLETON RD
10 ALEXANDRA CR
11 NORTH CROFT GR
12 BOLTON BRIDGE RD
13 REGENT RD
14 All Saints CE Prim Sch
15 Victoria Arcade

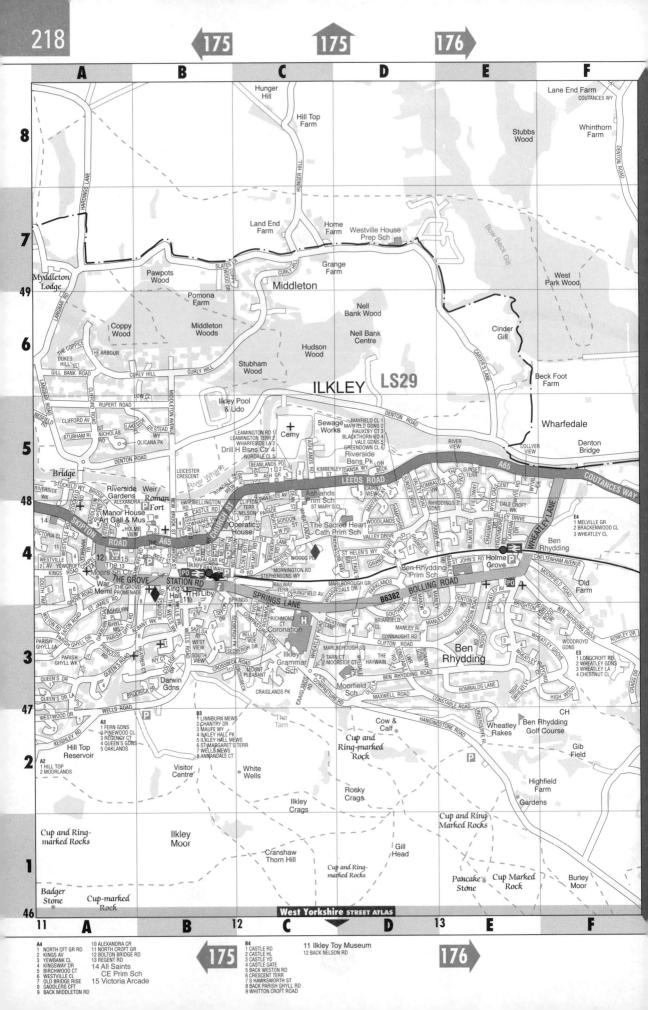

B4
1 CASTLE RD
2 CASTLE HL
3 CASTLE YD
4 CASTLE GATE
5 BACK WESTON RD
6 CRESCENT TERR
7 S HAWKSWORTH ST
8 BACK PARISH GHYLL RD
9 WHITTON CROFT ROAD
11 Ilkley Toy Museum
12 BACK NELSON RD

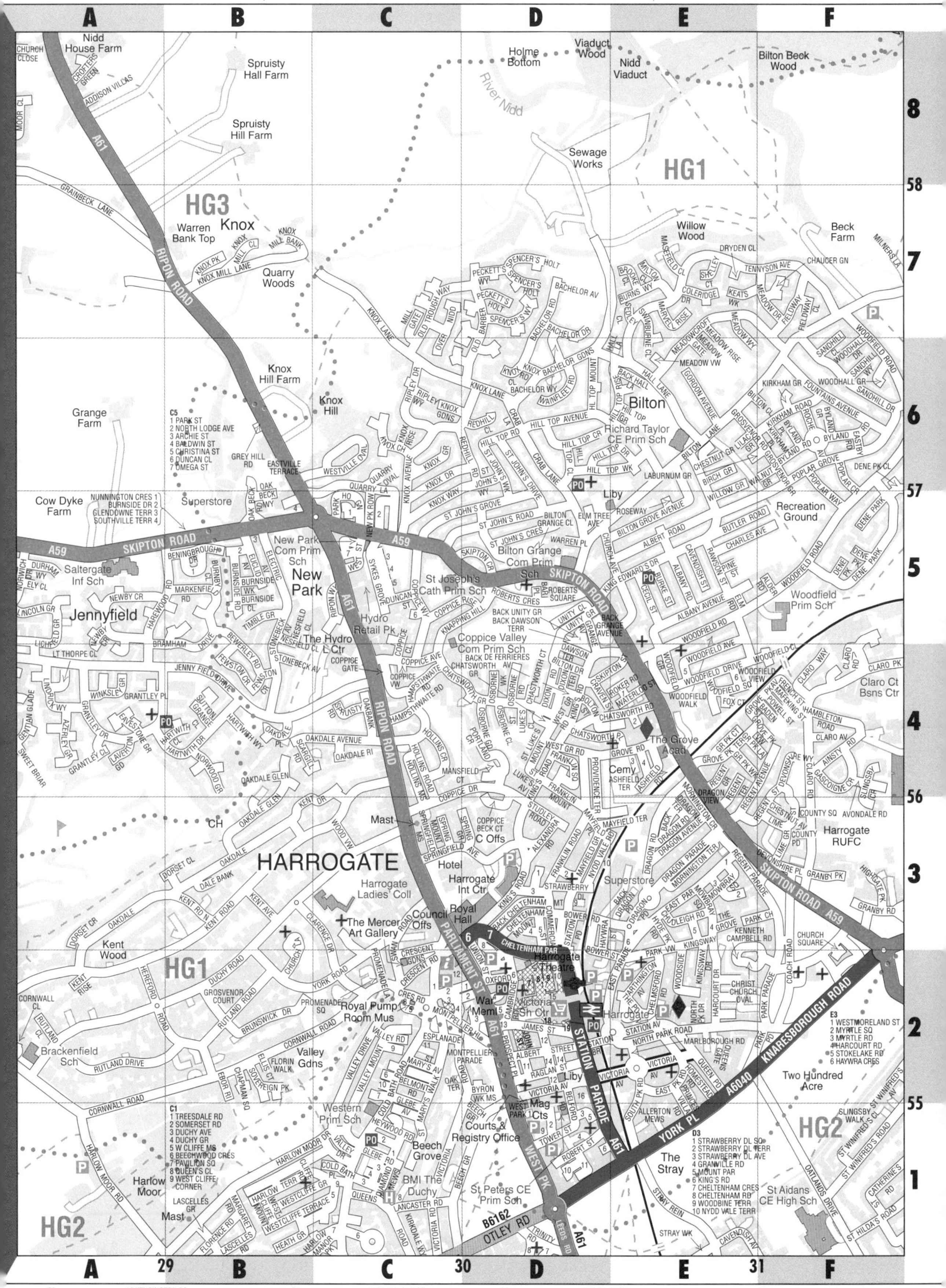

C2
1 MONTPELLIER RD
2 MONTPELLIER GDNS
3 MONTPELLIER MEWS
4 MONTPELLIER ST
5 BACK ROYAL PAR
6 WELLINGTON SQ
7 ST PETER'S SQ
8 ROYAL PAR
9 WELLINGTON CT
10 KENSINGTON SQ
11 MONTPELLIER CT
12 Turkish Baths & Health Spa

D1
1 BRUNSWICK PL
2 OXFORD TERR
3 BELFORD PL
4 ST ROBERTS MEWS
5 ALBERT TERR
6 BACK YORK PL
7 PARK DR
8 PARK RD
9 BELFORD SQ
10 TRAFALGAR CT
11 TRAFALGAR RD

D2
1 THE GINNEL
2 PARLIAMENT TERR
3 MONTPELLIER SQ
4 CAMBRIDGE TERR
5 CAMBRIDGE CRES
6 CHELTENHAM CRES
7 OXFORD PL
8 CAMBRIDGE PL
9 EBENEZER TERR
10 BEULAH ST
11 JOHN ST
12 ST PRINCES ST
13 PROSPECT CRES
14 PRINCES SQ
15 CAMBRIDGE ST
16 ROGERS SQ
17 NORTHUMBERLAND CT
18 MARKET PL
19 STATION SQUARE

E4
1 WEYMOUTH RD
2 CHATSWORTH TERR
3 BACK ELMWOOD ST
4 ELMWOOD ST
5 WOODFIELD GDNS
6 WOODFIELD PL

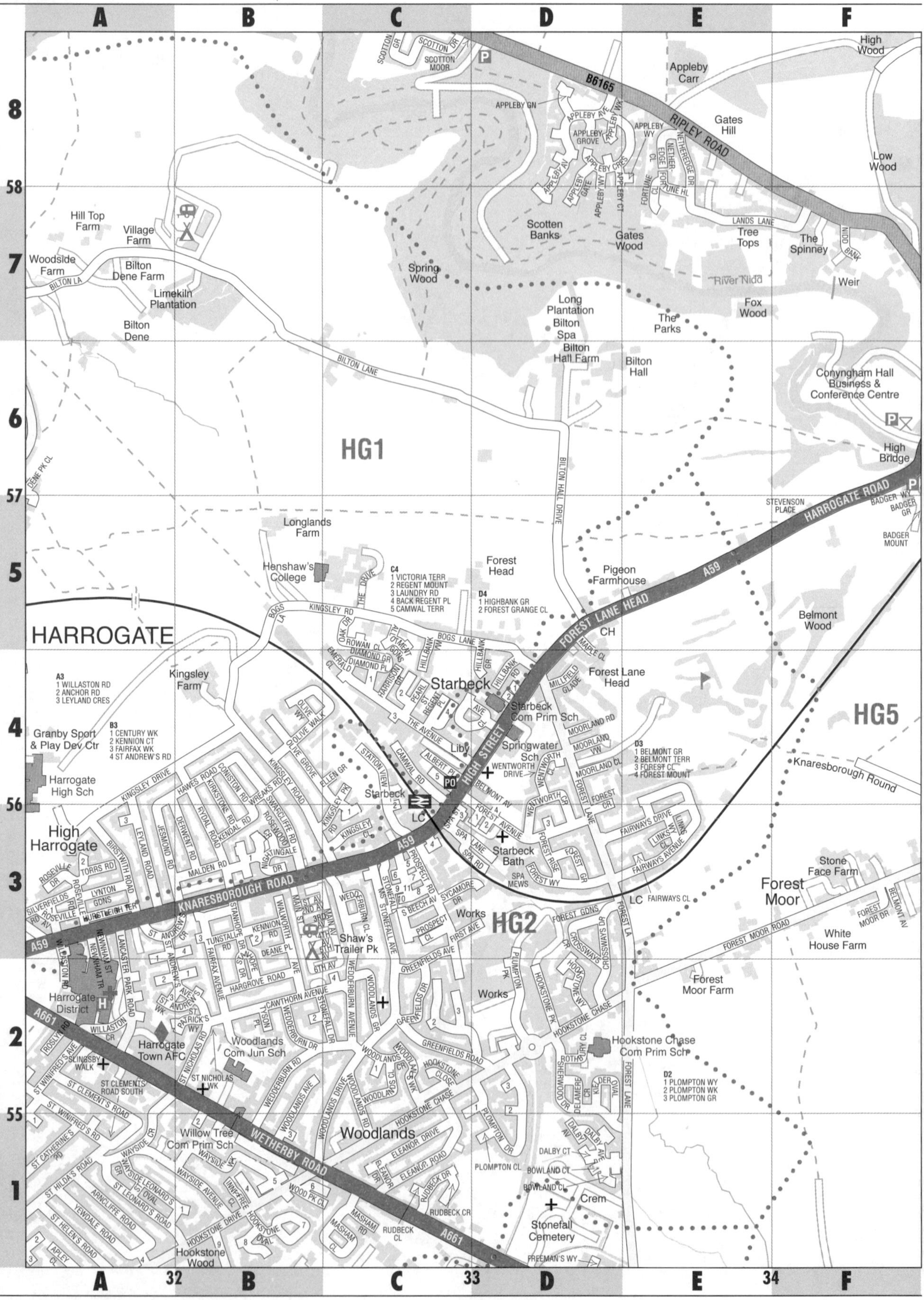

A1
1 NEWLAND AVE
2 ST RONAN'S RD
3 ST RONAN'S CL
4 WINDSOR RD

A2
1 ST ANDREW'S ST
2 ST ANDREW'S PL
3 ST ANDREW'S PAR

C2
1 WOODLANDS RI
2 HOOKSTONE GRANGE WY
3 HOOKSTONE GRANGE COURT
4 CAWTHORN PL

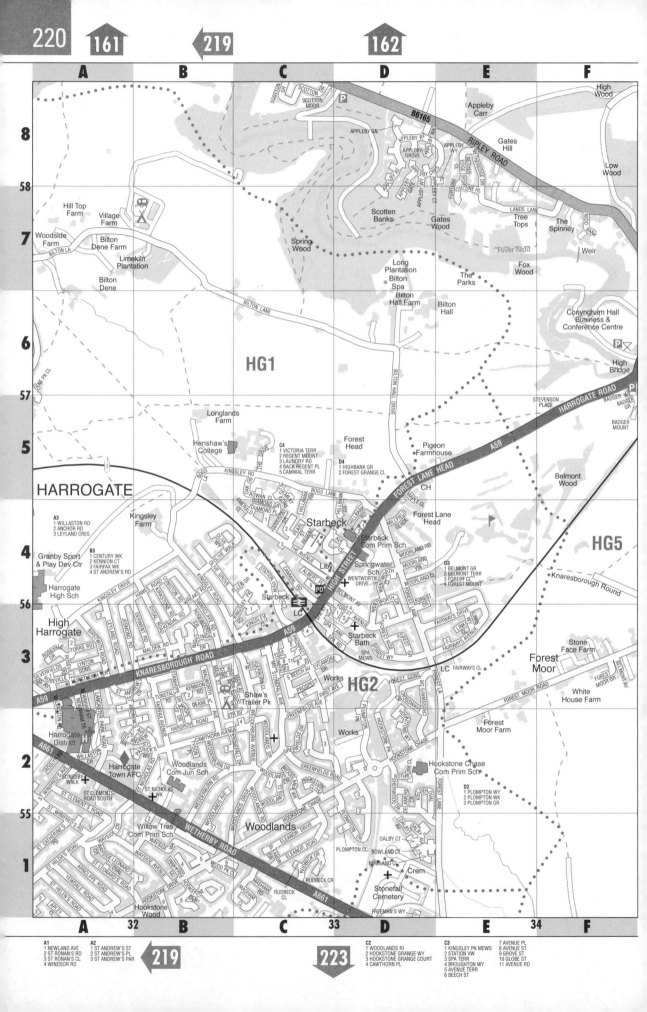

C3
1 KINGSLEY PK MEWS
2 STATION VW
3 SPA TERR
4 BROUGHTON WY
5 AVENUE TERR
6 BEECH ST
7 AVENUE PL
8 AVENUE ST
9 GROVE ST
10 GLOBE ST
11 AVENUE RD

A6
1 ST MARGARET'S GDNS
2 ST MARGARET'S GARTH
3 ST MARGARET'S CL
4 PUMP HL
5 JOCKEY LA
6 BEECH HL
8 WATER BAG BANK
9 STATION RD
10 VICARAGE LA
11 THE PARSONAGE
12 FINKLE ST
13 BOWLING GREEN YD
14 FINKLE KEEP
15 PROSPECT TERR
16 WEST VIEW TERR
17 SAVAGE YD
18 WHITELEY YD

B5
1 WELLINGTON ST
2 CHEAPSIDE
3 CASTLEGATE
4 SILVER ST
5 HIGH ST
6 FISHER ST
7 GRACIOUS ST
8 ORCHARD CT
9 STOCKDALE CL
10 TANNERY CT
11 PINFOLD CL

162

B6
1 COMMERCIAL YD
2 PARK SQ
3 MARKET PL
4 PARK PL
5 BERRY'S AVE
6 WHINCUP CL
7 WHINCUP GR
8 PARK CL
9 STOCKWELL CT
10 CHARLTON CT
11 HOLLY CT
12 CHARLTON GR
13 CHARLTON MANOR DR
14 PARK TERR
15 MANOR GDNS
16 BERRYS CT
17 Frazer Theatre

162

B7
1 NORWOOD CT
2 HAWTHORN AVE
3 PASTURE CRES
4 FROGMIRE CL
5 STOCKWELL CRES
6 SOMERLEY LA

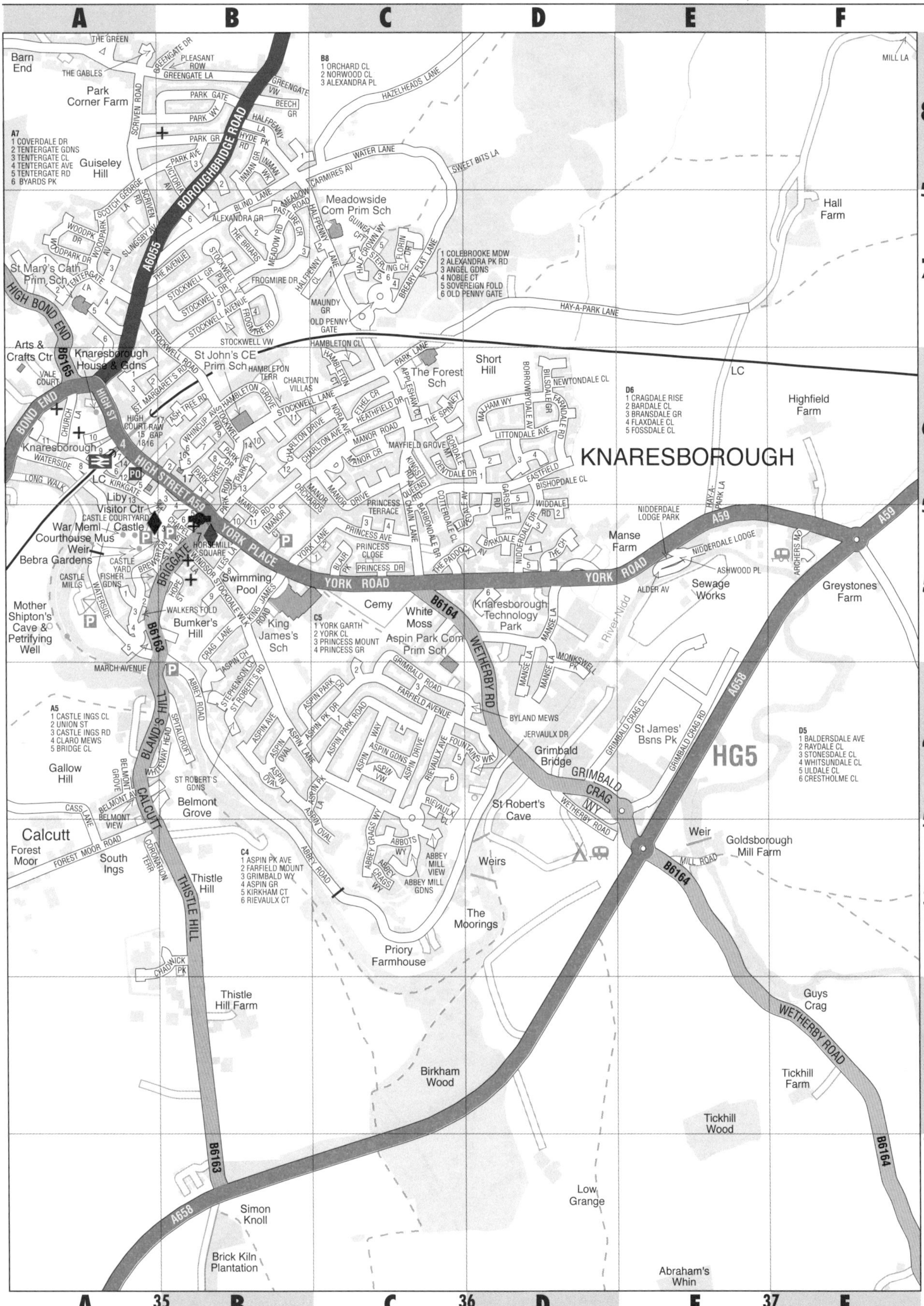

162 162

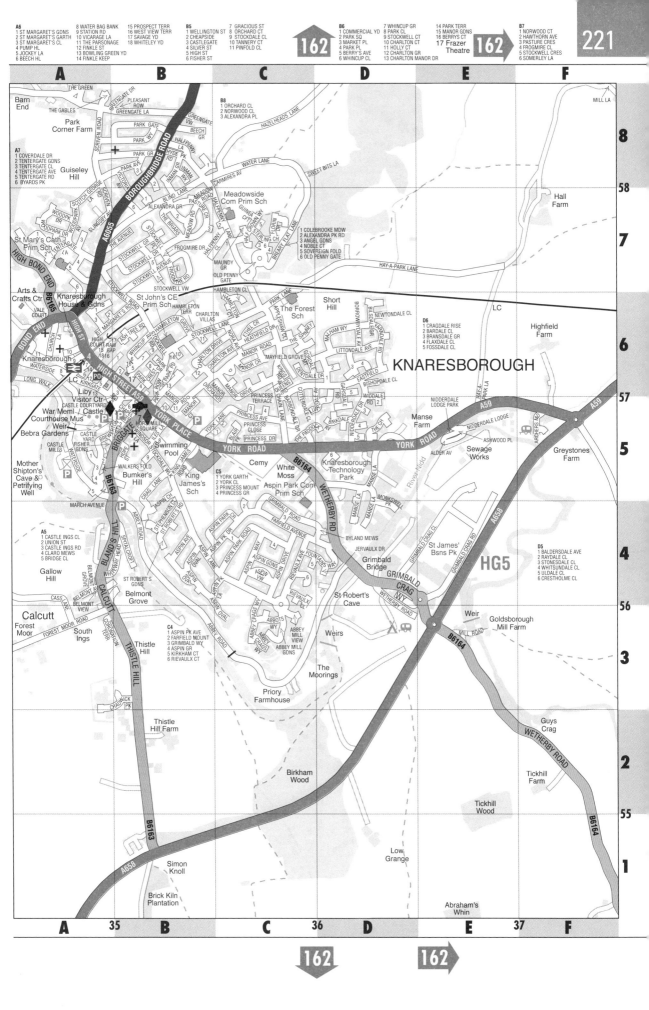

161
219

178
178

220
162

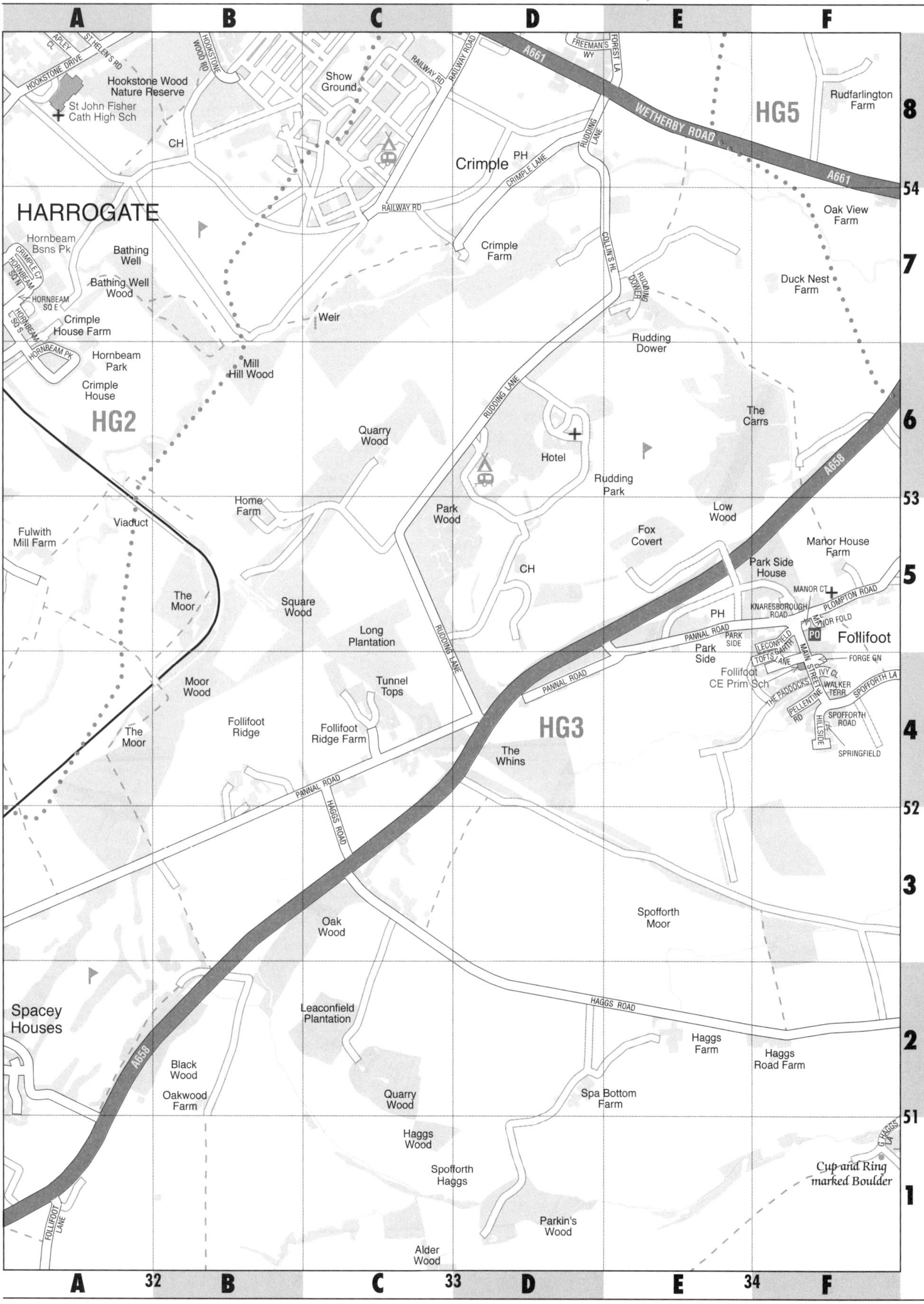

178
179
179

165
166

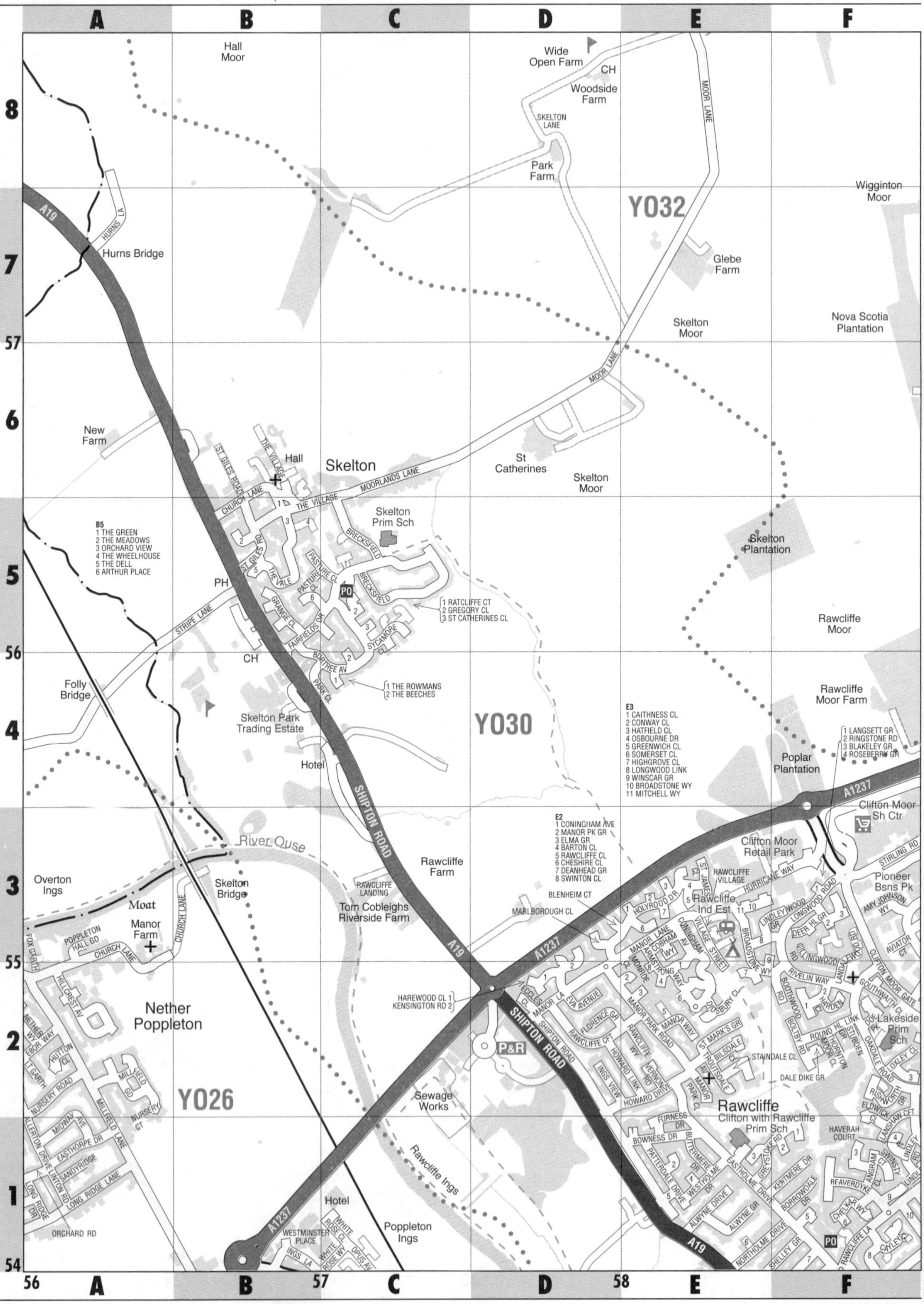
A
B
C
D
E
F
8
7
57
6
5
56
4
3
55
2
1
54
56
57
58
Hall Moor
Wide Open Farm
CH
Woodside Farm
SKELTON LANE
MOOR LANE
Park Farm
YO32
Wigginton Moor
Glebe Farm
HURNS LA
Hurns Bridge
A19
Skelton Moor
Nova Scotia Plantation
MOOR LANE
New Farm
Hall
Skelton
THE VILLAGE
ST GILES ROAD
MOORLANDS LANE
St Catherines
Skelton Moor
CHURCH LANE
THE VILLAGE
Skelton Prim Sch
B5
1 THE GREEN
2 THE MEADOWS
3 ORCHARD VIEW
4 THE WHEELHOUSE
5 THE DELL
6 ARTHUR PLACE
Skelton Plantation
BRECKSFIELD
ST GILES RD
PASTURE CL
THE VALE
PH
PO
1 RATCLIFFE CT
2 GREGORY CL
3 ST CATHERINES CL
STRIPE LANE
GRANGE CL
FAIRFIELDS DR
SYCAMORE CL
Rawcliffe Moor
CH
BURTREE AV
Folly Bridge
PARK CL
1 THE ROWMANS
2 THE BEECHES
Rawcliffe Moor Farm
Skelton Park Trading Estate
YO30
E3
1 CAITHNESS CL
2 CONWAY CL
3 HATFIELD CL
4 OSBOURNE DR
5 GREENWICH CL
6 SOMERSET CL
7 HIGHGROVE CL
8 LONGWOOD LINK
9 WINSCAR GR
10 BROADSTONE WY
11 MITCHELL WY
1 LANGSETT GR
2 RINGSTONE RD
3 BLAKELEY GR
4 ROSEBERRY GR
Poplar Plantation
Hotel
A1237
Clifton Moor Sh Ctr
E2
1 CONINGHAM AVE
2 MANOR PK GR
3 ELMA GR
4 BARTON CL
5 RAWCLIFFE CL
6 CHESHIRE CL
7 DEANHEAD GR
8 SWINTON CL
Clifton Moor Retail Park
River Ouse
SHIPTON ROAD
Rawcliffe Farm
RAWCLIFFE VILLAGE
HURRICANE WAY
STIRLING RD
Pioneer Bsns Pk
Overton Ings
Skelton Bridge
RAWCLIFFE LANDING
Tom Cobleighs Riverside Farm
BLENHEIM CT
Rawcliffe Ind Est
AMY JOHNSON WY
Moat
MARLBOROUGH CL
HOLYROOD DR
Manor Farm
CHURCH LANE
POPPLETON HALL GD
CHURCH LANE
FOX GARTH
A1237
MANOR LANE
COBHAM WY
CONINGHAM AV
VILLAGE STREET
BROADSTONE WY
LINDLEY WOOD GR
LONGWOOD ROAD
DEER HL GR
AVIATOR CT
GILLINGWOOD RD
LANDALEWOOD RD
CLIFTON MOOR GATE
HILLCREST AV
ARMSTRONG WAY
MONKROE CL
A19
RIVELIN WAY
SOUTHWAITH CL
HAREWOOD CL 1
KENSINGTON RD 2
EVA AVENUE
MANOR PARK ROAD
DUNSBURY CL
BOOTHWOOD RD
HAYDEN CL
Nether Poppleton
EBOR WAY
ECCLES CL
MANOR LA
FLORENCE GR
MANOR WAY
ST MARK'S GR
BOLTBY RD
ROUND HL LINK
THORNTON MOOR CL
STUBDEN GR
OAKDALE ROAD
Lakeside Prim Sch
SHIPTON ROAD
RAWCLIFFE CFT
RAWCLIFFE AV
BILSDALE CL
STAINDALE CL
P&R
SHIPTON ROAD
HOWARD LINK
OXLEY CL
MILLFIELD GD
MIDWAY AVE
MILLFIELD LANE
NURSERY ROAD
NURSERY CT
YO26
INGS VIEW
VERNON RD
TROUTSDALE AV
MANOR PARK CL
DALE DIKE GR
HOWARD DRIVE
Sewage Works
FURNESS DR
Rawcliffe
Clifton with Rawcliffe Prim Sch
ELDWICK CL
LANSHAW CFT
HAVERAH COURT
ALLERTON DRIVE
EASTHORPE DR
BOWNESS DR
BUTTERMERE DR
SANDYRIDGE
PATTERDALE DRIVE
EASTHOLME DRIVE
GREYSTOKE RD
KENTMERE DR
ANGRAM CL
LINDLEY
Rawcliffe Ings
LONG RIDGE DR
LINTON RD
LONG RIDGE LANE
WESTHOLME DR
BORROWDALE DR
RFAVERDYKE
Hotel
ALWYNE DRIVE
ALWYNE GR
CHELKAR WY
A1237
WESTMINSTER PLACE
WHITE ROSE CL
Poppleton Ings
NORTHOLME DRIVE
ORCHARD RD
INGS LA
WHITE ROSE WY
OPUS AV
A19
SHELLEY GR
RAWCLIFFE LA
PO
CAYLEY CL

165
227

E1
1 CONISTON CL
2 WASDALE CL
3 GARBURN GR
4 SCAFELL CL
5 LOWESWATER RD
6 FYLINGDALES AVE

F1
1 EMBLETON DR
2 COLEDALE CL
3 LEIGHTON CFT
4 BARMBY CL
5 GRASMERE GR
6 BARDEN CT
7 SOUTHOLME DR
8 MILTON CARR
9 FEWSTON DR
10 REIGHTON DR

F2
1 MOREHALL CL
2 WHARNSCLIFFE DR
3 RYBURN CL

C7
1 PLOUGHLANDS
2 THE GREENWAY
3 FOXCROFT

C8
1 DEALTRY AVE
2 ARENHALL CL
3 MINSTER CL
4 UPPERCROFT
5 BECKS CL
6 THE CHESTNUTS
7 COPWOOD GR
8 HESLIN CL
9 RUDDINGS CL
10 HUNTERS CL
11 CORNWOOD WY

166

D8
1 MEADOW LN
2 CHERRY ORCHARD
3 ORCHARD PADDOCK
4 CHERRY PADDOCK

226

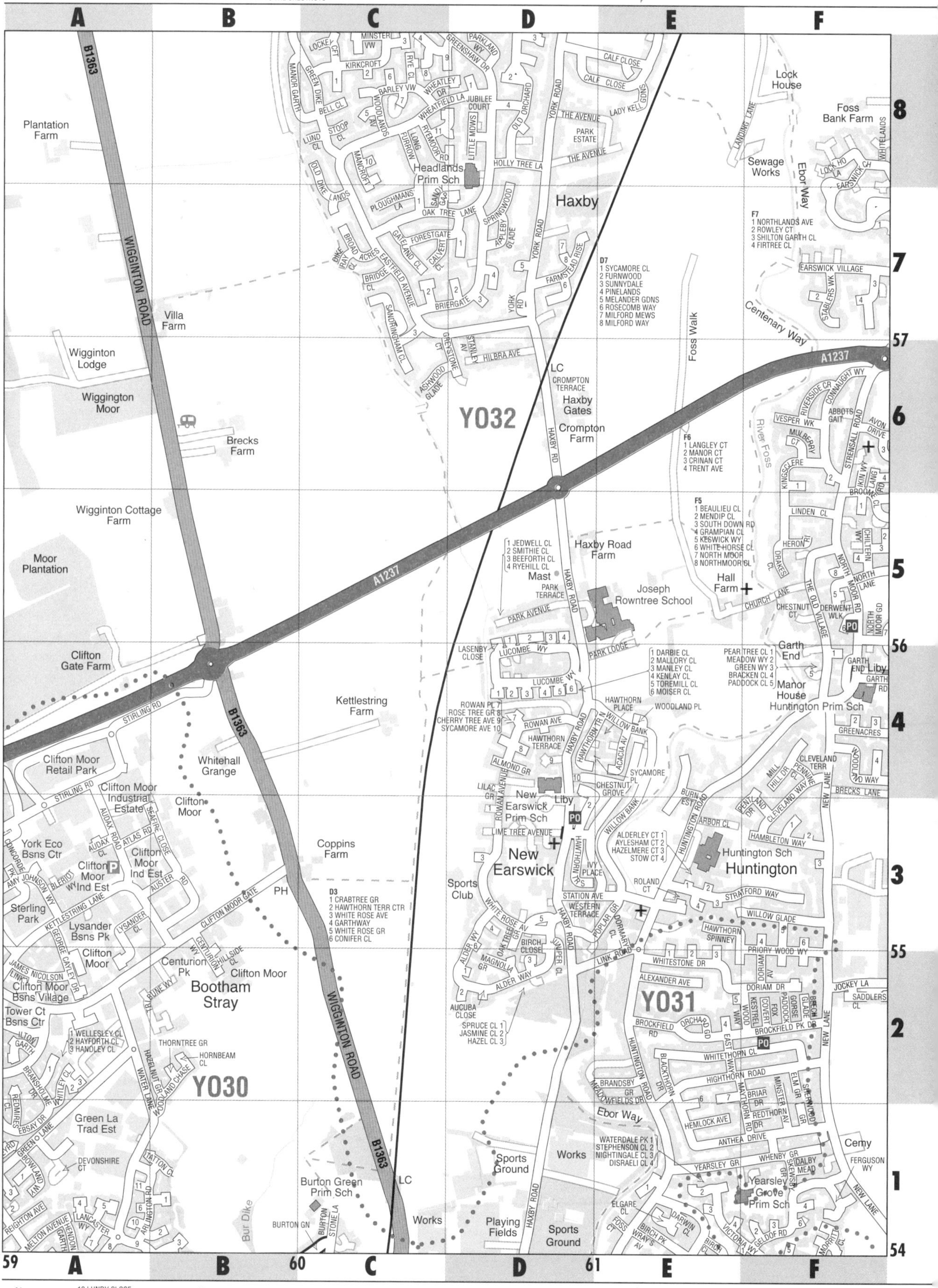

228

A1
1 CALDBECK CL
2 STONELANDS CT
3 BELMONT CL
4 HASTINGS CL
5 HARROW GLADE
6 WIMPOLE CL
7 HALIFAX CT
8 WATER LA
9 TAMWORTH RD
10 LUNDY CLOSE
11 PENTIRE CLOSE

B1
1 HERDWICK CL
2 HEADLEY CL
3 MINCHIN CL

226

E2
1 SCAWTON AVE
2 GORMIRE AVE
3 ROLSTON AVE
4 HEATHER CFT
5 BADGER PADDOCK
6 PINEWOOD GR
7 THORNFIELD DR

F1
1 DICKENS CL
2 HOMESTEAD CL
3 CARRNOCK CT
4 ANDREW DR
5 MONKTON RD
6 THERESA CL

F3
1 CHEVIOT CL
2 CAMBRIAN CL
3 KENDREW CL
4 MERLIN COVERT
5 FIRWOOD WHIN
6 OAK GLADE

225 167 167

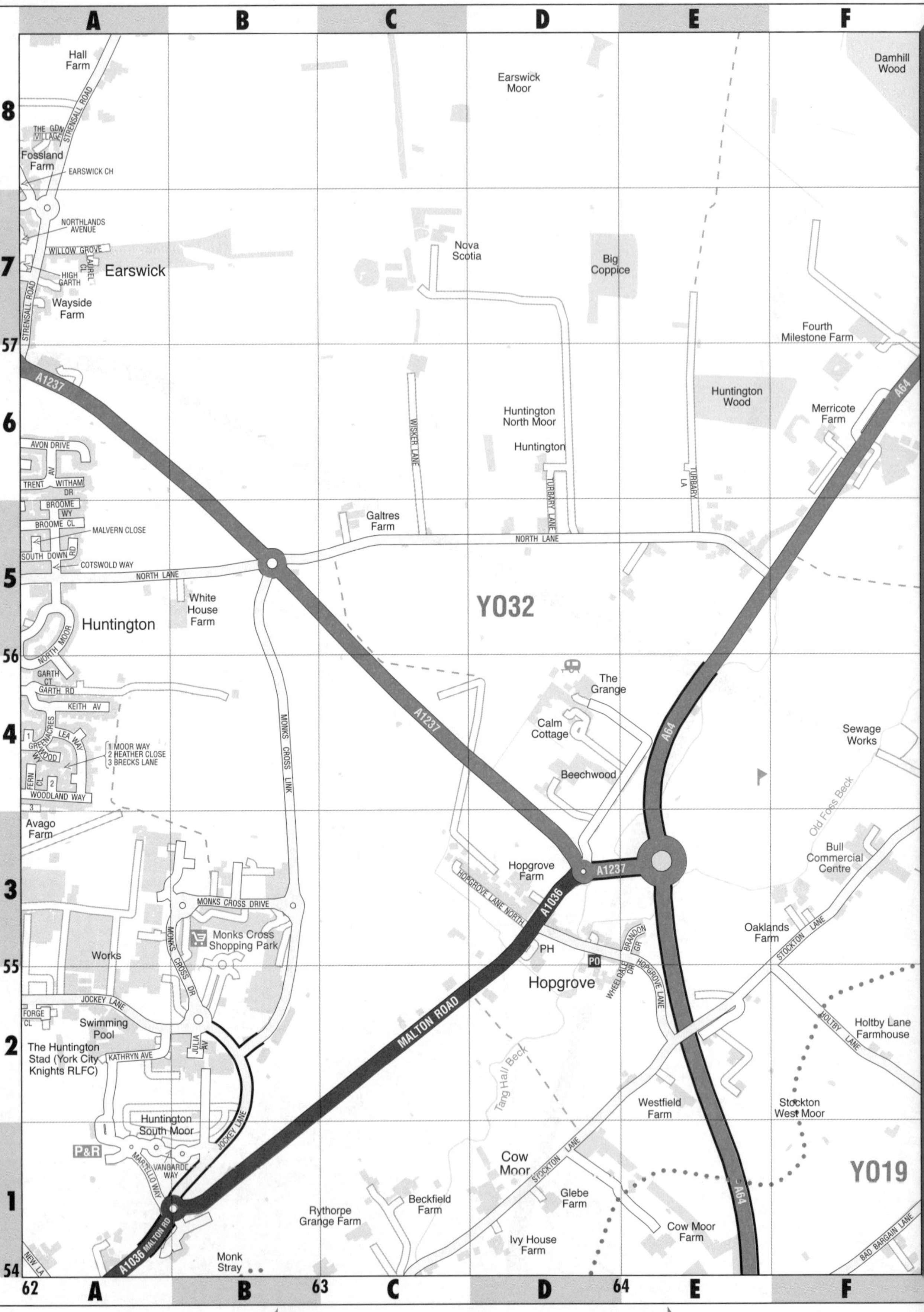

225 229 167

Poppleton Ings
Rawcliffe Ings
Clifton Park
Millfield La Ind Est
Park Side
Works
Manor CE Acad
Acomb Ings
River Ouse
York & Selby Path
YO30
Clifton Park (York CC & York RUFC)
Clifton Without Jun Sch
Clifton Ings
YO26
Lidgett Grove
North Field
Knapton
Golden Farm
Primrose Farm
Tenthorne Farm
Carr Inf Sch
Poppleton Rd Prim Sch
St Barnabas CE VC Prim Sch
Water Tower
Station Bsns Pk
Marquis Court
A59
BOROUGHBRIDGE RD
POPPLETON ROAD
HOLGATE ROAD
B1224
WETHERBY ROAD
YORK RD
ACOMB ROAD
A1237
A19
SHIPTON ROAD
Chapel Fields
Acomb
West Bank Pk
Holgate
Acomb Prim Sch
Melton College
Our Lady Queen of Martyrs RC VA Prim Sch
Birch Copse
Westfield Prim Com Sch
YO23
West Field
Hob Moor Oaks Sch
Hob Moor Prim Sch
YO24
York High Sch
Oaklands Sports Centre
Hob Moor
Edmund Wilson Swimming Pool
Acomb Moor
St Helen's Rehab
TADCASTER RD
A1036
B5
1 SUNNINGDALE CL
2 TROON CL
3 GREENSBOROUGH AVE
4 BIRKDALE GR
5 KENRICK PL
6 MUIRFIELD WAY
B4
1 CARNOUSTIE CL
2 LOCHRIN PL
3 GRESLEY CT
4 STAITHES CL
E5
1 CARRINGTON AVE
2 YARBURGH GR
3 OAK ST
4 AMBERLY ST
5 LINTON ST
6 THOMPSON PL
A3
1 BRIDLE WY
2 HESSAY PL
3 BARKSTON CL
B3
1 CROFTSIDE
2 CROFTWAY
3 HAMMERTON CL
F2
1 HARLOW CL
2 HEATH CL
3 HOLLY BANK GR
4 JENNIFER GR
5 MILDRED GR
6 ANDERSON GR
7 NIGEL GR
8 TREVOR GR
9 TOWTON AVE
10 MOORGARTH AVE
B1
1 ASKHAM CROFT
2 MINTER CL
3 WATERMAN CT
4 SALMOND RD
5 OTTERWOOD BK
6 BEECHWOOD GLADE
7 CEDARWOOD CL
8 APPLE BLOSSOM CT
9 ST JOSEPHS CT
10 ST MICHAELS CT
8
7
53
6
5
52
4
3
51
2
1
50

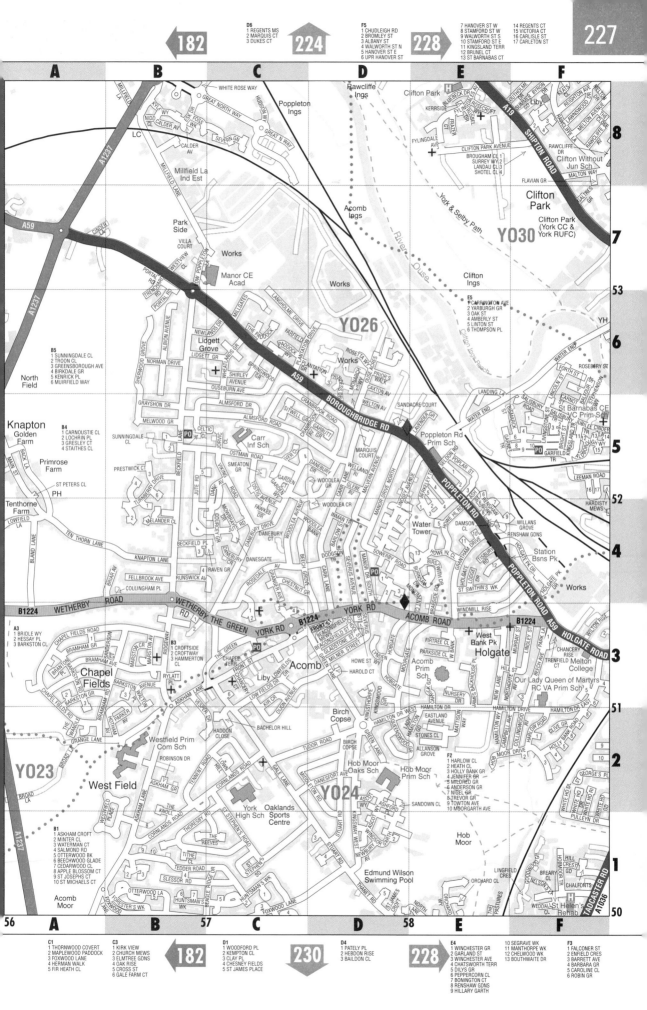

A8
1 LINDEN GROVE
2 MARTEN CLOSE
3 RAINSBOROUGH WAY
4 LOCKYER CL

A7
1 BELCOMBE WAY
2 HUDSON CRESCENT
3 CLIFTON PLACE
4 PINFOLD COURT

227

C7
1 UPR NEWBOROUGH ST
2 ALLAN ST
3 MURROUGH WILSON PL
4 FEVERSHAM CRES
5 HILLSBOROUGH TERR
6 HUDSON ST

225

E8
1 KIRKHAM AVE
2 THE CROSSWAY
3 LILLING AVE
4 PINSENT CT

E5
1 HAWTHORN ST
2 EMMERSON ST
3 FLEMING AVE
4 SCROPE AVE

F8
1 ALBERT CL
2 VICTORIA WY
3 MORRITT CL
4 FOSTON GR
5 THORNFIELD AVE
6 LABURNUM GARTH

For full street detail of the highlighted area see page 233.

A2
1 TOWTON AVE
2 TRENTHOLME DR
3 MOORGARTH AVE
4 WHITE HO GDNS

A3
1 ENFIELD CRES
2 WATSON TERR
3 CECILIA PL
4 CAMBRIDGE ST
5 OXFORD ST
6 MOUNT EPHRAIM
7 HOLGATE BR GDNS
8 St Paul's Nursery Sch

227

B1
1 WINDSOR ST
2 HUBERT ST
3 RUBY ST
4 COUNT DE BURGH TERR
5 BALMORAL TERR
6 LICHFIELD CT

231

B2
1 TELFORD TERR
2 PHILADELPHIA TERR
3 ADELAIDE ST

E3
1 BRINKWORTH TERR
2 THOMAS ST
3 HILDA ST
4 GRANVILLE TERR
5 LANSDOWNE TERR
6 HERBERT ST
7 CHAUCER ST
8 DAYSFOOT CT
9 APOLLO ST
10 THE TANNERY
11 LAWRENCE CT
12 LEAKE ST

F3
1 ST NICHOLAS PL
2 ARNSIDE PL

A5
1 MELROSE CL
2 APPLEBY PL
3 INGLETON WK
4 WOODHOUSE GR
5 HORNBY CT

226
184

A3
1 HEATHFIELD RD
2 OWSTON AVE
3 WAYNEFLEET GR
4 CYCLE ST
5 NORMAN ST

B1
1 ENCLOSURE GDNS
2 HESLINGTON CT
3 HOLBURNS CFT

C3
1 SHALLOWDALE GR
2 BRACKEN HILL
3 KIMBERLOWS WOOD HILL
4 PINEWOOD HILL

C4
1 VICARAGE GDNS
2 ST THOMAS'S CL
3 GIVENDALE GR

184
184

182
227

C8
1 HINTON AVE
2 LYDHAM CT
3 MARTIN CHEESEMAN CT
4 CRANFIELD PL
5 DOHERTHY WLK
6 BURGESS WLK

D8
1 FARMLANDS RD
2 DRINGFIELD CL
3 HERDSMAN RD
4 SANDCROFT CL
5 DEEPDALE

E8
1 TURNMIRE RD
2 SOUTHFIELD CRES
3 MEADOW CT
4 THE PASTURES
5 ST HELEN'S RD
6 RAILWAY VW

F8
1 KENSINGTON CT
2 REGENCY MEWS
3 CALCARIA CT

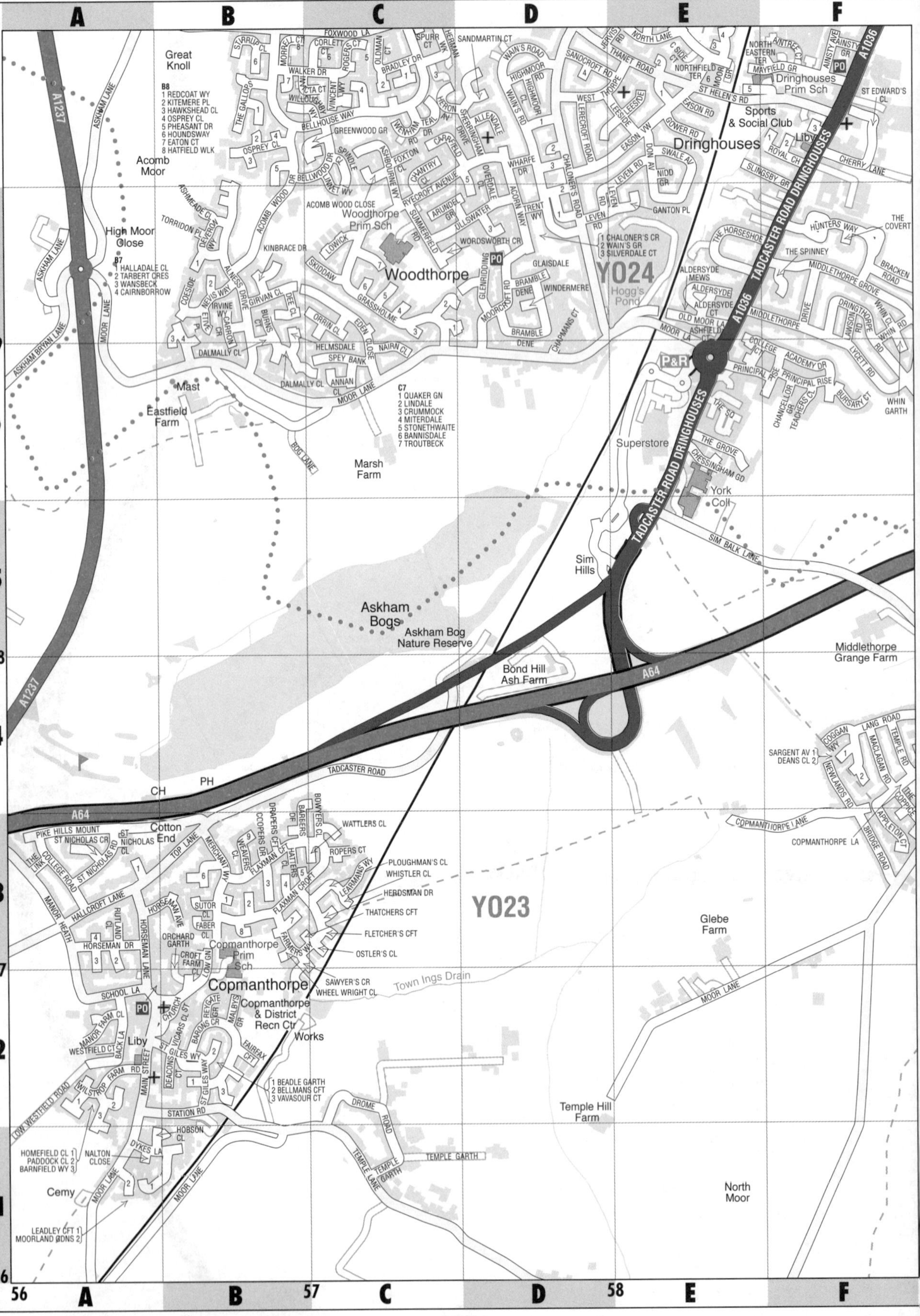
A
B
C
D
E
F
8
7
49
6
5
48
4
3
47
2
1
46
56
57
58
Great Knoll
Acomb Moor
High Moor Close
Mast
Eastfield Farm
Marsh Farm
Woodthorpe
Woodthorpe Prim Sch
Dringhouses
Dringhouses Prim Sch
Sports & Social Club
YO24
Hogg's Pond
Superstore
York Coll
Sim Hills
Askham Bogs
Askham Bog Nature Reserve
Bond Hill Ash Farm
Middlethorpe Grange Farm
YO23
Glebe Farm
Temple Hill Farm
North Moor
Cotton End
Copmanthorpe
Copmanthorpe Prim Sch
Copmanthorpe & District Recn Ctr
Works
Cemy
Town Ings Drain
A1237
A64
A1036
TADCASTER ROAD DRINGHOUSES
TADCASTER ROAD
MOOR LANE
SIM BALK LANE
ASKHAM LANE
ASKHAM BRYAN LANE
COPMANTHORPE LANE
LOW WESTFIELD ROAD
TEMPLE LANE
TEMPLE GARTH
DROME ROAD
B8
1 REDCOAT WY
2 KITEMERE PL
3 HAWKSHEAD CL
4 OSPREY CL
5 PHEASANT DR
6 HOUNDSWAY
7 EATON CT
8 HATFIELD WLK
B7
1 HALLADALE CL
2 TARBERT CRES
3 WANSBECK
4 CAIRNBORROW
C7
1 QUAKER GN
2 LINDALE
3 CRUMMOCK
4 MITERDALE
5 STONETHWAITE
6 BANNISDALE
7 TROUTBECK
1 CHALONER'S CR
2 WAIN'S GR
3 SILVERDALE CT
1 BEADLE GARTH
2 BELLMANS CFT
3 VAVASOUR CT
HOMEFIELD CL 1
PADDOCK CL 2
BARNFIELD WY 3
LEADLEY CFT 1
MOORLAND GDNS 2
SARGENT AV 1
DEANS CL 2

A3
1 LARKFIELD CL
2 HORSEMAN CL
3 LYNWOOD AVE
4 LYNWOOD VW

B3
1 SADDLERS CL
2 FARRIERS CFT
3 WAGGONERS DR
4 POTTERS DR
5 WAINERS CL
6 MILLERS CFT
7 LORINERS DR
8 GARDENERS CL
9 WEAVERS PK

182
191

228
184
D8
1 STOCKHOLM CL
2 DANES CFT
E8
1 ENDFIELDS RD
2 CROSSLANDS RD
3 BROADWAY GR
F8
1 WILSTHORPE GR
2 TILMIRE CL
3 LOW MOOR AVE

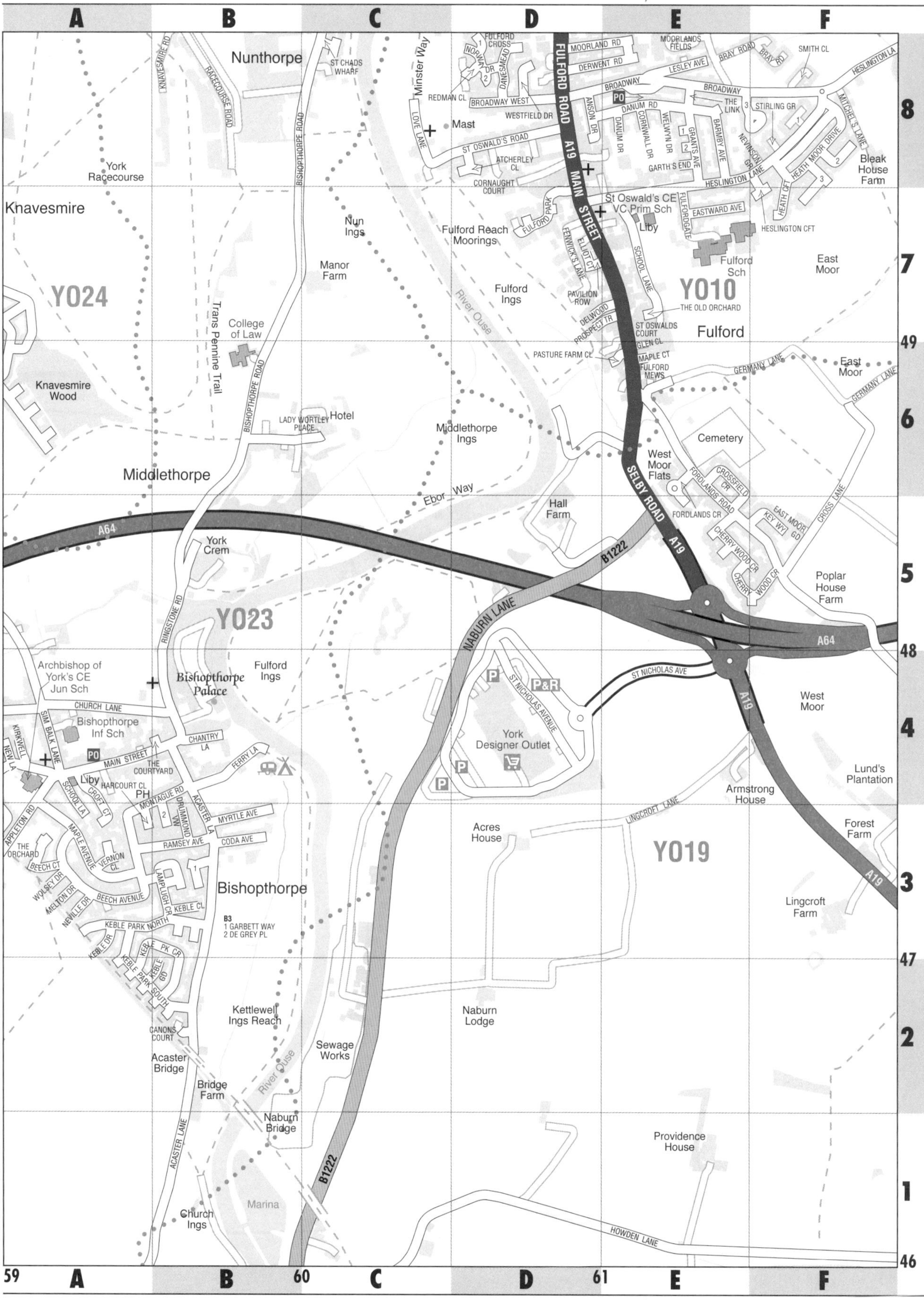

197 197 198 198

C5
1 YORK ST
2 HARPER ST
3 DOUGLAS ST
4 RAINCLIFFE ST
5 LONDESBOROUGH ST
6 HILDA ST
7 PORTHOLME CRES
8 SOUTH PAR
9 TURNERS SQ
10 AUDUS ST
11 MARKET PL
12 NEW CHURCH TERR
13 Market Cross Shop Ctr
14 MARKET LA

D5
1 MICKLEGATE
2 WREN LA
3 CHURCH HL
4 CHURCH LA
5 CORUNNA CT
6 CHURCH AVE
7 GANT WK
8 ABBEY PL

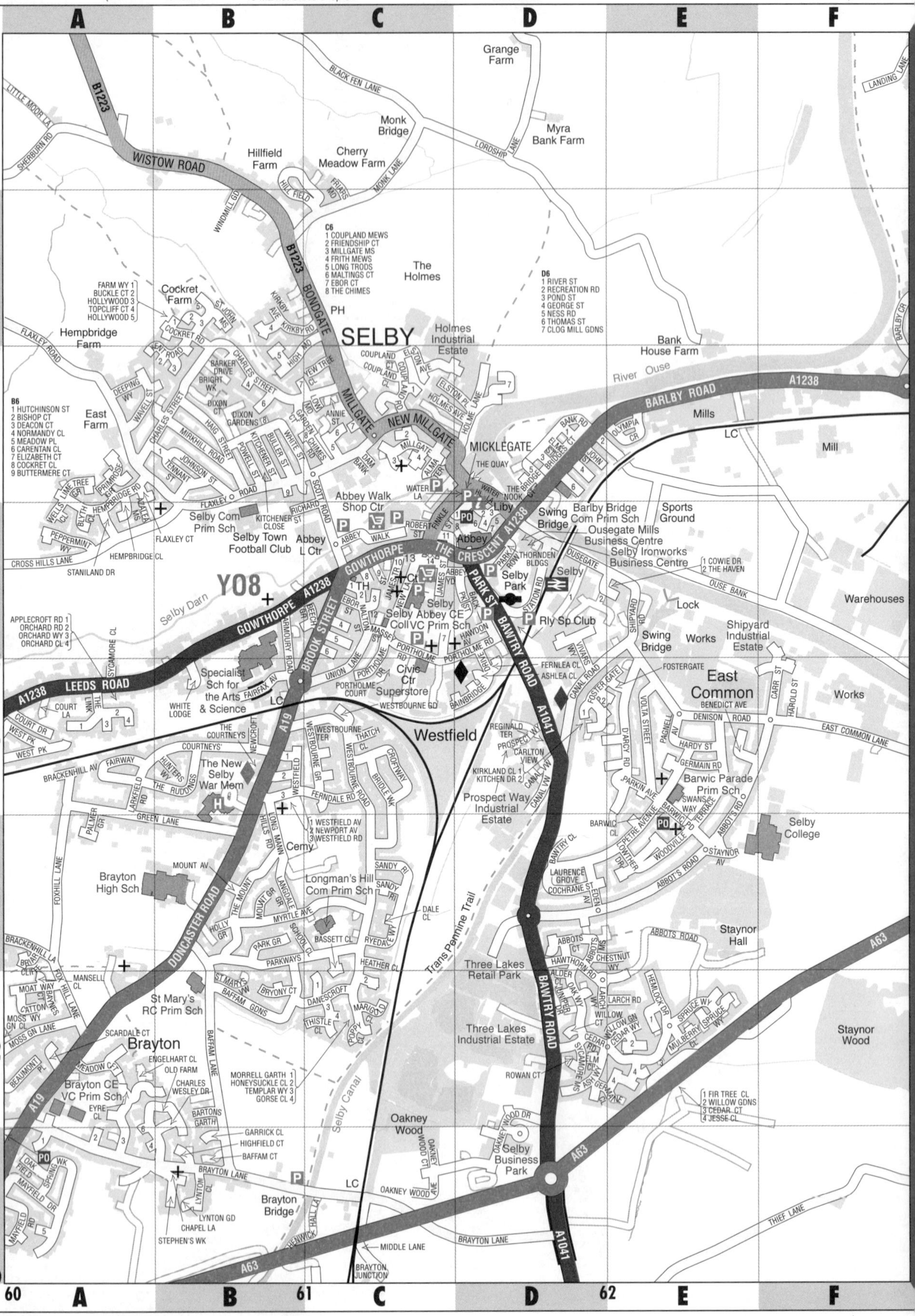

A1
1 MANOR FARM CL
2 HOLMEFIELD CT
3 HOLMEFIELD CL
4 CHILVERS CT
5 MAYFIELD DR
6 MIDDLEBROOK GDNS

197 203 204 198

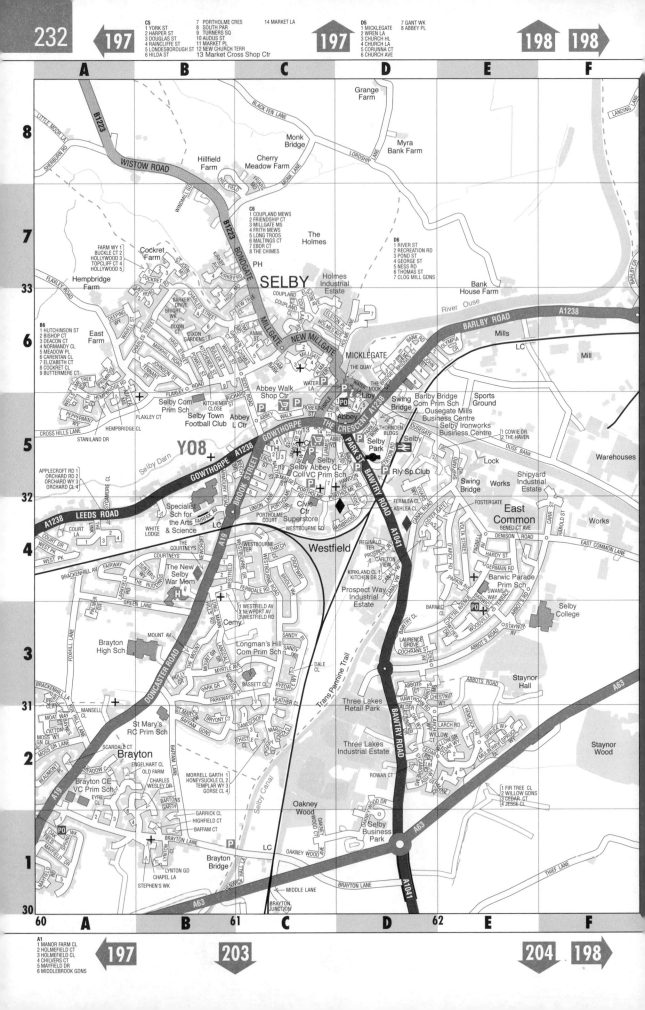

A B C

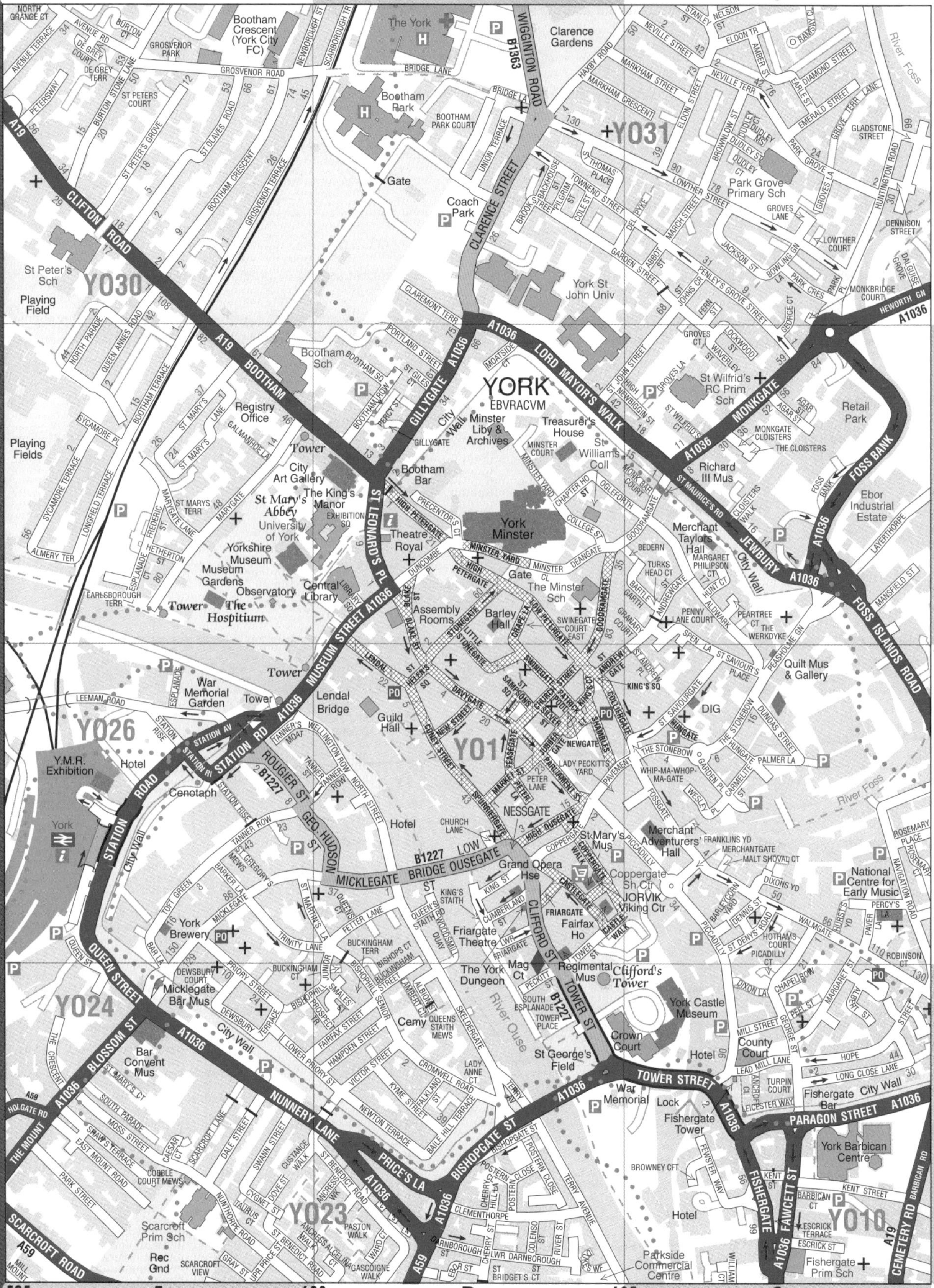

4
525
3
520
2
515
1
510

B1
1 VICTORIA ST
2 DRAKE ST
3 SPENCER ST
4 CLEMENT ST

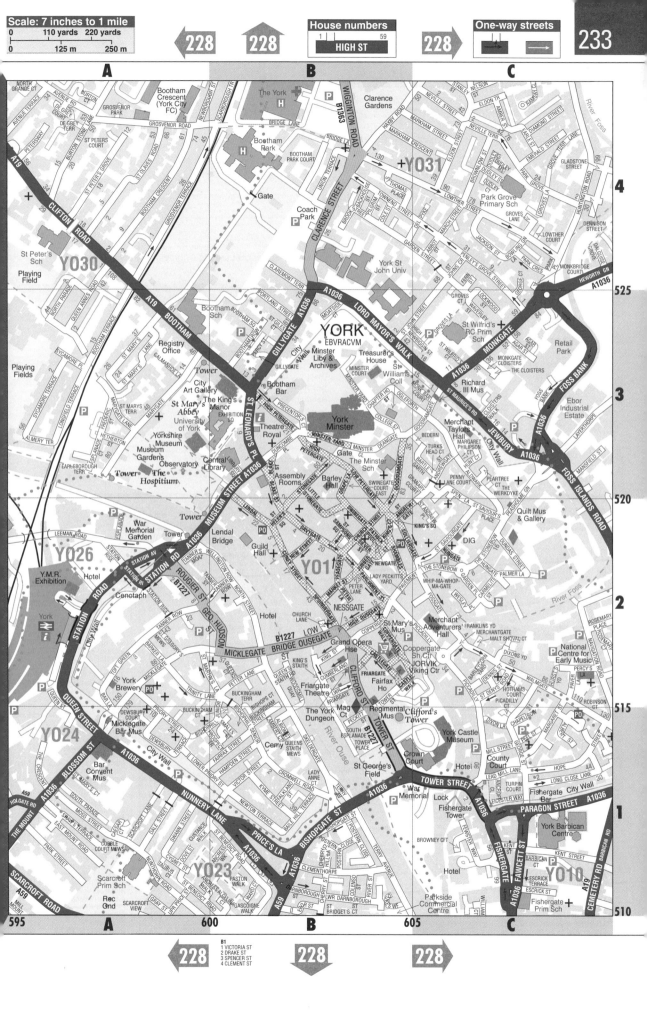

Index

Place name May be abbreviated on the map

Location number Present when a number indicates the place's position in a crowded area of mapping

Locality, town or village Shown when more than one place has the same name

Postcode district District for the indexed place

Page and grid square Page number and grid reference for the standard mapping

Church Rd [6] Beckenham BR2..........**53** C6

Cities, towns and villages are listed in CAPITAL LETTERS

Public and commercial buildings are highlighted in **magenta** **Places of interest** are highlighted in blue with a star★

Abbreviations used in the index

Acad	**Academy**	Comm	**Common**	Gd	**Ground**	L	**Leisure**	Prom	**Promenade**
App	**Approach**	Cott	**Cottage**	Gdn	**Garden**	La	**Lane**	Rd	**Road**
Arc	**Arcade**	Cres	**Crescent**	Gn	**Green**	Liby	**Library**	Recn	**Recreation**
Ave	**Avenue**	Cswy	**Causeway**	Gr	**Grove**	Mdw	**Meadow**	Ret	**Retail**
Bglw	**Bungalow**	Ct	**Court**	H	**Hall**	Meml	**Memorial**	Sh	**Shopping**
Bldg	**Building**	Ctr	**Centre**	Ho	**House**	Mkt	**Market**	Sq	**Square**
Bsns, Bus	**Business**	Ctry	**Country**	Hospl	**Hospital**	Mus	**Museum**	St	**Street**
Bvd	**Boulevard**	Cty	**County**	HQ	**Headquarters**	Orch	**Orchard**	Sta	**Station**
Cath	**Cathedral**	Dr	**Drive**	Hts	**Heights**	Pal	**Palace**	Terr	**Terrace**
Cir	**Circus**	Dro	**Drove**	Ind	**Industrial**	Par	**Parade**	TH	**Town Hall**
Cl	**Close**	Ed	**Education**	Inst	**Institute**	Pas	**Passage**	Univ	**University**
Cnr	**Corner**	Emb	**Embankment**	Int	**International**	Pk	**Park**	Wk, Wlk	**Walk**
Coll	**College**	Est	**Estate**	Intc	**Interchange**	Pl	**Place**	Wr	**Water**
Com	**Community**	Ex	**Exhibition**	Junc	**Junction**	Prec	**Precinct**	Yd	**Yard**

Index of towns, villages, streets, hospitals, industrial estates, railway stations, schools, shopping centres, universities and places of interest

1st–Alb

1st Ave HG2 .... **220** B3
2nd Ave HG2 .... **220** B3
3rd Ave HG2 .... **220** B3
4th Ave HG2 .... **220** B3
5th Ave HG2 .... **220** C3
6th Ave HG2 .... **220** B2

A

Abber La LS24 .... **182** A2
Abbeville Ave [1] YO21 ... **208** B6
Abbey Cl [12] LS29 .... **175** A4
Abbey Crags Way HG5 ... **221** C3
Abbeyfield Dr [10] TS16 ..... **5** D5
Abbey Gdns WF8 .... **201** B2
Abbey Hill BD23 .... **155** C5
Abbey Infants' Sch DL3 ..... **3** B5
Abbey Junior Sch DL3 ..... **3** B5
Abbey La YO22 .... **208** E7
Abbey L Ctr YO8 .... **232** C5
Abbey Mews WF8 .... **201** B2
Abbey Mill Gdns HG5 .... **221** C3
Abbey Mill View HG5 .... **221** C3
Abbey Pl [9] YO8 .... **232** D5
Abbey Rd
Darlington DL3 .... **3** B5
Knaresborough HG5 ..... **221** B3
Sadberge DL2 .... **4** C7
Abbey St YO30 .... **228** A7
Abbeystone Way [12] LS25 **202** A8
Abbey Terr [16] YO21 ..... **208** D7
Abbey Walk Sh Ctr YO8 .. **232** C6
Abbey Wlk
Pontefract WF8 .... **201** B2
Selby YO8 .... **232** C5
Abbey Yd YO8 .... **232** C5
Abbots Ct YO8 .... **232** D3
Abbotsford Ct [7] TS17 ..... **5** F5
Abbotsford Rd YO10 ..... **228** F3
Abbots Gait YO32 .... **225** F6
Abbot's Garth YO12 ...... **99** D6
Abbots Rd YO8 .... **232** E3
Abbot's Rd
Selby YO8 .... **232** E3
Whitby YO22 .... **208** E5
Abbot St YO31 .... **233** C4
Abbotsway YO31 .... **228** E8
Abbots Way HG5 .... **221** C3
Abbot's Wlk YO22 .... **208** E5
Abbotts Cl LS25 .... **194** F8
Abbotts Ct YO17 .... **215** E4
Abbotts Gdns YO8 .... **197** A8
Abbotts Mews YO8 ...... **232** D3
Abel Cl [14] YO51 .... **141** B4
Abelton Gr [33] YO32 ..... **166** E5
Aberbran Ct [41] TS17 .... **5** F4
Aberdeen La [19] YO11 .... **213** A6
Aberdeen Pl [20] YO11 .... **213** A6
Aberdeen Rd DL1 .... **3** E8
Aberdeen St [17] YO11 .... **213** A6
Aberdeen Terr [21] YO11 .. **213** A6
Aberdeen Wlk [16] YO11 .. **213** A6
ABERFORD **194** F7
Aberford CE Prim Sch
LS25 .... **194** F8
Aberford Rd
Barwick in Elmet & Scholes
LS15 .... **194** C8
Bramham cum Oglethorpe
LS23 .... **188** E5
Garforth LS25 .... **194** D4
Abrahams Quay YO22 ... **208** E5
Abram's View YO11 ..... **213** B2
Acacia Ave YO32 .... **225** E4
Acacia Dr WF10 .... **201** B3
Acacia Gr [36] YO32 ...... **166** E5
Academy Dr YO24 .... **230** F6
Academy Gdns DL2 .... **1** D8
Acaster Ave YO23 .... **191** A3
Acaster Dr LS25 .... **194** D3
Acaster La
Acaster Malbis YO23 ..... **231** B1
Acaster Selby YO23 ...... **191** A4
ACASTER MALBIS **191** D8
ACASTER SELBY **191** B4
Accommodation Rd
YO25 .... **151** D6
Acer Cl [4] BD20 .... **187** F7
ACKLAM
Middlesbrough **6** E8
Ryedale **169** E8
Acklam Grange Sch TS5 ... **6** D7
Acklam Rd TS17 .... **6** C8
Acklam Whin Prim Sch TS5 **6** D6
Ackton La WF7 .... **200** D1
Ackton Pasture La WF7 . **200** D2
Ackton Pastures Prim Sch
WF10 .... **200** D3
Ackworth St [3] YO12 .... **212** E4
ACOMB **227** C3
Acomb Prim Sch YO24 .. **227** E3
Acomb Rd YO24 .... **227** D3
Acomb Wood Cl YO24 ... **230** C7
Acomb Wood Dr YO24 ... **230** B7
Acorn Bsns Pk BD23 .... **173** D4
Acorn Cl
[6] Barlby YO8 .... **198** B4
Middleton St George DL2 ... **4** D4
Acorn Way
Gateforth YO8 .... **197** B1
York YO24 .... **230** D7
Acre Fold [21] LS29 .... **174** F4
Acre La [12] BD23 .... **134** E2
Acre Mdw [1] BD22 ...... **187** B6
Acre Rd [2] BD22 .... **187** B6
Acres Cl [24] YO62 .... **92** F6
Acresfield [6] BB8 .... **186** A3
Acres La
Brompton YO13 .... **98** C4
Helmsley YO62 .... **93** A6
Scrayingham YO41 ...... **169** B8
Acres The
Addingham LS29 .... **175** A5
Glusburn BD20 .... **187** E6
Stokesley TS9 .... **26** C8
Adam's Field La YO61 ... **117** F4
Adcott Rd TS5 .... **6** E7
ADDINGHAM **174** F5
Addingham Prim Sch
LS29 .... **174** F5
Addingham Wharfedale Rd
LS29 .... **174** E4
Addison Ave [18] WF6 .... **200** B1
Addison Rd TS9 .... **8** A1
Addison Villas HG3 ...... **219** A8
Addlethorpe La LS22 .... **179** C3
Adelaide Rd
Middlesbrough TS7 .... **7** B6
[6] Norton DN6 .... **206** E2
Adelaide St [3] YO23 ..... **228** B2
Adlington Cl [8] YO32 .... **167** A7
Admirals Ct YO7 .... **211** A2
Admirals' Ct YO7 .... **211** A2
Agar St YO31 .... **233** C3
AGGLETHORPE **60** A1
Agnesgate HG4 .... **214** D5
Agnesing La LA2 .... **128** A7
Agnes Ing La LA2 .... **128** A7
Aikengill Rd LA2 .... **129** A4
Ailcey Rd HG4 .... **214** D5
Ainderby Gdns DL7 ...... **210** C3
AINDERBY QUERNHOW ... **88** C4
Ainderby Rd DL7 .... **210** B2
Ainderby Steepe CE Prim Sch
DL7 .... **64** A7
AINDERBY STEEPLE **64** B7
Ainsford Way TS7 .... **7** D8
Ainstable Rd TS7 .... **7** D8
Ainsty Ave YO24 .... **230** F8
Ainsty Dr [2] LS22 .... **180** C4
Ainsty Garth YO23 ...... **190** E5
Ainsty Gr YO24 .... **230** F8
Ainsty Rd
Harrogate HG1 .... **219** F4
Wetherby LS22 .... **180** C4
Ainsty View
Acklam YO17 .... **169** E8
Whixley YO26 .... **164** A4
Ainsworth Way TS7 .... **7** D8
AINTHORPE **29** C6
Ainthorpe La YO21 .... **29** C7
Aintree Cl LS25 .... **194** C1
Aintree Ct
[9] Darlington DL1 .... **3** F6
York YO24 .... **230** F8
Aire & Calder Ind Pk
WF10 .... **200** E5
Aire Cres BD20 .... **187** E7
AIREDALE **201** B4
Airedale Acad WF10 ..... **201** B4
Airedale Ave
Gargrave BD23 .... **155** D1
Skipton BD23 .... **217** B4
Airedale Bsns Ctr BD23 .. **173** D4
Airedale Dr WF10 .... **201** B5
Airedale Ings BD20 ...... **173** D1
Airedale Mews [1] BD23 . **216** E3
Airedale Rd
Castleford WF10 .... **201** A4
Scotton DL9 .... **40** D4
Airedale Terr BD23 ...... **216** E3
Airedale Trading Pk
BD20 .... **187** F8
Airedale View [1] BD20 .. **187** F8
Aire Rd LS22 .... **180** B4
Aireside Ave BD20 ...... **173** D1
Aireside Terr BD20 ...... **173** D2
Aire St
Castleford WF10 .... **200** E4
Glusburn BD20 .... **187** F7
[12] Knottingley WF11 ...... **202** A3
Knottingley WF11 .... **202** A3
Aire Valley Cl BD20 ..... **173** D3
Aire Valley Dr BD20 ..... **173** D3
Aire Valley Mount WF10 . **201** A4
AIRE VIEW **173** D1
Aire View BD23 .... **216** C1
Aire View Infants Sch [13]
BD20 .... **174** C1
Aireville Dr BD20 .... **174** C1
Aireville Grange BD23 ... **216** D5
Aireyholme La TS9 .... **8** B2
Airfield Ind Est YO41 .... **184** F3
AIRMYN **205** E4
Airmyn Ave [5] DN14 ..... **205** F3
Airmyn Park Prim Sch
DN14 .... **205** E4
Airmyn Rd DN14 .... **205** D3
AIRTON **155** A6
AIRY HILL **208** D4
Airy Hill YO21 .... **208** D5
Airy Hill La TS12 .... **9** D8
AISKEW **63** A3
Aislabie Cl HG4 .... **214** A5
Aislabie Garth HG4 ...... **214** A5
AISLABY
Egglescliffe **5** C3
Pickering **95** D8
Whitby **31** F7
Aislaby Carr La YO18 ..... **95** C7
Aislaby La
Aislaby YO18 .... **95** C6
Aislaby YO21 .... **32** A8
Aislaby Rd TS16 .... **5** D4
Aismunderby Cl HG4 .... **214** C3
Aismunderby Rd HG4 ... **214** C4
Aisne Rd DL9 .... **209** C1
Aketon Cft [24] WF10 ..... **200** D3
Aketon Rd WF10 .... **200** D3
Alanbrooke Ind Est YO7 . **115** B8
Alanbrooke Sch YO7 ...... **89** A1
Alandale Cres LS25 ..... **194** B3
Alandale Rd LS25 .... **194** B4
Alan Farnaby Way YO60 . **145** C4
Albany Ave HG1 .... **219** E5
Albany Rd
Harrogate HG1 .... **219** E5
Middlesbrough TS7 .... **7** B6
Albany St [3] YO26 .... **227** F5
Albany Wlk LS29 .... **218** A3
Albatross Way DL1 .... **3** E5
Albemarle Back Rd [10]
YO11 .... **212** F6
Albemarle Cres [18] YO11 . **213** A6
Albemarle Rd YO23 ..... **228** B2
Albermarle Dr [3] DL9 .... **40** F5
Albert Cl [1] YO32 .... **228** F8
Albert Hill BD24 .... **131** E2
Albert Pl
Harrogate HG1 .... **220** C4

Albert Pl *continued*
1 Whitby YO21 . . . 208 D7
Albert Rd
Eaglescliffe TS16 . . . 5 E5
12 Glusburn BD20 . . . 187 E7
Harrogate HG1 . . . 219 E5
1 Scarborough YO12 . . . 213 A7
Albert Simmons Way St 44 LS29 . . . 176 C1
Albert Sq BD23 . . . 216 F4
Albert St
Airmyn DN14 . . . 205 F1
Darlington DL1 . . . 3 D6
33 Earby BB18 . . . 172 A1
Glusburn BD20 . . . 187 F7
Harrogate HG1 . . . 219 D2
Normanton South WF6 . . . 200 B2
8 Scarborough YO12 . . . 213 A7
York YO10 . . . 233 C1
Albert Terr
5 Harrogate HG1 . . . 219 D1
Skipton BD23 . . . 216 F4
Albion Ave YO26 . . . 227 B6
Albion Cres 3 YO11 . . . 213 A4
Albion Pl 14 YO21 . . . 208 D6
Albion Rd
25 Earby BB18 . . . 172 A1
Scarborough YO11 . . . 213 A4
Albion St
Boosbeck TS12 . . . 9 E7
Boston Spa LS23 . . . 188 E7
Castleford WF10 . . . 200 E4
28 Earby BB18 . . . 172 A1
York YO1 . . . 233 B1
Albion Terr
9 Boston Spa LS23 . . . 188 E7
23 Whitby YO21 . . . 208 D6
Alcelina Ct YO23 . . . 233 B1
Alcuin Ave YO10 . . . 229 A4
Alcuin Way YO10 . . . 229 B2
ALDBOROUGH . . . 141 C5
Aldborough Gate 13 YO51 . . . 141 B4
Aldborough Roman Town & Mus* YO51 . . . 141 C5
Aldborough Way YO26 . . . 227 F5
ALDBROUGH ST JOHN . . . 2 A2
Aldenham Rd TS14 . . . 8 E5
Alder Ave HG5 . . . 221 E5
Alder Carr La YO18 . . . 49 E2
Alder Cl
8 Leeming DL7 . . . 63 F3
Selby YO8 . . . 232 D2
Alder Ct 25 YO18 . . . 95 F6
Alder Hill St 1 BB18 . . . 172 B1
Alderley Ct YO32 . . . 225 E3
Alderman Best Rd DL1 . . . 4 A4
Alderman Leach Dr 13 DL2 3 A7
Alder Rd HG1 . . . 219 F5
Aldersley Ave BD23 . . . 217 B3
Alderson Cres YO12 . . . 99 E7
Alderson Rd HG2 . . . 222 E8
Alderson Sq HG2 . . . 222 E8
Alders Rd YO18 . . . 49 C4
Aldersyde YO24 . . . 230 E7
Aldersyde Ct YO24 . . . 230 E7
Aldersyde Mews YO24 . . . 230 E7
Alder Way YO32 . . . 225 D2
ALDFIELD . . . 139 A8
Aldreth Gr YO23 . . . 228 C2
Aldridge Rd TS3 . . . 7 B8
ALDWARK . . . 142 C2
Aldwark YO1 . . . 233 C3
Aldwych Cl TS6 . . . 7 E8
Alec Hare Cl YO17 . . . 215 E4
Alexander Ave
6 East Ayton/West Ayton YO13 . . . 99 B8
York YO31 . . . 225 E2
Alexander Cl YO7 . . . 211 C4
Alexander Rd DL9 . . . 209 C2
Alexandra Cres 10 LS29 . . . 218 A4
Alexandra Ct
Skipton BD23 . . . 216 F2
York YO10 . . . 228 E4
Alexandra Gr HG5 . . . 221 B7
Alexandra Park Rd HG5 . . . 221 C7
Alexandra Pk YO12 . . . 212 D5
Alexandra Pl
Ilkley LS29 . . . 218 A4
3 Knaresborough HG5 . . . 221 B8
Alexandra Rd
Harrogate HG1 . . . 219 D3
Strensall YO32 . . . 167 A6
Alexandra Terr BD23 . . . 216 F2
Alexandra Ville BD23 . . . 216 F2
Alexandra Way DL10 . . . 209 C7
Alexandria Dr DL2 . . . 4 D4
Alfreda Terr 1 YO22 . . . 208 E6
Algarth Rd YO31 . . . 229 B7
Algarth Rise YO31 . . . 229 B7
Alga Terr YO11 . . . 213 A4
Allans Ct DL10 . . . 209 B6
Allanson Gr YO24 . . . 227 E2
Allan St
Darlington DL1 . . . 3 D6
2 York YO30 . . . 228 C7
Allenby Rd
20 Helmsley YO62 . . . 92 F6
Hipswell DL9 . . . 209 C1
Allen Cl YO10 . . . 229 A4
Allendale YO24 . . . 230 D8
Allendale Rd
Middlesbrough TS7 . . . 7 D8
Thirsk YO7 . . . 211 D3
Allen Gr TS9 . . . 26 B7
Allensway TS17 . . . 6 C7
Allens West Sta TS16 . . . 5 D5
Allerdale Cl YO7 . . . 211 C4
ALLERSTON . . . 97 C5
Allerston La YO18 . . . 97 C4
Allerston Way 5 TS14 . . . 8 F7
Allerton Balk TS15 . . . 5 D2
ALLERTON BYWATER . . . 200 D6
Allerton Bywater Bsns Pk WF10 . . . 200 E6
Allerton Bywater Prim Sch WF10 . . . 200 D7
Allerton Castle* HG5 . . . 163 D4
Allerton Cl DL7 . . . 210 C4
Allerton Dr 22 YO26 . . . 165 F1
Allerton La HG5 . . . 163 D4
ALLERTON MAULEVERER . . . 163 E4
Allerton Mews HG1 . . . 219 E1
Allertonshire Sch DL6 . . . 210 D6
Allerton Wath Rd YO7 . . . 65 D4
Allhallowgate HG4 . . . 214 C5
Alliance Ind Est DL1 . . . 3 E6
Allington Dr YO31 . . . 229 B6
Allington Way
Darlington DL1 . . . 3 F5
Great Burdon DL1 . . . 4 A5
Allison Ave TS17 . . . 6 B4
Allison St TS14 . . . 8 E6
Allotment Gdns HG1 . . . 220 C5
Alloway Gr TS8 . . . 6 F5
All Saints Acad TS17 . . . 6 A4
All Saints CE Junior & Infants Sch WF7 . . . 200 E1
All Saints CE Prim Sch 12 LS29 . . . 218 A4
All Saints CE Sch HG3 . . . 179 A4
All Saints Cl YO51 . . . 141 B7
All Saints RC Prim Sch YO7 . . . 211 B2
All Saints RC Sch YO29 . . . 228 B2
All Saints Rd 1 YO12 . . . 212 F4
All Saints Sq HG4 . . . 214 D5
Alma Gdns HG4 . . . 214 D4
Alma Gr YO10 . . . 228 D2
Alma Par 2 YO11 . . . 212 F5
Alma Pl DL10 . . . 209 C7
Alma Rd BB8 . . . 186 B3
Alma Sq 3 YO11 . . . 212 F5
Alma Terr
Selby YO8 . . . 232 C6
3 Skipton BD23 . . . 217 A4
York YO10 . . . 228 D2
Alma Way 2 YO18 . . . 96 A6
Almery Terr YO30 . . . 233 A3
Almond Cl
7 Filey YO14 . . . 101 B4
Hambleton YO8 . . . 197 B1
Almond Ct 4 TS4 . . . 6 F8
Almond Gr
11 Filey YO14 . . . 101 B4
Northallerton DL7 . . . 210 D3
Scarborough YO12 . . . 212 D5
York YO32 . . . 225 D4
Almond Tree Ave
4 Carlton DN14 . . . 204 C3
Malton YO17 . . . 215 D6
Almscliffe Dr LS17 . . . 178 B2
Almscliffe Garth LS17 . . . 178 B4
Almsford Ave HG2 . . . 222 E6
Almsford Bank HG2 . . . 222 E5
Almsford Cl HG2 . . . 222 F6
Almsford Dr
Harrogate HG2 . . . 222 F6
York YO26 . . . 227 C5
Almsford End HG2 . . . 222 E6
Almsford Oval HG2 . . . 222 F6
Almsford Pl HG2 . . . 222 E6
Almsford Rd
Harrogate HG2 . . . 222 F6
York YO26 . . . 227 C5
Almsford Wlk HG2 . . . 222 F6
Almshouse Hill 1 LS23 . . . 188 E5
ALNE . . . 142 F4
Alne Prim Sch YO61 . . . 142 F4
Alne Rd
Easingwold YO61 . . . 143 B8
Tollerton YO61 . . . 143 A3
Alness Dr YO24 . . . 230 B7
ALNE STATION . . . 143 A5
Alne Terr YO10 . . . 228 E2
Alpine Ct 5 WF10 . . . 200 F3
Altofts La WF10 . . . 200 B3
Altofts Rd WF6 . . . 200 A1
Alum House La TS9 . . . 26 B2
Alverton Cl YO17 . . . 121 B7
Alverton Dr DL3 . . . 3 B8
Alverton La DL7 . . . 210 D4
Alverton Prim Sch DL6 . . . 210 F6
Alvin Wlk 9 YO41 . . . 185 B2
Alvis Gr YO10 . . . 229 D4
Alwyne Dr YO30 . . . 224 E1
Alwyne Gr YO30 . . . 224 E1
Alwyn Rd DL3 . . . 3 D8
Amber Ct YO31 . . . 233 C4
Amberly St 4 YO26 . . . 227 E5
Amber St YO31 . . . 233 C4
Amble Cl YO62 . . . 70 B2
Ambler Ct 23 WF6 . . . 200 A1
Ambler's La YO30 . . . 165 F7
Ambler St WF10 . . . 200 E4
Ambleside Ave
10 Barnoldswick BB18 . . . 171 D2
York YO10 . . . 229 B4
Ambleside Gr TS5 . . . 6 E8
Ambleside Wlk DL1 . . . 3 D4
Ambrey Cl 16 YO14 . . . 126 F8
Ambrose Rd HG4 . . . 214 C4
Ambrose St YO10 . . . 228 D1
America La BD20 . . . 187 F4
Amesbury Cres TS8 . . . 6 F5
Amiens Cres DL9 . . . 209 D1
AMOTHERBY . . . 121 B4
Amotherby Com Prim Sch YO17 . . . 121 A4
Amotherby La YO17 . . . 121 A6
Amplecarr YO61 . . . 117 B5
AMPLEFORTH . . . 92 C1
Ampleforth Coll YO62 . . . 92 D1
Amy Busfield Gn 40 LS29 176 C1
Amy Johnson Way YO30 . . . 225 A3
Anchorage Hill DL10 . . . 209 D7
Anchorage La DL7 . . . 210 C5
Anchorage Way YO21 . . . 208 C5
Anchorite La 7 YO18 . . . 95 F7
Anchor Rd 2 HG1 . . . 220 A3
Ancress Wlk YO23 . . . 233 A1
Ancroft Cl YO1 . . . 233 C1
Anderson Gr 6 YO24 . . . 227 F2
Anderson St 6 WF8 . . . 201 B1
Anderton St 18 BD20 . . . 187 E8
Andrew Dr 4 YO32 . . . 225 F1
Andrew La YO18 . . . 71 B4
Anfield Ct 8 DL1 . . . 3 F6
Angel Ct 8 TS9 . . . 26 C7
Angel Gdns HG5 . . . 221 C7
Angelica Cl 12 HG3 . . . 161 B3
Angel Yd 1 YO21 . . . 208 D6
ANGRAM
Keld . . . 35 E6
York . . . 182 C3
Angram Cl YO30 . . . 224 F1
Angram La
Barlby with Osgodby YO8 . 198 A6
Muker DL11 . . . 35 E6
Tollerton YO61 . . . 143 B3
Angram Rd YO26 . . . 182 A5
Angrove Cl TS9 . . . 7 F1
Angrove Dr TS9 . . . 7 F1
Annan Cl YO24 . . . 230 C6
Annandale Ct 8 LS29 . . . 218 B2
Annandale Gr 1 YO13 . . . 75 D5
Annas Garth DL8 . . . 60 F4
Annas Garth Cl DL8 . . . 60 F4
Anne St YO23 . . . 228 C2
Annie St YO8 . . . 232 C6
Annumhills Rd YO8 . . . 199 D7
Anserdale La YO62 . . . 70 E5
Anson Croft 5 YO8 . . . 196 E1
Anson Dr YO10 . . . 231 D8
Anson Gr YO8 . . . 191 B1
Anstruther Dr DL1 . . . 3 D8
Anteforth View DL10 . . . 20 E3
Anthea Dr YO31 . . . 225 E1
Anthony La HG4 . . . 114 E1
Anvil Sq 3 DL11 . . . 38 B6
Anvil Way DL7 . . . 22 C2
Anzio Rd DL9 . . . 209 C1
Apedale Rd
Castle Bolton with East & West Bolton DL8 . . . 37 F1
Redmire DL8 . . . 59 C8
Apley Cl HG2 . . . 220 A1
Apollo St 9 YO10 . . . 228 E3
APPERSETT . . . 56 C5
Apple Blossom Ct 8 YO24 . . . 227 B1
Appleby Ave HG5 . . . 220 D8
Appleby Cres HG5 . . . 220 D8
Appleby Ct HG5 . . . 220 D8
Appleby Gate HG5 . . . 220 D7
Appleby Glade YO32 . . . 225 D7
Appleby Gn HG5 . . . 220 D8
Appleby Gr HG5 . . . 220 D8
Appleby La
Aldbrough DL11 . . . 1 F1
Kirkby Malzeard HG4 . . . 112 B4
Appleby Pl 2 YO31 . . . 229 A5
Appleby Way HG5 . . . 220 D7
Appleby Wlk HG5 . . . 220 D8
Applecroft Rd
Selby YO8 . . . 232 A4
York YO31 . . . 229 B7
Applefields Sch YO31 . . . 229 B5
Applegarth
Barnoldswick BB18 . . . 171 E2
Coulby Newham TS8 . . . 7 A4
Apple Garth
10 Easingwold YO61 . . . 117 D1
15 Poppleton YO26 . . . 165 F1
Applegarth Ct DL7 . . . 210 D5
Applegarth Prim Sch DL7 . . . 210 D4
Applegarth St 15 BB18 . . . 172 A1
Appleshaw Cl HG5 . . . 221 C6
Appleton Cl 13 TS14 . . . 8 F7
Appleton Ct YO23 . . . 230 F3
Appleton La
Appleton-le-Street with Easthorpe YO17 . . . 120 F4
Coneysthorpe YO60 . . . 120 E2
APPLETON-LE-MOORS . . . 70 F2
APPLETON-LE-STREET . . . 120 F4
Appleton Rd YO23 . . . 231 A3
APPLETON ROEBUCK . . . 190 F5
Appleton Roebuck Prim Sch 1 YO23 . . . 190 F5
APPLETON WISKE . . . 24 B3
Appleton Wiske Com Prim Sch DL6 . . . 24 B3
Appletree Dr YO8 . . . 196 E1
Appletree Gdns 2 TS7 . . . 7 D8
Apple Tree Gdns 2 LS29 175 C2
Apple Tree La
Great Preston LS25 . . . 200 D8
4 Kippax LS25 . . . 194 D1
Apple Tree Mews 5 LS25 . . . 194 D1
Appletree Way
Malton YO17 . . . 215 B4
10 Sherburn in Elmet LS25 195 F4
APPLETREEWICK . . . 157 D7
Appletreewick Stone Circ* BD23 . . . 135 E2
Apple Tree Wlk 7 LS25 . . . 194 D1
Appley Cl TS16 . . . 5 E7
Apron La HG3 . . . 140 B2
Apsley Way 6 TS17 . . . 5 F5
Arbor Cl YO32 . . . 225 E3
Arbour The
4 Glusburn BD20 . . . 173 E1
Ilkley LS29 . . . 218 A6
Arbour Way YO17 . . . 215 E4
Arcade Sh Ctr* HG4 . . . 214 C5
Arcade The LS29 . . . 218 B4
Archaeology Store* YO62 92 F6
Archbishop Holgate's Sch YO10 . . . 229 B3
Archbishop of York's CE Jun Sch YO23 . . . 231 A4
ARCHDEACON NEWTON . . . 2 F7
Archer La HG3 . . . 140 B3
Archer Rd DL2 . . . 4 D3
Archers Green The DL10 . . 41 C7
Archers Mdw HG5 . . . 221 F5
Archie St 3 HG1 . . . 219 C5
Archway La 13 YO18 . . . 96 D5
Archways Comm Intermediate Care Inpatient Facility YO31 . . . 228 C7
Arden Ct DL7 . . . 210 D5
Arden La YO62 . . . 92 B8
Arden Mews DL7 . . . 210 D5
Arena View 11 DL10 . . . 41 D5
Arenhall Cl 2 YO32 . . . 225 C8
Arennig Ct 43 TS17 . . . 5 F4
Argam Dikes* YO25 . . . 127 B2
Argam La YO25 . . . 126 F1
Argill DL8 . . . 60 F5
Argyle Rd YO21 . . . 208 C7
Argyle St YO23 . . . 228 B1
ARKENDALE . . . 163 B8
Arkendale La HG5 . . . 141 A2
Arkendale Rd HG5 . . . 162 F8
Arkengarthdale CE Prim Sch DL11 . . . 17 D1
Arkengarthdale Rd DL11 . . 38 B7
Arkle Cres DL1 . . . 3 C3
Arlington Rd
Middlesbrough TS5 . . . 6 F8
York YO30 . . . 225 A1
Armoury Rd YO8 . . . 232 B5
Armstrong Cl 7 WF6 . . . 200 A2
Armstrong Way YO32 . . . 224 E3
Army Foundation Coll HG3 . . . 161 A2
ARNCLIFFE . . . 107 D2
Arncliffe Dr WF11 . . . 201 D2
Arncliffe Gr DL3 . . . 2 F5
Arncliffe Rd HG2 . . . 220 A1
Arndale Way 8 YO14 . . . 101 B4
Arnold Rd DL1 . . . 3 E6
Arnside Cres WF10 . . . 201 B4
Arnside Pl 2 YO10 . . . 228 F3
Arran Cl 1 TS17 . . . 6 B6
Arran Ct LS25 . . . 194 C3
Arran Dr LS25 . . . 194 C3
Arran Pl YO31 . . . 228 D7
ARRATHORNE . . . 62 A8
Arrathorne Rd 10 TS18 . . . 5 D8
Arrows Cres 10 YO51 . . . 141 B5
Arrows Terr 9 YO51 . . . 141 B5
Arthington Ave HG1 . . . 219 E2
Arthur Pl 6 YO30 . . . 224 B5
Arthurs Ave HG2 . . . 222 C7
Arthurs Cl HG2 . . . 222 C7
Arthurs Gr HG2 . . . 222 C7
Arthur St
6 Barnoldswick BB18 . . . 171 D2
Earby BB18 . . . 186 A8
Great Ayton TS9 . . . 8 A2
York YO10 . . . 228 E4
Arts Ctr The* YO22 . . . 208 E7
Arundel Ct 1 TS17 . . . 5 F5
Arundel Gr YO24 . . . 230 C7
Arundel Pl
12 Scarborough YO11 . . . 212 F5
9 Whitby YO21 . . . 208 C6
Arundel Rd 5 DN6 . . . 206 E2
Ascot Ave 6 DL9 . . . 40 F4
Ascot Cl DL6 . . . 210 D3
Ascot Rd
Kippax LS25 . . . 194 C1
Wigginton YO32 . . . 166 D5
Ascot Way YO24 . . . 227 D1
Ascough Wynd DL8 . . . 63 D3
ASENBY . . . 115 B6
Ash Bank Ave 2 HG4 . . . 113 D2
Ash Bank Cl 1 HG4 . . . 113 D2
Ashbank La
Firby DL8 . . . 62 F1
Sheriff Hutton YO60 . . . 145 F6
Ash Bank Rd HG4 . . . 113 D2
Ashbourne Cl 12 YO51 . . . 141 B4
Ashbourne Rd 10 YO51 . . . 141 B4
Ashbourne Way YO24 . . . 230 C8
Ashbrook Ct DL10 . . . 20 E3
Ashburnham Cl 4 DN6 . . 206 F2
Ashburnham Wlk 5 DN6 206 F2
Ashburn Pl LS29 . . . 218 A3
Ashburn Rise 10 YO11 . . . 212 E4
Ashburn Way LS22 . . . 180 B4
Ash Cl
1 Ilkley LS29 . . . 175 C2
Newton on Derwent YO41 . 185 E4
9 North Duffield YO8 . . . 199 A7
Ash Cl *continued*
York YO31 . . . 229 B7
Ash Croft 6 DL10 . . . 41 D5
Ashdale Cl DL2 . . . 4 E4
Ashdale La LS22 . . . 180 B4
Ashdale Rd
19 Dunnington YO19 . . . 184 F7
Helmsley YO62 . . . 92 F6
Ashdene Gr WF8 . . . 201 D2
Ashdowne Cl DL8 . . . 62 E5
Ashdowne Ct DL8 . . . 62 E5
Ashdown Rise YO13 . . . 75 C8
Ashes The
Barton DL10 . . . 21 C7
Hellifield BD23 . . . 154 A3
Ashfield LS22 . . . 180 C3
Ashfield Ave YO17 . . . 215 D5
Ashfield Cl
9 Constable Burton DL8 . . 61 C5
9 Pateley Bridge HG3 . . . 137 B4
Ashfield Court Rd 10 HG3 . . . 137 B4
Ashfield Cres BD23 . . . 216 F2
Ashfield Ct YO24 . . . 230 E7
Ashfield Prim Sch LS21 . 176 F1
Ashfield Rd
Danby YO21 . . . 29 B6
Harrogate HG1 . . . 219 E4
6 Pickering YO18 . . . 96 A6
Ashfield St WF6 . . . 200 A2
Ashfield Terr
Harrogate HG1 . . . 219 E4
Skipton BD23 . . . 216 F2
Ashford Ave TS5 . . . 6 D8
Ashford Pl YO24 . . . 227 D2
Ashgap La WF6 . . . 200 A2
Ashgarth Ct HG2 . . . 222 C5
Ashgarth Way HG2 . . . 222 C5
Ash Gn TS8 . . . 7 A4
Ash Gr
13 Barnoldswick BB18 . . . 171 D1
Danby YO21 . . . 29 A6
12 Filey YO14 . . . 101 B4
Glusburn BD20 . . . 187 E7
Ilkley LS29 . . . 218 C5
7 Kirkbymoorside YO62 . . . 70 B1
1 Kirklevington TS15 . . . 24 E8
Northallerton DL6 . . . 210 F5
1 Riccall YO19 . . . 197 F8
Ripon HG4 . . . 214 A6
Scarborough YO12 . . . 212 C7
Whitby YO21 . . . 208 B6
Ashgrove BD23 . . . 216 E4
Ashgrove Cres LS25 . . . 194 D2
Ash Hill TS8 . . . 7 B5
Ash La
Church Fenton LS24 . . . 196 B6
Garforth LS25 . . . 194 D4
8 Haxby YO32 . . . 166 E5
Little Fenton LS25 . . . 196 C5
Ashlands Cl DL6 . . . 210 F4
Ashlands Ct DL6 . . . 210 F4
Ashlands Dr DL7 . . . 63 C5
Ashlands Prim Sch LS29 218 C5
Ashlands Rd
Ilkley LS29 . . . 218 C5
Northallerton DL6 . . . 210 F4
Ash Lea
Danby YO21 . . . 29 A6
Fairburn WF11 . . . 201 D6
Ashlea Cl YO8 . . . 232 D4
Ashlea Rd DL7 . . . 210 D4
Ashley Ct 2 YO14 . . . 101 B3
Ashley Park Cres YO31 . . . 229 B6
Ashley Park Rd YO31 . . . 229 B7
Ashmead 4 LS23 . . . 188 E7
Ashmeade Cl YO24 . . . 230 B8
Ash Rd
13 Filey YO14 . . . 101 B4
Guisborough TS14 . . . 8 F7
Harrogate HG2 . . . 222 E6
Ash Ridge 5 DL6 . . . 210 E3
Ashridge Cl 4 TS17 . . . 6 B5
Ash St
11 Glusburn BD20 . . . 187 E7
Ilkley LS29 . . . 218 C5
Trawden BB8 . . . 186 B1
York YO26 . . . 227 E4
Ashton Ave YO30 . . . 228 B8
Ashton Ct BD23 . . . 154 B3
Ashton Gn 10 YO62 . . . 93 D7
Ashton Rd WF10 . . . 200 E3
Ash Tree Cl DL8 . . . 62 F2
Ashtree Dr YO8 . . . 197 D1
Ash Tree Garth LS24 . . . 195 E7
Ash Tree Gdns 4 YO23 . . 190 F5
Ash Tree Rd
8 Bedale DL8 . . . 63 A2
Knaresborough HG5 . . . 221 B6
Ashtree Way WF11 . . . 201 C4
Ash Tree Wlk 22 LS29 . . . 176 C1
Ash View HG2 . . . 222 B6
Ashville Ave
Eaglescliffe TS16 . . . 5 E6
Scarborough YO12 . . . 212 F6
Ashville Cl HG2 . . . 222 C5
Ashville Dr 9 DL2 . . . 22 E8
Ashville Gr HG2 . . . 222 C5
Ashville St YO31 . . . 228 D7
Ash Way YO8 . . . 232 D2
Ashwood Cl 5 YO62 . . . 92 F7
Ashwood Dr TS9 . . . 26 C8
Ashwood Glade YO32 . . . 225 C6
Ashwood Pl HG5 . . . 221 E5
Ashworth Rd WF8 . . . 201 C2

Askam Ave WF8 201 C2
Aske Ave DL10 209 E8
Aske Hall★ DL10 20 D2
Askern & Campsall Sports Ctr DN6 206 F1
Askew Dale TS14 8 D6
Askew Rigg La YO18 71 A5
Askham Bog Nature Reserve★ YO23 230 C5
ASKHAM BRYAN 182 F3
Askham Bryan Coll YO23 182 F2
Askham Bryan Coll (Guisborough Ctr) 17 TS14 8 F7
Askham Bryan Coll (Pickering Ctr) YO18 95 F8
Askham Bryan La YO23 230 A6
Askham Croft 1 YO24 227 B1
Askham Fields La YO23 182 F2
Askham Gr YO24 227 B2
Askham La
Askham Bryan YO24 230 A8
Woodthorpe YO23 230 A7
York YO24 227 B1
ASKHAM RICHARD 182 D3
ASKRIGG 57 F6
Askrigg Prim Sch DL8 57 E5
ASKWITH 176 D3
Askwith La LS21 176 D3
Askwith Moor Rd LS21 176 D5
Askwith Prim Sch LS21 176 D3
Aspen Cl
3 Dunnington YO19 184 F7
Pickering YO18 95 F7
Selby YO8 197 D2
Aspen Gr BB18 172 B1
Aspen La BB18 172 A1
Aspen Pk WF10 200 F2
Aspen Way
Slingsby YO62 120 B5
Tadcaster LS24 189 D6
Aspinall Rise 13 BD23 154 B3
Aspin Ave HG5 221 B4
Aspin Chase HG5 221 B4
Aspin Dr HG5 221 C4
Aspin Gdns HG5 221 C4
Aspin Gr 4 HG5 221 C4
Aspin La HG5 221 C3
Aspin Oval HG5 221 C4
Aspin Park Ave 1 HG5 221 C4
Aspin Park Com Prim Sch HG5 221 C5
Aspin Park Cres HG5 221 B4
Aspin Park Dr HG5 221 B4
Aspin Park La HG5 221 C4
Aspin Park Rd HG5 221 C4
Aspin View HG5 221 C4
Aspin Way HG5 221 C4
Asquith Ave
Scarborough YO12 212 E3
York YO31 229 A5
Asquith Ind Est BD23 155 D1
ASSELBY 205 D7
Assembly St 7 WF6 200 A1
Astbury TS8 7 C4
Asterley Dr TS5 6 D8
Astley Ave LS26 194 A1
Astley La
Great & Little Preston LS26 200 B8
Swillington LS26 194 A1
Astley Lane Ind Est LS26 200 B8
Astley Way LS26 200 A8
Atcherley Cl YO10 231 D8
Athelstan La 7 LS21 177 A1
Athelstan Prim Sch LS25 195 F3
Athelstans Ct LS25 195 F4
Athol Sq YO17 215 E4
Atkinson Ave DL10 209 D8
Atkinson Ct WF6 200 A1
Atkinson La WF8 201 C1
Atlas Rd YO30 225 A3
Atlas Wynd TS15 5 E3
Atlee Cl YO12 212 E2
Attermire Cave★ BD24 132 A3
Atterwith La YO26 182 A7
Auborough St 5 YO11 213 A6
Auckland Ave DL3 3 B6
Auckland Ave 2 DL3 3 B7
Auckland St TS14 8 F7
Auckland Way 7 YO21 208 C6
Aucuba Cl YO32 225 D2
Audax Cl YO30 225 A3
Audax Rd YO30 225 A3
Audby La LS22 180 C4
Audus St 10 YO8 232 C5
AUGHTON 193 C1
Aughton La YO42 193 C2
Augusta Cl DL1 3 F7
Aumit La YO62 92 E1
Aunums Cl 7 YO18 96 D5
Aunums Field YO18 96 C5
Auster Bank Ave LS24 189 F7
Auster Bank Cres LS24 189 F7
Auster Bank Rd LS24 189 F7
Auster Bank View LS24 189 F7
Auster Rd YO30 225 B3
Austfield La LS25 202 B8
Austin Dr DL9 41 A5
Austin Rd WF10 201 B4
AUSTWICK 130 E7
Austwick CE Prim Sch LA2 130 E7
Austwick Rd BD24 131 C8
Authitts Ct YO30 165 F5
Autumn Ave 8 LS22 8 C4
Avalon Ct TS8 6 F5
Ava Rd DL9 40 C4
Avens Way TS17 6 A5
Avenue A LS23 181 A2
Avenue B
Thorp Arch LS23 181 A1
Walton LS23 181 A1
Avenue Bank HG4 86 C4
Avenue C E LS23 181 B1
Avenue Cl HG2 220 D4
Avenue C W LS23 181 A1
Avenue D LS23 181 A1
Avenue E E LS23 181 B1
Avenue E W LS23 189 A8
Avenue F LS23 181 B1
Avenue G LS23 181 B1
Avenue House Ct HG5 162 F3
Avenue Pl
Guisborough TS14 8 F7
7 Harrogate HG2 220 C3
Avenue Prim Sch The TS7 7 D6
Avenue Rd
11 Harrogate HG2 220 C3
Scarborough YO12 212 E4
York YO30 233 A4
Avenue St 8 HG2 220 C3
Avenue Terr
5 Harrogate HG2 220 C3
York YO30 233 A4
Avenue The
Campsall DN6 206 E1
Collingham LS22 180 A1
Dalby-cum-Skewsby YO60 119 B2
Eaglescliffe TS16 5 E6
26 Filey YO14 101 B3
Gilling East YO62 118 E7
Great Ribston with Walshford LS22 180 C8
Guisborough TS14 8 D6
Harrogate HG1 220 C4
5 Haxby YO32 166 E5
Haxby YO32 225 D8
Knaresborough HG5 221 A7
Masham HG4 86 C3
Middlesbrough TS5 6 F8
Norton YO17 215 C2
Nun Monkton YO26 165 A4
Nunnington YO62 93 E1
8 Pateley Bridge HG3 137 C4
Richmond DL10 209 D7
Rufforth YO23 182 C6
Skipton BD23 217 B6
Skutterskelfe TS15 25 E6
1 Sleights YO22 32 A6
Snape with Thorp DL8 87 A7
South Milford LS25 195 F2
Stainton Dale YO13 54 A8
Stokesley TS9 26 C7
Thirkleby High & Low with Osgodby YO7 116 D8
West Hauxwell DL8 61 C8
Whitby YO21 208 B4
Wighill LS24 181 D2
York YO30 228 A6
Avenue Victoria YO11 213 A3
Aviation Rd LS25 196 A4
Aviation Way DL2 4 E4
Aviator Ct YO30 224 F3
Aviemore Ct 10 DL1 3 F6
Aviemore Rd TS8 6 F5
Avocet Cres 11 YO12 99 F6
Avocet Sh Ctr 8 YO12 99 E6
Avondale Rd HG1 219 F4
Avon Dr
Barnoldswick BB18 171 E2
Guisborough TS14 8 E6
York YO32 225 F6
Avon Garth LS22 180 B3
Avon Rd 8 DL2 22 D8
Avro Cl TS18 5 F7
Awnhams La YO42 169 D2
Axminster Rd TS8 6 F5
Axton Cl TS17 6 A6
Aylesham Ct YO32 225 E3
Aylton Dr TS5 6 E6
Aynham Cl 2 BD23 134 E2
Aynholme Cl 10 LS29 174 F4
Aynholme Dr 1 LS29 175 A4
Ayresome Way 1 DL1 3 F6
AYSGARTH 58 E3
Aysgarth Falls★ DL8 58 F3
Aysgarth Gr DL7 210 B2
Aysgarth Rd DL1 3 D4
Aysgarth Sch DL8 62 A4
Ayton Castle★ YO13 99 A8
Ayton Ct TS14 8 E7
Ayton Rd YO12 99 C7
Azalea Mews YO8 232 A5
AZERLEY 113 A5
Azerley Gr HG3 219 A4
Azerley La HG4 112 F3

B

Babyhouse La BD20 173 A1
Bachelor Ave HG1 219 D7
Bachelor Dr HG1 219 D6
Bachelor Gdns HG1 219 D6
Bachelor Hill YO24 227 C2
Bachelor Rd HG1 219 D6
Bachelor Way HG1 219 D6
Back Avenue Victoria 2 YO11 213 A3
Back Beck La LS29 174 F4
Back Bridge St BD23 216 F4
Back Chatsworth Gr HG1 219 D4
Back Cheltenham Mount HG1 219 D3
Back Colne Rd
9 Glusburn BD20 187 E7
Trawden BB8 186 A2
Back Dawson Terr HG1 219 D5
Back Dragon Par HG1 219 E3
Back Dragon Rd HG1 219 E3
Back Elmwood St 3 HG1 219 E4
Back Gate LA6 103 D3
Back Gladstone St HG2 222 D7
Back Gn BD23 153 F5
Back Grange Ave HG1 219 D5
Back Hall La HG1 219 E6
Back High St 13 HG3 137 B4
Backhouse St YO31 233 B4
Back La
Acaster Selby YO23 191 B3
Airton BD23 155 A6
Aiskew DL7 63 C5
Alne YO61 142 F4
Ampleforth YO62 92 C1
Appleton-le-Moors YO62 70 F2
Appleton Roebuck YO23 191 A5
Askwith LS21 176 D3
Asselby DN14 205 D6
Bagby YO7 90 B3
Barkston Ash LS24 195 F6
Barlby with Osgodby YO8 198 C4
Barton DL10 21 C7
Barton-le-Street YO17 120 E5
1 Bedale DL8 63 A3
Bilbrough YO23 182 D1
Birstwith HG3 160 D5
Bolton-on-Swale DL10 41 E5
7 Boroughbridge YO51 141 B5
Borrowby YO7 65 E4
Bradleys Both BD20 173 E4
10 Brafferton YO61 115 F1
Bramham LS23 188 E6
Brearton HG3 162 A8
Burley in Warfedale LS29 176 C1
Burnsall BD23 157 B7
Carthorpe DL8 87 E7
Cold Kirby YO7 91 C8
Copmanthorpe YO23 230 A2
Copt Hewick HG4 114 B2
Cottingwith YO42 193 C5
Crakehall DL8 62 E4
Crathorne TS15 24 F6
Dalton YO7 115 E7
Dishforth YO7 115 A4
Drax YO8 204 F5
Eaglescliffe TS16 5 E4
Easingwold YO61 117 D1
East Tanfield DL8 87 D2
Ebberston & Yedingham YO13 97 D5
Ellerton YO42 193 C1
Fewston HG3 159 F1
Giggleswick BD24 130 F2
Great & Little Broughton TS9 26 E5
Great Ouseburn YO26 164 A8
Great Preston WF10 200 D6
Gristlthorp YO14 100 E5
Guisborough TS9 8 A4
Hambleton YO8 196 F1
Harome YO62 93 C5
Hawsker-cum-Stainsacre YO22 32 F5
11 Haxby YO32 166 D5
Hebden BD23 135 A1
Hellifield BD23 154 B3
Hemingbrough YO8 198 F1
Hetton BD23 155 F5
Hirst Courtney YO8 203 F3
Holtby YO19 184 E8
Hunsingore LS22 180 E8
Hutton-le-Hole YO62 70 C4
Huttons Ambo YO60 147 B7
Kirby Wiske YO7 88 E7
Kirkby Malham BD23 154 F8
Kirkby Malzeard HG4 112 C5
Leavening YO17 147 E2
Lockton YO18 72 E4
Longnewton TS21 4 F8
Long Preston BD23 153 F5
Low Coniscliffe & Merrybent DL2 2 E4
Low Worsall TS15 24 C7
Luttons YO17 150 B8
Malham BD23 132 F2
Markington with Wallerthwaite HG3 139 C3
Marton cum Grafton YO51 141 D1
Marton YO62 94 F5
Melmerby HG4 114 B7
8 Middleham DL8 60 E2
Morton-on-Swale DL7 64 A6
Moulton DL10 21 E3
Newby Wiske DL7 64 D3
Newholm-cum-Dunsley YO21 13 A1
Newton-on-Ouse YO30 165 B6
North Cowton DL7 22 B3
North Duffield YO8 199 A7
Norton DN6 206 E2
Osmotherley DL6 45 B4
Raskelf YO61 116 F2
Rathmell BD24 153 C6
Reeth, Fremington & Healaugh DL11 38 B6
2 Riccall YO19 198 A8
Rookwith HG4 86 A8
Scorton DL10 41 E6
Settrington YO17 148 D8
Sicklinghall LS22 179 E3
Back La *continued*
Sinnington YO62 95 A8
Skelton HG4 140 E7
Sutton-under-Whitestonecliffe YO7 90 E5
Thirkleby High & Low with Osgodby YO7 116 D8
Thirsk YO7 211 B1
Tholthorpe YO61 142 D5
Thormanby YO61 116 F6
Thornton Steward DL8 61 C2
Topcliffe YO7 115 C7
Trawden BB8 186 A1
Tunstall DL10 41 B3
Tunstall LA6 102 A4
Wath HG3 137 A6
Weaverthorpe YO17 124 E1
Weeton LS17 178 C2
Wennington LA2 102 C2
Westerdale YO21 28 E5
West Tanfield HG4 87 A1
West Witton DL8 59 C4
Whixley YO26 164 A3
Whorlton DL6 45 D8
Wilberfoss YO41 185 F5
Wold Newton YO25 126 A4
Wombleton YO62 93 E7
Wray-with-Botton LA2 128 A6
York YO26 227 A5
Back Lane S
Middleton YO18 95 E8
Wheldrake YO19 192 F7
Back Mary St 3 BD20 173 F1
Back Middleton Rd 9 LS29 218 A4
Back Nelson Rd 12 LS29 218 B4
Back Newton La WF10 201 A7
Back Nook 1 DL8 58 F1
Back Northgate 18 WF8 201 B1
Back of Parks Rd YO62 70 C2
Back of the Beck 6 BD23 216 F4
Back O' Newton YO41 185 E3
Back Parish Ghyll Rd 8 LS29 218 B4
Back Park St YO8 232 D5
Back Rd
Birstwith HG3 160 B5
Thormanby YO61 116 F5
Back Regent Pl 4 HG1 220 C4
Back Royal Par 5 HG1 219 C2
Back Side YO17 149 B5
Backside La YO62 93 E6
Back St
Boroughbridge YO51 141 C5
Bramham LS23 188 E6
Burton Fleming YO25 126 E3
Langtoft YO25 151 D5
10 Middleham DL8 60 E2
Wold Newton YO25 126 A4
Back Station Rd 17 BD20 187 E8
Backstone La LS29 218 C3
Backstone Way LS29 218 C4
Back Street Hilda's Terr YO21 208 D7
Back Syke DL8 57 D5
Back Tewit Well Rd HG2 222 E8
Back Weston Rd 5 LS29 218 B4
Back West View 2 YO30 228 B7
Back York Pl 6 HG1 219 D1
Bacon Ave WF6 200 B2
Bad Bargain La YO31 229 A5
Baden St HG1 219 F4
Bader Ave TS17 6 B6
Bader Prim Sch TS17 6 B6
Badgerbeck Rd 2 DL9 209 B1
Badger Butt La BD23 155 B5
Badger Cl 33 LS29 175 C2
Badger Gate BD23 134 D3
Badger Gr HG5 220 F5
Badger Hill Dr 14 DL8 63 B3
Badger Hill Prim Sch YO10 229 B2
Badger La DN6 207 A3
Badger Mount HG5 220 F5
Badger Paddock 5 YO31 225 E2
Badgers Gate LS29 175 C6
Badger Way
Cliffe YO8 198 E3
Knaresborough HG5 220 F5
Badger Wood Glade LS22 180 C4
Badger Wood Wlk YO10 229 D3
Badminton Ct 18 DL1 3 F6
Baek Chapel St 26 BB18 171 D1
Baffam Ct YO8 232 B1
Baffam Gdns YO8 232 B2
Baffam La YO8 232 B2
BAGBY 90 C3
Bagby La YO7 90 B2
Bagdale YO21 208 C6
Bagdale Ct YO21 208 D6
Baghill La WF8 201 C1
Baildon Ave LS25 194 D2
Baildon Cl 3 YO26 227 D4
Baile Hill Terr YO1 233 B1
Bailey Ct
Northallerton DL7 210 C4
28 Walkerville DL9 41 A5
Bailey La BD23 152 E3
Bailey St BB18 172 B1
Bailey The BD23 217 A4
BAINBRIDGE 57 D5
Bainbridge CE Prim Sch DL8 57 D5
Bainbridge Dr YO8 232 C4
Bajan Pl HG4 214 A6
Bakersfield Dr DN14 202 F3
Baker St
Appleton Wiske DL6 24 A3
York YO30 228 C7
Bakewell Mews 6 DL2 3 A7
Bala Cl 2 TS17 5 F4
BALDERSBY 88 D1
Baldersby Garth
Baldersby YO7 88 D1
Rainton YO7 114 F6
BALDERSBY ST JAMES 114 E8
Baldersby St James CE Prim Sch YO7 114 E7
Baldersdale Ave 1 HG5 221 D5
Baldoon Sands TS5 6 D6
Baldwin St 4 HG1 219 C5
Balfour St YO26 227 F5
Balfour Terr TS5 6 D8
Balfour Way YO32 167 A6
Baliol Croft TS21 5 A7
Balk La DN14 207 F7
Balksyde YO62 120 B5
Balk The
Bishop Wilton YO41 169 C2
Marton-le-Moor HG4 114 E1
Slingsby YO62 120 B5
Balk Top YO7 115 B1
Ball Grove Dr BB8 186 A3
Ballhall La YO42 193 E6
Ballowfield Nature Reserve★ DL8 58 C4
Balmer Hill DL2 1 C8
Balmoral Ave TS17 6 C8
Balmoral Dr LS26 200 B6
Balmoral Rd
Barmpton DL1 3 E8
Lingdale TS12 9 F6
Middlesbrough TS3 7 C8
Ripon HG4 214 C3
Balmoral Sh Ctr YO11 213 A6
Balmoral Terr 5 YO23 228 B1
BALNE 207 C5
Balne Hall Rd DN14 207 F5
Balne Moor Rd DN14 207 B6
Balshaw Rd LA2 129 B3
Baltimore Way DL1 3 D7
Bamburgh Ct TS17 5 F5
Banbury Rd WF8 201 C2
Bancroft Fold 18 BB18 171 D1
Bancroft Mill Engine Steam Mus★ BB18 171 D1
Bands La DL8 56 C4
Bank Bottom LA6 103 D3
Bank Cl 2 YO22 32 A6
Bank Dike Hill HG3 159 A4
Bankfield La DN14 205 A7
Bankfield St BB8 186 A2
Bank Hall Cl LA6 103 D4
Bankhead Cl DL6 210 F4
Bankhead Rd DL6 210 F4
Bank House La LA6 103 B5
Bank La
Egton YO21 30 E5
Faceby TS9 25 F1
Grassington BD23 134 E3
Great & Little Broughton TS9 26 F3
Silsden BD20 174 C4
Banklands Ave BD20 174 C1
Banklands La BD20 174 C1
BANK NEWTON 172 B8
Bank Rd
Glusburn BD20 187 E8
Selby YO8 232 D6
Banks Bridge Cl BB18 171 E2
Banksfields Ct TS6 7 F8
Banks Hill 1 BB18 171 D2
Bank Side
2 Eastfield YO11 100 A7
Rawcliffe DN14 205 A2
Bankside Cl
3 Poppleton YO26 165 F1
Thirsk YO7 211 D2
Banks La
Knottingley WF11 201 F2
Scorton DL10 41 E7
Banks Rd
Brompton DL6 44 A2
Darlington DL1 3 E6
Banks Rise 4 LA2 129 A8
Bank St
Barnoldswick BB18 171 D1
Castleford WF10 200 E4
Trawden BB8 186 B1
11 Wetherby LS22 180 C3
Banks Way 3 LA2 129 A8
Bank The DL10 41 D4
Bank Top LA6 103 D3
Bank Top La 4 TS13 12 A7
Bankwell Cl BD24 131 D2
Bankwell Rd BD24 131 D2
Bank Wood Rd WF8 206 A6
Bank Yd DL10 209 C6
Bannisdale 6 YO24 230 C7
Bannister Cl BB8 186 B2
Bannister Wlk BD22 187 B6
Barbara Gr 4 YO24 227 F3
Barbeck YO7 211 C3
Barbeck Cl YO7 211 D3
Barberry TS8 7 B4
Barberry Cl
Ingleby TS17 6 B5
20 Killinghall HG3 161 B3
Barbers Dr YO23 230 B4
Barbican Ct YO10 233 C1
Barbican Mews YO10 228 E3
Barbican Rd YO10 233 C1
Barbondale Gr HG5 221 C5
Barbondale Rd LA6 77 A7
Bar Convent Mus★ YO24 233 A1

Bardale Cl 2 HG5 221 D6
BARDEN 61 A8
Barden Ct 6 YO30 224 F1
Barden Fell View 3
BD23 134 E2
Barden La DL8 40 B1
Barden Moor Rd DL1 3 E4
Barden Pl 9 YO14 101 A3
Barden Rd BD23 157 A1
Barden Twr★ BD23 157 C4
Bardney Rd 14 YO14 126 F8
Bardsley Cl TS16 5 E7
Barefoot St HG4 214 C4
Barf Bank DL8 61 A2
Barff Cl 10 YO8 197 D1
Barff Gr 6 YO8 197 B2
Barff La YO8 197 C1
Barff View YO8 203 D7
Barfield Rd YO31 228 F8
Barf La YO41 169 D4
Bargate DL10 209 B6
Barker Bsns Pk HG4 114 C6
Barker Dr YO8 232 B6
Barker La YO1 233 A2
Barkers Arc DL6 210 D4
Barker's La
Newholm-cum-Dunsley
YO21 13 A1
Snainton YO13 98 A4
Barkery The TS8 7 B3
Barkhouse Bank HG3 138 F4
Bark House La LA2 131 B8
Barkhouse Wood La
WF11 202 D6
Bark La
Addingham LS29 175 A5
Embsay with Eastby BD23 157 A1
Bar Knotts Terr YO17 215 C3
BARKSTON ASH 195 F7
Barkston Ash Cath Prim Sch
LS24 195 E7
Barkston Ave YO26 227 B3
Barkston Cl 3 YO26 227 A3
Barkston Gr YO26 227 A3
Barkston Rd YO26 227 A3
Bar La
Bramham cum Oglethorpe
LS23 188 F7
Garforth LS25 194 D4
Hambleton YO8 196 E1
Knaresborough HG5 162 D5
Roecliffe YO51 141 A5
York YO1 233 A2
BARLBY 198 B5
Barlby Bridge Com Prim Sch
YO8 232 D6
Barlby By-pass 2 YO8 198 B4
Barlby Com Prim Sch
YO8 198 B4
Barlby Cres YO8 232 F7
Barlby High Sch YO8 198 B5
Barlby Rd YO8 232 E6
Barley Cl YO17 215 D2
Barleycorn Yd YO1 233 C2
Barleycroft YO11 213 C1
Barleyfields La 5 LS22 180 C3
Barley Fields Prim Sch
TS17 6 A4
Barleyfields Rd 4 LS22 180 C3
Barley Hall★ YO1 233 B3
Barleyhill Rd LS25 194 B4
Barley Horn Rd LS24 190 B2
Barley Rise YO32 167 A6
Barley's Yd 1 YO7 211 B3
Barley View YO32 225 C8
Barley Wlk 16 LS25 195 F2
BARLOW 204 C7
Barlow CE VC Prim Sch
YO8 204 C7
Barlow Cl TS14 8 F6
Barlow Comm Nature
Reserve★ YO8 204 B7
Barlow Comm Rd YO8 204 B8
Barlow Rd YO8 204 B6
Barlow St YO26 227 D4
Barmby Ave YO10 231 E8
Barmby Cl 4 YO30 224 F1
Barmby Ferry Rd 1 YO8 198 F1
BARMBY ON THE
MARSH 205 B7
Barmby-on-the-Marsh Prim
Sch DN14 205 B7
Barmoor Cl YO13 75 D6
Barmoor Gn YO13 75 D6
Barmoor La YO13 75 C6
Barmpton La DL1 3 F7
Barnaby Pl TS14 8 E7
Barnaby Way YO51 141 B5
Barnard La YO13 98 C4
Barnard's Rd YO22 31 A4
Barnbow La LS15 194 A6
Barn Elms YO8 204 C5
Barnes Rd
Castleford WF10 200 E3
Darlington DL3 3 A4
Barney La YO60 146 A1
Barn Field Cl BB8 186 A3
Barnfield Way YO23 230 A2
Barnhill La DN14 205 F7
Barningham Rd DL11 18 G7
BARNOLDSWICK
Earby 171 D1
Ingleton 103 A2
Barnoldswick La LA6 103 A2
Barnsdale Est WF10 200 D3
Barnsdale Rd
Ledston WF10 200 E7
Mickletown LS26 200 B5
Barnsdale View DN6 206 E2
Barns Wray 2 YO61 117 D1
Barnwell Cres HG2 222 B5
Barnwood Cres BB18 172 B1
Barnwood Rd BB18 172 A1
Barnygate La YO60 147 A7
Barons Cres YO23 230 B2
Bar Pl HG1 219 D5
Barracks Bank DL10 21 A2
Barrack View DL10 209 C8
Barrel Sykes 3 BD24 131 D3
Barret St 13 BB18 172 A1
Barrett Ave 3 YO24 227 F3
Barrett Rd DL3 3 A5
Barrington Garth DN14 202 F3
Barr La YO32 167 D4
Barrowby La
Austhorpe LS15 194 A4
Kirkby Overblow HG3 179 A3
BARROWCLIFF 212 D7
Barrowcliff Rd YO12 212 D7
Barrowcliff Sch YO12 212 C7
Barry Bank YO21 11 F1
Barry's La YO12 212 E2
Barse Beck La HG3 160 D5
Bar St YO11 213 A6
Barstow Ave YO10 228 F3
Barstow Fall 2 WF8 201 C2
Bar The 6 DL10 209 C6
Bartholomew Ave 11
DN14 205 F3
Bartindale Rd YO14 127 A5
Bartle Garth YO1 233 C3
BARTON 21 D7
Barton CE Prim Sch DL10 21 D7
BARTON HILL 146 D3
BARTON-LE-STREET 120 E5
BARTON-LE-WILLOWS 146 D1
Barton Quarry Ind Est
DL10 20 B6
Bartons Garth YO8 232 B2
Barton St DL1 3 E6
Barton Way HG4 113 C8
Barugh La
Barugh (Great & Little)
YO17 95 B2
Normanby YO62 94 F4
Barugh Way HG4 114 B6
Barwic Cl YO8 232 E3
Barwick Cl 9 ts17 6 A5
Barwick Fields 8 TS17 6 A5
BARWICK IN ELMET 194 B8
Barwick in Elmet CE Sch
LS15 194 C8
Barwick La
Ingleby Barwick TS17 5 F5
Ingleby TS17 6 A4
Barwick Rd LS25 194 C5
Barwick St YO12 212 F5
Barwick Terr 1 YO12 212 F5
Barwick View 10 TS17 6 A5
Barwick Way TS17 6 A4
Barwic Parade YO8 232 E4
Barwic Parade Prim Sch
YO8 232 E4
Bassett Cl YO8 232 C3
Bassleton La TS17 6 A6
Baston La YO61 143 E4
Batemans Yd 3 YO7 211 B3
Bates Ave DL3 3 B7
Bateson Cl YO10 229 C1
Bath St LS29 218 C5
Battalion Ct DL9 41 A4
BATTERSBY 27 D6
Battersby Ave TS9 27 C7
Battersby Sta TS9 27 C6
Battery Par YO21 208 D7
Battle Cl 27 YO51 141 B5
Battleflats Way YO41 168 D2
Battle of Bramham Moor
(site of)★ LS24 188 F4
Battle of Marston Moor (site
of)★ YO26 181 F7
Battle of the Standard 1138
(site of)★ DL6 43 E4
Battle of Towton (site of)★
LS24 195 D8
Battling Hills La YO18 49 B5
Bawhead Rd 23 BB18 172 A1
Bawtry Cl YO8 232 D3
Bawtry Rd YO8 232 D3
Baxby Manor★ YO61 117 B6
Baxby Terr 2 DL2 22 D8
Baxtergate YO21 208 D6
Baxter Wood BD20 187 E8
Baxton's Sprunt 1 YO62 92 F7
Bay Bolton Ave DL8 59 F3
Bay Cres YO14 101 B2
Baydale Rd DL3 3 A4
Bay Horse Yd 9 BD23 216 F4
Baynes Ct YO8 232 A2
Baynes Way BD23 217 D8
Baysdale Ave YO10 229 D3
Baysdale Cl 3 TS14 8 F6
Baysdale Rd TS17 6 B7
Bazeley's La YO17 215 E1
Beach Rd The YO14 101 B3
Beach The YO14 101 B3
Beacon Bank YO62 92 D1
Beacon Brow Rd YO13 75 A7
Beacon Grange Pk DL2 4 C7
Beacon Hill DL1 4 B7
Beacon Park First Ave 10
YO18 95 F7
Beacon Park Second Ave 9
YO18 95 F7
Beacon Rd
Millington YO42 170 B1
Beacon Rd *continued*
Seamer YO12 99 D7
Beacon Rise 4 LS29 175 C2
Beaconsfield Mews
YO24 227 D3
Beaconsfield St
Northallerton DL7 210 D4
3 Scarborough YO12 212 E3
York YO24 227 D3
Beacons La 18 TS17 5 F4
Beacon St 5 LS29 175 A4
Beacon View 3 BD23 217 E8
Beacon Way YO22 32 D6
BEADLAM 93 C7
Beadlam Ave TS7 7 D6
Beadle Garth YO23 230 B2
Beadnell Cl 3 TS17 6 B5
Beagle Croft YO41 168 C1
Beagle Ridge Dr YO24 227 C1
Beagle Spinney YO41 168 C1
BEAL 202 D4
Beale Cl TS17 6 B5
Beal La
Beal DN14 202 D4
Cridling Stubbs WF11 202 C1
BEAMSLEY 174 F7
Beamsley Ct BD23 217 A2
Beamsley La BD23 174 F7
Beamsley View 13 LS29 175 C2
Beancroft Rd WF10 200 E3
Beancroft St WF10 200 E3
Beanland La YO32 167 D2
Beanlands Dr 7 BD20 187 E7
Beanlands Par LS29 218 C5
Beanlands Pl 8 BD20 187 E7
Bean Sheaf La YO17 96 A3
Bean's Way YO31 229 B8
Beatswell Lawn HG4 113 C8
Beaufighter Cl DL10 41 F6
Beaufort Cl
Guisborough TS14 8 F5
York YO10 229 B3
Beaulieu Cl 1 YO32 225 F5
Beaumont Ct 12 DN14 205 F3
Beaumont Hill DL1 3 D8
Beaumont Hill Acad DL1 3 E7
Beaumont Pl YO8 232 A2
Beaverdyke YO30 224 F1
Bebra Gdns★ HG5 221 A5
Becca La LS25 194 F8
Beckbridge La 2 WF6 200 B1
Beckbridge Rd WF6 200 B2
Beckbridge Way WF6 200 B1
Beck Cl 6 YO41 185 B2
Beckclose La DL8 87 F6
Beck Closes Rd YO26 142 A3
Beckdale Rd YO62 92 E7
BECKERMONDS 80 D3
Beckett Cl 8 YO62 93 D7
Beckett Dr YO10 229 D4
Beckfield Cl 6 BD20 187 F7
Beckfield La
Fairburn WF11 201 C7
York YO26 227 B5
Beckfield Pl YO26 227 B4
Beckfields Ave TS17 6 A4
Beck Hole 9 YO11 100 B6
Beck Hole Rd YO22 31 C1
Beck Holme YO22 32 B6
Beck Isle Mus★ YO18 95 F7
Beck La
Cloughton YO13 54 C1
Collingham LS22 180 A1
Farndale East YO62 48 F2
Leavening YO17 147 E1
Lebberston YO11 100 D5
South Kilvington YO7 211 B6
Wheldrake YO19 193 A8
Becklands Cl YO51 141 A5
Becklands La YO51 141 A4
Beck Mdw LS15 194 C7
Beck Mill Cl YO17 215 D3
Beck Row YO41 169 D5
Becks Brow BD23 153 C3
Becks Cl 5 YO32 225 C8
Beckside
Aberford LS25 194 F7
Catterick DL10 41 E4
7 Elvington YO41 185 B2
Malton YO17 215 F4
Northallerton DL7 210 B4
4 Staithes TS13 13 K2
Stillingfleet YO19 191 D3
Trawden Forest BB8 186 B2
Wilberfoss YO41 185 F6
Beck Side BD23 173 B4
Beckside Cl
13 Addingham LS29 174 F4
29 Burley in Warfedale
LS29 176 C1
Beck Side Cl BD20 173 D1
Beckside Ct 6 BD20 174 C1
Beckside Gdns YO10 228 F4
Beckwith Ave HG2 222 B7
Beckwith Cl
Harrogate HG2 222 A6
Heworth YO31 229 C7
Beckwith Cres HG2 222 B7
Beckwith Dr HG2 222 B6
Beckwith Hall Dr 7
YO19 198 A8
Beckwith Head Rd HG3 178 C8
Beckwith Rd HG2 222 A7
BECKWITHSHAW 178 A7
Beckwithshaw Comm Prim
Sch HG3 178 A8
Beckwith Wlk HG2 222 A7
BEDALE 63 B2
Bedale Ave
Scarborough YO12 212 E8
York YO10 229 D4
Bedale CE Prim Sch DL8 63 A2
Bedale High Sch DL8 63 A2
Bedale La HG4 114 A8
Bedale L Ctr DL8 63 A2
Bedale Mus★ DL8 63 A3
Bedale Rd
Aiskew DL7 63 C4
Hunton DL8 61 E7
Scotton DL9 40 F2
Well DL8 87 A4
Bedale Sta DL8 63 A3
Bedburn Dr DL3 2 F5
Bede Ave YO30 228 B7
Bedern YO1 233 C3
Bedern Bank 13 HG4 214 C5
Bedern Ct 16 HG4 214 C5
Bedford Rd TS7 7 D6
Bedfords Fold 6 LS25 202 A7
Bedford St 13 YO11 213 A6
BEDLAM 161 A8
Bedlam Hill YO7 65 E4
Bedlam La
Fewston HG3 159 F2
Staveley HG5 140 E1
Bedlington's La YO22 33 C4
Beech Ave
3 Airmyn DN14 205 E4
Bishopthorpe YO23 231 A3
1 Earby BB18 172 A1
Harrogate HG2 222 E6
4 Naburn YO23 191 C7
4 Topcliffe YO7 89 B1
York YO24 227 F3
Beech Cl
Baldersby YO7 88 D1
6 Eastfield YO11 100 A7
2 Elvington YO41 185 B2
Farnham HG5 162 D7
Great Ayton TS9 7 F1
Hunton DL9 40 E2
7 Leeming DL7 63 F3
Scruton DL7 63 E7
7 Sherburn in Elmet LS25 195 F4
Snape with Thorp DL8 87 A7
3 South Milford LS25 195 F2
Tadcaster LS24 189 F6
Beech Cres
Castleford WF10 201 B3
Whitwell-on-the-Hill YO60 146 E4
Beech Croft
Barlby with Osgodby YO8 198 B6
Pontefract WF8 201 C2
Beechcroft Cl TS12 9 F6
Beech Ct
Bishopthorpe YO23 231 A3
2 Castleford WF10 200 F3
Hellifield BD23 154 B3
Beech Dr
6 Kirkbymoorside YO62 70 B1
12 Scalby YO13 75 D5
South Milford LS25 195 F2
Beecher Stowe Dr 39 DL9 41 A5
Beeches Cl BD23 172 C8
Beeches End LS23 188 F8
Beeches The
Middleton St George DL2 4 D4
Skelton YO30 224 C4
11 Stokesley TS9 26 C7
26 Upper Poppleton YO26 165 F1
Wetherby LS22 180 D4
Beechfield
Coulby Newham TS8 7 A5
Hawsker-cum-Stainsacre
YO22 33 A6
Newby Wiske DL7 64 F2
Newton-on-Ouse YO30 165 B6
Beechfield Cl 15 YO8 197 B1
Beechfield Rd DL10 209 C8
Beech Glade YO31 225 F2
Beech Gr
1 Airmyn DN14 205 E4
Burton Salmon LS25 201 F6
Camblesforth YO8 204 C5
Harrogate HG2 219 C1
Knaresborough HG5 221 B8
Maltby TS8 6 C4
Northallerton DL6 210 E5
Selby YO8 232 C5
Sherburn in Elmet LS25 195 F4
Sowerby YO7 211 C1
Whitby YO21 208 B6
York YO26 227 C4
Beech Hill
Carleton BD23 173 A4
6 Knaresborough HG5 221 A6
5 Pontefract WF8 201 C1
Beech Hill Rd BD23 173 A4
Beechings Mews YO21 208 B7
Beech La
8 East Ayton/West Ayton
YO13 99 A7
3 Spofforth HG3 179 E6
Beechnut La WF8 201 B1
Beech Pk YO19 198 A8
Beech Pl 5 YO32 167 A6
Beech Rd
Boston Spa LS23 188 E8
Campsall DN6 206 E1
Darlington DL1 3 F7
Harrogate HG2 222 E6
Ripon HG4 214 B3
Beech Rise DL1 3 F7
Beech St
23 Barnoldswick BB18 171 D1
10 Glusburn BD20 187 E7
Beech St *continued*
6 Harrogate HG2 220 C3
Beech Tree Ct 2 YO30 164 F7
Beech Tree La YO8 204 C5
Beechtree Rd LS24 189 D5
Beech View
Aberford LS25 194 E8
Ferrybridge WF11 201 C4
Beechville Ave YO12 212 F6
Beech Way 25 YO26 165 F1
Beech Wlk
5 Eastfield YO11 100 A7
Tadcaster LS24 189 D6
Beechwood Ave 2 TS9 26 C8
Beechwood Cl
14 Bedale DL8 63 A2
Markington with Wallerthwaite
HG3 139 D4
Sherburn in Elmet LS25 195 F3
West Marton BD23 171 F5
Beechwood Cres 6 HG2 219 C1
Beechwood Croft LS25 195 F3
Beechwood Dr BD23 216 D5
Beechwood Glade
Sherburn in Elmet LS25 195 F3
6 York YO24 227 B1
Beechwood Gr
Harrogate HG2 222 F7
16 Ilkley LS29 175 C2
Beechwood Rd
Eaglescliffe TS16 5 E6
Norton YO17 215 D2
Beechwood Rise 1 LS22 180 C4
Beecroft La BD23 153 D3
Beeforth Cl YO32 225 D5
Beeston's La LS17 178 C4
Beeston Way WF10 200 E6
Beggarmans Rd DL8 80 C8
Belbrough Cl 3 TS15 25 C4
Belbrough La TS15 25 C4
Belcombe Way 1 YO30 228 A7
Belford La HG4 112 A3
Belford Pl 3 HG1 219 D1
Belford Rd HG1 219 D2
Belford Sq 9 HG1 219 D1
Belfry Way 30 WF6 200 B1
Belgrave Cres
Harrogate HG2 222 E8
15 Scarborough YO11 212 F5
Belgrave St
3 Skipton BD23 216 E4
York YO31 228 C7
Belgrave Terr
3 Hurworth-on-Tees DL2 22 D8
14 Scarborough YO11 212 F5
Thirsk YO7 211 B2
Bellaby Pk 7 YO62 93 D7
Bellburn La DL3 3 B7
BELL BUSK 155 A3
Bell Cl
Haxby YO32 225 C8
5 Seamer YO12 99 D6
Belle Hill BD24 131 D3
Bell End Gn YO18 49 D3
BELLERBY 60 D7
Bellerby Camp DL8 60 B7
Bellerbyhurn Rd YO17 95 F2
Bellerby Rd DL8 60 D6
Belle Vue LS29 218 C3
Belle Vue Cres 33 YO14 101 B3
Belle Vue Par 9 YO11 212 F5
Belle Vue Pl 10 YO11 212 F5
Belle Vue St
34 Filey YO14 101 B3
Scarborough YO12 212 F5
York YO10 228 E3
Bellevue Terr
Ripon HG4 214 C5
2 Skipton BD23 216 E4
Belle Vue Terr
Whitby YO21 208 D7
York YO10 228 E3
Bellfarm Ave YO31 228 E8
Bellflower Cl 16 WF10 200 D3
Bellground La YO30 165 D4
Bell Hall★ YO19 191 E6
Bell Horse Gate LA6 103 D4
Bellhouse La YO21 29 C7
Bellhouse Way YO24 230 B8
Bellingham Cl YO7 211 C3
Bell La
Cawood YO8 197 A7
Huby YO61 144 A4
Husthwaite YO61 117 B5
Rawcliffe DN14 205 A2
Ulleskelf LS24 190 C2
Bellmans Croft YO23 230 B2
Bellman Wlk 3 HG4 113 D2
Bell's Ct 15 YO62 92 F6
Bellwood Ave
Boston Spa LS23 188 E7
Lockwood TS12 9 E7
Bellwood Dr YO24 230 B8
Belmangate 2 TS14 8 F6
Belmont WF11 201 D5
Belmont Ave
Harrogate HG2 220 D4
10 Otley LS21 176 F1
Belmont Cl 3 YO30 225 A1
Belmont Gr
Calcutt HG5 221 A4
1 Harrogate HG2 220 D3
Belmont Grosvenor Sch
HG3 160 D6
Belmont Prim Sch 7 TS14 8 F6

Belmont Rd
Harrogate HG2 219 C2
Ilkley LS29 218 E4
Scarborough YO11 213 A4
Belmont St BD23 216 F4
Belmont Terr 2 HG2 220 D3
Belmont View HG5 221 A4
Belmont Wharf BD23 216 F4
Belthorpe La YO42 169 E1
Belton Park Dr 7 DL9 40 E4
Belvedere Cres 8 DN14 205 F3
Belvedere Pl YO11 213 A3
Belvedere Rd YO11 213 A3
Belvedere Terr YO11 213 A3
Belvoir Ave 8 YO41 185 B2
Belvoir Dr WF11 201 F2
Belvoir Terr 9 YO11 213 A5
Bence The YO42 170 C3
Benedict Ave YO8 232 E4
BENINGBROUGH 165 D4
Beningbrough Dr HG3 219 B5
Beningbrough Hall & Gdns* YO30 165 B5
Beningbrough La YO30 165 D5
Benjy La YO19 192 E7
Benkhill Dr 16 DL8 63 A2
Ben La BB18 171 E2
Bennett St 11 BD23 216 F3
Bennions Way 5 DL10 41 E4
Bennison La YO21 13 A1
Bennymoor La YO8 198 C4
BEN RHYDDING 218 E3
Ben Rhydding Dr LS29 218 F3
Ben Rhydding Prim Sch LS29 218 E4
Ben Rhydding Rd LS29 218 D3
Ben Rhydding Sta LS29 218 F4
Bensham Rd DL1 3 D8
Benson La WF6 200 B2
BENT 187 D7
Bentham Moor Rd LA6 103 A2
Bentham Rd LA6 103 B3
Bentham Sta LA2 129 A7
Bentinck Ave TS5 6 F8
Bent La
Colne BB8 186 A3
Sutton BD20 187 E7
Bentley Wynd TS16 5 D3
Benton Gap La BD22 187 B7
Bent Rigg La YO13 54 B7
Bents La YO18 71 A5
Beresford Cl 6 DL8 63 B2
Beresford Terr YO23 228 C1
Berghill La YO7 66 A7
Berkeley Terr YO26 227 E5
Berkley Dr TS14 8 F5
Bernard La YO26 164 B3
Bernica Gr TS17 6 A4
Berry Bank DL2 1 A6
Berrygate La HG4 214 E7
Berry La LS26 200 C8
Berry's Ave 5 HG5 221 B6
Berrys Ct 16 HG5 221 B6
Berwick Rd
Archdeacon Newton DL3 3 A7
18 Scotton DL9 40 E4
Bestmire La DL6 65 A4
Betteras Hill Rd LS25 202 A8
Betton Bsns Ctrtre YO13 99 C8
Betton Farm Visitor Ctr* YO13 99 C8
Betton Rise YO13 99 B8
Between Dikes Rd YO8 204 F8
Beulah St 10 HG1 219 D2
Beulah Terr YO11 212 F5
Beverley Balk YO41 168 B2
Beverley Cl 12 YO11 100 B6
Beverley Gate YO12 99 D1
Beverley Rd
11 Eastfield YO11 100 B6
Middlesbrough TS7 7 D6
Norton YO17 215 E3
Beverley Rise LS29 175 C2
BEWERLEY 137 B3
Bewerley Rd HG1 219 B5
Bewlay St YO23 228 C2
Bewley Gr TS5 6 E7
Bexhill Cl WF8 201 C1
Bexley Dr TS6 7 E8
BICKERTON 181 A5
Bickerton Way LS21 176 F1
Bickley Gate YO13 73 F6
Bickley Howe YO12 212 B4
Bickley Way TS8 7 A5
Bielby Cl
8 Bedale DL8 63 B3
33 Scalby YO12 75 D5
BIGGIN 196 E5
Biggin La LS25 196 C6
Big Meadow Dr 5 LS29 174 E4
Big Sheep & Little Cow Farm* DL8 63 B3
BILBROUGH 182 D1
Bilsdale Cl
Northallerton DL7 210 C2
York YO30 224 E2
Bilsdale Gr HG5 221 D6
Bilsdale Midcable Chop Gate CE VC Prim Sch TS9 46 F6
BILTON 219 E6
Bilton Cl HG1 219 E6
Bilton Dr HG1 219 D4
Bilton Grange Cl HG1 219 D5
Bilton Grange Com Prim Sch HG1 219 D5
Bilton Grove Ave HG1 219 E5
Bilton Hall Dr HG1 220 D6
BILTON IN AINSTY 181 E4
Bilton La HG1 219 E6
Binks Cl DL6 210 B7
Binnington Carr La YO12 99 B1
Binns La BD20 187 D7
Binsley La YO61 117 E2
BINSOE 86 F2
Binsoe La HG4 86 F3
Birch Ave
Malton YO17 215 D6
Sleights YO22 32 A6
Birch Cl
8 Filey YO14 101 B3
9 Hunton DL9 40 F2
2 Kirklevington TS15 24 E8
4 Thorpe Willoughby YO8 197 B1
York YO31 225 E1
York YO31 228 E8
York YO32 225 D3
Birch Copse YO24 227 D2
Birch Cres 10 YO22 32 A6
Birch Dr
2 Faceby TS9 25 F1
Kippax LS25 194 D2
Birchen Cl 7 WF10 200 D3
Birches The TS8 7 A5
Birchfield Dr TS16 5 D5
Birch Gr
Castleford WF10 201 B3
Harrogate HG1 219 E6
Kippax LS25 194 D1
Sleights YO22 32 A6
Birch Hall La BB18 172 B1
Birch La
13 Haxby YO32 166 E5
New York HG3 137 F1
Birch Park Ind Est YO31 228 E8
Birch Pk YO31 225 E1
Birch Rd DL1 3 D8
Birch Tree Cl 11 YO32 167 B6
Birch View 8 YO18 96 A6
Birch Way YO61 143 D8
Birchwood Cl 16 BD24 131 D2
Birchwood Ct 5 LS29 218 A4
Birchwood Gdns 13 YO61 115 F1
Birchwood Mews HG2 222 F7
Birchwood Rd TS7 7 C6
Birdale Field La LS22 188 B8
BIRDFORTH 116 E6
Birdforth Way 1 YO62 92 C1
Bird Gdn* LS25 195 B7
Bird La
Hensall DN14 203 D2
Kellington DN14 202 F4
Bird Ridding La DL8 60 B1
BIRDSALL 148 B4
Birds of Prey & Conservation Ctr* YO7 88 F7
Birdwood Cl DL9 209 C2
Birk Brow Rd TS12 9 D5
BIRKBY 23 B1
Birkby La DL7 23 B1
Birk-crag Ct 2 HG3 161 B2
Birk Crag Nature Reserve* HG3 161 B1
Birkdale Ave HG5 221 D5
Birkdale Gr 4 YO26 227 B5
Birkdale Rd 9 TS18 5 D8
Birker La
Newton on Derwent YO41 185 D4
Wilberfoss YO41 185 F6
Birkett La CA17 14 B7
Birk Field Bank YO21 28 F6
Birk Head La YO18 70 F4
Birkhills HG3 140 A3
BIRKIN 202 D6
Birkin La WF11 202 B4
Birkin Rd YO8 202 F5
Birk La YO8 199 D8
Birklands 1 YO62 93 D7
Birkwith La LA2 128 F7
BIRSTWITH 160 E6
Birstwith CE Prim Sch HG3 160 E6
Birstwith Dr YO26 227 E4
Birstwith Grange HG3 160 E6
Birstwith Rd HG1 220 A3
Birt Gr 16 DN14 205 F3
Birthwaite La HG3 161 C8
Birtley Ave TS5 6 E7
Bishop Cl 1 HG3 137 C4
Bishop Ct 2 YO8 232 B6
Bishopdale Cl HG5 221 D6
Bishopdale Ct 28 BD24 131 D2
Bishopdale Dr 7 LS22 180 A1
Bishopdike Rd
Cawood YO8 197 A6
Sherburn in Elmet LS25 196 A4
Bishop Garth 2 HG3 137 C4
Bishopgate St YO23 233 B1
Bishophill Jun YO1 233 A1
Bishophill Senior YO1 233 B1
BISHOP MONKTON 140 A5
Bishop Monkton CE Prim Sch HG3 140 A5
Bishop Monkton Railway Cutting Nature Reserve* HG3 139 F5
Bishop's Cl YO8 197 A8
Bishops Ct YO1 233 B1
Bishopsfields Dr YO26 228 A5
Bishopsgarth DL7 210 C4
Bishopsway YO10 229 C3
Bishops Way DL10 41 D5
BISHOP THORNTON 138 F2
BISHOPTHORPE 231 B3
Bishopthorpe Infant Sch YO23 231 A4
Bishopthorpe Palace* YO23 231 B4
Bishopthorpe Rd YO23 231 B5
BISHOPTON 113 D2
Bishopton HG4 214 A5
Bishopton La
Great Burdon DL1 4 A7
Ripon HG4 113 D2
Bishopton Pk HG4 214 A5
Bishop Way 3 HG3 137 C4
BISHOP WILTON 169 F2
Bishop Wilton CE VC Prim Sch YO42 169 F2
Bisley Ct 13 DL1 3 F6
Bismarck St YO26 227 E5
Bitterdale La YO62 70 A3
Black Abbey La 1 BD20 187 E8
Black Bank Rd LA2 130 B3
BLACK BANKS 3 D2
Blackberry Gdns YO19 184 E7
Blackbird Way 8 YO12 99 F6
Black Bull Wynd TS16 5 C3
Black Bull Yard 14 DL8 60 E2
Blackburn Ind Est 7 LS25 196 A4
Blackburn La WF11 202 B2
Black Diamond Way 3 TS16 5 D5
Black Dike La YO26 182 F8
Blackett Rd DL1 3 E6
Black Fen La YO8 232 C8
Black Gill La
Airton BD23 154 B8
Settle BD24 132 A1
Black Hill YO62 118 E5
Black Hill Rd HG3 157 F8
Black Horse La TS15 25 C3
Blacklee Cl 3 YO32 167 B8
Blackmore Cl TS14 8 F5
Black Sheep Brewery Visitor Ctr* HG4 86 C4
Black Sike La YO13 98 B4
Blacksmith Bank DL8 62 E5
Blacksmith Ct DL7 22 C2
Blacksmith Hill YO22 53 A7
Blacksmiths Cl 5 YO41 185 C2
Blacksmiths La 29 YO41 168 D2
Blackthorn TS8 7 B4
Blackthorn Cl DN14 207 A7
Blackthorn Dr YO31 225 E2
Blackthorn La HG3 222 C3
Blackthorn Rd LS29 218 D5
BLACKWELL 3 B4
Blackwell DL3 3 B3
Blackwell La DL3 3 B4
Black Wlk WF8 201 B1
Blackwood Hall Bsns Pk YO8 198 E7
Blackwood La YO8 198 F7
Blackwood Rd YO8 198 E8
BLADES 37 B5
Blair Ave TS17 5 F4
Blair Pk HG5 221 C5
Blake Ct YO19 193 A8
Blake Gate HG3 136 E1
Blakeley Cres 3 BB18 171 D2
Blakeley Gr YO30 224 F3
Blakeney Pl YO10 228 F3
Blake St YO1 233 B3
Blakey Bank YO62 49 A5
Blakey Cl YO7 211 C1
Blakey La YO7 211 C1
Blakey Rd YO62 70 B6
Blandford Rd DL9 40 E3
Bland La YO26 227 A4
Blands Ave WF10 200 D7
Bland's Cliff 27 YO11 213 A6
Blandscliff Gall* YO11 213 B6
Blands Cres 3 WF10 200 D7
Blands Gr 4 WF10 200 D7
Bland's Hill HG5 221 A4
Blands Terr WF10 200 D7
Blansby La YO17 121 C8
Blansby Park La YO18 96 A8
Blatchford YO30 228 B8
Blatchford Mews YO30 228 B8
Blawath Rd YO18 51 A2
Blayshaw La HG3 110 B4
BLAZEFIELD 137 E4
Blazefield Bank HG3 137 D3
Bleaberry La YO41 169 B5
Bleachfield YO10 228 F2
Blea Moor Rd LA6 78 E2
Blean La DL8 57 D3
Blea Pit La HG4 140 E8
Bleara Rd BB18 186 B8
Blenheim Ave 4 YO21 208 B7
Blenheim Cl DL10 41 F6
Blenheim Ct
Harrogate HG2 222 D7
Rawcliffe YO30 224 D3
Blenheim St 12 YO12 213 A7
Blenheim Terr YO12 213 A7
Blenheim Way HG2 222 C7
Bleriot Way YO30 225 A3
Blewhouse La DL8 61 E3
Blind La
Aiskew DL8 63 B3
Barton DL10 21 D7
Burton in Lonsdale LA6 102 F3
Guisborough TS14 8 C6
Hurworth DL2 22 E8
Knaresborough HG5 221 B7
Scorton DL10 42 B8
Tockwith YO26 181 B8
Blind Piece La YO7 116 A6
Bloe Beck La LA2 129 E6
Bloody Beck Hill YO13 54 A7
Blorenge Ct 22 TS17 5 F4
Blossomgate HG4 214 B5
Blossom St YO24 233 A1
Blossoms The LS26 200 B6
Blossom Way WF10 200 D3
BLUBBERHOUSES 159 D2
Blue Anchor Rd YO14 127 C8
Blue Bank YO22 32 A4
Blue Barn La TS15 25 C6
Bluebeck Dr YO30 227 E8
Blue Bell Farm Ct YO8 192 E1
Bluebell Gr YO22 208 E4
Blue Bell Gr TS5 6 F6
Bluebell Mdw 15 HG3 161 B3
Bluebell Mews WF10 200 C3
Bluebell Wlk 18 HG3 161 B3
Blue Bridge La YO10 228 D2
Blue Coat YO19 184 D7
Blue Nile Way 25 DL9 41 A5
Blue Ridge Pk WF10 200 E3
Blue Slates Cl YO19 193 A8
Blyth Cl YO8 232 A5
BMI The Duchy Hospl HG2 219 C1
BMI Woodlands Hospl DL1 4 A4
Board St YO23 228 C2
Boar La TS17 6 B5
Boatcliffe Rd YO14 127 D7
Boathouse La DL2 2 E4
Boat La
Barforth DL11 1 C7
Great Ouseburn YO26 164 C8
Kirby Hall YO26 142 C1
Mickletown LS26 200 D5
Bob La YO7 65 E3
Bodmin Dr WF6 200 A2
Bodner Hill YO61 118 F1
Boeing Way TS18 5 F7
Boggart La LS24 190 C2
Boggy La DL10 209 B5
Bog Hall YO21 208 D5
Boghole Bank DL6 45 B3
Boghouse La TS13 10 F3
Bog La
Askham Bryan YO24 230 B6
Barwick in Elmet & Scholes LS15 194 A7
Stirton with Thorlby BD23 216 D7
Bogs La
Bridge Hewick HG4 114 C1
Harrogate HG1 220 C5
Bolckow St TS14 8 F7
Boldron Cl 8 TS18 5 D8
Bold Venture St BD23 216 F2
Bolland St 16 BB18 171 D2
Bolling Rd LS29 218 D4
BOLTBY 66 F1
Boltby Rd YO30 224 F2
BOLTON ABBEY 174 E8
Bolton Abbey Sta BD23 174 D8
Bolton Ave DL10 209 B7
BOLTON BRIDGE 174 F8
Bolton Bridge Rd LS29 218 A4
Bolton Castle* DL8 59 B6
Bolton Cross DL10 41 F5
Bolton Ct 13 DL8 60 D5
Bolton Hall* BD23 157 F1
Bolton La YO42 169 E1
BOLTON-ON-SWALE 41 F6
Bolton-on-Swale Lake Nature Reserve* DL10 41 F5
Bolton-on-Swale St Mary's CE Prim Sch DL10 41 F6
BOLTON PERCY 190 D4
Bolton Percy Station Nature Reserve* YO23 190 C4
Bolton Priory (rems of)* BD23 157 F1
Bolton Rd
Draughton BD23 174 F7
Ellerton DL10 41 F5
Silsden BD20 174 D3
Bolton St HG1 219 D4
Bolton Way
12 Leyburn DL8 60 D5
Richmond DL10 209 C8
Bonby La YO8 192 E2
Bond End HG5 221 A6
Bondgate
Darlington DL1 3 C5
Helmsley YO62 92 F6
Pontefract WF8 201 C1
Ripon HG4 214 C4
Selby YO8 232 B7
Bondgate Ct HG4 214 C4
Bondgate Gn HG4 214 D4
Bondgate Green Cl 6 HG4 214 C4
Bondgate Green La HG4 214 C4
Bondings Rise 5 LS25 196 A4
Bond La
Appleton Roebuck YO23 190 F5
Settle BD24 131 D2
Bond St WF8 201 C1
Bonington Ct 17 YO26 227 E4
Bonney Croft La 25 YO61 143 C8
Bonnygate La YO61 118 F3
Bonny Gr TS8 7 C5
Bonnygrove Way TS8 7 B5
Bonnywell La YO7 114 E6
Boonhill Rd YO62 69 F4
BOOSBECK 9 E8
Boosbeck Rd TS12 9 D8
Bootham YO30 233 A3
Bootham Bar* YO31 233 B3
Bootham Crescent YO30 233 A4
Bootham Crescent (York City FC) YO31 228 B7
Bootham Park Ct YO31 233 B4
Bootham Park Hospl YO31 233 B4
Bootham Row YO30 233 B3
Bootham Sch YO30 233 A3
Bootham Sq YO30 233 B3
BOOTHAM STRAY 225 B2
Bootham Terr YO30 233 A3
Booth Bridge La BD23 172 A3
BOOTHFERRY 205 E5
Boothferry Prim Sch DN14 205 F2
Booth Ferry Rd DN14 205 F6
Booth St 27 LS29 176 C1
Boothwood Rd YO30 224 E2
Boot St 26 BB18 172 A1
Booty La DN14 206 F7
BOOZE 17 F1
Borage Rd 30 HG3 161 B3
BORDLEY 133 D3
Bore Tree Baulk YO19 184 D6
Borogate 9 YO62 92 F6
BOROUGHBRIDGE 141 C5
Boroughbridge High Sch YO51 141 B5
Boroughbridge L Ctr YO51 141 B5
Boroughbridge Prim Sch YO51 141 B5
Boroughbridge Rd
Bishop Monkton HG3 140 B5
Bridge Hewick HG4 114 B1
Dishforth YO7 115 A2
Knaresborough HG5 221 B7
Northallerton DL7 210 C1
North Otterington DL7 64 E6
Ripon HG4 214 E3
Scriven HG5 162 E6
Westwick YO51 140 D4
Whixley YO26 164 B4
York YO26 227 D5
Borough Mere La YO17 215 D8
Borough Rd
Darlington DL1 3 D5
Richmond DL10 208 D7
Borough Road Ind Est DL1 3 D5
Borrage Green La HG4 214 B4
Borrage La HG4 214 B4
BORROWBY
Northallerton 65 E4
Whitby 11 D6
Borrowby Ave DL6 210 F3
Borrowby Ct TS14 8 E7
Borrowbydale Ave HG5 221 D6
Borrowby La
Borrowby TS13 11 D7
Staithes TS13 13 J1
Borrowdale Dr
Castleford WF10 201 B5
York YO30 224 F1
Boscombe Gdns 2 TS8 6 F5
BOSSALL 168 D7
Boss Moor La BD23 155 F8
Boston Ave DL6 210 D4
Boston Dr TS7 7 B5
Boston Rd Clifford LS23 188 E7
Wetherby LS22 180 C2
BOSTON SPA 188 F8
Boston Spa Sch LS23 188 D8
Botheby Wood BD23 216 E5
Bottom House La YO22 33 B5
Bottoms La YO22 33 B6
BOTTON 29 B3
Botton Rd LA2 128 E2
Botton Village Sch YO21 29 B3
Boulby Bank YO22 208 E6
Bouldershaw La DL11 17 D1
Boulsworth Dr BB8 186 B1
Boulsworth Gr 4 BB8 186 A3
Boundary Ave BD20 187 E7
Boundary Way DL10 209 F8
Bourlon Rd DL9 209 A2
Bournemouth Ave 2 TS3 7 C8
Bournemouth Rd TS3 7 C8
BOUTHWAITE 110 E2
Bouthwaite Dr 13 YO26 227 E4
Bow Bridge Dr BD23 217 D7
Bowbridge La DL7 63 A8
Bow Bridge La YO21 29 A7
Bow Bridge View LS24 189 F7
Bowcarr La YO26 163 D8
Bowcliffe Rd LS23 188 E5
Bowe Cres 8 DL8 63 B2
Bowen Rd DL3 3 B7
Bower Rd HG1 219 D3
Bower St HG1 219 D2
Bowers Wharf BD23 216 F3
Bower Wlk YO17 215 E4
Bowes Ave YO31 228 E5
Bowes Ct DL1 3 D6
Bowesfield Cres TS18 6 A8
Bowesfield Ind Est TS18 6 A8
Bowesfield La TS18 6 A7
Bowes La YO14 100 F5
Bowes Pk HG2 222 D6
Bowland Cl HG2 220 D1
Bowland Ct HG2 220 D1
Bowland La YO42 193 E2
Bowland View LA6 103 E3
Bowland Way YO30 225 A1
Bowling Green Ct YO31 228 D8
Bowling Green La
9 Hunmanby YO14 126 F8
Manfield DL2 2 B4
York YO31 233 C4

Bowling Green Yd 13 HG5 221 A6
Bowling La YO17 215 E4
Bowling Terr BD23 216 D3
Bowling View BD23 216 D3
Bowman St DL3 3 D7
Bowness Dr YO30 224 E1
Bowood Cl 8 TS17 5 F5
Bow St TS14 8 F7
Bowthorpe La YO8 199 B4
Bowyers Cl YO23 230 C4
Box Hill YO12 212 C3
Box La WF8 201 C1
Boyle The LS15 194 B8
Boynton La
- Barton-le-Street YO17 120 F8
- Rawcliffe DN14 205 A1

Boynton Rd DL7 22 E2
Brabourn Gdns TS8 6 F5
BRACEWELL 171 C3
Bracewell La BD23 171 B4
Bracewell St 15 BB18 171 D2
Brackenber Cl BD24 131 C2
Brackenber La BD24 131 C1
BRACKENBOTTOM 105 E3
Bracken Cl
- 13 Sherburn in Elmet LS25 196 A4
- Whitby YO22 208 E4
- York YO32 225 F4

Bracken Cres TS14 8 D6
Bracken Field BD23 134 B3
Brackenfield Sch HG1 219 A2
Bracken Ghyll Dr BD20 174 B1
Bracken Hill
- Scarborough YO12 212 C7
- 2 York YO10 229 C3

Brackenhill Ave YO8 232 A4
Brackenhill Cl YO8 197 D2
Brackenhill La
- Brayton YO8 232 A3
- Church Fenton LS24 196 C8
- Sleights YO22 32 A5

Brackenhills YO26 165 F1
Brackenley Ave 2 BD23 217 C7
Brackenley Cl 3 BD23 217 C7
Brackenley Cres BD23 217 C7
Brackenley Ct BD23 217 C7
Brackenley Dr BD23 217 C7
Brackenley Gr 1 BD23 217 C7
Brackenley La BD23 217 A7
Bracken Rd YO24 230 F7
Brackenthwaite La HG3 222 A1
Brackenwell La LS17 178 B4
Brackenwood Cl 2 LS29 218 E4
Brackit La YO61 91 B2
Bracknell Rd TS17 6 C8
Bradfords Cl 8 LS23 188 E6
Bradley Ave
- Castleford WF10 200 E4
- Northallerton DL6 210 F2

Bradley Cres YO23 182 D6
Bradley Dr YO24 230 C8
Bradley Gr BD20 174 B1
Bradley La YO23 182 C5
Bradley Rd
- Pickering YO18 71 F4
- Silsden BD20 174 B2

Bradley Rise BD20 174 B1
Bradleys Both Com Prim Sch BD20 173 E3
Bradleys Terr 2 TS9 8 A2
Bradworth Cl 3 YO11 100 B7
Bradworth Dr 2 YO11 100 B7
Braeburn Infant Sch 14 YO11 100 A6
Braeburn Junior Sch 15 YO14 100 A6
Braegate La LS24 190 E7
Braemar Dr LS25 194 D4
Braeside 3 TS15 24 E8
Braeside Gdns YO24 227 E3
BRAFFERTON 116 A1
Brafferton Hall Gdn 3 YO61 115 F1
Braham La HG5 179 F7
BRAIDLEY 83 B2
Brailsford Cres YO30 228 A8
Braimber La YO51 141 C1
Braithegayte YO19 192 F8
Braithwaite Hall* DL8 84 D8
Braithwaite La
- Dacre HG3 159 A7
- East Witton Town DL8 84 E8

Braker La YO26 163 F4
Bramall La 6 DL1 3 F6
Bramble Ave 2 LS23 188 D8
Bramble Cl
- 13 Colburn DL9 41 A5
- 11 Killinghall HG3 161 B3

Bramble Ct 20 LS25 195 F4
Bramble Dene YO24 230 D7
Bramblefields DL6 210 F4
Brambles 8 YO8 197 B1
Brambles Ct LS25 202 B7
Brambles The 6 LS29 175 C2
Bramble Wlk YO17 215 B4
Brambling Fields La YO17 122 C2
Bramblings The 6 WF10 200 D3
Brame La HG3 177 A8
Bramfield Way 6 TS17 6 D6
BRAMHAM 188 F5
Bramham Ave YO26 227 A3
Bramham Dr HG3 219 A4
Bramham Gr YO26 227 A3
Bramham La LS23 188 A6
Bramham Park Gdns* LS23 188 C4
Bramham Prim Sch LS23 188 E6
Bramham Rd
- Boston Spa LS23 188 E7
- Thorner LS14 188 A3
- York YO26 227 A2

Bramley Ave YO8 198 B5
Bramley Garth YO31 229 B6
Bramley Head La HG3 158 E5
Bramper La DL7 42 E1
Brancepeth Av TS3 7 B8
Branch Rd BD23 216 F2
Brandon Gr YO32 226 E3
BRANDSBY 118 C3
Brandsby Bank YO61 118 D3
Brandsby Gr YO31 225 E2
Brandsby Rd YO61 118 A1
Brandsby St YO61 118 A1
Brankin Dr DL1 3 E4
Brankin Rd DL1 3 D3
Branklyn Gdns TS17 6 A4
BRANKSOME 2 F6
Branksome Gr 1 TS18 5 E8
Bransdale TS14 8 D6
Bransdale Ave
- Northallerton DL7 210 C2
- 11 Pontefract WF6 200 A2

Bransdale Cl 6 WF6 200 A2
Bransdale Gr 3 HG5 221 D6
Bransdale Mews 10 WF6 200 A2
Bransdale Rd YO62 48 B1
Bransdale Wlk WF6 200 A2
Bransholme Dr YO30 225 A2
Brant Bank La LS29 175 B3
Brantingham Dr 2 TS17 5 F5
Brant La LS24 189 D4
Branton Cl YO26 142 A1
Branton Ct YO26 142 A1
BRANTON GREEN 142 A1
Branton La YO26 142 A1
Branton Pl YO26 227 A3
Brass Castle La TS8 7 C3
Brat La LS21 177 A7
Bravener Ct YO30 165 B6
BRAWBY 94 F1
Brawby La YO17 94 E1
BRAWITH 26 A6
Bray Gate YO42 169 E2
Braygate Balk YO18 72 C5
Braygate La YO18 72 D5
Braygate St YO17 121 A2
Bray Rd YO10 231 F8
Brayshaw La BD23 135 A2
BRAYTHORN 177 E4
Braythorne La LS21 177 E4
BRAYTON 232 A2
Brayton CE VC Prim Sch YO8 232 A2
Brayton High Sch YO8 232 A3
Brayton Junc YO8 232 C1
Brayton La YO8 232 B1
Brazengate BD23 134 B3
Breakmoor Ave BD20 174 C2
Breamar Ct 2 DN14 203 A2
Brearlands BD23 172 A3
BREARTON 162 A7
Brearton La HG3 161 E8
Breary Cl YO24 227 F1
Breary Flat La HG5 221 C7
Brechin Dr TS17 6 B6
Breckenbrough La DL10 41 A3
Breckenbrough Sch YO7 89 A6
Breckney La YO17 122 D5
Breckon Hill YO62 49 A1
Brecksfield YO30 224 C5
Brecks Gdns LS25 194 C2
Brecks La
- Beadlam YO62 93 B8
- Kippax LS25 194 C2
- Pockley YO62 93 B8
- Strensall YO32 167 B7
- Swillington LS26 194 B2
- York YO32 225 F4

Brecon Cres TS17 5 F4
Breedycroft La YO17 121 C4
BREIGHTON 199 D5
Breighton Aerodrome* YO8 199 D5
Breighton Rd
- Bubwith YO8 199 D6
- Wressle YO8 199 C3

Brendon Gr TS17 6 A3
Brentwood DL8 60 D5
Brentwood Cres YO10 229 C2
Brewers Ct YO7 211 B3
Brewerton St HG5 221 A5
Brewery Cl HG4 114 C6
Brewery La
- 5 Ripon HG4 214 C4
- Skipton BD23 216 F4

Brewery Rd LS29 218 C4
Brewster Terr HG4 214 C6
Brexdale Ave LS25 194 C2
Briar Ave YO26 227 B4
Briar Cl DL8 59 C6
Briar Cliffe YO8 232 A3
Briardene Ave 9 YO12 75 E5
Briar Dr YO31 225 F2
Briarfield Cl LS29 218 D3
Briar Pk 5 YO62 93 D7
Briar Rd TS17 6 B7
Briars Ct YO23 190 E5
Briars Dr YO23 190 E5
Briars The HG5 221 B7
Briar Wlk DL3 3 B3
Briarwood Cl YO8 202 F7
Brickfield La YO51 141 D4
Brickhill La YO8 204 F4
Brickkiln La
- Aldbrough DL11 2 A3
- Forcett & Carkin DL11 20 C8

Brick Kiln La YO8 203 D6
Brick Lands La DN14 203 F4
Brickyard Rd YO51 141 A4
Bridge Beck La YO7 66 C7
Bridge Cl
- Burniston YO13 75 D7
- Church Fenton LS24 196 A7
- 3 Colburn DL9 41 A5
- Haxby YO32 225 C7
- 5 Knaresborough HG5 221 A5
- Newton-le-Willows DL8 62 B4

Bridge Cres YO8 205 C8
Bridge Ct YO8 232 D6
Bridge End DL6 65 B5
Bridge End Yd 6 BD24 131 D3
Bridge Farm DN14 207 F6
Bridge Farm Cl 27 YO62 92 F6
Bridge Foot LS23 188 F8
Bridge Garth
- 2 Boston Spa LS23 188 E7
- South Milford LS25 195 F2

Bridge Gn YO21 29 C7
BRIDGE HEWICK 114 B1
Bridge Hill LS21 176 C7
Bridge Holm La YO22 33 C2
BRIDGEHOUSE GATE 137 B4
Bridge La
- Ilkley LS29 218 A5
- Pollington DN14 207 F6
- York YO30 233 B4

Bridge Mews LA6 103 C4
Bridge Rd
- Bishopthorpe YO23 230 F3
- Boston Spa LS23 188 F8
- Brompton-on-Swale DL10 41 B6
- Glusburn BD20 187 E7
- Hurworth DL3 3 B3
- Malton YO17 215 C5
- Old Byland & Scawton YO7 91 F7
- 10 Stokesley TS9 26 C7

Bridges Ct YO8 232 D6
Bridges La YO42 193 E4
Bridge St
- 5 Bedale DL8 63 A3
- 9 Brafferton YO61 115 F1
- Castleford WF10 200 F4
- Egglescliffe TS16 5 D4
- 12 Helmsley YO62 92 F6
- 8 Normanton South WF6 200 B2
- 16 Pickering YO18 95 F7
- Richmond DL10 209 B6
- Skipton BD23 216 F4
- Tadcaster LS24 189 E6
- Thirsk YO7 211 B3
- Whitby YO22 208 D7
- York YO1 233 B2

Bridge Terr
- Northallerton DL7 210 C4
- Richmond DL10 209 B6

Bridge View Rd HG4 214 C7
Bridle Way 1 YO26 227 A3
Bridle Wlk YO8 232 C4
Bridlington Rd
- Hunmanby YO14 127 A7
- Sledmere YO25 150 C4
- 1 Stamford Bridge YO41 168 D2
- Wold Newton YO25 126 A4

Bridlington St YO14 126 F8
Briercliffe YO12 212 C7
Briergate YO32 225 C7
Brier Hill YO21 29 C7
Brier La YO8 205 A4
Brierlands Cl LS25 194 D4
Brierlands La LS25 194 E4
Brierley Rd YO12 99 E7
Briery Cl 18 LS29 175 C2
Brigantia Gdns 12 YO12 99 E6
Briggate HG5 221 B5
Brigg Farm Ct YO8 204 D5
Brigg La YO8 204 D5
Brigg Rd 55 YO14 101 B3
Brigg's Ave WF10 200 E3
Briggs St YO31 228 C7
BRIGGSWATH 32 B7
Brighton Rd LS29 218 E3
Bright St
- 18 Colne BB8 186 A3
- Darlington DL1 3 E5
- 1 Glusburn BD20 173 E1
- Skipton BD23 216 E4
- 15 Trawden BB8 186 A3
- York YO26 227 F5

Bright Terr BB8 186 A1
Bright Wlk YO8 232 B6
Brigshaw Dr WF10 200 C8
Brigshaw High Sch WF10 200 C8
Brigshaw La WF10 200 C8
Brimham Cl 2 TS17 6 B5
Brimham Rocks* HG3 138 B4
Brimham Rocks Rd HG3 138 B2
Brind La DN14 199 F2
Brindle Park Dr WF10 201 A3
Brindle Way YO17 215 F4
Brindley Ct 15 BD23 216 F3
Brindley Mill BD23 216 F3
Brindleys La DN14 199 F3
Brindley Wharf BD23 217 A3
Brinkburn Ave DL3 3 B7
Brinkburn Dr 1 DL3 3 B6
Brinkburn Rd
- Darlington DL3 3 B6
- 4 Scarborough YO12 212 E5

Brinklow Way HG2 222 B5
Brinkworth Rush YO41 185 A2
Brinkworth Terr 1 YO10 228 E3
Briscoe Ridge La HG3 177 F6
BRISCOERIGG 177 F5
Briscoe Way TS8 6 E5
Britannia Dr YO14 127 C8
Britannia St 2 YO12 212 E5
Broach La
- Heck DN14 203 D1
- Kellington DN14 202 F3

Broach Rd
- Heck DN14 207 D8
- Hensall DN14 203 C1

Broadacres DN14 204 D3
Broad Acres YO32 225 C7
Broadacres Ave DN14 204 D3
Broadacres Garth DN14 204 D3
Broad Balk YO17 149 A5
Broad Balk La YO7 115 B1
Broad Carr Rd HG3 110 D2
Broad Cl
- Askrigg DL8 57 E6
- Coulby Newham TS8 6 D5

Broad Dubb Rd HG3 177 C8
Broadfield La HG4 138 B8
Broadfield Way 9 LS29 174 E4
Broad Gate
- Brompton YO13 98 B7
- Hunsingore LS22 180 F8
- Marton cum Grafton YO26 141 F1

Broadgate Rd TS5 6 E8
Broad Gate Rd YO21 28 E4
Broad Head La BD22 187 E2
Broad Highway YO19 192 F8
Broad La
- Appleton Roebuck YO23 191 A6
- 6 Beal DN14 202 D4
- Catton YO41 185 C7
- Cawood YO8 197 A6
- Church Fenton LS25 196 D6
- Rufforth YO23 227 A2
- Upper Poppleton YO26 165 D2
- Wistow YO8 197 A5

Broadlands
- 2 Roundhill Village TS17 6 A5
- Wheldrake YO19 193 A8

Broadlands Dr 5 YO13 99 B8
Broadmanor YO8 199 A7
Broadmires La YO18 96 C5
Broad Oak La 13 YO32 166 E5
Broadrum La YO18 95 E6
Broadstone Way
- 10 Rawcliffe YO30 224 E3
- York YO30 224 E3

Broadway
- Scarborough YO12 212 D7
- York YO10 231 E8

Broadway Gr 3 YO10 231 E8
Broadway The DL1 3 E5
Broadway W YO10 231 D8
Broadwell Rd TS4 7 A8
Brockadale Nature Reserve* WF8 206 B4
Brockett Ind Est YO23 191 B6
BROCKFIELD 167 E2
Brockfield Park Dr YO31 225 F2
Brockfield Rd YO31 225 E2
Brockholme La DL6 65 A4
Brocklesby Rd TS14 8 F5
Brockley Cl LS24 196 B7
Brockrigg Ct TS14 8 E7
Broc-o-Bank 1 DN6 206 E2
Brodie Cl 9 TS17 5 F5
Brodrick Dr LS29 218 A3
Brogden La BB18 171 B1
Brogden View 19 BB18 171 D2
Brokes La DL11 40 B6
Bromley La TS8 7 B3
Bromley St 2 YO26 227 F5
BROMPTON 43 F3
Brompton Ave 4 TS14 8 F7
BROMPTON-BY-SAWDON 98 C5
Brompton Carr La YO13 98 B4
Brompton Com Prim Sch DL6 43 F3
Brompton Hall Sch YO13 98 C5
Brompton House Day Hospl DL6 210 E5
Brompton Ings Rd YO13 98 D3
Brompton La DL6 43 E4
BROMPTON-ON-SWALE 41 B7
Brompton-on-Swale CE Prim Sch DL10 41 B7
Brompton Pk DL10 41 B6
Brompton Rd
- Newton-le-Willows DL8 62 B4
- Northallerton DL6 210 D5
- York YO30 228 A7

Brompton & Sawdon Com Prim Sch YO13 98 C5
Bronaber Cl 1 TS17 5 F4
Bronte Cl
- Brompton on Swale DL10 41 C7
- Scarborough YO12 212 D5

Bronte Ct WF8 201 B1
Bronte Dr 33 DL9 41 A5
Bronte Rise WF10 201 B3
Brookacre 7 LA6 103 D3
Brooke Cl
- Harrogate HG1 219 E7
- 12 Kirkbymoorside YO62 70 B1

BROOKFIELD 6 E6
Brookfield Cl HG3 161 A5
Brookfield Cres HG3 161 A5
Brookfield Ct 5 WF6 200 B1
Brookfield Garth HG3 161 A5
Brookfield Way
- 7 Earby BB18 172 A1
- Hampsthwaite HG3 160 F5

Brook House Croft BD24 131 E6
Brook La
- Danby YO21 29 C6
- Halton West BD23 153 F1
- Thornton Dale YO18 96 D6
- Weeton LS17 178 C2

Brookland 1 LA6 102 F2
Brooklands
- 43 Filey YO14 101 B3
- York YO10 229 D4

Brooklands Cl 44 YO14 101 B3
Brooklands Cres DL6 210 E5
Brooklands Sch BD23 216 F2
Brooklands Terr BD23 216 F3
Brook Pk YO21 32 A7
Brooksbank Rd TS7 7 D7
Brookside
- Collingham LS22 188 A8
- Hovingham YO62 119 E6
- Hunton DL8 61 E7
- Skelton & Brotton TS12 9 D8
- Skipton BD23 217 A3
- Sleights YO22 32 B6
- Spennithorne DL8 60 F4

Brookside Ave 1 DL8 63 B2
Brookside Cl 2 DL8 63 B2
Brook St
- Castleford WF10 201 B6
- 18 Earby BB18 172 A1
- Hebden BD23 135 A2
- Hellifield BD23 154 B3
- Ilkley LS29 218 B4
- 12 Scarborough YO12 212 F6
- Selby YO8 232 C4
- Skipton BD23 216 F4
- York YO31 233 B4

Brook View BD23 173 B4
Brookwood Way TS16 5 E4
Broome Cl
- 14 Pontefract WF6 200 A2
- York YO32 225 F5

Broome Way YO32 226 A5
Broom Field HG3 160 E6
Broomfield Ave DL7 210 D2
Broomfield Sch DL7 210 D2
Broomfield Terr 18 YO21 208 D6
Broomhill WF10 201 A3
Broom Hill Ave 6 TS17 6 D5
Broomhill Cl 23 WF11 202 A2
Broomhill Cres 25 WF11 202 A2
Broomhill Dr 26 WF11 202 A2
Broomhill Gr 19 WF11 202 A2
Broomhill Pl 22 WF11 202 A2
Broomhill Sq 24 WF11 202 A2
Broomhill Wlk 21 WF11 202 A2
Broom House La
- Egton YO21 30 F4
- Ugthorpe YO21 12 B2

Broom Rd LS24 189 D5
Broom Wlk YO12 212 E7
Brootes La BD23 107 C2
Brotes La YO26 164 B5
BROTHERTON 201 D5
Brotherton & Byram Com Prim Sch WF11 201 E4
Brougham Cl
- 3 Egglescliffe TS17 5 F6
- York YO30 227 F8

Brougham St
- Darlington DL3 3 C7
- Skipton BD23 217 A3

Brough Ave 5 DL9 41 A5
Brough Field Cl 4 TS17 6 D6
Brough Hall* DL10 41 B4
Brough Mdws DL10 41 D5
Brough Rd 23 DL9 40 E4
BROUGHTON
- Malton 121 D4
- Skipton 172 E6

Broughton Ave BD23 216 D3
Broughton Cres BD23 216 C3
Broughton Gr BD23 216 D3
Broughton Green La YO17 121 C4
Broughton Mews BD23 216 D3
Broughton Rd
- Broughton YO17 121 C3
- 11 East Ayton/West Ayton YO13 99 A7
- Malton YO17 215 A5
- Skipton BD23 216 C3

Broughton Rise YO17 215 B5
Broughton Way
- 4 Harrogate HG2 220 C3
- York YO10 229 B4

Browcliff BD20 174 C2
Brow La LA2 129 D6
Brown Bank La BD20 174 D2
Brown Bank Rd
- Kirkby Malzeard HG4 111 F5
- Norwood HG3 177 B8

Brown Cow Rd YO8 204 C8
Browney Croft YO10 233 C1
Brown Howe Rd YO18 51 A1
Browning Cl 3 DL9 40 E4
Brown La YO26 141 F1
Brownlow St YO31 233 C4
Brown Moor 22 YO41 168 D2
Brownmoor La
- Huby YO61 144 A2
- Sutton-on-the-Forest YO32 166 B8

Brown Rigg Rd YO13 53 F5

Brownroyd 14 BB18 ... 172 B1
Browns Ct 4 BD20 ... 173 E3
Browns Fold 3 BD23 ... 134 E3
Brown's Terr 4 TS13 ... 11 F7
Brownswood Cotts YO21 . 31 A5
Browsfield Rd 24 LS29 ... 174 F4
BROXA ... 74 C6
Broxa Hill YO13 ... 74 C6
Broxa La YO13 ... 74 D5
Broxa Moor La YO13 ... 74 C7
Bruce St 21 BB18 ... 171 D2
Bruce Way 5 YO18 ... 95 F6
Bruche Dr YO7 ... 115 A2
Brunel Ct 12 YO26 ... 227 F5
Brunel Rd HG1 ... 220 D5
Brunel Way DL1 ... 3 D5
Brunsell La YO26 ... 163 F7
Brunswick Cl 2 YO32 ... 167 C8
Brunswick Dr HG1 ... 219 B2
Brunswick Pl 1 HG1 ... 219 D1
Brunswick Sh Ctr YO11 .. 213 A5
Brunswick St
Whitby YO21 ... 208 D6
York YO23 ... 228 B1
Brunt Acres Ind Est DL8 .. 56 D5
Brunt Acres Ind Est DL8 .. 56 D5
Brunt Acres Rd DL8 ... 56 D4
BRUNTHWAITE ... 174 D1
Brunthwaite La BD20 ... 174 E1
Brunton Bank DL8 ... 59 A5
Brunton La HG5 ... 163 B6
Brunton Rd LA2 ... 131 A6
Bryan Cl 13 DL2 ... 3 E1
Bryden Cl DL6 ... 210 E2
Bry Hills YO12 ... 99 D6
Brymor Ice Cream Palour★ HG4 ... 85 E7
Bryony Ct YO8 ... 232 B2
Bryony Rd 4 HG3 ... 161 B3
Bryony Way 5 HG3 ... 161 B3
BUBWITH ... 199 D7
Bubwith Com Prim Sch YO8 ... 199 D7
Buccaneer Ct YO41 ... 185 A3
Buccleugh Cl TS14 ... 8 F5
BUCKDEN ... 107 E8
Buckden Cl 13 YO61 ... 143 D8
Buckden Wood La BD23 107 D8
Buck Haw Brow BD24 ... 131 B4
Buckingham Ct YO1 ... 233 A1
Buckingham Sq 7 YO62 .. 92 F6
Buckingham St YO1 ... 233 B1
Buckingham Terr YO1 ... 233 B2
Buckingham Way WF11 . 201 F4
Buck La YO60 ... 147 B6
Buckle Cl YO8 ... 199 A8
Buckle Ct YO8 ... 232 B7
Buckle La WF6 ... 200 A1
Bucks La 1 BD24 ... 131 D2
Buck Stone La BD20 ... 187 C5
Buess La DL1 ... 4 A7
Buffet Hill La LA2 ... 129 D7
BUGTHORPE ... 169 D4
Bugthorpe CE VC Prim Sch YO41 ... 169 D4
Bugthorpe La YO41 ... 169 D5
Bull Alley La DN14 ... 204 B3
BULLAMOOR ... 44 B1
Bullamoor Cl DL6 ... 210 F5
Bullamoor Rd DL6 ... 210 E5
Bull Balk YO41 ... 185 E4
Bull Commercial Centre YO32 ... 226 F3
Buller St YO8 ... 232 B6
Bull Hill DL8 ... 61 E8
Bull Ing La BD23 ... 134 D3
Bull La
Huby YO32 ... 166 B7
York YO10 ... 228 F3
Bull Moor La YO60 ... 168 A8
Bullock La
Newsham with Breckenbrough YO7 ... 89 A5
Newsham YO7 ... 88 F8
Bull Piece La YO17 ... 122 D3
Bullytree La LS25 ... 195 E2
BULMER ... 146 B6
Bulmer Hill YO60 ... 146 B6
Bungalow Rd BD20 ... 187 D7
Bunkers Hill
Aberford LS25 ... 194 F7
1 Skipton BD23 ... 217 A4
Burdale Cl
8 Eaglescliffe TS16 ... 5 D5
Norton YO17 ... 215 F2
Burdike Ave YO30 ... 228 A8
Burdock Cl 10 HG3 ... 161 B3
Burdon Garth TS17 ... 6 D5
Burdon View 3 TS16 ... 5 D4
Burgate YO18 ... 95 F7
Burgess Wlk YO24 ... 230 C8
Burghley Dr 1 TS17 ... 6 A5
Burgoyne Cl HG4 ... 113 D3
Burke Rd YO17 ... 215 C5
Burke St HG1 ... 219 E5
Burlands La YO26 ... 182 F7
Burley Ave HG3 ... 161 A2
Burley Bank Cl HG3 ... 161 A3
Burley Bank Rd HG3 ... 161 A3
Burley Cl
12 South Milford LS25 ... 195 F2
Thornton-le-Street YO7 ... 65 B1
BURLEY IN WHARFEDALE ... 176 B1
Burley La HG3 ... 161 A3
Burley Oaks Prim Sch 42 LS29 ... 176 C1
Burlington Ave YO10 ... 228 F4
Burlyn Rd 3 YO14 ... 127 A8
Burma Rd DL2 ... 3 F2
BURN ... 203 D7
BURN BRIDGE ... 222 D3
Burn Bridge La HG3 ... 222 C2
Burn Bridge Oval HG3 ... 222 C3
Burn Bridge Rd HG3 ... 222 C3
Burnby Cl HG3 ... 219 B5
Burn Cl WF10 ... 200 C7
Burn Est YO32 ... 225 E4
BURNESTON ... 87 E7
Burneston CE VA Prim Sch DL8 ... 87 E8
Burneston Ct DL3 ... 2 F5
Burneston Hargill DL8 ... 87 F8
Burnett Cl HG3 ... 140 A2
Burn Hall Cl YO8 ... 203 D7
Burn Hall Cres YO8 ... 203 C7
Burnham Rd LS25 ... 194 C3
Burnholme Ave YO31 ... 229 B6
Burnholme Com Coll YO31 ... 229 A5
Burnholme Dr YO31 ... 229 A6
Burnholme Gr YO31 ... 229 A5
BURNISTON ... 75 C8
Burniston Gdns YO13 ... 75 D7
Burniston Gr YO10 ... 229 A4
Burniston Ind Est YO13 ... 75 D7
Burniston Rd YO12 ... 212 E8
Burn La YO8 ... 203 D6
Burnley Rd BB8 ... 186 A1
Burnleys Ct LS26 ... 200 B4
Burnleys Dr LS26 ... 200 B4
Burnleys Mews LS26 ... 200 B4
Burnleys View LS26 ... 200 B5
Burnmoor Cres LA6 ... 103 D3
Burnmoor Dr TS16 ... 5 D5
Burnroyd Ave 17 BD20 ... 187 E7
BURNSALL ... 157 B8
Burnsall Cl 6 YO14 ... 101 A3
Burnsall Dr YO26 ... 227 E4
Burnsall La BD23 ... 135 A1
Burnsall Mews BD20 ... 174 B2
Burnsall Prim Sch BD23 . 157 B8
Burns Ct YO24 ... 230 B7
Burns Hill 4 LS29 ... 174 F4
Burnside 4 YO11 ... 100 A6
Burnside Ave BD23 ... 216 F2
Burnside Cl HG1 ... 219 B5
Burnside Cres BD23 ... 216 F2
Burnside Dr HG1 ... 219 B5
Burnside Rd
Darlington DL1 ... 3 E4
Harrogate HG1 ... 219 B5
Burnside Wlk HG1 ... 219 B5
Burns Way
Boston Spa LS23 ... 188 E7
Harrogate HG1 ... 219 E7
Burnthouse Bank DL6 ... 45 B3
Burnt La HG4 ... 87 A1
BURNT YATES ... 160 F8
Burnt Yates CE Prim Sch HG3 ... 160 F8
Burn Wood Ct TS21 ... 5 A7
Burrard Ave DL10 ... 209 B7
Burr Bank 15 YO11 ... 213 B6
BURRILL ... 62 E2
Burrill Ave YO30 ... 228 B8
Burrill Dr 13 YO32 ... 166 D5
Burrill Rd DL8 ... 62 F2
Burrow Rd LA6 ... 102 B7
Bursary Ct YO24 ... 230 F6
Burstall Dr 2 DL9 ... 209 C1
BURTERSETT ... 56 E4
Burtersett Rd DL8 ... 56 D4
Burton Ave YO30 ... 228 B7
Burton Comm La LS25 ... 202 A6
Burton Ct YO30 ... 233 A4
Burtondale Rd 1 YO12 ... 99 F7
Burton Fields Cl 12 YO41 168 D2
Burton Fields Rd 4 YO41 ... 168 D2
BURTON FLEMING ... 126 E3
Burton Fleming Rd YO25 126 B3
Burton Gn YO30 ... 228 B8
Burton Green Prim Sch YO30 ... 225 C1
Burton Hill 3 LA6 ... 102 F3
BURTON IN LONSDALE ... 102 F3
Burton La YO61 ... 141 D8
BURTON LEONARD ... 140 B2
Burton Leonard CE Prim Sch HG3 ... 140 A2
Burton Leonard Lime Quarries Nature Reserve★ HG3 ... 140 A1
Burton Rd LA2 ... 128 E8
Burton Riggs Nature Reserve★ YO11 ... 99 F6
BURTON SALMON ... 201 F6
Burton Salmon Com Prim Sch LS25 ... 201 F6
Burton Stone La YO30 ... 233 A4
Burtree Ave YO30 ... 224 B4
Burtree La YO21 ... 29 B5
Burwains La BD23 ... 155 F5
Burwen Castle Rd BD23 . 172 C4
Burwen Castle (Roman Fort)★ BD23 ... 172 C4
BURYTHORPE ... 147 F3
Busby La TS9 ... 26 C4
Bushby Gill Wlk DL9 ... 40 E2
Bush Gdns YO17 ... 121 B4
Busk La LS24 ... 196 C8
Busky Dike La LS21 ... 159 E2
Butcher La
Potto DL6 ... 25 C2
Whitley DN14 ... 207 A6
Butcher's La YO25 ... 126 E3
Butcher Terr YO23 ... 228 C1
Bute Cl 2 TS17 ... 6 B6
Butler Rd HG1 ... 219 E5
Buttacre La YO23 ... 182 D2
Butterbergh 11 LA2 ... 129 A8
Butterbur Way 34 HG3 ... 161 B3
BUTTERCRAMBE ... 168 E5
Buttercrambe Rd
Gate Helmsley YO41 ... 168 C3
Sand Hutton YO41 ... 168 C5
Buttercup Cl 6 HG3 ... 161 B3
Butterfield Cl HG3 ... 140 B5
Butterfield Dr TS16 ... 5 D5
Butterfly World★ TS18 ... 5 E6
Buttermere Ave
Middlesbrough TS5 ... 6 E8
4 Wetherby LS22 ... 180 B3
Buttermere Ct 9 YO8 ... 232 B6
Buttermere Dr YO30 ... 224 E1
Butter Mkt 8 DN14 ... 204 C1
Butters Cl 20 YO32 ... 166 D5
BUTTERWICK
125 B2
Brawby ... 120 E8
Butterwick La YO17 ... 120 F8
Butterwick Rd
Barton-le-Street YO17 ... 120 E5
Foxholes YO17 ... 125 B1
Langtoft YO25 ... 151 C7
Butt Fields La DN14 ... 203 F1
Butt Hedge YO26 ... 182 A5
Butt Hill
22 Haxby YO32 ... 166 D5
Kippax LS25 ... 194 D1
Butthouse Rigg DL11 ... 35 F8
Butt La
Carlton Husthwaite YO7 .. 116 F7
Guisborough TS14 ... 9 A6
Wold Newton YO25 ... 126 A3
Buttle La 3 DN14 ... 204 C1
Butts BB18 ... 171 D1
Butts Cl 19 YO41 ... 168 D2
Butts Hill YO14 ... 127 C6
Butts La
Bainbridge DL8 ... 81 B8
Barton-le-Willows YO60 ... 146 D2
Bentham LA2 ... 129 A8
Eaglescliffe TS16 ... 5 D4
Monk Fryston LS25 ... 201 E8
South Milford LS25 ... 195 E1
Butts The 12 WF8 ... 201 B1
Buxton Ave TS7 ... 7 B5
Byards Pk 6 HG5 ... 221 A7
Byefield Gr YO13 ... 99 B8
Byemoor Ave TS9 ... 8 A1
Byemoor Cl TS9 ... 8 A1
BYLAND ABBEY ... 91 E1
Byland Abbey (rems of)★ YO61 ... 91 E1
Byland Ave
Northallerton DL6 ... 210 E5
Thirsk YO7 ... 211 C3
York YO31 ... 228 E8
Byland Ct 5 YO21 ... 208 B6
Byland Gr HG1 ... 219 F6
Byland Mews HG5 ... 221 D4
Byland Pl
Harrogate HG1 ... 219 F6
Northallerton DL6 ... 210 E5
Byland Rd
Harrogate HG1 ... 219 F6
Whitby YO21 ... 208 B6
Bylands Way DL3 ... 3 A6
Byng Rd DL9 ... 209 F1
Bypass Pk Ind Est LS25 .. 196 B7
BYRAM ... 201 F4
Byram Cl 3 DL6 ... 210 E3
Byram Ct 4 DL6 ... 210 E3
Byram Park Ave WF11 ... 201 F4
Byram Park Rd WF11 ... 202 A4
Byre Way YO25 ... 126 E3
Byron Ave 3 DN6 ... 206 E1
Byron Ct DL2 ... 22 D7
Byron Dr YO30 ... 227 F8
Byron St 2 BD23 ... 217 A3
Byron Wlk Mews HG2 ... 219 D2
Byward Dr YO12 ... 99 F7
Bywater Ct WF10 ... 200 E6
Byways HG2 ... 222 D6
Byway The DL1 ... 3 E5

C

Cabin La 2 HG3 ... 137 F1
Caburn Cl 2 YO12 ... 212 B5
Caedmon Ave YO21 ... 208 B8
Caedmon Cl YO31 ... 229 A7
Caedmon Coll Whitby YO21 ... 208 C5
Caesar Ct YO24 ... 233 A1
Cairnborrow 4 YO24 ... 230 B7
Cairn View LS29 ... 218 D5
Caithness Cl 1 YO30 ... 224 E3
Calcaria Cres LS24 ... 189 D5
Calcaria Ct 3 YO24 ... 230 F8
Calcaria Rd LS24 ... 189 E5
CALCUTT ... 221 A3
Calcutt HG5 ... 221 A4
Caldbeck Cl 1 YO30 ... 225 A1
CALDBERGH ... 84 B7
Calder Ave YO26 ... 227 B8
Calder Cres DN14 ... 207 F6
Caldey Gdns 39 TS17 ... 5 F4
CALDWELL ... 1 B4
Caledonian Way DL1 ... 3 F8
Caledonia St YO12 ... 212 E5
Calf Cl YO32 ... 225 D8
Calf Hall La BB18 ... 171 D1
Calf Wood La BD20 ... 172 E1
California Dr WF10 ... 200 B3
California Gr 7 TS9 ... 8 A2
California Rd YO22 ... 208 E5
California Terr YO22 ... 208 E5
Callum Cl DL3 ... 3 C7
CALTON ... 155 B6
Calton La BD23 ... 155 A6
Calton Terr BD23 ... 216 F3
Calvert Cl
Haxby YO32 ... 225 C7
Kippax LS25 ... 194 D2
Calvert Hos DL11 ... 36 C4
Calverts Garth YO60 ... 145 D5
Calvert Way 23 DL8 ... 63 A2
CAMBLESFORTH ... 204 D5
Camblesforth Com Prim Sch YO8 ... 204 C4
Cambrain Ct 10 TS17 ... 5 F4
Cambrian Cl 2 YO32 ... 225 F3
Cambridge Ave
4 Airmyn DN14 ... 205 F3
Middlesbrough TS7 ... 7 B5
Cambridge Cres 5 HG1 219 D2
Cambridge Pl
8 Harrogate HG1 ... 219 D2
1 Scarborough YO12 ... 212 E4
Cambridge Rd
Harrogate HG1 ... 219 D2
Middlesbrough TS5 ... 6 E8
Cambridge St
3 Castleford WF10 ... 200 E4
15 Harrogate HG1 ... 219 D2
Normanton South WF6 ... 200 A1
Scarborough YO12 ... 212 F6
4 York YO24 ... 228 A3
Cambridge Terr
4 Harrogate HG1 ... 219 D2
1 Scarborough YO11 ... 213 A4
Camden Rd WF10 ... 201 B4
Camela La YO8 ... 204 B6
Cameron Gr YO23 ... 228 C1
Cam Garth BD23 ... 108 A3
Cam Gill Rd
Kettlewell with Starbotton BD23 ... 108 B4
Woodale DL8 ... 83 A2
Cam High Rd BD23 ... 79 D5
Cam La BD23 ... 172 A3
Camm La DN14 ... 204 C3
Cammock La BD24 ... 131 D2
Campbell Ave
Ripon HG4 ... 113 D3
York YO24 ... 227 E2
Campbell St 11 BD20 ... 187 E8
CAMP HILL ... 87 F5
Camp Hill Cl HG4 ... 214 D3
Campion Cl YO13 ... 75 D5
Campion Dock YO22 ... 208 E5
Campion Dr TS14 ... 8 D6
Campion Gr
Coulby Newham TS7 ... 7 B6
6 Harrogate HG3 ... 161 B3
Campion La TS15 ... 25 B4
Campion Rd DL1 ... 3 D7
Campleshon Rd YO23 ... 228 B1
Campsall Balk DN6 ... 206 E1
Campsall Hall Rd 12 DN6 206 E1
Campsall Park Rd 11 DN6 ... 206 E1
Camwal Rd HG1 ... 220 C4
Camwal Terr 5 HG1 ... 220 C4
Canaan La DL8 ... 60 E2
Cana La HG4 ... 114 E2
Canal Garth DN14 ... 207 F6
Canal Rd
Cottingwith YO42 ... 193 C5
Ripon HG4 ... 214 D4
Selby YO8 ... 232 D4
Canal St BD23 ... 216 F4
Canal View YO8 ... 232 D3
Canal Yd 8 BD23 ... 216 F4
Canberra Rd TS7 ... 7 B6
Canby La 4 HG3 ... 179 E6
Candler Ave 12 YO13 ... 99 A7
Candler St YO12 ... 212 E5
Canham Gr YO10 ... 229 D3
Cannon Hall La DN14 ... 202 F1
Cannon St WF10 ... 200 F3
Canon Gr TS15 ... 5 E2
Canon Lee Sch YO30 ... 228 A8
Canons Ct YO23 ... 231 B2
Canons Garth La 2 YO62 . 92 F6
Canterbury Cl
9 Haxby YO32 ... 166 D5
Whitby YO21 ... 208 C5
Canterbury Ct 5 WF8 ... 201 C2
Canton Gdns TS5 ... 6 E6
CANTSFIELD ... 102 B4
Caper Hill YO21 ... 29 F1
Captain Cook Birthplace Mus★ TS7 ... 7 B7
Captain Cook Cres YO22 . 208 E6
Captain Cook Meml Mus★ YO22 ... 208 E7
Captain Cook Monumnet★ YO21 ... 208 D8
Captain Cook Prim Sch TS7 7 B6
Captain Cook Schoolroom Mus★ TS9 ... 8 A1
Captain Cook's Cl
Hinderwell TS13 ... 11 D8
Staithes TS13 ... 13 K1
Captain Cooks Cres 14 YO22 ... 208 E6
Captain Cook's Cres TS7 .. 7 C6
Captain Cook's Mon★ TS9 . 8 D1
Captain Cook & Staithes Heritage Ctr★ TS13 ... 13 K2
Captain Cook's Way TS9 ... 8 A1
Cardale Pk
Pannal HG3 ... 178 C8
Pannal HG3 ... 222 A6
Cardan Dr LS29 ... 218 E4
Cardinal Cl 13 LS25 ... 195 F4
Cardinal Gdns DL3 ... 3 B5
Cardinals Cl 3 YO8 ... 197 B8
Careless House La HG3 .. 138 E4
Carentan Cl 6 YO8 ... 232 B6
Carey St YO10 ... 228 D1
Cargate Hill 32 YO14 ... 101 B3
Cargo Fleet La TS3 ... 7 C8
Carla Beck La BD23 ... 173 B4
CARLBURY ... 2 B7
Carlbury Ave TS5 ... 6 D6
Carlbury Cres DL3 ... 3 A5
CARLESMOOR ... 111 E4
Carless La YO14 ... 100 F4
Carleton Ave BD23 ... 216 E3
Carleton Bsns Pk BD23 .. 216 E3
Carleton Cl 4 LS23 ... 188 D8
Carleton Dr
3 Boston Spa LS23 ... 188 D8
Darlington DL3 ... 3 A5
Carleton Endowed CE Prim Sch BD23 ... 173 B4
CARLETON IN CRAVEN ... 173 A4
Carleton La BD23 ... 173 A4
Carleton New Rd BD23 .. 216 E3
Carleton Rd BD23 ... 216 E1
Carleton St
3 Skipton BD23 ... 216 F3
17 York YO26 ... 227 F5
Carlile Hill TS8 ... 6 E5
Carline Mead 23 HG3 ... 161 B3
Carlisle St 16 YO26 ... 227 F5
Carlow Cl TS14 ... 8 F6
Carl St YO23 ... 228 C2
CARLTON
204 D3
Darlington ... 1 F3
Helmsley ... 68 E1
West Witton ... 83 E7
Carlton App 1 LS22 ... 180 B3
Carlton Ave
Thirsk YO7 ... 211 B1
York YO10 ... 229 B3
Carlton Cl
4 Carlton Miniott YO7 ... 89 C4
Eggborough DN14 ... 202 F1
11 Eggborough DN14 ... 202 F2
11 Guisborough TS14 ... 8 F7
19 Normanton South WF6 200 A1
Carlton Dr TS17 ... 6 A6
Carlton & Faceby CE Prim Sch TS9 ... 26 A3
Carlton Gdns 1 WF6 ... 200 B1
CARLTON HUSTHWAITE .. 116 F7
CARLTON IN CLEVELAND .. 26 A3
Carlton-in-Snaith Com Prim Sch DN14 ... 204 C3
Carlton La YO62 ... 92 F7
Carlton Lanes Sh Ctr WF10 ... 200 F4
CARLTON MINIOTT ... 89 C4
Carlton Miniott Com Prim Sch YO7 ... 89 B4
Carlton Moor Cres DL1 ... 3 E4
Carlton Rd
Carlton Miniott YO7 ... 89 A3
1 Catterick Garrison DL9 . 40 F4
9 Filey YO14 ... 101 B3
Harrogate HG2 ... 222 D7
Helmsley YO62 ... 92 F7
Skipton BD23 ... 217 F3
Sutton upon Derwent YO41 185 C1
Carlton St WF6 ... 200 A2
Carlton Terr 6 YO11 ... 213 A4
Carlton Twrs★ DN14 ... 204 D2
Carlton View
Great Preston WF10 ... 200 C7
Selby YO8 ... 232 D4
Carlton Way YO7 ... 89 C4
Carlyle Cres WF10 ... 201 A4
Carlyle Rd WF10 ... 201 A4
Carmel Coll DL3 ... 3 A5
Carmel Gdns TS5 ... 6 E6
Carmel Gr DL3 ... 3 B4
Carmelite St YO1 ... 233 C2
Carmel Road N DL3 ... 3 B5
Carmel Road S DL3 ... 3 B4
Carmires Ave
Haxby YO32 ... 166 F5
Knaresborough HG5 ... 221 C8
Carnagill Com Prim Sch DL9 ... 40 D4
Carnagil Rd DL9 ... 209 B1
Carney St TS12 ... 9 D7
Carnot St YO26 ... 227 F5
Carnoustie Cl 1 YO26 ... 227 B4
Carnoustie Dr TS16 ... 5 E5
Carnoustie Gdns 20 WF6 200 B1
Carnoustie Way TS8 ... 7 C5
Caroline Cl 5 YO24 ... 227 F3
Carousel Wlk LS25 ... 195 F4
Carpenters Yd 10 YO17 .. 215 C4
CARPERBY ... 58 E4
Carpley Green Rd DL8 ... 57 D3
Carr Ave LS25 ... 195 F4
Carrbank La YO32 ... 167 D2
Carr Beck Dr 11 WF10 ... 200 D3

Carr Beck Rd 2 WF10 ... 200 D3
Carr Beck View 5 WF10 200 D3
Carr Bridge Cl 4 TS16 ... 5 D4
Carr Bridge La DL6 ... 24 D3
Carr Cl
13 Hemingbrough YO8 ... 198 F1
Rainton with Newby YO7 .. 114 F6
Ripon HG4 ... 214 B3
Carrfield YO24 ... 230 C8
Carrfield Dr LS15 ... 194 B8
Carr Field La YO26 ... 141 F1
Carrfield Rd LS15 ... 194 B8
Carr Fields La YO13 ... 99 B5
Carr Head La BD22 ... 187 B7
Carr Hill YO60 ... 145 D5
Carr Hill La YO21 ... 32 B7
Carr Hill Ridge YO21 ... 32 B7
Carr House La
Cayton YO11 ... 100 A5
Heslerton YO17 ... 98 A1
Carriage Wlk 4 TS16 ... 5 D5
Carrick Gdns YO24 ... 227 E3
Carrier's Row BB8 ... 186 B2
Carr Infant Sch YO26 ... 227 C5
Carrington Ave 1 YO26 . 227 E5
Carr La
Ampleforth YO62 ... 92 B1
Azerley HG4 ... 113 A7
Barlow YO8 ... 204 C7
Castleford WF10 ... 200 F3
Cawton YO62 ... 119 C8
Cayton YO14 ... 100 B4
East Ayton YO13 ... 99 B7
Escrick YO19 ... 192 B5
Glaisdale YO21 ... 30 D4
Gristhorpe YO11 ... 100 E4
Heslerton YO17 ... 124 A8
Kilburn High & Low YO61 .. 91 B3
Little Ouseburn YO26 ... 164 A7
Long Drax YO8 ... 204 F6
Muston YO14 ... 100 F3
Newby & Scalby YO13 ... 75 C5
Newton on Derwent YO41 . 185 F4
Rainton with Newby YO7 .. 114 F6
Roecliffe YO51 ... 140 E3
Sheriff Hutton YO60 ... 145 E6
Stillington YO61 ... 144 C6
Sutton-on-the-Forest YO61 144 D2
Thirlby YO7 ... 90 F6
Thormanby YO61 ... 116 E4
Wetherby LS22 ... 180 D4
Wistow YO8 ... 197 A3
York YO26 ... 227 D5
Carr Leys La YO7 ... 66 A5
Carr Mill Mews BD22 ... 187 B5
Carrnock Ct 3 YO32 ... 225 F1
Carrol Cl DL6 ... 210 F2
Carroll Pl 2 DL2 ... 22 C8
Carron Cres YO24 ... 230 B7
Carr Rd 7 BB18 ... 171 D2
Carrside 2 YO11 ... 99 F6
Carr Side Rd YO26 ... 163 F8
Carrs Mdw YO19 ... 192 B5
Carr St YO8 ... 232 F4
Carrs The YO21 ... 208 A2
Carr The HG3 ... 222 E2
Carr Wood Rd WF10 ... 200 F3
Carseylands Hill BD23 ... 155 A4
Carter Ave YO31 ... 228 F5
Carter La 22 YO62 ... 70 B1
Carter's La
Ilkley LS29 ... 218 E6
Longnewton TS16 ... 5 A4
Carters Yd DL10 ... 209 B6
CARTHORPE ... 87 E6
Cartmell Terr DL3 ... 3 C6
Cart Riggin YO7 ... 66 A8
Cass House Rd TS8 ... 6 E4
Cass La
Knaresborough HG5 ... 221 A4
South Milford LS25 ... 195 E1
Castelo Gr 1 YO18 ... 96 A6
Castle Bank DL6 ... 25 E1
Castlebergh Hospl BD24 131 C2
Castlebergh La 5 BD24 . 131 E2
CASTLE BOLTON ... 59 A6
Castle Cl
Cawood YO8 ... 197 A8
1 Haxby YO32 ... 166 D5
Killinghall HG3 ... 161 C5
Middleton St George DL2 ... 4 C3
Northallerton DL7 ... 210 D5
2 Spofforth HG3 ... 179 E6
1 Thornton Dale YO18 ... 96 D5
Castle Cres YO11 ... 213 B7
Castle Ctyd HG5 ... 221 A5
Castle Dyke Wynd TS16 ... 5 E3
Castle End DL8 ... 59 B6
CASTLEFORD ... 200 E4
Castleford Acad WF10 ... 200 F4
Castleford Half Acres Primary School WF10 ... 200 E4
Castleford La
Featherstone WF7 ... 200 D1
Knottingley WF11 ... 201 D3
Castleford Mus* WF10 .. 220 E4
Castleford & Normanton District Hospl WF10 ... 200 D3
Castleford Park Junior Acad WF10 ... 200 F4
Castleford Rd WF6 ... 200 B2
Castleford Redhill Junior Sch WF10 ... 201 B4
Castleford Ret Pk WF10 . 200 E4
Castleford Sta WF10 ... 200 E4
Castle Garth
Pontefract WF8 ... 201 C1
4 Thornton Dale YO18 ... 96 D5
Castlegate
East Ayton/West Ayton YO13 ... 99 A7
6 Helmsley YO62 ... 92 F6
Kirkbymoorside YO62 ... 70 B1
3 Knaresborough HG5 ... 221 B5
Malton YO17 ... 215 C4
19 Pickering YO18 ... 95 F7
Scarborough YO11 ... 213 B7
Thirsk YO7 ... 211 B2
York YO1 ... 233 B2
Castle Gate 4 LS29 ... 218 B4
Castle Gdns YO11 ... 213 B6
Castle Hill
8 Hunmanby YO14 ... 126 F8
2 Ilkley LS29 ... 218 B4
Richmond DL10 ... 209 C6
4 Settle BD24 ... 131 E2
Castle Hill Cl HG2 ... 222 B6
Castle Hill Dr HG2 ... 222 B6
Castle Hill Glade HG2 ... 222 B6
Castle Hill Gr HG2 ... 222 B6
Castle Hill La YO8 ... 204 F5
Castle Howard* YO60 ... 120 D1
Castle Howard Dr YO17 . 215 A4
Castle Howard Rd YO17 . 215 A4
Castle Ings 1 HG3 ... 179 E5
Castle Ings Cl 1 HG5 ... 221 A5
Castle Ings Rd 3 HG5 ... 221 A5
Castlekeep Cl DL10 ... 209 C8
Castle La
Danby YO21 ... 29 D6
10 East Ayton/West Ayton YO13 ... 99 B8
Castle Mdws DL8 ... 87 A7
Castle Mills HG5 ... 221 A5
Castlemount Ave YO13 ... 75 D6
Castle Rd
Colne BB8 ... 186 A4
1 Ilkley LS29 ... 218 B4
Killinghall HG3 ... 161 C5
18 Pickering YO18 ... 95 F7
Scarborough YO11 ... 213 A6
Thornton Dale YO18 ... 96 D5
Whitby YO21 ... 208 A6
Castlereagh Cl TS21 ... 5 A7
Castle Rise 1 YO13 ... 99 A7
Castle Side YO60 ... 145 C5
Castle St
Skipton BD23 ... 217 A3
Spofforth HG3 ... 179 E6
Castle Steads* DL11 ... 19 D6
Castle Steads (Fort)* DL8 ... 84 C8
Castle Terr
Richmond DL10 ... 209 C6
16 Scarborough YO11 ... 213 B6
CASTLETON ... 29 A6
Castleton Ave
Middlesbrough TS5 ... 6 D8
Northallerton DL7 ... 210 C1
Castleton Com Prim Sch YO21 ... 29 A7
Castleton Moor Sta YO21 . 29 A7
Castleton Rd DL9 ... 40 F4
Castle View
7 Newby & Scalby YO13 .. 75 D5
Richmond DL10 ... 209 B6
Sheriff Hutton YO60 ... 145 C5
Castle View Terr BD23 .. 216 F4
Castle Wlk YO1 ... 233 C2
Castle Wynd 11 DL10 ... 209 C6
CASTLEY ... 178 A1
Castle Yard Stables 8 YO7 ... 211 B3
Castle Yd
3 Ilkley LS29 ... 218 B4
Knaresborough HG5 ... 221 A5
Castley La LS21 ... 178 A1
Cat Bank DL11 ... 39 C6
Cathcart Cl DN14 ... 206 F7
Cathedral CE Prim Sch HG4 ... 214 D5
Cathedral Cl HG4 ... 214 D5
Catherine Love Dr 15 YO61 ... 143 C8
Catherine St 2 TS12 ... 9 F7
Cat La
Balne DN14 ... 207 E5
Bilbrough YO23 ... 182 D1
Cat Pottery The* DL8 ... 58 F1
CATTAL ... 164 A1
Cattal Moor La YO26 ... 181 B8
Cattal St YO26 ... 164 A2
Cattal Sta YO26 ... 164 A2
CATTERICK ... 41 D5
Catterick AWS Football Ctr DL9 ... 209 D1
CATTERICK BRIDGE ... 41 D6
Catterick Bridge* DL10 ... 41 C6
CATTERICK GARRISON ... 209 D2
Catterick La DL10 ... 41 D3
Catterick Racecourse DL10 ... 41 C5
Catterick Rd DL9 ... 40 E4
CATTERTON ... 190 B8
Catterton La
Catterton LS24 ... 190 A8
Healaugh LS24 ... 182 A1
Cattlebank Cl YO25 ... 151 D5
Cattle La LS25 ... 194 F8
Cattlelaith La
Knottingley WF11 ... 201 E1
Knottingley WF11 ... 201 E2
CATTON ... 88 F1
Catton La YO7 ... 115 A7
Catton Moor La YO7 ... 114 F8
Catton Way YO8 ... 232 A2
Caudle Hill WF11 ... 201 C6
Causeway BD23 ... 81 E3
Causeway The
Darlington DL1 ... 3 E5
Lythe YO21 ... 12 E3
Cautley Dr HG3 ... 161 C5
Cautley Gr HG3 ... 161 C5
Cavalry Ct 9 YO12 ... 75 F5
Cavendish Ave
Harrogate HG2 ... 219 E1
8 Pontefract WF8 ... 201 C2
Cavendish Ct HG2 ... 222 F8
Cavendish Gr YO10 ... 229 D3
Cavendish Rd TS4 ... 7 A8
Cavendish St
Barnoldswick BB18 ... 171 D1
Harrogate HG1 ... 219 E5
Skipton BD23 ... 216 F3
Cavendish Terr 8 HG4 . 214 C4
Cavendish View BD23 ... 217 D7
Caversham Rd TS4 ... 7 A8
Cawcliff La YO18 ... 97 A5
Cawdel Cl 4 LS25 ... 195 F2
Cawdel Way 11 LS25 ... 195 F2
Cawder Ghyll BD23 ... 217 A1
Cawder Gn BD23 ... 217 A2
Cawder La BD23 ... 217 A1
Cawder Mews BD23 ... 217 A1
Cawder Rd BD23 ... 217 A1
CAWOOD ... 197 B8
Cawood CE VA Prim Sch YO8 ... 197 B8
Cawood Cres LS24 ... 190 C1
Cawood Dr TS5 ... 6 F7
Cawood Rd
Stillingfleet YO19 ... 191 D3
Wistow YO8 ... 197 C7
Cawthorn Ave HG2 ... 220 B2
CAWTHORNE ... 71 D4
Cawthorne Cres YO14 ... 101 A3
Cawthorne La YO18 ... 71 D3
Cawthorn Pl 4 HG2 ... 220 B3
CAWTON ... 119 C7
Cawton Rd YO62 ... 118 F8
Caxton Ave YO26 ... 227 D6
Caxton Cl 1 DL10 ... 41 C7
Caxton Gdns 4 WF8 ... 201 B2
Caxton View HG4 ... 214 C6
Caxton Way YO11 ... 99 F6
Caygill St 10 YO21 ... 208 C6
Cayley Cl YO30 ... 224 F1
Cayley La YO13 ... 98 C5
Caymer Rd YO11 ... 100 A7
CAYTON ... 100 C6
Cayton App YO11 ... 99 F6
Cayton Com Prim Sch YO11 ... 100 B6
Cayton Low Rd YO11 ... 99 F6
Cayton Low Road Ind Est YO11 ... 100 A6
Cecilia Pl 3 YO24 ... 228 A3
Cecil Rd 7 YO14 ... 127 A8
Cecil St
Barnoldswick BB18 ... 171 D2
Harrogate HG1 ... 219 E5
Cedar Cl
Hambleton YO8 ... 197 B1
Ripon HG4 ... 214 B3
Cedar Cres YO8 ... 197 D2
Cedar Ct
Newbiggin YO14 ... 100 F5
Selby YO8 ... 232 E2
Cedar Dr
Coulby Newham TS8 ... 6 D4
Tadcaster LS24 ... 189 D6
Cedar Glade YO19 ... 184 E7
Cedar Gr
Barton DL10 ... 21 C7
3 Filey YO14 ... 101 B4
Middleton One Row DL2 ... 4 D3
Sutton BD20 ... 187 E7
York YO31 ... 229 B7
Cedar Grange HG2 ... 222 D7
Cedarhurst Dr TS12 ... 9 F7
Cedar Mews 4 DL2 ... 22 D8
Cedar Pl 14 YO61 ... 117 D1
Cedar Rd
Darlington DL3 ... 3 B6
Selby YO8 ... 232 D2
Cedar Ridge LS25 ... 194 E5
Cedar Vale 8 YO62 ... 70 B1
Cedar Way YO8 ... 232 E2
Cedarwood 3 DL2 ... 4 C4
Cedarwood Ave 1 TS9 ... 26 C8
Cedarwood Cl 7 YO24 . 227 B1
Cedarwood Glade TS8 ... 6 E4
Celtic Cl YO26 ... 227 B5
Cemetery La DL3 ... 3 A5
Cemetery Rd
40 Earby BB18 ... 172 A1
Normanton South WF6 ... 200 B1
Thirsk YO7 ... 211 A3
York YO10 ... 233 C1
Cennon Gr 15 TS17 ... 5 F4
Centenary Row BD23 ... 217 D8
Central Arc DL7 ... 210 D5
Central Av 6 YO61 ... 143 D8
Central Dr
Castleford WF10 ... 200 C4
Northallerton DL6 ... 210 E4
Central St TS16 ... 5 E3
Central Way 6 TS9 ... 8 A2
Centre La LS24 ... 189 E6
Centrepoint Rd DL1 ... 3 F6
Centre Rd BD20 ... 186 D7
Centurian Cl 7 DL10 ... 41 E4
Centurion Pk YO30 ... 225 B2
Centurion Way
Clifton YO30 ... 225 B3
Crossgates YO12 ... 99 E6
Faverdale DL3 ... 3 B8
Century Wlk 1 HG2 ... 220 B3
Ceres Rd LS22 ... 180 C3
Chacksfield Rd 16 DL10 ... 41 E4
Chadderton Cl TS12 ... 9 E8
Chadderton Dr 2 TS17 ... 6 C7
Chadwell Ave 2 TS3 ... 7 B8
Chadwick Pk HG5 ... 221 B3
Chafer Wood Nature Reserve* YO13 ... 97 D6
Chain Bar La HG3 ... 161 A4
Chain La HG5 ... 221 C6
Chair Wlk HG4 ... 139 B8
Chaldon Cl 4 YO32 ... 167 A6
Chaldron Way TS16 ... 5 D6
Chalfield Cl TS17 ... 6 B4
Chalfonts YO24 ... 227 F1
Chalford Oaks TS5 ... 6 D8
Challacombe Cres TS17 ... 6 A3
Challoner Rd TS15 ... 5 D2
Chaloner Prim Sch 18 TS14 8 F7
Chaloner's Cres YO24 ... 230 D7
Chaloner's Rd YO24 ... 230 D8
Chaloner St 4 TS14 ... 8 F6
Chaly Fields LS23 ... 188 E8
Chamber End Fold 5 BD23 ... 134 E3
Champion Ave 6 WF10 . 200 F3
Champions Gate YO8 ... 199 A8
Chancellor Gr YO24 ... 230 F6
Chancel Way YO21 ... 208 A6
Chancery Ct YO24 ... 227 C3
Chancery Rise
Stockton-on-Tees TS18 ... 6 A6
York YO24 ... 227 F3
Chandler Cl DL10 ... 209 F8
Chandlers Ct YO11 ... 213 B2
Chandlers Ridge Academy TS7 ... 7 D5
Chandlers Wharf YO17 .. 215 C3
Chantilly Ave DL1 ... 3 F7
Chanting Hill Cl YO60 ... 146 E6
CHANTRY ... 59 D2
Chantry Ave 14 YO26 ... 165 F1
Chantry Bank DL8 ... 59 D3
Chantry Cl
1 Park End TS3 ... 7 B8
York YO24 ... 230 C8
Chantry Ct HG3 ... 161 C7
Chantry Dr
East Ayton/West Ayton YO13 ... 99 B8
2 Ilkley LS29 ... 218 B3
Chantry Gap 11 YO26 ... 165 F1
Chantry Garth DL8 ... 59 D3
Chantry Gdns DN14 ... 207 A7
Chantry Gr 13 YO26 ... 165 F1
Chantry La
Bishopthorpe YO23 ... 231 B4
Scotton HG5 ... 162 A6
Stutton with Hazlewood LS24 ... 189 B3
Chantry Rd
9 East Ayton/West Ayton YO13 ... 99 B8
Northallerton DL7 ... 210 B3
Chantry Wynd 7 DL10 .. 209 C6
Chapel Balk Rd YO8 ... 198 F1
Chapel Cl
Bilton-in-Ainsty with Bickerton LS22 ... 181 B5
Church Fenton LS24 ... 196 B8
21 Helmsley YO62 ... 92 F6
North Duffield YO8 ... 199 A7
Rawcliffe DN14 ... 205 A1
Chapel Cres DL7 ... 63 C8
Chapel Croft 7 BD23 ... 134 E3
Chapel Ct
Burton Fleming YO25 ... 126 E3
Gargrave BD23 ... 155 D1
Huby YO61 ... 144 A4
CHAPEL FIELDS ... 227 B3
Chapel Fields Rd YO26 ... 227 A3
Chapel Fold 6 BD23 ... 134 E3
Chapel Garth
Dalton YO7 ... 115 E7
Markington with Wallerthwaite HG3 ... 139 C3
Thrintoft DL7 ... 63 F7
Chapel Gate
Malham BD23 ... 132 F1
Sherburn YO17 ... 124 D6
CHAPEL HADDLESEY ... 203 C5
Chapel Haddlesey CE VC Prim Sch YO8 ... 203 B5
Chapel Hill
Boroughbridge YO51 ... 141 C5
Kearby with Netherby LS22 179 B1
Skipton BD23 ... 217 A5
Chapel Hill La LS21 ... 178 A1
Chapel House Mews 9 BD23 ... 173 B4
Chapel La
Askham Bryan YO23 ... 182 F3
Barwick in Elmet LS15 ... 194 C8
Boston Spa LS23 ... 188 E7
Brayton YO8 ... 232 B1
Brompton YO13 ... 98 B7
5 Burton in Lonsdale LA6 102 F3
13 Easingwold YO61 ... 143 C8
13 Eastfield YO11 ... 100 B6
Finghall DL8 ... 61 E4
Halton East BD23 ... 174 C8
Harome YO62 ... 93 C4
Hebden BD23 ... 135 A2
Chapel La *continued*
Horton in Ribblesdale BD24 ... 105 C3
Ilkley LS29 ... 218 A4
Langtoft YO25 ... 151 D5
Little Smeaton WF8 ... 206 B3
9 Malton YO17 ... 215 C4
Marton-le-Moor HG4 ... 114 F1
Rawcliffe DN14 ... 205 A2
Reighton YO14 ... 127 E5
3 Riccall YO19 ... 192 A1
2 Spofforth HG3 ... 179 E5
3 Thornton Dale YO18 ... 96 D5
Tollerton YO61 ... 143 A3
Westow YO60 ... 147 B4
CHAPEL-LE-DALE ... 104 C8
Chapel Mews YO7 ... 211 C2
Chapel Rd
23 Scarborough YO11 ... 213 A6
Settrington YO17 ... 122 D1
Chapel Riggs 4 DL10 ... 41 E4
Chapel Row YO10 ... 233 C1
Chapel Sq 7 BD24 ... 131 E2
Chapel St
8 Addingham LS29 ... 174 F4
6 Beadlam YO62 ... 93 D7
Carleton BD23 ... 173 B4
Cattal YO26 ... 164 A1
22 Earby BB18 ... 172 A1
27 Filey YO14 ... 101 B3
Grassington BD23 ... 134 E3
Hambleton YO8 ... 196 F1
Hillam LS25 ... 202 B7
Kirk Hammerton YO26 ... 164 C2
Knaresborough HG5 ... 221 B5
Middleton St George DL2 ... 4 C4
Nunnington YO62 ... 93 E2
12 Settle BD24 ... 131 D2
Tadcaster LS24 ... 189 E6
Thirsk YO7 ... 211 B2
Chapel Terr YO24 ... 227 C3
Chapel Wlk
Long Preston BD23 ... 153 F5
4 Riccall YO19 ... 192 A1
Chapman Cl 1 YO32 ... 167 C8
Chapman Ct BB18 ... 171 D2
Chapman La 8 HG4 ... 86 C3
Chapmans Ct YO24 ... 230 D6
Chapman's La YO30 ... 165 E7
Chapman Sq HG1 ... 219 B2
Chapter House St YO1 ... 233 B3
Chariot Pl 6 WF11 ... 201 D3
Charles Ave HG1 ... 219 E5
Charles Ct DL10 ... 209 F7
Charles Dr 14 DN14 ... 205 F3
Charles Moor YO31 ... 228 F7
Charles St YO8 ... 232 B6
Charles Wesley Dr YO8 .. 232 B2
Charlock TS8 ... 7 B4
Charlton Ave
Knaresborough HG5 ... 221 B6
2 Whitby YO21 ... 208 B7
Charlton Ct 10 HG5 ... 221 B6
Charlton Dr HG5 ... 221 B6
Charlton Gr 12 HG5 ... 221 B6
Charlton Manor Dr 13 HG5 ... 221 B6
CHARLTONS ... 9 C6
Charlton St YO23 ... 228 C2
Charlton Villas HG5 ... 221 B6
Charnwood Dr TS7 ... 7 D6
Charrington Ave TS17 ... 6 A6
Charter Ave DN14 ... 205 A1
Chartermark Way DL9 ... 41 A4
Charter Rd HG4 ... 214 E4
Charters The YO8 ... 198 B5
Chartwell Cl TS17 ... 6 B4
Chase Garth Rd 16 YO61 . 143 C8
Chase Side Ct YO24 ... 230 E8
Chase The
11 Boroughbridge YO51 .. 141 B4
Garforth LS25 ... 194 D4
Hurworth-on-Tees DL2 ... 3 E1
Knaresborough HG5 ... 221 D5
Norton YO17 ... 215 E2
17 Wetherby LS22 ... 180 C3
Chastworth Ct HG1 ... 219 D4
Chatham Rd HG4 ... 113 D2
Chatsworth Ave 7 WF8 . 201 C2
Chatsworth Dr
9 Airmyn DN14 ... 205 F3
16 Haxby YO32 ... 166 F5
2 Wetherby LS22 ... 180 B3
Chatsworth Gdns YO12 ... 212 E7
Chatsworth Gr
4 Boroughbridge YO51 .. 141 B5
Harrogate HG1 ... 219 C4
Chatsworth Pl HG1 ... 219 D4
Chatsworth Rd HG1 ... 219 D4
Chatsworth Terr
2 Harrogate HG1 ... 219 E4
4 York YO26 ... 227 E4
Chaucer Gn HG1 ... 219 F7
Chaucer La
Fadmoor YO62 ... 69 F5
Strensall YO32 ... 167 B8
Chaucer St 7 YO10 ... 228 E3
Chaumont Way 1 YO32 . 167 D2
Chauvel Cl DL9 ... 209 C2
Cheapside
2 Knaresborough HG5 ... 221 B5
12 Normanton South WF6 200 A1
11 Settle BD24 ... 131 D2
Cheapsides Rd YO17 ... 215 B8
Checker La YO19 ... 198 A7

Checkstone Ave 10
WF10 ... 200 D2
Chedworth Ct 4 TS17 ... 5 F6
Chelkar Way YO30 ... 224 F1
Chelmsford Rd HG1 ... 219 E2
Cheltenham Ave
Ilkley LS29 ... 218 E4
Middlesbrough TS7 ... 7 B5
Cheltenham Cres 6
HG1 ... 219 D2
Cheltenham Ct DL2 ... 4 C5
Cheltenham Mount HG1 219 D3
Cheltenham Par HG1 ... 219 D3
Cheltenham Rd 8 HG1 .. 219 D3
Chelwood Wlk 12 YO26 .. 227 E4
Chepstow Cl 9 DL9 ... 40 F4
Chepstow Ct 14 DL1 ... 3 F6
Cherry Ave
Malton YO17 ... 215 D6
Swinton YO17 ... 121 B4
Cherry Cl YO21 ... 208 B6
Cherry Farm Cl YO17 ... 121 D1
Cherry Garth YO31 ... 229 B5
Cherry Garth Rd DL7 ... 210 C3
Cherry Gr
7 Bedale DL8 ... 63 B3
2 Ilkley LS29 ... 175 C2
16 Poppleton YO26 ... 165 F1
Cherry Hill La YO23 ... 233 B1
Cherry La YO24 ... 230 F8
Cherry Orch 2 YO32 ... 225 D8
Cherry Paddock
4 Haxby YO32 ... 225 D8
Kexby YO41 ... 168 C2
Cherry Rd 4 YO14 ... 127 A8
Cherry St YO23 ... 233 B1
Cherry Tree Ave
Newton-on-Ouse YO30 ... 165 B6
1 Scarborough YO12 ... 212 B5
York YO32 ... 225 D4
Cherrytree Cl HG4 ... 140 E7
Cherry Tree Cl
13 Brayton YO8 ... 197 D1
9 Castleford WF10 ... 200 D3
Cherry Tree Ct
12 Barlby with Osgodby
YO8 ... 198 B4
Catterick DL10 ... 41 E4
Salton YO62 ... 94 D3
Cherrytree Dr YO8 ... 197 D6
Cherry Tree Dr
Gristhorpe YO14 ... 101 A4
5 Naburn YO23 ... 191 C7
Cherry Tree Way 14 DL9 .. 41 A5
Cherry Tree Wlk
Amotherby YO17 ... 121 A4
7 Barlby YO8 ... 198 B4
Knottingley WF11 ... 201 F2
Cherrywood Ave 4 TS9 .. 26 C8
Cherry Wood Cres YO19 . 231 E5
Chervil Ct TS8 ... 7 B4
Cherwell Croft YO8 ... 196 F1
Cherwell Ct YO8 ... 196 F1
Cheshire Ave YO32 ... 167 A6
Cheshire Cl 6 YO32 ... 224 E2
Cheshire Sq 5 YO7 ... 89 B1
Chesler-Pit La YO61 ... 117 F2
Chesney Fields 4 YO24 . 227 D1
Chessingham Gdns YO24 230 E6
Chessingham Pk YO19 ... 184 F6
Chester Court Rd YO8 ... 204 A6
Chester La DL6 ... 65 D8
Chesterton Ave TS17 ... 6 A6
Chestnut Ave
2 Airmyn DN14 ... 205 E4
3 Airmyn DN14 ... 205 F2
Harrogate HG1 ... 219 F3
10 Hemingbrough YO8 ... 198 F1
Malton YO17 ... 215 D5
Thornton Dale YO18 ... 96 D6
2 Topcliffe YO7 ... 89 A1
Welburn YO60 ... 146 E6
12 Wetherby LS22 ... 180 B3
York YO31 ... 228 F6
Chestnut Bank YO12 ... 212 D6
Chestnut Cl
Bedale DL8 ... 63 B3
3 Catterick DL10 ... 41 D5
4 Ilkley LS29 ... 218 E3
7 North Duffield YO8 ... 199 A7
Richmond DL10 ... 209 C8
Scarborough YO12 ... 212 D6
Chestnut Cres
6 Catterick Garrison DL9 . 40 F5
1 Catton YO7 ... 89 A1
Hipswell DL9 ... 40 F5
Chestnut Croft 7 YO8 ... 198 F1
Chestnut Ct
9 Hemingbrough YO8 ... 198 F1
York YO32 ... 225 F5
Chestnut Dr
17 Barnoldswick BB18 ... 171 D1
Firth Moor DL1 ... 3 F4
8 Hemingbrough YO8 ... 198 F1
Middlesbrough TS7 ... 7 C6
Chestnut Garth 4 YO8 ... 198 F1
Chestnut Gn 10 LS25 ... 202 A8
Chestnut Gr
Acomb YO26 ... 227 C4
Harrogate HG1 ... 219 E6
Huntington YO32 ... 225 E4
Norton YO17 ... 215 F2
Chestnut Mews YO8 ... 197 A8
Chestnut Rd
Cawood YO8 ... 197 A8
Chestnut Rd *continued*
Eaglescliffe TS16 ... 5 E6
Chestnut Rise 6 YO8 ... 198 F1
Chestnuts The
6 Haxby YO32 ... 225 C8
Hensall DN14 ... 203 D2
Pontefract WF8 ... 201 C2
Scarborough YO12 ... 212 B7
Chestnut Way YO8 ... 232 E3
Chevin Dr YO14 ... 101 A3
Cheviot Cl 1 YO32 ... 225 F3
Chew La
Gargrave BD23 ... 155 D1
Seamer YO12 ... 99 D6
Chichester Cl 18 YO13 ... 75 D5
Chieftain Rd DL9 ... 40 C4
Chiltern Ave WF10 ... 200 C3
Chiltern Way YO32 ... 225 F5
Chilvers Ct 4 YO8 ... 232 A1
Chimes Rd YO8 ... 232 C6
Chimes The 8 YO8 ... 232 C6
China St DL3 ... 3 D7
Chippendale Rise 8
LS21 ... 177 A1
Chippenham Rd TS4 ... 7 A7
Cholmley Way YO22 ... 208 F3
CHOP GATE ... 46 F6
Christ Church CE Prim Sch
Colne BB8 ... 186 A3
Skipton BD23 ... 216 F3
Christ Church Oval HG1 . 219 E2
Christina St 5 HG1 ... 219 C5
Christ's Hospl ★ DL8 ... 63 A1
Christ the King RC Prim Sch
TS17 ... 6 C6
Christy Gate Rd YO21 ... 28 E4
Chubb Hill Rd YO21 ... 208 C6
Chudleigh Rd
Harrogate HG1 ... 219 E3
1 York YO26 ... 227 F5
Church Ave
Clapham LA2 ... 130 C8
4 Dacre HG3 ... 137 F1
Harrogate HG1 ... 219 D5
6 Selby YO8 ... 232 D5
Church Balk YO19 ... 184 E7
Church Bank
Aysgarth DL8 ... 58 F3
Hunton DL8 ... 61 F7
Kirkby Malzeard HG4 ... 112 D5
West Witton DL8 ... 59 E3
Church Cl
Askham Bryan YO23 ... 182 F3
Bagby YO7 ... 90 C3
4 Bubwith YO8 ... 199 D7
Carleton BD23 ... 173 B4
18 Filey YO14 ... 101 B4
1 Hambleton YO8 ... 196 F1
Killinghall HG3 ... 219 A8
Kirby Hill YO51 ... 141 B7
Middleton St George DL2 ... 4 C3
Newby & Scalby YO13 ... 75 C5
Redmire DL8 ... 59 C5
10 Riccall YO19 ... 197 F8
Sawley HG4 ... 138 E6
Sharow HG4 ... 214 F7
4 Swillington LS26 ... 194 A1
5 Tollerton YO61 ... 143 B3
Wheldrake YO19 ... 193 A7
Church Cliff Dr 9 YO14 . 101 B4
Church Cres
Stutton with Hazlewood
LS24 ... 189 D4
Swillington LS26 ... 194 A1
Church Croft
Barkston Ash LS24 ... 195 F7
Gargrave BD23 ... 172 C8
Church Cswy LS23 ... 188 F8
Church Ct
18 Normanton South
WF6 ... 200 A1
Saxton LS24 ... 195 D7
Church Dike La YO8 ... 204 F5
Church Dr
Great Ayton TS9 ... 7 F1
Lockwood TS12 ... 9 E7
Church End
Cawood YO8 ... 197 B8
Sheriff Hutton YO60 ... 145 D5
Church Farm YO7 ... 211 A6
Church Farm Cl YO23 ... 182 C6
Church Farm Ct YO25 ... 126 E3
Church Farm View LS15 . 194 C8
CHURCH FENTON ... 196 B7
Church Fenton La LS24 .. 190 B3
Church Fenton Sta LS24 196 A8
Churchfield DN14 ... 204 C2
Churchfield Dr 28 YO32 . 166 E5
Churchfield La
Castleford WF10 ... 200 F3
6 Kippax LS25 ... 194 D1
Little Smeaton WF8 ... 206 C4
Church Field La 2 YO26 . 164 A8
Church Field Rd DN6 ... 206 E1
Churchfields DL6 ... 210 E4
Church Fields 17 WF6 ... 200 A1
Church Garth DL6 ... 23 C3
Church Gdns LS25 ... 194 C3
Church Gn 3 YO41 ... 185 C2
Church Hill
Blubberhouses LS21 ... 159 C2
4 Bramham LS23 ... 188 E5
Crayke YO61 ... 118 A1
Easingwold YO61 ... 117 C1
10 Hunmanby YO14 ... 126 F8
Hunsingore LS22 ... 180 E8
Malton YO17 ... 215 C4
Newby & Scalby YO13 ... 75 C5
Church Hill *continued*
North Rigton LS17 ... 178 B3
Reighton YO14 ... 127 C6
3 Selby YO8 ... 232 D5
Sherburn in Elmet LS25 ... 195 E4
5 Spofforth HG3 ... 179 E6
Stillingfleet YO19 ... 191 D3
Thorner LS14 ... 188 A3
Thornton Dale YO18 ... 96 D6
8 Wistow YO8 ... 197 D6
CHURCH HOUSES ... 48 F4
Churchill Cl 3 TS9 ... 8 A2
Churchill Dr 41 DL9 ... 41 A5
Churchill Way 4 BD20 . 187 F8
Church La
Allerston YO18 ... 97 B5
Appleton Roebuck YO23 ... 190 F4
Aysgarth DL8 ... 58 F3
Bagby YO7 ... 90 C3
Barton DL10 ... 21 C8
Bishopthorpe YO23 ... 231 A4
Bolton Percy YO23 ... 190 D4
Boroughbridge YO51 ... 141 B5
Brompton YO13 ... 98 C5
Burnsall BD23 ... 157 A8
Burton Leonard HG3 ... 140 A2
1 Carlton DN14 ... 204 C3
Catton YO41 ... 185 D8
Cayton YO11 ... 100 B6
Collingham LS22 ... 180 A1
Cropton YO18 ... 71 B4
Cundall with Leckby YO61 . 115 E3
Dunnington YO19 ... 184 E7
East Heslerton YO17 ... 124 A7
Elslack BD23 ... 172 D4
4 Elvington YO41 ... 185 C2
Faceby TS9 ... 25 F1
Fylingdales YO22 ... 33 C4
Garforth LS25 ... 194 C4
Gargrave BD23 ... 172 D8
Gateforth YO8 ... 202 F8
Gilling East YO62 ... 118 F7
Guisborough TS7 ... 7 E5
Harrogate HG1 ... 219 B2
17 Haxby YO32 ... 166 E5
Hebden BD23 ... 135 A1
Hensall DN14 ... 203 C1
Hutton Buscel YO13 ... 98 F7
Ingleby Greenhow TS9 ... 27 B5
Kelbrook & Sough BB18 .. 186 A8
Kellington DN14 ... 202 E3
Kirby Hall YO26 ... 164 B7
Kirby Hill YO51 ... 141 B7
Knaresborough HG5 ... 221 A6
Langtoft YO25 ... 151 C1
Low Worsall TS15 ... 24 A8
Marton cum Grafton YO51 141 D1
Martons Both BD23 ... 172 A5
Micklefield LS25 ... 194 F4
Mickletown LS26 ... 200 B5
Middlesbrough TS5 ... 6 E7
Middleton St George DL2 ... 4 C3
Middleton YO18 ... 95 E8
Milby YO51 ... 141 B7
4 Monk Fryston LS25 ... 202 A8
Moor Monkton YO26 ... 165 B2
Nether Poppleton YO26 ... 224 B3
New Earswick YO32 ... 225 F5
11 Normanton South WF6 200 A1
North Featherstone WF7 .. 200 E1
Pannal HG3 ... 222 D4
Poppleton YO26 ... 224 A3
Rainton YO7 ... 114 E6
Redmire DL8 ... 59 C5
Ripon HG4 ... 214 B5
Sadberge DL2 ... 4 C7
Scarborough YO11 ... 213 B7
4 Selby YO8 ... 232 D5
Sessay YO7 ... 116 C6
Settrington YO17 ... 122 D1
Sinnington YO62 ... 71 A1
Skelton YO30 ... 224 B5
Slingsby YO62 ... 120 B6
2 Snaith DN14 ... 204 C1
South Stainley with Cayton
HG3 ... 139 E2
9 Spofforth HG3 ... 179 E6
Stainburn LS21 ... 177 E3
Stainforth BD24 ... 131 E6
10 Stamford Bridge YO41 168 D2
Strensall YO32 ... 167 A7
Stutton with Hazlewood
LS24 ... 189 E4
Swillington LS26 ... 194 A1
Terrington YO60 ... 119 F1
Thormanby YO61 ... 116 F5
Thornton Dale YO18 ... 96 D6
Thwing YO25 ... 126 A1
Tunstall LA6 ... 102 B4
Welburn YO60 ... 146 E6
Weston LS21 ... 176 D1
Westow YO60 ... 147 B4
West Witton DL8 ... 59 E3
Wheldrake YO19 ... 193 A7
Whitby YO22 ... 208 E7
Whorlton DL6 ... 25 D1
Wigglesworth BD23 ... 153 D3
Wighill LS24 ... 181 D1
Wintringham YO17 ... 123 C4
York YO1 ... 233 B2
Church Lea DL7 ... 64 B7
Church Mdw
Barton DL10 ... 21 D8
Sherburn in Elmet LS25 ... 195 E4
Church Mdws 9 LS23 ... 188 E6
Church Mews
Barlby YO8 ... 198 A5
13 Boroughbridge YO51 .. 141 B5
Church Mews *continued*
Church Fenton LS24 ... 196 B7
Gainford DL2 ... 1 A7
Sherburn in Elmet LS25 ... 195 F4
2 York YO26 ... 227 C3
Church Rd
26 Glusburn BD20 ... 187 E7
Great Preston LS26 ... 200 C8
Linton BD23 ... 134 E2
Pontefract WF6 ... 200 A3
Scotton DL9 ... 40 E4
Stainton Dale YO13 ... 54 A7
Stamford Bridge YO41 ... 168 D2
Thornton in Craven BD23 . 171 F3
York YO10 ... 229 D4
Church Rise YO19 ... 167 F1
Church Row
Hurworth-on-Tees DL2 ... 3 E1
Melsonby DL10 ... 20 F7
Church Side LS26 ... 200 B5
Churchside Villas LS26 .. 200 B5
Church Sq
Harrogate HG1 ... 219 F3
Whitby YO21 ... 208 C7
Church St
Addingham LS29 ... 175 A4
Amotherby YO17 ... 121 B4
Asenby YO7 ... 115 B7
Barkston Ash LS24 ... 195 F7
Bellerby DL8 ... 60 D7
Bilton-in-Ainsty with Bickerton
YO26 ... 181 D5
Boston Spa LS23 ... 188 E8
Broughton BD23 ... 172 D7
Bubwith YO8 ... 199 D7
Carleton BD23 ... 173 B4
Church Fenton LS24 ... 196 B7
Copmanthorpe YO23 ... 230 B2
Danby YO21 ... 29 B7
Dunnington YO19 ... 184 E7
5 Easingwold YO61 ... 143 C8
5 Filey YO14 ... 101 B3
Gargrave BD23 ... 155 D1
13 Glusburn BD20 ... 187 E8
Goldsborough HG5 ... 163 A3
Guisborough TS14 ... 8 F7
5 Helmsley YO62 ... 92 F6
Heslerton YO17 ... 123 E7
Hovingham YO62 ... 119 E6
Ilkley LS29 ... 218 A4
Ingleton LA6 ... 103 D4
Kirkby Malzeard HG4 ... 112 D5
24 Kirkbymoorside YO62 ... 70 B1
Kirk Hammerton YO26 ... 164 C2
Knottingley WF11 ... 201 E4
Long Preston BD23 ... 153 F4
6 Masham HG4 ... 86 C3
6 Middleham DL8 ... 60 E2
Norton YO17 ... 215 D3
Nunnington YO62 ... 93 E2
3 Riccall YO19 ... 197 F8
2 Scarborough YO11 ... 213 B6
Settle BD24 ... 131 D3
4 Skipton BD23 ... 216 F3
5 Staithes TS13 ... 13 K2
Trawden BB8 ... 186 B1
Ulleskelf LS24 ... 190 C3
Well DL8 ... 87 A4
West Tanfield HG4 ... 87 A1
14 Wetherby LS22 ... 180 C3
Whitby YO22 ... 208 E6
Whittington LA6 ... 102 A7
Whixley YO26 ... 164 A5
York YO1 ... 233 B2
Church Stairs St 3 YO11 213 B6
Church View
12 Airmyn DN14 ... 205 E4
3 Brompton DL6 ... 43 F3
22 Hemingbrough YO8 ... 198 F1
16 Hurworth DL2 ... 3 E1
Kirby Hill YO51 ... 141 B7
Ledston LS25 ... 194 E1
Norton DN6 ... 206 E1
Sherburn in Elmet LS25 ... 195 F4
Sherburn YO17 ... 124 D8
South Milford LS25 ... 195 F2
Thirsk YO7 ... 211 A3
Church View Mews 7
LS23 ... 188 E7
Churchville LS25 ... 195 A4
Churchville Ave LS25 ... 194 F4
Churchville Dr LS25 ... 195 A4
Churchville Terr LS25 ... 195 A4
Church Wind
Alne YO61 ... 142 F4
Burneston DL8 ... 87 E7
Church Wlk
Lindrick with Studley Royal &
Fountains HG4 ... 139 B7
1 Willerby YO12 ... 99 D2
5 Wistow YO8 ... 197 D6
Churchwood Cl HG4 ... 140 E7
Church Wynd DL10 ... 209 C7
Churchyard 14 LS24 ... 189 E6
Churwell Cl WF10 ... 200 E3
Cinder Hill La BD22 ... 187 A6
Cinder La
Castleford WF10 ... 200 E4
Clifford LS23 ... 188 F7
Lindley LS21 ... 177 C3
Upper Poppleton YO26 ... 227 A7
York YO26 ... 227 F5
Cinder Mews YO26 ... 228 A5
Citadilla Cl 5 DL10 ... 41 C7
City Art Gallery ★ YO30 .. 233 B3
Clack La DL6 ... 45 A4
Clapdale Dr LA2 ... 130 C8
Clapdale Way 2 LA2 ... 130 C8
Clapgate Bank DL11 ... 39 D8
CLAPHAM ... 130 C8
Clapham CE Prim Sch
LA2 ... 130 C7
CLAPHAM GREEN ... 160 E5
Clapham Old Rd LA6 ... 103 E3
Clapham Sta LA2 ... 130 A6
Clare Ave DL3 ... 3 A5
Claremont 23 YO14 ... 101 B3
Claremont Dr TS7 ... 7 C5
Claremont La HG3 ... 140 B5
Claremont St BB8 ... 186 A3
Claremont Terr YO31 ... 233 B4
Clarence Ave 47 YO14 ... 101 B3
Clarence Dr
56 Filey YO14 ... 101 B3
Harrogate HG1 ... 219 B3
Clarence Pl
7 Scarborough YO11 ... 213 A6
2 Whitby YO21 ... 208 D7
Clarence Rd
Middlesbrough TS7 ... 7 D5
2 Scarborough YO12 ... 213 A7
Scorton DL10 ... 41 F7
Clarence St
2 Barnoldswick BB18 ... 171 E1
2 Colne BB8 ... 186 A3
1 Trawden Forest BB8 ... 186 B1
York YO31 ... 233 B4
Clarendon Ct YO31 ... 228 C7
Clarendon Rd
Boston Spa LS23 ... 188 E8
Great Burdon DL1 ... 3 F7
Thornaby TS17 ... 6 B7
Clarendon St 10 BB8 ... 186 A3
Clareton La HG5 ... 163 B6
Clark Beck Cl HG3 ... 222 E3
Clark Ct WF7 ... 200 E1
Clarke's Croft YO7 ... 115 A4
Clarkson Ct 12 WF6 ... 200 B1
Clarkson Dr LS25 ... 201 F6
Clarkson St 7 YO21 ... 208 D7
Clarkson Wynd DL8 ... 56 C4
Clark St 7 YO12 ... 213 A7
Clarks Terr YO31 ... 228 F6
Claro Ave HG1 ... 219 F4
Claro Bsns Ctr ... 219 F4
Claro Mews 4 HG5 ... 221 A5
Claro Pk HG1 ... 219 F4
Claro Rd
Harrogate HG1 ... 219 F3
Ripon HG4 ... 214 C4
Claro Way HG1 ... 219 F4
Claude Ave TS5 ... 6 E8
Claudius Gr YO12 ... 99 E6
Claver Cl DL6 ... 45 D8
Clavery Ley La YO62 ... 67 E1
CLAXTON ... 168 B7
Claxton Ave DL3 ... 3 A6
Clay Bank TS9 ... 27 A3
Claygate YO31 ... 229 B6
Clay Hill YO41 ... 169 C3
Clay La
Bubwith YO8 ... 199 C5
Camblesforth YO8 ... 204 C6
Cliffe YO8 ... 198 D4
Claypit La
Carlton DN14 ... 204 C3
Ledston WF10 ... 201 A8
Clay Pit La YO51 ... 141 A4
Clay Pl 3 YO24 ... 227 D1
Clayton Fold 5 BD20 ... 187 F7
Clayton Hall Rd BD20 ... 187 F7
Clayton Mews 8 WF6 ... 200 A2
Clayton Pl 9 WF6 ... 200 A2
Clayton St 7 BB18 ... 171 E1
CLEASBY ... 2 F4
Cleasby La DL2 ... 2 F1
Cleasby Way TS16 ... 5 D6
Cleatop Park Nature
Reserve ★ BD24 ... 153 D8
Clementhorpe YO23 ... 233 B1
Clement St 4 YO23 ... 233 B1
Clevegate TS7 ... 7 C5
Cleveland 1 TS16 ... 5 D4
Cleveland Ave
Darlington DL3 ... 3 C5
Knottingley WF11 ... 201 F2
Scalby YO12 ... 212 D8
Stokesley TS9 ... 26 C8
Cleveland Cl TS7 ... 7 D7
Cleveland College of Art &
Design TS5 ... 6 E8
Cleveland Dr
Middlesbrough TS7 ... 7 B6
Northallerton DL7 ... 210 D2
Cleveland Gdns YO32 ... 167 D3
Cleveland Ind Est DL1 ... 3 D6
Cleveland Rd
Boltby YO7 ... 91 B8
Catterick Garrison DL9 ... 40 F4
Scarborough YO12 ... 212 E6
Scorton DL10 ... 41 F7
Cleveland Rein YO7 ... 66 A3
Cleveland St
Darlington DL1 ... 3 D6
Great Ayton TS9 ... 8 A2
Guisborough TS14 ... 8 E6
York YO24 ... 228 A4
Cleveland Terr
Darlington DL3 ... 3 B5
8 Whitby YO21 ... 208 D5
York YO32 ... 225 F4
Cleveland Trad Est DL1 ... 3 D6
Cleveland View 1 TS9 ... 25 F1
Cleveland Way
1 Carlton Miniott YO7 ... 89 C4
Helmsley YO62 ... 92 E6

Cleveland Way *continued*
York YO32 . . . . **225** F3
Cliff Bridge Pl 6 YO11 . . **213** A5
Cliff Bridge Terr 7 YO11 **213** A5
Cliff Brow TS13 . . . . **11** C7
Cliff Cres LS25 . . . . **194** E1
Cliff Dr 23 DL8 . . . . **60** D5
CLIFFE
198 E2
Darlington **2** B6
Cliffe Mews YO60 . . . . **119** E1
Cliffe Rd HG2 . . . . **219** B1
Cliffe VC Prim Sch YO8 . . **198** E2
Cliff Gate Rd DL11 . . . . . . **35** E4
Cliff Hill Rd DN6 . . . . **206** D2
Cliff La
Newholm-cum-Dunsley
YO21 . . . . **13** B2
Snainton YO13 . . . . **97** F5
Whitwell-on-the-Hill YO60 . **146** E4
Wilton YO18 . . . . **97** A5
Wrelton YO18 . . . . **95** B8
CLIFFORD **188** E7
Clifford Ave LS29 . . . . **218** A5
Clifford Ct BD23 . . . . **216** D3
Clifford Moor Rd LS23 . . . **188** D8
Clifford Rd
Boston Spa LS23 . . . . **188** F8
Ilkley LS29 . . . . **218** A6
Clifford St
3 Barnoldswick BB18 . . . **171** E1
1 Skipton BD23 . . . . **216** F3
York YO1 . . . . **233** B2
Clifford's Terr 25 YO14 . . **101** B3
Clifford's Twr★ YO1 . . . . . . **233** B1
Cliff Rd
Stainton Dale YO13 . . . . **54** A8
Staithes TS13 . . . . **13** K2
Cliff St YO21 . . . . **208** D7
Cliff The YO22 . . . . **32** B6
CLIFTON
228 A7
Ilkley **176** F3
Clifton Ave TS18 . . . . **5** E6
Clifton Dale YO30 . . . . **228** A6
Clifton Gn YO30 . . . . **228** A6
Clifton Green Prim Sch
YO30 . . . . **228** B7
Clifton La LS21 . . . . **176** F3
Clifton Moor Bsns Village
YO30 . . . . **225** A2
Clifton Moorgate YO30 . . **225** B3
Clifton Moor Gate YO30 . **225** A2
Clifton Moor Ind Estate
YO30 . . . . **225** A3
Clifton Moor Retail Pk
YO30 . . . . **225** A4
Clifton Moor Sh Ctr
YO30 . . . . **224** F3
Clifton Park Ave YO30 . . . **227** E8
Clifton Park (York CC & York
RUFC) YO30 . . . . **227** F7
Clifton Pk Hospl YO30 . . . **227** E8
Clifton Pl 3 YO30 . . . . . . **228** A7
Clifton Rd
Darlington DL1 . . . . **3** D4
Ilkley LS29 . . . . **218** D3
York YO30 . . . . **233** A4
Clifton St
Earby BB18 . . . . **186** A8
5 Scarborough YO12 . . . . **212** F6
Trawden Forest BB8 . . . . . **186** A1
Clifton Terr LS29 . . . . **218** C4
Clifton Without Jun Sch
YO30 . . . . **227** F8
Clifton with Rawcliffe Prim
Sch YO30 . . . . **224** E1
CLINT **161** A6
Clint Bank HG3 . . . . **160** E6
Clint Bank La HG3 . . . . . . **160** F6
Clint Garth HG3 . . . . **160** F8
CLINTS **39** C7
Clipt La YO7 . . . . **65** D2
Clitheroe St 2 BD23 . . . . **216** D3
Clive Gr YO24 . . . . **227** F2
Clive Rd 1 HG3 . . . . **179** E6
Clockhill Field La YO26 . . **163** F3
Clock Twr★ HG4 . . . . **214** C6
Clockwood Gdns TS16 . . . . . **5** E3
Cloggerby Rigg DL11 . . . . . **35** E5
Clogger La BD23 . . . . **172** D3
Clog Mill Gdns 7 YO8 . . . **232** D6
Cloisters The
15 Hemingbrough YO8 . . . **198** F1
Wilberfoss YO41 . . . . **185** F6
York YO31 . . . . **233** C3
Cloisters Wlk YO31 . . . . . . **233** C3
Close La BD22 . . . . **187** B5
Close Rd WF10 . . . . **200** F4
Close The
9 Acaster Malbis YO32 . . **191** C7
Barwick in Elmet LS15 . . . . **194** B7
Boroughbridge YO51 . . . . . **141** A3
Boston Spa LS23 . . . . **188** E8
Cawood YO8 . . . . **197** A7
6 Collingham LS22 . . . . . . **188** A8
11 East Ayton/West Ayton
YO13 . . . . **99** B8
4 Fylingdales YO22 . . . . . . **33** D4
Hutton Rudby TS15 . . . . **25** C5
Kirkby Fleetham DL7 . . . . . . **42** C1
Longnewton TS21 . . . . **4** F7
Minskip YO51 . . . . **141** A3
Neasham DL2 . . . . **4** A1
Northallerton DL7 . . . . **210** B2
Norton DN6 . . . . **206** E2
Riccall YO19 . . . . **198** A8
Scalby YO12 . . . . **212** B8

Close The *continued*
Skipton BD23 . . . . **216** F3
Studley Roger HG4 . . . . . . **113** D1
Thirsk YO7 . . . . **211** C1
Thorner LS14 . . . . **188** A3
Thornton Dale YO18 . . . . **96** D5
Towton LS24 . . . . **189** E2
York YO30 . . . . **227** F8
Clotherholme Rd HG4 . . . **214** A5
CLOUGH **55** A7
CLOUGHTON **54** C1
CLOUGHTON NEWLANDS . . **54** C2
Clover Cl WF10 . . . . **200** C7
Clover Hill BD23 . . . . **217** B5
Cloverley Cl YO41 . . . . **168** C2
Clover Way 9 HG3 . . . . . . **161** B3
Clowbeck Ct DL3 . . . . **3** B8
Clydach Gr 24 TS17 . . . . **5** F4
Clyde Gr TS18 . . . . **5** F8
Coach La
10 Hurworth-on-Tees DL2 . . . **3** E1
Lindley LS21 . . . . **177** D3
Coachman's Ct 6 HG2 . . **220** B1
Coach Rd
Harrogate HG1 . . . . **219** F2
Sheriff Hutton YO60 . . . . . **145** D4
Sleights YO22 . . . . **32** A6
Coach St BD23 . . . . **216** F4
Coach Street Yd 13 BD23 **216** F4
Coalmire La DL6 . . . . **45** D7
Coal Pit La
Kirk Smeaton WF8 . . . . **206** A2
Rimington BB7 . . . . **171** A1
Coalpits La 10 DL2 . . . . **3** A7
Coarse La HG3 . . . . **159** A4
Coastal Rd YO13 . . . . **75** D7
Coastguard Hill YO14 . . . **127** E5
Coate Cl TS8 . . . . **6** E5
COATES **171** E2
Coates Ave BB18 . . . . **171** E2
Coates Fields BB18 . . . . . . **171** E2
Coates La
Barnoldswick BB18 . . . . . . **171** E2
Kettlewell with Starbotton
BD23 . . . . **107** F5
Coate's La BD20 . . . . **173** F2
Coates Lane Prim Sch
BB18 . . . . **171** E2
Coates Marsh La DN14 . . **204** B2
Coatham Ave DL2 . . . . **4** D3
Coatham La TS21 . . . . **5** B7
Cobble Carr TS14 . . . . **8** E8
Cobble Court Mews
YO24 . . . . **233** A1
Cobble Field YO25 . . . . . . **151** D5
Cobbler Hill 13 DN14 . . . . **205** F3
Cobblers La WF8 . . . . **201** C1
Cobbler's La WF8 . . . . **201** C1
COBBY SYKE **159** F2
Cobby Syke Rd HG3 . . . . . **159** F1
Cobcroft La WF11 . . . . **206** B8
Cobden St
Barnoldswick BB18 . . . . . . **171** D1
Darlington DL1 . . . . **3** E5
Thornaby TS17 . . . . **6** B8
Cobham Way YO32 . . . . **224** E3
Cob La BB18 . . . . **186** A6
Coble La YO60 . . . . **145** D5
Cobshaw La DL8 . . . . **62** F6
Cochrane St YO8 . . . . **232** D3
COCKAYNE **48** A5
Cockburn St 5 TS12 . . . . **9** F7
Cocked Hat HG4 . . . . **139** C8
Cocked Hat Pk YO7 . . . . . **211** A1
Cockerhill La YO62 . . . . **93** E7
COCKERTON **3** B6
Cockerton CE Prim Sch
DL3 . . . . **3** A6
Cockerton Gn DL3 . . . . **3** B6
Cock Garth YO17 . . . . **122** D1
COCK HILL **165** B2
Cockhill La BB8 . . . . **186** A4
Cocking La LS29 . . . . **174** E3
Cock La
Gainford DL2 . . . . **1** E8
Piercebridge DL2 . . . . **2** A7
Cocklakes La YO7 . . . . **114** F1
Cock Lodge (site of)★
YO7 . . . . **115** C6
Cockmoor Rd YO13 . . . . **74** A1
Cock Pit Cl HG4 . . . . **113** C7
Cockrah Rd YO13 . . . . **74** F2
Cockret Cl 8 YO8 . . . . **232** B6
Cockret Ct YO8 . . . . **232** B7
Cockret Rd YO8 . . . . **232** B7
Cockshaw Bank La HG4 . . **113** B4
Cockshott Pl 5 LS29 . . . . **174** F4
Coda Ave YO23 . . . . **231** B3
Codlin Rd 1 TS15 . . . . **25** C5
Coeside YO24 . . . . **230** B7
Coggan Cl YO23 . . . . **228** B2
Coggan Way YO23 . . . . **230** F4
Colbeck La 17 HG3 . . . . . . **137** B4
Colber La HG3 . . . . **138** F2
Colbert Ave LS29 . . . . **218** E5
COLBURN **41** A5
Colburn Com Prim Sch
DL9 . . . . **41** A5
Colburn Dr DL9 . . . . **40** F5
Colburn La DL9 . . . . **40** F6
Colburn Sidings DL9 . . . . . . **40** F4
Cold Bath Pl HG2 . . . . **219** C1
Cold Bath Rd HG2 . . . . **222** C8
COLD COTES **103** F2
Cold Cotes Rd HG3 . . . . . . **160** B4
Coldhill La LS25 . . . . **195** C6
Coldie Hill 11 TS15 . . . . **25** C5
COLD KIRBY **91** D7

Cold Kirby Rd YO7 . . . . **91** C8
Coldstone La YO7 . . . . **88** B2
Coldyhill La YO12 . . . . **212** B8
Colebrooke Mdws HG5 . . **221** C7
Coledale Cl 2 YO30 . . . . . **224** F1
Colenso St YO23 . . . . **233** B1
Coleridge Dr HG1 . . . . **219** E7
Coleridge Gdns DL1 . . . . **3** D3
Coleridge Way 1 WF8 . . . **201** B1
Colescliffe Cres YO12 . . . **212** C8
Colescliffe Rd YO12 . . . . . **212** C8
Cole St YO31 . . . . **233** B4
Colin St 14 BB18 . . . . **171** D2
Coliseum★ YO21 . . . . **208** D6
College Ave YO11 . . . . **213** A2
College Bsns Pk HG4 . . . . **214** B7
College Ct
1 Low Bradley BD20 . . . . **173** E3
4 Scarborough YO11 . . . . **212** F4
York YO24 . . . . **230** E6
College Dr LS29 . . . . **218** B3
College Farm Cl DN14 . . . **207** A8
College Farm La LS22 . . . **180** A2
College Gdns DL1 . . . . **3** B5
College Gr WF10 . . . . **200** D3
College La
5 Masham HG4 . . . . **86** C3
Scarborough YO11 . . . . **213** A1
College of Law YO23 . . . . **231** B7
College Rd
Bradleys Both BD20 . . . . . . **173** E3
Copmanthorpe YO23 . . . . . **230** A3
Harrogate HG2 . . . . **222** B8
Ripon HG4 . . . . **214** B6
College St
Harrogate HG2 . . . . **222** B8
York YO1 . . . . **233** B3
Colley Broach Rd YO61 . . **117** F7
Colliergate YO1 . . . . **233** B2
Collier Hag La YO23 . . . . . **182** B3
Collier La
Lotherton cum Aberford
LS25 . . . . **195** A6
West Layton DL11 . . . . **20** A8
Collin Ave TS4 . . . . **6** F8
Collin Bank HG3 . . . . **160** E6
Collinge Rd 9 BD22 . . . . **187** B6
COLLINGHAM **188** A8
Collingham Dr TS7 . . . . **7** D4
Collingham Lady Elizabeth
Hastings CE Sch LS22 . . **180** A1
Collingham Way 12 YO14 **101** A3
Collingsway 4 DL2 . . . . **3** A7
Collingwood Ave YO24 . . **227** F2
Collingwood Dr 4 LA2 . . **128** E8
Collingwood Gdns YO17 . **215** A3
Collingwood Rd WF6 . . . . **200** A2
Collin's Hill HG3 . . . . **223** D7
Collinsons La YO17 . . . . . . **122** F5
Colliwath La DL8 . . . . **60** F4
Collyer View LS29 . . . . **218** E5
Colne & Broughton Rd
BD23 . . . . **172** C4
Colne Rd
Barnoldswick BB18 . . . . . . **171** D1
Cowling BD22 . . . . **187** A5
Earby BB18 . . . . **172** A1
Kelbrook & Sough BB18 . . **186** A8
Sutton BD20 . . . . **187** C7
Trawden Forest BB8 . . . . . **186** A1
Colonel's Wlk 9 WF8 . . . . **201** B1
Colonley Bsns Pk BD20 . . **173** D1
Colorado Way WF10 . . . . . **200** F2
Colstan Rd DL6 . . . . **210** E3
COLSTERDALE **84** E4
COLTON **190** E7
Colton La YO23 . . . . **190** E6
Coltsfoot Ct 19 HG3 . . . . . **161** B3
Coltsgate Hill HG4 . . . . . . **214** B6
Columbine Gr 33 HG3 . . . **161** B3
Columbus Ravine YO12 . . **212** F7
Columbus Way DL10 . . . . . . **41** C7
Colville Cres 8 DL9 . . . . . . **41** A5
Colville Rd 12 DL9 . . . . **41** A5
Comercial St
9 Barnoldswick BB18 . . . **171** D1
Harrogate HG1 . . . . **219** D3
Norton YO17 . . . . **215** D3
Scarborough YO12 . . . . **212** E5
Tadcaster LS24 . . . . **189** E6
Comercial Yd 1 HG5 . . . . **221** B6
Comets Garth 11 DL2 . . . . . **3** A7
Comfort La DL10 . . . . **20** C5
Comfrey Cl 32 HG3 . . . . . . **161** B3
Comfrey Manor TS8 . . . . **7** B4
Commercial St 9 BD24 . . **131** E2
Common Croft La YO26 . . **165** E1
COMMONDALE **9** D1
Common La
Beal DN14 . . . . **202** D3
Burn YO8 . . . . **203** E7
Catton YO41 . . . . **185** E8
Dunnington YO19 . . . . **184** F5
Fangfoss YO41 . . . . **169** B1
Knottingley WF11 . . . . **202** B1
Norton DN6 . . . . **206** E2
Sutton upon Derwent YO41 **193** C8
Temple Hirst YO8 . . . . **203** F4
Thorganby YO19 . . . . **192** F5
Walden Stubbs DN6 . . . . . . **206** F4
Warthill YO19 . . . . **167** F2
York YO10 . . . . **229** B1
Common Rd
Dunnington YO19 . . . . **184** F7
Skipwith YO8 . . . . **192** E1
Comon Balk La HG3 . . . . . **140** A3
Comondale Sta YO21 . . . . **9** E1
Comon Holme La LS29 . . **175** C3

Comon La
Carlton Husthwaite YO7 . . **116** F8
Coverham with Agglethorpe
DL8 . . . . **60** A2
Glaisdale YO21 . . . . **29** F1
Hambleton YO8 . . . . **196** D2
Harome YO62 . . . . **93** E5
Hartley CA17 . . . . **14** A8
Scruton DL7 . . . . **63** E7
South Milford LS25 . . . . . . **195** F2
Ulleskelf LS24 . . . . **190** C2
West Witton DL8 . . . . **59** F2
Comon Rd
Barkston Ash LS24 . . . . . . **195** F7
Church Fenton LS24 . . . . . . **196** A7
Strensall YO60 . . . . **145** D1
Compton La LS22 . . . . **188** A7
Compton St YO30 . . . . **228** A6
Conan Dr DL10 . . . . **209** D8
Conan Gdns DL10 . . . . **209** D8
Concept Business Ct
YO7 . . . . **211** D3
Concorde Pk YO30 . . . . . . **225** A3
Concorde Way TS18 . . . . **5** F7
Coneycroft 10 YO19 . . . . . **184** F7
Coneygarth La
Dunnington YO19 . . . . **184** E5
Tunstall LA6 . . . . **102** A4
Coney Garth La YO7 . . . . . . **89** B3
Coney Garth View HG5 . . **162** C5
Coney Moor Gr LS26 . . . . **200** C6
Coney St YO1 . . . . **233** B2
CONEYSTHORPE **120** D2
CONEYTHORPE **163** A5
Conference Cl YO17 . . . . . **215** B4
Conifer Cl 6 YO32 . . . . . . **225** D3
Conifers Cl 2 YO8 . . . . . . **197** D1
Coningham Ave 1 YO30 . **224** E2
Coniscliffe Mews DL3 . . . . . **3** A4
Coniscliffe Rd DL3 . . . . **3** A4
Coniston Ave BB18 . . . . . . **171** D2
Coniston Cl 1 YO30 . . . . . **224** E1
CONISTON COLD **155** A1
Coniston Dr
Castleford WF10 . . . . **201** C4
York YO10 . . . . **229** B4
CONISTONE **134** C6
Conistone La BD23 . . . . . . **108** B3
Coniston Gdns 6 YO12 . . . **99** F7
Coniston Gr TS5 . . . . **6** E7
Coniston Rd HG1 . . . . **220** B4
Coniston Way
3 Eastfield YO12 . . . . **99** F7
Thirsk YO7 . . . . **89** C4
Connaught Rd
Ilkley LS29 . . . . **218** D3
Middlesbrough TS7 . . . . **7** D6
Connaught Way YO32 . . . **225** F6
CONONLEY **173** C2
Cononley Com Prim Sch
BD20 . . . . **173** D2
Cononley La BD20 . . . . **173** D1
Cononley Rd BD20 . . . . . . **187** D8
Cononley Sta BD20 . . . . . . **173** D1
CONONLEY WOODSIDE . . . **173** C3
Conowl Cl 23 YO62 . . . . **92** F6
Conroy Cl 11 YO61 . . . . . . **143** D8
Consort St BD23 . . . . **217** B4
CONSTABLE BURTON **61** C5
Constable Burton Hall Gdns★
DL8 . . . . **61** C6
Constable Rd
Hunmanby YO14 . . . . **127** A8
Ilkley LS29 . . . . **218** D3
Constable Ridge Rd HG3 **160** B2
Constantine Ave
10 Colburn DL9 . . . . **41** A5
York YO10 . . . . **229** A4
Constantine Cres 11 YO12 **99** E6
Constantine Gr 11 DL9 . . . **41** A5
Constitution Hill 3 BD24 **131** E2
Conway Cl 2 YO30 . . . . . . **224** E3
Conway Cres BB18 . . . . . . **171** E1
Conway Gr 8 TS17 . . . . **5** F4
Conyers Ave DL3 . . . . **3** A6
Conyers Cl
Richmond DL10 . . . . **209** D8
Yarm TS15 . . . . **5** D2
Conyers Ings YO13 . . . . **99** A7
Conyers La DL8 . . . . **61** D6
Conyers Rd DL7 . . . . **22** E2
Conyers Sch TS15 . . . . **5** E2
Conygarth Way DL7 . . . . . . **63** C5
Conyngham Hall HG5 . . . . **220** F6
Cook Cl DL10 . . . . **41** C7
Cookgate TS7 . . . . **7** C5
Cooks Cl 2 DL6 . . . . **45** A7
Cooks Gdns 3 YO13 . . . . . . **75** D5
Cookson Way 34 DL9 . . . . . **41** A5
Cook's Row 5 YO11 . . . . . **213** B6
Coolham La BB18 . . . . **186** B8
Coombe Dr DL1 . . . . **3** F6
Coombes Cl YO61 . . . . **144** C3
COOMBOOTS **75** B6
Coomboots Brow YO13 . . . **75** A6
Cooper Cl DL6 . . . . **25** D2
Cooper La
Blubberhouses LS21 . . . . . **159** C2
Potto DL6 . . . . **25** D2
Cooper Lane Shepherd
LS21 . . . . **159** C2
Cooper Rd
49 Filey YO14 . . . . **101** B3
18 Wetherby LS22 . . . . . . **180** C3
Coopers Dr YO23 . . . . **230** B3
COPGROVE **140** C2
Copgrove La HG5 . . . . **162** D8
Copgrove Rd HG3 . . . . **140** A2

Cophill La YO7 . . . . **66** A4
Copley La LS25 . . . . **195** B7
Copmanroyd LS21 . . . . **177** A2
COPMANTHORPE **230** B2
Copmanthorpe & District
Recreation Ctr YO23 . . . **230** B2
Copmanthorpe La YO23 . **230** E3
Copmanthorpe Prim Sch
YO23 . . . . **230** B3
Copper Beech Cl
9 Dunnington YO19 . . . . . **184** E7
Upper Poppleton YO26 . . . **182** F8
Copper Beech Dr DN14 . . **207** A8
Copper Beeches The 2
YO19 . . . . **184** E7
Copperbeech Way 44 DL9 **41** A5
Copperclay Wlk YO61 . . . . **117** D1
Copperfield Cl
Malton YO17 . . . . **215** C5
21 Sherburn in Elmet LS25 **195** F4
Coppergate
1 Riccall YO19 . . . . **191** F1
York YO1 . . . . **233** B2
Coppergate Sh Ctr YO1 . . **233** B2
Coppergate Wlk YO1 . . . . **233** B2
Coppertop Mews 4
WF8 . . . . **201** C2
Coppice Ave HG1 . . . . **219** C4
Coppice Beck Ct HG1 . . . **219** D3
Coppice Cl
Harrogate HG1 . . . . **219** C4
10 Haxby YO32 . . . . **166** E5
Coppice Dr HG1 . . . . **219** C3
Coppice Gate HG1 . . . . . . **219** C4
Coppice La
14 Hellifield BD23 . . . . . . **154** B3
Wrelton YO18 . . . . **71** B1
Coppice Rise HG1 . . . . **219** C5
Coppice The
Barwick in Elmet LS15 . . . . **194** B7
Bishopthorpe YO23 . . . . . . **230** F4
Brayton YO8 . . . . **197** C1
Ilkley LS29 . . . . **218** A6
Leeming DL7 . . . . **63** F3
14 Sherburn in Elmet LS25 **195** F4
19 Sutton BD20 . . . . **187** E7
Coppice Valley Com Prim Sch
HG1 . . . . **219** C5
Coppice View HG1 . . . . . . **219** C4
Coppice Way HG1 . . . . **219** C5
Coppy La
Cononley BD20 . . . . **173** C2
Sutton BD22 . . . . **187** E4
Coppy Rd LS29 . . . . **174** F4
Coppy Wood Dr LS29 . . . . **218** B7
Copse Hill 1 YO14 . . . . . . **101** A4
Copse La TS17 . . . . **6** A5
Copse The
Boston Spa LS23 . . . . **180** E1
3 North Featherstone
WF7 . . . . **200** E1
5 Scarborough YO12 . . . . **212** B5
Copsewood Wlk 5 TS9 . . . **26** C8
COPT HEWICK **114** C2
Copwood Gr 7 YO32 . . . . . **225** C8
Corban La YO32 . . . . **166** B6
Corban Way 21 YO32 . . . . **166** D5
Corber Hill 7 DL6 . . . . **43** F3
Corbie Way YO18 . . . . **96** A7
Corby Ave TS5 . . . . **6** D8
Cordike La
Birdsall YO17 . . . . **148** D6
Langton YO17 . . . . **147** F6
Cordilleras La DL11 . . . . . . **39** C8
Corlett Ct
Woodthorpe YO24 . . . . **230** C8
York YO24 . . . . **230** C8
Cormorant Cl 10 YO14 . . . **101** D4
Cornaught Ct YO10 . . . . . . **231** D8
Cornbell Gate 4 HG4 . . . . **113** D2
Cornborough Ave YO31 . . **228** F6
Cornborough Rd YO60 . . . **145** C5
Cornelian Ave YO11 . . . . . **100** B8
Cornelian Cl YO11 . . . . . . **213** C1
Cornelian Dr YO11 . . . . . . **213** C1
Cornelius Cswy YO8 . . . . . **198** E8
Cornel Rise 26 HG3 . . . . . . **161** B3
Corner Cl 17 YO32 . . . . . . **166** D5
Corners Terr 5 YO22 . . . . **208** E6
Cornerstones Cl LS29 . . . **175** A4
Corners Yd 5 YO22 . . . . . . **208** E6
Cornfield Rd TS17 . . . . **6** A8
Cornflower Way 1 HG3 . **161** B3
Cornforth Hill DL10 . . . . . **209** B6
Cornlands YO17 . . . . **215** D2
Cornlands Rd YO24 . . . . . . **227** B1
Cornmill Cl YO8 . . . . **197** B8
Corn Mill Ct 19 LS25 . . . . . **195** F4
Corn Mill Gdns YO12 . . . . **212** D7
Corn Mill La 39 LS29 . . . . **176** D1
Cornmill Pl 20 BB18 . . . . . **171** D2
Cornmill Sh Ctr DL1 . . . . **3** C5
Corn Mill Wlk BD20 . . . . . **187** F7
Cornwall Ave
Darlington DL1 . . . . **3** E6
Silsden BD20 . . . . **174** B1
Cornwall Cl HG1 . . . . **219** A2
Cornwall Dr YO10 . . . . **231** E8
Cornwall Rd HG1 . . . . **219** B2
Cornwood Way 11 YO32 . **225** C8
Coronation Ave
6 Colburn DL9 . . . . **41** A5
Harrogate HG2 . . . . **222** E7
1 Hinderwell TS13 . . . . **11** F7
Coronation Gr HG2 . . . . . . **222** E7

Coronation Hospl LS29 218 C3
Coronation Pl DL10 209 A7
Coronation Rd
Crakehall DL8 62 E5
Harrogate HG2 222 E7
Coronation St
8 Barnoldswick BB18 171 E1
Castleford WF6 200 B2
Coronation Terr HG5 221 A3
Corporation Rd DL3 3 C6
Corporation Rd Com Prim Sch DL3 3 C6
Corpse Rd
North Otterington DL7 64 E5
Thornton-le-Moor DL6 65 A4
Corunna Ct 5 YO8 232 D5
Cosmo Ave YO31 229 A5
Costa La YO18 95 D6
Costa Way YO18 95 E7
Cotchers La LS24 195 D8
Cotcliffe Ave DL6 210 F3
Cotcliffe Bank DL6 65 E5
Cote Hill Rd HG3 160 B4
Cote La
Healey HG4 85 D5
Sproxton YO62 92 C4
Cotescue Bank DL8 60 C1
Cotherstone Cl TS16 5 C5
Cotswold Dr LS25 194 C3
Cotswold Way YO32 226 A5
Cottage Cl DL6 210 E5
Cottage La YO60 145 C4
Cottagers La DL2 2 C3
Cottam La YO25 151 C5
Cottee Way 16 DL9 41 A5
COTTERDALE 55 F8
Cotterdale Cl HG5 221 C6
Cotterdale Gdns LS25 202 A6
Cotterdale Holt 9 LS22 180 A1
Cottom La YO42 193 C2
COTTON TREE 186 A2
Cotton Tree La BB8 186 A3
Coulby Farm Way TS8 7 A5
Coulby La YO18 97 A6
Coulby Manor Way TS8 6 F6
COULBY NEWHAM 7 A5
Coulby Newham Sch TS8 7 A5
Coulson Cl 5 YO32 167 C8
Coulter Beck La LA6 102 D7
COULTON 119 B5
Coulton La YO62 119 A6
Count De Burgh Terr 4 YO23 228 B1
COUNTERSETT 57 C2
Counting House Mews BD23 216 F4
County Par HG1 219 F3
County Sq HG1 219 F3
Coupland Cl YO8 232 C6
Coupland Ct YO8 232 C6
Coupland Mews 1 YO8 232 C6
Coupland Rd
Garforth LS25 194 C4
Selby YO8 232 C6
Courby Hill HG4 86 F2
Courcey Gr YO26 227 C4
Court Barton La LS23 188 F7
Court Dr YO8 232 A4
Court Green Cl YO13 54 D1
Court La BD23 217 A4
Court Moor La YO62 70 A4
Courtneys
Selby YO8 232 B4
Wheldrake YO19 193 A8
Courtneys The YO8 232 B4
Courts Cl 7 DN14 205 E4
Court Terr HG4 214 C5
Court The 6 DL8 63 A2
Courtyard The
Bishopthorpe YO23 231 B4
11 Pontefract WF8 201 C2
Coutances Way LS29 218 F5
Cove Rd BD23 132 F2
Coverdale Dr
1 Knaresborough HG5 221 A7
Scarborough YO12 212 B4
Coverdale Garth 2 LS22 188 A8
Coverdale La TS13 12 A4
COVERHAM 60 C1
Coverham Abbey (rems of)★ DL8 60 C1
Coverham Cl DL7 210 C2
Coverham La DL8 60 C1
Cover La
Carlton Town DL8 83 E7
Marton-le-Moor HG4 114 E1
Covert The
Mount Pleasant TS8 7 B4
9 Topcliffe YO7 89 B1
York YO24 230 F7
COWAN BRIDGE 102 D7
Cowbar Bank 1 TS13 13 K2
Cowbar La TS13 13 J2
Cow & Calf Rocks★ LS29 218 D2
Cowcliff Hill YO17 148 F6
Cow Cl La
Kirkby Malham BD23 154 E8
Lockwood TS12 10 B4
COWESBY 66 C4
Cowgarth La 15 BB18 172 B1
Cow Gate La BD23 171 B7
Cowgill St 17 BB18 172 A1
Cowhouse Bank YO62 68 F3
Cowie Dr YO8 232 D5
Cow La
Cowling BD22 187 B6
Knottingley WF11 202 A2
Lothersdale BD20 172 F1
Middleton Tyas DL10 21 E5
Womersley DN6 206 D6
Cowland La YO7 88 D3
Cowley Cl TS16 5 E7
Cowley Rd TS5 6 E7
COWLING
Bedale 62 D2
Glusburn 187 B6
Cowling Com Prim Sch BD22 187 A6
Cowling Hill La BD22 186 F7
Cowling La DL8 62 D3
Cowling Rd DL8 62 D2
Cowlings Cl 16 YO14 127 A8
Cow Pasture La YO42 193 C3
Cowpasture Rd LS29 218 C3
Cowper La YO23 191 C8
Cowper St 3 BD23 217 A3
Cowslip La 18 WF10 200 D3
COWTHORPE 180 E7
Cowton Castle★ DL7 22 D1
Cowton La YO14 127 C6
Cowton Way TS16 5 D6
Cow Wath Bank YO22 51 E8
Cow Wath Cl 30 YO12 75 D5
Coxlea Gr YO31 229 B6
Coxwain Cl YO14 101 B2
COXWOLD 117 D8
Coxwold Dr DL1 3 D4
Coxwold Hill 5 LS22 180 C4
Coxwold Pottery★ YO61 117 D7
Coxwold View 1 LS22 180 C3
Crab La
Harrogate HG1 219 D6
Seamer YO12 99 E6
Crabmill La YO61 143 D8
Crabtree Cl YO61 118 A1
Crabtree Gn LS22 188 A8
Crabtree Gr 1 YO32 225 D3
Crabtree Hill LS22 188 A8
CRACKPOT 37 B3
CRACOE 156 C7
Cracoe & Rylstone VC CE Prim Sch BD23 156 B6
Cradley Dr TS5 6 E6
Cradoc Gr 14 TS17 5 F4
CRAG 187 D6
Crag Bank YO21 28 B8
Crag Cl 33 BD20 187 E7
Cragdale 13 BD24 131 D2
Cragdale Rise 1 HG5 221 D6
Cragg Bottom Rd BD22 187 C1
Cragg Gdns LS23 188 E5
Cragg Dr LS29 218 F3
Cragg Hill Rd BD24 105 C3
Craggs La LA2 130 C4
Craggs La
Arrathorne DL10 41 A1
Tatham LA2 129 A3
Cragg The 21 YO21 208 D7
Crag Hill La HG3 161 B6
Crag La
Bradleys Both BD20 173 E2
Felliscliffe HG3 160 D4
Huby LS17 178 B2
Killinghall HG3 161 B1
Knaresborough HG5 221 B5
North Rigton LS17 178 B3
Pannal HG3 178 C8
Sutton BD20 187 D6
Crag Side Rd DL8 57 B2
Crag The 3 LS23 188 E5
Crag View
Cononley BD20 173 D1
Skipton BD23 217 B6
Threshfield BD23 134 B3
Weeton LS17 178 B2
Crag View Rd BD23 217 B3
Craiglands Pk LS29 218 C3
Craiglands Rd LS29 218 C3
Craig Miller Pk DL3 2 F5
Craigmore Dr LS29 218 E4
Craig St DL3 3 C6
Craigs Way YO7 211 C4
Crakehall Prim Sch DL8 62 E4
CRAKEHILL 115 E4
Crake La HG3 159 F6
CRAMBE 146 F3
CRAMBECK 146 F6
Crambeck Village YO60 146 F6
Cranberry TS8 7 B5
Cranbrook Ave YO26 227 C5
Cranbrook Cl YO19 192 F8
Cranbrook Rd YO26 227 C5
Cranbrooks The YO19 192 F8
Cranbrook Way 17 WF8 201 C2
Cranesbill Cl HG3 161 B3
Cranfield Pl 4 YO24 230 C8
Cranford Gdns TS5 6 D8
Crank La DL7 63 B7
Crankley La YO61 143 B7
Cranwell Gr TS17 6 B6
CRATHORNE 25 A6
Craven Bank La BD24 131 B3
Craven Coll (Aireville Campus) BD23 216 D4
Craven Coll (Snaygill Campus) BD23 173 D4
Craven Coll (The Academy of Hair) BD23 216 F4
Craven Coll (The Centre for Rural & Equine Studies) BD23 216 C4
Craven Coll (Tyro Training) BD23 216 F4
Craven Court Sh Ctr BD23 217 A4
Craven Cres 3 LS29 174 F4
Craven Ct
Cowling BD22 187 C6
Northallerton DL7 210 B3
Richmond DL10 209 B6
Silsden BD20 174 C1
Cravendale Rd 4 DL9 40 F5
Craven Dr BD20 174 C1
Craven Garth 5 DN14 202 D4
Cravengate DL10 209 B6
Craven Mus★ BD23 217 A4
Craven Ridge La BD24 131 A2
Craven Ridge Lane Ends BD24 131 B3
Craven's Hill YO13 54 C3
Craven St
3 Colne BB8 186 A3
Harrogate HG1 219 D4
Scarborough YO11 213 A4
Skipton BD23 216 F3
Craven Swimming Pool BD23 216 D4
Craven Terr BD23 216 F4
Craven Way
5 Boroughbridge YO51 141 B4
Dent LA10 78 B8
Crawford Cl YO26 181 C7
Crawley Way YO31 229 B6
CRAY 81 E2
CRAYKE 118 A1
Crayke Castle★ YO61 117 F1
Crayke CE Prim Sch YO61 117 F1
Crayke La YO61 117 F2
Crayke Manor★ YO61 118 A2
Cray Thorns Cres YO7 115 A4
Crescent Ave YO21 208 C7
Crescent Back Rd 8 YO11 213 A5
Crescent Ct LS29 218 B4
Crescent Gdns HG1 219 C2
Crescent Hill 53 YO14 101 B3
Crescent Par HG4 214 C6
Crescent Pl 20 YO21 208 D7
Crescent Rd
Harrogate HG1 219 C2
Ripon HG4 214 B6
Crescent Terr 6 LS29 218 B4
Crescent The
13 Bedale DL8 63 B3
Burton Fleming YO25 126 E3
Carlton TS9 26 A2
Dishforth YO7 115 A2
Eaglescliffe TS16 5 D4
Filey YO14 101 B3
Garforth LS25 194 D4
17 Helmsley YO62 92 F6
Ilkley LS29 218 E5
1 Kelfield YO19 191 D1
Kexby YO41 185 C5
Kippax LS25 194 D1
Micklefield LS25 195 A3
Middlesbrough TS7 7 D6
Middleton St George DL2 4 E4
Monk Fryston LS25 202 A8
Northallerton DL6 210 E4
North Rigton LS17 178 B3
Otley LS21 177 A1
6 Riccall YO19 197 F8
Richmond DL10 209 D7
Ripon HG4 214 B6
Scalby YO12 212 B7
Scarborough YO11 213 A5
Sicklinghall LS22 179 E3
Skipton BD23 217 B6
Stamford Bridge YO41 168 D2
2 Summerbridge HG3 138 A1
Thirsk YO7 211 C3
Thornaby TS17 6 B8
Thornton Dale YO18 96 D5
York YO10 229 C1
York YO24 233 A1
Crestbrooke DL7 210 D2
Crestholme Cl 6 HG5 221 D5
Crest The LS26 194 A1
Crewe Rd WF10 201 B4
Creyke View DN14 205 A1
Cribyn Cl 20 TS17 5 F4
Crichton Ave YO30 228 B8
Cricketers Cl LS25 194 D3
Cricketers Way
8 Sherburn in Elmet LS25 195 F4
Wilberfoss YO41 185 F5
Cricket La TS6 7 E8
Cridling Gdns DN6 206 F2
CRIDLING STUBBS 206 C8
CRIMPLE 223 D8
Crimple Ave LS22 180 A8
Crimple Ct HG2 223 A7
Crimple La HG3 223 D7
Crimple Mdws HG3 222 D3
Crinan Ct
Pontefract WF6 200 A2
3 York YO32 225 F6
Crindle Carr La DL7 65 B3
Cringle Moor Chase TS9 26 F4
CRINGLES 174 C3
Cringles La BD20 174 C4
Cringley La DL8 57 E5
CROCKEY HILL 184 A1
Crocus Ct 20 DL9 41 A5
Croft Ave
8 Knottingley WF11 202 A3
Croft Ave *continued*
Middlesbrough TS5 6 D8
4 Normanton South WF6 200 B2
Otley LS21 176 F1
Croft CE Prim Sch DL2 22 C8
Croft Cl
Carlton Husthwaite YO7 116 F7
14 Easingwold YO61 143 C8
Ingleton LA6 103 D3
Croft Ct YO23 231 A4
Croft Dr LS23 188 E6
Crofters Gn HG3 219 A8
Crofters Mill
Cross Hills BD20 187 B7
Cross Hills BD20 187 E7
Croft Farm Cl YO23 230 B3
Croft Gdns YO7 211 B1
Croft Heads YO7 211 B1
Croft Head Terr 2 BD20 187 E7
Croft Hill
Carthorpe DL8 87 E6
32 Glusburn BD20 187 E7
Croft Hills TS9 26 A7
Croft House Dr 8 LS21 176 F1
Croft House Fold 10 LS29 175 A4
Croft House La BD23 135 A1
Croft La
Carlton Husthwaite YO7 116 F8
Newton Kyme cum Toulston LS24 189 B7
Snainton YO13 97 F5
Walton LS23 181 A2
Croftlands 7 WF11 202 A3
Croft Motor Racing Circuit★ DL2 22 C5
CROFT-ON-TEES 22 D8
Croft Rd
Bramham cum Oglethorpe LS23 188 E6
Camblesforth YO8 204 D4
Catterick Garrison DL9 209 E1
Eaglescliffe TS16 5 D4
Hurworth DL2 3 B2
Ingleton LA6 103 D3
Crofts Ave
4 Pickering YO18 96 A6
Richmond DL10 209 B7
Croftside 1 YO26 227 B3
Croft St 1 BD20 187 E7
Crofts The
1 Glusburn BD20 173 F1
1 Sutton BD20 187 E6
Croft The
Beadlam YO62 93 D7
Burton in Lonsdale LA6 102 F3
Castleford WF10 200 F3
5 Collingham LS22 188 A8
Draughton BD23 174 B7
1 Filey YO14 101 B3
Grafton YO51 141 D2
Knottingley WF11 202 A3
Langthorpe YO51 141 A7
Scalby YO12 212 B7
Sheriff Hutton YO60 145 D5
Stirton with Thorlby BD23 216 C6
Thirsk YO7 211 B1
West Tanfield DL8 87 B3
Croft View 6 YO7 211 B3
Croftway
Barwick in Elmet LS15 194 C8
Camblesforth YO8 204 C5
Selby YO8 232 C4
Sherburn in Elmet LS25 195 F4
2 York YO26 227 B3
Crombie Ave YO30 228 B7
Cromer St YO30 228 B7
Crompton Terr YO32 225 D6
Cromwell Ave 22 YO14 101 B3
Cromwell Cl 5 WF11 201 E4
Cromwell Cres 6 WF8 201 C1
Cromwell Dr DL7 64 A6
Cromwell Gdns 6 YO11 212 F4
Cromwell Office Pk 22 LS22 180 C3
Cromwell Par 5 YO11 212 F4
Cromwell Rd
Harrogate HG2 222 E7
Scarborough YO11 212 F4
York YO1 233 B1
Cromwell Rise LS25 200 D8
Cromwell St 9 BD23 217 A3
Cromwell Terr 7 YO11 212 F4
Crook Bank La DL11 38 F6
Crooked La YO26 164 C2
Crook La HG4 85 E5
Crookland La YO32 166 F5
Crook Rise View BD23 217 B3
Croome Dale La YO17 150 C6
Croome Rd YO25 150 B4
Croom Medieval Village★ YO25 150 B4
Cropstones LS23 188 F5
CROPTON 71 B4
Cropton Brewery & Visitor Ctr★ YO18 71 B3
Cropton La YO18 71 B2
Cropton Rise YO12 212 B4
Cropton Way TS8 7 B5
CROSBY COURT 65 B6
Crosby Gdns DL6 210 E4
Crosby Rd DL6 210 E4
Crosby St DL3 3 C7
Crosland Cl 22 YO62 92 F6
Cross Bank BD23 217 B6
Crossbeck Cl LS29 218 B3
Crossbeck Rd
Ilkley LS29 218 B3
Crossbeck Rd *continued*
Northallerton DL6 210 F5
Crossbeck Way TS7 7 D8
Crosscliff TS8 6 F5
Crossdale Rd YO18 72 E3
Cross End Fold 3 LS29 175 A4
Crossfield Cl 2 DL2 3 E1
Crossfield Cres YO19 231 E6
Crossfields TS8 7 A4
Cross Gate YO13 97 D5
Crossgate La 22 YO18 95 F6
CROSSGATES 99 E7
Crossgates HG3 138 B5
Cross Haw La 3 LA2 130 C8
Cross Head Bank DL8 60 D7
Cross Hill
Fairburn WF11 201 D6
Sutton-under-Whitestonecliffe YO7 90 D5
Crosshill La DN14 207 E6
CROSS HILLS 187 E7
Cross Hills La YO8 232 A5
Crossings The 13 DN14 205 E4
Cross La
Bentham LA2 128 E8
Brompton YO13 98 C5
Burneston DL8 87 E8
Burniston YO13 75 D7
Farndale East YO62 48 E4
Flaxton YO60 167 E8
Fulford YO19 231 F5
Giggleswick BD24 130 F2
Great Ouseburn YO26 164 B8
Little Ayton TS9 27 A8
Pickhill with Roxby YO7 88 C6
Scalby YO12 212 C8
Sinnington YO62 95 A8
Snainton YO13 97 F3
Stonebeck Up HG3 110 B5
Crosslands Rd 2 YO10 231 E8
Cross Lane Ct BD20 173 E3
CROSS LANES 143 D3
Cross Lanes DL10 209 E7
Crossley Pl BD23 216 F4
Crossley St 8 LS22 180 C3
Crossley Street Prim Sch LS22 180 C3
Crossman Dr 2 WF6 200 B2
Crossmoor Cl 7 BD20 174 B1
Crossmoor La
Haxby YO32 166 E6
Haxby YO32 166 F7
Cross Queen St 9 WF6 200 A1
Cross Rd LA2 128 E7
Cross Rein Bank DL7 23 A1
Cross Row
Boosbeck TS12 9 E7
Swillington LS15 194 A3
Cross St
6 Cowling BD22 187 B6
14 Earby BB18 172 A1
Scarborough YO11 213 A6
Skipton BD23 216 F3
5 York YO24 227 C3
Cross The LS15 194 B8
Cross Top DL8 57 E7
Crossways YO10 229 C2
Crossways Cres HG2 220 D3
Crossways Dr HG2 220 D2
Crossways The LS21 177 A1
Crossway The
Darlington DL1 3 E5
2 York YO31 228 E8
Crosswell Pk 40 TS17 5 F4
Crowberry Dr HG3 161 B3
CROWDON 54 A4
Crowdy Cl YO22 208 E4
Crowfoot La DL6 43 D5
Crowgarth HG4 140 D7
Crow Hill La HG3 160 C4
Crown Close Back 14 YO11 213 A4
Crown Cres YO11 213 A4
Crow Nest Rd LA2 130 F6
Crown Gr YO17 215 E3
Crown Sq 26 YO62 70 B1
Crown St
34 Burley in Warfedale LS29 176 C1
Darlington DL1 3 C5
Crown Terr YO11 213 A4
Crowood Ave TS9 26 C8
Crowtrees 1 LA2 128 E8
Croyside Terr DN14 202 F1
Cruet Fold HG3 161 A5
Crummack La LA2 130 E8
Crummock 3 YO24 230 C7
CUBECK 57 F4
Cuddy Brown Cl 7 YO18 96 A6
Cuddy La DL6 45 B4
Culloden Twr★ DL10 209 B6
Culvert La BD23 216 A4
Cumberland Cl
Airmyn DN14 205 F2
6 Strensall YO32 167 B6
Cumberland Gdns DL10 21 C4
Cumberland Rd 1 WF10 201 C5
Cumberland St
6 Skipton BD23 216 F3
York YO1 233 B2
Cumbernauld Rd TS17 6 C7
Cumboots Brow YO13 75 B6
Cumbrian Ave 4 YO32 167 B6
CUNDALL 115 E3
Cundall Ave YO7 115 B6
Cundall Cl 6 YO32 167 C8
Cundall Dr 6 YO32 191 C7

Cundall Manor Prep Sch YO61 115 E3
Cundall Way HG2 222 C8
Cunliffe Rd LS29 218 B4
Cunningham Ave TS17 6 B6
Cunningham Rd 4 DL9 40 F4
Cupid's Alley YO17 149 B6
Curfew Rd HG4 214 C3
Curlew Cl
11 Ilkley LS29 175 C2
Leyburn DL8 60 E4
Curlew Cres 2 DL9 40 F2
Curlew Dr
13 Crossgates YO12 99 E6
3 Filey YO14 101 A3
Curlew Glebe 8 YO19 184 E7
Curly Hill LS29 218 C7
Currer La LS29 175 B6
Currie Cl DL9 209 C2
Curson Terr YO8 198 E3
Curtain La DL11 1 D5
Curtain The DL11 1 D4
Curteis Dr DL10 41 B6
Curzon Terr YO23 228 B1
Custance Wlk YO23 233 A1
Cutler La LS26 200 C6
Cutpurse La DL10 209 C8
Cut Rd WF11 201 D6
CUTSYKE 200 E3
Cutsyke Ave WF10 200 D3
Cutsyke Crest 22 WF10 200 D3
Cutsyke Rd WF10 200 D2
Cut Throat La HG3 138 F1
Cycle St 4 YO10 229 A3
Cygnet Cl 7 YO14 101 A4
Cygnet Dr TS18 6 A7
Cygnet Mews 29 YO51 141 B5
Cygnet St YO23 233 A1
Cyndor Ct WF10 201 C3
Cypress Cl DL3 3 B4
Cypress Gdns HG4 214 B2
Cypress Rd TS7 7 C6
Cyprus Gr 37 YO32 166 E5

D

DACRE 159 F7
DACRE BANKS 159 F8
Dacre Braithwaite CE Prim Sch HG3 159 B7
Dacre Ct LS24 195 D7
Dacre Hall Pk HG3 159 F7
Dacre La HG3 159 D7
Dacre Pasture La HG3 159 D6
Daffy La YO61 117 E1
Dairy La
Cayton YO11 100 B5
Dacre HG3 159 E6
Dairy Way YO17 215 F2
Daisy Cl DL9 41 A5
Daisy Hill BD20 174 C1
Dakyn Cl DL7 22 F2
Dalacres Cres BD23 217 D8
Dalacres Dr BD23 217 D8
DALBY 119 B2
Dalby Ave HG2 220 D1
Dalby Bank YO60 119 C2
Dalby Cl YO12 212 B5
Dalby Ct HG2 220 D1
Dalby Forest Dr YO18 96 E8
Dalby Mead YO32 225 F1
Dalby Way TS8 7 A5
Dale Ave YO13 75 C8
Dale Bank HG1 219 B3
Dale Cl
Burniston YO13 75 C8
Hampsthwaite HG3 161 A5
7 Hurworth-on-Tees DL2 3 E1
Selby YO8 232 C3
Thornton Watlass HG4 86 D8
Dale Cres BD23 173 A4
Dale Croft 20 LS29 175 C2
Dale Croft Wlk LS29 218 E5
Dale Dike Gr YO30 224 F2
Dale Edge 11 YO11 99 F7
Dale End
Danby YO21 29 C7
Kirkbymoorside YO62 70 B1
Dale End Rd YO62 70 A7
Dalefield Ave WF6 200 A1
Dalefield Rd WF6 200 A1
Dale Garth YO12 212 D4
Dale Gr DL8 60 D6
Dalehouse Bank TS13 13 J1
Dale Rd
Carleton BD23 173 A4
Darlington DL3 3 B5
Sadberge DL2 4 C7
Dale Rise YO13 75 C8
Dales Ave BD23 217 C7
Dalesbridge Outdoor Ctr* LA2 130 E6
Dales Countryside Mus* DL8 56 D5
Dales Ct YO19 191 D3
Daleside Ave HG2 222 E5
Daleside Dr HG2 222 E5
Daleside Gdns HG2 222 E5
Daleside Pk HG3 160 A6
Daleside Rd
Farndale East YO62 48 C7
Farndale West YO62 48 B6
Harrogate HG2 222 E5
Rosedale East Side YO18 49 C5
Rosedale West Side YO18 49 C3
Dale's La YO31 228 F6
Dales Park Rd TS8 6 E5
Dales Sch The DL7 64 A7
Dale St
Earby BB18 172 B1
York YO23 233 A1
Dale Stone Cl WF11 201 D5
Dales View DL7 64 A6
Dale The LS25 188 F1
Dale View
6 Earby BB18 172 A1
Ilkley LS29 175 C2
Weaverthorpe YO17 124 E1
Dale Way 2 DL8 60 D5
Dalewood Wlk 3 TS9 26 C8
Dalguise Gr YO31 233 C4
Dallamires Cl HG4 214 D3
Dallamires Ind Est HG4 214 D4
Dallamires La HG4 214 E3
Dallamires Way N HG4 214 D4
Dallamires Way S HG4 214 D3
Dallas Ct TS8 6 F5
DALLOW 111 F2
Dalmally Cl YO24 230 B6
DALTON
Newsham 19 D7
Topcliffe 115 F7
Dalton Airfield Industrial Estate YO7 115 D6
DALTON GATES 22 D4
Dalton Hill YO19 193 A8
Dalton La
Dalton YO7 115 D7
Wothersome LS23 188 C5
DALTON-ON-TEES 22 E6
Dalton Terr YO24 228 A3
Dam Bank YO8 232 C6
Dame La DL8 58 F1
Dam Head Rd 14 BB18 171 D1
Dam Hill YO23 182 B4
Dam La
Appleton Roebuck YO23 190 F4
Markington with Wallerthwaite HG3 139 C3
Saxton with Scarthingwell LS24 195 C7
Selby YO8 197 B3
Damson Cl YO26 227 E4
DANBY 29 C7
Danby Castle* YO21 29 D6
Danby CE Sch YO21 29 B6
Danby La DL7 43 C5
Danby St 3 DL9 40 F4
Danby Sta YO21 29 C7
DANBY WISKE 43 C5
Dandy Mill Ave WF8 201 C1
Dandy Mill Croft 8 WF8 201 C1
Dandy Mill View WF8 201 C1
Dane Ave
Thorpe Willoughby YO8 197 B1
York YO26 227 C5
Danebury Cres YO26 227 C4
Danebury Ct YO26 227 C4
Danebury Dr YO26 227 C4
Danelaw Fields 1 DL6 43 F3
Danelaw Rd 2 DL6 43 F3
Dane Rd DL9 209 E1
Danescroft YO8 232 C2
Danes Croft 2 YO10 231 D8
Danes Ct 5 YO19 198 A8
Danes Dyke 34 YO12 75 D5
Danesfort Ave YO24 227 D2
Danesgate YO26 227 C4
Dane's Graves (Tumuli)* YO25 151 D2
Danes Hills (Tumuli)* YO8 192 E2
Danesmead YO10 231 D8
Danesmoor Cres DL3 3 B5
Daneswell Cl 3 YO41 168 D2
Dangerous Cnr HG3 160 A2
Dansk Way LS29 218 D5
Danum Ave YO7 211 A1
Danum Dr YO10 231 E8
Danum Rd YO10 231 E8
Darbie Cl YO32 225 D4
D'arcy Ct DL9 40 F4
D'arcy Rd YO8 232 E4
Darfield Cl YO32 167 B8
Darkfield La WF8 201 C2
Dark La
Brompton YO13 98 C5
Earby BB18 172 B1
Newsham DL11 19 C8
Sinnington YO62 71 A1
Spofforth with Stockeld HG5 179 F7
Stainburn LS21 177 E2
Sutton BD22 187 F1
DARLEY 160 A6
Darley Carr HG3 159 F6
Darley Cl 7 YO41 168 D2
Darley Mill Ctr* HG3 159 F6
Darley Prim Sch HG3 160 A6
Darley Rd HG3 160 D6
Darling La YO23 191 C8
DARLINGTON 3 E6
Darlington Arts Ctr* 2 DL3 3 C5
Darlington Back La DL2 4 E8
Darlington (Bank Top) Sta DL1 3 D4
Darlington Civic Theatre* DL1 3 D5
Darlington Coll DL1 3 D6
Darlington Coll at Catterick Garrison 28 DL9 40 E4
Darlington Meml Hospl DL3 3 C6
Darlington Rd
Easby DL10 20 F1
Longnewton TS21 5 A7
Northallerton DL6 210 C7
Richmond DL10 209 E8
Sadberge DL2 4 B7
Stockton-on-Tees TS18 5 E8
Darlington Ret Pk DL1 3 F5
Darlington Sch of Maths & Science DL3 3 A6
Darlington Sta DL1 3 D4
Darnborough Gate HG4 214 B6
Darnborough St YO23 233 B1
Darnbrook Rd 2 BB18 171 D1
Darnbrook Wlk YO31 229 B5
Darnholme La YO22 51 D8
Darnton Dr TS4 7 A7
Darrowby Cl YO7 211 C4
Darrowby Dr DL3 3 C6
Darwin Cl YO31 225 E1
Darwin Dr 40 DL9 41 A5
Daskett Hill YO60 145 D5
Dauby La YO41 185 B3
Davenport Rd TS15 5 D2
David La YO18 72 F5
Davis Ave WF10 201 B3
Davison Rd DL1 3 D7
Davison St TS12 9 F7
Davygate YO1 233 B2
Davy Rd WF10 200 E6
DAW CROSS 222 B3
Dawcross Rise HG3 222 B3
Dawes Ave WF10 201 A3
Daw La YO23 191 A5
Dawnay Cl 5 YO12 99 F7
Dawnay Garth
Shipton YO30 165 E5
2 Snaith DN14 204 B1
Dawney La YO61 143 B6
Dawson Ct HG3 161 A5
Dawson's La HG4 85 F4
Dawson St 16 BD23 217 A3
Dawson Terr HG1 219 D4
Dawtrie St WF10 201 B4
Day La HG3 159 E4
Daysfoot Ct 8 YO10 228 E3
Deacon Ct 3 YO8 232 B6
Deacons Ct YO23 230 B2
Dealtry Ave 1 YO32 225 C8
Dean Edge Rd BD22 187 D1
Deane Pl HG2 220 B3
Deangate YO1 233 B3
Dean Hall Brow YO22 32 C5
Deanhead Gr 7 YO30 224 E2
Dean La BD22 187 F3
Dean Rd
Norton YO17 215 E3
Scarborough YO12 212 E6
Deans Cl YO23 230 F4
Deans Sq YO7 115 C7
Dean St
Ilkley LS29 218 C5
Trawden Forest BB8 186 A1
De Bruce Rd DL6 210 D8
Debruse Ave TS15 5 D2
De Brus Pk TS8 7 C4
De Brus Way TS14 8 F7
De Burgh Ct DL9 41 A5
Dee Cl YO24 230 B7
DEEPDALE 80 F2
Deepdale
Guisborough TS14 8 D6
7 Hutton Rudby TS15 25 C5
5 York YO24 230 D8
Deep Dale LS23 180 E1
Deepdale Ave
Eastfield YO11 100 A8
Middlesbrough TS4 7 A8
Scarborough YO11 213 A1
Deepdale La
Boston Spa LS23 180 D1
Dent LA10 77 F8
Deepdale Way 7 DL1 3 F6
Deep Ghyll Croft HG4 214 C3
Deep Ghyll Wlk HG4 214 C3
Deeping Way YO8 232 A6
Deer Hill Gr YO30 224 F3
Deer Park Ct 1 LS25 202 A8
DEERSTONES 175 B8
Deerstone Way 22 YO19 184 F7
De Ferrers Rd DL6 210 D8
De Ferrieres Ave HG1 219 D4
De Gaunte Rd DL6 210 E8
De Grey Ct YO30 233 A4
De Grey Pl 2 YO23 231 B3
DEIGHTON
192 A7
Brompton 44 A8
Deighton Ave 18 LS25 195 F4
Deighton Cl LS22 180 C3
Deighton Grove La YO19 184 A1
Deighton La
Brompton DL6 43 E5
Little Smeaton DL6 23 E1
Deighton Rd
Coulby Newham TS4 7 A7
Spofforth with Stockeld HG3 179 F6
Wetherby LS22 180 C4
Deigton Gates Prim Sch 7 LS22 180 C4
Deira Ct 25 YO61 143 D8
De Lacy Acad WF11 202 A2
De Lacy Ave 1 WF7 200 E1
Delacy Cres WF10 201 B5
Delamere Cl 6 YO32 166 D5
Delamere Cres HG2 220 D1
Delamere Rd TS3 7 B8
Delaney Cl 19 BD24 131 D2
Delf La YO7 66 A4
De Lisle Cres DL9 209 C2
Dell The
Langtoft YO25 151 C5
5 Skelton YO30 224 B5
Del Pyke YO31 233 C4
Delves La YO22 30 F3
Delwood YO10 231 D7
De Mowbray Ct YO23 182 D3
Dene Cl DN14 203 C2
Dene Gr DL3 3 C6
Dene Mdw 1 YO13 99 B8
Dene Park Cl HG1 219 F6
Dene Pk HG1 219 F5
Dene Rd DL6 210 E5
Deneside Rd DL3 3 B6
Denesway LS25 194 D3
Dene The YO12 212 E7
Denevale TS15 5 E3
Denison Ave 8 YO12 99 D6
Denison Rd YO8 232 E4
Dennis La BD20 174 A2
Dennison St YO31 233 C4
Dennis St YO1 233 C2
Dentdale Dr HG5 221 C6
DENTON 176 A3
Denton Rd LS29 218 A5
Denton Terr WF10 200 F4
Denver Dr DL2 4 D4
Denver Rd 6 DN6 206 F2
Denwell Terr WF8 201 B1
Depot La 11 YO12 212 E4
Deramore Dr YO10 229 C3
Deramore Drive W YO10 229 C3
Derby Cl DL9 209 C1
Derby Rd TS14 8 E6
Derby The TS7 7 B6
Derby Way 8 DL9 40 F4
Dere St DL7 63 D3
Dere Street Roman Rd* DL11 2 B2
Derrings La YO61 142 D6
Derventio Roman Fort* YO17 215 D4
Derwent Ave
Garforth LS25 194 C3
5 Scarborough YO12 212 E4
York YO31 228 F4
Derwent Chase DN14 205 B7
Derwent Cl
East Cottingwith YO42 193 C5
Elvington YO41 185 B3
2 Stamford Bridge YO41 168 D2
Derwent Ct YO41 185 C2
Derwent Dr
4 Barlby YO8 198 B5
Castleford WF10 201 C5
Wheldrake YO19 192 F7
Derwent Est YO19 184 E7
Derwent La YO19 184 E7
Derwent Park Cl YO41 185 C1
Derwent Pk YO19 193 A8
Derwent Pl WF11 201 F1
Derwent Pool & Fitness Ctr YO17 215 D4
Derwent Rd
Harrogate HG1 220 B3
Huttons Ambo YO17 215 A2
Whitby YO21 208 A7
York YO10 231 D8
Derwent St 7 YO12 212 E4
Derwent Terr YO17 215 D3
Derwent Valley Ind Est YO19 184 F6
Derwent Wlk YO32 225 F5
Desmond Rd DL2 4 C3
Desmond Way DL3 3 C6
Deveron Way YO24 230 B7
Devilliers Wy WF6 200 C1
Devil's Arrows Standing Stones* YO51 141 B5
Devon Ct 8 DL9 209 C1
Devon Pl YO10 228 F3
Devonshire Ct YO30 225 A1
Devonshire Dr
6 Airmyn DN14 205 F3
Scarborough YO12 212 E7
Devonshire Gn HG4 114 F1
Devonshire Pl
Harrogate HG1 219 E3
12 Skipton BD23 216 F4
Devonshire Rd DL1 3 E6
Devonshire St 13 BD23 217 A3
Devonshire Way HG1 219 F4
Dewberry TS8 7 B4
Dew La TS7 7 D7
Dewsbury Ct YO1 233 A1
Dewsbury Terr YO1 233 A1
Dexta Way DL7 210 C3
Dialstone The YO7 211 A2
Diamond Ct TS18 5 F7
Diamond Gr HG1 220 C4
Diamond Pl HG1 220 C4
Diamond Rd TS17 6 B8
Diamond St YO31 233 C4
Dibble Bridge Bank YO21 28 F6
Dibdale Rd DL2 4 A1
Dickens Cl 1 YO32 225 F1
Dickens Dr 32 DL9 41 A5
Dickens Rd YO17 215 C6
Dickey La YO8 197 D5
Dick La BD22 187 B6
Dick Pieck La DL7 42 E1
Dick Scot La DL11 19 D7
Dicky Grounds La YO17 121 D8
Didsbury Cl YO30 224 E2
DIG* YO1 233 C2
Dijon Ave YO24 227 C2
Dikehollin La DL8 58 E2
Dike La HG3 159 C8
Dikelands Cl 19 YO26 165 F1
Dikelands La YO26 165 F1
Dike Ray Cl YO32 225 C7
Dikes La TS9 8 C2
Diligence Way 2 TS16 5 D5
Dilys Gr 5 YO26 227 E4
Dimmingdale Rd TS12 10 A3
Dinas Ct 12 TS17 5 F4
Dinsdale Ave TS5 6 E7
Dinsdale Cl 7 DL2 4 C4
Dinsdale Cres DL1 3 D5
Dinsdale Ct 6 DL2 4 C4
Dinsdale Dr TS16 5 E5
Dinsdale Sta DL2 4 C4
Diomed Ct TS7 7 B7
DISHFORTH 115 A4
Dishforth Airfield YO7 115 A2
Dishforth Airfield Com Prim Sch YO7 115 B2
Dishforth CE Prim Sch YO7 114 F4
Dishforth Rd
Copt Hewick HG4 114 B2
Sharow HG4 214 F6
Disraeli Cl YO32 225 E1
Dixon Ct YO8 232 B6
Dixon Gdns YO8 232 B6
Dixon La YO1 233 C1
Dixon Rd HG1 219 D4
Dixons Bank TS8 7 C5
Dixon St BD20 187 F7
Dixons Yd YO1 233 C2
Dixon Terr HG1 219 D4
Dobella Ave DN14 205 A1
Dob Park Rd LS21 176 F4
Doctor Laithe 3 BD23 134 D2
Doctor's Hill 2 LA2 128 E8
Doctors La WF10 200 D7
Doctor's La TS15 25 C5
Dodder Carr Rd TS13 10 F3
Dodford Rd TS8 6 F5
Dodgson La
Lothersdale BD20 186 D8
Thornton in Craven BB18 172 C1
Dodgson Terr YO26 227 D4
Dodsworth Ave YO31 228 E7
Doe Park La YO41 169 B4
Doe Pk YO30 224 F2
Dog Hill DL8 60 E3
Dog Hill Brow BD24 131 D6
Dog Kennel La YO18 96 E5
Doherty Wlk YO24 230 C8
Dolegate YO41 168 F4
Dolly La DL7 64 C8
Dollyth Howe* YO17 149 F6
Dolphin Ctr The DL3 3 C5
Dolphin Way YO14 100 F5
Donald Smith Ct DL8 61 C5
Don Ave YO24 230 E8
Doncaster Rd
Brayton YO8 232 B3
Knottingley WF11 201 E2
North Elmsall WF8 206 A1
Dondeen Ave
Old Thirsk YO7 211 C4
Thirsk YO7 211 A2
Don Pedro Ave WF6 200 B1
Don Pedro Cl WF6 200 B1
Doran Cl 45 YO14 101 B3
Dorchester Rd LS24 189 D5
Doriam Ave YO31 225 F2
Doriam Dr YO31 225 F2
Dorkings The TS9 26 E5
Dormary Cl YO32 225 E3
Dorset Cl HG1 219 A3
Dorset Cres HG1 219 A3
Dorset Ct 9 DL9 209 C1
Dorset Rd TS14 8 E5
Dorset St BD23 217 A3
Dorts Cres LS24 190 C1
Dotcliffe Rd BB18 186 A7
Doublegates Ave 6 HG4 113 D2
Doublegates Cl 8 HG4 113 D2
Doublegates Ct 10 HG4 113 D2
Doublegates Gn 9 HG4 113 D2
Doublegates Wlk 7 HG4 113 D2
Doubting Castle* YO21 10 D1
Douglas Cl TS18 5 F7
Douglas St 3 YO8 232 C5
Douky Bottom Cave* BD23 133 F7
Dove Bank HG3 139 E3
Dove Cl LS22 180 B4
Dovecot Cl
Gristhorpe YO14 100 E4
Wheldrake YO19 192 F8
Dovecote Dr WF10 200 F7
Dovecote Garth 5 YO41 185 B2
Dove Cote Gdns DN14 203 D2
Dovecote Mews YO7 115 C7
Dovedale Ave YO12 212 D8
Dovelands 14 BD20 187 E6
Dove St YO23 233 A1
Dove Way YO62 94 C8
Dovey Ct 7 TS17 5 F4
Dowber Ct YO7 211 D3
Dowber Way YO7 211 D4
Dower Chase YO19 192 A6
Dower Pk YO19 192 B6
Dowkell La LS23 180 F1
Downdale Rd YO13 54 B4
Downdinner Hill YO21 208 C6

DOWNHOLME 39 D4
Downholme Rd DL9 209 B1
Downland Cres WF11 202 A1
Downside Rd TS5 6 D8
Dracula Experience★ YO21 208 D7
Dragon Ave HG1 219 E3
Dragon Par HG1 219 E3
Dragon Rd HG1 219 E3
Dragon Terr HG1 219 E3
Dragon View HG1 219 E4
Drake Cl YO21 208 B5
Drakes Cl
38 Colburn DL9 41 A5
York YO32 225 F5
Drake St 2 YO23 233 B1
Drapers Croft YO23 230 B4
DRAUGHTON 174 B7
DRAX 204 F5
Drax Castle Earthworks★ YO8 204 F4
Drax Com Prim Sch YO8 204 F5
Dreaken Fold 4 YO13 99 A7
DREBLEY 157 D6
Drebley La BD23 157 D6
Dresser Cl DL10 209 C8
Driffield Ave 27 YO61 143 C8
Driffield Rd YO25 151 C4
Driffield Terr YO24 228 A2
Drift La HG4 138 B8
Drill Hall Bsns Ctr LS29 218 C5
Dringfield Cl 2 YO24 230 D8
DRINGHOUSES 230 E8
Dringhouses Prim Sch YO24 230 F8
Dringhouses Sports Club YO24 230 F8
Dringthorpe Rd YO24 230 F7
Drive The
Harrogate HG1 220 C5
7 High & Low Bishopside HG3 137 C4
Kippax LS25 194 D1
Middlesbrough TS17 6 A6
Skipton BD23 217 B5
12 Swillington LS26 194 A1
Threshfield BD23 134 B3
Drome Rd YO23 230 C2
Drovers Ct 8 YO61 143 C8
Drovers Way YO7 211 D4
Drovers Wlk BD23 154 B3
Druggist La 16 LS29 174 F4
Druggon Rd DL9 40 E3
Druids Mdw 8 YO51 141 B5
Drummond View YO23 231 B4
Drury Cl HG3 222 F2
Drury La
Humberton YO61 141 F8
Pannal HG3 222 F2
Drury St DL3 3 C6
Dryden Cl HG1 219 E7
Dryhurst Cl 9 DN6 206 F2
Dubbing Garth La DL11 37 B4
Dubb's La BD23 81 C1
Duchy Ave
3 Harrogate HG2 219 C1
11 Scalby YO13 75 D5
Duchy Gr 4 HG2 219 C1
Duchy Rd HG1 219 B2
Duckett Cl DL10 209 F8
Duckett St BD23 217 A3
Duck Hill HG4 214 C5
Duckhill La YO7 115 A4
Duck La YO12 125 A8
Duck St LA2 128 A6
Duck Street La HG3 136 D2
Dudley Ct YO31 233 C4
Dudley Mews YO31 233 C4
Dudley Rd DL1 4 A5
Dudley St YO31 233 C4
Dudley Wlk HG4 214 B3
Duffield Cres 1 LS25 195 F4
Dugdale La BD23 152 C1
DUGGLEBY 149 B6
Duggleby Howe★ YO17 149 C5
Dukes Chase 7 WF8 201 B2
Dukes Ct 3 YO26 227 D6
Dukes Hill LS29 218 A6
Duke's La YO25 126 A1
Duke St
6 Burton in Lonsdale LA6 102 F3
High Bentham LA2 129 A8
Settle BD24 131 D2
Skipton BD23 217 A4
14 Trawden Forest BB8 186 A3
Dukesway TS17 6 B5
Dukes Wharf YO23 233 B1
Dulverton Cl
2 High Leven TS17 6 A3
13 Pontefract WF8 201 C2
Dulverton Rise WF8 201 C2
Dulverton Way
5 Guisborough TS14 8 F6
12 Pontefract WF8 201 C2
Dumb Tom's La LA6 103 B1
Dumfries Sq 8 DL9 40 E4
Duna Way 6 YO62 70 C1
Dunbar Ct LS26 200 B6
Duncan Cl 6 HG1 219 C5
Duncan St HG1 219 C5
Dunce Mire Rd LS25 202 A8
Duncombe Cl
2 Eastfield YO12 99 F7
Malton YO17 215 A3
Duncombe Dr
24 Pickering YO18 95 F7
Strensall YO32 167 B8
Duncombe La YO32 167 B8
Duncombe Park National Nature Reserve★ YO62 92 E6
Duncombe Pl YO1 233 B3
Dundas Gdns YO21 208 B6
Dundas St
Richmond DL10 209 C7
York YO1 233 C2
Dunderdale Cres WF10 201 B5
Dunelm Wlk DL1 3 E7
Dunholm Ave 1 TS3 7 D8
DUNKESWICK 178 E2
Dunkeswick La LS17 178 D4
Dunn Gr 3 YO11 100 A7
DUNNINGTON 184 F7
Dunnington CE VC Prim Sch YO19 184 E7
Dunnington Dr YO8 196 E1
Dunniwood Cl 4 WF10 200 D3
Dunniwood Dr 3 WF10 200 D3
Dunroyal YO61 141 F8
Dunroyal Cl YO61 141 F8
DUNSLEY 12 F2
Dunsley Cres YO21 208 A8
Dunsley La YO21 32 A8
Dunslow Ct YO11 99 F6
Dunslow Rd YO11 99 F6
Dunsmore Cl TS8 6 C4
Dunwell Ave 2 YO12 212 B7
Durham Cl 18 YO8 198 F1
Durham La TS16 5 D5
Durham Lane Ind Pk TS16 5 D6
Durham Lane Prim Sch 13 TS16 5 D5
Durham Pl 5 YO12 213 A7
Durham St
Castleford WF10 200 F3
6 Scarborough YO12 212 F7
Durham Tees Valley Airport DL2 4 F4
Durham Way HG3 219 A5
Durlston Dr YO32 167 A7
Duxbury St 11 BB18 172 B1
Dyke Hall La LA10 78 A8
Dykelands Cl YO19 192 F7
Dykes La YO23 230 A1
Dyon La YO8 199 B3
Dyon Rd YO8 199 D7
Dyon Way YO8 199 D7
Dyson La DL11 18 G7

E

Eagle Pk TS8 7 C5
EAGLESCLIFFE 5 E5
Eaglescliffe Sta TS16 5 E6
EARBY 172 B1
Earby Springfield Prim Sch BB18 172 B1
Earfit La YO23 191 A8
Earl Crag View BD22 187 C6
Earl Edwin Dr DL10 209 D8
Earlesdon Ave BB18 172 A1
Earle St YO31 233 C4
Earlham St 10 BB18 172 B1
Earlsborough Terr YO30 233 A3
Earls Chase WF8 201 B2
Earls Court Rd TS8 6 F5
Earlsdon Ave TS5 6 D7
Earls View 3 BD20 187 E6
Earlsway TS17 6 C5
Earlswood Cres LS25 194 C1
EARSWICK 226 A7
Earswick Chase YO32 225 F7
Earswick Village YO32 225 F7
EASBY
Richmond 209 F5
Stokesley 27 B7
Easby Abbey (rems of)★ DL10 209 E5
Easby Ave TS5 6 F8
Easby Cl
4 Bedale DL8 63 B2
7 Ilkley LS29 175 C2
Easby Ct DL10 209 F5
Easby Dr LS29 175 C2
Easby La
Easby TS9 27 A8
Great Ayton TS9 7 F1
Easby Low Rd DL10 209 D7
EASINGTON 11 A8
EASINGWOLD 143 D8
Easingwold Bsns Pk YO61 143 D8
Easingwold Com Prim Sch YO61 117 C1
Easingwold Sch YO61 143 C8
Eason Rd YO24 230 E8
Eason View YO24 230 E8
Easson Rd DL3 3 C5
East Acres WF11 201 F4
EAST APPLETON 41 D2
East Ave
8 Easingwold YO61 143 D8
13 Glusburn BD20 187 E7
21 Scalby YO13 75 D5
EAST AYTON 99 B8
East Ayton Com Prim Sch YO13 99 A8
East Bank 2 LS25 195 F4
EAST BARNBY 12 C3
East Barnby La YO21 12 C3
Eastbeck Cl YO17 124 E8
East Beck Ct LS21 176 C3
Eastborough YO11 213 B6
EASTBOURNE 3 E4
Eastbourne Comp Sch DL1 3 E5
Eastbourne Gdns TS3 7 C8
Eastbourne Gr YO31 228 F5
Eastbourne Rd DL1 3 D5
Eastbourne Sports Complex DL1 3 E5
East Brow Rd YO18 72 C4
EASTBURN 187 F7
Eastburn Junior & Infant Sch BD20 187 F7
Eastbury Cl TS17 6 B4
EASTBY 156 F1
Eastby Rd HG1 219 F6
East Carr 18 YO11 100 B6
East Castle St 6 BD23 217 A3
East Cl DL2 4 C7
East Cliff YO22 208 E7
East Comm La YO8 232 F4
EAST COMMON 232 E4
EAST COTTINGWITH 193 C5
EAST COWTON 22 F2
East Cowton CE Prim Sch DL7 22 E1
East Cres 19 YO21 208 D7
East Dene 11 BD20 174 C1
East Down WF10 201 A4
East End YO60 145 D5
Eastern Terr YO31 228 E6
Easter Pk TS17 6 C5
EASTERSIDE 7 A7
Easterside Academy TS4 7 A7
Easterside La YO62 67 F4
Easterside Rd TS4 7 A7
EASTFIELD 100 A7
Eastfield
Amotherby YO17 121 B4
Foxholes YO25 125 D3
Hunmanby YO14 126 F8
Knaresborough HG5 221 D6
Eastfield Ave
Haxby YO32 225 C7
Norton YO17 215 E3
Richmond DL10 209 D8
Eastfield Cl LS24 189 F7
Eastfield Cres YO10 229 C2
Eastfield Ct YO10 229 C2
Eastfield Dr 14 WF8 201 C1
Eastfield Gr WF6 200 B2
Eastfield Ind Est 15 YO11 99 F6
Eastfield La
Dunnington YO19 184 F8
Kellington DN14 202 F4
Spennithorne DL8 61 A3
Thoralby DL8 58 E2
Eastfield Rd
Norton YO17 215 E3
Pickering YO18 96 A6
Eastfields TS9 26 C7
EAST GARFORTH 194 E4
East Garforth Prim Sch LS25 194 D4
East Garforth Sta LS25 194 D3
Eastgate
16 Helmsley YO62 92 F6
Pickering YO18 96 A6
3 Seamer YO12 99 D6
East Gate YO13 98 D6
East Grange Cl DL7 63 E7
EAST HARLSEY 44 E6
EAST HAUXWELL 61 D8
EAST HESLERTON 124 A7
East Heslerton La YO17 124 A8
Eastholme Dr YO30 224 E1
Easthorpe Dr YO26 224 A1
East Ings La YO18 95 F4
EAST KNAPTON 123 C6
East La
Ampleforth YO62 92 D1
Castle Bolton with East & West Bolton DL8 59 B6
Cock Hill YO26 165 B3
Embsay BD23 217 D7
Yafforth DL7 43 C1
Eastland Ave YO24 227 E2
EAST LAYTON 20 C8
East Lea YO7 115 C7
East Lea View 21 YO11 100 B6
EAST LUTTON 150 C8
EAST MARTON 172 B6
East Moor Gdns YO19 231 F5
East Mount YO17 215 C4
Eastmount Rd DL1 3 D6
East Mount Rd YO24 233 A1
EAST NESS 94 B1
East Neville St 14 BD23 217 A3
EAST NEWTON 93 C2
Easton La YO21 29 D6
Easton Way
Catterick DL10 41 D5
29 Walkerville DL9 41 A5
East Par
Harrogate HG1 219 E2
Ilkley LS29 218 C4
East Parade YO31 228 F6
East Park Rd
Harrogate HG1 219 E2
15 Scalby YO13 75 D5
5 Spofforth HG3 179 E5
Eastpoint Rd DL1 3 F6
East Rd
Melsonby DL10 20 F7
Northallerton DL6 210 E4
Norton YO17 215 E3
EAST ROUNTON 24 E2
EAST ROW 13 A3
East Sandgate 14 YO11 213 B6
East Side 5 TS15 25 D5
East St
Gargrave BD23 155 D1
Gayles DL11 19 E6
Swinton YO17 121 B4
East Terr YO21 208 D7
East Terrace Cres YO21 208 D7
East View
Barton DL10 21 D8
7 Campsall DN6 206 E1
Kippax LS25 194 D1
10 Knottingley WF11 202 A2
Langthorpe YO51 141 A6
3 Low Bentham LA2 128 E8
Middleton St George DL2 4 D3
Northallerton DL6 210 E3
Sherburn in Elmet LS25 195 F3
South Kilvington YO7 211 B6
3 Trawden BB8 186 B1
East View Ct HG5 162 F3
Eastville Terr HG1 219 B6
East Vw LS25 195 A3
Eastward Ave YO10 231 E7
Eastway YO11 100 A7
East Way
Whitby YO21 208 B7
York YO31 225 E2
Eastway Cl 2 YO62 70 C1
East Whitby Com Prim Sch YO22 208 F4
EAST WITTON 61 A1
East Witton Rd DL8 60 E2
Eaton Ct 7 YO24 230 B8
Eaton Rd LS29 218 A3
EAVESTONE 138 B7
Eavestone Gr HG3 219 A4
EBBERSTON 97 E5
Ebberston Hall★ YO13 97 D6
Ebenezer Terr 9 HG1 219 D2
Ebor Cl DL10 21 A1
Ebor Ct
Northallerton DL7 210 D3
7 Selby YO8 232 C6
Ebor Ind Est YO31 233 C3
Ebor Mount LS25 194 D1
Ebor Prep Sch YO30 228 A7
Ebor Rise HG1 219 B2
Ebor St
Selby YO8 232 C5
York YO23 233 B1
Ebor Way YO26 224 A2
Ebsay Dr YO30 225 A1
Eccles Cl YO30 224 D2
Echo Hill YO22 32 B7
Eddison Way 1 TS8 6 F5
Eden Ave YO8 232 D3
Eden Camp Modern History Theme Mus★ YO17 215 E8
Eden Cl
2 Hurworth-on-Tees DL2 3 D1
1 Hutton Rudby TS15 25 C4
York YO24 230 C7
Eden Cres DL1 3 C4
Eden Crest DL2 1 D7
Edendale WF10 200 F4
Edenhouse Rd YO17 215 E8
Eden La DL2 1 D8
Eden Park Rd 2 TS15 25 C4
Eden Pk DL2 1 D7
Eden Rd DL7 210 B2
Edens Way HG4 214 C2
Edgecombe Dr DL3 3 A6
Edge Dell YO12 99 E8
Edgehill Rd YO12 212 F2
Edge La
Grassington BD23 134 F3
Long Preston BD23 153 E6
Edgemoor Rd
Darlington DL1 3 E3
2 Firth Moor DL1 3 E4
Edgerton Cl LS24 189 D6
Edgerton Ct 11 LS24 189 D6
Edgerton Dr LS24 189 D6
Edgerton Garth LS24 189 D6
Edgware Rd YO10 228 E2
Edinburgh Dr DL3 3 A4
Edmondson's La BD23 172 C5
Edmondson St 17 BB18 171 D2
Edmund Wilson Swimming Pool YO24 227 D1
Edston Dr 9 TS14 8 F7
Edward Kitching Terr 14 TS9 8 A2
Edward Pease Way DL3 3 A7
Edwards Street Ind Est DL1 3 D6
Edward St
27 Earby BB18 172 A1
Pontefract WF6 200 A3
EGGBOROUGH 202 F2
EGGLESCLIFFE 5 E4
Egglescliffe CE Sch TS16 5 E4
Egglescliffe Sch TS16 5 D4
Eggleston View DL3 3 A6
Eggshell La LA2 130 C8
Eglington Ave TS14 8 F6
Egremont Cl 11 YO41 168 D2
EGTON 31 B5
Egton Ave TS7 7 C5
EGTON BRIDGE 31 A4
Egton CE VA Prim Sch YO21 31 B5
Egton Cliff YO21 31 A4
Egton La YO21 30 F5
Egton Sta YO21 31 A4
Eight Acre La HG4 113 A5
Eighth Ave YO31 228 F5
El Alamein Rd 5 DL9 209 C1
Elbolton Cave★ BD23 156 E8
Elbow Terr 4 YO22 208 E6
Elderberry View 17 WF10 200 D3
Elder Gr 38 YO32 166 E5
Elder Rd DL7 210 D4
Elder's St YO11 213 A6
Eldmire La YO7 115 D6
Eldon St YO31 233 C4
Eldon Terr YO31 233 C4
ELDROTH 130 E4
Eldroth Rd LA2 130 C5
Eldwick Cl YO30 224 F2
Eleanor Dr HG2 220 C1
Eleanor Rd HG2 220 C1
Electric Ave HG1 219 B5
Elgar Cl YO31 225 E1
Elgin Rd TS17 6 B6
Elgin St 16 YO21 208 D6
Elizabethan Ct 4 WF8 201 C1
Elizabeth Ct
7 Selby YO8 232 B6
Sherburn in Elmet LS25 195 E4
Elizabeth Dr WF10 201 B4
Elizabeth Rd WF10 200 C7
Elland Ct 12 DL1 3 F6
Ellarfield La LS25 195 F5
Ellen Gr HG1 220 C4
Ellenthorpe La YO51 141 D6
ELLERBECK 44 F3
Ellerbeck Ct TS9 26 D6
Ellerbeck Way
Great & Little Broughton TS9 26 D6
Middlesbrough TS7 7 D8
Whitby YO22 208 E4
ELLERBURN 96 E7
Ellerburn Bank Nature Reserve★ YO18 72 F1
Ellerburn Rd YO18 96 F7
Ellerby Bank TS13 11 F4
Ellerby La TS13 11 F5
Ellerclose Rd 22 DL8 60 D5
Eller Gates YO21 30 C6
Eller Gill La BD23 172 D4
Ellerholme La DL11 38 F5
Ellerington Cl 5 LA6 103 D3
Ellerker La LS14 188 A3
Ellerker Rd LS14 188 A3
Eller Mews 3 BD23 216 E3
Ellers La DL8 59 A2
Ellers Rd BD20 187 E6
ELLERTON
193 C2
Catterick 41 F4
Ellerton Priory (rems of)★ DL11 39 A4
Ellerton Rd TS18 5 D8
ELLINGSTRING 85 D6
Elliot Ct YO10 231 D7
Elliot St BD23 216 F4
Elliott St BD20 174 B1
Ellis Ct HG1 219 B2
Ellis Gdns 6 YO13 75 D5
Ellis La LS25 194 C5
Ellison Ave 32 YO12 75 D5
Ellwood Cotts BD24 131 D4
Ellwood Ct YO10 228 D2
Elma Gr 3 YO30 224 E2
Elm Ave
Airmyn DN14 205 F2
Kippax LS25 194 C2
Northallerton DL6 210 F5
Elm Avenue 10 YO32 191 C7
Elm Cl
Barnoldswick BB18 171 D1
10 Filey YO14 101 B4
Hipswell DL9 209 F1
Northallerton DL6 210 F5
Selby YO8 232 D2
Elm Ct DL6 210 E5
Elm Dr TS7 7 B6
Elm End 9 YO32 166 E5
Elmet Dr LS15 194 C8
Elmete Ave LS25 195 F4
Elmete Rd WF10 201 B5
Elmet Rd LS15 194 C7
Elmfield Ave YO31 228 F8
Elmfield Rd
3 Glusburn BD20 187 F8
Hurworth DL2 3 D1
Hurworth-on-Tees DL2 22 D8
Elmfield Terr YO31 228 F7
Elm Gn 7 YO62 92 F7
Elm Gr
Robin Hood's Bay YO22 33 D4
Sherburn YO17 124 D8
Thornaby TS17 6 B8
4 Whitby YO21 208 B6
York YO31 225 F2
Elmhurst Gdns 8 BD24 131 D3
Elmlands Gr YO31 228 F8
Elmpark Vale YO31 229 A8
Elmpark View YO31 229 A8
Elmpark Way YO31 229 A8
Elm Pl WF11 201 F2
Elm Rd
34 Glusburn BD20 187 E7
Guisborough TS14 8 F7
Harrogate HG1 219 E5
Ripon HG4 214 B2
9 Scarborough YO12 212 E4
3 Topcliffe YO7 89 B1
Elms Cl 2 YO19 191 F1
Elmslac Cl 1 YO62 92 F6
Elmslac Rd 3 YO62 92 F7
Elm St YO8 232 D6
Elms The YO32 167 D2

Elm Tree Ave
46 Colburn DL9 41 A5
Harrogate HG1 219 D5
9 Poppleton YO26 165 F1
Elmtree Gdns 3 YO24 227 C3
Elm Tree Rise HG3 140 B5
Elm Tree Sq BD23 217 D8
Elm View YO18 96 A6
Elmville Ave YO12 212 E6
Elm Wlk 5 DL10 41 D5
Elmwood Ave LS15 194 B8
Elmwood Chase LS15 194 B8
Elmwood Cl 6 TS9 26 C8
Elmwood La LS15 194 B8
Elmwood Rd TS16 5 E6
Elmwood St 4 HG1 219 E4
Elphin Bridge La YO61 117 B6
Elslack La BD23 172 C4
Elston Ave YO8 232 C6
Elston Cl YO30 228 A8
Elston Pl YO8 232 C6
Eltham Cres TS17 6 C6
ELTON 5 C8
Elton La HG3 160 E6
Elton Par DL3 3 B5
Elton Rd DL3 3 B5
ELVINGTON 185 B2
Elvington CE VC Prim Sch YO41 185 B3
Elvington Ind Est YO41 185 A3
Elvington La YO19 184 E5
Elvington Pk YO41 185 A3
Elvington Terr YO10 228 E4
Elwick Ave TS5 6 E7
Elwick Gr YO10 229 C4
Elwick La YO26 164 B7
Ely Cl HG3 219 A5
Embleton Dr 1 YO30 224 F1
Embleton Rd LS26 200 B4
EMBSAY 217 D8
Embsay & Bolton Abbey Steam Rly★ BD23 217 E7
Embsay CE Prim Sch BD23 217 D8
Embsay Sta BD23 217 D7
Emerald Cl HG1 220 C4
Emerald St YO31 233 C4
Emerson Ave TS5 6 F8
Emerson Cl 2 DL6 25 D1
Emerson Rd DL2 3 E1
Emery Cl DL2 3 E1
Emgate 2 DL8 63 A3
Emily Mews YO10 228 E4
Emley Moor Rd DL1 3 E4
Emley View LS25 194 C2
Emmerson St 2 YO31 228 E5
Emmet La HG3 160 C5
Emmott Ct BB8 186 C3
Emmott La BB8 186 B4
Emsworth Dr TS16 5 D5
Enclosure Gdns 1 YO10 229 B1
Endcliff Cres YO12 212 D8
Endeavour Wharf 6 YO21 208 D6
Endfields Rd 1 YO10 231 E8
Endican La DL7 65 D3
Endsleigh Dr TS5 6 D8
Enfield Chase TS14 8 F5
Enfield Cl 4 DL9 40 E4
Enfield Cres 1 YO24 228 A3
Enfield Gr TS7 7 D8
Engelhart Cl YO8 232 A2
Engine Shed La BD23 216 D3
Engine Shed Lane Ind Est BD23 216 D3
England La WF11 201 F2
England Lane Acad WF11 201 F2
Ennerdale Ave YO31 229 B5
Ennerdale Dr 4 WF11 201 F1
Enter La LA6 103 D3
ENTERPEN 25 C4
Enterpen TS15 25 C4
Enterprise Way
Bradleys Both BD20 173 D4
Pickering YO18 96 A6
Sherburn in Elmet LS25 196 B4
Whitby YO22 32 F8
EPPLEBY 1 E4
Eppleby Forcett CE Prim Sch DL11 1 D4
Epsom Ct 11 DL1 3 F6
Eridge Rd TS14 8 F6
Ermysted's Gram Sch BD23 216 F4
Ermysted St 4 BD23 217 A4
ERYHOLME 23 A7
Eryholme La DL2 22 F7
ESCRICK 192 B5
Escrick Bsns Pk YO19 192 A3
Escrick CE VC Prim Sch YO19 192 A5
Escrick Ct YO19 192 B5
Escrick Park Gdns YO19 192 B5
Escrick St YO10 233 C1
Escrick Terr YO10 233 C1
Esher Ave TS6 7 E8
Eshington La DL8 58 F2
ESHTON 155 D3
Eshton Rd BD23 155 D2
Eskdale Ave
Normanton WF6 200 A2
York YO10 229 C3
Eskdale Cl
5 Pontefract WF6 200 A2
Sleights YO22 32 A5
Eskdale Croft WF6 200 A2
Eskdale Ct 12 WF6 200 A2
Eskdale Rd YO22 208 F3
Eskdale Sch YO22 208 E3
Eskdaleside YO22 31 F5
Esk Dr YO26 227 B8
Eskew Cres LA2 128 E7
Eskew La
Bentham LA2 128 E7
Low Bentham LA2 128 E8
Eskitt Hill YO12 212 D4
Esk Rd DL1 3 D3
Esplanade
Harrogate HG2 219 C2
Scarborough YO11 213 A4
Whitby YO21 208 D7
York YO26 233 A2
Esplanade Cres YO11 213 B2
Esplanade Ct YO30 233 A3
Esplanade Gdns YO11 213 A4
Esplanade Rd YO11 213 A3
Esplande La BB18 171 C1
Estell La YO13 74 C5
Estill Cl 2 YO11 100 B6
Estoril Road S DL1 3 F4
Ethel Cres HG5 221 C6
Ethel St 12 BB18 171 E1
Etive Pl YO24 230 B7
Eton Dr 7 YO32 166 D5
Eton Rd TS5 6 E8
Ettersgill Cl TS16 5 D5
Ettersgill Dr DL3 3 A5
Ettington Ave TS3 7 B8
Etty Ave YO10 229 A4
Etty Cl 24 YO41 168 D2
Euclid Ave HG1 219 B5
Eva Ave YO30 224 D2
Evaglades Sch LA2 128 E8
Evelyn Cres YO30 228 B7
Evelyn Ct 5 HG3 161 B2
Evelyn Dr YO12 212 D4
Evergreen Way 1 YO8 197 D1
Evergreen Wlk 2 TS4 6 F8
Everingham Rd TS15 5 D2
EVERLEY 74 F4
Eversley Ave LS25 195 F3
Eversley Ct LS25 195 F4
Eversley Garth Cres LS25 195 F4
Eversley Mount LS25 195 F3
Evesham Rd TS3 7 B8
Evron Ctr YO14 101 B3
Ewart St YO12 212 E3
Ewden Cl 16 YO14 101 A3
Ewelands Hill YO7 90 C7
Ewe Leys La YO7 66 A5
Exchange St 8 WF6 200 A1
EXELBY 63 D1
Exelby Cl DL8 63 D1
Exelby La DL7 63 D3
Exeter Cres 10 HG3 161 B3
Exeter Dr DL1 3 F7
Exford Cl 8 TS17 6 A3
Exhibition Sq YO1 233 B3
Express Way WF6 200 A3
Eyre Cl
Brayton YO8 232 A2
Selby YO8 232 A2

F

Faber Cl YO23 230 B3
Faber St YO31 228 E5
FACEBY 25 F2
Faceby Rd TS9 26 A2
FADMOOR 69 F4
Fadmoor Bank YO62 69 E6
Fadmoor La YO62 69 F4
FAIRBURN 201 D7
Fairburn Com Prim Sch WF11 201 D6
Fairburn Dr LS25 194 D3
Fairburn St WF10 200 E4
Fairfax 15 YO41 168 D2
Fairfax Ave
Harrogate HG2 220 B2
North Featherstone WF7 200 E1
Selby YO8 232 B4
Fairfax Cl
2 Ampleforth YO62 92 C1
5 Appleton Roebuck YO23 190 F5
Bolton Percy YO23 190 D4
Gilling East YO62 118 F8
Fairfax Cres YO26 181 C7
Fairfax Croft YO23 230 B2
Fairfax Dr 19 WF8 201 B1
Fairfax House★ YO1 233 C2
Fairfax Rd DL2 4 D4
Fairfax St
1 Scarborough YO12 212 E5
10 Skipton BD23 217 A3
York YO1 233 B1
Fairfax Wlk 3 HG2 220 B3
Fairfield
Fairburn WF11 201 D7
Thirsk YO7 211 C4
Fairfield Ave TS7 7 D7
Fairfield Cl 16 LS25 195 F4
Fairfield Cres YO12 212 B8
Fairfield La LS25 202 A6
Fairfield Link LS25 195 F4
Fairfield Rd
Staithes TS13 13 K2
Stokesley TS9 26 B7
Tadcaster LS24 189 E6
Fairfields Dr YO30 224 B5
Fairfield St DL3 3 C6
Fairfield Way
Richmond DL10 209 B8
9 Tadcaster LS24 189 E6
Fairfield Way *continued*
Whitby YO22 208 F3
Fairgrey Cl HG4 214 B6
Fair Head La YO22 31 D4
Fairheath Rd LA2 128 E5
Fairholme La DL7 64 A4
Fairmead Ct YO22 208 E4
Fairmead Way YO22 208 E4
Fairview TS21 5 A7
Fair View WF10 201 A5
Fairview Gdns DL10 209 C8
Fairway
Normanton South WF6 200 B1
4 Scalby YO12 75 E5
Selby YO8 232 A4
York YO30 228 A8
Fairway App WF6 200 B1
Fairway Ave WF6 200 B1
Fairway Cl
8 Normanton South WF6 200 B1
15 Sherburn in Elmet LS25 195 F4
Fairway Dr
Normanton South WF6 200 B1
18 Poppleton YO26 165 F1
Fairway Gdns 4 WF6 200 B1
Fairway Mdws 9 WF6 200 B1
Fairways Ave HG2 220 E3
Fairways Cl HG2 220 E3
Fairways Dr HG2 220 D3
Fairways The LS24 189 E5
Fairway The
Darlington DL1 3 E5
Middlesbrough TS8 7 C5
Northallerton DL7 210 C3
8 North Featherstone WF7 200 E1
Sherburn in Elmet LS25 195 F4
Fairwood Pk TS8 7 C5
Fairy Hill La WF8 201 B3
Fairy La YO18 71 C3
Falcon Ave 7 YO12 99 E6
Falconberg Way TS15 5 D2
Falcon Cl
10 Haxby YO32 166 F5
1 Scotton DL9 40 F2
17 Settle BD24 131 D2
Falcon Dr WF10 200 E3
Falconers Rd YO11 213 A5
Falconers Sq 10 YO11 213 A5
Falconer St 1 YO24 227 F3
Falcon Gdns 20 BD24 131 D2
Falcon Terr 11 YO21 208 D6
Falcon Way TS14 8 D6
Falcon Wlk TS15 6 C2
Falkland Rd 2 DL9 40 F5
Falkland St YO1 233 B1
Falling Foss (Waterfall)★ YO22 32 C2
Fall La
Pannal HG3 222 B2
Thornthwaite with Padside HG3 159 A6
Fallow Field 1 BD23 217 B5
Falmer Rd DL1 3 D4
Falmouth Ave WF6 200 A2
Falmouth Cres 20 WF6 200 A2
Falmouth Dr DL3 3 C8
Falmouth Rd WF6 200 A2
FALSGRAVE 212 D3
Falsgrave Cres YO30 228 B7
Falsgrave Mews 6 YO12 212 E5
Falsgrave Rd YO12 212 F5
Fanacurt Rd TS14 8 D6
Fancy Bank TS14 9 B6
Fane Gr TS5 6 E7
FANGDALE BECK 47 A1
Fanny La
Knayton with Brawith YO7 65 F2
Knayton YO7 65 F2
Stutton with Hazlewood LS24 189 D4
Farfield YO26 227 C6
Farfield Ave HG5 221 C4
Farfield La YO19 184 E8
Farfield Mount 2 HG5 221 C4
Farfields Cl TS21 4 F6
Far La
Hutton Buscel YO13 98 F8
Kettlewell with Starbotton BD23 108 A3
Farley Dr TS5 6 D7
FARLINGTON 144 F6
Farmanby Cl 12 YO18 96 D5
Farmbank Rd TS7 7 E7
Farm Cl
Walton LS23 181 A2
Whitby YO21 208 A7
Farmcote Ct TS8 6 E5
Farm Croft BD23 216 F1
Far Mead Croft 3 LS29 176 C1
Farmers Way YO23 230 B3
Farm Garth TS9 8 A2
Farm La TS17 6 A5
Farmlands Rd 1 YO24 230 D8
Farmside Mews TS8 7 C4
Farmstead Rise YO32 225 D7
Farm View YO17 215 F2
Farm Way YO8 232 B7
Farnborough Ct 10 DL2 4 C4
Farndale Ave
Northallerton DL7 210 C2
York YO10 229 D4
Farndale Cl 1 YO32 166 F5
Farndale Cres DL3 3 B6
Farndale Dr TS14 8 D6
Farndale Rd HG5 221 D6
Farndale St YO10 228 D2
FARNHAM 162 D7
Farnham La HG5 162 D7
FARNHILL 173 E1
FARNLEY 177 B2
Farnley CE Prim Sch LS21 177 B3
Farnley Hall★ LS21 177 B2
Farnley La LS21 177 B2
Farnley Pk LS21 177 C2
Farrar St YO10 228 E3
Farriers Croft 2 YO23 230 B3
Farriers Ct 16 LS22 180 C3
Farrow House Sch 19 YO11 212 F5
Farside Garth YO13 75 D6
Farside Rd YO13 99 A7
Farthingale Way TS8 6 E4
Favell Ave WF6 200 A1
Faven Field Rd YO7 211 D4
FAVERDALE 3 B8
Faverdale DL3 3 B7
Faverdale Ind Est DL3 3 B7
Faverdale N DL3 3 B7
Faverdale Rd DL3 3 B7
Faverdale W DL3 3 B7
Faversham Cl TS8 6 F4
Favordale Rd BB8 186 A3
Fawcett Ave TS8 6 E4
Fawcett St YO10 233 C1
FAWDINGTON 115 F3
Fawdington Rd YO61 115 F2
Fawkes Dr YO26 227 C4
FEARBY 85 F4
Fearby Rd
Fearby HG4 85 F4
Masham HG4 86 A4
7 Stockton-on-Tees TS18 5 D8
Fearby Road Ind Est HG4 86 B3
Fearnhead TS8 7 C5
Feasegate YO1 233 B2
Featherbeck Cl 8 LA6 103 D3
Featherbed La
Bilton-in-Ainsty with Bickerton LS24 181 C3
Ellerbeck DL6 44 E4
Feather Bed La YO21 32 A7
Federation St 12 BB18 171 D1
Feeding Pasture La YO60 147 B7
FEETHAM 37 C5
Feetham Ave DL1 3 F7
FEIZOR 131 B6
Felbrigg La TS17 6 A4
Feldom La DL11 19 E1
FELIXKIRK 90 C7
Felixkirk Rd YO7 211 F4
Felixstowe Dr 10 DL9 40 E4
Fellbrook Ave YO26 227 B4
Fell La
Cracoe BD23 156 B7
Ingleton LA6 103 E4
Winton CA17 14 C8
Fell Rd LA6 77 A4
Fell View BD23 217 E8
Fell View Sq 4 BD23 134 E2
Fenby Ave DL1 3 E4
Fenby Gdns YO12 212 C4
Fence Dike La DL7 63 C7
Fennel Ct LS26 200 B6
Fennel Gr HG4 214 B6
Fenton Ave BB18 171 E2
Fenton Cl 10 YO11 100 B7
Fenton La
Malton YO17 215 C8
Sherburn in Elmet LS25 196 A5
Fenton St
Boosbeck TS12 9 D7
33 Burley in Warfedale LS29 176 C1
FENWICK 207 D3
Fenwick Cl 1 YO11 100 B6
Fenwick Common La DN6 207 D2
Fenwick La DN6 207 B1
Fenwick's La YO10 231 D7
Fenwick St YO23 228 C2
Ferguson Cl DL7 210 C3
Ferguson Way YO32 225 F1
Fern Bank Ave BB18 171 D2
Fern Cl YO32 226 A4
Fern Ct 6 YO19 192 A1
Ferndale Rd YO8 232 C4
Fern Gdns 1 LS29 218 A3
Fernie Rd TS14 8 F5
Fernlea Cl YO8 232 D4
Fernley Green Cl 6 WF11 202 A2
Fern St YO31 233 C4
Ferns The YO19 191 D1
Fernway YO10 229 C3
Fernwood TS8 7 A4
Fernwood Cl 9 DL6 43 F3
FERRENSBY 162 F7
FERRYBRIDGE 201 D3
Ferrybridge By-pass WF11 201 E3
Ferrybridge Infant Sch WF11 201 E3
Ferrybridge Rd
Castleford WF10 200 F4
Pontefract WF8 201 C1
Ferry Cl 11 YO8 198 F1
Ferry Farm Cl 2 YO19 191 D8
Ferry La
Bishopthorpe YO23 231 B4
Bubwith YO8 199 C5
Snaith & Cowick DN14 204 C1
Thorganby YO19 193 B5
Ferrymans Wlk YO26 165 F2
Fetter La YO1 233 B2
Feversham Cres 4 YO31 228 C7
Feversham Dr 16 YO62 70 B1
Feversham Rd YO62 92 F7
Fewster Way YO10 233 C1
FEWSTON 159 F1
FEWSTON BENTS 159 F1
Fewston Cl 11 YO14 101 A3
Fewston Cres HG1 219 B4
Fewston Dr 9 YO30 224 F1
Field Ave YO8 197 B1
Field Cl YO21 208 A7
Field Cl Rd 16 YO13 75 D5
Field Dr
1 Pickering YO18 95 F6
Tadcaster LS24 189 F7
Fieldfare Dr WF10 200 E6
Field Gr 7 DL9 40 E3
Field Head YO41 185 F6
Fieldhead Cl 12 WF8 201 C1
Fieldhead Dr
Barwick in Elmet LS15 194 C8
15 Glusburn BD20 187 E7
Fieldhead Paddock LS23 188 E8
Field House Rd 2 YO21 208 C7
Fielding's Yd DL10 209 A7
Field La
Aberford LS25 194 F8
Burniston YO13 75 D8
Gowdall DN14 207 F8
Hambleton YO8 196 F1
Hensall DN14 203 D2
Heslington YO10 229 C2
Newby & Scalby YO13 75 E5
Rawcliffe DN14 205 A1
Wistow YO8 197 C7
Field Lane Sports Club YO8 197 B1
Field Rd HG3 203 A5
Fieldside YO12 212 D7
Fieldside Ct LS24 196 B8
Fieldstead Cres YO12 212 B8
Field View
Norton YO17 215 E2
24 South Milford LS25 195 F2
York YO31 228 C7
Fieldway
Harrogate HG1 219 F7
Ilkley LS29 218 E4
Fieldway Cl HG1 219 F7
Fifth Ave
24 Colburn DL9 41 A5
York YO31 228 F4
FILEY 101 C3
Filey Ave HG4 214 A6
Filey CE Infant Sch YO14 101 B3
Filey Cl 12 DL9 40 E4
Filey Dams Nature Reserve★ YO14 101 A3
Filey Junior Sch YO14 101 B3
Filey Mus★ YO14 101 B3
Filey Rd
Folkton YO11 100 A2
Hunmanby YO14 127 A8
Scarborough YO11 213 A2
Filey Sch YO14 101 A3
Filey Sta YO14 101 B3
Filey Terr YO30 228 C7
Finchley Ct TS5 6 E6
Finden Gdns HG3 160 F5
Fine Garth Cl LS23 188 E6
FINGHALL 61 D4
Finghall Sta DL8 61 E5
Finkills Way DL7 210 C6
Finkle Cl 4 HG4 214 C5
Finkle Hill LS25 195 F5
Finkle Keep 14 HG5 221 A6
Finkle St
Hensall DN14 203 D2
12 Knaresborough HG5 221 A6
Malham BD23 133 A1
3 Malton YO17 215 C4
8 Richmond DL10 209 C6
5 Ripon HG4 214 C5
Selby YO8 232 C5
Sheriff Hutton YO60 145 C5
Thirsk YO7 211 C3
Finsbury Ave YO23 228 C1
Finsbury St YO23 228 C1
Firbank Cl 9 YO32 167 A7
Firbeck Rd LS23 188 E6
Firbeck Wlk TS17 6 B6
FIRBY
Bedale 63 A1
Westow 147 A5
Firby La HG4 214 B5
Firby Rd
Bedale DL8 63 A2
Richmond DL10 209 B8
Fir Gr TS17 6 B8
Fir Heath Cl 5 YO24 227 C1
Firs Ave
Harrogate HG2 222 E6
Ripon HG4 214 D4
Firs Cl HG2 222 E6
Firs Cres HG2 222 E5
Firs Dr HG2 222 E6
Firs Garth La 28 YO41 168 D2
Firs Gate HG2 222 E5
Firs Gr HG2 222 E5
Firs Pk HG2 222 E6
Firs Rd HG2 222 E6
First Ave
23 Colburn DL9 41 A5
Harrogate HG2 220 C3

First Ave *continued*
Menwith with Darley HG3 160 A4
Sherburn in Elmet LS25 196 A4
9 Wetherby LS22 180 C3
York YO31 228 F6
First Common La YO8 197 D4
Firs View HG2 222 E5
Firthfields LS25 194 D4
Firthland Rd YO18 95 F7
FIRTH MOOR 3 F4
Firthmoor Cres DL1 3 E4
Firthmoor Prim Sch DL1 3 F4
Firth St BD23 217 A2
Firtree Ave TS6 7 E8
Firtree Cl
4 Earswick YO32 225 F7
York YO24 227 E3
Fir Tree Cl
Hilton TS15 6 C2
Selby YO8 232 E2
Thorpe Willoughby YO8 197 B2
Firtree Cres LS24 189 D5
Fir Tree Ct LS24 195 F7
Fir Tree Dr
Filey YO14 101 B4
11 Norton DN6 206 E2
Fir Tree La YO8 197 B2
Fir Trees The YO8 197 B2
Fir Tree View LS26 200 C6
Fir Tree Way YO8 197 B2
Firville Ave WF6 200 A1
Firwood Whin 5 YO31 225 F3
Fishbeck La BD20 174 D2
Fishbourne Gr 2 TS17 5 F6
Fishburn Rd 4 YO21 208 D5
Fishergate
3 Boroughbridge YO51 141 B5
Knottingley WF11 201 E3
17 Ripon HG4 214 C5
York YO10 233 C1
Fishergate Prim Sch
YO10 233 C1
Fisher Gdns HG5 221 A5
Fishergreen HG4 214 D4
Fisher Green La HG4 214 F4
Fisher Row 14 HG4 86 C3
Fishers Ct HG4 214 C5
Fishers Garth 10 YO18 95 F6
Fisher St 6 HG5 221 B5
FISHPOOL 177 C2
Fitzalan Rd 18 DL8 63 A2
Fitzjohn Cl YO17 215 C6
Fitzwilliam Dr
Darlington DL1 3 D7
Malton YO17 215 A4
Five Hills La DL10 21 D5
Five Lane Ends HG4 86 D5
Flake La TS13 12 A3
Flamingo Land Theme Pk & Zoo* YO17 95 D2
FLASBY 155 E3
Flashley Carr La DN6 207 F1
Flask La DL8 87 C3
Flass La WF10 200 E3
Flat Cliffs YO14 101 C1
Flat La
Bolton-on-Swale DL10 41 E6
Hellifield BD23 153 F3
Flats Bank DL11 19 F6
Flats La
Barwick in Elmet LS15 194 B7
Thirkleby High & Low with Osgodby YO7 90 D1
West Witton DL8 59 D4
Flatts La
Eston & South Bank TS6 7 F7
Welburn YO62 94 A7
Wombleton YO62 93 F6
Flavian Gr YO30 227 F8
FLAWITH 142 E4
FLAXBY 163 B4
Flaxdale Cl 4 HG5 221 D6
Flaxley Ct YO8 232 B5
Flaxley Rd YO8 232 A7
Flaxman Ave YO10 229 A4
Flaxman Croft YO23 230 B3
Flaxmill Cl DL11 18 G7
FLAXTON 145 F1
Flaxton Rd YO32 167 B7
Flaxton Terr HG3 222 E3
Fleck Way TS17 6 B5
Fleet Bank La YO61 143 C1
Fleetham La
Cundall with Leckby YO7 115 C4
Kirkby Fleetham with Fencote DL7 63 C8
Fleet La
Barmby on the Marsh DN14 205 A7
Mickletown LS26 200 A6
Tockwith YO26 181 C7
FLEETS 156 A7
Fleets La BD23 156 A6
Fleming Ave 3 YO31 228 E5
Fletcher Ct 14 YO32 166 E5
Fletcher's Croft YO23 230 C3
Fletton Rd YO17 215 F4
Flintmill La LS23 180 E2
Flints Terr DL10 209 C7
FLIXTON 99 F2
Flixton Carr La YO11 99 F4
Floats Mill BB8 186 B1
Flock Leys 24 YO13 75 D5
Flora Ave DL3 3 B5
Florence Ct 12 YO51 141 B5
Florence Gr YO30 224 D2
Florence Rd HG2 219 B1
Florentine's Ct HG4 214 C5
Florin Dr HG5 221 C7
Florin Wlk HG1 219 B2
Flotmanby La YO14 100 D2
Flow Edge DL8 57 F7
Flower Ct 19 YO11 100 B6
Flower Garth
40 Filey YO14 101 B3
Scarborough YO12 212 C6
Flowergate 12 YO21 208 D7
Flywheel St DL10 41 F7
Fog La YO42 193 E4
Fold La BD22 187 B6
Foldshaw La HG3 159 C8
Fold The
Filey YO14 101 B1
Thornton in Craven BD23 172 A3
Fold Wlk YO32 167 B8
Folks Cl 13 YO32 166 F5
FOLKTON 100 B2
FOLLIFOOT 223 F5
Follifoot CE Prim Sch
HG3 223 F4
Follifoot Rd HG3 222 F3
Folliott Ward Cl YO17 215 B5
Folly La LS23 188 E5
Folly View 2 LS23 188 E5
Fontenay Rd DL10 209 D8
Fonteyn Ct TS8 6 F5
Forbes Ct 42 DL9 41 A5
Forbidden Cnr The* DL8 60 B1
FORCETT 1 D3
Forcett Cl
East Layton DL11 20 C8
Middlesbrough TS5 6 E7
Forcett Gdns DL11 1 D3
Forcett La DL10 20 D5
Ford Dike La DL2 1 D8
Fordgreen HG4 214 E4
Fordlands YO8 197 B2
Fordlands Cres YO19 231 E5
Fordlands Rd YO19 231 E6
FORDON 126 A6
Fordon La
Willerby YO12 125 E7
Wold Newton YO25 126 A6
Fordon Pl TS4 7 A8
Fordyce Rd TS8 6 E4
FOREDALE 131 C8
Fore La
Cowesby YO7 66 B4
West Tanfield DL8 87 D3
Whorlton TS9 25 F1
Foreshore Rd YO11 213 A5
FOREST 42 B7
Forest Ave HG2 220 D3
Forest Cl
3 Harrogate HG2 220 D3
27 Haxby YO32 166 E5
Forest Cres HG2 220 D4
Forest Ct 11 HG3 137 C4
Forest Dr
Colburn DL9 41 A5
Dishforth YO7 115 A4
Middlesbrough TS7 7 D7
Middlesbrough TS7 7 D7
Foresters Ct 5 YO12 75 F5
Foresters Wlk YO41 168 C1
Forester's Wlk YO24 227 B1
Forestgate YO32 225 C7
Forest Gdns HG2 220 D3
Forest Gr
Barlow YO8 204 D7
Harrogate HG2 220 D3
York YO31 228 F6
Forest Grange Cl 2 HG2 220 D4
Forest La
Alne YO61 143 B5
Fulford YO19 184 A2
Harrogate HG2 220 D3
Kirklevington TS15 24 D8
Strensall YO32 167 A8
Forest Lane Head HG2 220 D5
FOREST MOOR 220 F3
Forest Moor Dr HG5 220 F3
Forest Moor Rd HG5 220 E3
Forest Mount 4 HG2 220 D3
Forest of Galtres Anglican Methodist Prim Sch
YO30 165 E5
Forest Rd
Appletreewick HG3 157 F8
Northallerton DL6 210 E5
Pickering YO18 96 A6
Forest Rise HG2 220 D3
Forest Sch The HG5 221 C6
Forest Way
Harrogate HG2 220 D3
York YO31 228 F6
Forge Cl
Cayton YO11 100 B5
Huntington YO32 226 A2
Wheldrake YO19 193 A7
Forge Gn HG3 223 F4
Forge Hill La WF11 201 F3
Forge La
Deighton YO19 192 A7
Kirkby Fleetham with Fencote DL7 42 C1
Tollerton YO61 143 A3
Forge Valley Wood National Nature Reserve* YO12 75 A1
Forge Way DL1 3 D6
Forkers La YO17 122 D2
Forrester Cl YO8 197 D1
Forrester's Cl 3 DN6 206 E2
Forth St YO26 227 F6
Fort's Bldgs 5 BB18 186 A7
Fortune Cl HG5 220 E7
Fortune Hill HG5 220 E8
Fossards Cl 8 LS23 188 E5
Foss Ave LS22 180 B4
Foss Bank YO31 233 C3
Foss Ct YO31 225 E1
Fossdale Cl 5 HG5 221 D6
Fossel Island Retail Park
YO31 228 E5
Fosse Way LS25 194 D3
Foss Field La YO23 191 B8
Foss Garth YO41 185 F5
Fossgate YO1 233 C2
Foss Islands Rd YO31 233 C3
Foss La YO22 32 C2
Fossland View 4 YO32 167 A7
Fossview Cl YO33 167 B8
Fossway
Stamford Bridge YO41 168 D1
York YO31 228 D7
Foss Way 30 DL9 41 A5
Foss Wlk YO26 227 B8
Foster Ave
Normanton South WF6 200 A1
Silsden BD20 174 B1
Foster Cl 31 LS29 176 C1
Fostergate YO8 197 A8
Foster Gate YO8 232 D4
Foster Rd 4 BB18 171 D2
Foster Wlk LS25 195 F4
FOSTON 146 B4
Foston CE Prim Sch
YO60 146 A3
Foston Gr 4 YO31 228 F8
Foston La YO60 146 B2
Fothergill Way 3 YO51 141 B4
Fother Ingay Dr DL1 3 F8
Fothill La YO13 98 E6
Foulbridge La YO13 97 F3
Foulds Rd BB8 186 A1
Foulgate Nook La HG4 112 B6
FOUL GREEN 9 E1
Foundry Ct WF11 202 A2
Foundry La
5 Knottingley WF11 202 A2
6 Summerbridge HG3 138 A1
Fountains Abbey & Studley Royal* HG4 139 B7
Fountains Ave
Boston Spa LS23 188 E8
Harrogate HG1 219 F6
Ingleby TS17 6 B5
Fountains CE Prim Sch
HG4 138 D8
Fountains Cl
1 Guisborough TS14 8 F6
1 Whitby YO21 208 C6
Fountains Ct YO7 90 E5
Fountains Dr TS5 6 E8
Fountains Earth, Lofthouse CE Endowed Prim Sch
HG3 110 B4
Fountains Gate HG4 112 F1
Fountains La HG4 139 B7
Fountains Mill* HG4 139 B7
Fountains Pl DL6 210 E6
Fountains Rd
Hardgate HG3 139 B2
Northallerton DL6 210 E6
Ripley HG3 161 B8
Fountain St TS14 8 F6
Fountains View DL3 3 A6
Fountains Way
Knaresborough HG5 221 C4
Morton-on-Swale DL7 64 A7
Fountayne Rd 13 YO14 126 F8
Fountayne St YO31 228 C7
Fouracre Dr 11 YO22 32 A6
Four Lane Ends
Burythorpe YO16 147 D4
Lawkland BD24 130 F3
Four Lanes Ends BB7 152 C1
Four Riggs DL3 3 C5
Fourth Ave
26 Colburn DL9 41 A5
York YO31 228 E5
Foxberry Ave TS5 6 D6
Foxbridge Way WF6 200 C2
Fox Cl 6 DL2 22 D8
Foxcliff WF11 201 E5
Fox Covert YO31 225 F2
Fox Covert Cl 15 DL8 63 B3
Fox Covert Rd WF8 206 C1
Foxcroft 3 YO32 225 C7
Fox Ct HG1 219 E4
Foxdale Ave YO8 197 B1
Foxe Howe TS8 7 A6
Fox Furniture Workshop*
YO7 116 F7
Fox Garth
5 Brafferton YO61 115 F1
Poppleton YO26 224 A3
Fox Glade YO41 168 C2
Foxglove Cl
2 Killinghall HG3 161 B3
Northallerton DL7 210 C1
Foxglove Covert Nature Reserve* DL9 40 B4
Foxglove Ct 10 DL9 41 A5
Foxglove Fold 19 WF10 200 D3
Foxhill La YO8 232 A3
Fox Hill La YO8 232 A3
FOXHOLES 125 D3
Foxholme La HG4 86 B3
Foxhunter Ave 7 DL9 40 F4
Fox La
Chapel Haddlesey YO8 203 C5
Hambleton LS25 202 D8
Thornton-le-Dale YO18 96 C3
Thorpe Willoughby YO8 197 B1
Fox Terr WF8 201 C1
Foxthorn Paddock YO10 229 D3
FOXTON 44 E3
Foxton Cl YO24 230 C8
Foxton La DL6 44 E2
FOXUP 106 C7
Foxwood La 3 YO24 227 C1
Frances Rd DL10 209 C7
Frances St YO10 228 D1
Francis Ct 7 YO8 197 B2
Francis Dr 27 DL9 41 A5
Frankfield Mews TS9 8 D1
Frank La YO26 164 F4
Franklin Mount HG1 219 D4
Franklin Rd HG1 219 D3
Franklin Sq HG1 219 D4
Franklin St 7 YO12 212 F6
Frank's La YO26 164 A5
Frank St 9 BB18 171 E1
Franks Terr 2 YO22 208 E6
Fraser Rd 8 TS18 5 E8
Frazer Ct YO30 227 E8
Frazer Theatre* HG5 221 B6
Frederick St 23 BB18 171 D2
Frederic St YO30 233 A3
Freebrough Rd TS12 10 A4
Freeholder's Wood & Riddings Field Nature Reserve* DL8 58 F3
Freehold La YO17 215 D8
Freely Fields 7 LS23 188 E5
Freely La LS23 188 E5
Freemans Way
Leeming DL7 63 C4
New Thirsk YO7 211 A2
Wetherby LS22 180 D3
Freeman's Way HG3 223 D8
Freemantle Pl HG4 214 C6
Freers Yd YO17 215 D3
Freeston Ct 18 WF6 200 A2
Freeston Dr 18 WF6 200 A2
Freeway Dr WF10 200 B3
FREMINGTON 38 D6
Frenchgate DL10 209 C6
French Rd DL9 209 C2
French St HG1 219 F4
Friarage 20 YO11 213 B6
Friarage Ave DL6 210 D5
Friarage Com Prim Sch
YO11 213 B6
Friarage Gdns DL6 210 D5
Friarage Hospl DL6 210 E5
Friarage Mount DL6 210 D5
Friarage St DL6 210 D5
Friarage Terr DL6 210 D5
Friargate
Scarborough YO11 213 A6
York YO1 233 B2
Friargate Theatre YO1 233 B2
Friars Cl YO19 184 D7
Friar's Gdns 10 YO11 213 A6
Friars Hill YO62 95 A8
Friars Mdw YO8 232 C8
Friars Pardon DL2 3 E1
Friar's Way 11 YO11 213 A6
Friar's Wlk YO31 228 E8
Friary Com Hospl DL10 209 B7
Friendship Ct 2 YO8 232 C6
Frith Mews 4 YO8 232 C6
Frobisher Dr
37 Colburn DL9 41 A5
5 Whitby YO21 208 C5
Frogmire Cl 4 HG5 221 B7
Frogmire Dr HG5 221 B7
Frogmire Rd HG5 221 B7
Front Nook 2 DL8 58 F1
Front St
Appleton Wiske DL6 24 B3
6 Bramham LS23 188 E5
Burton Fleming YO25 126 E3
Burton Leonard HG3 140 A2
Castleford WF10 200 F3
Grosmont YO22 31 C4
Langtoft YO25 151 C5
Lastingham YO62 70 E5
Naburn YO19 191 D8
Thirsk YO7 211 C1
Topcliffe YO7 115 C7
Wold Newton YO25 126 A4
York YO24 227 C3
Front The DL2 4 D3
Fryer Cres DL1 3 F7
Fryors Cl YO19 184 D7
Fryston Comm La LS25 202 A8
Fryston La WF11 201 C3
Fryston Rd WF10 201 B5
FRYTON 120 A6
Fryton La YO62 120 A7
Fryup Cres TS14 8 E5
Fulbeck Rd TS3 7 D8
FULFORD 231 E7
Fulford Cross YO10 228 D1
Fulfordgate YO10 231 E7
Fulford Ind Est YO10 228 C1
Fulford La 8 YO11 212 F3
Fulford Mews
7 Scarborough YO11 212 F3
York YO10 231 E6
Fulford Pk YO10 231 D7
Fulford Rd
Scarborough YO11 212 F3
York YO10 231 D8
Fulford Sch YO10 231 E7
Fulham La DN14 206 E7
Fuller-Good Rd 17 DL10 41 E4
Fullicar La DL6 43 F3
FULL SUTTON 169 A2
Fulmar Head TS14 8 D6
Fulthorpe Ave DL3 3 A5
Fulthorpe Gr DL3 3 A5
Fulwith Ave HG2 222 E5
Fulwith Cl HG2 222 F5
Fulwith Dr HG2 222 F5
Fulwith Gate HG2 222 F5
Fulwith Gr HG2 222 F5
Fulwith Mill La HG2 222 F5
Fulwith Rd HG2 222 F5
Fummerber La LA2 130 C5
Furlong Rd 23 YO41 168 D2
Furlongs Ave YO17 215 F3
Furnace La HG4 87 A1
Furness Dr
Bentham LA2 129 A8
York YO30 224 E1
Furnessford Rd LA2 128 D6
Furnwood 2 YO32 225 D7
Furrows The 16 YO11 100 B7
Fushetts La LA2 129 A8
Fusion Ct LS25 194 D4
Futurist Theatre* YO11 213 A6
Fylingdales Ave 6 YO30 224 E1
Fylingdales CE Prim Sch
YO22 33 C4
Fyling Hall Sch YO22 33 B3
Fyling Rd YO21 208 A6
FYLINGTHORPE 33 B3

G

Gable Pk YO23 182 C6
Gables Cl 8 DN14 202 D4
Gables Ct YO7 115 A4
Gables The
15 Hurworth-on-Tees DL2 3 E1
Knaresborough HG5 221 A8
Middlesbrough TS7 7 B6
Scriven HG5 162 C5
Gadwall Dr WF10 200 D6
GAINFORD 1 D8
Gainford CE Prim Sch DL2 1 C7
Gainforth Wath Rd YO13 53 F5
Gainsborough Cl YO32 167 B8
Gainsborough Ct BD23 216 E4
Gaits DL8 56 C4
Gale Bank DL8 60 B3
Gale Farm Ct 6 YO24 227 C3
Gale Garth YO61 142 F4
Gale Gate YO26 142 A1
Gale La
Beadlam YO62 93 D6
Stainburn LS21 177 E3
Thorganby YO19 192 F4
York YO24 227 C2
Gale Rd YO61 142 F4
Gale The YO19 191 D4
Gallabar La YO51 141 E1
Galley Hill Prim Sch 3
TS14 8 D6
Galligap La YO10 229 C4
Gallogate La LS17 178 C1
Gallops The
Norton YO17 215 E2
York YO24 230 B8
Gallowfields Rd DL10 209 B7
Gallowfields Trad Est
DL10 209 B8
Gallowgate DL10 209 C7
Gallowheads La YO18 95 A6
Gallows Hill
Castleford WF10 201 B4
Ripon HG4 214 C2
Gallows Hill Dr HG4 214 C2
Gallows Hill La YO13 98 D5
Gallows Hill Pk HG4 214 D2
Gallows La YO7 211 B4
Galmanhoe La YO30 233 A3
GALPHAY 112 F3
Galphay La HG4 113 A3
Galtres Ave YO31 229 B7
Galtres Dr 7 YO61 143 D8
Galtres Gr YO30 227 F7
Galtres Rd
Northallerton DL6 210 E6
York YO31 229 B7
GAMMERSGILL 83 C5
GANTHORPE 120 A1
GANTON 125 A8
Ganton Cl 1 YO21 208 C5
Ganton Hill YO12 125 B7
Ganton Pl YO24 230 F7
Ganton Rd YO25 125 C4
Gant Wlk 7 YO8 232 D5
Gaol The YO61 144 E7
Gap Cres YO14 127 D7
Gap Rd YO14 127 D8
Garbett Way 1 YO23 231 B3
Garburn Gr 3 YO30 224 E1
Garbutt Gr YO26 227 D5
Garbutt La 1 DL6 25 D1
Garbutts La TS15 25 B5
Garbutt Wood Nature Reserve* YO7 91 A6
Garden Cl
3 Glusburn BD20 187 D7
Sherburn in Elmet LS25 195 E4
Garden Ct
Selby YO8 232 B6
York YO26 227 C5
Gardeners Cl 8 YO23 230 B3
Gardeners Row YO25 150 B3

Garden Flats La YO19 . . . 184 E7
Garden House Cl LS26. . . 200 B6
Garden La
11 Knottingley WF11. . . . . 202 A3
Sherburn in Elmet LS25. . . 195 E4
Garden Mews HG2 . . . . . . 222 B8
Garden Pl YO1. . . . . 233 C2
Gardens Rd BD23 . . . . 155 D2
Garden St
Castleford WF10 . . . . 200 E3
13 Normanton South WF6 200 A1
York YO31 . . . . 233 B4
Gardens The 15 YO14. . . . 101 B4
Garden Terr
10 Carleton in Craven
BD23. . . . . 173 B4
Lothersdale BD20 . . . . 186 F8
Garden Village LS25. . . . . 195 A3
Garden Village The YO32 226 A8
Garden Way
3 Pickering YO18. . . . . 95 F6
York YO26 . . . . 227 C5
Garfield Rd YO12. . . . . . . 212 E6
Garfield Terr YO26 . . . . . . 227 F5
GARFORTH 194 C4
Garforth Acad LS25 . . . . . 194 C3
Garforth Squash & L Ctr
LS25 . . . . 194 D3
Garforth Sta LS25. . . . . . . 194 C4
GARGRAVE 155 D1
Gargrave CE Prim Sch
BD23. . . . . 155 C1
Gargrave House Gdn
BD23 . . . . 155 C1
Gargrave Rd
Broughton BD23 . . . . 172 D6
Skipton BD23. . . . . 216 D4
Gargrave Sta BD23. . . . . . 172 C8
Garibaldi St 1 YO11 . . . 213 B6
Garlands Hill 3 YO11 . . . 212 F3
Garland St 2 YO26. . . . . . 227 E4
Garlands The
Scarborough YO11. . . . . . . 212 F3
York YO30 . . . . 228 A8
Garman Carr La YO8 . . . . 197 D6
Garnet Brow La LA2. . . . . . 130 D2
Garnet La 1 LS24. . . . . . . 189 D5
Garnet Rd TS17. . . . . 6 B8
Garnet Terr YO26 . . . . . . 227 E5
Garrick Cl YO8. . . . . 232 B1
GARRISTON. 61 B7
Garroway Way YO10. . . . . 184 A4
Garrowby Hill YO41 . . . . . 169 F3
Garrowby Rd YO42 . . . . . . 169 F2
Garrowby St YO41. . . . . . . 169 E3
Garrowby View 5 YO41 . 168 D2
Garrow Hill YO10 . . . . 228 F2
Garrow Hill Ave YO10 . . . . 229 A3
Garrs End La BD23 . . . . . . 134 E3
Garrs La 10 BD23. . . . . 134 E3
Garsbeck Way TS7 . . . . 7 D8
Garsdale Fold 8 LS22. . . . 180 A1
Garsdale Rd HG5. . . . . 221 D6
Garsdale Sta LA10 . . . . 55 A6
Gars End LA2 . . . . 128 A6
Gars The LA2 . . . . 128 A6
Garth Ave
Collingham LS22 . . . . 188 A8
4 North Duffield YO8. . . . 199 A7
Garth Cl
10 Catterick DL10. . . . . 41 D5
Hambleton YO8 . . . . 196 E1
6 Wistow YO8 . . . . 197 D6
Garth Ct YO32 . . . . 226 A4
Garth Dr YO8 . . . . 196 E1
Garth End
Collingham LS22 . . . . 188 A8
Kirk Deighton LS22 . . . . . . 180 B5
York YO32 . . . . 225 F4
Garth End Rd YO13. . . . . . . 99 A7
Garthends La 3 YO8. . . . . 198 F1
Garth Fold BD20 . . . . 173 C1
Garth La
Hambleton YO8 . . . . 196 E1
Snainton YO13. . . . . 98 A5
Garth Mdws 12 DL10 . . . . . 41 D5
Garth Mill 1 DN14 . . . . . . 202 D4
Garthorne Ave DL3. . . . . 3 A5
Garth Rd
4 Hambleton YO8 . . . . . . 196 E1
York YO32 . . . . 225 F4
Garths End 20 YO32 . . . . . 166 F5
Garth's End YO10 . . . . 231 E8
Garthside DL10 . . . . 41 F6
Garths La DL8 . . . . 58 E3
Garth Terr YO30 . . . . 228 B7
Garth The
8 Collingham LS22. . . . . . 188 A8
Mount Pleasant TS8. . . . . . . 7 A4
Sinnington YO62 . . . . 95 A8
4 Stokesley TS9. . . . . 26 C7
Tunstall DL10. . . . . 41 B2
Whitby YO21 . . . . 208 B7
Garth View YO8. . . . . 196 E1
Garthway 4 YO32. . . . . . . 225 D3
Garth Way Arc DL7. . . . . . 210 D5
Garton La 22 YO14 . . . . . . 126 F8
Gascoigne Ave LS15. . . . . 194 B7
Gascoigne Cres HG1 . . . . . 219 F4
Gascoigne Ct LS15 . . . . . . 194 B7
Gascoigne Rd LS15. . . . . . 194 B7
Gascoigne View LS15 . . . 194 B7
Gascoigne Wlk YO23 . . . . 233 B1
Gascoigne Wood Mine
LS25. . . . . 196 C2
Gas House La 9 LA2 . . . . 129 A8
Gaskell Cl DL6. . . . . 210 C6
Gas St BD23 . . . . 216 F3
Gas Works La LS23. . . . . . 188 F8
Gate Bridge Rd HG4. . . . . . 112 D2
Gatecliff Brow BD23 . . . . 155 F4
GATEFORTH 203 A7
Gateforth Ct YO8. . . . . 196 F1
Gateforth La YO8 . . . . 196 F1
Gateforth Mews YO8. . . . . 202 F8
Gateforth New Rd YO8 . . 203 A8
Gate Grains La 23 YO61. . 143 C8
Gatehead La YO42 . . . . . . 193 D7
GATE HELMSLEY 168 B2
Gatehowe Rd YO17. . . . . . 170 A7
Gate La
Borrowby YO7 . . . . 65 E4
Low Coniscliffe & Merrybent
DL2. . . . . 2 E4
Gateland Cl YO32 . . . . 225 C7
Gateland Field La DN14 . 205 B6
Gatela Rd YO13 . . . . 53 D2
GATENBY 64 A2
Gatenby Garth YO61. . . . . 143 B8
Gatering La 45 BD22 . . . . 187 E7
Gatesgarth Cl YO12 . . . . . 212 B8
Gate Way YO21 . . . . 29 B4
Gatherley Rd DL10 . . . . 41 C7
Gatherley Road Ind Est
DL10. . . . . 41 C7
GAUBER. 78 F1
Gauber Rd LA6. . . . . 78 F1
Gaudy La DL8. . . . . 56 C3
Gauk St WF11. . . . . 201 D6
Gaul Rd DL9. . . . . 209 E1
Gault Cl YO17. . . . . 215 F4
Gaw La BD23 . . . . 174 C8
Gawtersike La YO62. . . . . . 94 B8
Gay La LS24 . . . . 196 C7
Gaylands La BB18. . . . . . . 172 B1
GAYLE 56 D4
Gayle La DL8. . . . . 56 C4
Gayle Moor Cl 9 TS17 . . . . 6 A3
GAYLES 19 E6
Gay Mdws YO32. . . . . 167 D2
Gayton Sands TS5. . . . . 6 D6
Gazelle Way YO7. . . . . 115 B1
Geecroft La LS22. . . . . 179 D3
Geldof Rd YO32 . . . . 225 F1
General La YO42 . . . . 193 E6
Geneva Cres DL1. . . . . 3 D4
Geneva La DL1. . . . . 3 D4
Geneva Rd DL1 . . . . 3 E5
Gennell La YO60 . . . . 145 E1
Gentian Glade HG3. . . . . . 219 A4
George Cartwright Cl
YO17 . . . . 215 E4
George Cayley Dr YO30. . 225 A3
George Ct YO31. . . . . 233 C3
George Hudson St YO1 . . 233 B2
George Long Mews 19
YO61 . . . . 143 D8
George Pindar Sch YO11 100 A6
George St
15 Addingham LS29. . . . . . 174 F4
Carleton BD23. . . . . 173 B4
19 Earby BB18. . . . . 172 A1
Great Preston WF10 . . . . . 200 C7
3 Scarborough YO12 . . . . 213 A6
4 Selby YO8. . . . . 232 D6
17 Skipton BD23 . . . . 217 A3
Snaith DN14. . . . . 204 C1
12 Whitby YO21. . . . . 208 D6
7 Wistow YO8 . . . . 197 D6
York YO1 . . . . 233 C1
George Terr 1 YO8. . . . . . 198 B4
Georgian Theatre Royal*
DL10. . . . . 209 C6
Gerard Ave YO31. . . . . 229 A5
Germaine Cl YO8 . . . . 232 D2
Germain Rd YO8 . . . . 232 E4
Germany La YO10 . . . . 231 E6
GERRICK 10 C3
Gerrick La TS12. . . . . 10 C3
Ghyll Brow YO21 . . . . 30 D4
Ghyll Field YO14 . . . . 127 D7
Ghyll La BB18. . . . . 171 E2
Ghyll Mdws BB18 . . . . 171 E2
Ghyll Mews LS29. . . . . 218 A3
Ghyll Royd Prep Sch
LS29 . . . . 176 B2
Ghyll The DL10. . . . . 209 D8
Ghyll Way BD23. . . . . 173 D4
Ghyll Wood 28 LS29. . . . . 175 C2
Gibbet Hill YO61 . . . . 117 C5
Gibb St 13 BD22. . . . . 187 B6
Gibside La BD20 . . . . 173 C1
Gibson Cl 2 YO8 . . . . 196 F1
Gibson La LS25 . . . . 194 D1
GIGGLESWICK 131 C2
Giggleswick Prim Sch
BD24. . . . . 131 C3
Giggleswick Sch BD24 . . 131 C3
Giggleswick Sta BD24. . . . 131 C1
Gilcar St WF6. . . . . 200 B2
Gilcar Way WF10. . . . . 200 B3
Gildercliffe YO12. . . . . 212 C7
Giles Ave YO31. . . . . 229 A5
GILL 187 A6
GILLAMOOR 70 A5
Gillamoor Ave YO31. . . . . . 229 B5
Gillamoor Bank YO62 . . . . . 70 A5
Gillamoor CE Prim Sch
YO62. . . . . 70 A4
Gillamoor Rd YO62. . . . . 70 A2
Gillann St 15 WF11 . . . . . . 202 A2
Gill Bank Rd LS29 . . . . 218 A6
Gill Cl 6 LS29 . . . . 174 E4
Gill Croft YO61. . . . . 117 C1
Gillgate Rd HG4. . . . . 112 B4
Gilling Castle* YO62 . . . . 118 E7
Gilling Cres DL1 . . . . 3 E4
GILLING EAST. 118 F8
Gilling Rd
Aske DL10 . . . . 20 E1
Richmond DL10 . . . . 209 D7
Gillings Ct 4 YO7. . . . . . . 211 B3
Gilling Way YO17 . . . . 215 C5
GILLING WEST 20 E4
Gillingwood Cl DL10 . . . . 209 C8
Gillingwood Rd YO30. . . . 224 F3
Gill La
Cowling BD22 . . . . 187 A6
Kearby with Netherby LS22179 C1
Nesfield with Langbar LS29175 B4
Rosedale West Side YO18 . . 49 E2
Gills Fold 8 BD23. . . . . . . 134 E2
Gills The LS21 . . . . 177 A1
Gillygate YO31 . . . . 233 B3
Gillylees YO12 . . . . 212 C5
Gilmonby Rd TS3 . . . . 7 B8
Gilsforth Hill YO26 . . . . . . 164 A3
Gilsforth La YO26 . . . . 164 A3
Gilstead Way LS29 . . . . . . 218 B5
Gilsthwaite La YO26. . . . . 164 A3
Gilwern Ct 23 TS17. . . . . 5 F4
Gindhill La LS17 . . . . 178 A4
Ginnel Mews The BD23. . 217 A4
Ginnel The 1 HG1 . . . . . . 219 D2
Gipsey Cnr YO19 . . . . 184 E3
Girrick Cl 3 TS8. . . . . 6 E5
GIRSBY 23 D7
Girton Wlk DL1 . . . . 3 D7
Girvan Cl YO24. . . . . 230 B7
Gisburn Rd
Barnoldswick BB18 . . . . . . 171 D2
Hellifield BD23. . . . . 154 B3
Gisburn Road Com Prim Sch
BB18. . . . . 171 D1
Gisburn St
Barnoldswick BB18 . . . . . . 171 D2
Skipton BD23. . . . . 216 D3
Givendale Gr 3 YO10 . . . 229 C4
Givendale Rd YO12. . . . . . 212 D8
Glade Rd YO19. . . . . 192 B2
Glade The
Escrick YO19 . . . . 192 A6
Scarborough YO11. . . . . . . 212 F3
York YO31 . . . . 229 B7
Gladstone La YO12. . . . . . 212 E5
Gladstone Rd YO12. . . . . . 212 E5
Gladstone Rd Prim Sch
YO12. . . . . 212 E5
Gladstone St
Acomb YO24. . . . . 227 D3
Darlington DL3. . . . . 3 C5
Harrogate HG2 . . . . 222 E7
Normanton South WF6 . . . 200 B2
Scarborough YO12. . . . . . . 212 E6
14 Skipton BD23 . . . . 216 F4
York YO24 . . . . 227 D3
York YO31 . . . . 233 C4
Gladstone Terr 10 HG4 . . 214 C4
Glaisby Ct YO31. . . . . 229 A6
GLAISDALE 30 D4
Glaisdale YO24 . . . . 230 D7
Glaisdale Ave TS5. . . . . 6 F8
Glaisdale Ct DL3 . . . . 3 B5
Glaisdale Hall La YO21 . . . 30 C5
Glaisdale Prim Sch YO21 . 30 D4
Glaisdale Rd
Egglescliffe TS15 . . . . 5 F3
Knapton YO26 . . . . 182 F7
Glaisdale Sta YO21. . . . . . . 30 E4
Glasgow Dr 3 DL9. . . . . . 209 C1
GLASS HOUGHTON 201 A3
Glasshoughton Infant Sch
WF10 . . . . 200 F4
Glasshoughton Sta WF10 200 F2
GLASSHOUSES. 137 D4
Glasshouses Com Prim Sch
HG3. . . . . 137 D3
Glaves Cl YO13. . . . . 99 B7
Glebe Ave
Full Sutton YO41 . . . . 169 A2
Harrogate HG2 . . . . 219 C2
York YO26 . . . . 227 D5
Glebe Cl
15 Bedale DL8. . . . . 63 A2
Bolton Percy YO23. . . . . . . 190 D4
Kirby Hill YO51. . . . . 141 B7
Manfield DL2 . . . . 2 C4
3 Strensall YO32 . . . . 167 B7
Glebe Ct DL10 . . . . 21 A7
Glebe Field Dr 11 LS22 . . 180 B3
Glebe Garth 8 YO8 . . . . . 198 B5
Glebe Gdns TS13. . . . . 11 A8
Glebe La DL2 . . . . 2 C4
Glebe Mdw HG4 . . . . 214 F6
Glebe Rd
Campsall DN6 . . . . 206 E1
Darlington DL1. . . . . 3 D8
Harrogate HG2 . . . . 219 C1
Stokesley TS9. . . . . 26 C7
Glebe Sq DL7 . . . . 63 C5
Glebe St WF10. . . . . 200 E4
Glebe Way 26 YO32 . . . . . 166 E5
Gledhill Dr 10 YO21 . . . . . 208 D5
Gledstone Rd BD23 . . . . . 171 E5
Gledstone View 8 BB18 171 D2
Glen Ave YO31. . . . . 228 E5
Glen Cl
Newby & Scalby YO13 . . . . . 75 C5
York YO10 . . . . 231 E6
Glencoe Cl LS25 . . . . 200 C8
Glencoe Croft LS25 . . . . . . 200 C8
Glencoe Gdns LS25 . . . . . . 200 C8
Glencoe St 1 YO30 . . . . . 228 B7
Glencoe Terr LS25 . . . . 200 C8
Glendale
Guisborough TS14 . . . . 8 D5
9 Hutton Rudby TS15. . . . . . 25 C5
Glendale Rd TS5 . . . . 6 F8
Glendowne Terr HG1. . . . 219 B5
Gleneagles Ct
28 Castleford WF6 . . . . . . 200 B1
Spofforth HG3 . . . . 179 E5
Gleneagles Dr 29 WF6. . . 200 B1
Gleneagles Rd
Darlington DL1. . . . . 3 F8
Middlesbrough TS4 . . . . 7 A8
North Featherstone WF7. . 200 E1
Glen Esk Rd YO22 . . . . 208 C3
Glenfield Ave LS22 . . . . . . 180 C2
Glenmore Dr YO17 . . . . . . 215 E2
Glenn Cres TS7 . . . . 7 B5
Glen Rd YO31. . . . . 228 E5
Glenridding YO24 . . . . 230 D7
Glenside YO12 . . . . 212 E7
Globe St
10 Harrogate HG2. . . . . . . 220 C3
9 Scarborough YO11 . . . . 213 B6
Gloucester Ave 2 BD20 . 174 B1
GLUSBURN 187 D8
Glusburn Com Prim Sch 37
BD20. . . . . 187 E7
Glyder Ct 6 TS17 . . . . 5 F4
Glynndale Dr YO12 . . . . . . 212 A8
Glynwed Ct 2 BD23. . . . . 216 E3
Gn La TS18 . . . . 6 A7
GOATHLAND. 51 E8
Goathland Gr TS14 . . . . 8 E5
Goathland Prim Sch YO22 51 C8
Goathland Sta YO22. . . . . . 51 D8
Goat La BD24 . . . . 131 F7
Goats Rd DL11. . . . . 18 D2
Godfrey Way 12 DL10. . . . . 41 E4
Godley Cl DL9 . . . . 209 C2
Godwinsway 18 YO41. . . . 168 D2
Goffa Mill BD23. . . . . 172 D8
Goker La YO51. . . . . 141 E1
Goldcrest Rd WF10. . . . . . 200 D6
Golden Acres DL7. . . . . 22 E2
Golden Butts Rd LS29 . . . 218 C4
Goldenfields YO13 . . . . 75 C5
Golden Gr YO22. . . . . 208 E2
Golden Lion Bank 25
YO21 . . . . 208 D7
Golden Lion Yd YO7. . . . . . 211 C3
Goldhill La YO7 . . . . 90 D6
GOLDSBOROUGH
Knareborough 163 A2
Whitby 12 D5
Goldsborough CE Prim Sch
HG5. . . . . 162 F3
Goldsborough Ct HG5 . . . 163 A3
Goldsborough Way YO21. . . 12 C4
Gold Thread La 5 YO8. . . 197 B8
Golf Links Ave 5 LS24 . . . 189 D5
Golf Links Cres 4 LS24. . 189 D5
Golf Links Ct LS24. . . . . . . 189 E5
GOLLINGLITH FOOT. 85 B3
Goodall Cl 31 BB18. . . . . . 172 A1
Goodenber Cres 2 LA2 . . 129 A8
Goodenber Rd LA2 . . . . . . 129 A8
Good Hope Cl WF6. . . . . . . 200 B2
Goodramgate YO1 . . . . 233 B2
Goodrick Cl HG2. . . . . 222 B5
Goodricke Way 5 YO10 . . 229 A1
Goods Yd The YO8 . . . . . . 232 D5
Goodwood Ave LS25 . . . . 194 C1
Goodwood Cl
Sadberge DL2 . . . . 4 B8
Scalby YO12 . . . . 212 B6
Goodwood Gr YO24 . . . . . 227 F1
Goodwood Rd 3 DL9 . . . . . 40 E3
Goody Cross LS26. . . . . . . 194 B1
Goody Cross La LS26. . . . . 194 A1
Goody Cross Vale LS26. . 194 A1
Goosecroft Gdns DL6 . . . . 210 D5
Goosecroft La
East Harlsey DL6. . . . . 44 D6
Northallerton DL6 . . . . 210 D5
Goose Green Cl 2 DL9. . . . 40 E3
Goose Green La BB8 . . . . . 186 A1
Goose La YO61. . . . . 144 C1
Gooselands BD24 . . . . 153 C6
Gooselands Hill BD23 . . . 107 D2
Goose Mire La YO12. . . . . . 99 C6
Goosepastures TS16 . . . . . . 5 E3
Goose Track La YO60. . . . . 145 C3
Gordale Cl
3 Barnoldswick BB18 . . . 171 D1
Skirethorns BD23 . . . . 134 B4
Gordale La BD23. . . . . 133 A2
Gordale Mount HG5. . . . . 221 C6
Gordon Ave
Harrogate HG1 . . . . 219 E6
Ripon HG4 . . . . 113 C3
Gordon Cres DL10. . . . . . . 209 D8
Gordon St
28 Glusburn BD20. . . . . . . 187 E7
Ilkley LS29. . . . . 218 C4
Scarborough YO12. . . . . . . 212 E5
York YO10 . . . . 228 E3
Gordon Terr BD20. . . . . . . 173 C1
Gore La DN14. . . . . 207 B5
Gore Sands TS5. . . . . 6 D6
Gorman Cl 9 TS17. . . . . 5 F4
Gormire Ave 2 YO31. . . . . 225 E2
Gormire Cl YO7. . . . . 211 D3
Gorse Cl YO8 . . . . 232 C2
Gorse Hill 1 YO19 . . . . . . 184 F7
Gorse La LS25 . . . . 195 D3
Gorse Paddock YO32. . . . . 225 F2
Goschen St 8 BD23. . . . . . 217 A3
Goslipgate 9 YO18 . . . . 95 F6
Gosside Gr 31 WF6. . . . . . 200 B1
Gough Rd DL9 . . . . 40 D4
Gouldings Cl YO11 . . . . . . 100 A7
GOULTON 25 E3
Goulton La TS9 . . . . 25 E3
Gouthwaith Cl YO30. . . . . 224 F2
Government House Rd
YO30 . . . . 228 A6
Gowans The YO61. . . . . . . 144 C3
GOWDALL 204 A1
Gowdall Broach DN14. . . . 207 E8
Gowdall La
Pollington DN14. . . . . 207 F7
Snaith & Cowick DN14. . . . 204 B1
Gowdall Rd DN14 . . . . 203 E2
Gower Rd
Aske DL10 . . . . 20 D1
Richmond DL10 . . . . 209 C8
York YO24 . . . . 230 E8
Gowland La YO13 . . . . 54 B2
GOWTHORPE 169 C1
Gowthorpe YO8. . . . . 232 C5
Gracious St
Huby YO61. . . . . 144 A4
7 Knaresborough HG5. . . 221 B5
GRAFTON 141 D2
Grafton Cl TS14. . . . . 8 F6
Grafton La YO51 . . . . 141 C3
Grafton St WF10 . . . . 200 F3
Graham Cl YO11 . . . . 213 B7
Graham Cres YO12. . . . . . . 212 C5
Graham Dr WF10. . . . . 201 A4
Graham Rd HG4 . . . . 113 D3
Graham Sch YO12. . . . . 212 B5
Grainary The* YO13. . . . . . . 53 E3
Grainbeck La HG3. . . . . . . 219 A7
Grainger Cl 6 TS16. . . . . 5 D5
Grainger Row HG4 . . . . . . 214 D5
Grainger St DL1. . . . . 3 D4
Grains La BD23 . . . . 154 E8
Grammar Sch La
Northallerton DL6 . . . . 210 D3
Yarm TS15 . . . . 5 E3
Grampian Cl 4 YO32. . . . 225 F5
Granary Ct
13 Pickering YO18. . . . . 96 A6
York YO1 . . . . 233 B3
Granby Pk HG1 . . . . 219 F3
Granby Rd HG1 . . . . 219 F3
Granby Sport & Play
Development Ctr HG1. . 220 A4
Grandage La BD22 . . . . . . 187 A7
Grand Opera House York*
YO1. . . . . 233 B2
GRANGE. 57 D5
Grange Ave
Aiskew DL7 . . . . 63 C4
Filey YO14 . . . . 101 B3
Garforth LS25 . . . . 194 C3
Harrogate HG1 . . . . 219 D5
3 Hurworth-on-Tees DL2. . . 3 D1
Ilkley LS29. . . . . 218 D4
Scarborough YO12. . . . . . . 212 E4
Spofforth HG3 . . . . 179 E6
Tadcaster LS24 . . . . 189 F6
Thorp Arch LS23 . . . . 181 A2
3 Willerby YO12. . . . . 99 D2
Grange Cl
10 Bedale DL8. . . . . 63 A2
Bishop Thornton HG3. . . . . 138 F1
Dishforth YO7 . . . . 114 F4
Full Sutton YO41 . . . . 169 A2
Ilkley LS29. . . . . 218 D4
Lebberston YO11 . . . . 100 D5
Northallerton DL7 . . . . 210 C3
Skelton YO30 . . . . 224 B5
Grange Close E DL7 . . . . 63 E7
Grange Cres
Middlesbrough TS7 . . . . 7 B5
10 Tadcaster LS24. . . . . . . 189 E6
Grange Ct YO12. . . . . 99 D7
Grange Dr TS9. . . . . 26 C7
Grange Est LS29 . . . . 218 D4
Grange Farm Cl YO8 . . . . 198 B5
Grangefield Ave 32 LS29. 176 C1
Grange Garth
3 Linton-on-Ouse YO30 . . 164 F7
10 Wistow YO8 . . . . 197 D6
York YO10 . . . . 228 D2
Grange La
1 Dacre HG3 . . . . 137 F1
Rufforth YO26 . . . . 227 A2
Scackleton YO62 . . . . 119 C3
Stonebeck Down HG3 . . . . 137 A6
Sutton BD22. . . . . 187 F2
Grangemoor Cl 5 DL1 . . . . . 3 E4
Grange Park Cl WF10 . . . . 200 D7
Grange Park Rd HG4 . . . . . 214 B2
Granger Ave YO26 . . . . 227 C4
Grange Rd
19 Bedale DL8. . . . . 63 A2
Brompton-on-Swale DL10. . 41 B6
Burley in Warfedale LS29 . 176 C1
8 Campsall DN6. . . . . 206 E1
Castleford WF10 . . . . 201 B5
Colburn DL9. . . . . 40 F5
Darlington DL1. . . . . 3 C4
Farnhill BD20. . . . . 173 E1
Tadcaster LS24 . . . . 189 E6
Thornaby TS17. . . . . 6 B8
Grangeside DL3. . . . . 3 B4
Grange St YO10. . . . . 228 D2
Grange Terr HG4. . . . . 114 B8
Grange The
Kirby Hill YO51. . . . . 141 A7

Grange The *continued*
Leeming DL7 ... 63 D4
Thirsk YO7 ... 211 B2
Grange View
11 Otley LS21 ... 176 F1
Towton LS24 ... 189 E2
Granholme Cl 44 BD22 .. 187 E7
Grant Cl DL6 ... 45 B4
Grantham Dr YO26 ... 227 E4
Grantley Cl HG3 ... 219 A4
Grantley Dr HG3 ... 219 A4
Grantley Pl HG3 ... 219 A4
Grantly 3 DL3 ... 3 B6
Grants Ave YO10 ... 231 E8
Granville Rd
21 Filey YO14 ... 101 B3
4 Harrogate HG1 ... 219 D3
Scarborough YO11 ... 213 A3
Granville Sq 3 YO11 ... 213 A3
Granville St
20 Normanton South WF6 ... 200 A1
Skipton BD23 ... 216 E4
Granville Terr 4 YO10 .. 228 E3
Grape La
Whitby YO22 ... 208 E7
York YO1 ... 233 B3
Grasmere Ave LS22 ... 180 A3
Grasmere Cres HG2 ... 222 C7
Grasmere Dr
6 High Bentham LA2 ... 129 A8
York YO10 ... 229 B4
Grasmere Gr 5 YO30 ... 224 F1
Grass Croft TS21 ... 5 A7
Grassfield Cl 8 HG3 ... 137 B4
Grassgill La DL8 ... 59 E3
Grassholme YO24 ... 230 C7
Grassholme Way TS16 ... 5 D5
GRASSINGTON ... 134 E3
Grassington Ave DL7 ... 210 C2
Grassington CE Prim Sch BD23 ... 134 E2
Grassington Rd
Middlesbrough TS4 ... 7 A8
Skipton BD23 ... 216 F5
Grass Wood La BD23 ... 134 C3
Grass Wood Nature Reserve★ BD23 ... 134 C4
Gravelhill La DN14 ... 206 F7
Gravel Hole La
Sowerby YO7 ... 89 E3
Thirsk YO7 ... 211 C1
Gravelly Hill La LS17 ... 178 A2
Gray La YO62 ... 70 D1
Grayshon Dr YO26 ... 227 B5
Grays Rd YO62 ... 69 F6
Gray St
13 Whitby YO21 ... 208 D6
York YO23 ... 233 A1
Graystonber La LA2 ... 130 E7
Graystone Ct 12 YO18 ... 96 A6
Grayston Plain La HG3 .. 160 F4
Great Auk TS14 ... 8 D6
Great Ave DL10 ... 209 A7
GREAT AYTON ... 7 F2
Great Ayton Sta TS9 ... 8 B1
GREAT BARUGH ... 95 A1
GREAT BROUGHTON ... 26 E5
GREAT BURDON ... 3 F8
GREAT BUSBY ... 26 C4
Great Cl YO8 ... 197 B8
Great Close La BD24 ... 153 A6
GREAT CRAKEHALL ... 62 E4
Great Croft Cl 9 BB18 .. 171 D2
GREAT EDSTONE ... 94 C7
GREAT FENCOTE ... 63 C8
GREAT HABTON ... 121 C7
GREAT HECK ... 207 D7
Great Hill YO11 ... 99 F6
GREAT LANGTON ... 42 D3
Great Moor Rd YO13 ... 74 D2
Great North Rd
5 Fairburn WF11 ... 201 D6
Ledsham LS25 ... 195 C1
Micklefield LS25 ... 194 F5
Great North Way YO26 .. 227 B8
GREAT OUSEBURN ... 164 B8
Great Ouseburn Prim Sch YO26 ... 164 B8
Great Pasture LS29 ... 176 C1
GREAT PRESTON ... 200 C8
Great Preston CE Prim Sch LS26 ... 200 C8
Great Sike Rd YO17 ... 215 D8
GREAT SMEATON ... 23 C3
Great Smeaton Acad Prim Sch DL6 ... 23 C3
GREAT THIRKLEBY ... 90 D1
Greatwood Ave BD23 ... 217 A3
Greatwood Cl BD23 ... 217 B3
Greatwood Com Prim Sch BD23 ... 217 A2
Greaves Smithy LS29 ... 175 B4
Grebe Ave DL9 ... 40 E2
Grebe Way YO18 ... 95 F7
Greenacre Cl TS9 ... 7 F1
Greenacres
Hunton DL8 ... 61 E7
Morton-on-Swale DL7 ... 64 A6
Skipton BD23 ... 217 B5
Stainton & Thornton TS8 ... 6 D5
York YO32 ... 225 F4
Greenacres Cl 8 YO8 ... 197 D1
Greenacres Cres 7 YO8 197 D1
Greenacres Dr
Airedale WF10 ... 201 A4
4 Brayton YO8 ... 197 D1
Greenacres Gr 3 YO8 ... 197 D1
Green Ave LS25 ... 194 C2
Green Balk
Great & Little Broughton TS9 ... 26 F5
Millington YO42 ... 170 D1
Greenbank 5 DL6 ... 210 E2
Green Bank BB18 ... 171 E2
Greenbank Cl 12 WF10 .. 200 D3
Green Bank La
Sawley HG4 ... 139 A6
27 Stamford Bridge YO41 168 D2
Greenbank Rd DL3 ... 3 C6
Greenberfield La BB18 .. 171 E2
Green Cl
Bradleys Both BD20 ... 173 D3
Hunmanby YO14 ... 127 B8
2 Linton-on-Ouse YO30 .. 164 F8
Middlesbrough TS7 ... 7 D5
Steeton with Eastburn BD20 ... 187 F7
York YO30 ... 228 A8
Greencliffe Dr YO30 ... 228 A6
GREEN CLOSE ... 130 A8
Green Cres The YO62 ... 120 B5
Greencroft Ct 14 YO19 ... 184 F7
Green Croft Gdns 24 YO11 ... 100 B6
Greencroft La 17 YO19 .. 184 F7
Green Dike YO32 ... 225 C8
Green Dikes La YO25 ... 151 F1
Greendown Cl LS29 ... 218 D4
Green Dyke La YO62 ... 120 C5
Green Dykes YO17 ... 215 A3
Green Dykes La YO10 ... 228 F3
Green End Ave 35 BB18 .. 172 A1
Green End Rd 34 BB18 .. 172 A1
Greenfield Ave LS25 ... 194 D1
Greenfield Cl DL2 ... 3 E1
Greenfield Dr
6 Brayton YO8 ... 197 D1
Eaglescliffe TS16 ... 5 D5
Greenfield Gdns BD20 ... 187 F7
Greenfield Park Dr YO31 229 A7
Greenfield Rd 8 YO11 .. 213 A4
Greenfields
Pollington DN14 ... 207 F6
York YO31 ... 228 D7
Greenfields Ave HG2 ... 220 C2
Greenfields Dr HG2 ... 220 C2
Greenfields Rd HG2 ... 220 C2
Greenfield St 5 BD23 ... 216 D3
Greenfinch Cl 1 YO12 ... 99 E6
Greenfoot La LA2 ... 128 E8
Greengales Ct YO19 ... 193 A8
Greengales La YO19 ... 193 A8
Greengate
Malton YO17 ... 215 C4
Scarborough YO12 ... 212 D4
Green Gate
Exelby, Leeming & Newton DL7 ... 63 D2
Hawsker-cum-Stainsacre YO22 ... 33 A6
Kirkby Malham BD23 ... 154 F8
West Witton DL8 ... 59 C3
Greengate Dr HG5 ... 221 B8
Greengate La
Cliffe YO8 ... 198 F6
Kirkby Fleetham with Fencote DL7 ... 42 B1
Knaresborough HG5 ... 221 B8
Thornton-le-Dale YO18 ... 96 C6
Green Gate La
Crakehall DL8 ... 62 E5
Kildale YO21 ... 27 F8
Long Preston BD23 ... 153 F5
Greengate Rd WF8 ... 206 C1
Greengates La YO61 ... 142 E3
Greengate View HG5 ... 221 B8
Green Haggs La HG3 ... 223 F1
GREEN HAMMERTON ... 164 C3
Green Hammerton CE Prim Sch YO26 ... 164 B3
Green Head La BD24 ... 131 E2
GREEN HILL ... 194 F8
Green Hill YO62 ... 118 E6
Greenhill Cres DL6 ... 210 E3
Greenhill La YO7 ... 66 B4
Green Hill La BD22 ... 187 A5
Green Hills YO60 ... 168 B7
Green Hills La DL7 ... 64 B6
Greenholme Cl
1 Boroughbridge YO51 .. 141 B6
7 Burley in Warfedale LS29 ... 176 C1
GREENHOW ... 136 D3
Green Howards Dr DL10 . 209 C8
Green Howard's Dr 8 YO12 ... 75 F5
Green Howards Rd
Pickering YO18 ... 96 A6
Richmond DL10 ... 209 B8
Green Howards Regimental Mus The★ DL10 ... 209 C6
Greenhow Hill HG3 ... 136 C2
Greenhow Hill Rd HG3 .. 159 B6
Greenhow Pk LS29 ... 176 B1
Greenhowsyke La DL6 ... 210 E4
Green Island YO12 ... 99 D7
Green La
Acomb YO24 ... 227 D2
Addingham LS29 ... 174 F4
Appleton Roebuck YO23 ... 191 B6
Green La *continued*
Barmby on the Marsh DN14 ... 205 A6
Barton-le-Street YO17 ... 120 E8
Bedale DL8 ... 62 F3
Boston Spa LS23 ... 188 F7
Bradleys Both BD20 ... 174 A3
Burton Leonard HG3 ... 140 B2
Burton-on-Yore DL8 ... 86 D6
Castleford WF10 ... 200 E3
Cawton YO62 ... 119 B6
Collingham LS22 ... 188 A8
Coneythorpe & Clareton HG5 ... 163 B5
Constable Burton DL8 ... 61 A6
Cottingwith YO42 ... 193 C5
Darlington DL1 ... 3 D8
Dishforth YO7 ... 115 A2
East Rounton DL6 ... 24 F4
Fadmoor YO62 ... 69 E3
Farndale West YO62 ... 48 E1
Ferrensby HG5 ... 162 F8
Flixton YO11 ... 99 F1
Garforth LS25 ... 194 D4
Glusburn BD20 ... 187 D7
Great Ouseburn YO26 ... 142 A1
Halton East BD23 ... 157 C1
Harome YO62 ... 93 C5
Harrogate HG2 ... 222 C6
Heck DN14 ... 207 D8
Horton BD23 ... 171 B5
Hudswell DL11 ... 39 F5
Hurgill DL10 ... 40 B8
Hutton Rudby TS15 ... 25 B4
Ilkley LS29 ... 176 C2
Ingleton LA6 ... 103 E2
Kippax LS25 ... 194 C1
Kippax LS25 ... 194 C2
Kirby Wiske YO7 ... 88 F7
Kirkby Overblow LS17 ... 178 D2
Kirklevington TS15 ... 5 E2
Langtoft YO25 ... 151 D5
Lebberston YO11 ... 100 D5
Ledston WF10 ... 200 E7
Little Ayton TS9 ... 27 A8
Littlethorpe HG4 ... 140 A7
Marrick DL11 ... 38 E7
Maunby YO7 ... 64 D1
Menwith with Darley HG3 160 A6
Mickletown LS26 ... 200 C5
Middlesbrough TS5 ... 6 E8
Moor Monkton YO26 ... 164 F1
Newby TS7 ... 7 C3
North Cowton DL7 ... 22 B2
North Duffield YO8 ... 198 F8
North Lees HG4 ... 113 D5
Otley LS21 ... 176 F1
Rawcliffe YO30 ... 225 A1
Ripon HG4 ... 113 C3
Rylstone BD23 ... 156 A5
Sawley HG4 ... 138 E7
Scalby YO12 ... 212 C8
Selby YO8 ... 232 A3
South Stainley with Cayton HG3 ... 161 E8
Stutton with Hazlewood LS24 ... 189 D4
Sutton BD22 ... 187 F2
Sutton-on-the-Forest YO61 144 E4
Thirsk YO7 ... 211 F3
Weaverthorpe YO17 ... 124 F1
Welburn DL6 ... 44 C8
Wensley DL8 ... 60 A4
Whitby YO22 ... 208 E5
Whorlton DL6 ... 45 F7
Wigginton YO32 ... 166 D5
Winksley HG4 ... 112 F2
Wressle DN14 ... 205 D8
Greenland La YO17 ... 95 B3
Greenlands TS15 ... 25 C6
Greenlands La YO8 ... 197 C3
Greenlands Rd YO18 ... 95 F6
Green Lane E YO7 ... 211 B1
Green Lane Prim Acad LS25 ... 194 D3
Green Lane Prim Sch TS5 .. 6 E8
Green Lane Trading Est YO30 ... 225 A1
Green Lane Villas LS25 .. 194 D4
Green Lane W YO7 ... 211 A1
Green Lea Cl LS23 ... 188 F8
Greenless La DL11 ... 1 A2
Green Mdw BB8 ... 186 A1
Green Mdws YO31 ... 229 A7
Green Meadow Cl 11 LA6 ... 103 D3
Greenmires La LS21 ... 177 E4
Green Park Ave 15 YO11. 100 B6
Green Park Rd 14 YO11 .. 100 B6
Green Pastures DL8 ... 62 C5
Green Row LS26 ... 200 B5
Greenroyd Cl 46 BD20 ... 187 E7
Greenroyd Gr 13 BD20 ... 187 E6
Greensborough Ave 3 YO26 ... 227 B5
Greensforge Dr TS17 ... 5 F5
Greenshaw Dr YO32 ... 225 C8
Greenside 18 YO19 ... 184 F7
Greenside Cl 24 YO19 ... 184 F7
Greenside Ct 9 DL2 ... 3 E1
Greenside View TS12 ... 9 D8
Greenside Wlk 23 YO19 .. 184 F7
Green St
Castleford WF10 ... 200 E5
7 Cowling BD22 ... 187 B6
Darlington DL1 ... 3 D5
Greenstead Rd YO12 ... 212 B8
Green Sward YO31 ... 229 A8
Greens Yd YO22 ... 208 E7
Green Sykes Rd BD22 ... 187 F4
Green The
Brompton DL6 ... 43 F3
Castleford WF10 ... 201 B4
1 Clapham LA2 ... 130 C8
Cleasby DL2 ... 2 F4
Conistone with Kilnsey BD23 ... 134 B6
20 Dunnington YO19 ... 184 F7
Garforth LS25 ... 194 D3
Hellifield BD23 ... 154 B3
High Coniscliffe DL2 ... 2 C6
Kettlewell with Starbotton BD23 ... 108 B3
Kirkby Malzeard HG4 ... 112 D5
8 Kirklevington TS15 ... 24 E8
Knaresborough HG5 ... 221 A8
Linton-on-Ouse YO30 ... 164 F8
Longnewton TS21 ... 5 A7
Middlesbrough TS17 ... 6 D7
Northallerton DL7 ... 210 C3
North Deighton LS22 ... 180 A6
9 Otley LS21 ... 176 F1
Rawcliffe DN14 ... 205 A1
Richmond DL10 ... 209 B6
Scalby YO12 ... 212 B7
Seamer TS9 ... 6 F1
6 Seamer YO12 ... 99 D6
Sheriff Hutton YO60 ... 145 D5
1 Skelton YO30 ... 224 B5
Skipton BD23 ... 217 B6
Slingsby YO62 ... 120 B5
Stillingfleet YO19 ... 191 D3
10 Thirsk YO7 ... 211 C3
Thornaby-on-Tees TS17 ... 6 B7
Tockwith YO26 ... 181 C7
2 Tollerton YO61 ... 143 B3
7 Topcliffe YO7 ... 89 B1
Wistow YO8 ... 197 D6
York YO26 ... 227 C3
Green Village YO7 ... 88 C5
Green Way
Glusburn BD20 ... 187 E8
Harrogate HG2 ... 222 C6
Middlesbrough TS7 ... 7 D5
York YO32 ... 225 F4
Green Ways Ct 2 YO8 ... 197 D6
Greenways Dr 1 YO8 ... 197 D6
Greenways The DL7 ... 63 C8
Greenway The
2 Haxby YO32 ... 225 C7
2 Middleton St George DL2. 4 C4
Greenwich Cl 5 YO30 ... 224 E3
Green Wlk 5 BB18 ... 172 A1
Greenwood Ave 7 HG3 . 137 B4
Greenwood Gr YO24 ... 230 C8
Greenwood Rd 6 HG3 .. 137 B4
Greet's Hill YO17 ... 169 E7
Gregory Cl YO30 ... 224 C5
Grenadier Dr DL6 ... 210 F3
Grendon Gdns 1 DL2 ... 4 C4
Grenley St 8 WF11 ... 202 A2
Grenville Rd TS17 ... 6 B6
Gresham Cl DL1 ... 3 D7
Gresley Ct 3 YO26 ... 227 B4
Greta Ave DL10 ... 209 D7
Greta Heath 2 LA6 ... 102 F2
GREWELTHORPE ... 112 D7
Grewelthorpe CE Prim Sch HG4 ... 112 C7
Grey Cl YO61 ... 144 C3
GREYGARTH ... 111 F3
Grey Hill Rd HG1 ... 219 B6
Greylands Park Ave YO12 ... 212 C8
Greylands Park Dr YO12. 212 C8
Greylands Park Gr 3 YO12 ... 212 C8
Greylands Park Rd YO12. 212 C8
Grey St HG2 ... 222 E7
Greystoke Rd YO30 ... 224 E1
Greystone Cl 2 LS29 ... 176 C1
Greystone Com Prim Sch HG4 ... 214 C2
Greystone Ct YO32 ... 225 C7
GREYSTONEGILL ... 129 C8
Greystonegill La LA2 ... 129 D7
Greystone Head HG4 ... 112 A4
Greystone La DL11 ... 1 E4
Greystone Pk LS25 ... 188 F1
Greystones Ave HG3 ... 161 B4
Greystones Cl LS25 ... 188 F1
Greystones Dr 2 DL3 ... 3 B6
Greystones La BD22 ... 187 E4
Grey Thorn La HG5 ... 163 D3
Grey Towers Dr TS7 ... 7 D5
Grimbald Crag Cl HG5 ... 221 D4
Grimbald Crag Rd HG5 ... 221 E4
Grimbald Crag Way HG5 221 D4
Grimbald Rd HG5 ... 221 C5
Grimbald Way 3 HG5 ... 221 C4
GRIMSTON ... 229 E3
Grimston Bar YO19 ... 229 F4
Grimston La YO17 ... 148 D7
Grimston Rd 12 YO14 ... 127 A8
Grimwith Garth YO30 ... 224 F2
Grimwith Rd BD23 ... 135 E2
GRINDALE ... 127 D2
Grindale Rd YO16 ... 127 E2
Grinkle La TS13 ... 10 F5
GRINTON ... 38 C5
Grinton Rd TS18 ... 5 D8
Grisedale Cres TS16 ... 5 E4
GRISTHORPE ... 100 E4
Gristhwaite La YO7 ... 89 D1
Gritstone Cl 45 LS29 ... 176 C1
GROSMONT ... 31 D3
Grosmont Gall★ YO22 ... 31 C4
Grosmont Sta YO22 ... 31 C4
Grosvenor Ave 1 DN14 . 205 F3
Grosvenor Cres 2 YO11. 213 A4
Grosvenor Ct HG1 ... 219 B2
Grosvenor Gdns LS17 ... 178 B2
Grosvenor Gr HG1 ... 219 F6
Grosvenor House YO30 .. 233 A4
Grosvenor Pk YO30 ... 233 A4
Grosvenor Pl TS14 ... 8 E6
Grosvenor Rd
Harrogate HG1 ... 219 E6
Scarborough YO11 ... 212 F4
York YO30 ... 233 A4
Grosvenor Sq 3 YO30 ... 164 F8
Grosvenor Terr YO30 ... 233 A4
Grove Ave 25 LS29 ... 175 C2
Grove Bank 4 TS15 ... 24 E8
Grove Cl HG4 ... 214 C3
Grove Cres
Boston Spa LS23 ... 188 F8
South Milford LS25 ... 195 F2
Grove Gdns 12 YO26 ... 165 F1
Grove Hill Rd 4 YO14 ... 101 B4
Grove La
Knottingley WF11 ... 201 F2
Ripon HG4 ... 214 C3
Grove Park Ave HG1 ... 219 E4
Grove Park Ct HG1 ... 219 E4
Grove Park Gdns 25 BD24 ... 131 D2
Grove Park La HG1 ... 219 E4
Grove Park Terr HG1 ... 219 E4
Grove Park View HG1 ... 219 E4
Grove Park Wlk HG1 ... 219 E4
Grove Pk 7 YO8 ... 198 B5
Grove Prom The LS29 ... 218 A4
Grove Rd
Boston Spa LS23 ... 188 F8
14 Filey YO14 ... 101 B4
Harrogate HG1 ... 219 D4
Ilkley LS29 ... 218 A3
Groves Ct YO31 ... 233 C3
Groves La YO31 ... 233 C3
Grove Sq DL8 ... 60 D5
Grove St
38 Earby BB18 ... 172 A1
9 Harrogate HG2 ... 220 C3
Norton YO17 ... 215 E3
15 Whitby YO21 ... 208 D6
Grove Terr 11 DL8 ... 60 E2
Grove Terrace La YO31 .. 233 C4
Grove The
Eaglescliffe TS15 ... 5 E2
Guisborough TS14 ... 8 D5
Harrogate HG1 ... 219 E3
1 Hutton Rudby TS15 ... 25 D5
Ilkley LS29 ... 218 A4
Kellington DN14 ... 203 A3
Kippax LS25 ... 194 D1
Middlesbrough TS5 ... 6 E6
Normanton South WF6 ... 200 A1
Norton YO17 ... 215 E2
1 Seamer YO12 ... 99 D6
Skipton BD23 ... 217 C3
Swillington LS26 ... 194 A1
York YO24 ... 230 E6
Grove View YO30 ... 228 A6
Grundy Way 11 DL10 ... 41 E4
GRUNSAGILL ... 153 A1
Grunton La DL2 ... 2 C4
Grysedale La BD23 ... 134 B2
Guadaloupe Rd DL9 ... 40 C4
Guards Ct 10 YO12 ... 75 F5
Guildford Rd TS6 ... 7 E8
Guinea Croft HG5 ... 221 C7
GUISBOROUGH ... 8 D7
Guisborough Forest & Walkway Ctry Pk★ TS14 .. 8 C6
Guisborough Mus★ TS14 ... 8 F7
Guisborough Primary Care Hospl TS14 ... 8 F7
Guisborough Priory★ TS14 .8 F7
Guisborough Rd
Aislaby YO21 ... 31 F8
Great Ayton TS9 ... 7 F1
Lockwood TS12 ... 10 A5
Middlesbrough TS7 ... 7 D5
6 Thornaby TS17 ... 6 B8
Whitby YO21 ... 208 A5
Guisborough Swimming Pool TS14 ... 8 E7
Guiseley Way TS16 ... 5 D6
GUNBY ... 199 D6
Gunby Rd YO8 ... 199 D5
Gunbywood Rd YO8 ... 199 D6
Guncroft La YO62 ... 69 D1
Guning La DL11 ... 36 B4
Gunnergate La TS8 ... 7 B5
GUNNERSIDE ... 36 F4
Gunnerside Methodist Prim Sch DL11 ... 36 E5
Gurney Pease Acad DL1 ... 3 D6
Gurney St DL1 ... 3 D6
Guy La HG4 ... 114 F2
Gyll Hall La DL10 ... 41 E1
Gypsy La
Castleford WF10 ... 201 B3
Middlesbrough TS7 ... 7 C6
Gypsy Lane Sta TS7 ... 7 D6

H

Haakon Cl DL10 ... 209 C7
Habton La YO17 ... 121 B7
Habton Rd YO17 ... 95 D1
HACKFORTH ... 62 E8

Hackforth & Hornby CE Prim Sch DL8 . . . 62 E8
Hackforth Rd 2 TS18 . . . 5 D8
HACKNESS . . . 74 F5
Hackness CE Prim Sch YO13 . . . 74 E5
Hackness Dr YO12 . . . 212 A8
Hackness Rd YO12 . . . 212 A8
Haddlesey Rd WF11 . . . 202 D5
Haddocks La YO61 . . . 142 B4
Haddon Cl YO24 . . . 227 C2
Hadrian Ave YO10 . . . 229 B3
Hadrians Wlk YO12 . . . 99 E6
Hadrian Way TS17 . . . 5 F5
Haggersgate 10 YO21 . . . 208 D7
Haggitt Hill La DL6 . . . 24 E3
Hagg La
Colton LS24 . . . 190 E8
Cottingwith YO42 . . . 193 E8
Cowesby YO7 . . . 66 C4
Dunnington YO19 . . . 184 F6
Hemingbrough YO8 . . . 198 F3
South Milford YO8 . . . 196 C2
Hagg Rd YO62 . . . 69 F2
Hagg Side La YO13 . . . 97 D6
Haggs La DN6 . . . 207 D2
Haggs Rd HG3 . . . 223 C4
Haggwood Wlk YO19 . . . 184 F1
Hag La
Cottingwith YO42 . . . 193 C4
Raskelf YO61 . . . 142 E8
South Kilvington YO7 . . . 211 D6
Sproxton YO62 . . . 92 D4
Youlton YO61 . . . 142 F2
Hague Ave 31 YO12 . . . 75 D5
Hagworm Hill★ YO12 . . . 75 C2
Haigh La DN14 . . . 207 A6
Haigh Moor Way WF10 . . . 200 E6
Haig Rd DL9 . . . 209 C2
Haig St YO8 . . . 232 B6
Hailsham Ave TS17 . . . 6 B5
Hailstone Dr DL6 . . . 210 F5
Hales Ct WF8 . . . 201 B2
Hales La YO8 . . . 204 E5
Haley's Terr YO31 . . . 228 D8
Half Crown Way HG5 . . . 221 C7
Half Moon St 1 YO30 . . . 164 F7
Halfpenny Cl HG5 . . . 221 C7
Halfpenny La HG5 . . . 221 B7
Halifax Cl YO41 . . . 169 A2
Halifax Ct 7 YO30 . . . 225 A1
Halifax Way YO41 . . . 185 A3
Halladale Cl 1 YO24 . . . 230 B7
Hallam Cl 41 YO14 . . . 101 B3
Hallam La LS21 . . . 176 D3
Hallam's Yd 4 BD23 . . . 216 F4
Hallard Way 7 YO32 . . . 167 B7
Hall Arm La YO51 . . . 141 D5
Hall Ave 10 BD20 . . . 187 E6
Hall Brow BD23 . . . 155 A5
Hall Cl
5 Airmyn DN14 . . . 205 E4
Austwick LA2 . . . 130 E7
Burley in Warfedale LS29 . . . 176 B1
Cawood YO8 . . . 191 D1
11 Glusburn BD20 . . . 187 E6
Wheldrake YO19 . . . 193 A7
Hall Croft BD23 . . . 216 E4
Hallcroft Dr 13 LS29 . . . 175 A4
Hallcroft La YO23 . . . 230 A3
Hall Ct WF11 . . . 201 E4
Hall Dr
Burley in Warfedale LS29 . . . 176 B1
Glusburn BD20 . . . 187 E6
Middlesbrough TS5 . . . 6 F7
Hall Farm Cl 4 YO19 . . . 197 F8
Hall Farm Ct YO42 . . . 169 F2
Hall Farm Pk LS25 . . . 194 F4
Hallfield Ave LS25 . . . 194 F4
Hallfield La
Nawton YO62 . . . 69 C3
Wetherby LS22 . . . 180 C3
Hallfield Rd YO31 . . . 228 E5
Hallfield Terr LS25 . . . 194 F4
HALL GARTH . . . 184 F6
Hallgarth
Alne YO61 . . . 142 F4
Great & Little Broughton TS9 . . . 26 E5
Hipswell DL9 . . . 209 F1
Hall Garth
Osgodby YO8 . . . 198 C4
25 Pickering YO18 . . . 95 F7
Hall Garth★ LS25 . . . 195 E4
Hall Garth Cl LS24 . . . 190 C3
Hall Garth Com Arts Coll TS5 . . . 6 E7
Hallgarth Ct DL11 . . . 18 G7
Hall Garth Mews 24 LS25 . . . 195 F4
Hall Gdns
Ellerburn YO18 . . . 96 E7
Farnhill BD20 . . . 173 F1
Rawcliffe DN14 . . . 205 B2
Hall Green La LS17 . . . 178 C4
Hallikeld Cl HG4 . . . 114 B6
Hall Ings La YO62 . . . 70 E4
Hall La
Askwith LS21 . . . 176 C4
Bilton HG1 . . . 219 E6
Blubberhouses LS21 . . . 159 C2
4 Brafferton YO61 . . . 115 F1
Caldwell DL11 . . . 1 C4
Church Fenton LS24 . . . 196 C7
Cock Hill YO26 . . . 165 C3
Harome YO62 . . . 93 C4
Harrogate HG1 . . . 219 E6
Hawnby DL6 . . . 46 B1
Huddleston with Newthorpe LS25 . . . 195 C3
Hall La *continued*
Leathley LS21 . . . 177 D1
Ledston WF10 . . . 200 F7
Myton-on-Swale YO61 . . . 142 A6
Hall Mdws BB8 . . . 186 A2
Hall Moor Cl 7 TS15 . . . 24 E8
Hall Orchards Ave LS22 . . . 180 D3
Hall Park Cl 23 YO13 . . . 75 D5
Hall Park Croft LS25 . . . 200 D8
Hall Park Gr 25 YO13 . . . 75 D5
Hall Park Mdws LS25 . . . 200 D8
Hall Park Orch LS25 . . . 200 D8
Hall Park Rd
Hunmanby YO14 . . . 126 F8
Walton LS23 . . . 181 A2
Hall Pasture 9 YO22 . . . 32 A6
Hall Pk
Wistow YO8 . . . 198 A5
York YO10 . . . 229 B1
Hall Rd
Swillington LS26 . . . 194 A1
Trawden Forest BB8 . . . 186 A2
Hall Rise
Burley in Warfedale LS29 . . . 176 B1
12 Haxby YO32 . . . 166 F5
Hall Sq 5 YO51 . . . 141 B5
Hall Tower Hill★ LS15 . . . 194 B8
Hall View Gr DL3 . . . 3 A6
Hall Way 9 BD20 . . . 187 E6
Hallwith Rd DL8 . . . 61 A3
Halnaby Ave DL3 . . . 2 F5
Halstead Rd HG2 . . . 222 E7
HALTON EAST . . . 174 C8
HALTON GILL . . . 106 E7
HALTON WEST . . . 154 A1
HAMBLETON
Selby . . . 196 F1
Skipton . . . 174 D8
Hambleton Ave
Northallerton DL7 . . . 210 C2
Thirsk YO7 . . . 211 D3
York YO10 . . . 229 C4
Hambleton CE Prim Sch YO8 . . . 196 F1
Hambleton Cl
12 Easingwold YO61 . . . 143 D8
Knaresborough HG5 . . . 221 C6
11 Thirsk YO7 . . . 211 C3
Hambleton Ct
Great Smeaton DL6 . . . 23 C3
Knaresborough HG5 . . . 221 C6
Old Thirsk YO7 . . . 211 D3
Hambleton Dr YO7 . . . 211 C3
Hambleton Forum★ DL6 . . . 210 E5
Hambleton Garth 21 YO61 . . . 143 C8
Hambleton Gate TS9 . . . 26 C7
Hambleton Gr HG5 . . . 221 B6
Hambleton La YO61 . . . 91 F2
Hambleton L Ctr DL6 . . . 210 D6
Hambleton Pl YO7 . . . 211 C3
Hambleton Rd
6 Catterick Garrison DL9 . . . 40 E3
Harrogate HG1 . . . 219 F4
Hawnby YO7 . . . 67 A3
Norton YO17 . . . 215 E2
Hambleton Row YO7 . . . 211 D4
Hambleton Terr
Knaresborough HG5 . . . 221 B6
York YO31 . . . 228 C7
Hambleton View
10 Haxby YO32 . . . 166 D5
Thirsk YO7 . . . 211 D3
4 Tollerton YO61 . . . 143 B3
Hambleton Way
20 Easingwold YO61 . . . 143 D8
York YO32 . . . 225 F3
Hamer Bank YO18 . . . 49 F4
Hamerton Cl 11 YO14 . . . 127 A8
Hamerton Rd 10 YO14 . . . 127 A8
Hamhall La DL7 . . . 63 D6
Hamilton Ave HG2 . . . 222 E8
Hamilton Cl YO13 . . . 75 C5
Hamilton Ct WF6 . . . 200 A2
Hamilton Dr
Darlington DL1 . . . 3 D8
York YO24 . . . 227 E2
Hamilton Drive E YO24 . . . 227 F2
Hamilton Drive W YO24 . . . 227 D2
Hamilton Gn YO17 . . . 215 B3
Hamilton Way YO24 . . . 227 E2
Hamlet The 8 DN14 . . . 202 F2
Hamley La YO62 . . . 70 F3
Hammer Rd HG4 . . . 85 B7
Hammersike Rd
Cawood LS25 . . . 196 F5
Wistow YO8 . . . 197 A4
Hammerton Cl
Green Hammerton YO26 . . . 164 D3
3 York YO26 . . . 227 B3
Hammerton Dr
Garforth LS25 . . . 194 D3
Hellifield BD23 . . . 154 B3
Hammertonlane Kirk YO26 . . . 164 C3
Hammerton Sta YO26 . . . 164 D2
Hammond Dr DL1 . . . 3 C4
Hammond Rd YO13 . . . 54 A8
Hampden Cl 4 WF11 . . . 201 D3
Hampden St YO1 . . . 233 B1
Hampden Way TS17 . . . 6 B6
Hampshire Cl
Ilkley LS29 . . . 218 D4
6 Pontefract WF8 . . . 201 C2
Hampson Gdns YO30 . . . 228 B8
HAMPSTHWAITE . . . 160 F5
Hampsthwaite CE Prim Sch HG3 . . . 161 A5
Hampsthwaite Rd HG1 . . . 219 C4
Hampton Gdns YO30 . . . 228 C8
Hampton Rd YO12 . . . 212 E5
Hampton Row LS25 . . . 196 A1
Hanbury Gdns LS25 . . . 194 C4
Hancow Rd
Hartoft YO18 . . . 50 A1
Rosedale East Side YO18 . . . 49 F3
Handale Cl TS14 . . . 9 A6
Handley Cl
Stockton-on-Tees TS18 . . . 5 F7
York YO30 . . . 225 A2
Hang Bank DL10 . . . 21 B8
Hanger La DN14 . . . 204 B3
Hanghow La DL8 . . . 84 C8
Hanging Stone La YO18 . . . 49 E4
Hangingstone Rd LS29 . . . 218 D2
Hankins La YO42 . . . 193 D1
HANLITH . . . 155 A8
Hanover Pl
2 Kippax LS25 . . . 194 D1
Knottingley WF11 . . . 201 D4
Hanover Rd 6 YO11 . . . 212 F5
Hanover St 2 BD20 . . . 173 E1
Hanover Street E 5 YO26 . . . 227 F5
Hanover Street W 7 YO26 . . . 227 F5
Hanover Terr YO21 . . . 208 C6
Hansom Pl YO31 . . . 228 C7
Hanson Ave WF6 . . . 200 A1
Hanson Ct 24 WF6 . . . 200 A1
Harborough Cl 20 YO14 . . . 126 F8
Harbour Rise 5 DL8 . . . 63 A2
Harbour View 7 DL8 . . . 63 A3
Harclay Garth 28 YO51 . . . 141 B5
Harcourt Ave YO12 . . . 212 E3
Harcourt Cl
Bishopthorpe YO23 . . . 231 A4
Wheldrake YO19 . . . 192 F7
Harcourt Dr
Addingham LS29 . . . 174 F5
Harrogate HG1 . . . 219 E2
Harcourt Pl 4 YO11 . . . 213 A5
Harcourt Rd 4 HG1 . . . 219 E3
Harcourt St YO31 . . . 228 E5
Hardcastle Ave 8 WF8 . . . 201 B1
Harden Cl YO30 . . . 224 F2
Harden Rd BB18 . . . 186 A7
Hardenshaw La YO8 . . . 204 B4
HARDGATE . . . 139 A1
Hard Gate BD23 . . . 134 A3
Hardgroves Hill HG3 . . . 159 F5
Hardigate Rd YO18 . . . 72 B7
Hardings La
Glusburn BD20 . . . 187 F8
Middleton LS29 . . . 218 A8
Harding's Yd YO17 . . . 95 E2
Hardistry-le-Court WF8 . . . 201 D2
Hardisty Hill HG3 . . . 159 C3
Hardisty Mews YO26 . . . 228 A4
Hardrada Way 3 YO41 . . . 168 D1
HARDRAW . . . 56 C6
Hard Stiles DL11 . . . 39 B7
Hardy Mdws 11 BD23 . . . 134 E2
Hardy St YO8 . . . 232 E4
Harebell Cl
17 Harrogate HG3 . . . 161 B3
Northallerton DL7 . . . 210 C1
Harecroft Rd 9 LS21 . . . 177 A1
Haregill Bank HG4 . . . 85 E6
Harehills La BD22 . . . 187 E1
Haresfield Way TS17 . . . 6 A5
Harewell Cl HG3 . . . 137 D3
Harewell La 3 HG3 . . . 137 F1
Harewood Ave
5 Normanton South WF6 . . . 200 B2
1 Scalby YO12 . . . 212 D8
Harewood Chase DL7 . . . 210 B2
Harewood Cl
Morton-on-Swale DL7 . . . 64 A6
Rawcliffe YO30 . . . 224 D2
5 Wigginton YO32 . . . 166 D5
Harewood Dr 4 YO14 . . . 101 A3
Harewood La DL7 . . . 210 C3
Harewood Prim Sch TS17 . . . 6 B8
Harewood Rd
Collingham LS22 . . . 188 A8
Harrogate HG3 . . . 219 A5
Ripon HG4 . . . 214 B3
Skipton BD23 . . . 216 E4
Harewood Way YO10 . . . 229 A2
Harford Rd YO11 . . . 100 B6
Hargill
Gilling with Hartforth & Sedbury DL10 . . . 20 E4
Harmby DL8 . . . 60 E4
West Witton DL8 . . . 59 C3
Hargill Cl DL8 . . . 60 E4
Hargill La
Finghall DL8 . . . 61 E4
6 Leeming DL7 . . . 63 D4
Redmire DL8 . . . 59 C7
Hargill Rd DL8 . . . 61 A3
Hargreaves St 8 BD20 . . . 187 F8
Hargrove Rd HG2 . . . 220 B2
Harington Ave YO10 . . . 228 F4
Harker Hill DL8 . . . 56 C4
Harker St
42 Cross Hills BD20 . . . 187 E7
12 Knottingley WF11 . . . 202 A2
Harkness Cl DL7 . . . 63 C4
Harkness Dr DL7 . . . 63 C4
Harland Cl YO61 . . . 144 C3
Harland Mount Nature Reserve★ YO12 . . . 212 B3
Harlech Ct 11 TS17 . . . 5 F4
Harlech Way HG2 . . . 222 B5
Harley Cl
3 Low Bentham LA2 . . . 128 F8
Scarborough YO12 . . . 212 E5
Harley Cres DL9 . . . 40 F4
Harley La 2 DL9 . . . 40 F4
Harley St 5 YO12 . . . 212 E5
Harlow Ave HG2 . . . 222 B7
Harlow Carr RHS Gdn★ HG3 . . . 161 B1
Harlow Cl 1 YO24 . . . 227 F2
Harlow Cres HG2 . . . 222 B7
Harlow Ct 9 YO32 . . . 167 A6
Harlow Grange Pk HG3 . . . 178 C8
HARLOW HILL . . . 222 A8
Harlow Manor Pk HG2 . . . 222 B8
Harlow Moor Dr HG2 . . . 219 B1
Harlow Moor Rd HG2 . . . 219 A1
Harlow Oval HG2 . . . 222 B8
Harlow Oval Mews HG2 . . . 222 B8
Harlow Park Cres HG2 . . . 222 B7
Harlow Park Dr HG2 . . . 222 B7
Harlow Park Rd HG2 . . . 222 B7
Harlow Pines HG3 . . . 222 A7
Harlow Rd YO24 . . . 227 F2
Harlow Terr HG2 . . . 219 B1
Harlow View HG2 . . . 222 B6
Harlsey Castle★ DL6 . . . 44 D5
Harlsey Cres TS18 . . . 5 E8
Harlsey Rd TS18 . . . 5 E8
HARMBY . . . 60 E4
Harmby Rd 11 DL8 . . . 60 D5
Harness La 9 YO51 . . . 141 B4
Harold Ct YO24 . . . 227 D3
Harold St YO8 . . . 232 F4
Harolds Way 1 YO41 . . . 168 D1
HAROME . . . 93 C4
Harome Heads La YO62 . . . 93 B6
Harome Heads Rd YO62 . . . 93 C6
Harper Gr BD20 . . . 187 E6
Harper La HG3 . . . 159 C6
Harpers Sq 7 BD20 . . . 187 E6
Harper St
Barnoldswick BB18 . . . 171 C1
2 Selby YO8 . . . 232 C5
Harpers Terr DL2 . . . 4 B5
Harper Terr 7 TS18 . . . 5 E8
Harr Gill DL8 . . . 58 A6
Harrier Ct YO41 . . . 185 A3
Harriers Croft YO7 . . . 115 E7
Harringay Cres 20 DL1 . . . 3 F6
Harris Dr 9 DL10 . . . 41 E4
Harrison Gr HG1 . . . 220 C4
Harrison St
Barnoldswick BB18 . . . 171 E1
York YO31 . . . 228 F6
Harris St DL1 . . . 3 E4
HARROGATE . . . 219 D1
Harrogate District Hospl HG2 . . . 220 A2
Harrogate Gram Sch HG2 . . . 222 C8
Harrogate High Sch HG1 . . . 220 A4
Harrogate Hill Sch DL3 . . . 3 D7
Harrogate Int Ctr★ HG1 . . . 219 D3
Harrogate Ladies' Coll HG1 . . . 219 C3
Harrogate Rd
Bishop Monkton HG3 . . . 139 E5
Boroughbridge HG5 . . . 141 A2
Ferrensby HG5 . . . 162 E7
Green Hammerton YO26 . . . 164 B3
Kirkby Overblow HG3 . . . 222 D1
Knaresborough HG5 . . . 220 F5
Littlethorpe HG4 . . . 214 C1
Spofforth with Stockeld LS22 . . . 180 A4
Weeton LS17 . . . 178 B2
Harrogate Sta HG1 . . . 219 D2
Harrogate Theatre★ HG1 . . . 219 D2
Harrow Cliff La YO18 . . . 96 E4
HARROWGATE HILL . . . 3 C8
HARROWGATE VILLAGE . . . 3 E8
Harrow Glade 5 YO30 . . . 225 A1
Harrowing Dr 2 YO21 . . . 208 C6
Harrow Rd TS5 . . . 6 E8
Harryfield La
Marton-cum-Moxby YO61 . . . 144 C8
Marton-in-the-Forest YO61 . . . 144 D7
Harry Moor La YO8 . . . 197 B2
Hartburn Village TS18 . . . 5 E8
HARTFORTH . . . 20 D5
Hartforth La DL10 . . . 20 E4
Hart Hill Cres YO41 . . . 169 A2
Harthorn Ct DL11 . . . 2 A2
Hartington St 13 BB8 . . . 186 A3
Hartington Way DL3 . . . 3 C7
HARTLEY . . . 14 A7
Hartley Gn 4 BD23 . . . 153 F5
Hartley La CA17 . . . 14 A7
Hartley Pl BD22 . . . 187 B6
Hartley Rd HG2 . . . 222 B7
Hartley St
12 Earby BB18 . . . 172 A1
2 Glusburn BD20 . . . 187 D7
HARTLINGTON . . . 157 C8
Hartlington Moor La BD23 . . . 135 C3
Hartlington Raikes BD23 . . . 157 B8
Hartoft St YO10 . . . 228 D2
HARTON . . . 168 C8
Hart Rhydding La LS29 . . . 174 F4
HARTWITH . . . 160 B8
Hartwith Ave 3 HG3 . . . 138 A1
Hartwith Bank HG3 . . . 138 A1
Hartwith Cl HG3 . . . 219 A4
Hartwith Dr HG3 . . . 219 B4
Hartwith Gn 4 HG3 . . . 138 A1
Hartwith View HG3 . . . 159 F8
Hartwith Way HG3 . . . 219 B4
Harvard Ct YO12 . . . 212 A8
Harvest Cl
10 Pontefract WF8 . . . 201 C2
11 Strensall YO32 . . . 167 B7
Harvest Croft LS29 . . . 176 B1
Harvester Way 18 LS25 . . . 195 F2
Harvest Way YO11 . . . 100 B7
HARWOOD DALE . . . 53 E2
Harwood Dale Rd YO13 . . . 54 A1
Harwood Rd YO26 . . . 182 F7
Hasguard Way 37 TS17 . . . 5 F4
Hassacarr La YO19 . . . 184 F6
Hastings Cl 4 YO30 . . . 225 A1
Hastings Cres WF10 . . . 201 A4
Hatcase La 23 YO18 . . . 95 F7
Hatfield Ave TS5 . . . 6 E8
Hatfield Cl 3 YO30 . . . 224 E3
Hatfield Rd DL7 . . . 210 D3
Hatfield Wlk YO24 . . . 230 B8
Hatkill La YO41 . . . 169 B1
Hatterall Ct 44 TS16 . . . 5 E4
Hatterboard Dr YO12 . . . 212 C6
Hatters Cl YO23 . . . 230 B3
Haugh La YO8 . . . 202 F8
HAUGHTON LE SKERNE . . . 3 F6
Haughton Rd
Darlington DL1 . . . 3 D6
York YO30 . . . 228 C7
Hauling La YO23 . . . 191 C8
Hauxley Ct LS29 . . . 218 D5
Havelock Pl 17 YO21 . . . 208 D7
Haven The
Selby YO8 . . . 232 D5
5 South Milford LS25 . . . 195 F2
Haverah Ct YO30 . . . 224 F1
Havercroft Rd 15 YO14 . . . 127 A8
Havernook La HG4 . . . 86 A3
Havers Hill YO11 . . . 100 A6
Haverthwaites Dr LS25 . . . 188 F1
Havertop La WF6 . . . 200 C1
Havikil La HG5 . . . 162 A5
Havikil Pk HG5 . . . 162 A6
Havilland Rd TS17 . . . 6 B6
Havre Pk 11 BB18 . . . 171 E1
Haw Bank Ct BD23 . . . 217 B5
Hawber Cote Dr BD20 . . . 174 C1
Hawber La
Earby BB18 . . . 172 C2
Silsden BD20 . . . 174 C1
Hawdon Ave YO8 . . . 232 D5
HAWES . . . 56 D4
Hawes Com Prim Sch DL8 . . . 56 D4
Hawes Rd HG1 . . . 220 B4
Hawford Cl 1 TS17 . . . 6 B5
Haw Gr BD23 . . . 154 B3
Haw Hill View WF6 . . . 200 A2
Hawkcliffe Vw 6 BD20 . . . 174 B1
Hawk Creative Bsns Pk YO61 . . . 143 D6
Hawke Garth 5 YO14 . . . 127 A8
Hawkins Dr 36 DL9 . . . 41 A5
Hawkridge Cl TS17 . . . 6 A3
Hawkshead Cl 3 YO24 . . . 230 B8
Hawksmoor Ct HG4 . . . 214 C6
Hawkstone TS8 . . . 7 C4
Hawkstone Cl TS14 . . . 8 E6
Hawkswell La DL9 . . . 40 E1
HAWKSWICK . . . 107 F1
Hawkswood 1 DL2 . . . 3 D1
Haw La
Hellifield BD23 . . . 154 B3
Thoralby DL8 . . . 58 C1
Hawley St BB8 . . . 186 B3
HAWNBY . . . 67 E4
Haw Pk 1 BD23 . . . 217 E8
Hawse Rd YO8 . . . 204 E8
Hawshaw Rd BD22 . . . 186 E7
Hawsker Cum Stainsacre CE VC Prim Sch YO22 . . . 33 A7
Hawsker Intake Rd YO22 . . . 32 F5
Hawsker La
Hawsker-cum-Stainsacre YO22 . . . 13 F1
Whitby YO22 . . . 208 F6
Hawson Cl 9 YO11 . . . 100 B7
Hawswater Pl 3 WF11 . . . 201 F1
Hawthorn Ave
2 Knaresborough HG5 . . . 221 B7
Knottingley WF11 . . . 201 E2
Malton YO17 . . . 215 D5
Tadcaster LS24 . . . 189 D5
Hawthorn Cl
11 Addingham LS29 . . . 174 E4
Hellifield BD23 . . . 154 B3
3 Leeming DL7 . . . 63 F3
24 Leyburn DL8 . . . 60 D5
3 Pickering YO18 . . . 96 A6
Stutton with Hazlewood LS24 . . . 189 E5
Hawthorn Cres TS7 . . . 7 C6
Hawthorn Croft 6 LS24 . . . 189 D5
Hawthorn Dr
2 Topcliffe YO7 . . . 89 B1
Wilberfoss YO41 . . . 185 E5
Wistow YO8 . . . 198 A5
Hawthorne Ave
12 Haxby YO32 . . . 166 E5
10 Scotton DL9 . . . 40 F2
Hawthorne Cl
Burniston YO13 . . . 75 D7
10 Thorpe Willoughby YO8 . . . 197 B2

Hawthorne Dr
Barnoldswick BB18 . . . . . . 171 E2
Guisborough TS14 . . . . 8 E6
Hawthorne Gr YO31 . . . . . 228 E5
Hawthorne Mews YO32. . 167 B7
Hawthorne St 1 BD20 . . 174 B1
Hawthorn Garth DN14. . . 202 F4
Hawthorn Gr YO31 . . . . . . 228 E5
Hawthorn La
9 Bedale DL8. . . . . 63 B2
Pickering YO18 . . . . 96 A6
Hawthorn Pl YO32 . . . . . . 225 E4
Hawthorn Rd YO8. . . . . . . 232 D3
Hawthorns 2 YO19 . . . . . 197 F8
Hawthorns La BD23 . . . . . 133 B2
Hawthorn Spinney YO31. 225 E3
Hawthorn St 1 YO31. . . . 228 E5
Hawthorns The
20 Glusburn BD20. . . . . . . 187 E7
10 Great Ayton TS9. . . . . 8 A2
Hawthorn Terr YO32 . . . . 225 D4
Hawthorn Terrace Ctr 2
YO32 . . . . 225 D3
Hawthorn Terrace N
YO32 . . . . 225 D4
Hawthorn Terrace S
YO32 . . . . 225 D3
Hawthorn Wlk 1 YO11. . 100 A7
HAXBY. 225 D7
Haxby Moor Rd
Haxby YO32 . . . . 166 F7
Towthorpe YO32 . . . . 167 A7
Haxby Rd
Clifton YO31. . . . . 225 D1
Middleton St George DL2 . . . 4 C5
New Earswick YO32. . . . . . 225 D6
York YO31 . . . . 233 B4
Haxby Rd Prim Acad
YO31. . . . . 228 D7
Hay-a-Park La HG5 . . . . . 221 D7
Hay Brow Cl YO13. . . . . 75 C5
Hay Brow Cres YO13 . . . . . 75 C5
Hayfield Ave LS23. . . . . . . 188 E8
Hayforth Cl YO30. . . . . . . 225 A2
Haygate La YO18. . . . . 95 F5
Haygill Nook BD20 . . . . . . 174 B5
Hayhills La BD20. . . . . 174 B2
Hayhills Rd 10 BD20. . . . . 174 C1
Hay La YO13 . . . . 75 C5
Hayton Wood View LS25. 194 F8
Haywain The
Ilkley LS29. . . . . 218 D3
17 South Milford LS25. . . . 195 F2
Haywra Cres 6 HG1 . . . . 219 E3
Haywra St HG1 . . . . 219 D3
Hazel Bank HG5 . . . . 162 D6
Hazel Brow Farm* DL11 . 37 C4
Hazel Cl
Pannal HG3 . . . . 222 C3
York YO32 . . . . 225 D2
Hazel Ct
11 Bedale DL8. . . . . 63 B3
York YO10 . . . . 228 E4
Hazel Dr HG3. . . . . 222 C3
Hazel Garth YO31 . . . . 229 B7
Hazel Gr
Middlesbrough TS7 . . . . 7 C6
Pontefract WF8 . . . . 201 C1
Sutton BD20. . . . . 187 E7
Hazel Grove Rd BD20. . . . 187 E7
Hazelheads La HG5 . . . . . 221 C8
Hazel Hill YO12 . . . . 75 A2
Hazel Lodge Pupil Referral Unit DN14 . . . . 205 A2
Hazelmere Ct YO32 . . . . . 225 E3
Hazelnut Gr YO30 . . . . . . 225 B2
Hazel Old La DN14 . . . . . . 203 C2
Hazel Rd
2 Boroughbridge YO51 . . 141 B4
2 Filey YO14 . . . . 101 A4
Knottingley WF11. . . . . 201 F1
Hazel Rise LS26. . . . . 200 B5
Hazelwood Ave
Garforth LS25 . . . . 194 D3
York YO10 . . . . 229 D4
Hazing La DN14. . . . . 207 B6
Hazler La BD23 . . . . 157 D7
HAZLEWOOD 175 A8
Headingley Cres 3 DL1 . . . . 3 F6
Headingley Rd 7 DN6. . . 206 E2
Headland Cl 30 YO32 . . . . 166 E5
Headland La YO18 . . . . 72 B4
Headlands La
Howgrave DL8. . . . . 87 F2
Knottingley WF11. . . . . 201 F2
Pontefract WF8 . . . . 201 B1
Headlands Prim Sch
YO32. . . . . 225 D8
Headlands Rd YO62 . . . . . . 70 E2
Headlands The DL3 . . . . 3 A5
Headley Cl 2 YO30 . . . . . 225 B1
Headley La LS23 . . . . 188 F5
Head of Steam-Darlington Railway Mus DL3 . . . . 3 C6
Heads Bank DL8 . . . . 58 F3
Heads La BB18. . . . . 186 A7
Heads Rd
Newton YO18. . . . . 51 B1
Pickering YO18 . . . . 71 F8
Headwell La LS24 . . . . 195 E7
HEALAUGH 37 F6
Healaugh La YO26 . . . . . . 181 F4
Healaugh Pk TS15 . . . . 5 E2
Healaugh Priory* LS24 . 181 E1
Heald Brow BB18 . . . . 171 D2
Healdfield Rd WF10. . . . . 201 A4
Heald St WF10. . . . . 200 F4
Healdwood Rd WF10. . . . 200 F4
HEALEY 85 E3
Healey Gr YO31. . . . . 228 F8
Healthfield Prim Sch DL1 . . 3 E5
Heath Cl 2 YO24 . . . . 227 F2
Heathcliff Gdns 5 YO12. 212 C8
Heath Cres BD20. . . . . 173 E3
Heath Croft YO10 . . . . 231 F7
Heath Gr 11 BD20 . . . . 173 E3
Heath Dr
Boston Spa LS23 . . . . 188 D8
7 Low Bradley BD20 . . . . 173 E3
Heather Bank
13 Stamford Bridge YO41. . . . . 168 D2
York YO10 . . . . 229 C4
Heather Brow 16 BB18 . . 172 B1
Heather Cl
Selby YO8. . . . . 232 C3
3 Whorlton DL6 . . . . 25 D1
York YO32 . . . . 226 A4
Heather Croft 4 YO31 . . 225 E2
Heather Ct LS29 . . . . 218 B3
Heatherdene LS24 . . . . . . 189 E6
Heatherdene Rd 1 DL9 . . 40 E4
Heather Dr
9 Sherburn in Elmet LS25. . . . . 196 A4
Whitby YO22 . . . . 208 E3
Heather View BD23 . . . . . 217 B3
Heather Way 16 HG3 . . . . 161 B3
HEATHFIELD. 136 F6
Heathfield Dr HG5 . . . . . . 221 C6
Heathfield La 1 LS23 . . . 188 D8
Heathfield Pk DL2 . . . . 4 C5
Heathfield Rd 1 YO10 . . 229 A3
Heath Gr HG2. . . . . 219 B1
Heath Moor Dr YO10 . . . . 231 F8
Heathness Rd LS29. . . . . . 174 E5
Heath Pk 27 LS29 . . . . 175 C2
Heath Ride YO32. . . . . 167 B8
Heathrow TS17 . . . . 6 C7
Heathrow Cl 13 DL2. . . . . . . 4 C4
Heaths Ct HG4 . . . . 214 C5
HEATHWAITE 45 E8
HEBDEN. 135 A1
Hebden Bank HG4 . . . . . . 138 F4
Hebden Rd BD23. . . . . 134 E2
Hebdon Rise 2 YO26. . . . 227 D4
Heber Dr BD23. . . . . 172 A5
Hebers Ghyll Dr 24 LS29. 175 C2
Hebers Gr 21 LS29 . . . . . . 175 C2
Hebron Ct TS9. . . . . 26 B7
Hebron Rd TS9 . . . . 26 B7
Heck Gill La HG3. . . . . 160 A5
Heck La
Heck DN14. . . . . 207 C7
Hensall DN14. . . . . 203 D1
Heckler Cl 3 HG4 . . . . . . 214 C4
Heckler La HG4 . . . . 214 C4
Heck & Pollington Lake
DN14 . . . . 207 E7
Heddon Gr TS17 . . . . 6 A3
Hedgerows The YO8 . . . . 198 E3
Hedley St TS14 . . . . 8 F7
Height La BD23 . . . . 174 C6
Height Lands La YO23 . . . 182 D6
Heights La BD20 . . . . 174 A2
Helena St LS25 . . . . 200 C8
Helios 47 LS25. . . . . 194 D5
Helks Brow LA2. . . . . 128 E2
HELLIFIELD. 154 B3
Hellifield Com Prim Sch
BD23. . . . . 154 B3
HELLIFIELD GREEN 154 B3
Hellifield Rd BD23 . . . . . . 155 A6
Hellifield Sta BD23. . . . . . 154 B4
Hell Wath Gr HG4. . . . . . . 214 A2
Hell Wath La
Littlethorpe HG4 . . . . 214 A2
Markingfield Hall HG4. . . . 139 E6
Hell Wath Nature Reserve*
HG4. . . . . 214 A4
HELM. 57 D6
Helmsdale YO24 . . . . 230 C6
HELMSLEY 92 F7
Helmsley Castle* YO62. . . . 92 E6
Helmsley Com Prim Sch
YO62. . . . . 92 F7
Helmsley Dr TS14. . . . . 8 E7
Helmsley Gr 16 YO32 . . . . 166 D5
Helmsley Rd TS9. . . . . 26 C7
Helmsley Walled Gdn*
YO62. . . . . 92 E6
Helmsley Way DL7 . . . . . . 210 C2
HELPERBY. 142 A8
Helperby La YO51. . . . . . . 141 C7
Helperby & Myton La
YO61 . . . . 142 A7
HELPERTHORPE. 124 D1
Helredale Gdns YO22. . . . 208 E4
Helredale Rd YO22. . . . . . 208 E4
Helston Rd WF6 . . . . 200 A2
Helwath Rd YO13 . . . . 53 D5
HELWITH BRIDGE 131 D8
Helwith Rd DL11. . . . . 38 E7
HEMINGBROUGH. 198 F1
Hemingbrough Com Prim Sch YO8. . . . . 198 F1
Hemingford Gdns TS15. . . . . 5 E2
Hemishor Dr LS26. . . . . . . 200 C8
HEMLINGTON. 6 F4
Hemlington Hall Prim Sch
TS8. . . . . 6 E5
Hemlington Hall Rd TS8. . . . 6 E5
Hemlington Lake & Recn Ctr
TS8. . . . . 6 E5
Hemlington Rd TS8 . . . . 6 E5
Hemlington Village Rd TS8 7 A5
Hemlock Ave YO31. . . . . . 225 E1
Hemlock Dr YO8 . . . . 232 E2
Hempbridge Cl YO8 . . . . . 232 A5
Hempbridge Rd YO8 . . . . 232 A5
Hempland Ave YO31 . . . . 228 F6
Hempland Dr YO31. . . . . . 229 A7
Hempland La YO31. . . . . . 229 A7
Hempland Prim Sch
YO31. . . . . 229 B6
Hemsby Rd WF10 . . . . 200 E3
Hemsworth Wlk HG4. . . . 214 B7
Henbusk La LA2 . . . . 130 A8
Hendon Garth YO30. . . . . 225 A1
Henlow La YO60 . . . . 147 B4
Henrhyd Cl 26 TS17 . . . . 5 F4
Henrietta Cl
Richmond DL10 . . . . 209 F8
3 Thornaby-on-Tees TS17 . . 6 B8
Henrietta St YO22. . . . . . . 208 E7
Henry Moore Pl WF10. . . 200 F3
Henry's Mews 22 LS25. . . 195 F4
Henry St
2 Airmyn DN14 . . . . 205 F2
Skipton BD23. . . . . 216 F1
HENSALL. 203 D2
Hensall Com Prim Sch
DN14. . . . . 203 C1
Hensall Sta DN14 . . . . 203 C1
Hensfield Gr DL3. . . . . 3 C7
Henshaw's Coll HG1 . . . . 220 B5
Henside La BD24. . . . . 132 A5
Henside Rd BD24 . . . . 132 B6
Henson Gr WF10. . . . . 201 A4
Henson Rd DL1 . . . . 3 F5
Henwick Hall La YO8. . . . 232 C1
Hepton Hill YO17 . . . . 120 F2
Hepworth's La DN14 . . . . 204 C2
Herbert St 6 YO10. . . . . . 228 E3
Herberts Way YO31 . . . . . 228 F7
Hercules St DL1 . . . . 3 E7
Herdborough Rd YO11 . . 100 A7
Herdsman Dr YO23. . . . . . 230 C3
Herdsman Rd 3 YO24. . . . 230 D8
Herdwick Cl 1 YO30 . . . . 225 B1
Hereford Rd HG1 . . . . 219 A2
Hergill La
Baldersby HG4. . . . . 88 C1
Kirkby Fleetham with Fencote DL7 . . . . 63 C8
Herisson Cl 20 YO18. . . . . . 95 F7
Herman Wlk YO24. . . . . . . 230 C8
Hermitage Ct DL10. . . . . . 209 A7
Hermitage The* HG4 . . . . 86 C8
Hermitage Way YO22. . . . . 32 A5
Heron Ave YO24 . . . . 230 C8
Heron Cl
1 Bedale DL8. . . . . 63 B3
11 Thornton Dale YO18 . . . . 96 D5
Heron Ct
6 Filey YO14 . . . . 101 A4
6 Hunton DL9 . . . . 40 F2
Heron Dr DL1. . . . . 3 E5
Herongate YO18 . . . . 95 F6
Heron Gate TS14. . . . . 8 D6
Heron La YO12. . . . . 99 E6
Heron Rise YO32. . . . . 225 F5
Heron Tree Cl DL8 . . . . 60 D7
Heron Way YO17 . . . . 215 D2
Herriot Ct DL8 . . . . 60 D5
Herriot Dr DL9. . . . . 41 A5
Herriot Way YO7. . . . . 211 C4
Hertford Cl 4 YO11 . . . . . 100 A7
Hertford Vale CE Prim Sch
YO12. . . . . 99 D2
Hesketh Ave TS4. . . . . 7 A7
Hesketh Bank YO10 . . . . . 229 D3
Heslaker La BD23 . . . . 216 C1
Hesleden Ave TS5. . . . . 6 D6
Hesley La BD24 . . . . 153 A6
Heslin Cl 8 YO32 . . . . 225 C8
HESLINGTON 229 B1
Heslington Croft YO10 . . 231 F7
Heslington Ct 2 YO10. . . 229 B1
Heslington Gdns 2 TS14 . . . 8 F7
Heslington La
Heslington YO10 . . . . 229 A1
York YO10 . . . . 228 F3
Heslington Rd YO10. . . . . 228 E3
HESSAY. 182 C8
Hessay Ind Est YO26. . . . . 182 C8
Hessay Pl 2 YO26 . . . . . . 227 A3
Hetherton St YO30 . . . . . . 233 A3
HETTON. 155 F5
Hetton Garth 17 DL8 . . . . . 60 D5
HEW GREEN 160 D5
Hewitson Rd DL1 . . . . 3 E5
Hewitts La BD20 . . . . 172 F2
Hewley Ave YO10 . . . . 229 A4
Hewley Dr 9 YO13. . . . . 99 A7
HEWORTH. 228 F6
Heworth YO31 . . . . 229 A6
Heworth CE VA Prim Sch
YO31. . . . . 228 F6
Heworth Dr YO21 . . . . 208 B6
Heworth Gn YO31. . . . . . . 233 C4
Heworth Hall Dr YO31. . . 228 F6
Heworth Mews YO31. . . . 228 E6
Heworth Pl YO31. . . . . 228 F6
Heworth Rd YO31 . . . . 228 F6
Heworth Village YO31. . . . 229 A6
Heyford Rd YO7. . . . . 115 B1
Heygate Bank YO18 . . . . . . 49 F3
Heygate La LS23 . . . . 188 F6
Heys Cl WF11. . . . . 202 A2
HEYSHAW. 159 D8
Heyshaw Rd HG3. . . . . 159 C8
Heythrop Dr
Guisborough TS14 . . . . 8 F6
Middlesbrough TS5 . . . . 6 D7
Heywood Rd HG2 . . . . 219 C1
Hibernia St YO12. . . . . 212 E5
Hicks La LS26. . . . . 200 B6
Hickstead Ct 16 DL1. . . . . . . 3 F6
Hidcote Gdns TS17. . . . . 6 A4
High Back Side YO18. . . . . . 95 E8
High Bank
Ampleforth YO62 . . . . 92 B2
Bradleys Both BD20. . . . . . 173 E3
5 Threshfield BD23 . . . . . . 134 D2
High Bank Cl 7 LS29. . . . 174 F4
Highbank Gr 1 HG2 . . . . 220 D4
Highbank Rd TS7 . . . . 7 D7
High Barmer YO13 . . . . 75 B7
HIGH BENTHAM 129 B8
High Bentham Com Prim Sch
LA2. . . . . 129 B8
HIGH BIRSTWITH. 160 D5
High Bond End HG5. . . . . 221 A7
HIGH BRADLEY. 173 E4
High Bradley La BD20 . . . 173 E4
Highbury Ave TS5. . . . . 6 F8
HIGH CATTON. 185 D8
High Catton Rd YO41. . . . 185 D8
High Church Wynd TS16. . . 5 D3
High Cleugh HG4 . . . . 214 A4
Highcliffe Ct YO30 . . . . . . 228 A6
Highcliffe Prim Sch TS14. . . 8 E5
Highcliff Rd TS14 . . . . 8 E4
HIGH CONISCLIFFE 2 C6
High Coniscliffe CE Sch
DL2. . . . . 2 C6
High Cragwell YO21. . . . . . 31 F7
High Crest 6 HG3 . . . . . . 137 C4
Highcroft
Collingham LS22 . . . . 188 A8
9 Grassington BD23 . . . . 134 E3
12 High Bentham LA2. . . . . 129 A8
High Croft 7 YO14. . . . . . 126 F8
High Croft Way 5 BD20 . 173 E1
High Ct HG5 . . . . 221 A6
Highdale Ave 5 YO12. . . . 212 D8
Highdale Rd YO12. . . . . . . 212 E7
High Eggborough La
DN14 . . . . 203 A1
HIGH ELLINGTON. 85 F6
Higher Hartley St 5
BD20 . . . . 187 D7
Higherlands Cl BD23 . . . . 155 D1
Higher Lodge St 1
BD20 . . . . 187 D7
Higher Rd BD23. . . . . 152 F4
High Fell Cl BD24 . . . . 131 D1
HIGHFIELD 199 E7
Highfield
Pollington DN14. . . . . 207 F7
Scarborough YO12. . . . . . . 212 E4
High Field YO10. . . . . 229 D4
Highfield Ave WF8 . . . . . . 201 D2
Highfield Cl YO25 . . . . 126 A4
Highfield Cres YO8. . . . . . 198 B5
Highfield Ct YO8. . . . . 232 B1
Highfield Dr
Allerton Bywater WF10 . . . 200 C7
Garforth LS25 . . . . 194 C3
Highfield Gn
Allerton Bywater WF10 . . . 200 C7
Sherburn in Elmet LS25 . . . 195 F3
Highfield Gr
Great Preston WF10 . . . . . 200 C7
Highfield YO8. . . . . 199 E7
Highfield La
Barwick in Elmet & Scholes LS15 . . . . 194 B7
Fangfoss YO41. . . . . 169 B1
Gillamoor YO62 . . . . 69 F5
Huddleston with Newthorpe LS25 . . . . 195 C3
Nawton YO62. . . . . 69 C2
Scagglethorpe YO17 . . . . . 122 E2
Womersley DN6. . . . . 206 D5
Highfield Pl 1 WF10. . . . 200 D7
Highfield Rd
Aberford LS25 . . . . 194 F8
29 Earby BB18. . . . . 172 A1
Highfield YO8. . . . . 199 D7
Malton YO17 . . . . 215 C5
Ripon HG4 . . . . 214 B3
Whitby YO21 . . . . 208 A7
Highfields La YO7. . . . . . . 115 A1
Highfield Terr BD23. . . . . 216 F3
Highfield View 3 YO8. . . 198 B4
Highfield Villas LS25. . . . 195 F3
High Fold BB18 . . . . 186 A7
High Garth
Earswick YO32. . . . . 226 A7
Eastfield YO11 . . . . 100 A7
Markington with Wallerthwaite HG3. . . . . 139 C3
Richmond DL10 . . . . 209 B8
Highgate
Balne DN14 . . . . 207 D6
Glusburn BD20. . . . . 187 D8
Highgate Pk HG1 . . . . 219 F3
High Gill Rd TS7 . . . . 7 D6
High Gn
Catterick DL10. . . . . 41 D4
Hebden BD23. . . . . 135 A2
HIGH GRANTLEY 138 D8
High Green Dr BD20. . . . . 174 B1
Highgrove Cl 7 YO30 . . . . 224 E3
HIGH HARROGATE. 220 A3
HIGH HAWSKER. 33 B6
High Hill Grove St 14
BD24 . . . . 131 D2
High Hill La BD24 . . . . 131 E2
HIGH HUTTON 147 B7
HIGH KILBURN. 91 B2
High La
Beadlam YO62 . . . . 93 C8
Birstwith HG3 . . . . 160 C5
Cowling BD22 . . . . 187 A4
Cropton YO18. . . . . 71 C4
Dalby-cum-Skewsby YO60 119 A2
Dalton DL11. . . . . 19 D7
Fylingdales YO22 . . . . 33 C5
Gillamoor YO62 . . . . 70 A6
Grassington BD23 . . . . 134 E3
Grinton DL11 . . . . 37 D4
Hawes DL8. . . . . 56 F4
Howsham YO60 . . . . 147 B1
Kirby Sigston DL6 . . . . 44 E1
Leake DL6 . . . . 65 E6
Maltby TS8. . . . . 6 C4
Muston YO14 . . . . 100 F1
Myton-on-Swale YO61 . . . . 142 B6
Newsham DL11 . . . . 18 G7
Reeth, Fremington & Healaugh DL11 . . . . 37 F5
Spofforth with Stockeld HG3. . . . . 179 C4
Sutton upon Derwent YO41 185 D3
Thirlby YO7 . . . . 90 D6
Thornton Watlass DL8. . . . . 62 C2
West Scrafton DL8. . . . . 83 F6
West Witton DL8 . . . . 59 D2
Highland Cl 9 WF8 . . . . . 201 C1
Highlands Ave 5 YO32 . . 167 B7
Highlands Cl YO14 . . . . . . 101 B1
High Leir La YO7. . . . . 67 D1
HIGH LEVEN 6 A3
HIGH MARISHES. 96 B1
High Market Pl 27 YO62 . . 70 B1
High Mdw
Gowdall DN14 . . . . 204 A1
Selby YO8. . . . . 232 B6
Highmead Wlk 3 TS3. . . . . . 7 B8
High Mill Dr 1 YO12 . . . . . 75 E5
High Mill La LS29 . . . . 175 A5
Highmoor Cl YO24 . . . . . . 230 D8
High Moor Edge YO12. . . 212 A7
High Moor La
Boroughbridge HG5. . . . . . 141 A2
Brearton HG3 . . . . 161 F8
Newton-on-Ouse YO30 . . . 165 C8
Scotton HG5. . . . . 162 A5
Highmoor Rd YO24. . . . . . 230 D8
High Moor Rd
North Rigton HG3 . . . . 178 A5
Skelton YO51 . . . . 140 F7
High Moor Way 11 YO11. 100 A6
HIGH MOWTHORPE. 149 D7
High Newbiggin St YO31 233 B3
High Oaks YO31. . . . . 229 B7
High Ousegate YO1 . . . . . 233 B2
High Peak TS14. . . . . 8 F5
High Petergate YO1. . . . . 233 B3
High Peter La HG3 . . . . . . 140 A3
High Rd LA2 . . . . 128 F5
High Riding
Aske DL10 . . . . 20 D1
Richmond DL10 . . . . 209 C8
High Rifts TS8 . . . . 6 E5
High Riggs La YO18 . . . . . . 96 C3
High Row
Bugthorpe YO41. . . . . 169 D4
Caldwell DL11 . . . . 1 C4
Darlington DL1. . . . . 3 C5
Gainford DL2 . . . . 1 C7
Melsonby DL10 . . . . 20 F7
HIGH SHAW 56 D7
High Skellgate 7 HG4 . . 214 C5
High St
Airmyn DN14 . . . . 205 E3
Ampleforth YO62 . . . . 92 C3
Aske DL10 . . . . 20 E2
Austwick LA2. . . . . 130 E7
Barmby on the Marsh DN14. . . . . 205 A7
Barnby YO21 . . . . 12 C4
Barton-le-Street YO17 . . . . 120 E5
Beadlam YO62 . . . . 93 D7
Boosbeck TS12. . . . . 9 D8
6 Boroughbridge YO51 . . 141 B5
Boston Spa LS23 . . . . 188 E8
Bramham LS23 . . . . 188 E5
Buckton/Bempton YO13 . . . 97 D6
Burniston YO13 . . . . 75 C8
Burton in Lonsdale LA6 . . . 102 F3
Carlton DN14. . . . . 204 C2
Castleford WF10 . . . . 200 E4
Catterick DL10. . . . . 41 D5
Cawood YO8. . . . . 197 B8
Cottam YO25 . . . . 150 E5
Cropton YO18. . . . . 71 B4
Danby YO21 . . . . 29 A6
Eaglescliffe TS15. . . . . 5 D4
13 Eastfield YO11 . . . . 100 A6
Gargrave BD23 . . . . 155 D1
Glaisdale YO21. . . . . 30 D4
Glusburn BD20. . . . . 187 E6
Great Ayton TS9. . . . . 7 F1
Great Broughton TS9. . . . . . . 26 E4
Hampsthwaite HG3 . . . . . . 160 F5
Harrogate HG2 . . . . 220 C4
4 Helmsley YO62 . . . . 92 F6
Heslerton YO17 . . . . 123 F6
Hinderwell TS13. . . . . 11 F7
Hovingham YO62 . . . . 119 E6
Husthwaite YO61 . . . . 117 B6
Ingleton LA6 . . . . 103 D4

High St *continued*
Kippax LS25 194 D1
Kirby Grindalythe YO17 149 D8
5 Knaresborough HG5 221 B5
Knottingley WF11 201 E5
Langtoft YO25 151 C8
Lastingham YO62 70 E5
8 Leyburn DL8 60 D5
Lingdale TS12 9 F7
Lockwood TS12 10 A5
Markington with Wallerthwaite HG3 139 C4
Mickleby TS13 12 A4
Middlesbrough TS7 7 C8
Newton Mulgrave TS13 11 E4
Normanton South WF6 200 A1
Northallerton DL7 210 D6
14 Norton DN6 206 E1
Old Byland & Scawton YO62 92 A4
Oldstead YO7 91 E5
Pateley Bridge HG3 137 B4
Rawcliffe DN14 205 A1
Rillington YO17 122 F5
Scalby YO13 75 D5
6 Settle BD24 131 E2
Settrington YO17 122 F1
Sherburn YO17 124 D7
Skipton BD23 217 A4
Slingsby YO62 120 B5
Snainton YO13 98 A5
Snaith DN14 204 B1
South Milford LS25 195 E2
Spofforth HG3 179 E5
3 Staithes TS13 13 K2
Stillington YO61 144 B6
Stokesley TS9 26 C7
Swinton YO17 121 B4
Tadcaster LS24 189 E6
Thornton Dale YO18 96 E6
Thornton-le-Clay YO60 146 A4
Wharram YO17 149 A6
Whitby YO21 208 B3
Whixley YO26 164 A4
Whorlton DL6 45 D8
Wombleton YO62 93 E7
Wrelton YO18 71 C1
HIGH STAKESBY 208 B5
High Stakesby Rd YO21 208 A6
High Stell DL2 4 C4
High Street Agnesgate HG4 214 C5
Highthorne La YO61 117 B5
Highthorn Rd YO31 225 E2
High Town Bank Rd YO7 91 C5
High Trace DL6 210 E2
High Trees Ct LS25 195 F4
High View HG3 160 F8
Highway BD24 131 E3
High Wheatley LS29 218 E3
High Wlk YO12 212 E7
High Wood LS29 218 F3
HIGH WORSALL 24 A8
Hilbeck Gr YO31 229 B6
Hilbra Ave YO32 225 D6
Hilda St
6 Selby YO8 232 C5
3 York YO10 228 E3
Hildenley Cl 6 YO12 212 B5
Hilderthorpe TS7 7 C6
Hildewell 3 TS13 11 F7
Hildyard Cl TS9 26 C8
HILLAM 202 A7
Hillam Comm La LS25 202 B7
Hillam Hall La 4 LS25 202 A7
Hillam Hall View 3 LS25 202 A7
Hillam House Cl 5 LS25 202 A7
Hillam La
Burton Salmon LS25 201 F7
Hillam LS25 202 A7
Hillam Rd YO8 202 F8
Hillary Garth 9 YO26 227 E4
Hill Bank HG5 163 B7
Hillbank Gr HG1 220 D4
Hillbank Rd HG1 220 D4
Hillbank View HG1 220 C4
Hillbrook Cr TS17 6 A5
Hill Cl DL11 38 B6
Hillcrest
8 Monk Fryston LS25 202 A8
Tadcaster LS24 189 D5
Hill Crest YO19 167 F1
Hillcrest
Newby & Scalby YO12 75 E5
Poppleton YO26 224 A2
Silsden BD20 174 C1
Hillcrest Cl WF10 201 B3
Hillcrest Ct 2 LS24 189 D5
Hillcrest Dr
Castleford WF10 201 B3
Loftus TS13 10 D8
Middlesbrough TS7 7 D6
Hillcrest Gdns YO51 141 A7
Hill Crest Gdns YO24 227 F1
Hillcrest Gr 2 YO12 75 E5
Hillcrest Mount WF10 201 B3
Hillcroft 4 LA2 129 A7
Hill End La BD22 186 F5
Hill Field YO8 232 B8
Hill Foot La HG3 222 B2
Hillgarth WF11 201 F2
Hillgarth Ct 4 YO41 185 B2
Hillhouse La DL2 4 C7
Hill House La DL2 4 C8
Hillingdon Rd TS4 7 B8
Hill La BB8 186 B4
Hillocks La TS12 10 A5
Hill Rd WF10 200 F3
Hill Rise
Middleton St George DL2 4 D3
Skipton BD23 216 E5
Hill Rise Ave HG2 222 B8
Hill Rise Cl HG2 222 B8
Hillsborough Terr 5 YO30 228 C7
Hillshaw Parkway HG4 214 D5
Hillside
Byram WF11 201 E4
Follifoot HG3 223 F2
3 Ingleby Arncliffe DL6 45 A7
Skipton BD23 217 B6
Hill Side DL2 3 A3
Hillside Cl
18 Addingham LS29 174 F4
Bootham Stray YO30 225 B2
9 Monk Fryston LS25 202 A8
Skipton BD23 217 B6
Threshfield BD23 134 B3
Hillside Cres BD23 217 C3
Hillside Dr BD23 134 B3
Hillside Gdns
Langtoft YO25 151 D5
Scarborough YO12 212 E1
Hillside Rd
2 Low Bentham LA2 128 F8
Pannal HG3 222 E3
Hillside Way YO17 150 B8
Hills La BD23 155 E5
Hill St
6 Barnoldswick BB18 171 E1
York YO24 227 E3
Hill The DL8 56 D4
Hill Top
24 Burley in Warfedale LS29 176 C1
Castleford WF10 200 C4
Ilkley LS29 218 A2
Knottingley WF11 201 F2
Hill Top Ave HG1 219 D6
Hill Top Cl
Embsay BD23 217 C8
Harrogate HG1 219 D6
Stutton with Hazlewood LS24 189 D4
Hilltop Cres DL9 40 E4
Hill Top Cres HG1 219 D6
Hill Top Ct DL7 22 C3
Hill Top Dr HG1 219 D6
Hill Top Gr HG1 219 E6
Hill Top La
Earby BB18 172 A1
Pannal HG3 222 A4
Hill Top Mount HG1 219 D6
Hill Top Rd
Harrogate HG1 219 D6
4 Wistow YO8 197 D6
Hill Top Rise HG1 219 E6
Hill Top View HG3 159 F8
Hill Top Wlk HG1 219 D6
Hill View
Langthorpe YO51 141 A6
Stillington YO61 144 C6
York YO31 229 C7
Hillway 7 TS17 6 A5
HILTON 6 C2
Hilton Cl DL6 210 E8
Hilton Gn DL6 210 D8
Hilton Grange DL6 210 E8
Hilton La 7 HG5 221 A6
Hilton Rd TS9 6 F1
Hilton Sq DL6 210 E8
Hincks Hall La HG3 139 C3
HINDERWELL 11 F7
Hinderwell Ind Pk TS13 11 F7
Hinderwell La
Hinderwell TS13 11 E8
Staithes TS13 13 K1
Hinderwell Pl YO12 212 E2
Hinderwell Rd YO12 212 E1
Hindle Dr 39 YO14 101 B3
Hinsley La DN14 204 C2
Hinton Ave 1 YO24 230 C8
Hinton Cl 9 WF8 201 C2
Hinton La WF11 201 D3
HIPSWELL 209 F1
Hipswell CE Prim Sch DL9 209 F1
Hipswell Rd DL9 209 E1
Hipswell Road W DL9 209 C1
Hird Ave 22 DL8 63 A2
Hird Rd TS15 5 D2
Hirds Yd 2 BD23 216 F3
HIRST COURTNEY 203 F3
Hirstead Gdns YO12 212 B8
Hirstead Rd YO12 212 B8
Hirst La HG3 160 E5
Hirst Rd DN14 204 A3
Hirst St WF10 200 C8
Hobart Rd WF10 201 B5
Hobb Nook La LS21 176 D4
Hobbs Cl DL9 209 C2
Hob Cote La BD22 187 F1
Hobgate YO24 227 D3
Hob Moor Dr YO24 227 E2
Hob Moor Oaks Sch YO26 227 D2
Hob Moor Prim Sch YO24 227 E2
Hobmoor Terr YO24 227 F1
Hobson Cl YO23 230 B1
Hoctun Cl WF10 200 F3
Hodge La WF8 206 B3
Hodgson Fold LS29 174 E5
Hodgson Hill YO13 54 B4
Hodgson La YO26 182 F8
Hodgson's La LS25 196 A5
Hogg La YO17 148 E6
Holbeck Ave
Middlesbrough TS5 6 E6
Scarborough YO11 213 B2
Holbeck Cl YO11 213 B2
Holbeck Hill YO11 213 B1
Holbeck Rd YO11 213 A2
Holbeck's La YO26 141 F3
Holburns Croft 3 YO10 229 B1
Holden Gdns YO8 197 D2
Holderness Dr
7 Darlington DL2 3 A7
4 Faverdale DL2 3 B7
HOLE BOTTOM 135 A3
Hole House La BB7 152 B2
Hole La BD20 174 A2
Holes La WF11 201 E2
HOLGATE 227 F3
Holgate DL6 45 E8
Holgate Bank HG5 163 A8
Holgate Bridge Gdn 7 YO24 228 A3
Holgate Cl YO17 215 C5
Holgate La LS23 188 E8
Holgate Lodge Dr YO26 227 E4
Holgate Park Dr YO26 227 F4
Holgate Rd YO24 233 A1
Holl Gate DL8 59 E3
Hollicarrs Cl YO19 192 A2
Hollies The
Barlby with Osgodby YO8 198 C4
Stockton on the Forest YO19 167 D3
Hollin Gate LS21 176 E1
Hollings The LS26 200 A6
Hollington St 9 BB8 186 A3
Hollingwood Gate 31 LS29 175 C2
Hollingwood Pk 37 LS29 175 C2
Hollingwood Rise 32 LS29 175 C2
Hollingworth Cl BD23 217 B3
Hollin Hall Dr LS29 175 C2
Hollinhurst Brow LA2 128 F2
Hollin La LA2 129 F6
Hollins DL8 60 B3
Hollins Beck Cl LS25 200 D8
Hollins Cl HG3 161 A5
Hollins Cres HG1 219 C4
Hollins Gr WF10 200 C7
Hollins Hall HG3 161 A4
Hollins La
Firby DL8 63 B1
Hampsthwaite HG3 161 A5
Melmerby HG4 114 B8
Middleton Quernhow HG4 88 C1
Rosedale East Side YO18 49 D4
Hollins Mews HG1 219 C4
Hollins Rd
10 Barnoldswick BB18 171 D1
Harrogate HG1 219 C4
HOLLINTHORPE 194 A2
Hollin Top La YO21 29 C7
Hollis Cres YO32 167 B6
Hollow Gill Brow BD24 153 C5
Hollow Moor La DL8 62 E7
Holly Bank Gr 3 YO24 227 F2
Hollybank La HG3 161 B6
Holly Bank Rd YO24 227 F2
Hollybush Ave TS17 6 B5
Hollybush Cl DN14 207 A7
Hollybush Gn LS22 188 B8
Holly Cl
Acaster Malbis YO23 191 C8
Firth Moor DL1 3 F4
Full Sutton YO41 169 A2
5 Leeming DL7 63 F3
Thirsk YO7 211 B2
Wrelton YO18 71 C1
Holly Ct 11 HG5 221 B6
Holly Garth 1 YO61 115 F1
Holly Garth Cl TS9 7 F1
Hollygarth La DN14 202 D4
Holly Gr
Selby YO8 232 B3
8 Thorpe Willoughby YO8 197 B2
HOLLY HILL 209 B5
Holly Hill DL10 209 C5
Holly Hill Cl TS7 7 D7
Hollyhocks La LS24 195 F7
Hollyhurst Ave 1 TS4 6 F8
Hollyhurst Rd DL3 3 C6
Hollymead Ct YO8 197 D2
Holly Pk LS17 178 B3
Holly Rd
10 Bedale DL8 63 B3
Boston Spa LS23 188 D8
Holly Terr YO10 228 D1
Holly Tree Croft 2 YO19 184 F7
Holly Tree Ct
5 Hambleton YO8 196 F1
2 Whitby YO21 208 B6
Holly Tree Garth YO32 167 E3
Holly Tree La
Dunnington YO19 184 F7
Haxby YO32 225 D8
Hollytree Way YO8 197 D1
Hollywalk Ave TS6 7 E8
Holly Wlk YO12 212 D7
Hollywood YO8 232 B7
HOLME 88 D5
Holmebeck La HG4 88 B1
Holme Cl
Earby BB18 186 A8
23 Sutton BD20 187 E7
Holme Cres BB8 186 A2
Holme Farm La LS23 188 A5
Holmefield Cl 3 YO8 232 A1
Holmefield Cres HG4 214 C3
Holmefield Ct 2 YO8 232 A1
Holmefield La YO10 229 A1
Holmefield Rd
Glusburn BD20 187 E7
Ripon HG4 214 C3
Holmefields Rd TS6 7 E8
HOLME GREEN 190 F4
Holme Green Rd YO23 190 F4
Holmehead BD24 131 D4
Holme Hill 2 YO11 100 A6
Holme Hill La YO10 184 C4
Holme Ings LS29 175 B4
Holme La
Glusburn BD20 187 E7
Halton East BD23 174 B8
Newbiggin DL8 58 E1
Rudby TS9 25 E7
Selby YO8 232 D6
Holmemead TS9 26 E5
Holme Pk 3 LA2 129 A7
Holmes Ave YO8 232 C6
Holmes Cres YO60 146 E6
Holmes Dr 2 YO19 192 A1
Holmes Ind Est YO8 232 D6
Holme St 12 BB8 186 A3
Holme The TS9 26 E4
Holme View LS29 218 A4
Holmfield HG4 112 D7
Holmfield Cl WF8 201 C2
Holmfield Ct WF8 201 D2
Holmfield La WF8 201 C2
Holm Hill YO13 54 C2
Holm La LA2 130 E6
Holmstead Ave YO21 208 A5
Holmtree La HG4 113 B8
Holmwood Ave TS5 6 F8
Holmwood Sch TS4 7 A7
Holnicote Cl 3 TS17 6 A3
Holray Pk DN14 204 C2
Holroyd Ave YO31 229 A5
HOLTBY 167 F1
Holtby Gr YO12 212 D5
Holtby La
Holtby YO19 167 D1
Stockton on the Forest YO19 226 F2
Holy Family Catholic High Sch DN14 204 C3
Holy Family RC Prim Sch 1 DL3 3 B6
Holyrood Ave DL3 3 A5
Holyrood Cl TS17 6 B8
Holyrood Dr YO30 224 E3
Holy Rood La LS25 201 C8
Holystone Dr TS17 6 A4
Holy Trinity CE Infant Sch HG4 214 B6
Holywell Ave WF10 201 A3
Holywell Gn TS16 5 E5
Holywell Halt BD23 174 A8
Holywell La
Castleford WF10 201 A3
North Cowton DL7 22 C2
Home Croft 1 BD23 134 D2
Home Farm Cl
Hensall DN14 203 D2
Wray-with-Botton LA2 128 A6
Homefield Cl YO23 230 A2
Homelea YO32 167 A6
Homestead Cl
Eggborough DN14 203 A2
2 York YO32 225 F1
Homestead Garth 1 TS17 6 D6
Homestead Rd HG1 219 E2
Honey Pot 5 YO8 199 D7
Honeypot La
Darlington DL3 3 C7
8 Faverdale DL2 3 B7
Honey Pot Rd 2 DL10 41 C6
Honeysuckle Cl
New Micklefield LS25 195 A3
Romanby DL7 210 C1
Selby YO8 232 C2
Honeysuckle Way 20 WF10 200 D3
Honister Gr TS5 6 D7
Honoldu Ct 29 TS17 5 F4
Hood Gr 15 DN14 205 F3
Hood La YO13 54 D2
Hoodstorth La HG3 158 F6
Hookstone Ave HG2 222 E7
Hookstone Chase HG2 220 D2
Hookstone Chase Com Prim Sch HG2 220 D2
Hookstone Cl HG2 220 C2
Hookstone Dr HG2 223 A8
Hookstone Garth HG3 159 E5
Hookstone Grange Ct 3 HG2 220 C2
Hookstone Grange Way 2 HG2 220 C2
Hookstone Oval 7 HG2 220 B1
Hookstone Pk HG2 220 D2
Hookstone Rd HG2 222 E7
Hookstone Way HG2 220 D2
Hookstone Wood Nature Reserve* HG2 223 A3
Hookstone Wood Rd 9 HG2 220 B1
Hope St
30 Filey YO14 101 B3
Knaresborough HG5 221 B5
Scarborough YO12 213 A6
York YO10 233 C1
Hope Terr 7 YO21 208 D5
HOPETOWN 200 C2
Hopetown La DL3 3 C6
HOPGROVE 226 D2
Hopgrove Lane N YO32 226 C3
Hopgrove Lane S YO32 226 E3
Hopper Hill Rd YO11 99 F6
Hopper La LS21 159 C2
HOPPERTON 163 E3
Hopperton St HG5 163 E4
Hopps's Rd 6 BD20 187 E8
Horcum Ct 4 TS8 6 E5
Hornbeam Bsns Pk HG2 223 A7
Hornbeam Cl YO30 225 B2
Hornbeam Cres HG2 222 F8
Hornbeam Park Ave HG2 222 F7
Hornbeam Park Oval HG2 222 F7
Hornbeam Park Rd HG2 222 F7
Hornbeam Park Sta HG2 222 F7
Hornbeam Pk HG2 222 F7
Hornbeam Pk HG2 223 A6
Hornbeam Square N HG2 223 A7
Hornbeam Square S HG2 223 A7
Hornbeam Square W HG2 222 F7
Hornblower Cl 5 HG4 113 D2
HORNBY
Bedale 62 B8
Croft-on-Tees 23 E4
Hornby Castle* DL8 62 C8
Hornby Cl 1 DL2 3 E1
Hornby Ct 5 YO31 229 A5
Hornby Rd
Appleton Wiske DL6 24 A3
Roeburndale LA2 128 A2
Wray-with-Botton LA2 128 A6
Horndale Rd 5 YO14 101 B4
Horner Ave YO61 144 A5
Horner Cl YO61 144 A5
Horne Rd DL9 40 F4
Horner St YO30 228 B7
Horners Terr 13 YO22 208 E6
Horn La BD20 174 B3
Hornsea Rd TS8 6 E5
Hornsey Garth 25 YO32 166 E5
Horse Course La YO17 122 E1
Horsefair 2 YO51 141 B5
Horsefair Sh Ctr LS23 180 C3
HORSEHOUSE 83 C4
Horseman Ave YO23 230 A3
Horseman Cl 2 YO23 230 A3
Horseman Dr YO23 230 A3
Horseman La YO23 230 A3
Horsemarket Rd YO17 215 B4
Horse Mill La HG3 139 D5
Horsemill Sq HG5 221 B5
Horse Rd 12 YO22 208 E6
Horseshoe Cave* BD24 132 A3
Horseshoe Cl DL9 40 F4
Horseshoe The YO24 230 E7
Horseway Gn YO18 49 D4
Horsfield Way YO19 184 F7
Horsman Ave YO10 233 C1
HORTON 171 B5
HORTON IN RIBBLESDALE 105 C3
Horton-in-Ribblesdale Prim Sch BD24 105 D3
Horton-in-Ribbleside Sta BD24 105 C3
Hoskins La TS4 7 A8
Hospital Fields Rd YO10 228 D1
Hospital La YO8 197 B4
Hospital Rd YO17 215 B4
Hospitium The* YO1 233 A3
Hostess La YO18 72 E4
Hotham Ave YO26 227 B2
Hothams Ct YO1 233 C2
Hothfield Junior Sch 5 BD20 174 C1
Hothfield Terr BD23 216 F3
Houghton Ave WF11 201 D2
Houghton Banks 3 TS17 6 D6
HOULSYKE 29 F6
Houndgate DL1 3 C5
Houndsway 6 YO24 230 B8
HOVINGHAM 119 F6
Hovingham CE VC Prim Sch YO62 119 E6
Hovingham Dr
6 Guisborough TS14 8 F7
Scarborough YO12 212 B4
Hovingham Hall* YO62 119 E6
Howard Cl DL10 41 F7
Howard Dr YO30 224 E2
Howard Link YO30 224 D2
Howard Rd
Catterick Garrison DL9 209 E1
Towthorpe YO32 167 B6
Howard St
3 Scarborough YO12 213 A7
York YO10 228 D2
Howden Dike TS15 5 E2
Howden La YO19 231 E1
Howden Rd
4 Barlby YO8 198 B4
Romanby DL7 210 B2
Silsden BD20 174 C1
Howdenshire Way DN14 205 F6
Howdlands La HG4 140 E7
HOWE 88 E3
Howe Ave DL10 41 E4
Howe Bank YO21 29 B7
Howe End YO62 70 B1
Howe Field Rd YO26 142 A2
Howe Hill Bank TS8 7 B2

Howe Hill Cl
Yafforth DL7 .... 43 C1
York YO26 .... 227 E4
Howe Hill La DL10 .... 41 C6
Howe Hill Rd YO26 ...... 227 E4
Howe La YO41 .... 170 A5
Howe Rd
Malton YO17 .... 122 A6
Norton YO17 .... 215 E3
Howes Rd 8 YO14 ...... 127 A8
Howe St YO24 .... 227 D3
Howgate DL8 .... 57 F6
HOWGILL 157 E6
Howgill La
Barden BD23 .... 157 E6
Rimington BB7 .... 171 A1
Howhill Quarry Rd HG3 .. 178 B7
Howhill Rd HG3 .... 178 B8
How Hill Rd HG4 .... 139 B6
Howker La YO61 .... 116 F2
Howlbeck Rd TS14 .... 8 E7
Howldale La
Appleton-le-Moors YO62 ... 70 F4
3 Beadlam YO62 .... 93 D7
Howlett Cl 21 YO61 ...... 143 D8
Howl Gate YO41 .... 185 E8
Howlgate La YO21 .... 13 A1
HOWSHAM 146 F1
Howsham Hall★ YO60 ... 146 F2
Howson La BD24 .... 131 E4
How Stean Gorge★ HG3. 110 B4
Hoxton Rd YO12 .... 212 F6
Hoylake Rd TS4 .... 6 F8
Hoylake Way TS16 .... 5 E4
Hubback Sq 5 DL2 .... 3 A7
HUBBERHOLME 81 C1
Hubert St 2 YO23 ...... 228 B1
HUBY
Harrogate 178 B2
Stillington 144 A4
Huby CE Prim Sch YO61 144 A4
Huby Ct
3 Guisborough TS14 .... 8 F7
York YO10 .... 228 E3
Huby Rd YO61 .... 144 B3
Hudgin La
Lockton YO18 .... 72 E4
Wykeham YO13 .... 98 D4
Hudson Cl
Malton YO17 .... 215 C6
Stamford Bridge YO41 .... 168 D2
2 Tadcaster LS24 .... 189 E6
13 Wetherby LS22 .... 180 C3
Hudson Cres 2 YO30 ... 228 A7
Hudson Rd YO14 .... 127 B8
Hudson St
Whitby YO21 .... 208 D7
6 York YO30 .... 228 C7
Hudson View 1 LS24 ... 189 E6
Hudson Way
Clifton Park YO26 .... 227 C8
Tadcaster LS24 .... 189 E6
HUDSWELL 40 A7
Hudswell La DL10 .... 209 C5
Hugden Cl YO18 .... 96 A6
Hugden Way YO17 ...... 215 F4
Huggate Dikes★ YO42 ... 170 F2
Huggate Hill YO17 ...... 170 E7
Hugh Field La YO8 ...... 199 A8
Hugh Field North La YO8 193 A1
Hugh St WF10 .... 200 E4
Hull Rd
Cliffe YO8 .... 198 E2
Hemingbrough YO8 ...... 199 B1
Osbaldwick YO10 .... 229 D3
York YO10 .... 229 B3
Humber Dr 5 YO32 ..... 167 B6
Humber Rd TS17 .... 6 B7
HUMMERSKNOTT 3 A5
Hummersknott Acad DL3 .. 3 A4
Hummersknott Ave DL3 ... 3 A5
Humphrey Balk La YO7 .. 114 D8
Humphrey Hill DL8 .... 58 D1
Hundale Rd 5 TS15 .... 25 C5
Hunday Field Rd YO51 ... 141 E2
Hundens Day Hospl DL1 ... 3 E5
Hundens La DL1 .... 3 D6
Hungate
Bishop Monkton HG3 ..... 140 A5
Brompton YO13 .... 98 C5
Pickering YO18 .... 95 F6
York YO1 .... 233 C2
Hungate Cl LS24 .... 195 D8
Hungate Ct 11 YO14 ..... 126 F8
Hungate La YO14 .... 126 F8
Hungate Prim Sch 23
LS25 .... 195 F4
Hungate Rd LS25 .... 195 F4
Hunger Hill LS29 .... 218 C7
Hungerhill La YO62 ...... 93 F6
HUNMANBY 126 F8
Hunmanby Ind Est YO14 127 A1
Hunmanby Prim Sch
YO14 .... 126 F8
Hunmanby Rd
Burton Fleming YO25 ..... 126 E3
Reighton YO14 .... 127 C6
Hunmanby St YO14 ...... 100 F2
Hunmanby Sta YO14 .... 127 A7
HUNSINGORE 180 F8
Hunt Ct YO31 .... 233 C3
Hunter Dr YO41 .... 185 A2
Hunters Cl
Dunnington YO19 .... 184 E7
19 Easingwold YO61 ..... 143 C8

Hunters Cl *continued*
10 Haxby YO32 .... 225 C8
4 Hurworth-on-Tees DL2 ... 3 D1
Osgodby YO11 .... 100 B7
Hunters Croft BD23 ..... 156 F1
Hunters Gn
Eaglescliffe TS16 .... 5 D5
Low Dinsdale DL2 .... 4 C3
Hunters Ride DL6 .... 24 B3
Hunters Row 6 YO51 ... 141 B4
Hunter St 8 YO21 ...... 208 D7
Hunters Way
Norton YO17 .... 215 D2
Selby YO8 .... 232 B4
York YO24 .... 230 F7
Hunters Wlk
Barlow YO8 .... 204 D7
Kirk Deighton LS22 ...... 180 C4
Hunters Wood Way 21
YO19 .... 184 F7
Hunt House Rd YO22 ..... 51 B6
HUNTINGTON 225 E3
Huntington Mews YO31 . 228 D7
Huntington Prim Sch
YO32 .... 225 F4
Huntington Rd YO31 .... 233 C4
Huntington Sch YO32 .... 225 E3
Huntington Stadium (York City Knights RLFC) The
YO32 .... 226 A2
HUNTON 61 E7
Hunton & Arrathorne Com Prim Sch DL8 .... 61 F7
Hunton Rd DL9 .... 40 E1
Huntriss Row YO11 ...... 213 A6
Huntsmans La YO41 ..... 168 C2
Huntsman's Wlk YO24 ... 227 B1
Hunt St WF10 .... 200 D4
Hurdle Cl YO17 .... 215 E2
HURGILL 209 A7
Hurgill Rd DL10 .... 209 A7
Hurn Rd YO61 .... 144 A4
Hurns La YO30 .... 224 A7
Hurrell La YO18 .... 96 E5
Hurricane Cl LS25 .... 196 B4
Hurricane Way YO30 ..... 224 E3
Hurrs Rd 3 BD23 .... 217 B4
Hurstleigh Terr HG1 .... 220 A3
Hurst's Yd YO1 .... 233 C2
HURWORTH-ON-TEES 3 E1
HURWORTH PLACE 3 D1
Hurworth Prim Sch DL2 .... 3 E1
Hurworth Rd
Hurworth DL2 .... 3 F1
Hurworth-on-Tees DL2 .... 22 D8
Neasham DL2 .... 4 A1
Hurworth Sch DL2 .... 22 D8
Hussars Ct 6 YO12 ...... 75 F5
Husthwaite CE Prim Sch
YO61 .... 117 B5
Husthwaite Rd
Coxwold YO61 .... 117 D7
Easingwold YO61 .... 117 B2
Hutchinson Dr DL6 ...... 210 E3
Hutchinson St 1 YO8 ... 232 B6
HUT GREEN 203 A2
Hutton Ave DL1 .... 3 E7
Hutton Bank
3 Hutton Rudby TS15 ..... 25 D5
Ripon HG4 .... 214 D7
HUTTON BONVILLE 43 C7
HUTTON BUSCEL 98 E7
Hutton Cl YO26 .... 224 A2
HUTTON CONYERS 114 A4
Hutton Cross Rd YO13 .... 98 E8
HUTTON GATE 8 D6
Hutton Gate HG2 .... 222 D6
HUTTON HANG 61 D3
Hutton La
Guisborough TS14 .... 8 E5
Hutton Conyers HG4 ..... 114 A4
Sharow HG4 .... 214 E8
HUTTON-LE-HOLE 70 C5
HUTTON MULGRAVE 12 D1
Hutton Rae La YO7 ...... 116 D7
HUTTON RUDBY 25 C5
Hutton Rudby Prim Sch
TS15 .... 25 C5
HUTTONS AMBO 147 B6
HUTTON SESSAY 116 D7
Hutton's Mon★ DL11 ..... 39 C6
Hutton St YO26 .... 182 A5
Hutton View Rd HG4 .... 214 C7
HUTTON VILLAGE 8 E4
Hutton Village Rd TS14 .... 8 D5
HUTTON WANDESLEY 182 A5
Hutts La HG4 .... 112 C7
HW Baines Ind Est HG4 . 214 D4
Hyde Park Rd
Harrogate HG1 .... 219 E3
Knaresborough HG5 ..... 221 B8
Hydro Cl LS29 .... 218 F3
Hydro L Ctr The HG2 .... 219 C5
Hydro Ret Pk 219 C5
Hyrst Gr YO31 .... 228 E6

I

I'Anson Cl DL8 .... 60 D6
I'Anson Rd DL10 .... 209 D7
Ian St TS17 .... 6 B8
Ibbetson Cl 16 HG4 .... 86 C3
Iburndale La YO22 .... 32 A6
ICKORNSHAW 187 A6
Iddison Dr DL8 .... 63 A2
Ikin Way YO32 .... 225 F6
ILKLEY 218 B4
Ilkley Gr TS14 .... 8 E5
Ilkley Gram Sch LS29 .... 218 C3
Ilkley Hall Mews 5 LS29 218 B3
Ilkley Hall Pk 4 LS29 ... 218 B3
Ilkley Pool & Lido LS29 .. 218 B5
Ilkley Rd
Addingham LS29 .... 175 A4
Ilkley LS29 .... 176 C1
Ilkley Sta LS29 .... 218 B4
Ilkley Toy Mus★ 9 LS29 . 218 B4
ILTON 85 E1
Ilton Bank HG4 .... 85 E1
Ilton Garth YO30 .... 225 A2
Imperial Ave TS17 .... 6 B8
Ind Est The YO60 .... 145 C4
Ingdale Howl YO62 .... 92 C7
Ingdale La YO7 .... 66 C3
Ing Dene Ave 16 BB8 .... 186 A3
Ing Dene Cl BD23 .... 155 E3
INGERTHORPE 139 C5
Ingfield Cres BD24 ...... 131 D1
Ingfield Est BD24 .... 131 D2
Ingfield La BD24 .... 131 D2
Ingfield Mews BD24 ..... 131 D1
Ingham Cl YO22 .... 32 A6
Ingleborough Ave YO10 . 229 B4
Ingleborough Cave★
LA2 .... 104 D2
Ingleborough Dr 4
BB18 .... 171 D1
Ingleborough National Nature Reserve★ LA6 .. 104 D8
Ingleborough Park Cl 3
LA6 .... 103 D3
Ingleborough Park Dr 2
LA6 .... 103 D3
INGLEBY ARNCLIFFE 45 B8
Ingleby Arncliffe CE Prim Sch
DL6 .... 45 A8
Ingleby Ave TS9 .... 27 B6
INGLEBY BARWICK 6 B4
INGLEBY CROSS 45 A7
Ingleby Dr LS24 .... 189 E6
INGLEBY GREENHOW 27 C5
Ingleby Greenhow CE Prim Sch TS9 .... 27 C5
Ingleby Manor★ TS9 ..... 27 C4
Ingleby Manor Free Sch
TS17 .... 6 C4
Ingleby Mill Prim Sch TS17 6 A3
Ingleby Rd
Great Broughton TS9 ...... 26 E5
Great & Little Broughton TS9 27 A5
Ingleby Way TS17 .... 6 B5
Ingle Cl YO12 .... 212 E1
Inglenook Cl 15 LS25 .... 195 F2
Ingles The 10 LA6 ...... 103 D3
INGLETON 103 D3
Ingleton Dr 16 YO61 .... 143 D8
Ingleton Ind Est LA6 .... 103 D3
Ingleton Prim Sch LA6 .. 103 D3
Ingleton Wlk 3 YO31 ... 229 A5
Ingman Lodge Rd BD24 ... 78 F1
INGMANTHORPE 180 E5
Ingramgate YO7 .... 211 C3
Ingrish La YO23 .... 182 C1
Ings Ave BD23 .... 216 D3
Ings Cl
6 Pickering YO18 .... 95 F6
5 Willerby YO12 .... 99 D2
Ings Com Prim Sch BD23 216 D3
Ings Ct DN14 .... 202 F4
Ings Dr
Low Bradley BD20 .... 173 E3
Mickletown LS26 .... 200 C6
Ings Field Rd YO26 ...... 142 A3
Ingsgarth YO18 .... 95 F6
Ings La
Ainderby Quernhow YO7 ... 88 D4
Beal DN14 .... 202 D4
Bishop Monkton HG3 ..... 140 B5
Bishop Wilton YO42 ..... 169 D2
Bradleys Both BD20 ..... 173 E3
Brompton YO13 .... 98 C4
Carlton DN14 .... 204 E2
Cawood YO19 .... 197 D8
Cononley BD20 .... 173 D2
Cottingwith YO42 .... 193 C5
Crakehall DL8 .... 62 F5
Ebberston & Yedingham
YO13 .... 97 E4
Great Preston WF10 ..... 200 E6
Harome YO62 .... 93 D4
Hensall DN14 .... 203 D2
Husthwaite YO61 .... 117 A6
Hutton Buscel YO13 ...... 99 A3
Kellington DN14 .... 202 F4
21 Kirkbymoorside YO62 ... 70 B1
Kirkbymoorside YO62 ..... 94 B7
Lastingham YO62 .... 70 F5
Lillings Ambo YO32 ..... 145 C2
Nether Poppleton YO26 .. 224 B1
Pickering YO18 .... 95 E4
Riccall YO19 .... 197 E8
Roundhill Village TS15 ..... 5 D2
Skipton BD23 .... 216 D2
Snape with Thorp DL8 .... 87 B7
Stillington YO61 .... 144 A6
Thorganby YO19 .... 193 B5
Thorp Arch LS23 .... 189 A8
Tollerton YO61 .... 143 B2
Welburn YO62 .... 94 A5
Wheldrake YO19 .... 193 B7
Wighill LS24 .... 189 D8
4 Willerby YO12 .... 99 D2
Wistow YO8 .... 198 A6
Ings Mere Ct WF11 ...... 201 C6

Ings Rd
Cliffe YO8 .... 198 D2
Dunsforths YO26 .... 142 A3
Thorganby YO19 .... 193 B4
Ulleskelf LS24 .... 190 C3
West Ayton YO13 .... 99 B6
Wilberfoss YO41 .... 185 E6
Ings Terr YO22 .... 31 C4
Ings View
2 Bedale DL8 .... 63 B3
Castleford WF10 .... 201 A4
Mickletown LS26 .... 200 C6
Tollerton YO61 .... 143 A2
York YO30 .... 224 D2
Ingthorne La LS25 ...... 195 F1
Ingthorns La LS25 ...... 195 F1
Ingthorpe La
Martons Both BD23 ..... 171 E7
Monk Fryston LS25 ...... 196 A1
Inhams La YO26 .... 141 F2
INHOLMES 189 C6
Inholmes La
Tadcaster LS24 .... 189 D6
Walton LS23 .... 181 B2
Inman Gr HG5 .... 221 B8
Inman Terr YO26 .... 227 D4
Inman Wlk HG5 .... 221 B8
In Moor La HG3 .... 109 F6
Innisfree Cl HG2 .... 220 B1
Innovation Cl YO10 ..... 229 B2
Innovation Way YO10 .... 229 B2
Institute St 4 BD20 .... 187 E7
Intake Ave YO30 .... 228 C8
Intakefield Rd YO8 ..... 199 D7
Intake La
Acaster Malbis YO23 .... 191 C7
Beal WF11 .... 202 D5
Dunnington YO19 .... 184 F7
Grassington BD23 .... 134 E3
Habton YO17 .... 121 E7
Heck DN14 .... 207 C8
Tollerton YO61 .... 143 B4
West Haddlesey YO8 .... 202 F6
Intake The
3 Kippax LS25 .... 194 D1
Osgodby YO11 .... 100 B7
Invicta Ct YO24 .... 230 B8
IREBY 102 F6
Ireby Rd LA6 .... 102 F3
Ireton St 3 YO12 .... 212 E5
Iron Row LS29 .... 176 C1
IRTON 99 D6
Irton Moor La YO12 ..... 212 A1
Irvine Way YO24 .... 230 B7
Irwin Ave YO31 .... 228 E6
Isabella Rd LS25 .... 194 D5
Island Heritage★ HG4 ... 111 B8
Islebeck La YO7 .... 115 F8
IVELET 36 D5
Iver Cl YO26 .... 227 C5
Ivy Bank Ct 4 YO13 ...... 75 D5
Ivy Cl
Carlton DN14 .... 204 C2
Follifoot HG3 .... 223 F4
2 Leeming DL7 .... 63 F3
Marton YO51 .... 141 D1
Ivy Cotts DL7 .... 210 D4
Ivy Cres
Newton-le-Willows DL8 .... 62 B4
Newton-le-Willows DL8 .... 62 B4
Ivy Ct LS29 .... 218 B3
Ivy Dene Cl 26 BD24 .... 131 D2
Ivy House Cl 6 YO11 .... 100 B6
Ivy House Gdns BD23 .... 155 D1
Ivy La LS23 .... 188 E8
Ivy Pl
22 Cross Hills BD20 ..... 187 E8
York YO32 .... 225 D3
Ivy Yd 16 YO22 .... 208 E6

J

Jack Field La BD20 ..... 187 D6
Jack Hill La LS21 .... 176 F6
Jack Hole YO61 .... 142 F4
Jack La
Crayke YO61 .... 118 A1
Stillington YO61 .... 144 C7
Wigglesworth BD23 ..... 153 C4
Jackson Cl YO11 .... 100 B6
Jackson Dr TS9 .... 26 C8
Jackson La YO41 .... 185 E4
Jackson's La
Bradleys Both BD20 ..... 173 F3
Eastfield YO11 .... 100 A8
Kirk Smeaton WF8 ...... 206 A4
Scarborough YO11 ...... 213 A1
Jackson St
24 Glusburn BD20 ...... 187 E7
York YO31 .... 233 C4
Jackson's Wlk
Askham Richard YO23 .... 182 D2
Askham Richard YO23 .... 182 D3
Jacobi Cl YO30 .... 228 A7
Jacques Gr BD20 .... 174 C1
Jaffa Rd DL9 .... 209 E2
Jagger La DL10 .... 20 E6
Jagoe Rd 8 BB18 .... 172 A1
James Backhouse Pl
YO24 .... 227 E3
James Cl LS25 .... 194 D4
James Cook Univ Hospl The
TS4 .... 7 B8
James Ct DL10 .... 209 F7
James La DL10 .... 41 A2
James Nicolson Link
YO30 .... 225 A2

Jameson Cres YO12 ..... 212 D5
James Pl 2 YO12 .... 213 A6
James St
Castleford WF10 .... 200 E5
20 Earby BB18 .... 172 A1
10 Glusburn BD20 ...... 187 E8
Harrogate HG1 .... 219 D2
Scarborough YO12 ...... 213 A6
Selby YO8 .... 232 C5
York YO10 .... 228 E4
Jamesville Way YO7 .... 115 B6
James Way YO10 .... 229 A1
Jamieson Terr YO23 .... 228 B1
Janesway LS25 .... 194 C1
Janet's Foss★ BD23 ..... 133 B2
Jasmine Cl
5 Snaith DN14 .... 204 C1
York YO32 .... 225 D2
Jasmine Fields 1 TS15 ... 24 F8
Jasmine Garth 6 YO41 .. 185 C2
Jasmine Gdns 13 WF10 .. 200 D3
Jasper La HG3 .... 179 A3
Jay Ave TS17 .... 6 B4
Jaywick Cl YO32 .... 167 B8
Jedburgh Dr DL3 .... 2 F7
Jedwell Cl YO32 .... 225 D5
Jeffry Bog Nature Reserve★
YO60 .... 147 C5
Jenkins Fold
Ingleton LA6 .... 103 D3
Thornton in Lonsdale LA6 . 103 D3
Jennifer Gr 4 YO24 ..... 227 F2
JENNYFIELD 219 A5
Jenny Field Dr HG3 ..... 219 B4
Jenny Frisk Rd TS12 ...... 9 E6
Jenny Gill Cres BD23 .... 217 B3
Jenny La DN14 .... 207 B5
Jerry Carr Bank YO62 .... 92 B1
Jerry Croft 2 BD23 ..... 217 A4
Jerry La BD20 .... 174 F1
Jersey Ct YO12 .... 99 C7
Jervaulx Abbey★ HG4 .... 85 D8
Jervaulx Dr HG5 .... 221 D4
Jervaulx Rd DL7 .... 64 A6
Jervis Ct YO41 .... 185 C1
Jervis Rd YO24 .... 230 E8
Jesmond Ct YO17 .... 215 E3
Jesmond Gr 5 TS18 .... 5 E8
Jesmond Rd
Darlington DL1 .... 3 F7
Harrogate HG1 .... 220 A3
Jessamine Pl 1 BD20 ... 187 F7
Jesse Cl YO8 .... 232 E2
Jewbury YO31 .... 233 C3
Jewitt La LS22 .... 188 B8
Jew Leys La YO23 .... 190 E3
Jin Whin Ct WF10 ...... 200 D4
Jin-Whin Hill WF10 ..... 200 C4
Jobbing Cross YO61 ..... 116 C3
Jockey La
Huntington YO32 .... 225 F2
5 Knaresborough HG5 ... 221 A6
Joffre Ave WF10 .... 200 F3
John Breckon Rd YO21 ... 28 D5
John Dixon La DL1 .... 3 D5
John Fowler Way 14 DL2 .. 3 A7
John of Gaunt's Castle★
HG3 .... 160 B1
John Smiths Brewery★
LS24 .... 189 E6
Johnson Cl
Brompton on Swale DL10 .. 41 C7
1 Thirsk YO7 .... 211 C3
Johnson St YO8 .... 232 B6
Johnson Way YO7 .... 211 D2
John St
Darlington DL1 .... 3 D6
11 Earby BB18 .... 172 A1
35 Filey YO14 .... 101 B3
Great Ayton TS9 .... 8 A2
11 Harrogate HG1 .... 219 D2
Selby YO8 .... 232 D6
Whitby YO21 .... 208 D7
York YO31 .... 228 E6
John Ward Cl 31 YO41 ... 168 D2
Jolby La
Cleasby DL10 .... 2 E1
Croft-on-Tees DL2 .... 22 B8
Newton Morrell DL2 ...... 21 F8
Jonah's La HG3 .... 160 B1
Jonathan Garth 17 LS29 . 174 F4
Jorvik Cl YO26 .... 227 C5
JORVIK Viking Ctr★ YO1 233 C2
Joseph Rowntree Sch
YO32 .... 225 E5
Jowett's La BD20 .... 174 B4
Jowland Winn La YO8 ... 204 A4
Jubber Gate YO1 .... 233 B2
Jubilee Bank TS7 .... 7 C8
Jubilee Cave★ BD24 ..... 131 F4
Jubilee Cl BD23 .... 216 D3
Jubilee Croft 1 BD23 .... 153 F5
Jubilee Ct
Richmond DL10 .... 209 E8
6 Tollerton YO61 .... 143 B3
Wigginton YO32 .... 225 D8
Jubilee Gdns DL6 .... 210 F3
Jubilee Rd
18 Bedale DL8 .... 63 B3
Norton YO17 .... 215 E3
Wistow YO8 .... 197 D6
Jubilee Terr YO26 ...... 227 F5
Judson Cl HG4 .... 214 C4
Julia Ave YO32 .... 226 B2
JUNCTION 187 F8
Junction 32 Sh Village★
WF10 .... 200 F3

Junction Farm Prim Sch TS16 ... 5 D5
Jungle (Castleford Tigers RFC) The WF10 ... 200 F5
Juniper Cl YO32 ... 225 D3
Juniper Dr YO8 ... 232 D2
Juniper Gr TS21 ... 5 C8
Juniper Way 23 HG3 ... 161 B3
Jura Dr DL1 ... 3 E8
Jute Rd YO26 ... 227 B5
Jutland Rd DL9 ... 209 C2

K

Kader Ave TS5 ... 6 D7
Kader Prim Sch TS5 ... 6 E7
Kail La BD23 ... 156 F8
Kangel Cl HG4 ... 214 E3
Kareen Ave 3 YO12 ... 99 E6
Kathryn Ave YO32 ... 226 A2
Kaye Dr YO8 ... 198 B4
Kay House La TS15 ... 24 D5
Kays Bank YO61 ... 117 C5
Kearby Cliff LS22 ... 179 B1
Kearsley Cl TS16 ... 5 E7
Kearsley Rd HG4 ... 214 B7
Kearton DL11 ... 37 D6
KEASDEN ... 130 A5
Keasden Rd LA2 ... 130 A3
Keats Cl
4 Pontefract WF8 ... 201 B1
York YO30 ... 227 F8
Keats Wlk HG1 ... 219 E7
Keble Cl YO23 ... 231 B3
Keble Dr YO23 ... 231 A2
Keble Garth LS25 ... 194 E1
Keble Gdns YO23 ... 231 B2
Keble Park Cres YO23 ... 231 A2
Keble Park N YO23 ... 231 A3
Keble Park S YO23 ... 231 A2
Keeper's Cl YO61 ... 118 A1
Keepers Gate 18 YO18 ... 95 F6
Keeper's Hill YO25 ... 150 A1
Keepers Way 11 YO19 ... 184 F7
Keesbury Pk 10 YO8 ... 197 B8
Keighley Rd
Bradleys Both BD23 ... 173 D3
1 Colne BB8 ... 186 A3
Cowling BD22 ... 187 B6
2 Glusburn BD20 ... 187 F7
Ilkley LS29 ... 218 A2
Laneshaw Bridge BB8 ... 186 D3
Skipton BD23 ... 216 F2
Trawden Forest BB8 ... 186 B3
Keilder Rise TS8 ... 6 F5
Keith Ave YO32 ... 226 A4
Keith Rd TS4 ... 6 F8
KELBROOK ... 186 A8
Kelbrook Prim Sch BB18 186 A7
Kelbrook Rd BB18 ... 171 D1
Kelcbar Cl LS24 ... 189 D6
Kelcbar Hill LS24 ... 189 D6
Kelcbar Way LS24 ... 189 D6
Kelcow Caves* BD24 ... 131 D3
KELD ... 35 E8
Keldale 4 YO32 ... 166 F5
Keldale Gdns HG4 ... 214 F6
Keld Cl
Melmerby HG4 ... 114 B6
Pickering YO18 ... 95 E7
Scalby YO12 ... 212 B8
Keldgate Rd YO18 ... 72 A3
Keldhead YO18 ... 95 E8
Keld Head Orch 1 YO62 ... 70 B1
Keld Head Rd YO62 ... 70 A1
Keldheads La DL8 ... 59 F5
KELDHOLME ... 70 D1
KELD HOUSES ... 136 C2
Keld La
Hutton-le-Hole YO62 ... 70 C5
Newton YO18 ... 72 A5
Thorpe Bassett YO17 ... 123 A3
Keld Runnels Rd YO13 ... 75 A4
KELFIELD ... 191 D1
Kelfield Rd 9 YO19 ... 197 F8
Kellaw Rd DL1 ... 3 F5
Kell Bank HG4 ... 85 E3
Kell Bank CE Prim Sch HG4 ... 85 E3
Kell Beck 1 LS21 ... 176 F1
KELLINGLEY ... 202 C2
KELLINGTON ... 202 F4
Kellington Ct 9 DN14 ... 202 F2
Kellington La DN14 ... 202 F2
Kellington Prim Sch
HutGreen DN14 ... 203 A3
Kellington DN14 ... 202 F3
Kell Syke La BD23 ... 155 A6
Kelvin Terr DL7 ... 210 D4
Kemmel Cl DL9 ... 40 E2
Kempton Cl 2 YO24 ... 227 D1
Kempton Ct 15 DL1 ... 3 F6
Kendal Cl
6 Dunnington YO19 ... 184 F7
Hellifield BD23 ... 154 B3
Kendal Dr WF10 ... 201 B4
Kendal Gdns YO26 ... 181 D7
Kendal La YO26 ... 181 D7
Kendalmans 4 BD24 ... 131 D2
Kendal Rd
Harrogate HG1 ... 220 B3
Long Preston BD23 ... 154 A3
Kendrew Cl
11 Bedale DL8 ... 63 A2
3 York YO32 ... 225 F3
Kenilworth Ave HG2 ... 222 D7
Kenilworth Dr 3 BB18 ... 172 A1
Kenlay Cl YO32 ... 225 D4
Kennedy Dr 32 YO32 ... 166 E5
Kennels La LS14 ... 188 A4
Kenneth Campbell Rd HG1 ... 219 E2
Kennet La LS25 ... 194 D3
Kennion Ct 2 HG2 ... 220 B3
Kennion Rd HG2 ... 220 B3
KENNYTHORPE ... 147 F5
Kenrick Pl 5 YO26 ... 227 B5
Kensal Rise YO10 ... 228 D2
Kensington Ave
Eston & South Bank TS6 ... 7 E8
Thorner LS14 ... 188 A3
Kensington Ct 1 YO24 ... 230 F8
Kensington Gdns DL1 ... 3 E5
Kensington Rd YO30 ... 224 D2
Kensington Sq 10 HG2 ... 219 C2
Kensington St YO23 ... 228 B1
Kent Ave HG1 ... 219 B3
Kent Cl HG4 ... 214 A2
Kent Ct 7 DL9 ... 209 C1
Kent Dr HG1 ... 219 B3
Kentmere Dr YO30 ... 224 F1
Kenton Cl 4 TS18 ... 5 E8
Kent Rd
Guisborough TS14 ... 8 E5
Harrogate HG1 ... 219 B3
Selby YO8 ... 232 A6
Kent Rise HG1 ... 219 A2
Kent Road N HG1 ... 219 B3
Kent St YO10 ... 233 C1
Kenwood Cr TS17 ... 6 A5
KEPWICK ... 66 C6
Kerrside YO30 ... 227 E8
Kershaw Ave WF10 ... 201 A4
Kerver La YO19 ... 184 F7
Kesteven Rd TS4 ... 7 A7
Kestrel Dr 7 DL9 ... 40 F2
Kestrel Mews 21 WF6 ... 200 A1
Kestrel View 2 YO12 ... 99 E6
Kestrel Wood Way YO31 ... 225 F2
Keswick Dr WF10 ... 201 C5
Keswick Gr
4 Darlington DL1 ... 3 D4
Middlesbrough TS5 ... 6 D7
Keswick Way 5 YO32 ... 225 F5
Kettle End DL10 ... 21 C7
KETTLENESS ... 12 D6
Kettlesbeck Brow LA2 ... 130 C5
KETTLESING ... 160 C3
KETTLESING BOTTOM ... 160 D4
Kettlesing Felliscliffe Prim Sch HG3 ... 160 C4
Kettle Spring La HG3 ... 139 B1
Kettlestring La YO30 ... 225 A3
KETTLEWELL ... 108 B3
Kettlewell La DL8 ... 57 A5
Kettlewell Prim Sch BD23 ... 108 A3
Kew at Castle Howard* YO60 ... 146 C8
KEXBY ... 185 C6
Kexby Ave YO10 ... 228 F3
Kexby Stray YO41 ... 185 A5
Kex Gill Rd BD23 ... 158 D1
KEY GREEN ... 31 A3
Key La YO61 ... 118 A1
Keys Beck Rd YO18 ... 71 F8
Keystone Ave 3 WF10 ... 200 F3
Key Way YO19 ... 231 F5
Khyber Pass YO21 ... 208 D7
Kiddal La LS15 ... 188 C2
Kidstones Bank DL8 ... 81 E3
Kielder Dr DL1 ... 3 E7
Kielder Oval HG2 ... 220 D2
KILBURN ... 91 B2
Kilburn Rd YO10 ... 228 D2
KILDALE ... 27 E8
Kildale Sta YO21 ... 27 E8
Kildare Garth 5 YO62 ... 70 C1
KILDWICK ... 187 F8
Kildwick CE Prim Sch BD20 ... 187 F8
Kilgram La HG4 ... 85 E8
Kilham Rd YO25 ... 151 D5
KILLERBY ... 100 C5
Killerby Dr 2 DL10 ... 41 E4
Killerby La YO11 ... 100 C5
KILLINGHALL ... 161 C5
Killinghall CE Prim Sch HG3 ... 161 C5
Killin Rd DL1 ... 3 E7
Kilmarnock Rd DL1 ... 3 E8
Kiln Dr BD23 ... 134 B3
Kilners Croft 11 LS29 ... 174 F4
Kiln Hill La
Lawkland LA2 ... 131 A6
Silsden BD20 ... 174 A3
Kiln La
Wray LA2 ... 128 A6
Wray-with-Botton LA2 ... 128 A6
KILNSEY ... 134 B6
Kilnsey Fold BD20 ... 174 A1
Kilnsey Pk* BD23 ... 134 B6
Kilnwick Ct DL7 ... 210 D3
Kilton Ct DL11 ... 2 A2
Kilton La TS12 ... 9 F7
KILTON THORPE ... 10 B8
Kilton Thorpe La TS12 ... 10 B8
Kimberley St LS29 ... 218 C5
Kimberlows Wood Hill 3 YO10 ... 229 C3
Kinbrace Dr YO24 ... 230 B7
King Edward Ave WF10 ... 200 C7
King Edward Rd HG4 ... 214 C3
King Edward's Dr HG1 ... 219 D5
King Edward St
27 Glusburn BD20 ... 187 E7
Normanton South WF6 ... 200 A1
Kingfisher Cl 7 YO12 ... 99 F6
Kingfisher Ct
22 Castleford WF10 ... 200 A1
3 Scotton DL9 ... 40 F2
Kingfisher Dr
3 Bedale DL8 ... 63 B3
Guisborough TS14 ... 8 D6
14 Pickering YO18 ... 95 F6
Whitby YO22 ... 208 E3
Kingfisher La LS25 ... 194 F8
Kingfisher Reach
17 Boroughbridge YO51 ... 141 B5
5 Collingham LS22 ... 180 A1
King Garth 3 DL8 ... 58 F1
King George Rd 1 HG4 ... 214 C3
King Hill YO14 ... 101 A2
King James Rd HG5 ... 221 B5
King James's Sch HG5 ... 221 B5
King Rudding Cl 6 YO19 198 A8
King Rudding La YO19 ... 198 B8
King's Acad The TS8 ... 7 A5
Kings Acre YO31 ... 229 B6
Kings Arms Ct YO7 ... 211 B3
Kings Ave 2 LS29 ... 218 A4
Kings Cl
5 Barlby YO8 ... 198 B5
19 Ilkley LS29 ... 175 C2
15 Pateley Bridge HG3 ... 137 B4
King's Cl 8 DL10 ... 41 D5
Kingsclere YO32 ... 225 F6
Kings Ct YO1 ... 233 B2
King's Gate LA2 ... 130 D3
King's Gdns YO7 ... 211 B1
Kings Keld Bank DL8 ... 86 F8
Kings La YO13 ... 97 D5
Kingsland Terr 11 YO26 ... 227 F5
Kings Lea YO8 ... 199 A8
Kingsley Ave WF11 ... 201 D3
Kingsley Cl HG1 ... 220 C3
Kingsley Croft 7 BD20 ... 187 F8
Kingsley Dr
Castleford WF10 ... 201 B3
Harrogate HG1 ... 220 A4
2 Middleham DL8 ... 60 E2
Kingsley Park Mews 1 HG1 ... 220 C3
Kingsley Park Rd HG1 ... 220 C3
Kingsley Rd
Harrogate HG1 ... 220 B5
Trawden Forest BB8 ... 186 B3
Kings Mdws YO7 ... 89 E3
Kings Mead HG4 ... 214 B7
Kings Mill La 8 BD24 ... 131 D2
Kings Moor Rd YO32 ... 167 D2
King's Mount 2 WF11 ... 201 D3
Kings Rd
Ilkley LS29 ... 218 A4
Knaresborough HG5 ... 221 C6
King's Rd 6 HG1 ... 219 D3
King's Sq YO1 ... 233 C2
King's St 7 BD23 ... 217 B4
King's Staith YO1 ... 233 B2
King St
Castleford WF10 ... 200 F3
6 Cawood YO8 ... 197 B8
7 High Bentham LA2 ... 129 A8
Hopperton LS22 ... 163 E3
Muston YO14 ... 100 F2
Normanton South WF6 ... 200 A1
Pateley Bridge HG3 ... 137 B4
Richmond DL10 ... 209 C6
Ripon HG4 ... 214 C4
Scarborough YO11 ... 213 A6
3 Silsden BD20 ... 174 C1
York YO1 ... 233 B2
Kingsthorpe YO24 ... 227 D2
Kingsthorpe Pk 11 YO8 ... 197 D6
Kingston Ave HG4 ... 214 C3
Kingston Cres YO8 ... 196 E2
Kingston Dr
24 Castleford WF6 ... 200 B1
Hambleton YO8 ... 196 E1
16 Normanton WF6 ... 200 B1
Norton YO17 ... 215 E2
Kingston Garth 2 YO22 ... 33 C3
Kingston Gr 5 YO12 ... 212 B7
Kingstonia Gdns 3 HG4 ... 214 C3
Kingstonia Pl HG4 ... 214 C2
Kingsway
Garforth LS25 ... 194 B3
Harrogate HG1 ... 219 E3
Pontefract WF8 ... 201 B2
Scalby YO12 ... 212 C8
Skipton BD23 ... 217 B5
6 Stamford Bridge YO41 168 D2
Weeton LS17 ... 178 B2
Kingsway Dr
Harrogate HG1 ... 219 E2
4 Ilkley LS29 ... 218 A4
Kingsway Garth LS25 ... 194 B3
Kingsway N YO30 ... 228 B7
Kingsway W YO24 ... 227 D1
Kingswood Gr YO24 ... 227 D3
Kinloss Cl TS17 ... 6 C7
Kinsey Cave* BD24 ... 131 C4
Kintyre Dr TS17 ... 6 B6
KIPLIN ... 42 B4
Kiplin Dr 13 DN6 ... 206 E2
Kipling Dr 35 DL9 ... 41 A5
Kipling Gr WF8 ... 201 B2
Kiplin Hall* DL10 ... 42 B4
KIPPAX ... 194 E1
Kippax Ash Tree Prim Sch LS25 ... 194 D1
Kippax Greenfield Prim Sch LS25 ... 194 D1
Kippax L Ctr LS25 ... 200 D8
Kippax North Jun & Inf Sch LS25 ... 194 C2
KIRBY GRINDALYTHE ... 149 E6
KIRBY HILL
Boroughbridge ... 141 B7
Moulton ... 20 A5
Kirby Hill CE Prim Sch YO51 ... 141 B7
KIRBY KNOWLE ... 66 C2
Kirby La
Ebberston & Yedingham YO17 ... 97 E1
Sledmere YO25 ... 150 A4
KIRBY MISPERTON ... 95 D2
Kirby Misperton La YO17 121 C7
Kirby Misperton Rd YO17 . 95 F2
KIRBY SIGSTON ... 44 D1
KIRBY UNDERDALE ... 170 A5
KIRBY WISKE ... 88 F8
Kir Cres YO24 ... 227 C3
Kirk Balk YO17 ... 169 E8
Kirk Balk La YO60 ... 168 B7
Kirk Bank
Conistone with Kilnsey BD23 ... 134 B4
Kirkby Malzeard HG4 ... 112 A5
Kirkbank La CA17 ... 14 A8
Kirkbride Way TS17 ... 5 F5
KIRKBRIDGE ... 62 F5
KIRKBY ... 26 D5
Kirkby Ave
Ripon HG4 ... 214 A6
Selby YO8 ... 232 B7
Kirkby Brow
Kirkby Malham BD23 ... 154 F8
Malham BD23 ... 132 F1
Kirkby Cl HG4 ... 214 A6
Kirkby Dr HG4 ... 214 A6
KIRKBY FLEETHAM ... 42 D1
Kirkby Fleetham CE Prim Sch DL7 ... 42 C1
Kirkby & Great Broughton CE Prim Sch TS9 ... 26 E5
Kirkby La
Gillamoor YO62 ... 70 A3
Kearby with Netherby HG3 179 B2
Kirkby Fleetham with Fencote DL7 ... 42 C2
Kirkby TS9 ... 26 D6
Sicklinghall LS22 ... 179 D3
KIRKBY MALHAM ... 154 F8
Kirkby Malham Prim Sch BD23 ... 154 F8
KIRKBY MALZEARD ... 112 D5
Kirkby Malzeard CE Prim Sch HG4 ... 112 D5
KIRKBY MILLS ... 94 C8
Kirkby Mills Ind Est YO62. 94 C8
KIRKBYMOORSIDE ... 70 B1
Kirkbymoorside Com Prim Sch YO62 ... 70 A1
KIRKBY OVERBLOW ... 179 A4
Kirkby Rd
North Stainley with Sleningford HG4 ... 113 C4
Ripon HG4 ... 214 A6
Selby YO8 ... 232 B7
KIRKBY WHARFE ... 190 A3
Kirkcaldy Fold WF6 ... 200 B1
Kirkcroft YO32 ... 225 C8
Kirkdale La YO62 ... 93 F8
Kirkdale Rd YO10 ... 229 D4
Kirkdale Way HG2 ... 219 C1
KIRK DEIGHTON ... 180 B5
Kirk Fenton Parochial CE VC Prim Sch LS24 ... 196 B8
Kirkfield Ave LS14 ... 188 A3
Kirkfield Cres LS14 ... 188 A3
Kirkfield La LS14 ... 188 A3
Kirkfield Rd DL3 ... 3 D8
Kirkgate
9 Glusburn BD20 ... 187 F8
Knaresborough HG5 ... 221 A6
7 Middleham DL8 ... 60 E2
12 Ripon HG4 ... 214 C5
Settle BD24 ... 131 D2
Sherburn in Elmet LS25 ... 195 E4
Silsden BD20 ... 174 C1
Thirsk YO7 ... 211 B3
Kirk Gate
Brompton YO13 ... 98 C7
Silpho YO13 ... 74 E6
Kirkgate La YO62 ... 70 F4
KIRKHAM ... 147 A4
Kirkham Ave 1 YO31 ... 228 E8
Kirkham Bridge* YO60 ... 146 F4
Kirkham Cl 6 YO21 ... 208 C6
Kirkham Ct 5 HG5 ... 221 C4
Kirkham Gr HG1 ... 219 F6
KIRK HAMMERTON ... 164 C2
Kirk Hammerton CE Prim Sch YO26 ... 164 C2
Kirk Hammerton La YO26 ... 164 C3
Kirkham Mews 12 YO8 ... 197 D6
Kirkham Pl HG1 ... 219 F6
Kirkham Priory (rems of)* YO60 ... 146 F4
Kirkham Rd
Harrogate HG1 ... 219 F6
Middlesbrough TS7 ... 7 D6
Whitby YO21 ... 208 C6
Kirkham View YO60 ... 147 B4
Kirkhaw La WF11 ... 201 D4
Kirk Hills LS14 ... 188 A3
Kirk Ings La YO7 ... 66 B7
Kirk La
Embsay with Eastby BD23 ... 217 E8
Tockwith YO26 ... 181 C7
Kirkland Cl YO8 ... 232 D4
Kirklands YO32 ... 167 B6
Kirklands La YO41 ... 169 C2
Kirkleavington Hall Dr TS15 ... 5 E1
KIRKLEVINGTON ... 24 F8
Kirklevington Prim Sch TS15 ... 24 F8
KIRKLINGTON ... 88 A4
Kirk Rd
Eaglescliffe TS15 ... 5 F2
Northallerton DL7 ... 210 B3
KIRK SMEATON ... 206 B3
Kirk Smeaton CE Prim Sch WF8 ... 206 B3
Kirkstall Dr BB18 ... 171 E2
Kirkstone Dr YO31 ... 229 A6
Kirkstone Rd HG1 ... 220 B4
Kirk Syke La BD23 ... 155 A5
Kirk View 1 YO26 ... 227 C3
Kirkwell YO23 ... 231 A4
Kitchen Dr YO8 ... 232 D4
Kitchener Cl YO8 ... 232 B5
Kitchener Rd
Ripon HG4 ... 113 D3
Scotton DL9 ... 40 E4
Kitchener St
Selby YO8 ... 232 B6
York YO31 ... 228 D7
Kitemere Pl 2 YO24 ... 230 B8
Kit La BD20 ... 174 B3
Kitter La YO21 ... 31 C8
Kitty Garth YO19 ... 193 A7
Kitty Hill (Tumulus)* YO41 ... 169 E3
Knapping Hill HG1 ... 219 C5
KNAPTON ... 227 A5
Knapton Cl 1 YO32 ... 167 B6
Knapton La YO26 ... 227 B4
Knapton Wold Rd YO17 .. 123 C5
KNARESBOROUGH ... 221 A6
Knaresborough Ave TS7 ... 7 B5
Knaresborough Castle* HG5 ... 221 A5
Knaresborough House & Gdns* HG5 ... 221 A6
Knaresborough Mus* HG5 ... 221 A5
Knaresborough Rd
Bishop Monkton HG3 ... 140 B4
Follifoot HG3 ... 223 F5
Harrogate HG1 ... 219 F2
Little Ribston LS22 ... 180 A8
Ripon HG4 ... 214 C3
Knaresborough Sta HG5 ... 221 A6
Knaresborough Swimming Pool HG5 ... 221 B5
Knaresborough Technology Pk HG5 ... 221 D5
KNAVESMIRE ... 231 A7
Knavesmire Cl YO62 ... 93 C5
Knavesmire Cres YO23 .. 228 B1
Knavesmire Prim Sch YO23 ... 228 B1
Knavesmire Rd
Nunthorpe YO23 ... 231 B8
York YO23 ... 228 A1
KNAYTON ... 65 F2
Knayton CE Prim Sch YO7 ... 65 E3
KNEDLINGTON ... 205 E6
Kneeton Cl DL10 ... 21 C5
Kneeton La DL10 ... 21 C5
Knightsway LS25 ... 194 B3
Knipe Point Dr 8 YO11 ... 100 B8
Knolls Cl 11 YO11 ... 100 B7
Knolls La YO62 ... 67 F5
Knoll The
3 Bramham LS23 ... 188 E6
York YO24 ... 227 B2
Knot La BB7 ... 171 A5
KNOTTINGLEY ... 201 F3
Knottingley Rd WF8 ... 201 D1
Knottingley St Botolphs CE Acad 28 WF11 ... 202 A2
Knottingley Sta WF11 ... 201 F2
Knott La
Easingwold YO61 ... 143 C8
Steeton with Eastburn BD20 ... 187 F7
Knotto Bottom Cl DL6 ... 210 F3
Knotto Bottom Way DL6. 210 F3
Knott Rd YO18 ... 49 D5
Knotts La BD23 ... 152 E1
Knowle La
Ilton-cum-Pott HG4 ... 85 D1
Kirkby Knowle YO7 ... 66 C2
Knowles Cl 5 TS15 ... 24 E8
KNOX ... 219 B7
Knox Ave HG1 ... 219 C5
Knox Chase HG1 ... 219 C6
Knox Cl HG1 ... 219 D6
Knox Dr HG1 ... 219 C6
Knox Gdns HG1 ... 219 C6
Knox Gr HG1 ... 219 C6
Knox La
Harrogate HG1 ... 219 D6
Scarborough YO11 ... 213 B1
Knox Mill Bank HG3 ... 219 B7

Knox Mill Cl HG3 219 B7
Knox Mill La HG3 219 B7
Knox Pk HG3 219 B7
Knox Rd HG1 219 D6
Knox Rise HG1 219 C6
Knox Way HG1 219 C5
Kyle Cl 3 YO61 143 B3
Kyle Way YO26 227 B8
Kyme Castle* LS24 189 C7
Kyme St YO1 233 B1

L

La Bassee Rd DL9 209 D1
Laburnum Ave
Fylingdales YO22 33 C4
Thornaby TS17 6 B7
Laburnum Cl
Rufforth YO23 182 C6
3 Thorpe Willoughby YO8 197 B1
Laburnum Ct
Barlow YO8 204 D7
1 Castleford WF10 200 F3
Laburnum Dr HG3 140 A5
Laburnum Farm Cl YO26 182 C8
Laburnum Garth 6 YO31 228 F8
Laburnum Gr
Harrogate HG1 219 E6
Richmond DL10 209 D8
Stillingfleet YO19 191 D4
Whitby YO21 208 B6
Laburnum Rd TS7 7 D8
Lacey Ave YO12 99 D7
Lachman Rd BB8 186 A2
Lack La YO62 93 C2
Lackon Bank HG3 160 D6
Lacy Gr LS22 180 C2
Ladgate La TS5 6 F6
Lady Anne Ct YO1 233 B1
Lady Balk La WF8 201 B1
Ladycarr La YO61 143 E8
Lady East Hastings CE Prim Sch WF10 200 F7
Lady Edith's Ave YO12 212 B6
Lady Edith's Cres YO12 212 B6
Lady Edith's Dr YO12 212 A6
Lady Edith's Pk YO12 212 B7
Lady Elizabeth Hastings CE Prim Sch LS23 180 F1
Lady Grace's Ride YO12 212 A3
Lady Hamilton Gdns YO24 227 E2
Lady Hartley Ct BB8 186 B3
Lady Hullocks Ct 12 TS9 26 C7
Lady Kell Gdns YO32 225 E8
Lady La HG3 222 A5
Lady Lumley's Sch YO18 95 F7
Lady Mill Garth YO30 228 B8
Lady Peckitts Yd YO1 233 B2
Lady Rd YO30 228 B7
Ladysmith Ave YO21 208 C7
Ladysmith Mews 13 YO32 167 A7
Ladysmith Rd DL9 40 C4
Ladywell La YO51 141 C5
Ladywell Rd YO51 141 B5
Lady Wortley Pl YO23 231 B6
Lagentium Plaza
9 Castleford WF10 200 F3
8 Castleford WF10 200 F3
Lairs Cres YO13 98 A5
Lairs La YO13 98 A5
Lairum Rise LS23 188 E7
Laithe Cl 9 BD20 174 C1
Laith Staid La LS25 195 D4
Lakeber Ave LA2 129 A8
Lakeber Dr LA2 129 A8
Lakeber St 8 LA2 129 A8
Lakeside
Acaster Malbis YO23 191 C7
Darlington DL1 3 C4
Hunmanby Sands YO14 101 B1
Scarthingwell LS24 195 F7
Lakeside App LS24 195 E7
Lakeside Cl LS29 218 A5
Lakeside Ct 26 WF6 200 B1
Lakeside Gr 1 YO32 167 B8
Lakeside Mdws 1 WF8 201 B2
Lakeside Prim Sch YO30 224 F2
Lakeside Way YO17 215 D2
Lake Terr HG4 112 D7
Lake View WF8 201 B2
Laking La YO25 126 A3
Lambert Ct YO1 233 B1
Lambert Meml Hospl YO7 211 B2
Lambert St
11 Skipton BD23 217 A3
2 Trawden BB8 186 B1
Lambeth St 8 BB8 186 A3
Lambfield Way 8 TS17 6 A6
Lamb Inn Rd 9 WF11 202 A2
Lamb La TS17 6 A4
Lambourne Dr TS7 7 C6
Lambs La 12 YO18 95 F7
Lamb's La TS9 27 B4
Lamel St YO10 229 A3
Lamplugh Cres YO23 231 B3
Lanacar La DL8 56 A4
Lancar Cl 18 YO32 166 D5
Lancaster Cl
9 Scalby YO13 75 D5
Sherburn in Elmet LS25 196 B4
Lancaster Ct 24 YO51 141 B5
Lancaster Park Rd HG2 220 A3
Lancaster Rd
Harrogate HG2 219 C1
North Cowton DL7 22 C2
Lancaster St 6 YO11 213 A6
Lancaster Way
Middlesbrough TS17 6 B6
17 Scalby YO13 75 D5
York YO30 225 A1
Lancers Ct 4 YO12 75 F5
Landalewood Rd YO30 224 F2
Landau Cl YO30 227 F8
Landing La
Asselby DN14 205 D6
Barlby with Osgodby YO8 232 F8
22 Haxby YO32 166 F5
Hemingbrough YO8 204 F8
Riccall YO19 197 F8
York YO26 227 E6
Landing Rd YO8 203 A7
Landings The 21 YO32 166 F5
Landsdowne Rd YO21 208 B7
Lands La HG5 220 E7
LANE END 171 C2
LANE ENDS 187 C6
Lane Ends La BD22 187 B7
Lane Foot Rd HG3 159 E8
Lane Head LA2 128 A6
Lanehead La DL11 18 H8
Lane House La BB8 186 B1
Lanehouse Rd TS17 6 B8
Lane House Rd BD22 187 A6
LANESHAW BRIDGE 186 C4
Laneshaw Bridge Prim Sch BB8 186 B3
Lane The
Gate Helmsley YO41 168 B2
Mickleby TS13 12 A4
Lang Ave YO10 229 A4
LANGBAR 175 B6
Langbar Rd LS29 218 A6
LANGBAURGH 7 F2
Langbaurgh Cl TS9 8 A2
Langbaurgh Rd TS15 25 C4
Langber End La LA6 103 D1
Langber La BD23 154 A6
Langborne Rd 19 YO21 208 D6
Langbourne Rd YO21 208 D6
Langburn La YO21 29 A7
Langburn's Bank YO21 29 A7
LANGCLIFFE 131 E3
Langcliffe & Attermire Nature Reserve* BD24 132 A3
Langcliffe Ave HG2 222 E8
Langcliffe Avenue E HG2 222 E8
Langcliffe Garth BD23 108 B3
Langcliffe Rd BD24 131 D3
Langdale TS14 8 D6
Langdale Ave
3 Pontefract WF6 200 A2
York YO31 229 B6
Langdale Dr 2 WF6 200 A2
Langdale Gr YO8 232 B3
Langdale Mews 4 WF6 200 A2
Langdale Rd 3 YO12 212 F7
Langdale Terr YO21 208 C7
Langdon Way TS16 5 D5
Langer Hill La HG3 160 B5
Langford Cl 21 LS29 176 C1
Langford Ct 17 LS29 176 C1
Langford La LS29 176 C1
Langford Mews 19 LS29 176 C1
Langford Rd LS29 176 C1
Langford Ride 30 LS29 176 C1
Lang Gate YO13 74 E4
Langholm Cres DL3 3 C5
Langholme Dr YO26 227 C6
Langhorne Dr 2 DL11 38 B6
Lang Kirk Cl 2 BD20 173 F1
Langley Ave TS17 6 B8
Langley Ct 1 YO32 225 F6
Langley Dr YO17 215 E1
Langleys Rd 6 DN6 206 E1
Langold Dr 15 DN6 206 E2
Lang Rd
Bishopthorpe YO23 230 F4
York YO32 225 F6
Langrickgate La YO42 193 C5
Langsett Ave 7 YO14 101 A3
Langsett Gr YO30 224 F3
Langstrothdale Rd BD24 105 D7
LANGTHORNE 62 F6
LANGTHORPE 141 A6
LANGTHWAITE 17 E1
Langthwaite La DL8 59 C3
LANGTOFT 151 D5
Langtoft Prim Sch YO25 151 C5
LANGTON 147 F6
Langton Crossroads YO17 148 B6
Langton Ct 1 YO32 167 A6
Langton La YO17 148 C8
Langton Prim Sch YO17 147 F5
Langton Rd
Langton YO17 148 A7
Norton YO17 215 E2
Langwith Ave LS22 188 A8
Langwith Stray YO10 184 C2
Lansdowne Rd TS15 5 E3
Lansdowne Terr 5 YO10 228 E3
Lansdown Way 7 YO32 166 F5
Lanshaw Bank BD23 175 A7
Lanshaw Croft YO30 224 F1
Lantsbury Dr TS13 10 D8
Larch Ct DL1 3 F4
Larchfield YO31 229 C7
Larchfield Com TS8 6 F4
Larchfield Sports Ctr DL3 3 C5
Larchfield St DL3 3 C5
Larch Gr
1 Filey YO14 101 B4
Pannal HG3 222 E2
Larch Rd
Guisborough TS14 8 E7
Selby YO8 232 E2
6 Topcliffe YO7 89 A1
Larch Rise 4 YO61 117 D1
Larch Way
35 Haxby YO32 166 E5
Selby YO8 232 D2
Larkfield Cl
1 Copmanthorpe YO23 230 A3
Harrogate HG2 222 A7
Larkfield Dr HG2 222 A7
Larkfield Rd
Harrogate HG2 222 A7
Selby YO8 232 A4
Larkfield Way HG2 222 A7
Lark Hill HG4 214 A7
Larkhill Cl HG4 214 A6
Lark Hill Cres 13 HG4 113 D2
Lark Hill Dr HG4 214 A6
Lark La HG4 214 A6
Larkspur Dr DL1 3 E5
Larkspur Gr 14 HG3 161 B3
Larkspur Rd TS7 7 A6
Larpool Cres YO22 208 E4
Larpool Dr YO22 208 D3
Larpool La YO22 208 D4
Larpool Lane Ind Est YO22 208 D5
Larth Cl DN14 207 A7
Lartington Way TS16 5 D5
Larun Beat The TS15 5 E2
Lascelles Ct DL6 210 E4
Lascelles Gr HG2 219 B1
Lascelles La
Malton YO17 215 E6
Northallerton DL6 210 E4
Lascelles Rd HG2 222 B8
Lasenby Cl YO32 225 D5
LASTINGHAM 70 F5
Lastingham Terr YO10 228 D2
Latimer La TS14 8 E6
Latimer Rd DL1 3 E7
Lauderdale Dr TS14 8 F6
Laughton Ave YO12 212 C5
Laundry La LA6 103 D3
Laundry Rd
4 Filey YO14 101 B3
3 Harrogate HG1 220 C4
Lauradale La BD23 134 D1
Laurel Ave TS4 7 A8
Laurel Cl
Burniston YO13 75 D8
Earswick YO32 226 A7
Embsay BD23 217 D8
Gateforth YO8 197 B1
4 Leeming DL7 63 F3
Laurel Croft BD23 217 D8
Laurel Rise YO14 101 C1
Laurels Garth YO60 145 C5
Laurels The
Barlby YO8 198 B5
6 Northallerton DL6 210 E2
Laurence Gr YO8 232 D3
Laurence Jackson Sch TS14 8 F7
Lavender Ct 21 DL9 41 A5
Lavender Gr YO26 227 E5
Laveracks Ind Est YO41 185 B3
Laverick Terr 9 YO22 208 E6
LAVERTON 112 D4
Laverton Gdns HG3 219 A4
LAWKLAND 130 F5
LAWKLAND GREEN 131 A4
Law La HG3 138 F1
Lawn Ave LS29 176 C1
Lawnfield Dr HG3 140 B5
Lawnfield Rd HG3 140 B5
Lawn La DN6 207 E3
Lawn Rd 35 LS29 176 C1
Lawns Rd YO21 29 E6
Lawns The HG2 222 C8
Lawnswood Dr YO30 227 F8
Lawnway YO31 229 A7
Lawrence Cl YO12 212 A8
Lawrence Cres DL10 209 E8
Lawrence Ct 11 YO10 228 E3
Lawrence Gr YO12 212 A8
Lawrence Sq YO10 228 F3
Lawrence St YO10 228 E3
Lawsings Brow LA2 130 B5
Lawson Ave 1 YO51 141 B4
Lawson Rd YO24 230 F7
Lawsons Cl YO14 126 F7
Lawson's Ct DL2 2 C6
Laycock Fields 11 BD22 187 B6
LAYERTHORPE 228 E4
Layerthorpe YO31 233 C3
Layfield Prim Sch TS15 5 D2
Lazenby Dr 10 LS22 180 B3
Lea Croft LS23 188 E7
Leadhall Ave HG2 222 D6
Leadhall Cl HG2 222 D6
Leadhall Cres HG2 222 E6
Leadhall Dr HG2 222 D7
Leadhall Gdns HG2 222 D6
Leadhall Gr HG2 222 D6
Leadhall La HG2 222 D6
Leadhall Rd HG2 222 C6
Leadhall View HG2 222 C5
Leadhall Way HG2 222 C6
Leading Post St 8 YO11 213 B6
Lead La
Brompton DL6 43 F3
Lead La *continued*
Nether Silton YO7 66 B7
Ripon HG4 214 B3
Westerdale YO21 28 E4
Leadley Croft YO23 230 A1
Lead Mill La YO1 233 C1
Leafield Rd DL1 3 D4
Leahope Ct TS17 6 C6
Leahurst Cl YO17 215 E2
LEAKE 65 F5
Leake La YO7 65 F6
Leake St
Castleford WF10 200 F4
12 York YO10 228 E3
Lea La YO61 143 F4
LEALHOLM 30 B6
Lealholm Cres TS3 7 C8
Lealholm La YO21 30 B5
Lealholm Prim Sch YO21 30 C6
LEALHOLM SIDE 30 D7
Lealholm Sta YO21 30 B6
Leamington Rd LS29 218 C5
Leamington Terr LS29 218 C5
Learmans Way YO23 230 C3
Learning La DN14 202 F1
Lease Rigg La YO22 31 A3
Leases La DL10 41 E2
Leases Rd DL7 63 C5
Leas Head Rd YO22 32 B2
Leas La YO18 95 F5
Leasmires Ave 10 YO61 143 D8
Leas The
11 Brafferton YO61 115 F1
Darlington DL1 3 D8
8 Eastfield YO11 99 F7
Leat Cl YO17 215 D2
Leather Bank LS29 176 C1
LEATHLEY 177 D2
Leathley La LS21 177 D1
LEAVENING 147 E1
Leavening Com Prim Sch YO17 147 E2
Lea Way YO32 226 A4
Leazon Hill 5 TS17 6 D6
LEBBERSTON 100 D5
Le Cateau Com Prim Sch DL9 40 F4
Le Cateau Rd DL9 40 E4
LECK 102 E7
Leck St Peter's CE Prim Sch LA6 102 E7
Leconfield DL3 3 B5
Leconfield Garth HG3 223 F5
Ledbury Way TS14 8 E6
Ledgate La LS25 201 E6
LEDSHAM 201 B8
LEDSTON 200 F7
Ledston Ave LS25 194 D3
Ledston Hall* WF10 200 F8
LEDSTON LUCK 194 F1
Ledston Mill La WF10 200 F8
Leech La DL10 41 E4
Lee Ct DN14 207 A7
Leeds Barnsdale Rd WF10 200 D3
Leeds La LS15 194 A3
Leeds Rd
Allerton Bywater WF10 200 D7
Barwick in Elmet & Scholes LS15 194 A7
Castleford WF10 200 E3
Collingham LS22 188 A8
Great Preston WF10 200 C7
Harrogate HG2 219 D1
Ilkley LS29 218 D5
Kippax LS25 194 C2
Mickletown LS26 200 A6
Pannal HG3 222 F3
Selby YO8 232 A4
Tadcaster LS24 189 D5
Leeman Rd YO26 233 A2
LEEMING 63 D4
LEEMING BAR 63 C5
Leeming Bar CE Prim Sch DL7 63 C4
Leeming Bar Ind Est DL7 63 C5
Leeming Bar Sta DL7 63 C5
Leeming La
Brough with St Giles DL10 41 D5
Burneston DL8 87 F8
4 Burton in Lonsdale LA6 102 F3
Catterick DL10 41 E4
Kirklington-cum-Upsland YO7 88 A6
Langthorpe YO51 141 B6
Leeming DL7 63 C4
Melmerby YO7 114 D8
Theakston DL7 63 E1
Thornthwaite with Padside HG3 159 D5
Leeming & Londonderry Com Prim Sch DL7 63 D4
Leeming RAF Com Prim Sch DL7 63 F3
Leeside YO24 230 E8
Lees La DL7 210 B1
Lee View DN14 207 A7
Lee Way WF10 200 F3
Legion Ave DL3 3 B8
Legion St LS25 195 F2
Legram La YO26 163 D8
Legram Rd YO26 163 D8
Leicester Cres LS29 218 B5
Leicester Way
Aislaby TS16 5 D4
York YO1 233 C1
LEIGHTON 85 C2
Leighton Cl YO12 99 E6
Leighton Croft 3 YO30 224 F1
Leighton Rd 6 TS18 5 D8
Leith Rd DL3 3 A5
Lendal YO1 233 B2
Lendales La YO17 95 E3
Lennerton La LS25 196 C3
Lennox Ave DL10 209 D7
Lennox Cl 2 YO14 127 A8
Lennox Pl HG4 113 D3
Leonard St 15 BB18 171 D1
LEPPINGTON 169 C8
Leppington Dr YO12 212 C4
Leppington La YO60 147 D1
Lerecroft Rd YO24 230 D8
Lesley Ave YO10 231 E8
L'Espec St DL7 210 D3
Leven Bank Rd TS15 5 F2
Leven Cl TS16 5 D4
Leven Ct TS9 8 A1
Levendale 6 TS15 25 C5
Levendale Prim Sch TS15 5 F3
Leven Rd
Eaglescliffe TS15 5 E3
Stokesley TS9 26 B7
York YO24 230 D7
Levens Cl HG3 161 B4
Levenside
Great Ayton TS9 7 F1
4 Hutton Rudby TS15 25 D5
Stokesley TS9 26 C7
Leven Wynd 9 TS9 26 C7
Levick Cres TS5 6 D8
Levington Ct 3 TS15 24 F8
Levington Mews 4 TS15 24 F8
LEVISHAM 72 D5
Levisham St YO10 228 D2
Levisham Sta YO18 72 B5
Lewes Rd DL1 3 D4
Lewis Cl
1 Croft-on-Tees DL2 22 C8
Northallerton DL6 210 F5
Lewis Rd DL6 210 F5
Lexden Ave TS5 6 D8
LEYBURN 60 D5
Leyburn Bsns Pk DL8 60 D5
Leyburn Com Prim Sch DL8 60 D5
Leyburn Gr 1 TS18 5 D8
Leyburn Old Glebe Field Nature Reserve* DL8 60 B4
Leyburn Pl 8 YO14 101 A3
Leyburn Rd
Askrigg DL8 57 F6
Darlington DL1 3 D7
Hunton DL8 61 E7
Masham HG4 86 B4
Middleham DL8 60 E3
Scotton DL9 40 C4
Leyburn Sta DL8 60 D5
Leyes The YO10 229 C4
Leyfield Cl 1 YO32 167 A7
Leyland Cl BB8 186 A2
Leyland Cres 3 HG1 220 A3
Leyland Rd
Harrogate HG1 220 A3
York YO31 229 A5
Leys La
Boston Spa LS23 188 D8
Darrington WF11 206 A8
Glusburn BD20 187 B8
Knottingley WF11 201 F1
Little Smeaton WF8 206 B4
Leys Rd WF11 206 A7
LEYSTHORPE 93 B1
Leysthorpe La YO62 93 B2
Liardet Rd 19 DL10 41 E4
Libanus Ct 18 TS17 5 F4
Library Sq YO1 233 B3
Libra Way 9 WF8 201 B2
Lichfield Ct 6 YO23 228 B1
Lichfield Gr HG3 219 A4
Lickley St HG4 214 D5
Lidget Croft 10 BD20 173 E3
Lidget La HG5 163 B5
Lidget Rd BD20 173 E3
Lidgett Gr YO26 227 B6
Lidgett La LS25 194 C3
Lidice Rd DN14 205 E2
Lidsty Hill YO62 70 E5
Light Bank La BD20 174 E2
Lightfoots Ave YO12 212 D3
Lightfoots Cl YO12 212 C3
Lightfoot's La YO12 212 D3
Lightfoots Rd YO12 212 D3
Light La DL8 59 E5
Lightmire La YO26 142 A1
Lightwater Sh Village HG4 113 C6
Lightwater Valley Bird of Prey Ctr* HG4 113 C7
Lightwater Valley Miniature Rly* HG4 113 C6
Lightwater Valley Theme Pk* HG4 113 C6
Lilac Ave
2 Appleton Roebuck YO23 190 F5
2 Naburn YO19 191 D8
Thornaby TS17 6 B7
York YO10 229 B3
Lilac Cl 7 LS29 175 A4
Lilac Gr
Harrogate HG1 219 E6
New Earswick YO32 225 D4
Lilac Rd TS7 7 D7
Lilac Wlk YO12 212 D7
Lilbourne Dr YO30 228 A8
Lile Cl DL10 209 C7

Lilla Cl YO21 208 A6
Lilling Ave 3 YO31 228 E8
Lilling La YO60 145 E3
Lilling Low La YO32 145 C2
Lilly Gate La HG3 162 A8
Limber Hill YO21 30 E4
Lime Ave YO31 228 F7
Limebar Bank Rd YO51 141 D1
Limebar La YO51 141 C2
Lime Chase 10 YO62 70 B1
Lime Cl
10 Addingham LS29 174 E4
8 North Duffield YO8 199 A7
Limegarth 10 YO26 165 F1
Lime Gr
Harrogate HG1 219 F3
4 Whitby YO21 208 C6
Limehouse La BD23 216 E1
Limekiln Bank HG4 113 C1
Limekiln Cottages 1
HG4 214 D5
Limekiln Hill YO25 150 B3
Limekiln La
Burton Leonard HG3 140 A1
8 Eastfield YO11 100 B6
East Layton DL11 1 B1
Halton West BD23 154 A1
North Stainley with Sleningford HG4 113 C5
Snape with Thorp HG4 86 D5
Lime Kiln La LS22 180 B5
Limekiln Rd YO7 65 F5
Lime La DL8 87 F2
Lime Rd
Eaglescliffe TS16 5 E6
Guisborough TS14 8 E7
Sinnington YO62 94 D8
Limes Ct YO31 228 F6
Lime St HG1 219 F3
Limes The
Burniston YO13 75 C8
Helmsley YO62 92 F6
13 South Milford LS25 195 F2
Stockton on the Forest YO32 167 D2
Limestone Gr YO13 75 C8
Limestone La YO13 75 A5
Limestone Rd YO13 75 B7
Limestone Way YO13 75 C8
Lime Tree Ave
Boston Spa LS23 188 E8
8 Easingwold YO61 117 D1
Malton YO17 215 D6
York YO32 225 D3
Limetree Cl 2 YO8 197 B1
Lime-Tree Cres LS25 194 E1
Lime Tree Dr DN14 207 A7
Lime Tree Gdns LS23 188 E8
Lime Tree Gr YO8 232 A6
Lime Tree Mews 15 YO19 184 F7
Limetrees WF8 201 D2
Lime Wlk HG4 214 B2
Limpsey Gate La YO18 72 D6
Limpton Gate TS15 5 E2
Linacre Way DL1 3 D7
Lincoln Gr HG3 219 A5
Lincoln Pl 1 TS17 6 B8
Lincoln Rd 30 BB18 172 A1
Lincoln St YO26 227 F5
Lincoln Way LS25 196 A4
Lindale 2 YO24 230 C7
Linden Ave
Darlington DL3 3 B5
Great Ayton TS9 7 F1
Linden Cl
Great Ayton TS9 7 F2
4 Hutton Rudby TS15 25 C4
Richmond DL10 209 D7
Sleights YO21 32 B7
York YO32 225 F5
Linden Cres
Great Ayton TS9 7 F1
5 Hutton Rudby TS15 25 C4
Middlesbrough TS7 7 B6
Linden Dr
Hurworth DL2 3 D1
1 Hurworth-on-Tees DL2 22 D8
Linden Gdns DL10 209 D7
Linden Gr
Great Ayton TS9 7 F1
Thornaby TS17 6 B8
1 York YO30 228 A8
Linden Rd
9 Earby BB18 172 A1
Great Ayton TS9 7 F1
Northallerton DL6 210 E4
Scalby YO12 212 A8
Linden Way
9 Thorpe Willoughby YO8 197 B1
Wetherby LS22 180 B4
Lindhead Rd YO13 75 B8
Lindhead Sch YO13 75 C8
Lindisfarne Ave 4 TS17 6 B8
Lindisfarne Rd TS3 7 C8
LINDLEY 177 C4
Lindley Rd YO30 224 F1
Lindley St
Skipton BD23 216 F2
York YO24 227 F3
Lindley Wood Gr YO30 224 E3
Lindon Rd DL10 20 F1
Lindrick Cl
32 Castleford WF6 200 B1
3 Ripon HG4 214 B2
Lindrick Way HG3 219 A4
Lindsay Rd LS25 194 C3
Lindsey Ave YO26 227 D4
Linen Way 10 DL6 43 F3
Linfield Ct YO14 101 B1
Lingcrag Gdns BD22 187 B6
Ling Croft LS23 188 D8
Lingcroft Cl YO8 204 D4
Lingcroft La
Naburn YO19 231 E3
Tockwith LS22 181 A6
LINGDALE 9 F7
Lingdale Prim Sch TS12 9 F7
Lingdale Rd
Lockwood TS12 9 E7
Thornaby TS17 6 C7
LINGERFIELD 162 B6
LINGFIELD 3 F5
Lingfield Ash TS8 7 A5
Lingfield Cl
Great Burdon DL1 3 F5
10 Hipswell DL9 40 F4
Lingfield Cres YO24 227 F1
Lingfield Prim Sch TS7 7 B5
Lingfield Rd TS15 5 F3
Ling Fields BD23 216 C4
Lingfield Way DL1 4 A5
Ling Gill National Nature Reserve★ BD24 79 C1
Lingham La YO7 115 A3
Linghaw La LA2 129 C7
Ling Hill YO12 212 B7
Lingholm Cres 9 YO11 99 F7
Lingholm La YO11 100 D4
Ling La YO41 185 F6
Lingrow Cl 3 TS13 12 A7
Ling Trod YO17 123 D4
Link Ave YO30 228 C8
Link Bsns Pk YO10 229 D4
Linkfoot La YO62 93 A6
Link Rd YO32 225 E2
Link Road Ct YO10 229 D4
Links Cl HG2 220 E3
Links Dr LA2 129 A8
Links Prim Sch The TS16 5 E5
Links The
7 North Featherstone WF7 200 E1
Tadcaster LS24 189 E5
Links Way HG2 220 E3
Link The
Copmanthorpe YO23 230 A3
Middlesbrough TS3 7 C8
Northallerton DL7 210 B2
Selby YO8 232 A4
York YO10 231 E8
Linkway DN6 206 E2
Link Wlk 5 YO11 100 A6
Linley Ave 24 YO32 166 F5
Linnburn Mews 1 LS29 218 B3
Linnet Way YO24 230 C8
LINTON
Grassington 134 D1
Wetherby 180 A1
Linton Ave 9 LS22 180 B3
Linton Cl
Cloughton YO13 54 D1
19 Filey YO14 101 B3
Linton Com LS22 179 F1
Linton Ct 8 BD23 216 F3
Linton Falls 1 BD23 134 E2
Linton La LS22 180 B2
Linton Mdw 5 YO30 164 F7
Linton Mdws 7 LS22 180 B3
LINTON-ON-OUSE 164 E7
Linton-on-Ouse Prim Sch YO30 165 A7
Linton Pl 4 YO30 164 F7
Linton Rd
Collingham LS22 180 A1
Poppleton YO26 224 A1
Wetherby LS22 180 B3
Linton Rise 17 DL9 40 E4
Linton St 5 YO26 227 E5
Linton Woods YO30 165 A7
Linton Woods La YO30 165 A8
Linwith La DN14 204 C3
Linwood Ave TS9 26 C8
Lion Ct 43 LS29 176 C1
Lippersley La
Cringles LS29 174 D3
Silsden BD20 174 D2
Lisheen Ave WF10 200 F4
Lismore Pl YO12 212 E1
Lismore Rd YO12 212 E1
Lister Croft BD23 172 A3
Lister Hill 5 BD20 187 E6
Lister St LS29 218 A4
Lister Way YO30 228 A7
Lisvane Ave YO12 212 D4
Litley Bank YO7 66 B5
Litter La BD23 153 E5
LITTLE AIRMYN 205 E4
Little Ave YO30 228 B8
LITTLE AYTON 8 B1
Little Ayton La
Great Ayton TS9 8 A1
27 Roundhill Village TS17 5 F4
LITTLE BARUGH 95 C2
Little Beck Bank YO22 32 C4
Littlebeck Dr DL1 3 E7
Little Beck La YO22 32 B3
Little Beck Wood Nature Reserve★ YO22 32 B3
Littleboy Dr TS17 6 C8
Little Brook BD23 217 B4
Little Catterton La LS24 190 A7
Little Church La LS26 200 B5
Little Common La DN14 207 C5
LITTLE CRAKEHALL 62 D5
Little Croft HG3 139 C4
Little Crossing HG4 214 E2
Littledale YO18 95 F7
LITTLE FENCOTE 63 C8
LITTLE FENTON 196 B6
Littlefield Cl 5 YO26 165 F1
Little Field La YO18 72 C5
Little Garth YO26 224 A2
LITTLE HABTON 121 A8
Little Hallfield Rd YO31 228 E5
Little Harries La HG4 214 A7
LITTLE HECK 203 D1
Little Heck Common La DN14 203 D1
Little Hoppers Adventure World★ YO11 99 F6
LITTLE HUTTON 116 B7
Little Hutton La DL11 1 A4
Little Ings Cl LS24 196 C8
Little Ings La YO51 141 C5
Little King St 5 HG3 137 B4
Little La
Brompton DL6 44 A3
12 Easingwold YO61 143 C8
Ellerton YO42 193 C1
11 Haxby YO32 166 E5
Ilkley LS29 218 C4
Little Smeaton WF8 206 D4
North Stainley with Sleningford HG4 113 C4
Little Market Pl 17 HG4 86 C3
Little Mdws YO32 225 D8
Little Moor Cl YO13 54 C1
Little Moor La YO8 232 A8
LITTLE OUSEBURN 164 A7
Little Pasture 3 TS17 6 D5
LITTLE PRESTON 194 B1
LITTLE RIBSTON 180 A8
LITTLE SESSAY 116 C5
Little Shambles YO1 233 B2
Littleside DL8 83 E7
LITTLE SKIPWITH 192 D1
LITTLE SMEATON 206 C3
North Cowton 23 C2
LITTLE STAINFORTH 131 D6
Little Stonegate YO1 233 B3
LITTLE STUDLEY 214 C7
Little Studley Cl HG4 214 C7
Little Studley Pk HG4 214 C8
Little Studley Rd HG4 214 C7
LITTLETHORPE 214 F1
Littlethorpe Cl
Harrogate HG3 219 A4
6 Strensall YO32 167 B8
Littlethorpe La HG4 214 D2
Littlethorpe Pk HG4 214 E3
Littlethorpe Potteries★ HG4 140 A7
Littlethorpe Rd HG4 214 E3
Little Westfield YO25 151 C3
Little Wood St YO17 215 E3
LITTON 107 A5
Littondale Ave HG5 221 D6
LIVERTON 10 D6
Liverton La TS13 10 D6
Liverton Mill Bank TS12 10 B6
LIVERTON MINES 10 C8
Liverton Rd TS13 10 D7
Livingstone Rd YO12 212 E6
Livingstone St YO26 227 F5
Lloyd Cl YO10 229 B1
Lob La YO41 168 D2
Lochranza Rd YO7 211 A2
Lochrin Pl 2 YO26 227 B4
Lock Cl DN14 207 F6
Locker La HG4 214 C4
Lockey Croft YO32 225 C8
Lockeys Terr 3 YO22 208 E6
Lockfield Dr BB18 171 E2
Lockgate Rd DN14 207 C4
Lockheed Cl TS18 5 F7
Lock House La YO32 225 F8
Lock La
Castleford WF10 200 E5
Lower Altofts WF6 200 A3
Lock Lane Sports Ctr WF10 200 F5
Locks Barn BD24 131 D4
LOCKTON 72 D4
Lockton Cres TS17 6 A6
Lockton Ct LS24 196 B7
Lockton La YO18 72 E4
Lockton Rd YO21 208 A6
Lock Walk DL10 41 E4
Lockwood Chase YO13 54 D1
Lockwood La YO61 117 C1
Lockwood Prim Sch TS12 9 D7
Lockwood St YO31 233 C3
Lockyer Cl 4 YO30 228 A8
Locomotion Ct 5 TS16 5 D5
Locomotion La 7 DL3 3 B7
Loders Gn 5 YO11 99 F6
Lodge Cl 7 YO11 100 B6
Lodge Gdns YO14 100 E4
LODGE GREEN 36 F5
Lodge La
5 Brompton DL6 43 F3
Danby YO21 29 D7
Gowdall DN14 203 F1
Newby with Mulwith HG4 140 E6
Wennington LA2 102 B1
Wetherby LS22 180 C2
Lodge Rd
Hutton-le-Hole YO62 70 C5
Lythe YO21 12 E3
Settle BD24 153 E8
Lodge St 4 BD20 187 D7
Lodore Gr TS5 6 D7
LOFTHOUSE 110 C4
Lofthouse La YO41 185 D7
Loftus Cl YO12 212 B4
Lombards Wynd DL10 209 C7
Londesborough Gr 5 YO8 197 B2
Londesborough Pk 10 YO12 99 D6
Londesborough Rd YO12 212 E4
Londesborough St 5 YO8 232 C5
LONDONDERRY 63 E2
London La DN6 207 D1
Longacre WF10 200 E3
Long Acre YO8 204 D5
Long Acre Ct HG3 222 E2
Long Acre Wlk HG3 222 E2
Long Ashes L & Beauty Club BD23 134 B3
Long Band DL8 58 A8
Long Bank DL11 19 C6
Long Bank La BD23 153 E1
Longbank Rd TS7 7 D7
Longber La LA6 102 D4
Longbow Ave LS26 200 B6
Longbridge Cl 22 YO61 143 D8
Longbridge Dr 23 YO61 143 D8
Long Cl La YO10 233 C1
Long Crag View 1 HG3 161 B2
Longcroft 2 YO32 166 E5
Longcroft Rd 1 LS29 218 E3
Long Cswy
Arkengarthdale DL11 16 C6
Halton East BD23 174 B8
Thirkleby High & Low with Osgodby YO7 90 D1
Long Cswy Rd
Danby YO21 29 E3
Hutton Buscel YO13 99 A4
Longdale Ave 18 BD24 131 D2
Longdike La
Kippax LS25 200 E8
Thornton Steward HG4 61 E1
LONG DRAX 205 A6
Longfield Ct 21 BB18 171 D1
Longfield Rd DL3 3 C7
Longfield Sch DL3 3 C8
Longfield Terr YO30 233 A3
Long Furrow YO32 225 C8
Long Gate BD22 187 D4
Long Gn 7 BB18 172 B1
Long Heads La LS25 195 F1
Long Hill End BD22 187 B5
Long Ing La BB18 171 E1
Long La
Barwick in Elmet LS15 194 C7
Borrowby YO7 65 E5
Brompton DL6 44 A6
Catton YO41 185 D6
Cawood YO8 197 A6
Cowling BD22 187 B7
East Ayton YO13 99 B7
Ellerton YO42 193 F1
Farndale East YO62 48 F4
Felliscliffe HG3 160 E3
Gayles DL11 19 E6
Heck DN14 207 D8
Heslington YO10 184 C3
Kirk Smeaton WF8 206 B1
Laneshaw Bridge BB8 186 B4
Lockwood TS12 10 B5
Normanby YO62 95 A4
Picton TS15 24 E6
Seamer YO12 99 E6
Slingsby YO62 120 D6
Tatham LA2 128 E7
Well DL8 87 C4
Longland La YO26 164 A3
Longlands Field Rd YO26 163 D8
Longlands La
Boroughbridge YO51 141 A3
Danby YO21 29 B6
Hetton BD23 155 F5
Sicklinghall LS22 179 E3
Thornton-le-Dale YO18 96 E5
Longlands Rd YO17 123 B3
LONG LEASE 33 A7
Long Level LA6 102 C8
Long Mann Hills Rd YO8 232 B4
Longman's Hill Com Prim Sch YO8 232 C3
LONG MARSTON 182 A6
Long Marston CE VC Prim Sch YO26 182 A6
Long Mdw
7 Colne BB8 186 A3
Skipton BD23 217 B5
Long Mdws
Garforth LS25 194 C3
6 Ilkley LS29 176 C1
Rillington YO17 122 F5
Long Meadow Gate LS25 194 C2
LONGNEWTON 5 A7
Long Newton La TS21 5 A6
LONG PRESTON 153 F5
Long Preston Endowed Prim Sch BD23 153 F5
Long Preston Sta BD23 153 F4
Long Rampart YO42 193 D3
Long Riddings LS29 174 F5
Long Ridge Dr YO26 224 A1
Longridge Gdns 27 YO26 165 F1
Long Ridge La YO26 224 A1
LONGSCALES 160 C4
Long St
Asenby YO7 115 B6
Easingwold YO61 143 C8
Thirsk YO7 211 C3
Long St *continued*
Topcliffe YO7 115 C6
Long Stoop Standing Stone★ HG3 160 A2
Long Stps 8 YO22 208 E6
Long Swales La HG4 112 D5
Longtons La BD23 152 E3
Long Trods 5 YO8 232 C6
Longwestgate YO11 213 B6
Long Wlk
Knaresborough HG5 221 A6
Scarborough YO12 212 D7
Longwood Bank DL10 209 D5
Longwood Link 8 YO30 224 E3
Longwood Rd YO30 224 F3
Longwoods Wlk 13 WF11 202 A3
Lonsdale Mdws LS23 188 E8
Lonsdale Pl 12 YO13 99 B8
Lonsdale Rd YO11 213 A3
Loos Rd DL9 40 F3
Loraine Cres DL1 3 C4
Lord Ave TS17 6 B5
Lord Deramore's Prim Sch YO10 229 C1
Lord Mayor's Wlk YO31 233 B3
Lords Chase 8 WF8 201 B2
Lord's Cl 23 BD24 131 D2
Lord's Close Rd LA2 129 B3
Lordship La
5 Barlby YO8 198 A4
Wistow YO8 232 D8
Lords La
Ainderby Mires with Holtby DL8 41 F1
Hackforth DL8 62 E8
Upper Poppleton YO26 165 E2
Lord's La DL8 63 C2
Lords Moor La YO32 167 C7
Loriners Dr 7 YO23 230 B3
Loring Rd YO13 54 A7
Lorne St YO23 228 B1
Lorraine Ave 3 YO41 185 B2
LOSCOE 200 C1
Loscoe Cl WF6 200 C2
Loshpot La LS22 180 C5
LOTHERSDALE 187 A8
Lothersdale Com Prim Sch BD20 186 F8
Lothersdale Rd BD20 187 B8
Lotherton La LS25 195 A7
Lotherton Way LS25 194 C4
Louisa St DL1 3 D5
Lousy Hill La YO22 32 C3
Louvain St 5 BB18 171 D2
Love La
Bedale DL8 63 B3
Brawby YO17 94 F1
Castleford WF10 200 E3
Easby DL10 209 E4
Nunthorpe YO10 231 C8
Whitby YO21 208 A7
York YO24 228 A2
Lovers' La DL7 64 F2
Low Bank
4 Embsay BD23 217 E8
Over Silton DL6 66 A8
Low Beck LS29 218 D5
LOW BENTHAM 128 F8
Low Bentham Rd LA2 128 F8
LOW BRADLEY 173 E3
LOW CATTON 185 C8
Low Catton Rd YO41 185 C8
Low Cl LS29 218 A5
Low Comm LS26 200 C4
LOW CONISCLIFFE 2 F4
Lowcroft
9 Collingham LS22 188 A8
High Bentham LA2 129 B8
Low Croft 6 YO32 167 A7
Lowcross Ave TS14 8 E5
Lowcross Dr TS9 26 E5
LOW DALBY 72 F2
Lowdale Ave YO12 212 E8
Lowdale Ct 4 YO22 32 A6
Low Demesne LA6 103 D3
Low Demesne Cl 4 LA6 103 D3
LOW DINSDALE 4 C1
LOW ELLINGTON 86 A6
LOWER ALTOFTS 200 A3
Lower Clark St
2 Scarborough YO12 212 F6
13 Scarborough YO12 213 A7
Lower Clark Street Ind Est 14 YO12 213 A7
Lower Constable Rd LS29 218 D3
Lower Croft St 39 BB18 172 A1
Lower Darnborough St YO23 233 B1
Lower Derwent Valley Nat Nature Reserve★ YO42 199 C8
LOWER DUNSFORTH 142 A4
Lower Flat Cliffs YO14 101 C1
Lower Friargate YO1 233 B2
Lower Greenfoot 15 BD24 131 D2
LOWER MICKLETOWN 200 D6
Lower Mickletown LS26 200 C6
Lower Oxford St WF10 200 E4
Lower Park St 15 BB18 171 E1
Lower Pk Gn 8 BD20 174 B1
Lower Priory St YO1 233 A1
Lower Station Rd 3 WF6 200 A1
Lower Union St BD23 216 F3

Lower Wellington Rd
LS29 218 B4
LOWER WESTHOUSE 103 B4
Lower William St 3
YO12 212 F6
Lower York Ct HG1 220 D6
Loweswater Rd 5 YO30 224 E1
Low Farm LS26 200 C8
Low Farm Cl
Bolton Percy YO23 190 D4
Thornton TS8 6 D4
Low Farm Ct DN6 206 D6
Lowfield
3 Eastfield YO11 100 A6
Hawes DL8 56 C4
Lowfield Dr YO32 166 E5
Lowfield La
Beamsley BD23 174 F7
Bilbrough YO23 182 E1
Kirkby Fleetham with Fencote
DL7 42 D2
Rufforth YO26 227 A4
Scrayingham YO41 169 A7
Sharow HG4 214 F6
Snape with Thorp DL8 87 A7
Low Field La
Cold Kirby YO7 91 D7
Goldsborough HG5 163 A1
Marton cum Grafton YO51 141 E2
Staveley HG5 140 E1
Lowfield Rd
Barlby with Osgodby YO8 198 B5
Hillam LS25 202 C8
Malton YO17 215 C6
Lowfields 2 YO12 99 D2
Lowfields Ave
Ingleby Barwick TS17 6 A5
Roundhill Village TS17 6 D5
Low Fields Dr YO24 227 C3
Lowfields La YO7 88 C6
Low Fold 4 BB18 186 A7
LOW GARTH 29 F4
Low Garth YO22 32 A6
Low Garth Link 17 LS25 195 F4
Low Garth Rd LS25 195 F4
LOW GATE 138 F6
Lowgate DN14 207 D5
Low Gate DL8 57 F5
Low Gate La HG4 138 F7
LOW GATHERLEY 21 D1
LOWGILL 128 F3
Lowgill La LA2 128 F4
Low Gn
Catterick DL10 41 D4
Copmanthorpe YO23 230 B2
13 Knottingley WF11 202 A2
Menwith with Darley HG3 160 A6
LOW GRANTLEY 112 E1
LOW GREEN 160 A6
LOW HAWSKER 33 A6
Low Holland WF11 201 C6
Low Hospital Yd 6 YO22 208 E6
Low House La
Carlton Miniott YO7 89 C2
Dishforth YO7 115 B2
LOW HUTTON 147 C6
Low Hutton Pk YO60 147 C6
Lowick YO24 230 C7
Lowkber La LA6 103 E2
Low La
Askrigg DL8 58 B4
Carperby-cum-Thoresby DL8 58 F4
Cononley BD20 173 C2
Cowling BD22 187 A8
Cropton YO18 71 B4
Dalby-cum-Skewsby YO60 119 B2
Dalton DL11 19 D7
Embsay with Eastby BD23 217 E8
Grassington BD23 134 E3
Grinton DL11 37 E5
Heslington YO10 229 D1
Howsham YO60 147 A1
Hutton-Sessay YO7 116 B7
Leck LA6 102 D7
Leyburn DL8 60 C4
Lythe YO21 12 D3
Maltby TS17 6 B3
Menwith with Darley HG3 159 F6
Mickleby TS13 12 A3
Middlesbrough TS5 6 E6
Muker DL11 36 C4
Newsham DL11 18 H7
Reeth, Fremington & Healaugh
DL11 37 F5
Sawdon YO13 98 C7
Silsden BD20 174 B3
Spofforth with Stockeld
HG3 179 C4
Stainburn LS21 177 F3
Sutton-under-Whitestonecliffe
YO7 90 E6
Swinton YO17 121 C4
Thirkleby High & Low with
Osgodby YO7 90 C1
Westow YO60 147 C4
West Rounton DL6 24 D3
Wigglesworth BD23 153 D3
LOW LAITHE 137 F2
Lowlands Dr DL7 63 C5
LOW MARISHES 122 C8
Low Mdw YO8 232 C6
Low Mdws YO11 99 F5
Low Medstone Dr YO61 117 C1
LOW MILL 48 E2
Low Mill LS29 175 A4
Low Mill Cl YO10 229 D3
Low Mill Ct HG3 138 F1
Low Mill Est HG4 214 E5
Low Mill La LS29 175 A4
Low Mill Rd HG4 214 D4
Low Moor Ave 3 YO10 231 F8
Low Moorgate La YO17 122 F5
Low Moor La
Askham Richard YO23 182 D3
Brearton HG5 162 B7
East Harlsey DL6 44 C7
Fearby HG4 85 F3
Hessay YO26 182 C8
Rillington YO17 122 E6
Lowmoor Rd YO8 198 E6
Low Moor Rd YO18 71 F5
Low Moor South La
YO17 122 D6
LOWNA 70 A6
Lowna Rd YO62 70 B5
Lown Hill YO24 227 C2
Lownorth Rd YO13 53 C2
Low Ousegate YO1 233 B2
Low Park Rd LS29 176 A3
Low Petergate YO1 233 B3
Low Peter La HG3 140 A3
Low Poppleton La YO26 227 B7
Low Rd
Gainford DL2 1 C7
Gowdall DN14 204 A1
Irton YO12 75 B3
Kellington DN14 202 F4
Kirby Grindalythe YO17 149 F7
Newby & Scalby YO12 212 A6
Thirkleby High & Low with
Osgodby YO7 116 E8
LOW ROW 37 C4
Low Row DL11 37 E5
Low Skellgate HG4 214 C5
Low Sleights Rd LA6 104 B7
LOW SNAYGILL 173 D4
Low St
Aiskew DL7 63 C6
Austwick LA2 130 E7
Burton in Lonsdale LA6 102 F3
Carlton DN14 204 C2
Husthwaite YO61 117 B6
Kirkby Fleetham with Fencote
DL7 41 F2
Knottingley WF11 201 E4
Lastingham YO62 70 E5
Nunnington YO62 93 E2
Oswaldkirk YO62 92 F3
Ripon HG4 214 D5
22 Scalby YO13 75 D5
Sherburn in Elmet LS25 195 F4
Thornton-le-Clay YO60 146 A4
Low Stanghow Rd TS12 9 F6
Low Street Agnesgate
HG4 214 D4
Lowswater Rd WF11 201 F1
Lowther Cres 3 LS26 194 A1
Lowther Ct YO31 233 C4
Lowther Dr
Garforth LS25 194 C3
Selby YO8 232 E3
2 Swillington LS26 194 A1
Lowther St YO31 233 C4
Lowther Terr YO24 228 A3
Low Thorpe DL8 85 D8
LOW TOWN 5 B1
Low Town Bank Rd YO7 91 B4
Low Tun Way YO62 69 A2
Low Wath Rd HG3 137 B4
Low Way 5 LS23 188 E5
Low Well Pk YO19 192 F7
Low Westfield Rd YO23 230 A1
LOW WHITA 37 D5
Low Wood La
Glaisdale YO21 30 C6
Leyburn DL8 60 C4
Low Wood Rise LS29 218 F3
LOW WORSALL 24 A8
Loxley Cl YO30 224 F2
Loy La TS13 10 F8
Loyne Pk LA6 102 A7
Lucas Ave YO30 228 C8
Lucas Grove N YO26 181 C7
Lucas Grove S YO26 181 C7
Lucas Rd YO26 181 C7
Luccombe Cl 7 TS17 6 A3
Lucerne Cl YO19 192 A1
Lucerne Dr TS14 8 E6
Lucia La TS14 8 E6
Lucky La YO7 89 E8
Lucombe Way YO32 225 D4
Luddith Rd YO17 148 D5
Ludlow Ave LS25 194 D4
Lufton Cl 4 TS17 5 F5
Lullingstone Cres TS17 5 F6
Lulsgate TS17 6 C7
LUMB 187 A4
Lumb Gill La LS29 175 A3
Lumb La
Cowling BD22 187 A5
Topcliffe YO7 89 B1
Lumb Mill Way BD23 157 E7
LUMBY 195 E1
Lumby Hill LS25 202 A8
Lumby La
Monk Fryston LS25 202 A8
South Milford LS25 196 A1
Lumley Cl YO7 211 D2
Lumley La
Azerley HG4 112 D2
Kirkby Fleetham with Fencote
DL7 42 B1
Lumley Rd YO30 228 B7
Lumley St WF10 200 D3
Luna Pk* YO11 213 C6
Luncarr La HG4 114 B2
LUND 198 D3
Lund Cl YO32 225 C8
Lundgreen La YO61 144 A3
Lund Head La HG3 179 B2
Lund La
Bubwith YO8 199 C4
Cliffe YO8 198 D4
Hampsthwaite HG3 161 B4
Lund Rd YO62 70 B7
Lund Sand La
Easingwold YO61 143 A8
Raskelf YO61 117 A1
Lund Sike La LS25 195 F2
Lund's Twr* BD20 187 D6
Lundy Cl 10 YO30 225 A1
Lunebeck Wlk TS17 6 C6
Lunedale Ave
Knaresborough HG5 221 C5
Middlesbrough TS5 6 E8
Lunedale Rd DL3 3 A6
Lunnfields La WF11 201 E6
Lunn La DN14 202 D3
Lupton Bank HG3 137 D3
Lupton Cl HG3 137 D3
Lupton Springs HG3 137 D3
Lutton La YO17 123 F4
Luttons Com Prim Sch
YO17 150 B8
Lutyens The 22 LS29 175 C2
Lycett Rd YO24 230 F6
Lych Gate 14 DL2 3 E1
Lydford Rd 18 DL10 41 E4
Lydham Ct 2 YO24 230 C8
Lyell St YO12 212 E6
Lynbrook Cl YO7 211 B4
Lyndale
Guisborough TS14 8 D5
Kippax LS25 200 D8
Lyndale Ave YO10 229 C3
Lyndale Gr 14 WF6 200 B1
Lynden Cl HG4 214 E4
Lynden Way YO24 227 D3
Lyndhurst Cl
2 Norton DN6 206 F2
9 Whitby YO21 208 D6
Lyndhurst Dr 1 DN6 206 F2
Lyndhurst Rise 3 DN6 206 F2
Lyndon Ave
Bramham LS23 188 E6
Garforth LS25 194 C4
Lyndon Cl 1 LS23 188 E6
Lyndon Cres 4 LS23 188 E6
Lyndon Rd LS23 188 E6
Lyndon Sq 2 LS23 188 E6
Lyndon Way LS23 188 E6
Lynmouth Cl 2 TS8 6 E5
Lynndale Ave 6 BD20 187 F8
Lynton Ave LS23 188 E8
Lynton Cl YO8 232 B1
Lynton Gdns
Brayton YO8 232 B1
Darlington DL1 3 E5
Harrogate HG1 220 A3
Lynton Way DL6 210 D3
Lynwith Cl DN14 204 C3
Lynwith Ct DN14 204 C3
Lynwith Dr
5 Carlton DN14 204 C3
Carlton DN14 204 C3
Lynwood Ave 3 YO23 230 A3
Lynwood Cl YO32 167 A7
Lynwood View 4 YO23 230 A3
Lynx La YO7 115 B1
Lyonette Rd DL1 3 E7
Lyon Rd BD20 187 F7
Lyons Rd DL10 209 C8
Lysander Bsns Pk YO30 225 A3
Lysander Cl YO30 225 A3
Lys Cres DL9 209 D1
Lytham Cl BD23 217 C3
Lytham Gdns BD23 217 C3
Lytham Rd DL1 3 D8
LYTHE 12 E4
Lythe Bank
Lythe YO21 12 F4
Sutton with Howgrave DL8 87 F2
Lythe CE Prim Sch YO21 12 E3
Lythe Fell Rd LA2 129 B2
Lythe La LA2 129 A2

M

Mcan Cl YO10 229 D4
MacArthurs Cl YO7 211 B2
McBean Steps* YO11 213 A5
McCain Stad (Scarborough
FC) YO11 212 E2
McDonald Rd HG4 113 D3
MacDonell Cl 1 DL9 209 C1
MacKeridge La YO62 48 F4
Mackie Dr TS14 8 F7
MacKinnon Ave 1 WF6 200 B2
MacLagan Rd YO23 230 F4
McMullen Rd DL1 3 E6
Madeley Sq WF10 201 B5
Mafeking St HG1 219 F4
Magazine La YO8 198 C4
Magazine Rd YO8 198 B4
Magdalen's Cl HG4 214 D6
Magdalen's Rd HG4 214 D6
Magister Rd TS17 6 B7
Magnolia Gr YO32 225 D2
Magpie Garth YO12 99 E6
Magpie Wlk 28 DL9 41 A5
Maida Gr YO10 228 D2
Maiden Bower (Motte &
Bailey)* YO7 115 D5
Maiden Castle* DL11 38 A5
Maiden Greve YO17 215 A4
Maidensgrave Henge*
YO25 126 F1
Maidstone Dr TS7 7 C6
Main Ave
Woodlands HG2 220 C3
York YO31 228 F5
Main Rd
Drax YO8 204 F5
Gainford DL2 1 D7
Hambleton YO8 196 E1
Hellifield BD23 154 B3
Stainforth BD24 131 E6
Steeton with Eastburn
BD20 187 F7
Weaverthorpe YO17 124 E1
Mainsfield Cl 1 BD24 131 D3
Mainsfield Rise 2 BD24 131 D3
Mains La
Bishop Monkton HG3 140 A5
Leyburn DL8 60 C7
Whitwell-on-the-Hill YO60 146 D5
Main St
Aberford LS25 194 F8
Addingham LS29 174 F4
Allerston YO18 97 B5
Alne YO61 142 F4
Amotherby YO17 121 A4
Appleton Roebuck YO23 190 F5
Askham Bryan YO23 182 F3
Askrigg DL8 57 E6
Asselby DN14 205 D7
Austwick LA2 130 E7
Aysgarth DL8 58 E3
Barkston Ash LS24 195 E7
Barwick in Elmet LS15 194 B8
3 Beal DN14 202 D4
Bentham LA2 128 E8
Bilbrough YO23 182 C1
Bilton-in-Ainsty with Bickerton
LS22 181 A5
Bishop Monkton HG3 140 B5
Bishopthorpe YO23 231 A4
Boroughbridge YO51 141 A3
Brafferton YO61 141 F8
Bubwith YO8 199 C7
Bugthorpe YO41 169 D4
Burley in Warfedale LS29 176 C1
Burton Salmon LS25 201 F6
Church Fenton LS24 196 B7
Cliffe YO8 198 E2
Cononley BD20 173 D1
Copmanthorpe YO23 230 A2
Cottingwith YO42 193 C5
Darley HG3 160 A6
Deighton YO19 192 A7
Earby BB18 186 A7
East Ayton/West Ayton
YO13 99 A7
Eastfield YO11 100 B6
Ebberston & Yedingham
YO13 97 D5
Ellerton YO42 193 C1
Elvington YO41 185 C2
Embsay BD23 217 E8
Escrick YO19 192 B5
Farnhill BD20 173 E1
Folkton YO11 100 A2
Follifoot HG3 223 F5
Ganton YO12 125 A8
Garforth LS25 194 C3
Gillamoor YO62 70 A4
Gilling East YO62 118 F7
Glusburn BD20 187 E7
Gowdall DN14 204 A1
13 Grassington BD23 134 E3
Great Ouseburn YO26 164 B8
Great Preston WF10 200 D6
Gristlthorp YO14 100 E4
Harome YO62 93 C5
Healaugh LS24 181 F2
Hebden BD23 135 A1
Heck DN14 207 C8
Helperby YO61 142 A8
Hemingbrough YO8 198 F1
Hensall DN14 203 D2
Heslington YO10 229 B1
Hessay YO26 182 B8
High Bentham LA2 129 A8
Hovingham YO62 119 E6
Huby YO61 144 A4
Ingleton LA6 103 D3
Irton YO12 99 C6
Kelfield YO19 191 D1
Kellington DN14 202 F3
Kirkby Malham BD23 154 F8
Kirkby Malzeard HG4 112 C5
Kirk Deighton LS22 180 B5
Kirk Smeaton WF8 206 B3
Knapton YO26 227 A5
Langcliffe BD24 131 E4
Ledston WF10 200 F7
Linton LS22 180 A1
Little Ouseburn YO26 164 A7
Long Preston BD23 153 F5
Low Bradley BD20 173 E3
Menwith with Darley HG3 160 A4
Mickletown LS26 200 B6
Middleton YO18 95 E8
Monk Fryston LS25 201 F8
Monk Fryston LS25 202 A8
1 Naburn YO19 191 D8
Newton Kyme cum Toulston
LS24 189 C7
Main St *continued*
North Duffield YO8 199 A8
Nunthorpe YO10 231 D8
Pannal HG3 222 D3
Pollington DN14 207 F6
Poppleton YO26 165 F1
Rathmell BD24 153 C6
Reighton YO14 127 E5
Riccall YO19 198 A8
Ryther cum Ossendyke
LS24 190 E2
Saxton with Scarthingwell
LS24 195 D7
Scholes LS15 194 A7
Scotton HG5 162 A6
Seamer YO12 99 D6
Sheriff Hutton YO60 145 D5
Shipton YO30 165 F5
Sicklinghall LS22 179 D3
Sinnington YO62 95 A8
Stainforth BD24 131 E6
Stamford Bridge YO41 168 D2
Staveley HG5 140 E1
Stillington YO61 144 C6
Sutton-on-the-Forest YO61 144 C3
Threshfield BD23 134 C2
Thwing YO25 126 B1
Tollerton YO61 143 A3
Ulleskelf LS24 190 C3
Walton LS23 181 A2
Wath HG4 114 A8
Weeton LS17 178 C1
Westow YO60 147 B4
West Tanfield HG4 87 A1
Wheldrake YO19 192 F7
Whittington LA6 102 A7
Wilberfoss YO41 185 E5
Wombleton YO62 93 E6
Womersley DN6 206 C6
Woodlands HG2 220 B3
Wray-with-Botton LA2 128 A6
Mains The BD24 131 D3
Maison Dieu DL10 209 D7
Major St DL3 3 C6
Malais La BD20 187 D7
Malbys Gr YO23 230 B2
Malden Rd HG1 220 B3
MALHAM 133 A1
Malham Gr YO31 229 B5
Malham Moor La BD23 133 F4
Malham Rakes BD23 133 A2
Malham Tarn Field Ctr*
BD24 132 F6
Malham Tarn National Nature
Reserve* BD24 132 E5
Malham View Cl 28 BB18 171 D1
Malham Way HG5 221 D6
Malim Rd DL1 3 F5
Mallard Cl
8 Filey YO14 101 A4
12 Pickering YO18 95 F6
15 Ripon HG4 214 C5
Mallard Landings YO31 228 D8
Mallard Rd 4 DL9 40 F2
Mallard View YO17 215 D2
Mallard Way
4 Eastfield YO12 99 F6
11 Haxby YO32 166 F5
Mallard Wlk 14 YO51 141 B5
Mallinson Cl HG2 222 D6
Mallinson Cres HG2 222 E6
Mallinson Gate HG2 222 E6
Mallinson Gr HG2 222 D6
Mallinson Oval HG2 222 D6
Mallinson Way HG2 222 D6
Mallison Hill Dr 5 YO61 117 D1
Mallorie Cl HG4 214 A5
Mallorie Ct HG4 214 B5
Mallorie Park Dr HG4 214 A4
Mallory Cl YO32 225 D4
Mallory Ct 17 DL1 3 F6
Mallowdale TS7 7 C5
Malltraeth Sands TS17 6 D6
Malpas Dr DL7 210 D4
Malpas Rd
Brompton YO13 98 C4
Northallerton DL7 210 D3
Malsis Sch BD20 187 C7
MALTBY 6 C4
Maltby Pl 2 TS17 6 B8
Maltby Rd TS8 6 D4
Malt Dubs Cl LA6 103 D3
Malthouse Cl WF10 200 E4
Malthouse La HG3 222 D2
Maltings Bsns Ctr The
YO17 215 C3
Maltings Ct
Alne YO61 143 A5
6 Selby YO8 232 C6
Maltings Ind Est The
DN14 202 F1
Maltings The
8 Brafferton YO61 115 F1
Cliffe YO8 198 E3
13 Pontefract WF8 201 B1
Thirsk YO7 211 B2
Maltkiln La
Castleford WF10 200 F4
Killinghall HG3 161 C6
Malt Kiln La YO23 190 F5
Malt Kiln Terr LS24 189 D4
Maltings The LA6 102 A7
MALTON 215 C4
Malton Ave YO31 228 E6
Malton Gate YO18 96 D5
Malton La
Allerston YO18 97 B4
Flaxton YO60 146 A1

Malton La *continued*
Kirby Grindalythe YO17 150 A8
Malton Mus★ YO17 215 C4
Malton & Norton District Hospl YO17 215 B4
Malton Rd
Hunmanby YO14 126 F8
Huntington YO32 226 A1
Leavening YO17 147 E2
Pickering YO18 95 F6
Rillington YO17 122 E4
Scampston YO17 123 B7
Slingsby YO62 120 B5
Swinton YO17 121 C4
York YO31 228 F7
Malton Sch YO17 215 A5
Malton St YO61 117 D6
Malton Sta YO17 215 C3
Malton Way YO30 227 F8
Malt Shoval Ct YO1 233 C2
Malvern Ave YO26 227 D5
Malvern Cl
Huntington YO32 226 A5
8 Hurworth-on-Tees DL2 3 E1
Stokesley TS9 26 C7
Malvern Cres
Darlington DL3 2 F7
Scarborough YO12 212 D5
Malvern Dr
Middlesbrough TS5 6 E6
Stokesley TS9 26 C7
Malvern Rd WF11 201 F2
Manchester Rd BB18 171 D1
Mancroft YO32 225 C8
Mandale Mill Prim Sch TS17 6 B8
Mandale Rd TS5 6 D8
MANFIELD 2 B4
Manfield CE Prim Sch DL2 2 B4
Mangrill La LS14 188 C3
Manham Hill YO11 99 F7
Mankin La HG4 214 D1
Manley Cl YO32 225 D4
Manley Dr LS22 180 A3
Manley Gr LS29 218 D4
Manley Rd LS29 218 E4
Manley Rise LS29 218 D3
Manor Ave YO12 212 D6
Manor Beeches The 3 YO19 184 E7
Manor CE Acad YO26 227 C7
Manor Chase YO26 181 F6
Manor Cl
Burton in Lonsdale LA6 102 F3
Camblesforth YO8 204 C4
5 Hemingbrough YO8 198 F1
Ingleton LA6 103 D3
13 Kirkbymoorside YO62 70 B1
Kirk Smeaton WF8 206 B3
Low Worsall TS15 24 B8
6 North Duffield YO8 199 A7
12 Norton DN6 206 E2
5 Stokesley TS9 26 C7
Topcliffe YO7 115 C6
Upper Poppleton YO26 182 F8
Wath HG4 114 B7
Whitby YO21 208 B6
Manor Cres HG5 221 C6
Manorcroft WF6 200 A1
Manor Croft YO42 169 F1
Manor Ct
6 Bubwith YO8 199 D7
14 Eastfield YO11 99 F6
Fairburn WF11 201 D7
Follifoot HG3 223 F5
Kirkby Malzeard HG4 112 D5
Knaresborough HG5 221 B5
York YO10 228 F3
2 York YO32 225 F6
Manor Dr
2 Brafferton YO61 115 F1
Camblesforth YO8 204 C4
4 Dunnington YO19 184 E7
Harrogate HG2 222 C8
Hilton TS15 6 C2
Kirby Hill YO51 141 A7
Knaresborough HG5 221 C6
5 North Duffield YO8 199 A7
North Featherstone WF7 200 E1
Pickering YO18 95 E7
Scotton HG5 162 A6
Manor Drive N YO26 227 D4
Manor Drive S YO26 227 D4
Manor Farm LA6 102 A7
Manor Farm Cl
1 Brayton YO8 232 A1
Carlton DN14 204 C2
Copmanthorpe YO23 230 A2
Kellington DN14 202 F3
Manor Farm Ct
Chapel Haddlesey YO8 203 C4
Colton LS24 190 E7
Manor Farm Way
Coulby Newham TS8 6 F5
Scotton HG5 162 A6
Manorfields 11 DL2 3 E1
Manor Fields DN14 205 B2
Manor Fold HG3 223 F5
Manor Garth
13 Eastfield YO11 99 F6
Haxby YO32 225 B8
Kellington DN14 202 F3
12 Kirklevington TS15 24 E8
Ledsham LS25 201 B8
7 Norton DN6 206 F2
1 Riccall YO19 198 A8
7 Spofforth HG3 179 E6
Manor Garth Rd LS25 194 E1
Manor Gdns
6 Hunmanby YO14 127 A8
Killinghall HG3 161 C5
Kirkbymoorside YO62 70 B1
15 Knaresborough HG5 221 B6
Scarborough YO12 212 E6
Thorner LS14 188 A3
Manor Gn
Northallerton DL7 210 C3
Patrick Brompton DL8 62 C6
Manor Gr
Colburn DL9 40 F5
Great Broughton TS9 26 E5
Manor Heath YO23 230 A3
Manor House Art Gall & Mus★ LS29 218 B4
Manor House Wlk DL8 87 E7
Manor La
Healaugh LS24 181 E1
Rawcliffe YO30 224 D2
Manor Orchards HG5 221 B6
MANOR PARK 176 B2
Manor Park Ave
Great Preston WF10 200 D7
Pontefract WF8 201 C2
Manor Park Cl YO30 224 E2
Manor Park Gr 2 YO30 224 E2
Manor Park Rd YO30 224 E2
Manor Pk
Arkendale HG5 163 A7
Cowling BD22 187 B6
Ledston WF10 200 F7
Swinton YO17 121 C4
Manor Rd
Beal DN14 202 C4
Darlington DL3 3 C4
Easingwold YO61 117 C1
Fylingdales YO22 33 C4
Harrogate HG2 222 B8
Hurworth-on-Tees DL2 3 D1
Killinghall HG3 161 C5
Knaresborough HG5 221 B6
Scarborough YO12 212 E5
Stutton with Hazlewood LS24 189 D4
Manor Rise LS29 218 D4
Manor Vale La 28 YO62 70 B1
Manor View
Castleford WF10 200 F3
Oswaldkirk YO62 93 A1
Rillington YO17 122 F5
Manor View Rd YO11 100 D5
Manor Way
Glusburn BD20 187 E6
York YO30 224 E2
Manor Wood TS8 6 F6
Manse Cres 23 LS29 176 C1
Manse La HG5 221 D4
Mansell Cl YO8 232 A2
Manse Rd LS29 176 C1
Manse Way BD20 187 E7
Mansfield Ave TS17 6 B8
Mansfield Ct HG1 219 C4
Mansfield Rd LS29 176 B1
Mansfield St YO31 233 C3
Manston Ct 14 DL2 4 C4
Manston La LS15 194 A5
Manton Ave TS5 6 D8
Manuel St 1 DN14 205 F2
Maple Ave
Bishopthorpe YO23 231 A3
Malton YO17 215 D6
Walkerville DL9 41 A5
Maple Cl
5 Colburn DL9 40 F5
Hambleton YO8 197 B1
Harrogate HG2 220 D5
1 Leeming DL7 63 F3
2 South Milford LS25 195 F2
Maple Croft YO61 144 A5
Maple Ct
Wheldrake YO19 192 D8
York YO10 231 E6
Maple Dr YO12 212 D7
Maple Garth HG4 114 B7
Maple Gr
12 Brayton YO8 197 D1
7 Linton-on-Ouse YO30 164 F7
York YO10 228 D1
Maplehurst Ave YO31 228 D7
Maple La YO61 144 A5
Maple Rd DL10 209 A8
Maple Tree Ave 10 YO8 198 B4
Maple Wlk HG4 214 B2
Maplewood Paddock 2 YO24 227 C1
Marage Rd YO7 211 B3
Marazion Dr DL3 3 C8
March Ave HG5 221 A4
Marchbank Free Sch DL3 3 A6
Marchlyn Cres TS17 5 F4
March St
Normanton South WF6 200 A1
York YO31 233 C4
Marderby La YO7 90 C7
Maresfield Rd DL9 40 E3
Margaret Philipson Ct YO1 233 C3
Margaret Rd HG2 219 B1
Margaret St YO10 233 C1
Margerison Cres LS29 218 E3
Margerison Rd LS29 218 E3
Margrove Heritage Ctr★ TS12 9 D6
MARGROVE PARK 9 D6
Marhead Balk HG5 163 A7
Marias Ct 9 YO11 213 A6
Maria St 15 LS29 176 C1
Marigold Cl YO8 232 C2
Marina Cres BD23 216 D3
Marina Rd DL3 3 D8
Marina Way HG4 214 A2
Marine Dr YO11 213 C7
Marine Espl YO13 54 A8
Marine Par 24 YO21 208 D7
Mariner's Terr 16 YO14 101 B3
Marine Villa Rd WF11 201 F2
Marion Ave TS16 5 D4
Marishes La
Allerston YO17 97 A2
Thornton-le-Dale YO17 96 E1
Marishes Low Rd YO17 122 B8
Marjorie Waite Ct YO30 228 B7
Markenfield Hall★ HG4 139 D6
Markenfield Rd HG3 219 B5
Market Cross Sh Ctr 13 YO8 232 C5
Market Flat La HG5 162 C6
Market Hall YO11 213 B6
Market Hill 5 YO51 141 B6
Market La 14 YO8 232 C5
Market Pl
Askrigg DL8 57 E5
4 Bedale DL8 63 A3
2 Cawood YO8 197 B8
7 Easingwold YO61 143 C8
Harrogate HG1 219 D2
Hawes DL8 56 C4
10 Helmsley YO62 92 F6
25 Kirkbymoorside YO62 70 B1
3 Knaresborough HG5 221 B6
Malton YO17 215 C4
9 Masham HG4 86 C3
9 Middleham DL8 60 E2
6 Normanton South WF6 200 A1
Pickering YO18 95 F7
Richmond DL10 209 C6
11 Selby YO8 232 C5
10 Settle BD24 131 D2
7 Snaith DN14 204 C1
Thirsk YO7 211 B3
12 Wetherby LS22 180 C3
11 Whitby YO22 208 D7
Market Place E 19 HG4 214 C5
Market Place N 23 HG4 214 C5
Market Place S 20 HG4 214 C5
Market Place W 21 HG4 214 C5
Market Row DL7 210 D4
Market Sq 13 DL10 209 C6
Market St
Malton YO17 215 C4
Normanton South WF6 200 A1
24 Scarborough YO11 213 A6
York YO1 233 B2
Market Way 25 YO11 213 A6
Market Weighton Rd YO8 198 B6
Markham Cres YO31 233 B4
Markham St YO31 233 B4
Mark House La BD23 155 C1
MARKINGTON 139 D3
Markington CE Prim Sch HG3 139 C3
Mark La
Fylingdales YO22 33 C3
Kirk Deighton LS22 180 B5
Marlborough Ave
3 Byram WF11 201 F4
Tadcaster LS24 189 D5
3 Whitby YO21 208 B7
Marlborough Cl YO30 224 D3
Marlborough Dr
Darlington DL1 3 C4
Tadcaster LS24 189 D5
Marlborough Gr
Ilkley LS29 218 D3
Ripon HG4 214 B6
York YO10 228 D2
Marlborough Rd HG1 219 E2
Marlborough Sq LS29 218 C3
Marlborough St 11 YO12 213 A7
Marlborough Villas YO10 228 D2
Marl Hill La BD20 186 D8
Marmiam Dr 2 YO32 167 D2
Marmion Ct HG4 87 A1
Marmion Twr★ HG4 87 A1
Marne Cl 1 DL9 209 B1
Marne Rd DL9 209 D1
Marquis Ct 2 YO26 227 D6
MARRICK 38 F5
Marrick Priory Outdoor Ctr★ DL11 38 E4
Marrick Rd TS18 5 D8
Marridales DL8 56 D4
Marriforth La HG4 61 F2
Marriner St 13 LS21 176 F1
Marr The YO14 100 F5
Marrtree Bsns Pk WF10 200 E3
Marsdens Pl 7 YO22 208 E6
Marsden Wlk DL3 3 C8
MARSETT 57 A1
Marsett La DL8 57 B2
Marshall Dr YO18 96 A7
Marshall Mews 2 WF10 200 E4
Marshall Way HG4 214 C5
Marsh Croft WF11 201 E4
Marsh End WF11 202 A3
Marshfield Rd 7 BD24 131 D2
Marsh La
Asselby DN14 205 D7
Barlow YO8 204 B8
2 Beal DN14 202 D4
Bolton Percy YO23 190 D3
Byram cum Sutton WF11 201 F4
Cawood YO8 197 D8
Ingleby Greenhow TS9 27 B5
Marsh La *continued*
35 Kirkbymoorside YO62 70 B1
Knottingley WF11 202 A2
West Haddlesey YO8 202 F5
Marsh Lane Gdns DN14 202 F4
Marsh Rd WF10 200 D3
MARSKE 39 C7
Mars La TS13 11 A4
Marston Ave YO26 227 B3
Marston Bsns Pk YO26 181 B7
Marston Cres YO26 227 B3
Marston La
Long Marston YO26 182 A8
Moor Monkton YO26 165 A1
Marston Moor Rd 4 DL1 3 F4
Marston Rd YO26 181 D7
Marston Way 3 LS22 180 B3
Martello Way YO32 226 A1
Marten Cl 2 YO30 228 A8
Martin Cheeseman Ct 3 YO24 230 C8
Martindale Rd DL1 3 D7
Martinet Ct TS17 6 A7
Martinet Rd TS17 6 B7
Martinhoe Cl 4 TS17 6 A3
Martins Ct YO26 228 A5
MARTON
Boroughbridge 141 D1
Middlesbrough 7 B7
Pickering 94 F6
Marton Abbey (Priory)★ YO61 144 C8
Marton Ave TS4 7 B8
Marton Cl BD23 172 C8
Marton Ct YO21 208 B6
Marton-Cum-Grafton CE VA Prim Sch YO51 141 D1
Marton Gr 1 TS3 7 C8
MARTON-IN-THE-FOREST 144 E7
Marton La
Arkendale HG5 163 B8
Wrelton YO18 95 C7
MARTON-LE-MOOR 114 F1
Marton Manor Prim Sch TS7 7 B6
Marton Moor Rd TS7 7 D5
Marton Rd
Coulby Newham TS4 7 A7
Gargrave BD23 172 C8
Marton YO62 94 F6
Sinnington YO62 95 A7
Martonside Way TS4 7 A8
Marton St BD23 216 D3
Marton Sta TS7 7 C7
Marvell Rise HG1 219 E7
Marwood CE VC Infant Sch TS9 7 F1
Marwood Dr TS9 7 F1
Marygate
Barton DL10 21 D7
York YO30 233 A3
Marygate La YO30 233 A3
Marykirk Rd TS17 6 B6
Mary La YO26 141 F3
Masefield Cl HG1 219 E7
MASHAM 86 B3
Masham Bank HG4 85 D8
Masham CE Prim Sch HG4 86 C3
Masham Cl HG2 220 C1
Masham La DL8 87 A4
Masham Rd
Firby DL8 62 F1
Harrogate HG2 220 C1
Snape with Thorp DL8 86 E8
Mask La YO41 185 D4
MASONGILL 103 A6
Masongill Fell La LA6 103 A6
Masonic La YO7 211 B3
Masons Way BB18 171 D2
Maspin Moor Rd LS25 202 C7
Massa Flatts Wood BD23 216 E5
Massey St YO8 232 C5
Master Rd TS17 6 B7
Master's Gate YO18 49 D4
Mastil Cl DL8 62 D5
Mastiles La BD23 134 A6
Mastil La DL8 62 D5
Matfen Ave TS7 7 D6
Matthew La
Bradleys Both BD20 173 E3
Green Hammerton YO26 164 C4
Mattison Way YO24 227 E2
Maude Rd DL9 209 A1
Maud La LS21 177 A6
Maudon Ave YO18 96 A6
Maudon Gr YO17 215 F4
Maufe Way 3 LS29 218 B3
MAUNBY 64 D1
Maunby La YO7 64 D1
Maundy Gr HG5 221 C7
Mawson Gr DL6 65 B5
Mawson La HG4 214 C4
Maxim Cl 5 DL9 40 E4
Maxwell Rd LS29 218 D3
Mayfair Ave TS6 7 E8
Mayfair Rd DL1 3 D8
Mayfield DL7 64 F2
Mayfield Ave
Ilkley LS29 218 D4
7 Scalby YO12 75 E5
Mayfield Cl
3 Glusburn BD20 187 E7
Ilkley LS29 218 D4
Mayfield Cres TS16 5 D5
Mayfield Ct YO8 204 C7
Mayfield Dr
5 Brayton YO8 232 A1
4 Seamer YO12 99 D6
Mayfield Gdns LS29 218 D5
Mayfield Gr
Harrogate HG1 219 D3
Knaresborough HG5 221 C6
York YO24 230 E8
Mayfield Pl
Harrogate HG1 219 D3
3 Whitby YO21 208 C5
Mayfield Rd
Brayton YO8 232 A1
1 High Bentham LA2 129 A7
Ilkley LS29 218 C4
Middlesbrough TS7 7 D6
Whitby YO21 208 B5
Mayfield Terr HG1 219 D3
Mayfly Ct 26 YO18 95 F6
Maypole Gdns YO8 197 B8
Maypole Gr 3 YO19 191 D8
Maypole Mews LS15 194 B8
Maythorne 6 DL8 60 D5
Maythorn Rd YO31 225 E2
Maythorpe YO23 182 C6
Mayville Ave YO12 212 E6
Mead Cres TS17 6 C8
Meadlands YO31 229 B6
Meadow Ave 5 HG4 214 B2
Meadowbank Rd TS7 7 D7
Meadowbeck Cl YO10 229 B4
Meadow Brook Chase 19 WF6 200 B1
Meadow Cl
Cononley BD20 173 D2
7 Eastfield YO11 100 A6
Hampsthwaite HG3 160 F5
Northallerton DL7 210 D2
Thorpe Willoughby YO8 197 C2
Meadowcroft
Draughton BD23 174 B7
Harrogate HG1 219 E6
Meadow Croft
Brayton YO8 232 A2
Colonley BD20 173 C2
Meadowcroft Dr HG3 140 A5
Meadow Ct
Carlton DN14 204 C2
Rillington YO17 122 F5
Scruton DL7 63 E7
6 Willerby YO12 99 D2
3 York YO24 230 E8
Meadow Dale Ct TS12 9 F7
Meadow Dr
7 East Ayton/West Ayton YO13 99 B8
Harrogate HG1 219 E7
Scruton DL7 63 E7
Thorpe Willoughby YO8 197 B2
Meadowfield
Amotherby YO17 121 A4
9 Bedale DL8 63 B3
1 Bubwith YO8 199 D7
Lythe YO21 13 A3
8 Stokesley TS9 26 C8
Meadowfield Cl YO17 121 B4
Meadowfield Dr
Eaglescliffe TS16 5 D5
South Duffield YO8 199 A4
Meadowfield Rd
9 Colburn DL9 41 A5
Darlington DL3 3 A7
Meadowfields YO21 208 C6
Meadowfields Cl 9 YO61 143 D8
Meadowfields Ct 17 YO21 208 D6
Meadowfields Dr YO31 225 D2
Meadow Garth
2 Tadcaster LS24 189 F6
Thirsk YO7 211 B1
Thorpe Willoughby YO8 197 C2
Meadow Gate HG1 219 E6
Meadow Gr 20 DL8 63 A2
Meadowings The TS15 5 D2
Meadow La
Cononley BD20 173 C2
2 Darley HG3 160 A6
8 Eastfield YO11 100 A6
1 Haxby YO32 225 D8
Hellifield BD23 154 A3
Northallerton DL6 210 E6
Snape DL8 87 A7
Meadowlands Cl 2 TS13 11 A8
Meadow Lea 21 BD20 187 E7
Meadow Pl 5 YO8 232 B6
Meadow Rd
23 Castleford WF10 200 D3
Garforth LS25 194 D4
Knaresborough HG5 221 B7
2 Pickering YO18 95 F7
Meadow Rise
Harrogate HG1 219 E7
7 Settle BD24 131 D3
2 Skipton BD23 217 B5
Meadowside Com Prim Sch HG5 221 C7
Meadows Pk YO8 202 F8
Meadow Springs Way 3 YO61 143 D8
Meadows The
3 Carlton DN14 204 C3
Castleford LS25 200 C7
Coulby Newham TS8 7 B5
Hambleton YO8 196 F1

Meadows The *continued*
[8] Middleton St George DL2 4 C4
[7] Monk Fryston LS25 202 A8
Northallerton DL6 210 E5
Riccall YO19 197 F8
Richmond DL10 209 E7
Scalby YO12 212 B7
[2] Skelton YO30 224 B5
South Milford LS25 195 F2
Meadow Vale
Green Hammerton YO26 164 C3
[2] Ripon HG4 214 B2
Meadow View
Barwick in Elmet & Scholes LS15 194 B8
Gristhorpe YO14 100 E4
Harrogate HG1 219 E6
Sherburn in Elmet LS25 195 F4
Meadow Way
Barnoldswick BB18 171 E2
Harrogate HG1 219 E7
Heworth YO31 228 F7
Huntington YO32 225 F4
[3] Tadcaster LS24 189 F6
Meads La YO12 99 E5
Meads The [3] YO11 99 F6
Mead The DL1 3 E5
Meadway YO8 197 D2
Meadway Dr YO8 197 D2
MEAGILL 159 D3
Meagill La LS21 159 E2
Meagill Rise LS21 176 E1
Meam Cl YO10 229 D4
Meanee Rd [11] DL9 40 F2
MEARBECK 153 D7
Medbourne Gdns TS5 6 E7
Megson Pl YO7 211 C4
Megsons Ct BD23 217 C7
Melander Cl YO26 227 B4
Melander Gdns [5] YO32 225 D7
Melbourne Dr YO7 90 E5
Melbourne Pl YO7 211 B2
Melbourne St YO10 228 D2
Melcombe Ave [11] YO32 167 A7
Meldyke La TS8 6 D5
Mellersh Rd [15] DL10 41 E4
Melling St Wilfrid CE Prim Sch LA6 102 A2
Melltown's Gn YO7 88 C6
MELMERBY
Carlton 83 F8
Ripon 114 C7
Melmerby Green La HG4 114 C6
Melmerby Green Rd HG4 114 B6
Melmerby Ind Est HG4 114 B6
Melrose Cl [1] YO31 229 A5
Melrose Cres
Bishop Monkton HG3 140 A5
Guisborough TS14 9 A6
Melrose Dr [16] LS29 176 C1
Melrosegate YO31 228 F5
Melrose Rd HG3 140 A5
Melrose St [4] YO12 212 F6
MELSONBY 21 A7
Melsonby Methodist Prim Sch DL10 20 F7
Melton Ave YO30 227 F8
Melton Coll YO24 227 F3
Melton Dr
Bishopthorpe YO23 231 A3
York YO30 227 F8
Melville Gr [1] LS29 218 E4
Melville Terr [52] YO14 101 B3
Melwood Gr YO26 227 B5
Memorial Dr TS7 7 B6
Mendip Cl [2] YO32 225 F5
MENETHORPE 147 D6
Menethorpe La YO17 147 D7
Menin Rd DL9 209 B1
MENTHORPE 199 C5
Menwith Hill Rd HG3 159 D4
Mercer Art Gall The★ HG2 219 C3
Mercer Dr DL9 209 C1
Merchant Adventurers' Hall★ YO1 233 C2
Merchantgate YO1 233 C2
Merchants Ct YO31 228 E5
Merchant's Row [10] YO11 213 B6
Merchant Way YO23 230 B3
Mercury Pk DL7 63 C5
Mercury Rd DL10 209 A8
Merefield Way WF10 200 E2
Mere La YO11 212 F1
Mere View Gdns YO12 99 F8
Merewood Rd WF10 200 C4
Merioneth Cl [5] TS17 5 F4
Merlin Cl DL9 209 D1
Merlin Covert [4] YO31 225 F3
Merlinwood BD23 172 B4
Merrington Ave TS17 6 D6
Merrybank La LS17 178 A3
MERRYBENT 2 E5
Merrybent Dr DL2 2 F5
Merry Dale YO11 100 A7
Merryfield HG2 222 B7
Messines Rd DL9 40 E3
Metcalfe La YO19 229 C5
Metcalfes Ct HG4 214 C6
Metes La YO12 99 E5
METHLEY 200 B5
METHLEY JUNCTION 200 A4
Methley La LS26 200 A6
Methley Park Hospl LS26 200 A6
Methley Prim Sch LS26 200 B6
Methley Rd WF10 200 D4
Meuse Cl [4] DL9 209 C1
Mewburn Rd DL3 3 C8
MEWITH HEAD 129 E6
Mewith La LA2 129 B6
Mews The WF6 200 A2
Meynell Rd DL3 3 C7
Meyrick Ave LS22 180 D4
Michael Mount Rd YO11 213 C1
Michael Syddall CE Prim Sch DL10 41 E5
Micklebury La HG4 86 A3
MICKLEBY 12 A4
Mickleby Dr YO21 208 B6
Mickleby La TS13 11 F4
Mickledale La YO26 163 D8
MICKLEFIELD 194 F4
Micklefield CE Prim Sch LS25 195 A4
Micklefield Sta LS25 195 A3
Micklegate
[17] Pontefract WF8 201 B1
[1] Selby YO8 232 D5
York YO1 233 A2
Micklegate Bar Mus★ YO24 233 A1
Mickle Hill Mews BD23 155 D1
Micklethwaite View LS22 180 C2
MICKLETOWN 200 B5
Mickletown Rd LS26 200 B6
Micklewaite Gr LS22 180 C2
MICKLEY 112 F7
Middle Bank Rd TS7 7 D7
Middle Banks [24] YO32 166 E5
Middlebrook Gdns YO8 232 A2
MIDDLECAVE 215 A5
Middlecave Cl YO17 215 A4
Middlecave Dr YO17 215 A4
Middlecave Rd YO17 215 B4
Middle Craven Rd [27] BD24 131 D2
Middlecroft YO41 185 F5
Middlecroft Dr YO32 167 A7
Middlecroft Gr [2] YO32 167 B7
Middlefield Cl
[19] Osgodby YO11 100 B7
Weaverthorpe YO17 124 E1
Middlefield La
Kirk Smeaton WF8 206 A2
Melmerby DL8 84 A8
MIDDLEHAM 60 E2
Middleham Ave YO31 228 E8
Middleham Castle★ DL8 60 E2
Middleham CE Prim Sch DL8 60 E2
Middleham La DL8 60 E4
Middleham Rd [20] DL8 60 D5
Middle Head Rd
Pickering YO18 71 E8
Stape YO18 71 E8
Middle La
Brayton YO8 232 C1
Brompton YO13 98 C7
Collingham LS22 180 B1
Hutton Buscel YO13 74 E1
Kettlewell with Starbotton BD23 108 A3
[4] Knottingley WF11 202 A2
Snainton YO13 97 F4
Middle Moor Bsns Pk YO7 116 A7
Middle Moor La DL11 39 F5
Middle Oxford St WF10 200 E4
Middle Rd TS17 6 A5
Middlesbrough Rd TS7 7 E6
MIDDLESMOOR 110 B5
Middle St
Gayles DL11 19 E6
Swinton YO17 121 B4
Wilberfoss YO41 185 F6
MIDDLETHORPE 231 B6
Middlethorpe Dr YO24 230 E7
Middlethorpe Gr YO24 230 F7
MIDDLETON
Glusburn 187 A6
Ilkley 218 C7
Pickering 95 E8
Middleton Ave
Ilkley LS29 218 B6
Thornaby TS17 6 B6
Middleton Carr La YO18 95 D7
Middleton Cl
Egglescliffe TS16 5 C5
Settrington YO17 122 D1
Middleton La
Middleton St George DL2 4 C3
Middleton YO18 95 E8
MIDDLETON ONE ROW 4 D3
MIDDLETON-ON-LEVEN 25 D8
MIDDLETON QUERNHOW 88 B1
Middleton Rd
Hutton Rudby TS15 25 D6
Ilkley LS29 218 A4
Pickering YO18 95 E7
Sadberge DL2 4 C7
York YO24 227 C2
MIDDLETON ST GEORGE 4 B4
MIDDLETON TYAS 21 D5
Middleton Tyas CE Prim Sch DL10 21 C5
Middleton Tyas La DL10 21 B4
Middleway BD20 174 C1
Middle Wlk YO12 212 E7
Middlewood Cl
[3] Fylingdales YO22 33 C3
Rufforth YO23 182 C6
Middlewood Cres [5] YO22 33 C3
Middlewood Garth [4] YO22 33 C3
Middlewood La YO22 33 C3
Middycar Bank HG4 138 F6
Midge Hall Cl [18] LS29 176 C1
Midgeley Gate HG5 162 F2
Midgeley La HG5 163 A3
Midgley Cl
[4] Embsay BD23 217 C7
[21] Stamford Bridge YO41 168 D2
Midgley Rd LS29 176 C1
Midgley Rise [2] WF8 201 B2
Midhope Way [15] YO14 101 A3
Midland St BD23 216 E3
Midway Ave YO26 224 A1
Mightens' Bank DL8 60 D4
Milbank Rd DL3 3 B5
Milburn La YO7 89 D3
MILBY 141 B6
Mildred Gr [5] YO24 227 F2
Mildred Sylvester Way WF6 200 B1
Mile Hill Coldhill La LS25 195 E5
Mile House Bsns Pk DL6 210 B7
Mile Planting DL10 209 F8
Milestone Ave YO23 182 C6
Milford Mews [7] YO32 225 D7
Milford Rd LS25 195 F3
Milford Way
[8] Haxby YO32 225 D7
[19] South Milford LS25 195 F2
Milking Hill YO61 118 B4
Mill Balk DN14 207 C8
Mill Bank
Bishop Thornton HG3 138 F1
Fylingdales YO22 33 D2
Lindrick with Studley Royal & Fountains HG4 113 A3
Norton YO17 215 E3
Millbank Ct YO7 89 D4
Millbank La TS17 6 B7
Mill Bank Rd YO18 72 D5
Millbeck Gn LS22 188 A8
Millbeck La BB18 186 A7
Millbeck View WF8 201 B2
Mill Bridge BD23 216 F4
Millbrook Ct [17] BB8 186 A3
Mill Brow LA2 128 E2
Mill Brow Rd BB18 172 B1
Mill Cl
Monk Fryston LS25 202 A8
Ravensworth DL11 19 F6
Settle BD24 131 D2
[6] Spofforth HG3 179 E6
Mill Close La DL8 62 D6
Mill Cotts YO17 215 D4
Millcroft [15] YO8 197 D1
Mill Croft
Cowling BD22 187 B6
Richmond DL10 209 A7
MILL DAM 129 C6
Mill Dam LS23 188 F7
Mill Dam La WF8 201 C1
Mill Dike La YO7 116 F8
Millenium Rd BD20 173 D4
Millers Cl YO17 215 D2
Millers Croft [6] YO23 230 B3
Millers Dr [10] DN14 202 F2
Millers Ford LA2 128 E8
Millers La TS12 9 F6
Millers Rd [2] YO7 211 C3
Millfield YO51 141 D2
Millfield Ave
Northallerton DL6 210 E3
York YO10 228 F3
Millfield Cl
Eaglescliffe TS16 5 D4
[1] Leeming DL7 63 D4
Pickering YO18 95 F6
Wilberfoss YO41 185 E5
Millfield Cres DL6 210 E3
Millfield Ct YO19 192 F7
Mill Field Ct [5] BD20 174 C1
Millfield Dr YO8 204 D4
Millfield Gdns YO26 224 A2
Millfield Glade HG2 220 D4
Millfield Ind Est YO19 192 F7
Millfield La
Easingwold YO61 117 C1
Nether Poppleton YO26 227 B8
Poppleton YO26 224 A2
York YO10 229 A3
Mill Field La YO61 91 B1
Millfield Lane Ind Est YO10 227 B8
Millfield Rd
[17] Hemingbrough YO8 198 F1
Hemingbrough YO8 204 F8
York YO23 228 B2
Mill Field Rd YO8 203 B5
Millfield Rise YO61 117 C1
Millfields [2] BD20 174 C1
Millfield St [4] HG3 137 B4
Mill Flats La DL8 60 F3
Mill Garth [14] YO8 198 F1
Millgarth Ct [7] LS22 188 A8
Millgate
[10] Masham HG4 86 C3
Richmond DL10 209 C6
Selby YO8 232 C6
Thirsk YO7 211 B3
Mill Gate
Gilling with Hartforth & Sedbury DL10 20 E3
Harrogate HG1 219 C7
Knayton with Brawith YO7 65 E2
Millgate House Gdn★ DL10 209 C6
Millgate Mews [3] YO8 232 C6
Millgates YO26 227 C6
Mill Green Way The YO22 51 D8
Mill Hill
Escrick YO19 192 B5
[16] Normanton South WF6 200 A1
Mill Hill Cl [8] DL6 43 F3
Mill Hill Com Prim Sch DL6 210 E4
Mill Hill Cres DL6 210 E3
Mill Hill Dr YO32 225 F4
Mill Hill La
Giggleswick BD24 131 C3
Northallerton DL6 210 E3
MILL HIRST 159 F7
Millholme Dr [2] LA2 129 A7
Millholme Rise BD23 217 C8
Mill House YO7 65 D1
Mill Hurst HG3 159 F7
Millings La YO51 141 B7
Mill La
Acaster Malbis YO23 191 C8
Ampleforth YO62 118 C8
Askham Richard YO23 182 D2
Askrigg DL8 57 E6
Aysgarth DL8 58 E3
Barlow YO8 204 B7
Bellerby DL8 60 E8
Bentham LA2 128 F7
[3] Bewerley HG3 137 B4
Boroughbridge YO51 141 B5
Brayton YO8 203 C8
Buckton/Bempton YO13 97 D5
Burniston YO13 75 C8
Burton Leonard HG3 140 B2
Carlton DN14 204 D3
Castleford WF10 200 E5
Cayton YO11 100 C6
Constable Burton DL8 61 C5
Darlington DL1 3 F6
Drax YO8 204 F5
Earby BB18 172 B1
Easingwold YO61 117 D1
[3] East Ayton/West Ayton YO13 99 A7
Eskdaleside cum Ugglebarnby YO22 32 B6
Exelby, Leeming & Newton DL7 63 D3
Faceby TS9 25 F2
Farndale East YO62 48 E4
Gargrave BD23 155 D1
Great Ouseburn YO26 164 C8
Hambleton YO8 196 F1
Haxby YO32 166 D5
Hebden BD23 135 A1
[2] Hemingbrough YO8 198 F1
Hessay YO23 182 B7
High Coniscliffe DL2 2 C6
Kearby with Netherby LS22 179 C2
Kirk Hammerton YO26 164 C2
Knaresborough HG5 221 F8
Langtoft YO25 151 C7
Leyburn DL8 60 E4
[6] Linton-on-Ouse YO30 164 F7
Longnewton DL2 4 F6
Long Preston BD23 153 F4
Low Bradley BD20 173 E3
Low Hawsker YO22 33 A6
Mickletown LS26 200 B6
Middleton St George DL2 4 D5
Muston YO14 101 A2
Nether Burrow LA6 102 B6
Nether Silton YO7 66 B7
Newland YO8 205 A3
Northallerton DL7 210 C3
Pannal HG3 222 E2
Pickering YO18 95 F6
Pontefract WF8 201 C2
Rawcliffe DN14 204 F1
Redmire DL8 59 C5
[1] Riccall YO19 192 A1
Richmond DL10 209 A6
Ryther cum Ossendyke LS24 190 E1
[1] Scarborough YO12 212 E3
Scruton DL7 63 E5
Sherburn in Elmet LS25 195 F2
Skipton BD23 216 F3
Sledmere YO25 149 F3
Snape with Thorp DL8 87 B7
South Milford LS25 195 F2
Spofforth with Stockeld HG3 179 E6
Stillington YO61 144 C6
Stutton with Hazlewood LS24 189 E4
Swinden BD23 154 B1
Thirkleby High & Low with Osgodby YO7 90 D2
Thormanby YO61 116 E5
Thrintoft DL7 63 F8
Whitwood WF10 200 B2
Wilberfoss YO41 185 E6
York YO31 228 E6
Youlton YO61 142 F2
Mill Lane Ave YO60 145 C5
Mill Mount YO24 228 A3
Mill Mount Ct YO24 228 A3
Millrace Cl YO17 215 D2
Mill Race The [4] DL2 22 C8
Mill Rd
Burton Fleming YO25 126 D4
Gillamoor YO62 70 A5
Goldsborough HG5 221 F3
Mill Riggs TS9 26 D7
Mill Rise DL6 210 E2
Mill Row BD20 187 F7
Millside YO17 215 D2
Mill St
[6] Barnoldswick BB18 171 D1
[8] Eastburn BD20 187 F7
[41] Glusburn BD20 187 F7
Guisborough TS14 8 F6
Harome YO62 93 C4
Malton YO17 215 E3
Scarborough YO12 212 F5
York YO1 233 C1
Millthorpe Sch YO23 228 B2
Mill View
[5] Burley in Warfedale LS29 176 C1
Hut Green DN14 203 A2
Knottingley WF11 201 D2
Millway YO62 92 C1
Mill Wynd TS16 5 E3
Milner La LS24 195 D8
Milner Rd DL1 3 D4
Milners La HG1 219 F7
Milner St YO24 227 D3
Milnthorpe Cl [6] LS23 188 E6
Milnthorpe Garth [7] LS23 188 E6
Milnthorpe Gdns [5] LS23 188 E6
Milnthorpe La LS23 188 E6
Milnthorpe Way LS23 188 D5
Milson Gr YO10 229 A3
Milton Ave
Malton YO17 215 D5
Scarborough YO12 212 E3
Milton Carr [8] YO30 224 F1
Milton Cl HG1 219 E7
Milton Gr [11] BB18 171 D2
Milton Rd
Malton YO17 215 C5
Pannal HG3 222 E3
Milton St
Darlington DL1 3 E5
[4] Skipton BD23 217 A3
York YO10 228 F3
Minchin Cl [3] YO30 225 B1
Miniskip Cl [12] TS14 8 F7
Minors Cres DL3 3 A7
MINSKIP 141 A3
Minskip Rd HG5 140 F2
Minster Ave YO31 225 F2
Minster Cl
[3] Haxby YO32 225 C8
[23] Ripon HG4 214 C5
[40] Wigginton YO32 166 E5
York YO1 233 B3
Minster Ct YO1 233 B3
Minsterley Dr TS5 6 D7
Minster Rd HG4 214 C5
Minster Sch The YO1 233 B3
Minster View YO32 225 C8
Minster Wlk [12] DL2 3 E1
Minster Yd YO1 233 B3
Minter Cl [2] YO24 227 B1
Mire Bank La DL8 56 F4
Mire Close La BD22 187 A8
Mire Ridge BB8 186 A2
Mires La
Carthorpe DL8 87 D6
Ulleskelf LS24 190 B1
Mire Syke La HG5 162 A5
Mirey Butt La WF11 201 E2
Mirkhill Rd YO8 232 B6
Miry La LS15 188 C1
Missies La HG4 112 C3
Mistral Ct YO31 228 E8
Mitchell Ave TS17 6 B7
Mitchell Gr [43] DL9 41 A5
Mitchell La
Alne YO61 142 F4
Catton YO41 185 D8
Settle BD24 131 E1
Mitchell Way [11] YO30 224 E3
Mitchel's La YO10 231 F8
Miterdale [4] YO24 230 C7
Mitford Cl [3] YO14 126 F8
Mitford Rd [2] YO14 126 F8
Mitford St [24] YO14 101 B3
Mitton La BD20 172 D1
MLS Bsns Centres YO30 225 A2
Moat Field YO10 229 C4
Moatside Ct YO31 233 B3
Moat Way YO8 232 A2
Mock Beggar Hall★ BD23 157 D7
Moins Ct YO10 229 D4
Moiser Cl YO32 225 D4
Mole End [15] YO18 95 F6
Monarch Way YO26 227 D6
Monash Ave DL9 209 C1
Monckton Dr WF10 201 B3
Monk Ave YO31 228 F7
Monk Bar Ct YO1 233 B3
Monkbridge Ct YO31 233 C4
Monket House Bank YO62 48 C4
MONK FRYSTON 202 B8
Monk Fryston CE Prim Sch LS25 202 A8
Monk Gardens La YO62 93 A7
Monkgate YO31 233 C3
Monkgate Cloisters YO31 233 C3
Monk Gn YO61 142 F4
MONKHILL 201 B1
Monkhill Ave WF8 201 B1
Monkhill Dr WF8 201 B1
Monkhill La WF8 201 B2
Monkhill Mount WF8 201 B1
Monkholme La BD23 134 C2
Monk Ing Rd HG3 159 E8
Monk La YO8 232 C7

Monkmans Wharfe 1 BD20 174 C1
Monk Park Farm★ YO7 90 D4
MONKROYD 186 D4
Monkroyd Ave BB18 171 D1
Monks Cross Dr YO32 226 A3
Monks Cross Link YO32 226 B4
Monks Cross Sh Pk YO32 226 B3
Monk's Rd BD23 107 D2
Monkswell Pk HG5 221 D5
Monkton Rd 5 YO31 225 F1
Monkton Rise 7 TS14 8 F7
Monmouth Dr TS16 5 E5
Monmouth St 5 BB8 186 A3
Monroe Cl YO30 224 E2
Mons Cl 3 DL9 209 B1
Mons Rd DL9 40 F4
Montage Studio Gall★ YO21 29 A7
Montague Cres LS25 194 D4
Montague Rd YO23 231 A3
Montague St YO23 228 C1
Montague Wlk 6 YO26 165 F1
Montagu La LS22 180 E5
Montagu Mews LS22 180 E5
Montagu's Harrier TS14 8 D6
Montagu Way LS22 180 E5
Montgomery Rd DL9 209 C2
Montgomery St BD23 217 A3
Montpellier Ct 11 HG2 219 C2
Montpellier Gdns 2 HG1 219 C2
Montpellier Hill HG2 219 C2
Montpellier Mews 3 HG1 219 C2
Montpellier Par HG1 219 C2
Montpellier Rd 1 HG1 219 C2
Montpellier Sq 3 HG1 219 D2
Montpellier St 4 HG1 219 C2
Montrose Ave YO31 228 D8
Montrose Gdns WF10 200 D4
Monument Cl YO24 227 E3
Moody Sty La 4 BD23 134 E3
Mook St YO60 169 B8
Moons Acre LA2 129 A8
Moor Ave 1 LS23 188 E7
Moorber La BD23 171 F8
Moorberries TS15 6 C2
Moorbridge Croft 6 LS25 196 A4
Moor Carr La
Barlby with Osgodby YO8 198 B5
Barlby YO8 198 B5
Moor Cl
Killinghall HG3 219 A8
10 Kirklevington TS15 24 E8
Lockwood TS12 10 A5
Wheldrake YO19 192 F8
Moorcock La HG3 159 F5
Moor Cres BD23 217 B4
Moor Croft 8 BD23 134 E3
Moorcroft Rd YO24 230 D7
Moore Ave YO10 229 B4
MOOR END 188 D8
Moor End Gdns LS23 188 D8
Moor End La
Crakehall DL8 62 C3
Sowerby YO7 90 A2
Moor End Rd YO13 53 F2
Moorfield Cl 6 DL1 3 E4
Moorfield Dr YO41 185 E6
Moorfield Rd LS29 218 F4
Moorfields
Raskelf YO61 116 F2
3 Wistow YO8 197 D6
Moorfield Sch LS29 218 C3
Moorfields La YO62 93 E5
Moorfield Way YO41 185 E6
Moorfoot La BD20 173 D2
Moorgarth LA6 103 D2
Moorgarth Ave 10 YO24 227 F2
Moorgate YO24 227 D3
Moorgate Dr LS25 194 D1
Moorgate Rd LS25 194 D2
Moor Gn TS7 7 D5
Moor Gr YO24 230 E8
Moor Hill YO17 147 E7
Moorhill La YO17 147 E6
Moorhills DL8 56 C4
Moorhouse Cl 3 WF6 200 B2
Moorhouse La YO7 89 E8
Moor House La YO61 116 B1
Moor La
Addingham LS29 174 D5
Aislaby YO21 31 F7
Aldfield HG4 138 F8
Arkendale HG5 162 F7
Arrathorne DL10 41 A2
Askwith LS21 176 D4
Bagby YO7 90 C4
6 Barlby YO8 198 B5
Bilbrough LS24 182 B1
Bilton-in-Ainsty with Bickerton YO26 181 D5
Bishopthorpe YO23 230 E2
Borrowby TS13 11 C6
Brawby YO17 94 F2
Brompton YO13 74 B1
Broughton YO17 121 C4
Burton Leonard HG3 140 B4
Carthorpe DL8 87 D4
Catterton LS24 190 A8
Cleasby DL2 2 F2
Cliffe YO8 198 F4
Cloughton YO13 54 C1
Collingham LS23 188 C8
Coneythorpe & Clareton HG5 163 B6
Moor La *continued*
Copmanthorpe YO23 230 A1
Cropton YO18 71 B6
Crosby DL6 65 C5
Dalton DL11 19 C6
Dalton YO7 116 B8
Dishforth YO7 114 F3
Earswick YO32 226 C8
East Ayton/West Ayton YO13 99 B8
Eastfield YO11 100 A6
East Layton DL11 20 B8
Elslack BD23 172 D3
Embsay with Eastby BD23 156 F1
Full Sutton YO41 168 F1
Grassington BD23 134 E3
Great Ouseburn YO26 163 D7
Great Ribston with Walshford LS22 180 E8
Halton East BD23 157 B1
Haxby YO32 166 D7
Hunton DL8 61 E8
Hutton-le-Hole YO62 70 C5
Kearby with Netherby HG3 179 B2
Kelfield YO19 191 E2
Kirby Hill HG4 140 F8
Kirby Hill YO51 141 A8
Knapton YO26 182 E6
Long Preston BD23 153 F5
Milby YO51 141 C7
Murton YO19 229 F8
Myton-on-Swale YO61 142 B5
Naburn YO19 191 D8
Nether Silton DL6 66 C8
Newsham DL11 19 A7
Newsham with Breckenbrough YO7 65 A1
Newton-on-Ouse YO30 165 C7
Rufforth YO26 182 E6
Ryther cum Ossendyke LS24 196 E8
Scalby YO12 212 A8
Settrington YO17 122 C1
Sherburn in Elmet LS25 195 F4
Skelton YO30 224 D6
Snape with Thorp DL8 86 E6
Steeton with Eastburn BD20 187 F7
Stillington YO61 143 F6
Strensall YO32 167 B7
Stutton with Hazlewood LS24 189 D4
Thirkleby High & Low with Osgodby YO7 90 C1
Thirsk YO7 89 D5
Tholthorpe YO61 142 D6
Thormanby YO61 116 E5
Thornton-le-Clay YO60 145 F2
Thornton Steward HG4 61 E2
Thorp Arch LS23 180 E3
Threshfield BD23 134 B2
Welburn YO62 94 A5
Weston LS21 176 E2
West Tanfield HG4 87 B2
Wilstrop YO26 181 D8
Yafforth DL7 43 B2
York YO24 230 C6
Moorland Ave
6 Earby BB18 172 B1
Skipton BD23 217 A4
Moorland Cl
5 Embsay BD23 217 E8
Harrogate HG2 220 D4
Moorland Garth 2 YO32 167 A7
Moorland Gdns
Copmanthorpe YO23 230 A1
York YO23 230 A1
Moorland Rd
Harrogate HG2 220 D4
Scarborough YO12 212 F7
14 Sherburn in Elmet LS25 196 A4
York YO10 231 D8
Moorland Rise BD23 217 E8
Moorlands
Ilkley LS29 218 A2
Skelton YO32 166 B5
Moorlands Cl YO10 229 C4
Moorlands Fields YO10 231 E8
Moorlands La
Skelton YO30 224 C6
1 Tollerton YO61 143 B3
Moorlands Nature Reserve★ YO32 166 B5
Moorlands Pk YO21 29 A6
Moorland Terr BD23 217 B4
Moorland View HG2 220 D4
Moorland Way 8 LS25 196 A4
Moor Lane Ind Est YO61 142 D6
Moor Lane Trad Est LS25 196 A3
Moor Lee La
Eggborough DN14 207 B8
Heck DN14 203 B1
MOOR MONKTON 165 A3
Moor Park Cl
2 Addingham LS29 174 E4
Pannal HG3 178 A8
Moor Park Cres 3 LS29 174 E4
Moor Park Dr LS29 174 E4
Moor Park Gr 2 LS29 174 F4
Moor Park Way 1 LS29 174 F4
Moor Pk TS7 7 D5
Moor Rd
Askrigg DL8 57 E6
Bishop Monkton HG3 139 F5
Filey YO14 101 B1
Hunmanby YO14 127 B7
Ilkley LS29 218 F1
Knayton with Brawith YO7 65 F3
Moor Rd *continued*
Leyburn DL8 60 C5
Marton cum Grafton YO51 141 C2
Melsonby DL10 20 F6
Muston YO14 101 A2
9 Sherburn in Elmet LS25 195 F4
Stamford Bridge YO41 168 D2
Wykeham YO13 74 B4
Moors Ctr The★ YO21 29 D7
MOORSHOLM 10 B5
Moorsholm La TS12 10 C6
Moorside
Melling-with-Wrayton LA6 102 A2
Scalby YO12 212 A8
Moor Side LS23 188 D8
Moorside Ave HG4 214 B2
Moorside Cl LA6 102 A2
Moorside Ct LS29 218 C3
Moorside Dale 6 HG4 214 B2
Moorside Jun Sch HG4 214 B3
Moorside La
Addingham LS29 175 A2
Askwith LS21 176 C4
Moorside Rd DL10 209 E8
Moorside View HG4 214 C2
Moors Shop Ctr The LS29 218 A4
Moor View
Hebden BD23 135 A2
2 Hinderwell TS13 11 F7
Moorview Rd
Northallerton DL6 210 F5
Skipton BD23 217 B3
Moorview Way BD23 217 B4
Moor Way YO32 226 A4
Morcar Rd YO41 168 D1
Morehall Cl YO30 224 F2
Morgan Dr TS14 8 E6
Morgan St 4 YO12 212 F5
Morlais Ct 28 TS17 5 F4
Morley Ave 29 WF11 202 A2
Morley Dr 10 YO13 99 A7
Morley Gate DL11 37 E5
Mornington Cres HG1 219 E4
Mornington Rd LS29 218 C4
Mornington Terr HG1 219 E3
Morpeth Ave
Coulby Newham TS4 7 A7
Darlington DL1 3 E7
Morpeth Gate DL8 58 F1
Morrell Ct
Woodthorpe YO24 230 B8
York YO24 230 B8
Morrell Garth YO8 232 C2
Morrell Way YO10 229 A2
Morrets La YO8 197 A1
Morris Fields 22 WF6 200 B1
Morrison Rd TS14 8 F7
Morritt Cl 3 YO31 228 F8
Morton Carr La TS7 7 E6
Morton La YO8 203 A8
MORTON-ON-SWALE 64 A6
Morton Rd DL1 4 A5
Mosber La BD23 172 C8
MOSS 207 D1
Moss Arc HG4 214 C5
Mossburn Dr YO62 119 E6
Mossdale BD23 134 B3
Mossdale Gr TS14 8 D6
Moss End La BD22 186 F5
Moss Green Cl YO8 232 A2
Moss Green La
Brayton YO8 232 A2
Hirst Courtney YO8 203 F3
Moss Haven DN6 207 D1
Moss Hill La YO26 164 D5
Mossra La HG4 85 F4
Moss Rd DN6 207 B1
Moss Side BB18 171 E1
Moss St YO23 233 A1
Moss Way TS18 5 F7
Mosswood Cres TS5 6 D7
Mosswood La YO61 118 A1
Mossy La DL8 56 C4
Mostyn Ave 43 BB18 172 A1
Mother Shipton's Cave & Petryfying Well★ HG5 221 A5
Moule Rise LS25 194 E5
MOULTON 21 D3
Moulton Hall★ DL10 21 D2
Moulton La DL7 22 C3
Mounstrall La DL7 43 C1
Mount Ave YO8 232 B3
Mount Bank DL6 45 A5
Mount Cres YO17 215 B5
Mount Dr DL8 60 D5
Mount Ephraim 6 YO24 228 A3
Mount Farm Cl YO22 208 E3
Mount Gdns HG2 222 E7
Mount Gr YO8 232 B3
Mount Grace Priory★ DL6 45 B5
Mount Leven Rd TS15 5 F3
Mount Par
5 Harrogate HG1 219 D3
York YO24 228 A3
Mount Park Ave YO12 212 E5
Mount Park Rd 2 YO12 212 E4
Mount Pk YO19 198 A8
MOUNT PLEASANT 7 B5
Mount Pleasant
26 Addingham LS29 174 F4
High Bentham LA2 129 A8
Ilkley LS29 218 C3
Kippax LS25 200 D8
Little Smeaton WF8 206 D3
Newby & Scalby YO13 75 C5
Whitby YO22 208 F3
Mount Pleasant Cl 9 DL2 4 C4
Mount Pleasant E 2 YO22 33 D4
Mount Pleasant Grange TS18 6 A8
Mount Pleasant N 1 YO22 33 D4
Mount Pleasant Prim Sch DL3 3 A7
Mount Pleasant S 3 YO22 33 D4
Mount Pleasant Way TS9 26 D6
Mount Rd
Malton YO17 215 B4
Northallerton DL6 210 F6
Mount Sch The YO24 228 A3
Mountside YO11 212 F3
Mount Side Pk YO11 212 E2
Mount St HG2 222 E7
Mount Terr YO24 228 A3
MOUNT THE 214 D3
Mount The
Barwick in Elmet & Scholes LS15 194 B7
Castleford WF10 201 B4
Malton YO17 215 B4
Middlesbrough TS6 7 E8
Selby YO8 232 B3
8 Thornton Dale YO18 96 D5
York YO24 233 A1
Mount Vale YO24 228 A2
Mount Vale Dr YO24 228 A2
Mount View
Muston YO14 101 A2
Northallerton DL6 210 C6
Mount View Ave YO12 212 E3
Mountview Bsns Pk YO12 212 E8
Mount View Cl 4 YO12 212 E3
Mount View Rd 3 YO11 100 B6
Mouseman Visitor Ctr★ YO61 91 B2
Mowbray Castle (site of)★ HG4 112 D5
Mowbray Cres
17 Bedale DL8 63 A2
Hovingham YO62 119 E6
Kirkby Malzeard HG4 112 D5
Mowbray Dr
4 Hurworth-on-Tees DL2 3 E1
York YO26 227 C4
Mowbray Pl YO7 211 B2
Mowbray Rd
4 Catterick DL10 41 D5
Northallerton DL6 210 E6
Mowbray Sch DL8 63 A2
Mowbray Sq HG1 219 E3
Mowbray Terr
Thirsk YO7 211 B2
West Tanfield HG4 87 A2
MOWDEN 3 A6
Mowden Infants' Sch DL3 3 A6
Mowthorpe La YO60 145 F8
Mowthorpe Medieval Village★ YO17 149 C6
Mowthorp Rd YO12 75 A3
MOXBY 144 D5
Moxby La YO61 144 D5
Moxby Priory★ YO61 144 D5
Muddy La LS22 180 A1
Muff La TS8 7 A3
Muirfield TS7 7 D5
Muirfield Ave WF7 200 E1
Muirfield Rd TS16 5 E5
Muirfield Way 6 YO26 227 B5
MUKER 36 A5
Mulberry Cl YO8 232 E2
Mulberry Ct
10 South Milford LS25 195 F2
York YO32 225 F6
Mulberry Dr 7 YO32 166 E5
Mulberry Garth LS23 188 F8
Mulgrave Castle★ YO21 12 E2
Mulgrave Cres YO21 208 B8
Mulgrave Dr 6 DL7 210 D2
Mulgrave Pl YO11 213 B7
Mulgrave Rd YO21 208 A8
Mulgrave View YO22 32 F7
Mullberry Gdns LS26 200 A5
Mulwith Cl YO31 229 A6
Mulwith La HG4 140 E6
Muncastergate YO31 228 E7
Muncaster Way YO22 208 E3
Murchison Pl 8 YO12 212 F6
Murchison St YO12 212 E6
Murrayfield Gdns YO21 208 B7
Murrayfield Way 5 DL1 3 F6
Murray St
31 Filey YO14 101 B3
Scarborough YO12 212 F5
York YO24 227 F3
Murray Wlk DL3 3 A5
Murrough Wilson Pl 3 YO31 228 C7
MURTON 184 D7
Murton Bank YO62 67 E3
Murton Garth YO19 229 F6
Murton La YO19 184 D7
Murton Lane Ind Est YO19 184 D7
Murton Way YO19 229 E5
MUSCOATES 94 A3
Muscoates La YO62 93 F3
Museum of North Craven Life★ BD24 131 E2
Museum of Victorian Science★ YO22 208 D7
Museum St YO1 233 B2
Musham Bank Rd YO12 99 F7
Music in Miniature★ YO22 33 D3
Musterfield La HG4 113 B7
MUSTON 100 F2
Muston Rd
Filey YO14 101 A3
Hunmanby YO14 126 F8
Mutton Scalp Rd TS12 9 E7
Myer's Green La HG3 161 B5
Myers La DL7 64 A8
My Love La HG3 159 C5
Myra Bank La YO61 117 F3
Myron Rd TS17 5 F5
Myrtle Ave
Bishopthorpe YO23 231 B3
Selby YO8 232 B3
Myrtle Farm Dr DN14 203 D2
Myrtle Gdns DL1 3 D8
Myrtle Rd
Eaglescliffe TS16 5 E6
3 Harrogate HG1 219 E3
Myrtle Sq 2 HG1 219 E3
Myson Ave WF8 201 C2
Myton La YO61 142 C5
MYTON-ON-SWALE 141 F5
Myton Park Prim Sch TS17 5 F4
Myton Rd TS17 6 A4

N

Nabs View YO12 212 A7
NABURN 191 D8
Naburn CE Prim Sch YO19 191 D8
Naburn La
Deighton YO19 192 A7
Fulford YO19 231 D4
Naburn Park Mews YO19 191 E8
Nab View BD20 174 C2
Nairn Cl YO24 230 C6
Nairnhead Cl
1 Coulby Newham TS8 6 E5
5 Stainton TS8 6 E5
Nalton Cl YO23 230 A1
Nalton St YO8 232 C5
Nanny Goat La
Barwick in Elmet & Scholes LS25 194 B4
Hunton DL8 61 F8
Nanny La LS24 196 C7
Nan Scar BD22 187 A5
Nansen St YO12 212 E6
Nap Cote La HG4 112 E4
Napier Cres YO12 99 D7
Napier Rd HG4 113 D3
NAPPA 171 B8
Nares St YO12 212 E6
Narrowfield 8 YO22 32 A6
Narrow La
Cottingwith YO42 193 D7
Skipwith YO8 192 E3
Wigginton YO32 166 D6
National Ctr for Early Music★ YO1 233 C2
National Rly Mus★ YO26 228 A4
Nat La LS17 178 A3
Nattrass Wlk 7 DL8 63 B2
Navigation Rd YO1 233 C2
Navigation Sq BD23 216 F4
Navigation Way HG4 214 E4
Navigator Ct TS18 6 D8
NAWTON 93 E7
Nawton Com Prim Sch YO62 93 D7
Nawton Rd YO62 93 E7
NEASHAM 4 A1
Neasham Ct TS9 26 C8
Neasham Hill DL2 4 B1
Neasham Rd
Darlington DL1 3 D4
Low Dinsdale DL2 4 B3
Needham Garth DL8 58 E4
Neile Cl DL7 210 B4
Nell Bank Ctr★ LS29 218 D6
Nelson Ct LS29 218 C4
Nelson Rd LS29 218 B4
Nelson's La YO24 227 F1
Nelson St
7 Normanton South WF6 200 B2
Scarborough YO12 212 F6
Skipton BD23 217 A3
York YO31 233 C4
NESFIELD 175 B4
Nesfield Cl
17 Eastfield YO11 100 B6
Harrogate HG1 219 B5
Nesfield Rd LS29 218 A5
Nesfield View 12 LS29 175 C2
Nessgate YO1 233 B2
Ness La
Pickhill with Roxby YO7 88 B6
Tockwith YO26 181 C8
Ness Rd 5 YO8 232 D6
Nestfield Cl WF8 201 B2
Nestfield Ind Est DL1 3 D6
NETHER BURROW 102 B6
NETHERBY 179 B1
Netherby Cl 6 YO22 32 A6
Netherby La
Huttons Ambo YO60 147 B6
Sinnington YO62 71 A1
Netherdale Ct LS22 180 D4

Netheredge Cl HG5 220 E8
Netheredge Dr HG5 220 E8
Netherfield Cl WF10 200 C3
Nethergill La BD20 173 B1
NETHER POPPLETON 224 A2
Netherside Hall Sch
BD23 134 C4
NETHER SILTON 66 B7
Nether Way 20 YO26 165 F1
Netherwindings 18 YO32 166 F5
Netherwoods 5 YO32 167 B8
Nettledale Cl 1 TS13 12 A7
Nettledale La YO13 97 F6
Nevern Cres TS17 5 F4
Neville Cl DL2 1 D8
Neville Cres BD23 155 D1
Neville Dr YO23 231 A3
Neville Gr LS26 194 A1
Neville Pits La DN14 207 B4
Neville Rd
Darlington DL3 3 B5
Gargrave BD23 155 D1
Neville Row DL8 87 D7
Neville St
Normanton South WF6 200 A1
Skipton BD23 217 A4
York YO31 233 C4
Neville Terr YO31 233 C4
Neville Wlk
31 Kirkbymoorside YO62 70 B1
Richmond DL10 209 D7
Nevinson Gr YO10 231 E8
Nevison Ave WF8 201 C2
Nevis Way YO24 230 B7
NEWALL 176 F1
Newall Ave LS21 176 F1
Newall Carr Rd LS21 176 F3
Newall Cl 14 LS21 176 F1
Newall Hall Pk 10 LS21 177 A1
NEWBIGGIN
Askrigg 57 F6
Filey 101 A5
Thoralby 82 D8
Newbiggin
Malton YO17 215 B5
Richmond DL10 209 B6
Newbiggin Cl TS16 5 C5
Newborough YO11 213 A6
Newborough St YO30 233 A4
NEWBRIDGE 96 A8
Newbridge La BD23 174 B8
New Brook St LS29 218 B5
Newburgh Priory★ YO61 117 E7
Newbury Ave YO24 227 D1
NEWBY
Ingleton 104 A1
Middlesbrough 7 A3
Ripon 140 D6
Scarborough 75 E5
Newby Cl HG4 214 D4
NEWBY COTE 104 B1
Newby Cres HG3 219 A4
Newby Dr
23 Cross Hills BD20 187 E8
Dishforth YO7 115 A2
Newby Farm Cl 35 YO12 75 D5
Newby Farm Cres 36
YO12 75 D5
Newby Farm Rd YO12 75 D5
Newby Hall & Gdns★
HG4 140 C6
Newby La DN14 207 F8
Newby Pk★ HG4 140 D6
Newby & Scalby Prim Sch
YO12 212 B8
Newby St HG4 214 D4
Newby Terr YO31 228 C7
NEWBY WISKE 64 E2
Newcastle Farm Ct 4
WF11 201 D6
Newchase Ct YO11 99 F6
New Church Terr 12 YO8 232 C5
New Cl La LA2 130 C7
New Coll WF8 201 A1
Newcoln Rd YO12 212 E1
Newcroft YO8 232 B4
Newdale 3 YO32 166 F5
New Dales La
Bradleys Both BD20 173 D4
Low Snaygill BD20 173 D4
NEW EARSWICK 225 D3
New Earswick Prim Sch
YO32 225 D4
New Earswick Sports Club
YO32 225 D3
Newfield Ave 6 WF6 200 B1
Newfield Cl 7 WF6 200 B1
Newfield Cres
Middlesbrough TS17 6 D7
Normanton South WF6 200 B1
Newfield Ct 3 WF6 200 B1
Newfield La LS25 201 B8
New Forge Ct 15 YO32 166 F5
NEW FRYSTON 201 B6
Newgate
2 Malton YO17 215 C4
York YO1 233 B2
Newgate Bank YO62 68 A4
Newgate Cl 36 TS17 5 F4
Newgate Ct YO1 233 B2
New Hall Rd WF8 201 C2
Newham Bridge Prim Sch
TS5 6 F8
Newham Way TS8 7 B5
Newhay La YO8 198 E1
Newhold LS25 194 D4
Newhold Ind Est LS25 194 D4
NEWHOLM 13 A1
New House Farm Malham
National Nature Reserve★
BD23 133 D3
New House La BD23 153 F5
NEW HOUSES 105 C4
New Ings La YO18 96 E4
Newington Rd TS4 7 A8
New Inn La
Carthorpe DL8 87 F6
10 Easingwold YO61 143 C8
Newkin DL8 57 D5
New La
Aislaby YO18 95 D8
Beal DN14 202 D3
Bishopthorpe YO23 231 A4
Burton Salmon WF11 201 E6
Green Hammerton YO26 164 C3
Hawes DL8 56 E4
Holgate YO24 227 E3
Huntington YO32 225 F1
Kildwick BD20 173 F1
Lillings Ambo YO60 145 C3
Little Ouseburn YO26 164 A8
Long Marston YO23 182 B3
Neasham DL2 4 A1
Newland YO8 205 A3
Ravensworth DL11 20 A7
Selby YO8 232 C5
Sherburn in Elmet LS25 195 F3
Sheriff Hutton YO60 145 D5
Stainburn LS21 177 E4
Strensall YO32 167 B8
West Tanfield DL8 87 C2
New Laithe Cl 5 BD23 217 B5
Newlaithes Cres WF6 200 B1
NEWLAND 205 B3
Newland Ave 1 HG2 220 A1
Newland Park Cl YO10 229 A3
Newland Park Dr YO10 228 F3
Newlands DL6 210 F4
Newlands Ave
Scarborough YO12 212 E8
3 Whitby YO21 208 C7
Newlands Ct YO7 211 D3
Newlands Dr
2 Glusburn BD20 187 F8
Ripon HG4 214 B3
York YO26 227 B6
Newlands La
Burniston YO13 54 D1
Upper Poppleton YO26 182 E8
Wintringham YO17 123 F3
Newlands Park Ave
YO12 212 D8
Newlands Park Cres
YO12 212 D8
Newlands Park Dr YO12 212 D8
Newlands Park Gr 2
YO12 212 D8
Newlands Park Rd YO12 212 D8
Newlands Rd
Bishopthorpe YO23 230 F4
Boosbeck TS12 9 D8
Darlington DL3 3 B6
New Lennerton La LS25 196 C3
Newlyn Dr DL3 3 C8
Newmarket St BD23 217 A4
NEW MICKLEFIELD 195 A3
New Millgate YO8 232 C6
New Mill La LS23 188 F7
Newnham St HG2 220 A3
Newnham Terr HG2 220 A3
NEW PARK 219 B5
New Park Com Prim Sch
HG1 219 C5
New Park Rd 4 YO12 212 E4
New Park Row HG1 219 C5
New Parks Cres 8 YO12 212 E4
Newport Ave YO8 232 B4
Newport Cl 42 TS17 5 F4
Newport St 5 WF8 201 B1
New Potter Grange Rd
DN14 205 E2
New Quay Rd YO21 208 D6
New Queen St 10 YO12 213 A7
New Rd
Allerston YO13 73 D6
Allerton Mauleverer with
Hopperton HG5 163 E4
Appleton Roebuck YO23 190 E5
Appletreewick BD23 157 E8
Beningborough YO30 165 C6
Birstwith HG3 160 D6
Bramham LS23 188 E6
Earby BB18 172 A1
Fylingdales YO22 33 D4
Glaisdale YO21 29 F3
Guisborough TS14 8 F6
Heck DN14 203 D1
Hessay YO26 182 C8
Hunmanby YO14 126 F7
Kirby Grindalythe YO17 149 B6
Kirby Hall YO26 164 B8
Kirkbymoorside YO62 70 B1
Knottingley WF11 201 D3
Ledsham LS25 201 B8
Lillings Ambo YO60 145 D3
Long Drax YO8 204 E6
Newsham DL11 18 J8
North Stainley with Sleningford
HG4 113 B8
Norton DN6 206 F2
Raskelf YO7 116 E3
Reighton YO14 127 E5
Richmond DL10 209 C6
New Rd *continued*
Rosedale East Side YO18 49 E3
Scotton HG5 162 A5
24 Settle BD24 131 D2
Settrington YO17 122 D1
Spaunton YO62 70 E5
Stapleton WF8 206 B5
Terrington YO60 119 E2
Thornton in Lonsdale LA6 103 B4
Ulleskelf LS24 190 B3
Westerdale YO21 28 F6
Wheldrake YO19 192 C7
Whixley YO26 164 A4
Newroad End WF8 206 A6
NEW ROAD SIDE 187 B5
NEW ROW 8 F1
New Row
15 Boroughbridge YO51 141 B5
Eppleby DL11 1 D4
Trawden Forest BB8 186 B2
Newsam Rd TS16 5 D5
NEWSHAM
Barnard Castle 19 D8
Thirsk 89 A8
Newsham Hill DL11 18 J8
Newsham La
Barugh (Great & Little)
YO17 95 A1
Habton YO17 121 A8
Newsham Rd YO7 211 A3
Newsham Way DL7 210 B1
NEWSHOLME
205 E8
Barnoldswick 171 A6
New St
Carleton BD23 173 B4
Kippax LS25 194 D1
Langcliffe BD24 131 E4
Tadcaster LS24 189 E6
York YO1 233 B2
Newstead La HG4 85 C7
Newsteads 12 DL8 63 B3
New Sturton La LS25 194 D4
NEW THIRSK 211 A3
NEWTHORPE 195 D3
Newthorpe Rd 2 DN6 206 E2
Newton Cres 4 DL7 63 D4
Newtondale Cl HG5 221 D6
Newtondale Forest Dr
YO18 72 B6
Newtondale Halt YO18 51 D1
Newton Dr TS17 6 B6
Newton Gdns HG4 214 C4
Newton House Ct YO61 144 B3
NEWTON KYME 189 B7
Newton La
Archdeacon Newton DL2 2 F8
Ledsham WF10 201 A6
Newton Mulgrave TS13 11 F6
NEWTON-LE-WILLOWS 62 B4
NEWTON MORRELL 21 E8
NEWTON MULGRAVE 11 E6
NEWTON-ON-OUSE 165 B6
NEWTON-ON-
RAWCLIFFE 72 A5
Newton Pk YO30 165 B7
Newton Rd
Great Ayton TS9 8 A2
Tollerton YO61 143 B3
Newton St YO21 208 D6
Newton Terr YO1 233 B1
NEWTON UNDER
ROSEBERRY 8 B4
NEWTON UPON
DERWENT 185 E4
Newton Way
15 Hellifield BD23 154 B3
10 Strensall YO32 167 B6
NEW TOWN 201 B2
New Walk Terr YO10 228 D2
New Way YO21 29 C4
NEW YORK 137 F1
New York Ind Est HG3 137 F1
Nicholas Gdns YO10 228 F3
Nicholas St YO10 228 F3
Nicholson Ave HG4 113 D3
Nichols Way LS22 180 A3
Nickey Nackey La YO8 197 B8
Nicklaus Dr TS16 5 E5
Nickstream La DL3 3 A7
Nicky Nacky La 11 YO8 197 B8
Nicolsons Pl 8 BD20 174 C1
NIDD 161 E6
Nidd Bank HG5 220 F7
Nidd Cl YO26 227 B8
Nidd Dr HG3 160 E6
Nidderdale Dr HG5 221 D5
Nidderdale High Sch & Com
Coll HG3 137 B4
Nidderdale Lodge HG5 221 E5
Nidderdale Lodge Pk
HG5 221 E5
Nidderdale Mus★ HG3 137 B4
Nidderdale Pool & L Ctr
HG3 137 A5
Nidd Gr YO24 230 E8
Nidd La
Birstwith HG3 160 E7
Darley HG3 160 B6
Ripley HG3 161 D7
Nidd Orch 4 HG3 160 A6
Nidd Rise HG3 160 E6
Niddside HG3 160 A6
Nidd Valley Ind Est HG5 162 B6
Nidd Viaduct★ HG3 219 E8
Nidd Wlk 1 HG3 137 B4
Niffany Gdns 7 BD23 216 D3
Nigel Gr 7 YO24 227 F2
Nightingale Cl YO32 225 E1
Nightingale Dr HG1 220 B3
Nightingale La 9 YO12 99 F6
Nile Rd LS29 218 B4
Ninelands La LS25 194 D3
Ninelands Prim Sch
LS25 194 D3
Ninelands Spur LS25 194 C3
Ninevah La WF10 200 C7
Ninth Ave YO31 228 F5
Nipcroft La DL8 87 E6
Niso Terr YO11 213 A6
Noble Ct HG5 221 C7
Noel's Ct DL10 41 E5
Nolton Ct 35 TS17 5 F4
No Man's Moor La DL8 61 E3
Nook Croft 12 BB18 172 B1
Nookfield Cl YO22 33 C4
Nooking The YO61 117 B6
Nook Rd LS15 188 A1
Nook The
Selby YO8 232 D6
South Milford LS25 195 F2
Nora Ave HG5 221 C6
NORBY 211 A4
Norby YO7 211 B3
Norby Est YO7 211 B4
Norby Front St YO7 211 B4
Nordale Cl LS29 218 C5
Norfolk Cl WF11 201 E4
Norfolk Cres TS3 7 C8
Norfolk Gdns YO26 181 C7
Norfolk Rd HG2 222 D7
Norfolk St YO23 228 C2
NORMANBY 94 F4
Normanby Prim Sch TS6 7 F8
Normanby Rd
Middlesbrough TS7 7 D8
Northallerton DL7 210 D2
Normanby Terr 18 YO21 208 D7
Norman Cl
22 Pickering YO18 95 F7
7 Thorpe Willoughby YO8 197 B1
Norman Cres 11 YO14 101 B3
Norman Dr YO26 227 B6
Normandy Cl 4 YO8 232 B6
Normandy Ct WF6 200 B3
Norman Rd
Aske DL10 20 D1
Catterick Garrison DL9 209 E1
Richmond DL10 209 C8
Norman Sq DL10 209 D8
Norman St 5 YO10 229 A3
NORMANTON 200 C1
Normanton All Saints CE Inf
Sch 26 WF6 200 A1
Normanton Com Prim Sch
WF6 200 B2
Normanton Ind Est WF6 200 B1
Normanton Junior Sch
WF6 200 A1
Normanton Sta WF6 200 A2
Norseman Cl 7 YO19 197 F8
Norseway 2 YO41 168 D1
NORTHALLERTON 210 C5
Northallerton Coll DL6 210 E4
Northallerton Rd
Brompton DL6 210 E7
Dalton-on-Tees DL2 22 E6
Leeming DL7 63 C4
Thirsk YO7 211 A6
5 Thornaby TS17 6 B7
Northallerton Rigg DL6 43 D4
Northallerton Sta DL7 210 C3
North App LS24 189 A2
North Ave
Castleford WF10 200 C4
12 Glusburn BD20 187 E6
North Back La
Stillington YO61 144 C6
Terrington YO60 119 E1
North Baileygate WF8 201 B1
North Bay Prom YO12 212 F8
North Bay Rly★ YO12 212 E8
North Bglws HG4 214 D6
North Burton La YO14 127 B4
Northcarrs La YO61 144 A4
North Cliff Ave YO12 75 F5
North Cliff Ctry Pk★
YO14 101 C4
Northcliffe Gr 3 TS15 25 C5
Northcote Ave YO24 227 E3
Northcote Fold 3 LS22 180 A1
North Cotes Rd
Hunmanby YO25 126 C5
Wold Newton YO25 125 E5
NORTH COWTON 22 C3
North Cres LS25 195 F5
Northcroft 5 YO32 166 F5
Northcroft Gr 11 LS29 218 A4
North Croft Grove Rd 1
LS29 218 A4
NORTH DEIGHTON 180 B6
North Dr
Kippax LS25 194 D2
Sherburn in Elmet LS25 195 F5
NORTH DUFFIELD 199 A8
North Duffield Com Prim Sch
YO8 199 A8
North Eastern Terr YO24 230 E8
North End
Bedale DL8 63 A3
2 Hutton Rudby TS15 25 C5
Osmotherley DL6 45 B4
Northern Ryedale L Ctr
YO18 95 F7
NORTH FEATHERSTONE 200 E1
Northfield 3 YO8 198 B5
North Field Ave YO23 190 F5
Northfield Cl
Stokesley TS9 26 C7
Womersley DN6 206 C6
North Field Cl YO23 190 F5
Northfield Ct LS24 196 B8
Northfield Dr
Pontefract WF8 201 C1
Stokesley TS9 26 C8
Northfield La
Church Fenton LS24 196 B8
Pockley YO62 69 B2
3 Riccall YO19 191 F1
South Milford LS25 195 E2
Womersley DN6 206 C7
North Field La
Askham Bryan YO23 182 F3
Upper Poppleton YO26 182 F7
Northfield Mews 15 LS22 180 C2
Northfield Pl LS22 180 C3
Northfield Rd YO8 199 E8
Northfields
Bickerton LS22 181 B5
4 Hutton Rudby TS15 25 C5
4 Strensall YO32 167 B8
Walton LS23 181 A2
Northfields Ave 4 BD24 131 D3
Northfields Cres 5
BD24 131 D3
Northfields La YO61 142 C6
Northfield Terr YO24 230 E8
Northfield Way YO13 75 D6
North Field Way YO23 190 F5
North Garth La YO60 145 D5
Northgate
Darlington DL1 3 D5
Guisborough TS14 8 F7
Hunmanby YO14 126 F8
Muston YO14 100 F1
Pontefract WF8 201 B1
Northgate Cl 15 WF8 201 B1
Northgate La
1 Linton LS22 180 A1
Warthill YO41 168 A3
Northgate Lodge 11 WF8 201 B1
Northgate Rise 2 LS22 180 A1
North Gr 2 LS22 180 C3
North Grange Ct YO30 233 A4
NORTH GRIMSTON 148 E6
North Grove Ave 6 LS22 180 C4
North Hill Rd YO7 115 B2
NORTH INGS 119 D1
NORTH KILVINGTON 89 E8
North La
Dringhouses YO24 230 E8
Eastfield YO11 100 B6
Gainford DL2 1 D8
Great Timble LS21 176 E8
Huntington YO32 225 F5
Hutton Hang DL8 61 C4
Wheldrake YO19 192 F7
Northlands Ave 1 YO32 225 F7
Northleach Dr TS8 6 F5
North Leas Ave YO12 212 D8
NORTH LEES 113 E4
North Lodge Ave 2 HG1 219 C5
North Marine Rd YO12 212 F7
Northminster Bsns Pk
YO26 182 F7
North Moor 7 YO32 225 F5
Northmoor Cl 8 YO32 225 F5
North Moor Gdns YO32 225 F5
North Moor La YO61 118 C5
North Moor Rd
Blubberhouses HG3 158 F2
Easingwold YO61 117 B2
York YO32 225 F5
Northolme Dr YO30 224 E1
NORTH OTTERINGTON 64 D4
North Parade
10 Burley in Warfedale
LS29 176 C1
Ilkley LS29 218 C4
Skipton BD23 217 A2
York YO30 233 A3
North Park Dr HG1 219 E2
North Park Rd HG1 219 E2
North Prom YO21 208 C7
North Rd
Darlington DL1 3 D7
Glusburn BD20 187 E7
Grosmont YO22 31 C4
Hackforth DL8 62 E8
3 Middleham DL8 60 E2
Norton YO17 215 E3
Ripon HG4 214 D6
Stokesley TS9 26 C7
Whitby YO21 208 D6
North Riding Rise DL7 65 B3
NORTH RIGTON 178 B5
North Rigton CE Prim Sch
LS17 178 C4
North Road Ind Est DL3 3 C7
North Road Sta DL1 3 D6
North Side
Hutton Rudby TS15 25 C5
2 Staithes TS13 13 K2
Northside Ind Pk DN14 202 F1
North & South Cowton Com
Prim Sch DL7 22 C3
North St
Addingham LS29 175 A4
Barmby on the Marsh
DN14 205 A7
Barnoldswick BB18 171 D1
Castleford WF10 201 B6
Folkton YO11 100 A2
Gargrave BD23 155 D1

North St *continued*
31 Glusburn BD20 187 E7
Newby & Scalby YO13 75 C6
Ripon HG4 214 C6
Scarborough YO11 213 A6
Silsden BD20 174 C1
Wetherby LS22 180 C3
York YO1 233 B2
NORTH STAINLEY 113 D7
North Stainley CE Prim Sch HG4 113 C8
Northstead Com Prim Sch YO12 212 D8
Northstead Flats YO12 212 D7
Northstead Manor Dr YO12 212 E7
North Street La 22 YO11 213 A6
North Sweeming Ct LS25 196 D5
North Terr
Gainford DL2 1 D7
4 Scarborough YO11 213 A6
Whitby YO21 208 C7
Northumberland Ct 17 HG1 219 D2
Northumberland Rd TS17 6 B8
North View
Knottingley WF11 201 F2
Little Ribston LS22 180 A8
Northway
Airmyn DN14 205 F3
Pickering YO18 95 E7
11 Scarborough YO12 212 F6
6 Whitby YO21 208 B7
Northwell Gate LS21 176 F1
Northwold Rd YO11 100 A7
Northwood Prim Sch DL1 3 D7
North Yorkshire Moors Rly* YO18 95 F7
NORTON 206 E2
Norton Back La DL2 4 D8
Norton Cl HG4 114 A8
Norton Coll YO17 215 E2
Norton Comm La DN6 206 F2
Norton Comm Rd DN6 207 A1
Norton Com Prim Sch YO17 215 E3
Norton Conyers* HG4 113 F7
Norton Cres DL2 4 C8
Norton Grove Ind Est YO17 215 F4
Norton Inf Sch DN6 206 E2
Norton & Kirk Smeat WF8 206 C3
NORTON-LE-CLAY 115 C2
Norton Mill La DN6 206 E2
NORTON-ON-DERWENT 215 D3
Norton Priory DN6 206 E2
Norton Rd
Norton YO17 215 C3
Sadberge DL2 4 C7
Norton Twr* BD23 156 B4
Norway Dr YO10 231 D8
Norwich Cl YO13 75 D6
Norwich Dr HG3 219 A5
Norwood Ave LS29 176 C1
Norwood Bottom Rd LS21 177 A5
Norwood Cl
36 Burley in Warfedale LS29 176 C1
2 Knaresborough HG5 221 B8
Norwood Ct 1 HG5 221 B7
Norwood Gr HG3 219 B4
Norwood La
Glusburn BD20 187 B8
Pannal HG3 177 E7
Norwood Mews 18 YO12 212 F5
Norwood Pl 8 YO12 212 F5
Norwood St
Normanton WF6 200 B2
Scarborough YO12 212 F5
Nossill La DL8 59 C3
NOSTERFIELD 87 B3
Nosterfield Nature Reserve* HG4 87 B2
Nosterfield Rd HG4 87 B2
Notagreen Rd DL11 39 F6
Nought Bank Rd HG3 137 B3
Nought Moor Rd HG3 137 B2
Nova Scotia Way 4 YO19 198 A8
Nuffield Health York Hospl YO31 228 D8
NUN APPLETON 190 F3
Nuneaton Dr TS8 6 E5
Nunmill St YO23 228 C2
NUN MONKTON 165 A4
Nun Monkton Foundation Prim Sch YO26 165 A5
Nunnery La
Darlington DL3 3 A5
York YO23 233 B1
Nunnery Way LS23 188 E7
NUNNINGTON 93 E2
Nunnington Cl TS17 6 B5
Nunnington Cres HG3 219 A5
Nunnington Hall* YO62 93 F2
Nunnington Studios* YO62 93 E2
Nun's Cl DL10 209 B7
Nuns Green La YO21 29 E3
NUNTHORPE 231 C8
Middlesbrough 7 D5
Nunthorpe Ave YO23 228 B2
Nunthorpe Cres YO23 228 B1
Nunthorpe Gdns TS7 7 D5
Nunthorpe Gr YO23 228 B2
Nunthorpe Prim Sch TS7 7 E6
Nunthorpe Rd YO23 233 A1
Nunthorpe Sch TS7 7 E6
Nunthorpe Sta TS7 7 E7
NUNWICK 114 A5
Nurseries The
Asselby DN14 205 D7
3 Easingwold YO61 143 C8
East Ayton YO13 99 C8
9 Leyburn DL8 60 D5
3 Whitby YO21 208 B6
Nursery Cl
19 Hemingbrough YO8 198 F1
23 South Milford LS25 195 F2
Nursery Ct
Low Catton YO41 185 C8
Nether Poppleton YO26 224 A2
Nursery Dr YO24 227 E3
Nursery Gdns
Thirsk YO7 211 C3
York YO10 229 C3
Nursery La
4 Addingham LS29 175 A4
Merrybent DL2 2 E5
Nursery Rd YO26 224 A2
Nursery Way 8 LS23 188 E7
Nusery Gdn DL10 41 B4
Nutgill La
Bentham LA2 129 D8
Ingleton LA6 103 D1
Nutwith La HG4 112 B8
Nydd Vale Rd HG1 219 D3
Nydd Vale Terr 10 HG1 219 D3

O

Oak Ave
Appleton Roebuck YO23 190 E3
Garforth LS25 194 C4
Killinghall HG3 161 B2
Oakbank HG1 219 C4
Oak Beck Rd HG1 219 B5
Oak Beck Way HG1 219 B6
Oakburn Rd LS29 218 A3
Oak Busk La YO60 145 F1
Oakbusks La YO61 142 F4
Oak Cl
Filey YO14 101 B4
9 Kirkbymoorside YO62 70 B1
6 Leeming DL7 63 F3
Oak Cres LS25 194 C4
OAKDALE 161 B2
Oakdale HG1 219 A3
Oakdale Ave HG1 219 B4
Oakdale Glen HG1 219 B3
Oakdale Manor HG1 161 B2
Oakdale Pl HG1 219 B4
Oakdale Rd YO30 224 F2
Oakdale Rise HG1 219 C4
Oak Dr
8 Acaster Malbis YO32 191 C7
Garforth LS25 194 C4
Harrogate HG1 220 C5
THIRSK YO7 89 E3
5 Thorpe Willoughby YO8 197 B1
3 Topcliffe YO7 89 A1
Oakenshaw Dr TS5 6 E7
Oaker Bank HG3 161 B2
Oak Farm YO8 197 D6
Oak Field YO8 232 A1
Oak Field Ave YO22 51 D8
Oakfield La 21 YO8 198 F1
Oakfields DL10 21 D4
Oak Glade 6 YO31 225 F3
Oak Gr
Harrowgate Village DL1 3 D8
Northallerton DL6 210 E6
Oak Hill TS8 7 B5
Oakhill Cres 3 YO32 167 A6
Oak La HG3 159 F8
Oakland Ave YO31 229 A7
Oakland Dr YO31 229 A7
Oakland Hills 23 WF6 200 B1
Oaklands
Camblesforth YO8 204 C5
9 Great Ayton TS9 8 A2
5 Ilkley LS29 218 A3
5 Pickering YO18 96 A6
6 Strensall YO32 167 B7
Oaklands Cres YO8 204 C5
Oaklands Rd TS6 7 F8
Oaklands Sports Ctr YO24 227 C2
Oaklands The DL2 4 D3
Oaklands Way YO61 143 D8
Oakley Bank YO22 208 B2
Oakley Cl TS14 8 F5
Oakley Rd TS12 9 E7
Oakmont Cl 21 WF6 200 B1
Oakmoor Cl 7 DL1 3 E4
Oak Mount Ct 6 DL6 210 E3
Oakney Wood Ave YO8 232 C1
Oakney Wood Ct YO8 232 C1
Oakney Wood Dr YO8 232 D1
Oak Rd
Garforth LS25 194 C4
Guisborough TS14 8 F7
2 North Duffield YO8 199 A7
Ripon HG4 214 B2
Scarborough YO12 212 D4
Tockwith LS22 180 E7
Whitby YO21 208 B6
Oak Ridge 6 LS22 180 B3
Oakridge Com Prim Sch TS13 11 F7
Oakridge View 3 HG3 161 B3
Oak Rise 4 YO24 227 C3
Oaksfield LS26 200 B5
Oaks La LS23 188 E8
Oak St 3 YO26 227 E5
Oaks The
Coulby Newham TS8 6 E5
Dalton YO7 115 F7
Hellifield BD23 154 A3
7 Masham HG4 86 C3
Oak Tree DL2 4 E4
Oak Terr HG2 219 C2
OAK TREE 4 E4
Oaktree Ave DL9 40 E2
Oaktree Bank YO7 65 F3
Oak Tree Cl
2 Bedale DL8 63 A2
Strensall YO32 167 B7
Tees-side Airport DL2 4 E4
Oak Tree Ct
Bubwith YO8 199 D7
4 Wigginton YO32 225 D7
Oaktree Dr DL7 210 C1
Oak Tree Dr DL8 62 F2
Oaktree Gr 5 TS18 5 D8
Oak Tree Gr YO32 225 D3
Oaktree Hill DL6 43 D6
Oaktree Junc DL2 4 D4
Oak Tree La YO32 225 C7
Oak Tree Rd 7 DL8 63 A2
Oak Tree Way 10 YO32 167 B7
Oakville Ave YO12 212 E6
Oakville St YO31 228 D7
Oak Way YO8 232 D2
Oakwood Cl
Church Fenton LS24 196 B7
Ferrybridge WF11 201 C4
Oakwood Pk DN14 207 F6
Oakwood Rd LS22 180 B4
OATLANDS 222 F6
Oatlands Com Inf Sch HG2 222 E7
Oatlands Com Jun Sch HG2 222 F7
Oatlands Dr
Harrogate HG2 222 F8
11 Otley LS21 177 A1
Oatlands Gr 3 TS13 11 A8
Occaney La HG3 162 D8
Occupation La LS24 188 E2
Occupation Rd TS6 7 F8
Ocean Rd YO21 208 C7
Ocean Terr YO14 100 F6
Ochrepit Hill YO42 170 A2
OCTON 151 F8
Oddie's La LA6 103 D5
Offerton Dr TS8 6 F5
Ogleforth YO1 233 B3
Okehampton Dr TS7 7 B6
Olav Rd DL10 209 C7
Old Barber HG1 219 D6
Old Borough Steadings DL11 2 A2
Old Boys Sch La 4 YO8 197 B8
Old Brewery Gdns 5 LS24 189 F6
Old Bridge Rise 7 LS29 218 A4
OLD BYLAND 91 F8
Old Chapel Cl 7 HG3 161 B2
Old Church Gn YO26 164 C2
Old Church La 9 HG3 137 C4
Old Coach Rd HG3 137 F2
Old Coastguard Sta* YO22 33 D3
Old Coppice 14 YO32 166 F5
Old Corn Mill The BD20 187 D7
Old Court Cl
Malton YO17 215 D4
Norton-on-Derwent YO17 215 E3
Old Courthouse Rural Arts The* YO7 211 B2
Old Cricket Field La YO7 116 B6
Old Dike Lands YO32 225 C8
Olde Mkt The TS16 5 D3
Old Farm Cl 5 YO18 95 F7
Old Farm Way YO8 232 B2
Old Farmyard* HG3 161 C7
Old Favourites Wlk 8 DL2 3 A7
Oldfield Cl LS25 195 A4
Oldfield La
Collingham LS22 180 C1
Spaunton YO62 70 E4
Sutton BD22 187 F1
Old Garth Croft 3 WF11 201 D6
Oldgate La LS24 195 E6
Old Gayle La DL8 56 D4
Old Great North Rd WF11 201 E4
Old Hall Cl BD20 187 D7
Old Hall Croft BD23 155 D1
Old Hall Ct LS25 201 F6
Old Hall La
Gilling with Hartforth & Sedbury DL10 20 D3
Kexby YO41 185 C5
Old Hall Rd BD20 187 D7
Old Hall Way BD20 187 D7
Oldham Cl TS12 9 E8
Oldham St TS12 9 D7
Old Highway The 9 YO32 167 B6
Old Hospital Compound 25 DL9 40 E3
Old House Gdns YO8 203 A5
Oldhouse La YO13 74 F1
Old La
Addingham LS29 175 B3
Broughton BD23 172 D5
Cowling BD22 187 B5
Old La *continued*
Earby BB18 172 A2
Hambleton YO8 196 E1
Hirst Courtney YO8 203 F3
Horton in Ribblesdale BD24 105 A7
Ilkley LS29 218 D3
Kelbrook & Sough BB18 186 A6
Long Marston YO26 182 A6
Old Lane Ct LS24 190 E7
Old Laundry Mews 12 LA6 103 D3
Old London Rd LS24 189 D3
OLD MALTON 215 E7
Old Maltongate YO17 215 C4
Old Malton Rd
Malton YO17 215 D5
7 Willerby YO12 99 D2
Oldman Ct
Woodthorpe YO24 230 C8
York YO24 230 C8
Old Market Pl 6 HG4 214 C5
OLD MICKLEFIELD 194 F4
Old Mill Cl 8 LS29 176 C1
Old Mill La LS23 188 F7
Old Mill Row 3 YO7 211 C3
Old Mill View YO60 145 C5
Old Mill Wynd TS9 8 A1
Old Moor La YO24 230 E7
Old Moor Rd LA2 128 B8
Old Oliver La BD24 152 F6
Old Orchard YO32 225 D8
Old Orchard The
1 Easingwold YO61 143 C8
Fulford YO10 231 E7
14 Hutton Rudby TS15 25 C5
Shipton YO30 165 F5
Old Park La YO21 31 D6
Old Park Mews HG4 214 B5
Old Penny Gate
Knaresborough HG5 221 C7
Knaresborough HG5 221 C7
Old Quarry La LS25 195 E1
Old Raike BD23 152 F4
Old Rd
Appleton Roebuck YO23 190 E5
Clapham LA2 130 C8
Garsdale LA10 55 A6
Kirkbymoorside YO62 70 B1
Kirkby Overblow LS17 178 E1
Thornton in Craven BD23 172 A3
Old St The LS24 190 C8
Old Sawmill The
Lane Ends BD22 187 C6
Rathmell BD24 153 B7
Old School Cl
Osbaldwick YO10 229 B4
Settle BD24 131 E2
West Witton DL8 59 D3
Old School La YO8 198 B5
Old Station Rd 4 YO62 92 C1
Old Station Way 20 LS29 174 F4
OLDSTEAD 91 C3
Oldstead Rd YO61 91 B3
Old Stone Trough La BB18 186 A6
Old Stubble The 6 TS13 13 K2
Old Sutton Rd YO7 211 E3
OLD THIRSK 211 C4
Old Trough Way HG1 219 C6
Old Vicarage La 5 LS25 202 A8
Old Village The YO32 225 F5
Old Wife's Way YO18 73 A8
Olicana Pk LS29 218 B5
Olive Gr HG1 220 B4
Oliver La YO17 121 C8
Oliver's Cl 18 YO14 126 F8
Oliver's Mount Rd YO11 212 F2
Oliver St 4 YO11 213 A4
Olive Way HG1 220 B4
Olive Wlk HG1 220 B4
Olliver La DL10 20 F1
Olliver Rd DL10 209 E8
Olympia Cres YO8 232 E6
Olympian Ct YO10 228 F4
Olympian Trad Est YO11 100 A6
Olympic Way DL10 209 B8
Omega Bus Village DL6 210 C7
Omega St 7 HG1 219 C5
Onams La YO62 69 F4
One Acre Garth 2 YO8 196 E1
Onhams La YO60 146 E4
OPSA Bsns Ctr YO1 233 B2
Opus Ave YO26 224 C1
Oran La DL10 41 E4
Orcaber La LA2 130 E6
Orchard Cl
Appleton Roebuck YO23 190 F5
Barkston Ash LS24 195 E7
Dalton-on-Tees DL2 22 D7
15 Easingwold YO61 117 D1
Eggborough DN14 202 F2
1 Great Ayton TS9 8 A2
6 Hartwith cum Winsley HG3 137 F1
Kirby Misperton YO17 95 D2
1 Knaresborough HG5 221 B8
6 Monk Fryston LS25 202 A8
9 Norton DN6 206 E2
Selby YO8 232 A4
Sharow HG4 214 F6
6 South Milford LS25 195 F2
Wilberfoss YO41 185 E6
York YO24 227 E1
Orchard Cotts 4 YO19 184 F7
Orchard Ct
Bramham cum Oglethorpe LS23 188 F5
Orchard Ct *continued*
8 Knaresborough HG5 221 B5
Northallerton DL7 210 C2
Orchard Dr
Fairburn WF11 201 D7
Hambleton YO8 196 F2
Linton LS22 180 A2
Orchard End 20 YO8 198 F1
Orchard Garth YO23 230 B2
Orchard Gdns
Malton YO17 215 B4
York YO31 225 E2
Orchard Gr
4 Brompton DL6 43 F3
1 Castleford WF10 200 D3
Orchard Head Cres WF8 201 C2
Orchard Head Dr WF8 201 C2
Orchard Head La WF8 201 B2
Orchard Head Prim Sch WF8 201 C2
Orchard La
8 Addingham LS29 175 A4
Barkston Ash LS24 195 F6
Hebden BD23 135 A2
Ripley HG3 161 C7
Ripon HG4 214 E1
Thirsk YO7 211 B1
Orchard Mews 9 DL9 40 E3
Orchard Paddock
34 Haxby YO32 166 E5
3 Haxby YO32 225 D8
Orchard Rd
Malton YO17 215 B4
Selby YO8 232 A4
3 Sleights YO22 32 A6
Thornaby-on-Tees TS18 6 A7
Upper Poppleton YO26 224 A1
Orchards The
2 Beadlam YO62 93 D7
6 Brafferton YO61 115 F1
Leavening YO17 147 E1
Mickletown LS26 200 B5
Ripon HG4 214 C6
Westow YO60 147 B4
Orchard The
5 Ampleforth YO62 92 C1
Ampleforth YO62 92 C1
Bishopthorpe YO25 231 A3
Burniston YO13 75 D8
Burton Leonard HG3 140 A2
Heslington YO10 229 A1
6 North Featherstone WF7 200 E1
11 Pickering YO18 96 A6
5 Roundhill Village TS17 6 D5
Sadberge DL2 4 C7
Scalby YO12 212 C7
Snainton YO13 98 A4
Thirsk YO7 211 C4
Tholthorpe YO61 142 D5
Wray LA2 128 A6
Orchard View
Markington with Wallerthwaite HG3 139 E3
3 Skelton YO30 224 B5
Orchard Way
Hensall DN14 203 C2
Middlesbrough TS7 7 D8
Selby YO8 232 A4
1 Strensall YO32 167 B7
Thorpe Willoughby YO8 197 B2
York YO24 227 E1
Orchid Ct 17 DL9 41 A5
Orchid Way 8 HG3 161 B3
Ordmerstones La YO18 96 C4
Ordnance La YO10 228 D1
Oriel Bank YO11 212 F3
Oriel Cl YO11 212 F3
Oriel Cres YO11 212 F3
Oriel Gr YO30 228 A8
ORMESBY 7 C8
Ormesby Bank TS7 7 D7
Ormesby Cres DL7 210 D2
Ormesby Rd TS3 7 C8
Orms Gill Green La BD23 154 D6
Orpington Rd TS3 7 C8
Orr Cres 10 YO7 89 B1
Orrin Cl YO24 230 C7
OSBALDWICK 229 C4
Osbaldwick Ind Est YO19 229 D5
Osbaldwick La YO10 229 B4
Osbaldwick Link Rd YO10 229 D4
Osbaldwick Prim Sch YO10 229 C4
Osbaldwick Village YO10 229 C4
Osborne Cl HG1 219 D4
Osborne Gdns HG1 219 D4
Osborne Pk YO12 212 D5
Osborne Rd HG1 219 D4
Osborne Terr 9 YO21 208 D5
Osborne Wlk HG1 219 D4
Osbourne Dr 4 YO30 224 E3
OSGODBY
Seamer 100 B7
Selby 198 C4
Osgodby Cl 9 YO11 100 B8
OSGODBY COMMON 198 C6
Osgodby Cres YO11 100 B7
Osgodby Gr 10 YO11 100 B8
Osgodby Hall Rd YO11 100 B7
Osgodby Hill YO11 100 B7
Osgodby La 12 YO11 100 B8
Osgodby Way 11 YO11 100 B8
Osgoodby Bank YO7 90 F3

Osmington Gdns 10 YO32 ... 167 A7
OSMOTHERLEY ... 45 C4
Osmotherley Prim Sch DL6 ... 45 B4
Osprey Cl
4 Collingham LS22 ... 180 A1
Guisborough TS14 ... 8 D6
5 Scotton DL9 ... 40 F2
4 York YO24 ... 230 B8
Osprey Garth 4 YO12 ... 99 E6
Ostler's Cl YO23 ... 230 C3
Ostman Rd YO26 ... 227 C5
Oswaldene DL6 ... 45 B4
OSWALDKIRK ... 93 A1
Oswaldkirk Bank YO62 ... 93 A1
Oswestry Gn TS4 ... 7 A7
Oswin Gr DL10 ... 20 E4
Oswy Cotts YO21 ... 208 D5
Oswy St 5 YO21 ... 208 D5
Otley Rd
Harrogate HG2 ... 222 B8
Killinghall HG3 ... 161 B4
Pannal HG3 ... 178 A7
Skipton BD23 ... 217 B4
Stainburn HG3 ... 177 F6
Otley St BD23 ... 217 A4
Otterbeck Way 16 DL8 ... 63 B3
OTTERBURN ... 154 E4
Otter Dr 13 YO18 ... 95 F6
Otter Way TS17 ... 6 A5
Otterwood Bank 5 YO24 227 B1
Otterwood La YO24 ... 227 B1
Otterwood Paddock YO41 ... 168 C2
Oucher La HG3 ... 140 B2
OUGHTERSHAW ... 80 C4
Oughtershaw Rd BD23 ... 80 B6
OULSTON ... 117 E5
Oulston Rd YO61 ... 117 D1
Our Lady Queen of Martyrs RC VA Prim Sch YO24 ... 227 F3
Ouse Acres YO26 ... 227 D6
Ouse Bank YO8 ... 232 E5
Ouseburn Ave YO26 ... 227 C6
Ousecliffe Gdns YO30 ... 228 A6
Ousegate YO8 ... 232 D5
Ousegate Mills Business Centre YO8 ... 232 D5
Ouse Lea YO30 ... 228 A7
Ouston Cl LS24 ... 189 F6
Ouston La LS24 ... 189 F6
Out Croft La YO18 ... 95 C8
Outgaits Cl 4 YO14 ... 126 F8
Outgaits La
Hunmanby YO14 ... 127 A8
Muston YO14 ... 100 F1
Outgang La
Osbaldwick YO19 ... 229 D6
21 Pickering YO18 ... 95 F6
Thornton-le-Dale YO18 ... 96 E6
Out Gang La BD23 ... 107 F1
Outgang Rd
Malton YO17 ... 215 B5
Pickering YO18 ... 96 A6
Scampston YO17 ... 122 F7
Outgang The YO17 ... 122 F4
Outgate Cnr DL6 ... 23 F4
OUTHGILL ... 34 A8
Outwood Academy Acklam TS5 ... 6 E7
Outwood Academy Ripon HG4 ... 214 A5
Outwood La LS24 ... 190 C2
Oval The
Harrogate HG2 ... 222 D8
Hurworth DL2 ... 3 F1
Kellingley DN14 ... 202 C3
Middlesbrough TS5 ... 6 E6
Otley LS21 ... 176 F1
3 Scarborough YO11 ... 100 B8
Skipton BD23 ... 217 B3
Overburn Rd 8 BD20 ... 187 E6
OVER BURROW ... 102 B7
Overdale YO11 ... 100 A7
Overdale Cl YO24 ... 230 D8
Overdale Com Prim Sch 7 YO11 ... 100 A7
Overdale Ct BD23 ... 217 A5
Overdale Grange 3 BD23 ... 217 B5
Overdale Rd TS3 ... 7 C8
Overfields Prim Sch TS3 ... 7 D8
Overgreen Cl YO13 ... 75 D8
Overgreen La YO13 ... 75 C8
Overgreen View YO13 ... 75 D8
Over Nidd HG1 ... 219 C6
Overscar La YO18 ... 72 E3
OVER SILTON ... 66 B8
OVERTON ... 165 F2
Overton Rd YO30 ... 165 F3
Overton Terr YO11 ... 213 B6
OVERTOWN ... 102 C7
Ovington La DL11 ... 1 A6
Ovington Terr YO23 ... 228 B2
Owler Park Rd LS29 ... 175 C3
Owlwood Ct 7 YO19 ... 184 E7
Owlwood La 6 YO19 ... 184 E7
Owmen Field La YO62 ... 93 C5
Owston Ave 2 YO10 ... 229 A3
Owston Rd 1 YO14 ... 126 F8
Ox Calder Cl 16 YO19 ... 184 F7
Ox Carr La YO32 ... 167 B6
Ox Cl YO41 ... 168 D2
Oxcliff YO12 ... 212 C8
Oxclose La YO62 ... 70 C4
Ox Close La
Eldmire with Crakehill YO7 ... 115 E5
Grimston YO10 ... 184 C4
Myton-on-Swale YO61 ... 141 F5
North Deighton LS22 ... 180 B7
Whixley YO26 ... 163 F5
Oxcroft 23 YO62 ... 70 B1
Oxenby Pl 12 YO61 ... 117 D1
Oxen La YO8 ... 198 E3
Oxford Dr LS25 ... 194 D1
Oxford Pl 7 HG1 ... 219 D2
Oxford St
Harrogate HG1 ... 219 D2
6 Normanton South WF6 ... 200 B2
Scarborough YO12 ... 212 F6
Skelton & Brotton TS12 ... 9 D7
5 York YO24 ... 228 A3
Oxford Terr 2 HG1 ... 219 D1
Oxmoor La LS24 ... 196 D7
Ox Moor La
Cattal YO26 ... 164 A1
Hunsingore LS22 ... 180 E8
Oxmoor Pl 24 YO61 ... 143 D8
Oxpasture Cl YO12 ... 212 C4
Ox Pasture La YO62 ... 67 D2
OXTON ... 190 A6
Oxton Dr LS24 ... 189 F6
Oxton La LS24 ... 189 F6
Oyster Park Prim Sch WF10 ... 201 B5
Oyster Way YO14 ... 127 C8
Ozone Pk DN14 ... 205 F6
Ozone Way DN14 ... 205 F6

P

Packhorse Bridge*
Dacre HG3 ... 159 D6
Romanby DL7 ... 210 B4
Padbury Ave 50 YO14 ... 101 B3
Padbury Cl 46 YO14 ... 101 B3
Pad Cote La BD22 ... 187 A5
Paddock Cl
Askham Richard YO23 ... 182 D3
Copmanthorpe YO23 ... 230 A2
Helmsley YO62 ... 92 F6
Huntington YO32 ... 225 F4
Norton YO17 ... 215 D3
2 Pickering YO18 ... 95 F6
Wilberfoss YO41 ... 185 E5
Paddock Farm Water Gdns* DL2 ... 22 D4
Paddock Hill YO17 ... 215 A4
Paddock House La LS22 ... 179 E1
Paddock Rise 13 YO61 ... 117 D1
Paddocks The
Follifoot HG3 ... 223 F4
Wheldrake YO19 ... 193 A7
Paddock The
14 Airmyn DN14 ... 205 E4
Appleton Wiske DL6 ... 24 B3
Burton Salmon LS25 ... 201 F6
Catterick DL10 ... 41 D4
Fairburn WF11 ... 201 D6
Knaresborough HG5 ... 221 C5
Leeming DL8 ... 63
1 Linton-on-Ouse YO30 ... 164 F8
Melmerby HG4 ... 114 B7
Middleton St George DL2 ... 4 C3
Newby Wiske DL7 ... 64 E2
Normanton South WF6 ... 200 A1
Stokesley TS9 ... 26 C8
9 Whitby YO21 ... 208 D7
Wilberfoss YO41 ... 185 E5
York YO26 ... 227 C6
Paddock View WF10 ... 201 A3
Paddock Way YO26 ... 227 C6
PADSIDE ... 159 B6
PADSIDE GREEN ... 159 C6
Page La YO62 ... 93 E6
Pagnell Ave YO8 ... 232 E4
PAINSTHORPE ... 170 B5
Painsthorpe La YO41 ... 170 B5
Painter La YO8 ... 196 E2
Palace Rd HG4 ... 214 B7
Palace Theatre Sh Mall YO17 ... 215 C4
Pale La
Carleton BD23 ... 216 E1
Gateforth YO8 ... 202 F7
Paley Green La BD24 ... 131 B2
Pallet Hill 9 DL10 ... 41 D5
Palmer Gr YO8 ... 232 A3
Palmer La YO1 ... 233 C2
Palmers La LS22 ... 180 E4
Palmes Cl YO19 ... 191 E8
Palms Ct DL2 ... 4 A5
Panman La YO19 ... 184 F8
PANNAL ... 222 E3
PANNAL ASH ... 222 B5
Pannal Ash Cl HG2 ... 222 C8
Pannal Ash Cres HG2 ... 222 B7
Pannal Ash Dr HG2 ... 222 B7
Pannal Ash Gr HG2 ... 222 B7
Pannal Ash Rd HG2 ... 222 B7
Pannal Ave HG3 ... 222 E2
Pannal Bank HG3 ... 222 E2
Pannal Cl 3 YO21 ... 208 B5
Pannal Gn HG3 ... 222 E3
Pannal Prim Sch HG3 ... 222 E3
Pannal Rd HG3 ... 223 B4
Pannal Sta HG3 ... 222 E2
Pannett Art Gall* YO21 ... 208 C6
Pannett Way 8 YO21 ... 208 D6
Pannierman La TS7 ... 7 E2
Panorama Cl 10 HG3 ... 137 C4
Panorama Dr LS29 ... 175 C1
Panorama Walk HG2 ... 222 A8
Panorama Wlk HG3 ... 137 C4
Pant La LA2 ... 130 E7
Parade Ct YO31 ... 228 F6
Parade The
Harrogate HG1 ... 219 E2
Hunmanby YO14 ... 127 B8
Whitby YO21 ... 208 B7
Paradise YO11 ... 213 B7
Paradise Cotts YO17 ... 170 F8
Paradise Field Est 2 YO61 ... 143 D8
Paradise La
Dalton YO7 ... 115 F8
Stutton with Hazlewood LS24 ... 189 A3
Paradise Rd YO7 ... 67 A2
Paradise Way 6 DL2 ... 3 B7
Paragon St YO10 ... 233 C1
Parcevall Hall Gdns* BD23 ... 157 E8
Parish Ghyll Dr LS29 ... 218 A3
Parish Ghyll La LS29 ... 218 A3
Parish Ghyll Rd LS29 ... 218 A3
Parish Ghyll Wlk LS29 ... 218 A3
Parison Ct WF10 ... 200 F3
PARK ... 186 F5
Park Ave
2 Airmyn DN14 ... 205 F3
Barlow YO8 ... 204 C7
Castleford WF10 ... 200 F4
Glusburn BD20 ... 187 F7
Great Preston WF10 ... 200 E6
Harrogate HG2 ... 219 C1
Hellifield BD23 ... 154 B3
Kippax LS25 ... 194 E1
Knaresborough HG5 ... 221 B8
New Earswick YO32 ... 225 D5
Normanton South WF6 ... 200 A1
Scarborough YO12 ... 212 D4
Sherburn in Elmet LS25 ... 195 E4
Skipton BD23 ... 216 F4
Swillington LS26 ... 194 A1
Thornaby TS17 ... 6 B8
Park Avenue S HG2 ... 222 D8
Park Bank YO21 ... 29 E7
Park Chase
Harrogate HG1 ... 219 E3
Hornby DL8 ... 62 C8
Park Cl
6 Airmyn DN14 ... 205 E4
1 Easingwold YO61 ... 143 D8
8 Knaresborough HG5 ... 221 B6
Skelton YO30 ... 224 B4
Park Cres
6 Addingham LS29 ... 175 A4
Castleford WF10 ... 201 B4
Darlington DL1 ... 3 D4
Embsay BD23 ... 217 C7
Hellifield BD23 ... 154 B3
York YO31 ... 233 C4
Park Crest HG5 ... 221 B6
Park Dale WF10 ... 201 B5
Park Dr
Campsall DN6 ... 206 E1
Glusburn BD20 ... 187 E7
Harrogate HG2 ... 222 D8
Knaresborough HG5 ... 221 B6
13 Masham HG4 ... 86 C3
Park Edge HG2 ... 222 F8
PARK END ... 7 B8
Park End Prim Sch TS3 ... 7 C8
Parker Ave YO26 ... 227 B2
Parker Dr 21 DL8 ... 63 A2
Parker La YO26 ... 164 C3
Parkers Mount 20 YO62 ... 70 B1
Parker St
Barnoldswick BB18 ... 171 C2
15 Glusburn BD20 ... 187 E8
Park Est YO32 ... 225 D8
Parkfield YO61 ... 144 C6
Parkfield Ave TS5 ... 6 E8
Parkfield Cl YO12 ... 212 D4
Parkfield Gdns YO12 ... 212 D4
Parkfield La WF7 ... 200 E1
Parkgate DL1 ... 3 D5
Park Gate
Knaresborough HG5 ... 221 B8
Strensall YO32 ... 167 B8
Parkgate La DL10 ... 41 B7
Park Gr
Knaresborough HG5 ... 221 B8
Norton YO17 ... 215 C3
Selby YO8 ... 232 B3
Swillington LS26 ... 200 A8
York YO31 ... 233 C4
Park Grove Prim Sch YO31 ... 233 C4
Park Hill BB18 ... 171 E1
Park House Gn
Harrogate HG1 ... 219 C5
7 Spofforth HG3 ... 179 E5
Park House La LA2 ... 128 D5
Parkin Ave YO8 ... 232 E4
Parkins Garth DL8 ... 57 F6
Parkinson App LS25 ... 194 C4
Parkinson's La LS21 ... 159 E2
Parkinson's Yd 5 DL10 ... 209 C6
Park La
Balne DN14 ... 207 C5
Barlow YO8 ... 204 C7
Bishop Wilton YO42 ... 169 F1
Borrowby YO7 ... 65 E4
Buckden BD23 ... 81 E2
Burn YO8 ... 203 D7
Carleton BD23 ... 173 A3
Park La *continued*
Cowling BD22 ... 186 F5
Darlington DL1 ... 3 D4
5 Easington TS13 ... 11 A8
Glusburn BD20 ... 187 E7
Great Preston WF10 ... 200 E7
Guisborough TS14 ... 8 E6
Kippax LS25 ... 200 E8
Kirkbymoorside YO62 ... 70 B1
Knaresborough HG5 ... 221 C6
Ledsham LS25 ... 201 B8
Luttons YO17 ... 150 C8
Mickletown LS26 ... 200 A5
5 Middleham DL8 ... 60 E2
North Featherstone WF8 ... 200 F1
North Stainley with Sleningford HG4 ... 113 E5
Spofforth with Stockeld HG3 ... 179 D5
Tatham LA2 ... 128 B8
West Tanfield HG4 ... 113 A8
Wilberfoss YO41 ... 185 E5
Womersley DN6 ... 206 D6
York YO24 ... 227 F3
Parkland Dr
Darlington DL3 ... 3 A6
Tadcaster LS24 ... 189 F6
Parklands
3 Airmyn DN14 ... 205 F3
Castleford WF10 ... 200 F4
Ilkley LS29 ... 218 D4
Park Lands 4 HG3 ... 179 E5
Parklands The
1 Ingleby Arncliffe DL6 ... 45 A7
Scruton DL7 ... 63 D7
Parkland Way YO32 ... 225 D8
Park Lane Cl YO42 ... 169 F1
Park Lodge YO32 ... 225 D4
Park Mount 6 HG3 ... 179 E5
Park Nook Rd LS25 ... 196 F4
Park Par
Harrogate HG1 ... 219 F2
Knaresborough HG5 ... 221 B6
Park Pl
Darlington DL1 ... 3 D5
Hellifield BD23 ... 154 B3
4 Knaresborough HG5 ... 221 B6
York YO31 ... 233 C4
Park Rd
Airmyn DN14 ... 205 E4
Asenby YO7 ... 115 B6
Barlow YO8 ... 204 C7
Castleford WF10 ... 201 A3
Cowling BD22 ... 187 B6
Glusburn BD20 ... 187 E8
8 Harrogate HG2 ... 219 D1
Norton-on-Derwent YO17 ... 215 C3
16 Pateley Bridge HG3 ... 137 B4
Pontefract WF8 ... 201 A1
6 Scarborough YO12 ... 212 E4
Spofforth HG3 ... 179 E5
Park Rise 17 YO14 ... 126 F8
Park Row
Knaresborough HG5 ... 221 B5
Selby YO8 ... 232 D5
Parkshill Ct DL10 ... 20 F7
Parkside DL1 ... 3 C4
Park Side
Earby BB18 ... 186 A8
Follifoot HG3 ... 223 E5
Parkside Cl YO24 ... 227 E3
Parkside Commercial Ctr YO23 ... 233 C1
Parkside La YO62 ... 119 E6
Parkside Prim Sch DN14 205 F3
Park Sq
2 Knaresborough HG5 ... 221 B6
9 Ripon HG4 ... 214 C4
Park St
16 Glusburn BD20 ... 187 E8
1 Harrogate HG1 ... 219 C5
Hovingham YO62 ... 119 E6
Masham HG4 ... 86 C3
Pickering YO18 ... 95 F7
Ripon HG4 ... 214 B5
Scarborough YO12 ... 212 D4
Selby YO8 ... 232 D5
1 Skipton BD23 ... 216 F4
York YO24 ... 233 A1
Parkstone Pl TS16 ... 5 E4
Park Terr
14 Knaresborough HG5 ... 221 B6
Whitby YO21 ... 208 D6
York YO32 ... 225 D5
Park The 14 YO13 ... 75 D5
Park View
Castleford WF10 ... 201 B3
Glaisdale YO21 ... 30 D4
Harrogate HG1 ... 219 E2
21 Leyburn DL8 ... 60 D5
Middleton Tyas DL10 ... 21 C4
Skipton BD23 ... 216 D4
Swillington LS26 ... 194 A1
Park View Dr BD23 ... 134 B3
Park Way
Kirk Hammerton YO26 ... 164 C2
Knaresborough HG5 ... 221 B8
Parkways YO8 ... 232 B3
Parkway The YO12 ... 212 B7
Park Wood BD23 ... 216 D5
Park Wood Cl BD23 ... 216 E5
Park Wood Cres BD23 ... 216 D5
Parkwood Dr 6 TS18 ... 5 E8
Park Wood Way BD23 ... 216 D5
Park Wynd DL10 ... 209 C6
Parliament Ave YO17 ... 215 E4
Parliament St
Harrogate HG1 ... 219 C3
Parliament St *continued*
Norton YO17 ... 215 E3
York YO1 ... 233 B2
Parliament Terr 2 HG1 ... 219 D2
PARLINGTON ... 194 E6
Parlington Ct LS15 ... 194 C8
Parlington Dr LS25 ... 194 E8
Parlington La LS25 ... 194 E7
Parlington Mdw LS15 ... 194 C7
Parlington Villas LS25 ... 194 E8
Parracombe Cl 6 TS17 ... 6 A3
Parrock St 7 BB18 ... 171 D1
Parsley Mews LS26 ... 200 B6
Parsonage Rd LS26 ... 200 C6
Parsonage The 11 HG5 ... 221 A6
Parson Back La DL6 ... 25 B2
Parsons Cl 10 DN14 ... 205 E4
Parson's Cl YO21 ... 208 A7
Parsons Close La BD24 ... 131 A2
Parsons Ct DL10 ... 209 F7
Parsons La YO26 ... 165 E1
Parson's La
1 Addingham LS29 ... 174 E4
Hutton Rudby DL6 ... 25 A2
Parson's Wlk 11 DN14 ... 205 E4
Pasley Rd HG4 ... 113 D3
Paston Wlk YO23 ... 233 B1
Pasture Ave LS25 ... 196 A4
Pasture Cl
Barnoldswick BB18 ... 171 E2
4 Sherburn in Elmet LS25 196 A4
Skelton YO30 ... 224 B5
Skipton BD23 ... 217 B5
2 Strensall YO32 ... 167 B6
Wistow YO8 ... 197 D6
Pasture Cres
Filey YO14 ... 101 A4
3 Knaresborough HG5 ... 221 B7
Pasture Ct LS25 ... 195 F4
Pasture Dr
Bedale DL8 ... 63 A2
Castleford WF10 ... 200 D3
Pasture Farm Cl YO10 ... 231 D6
Pasture Field La YO22 ... 32 C5
Pasture Fold 4 LS29 ... 176 C1
Pasture Gdns DN6 ... 206 F2
Pasture Gr 27 LS25 ... 195 F4
Pasture Hill YO17 ... 169 E8
Pasture La
Ellerton YO42 ... 193 C1
Helperby YO61 ... 142 B8
Heworth YO31 ... 229 B8
Hovingham YO62 ... 119 E6
Kearby with Netherby LS22 179 C1
Malton YO17 ... 215 C5
Marton-le-Moor HG4 ... 140 D8
2 Seamer YO12 ... 99 D6
Pasture Rd
Embsay with Eastby BD23 ... 217 C8
Lockton YO18 ... 73 A5
Pastures Gn DL8 ... 62 C5
Pastures The
2 Carlton DN14 ... 204 C3
Coulby Newham TS8 ... 7 B5
16 Eastfield YO11 ... 100 B6
Sherburn YO17 ... 124 D7
4 York YO24 ... 230 E8
Pasture The 4 TS17 ... 6 D5
Pasture View
Malton YO17 ... 215 C6
Sherburn in Elmet LS25 ... 195 F4
Pasture Way
Castleford WF10 ... 200 D3
Sherburn in Elmet LS25 ... 195 F4
Whitwood WF10 ... 200 D3
Wistow YO8 ... 197 D6
PATELEY BRIDGE ... 137 C4
Pateley Moor Cres DL2 ... 3 E3
Pately Pl 1 YO26 ... 227 D4
Paterson Cres DL6 ... 210 E4
Patience La HG4 ... 114 D3
PATRICK BROMPTON ... 62 C5
Patrick Pool YO1 ... 233 B2
Patterdale Dr YO30 ... 224 E1
Patterham La DL8 ... 59 D4
Pavement YO1 ... 233 B2
Paver La YO1 ... 233 C2
Pavilion Row YO10 ... 231 D7
Pavilion Sq
7 Harrogate HG2 ... 219 C1
11 Scarborough YO11 ... 213 A5
Pavilion Terr 12 YO11 ... 213 A5
Peacocks Cl TS9 ... 26 C8
Peacock's Cl DL7 ... 63 E7
Peak Alum Works* YO13 ... 53 F8
Peak Scar Rd YO62 ... 67 C3
Pearl Rd TS17 ... 6 B8
Pearl St HG1 ... 220 C4
Pearson Garth YO13 ... 99 A7
Pearson St WF6 ... 200 A3
Pearsons Yd YO17 ... 121 C4
Peart La BD23 ... 154 C8
Pear Tree Acre LS23 ... 180 F1
Pear Tree Ave
Long Drax YO8 ... 204 F7
8 Poppleton YO26 ... 165 F1
Pear Tree Cl
Skeeby DL10 ... 20 F1
York YO32 ... 225 F4
Peartree Ct YO1 ... 233 C3
Pear Tree Gdns
Asenby YO7 ... 115 C6
Barwick in Elmet LS15 ... 194 D7
Pear Tree Wlk YO17 ... 215 B4
Pease Ct
1 Eaglescliffe TS16 ... 5 D5
Guisborough TS14 ... 8 D5

Pease Ct *continued*
4 Lingdale TS12 .... 9 F7
Pease St
Darlington DL1 .... 3 E5
6 Lingdale TS12 .... 9 F7
Peasey Hills Rd YO17 .... 215 C5
Peasholm Ave YO12 ..... 212 F7
Peasholm Cres YO12 .... 212 F7
Peasholm Dr YO12 ...... 212 E7
Peasholme Bridge YO12. 212 E7
Peasholme Gn YO1 ...... 233 C2
Peasholm Gap YO12 ..... 212 F8
Peasholm Gdns YO12 .... 212 F7
Peasholm Rd YO12 ...... 212 F8
Peasland La YO7 .... 66 B5
Peaslands La YO18 .... 96 D5
Peat La HG3 .... 137 B3
Peatmoor La DL8 .... 58 E5
Pebble La 58 YO14 ...... 101 B3
Peckett's Holt HG1 ...... 219 D7
Peckett's Way HG1 ...... 219 D7
Peckfield HG4 .... 214 C2
Peckfield Bsns Pk LS25 . 194 F3
Peckfield Cl HG3 .... 160 F5
Peckitt St YO1 .... 233 B1
Peel Cl YO10 .... 229 A1
Peel Gn BD23 .... 154 B2
Peel Pl 11 LS29 .... 176 C1
Peel St
Thornaby TS17 .... 6 B8
York YO1 .... 233 C1
Peel Terr YO12 .... 213 A7
Pefham La YO25 .... 170 F4
Pegman Cl TS14 .... 8 F7
Peirse Cl DL8 .... 63 A2
Pelham Pl 15 YO32 ...... 167 A7
Pellentine Rd HG3 ...... 223 F4
Pemberton Cres TS4 ...... 7 A8
Pemberton Rd WF10 .... 201 A4
Pembroke St
10 Skipton BD23 .... 216 F3
York YO30 .... 228 B7
Pembroke Way YO21 .... 208 C5
Pembury Mews DL10 ..... 41 B6
Penberry Gdns 33 TS17 ..... 5 F4
Penders La TS15 .... 5 E1
Penderyn Cres TS17 .... 5 F4
Pendle St 4 BD23 .... 216 D3
Pendleton Rd DL1 .... 3 D7
Pendragon Castle* CA17. 14 A1
Pendragon Way HG2 .... 222 B8
Penfold Ct BD23 .... 154 B3
Penhill Ct DL7 .... 210 C1
Penhowe La YO17 .... 147 D4
Penistone Rd TS3 .... 7 C8
Penley's Grove St YO31 . 233 C4
Pennine Cl YO32 .... 225 F4
Pennine View
Burneston DL8 .... 87 E8
Northallerton DL7 .... 210 B2
Pennine Way
11 Barnoldswick BB18 ... 171 D1
Ingleby TS17 .... 6 A4
Lothersdale BD20 .... 172 E2
Penniston La YO13 .... 97 C4
Penn La DL8 .... 56 D4
Penn Rd DL10 .... 209 B7
Pennycarr La YO61 ..... 143 D7
Penny Gn BD24 .... 131 D1
Penny La
Burton Fleming YO25 .... 126 E2
Darlington DL1 .... 3 C4
1 Easingwold YO61 ..... 117 D1
Ripon HG4 .... 214 C7
Penny La Ct YO1 .... 233 C3
Pennyman Gn TS8 .... 6 C4
Pennyman Prim Acad TS3 . 7 D8
Penny Pot Gdns 4 HG3 . 161 B2
Pennypot La TS18 .... 5 E7
Penny Pot La HG3 .... 160 D2
Penny Pot La or Rough Rd
HG3 .... 161 A2
Penny Royal Cl 7 HG3 .. 161 B3
Pennywort Gr 15 HG3 ... 161 B3
Penrith Cres WF10 ...... 201 B5
Penrith Rd TS3 .... 7 B8
Pentire Cl 11 YO30 ...... 225 A1
Pentland Dr YO32 .... 225 E3
Penton Rd 20 YO11 ...... 100 B6
Penyghent Ave YO31 .... 229 A5
Penyghent Way TS17 ...... 6 A3
Pen-y-Ghent Way 5
BB18 .... 171 D1
Peplow Cl LS25 .... 201 F6
Peppercorn Cl 6 YO26 . 227 E4
Peppergarth The DL7 ... 210 B3
Peppermint Dr 15 DL9 .... 41 A5
Peppermint Way YO8 ... 232 A5
Per Ardua Way 6 DL10 ... 41 E4
Percy Cross Rigg YO21 .... 9 A1
Percy Ct HG5 .... 162 A6
Percy Dr
4 Airmyn DN14 .... 205 E4
Norby YO7 .... 211 B4
Percy Rd
Darlington DL3 .... 3 C7
14 Hunmanby YO14 ..... 127 A8
Percy's La YO1 .... 233 C2
Percy St YO31 .... 233 B3
Peregrine Ct 2 TS14 ...... 8 D6
Perie Ave HG4 .... 113 D3
Perran Ct YO14 .... 127 C8
Perry Ave TS17 .... 6 B5
Petch Garth 34 YO62 ..... 70 B1
Petercroft Cl 5 YO19 .... 184 F7
Petercroft La YO19 ..... 184 F7
Peter Hill Dr YO30 ...... 228 A8
Peterhouse Cl DL1 .... 3 D7
Peter La
Burton Leonard HG3 ..... 140 A2
York YO1 .... 233 B2
Petersbottom La LA2 .... 129 B4
Petersway YO30 .... 233 A4
Petre Ave YO8 .... 232 E3
Petty Whin Cl 25 HG3 ... 161 B3
Petyt Gr BD23 .... 217 A4
Pew Tree Cl YO41 ...... 185 E6
Pheasant Dr 5 YO24 .... 230 B8
Pheasantry The 14 YO12 .. 99 E6
Pheasant Wy 12 YO32 ... 191 C7
Philadelphia Terr 2
YO23 .... 228 B2
Philip La YO8 .... 196 E2
Philippa's Dr HG2 ...... 222 D8
Philip St 27 BB18 .... 171 D1
Philpin La LA6 .... 104 C8
Phlashetts La DL8 .... 87 A4
Phoenix Ave LS25 .... 194 F3
Phoenix Bsns Ctr HG4 .. 214 D5
Phoenix Bvd YO26 ...... 228 A4
Phoenix Pk TS8 .... 6 F6
Piave Rd DL9 .... 40 D4
Picadilly Ct YO1 .... 233 C2
Piccadilly YO1 .... 233 C2
Pickard Cl BB18 .... 171 E2
Pickard La BD20 .... 174 C1
PICKERING 95 E6
Pickering Ave LS25 ..... 194 D4
Pickering Castle* YO18 .. 95 F7
Pickering Com Inf Sch
YO18 .... 96 A7
Pickering Com Junior Sch 26
YO18 .... 95 F7
Pickeringmoor La YO7 ... 64 C2
Pickering Rd
East Ayton/West Ayton
YO13 .... 99 A7
Thornaby TS17 .... 6 B8
Thornton-le-Dale YO18 .... 96 C6
Pickering Sta YO18 .... 95 F7
Pick Haven Garth DN14 .. 202 F3
PICKHILL 88 C6
Pickhill CE Prim Sch YO7. 88 C6
Picking Croft La HG3 .... 161 B5
Picks Ct 5 YO7 .... 211 B3
Pickwick Cl YO17 .... 215 C5
PICTON 24 D6
Picton Cr TS17 .... 6 A6
Piece Croft 2 BD23 ..... 134 D2
Piece Fields 4 BD23 .... 134 D2
PIERCEBRIDGE 2 A6
Piercy End YO62 .... 70 B1
Pier La 22 YO21 .... 208 D7
Pier Rd YO21 .... 208 D7
Pierremont Rd DL3 .... 3 B6
Piggy La
Barforth DL2 .... 1 C7
Bilbrough YO23 .... 182 D1
Gainford DL2 .... 1 C7
Pighill Nook Rd LS25 .... 202 C7
Pike Hills Mount YO23 .. 230 A3
Pike La BD24 .... 131 E4
Pikepurse La DL10 ...... 209 D8
Pike Rd 8 YO18 .... 95 F6
Piker Thorn La YO19 .... 167 D1
Pilgrim St YO31 .... 233 B4
Pill White La LS21 ...... 177 C3
Pilmoor Cl DL10 .... 209 E8
Pilmoor Dr DL10 .... 209 E8
Pilmore Mews DL2 .... 22 D8
Pindar L Ctr YO11 ...... 100 A6
Pindar Rd YO11 .... 100 A6
Pindars Way YO8 .... 198 B4
Pinder Cl DL10 .... 209 F8
Pinders Cres WF11 ...... 201 E3
Pinders Green Ct LS26 .. 200 B5
Pinders Green Dr LS26 .. 200 B5
Pinders Green Fold LS26 200 B5
Pinders Green Wlk LS26 . 200 B4
Pine Cl
Castleford WF10 .... 200 F3
Skipton BD23 .... 216 E4
Pine Croft HG4 .... 112 F2
Pine Gr 1 DL6 .... 210 E3
Pine Hill TS8 .... 7 B5
Pinelands 4 YO32 .... 225 D7
Pinelands Way YO10 .... 229 C3
Pine Rd
Guisborough TS14 .... 8 E7
Middlesbrough TS7 .... 7 D8
Pines Gdns 29 LS29 ..... 175 C2
Pine St HG1 .... 219 E5
Pines The LS17 .... 178 B2
Pine Tree Ave YO17 ..... 122 F5
Pine Tree Cl YO8 .... 197 B2
Pinetree Gr DL2 .... 4 C4
Pine Tree La 1 LS25 .... 202 A7
Pine Wlk HG4 .... 214 D2
Pinewood Ave YO14 ..... 101 B4
Pinewood Cl
5 Easington TS13 .... 11 A8
3 Firth Moor DL1 .... 3 E4
2 Ilkley LS29 .... 218 A3
5 Whitby YO21 .... 208 C6
Pinewood Dr
Camblesforth YO8 .... 204 D4
Scarborough YO12 ...... 212 D5
Pinewood Gate HG2 ..... 222 A7
Pinewood Gr
13 Bedale DL8 .... 63 A2
6 York YO31 .... 225 E2
Pinewood Hill 4 YO10 .. 229 C3
Pinewood Rd TS7 .... 7 C6
Pinewood Wlk 7 TS9 ..... 26 C8
Pinfield Cl 37 YO13 ...... 75 D5
Pinfold Ave LS25 .... 195 F4
Pinfold Cl
Bilton-in-Ainsty with Bickerton
LS22 .... 181 B5
11 Knaresborough HG5 ... 221 B5
5 Riccall YO19 .... 192 A1
3 Sherburn in Elmet LS25 195 F4
Pinfold Croft BD23 ...... 155 D1
Pinfold Ct
Kirkby Malzeard HG4 ..... 112 D5
4 Sherburn in Elmet LS25 195 F4
4 York YO30 .... 228 A7
Pinfold Dr DL6 .... 210 E5
Pinfold Garth
Malton YO17 .... 215 A4
6 Sherburn in Elmet LS25 195 F4
Pinfold Gn HG5 .... 140 E1
Pinfold Hill YO8 .... 197 D6
Pinfold La
Kirk Smeaton WF8 .... 206 B3
Mickletown LS26 .... 200 C5
Moss DN6 .... 207 D1
Norton DN6 .... 206 E2
Norwood HG3 .... 177 A8
Pollington DN14 .... 207 F6
Pinfold Pl YO7 .... 211 C3
Pinfold Rise LS25 .... 194 F8
Pinfold The 5 BD23 ..... 216 F4
Pinfold View DN14 ...... 207 F6
Pinfold Way 5 LS25 .... 195 F4
Pinhaw Rd BD23 .... 217 A2
Pinnacle View BD22 ..... 187 A5
Pinsent Ct 4 YO31 ...... 228 E8
Pioneer Bsns Pk YO30 ... 224 F3
Pioneer Ct DL1 .... 4 A4
Pioneer Way WF10 ...... 200 C2
Piper Hill 1 WF11 ...... 201 D6
Piper Hill Cl DL10 .... 21 D7
Piper La
Cowling BD22 .... 187 B5
Thirsk YO7 .... 211 C3
Piper Rd DL6 .... 45 F6
Pipers Acre 4 YO18 ...... 95 F7
Pipers La YO26 .... 141 F1
Pippin Rd YO17 .... 215 B4
Pippin's App 17 WF6 .... 200 A2
Pit Ings La YO7 .... 115 F6
Pit La
Ledston Luck LS25 .... 194 F1
Micklefield LS25 .... 195 A4
Mickletown LS26 .... 200 B6
Pitman Rd YO17 .... 215 C5
Pittfields Corner DL7 ..... 63 D7
Place Hill DL11 .... 38 B6
PLACE NEWTON 123 C3
Planetree La
Kirkby Fleetham with Fencote
DL7 .... 42 A1
Thornville YO26 .... 164 A1
Plane Tree Way YO14 ... 101 A4
Plantation Ave HG3 ..... 222 A8
Plantation Cl HG2 .... 222 A8
Plantation Dr
Barlby with Osgodby YO8 . 198 B5
York YO26 .... 227 C6
Plantation Gr YO26 ..... 227 C6
Plantation Rd HG2 ...... 222 A8
Plantation Terr HG2 ..... 222 A8
Plantation The
Birstwith HG3 .... 160 E6
Gisburn Forest BD23 ..... 152 E3
Plantation Way 23 YO32 . 166 E5
Plaxton Ct YO12 .... 212 B5
Plaxton Pk Ind Est YO11 100 A6
Player Ct TS16 .... 5 E5
Pleasance The 6 LS26 .. 194 A1
Pleasant Ave 3 YO19 ... 191 D8
Pleasant Row HG5 ...... 221 B8
Pleasant View 5 BB18 .. 172 B1
Plews Way DL7 .... 63 C5
Plompton Cl HG2 .... 220 D1
Plompton Dr HG2 .... 220 D2
Plompton Gr 3 HG2 .... 220 D2
Plompton Rd HG3 .... 223 F5
Plompton Way 1 HG2 .. 220 D2
Plompton Wlk 2 HG2 ... 220 D2
Plough Garth The DN14 . 202 F3
Ploughlands 1 YO32 .... 225 C7
Ploughman's Cl YO23 ... 230 C3
Ploughmans Ct 14 YO11 . 100 B7
Ploughmans' La YO32 ... 225 C7
Plover Gdns 1 YO12 ...... 99 F6
Plumer Ave YO31 .... 229 A5
Plumer Rd DL9 .... 209 B1
Plumpton La HG4 .... 139 D8
Plumpton Pk HG2 .... 220 D3
Plumpton Rocks* HG5 .. 179 D8
Plum St YO17 .... 215 D3
Pluntrain Dale La YO18 ... 96 B7
Poachers The YO8 ...... 199 C5
POCKLEY 69 B1
Pocklington La YO42 ... 169 F2
Pockthorpe La YO25 .... 151 F2
Pocock Pl DL10 .... 41 E4
Polam Hall Sch DL1 .... 3 C4
Polam La DL1 .... 3 C4
Polam Rd DL1 .... 3 C4
Pole Rd BD22 .... 187 F4
Pollard Gdns YO12 ..... 212 C4
Pollard Rd YO31 .... 53 F8
Pollard's Fields 1 WF11 201 D3
POLLINGTON 207 F6
Pollington-Balne CE Prim
Sch DN14 .... 207 F6
Polperro Cl 21 WF6 ..... 200 A2
Pond Farm Cl TS13 .... 11 F7
Pond Field Cl DL3 .... 3 A4
Pondfields Dr LS25 ...... 194 D1
Pond St 3 YO8 .... 232 D6
Pond View DL6 .... 65 F7
Pontefract Monkhill Sta
WF8 .... 201 B1
Pontefract Park
Racecourse*
WF8 .... 200 F2
Pontefract Rd
Castleford WF10 .... 200 F4
Knottingley WF11 .... 201 D2
Normanton South WF6 ... 200 B2
Pontefract Tanshelf Sta
WF8 .... 201 A1
Pool Ct 20 YO18 .... 95 F6
POOLE 201 F5
Poole La LS25 .... 201 F6
Pool La YO26 .... 164 E4
Pope St WF6 .... 200 B3
Poplar Ave
Castleford WF10 .... 201 B4
Garforth LS25 .... 194 C3
6 Hutton Rudby TS15 ..... 25 D5
4 Kirkbymoorside YO62 ... 70 B1
3 Wetherby LS22 .... 180 C4
Poplar Cres
Harrogate HG1 .... 219 F6
Northallerton DL7 .... 210 C2
Poplar Ct YO8 .... 204 F5
Poplar Dr WF6 .... 200 A3
Poplar Gdns YO8 .... 204 F5
Poplar Gn HG5 .... 162 A6
Poplar Gr
Harrogate HG1 .... 219 F6
1 Knottingley WF11 ..... 201 F1
York YO32 .... 225 E3
Poplar Pl TS14 .... 8 E7
Poplar Row 6 YO21 ..... 208 D7
Poplars Adventure Mega
Maze* HG5 .... 162 F6
Poplars La YO17 .... 123 A7
Poplar St YO26 .... 227 E5
Poplars The
11 Brayton YO8 .... 197 D1
2 Glusburn BD20 .... 187 E6
Knottingley WF11 .... 202 A1
Poplar View YO17 ...... 215 F4
Poplar Way HG1 .... 219 F6
Poppleton Hall Gdn
YO26 .... 224 A3
Poppleton Ousebank Prim
Sch YO26 .... 165 F1
Poppleton Rd YO26 ..... 227 E4
Poppleton Rd Prim Sch
YO26 .... 227 E5
Poppleton Sta YO26 ..... 182 F8
Poppy Cl YO8 .... 232 C2
Poppy Ct DL9 .... 41 A5
Porchester Cl 3 TS17 ...... 5 F5
Porch Farm Cl YO62 ..... 120 B5
Porch The DL10 .... 21 D7
Pornic Ave YO13 .... 75 D5
Porritt La YO12 .... 99 D7
Portal Rd
Knapton YO26 .... 227 B7
York YO26 .... 227 B6
Portholme Cres 7 YO8 .. 232 C5
Portholme Ct YO8 ...... 232 C4
Portholme Dr YO8 ...... 232 C4
Portholme Rd YO8 ...... 232 C5
Portisham Pl 12 YO32 ... 167 A7
Portland Cres HG1 ...... 219 D4
Portland St YO31 .... 233 B4
Portland Way DL7 .... 63 C5
Portman Rise TS14 .... 8 F5
PORT MULGRAVE 11 F8
Postern Cl YO23 .... 233 B1
Postern La YO42 .... 193 D6
Post Office Row DN14 ... 205 A1
Post Office Slip 24 YO61 . 143 C8
Pot Bank HG3 .... 178 A8
Potlands DL7 .... 63 C4
Pott Bank HG4 .... 85 A1
Potter Cl YO13 .... 99 B8
Pottergate
Gilling East YO62 .... 118 F7
14 Helmsley YO62 .... 92 F6
Richmond DL10 .... 209 C7
Potter Hill 11 YO18 .... 95 F7
Potter La DL7 .... 64 A5
Potters Dr 4 YO23 ...... 230 B3
Potter's Side La YO21 ..... 9 D1
POTTERTON 188 C1
Potterton Cl LS15 .... 194 C8
Potterton La
Barwick in Elmet LS15 .... 194 C8
Barwick in Elmet & Scholes
LS15 .... 188 C1
Pottery La
Bishop Monkton HG4 ..... 140 A6
Knottingley WF11 .... 201 E3
Littlethorpe HG4 .... 214 E1
Strensall YO32 .... 145 A1
Strensall YO32 .... 167 A8
York YO31 .... 228 E7
Pottery St WF10 .... 200 D4
Potticar Bank YO62 ..... 119 D4
Pott Moor High Rd HG4 . 110 F8
POTTO 25 D2
Pounteys Cl 4 DL2 .... 4 C4
Powell St
Harrogate HG1 .... 219 F4
Selby YO8 .... 232 B6
Prail Cl 13 WF8 .... 201 C1
Prebendal Cl 11 LS25 ... 202 A8
Precentor's Ct YO31 .... 233 B3
Preen Dr TS5 .... 6 D8
Premiere Pk 30 LS29 .... 175 C2
Premier Rd TS7 .... 7 D7
Premier Way North WF6 200 C1
Preseli Gr 31 TS17 .... 5 F4
Preston Field Cross Rd
YO13 .... 74 E1
Preston Hall Mus* TS18 .... 5 F6
Preston La
Great Preston WF10 ..... 200 C7
Preston-on-Tees TS18 ...... 5 E7
PRESTON-ON-TEES 5 F7
Preston Prim Sch TS16 ..... 5 E6
PRESTON-UNDER-SCAR .. 59 E6
Preston View LS26 ...... 194 A1
Preston Way TS9 .... 26 C8
Prestwick Ct
15 Middleton St George DL2. 4 C4
Rufforth YO26 .... 227 B5
Pretoria St WF10 .... 200 F4
Price's La YO23 .... 233 B1
Priest Bank Rd 4 BD20 . 173 F1
Priestcarr La YO26 ..... 163 D8
Priest Cl YO14 .... 126 F8
Priest Gill Bank DL11 ..... 19 F5
Priest La
Dunnington YO19 .... 184 F5
Ripon HG4 .... 214 D4
Primrose Ave
Hunmanby Sands YO14 ... 101 B1
Hunmanby YO14 .... 127 B8
Swillington LS26 .... 194 A1
Primrose Cl
Guisborough TS14 .... 8 E6
13 Killinghall HG3 .... 161 B3
Ripon HG4 .... 214 C6
Primrose Ct 18 DL9 .... 41 A5
Primrose Dene WF11 .... 201 E4
Primrose Dr
Castleford WF10 .... 201 D3
Filey YO14 .... 101 B1
Ripon HG4 .... 214 C6
Primrose Gr YO8 .... 232 A6
Primrose Hill
9 Knottingley WF11 ..... 202 A3
2 Skipton BD23 .... 216 F4
Primrose Hill Cl LS26 .... 194 A1
Primrose Hill Dr
Great & Little Preston
LS26 .... 200 A8
15 Swillington LS26 ...... 194 A1
Primrose Hill Garth LS26 200 A8
Primrose Hill Gdns LS26. 194 A1
Primrose Hill Gn LS26 ... 200 A8
Primrose Hill Gr 16 LS26 194 A1
Primrose La LS23 .... 188 E8
Primrose Lane Prim Sch 5
LS23 .... 188 E8
Primrose Vale 1 WF11 .. 202 A2
PRIMROSE VALLEY 101 C1
Primrose Valley Rd YO14 101 B1
Prince Bishop Sch TS4 ...... 6 F8
Prince Henry Rd LS21 ... 177 A1
Prince Henrys Ct 12
LS21 .... 177 A1
Prince Henrys Gram Sch
LS21 .... 177 A1
Prince of Wales Terr
YO11 .... 213 A4
Prince Rupert Dr YO26 .. 181 C7
Princes Cres BD23 ...... 217 B4
Princes Dr BD23 .... 217 A4
Princess Ave HG5 .... 221 C5
Princess Cl
Knaresborough HG5 ..... 221 C5
Ripon HG4 .... 214 C6
Princess Ct 11 WF6 ..... 200 B1
Princess Dr
Knaresborough HG5 ..... 221 C5
West Haddlesey YO8 ..... 203 A5
York YO26 .... 227 D6
Princess Gr 4 HG5 ..... 221 C5
Princess La 12 YO11 .... 213 B6
Princess Mead HG5 ..... 163 A3
Princess Mount 3 HG5 . 221 C5
Princess Pl
1 Ripon HG4 .... 214 C6
5 Whitby YO21 .... 208 D6
Princes Sq
14 Harrogate HG1 ...... 219 D2
Thornaby TS17 .... 6 B6
Princess Rd
Darlington DL3 .... 3 D8
Ilkley LS29 .... 218 A3
Malton YO17 .... 215 C4
Ripon HG4 .... 214 C6
Strensall YO32 .... 167 B7
Princess Royal La 4
YO11 .... 212 F3
Princess Royal Pk 1
YO11 .... 213 A3
Princess Royal Rd HG4 . 214 C3
Princess Royal Terr
YO11 .... 213 A3
Princess Royal Way HG3 222 E1
Princess Sq 11 YO11 .... 213 B6
Princess St
Castleford WF10 .... 200 F5
Normanton South WF6 ... 200 A1
Scarborough YO11 ...... 213 B6
Princess Terr
Knaresborough HG5 ..... 221 C6
17 Scarborough YO11 ... 213 B6
Prince St WF10 .... 200 C8
Princes Villa Rd HG1 .... 219 E2
Principal Rise YO24 ..... 230 E6
Prior Ave DL10 .... 209 B7
Priorpot Way YO17 ..... 215 F4

Prior Pursglove Coll 16 TS14 ... 8 F7
Prior's La BD23 ... 174 C8
Prior's Wlk YO26 ... 227 D6
Prior Wath Rd YO13 ... 54 A5
Priorwood Gdns TS17 ... 6 A4
Priory Cl
Guisborough TS14 ... 8 F7
Northallerton DL6 ... 210 E5
Redmire DL8 ... 59 C6
Wilberfoss YO41 ... 185 F6
Priory Dr YO21 ... 208 A6
Priory Hospl Middleton St George DL2 ... 4 E4
Priory Hurworth Ho Sch DL2 ... 3 E1
Priory La 1 DN14 ... 204 C1
Priory Park Cl 3 LS25 ... 202 A8
Priory Park Gr 2 LS25 ... 202 B8
Priory Pk YO22 ... 31 C4
Priory Pl YO11 ... 100 B7
Priory Road or House DN6 ... 206 E2
Priory St YO1 ... 233 A1
Priory View 2 BD23 ... 217 E8
Priory Villas DL10 ... 209 D6
Priory Way
Barnoldswick BB18 ... 171 D1
4 Ingleby Arncliffe DL6 ... 45 A7
1 Snaith DN14 ... 204 B1
Priory Wood Way YO31 ... 225 F2
Prison & Pol Mus★ HG4 214 D5
Pritchett Rd TS3 ... 7 C8
Privet Dr YO8 ... 197 B2
Promenade La HG1 ... 219 C3
Promenade Sq HG1 ... 219 C2
Prospect Ave
Easingwold YO61 ... 117 C1
Normanton South WF6 ... 200 A2
Sherburn in Elmet LS25 ... 195 F4
Prospect Bank
Bramham cum Oglethorpe LS23 ... 188 F6
Scarborough YO12 ... 212 D6
Prospect Cl
Camblesforth YO8 ... 204 D5
Harrogate HG2 ... 220 C3
Monk Fryston LS25 ... 202 A8
Pollington DN14 ... 207 F6
Prospect Cotts 6 HG3 ... 160 A6
Prospect Cres
13 Harrogate HG1 ... 219 D2
Scarborough YO12 ... 212 D6
Prospect Ct 3 LS24 ... 189 E6
Prospect Dr LS24 ... 189 E6
Prospect Field 5 YO22 ... 33 D4
Prospect Hill YO21 ... 208 C5
Prospect Mount Rd YO12 ... 212 C6
Prospect Pk YO12 ... 212 D6
Prospect Pl
Harrogate HG1 ... 219 D2
Northallerton DL6 ... 210 F4
28 Scarborough YO11 ... 213 A6
Skipton BD23 ... 216 F4
Thornton-le-Dale YO18 ... 96 D6
10 Whitby YO22 ... 208 E6
Wistow YO8 ... 197 D6
Prospect Rd
Harrogate HG2 ... 220 C3
9 Scarborough YO12 ... 212 F6
Prospects Cotts YO61 ... 117 C6
Prospect St 14 BD20 ... 187 E7
Prospect Terr
Fulford YO10 ... 231 D6
15 Knaresborough HG5 ... 221 A6
1 Lingdale TS12 ... 9 F7
Micklefield LS25 ... 195 A3
York YO1 ... 233 B1
Prospect View
Appleton Wiske DL6 ... 24 B3
Northallerton DL6 ... 210 E4
Prospect Way
5 Leeming DL7 ... 63 D4
Selby YO8 ... 232 D4
Prospect Way Ind Est YO8 ... 232 D4
Providence Gn 16 WF8 ... 201 C2
Providence Pl
13 Filey YO14 ... 101 B3
Mickletown WR10 ... 200 D6
15 Scarborough YO11 ... 213 A6
Skipton BD23 ... 217 A4
Providence Terr HG1 ... 219 D4
Pry Hills La
Hartoft YO18 ... 71 A8
Rosedale East Side YO18 ... 49 F2
Pudding Hill Rd DL11 ... 1 B6
Pudding La YO13 ... 97 F5
Pudding Pie Hill★ YO7 ... 211 D1
Pudsey Wlk 3 DL1 ... 3 D4
Pudsley Wlk DL1 ... 3 D4
Pulleyn Cl 3 YO32 ... 167 C8
Pulleyn Dr YO24 ... 227 F1
Pump Hill 4 HG5 ... 221 A6
Pump La
Kirklevington TS15 ... 24 F8
4 Malton YO17 ... 215 C4
Pye Busk Cl LA2 ... 129 B8
Pye La HG3 ... 160 F8
Pysbury Wlk 23 YO51 ... 141 B5

Q

Quaker Cl
1 Reeth, Fremington & Healaugh DL11 ... 38 B6
Scarborough YO12 ... 212 C5
Quaker Gn 1 YO24 ... 230 C7
Quaker La DL6 ... 210 D5
Quakers La DL10 ... 209 B7
Quaker's La DL6 ... 44 D7
Quant Mews YO10 ... 229 B3
Quarry Ave 20 WF11 ... 202 A2
Quarry Bank YO17 ... 215 D5
Quarry Banks YO7 ... 116 E7
Quarry Dr TS8 ... 6 E5
Quarry Gate YO13 ... 74 C1
Quarry Hill YO17 ... 120 F4
Quarry Hill La LS22 ... 180 B3
Quarry Hills La 25 DL8 ... 60 D5
Quarry La
Harrogate HG1 ... 219 C6
Osmotherley DL6 ... 45 C5
Pateley Bridge HG3 ... 137 C4
Quarry Moor La HG4 ... 214 C3
Quarry Moor Nature Reserve★ HG4 ... 214 B1
Quarry Mount YO12 ... 212 E3
Quarry Oval HG1 ... 219 C6
Quarry Rd
Eaglescliffe TS18 ... 5 F7
Norton DN6 ... 206 F2
Richmond DL10 ... 209 B7
Ripon HG4 ... 214 B2
Quay St YO11 ... 213 B6
Quay The YO8 ... 232 D6
Queen Anne's Ct 3 DL8 ... 63 A2
Queen Anne's Dr 4 DL8 ... 63 A2
Queen Annes Rd YO30 ... 233 A3
Queen Elizabeth Dr 10 YO13 ... 75 D5
Queen Elizabeth's Sixth Form Coll 1 DL3 ... 3 C5
Queen Elizabeth Way TS18 6 D6
Queen Ethelburga's Coll YO26 ... 164 C6
Queen Ethelburga's Gdns 6 HG3 ... 161 B2
Queen Ethelburga's Par 8 HG3 ... 161 B2
Queen Ethelburga's Pk 9 HG3 ... 161 B2
Queen Margarets Ave 4 WF11 ... 201 E4
Queen Margarets Cl 3 WF11 ... 201 E4
Queen Margaret's Dr WF11 ... 201 E4
Queen Margaret's Ind Est YO11 ... 212 E2
Queen Margaret's Rd 6 YO11 ... 212 F3
Queen Margaret's Sch YO19 ... 192 A5
Queen Mary's Sch YO7 ... 115 A7
Queens Ave DL9 ... 40 E3
Queensbury Ct 15 WF6 ... 200 B1
Queens Cl DL10 ... 41 E5
Queen's Cl 8 HG2 ... 219 C1
Queens Ct
Gainford DL2 ... 1 D7
Great Preston LS26 ... 200 C7
Malton YO17 ... 215 D6
Richmond DL10 ... 209 C7
Queen's Ct YO1 ... 233 B2
Queens Dr
9 Stokesley TS9 ... 26 C8
Whitby YO22 ... 208 E3
Queen's Dr LS29 ... 218 A3
Queen's Drive La LS29 ... 218 A3
Queens Garth BD23 ... 172 A3
Queens Gate HG1 ... 219 E2
Queens Gdns YO7 ... 211 C1
Queen's Gdns
4 Ilkley LS29 ... 218 A3
Tadcaster LS24 ... 189 E6
Queen's Par YO12 ... 213 A7
Queen's Park Dr WF10 ... 201 A4
Queens Rd
Knaresborough HG5 ... 221 C6
Richmond DL10 ... 209 C7
Queen's Rd
Harrogate HG2 ... 219 C1
Ilkley LS29 ... 218 A3
Queen's St 6 BD23 ... 217 B4
Queens Staith Mews YO1 233 B1
Queen's Staith Rd YO1 ... 233 B2
Queen St
10 Cowling BD22 ... 187 B6
Great Preston LS26 ... 200 C7
Normanton South WF6 ... 200 A1
18 Ripon HG4 ... 214 C5
Scarborough YO11 ... 213 A6
4 Silsden BD20 ... 174 C1
Skelton & Brotton TS12 ... 9 D7
York YO24 ... 233 A2
Queen's Terr
3 Filey YO14 ... 101 B3
Scarborough YO12 ... 213 A7
Queensway
Garforth LS25 ... 194 B4
Pontefract WF8 ... 201 C2
Queen's Way YO62 ... 70 B1
Queenswood Gr YO24 ... 227 D2
Queen Victoria St YO23 ... 228 B1
Quentin Rd 19 DL9 ... 40 E4
Quernmore Dr BB18 ... 186 A7
Quilt Mus & Gall The★ YO1 ... 233 C2

R

Raby La DL7 ... 22 E3
Raby Pk LS22 ... 180 B3
Raby Terr DL3 ... 3 C5
Racca Ave 11 WF11 ... 202 A2
Racca Gn WF11 ... 202 A2
Racecourse Ct DL10 ... 209 A8
Racecourse La DL7 ... 210 D3
Racecourse Mews YO7 ... 211 A2
Racecourse Rd
East Ayton/West Ayton YO13 ... 99 B8
Irton YO12 ... 212 A1
Richmond DL10 ... 209 B8
York YO23 ... 231 B8
Race La
Carlton DN14 ... 204 B4
Sessay YO61 ... 116 C4
Rachel La DL11 ... 20 B5
Radley Ct 10 YO32 ... 167 A6
Raghill La YO61 ... 142 A8
Raglan St HG1 ... 219 D2
Raglan Terr 3 YO21 ... 208 D5
Rag Robin Turn YO7 ... 66 D6
Raikes Ave BD23 ... 216 F5
Raikes La BD23 ... 156 A6
Raikes' La YO22 ... 32 E3
Raikes Rd BD23 ... 216 F5
Raikes The HG3 ... 137 E3
Raikeswood Cres BD23 ... 216 E5
Raikeswood Dr BD23 ... 216 E5
Raikeswood Rd BD23 ... 216 E5
Railer Bank HG4 ... 112 E6
Railway Ave WF8 ... 201 B1
Railway Cotts HG4 ... 214 D1
Railway Rd
Follifoot HG3 ... 223 C7
Ilkley LS29 ... 218 B4
Railway St
15 Leyburn DL8 ... 60 D5
Norton YO17 ... 215 C3
Slingsby YO62 ... 120 B5
Railway Terr
Hurworth-on-Tees DL2 ... 22 D8
Ilkley LS29 ... 218 C4
5 Normanton South WF6 200 A1
Thirsk YO7 ... 211 B2
York YO24 ... 228 A4
Railway View
19 Bedale DL8 ... 63 B3
Darlington DL1 ... 3 D4
Northallerton DL7 ... 210 D3
York YO24 ... 230 E8
Raincliffe Ave
29 Filey YO14 ... 101 B3
Scarborough YO12 ... 212 C5
Raincliffe Cres YO12 ... 212 C5
Raincliffe Gr YO12 ... 212 C4
Raincliffe St 4 YO8 ... 232 C5
Raindale Rd YO18 ... 71 F6
Raines Dr 5 BD20 ... 173 E3
Raines Garth 29 BD24 ... 131 D2
Raines La BD23 ... 134 D3
Raines Lea BD23 ... 134 D3
Raines Mdws 6 BD23 ... 134 D2
Raines Rd BD24 ... 131 C1
Rainford Cl 7 YO12 ... 99 D6
Rainhall Cres BB18 ... 171 E1
Rainhall Rd BB18 ... 171 D1
Rainham Cl TS17 ... 6 B4
Rainhill Way 5 DL2 ... 3 B7
Rainsborough Way 3 YO30 ... 228 A8
Rainsburgh La YO25 ... 126 A3
RAINTON ... 114 E6
Raisdale Rd TS9 ... 26 D1
Rakehill Rd LS15 ... 194 B8
Rake La YO21 ... 30 D6
Raker Cl YO19 ... 192 F7
Rakes La BD23 ... 171 B5
Rake The LA6 ... 103 D4
Raleigh St YO12 ... 212 E6
Ralph Butterfield Prim Sch YO32 ... 166 F5
Ralph Garth YO26 ... 181 D7
Rampart The YO23 ... 190 D4
Ramsay Cl YO31 ... 233 C4
Ramsden Cl WF11 ... 201 D4
Ramsden St LS25 ... 200 C8
Ramsey Ave YO23 ... 231 B3
Ramsey Gdns 33 TS17 ... 5 F4
Ramsey St YO12 ... 212 E6
RAMSGILL ... 110 E1
Ramsgill DL1 ... 3 E4
Ramshaw Dr BD23 ... 217 A1
Ramshill Rd YO11 ... 213 A4
Randal La HG3 ... 160 D4
Range Rd DL9 ... 40 A2
Rankin's Well Rd 4 BD23 ... 217 B4
Rantreefold Rd LA2 ... 128 F4
Rape Close La YO62 ... 118 E4
Rape La YO62 ... 93 B7
Raper La YO61 ... 117 B3
Raper View LS25 ... 194 F8
Rarber Top La LA6 ... 103 D2
Rarey Dr YO17 ... 124 E1
RASKELF ... 116 E2
Raskelf Rd
7 Brafferton YO61 ... 115 F1
Easingwold YO61 ... 117 B1
Ratcliffe Ct YO30 ... 224 C5
Ratcliffe St YO30 ... 228 B7
Rathmall La YO26 ... 164 C2
RATHMELL ... 153 C6
Rathmell CE Prim Sch BD24 ... 153 B7
Rattan Row YO25 ... 151 C6
Ratten Row
Hunton DL8 ... 61 E7
Seamer YO12 ... 99 C5
Raven Cl 10 YO12 ... 99 F6
Raven Gr YO26 ... 227 C4
Raven Hall Rd YO13 ... 53 F7
RAVENSCAR ... 54 A8
Ravens Cl Brow LA2 ... 102 C1
Ravenscroft Way BB18 ... 171 E2
Ravensdale Rd DL3 ... 3 B4
RAVENSEAT ... 15 C2
Ravensville 1 BD20 ... 187 F7
RAVENSWORTH ... 20 A7
Ravensworth Castle★ DL11 ... 20 A6
Ravensworth CE Prim Sch DL11 ... 20 A6
Ravine Hill 17 YO14 ... 101 B4
Ravine Rd YO14 ... 101 B4
Ravine Top 7 YO14 ... 101 B3
RAW ... 33 B4
Raw Bank DL11 ... 37 E8
RAWCLIFFE
Goole ... 205 A1
York ... 224 E2
Rawcliffe Ave YO30 ... 227 F8
Rawcliffe Cl 5 YO30 ... 224 E2
Rawcliffe Croft YO30 ... 224 D2
Rawcliffe Dr YO30 ... 227 F8
Rawcliffe Ind Est YO30 ... 224 E3
Rawcliffe La YO30 ... 224 F1
Rawcliffe Landing YO30 ... 224 C3
Rawcliffe Prim Sch DN14 ... 205 A1
Rawcliffe Village YO30 ... 224 E3
Rawcliffe Way YO30 ... 224 E2
Rawcliff Rd YO18 ... 72 A5
Rawdon Ave YO10 ... 228 F4
Rawfield La WF11 ... 201 D7
Raw Gap HG5 ... 221 A6
Raw La
Fylingdales YO22 ... 33 B4
Kirkby Wharfe with North Milford LS24 ... 190 A3
Towton LS24 ... 189 F3
Rawlinson Rd DL9 ... 209 D2
Raw Pasture Bank YO22 ... 33 B5
Raw Pasture La YO22 ... 33 C5
Rawson St HG1 ... 219 E5
Ray Bridge La BD23 ... 155 D1
RAYDALE ... 57 A1
Raydale Cl 2 HG5 ... 221 D5
RAYGILL ... 186 E8
Raygill La BD20 ... 186 E8
Ray La HG4 ... 114 B1
Rayleigh Rd HG2 ... 222 E8
Raylton Ave TS7 ... 7 B5
Rayner St HG4 ... 214 C5
Raynes Ct DL8 ... 56 D5
Read Cl YO8 ... 204 F5
Read Sch YO8 ... 204 F5
Reas La YO51 ... 141 D1
Reasty Hill YO13 ... 53 E1
Reasty Rd YO13 ... 53 D2
Recreation Rd
17 Pickering YO18 ... 95 F6
2 Selby YO8 ... 232 D6
Rectory Cl
Bolton Percy YO23 ... 190 D4
Heslerton YO17 ... 123 F6
Rectory Gdns YO23 ... 228 B1
Rectory La
Guisborough TS14 ... 8 E6
3 Hurworth-on-Tees DL2 ... 22 C8
Longnewton TS21 ... 5 A7
Skipton BD23 ... 217 A4
Thornton-le-Dale YO18 ... 96 E5
Red Bank Cl HG4 ... 214 A3
Red Bank Dr HG4 ... 214 A3
Red Bank La HG4 ... 214 A3
Red Bank Rd HG4 ... 214 A3
Redbarn Dr YO10 ... 229 D4
Red Barnes Way DL1 ... 3 E6
Red Brae Bank HG3 ... 137 A3
Red Brow YO13 ... 74 C5
Redcap La YO42 ... 193 C5
Redcar Rd
Guisborough TS14 ... 8 F7
Thornaby TS17 ... 6 B7
Redcliff Cl 12 YO11 ... 100 B7
Redcliffe Ct YO12 ... 212 D7
Redcliffe Gdns YO12 ... 212 C6
Redcliffe La YO11 ... 100 D6
Redcliffe Rd YO12 ... 212 D6
Redcoat Way 1 YO24 ... 230 B8
Redeness St YO31 ... 228 E5
Redfearn Mews HG2 ... 222 D6
Red Gate DL8 ... 57 C6
Redgrave Cl 4 YO31 ... 228 E8
Red Hall La TS15 ... 6 A1
Red Hall Prim Sch DL1 ... 3 F6
RED HILL ... 201 A4
Redhill Ave WF10 ... 201 A3
Redhill Bank DL6 ... 43 E4
Redhill Cl HG1 ... 219 D6
Redhill Dr WF10 ... 201 A3
Redhill Field La YO23 ... 182 D1
Redhill Infant Sch WF10 ... 201 B4
Redhill Junior Sch WF10 201 B4
Red Hill La LS25 ... 201 D8
Red Hill La LS25 ... 195 E1
Redhill Rd
Castleford WF10 ... 201 A4
Redhill Rd *continued*
Harrogate HG1 ... 219 C6
Red Hills La HG3 ... 140 B3
Red Hills Rd HG4 ... 214 B7
Redhill Wlk WF10 ... 201 A3
Redhouse La YO8 ... 204 F6
Red House La YO26 ... 165 B2
Red La
Green Hammerton YO26 ... 164 C3
4 Masham HG4 ... 86 C3
Red Lion St BB18 ... 172 B1
Redlish Rd HG3 ... 136 E1
Redman Cl YO10 ... 231 C8
Redmayne Sq YO32 ... 167 B8
REDMIRE ... 59 C6
Redmires Cl YO30 ... 225 A2
Redmire Sta DL8 ... 59 C6
Redpoll Dr WF10 ... 200 D6
Red Rose Cl 3 DL2 ... 3 A7
Redruth Dr 22 WF6 ... 200 A2
Red Scar Dr YO12 ... 212 A7
Red Scar La
Newby & Scalby YO12 ... 75 C4
Scalby YO12 ... 212 A8
Redshaw Cl 1 HG4 ... 214 C4
Redshaw Gr 2 HG4 ... 214 C4
Redthorn Dr YO31 ... 225 F1
Red Twr★ YO1 ... 228 E4
Red Way
Brompton DL6 ... 43 F6
Danby YO21 ... 29 E6
Farndale East YO62 ... 48 E4
Nether Silton DL6 ... 45 D1
Redwing Rising 1 TS14 ... 8 D6
Redwood Cl DL1 ... 3 F4
Redwood Dr 6 YO32 ... 166 E5
Reebys La LA2 ... 129 F5
Reedshaw La BD22 ... 186 F5
REETH ... 38 B6
Reeth Com Prim Sch DL11 38 B6
Reeth Rd
Middlesbrough TS5 ... 6 E8
Richmond DL10 ... 209 A7
2 Stockton-on-Tees TS18 ... 5 E8
Reeval Cl 13 BB18 ... 172 B1
Reeves The YO24 ... 227 C1
Regency Ave TS6 ... 7 E8
Regency Ct
3 Ilkley LS29 ... 218 A3
Northallerton DL6 ... 210 F3
Regency Mews
Northallerton DL7 ... 210 D4
2 York YO24 ... 230 F8
Regency Pk TS17 ... 6 B4
Regent Ave
Harrogate HG1 ... 219 E3
Skipton BD23 ... 217 B5
Regent Cres BD23 ... 217 B5
Regent Dr BD23 ... 217 B5
Regent Gr HG1 ... 219 E4
Regent Mount 2 HG1 ... 220 C4
Regent Par HG1 ... 219 E3
Regent Pl HG1 ... 220 C4
Regent Rd
Ilkley LS29 ... 218 A4
Skipton BD23 ... 217 B5
Regents Ct
Walkerville DL9 ... 41 A4
14 York YO26 ... 227 F5
Regents Mews 1 YO26 ... 227 D6
Regent St
Castleford WF10 ... 200 E4
Harrogate HG1 ... 219 F3
Normanton WF6 ... 200 B2
1 Scarborough YO12 ... 213 A6
York YO10 ... 228 E3
Regent Terr HG1 ... 219 E3
Regimental Mus★ YO1 ... 233 B1
Reginald Gr YO23 ... 228 C1
Reginald Terr YO8 ... 232 D4
Reid Pk YO32 ... 166 E5
Reid St Prim Sch DL3 ... 3 C6
Reid Terr TS14 ... 8 F6
REIGHTON ... 127 D6
Reighton Ave YO30 ... 227 F8
Reighton Ct YO14 ... 127 D5
Reighton Dr 10 YO30 ... 224 F1
Rein Ct LS25 ... 194 F8
Reins HG5 ... 163 A7
Reivaulx Dr TS5 ... 6 F8
Renfield Gr WF6 ... 200 B2
Renshaw Gdns 8 YO26 ... 227 E4
Renton Cl HG3 ... 140 B5
Reservoir La 7 YO11 ... 100 B8
Residence La HG4 ... 214 D5
Resolution Way YO21 ... 208 B5
Retreat Hospl The YO10 ... 228 F2
Reygate Gr YO23 ... 230 B2
Reynard Crag La HG3 ... 160 C6
Reynolds St 15 YO14 ... 101 B3
Rhobell View 3 TS17 ... 5 F4
Rhodes Dr HG2 ... 222 D6
Rhode's Hill La LS23 ... 188 F6
Rhodes La LS23 ... 188 D7
Rhodes St WF10 ... 200 D4
Rhyddings Gdns LS29 ... 218 D4
Rianbow La YO17 ... 215 C6
Ribble Bank BD24 ... 131 E4
Ribble Dr DL1 ... 3 C3
Ribblehead Sta LA6 ... 78 E1
Ribblehead Viaduct★ LA6 78 D2
Ribstone Gr YO31 ... 229 B6
Ribston Rd
Little Ribston LS22 ... 180 A7
Spofforth with Stockeld HG3 ... 179 F6
Riccal Dr
25 Helmsley YO62 ... 92 F6

Riccal Dr *continued*
Huttons Ambo YO17 ... 121 C1
RICCALL ... 198 A8
Riccall Bsns Pk YO19 ... 198 B7
Riccall Com Prim Sch YO19 ... 191 F1
Riccall La
Kelfield YO19 ... 191 D1
Riccall YO19 ... 192 A2
Riccal Moor La YO62 ... 93 E4
Rice Gate YO13 ... 74 D8
Rice La
Aldwark YO61 ... 142 C2
Flaxton YO60 ... 145 F2
Richard Gossop Ct 41 LS29 ... 176 C1
Richard III Mus* YO31 ... 233 C3
Richardson Ct YO8 ... 196 F1
Richardson Rd TS17 ... 6 A7
Richardson St YO23 ... 228 C2
Richard St YO8 ... 232 B5
Richard Taylor CE Prim Sch HG1 ... 219 E6
Richard Thornton's CE VA Prim Sch LA6 ... 102 E3
RICHMOND ... 209 C7
Richmond Ave
22 Barnoldswick BB18 ... 171 D2
Harrogate HG2 ... 222 C7
Knottingley WF11 ... 201 D3
Richmond Castle* DL10 ... 209 C6
Richmond CE Prim Sch DL10 ... 209 D7
Richmond Cl HG2 ... 222 C7
Richmond Ct LS29 ... 218 C3
Richmondfield Ave LS15 ... 194 C7
Richmondfield Cl LS15 ... 194 C7
Richmondfield Cres LS15 ... 194 C7
Richmondfield Cross LS15 ... 194 C7
Richmondfield Dr LS15 ... 194 B7
Richmondfield Garth LS15 ... 194 C8
Richmondfield Gr LS15 ... 194 C7
Richmondfield La LS15 ... 194 C7
Richmondfield Mount LS15 ... 194 C7
Richmondfield Way LS15 ... 194 C8
Richmond Garth HG4 ... 112 C5
Richmond Gate DL8 ... 58 C4
Richmond Holt HG2 ... 222 C7
Richmond Methodist Prim Sch DL10 ... 209 E7
Richmond Pl LS29 ... 218 C3
Richmond Rd
12 Barnoldswick BB18 ... 171 D2
Barton DL10 ... 21 E6
Brompton-on-Swale DL10 ... 41 A6
Croft-on-Tees DL10 ... 21 F6
Harrogate HG2 ... 222 C7
Hipswell DL9 ... 209 D1
Leyburn DL8 ... 60 D5
Skeeby DL10 ... 20 F1
Richmond Rise DL7 ... 210 C3
Richmond Sch DL10 ... 209 D7
Richmondshire Mus* DL10 ... 209 C7
Richmond St YO31 ... 228 E5
Richmond Swimming Pool DL10 ... 209 D6
Richmond Way DL1 ... 3 F4
Ridding Cres DN14 ... 205 A1
Ridding Gate 5 LS21 ... 176 F1
Ridding La DN14 ... 205 A1
Riddings La HG4 ... 112 C7
Riddings Rd LS29 ... 218 B3
Riders La YO60 ... 146 F2
Ridgedale Mount WF8 ... 201 B2
Ridge Gn YO13 ... 75 D5
Ridge La
Roxby TS13 ... 11 A6
Silsden BD20 ... 174 B4
Sleights YO21 ... 32 B7
Staithes TS13 ... 13 H1
Ridge Rd LS25 ... 200 E8
Ridge The
Coulby Newham TS8 ... 7 A4
Linton LS22 ... 180 B2
Ridgeway
Coulby Newham TS8 ... 7 D5
Darlington DL3 ... 3 C8
10 Eastfield YO11 ... 99 F7
Skipton BD23 ... 216 E6
York YO26 ... 227 B3
Ridgeway The WF11 ... 201 F2
Ridgewood Cl DL1 ... 3 F4
Riding Cl 4 BB18 ... 171 E1
Ridings The
7 Boroughbridge YO51 ... 141 B4
Norton YO17 ... 215 D2
Ridley Ave TS5 ... 6 E8
Ridleys Fold 14 LS29 ... 174 F4
Ridsdale St DL1 ... 3 D5
RIEVAULX ... 92 B8
Rievaulx Abbey* YO62 ... 92 B8
Rievaulx Ave HG5 ... 221 C4
Rievaulx Bank YO62 ... 92 B8
Rievaulx Cl HG5 ... 221 C4
Rievaulx Ct 6 HG5 ... 221 C4
Rievaulx Dr DL7 ... 64 A6
Rievaulx Rd YO21 ... 208 C6
Rievaulx Terr & Temples* YO62 ... 92 B7
Rievaulx Way TS14 ... 8 F6
Riffa Bsns Pk LS21 ... 176 F1
Riffa La LS21 ... 177 E2
Rigg Bank HG4 ... 85 E3
Riggs Rd YO17 ... 121 F5
Riggs Spring 5 HG3 ... 137 F1
Rigg The TS15 ... 5 E2
Rigg View YO22 ... 32 F7
Rigton Hill LS17 ... 178 B4
Rileys Croft 3 BD23 ... 153 F5
Riley St 41 BB18 ... 172 A1
RILLINGTON ... 122 F5
Rillington Com Prim Sch YO17 ... 122 F5
Rimington Ave DL10 ... 209 D6
Rimington Way YO11 ... 100 B7
Ringing Keld Hill YO13 ... 54 A3
Rings The TS17 ... 5 F5
Ringstone Rd
Bishopthorpe YO23 ... 231 B5
York YO30 ... 224 F3
Ringstones La LA2 ... 129 A4
Ringway LS25 ... 194 B3
Ringway Gr 11 DL2 ... 4 C4
Ringwood Rd DL9 ... 40 F3
Riparian Way BD20 ... 187 F8
RIPLEY ... 161 C7
Ripley Bank HG3 ... 137 C4
Ripley Castle* HG3 ... 161 C7
Ripley Cl
11 Kirkbymoorside YO62 ... 70 B1
Normanton South WF6 ... 200 B1
Ripley Dr
Harrogate HG1 ... 219 C6
Normanton South WF6 ... 200 B2
Ripley Endowed CE Prim Sch HG3 ... 161 C7
Ripley Gr 3 YO32 ... 166 E5
Ripley Rd
Knaresborough HG5 ... 220 E8
Nidd HG3 ... 161 E6
Scotton HG5 ... 162 A5
Ripley's Rd YO13 ... 54 B1
Ripley Way HG1 ... 219 C6
RIPON ... 214 E5
Ripon Bsns Pk HG4 ... 214 E4
Ripon By-pass HG4 ... 214 C2
Ripon Cathedral* HG4 ... 214 C5
Ripon Courthouse Mus* HG4 ... 214 C5
Ripon & District Comm Hospl HG4 ... 214 B5
Ripon Dr DL1 ... 3 D4
Ripon Gram Sch HG4 ... 214 A6
Ripon Horn The* HG4 ... 214 C5
Ripon L Ctr HG4 ... 214 D3
Ripon Loop Nature Reserve* HG4 ... 113 F4
Ripon Racecourse* HG4 ... 214 F2
Ripon Rd
Harrogate HG3 ... 219 A7
Middlesbrough TS7 ... 7 E6
Ripley HG3 ... 161 D8
South Stainley with Cayton HG3 ... 139 E2
Ripon Spa Baths HG4 ... 214 B5
Ripon Way
Carlton Miniott YO7 ... 89 C4
Harrogate HG1 ... 219 C5
Riseber DL8 ... 60 C5
Risedale Rd DL9 ... 209 B1
Risedale Sports & Com Coll DL9 ... 209 F1
Riserber La DL8 ... 60 C5
Rise The
Huttons Ambo YO60 ... 147 C6
Kippax LS25 ... 194 D1
Knottingley WF11 ... 201 E4
Leavening YO17 ... 147 E1
Thornton Dale YO18 ... 96 D5
Whitby YO22 ... 208 E6
Risewood YO41 ... 168 B2
Rishworth Gr YO30 ... 224 F2
RISPLITH ... 138 E7
Rivadale View LS29 ... 218 B5
Rivelin Way
10 Filey YO14 ... 101 A3
York YO30 ... 224 F2
Rivendell BD23 ... 134 B3
Riverbank Trad Est DL1 ... 3 D7
River Cl 2 YO8 ... 198 B5
Riverdale 4 DN14 ... 202 D4
Riverdale Gdns LS23 ... 188 F8
Rivergarth DL1 ... 3 F7
River La
Brompton-on-Swale DL10 ... 41 B6
Kilburn High & Low YO61 ... 91 B2
West Haddlesey YO8 ... 203 A5
River Mdws YO13 ... 75 D8
River Pl BD23 ... 155 D1
River Rd YO61 ... 91 C2
Riversdale
17 Haxby YO32 ... 166 F5
5 Settle BD24 ... 131 D2
Riversdene TS9 ... 26 B7
Riverside
Clapham LA2 ... 130 C8
Gargrave BD23 ... 155 D1
Rawcliffe DN14 ... 205 A2
28 Scalby YO12 ... 75 D5
Riverside Ave LS21 ... 177 A1
Riverside Bsns Pk LS29 ... 218 D5
Riverside Cl
1 Elvington YO41 ... 185 C2
Farnley LS21 ... 177 A1
West Haddlesey YO8 ... 203 A5
Riverside Cres
5 Otley LS21 ... 177 A1
York YO32 ... 225 F6
Riverside Ct
9 Cawood YO8 ... 197 B8
Kelfield YO8 ... 191 B1
Riverside Ct *continued*
Rawcliffe DN14 ... 205 A2
Riverside Dr 3 LS21 ... 177 A1
Riverside Gdns
2 Boroughbridge YO51 ... 141 B6
2 Elvington YO41 ... 185 C2
2 Poppleton YO26 ... 165 F1
Riverside Mews 6 YO7 ... 211 C3
Riverside Pk 4 LS21 ... 177 A1
Riverside Prim Sch LS24 ... 189 E6
Riverside Rd DL10 ... 209 C6
Riverside View
Norton YO17 ... 215 B3
16 Tadcaster LS24 ... 189 E6
Riverside Way DL1 ... 3 E7
Riverside Wlk
Airton BD23 ... 155 A6
Ilkley LS29 ... 218 A5
1 Poppleton YO26 ... 165 F1
Ruswarp YO22 ... 208 C4
5 Strensall YO32 ... 167 A7
Riverslea TS9 ... 26 B7
River St
1 Selby YO8 ... 232 D6
Trawden BB8 ... 186 B2
York YO23 ... 233 B1
Riversvale Dr 21 YO26 ... 165 F1
Riversway BD23 ... 155 C1
River View
1 Barlby YO8 ... 198 B5
Boston Spa LS23 ... 188 F8
Ilkley LS29 ... 218 E5
Richmond DL10 ... 209 D6
Riverview Ind Est DL1 ... 3 D6
River View Rd HG4 ... 214 C7
RNLI Whitby Mus* YO21 ... 208 D7
Roach Grange Ave LS25 ... 194 D2
Roald Ct DL10 ... 209 E8
Roall La DN14 ... 202 F4
Robb Cl YO7 ... 211 A2
Roberts Cres HG1 ... 219 D5
Robertson Rd
Colburn DL9 ... 40 F4
Ripon HG4 ... 113 D3
Roberts Sq HG1 ... 219 D5
Robert St
Harrogate HG1 ... 219 D1
Selby YO8 ... 232 C5
Robert Wilkinson Prim Sch YO32 ... 167 A7
Robin Cl 6 WF8 ... 201 B2
Robin Gr 6 YO24 ... 227 F3
Robin Hood Cl YO21 ... 29 A6
Robin Hood Rd YO13 ... 53 F8
ROBIN HOOD'S BAY ... 33 D4
Robin Hood's Bay Mus* YO22 ... 33 D4
Robin Hood's Bay Rd YO22 ... 33 A3
Robin La
Bentham LA2 ... 103 A1
High Bentham LA2 ... 129 A8
Huby YO61 ... 144 A4
Robinson Ct
27 Pickering YO18 ... 95 F6
York YO1 ... 233 C2
Robinson Dr
Harrogate HG2 ... 222 B6
York YO24 ... 227 B2
Robinson Fold 18 BB18 ... 171 D2
Robinson Rd 13 DL10 ... 41 E4
Robinson St WF10 ... 200 D6
Robson Ave TS17 ... 6 B5
Roche Ave
Harrogate HG1 ... 219 F6
York YO31 ... 228 E8
Rockbourne Way 1 TS17 ... 5 F6
Rockcliff Ct 15 LS24 ... 189 E6
Rock Hill WF10 ... 201 A3
Rockingham Ave YO31 ... 229 A5
Rockingham Cl YO17 ... 215 A3
Rockingham Ct LS24 ... 189 E2
Rockingham Dr YO12 ... 212 B7
Rock La BB8 ... 186 B2
Rockland Gdns YO12 ... 212 D5
Rockley Grange Gdn LS25 ... 194 B3
Rocks La YO13 ... 75 D7
Rocks Lane Cl YO13 ... 75 D7
Rock Terr WF10 ... 201 A3
Rock View Terr BD23 ... 217 D8
Rockville Dr BD23 ... 217 C8
Rockwell Ave DL1 ... 3 E7
Rockwood Cl 1 BD23 ... 216 E4
Rockwood Dr BD23 ... 216 E5
Rodney Terr 15 HG4 ... 86 C3
Roebuck La LS21 ... 176 F2
ROECLIFFE ... 140 F4
Roecliffe CE Prim Sch YO51 ... 140 F4
Roecliffe Ct YO26 ... 182 C8
Roecliffe La YO51 ... 141 B5
Roedean Dr TS16 ... 5 E4
Roe La LS25 ... 202 C7
Roger La TS8 ... 6 C4
Rogers Ct
Woodthorpe YO24 ... 230 C8
York YO24 ... 230 C8
Rogers Sq 16 HG1 ... 219 D2
Roker Cl DL1 ... 3 F6
Roker Rd HG1 ... 219 E4
Roland Ct YO32 ... 225 E3
Rolston Ave 3 YO31 ... 225 E2
Roman Avenue N 17 YO41 ... 168 D2
Roman Avenue S YO41 ... 168 D1
ROMANBY ... 210 B3
Romanby Prim Sch DL7 ... 210 B2
Romanby Rd DL7 ... 210 C3
Roman Cl
Newby & Scalby YO12 ... 212 A7
4 Tadcaster LS24 ... 189 E6
Roman Cres DL9 ... 209 C1
Roman Fort of Olicana* LS29 ... 218 B4
Roman Garth YO17 ... 215 D4
Roman Rd
Leeming DL7 ... 63 D4
Middlesbrough TS5 ... 6 E8
Tadcaster LS24 ... 189 C5
Romans Cl YO19 ... 197 F8
Roman Signal Sta* YO21 ... 12 D6
Roman Way YO12 ... 212 A7
Romany Rd 11 TS9 ... 8 A2
Rombalds Dr BD23 ... 217 A2
Rombalds La LS29 ... 218 E3
Rombalds View LS21 ... 176 E1
Rombald's View LS29 ... 218 D5
Romille St 15 BD23 ... 217 A3
Ronaldshay Cl DL10 ... 209 E8
Ronaldshay Dr DL10 ... 209 E8
Ronway Ave HG4 ... 214 B2
Rooke La YO26 ... 165 A5
Rookery Rd BB18 ... 171 E1
Rook St
25 Barnoldswick BB18 ... 171 D1
Lothersdale BD20 ... 186 F8
ROOKWITH ... 62 A1
Rookwood Ave LS25 ... 200 C8
Rookwood Rd TS7 ... 7 D6
Roomer La HG4 ... 86 B1
Roper Ct DL10 ... 209 C7
Ropers Ct YO23 ... 230 C3
Ropery La YO17 ... 124 E1
Ropery The
15 Pickering YO18 ... 95 F7
Whitby YO22 ... 208 E6
Ropery Wlk YO17 ... 215 C4
Ropewalk The YO31 ... 228 E5
Rope Wlk
Knottingley WF11 ... 202 A2
Skipton BD23 ... 217 A4
Ropner Gdns DL2 ... 4 C3
Rosamund Ave 21 YO18 ... 95 F7
Roscoe St YO12 ... 212 F5
Rose Ave
Sherburn in Elmet LS25 ... 195 F3
Whitby YO21 ... 208 B7
Roseberry Ave
Great Ayton TS9 ... 8 A2
Stokesley TS9 ... 26 D8
Roseberry Cres TS9 ... 8 A2
Roseberry Ct TS9 ... 26 D6
Roseberry Dr 8 TS9 ... 8 A2
Roseberry Gn HG4 ... 113 C7
Roseberry Gr YO30 ... 224 F3
Roseberry La
Guisborough TS9 ... 8 B3
Stillington YO61 ... 144 B6
Roseberry Mount TS14 ... 8 E6
Roseberry Prim Sch TS9 ... 8 A2
Roseberry Rd TS9 ... 8 A2
Roseberry Topping* TS9 ... 8 C3
Rosebery Ave YO12 ... 212 E3
Rosebery St YO26 ... 227 F6
Rosebery Wood 30 YO41 ... 168 D2
Rosebud Way DL9 ... 41 A4
Rosecomb Way 6 YO32 ... 225 D7
Rose Cres
Richmond DL10 ... 209 B7
Sherburn in Elmet LS25 ... 195 F3
Rosecroft Ave TS13 ... 10 D8
Rosecroft La TS13 ... 10 D8
Rosecroft Way YO30 ... 227 E8
Rose & Crown Yd 20 YO21 ... 208 D6
Rose Ct LS25 ... 194 D4
Rosedale HG3 ... 222 D3
ROSEDALE ABBEY ... 49 E3
Rosedale Abbey Com Prim Sch YO18 ... 49 E2
Rosedale Ave YO26 ... 227 C4
Rosedale Chy Bank YO18 ... 49 E1
Rosedale Cl
Pannal HG3 ... 222 D3
3 Whitby YO21 ... 208 C6
Rosedale Cres
Darlington DL3 ... 3 A6
Guisborough TS14 ... 8 D6
Rosedale La
Hinderwell TS13 ... 11 F8
Staithes TS13 ... 13 L1
Rosedale Rd TS7 ... 7 D6
Rosedale Rise LS23 ... 188 E8
Rosedale St YO10 ... 228 D2
Rosegarth Ct TS9 ... 26 E5
Rosehill TS9 ... 8 A1
Rose Hill Dr 13 TS9 ... 26 C7
Rosehill Sq 11 HG5 ... 221 B5
Rose Hill Way TS9 ... 26 C7
Rosehurst Gr HG3 ... 222 E2
Rose La LS24 ... 196 A7
Roseland Dr TS7 ... 7 C7
Rose Lea Cl 2 LS25 ... 202 A7
Rosemary Ct
20 Easingwold YO61 ... 143 C8
6 Tadcaster LS24 ... 189 E6
York YO1 ... 233 C2
Rosemary La 1 DL10 ... 209 C6
Rosemary Pl YO1 ... 233 C2
Rosemary Row 5 LS24 ... 189 E6
Rosemoor Cl
Coulby Newham TS8 ... 7 B5
19 Hunmanby YO14 ... 126 F8
Rosemount Ct 4 BD20 ... 187 E6
Rosemount Dr WF6 ... 200 C1
Rosemount Rd 2 YO21 ... 208 C5
Rosendale Ave YO17 ... 215 F2
Rose St YO31 ... 228 C7
Rose Tree Gr YO32 ... 225 D4
Rosetta Way YO26 ... 227 D6
Rosevale Terr YO12 ... 212 E5
Roseville Ave
Harrogate HG1 ... 220 A3
Scarborough YO12 ... 212 E6
Roseville Dr HG1 ... 220 A3
Roseville Rd HG1 ... 220 A3
Roseway HG1 ... 219 E5
Rosewood Ave LS25 ... 194 C2
Rosewood Cres HG1 ... 220 B3
Rosewood Prim Sch TS8 ... 7 A4
Roseworth TS9 ... 26 E5
Rosie Rd WF6 ... 200 C1
Rosley St BB8 ... 186 B3
Roslyn Rd HG2 ... 220 A2
Rossett Acre Prim Sch HG2 ... 222 C7
Rossett Ave HG2 ... 222 C6
Rossett Beck HG2 ... 222 C6
Rossett Beck Cl HG2 ... 222 D6
Rossett Cres HG2 ... 222 D6
Rossett Dr HG2 ... 222 C6
Rossett Garth HG2 ... 222 C6
Rossett Gdns HG2 ... 222 C6
ROSSETT GREEN ... 222 D5
Rossett Green La HG2 ... 222 C5
Rossett Holt Ave HG2 ... 222 C7
Rossett Holt Cl HG2 ... 222 C8
Rossett Holt Dr HG2 ... 222 C7
Rossett Holt Gr HG2 ... 222 C7
Rossett Holt View HG2 ... 222 C7
Rossett Park Rd HG2 ... 222 D6
Rossett Sch HG2 ... 222 B6
Rossett Sports Ctr HG2 ... 222 C6
Rossett Way HG2 ... 222 C7
Rossiter Dr WF11 ... 201 E2
Rosslyn Ct TS18 ... 5 F8
Rosslyn St 1 YO30 ... 228 A6
Rossway DL1 ... 3 F8
Rostle Top Rd 10 BB18 ... 172 A1
Rotary Way
Faverdale DL3 ... 3 B8
Ripon HG4 ... 214 D6
Rothbury Cl HG2 ... 220 D2
Rothbury St YO12 ... 212 E5
Rothesay Gr TS7 ... 7 D6
Roth Hill La YO19 ... 192 E3
Rotunda Mus* YO11 ... 213 A5
Roughaw Cl BD23 ... 216 F2
Roughaw Rd BD23 ... 217 A2
Roughley Bank DL7 ... 63 C5
Rough Rd HG3 ... 161 A2
Rougier St YO1 ... 233 A2
Roundell Dr BD23 ... 171 F5
Roundell Rd BB18 ... 171 E2
Roundhill Ave TS17 ... 5 F4
Roundhill Cl 5 DL2 ... 3 E1
Round Hill Link YO30 ... 224 F2
Roundhill Rd DL2 ... 3 E1
ROUNDHILL VILLAGE ... 5 F5
Roundhouse Rd DL3 ... 3 B8
Routh Wlk 5 YO21 ... 208 D7
Rowan Ave
3 Filey YO14 ... 101 A4
Malton YO17 ... 215 D6
York YO32 ... 225 D4
Rowan Brook DL10 ... 41 E8
Rowan Cl
Gateforth YO8 ... 197 B1
Harrogate HG1 ... 220 C5
4 Hut Green DN14 ... 203 A2
Scarborough YO12 ... 212 C6
Rowan Ct
7 Catterick DL10 ... 41 D5
Leyburn DL8 ... 60 D5
Selby YO8 ... 232 D2
Rowan Dr 5 TS9 ... 8 A2
Rowan Fields YO12 ... 99 E7
Rowan Garth 22 BD20 ... 187 E7
Rowan La
16 Hellifield BD23 ... 154 B3
Skirethorns BD23 ... 134 B3
Rowan Lea HG2 ... 222 B7
Rowan Pl YO32 ... 225 D4
Rowans The
Dalton YO7 ... 115 F7
Hellifield BD23 ... 154 A3
Rowans Way DL7 ... 210 B4
Rowany Gdns LS29 ... 218 D3
ROWDEN ... 160 F4
Rowden La HG3 ... 160 F5
Rowedale Cl 15 YO14 ... 126 F8
Rowen Ave 6 YO61 ... 117 D1
Rowlandhall La DN14 ... 199 E1
Rowland Keld TS14 ... 8 E5
Rowland St 18 BD23 ... 217 A3
Rowley Ct 2 YO32 ... 225 F7
Rowley Dr LS29 ... 218 F3
Rowmans The YO30 ... 224 C4
Rowntree Ave YO30 ... 228 C8
Roxburghe Dale WF7 ... 200 C1
ROXBY ... 11 C7
Roxby Ave TS14 ... 8 E5
Roxby Gdns
4 Eastfield YO12 ... 99 F7
5 Thornton Dale YO18 ... 96 D5
Roxby La
Roxby TS13 ... 11 C7
Staithes TS13 ... 13 J1
Roxby Rd YO18 ... 96 D5
Roxby Terr 6 YO18 ... 96 D5

Royal Albert Dr YO12 212 F8
Royal Ave YO11 212 F4
Royal Chase YO24 230 F8
Royal Cres
Harrogate HG2 222 D8
12 Scarborough YO11 213 A4
Whitby YO21 208 C7
Royal Cres La 8 YO11 212 F4
Royal George Dr TS16 5 D5
Royal Hall★ HG1 219 D3
Royal Par
Filey YO14 101 B3
8 Harrogate HG1 219 C2
Royal Pump Room Mus★ HG2 219 C2
Royd Cl 18 BD20 187 E7
Royd Ct 12 BD22 187 B6
Royds Ave WF10 201 B4
Royd's Rd YO8 202 F6
Royd St BD22 187 B6
Royd The TS15 5 D2
Ruby St 3 YO23 228 B1
Rudbeck Cl HG2 220 C1
Rudbeck Cres HG2 220 C1
Rudbeck Dr HG2 220 C1
RUDBY 25 D5
Rudby Bank TS15 25 D5
Rudby Lea TS15 25 D6
Rudcarr La YO19 167 E1
Rudda Rd YO13 53 F6
Rudding Dower HG3 223 E7
Rudding La
Follifoot HG3 223 C5
North Rigton HG3 222 A1
Ruddings YO19 193 A8
Ruddings Cl 9 YO32 225 C8
Ruddings La
Cowesby YO7 66 C4
Crakehall DL8 62 D4
Ellerton YO42 193 E2
Ruddings Rd YO18 72 B3
Ruddings The
Selby YO8 232 A4
Wheldrake YO19 193 A8
Rudgate
Bilton-in-Ainsty with Bickerton YO26 181 B6
Newton Kyme cum Toulston LS24 189 B6
Walton LS23 181 B1
Rudgate Bsns Pk YO26 180 B7
Rudgate Ct LS23 181 B1
Rudgate Gr YO26 164 A4
Rudgate Pk LS23 181 A2
Rudstone Gr LS25 195 F4
Ruebury La DL6 45 B4
Rues La LS21 176 C8
Ruffa La YO18 96 A6
Ruffhams Cl YO19 192 F8
Ruffin La YO17 147 D5
Ruff La YO61 142 B5
Rufford Cl TS14 8 F5
RUFFORTH 182 C6
Rufforth Prim Sch YO23 182 C6
Rumford Way DL8 60 D6
Rumple Croft 4 LS21 176 F1
Runnymede TS7 7 D5
Runs Bank DL8 60 D8
Runswick Ave
Middlesbrough TS5 6 E6
Whitby YO21 208 B6
York YO26 227 B4
RUNSWICK BAY 12 A7
Runswick La TS13 11 F7
Rupert Rd LS29 218 A5
Rushmere TS8 7 B5
Rusholme La YO8 205 A5
RUSHTON 98 D6
Rushton Ave 21 BB18 172 A1
Rushwood Cl 6 YO32 166 F5
Ruskin Ave
Middlesbrough TS5 6 D7
6 Skipton BD23 216 D3
Ruskin Cl DL2 22 D7
Ruskin Dr WF10 201 A4
Russell Dixon Sq HG4 214 B3
Russell Dr YO30 227 E8
Russell Rd DN14 205 F2
Russell St
Harrogate HG2 222 E7
Skipton BD23 217 A3
York YO23 228 B2
Russell Terr DL7 63 D2
Russet Dr YO31 229 B5
Russet Gr YO12 212 C8
Russett Rd YO17 215 B4
Ruston La YO13 98 D7
RUSWARP 208 B3
Ruswarp Bank YO21 208 B3
Ruswarp CE Prim Sch YO21 208 B3
Ruswarp Fields YO22 208 C3
Ruswarp La YO21 208 B4
Ruswarp Pleasure Boats★ YO21 208 B3
Ruswarp Sta YO22 208 C3
Rutland Cl
Copmanthorpe YO23 230 A3
Harrogate HG1 219 A2
Waithwith Banks DL9 40 C4
Rutland Dr HG1 219 A2
Rutland Pl 4 YO62 92 F7
Rutland Rd HG1 219 B2
Rutland St 38 YO14 101 B3
Rutland Terr YO12 213 A7
Rutmoor Rd YO18 71 E8
Ryburn Cl YO30 224 F2
Rycroft Rd 3 YO12 75 E5
Rydal Ave
Middlesbrough TS5 6 E8
York YO31 229 A6
Rydal Cl 2 YO7 89 C4
Rydal Cres 7 YO12 99 F7
Rydal Rd
Darlington DL1 3 E4
Harrogate HG1 220 B3
Ryder Cres 3 YO62 70 B1
Ryder Sq YO17 215 C4
Ryder's Wynd 3 DL10 209 C6
Rye Cl
Haxby YO32 225 C8
Huttons Ambo YO17 121 C1
Ryecroft 7 YO32 167 A6
Ryecroft Ave
10 Norton DN6 206 E2
York YO24 230 C7
Ryecroft Cl YO31 229 C8
Ryecroft Gdns DN14 203 A2
Ryecroft Rd
Glusburn BD20 187 D8
Norton DN6 206 E1
Ryecroft Way 2 BD20 187 E8
Ryedale Ave 2 WF11 201 F1
Ryedale Cl
Helmsley YO62 92 F7
Norton YO17 215 F1
Pontefract WF6 200 A3
Ulleskelf LS24 190 B2
Ryedale Folk Mus★ YO62 70 C5
Ryedale Pk LS29 218 D3
Ryedale Pl WF6 200 A3
Ryedale Pool YO18 95 F6
Ryedale Sch YO62 93 D7
Ryedale State Pk YO17 215 C3
Ryedale View 2 YO62 70 B1
Ryedale Way YO8 232 C3
Ryefield Cl 12 YO11 99 F7
Ryefield Rd 1 YO11 100 A6
Ryegate 13 YO62 92 F6
Ryegrass Gdns 15 WF10 200 D3
Ryehill Cl YO32 225 D5
Rye Hill Way TS8 7 B4
Ryelands Pk 1 TS13 11 A8
Ryeland St 9 BD20 187 E8
Ryemoor Rd YO32 225 C8
Rylatt Pl YO26 227 B3
RYLSTONE 156 B5
Rylstone Dr 1 BB18 171 D1
Rymers Ct DL1 3 E7
Rymer Way 4 YO7 211 C3
Ryndle Cres YO12 212 E8
Ryndleside YO12 212 E7
Ryndle Wlk YO12 212 E8
Ryngwoode Dr YO17 215 C6
RYTHER 190 F1
Rythergate 8 YO8 197 B8
RYTON 121 F6
Ryton Old La YO17 121 F5
Ryton Stile Rd YO17 215 C7

S

Sackville Rd BD20 174 C1
Sackville St
20 Barnoldswick BB18 171 D1
Skipton BD23 217 A3
Sacred Heart Prim Sch The LS29 218 D4
Sacred Heart RC Prim Sch DL7 210 D2
SADBERGE 4 B8
Sadberge Ct YO10 229 C3
Sadberge Rd DL2 4 C5
Saddle Cl YO17 215 D2
Saddlers Cl
1 Copmanthorpe YO23 230 B3
Huntington YO32 225 F2
Saddlers Croft 8 LS29 218 A4
Saddlers La WF11 201 E5
Saddler's La WF11 201 E5
Saddlers Way YO26 182 A6
Saddlers Wlk YO19 192 A5
Sadler Dr TS7 7 B6
Sadler Forster Way TS17 6 B5
Sadlers Ct
Alne YO61 143 A5
26 Boroughbridge YO51 141 B5
Saffron Dr 6 DN14 204 C1
Saffron Mdw 19 HG3 161 B3
Sails Dr YO10 229 B3
St Aelreds Cl YO31 228 F4
St Aelred's RC Prim Sch YO31 229 B5
St Agathas DL10 209 C7
St Aidans CE High Sch HG2 219 F1
St Aidans Rd LS26 200 C8
St Aidan's Rd DL9 209 D1
St Alkelda's Rd 1 DL8 60 E2
St Andrewgate YO1 233 B2
St Andrew Pl YO1 233 C2
St Andrew's Ave HG2 220 A3
St Andrew's Cres HG2 220 A3
St Andrews Ct
Rillington YO17 122 F5
Sadberge DL2 4 C8
St Andrews Dr WF7 200 E1
St Andrews Gate HG4 112 D5
St Andrews Gr 2 DL7 210 D2
St Andrew's Gr 1 HG2 220 B2
St Andrews Mdws HG4 112 D5
St Andrew's Par 3 HG2 220 A2
St Andrew's Pl 2 HG2 220 A2
St Andrews Rd YO21 208 B5
St Andrew's Rd
Castleford WF10 201 B5
4 Harrogate HG2 220 B3
St Andrew's St 1 HG2 220 A2
St Andrew's Wlk HG2 220 A2
St Ann Ct YO10 228 E2
St Anne's Cres 3 DL10 41 E4
St Annes Gdns DL2 4 C3
St Ann's Ct YO10 228 D2
St Ann's Staith 13 YO21 208 D7
St Anthonys Ave 2 DL7 210 E2
St Athan's Wlk HG2 222 C7
St Aubyn's Pl YO24 228 A2
St Augustines RC Prim Sch TS8 7 B5
St Augustine's RC Prim Sch DL3 3 C5
St Augustine's RC Sch YO12 212 C4
St Barnabas CE VC Prim Sch YO26 227 F5
St Barnabas Ct 13 YO26 227 F5
St Bedes Ave 4 DL7 210 D2
St Bede's RC Prim Sch DL1 3 D8
St Benedict Rd YO23 233 A1
St Benedict's Catholic Prim Sch LS25 194 C4
St Benedict's RC Prim Sch YO62 92 C1
St Bernadettes RC Prim Sch TS7 7 D6
St Boltophs Cl 4 WF11 202 A2
St Brides Ct 30 TS17 5 F4
St Bridget's Ct YO23 233 B1
St Catherines Cl YO30 224 C5
St Catherines Pl YO24 228 A3
St Catherine's Rd HG2 219 F1
St Chads Wharf YO23 231 C8
St Christopher Cl 3 DL7 210 D2
St Christophers Dr 27 LS29 174 F4
St Clares Abbey DL3 3 B5
St Clares RC Prim Sch TS5 6 D6
St Clement's Gr YO23 228 C2
St Clement's Rd HG2 220 A2
St Clements Road S HG2 220 A2
St Cuthbert Ave TS7 7 C5
St Cuthbert Dr DL7 210 B3
St Cuthbert's Ave 4 DL9 41 A5
St Cuthberts CE Prim Sch HG3 137 B4
St Cuthberts Cl
15 Pateley Bridge HG3 137 B4
2 Ripon HG4 214 D5
St Cuthbert's Gn DL10 21 D8
St Cuthberts Wlk TS13 10 D8
St Davids Gr 34 TS17 5 F4
St Davids Rd LS21 176 F1
St David's View 9 DN14 205 E4
St Denys' Rd YO1 233 C2
St Edmunds YO41 168 D2
St Edmunds Cl 1 DL10 41 C6
St Edward's Catholic Prim Sch 3 LS23 188 E8
St Edwards Cl 2 WF11 201 F4
St Edward's Cl YO24 230 F8
St Edward's Wood LS23 188 F8
St Edwin's Cl DL2 2 C6
St Francis of Assisi CE Prim Sch TS17 6 A5
St Francis Xavier Sch DL10 209 E8
St Gabriel's Catholic VA Prim Sch TS7 7 D8
St George's Ave HG2 222 D7
St George's CE Acad DL2 4 C4
St George's Gate DL2 4 B5
St Georges Gr 8 DL7 210 E2
St George's Pl YO24 227 F2
St George's RC Prim Sch
Eastfield YO11 100 A7
York YO10 228 D2
St George's Rd HG2 222 D7
St Georges Terr TS13 10 D8
St George's Wlk HG2 222 D6
St Gerards RC Prim Sch TS8 6 F5
St Giles CE VA Prim Sch WF8 201 B1
St Giles Cl YO7 211 C3
St Giles' Cl 1 DL9 41 A5
St Giles Ct YO31 233 B3
St Giles Rd YO30 224 B5
St Giles Way YO23 230 A2
St Gregory's Cl DL8 62 E4
St Gregory's Mews YO1 233 A2
St Hedda's RC Prim Sch YO21 31 A4
St Helena 11 YO51 141 B5
St Helens Cl DL7 64 A7
St Helens Dr DL7 64 A7
St Helen's Dr LS25 194 F4
St Helen's La
Borrowby YO7 65 E4
Reighton YO14 127 C6
St Helen's Rd
Harrogate HG2 223 A8
5 York YO24 230 E8
St Helen's Rehabilitation Hospl YO24 227 F1
St Helen's Rise YO19 193 A7
St Helen's Sq
26 Scarborough YO11 213 A6
York YO1 233 B2
St Helen's Way LS29 218 D4
St Helens Wlk TS13 10 D8
St Hilary Cl DL10 209 B7
St Hilda's Ampleforth CE VC Prim Sch YO62 92 C1
St Hildas Bsns Ctr YO22 208 E6
St Hilda's Cres YO17 124 E8
St Hilda's Gdns 4 YO21 208 C7
St Hildas Mews YO10 229 B4
St Hilda's RC Prim Sch 11 YO21 208 D5
St Hildas Rd 5 DL7 210 D2
St Hilda's Rd HG2 219 F1
St Hilda's St YO17 124 D7
St Hilda's Terr YO21 208 D6
St Hilda's Wlk 6 YO62 92 C1
St Ians Croft 32 LS29 174 F4
St Ives Cl 3 WF8 201 B2
St Ives Cres WF10 201 B3
St James' Bsns Pk HG5 221 E4
St James Chapel Flats DL10 209 B6
St James Cl
Melsonby DL10 20 F7
York YO30 224 E3
St James Croft YO24 227 D1
St James Ct
Rawcliffe DN14 205 A1
Skipton BD23 217 B4
St James Dr DL7 210 D2
St James' Dr HG2 222 E8
St James Gn 9 YO7 211 C3
St James' Mdw 16 YO51 141 B5
St James Mount YO23 228 A2
St James Pl 5 YO24 227 D1
St James Rd
Northallerton DL7 210 B2
Scarborough YO12 212 E4
St James' Rd LS29 218 A3
St James's St 7 LS22 180 C3
St James Terr YO8 232 C5
St John Fisher Cath High Sch HG2 223 A8
St John Mews YO8 232 B7
ST JOHN'S 194 F8
St Johns Ave 25 LS29 174 F4
St John's Ave
42 Filey YO14 101 B3
Milby YO51 141 B7
Scarborough YO12 212 E5
St John's CE Acad DL1 3 E4
St John's CE Prim Sch HG5 221 B6
St Johns Cl
Northallerton DL7 210 E2
Sharow HG4 214 F7
St John's Cl
Aberford LS25 188 F1
Bishop Monkton HG3 140 B5
St John's Cres
Bishop Monkton HG3 140 A5
Harrogate HG1 219 D5
3 Leeming DL7 63 D4
York YO31 233 C4
St Johns Ct
Skipton BD23 217 A4
Ulleskelf LS24 190 C3
St John's Dr
Harrogate HG1 219 D6
North Rigton LS17 178 B4
St John's Garth
Aberford LS25 194 F8
Ingleby Arncliffe DL6 45 A8
St John's Gr HG1 219 C5
St Johns Mdws YO61 117 C1
St Johns Pk DL11 2 A1
St Johns RC Sch for the Deaf 7 LS23 188 E8
St Johns Rd DL9 209 F1
St John's Rd
Bishop Monkton HG3 140 A5
Clifford LS23 188 E7
Harrogate HG1 219 D5
Ilkley LS29 218 E4
2 Leeming DL7 63 D4
Scarborough YO12 212 E5
Scotton HG5 162 A6
9 Stamford Bridge YO41 168 D2
St John's St BD20 173 C1
St John St
Harrogate HG1 219 D2
York YO31 233 B3
St John's View LS23 188 E8
St John's Way
Bishop Monkton HG3 140 A5
Harrogate HG1 219 D6
St John's Wlk
Harrogate HG1 219 D6
Milby YO51 141 B7
St John the Baptist RC Prim Sch WF6 200 B1
St Joseph's Catholic Prim Sch
Barnoldswick BB18 171 D2
Bishop Thornton HG3 139 A2
Castleford WF10 200 F4
Harrogate HG1 219 C5
16 Tadcaster LS24 189 E6
St Joseph's Cl 2 YO12 212 C8
St Josephs Ct 9 YO24 227 B1
St Joseph's Ct LS25 194 C3
St Josephs RC Prim Sch
27 Pickering YO18 95 F7
Wetherby LS22 180 C3
St Joseph's RC Prim Sch TS13 10 D8
St Joseph's St LS24 189 E6
St Lawrence's CE Prim Sch YO10 228 E3
St Leonards Ave YO8 198 B4
St Leonards Cl 30 LS29 174 F4
St Leonard's Cl
1 Harrogate HG2 220 B1
7 Malton YO17 215 C4
St Leonard's Cres YO12 212 D8
St Leonard's Oval HG2 220 A1
St Leonard's Pl YO30 233 B3
St Leonards Rd TS14 8 E6
St Leonard's Rd HG2 220 A1
St Luke's Ave HG1 219 D4
St Lukes Cl DL7 22 C2
St Luke's Cl
6 Boston Spa LS23 188 E7
Harrogate HG1 219 D4
St Luke's Cres YO12 212 C6
St Luke's Gr YO30 228 B7
St Lukes Hospl TS4 7 A8
St Luke's Mount HG1 219 D4
St Margaret's Ave LS26 200 B6
St Margarets Cl DL2 4 C3
St Margaret's Cl 3 HG5 221 A6
St Margaret's Garth 2 HG5 221 A6
St Margaret's Gdns 1 HG5 221 A6
St Margaret's Rd
Knaresborough HG5 221 A6
Mickletown LS26 200 B6
St Margaret's Terr
6 Ilkley LS29 218 B3
York YO1 228 E4
St Mark's Ave HG2 222 D7
St Mark's Cl 1 YO12 212 C8
St Mark's Gr YO30 224 E2
St Martin's Ampleforth Sch YO62 118 F7
St Martins Ave 2 LS21 176 F1
St Martin's Ave YO11 213 A4
St Martin's CE VA Prim Sch YO11 213 C1
St Martins Cl
15 Catterick Garrison DL9 40 E4
Liverton Mines TS13 10 D8
St Martins Field 12 LS21 176 F1
St Martin's Gr 21 WF10 200 D3
St Martin's La YO1 233 A2
St Martin's Pl 10 YO11 213 A4
St Martin's Rd 9 YO11 213 A4
St Martin's Sq 5 YO11 213 A4
St Martins Way 11 TS15 24 E8
St Mary's YO30 233 A3
St Mary's Abbey★ YO1 233 A3
St Mary's App YO8 196 F1
St Mary's Ave
Barnoldswick BB18 171 E2
Harrogate HG2 219 C2
12 Hemingbrough YO8 198 F1
14 Swillington LS26 194 A1
Thirsk YO7 211 C4
St Marys Cath TS8 7 B5
St Mary's Catholic Prim Sch HG5 221 A7
St Mary's CE Aided Prim Sch TS21 5 A7
St Mary's CE Prim Sch YO23 182 D3
St Marys CE Sch 6 LS23 188 E8
St Mary's Chapel★ YO11 213 C7
St Marys Cl
Cottingwith YO42 193 C5
14 Stokesley TS9 26 C7
St Mary's Cl
Barton DL10 21 D7
15 Haxby YO32 166 E5
Ilkley LS29 218 C4
South Cowton DL7 22 E2
Strensall YO32 167 A7
Thirsk YO7 211 C4
St Mary's Cres YO22 208 E6
St Marys Ct
Bagby YO7 90 C3
7 Hambleton YO8 196 F1
North Stainley with Sleningford HG4 113 C8
St Mary's Ct
Allerton Bywater LS26 200 D6
York YO23 233 A1
St Mary's Dr YO7 211 C4
St Mary's Gate HG4 214 D5
St Mary's Gdns BD23 173 B4
St Mary's Gr YO10 229 C4
St Mary's La YO30 233 A3
St Mary's Mus★ YO1 233 B2
St Mary's RC Prim Sch
Malton YO17 215 D5
Richmond DL10 209 E7
Selby YO8 232 B2
St Mary's St 6 YO11 213 B6
St Marys Terr YO30 233 A3
St Mary's Terr YO30 233 A3
St Marys View YO8 232 B2
St Mary's Way YO7 211 C4
St Marys Wk 6 YO8 196 F1
St Mary's Wlk
Harrogate HG2 219 C1
Micklefield LS25 194 F4
Middlesbrough TS5 6 E8
Scarborough YO11 213 A7
Thirsk YO7 211 C4
St Matthew's Cl
19 Leyburn DL8 60 D5
4 Naburn YO19 191 D8
St Maurice's Rd YO31 233 C3
St Michaels Ct
1 Northallerton DL7 210 D2
10 West Field YO24 227 B1
St Michaels Gn 15 WF6 200 A1
St Michael's La YO11 213 C1

St Michael's Mead HG4 138 E6
St Michael St 6 YO17 215 C4
St Michaels Way 29 LS29 174 F4
St Mongahs Ct HG3 140 C2
St Mongahs La HG3 140 C2
St Monicas Ct 4 YO61 143 D8
St Monicas Garth 17
YO61 143 D8
St Monica's Hospl YO61 143 C8
St Nicholas Ave YO19 231 E4
St Nicholas CE Prim Sch
HG4 87 A1
St Nicholas Cl
Copmanthorpe YO23 230 A3
Richmond DL10 209 F8
St Nicholas Cliff 5 YO11 213 A5
St Nicholas Cres YO23 230 A3
St Nicholas Croft YO23 182 E3
St Nicholas Dr DL10 209 F7
St Nicholas Fields*
YO10 228 F4
St Nicholas Gdns TS15 5 F2
St Nicholas Pl 1 YO10 228 F3
St Nicholas Rd
Copmanthorpe YO23 230 A3
Harrogate HG2 220 B2
Ilkley LS29 218 A5
St Nicholas St
Norton YO17 215 D3
Scarborough YO11 213 A6
St Nicholas Way 22 YO32 166 E5
St Nicholas Wlk HG2 220 B2
St Olave's Cl HG4 214 A3
St Olave's Rd YO30 233 A4
St Oswald's CE VC Prim Sch
YO10 231 E7
St Oswalds Cl
14 Catterick Garrison DL9 40 E4
Sowerby YO7 89 F3
St Oswald's Cl
Catton YO41 185 F6
Oswaldkirk YO62 93 A1
St Oswalds Ct
6 Filey YO14 101 B3
York YO10 231 E7
St Oswalds Rd 13 DL9 40 E4
St Oswald's Rd YO10 231 D8
St Patrick's Catholic Coll
TS17 6 C7
St Patrick's RC Prim Sch
TS17 6 B8
St Patrick's Way HG2 220 B2
St Paulinus Dr DL7 210 B3
St Paulinus RC Prim Sch
TS14 8 D6
St Paul's CE Prim Sch
YO24 228 A3
St Pauls Cl 4 DL7 210 E2
St Paul's Cl DL10 41 B6
St Pauls Ct 3 WF8 201 C2
St Paul's Dr DL10 41 B6
St Paul's Gr LS29 218 D4
St Pauls Mews YO24 228 A3
St Paul's Nursery Sch
YO24 228 A3
St Paul's Rd TS17 6 B8
St Pauls Rise LS29 174 F4
St Paul's Sq YO24 228 A3
St Paul's Terr
Darlington DL3 3 C7
York YO30 228 A4
St Peter's Brafferton CE VA
Prim Sch YO61 115 F1
St Peters CE Prim Sch
HG2 219 D1
St Peters Cl
12 Brafferton YO61 115 F1
Rufforth YO26 227 A5
St Peter's Cl 2 DL9 41 A5
St Peter's Cres YO17 215 D3
St Peters Ct
31 Addingham LS29 174 F4
York YO30 233 A4
St Peter's Ct YO22 208 F4
St Peter's Garth LS14 188 A3
St Peter's Gr YO30 233 A4
St Peter's RC Prim Sch
YO12 212 D8
St Peter's Rd
Drax YO8 204 F5
Whitby YO22 208 F4
St Peter's Sch YO30 233 A4
St Peter's Sq 7 HG2 219 C2
St Peter St YO17 215 D3
St Philip's Gr YO30 228 A8
St Philip's Way 33 LS29 176 C1
St Princes St 12 HG1 219 D2
St Richards Rd 3 LS21 176 F1
St Robert Cl BD23 155 D1
St Robert Ct BD23 155 D1
St Robert's Cave* HG5 221 D4
St Robert's Gdns HG5 221 B4
St Roberts Mews 4 HG1 219 D1
St Robert's Rd HG5 221 B4
St Ronan's Cl 3 HG2 220 A1
St Ronan's Rd 2 HG2 220 A1
St Sampsons Sq YO1 233 B2
St Saviourgate YO1 233 C2
St Saviour's Pl YO1 233 C2
St Sepulchre St 7 YO11 213 B6
St Stephen's Catholic Prim
Sch 17 BD23 216 F4
St Stephen's Cl BD23 216 F4
St Stephens Gdns 1 DL7 210 E3
St Stephens Mews YO30 225 A2
St Stephen's Rd YO24 227 C2
St Stephen's Sq YO24 227 C1
St Swithin's Wlk YO26 227 E4
St Teresa's RC Prim Sch
DL1 3 E4
St Therese of Lisieux RC Prim
Sch TS17 6 A4
St Thomas A Beckett Wlk
HG3 161 A5
St Thomas More RC Prim Sch
TS4 7 A7
St Thomas' Pl YO31 233 B4
St Thomas's Cl 2 YO10 229 C4
St Thomas St YO11 213 A6
St Thomas's Way YO26 164 C3
St Trinians Cl DL10 209 F8
St Trinians Dr DL10 209 F8
St Vincent's Cl 8 YO41 185 C2
St Wilfred Dr DL7 210 B3
St Wilfrid's Catholic High
School WF7 200 E1
St Wilfrid's Cl 7 YO32 167 B6
St Wilfrid's Cres 9 YO8 197 D1
St Wilfrid's Ct YO31 233 C3
St Wilfrid's Gdns HG4 214 C6
St Wilfrid's Pl 2 HG4 214 C5
St Wilfrids RC Prim Sch
HG4 214 B5
St Wilfrid's RC Prim Sch
YO31 233 C3
St Wilfrid's Rd
1 Ripon HG4 214 C5
8 Strensall YO32 167 B6
St Williams Coll YO1 233 B3
St Winifred's Ave HG2 219 F1
St Winifred's Cl HG2 219 F1
St Winifred's Rd HG2 219 F1
St Wulstan Cl YO31 228 E7
Salents La
Birdsall YO17 148 C4
Duggleby YO17 149 B6
Salerno Cl 6 DL9 209 C1
Salisbury Cl 15 WF6 200 A2
Salisbury Dr 9 HG3 161 B3
Salisbury Rd YO26 227 F5
Salisbury St
Scarborough YO12 212 E3
Skipton BD23 216 E5
Salisbury Ter YO26 227 F5
Sallow Heath 16 HG3 161 B3
Salmond Rd 4 YO24 227 B1
Salmon La DL8 87 B6
Saltburn Rd TS17 6 B8
Salterforth La BB18 171 E1
Salterforth Rd BB18 172 A1
Saltergate Bank YO18 72 F8
Saltergate Dr HG3 161 B3
Saltergate Inf Sch HG3 219 A5
Saltergill La TS15 24 C8
Salter Rd YO11 99 F6
Salters Ave DL1 3 E6
Saltersgill Ave
Easterside TS4 7 A7
Middlesbrough TS4 6 F8
Saltersgill Cl 3 TS4 6 F8
Salters La DL1 3 F4
Salters Lane N DL1 3 D8
Salters Lane S DL1 3 E7
SALTON 94 D3
Salton La YO62 94 B1
Salt Pans Rd YO13 54 D2
Salt Pan Well Steps 11
YO22 208 E6
Salutation Rd DL3 3 A4
Samian Way DL3 3 C8
Sam La YO61 142 D8
Samuel Smith Old Brewery*
LS24 189 E6
San Carlos Cl 1 DL9 40 E3
Sandacre Ct YO26 227 D5
Sandbeck DL10 209 C5
Sandbeck Ind Est LS22 180 C4
Sandbeck La LS22 180 D4
Sandbeck Way LS22 180 C4
Sandcroft Cl 4 YO24 230 D8
Sandcroft Rd YO24 230 D8
Sanderson Ave WF6 200 A1
Sanderson Ct YO26 227 B3
Sanderson Rd DL2 3 F1
Sanders Way DL10 41 E4
Sandfield La YO7 88 D4
Sandfield Terr 4 LS24 189 F6
Sandgate 14 YO22 208 D7
Sandgate Dr LS25 194 D1
Sandgate La LS25 194 E2
Sandgate Oval YO7 115 A2
Sandgate Rd YO7 115 A1
Sandgate Rise LS25 194 E1
Sandgate Terr LS25 194 E1
Sandhill Bank YO21 9 E1
Sandhill Cl
Harrogate HG1 219 F6
Pontefract WF8 201 B2
Sandhill Dr HG1 219 F6
Sandhill La
17 Bedale DL8 63 B3
Brayton YO8 197 D2
Sutton upon Derwent YO41 185 E2
Sandhill Rise WF8 201 B2
Sandhill Way HG1 219 F6
Sand Hole La YO30 165 F5
Sandholme 2 YO32 166 F5
Sandholme Cl
14 Easingwold YO61 143 D8
22 Settle BD24 131 D2
Sandholmes La YO7 89 E3
Sandhurst Gdns 4 YO12 212 B7
SANDHUTTON 89 A4
SAND HUTTON 168 B5
Sand Hutton CE VC Prim Sch
YO41 168 B5
Sand Hutton Ct YO41 168 B5
Sandhutton La YO7 89 B4
Sandiacres 5 YO8 197 D1
Sand La
Barlby with Osgodby YO8 198 B4
Barlby with Osgodby YO8 198 B6
Bubwith YO8 199 D5
Heslerton YO17 123 F7
Huby YO61 144 A5
Oldstead YO61 91 D3
Sherburn YO17 124 D7
South Milford LS25 195 F2
Stillington YO61 144 A6
Wistow YO8 197 E6
Sandmartin Ct YO24 230 D8
Sandmoor Cl 5 YO21 208 B5
Sandown Cl
Bagby YO7 90 B3
York YO24 227 E2
Sandpiper Cl
6 Eastfield YO12 99 E6
1 Filey YO14 101 A3
Sandpit La YO62 69 B1
Sandriggs DL3 3 B7
Sandringham Cl YO32 225 C7
Sandringham Dr 10
DN14 205 F3
Sandringham Rd
Byram cum Sutton WF11 201 E4
Lockwood TS12 9 F6
Middlesbrough TS3 7 B8
2 Ripon HG4 214 C3
6 Wetherby LS22 180 C3
Sandringham St
4 Scarborough YO12 212 F7
York YO10 228 D2
Sandrock Rd 3 WF8 201 C1
Sands Cl YO14 127 D7
SANDSEND 13 A3
Sandsend Rd
Newholm-cum-Dunsley
YO21 13 A3
Whitby YO21 208 A8
Sandside
Scarborough YO11 213 B6
Whitby YO22 208 D7
Sands La
Hunmanby YO14 127 A8
Rillington YO17 122 F5
Sandsprunt La YO13 97 E6
Sands Rd YO14 127 B7
Sandstock Rd YO31 229 B7
Sandwath La LS24 196 A8
Sandway Ave 12 YO8 197 B1
Sandway Cl 11 YO8 197 B1
Sandway Dr
Camblesforth YO8 204 D4
1 Thorpe Willoughby YO8 197 B1
Sandwith La DN14 204 B4
Sandwood Pk TS14 8 D5
Sandy Bank
Farnham HG5 162 D7
Northallerton DL6 210 F3
Romanby DL6 65 A7
Sandybed Cres YO12 212 C4
Sandybed La
Scarborough YO12 212 C4
Wykeham YO13 98 F6
Sandy Flatts La TS5 6 F6
Sandyforth La BD22 186 E5
Sandy Gap YO32 225 C7
Sandy Gate HG3 159 A6
Sandy La
Alne YO61 143 A4
Dalton YO7 116 A8
5 Embsay BD23 217 C7
Harton YO60 168 B8
16 Haxby YO32 166 E5
High & Low Bishopside
HG3 137 D3
Humberton YO61 141 D8
North Duffield YO8 198 F8
Ripon HG4 214 B2
Scampston YO17 123 B5
Stockton on the Forest
YO32 167 E4
Sandyland 29 YO32 166 E5
Sandylands Bsns Ctr
BD23 216 E3
Sandylands Sports Ctr
BD23 216 F3
Sandy Leas La TS21 5 A8
Sandyridge YO26 224 A1
Sandy Rise YO8 232 C3
Sarah's Croft BD23 155 A1
Sargent Ave YO23 230 F4
SATRON 36 D4
Saunters Way WF6 200 A2
Savage Yd 17 HG5 221 A6
Savile Rd
Castleford WF10 200 E4
Mickletown LS26 200 B6
Saville Gr YO30 228 A8
Saville St YO17 215 C4
SAWDON 98 C7
SAWLEY 138 F6
Sawley Cl BD23 217 C7
Sawley Moor La HG4 138 D6
Sawley St 1 BD23 216 D3
Sawmill La YO62 92 F6
Saw Mill La 15 LS29 175 A4
Saw Wells Ct LS24 195 F6
Saw Wells La LS24 195 F6
Sawyer's Cres YO23 230 C2
Sawyers Garth 9 LS29 175 A4
Sawyers Wlk 9 YO19 184 F7
Saxford Way 8 YO32 166 D5
Saxon Cl 6 YO8 197 B1
Saxon Ct 10 LS25 196 A4
Saxon Dr YO17 122 F5
Saxonfield TS8 7 A6
Saxon Grange LS25 195 F3
Saxon Mews 11 LS25 196 A4
Saxon Pl YO31 228 E7
Saxon Rd
Catterick Garrison DL9 209 E1
Ripon HG4 214 D5
Stamford Bridge YO41 168 D2
Whitby YO21 208 B7
Saxon Vale YO30 165 F5
Saxon Way 12 LS25 196 A4
SAXTON 195 D8
Saxton CE Prim Sch
LS24 195 D7
Saxton Ct LS24 195 D8
Saxton La LS24 195 E8
Saxty Way YO7 211 A1
Sayers Wynd 47 DL9 41 A5
Scabbate Gate BD23 108 B3
SCACKLETON 119 C4
Scackleton Bank YO62 119 C4
Scackleton La YO62 119 C3
Scafell Cl 4 YO30 224 E1
Scaggiethorpe La YO26 165 D2
SCAGGLETHORPE 122 D3
Scagglethorpe La YO17 122 C4
Scaife Gdns YO31 228 C7
Scaife Mews YO31 228 C7
Scaife Shay La YO7 116 A7
Scaife St YO31 228 C7
SCALBY 75 D6
Scalby Ave YO12 212 C8
Scalby Beck Rd 27 YO13 75 D5
Scalby Mills Rd YO12 75 F5
Scalby Rd YO12 212 D5
Scalby Sch YO12 212 B8
Scaldhill La YO51 141 C7
Scalehaw La BD23 153 F5
Scale Hill LS21 177 D2
Scale The BD23 157 D3
SCALING 11 A4
SCALING DAM 11 A4
Scallow Bank La DL8 59 B6
Scalm La
Hambleton YO8 196 F2
Selby YO8 197 A4
SCAMPSTON 123 A6
Scampston Hall* YO17 123 A6
Scampton Cl TS17 6 A6
Scarah Bank HG3 161 B8
Scarah La HG3 140 A2
Scarbeck Bank DL11 19 D7
SCARBOROUGH 213 B5
Scarborough Art Gall & Cres
Art Studio* YO11 213 A5
Scarborough Bsns Pk
YO11 99 F6
Scarborough Castle*
YO11 213 C7
Scarborough Coll YO11 213 B2
Scarborough Hospl YO12 212 B6
Scarborough Indoor Pool*
YO12 212 E8
Scarborough Rd
Gristhorpe YO14 101 A4
Heslerton YO17 123 F6
Langtoft YO25 151 C7
Norton-on-Derwent YO17 122 A3
Norton YO17 215 F4
Seamer YO12 99 D6
Stainton Dale YO13 53 F8
Scarborough Sixth Form Coll
YO12 212 C4
Scarborough Sports Ctr
YO11 213 A2
Scarborough Sta YO11 212 F5
Scarborough Terr YO30 233 B4
Scarcroft Hill YO24 228 B2
Scarcroft La YO23 233 A1
Scarcroft Prim Sch YO23 233 A1
Scarcroft Rd YO24 233 A1
Scarcroft View YO23 233 A1
Scardale Cres YO12 212 E8
Scardale Ct YO8 232 A2
Scarer's La YO26 142 B2
Scar Field 9 BD23 134 E2
Scargill Rd HG1 219 B4
Scar Hos DL11 35 F5
Scarhouse La DL11 17 E2
Scarlet Balk La YO17 122 C1
Scar Rd BD23 171 E6
Scar St 2 BD23 134 E2
Scarth Cl 3 TS12 9 F7
SCARTHINGWELL 195 F7
Scarthingwell Cres LS24 195 D8
Scarthingwell La LS24 195 E8
Scarth Nick
Preston-under-Scar DL8 59 E6
Whorlton DL6 45 D6
Scate Moor La YO26 163 F3
Scaudercroft 13 YO19 184 F7
Scawling End Rd YO61 91 C3
Scawthorpe Cl WF8 201 C1
SCAWTON 91 E6
Scawton Ave 1 YO31 225 E2
Scholars Gate
Guisborough TS14 8 E5
West Garforth LS25 194 C3
Scholars Pk DL3 3 B5
Scholes La BD22 187 F1
Scholes Park Ave 3 YO12 75 F5
Scholes Park Cliff 1
YO12 75 F5
Scholes Park Dr 2 YO12 75 F5
Scholes Park Rd YO12 75 F5
Scholes Rd WF10 201 B5
Scholla La DL6 210 F5
Scholla View DL6 210 F5
School Bank DL10 21 C4
School Cl
Huby YO61 144 A4
Selby YO8 232 B3
16 Stamford Bridge YO41 168 D2
School Croft
Askrigg DL8 57 E6
Knottingley WF11 201 E4
School Fields BB18 172 A2
School Garth YO7 89 E3
Schoolgate LS15 194 C8
School Hill
Bainbridge DL8 57 D5
8 Settle BD24 131 E2
School House Dr YO12 99 D6
Schoolhouse Terr LS22 180 B5
School La
Addingham LS29 174 F5
Askham Richard YO23 182 D3
Bellerby DL8 60 D7
Bishopthorpe YO23 231 A4
Burton Fleming YO25 126 E3
Collingham LS22 188 A8
Copmanthorpe YO23 230 A2
Dacre HG3 159 F8
Earby BB18 172 A1
Easington BB7 152 B3
Eppleby DL11 1 D4
Great Ayton TS9 8 A1
Heslington YO10 229 B1
Laneshaw Bridge BB8 186 C3
Lawkland LA2 130 D3
Liverton Mines TS13 10 D8
Lotherton cum Aberford
LS25 194 F8
Malton YO17 215 C4
4 Nawton YO62 93 D7
Newton-le-Willows DL8 62 B4
Osmotherley DL6 45 B4
23 Poppleton YO26 165 F1
South Milford LS25 195 F2
8 Spofforth HG3 179 E6
Thornton-le-Beans DL6 65 B5
Topcliffe YO7 115 C7
Walton LS23 180 F2
Wray-with-Botton LA2 128 A6
York YO10 231 E7
School Rd
Hemingbrough YO8 198 F1
Wetherby LS22 180 C3
School St
Castleford WF10 200 F5
2 Earby BB18 186 A7
York YO24 227 D3
Scoreby La
Gate Helmsley YO41 168 B2
Kexby YO41 168 B1
Low Catton YO41 185 B8
Score Ray La YO26 164 A5
Scoresby Terr 2 YO21 208 D5
SCORTON 41 F7
Scoska Wood National
Nature Reserve* BD23 107 B3
Scosthrop La BD23 154 E6
Scotch Cnr
Middleton Tyas DL10 21 B4
Oldstead YO61 91 C4
Scotch George La HG5 221 A7
Scotchman La YO60 168 A8
Scot Gate DL8 59 D3
Scots Dike Terr DL10 209 D6
Scots Dyke Cl DL10 20 F7
Scott Cl
Catterick DL10 41 E4
35 Glusburn BD20 187 E7
13 Swillington LS26 194 A1
Scott Hill DL8 57 D5
Scott Moncrieff Rd YO32 167 B6
SCOTTON
Harrogate 162 A6
Richmond 40 F2
Scotton Bank DL8 40 D2
Scotton Ct HG5 162 A6
Scotton Dr HG5 220 C8
Scotton Gdns 8 DL9 40 E3
Scotton Gr
Knaresborough HG5 220 C8
Scotton HG5 162 A5
Scotton Lingerfield Com
Prim Sch HG5 162 B7
Scotton Moor HG5 220 C8
Scotton Pk DL9 40 E3
Scotton Rd DL9 40 E3
Scott Rd YO8 232 C6
Scotts Row DL7 64 F2
Scott St YO23 228 C2
Scraper La YO22 32 F7
SCRAYINGHAM 168 F7
Scriftain La LS22 180 C5
SCRIVEN 162 D5
Scriven Gr 8 YO32 166 F5
Scriven Rd HG5 221 A7
Scroggs La DL8 86 E7
Scrogs La DL8 59 B6
Scrope Ave 4 YO31 228 E5
SCRUTON 63 D7
Scugdale Rd DL6 45 E8
Scurragh House La DL10 21 C2
Scurragh La DL10 21 B2
Sea App YO14 100 F6
Sea Cliff Cres YO11 213 B2
Sea Cliff Rd YO11 213 B2
Seafield Ave 1 YO11 100 B7

Seafire Cl YO30 225 A3
Seaford Ave YO14 127 B8
Seafox Ct LS25 196 B4
Seagram Cres DL10 209 C8
Seakel La YO23 182 C2
Seal Bank BD23 81 D1
Sea Life & Marine Sanctuary★ YO12 75 F5
SEAMER
Middlesbrough 6 F1
Scarborough 99 E6
Seamer Carr Rd YO11, YO12 99 F5
Seamer & Irton Com Prim Sch YO12 99 D6
Seamer Moor Hill YO12 212 B1
Seamer Moor La YO12 212 B1
Seamer Rd
East Ayton YO13 99 B7
Eastfield YO12 99 F8
Hilton TS15 6 C2
Maltby TS8 6 E3
Scarborough YO12 212 E3
Thornton TS8 6 D4
Seamer Road Cnr YO12 212 E4
Seamer Road Ret Pk YO12 212 E1
Seamer St 2 YO12 212 E3
Seamer Sta YO11 99 F6
Seaton Cl
Staithes TS13 13 K2
York YO10 229 C4
Seaton Cres TS13 13 K2
Seaton Garth TS13 13 K2
Seave Close La YO26 164 D2
Seavegate 4 YO13 99 B8
Seavegate Cl 3 YO13 99 B8
SEAVE GREEN 47 A7
Sea View YO14 101 C1
Seaview Ave 5 YO12 75 E5
Sea View Cl
5 Scarborough YO11 100 B8
Whitby YO21 208 A6
Sea View Cres YO11 100 B8
Sea View Dr 13 YO11 100 B8
Sea View Gdns 6 YO11 100 B8
Sea View Gr 4 YO11 100 B8
Second Ave
Menwith with Darley HG3 160 A4
Wetherby LS22 180 C3
York YO31 228 F6
Second Comm La YO8 197 C4
Sedbergh Dr LS29 218 B3
Sedbergh Pk LS29 218 B3
Sedber La 5 BD23 134 E2
SEDBUSK 56 E6
Sedbusk La DL8 56 D6
Sedgefield Rd TS5 6 E6
Sedgemoor Rd TS6 7 F8
Sedge Rise LS24 189 D5
Sedley Cl HG1 219 E7
Seed Hill LA6 103 D4
Sefton Ave YO31 228 F8
Sefton Dr LS29 218 B3
Sefton Way TS15 5 D2
Seggans Rd YO26 142 A1
Seg La YO8 204 F3
Segrave Rd DL9 40 E4
Segrave Wlk 10 YO26 227 E4
Selaby Ct DL2 1 C8
Selbourne Terr 9 BB18 172 B1
SELBY 232 C6
Selby Abbey★ YO8 232 D5
Selby Abbey CE VC Prim Sch YO8 232 C5
Selby Bsns Pk YO8 232 D1
Selby Coll YO8 232 F3
Selby Coll (1811 Ctr) YO8 232 C5
Selby Coll (Tadcaster Learning Ctr) LS24 189 E6
Selby Com Prim Sch YO8 232 B5
Selby Cres DL3 3 A7
Selby Ironworks Bsns Ctr YO8 232 D5
Selby Rd
Eggborough DN14 202 F1
Fulford YO19 231 E6
Garforth LS15 194 A3
Ledston LS25 195 A2
Riccall YO19 198 A8
Snaith DN14 204 C1
Swillington LS15 194 A3
Wistow YO8 197 D6
Womersley DN14 207 A4
Selby Rly Sports Club YO8 232 D5
Selby Sta YO8 232 D5
Seldon Rd YO26 227 E5
Self Gdns YO62 70 F3
Selley Park Dr YO12 212 B4
SELLY HILL 32 A8
Selly Park Rd YO12 212 B4
SELSIDE 105 A6
Selside Shaw BD24 105 A7
Selstone Cres 7 YO22 32 A6
Semer Water Nature Reserve★ DL8 57 B1
Senhouse Rd DL1 3 F5
Seph Way YO17 215 A2
Sergeant Bank HG4 86 B8
Serinity Hallow TS12 9 E8
SESSAY 116 B6
Sessay CE Prim Sch YO7 116 C5
Sessions House Yd 10 WF8 201 B1
Seton Com Prim Sch TS13 13 K2
SETTLE 131 E3
Settle CE Prim Sch BD24 131 E2
Settle Coll BD24 131 D2
Settle Rd BD23 155 A6
Settle Sta BD24 131 D2
SETTRINGTON 122 D1
Settrington All Saints' CE VC Prim Sch YO17 122 D1
Settrington Rd YO12 212 B5
Seven St YO17 121 C1
Seventh Ave YO31 228 F5
Seven Wells YO17 121 A4
Severfield Cl YO7 211 D2
Severn Dr
Garforth LS25 194 D3
Guisborough TS14 8 E6
Severn Gn YO26 227 C8
Severn Way DL1 3 D3
Severus Ave YO24 227 D4
Severus St YO24 227 D3
Sewell's Cave★ LA2 131 A5
SEXHOW 25 D4
Sexhow La TS9 25 F4
Seymour Cres TS16 5 D4
Seymour Gr
Eaglescliffe TS16 5 D4
York YO31 228 F6
Shackleton Cl YO21 208 C5
Shady La BD20 173 C2
Shaftesbury Ave DN14 202 C3
Shaker Stile Rd YO18 96 B7
Shakespeare Ave 2 DN6 206 E1
Shakespeare Cl 3 DL10 41 C7
Shakespeare Cres WF10 201 B3
Shallowdale Gr 1 YO10 229 C3
Shambles La HG4 114 D5
Shambles The 8 YO17 215 C4
Shandon Pk TS8 7 B5
Shandy Hall★ YO61 117 D8
Shannon Cl 26 LS29 175 C2
Shannon Lea DL2 4 D4
SHAROW 214 F6
Sharow CE Prim Sch HG4 214 F7
Sharow La HG4 214 E6
Sharpe Howe★ YO11 126 A8
Sharphaw Ave BD23 217 A2
Sharphaw View BD23 155 D1
Sharphaw Vw BD23 155 D1
Sharp Hill Cl 13 DL8 60 E2
Sharp Hill La YO8 204 F6
Shaw Ave WF6 200 B1
Shaw Barn La LS22 180 B3
Shaw Cl
Garforth LS25 194 D3
Normanton South WF6 200 B1
Shawclose La YO62 67 E4
Shaw Cres YO61 144 A5
Shawcroft Ct DL10 209 E8
Shaw Dr YO62 70 B1
Shaw La
Farnham HG5 162 C7
Fenwick DN6 207 D2
North Rigton HG3 178 B6
Spofforth with Stockeld HG3 179 D7
Shawl Terr 10 DL8 60 D5
SHAW MILLS 138 F1
Shaw Rise WF6 200 B1
Shaws Cl YO7 211 B4
Shaws La
Barwick in Elmet & Scholes LS15 194 B7
Hawes DL8 56 E4
Shaw's Terr YO24 233 A1
Sheaflands La YO51 140 E5
Shearing Path LS29 174 F5
Sheepcote La HG3 159 F5
Sheepdyke La YO14 127 A8
Sheepfoot Hill YO17 215 D4
Sheep Rake La YO25 151 F4
Sheep St 11 BD23 216 F4
Sheepwalk La
Castleford WF10 201 B3
Kirby Grindalythe YO17 150 B7
Sheepwash Bank YO7 66 B5
Sheepwash La DN14 207 A7
Sheldrake Cl 9 YO14 101 A4
Sheldrake Rd WF10 200 E3
Shelley Cl YO11 100 B6
Shelley Ct HG1 219 E7
Shelley Dr WF11 201 D2
Shelley Gr YO30 224 F1
Shelley Rd TS4 6 F8
Shelton Ave 2 YO13 99 B8
Shepherd Ct TS12 9 E7
Shepherdfields La YO60 146 E5
Shepherd Gate LA2 130 F5
Shepherd Hill
Blubberhouses LS21 159 C1
Whorlton DL6 45 D8
Shepherdies The HG4 113 C8
Shepherds Dr 13 YO11 100 B7
Sherbrooke Cl 18 YO62 70 B1
SHERBURN 124 D8
Sherburn CE Prim Sch YO17 124 D7
Sherburn Enterprise Pk LS25 196 B4
Sherburn High Sch LS25 195 F3
SHERBURN IN ELMET 195 E5
Sherburn in Elmet Sta LS25 196 A4
Sherburn Rd YO8 232 A8
Sherburn St 1 YO8 197 B8
Sherburn Willows Nature Reserve★ LS25 195 E3
Sheridan Rd BB8 186 B3
SHERIFF HUTTON 145 C5
Sheriff Hutton Castle (rems of)★ YO60 145 D5
Sheriff Hutton Prim Sch YO60 145 C5
Sherriff Hutton House★ YO60 145 D4
Sherringham Dr YO24 230 D8
Sherwood Brow BD24 131 D7
Sherwood Cl
Hunton DL8 61 E7
13 Norton DN6 206 E1
Sherwood Dr HG2 220 D2
Sherwood Gr
Huntington YO32 225 F1
York YO26 227 B6
Sherwood Rd TS17 6 B6
Sherwood St 5 YO12 212 F5
Shetland Cl TS5 6 E6
Shilton Garth Cl 3 YO32 225 F7
SHIPTON 165 F5
Shipton Low Rd YO30 165 E5
Shipton Rd
Clifton YO30 227 F8
Rawcliffe YO30 224 D2
York YO30 228 A7
Shipton St 3 YO30 228 B7
Shipyard Ind Est YO8 232 E5
Shipyard Rd YO8 232 E5
Shirbutt La YO26 182 C8
Shire Cl 18 YO11 100 B7
Shire Croft 17 YO11 100 B7
Shire Fold YO11 100 B6
Shire Garth DL6 24 B1
Shire Gr YO17 95 D2
Shire Rd YO7 211 B4
Shires Croft BD23 217 E8
Shires La BD23 217 D8
Shirley Ave
Ripon HG4 214 B6
York YO26 227 C6
Shoebridge Ave BD20 187 F7
Shop Hill YO22 33 B4
Shop La
Cowling BD22 187 A6
Danby YO21 29 B3
Middleton YO18 95 D8
Shortacre La YO42 193 E2
Shortbank Cl BD23 217 B3
Shortbank Rd BD23 217 B3
Short Cl TS18 5 F7
Shorthorn La 1 DL2 3 A7
Short La
Acaster Selby YO23 191 A4
Farndale East YO62 48 F4
West Haddlesey YO8 202 F6
Short Lee La BD23 216 F6
Short Rd YO7 115 B2
Shortsill La HG5 163 B5
Shotel Cl YO30 227 F8
Showfield Cl LS25 195 F4
Showfield Dr 17 YO61 143 C8
Showfield Ind Est YO17 215 C6
Showfield La YO17 215 C6
Shrubberies The YO8 198 E2
Shute Rd DL9 209 E1
Shutt La DL8 56 E6
Shuttleworth St 36 BB18 172 A1
Shuttocks Fold LS25 194 D2
SICKLINGHALL 179 E3
Sicklinghall Com Prim Sch LS22 179 D3
Sicklinghall Rd LS22 179 F3
Side Gate YO12 99 D1
Sidegate La BD20 186 F8
Sidgwick Ct 7 BD23 217 A3
Siding La YO8 198 B5
Sidings Ind Est The BD24 131 D2
Sidings La YO61 143 B4
Sidings The
12 Bridgehouse Gate HG3 137 B4
5 Low Bentham LA2 128 F8
Settle BD24 131 D2
Skipton BD23 216 E3
Strensall YO32 167 B7
Sidmouth Cl TS8 7 D6
Sidmouth Sq 9 DL9 40 E4
Signals Ct 7 YO12 75 F5
Sigston Castle★ DL6 44 D2
Sike La YO7 115 B6
Silicar La HG4 88 B1
Silkstone Sq WF10 200 E6
Sills La YO30 165 B6
Silly La LA2 129 A2
SILPHO 74 E7
Silpho Forest Trail YO13 53 E1
SILSDEN 174 C2
Silsden Rd
Addingham LS29 174 D4
Low Bradley BD20 173 E3
Silverdale Cl 5 HG3 160 A6
Silverdale Ct YO24 230 D7
Silverdale Rd BD24 131 F8
Silverfields Rd HG1 220 A3
Silver Garth DL10 21 C7
Silver Hill DL7 22 C2
Silverlink Bsns Pk DL1 3 D6
Silver Mdws DL10 21 D7
Silversands Way YO14 127 C8
Silver St
Askrigg DL8 57 E5
Barton DL10 21 C7
Fairburn WF11 201 D6
Silver St *continued*
Hackforth DL8 62 E8
4 Knaresborough HG5 221 B5
Masham HG4 86 C3
Reeth, Fremington & Healaugh DL11 38 B6
3 Riccall YO19 198 A8
8 Scarborough YO11 213 A6
Thirsk YO7 211 C1
Whitby YO21 208 D7
Whitley DN14 207 A7
York YO1 233 B2
Silverton Rd TS14 8 F5
Silverwood Ave 5 YO14 101 A3
Simbach Cl BD23 217 B3
Sim Balk La YO23 230 E5
Simmons Cl 16 YO32 167 A7
Simon Howe
Ganton YO12 125 A5
Sherburn YO12 124 F6
SIMONSTONE 56 D6
Simpson Ave 6 YO14 126 F8
Simpson Cl BB18 171 E2
Simpsons La WF11 201 E2
Simpson's Lane Acad WF11 201 E2
Sinclair Ct YO12 212 E5
SINDERBY 88 C4
Sinderby La YO7 88 B4
Sinks La DL8 62 C4
SINNINGTON 95 A8
Sinnington Cl TS14 8 F6
Sinnington Cliff Rd YO62 95 A8
Sinnington Prim Sch YO62 94 F8
Sinnington Rd TS17 6 B6
Sir Douglas Pk TS17 6 A7
Sir John's La LS25 195 E4
Sirocco Ct YO31 228 D8
Sir William Hartley Ct BB8 186 B3
Siskin Way WF10 200 D6
Sissy Bank DL8 59 D6
Sitwell Gr YO26 227 C5
Sitwell St YO12 212 E5
Siwards Howe★ YO10 229 B1
Siward St YO10 229 A3
Siward's Way YO10 229 A2
Sixth Ave YO31 228 E5
Skates La YO61 144 B3
Sked Dale YO17 124 E6
SKEEBY 21 A1
Skeeby Cl 3 TS18 5 D8
Skegmer La YO60 145 F4
Skelda Rise LS29 218 B3
Skeldergate YO1 233 B2
Skelder Rd YO21 31 E8
Skelf St LS24 190 C1
Skelgate La DL11 38 B6
Skellbank HG4 214 B4
Skellbank Cl HG4 214 B4
Skelldale Cl HG4 214 E4
Skelldale Pk HG4 214 E4
Skelldale View HG4 214 E4
Skellfield Terr HG4 214 D4
Skellgarth HG4 214 C5
Skellgill La DL8 57 C6
SKELTON 224 C6
Skelton Ct
10 Guisborough TS14 8 F7
3 York YO30 228 A6
Skelton Ellers TS14 9 A8
Skelton La
Givendale HG4 140 C8
Marske DL11 39 B7
Skelton YO32 224 D8
Skelton Newby Hall CE Prim Sch HG4 140 E7
SKELTON ON URE 140 E7
Skelton Park Trading Est YO30 225 B4
Skelton Prim Sch YO30 224 C5
Skelton Rd
Skelton YO51 140 E6
Thornaby TS17 6 B8
Skelton Windmill★ YO51 140 F8
SKERNE PARK 3 C3
Skerne Park Acad DL1 3 D3
Skerningham Ave 9 DL2 3 A7
Skeugh Head La DL11 35 E6
Skeugh La YO61 144 D6
SKEWSBY 119 A1
Skewsby Gr YO31 225 F1
Skibeden BD23 217 E6
Skibeden Ct 4 BD23 217 B5
Skiddaw YO24 230 C7
Skiddaw Ct TS7 7 C6
Skinner La 14 WF8 201 B1
Skinner St YO21 208 D7
Skiplam Cl 4 YO12 212 B5
Skiplam Rd YO62 69 D2
Skipper La YO25 125 E3
SKIPTON 216 F4
Skipton Castle★ BD23 217 A5
Skipton Cres HG1 219 D5
Skipton General Hospl BD23 216 F3
Skipton Girls' High Sch BD23 216 E5
Skipton Little Theatre★ BD23 216 F3
Skipton Old Rd BB8 186 A3
SKIPTON-ON-SWALE 88 E2
Skipton Parish Church CE VC Prim Sch BD23 217 A3
Skipton Rd
Addingham LS29 174 E5
Barnoldswick BB18 171 E2
Bradleys Both BD20 173 D4
Skipton Rd *continued*
Colne BB8 186 A2
Cononley BD20 173 C2
Earby BB18 172 A2
Embsay with Eastby BD23 217 C7
Farnhill BD20 187 E8
Felliscliffe HG3 160 E3
Fewston LS21 159 D2
Gargrave BD23 155 D1
Glusburn BD20 187 F8
Harrogate HG3 219 A5
Hellifield BD23 154 B3
Ilkley LS29 218 A4
Silsden BD20 174 B1
Silsden BD20 174 B3
Skipton BD23 217 B6
Skipton St HG1 219 D4
Skipton Sta BD23 216 E3
SKIPWITH 192 E1
Skipwith Comm★ YO8 198 E8
Skipwith Rd YO19 192 B6
SKIRETHORNS 134 C2
SKIRPENBECK 169 A4
Skirt Bank YO7 66 C7
Skottowe Cres TS9 7 F2
Skottowe Dr TS9 7 F2
Skuff Rd BD23 157 B8
Skurkhill La YO62 92 E7
SKYREHOLME 157 E7
Skyreholme La BD23 157 E7
Slackgap La CA17 14 A8
Slack La HG3 160 B4
Sladeburn Dr 2 DL6 210 E3
Slaidburn Rd LA2 129 B4
SLAPEWATH 9 C6
Slate Hill YO21 29 D4
Slates La LS29 218 B7
Slayde The TS15 5 E2
Sledgate YO17 122 F5
Sledgate Garth YO17 122 F5
Sled Gates YO22 33 B3
Sled La DL10 41 F4
SLEDMERE 150 B4
Sledmere CE Prim Sch YO25 150 B3
Sledmere House★ YO25 150 B3
Sledmere Rd YO25 151 B6
Slee Gill DL10 209 C5
Sleigh La YO60 120 A1
Sleightholme Dale Rd YO62 69 D5
Sleightholme Moor Rd DL11 16 D7
SLEIGHTS 32 A6
Sleights CE Prim Sch YO22 32 A6
Sleights Ct 15 TS14 8 F7
Sleights La
Acklam YO17 169 E7
Amotherby YO17 121 A6
Birstwith HG3 160 C4
Rainton with Newby YO7 114 E5
Sleights Rd YO62 69 D6
Sleights Sta YO22 32 A7
Sleights The LS17 178 A2
Slessor Rd
8 Catterick DL10 41 E4
York YO24 227 B1
Slice La LS24 190 A6
Slim Rd DL9 209 C2
SLINGSBY 120 C6
Slingsby Ave HG5 221 A7
Slingsby Bank YO62 120 C4
Slingsby Castle (rems of)★ YO62 120 B5
Slingsby Com Prim Sch YO62 120 B5
Slingsby Cres HG1 219 F4
Slingsby Garth 19 YO62 70 B1
Slingsby Gdns DL7 210 B3
Slingsby Gr YO24 230 E8
Slingsby Wlk HG2 219 F1
Slip Inn Bank DL11 19 E6
Slippery Ford La BD22 187 E3
Slope La 8 YO12 99 D2
Smales' St YO1 233 B1
SMALL BANKS 174 F3
Smalldrink La 40 BD20 187 E7
Smary La
Murton YO19 184 D7
Murton YO19 184 D7
Smawthorne Ave WF10 200 E4
Smawthorne Gr WF10 200 E4
Smawthorne Henry Moore Prim Sch WF10 200 E3
Smawthorne La WF10 200 E4
Smay La YO22 33 D5
Smearbottoms La BD23 133 C3
Smeathorns Rd TS12 9 F4
Smeatley's La WF8 206 C4
Smeaton Gr
5 Swillington LS26 194 A1
York YO26 227 C5
Smeaton Rd YO41 185 D7
SMELTHOUSES 137 F3
Smiddyfields 5 YO22 32 A6
Smiddy Hill
19 Pickering YO18 95 F6
Walton LS23 181 A2
Smirthwaite View 14 WF6 200 A1
Smith Cl YO10 231 F8
Smithfield Cl 7 HG4 214 B2
Smithfield Rd DL1 3 D4
Smithgutter La DL10 21 C4
Smithie Cl YO32 225 D5
Smith La HG4 114 A4

Smith's La
Egton YO22 30 E3
Flaxton YO60 145 D1
Smithson Ave WF10 201 B3
Smithson Cl DL10 21 D2
Smithson Ct YO17 215 B5
Smithson Gr 4 YO51 141 B4
Smithsons Ct HG4 214 C5
Smithson's La HG3 177 A8
Smith St 19 BB18 171 D1
Smithy Croft Rd BD23 155 D1
Smithy Greaves LS29 175 B4
Smithy La
Denton LS29 176 A4
Scotton HG5 162 A6
Thornton in Lonsdale LA6 103 A4
Ulleskelf LS24 190 C2
Smuts Rd DL9 209 D1
Smythy La YO25 125 D4
SNAINTON 98 A5
Snainton CE Prim Sch
YO13 98 A5
Snainton La YO13 97 F7
SNAITH 204 C1
Snaith Rd
Pollington DN14 207 F7
Rawcliffe DN14 205 A1
Snaith Sta DN14 204 C1
Snaizeholme Rd DL8 55 E1
SNAPE 87 A7
Snape Castle* DL8 87 A7
Snape Com Prim Sch DL8 87 A7
Snape Hill YO62 93 E7
Snargate Hill YO61 118 E3
SNEATON 32 D6
Sneaton La YO22 208 B1
SNEATONTHORPE 32 F5
Sneaton Thorpe La YO22 32 E5
Sneck Gate La TS8 7 B2
Sneck Yate Bank YO7 67 A2
Snipe Cl 5 YO14 101 A4
Snipe La
Hurworth DL2 3 C3
Loftus TS13 11 A6
Snowden Carr Rd LS21 176 E5
Snowden Cl 4 HG4 214 B2
Snowdon Cl YO23 182 D3
Snowdon Gr 4 TS17 5 F4
Snowfield Ind Est YO17 215 C6
Snowfield La YO61 142 F5
Snydale Ave WF6 200 B1
Snydale Cl WF6 200 B1
Snydale Ct 10 WF6 200 B1
Snydale Gr WF6 200 B1
Snydale Rd WF6 200 A1
Sober Hall Ave TS17 6 A4
Socarrs La YO62 119 F7
SOCKBURN 23 C6
Sockburn La DL2 23 B8
Somerley La 6 HG5 221 B7
Somerset Cl
Hipswell DL9 40 D4
6 York YO30 224 E3
Somerset Rd
2 Harrogate HG2 219 C1
York YO31 228 D8
Somerset Terr YO11 213 A5
Somme Barracks DL9 40 F3
Sommerset Pastures
YO61 116 F2
Sopwith Cl TS18 5 F8
Sorrel Gr 29 HG3 161 B3
Sorrell Gr TS14 8 D6
Sough La BB18 186 A8
SOURBY 176 D8
Sourby La LS21 176 D7
Sour La DL8 216 B6
Soursikes Field Rd YO51 141 D5
Soutersfield YO61 144 C6
South App
Aberford LS25 188 F1
Bramham cum Oglethorpe
LS23 188 C5
Stutton with Hazlewood
LS25 189 A2
South Ave
Castleford WF10 200 C4
20 Scalby YO13 75 D5
South Back La
Stillington YO61 144 C6
Terrington YO60 119 E1
Tollerton YO61 143 B2
South Baileygate WF8 201 C1
SOUTH BANK 228 A1
South Bank Ave YO23 228 B1
South Beech Ave HG2 220 C3
South Cliff Dr YO14 101 B1
South Craven Sch 36
BD20 187 E7
South Cres
Ripon HG4 214 C4
Thirsk YO7 211 B2
South Cres Ave 54 YO14 101 B3
South Cres Cl 51 YO14 101 B3
South Cres Rd YO14 101 B3
Southdean Dr TS8 6 F6
Southdene 48 YO14 101 B3
South Down Rd 3 YO32 225 F5
South Dr HG2 222 E8
SOUTH DUFFIELD 199 A4
South Duffield Rd YO8 198 C4
South End
Bedale DL8 63 A3
Burniston YO13 75 D7
Osmotherley DL6 45 B3
Southend Ave DL3 3 C4
South End Ave 6 DL8 63 A3
South End Cl YO13 75 D7
Southend Gdns 8 YO21 208 C6
South End La DN14 207 B4
Southerscales Nature
Reserve* LA6 104 C7
South Esplande YO1 233 B1
Southey St 1 BD23 217 A3
Southfield YO17 122 D3
Southfield Ave HG4 214 B2
Southfield Cl
6 Hurworth-on-Tees DL2 3 E1
Rufforth YO23 182 D6
Southfield Cres 2 YO24 230 E8
Southfield Grange 3
YO23 190 F5
Southfield La
23 Addingham LS29 174 F4
Kellington DN14 202 E2
South Field La YO26 181 B6
Southfield Rd
28 Addingham LS29 174 F4
Burley in Warfedale LS29 176 C1
Littlethorpe HG4 214 B2
Southfields Rd YO32 167 B7
Southfield Terr
22 Addingham LS29 174 F4
7 Skipton BD23 216 F3
South Garth YO30 165 F5
Southgate
Eastfield YO12 99 E6
Pickering YO18 95 F7
Ripon HG4 214 C4
South Gate 18 YO62 92 F6
Southgate Ave HG4 214 C4
Southgate Cl 7 HG4 214 C4
South Grange Rd HG4 214 B2
South Hawksworth St 7
LS29 218 B4
SOUTH HOLME 120 B8
South House Pavement
Nature Reserve* BD24 104 F8
South Ings La YO62 70 F3
SOUTH KILVINGTON 211 B7
South Kilvington CE Prim Sch
YO7 211 A7
South La
Bishop Wilton YO42 169 F1
Burton Fleming YO25 126 E2
Cawood YO8 197 B7
Thornton Dale YO18 96 D6
Southlands
4 Haxby YO32 166 E5
19 Helmsley YO62 92 F6
16 Hemingbrough YO8 198 F1
2 High & Low Bishopside
HG3 137 B4
Southlands Ave 5 YO21 208 C7
Southlands Cl
Escrick YO19 192 B6
8 South Milford LS25 195 F2
Southlands Ct 21 LS25 195 F2
Southlands Dr TS7 7 D6
Southlands Gr YO12 212 B7
Southlands Rd YO23 228 B2
Southlea YO17 122 F5
SOUTH LOFTUS 10 E8
SOUTH MILFORD 195 F1
South Milford Prim Sch 9
LS25 195 F2
South Milford Sta LS25 195 F2
Southmoor La WF11 202 B1
South Moor La
Garriston DL8 61 A7
Sowerby YO7 89 F3
Southmoor Rd YO19 192 F5
Southolme Cl 22 YO51 141 B5
Southolme Dr 7 YO30 224 F1
Southolme Wlk 23 YO51 141 B5
SOUTH OTTERINGTON 64 F2
**South Otterington CE Prim
Sch** DL7 64 F2
South Parade
Hurworth-on-Tees DL2 22 C8
Ilkley LS29 218 A4
Northallerton DL7 210 D3
Norton YO17 215 E3
8 Selby YO8 232 C5
York YO23 233 A1
South Parade Ind Est
YO17 215 E3
South Park Ave TS6 7 E8
South Park La LS22 180 A8
South Park Rd HG1 219 E1
South Ridge LS25 194 D1
South Ruddings La YO19 192 F7
South Side TS15 25 C5
South St
Barmby on the Marsh
DN14 205 A7
Burton Fleming YO25 126 E2
Scalby YO13 75 D5
7 Scarborough YO11 213 A4
SOUTH STAINLEY 139 E2
South Terr YO7 211 B2
South Town La TS13 10 E8
South Vale DL6 210 E2
South View
Burniston YO13 75 D7
Castleford WF10 201 B5
2 Egglescliffe TS16 5 D4
3 Glusburn BD20 173 E1
Healaugh LS24 182 A2
Hunton DL8 61 E7
Ilkley LS29 218 B3
18 Leyburn DL8 60 D5
Northallerton DL6 210 F6
Ripon HG4 214 D2
2 Rudby TS15 25 D5
6 Whitby YO21 208 D5
South View Terr BD20 174 B1
Southville Terr HG1 219 B5
Southway
Harrogate HG2 222 C8
Ilkley LS29 218 D3
Manor Park LS29 176 B2
Southwold 7 YO11 100 B7
Southwold Cl 5 YO11 100 B7
Southwold Rise 6 YO11 100 B7
Southwood TS8 7 B4
South Wood La 11 BD23 134 E3
Southwood Rd YO41 193 C8
Sovereign Fold HG5 221 C7
Sovereign Gdns 2 WF6 200 A1
Sovereign Pk HG1 219 B2
Sowarth Field 21 BD24 131 D2
Sowarth Ind Est BD24 131 D2
SOWERBY 211 B1
Sowerby Com Prim Sch
YO7 211 B1
Sowerby Cres TS9 26 B7
Sowerby Rd
Thirsk YO7 211 B2
York YO26 227 D4
Sowerby Terr YO7 211 B2
Sowerby Way TS16 5 D5
Sowgate La WF8 201 D2
SPACEY HOUSES 223 A2
Spa Complex* YO11 213 B4
Spa Gdns* HG4 214 B5
Spa La
Harrogate HG2 220 C3
Middleton YO18 95 B6
Spalding Ave YO30 228 B7
Spa Mews HG2 220 D3
Spa Pk* HG4 214 B5
Spa Rd
Gainford DL2 1 C7
Harrogate HG2 220 C3
Sparrow Hall Dr DL1 3 E8
Spartal La LS25 200 F8
Spa St HG2 220 C3
Spa Terr 3 HG2 220 C3
SPA THE 213 B4
Spa The YO11 213 A4
SPAUNTON 70 E4
Spaunton Bank YO62 70 E5
Spaunton La YO62 70 E4
Spawd Bone La
Knottingley WF11 201 F2
27 Knottingley WF11 202 A2
**Specialist Sch for the Arts &
Science** YO8 232 B4
Speculation St YO1 228 E4
Speedwell Rd WF10 200 C3
SPEETON 127 F5
Speeton Ave TS5 6 F7
Spellow Cres HG5 140 E1
Spellow Gr HG5 140 E1
Spen Brow LA2 128 E6
Spence Ct 4 TS9 8 A2
Spenceley Pl DL11 2 A2
Spencer Cl 5 BD20 187 F8
Spencer's Holt HG1 219 D7
Spencer St
29 Glusburn BD20 187 E7
3 York YO23 233 B1
Spencer's Way HG1 219 D7
Spencer Wlk BD23 217 C3
Spen Comon La LS24 188 F3
Speng La YO23 182 B4
Spen La YO1 233 C3
SPENNITHORNE 60 F3
Spennithorne CE Prim Sch
DL8 60 F4
Spey Bank YO24 230 C6
Spiker's Hill La YO13 74 F2
Spindle Cl YO24 230 C8
Spindle Mill BD23 216 F4
Spink La WF8 201 B1
Spinksburn La HG3 159 F1
Spinner La HG3 161 A8
Spinners Ct BD23 216 F4
Spinney The
Darlington DL3 3 B4
Draughton BD23 174 B7
6 Easingwold YO61 143 C8
Knaresborough HG5 221 C6
3 Scarborough YO12 212 B5
Tees-side Airport DL2 4 D4
York YO24 230 F7
Spinniker Dr 4 YO21 208 C5
Spire View 21 YO8 198 F1
Spital Bridge YO22 208 E5
Spitalcroft HG5 221 B4
Spital Farm Craft Ctr*
YO12 99 E2
Spital Field Ct 1 YO17 215 C4
Spitalfields TS15 5 D2
Spital Rd YO12 99 E3
Spital St YO17 215 B4
Spital The TS15 5 D3
Spitfire Ct DL10 41 F6
Spitfire Way LS25 196 B4
Spitlands La HG5 163 B7
Spittal Hardwick La
WF10 201 B3
Spittlerush La DN6 206 D2
SPOFFORTH 179 E5
Spofforth Castle* HG3 179 D6
Spofforth CE Prim Sch
HG3 179 E5
Spofforth Hill LS22 180 B3
Spofforth La
Follifoot HG3 223 F4
North Deighton LS22 180 A6
Spofforth Rd HG3 223 F4
Spoffoth La LS22 180 A7
Spout La LA2 102 B2
Spreight Lane Steps
YO11 213 B7
Springbank
Marton cum Grafton
YO51 141 E2
Swillington LS25 194 B3
Spring Bank YO12 212 E3
Springbank Ave YO19 184 E7
Spring Bank Cl HG4 214 C7
Spring Bank Mdw HG4 214 C7
Spring Bank Rd HG4 214 C7
Spring Cl
Garforth LS25 194 D4
Middlesbrough TS18 6 B8
12 Sleights YO22 32 A6
Spring Ct HG3 160 E6
Springfield
Bentham LA2 129 B8
Clifford LS23 188 E7
Follifoot HG3 223 F4
4 Scarborough YO11 213 B6
Skeeby DL10 21 A1
Stokesley TS9 26 C7
Springfield Ave
4 Earby BB18 172 B1
Harrogate HG1 219 C3
Ilkley LS29 218 C4
11 Pontefract WF8 201 C1
Springfield Cl
Barlby with Osgodby YO8 198 B5
20 Boroughbridge YO51 141 B5
Heworth YO31 229 C7
1 Leyburn DL8 60 D5
5 Pateley Bridge HG3 137 C4
Ripon HG4 214 B7
Thirsk YO7 211 B4
Springfield Cres
Bentham LA2 129 B8
3 Kirk Smeaton WF8 206 C3
Springfield Ct
7 Grassington BD23 134 E2
Sherburn in Elmet LS25 195 F5
Springfield Dr
9 Barlby YO8 198 B5
19 Boroughbridge YO51 141 B5
Springfield Garth YO17 215 D3
Springfield Gdns 1 TS9 26 C7
Springfield Gr
21 Boroughbridge YO51 141 B5
Kirklevington TS15 5 F1
Springfield La
3 Kirkbymoorside YO62 70 C1
Tockwith YO26 181 C7
Springfield Mews HG1 219 C3
Springfield Mount LS29 174 F5
Springfield Pl LS25 194 B3
Springfield Rd
18 Boroughbridge YO51 141 B5
Darlington DL1 3 E7
6 Grassington BD23 134 E2
4 Poppleton YO26 165 F1
Sherburn in Elmet LS25 195 F5
Springfield Rise 1 YO26 164 A8
Springfields
18 Knottingley WF11 202 A2
5 Skipton BD23 217 B4
Springfields Ave 17
WF11 202 A2
Springfield Terr YO17 124 D7
Springfield Way
4 Pateley Bridge HG3 137 C4
York YO31 229 B7
Spring Gdns 10 YO11 100 B6
Spring Gr
Harrogate HG1 219 C3
Laneshaw Bridge BB8 186 B3
Whitby YO21 208 D6
Spring Hall Garth YO17 215 A3
Springhead Sch YO12 212 E2
Spring Hill
Stonegrave YO62 93 C1
Welbury DL6 24 B1
Whitby YO21 208 D6
Springhill Cl YO12 212 E4
Springhill Ct 7 LS24 189 E6
Springhill La YO12 212 D3
Springhill Rd YO12 212 E4
Spring Hill Sch HG4 113 E4
Spring Hill Terr 10 YO21 208 D6
Spring La
Birdforth YO7 116 F8
Kirkby Overblow HG3 179 A2
Long Marston YO26 182 A5
Pannal HG3 222 C3
Wetherby LS22 180 E3
York YO10 229 A1
Springmead Dr LS25 194 C3
Springmount 3 BB18 172 B1
Spring Mount HG1 219 C3
Spring Rise BD23 174 B7
Springs La
Ellerton-on-Swale DL10 41 F4
Ilkley LS29 218 C4
Walton LS23 180 F3
Whashton DL11 20 B4
Spring St 2 YO61 143 C8
Springs Terr LS29 218 B4
Springs The 4 DL8 60 E2
Spring Terr DL7 210 C4
Spring Vale YO21 208 C6
Springwater Sch HG2 220 D4
Spring Way TS18 5 F8
Springwell Ave 11 LS26 194 A1
Springwell Cl 8 BD22 187 B6
Springwell Gdns 3 DL7 210 D4
Springwell La DL7 210 B4
Springwell Rd 10 LS26 194 A1
Springwell Terrace E 1
DL7 210 D4
Springwell Terrace W 2
DL7 210 D4
Spring Wlk YO8 232 A1
Springwood YO32 225 D7
Springwood Gr YO26 227 C6
Spring Wood Rd TS14 8 F6
SPROXTON 92 F4
Spruce Cl YO32 225 D2
Spruce Gill Ave 4 DL8 63 B3
Spruce Gill Dr 5 DL8 63 B3
Spruce Way YO8 232 E2
Spruisty Rd HG1 219 C4
Spurr Ct YO24 230 C8
Spurriergate YO1 233 B2
Square The
Boston Spa LS23 188 F8
Castleford WF10 201 B4
Ingleton LA6 103 D4
Kippax LS25 194 D1
Knottingley WF11 201 E3
Leeming DL7 63 F3
Sheriff Hutton YO60 145 D5
1 Tadcaster LS24 189 F6
Stabler Cl 15 YO32 166 D5
Stable Rd YO8 204 D7
Stablers Wlk
Earswick YO32 225 F7
13 Pontefract WF6 200 A2
Stables La LS23 188 F8
Stables The LS24 189 E2
STACKHOUSE 131 D4
Stackhouse La
Giggleswick BD24 131 D4
Lawkland BD24 130 F2
Stags Way DL10 41 F7
STAINBURN 177 F3
Stainburn Ave WF10 201 A3
Stainburn La LS21 177 E2
Staindale TS14 8 D6
Staindale Cl YO30 224 E2
Staindrop Dr TS5 6 E7
Staindrop Rd DL3 3 A6
Stained Glass Ctr* YO11 100 C5
STAINFORTH 131 E6
Stainforth Gdns TS17 6 B5
Stainforth La BD24 131 D5
Stainforth Rd BD24 131 E4
STAINSACRE 32 F7
Stainsacre La
Hawsker-cum-Stainsacre
YO22 32 F6
Whitby YO22 208 F3
Stainsacre Lane Ind Est
YO22 208 F3
Stainsby Rd TS5 6 D8
Stainthorpe Row DL7 64 F2
STAINTON
Marrick 39 C3
Middlesbrough 6 D5
STAINTONDALE 54 B5
Staintondale Shire Horse
Farm* YO13 54 C5
Stainton Rd TS9 6 F1
Stainton Way
Coulby Newham TS8 7 A5
Stainton & Thornton TS8 6 E5
STAITHES 13 J2
Staithes Cl 4 YO26 227 B4
Staithes Gall* TS13 13 K2
Staithes La TS13 13 K2
Staithe St 3 YO8 199 D7
Stake Rd DL8 57 C1
Stakesby Com Prim Sch
YO21 208 B6
Stakesby Rd YO21 208 B6
Stakesby Vale YO21 208 C6
Stakesby Vale Ct YO21 208 B5
STALLING BUSK 81 B8
STAMFORD BRIDGE 168 E2
Stamford Bridge Prim Sch
YO41 168 D2
Stamford Bridge Rd
YO19 184 E7
Stamford Bridge W YO41 168 C2
Stamford Street E 10
YO26 227 F5
Stamford Street W 8
YO26 227 F5
Stammergate YO7 211 C3
Stammergate La LS22 180 A1
Stamp Hill Cl 7 LS29 174 E4
Standard Ct DL7 210 B6
Standard Way DL6 210 B6
Standard Way Ind Est
DL6 210 C6
Standridge Clough La
BB18 172 B1
Standroyd Dr BB8 186 A3
Standroyd Rd BB8 186 A3
Stanghow Rd TS12 9 F8
Stang La
Arkengarthdale DL11 17 E3
Farnham HG5 162 C7
Hope DL11 18 A8
Stangs La BD23 157 D6
Stang Top
Arkengarthdale DL11 17 F5
Hope DL11 18 A6
Stanhope Dr HG2 220 B2
Stanhope Gr TS5 6 E8
Stanhope Road N DL3 3 C5
Staniland Dr YO8 232 A5
Stanley Ave YO32 225 D7

Stanley Cl
4 Catterick Garrison DL9 . 40 E3
22 Eastfield YO11 . 100 B6
Stanley Gr
Aske DL10 . 20 D1
Great Ayton TS9 . 7 F1
Richmond DL10 . 209 D8
Stanley St
Castleford WF10 . 200 F4
4 Scarborough YO12 . 213 A7
York YO31 . 233 C4
Stansfield Brow BD20 . 187 A8
Stansfield Cl WF10 . 201 A4
Stansfield Dr WF10 . 201 B4
Stansfield Rd WF10 . 201 A4
Stanstead Way TS17 . 6 C7
Stansted Gr DL2 . 4 D4
Stan Valley 2 WF8 . 206 C3
STANWICK-ST-JOHN . 1 E2
Stanyforth Cres YO26 . 164 C2
STAPE . 71 F8
Stape Rd YO18 . 71 F7
STAPLETON . 3 A2
Stapleton Bank DL2 . 3 A2
Stapleton Cl
3 Bedale DL8 . 63 B2
11 Seamer YO12 . 99 D6
Stapley La DL8 . 87 F4
STARBECK . 220 C4
Starbeck Baths HG2 . 220 D3
Starbeck Cl 4 YO21 . 208 B5
Starbeck Com Prim Sch HG2 . 220 D4
Starbeck Sta HG2 . 220 C4
STARBOTTON . 107 F5
Star Carr La YO12 . 99 E4
Star Carr Rd YO11 . 100 B5
Starfits La
Fadmoor YO62 . 69 F3
Welburn YO62 . 94 A8
Stark Bank Rd HG4 . 85 C7
Starkey Cres YO31 . 229 A5
Starkey La 5 BD20 . 173 F1
Starmire BD22 . 187 A6
Starra Field La YO26 . 163 F5
Star Sh Prec DL6 . 210 E4
Station Ave
20 Filey YO14 . 101 B3
Harrogate HG1 . 219 E2
New Earswick YO32 . 225 D3
Whitby YO21 . 208 B7
York YO1 . 233 A2
Station Bridge HG1 . 219 D2
Station Bsns Pk YO26 . 227 F4
Station Cl
Dacre HG3 . 159 F8
6 East Ayton/West Ayton YO13 . 99 A7
Hambleton YO8 . 196 F2
Sharow HG4 . 214 D7
Station Ct
8 Spofforth HG5 . 179 E5
7 Tollerton YO61 . 143 B3
Station Dr HG4 . 214 D7
Station Fields LS25 . 194 C4
Station Gr 19 BD20 . 187 E8
Station La
Barmby on the Marsh DN14 . 205 B7
Burton Leonard HG3 . 139 F3
Cliffe YO8 . 198 E3
Cloughton YO13 . 54 D1
Gristhorpe YO14 . 100 E4
Hampsthwaite HG3 . 161 A6
Morton-on-Swale DL7 . 64 A7
Shipton YO30 . 165 E5
Station Par HG1 . 219 D2
Station Plaza* LS29 . 218 B3
Station Rd
Ampleforth YO62 . 92 C1
Beadlam YO62 . 93 D7
Brompton DL6 . 43 F3
Brompton-on-Swale DL10 . 41 B6
Burley in Warfedale LS29 . 176 C1
Carlton DN14 . 204 C3
Castleford WF10 . 200 E4
Cayton YO11 . 100 B5
Church Fenton LS24 . 196 B7
Clapham LA2 . 130 C7
Copmanthorpe YO23 . 230 B2
Danby YO21 . 29 A7
Eaglescliffe TS16 . 5 E6
Fylingdales YO22 . 33 C4
Gainford DL2 . 1 C8
Gilling East YO62 . 118 F8
Glusburn BD20 . 187 E8
Goldsborough HG5 . 163 A3
Great Ayton TS9 . 8 A1
Great Preston WF10 . 200 E6
Hambleton YO8 . 196 F1
Haxby YO32 . 166 F5
Hellifield BD23 . 154 B4
Helmsley YO62 . 92 F6
Hensall DN14 . 203 C1
Heslerton YO17 . 97 D1
High Bentham LA2 . 129 A8
Hinderwell TS13 . 11 F7
Horton in Ribblesdale BD24 . 105 C3
Ilkley LS29 . 218 B4
Kildale YO21 . 27 E8
Kippax LS25 . 200 C8
Kirk Hammerton YO26 . 164 D2
9 Knaresborough HG5 . 221 A6
Long Preston BD23 . 153 F4

Station Rd *continued*
Menwith with Darley HG3 160 A6
Mickletown LS26 . 200 A6
Middleton St George DL2 . 4 C5
Normanton WF6 . 200 A2
Norton DN6 . 206 F2
Nunnington YO62 . 93 E2
Pannal HG3 . 222 E2
24 Poppleton YO26 . 165 F1
Rawcliffe DN14 . 205 A1
Riccall YO19 . 198 A8
Richmond DL10 . 209 C7
Scalby YO13 . 75 D5
Scruton DL7 . 63 E6
Selby YO8 . 232 D5
Settle BD24 . 131 C2
Sleights YO22 . 32 A6
Snainton YO13 . 97 F4
South Otterington DL7 . 64 F2
Sowerby YO7 . 211 A2
Stainton Dale YO13 . 54 A8
Stokesley TS9 . 26 C7
Tadcaster LS24 . 189 D6
Thirsk YO7 . 89 D4
Threshfield BD23 . 134 D2
Tollerton YO61 . 143 B3
Wharram YO17 . 148 F4
Wharram YO17 . 149 A4
Whixley YO26 . 164 A3
Wistow YO8 . 197 C6
Womersley DN6 . 206 D5
Wood Row LS26 . 200 B6
York YO24 . 233 A2
Station Rise
8 Riccall YO19 . 198 A8
York YO1 . 233 A2
Station Road Ind Est
Brompton DL6 . 43 F3
Great Preston LS25 . 200 C8
Station Sq
4 Strensall YO32 . 167 B7
4 Whitby YO21 . 208 D6
Station Square
Harrogate HG1 . 219 D2
Ravenscar YO13 . 54 A8
Station Terr
4 Boroughbridge YO51 . 141 B6
Great Preston WF10 . 200 E6
Station View
Cliffe YO8 . 198 D3
Hambleton YO8 . 196 F2
2 Harrogate HG2 . 220 C3
Seamer YO12 . 99 E7
8 Skipton BD23 . 216 D3
Station Way YO17 . 215 C3
STAUPES . 160 C4
Staupes Rd HG3 . 160 B4
STAVELEY . 140 F1
Staveley Com Prim Sch HG5 . 140 E1
Staveley Nature Reserve* HG5 . 140 E2
STAXTON . 99 E2
Staxton Carr La YO12 . 99 D3
Staxton Hill YO12 . 125 C8
Staynor Ave YO8 . 232 E3
STEAD . 176 A1
Stead La LS14 . 188 A3
STEAN . 110 A4
Stean La HG3 . 110 A4
STEARSBY . 118 F2
Steelmoor La YO60 . 146 C2
Steeple Cl 4 YO32 . 166 D5
Steeton La LS24 . 190 D7
Steeton Way LS25 . 195 E2
Steincroft Rd 7 LS25 . 195 F2
Stella Gdns 10 WF8 . 201 C1
Stelling Rd DL11 . 38 E7
Stephen Bank DL11 . 18 H8
Stephen Joseph Theatre* YO11 . 212 F5
Stephenson Cl
Knaresborough HG5 . 221 B4
York YO31 . 225 E1
Stephenson Rd 2 DL10 . 41 C7
Stephenson's La YO26 . 164 A2
Stephensons Way LS29 . 218 C4
Stephenson Way YO26 . 227 F5
Stephen's Wlk YO8 . 232 B1
Stephenwath La YO41 . 169 C5
Stepin Turn YO62 . 49 B1
Stepney Ave YO12 . 212 D4
Stepney Cl YO12 . 212 C5
Stepney Dr YO12 . 212 C5
Stepney Gr YO12 . 212 C5
Stepney Hill YO12 . 212 B4
Stepney Rd YO12 . 212 D4
Stepney Rise YO12 . 212 D5
Steps The LS22 . 180 C2
Sterling Chase HG5 . 221 C7
Sterling Pk YO30 . 225 A3
Sterne Ave YO31 . 229 A5
Sterne Way YO61 . 144 C3
Stevenson Pl HG5 . 220 F5
Stevenson View YO7 . 114 F6
Steven Way HG4 . 214 B6
Steward Cl YO8 . 197 D1
Stewart Ct TS9 . 46 F6
Stewart La YO19 . 191 C4
STILLINGFLEET . 191 C3
STILLINGTON . 144 C6
Stillington Prim Sch YO61 . 144 C7
Stillington Rd
Easingwold YO61 . 143 D8
Huby YO61 . 144 A4
Stinton La
Boroughbridge YO51 . 141 C4

Stinton La *continued*
Helperby YO61 . 142 A8
Stirling Gr YO10 . 231 F8
Stirling Rd
Burley in Warfedale LS29 . 176 B1
York YO30 . 224 F3
Stirling Way TS17 . 6 B6
Stirrup Cl
Norton YO17 . 215 E2
York YO24 . 230 B8
STIRTON . 216 C6
Stirtonber BD23 . 216 E5
Stirton La BD23 . 216 C5
Stittenham Hill YO60 . 146 A6
Stobarts La TS15 . 5 B1
STOCK . 171 C3
Stockdale Cl 9 HG5 . 221 B5
Stockdale Ct DL6 . 210 F3
Stockdale La
12 Eastfield YO11 . 99 F6
Settle BD24 . 131 F2
Stockdale Wlk HG5 . 221 B5
Stockeld La LS22 . 179 E3
Stockeld Park House* LS22 . 179 F4
Stockeld Rd LS29 . 218 A4
Stockeld Way LS29 . 218 A5
Stockfield La YO51 . 141 D2
Stockhill Cl 1 YO19 . 184 E7
Stockholm Cl 1 YO10 . 231 D8
Stockinger La LS29 . 174 F4
Stocking Hill TS9 . 25 E2
Stocking La
Hambleton YO8 . 196 E1
Hillam LS25 . 202 B7
Knottingley WF11 . 202 B2
Lotherton cum Aberford LS25 . 195 A7
Stockings La YO62 . 92 F2
Stocks Cl YO17 . 215 F4
Stockshill YO12 . 99 D6
Stockshott La BD20 . 173 C2
Stocks La 1 HG3 . 160 A6
Stock Stile La HG3 . 160 D5
Stockton Hall Hospl YO32 . 167 D3
Stockton La
Heworth YO32 . 226 D1
York YO31 . 229 A7
STOCKTON ON THE FOREST . 167 D3
Stockton on the Forest Prim Sch YO32 . 167 D3
Stockton Rd
Darlington DL1 . 3 F7
Sadberge DL2 . 4 C7
South Kilvington YO7 . 211 B6
Stockwell Ave
Ingleby TS17 . 6 B5
Knaresborough HG5 . 221 B7
Stockwell Cres 5 HG5 . 221 B7
Stockwell Ct 9 HG5 . 221 B6
Stockwell Dr HG5 . 221 B7
Stockwell Gr HG5 . 221 B7
Stockwell La HG5 . 221 B6
Stockwell Pl HG5 . 221 B7
Stockwell Rd HG5 . 221 B6
Stockwell View HG5 . 221 B7
Stockwith La DN14 . 204 A4
Stokelake Rd 5 HG1 . 219 E3
STOKESLEY . 26 D7
Stokesley Com Prim Sch TS9 . 26 C7
Stokesley Ind Pk TS9 . 26 D6
Stokesley L Ctr TS9 . 26 D7
Stokesley Rd
Brompton DL6 . 44 A3
Coulby Newham TS7 . 7 B7
Guisborough TS14 . 8 C6
Middlesbrough TS7 . 7 B6
Northallerton DL6 . 210 E7
Stokesley Sch TS9 . 26 D7
Stonebeck Ave HG1 . 219 B4
Stonebeck Gate La YO21 . 29 D4
Stonebow The
Thornton-le-Beans DL6 . 65 B5
York YO1 . 233 C2
Stone Bramble 22 HG3 . 161 B3
Stonebridge Cres 2 TS17 . 6 D6
Stone Bridge Dr YO41 . 185 F5
Stonebridgegate HG4 . 214 D5
Stonecrop Ave 5 HG3 . 161 B3
Stonecrop Dr 1 HG3 . 161 B3
Stone Crop Dr 14 WF10 . 200 D3
Stone Cross Ct YO61 . 117 C1
Stonecross Rd YO21 . 208 A6
Stone Ct 6 YO13 . 75 D5
Stone Dale YO42 . 170 D3
Stoned Horse La YO26 . 164 C4
Stonefall Ave HG2 . 220 C3
Stonefall Dr HG2 . 220 B2
Stonefall Mews HG2 . 220 C3
Stonefall Pl 2 HG2 . 220 B2
Stonefield Ave YO61 . 143 C8
Stonefield Garth 9 YO61 . 143 C8
Stonefield La 4 YO61 . 143 C8
Stone Garth 3 YO62 . 92 F6
STONEGATE . 30 D8
Stonegate
Hunmanby YO14 . 126 F8
York YO1 . 233 B3
Stone Gate YO26 . 164 A4
STONEGRAVE . 119 D8
Stonehaven Way DL1 . 3 F8
Stone Head La BD22 . 186 E6
STONE HOUSE . 78 F8
Stonelands Cl YO60 . 145 D5

Stonelands Ct 2 YO30 . 225 A1
Stoneleigh Gate YO26 . 164 B3
Stone Man La DL11 . 19 C5
Stonepit Balk YO17 . 149 C5
Stonepit Hill YO17 . 149 C4
Stonepit La
Birdsall YO17 . 148 D6
Gristhorpe YO14 . 100 E5
Stone Quarry Rd YO13 . 75 C8
Stone Riggs YO32 . 167 D2
Stone Rings Cl HG2 . 222 E5
Stone Rings Grange HG2 222 E5
Stone Rings La HG2 . 222 E5
Stones Cl YO24 . 227 E2
Stonesdale Cl 3 HG5 . 221 D5
Stonesdale La DL11 . 35 E8
Stone Stoup Hill TS9 . 27 C5
Stonethwaite 1 YO24 . 230 C7
Stonewall Cottage La 25 YO41 . 168 D2
Stoney Bank Rd BB18 . 172 B1
Stoneyborough Cl YO7 . 211 C4
Stoneybrough La YO7 . 211 C4
Stoney Haggs Rd YO12 . 99 E7
Stony Cross YO62 . 93 E7
Stony Ct 5 YO13 . 75 D5
Stonygate Bank DL11 . 20 A5
Stony La
East Harlsey DL6 . 44 F5
8 Scalby YO13 . 75 D5
Stoop Cl YO32 . 225 C8
Stooperdale Ave DL3 . 3 B7
Stoopes Hill 8 BB18 . 172 B1
Storey Cl 26 YO62 . 92 F6
Storiths La BD23 . 175 A8
Storking La YO41 . 185 F6
Storr La YO13 . 74 E5
Storth Gill La BD24 . 131 A1
Stourton Rd LS29 . 175 C3
Stow Ct YO32 . 225 E3
Strafford Rd 14 DL10 . 41 E4
Straight La
Addingham LS29 . 174 E3
Aldwark YO61 . 142 C3
Burton Leonard HG3 . 140 A3
Holtby YO19 . 184 F8
Middleham DL8 . 60 F2
Straights The DL8 . 58 C4
Strait La
Copt Hewick HG4 . 114 B2
Danby YO21 . 29 C6
Hurworth DL2 . 3 F1
Stainton & Thornton TS8 . 6 D5
Weeton LS17 . 178 B2
Well DL8 . 87 A3
Straits La YO13 . 99 A3
STRANGHOW . 9 F6
Stranglands La WF11 . 201 C3
Stranton St TS17 . 6 B8
Stratford Way YO32 . 225 E3
Strathmore Dr 9 TS15 . 24 E8
Strathmore Rd LS29 . 218 E4
Strawberrry Fileds Prim Sch LS25 . 194 C3
Strawberry Ct YO12 . 212 D4
Strawberry Dale HG1 . 219 D3
Strawberry Dale Ave 3 HG1 . 219 D3
Strawberry Dale Sq 1 HG1 . 219 D3
Strawberry Dale Terr 2 HG1 . 219 D3
Straw Gate DL2 . 3 A2
Strawgate Gr DL2 . 3 A3
Stray Garth YO31 . 228 F7
Straylands Gr YO31 . 228 F8
Stray Rd
Harrogate HG2 . 222 D8
York YO31 . 229 B6
Stray Rein HG2 . 219 E1
Stray The
Darlington DL1 . 3 E5
Henderskelfe YO60 . 146 D8
Longnewton TS21 . 5 A7
Stray Wlk HG2 . 222 E8
STREET . 29 F3
Street 1 LS23 . 189 A8
Street 2 LS23 . 181 A1
Street 3 LS23 . 181 A1
Street 5 LS23 . 181 A1
Street 6 LS23 . 181 A2
Street 7 LS23 . 181 B1
Street 8 LS23 . 181 B1
Street Head La BD22 . 187 F1
STREET HOUSES . 190 C8
Street La
Bewerley HG3 . 137 B4
Bubwith DN14 . 199 F5
Colton LS24 . 190 D7
Glaisdale YO21 . 29 E3
Middleton YO18 . 95 E7
Pickhill with Roxby YO7 . 88 B6
STREETLAM . 42 F5
Street The 8 LS29 . 174 E4
STRENSALL . 167 A7
STRENSALL CAMP . 167 B6
Strensall Comm Nature Reserve* YO60 . 167 D8
Strensall Dr 11 YO12 . 75 F5
Strensall Pk YO32 . 167 A5
Strensall Rd
Earswick YO32 . 226 A7
York YO32 . 225 F6
Stretton Cl WF7 . 200 D1
Strickland Rd 13 YO14 . 127 A8
Strikes La BD20 . 187 F6
Stripe La
Greenhow HG3 . 136 C3

Stripe La *continued*
Hartwith cum Winsley HG3 160 B8
Skelton YO30 . 224 B5
Stripe The 6 TS9 . 26 C7
Stuart Ave DL10 . 209 C8
Stuart Cl
4 Scarborough YO11 . 100 B7
4 Strensall YO32 . 167 C8
Stuart Gr
Eggborough DN14 . 203 A2
1 Pontefract WF6 . 200 A2
9 Thorpe Willoughby YO8 . 197 B1
Stuart Rd YO24 . 227 D1
Stuart St
10 Barnoldswick BB18 . 171 E1
Pontefract WF8 . 201 B1
Stubbing La BD23 . 81 B1
Stubbing Nook La DL8 . 62 B2
Stubbs La
Cridling Stubbs WF11 . 206 A8
Norton DN6 . 206 E2
Stainton Dale YO13 . 53 F5
Stubbs Rd WF8 . 206 D3
Stubden Gr YO30 . 224 F2
Stubham Rise LS29 . 218 A5
Studdah Cl DL8 . 60 D7
STUDFOLD . 105 D1
Stud Fold Bank HG3 . 110 B3
Studford Ring* YO62 . 92 C2
Studley Cl DL7 . 210 B2
Studley La HG4 . 113 C1
Studley Rd
Harrogate HG1 . 219 D3
Ripon HG4 . 214 A4
Studley Roger HG4 . 113 D1
STUDLEY ROGER . 113 D1
STUDLEY ROYAL . 113 C1
Studley Terr 15 YO22 . 208 E6
Stump Cross TS14 . 8 E6
Stump Cross Caverns* HG3 . 136 A2
Stumpcross Ct 14 WF8 . 201 C2
Stumpcross La WF8 . 201 C2
Stumpcross Mdws WF8 . 201 D1
Stumpcross Way 15 WF8 201 C2
Stumps La HG3 . 160 A5
Stunstead Rd BB8 . 186 B2
Sturdee Gr YO31 . 228 D7
Sturdy House La
Marske DL11 . 19 E2
Whashton DL11 . 20 A4
Sturton Grange La LS25 . 194 D4
Sturton La LS25 . 194 D4
Stuteville Cl 4 YO62 . 70 C1
STUTTON . 189 D4
Stutton Rd LS24 . 189 D4
Stygate La DN6 . 206 E1
Sudforth La DN14 . 202 C3
SUFFIELD . 75 A5
Suffield Hill YO13 . 75 A5
Sugar Hill 9 LS29 . 174 F4
Sugar Loaf Ct 13 TS17 . 5 F4
Sumitt Pk WF10 . 200 F2
SUMMERBRIDGE . 138 A1
Summerbridge Com Prim Sch HG3 . 138 A1
Summerfield BD23 . 172 A3
Summerfield Cl 1 WF11 201 F4
Summerfield Dr WF11 . 201 F4
Summerfield La YO22 . 33 A7
Summerfield Rd YO24 . 230 C7
Summer Gdns YO30 . 227 F8
Summerhill Rd LS26 . 200 B6
Summer Hill Rd LS26 . 200 B6
SUMMERSCALES . 158 C1
Summers Fold 1 BD23 . 134 E3
Summer Way 57 YO14 . 101 B3
Sunderland Rd BD20 . 173 E3
Sundew Heath 24 HG3 . 161 B3
Sun Gdns TS17 . 6 A8
Sun La LS29 . 176 C1
Sunmoor Dr BD23 . 217 A4
Sunningdale LS25 . 194 F4
Sunningdale Cl
Knapton YO26 . 227 B5
1 York YO26 . 227 B5
Sunningdale Dr TS16 . 5 E5
Sunningdale Gr 1 YO21 . 208 B5
Sunningdales 27 WF6 . 200 B1
Sunnybank LS25 . 195 A3
Sunny Bank 3 WF11 . 202 A2
Sunnybank Rd LS25 . 195 A3
Sunny Bank Rd 6 BD20 . 187 E7
Sunnycrest Ave DL10 . 209 D8
Sunnydale 3 YO32 . 225 D7
Sunnyfield TS9 . 7 F1
Sunnyside
Coulby Newham TS8 . 7 D5
23 Wigginton YO32 . 166 D5
Sunnyside Acad TS8 . 7 A6
Sunny Way YO7 . 211 B4
Sunrise Dr YO14 . 127 C8
Sunset Dr LS29 . 218 D5
Sunset Terr LS29 . 218 E5
Sun St
Cononley BD20 . 173 C1
4 Cowling BD22 . 187 B6
Thornaby TS17 . 6 A8
Sunstar Gr TS7 . 7 B6
Sur Gate YO13 . 74 F8
Surrey Way YO30 . 227 F8
Surtees St
Darlington DL3 . 3 C6
York YO30 . 228 B7
Suskers Cl 26 YO61 . 143 C8
Sussex Cl
Bedale DL8 . 63 A2
York YO10 . 229 C2

Sussex Ct
10 Catterick Garrison DL9 209 C1
Thirsk YO7 211 D2
Sussex Rd YO10 229 C2
Sussex St
Bedale DL8 63 A2
14 Scarborough YO11 213 A6
Sussex Way 14 YO32 167 A7
Sutcliffe Ct 6 YO21 208 B6
Sutcliffe Gall★ YO21 208 D7
Sutherland Rd YO18 71 C6
Sutherland St YO23 228 B1
Sutor Cl YO23 230 B3
SUTTON 201 F4
Sutton Ave 7 DL9 41 A5
Sutton Bank YO7 91 A5
Sutton Bank Visitor Ctr★ YO7 91 B6
Sutton Bridge★ YO41 185 C2
Sutton Ct 5 YO7 211 C3
Sutton Dr DL7 210 C2
Sutton Grange Cl HG3 219 B4
SUTTON HOWGRAVE 87 F1
SUTTON-IN-CRAVEN 187 F6
Sutton in Craven CE Prim Sch 39 BD20 187 E7
Sutton in Craven Com Prim Sch 38 BD20 187 E7
Sutton La
Byram cum Sutton WF11 202 A4
Byram WF11 201 E4
Ellington High & Low HG4 86 A5
Fearby HG4 85 F4
Steeton with Eastburn BD20 187 F7
SUTTON-ON-THE-FOREST 144 C3
Sutton on the Forest CE VC Prim Sch YO61 144 C3
Sutton Pk★ YO61 144 C3
Sutton Pk 7 YO41 185 C2
Sutton Rd
Bagby YO7 211 E3
Huby YO61 144 A4
Wigginton YO32 166 D7
Sutton St YO17 215 D3
SUTTON-UNDER-WHITESTONECLIFFE 90 E5
SUTTON UPON DERWENT 185 C1
Sutton Upon Derwent CE VC Prim Sch YO41 185 C2
Sutton Way
Middlesbrough TS4 6 F8
York YO30 228 B8
Swadford St BD23 216 F4
SWAINBY 45 E8
Swainby Abbey★ DL8 88 B8
Swainby Ellers DL6 25 D1
Swainby La DL8 88 A8
Swainby & Potto CE Prim Sch DL6 45 D8
Swain Ct
Middleton St George DL2 4 D4
Northallerton DL6 210 D5
Swainsea Dr 8 YO18 95 F7
Swainsea La YO18 95 F8
Swainstead Raike BD24 153 B8
Swainston Cl TS5 6 E7
Swale App 25 WF6 200 B1
Swale Ave YO24 230 E8
SWALEDALE 37 C4
Swaledale Ave DL3 3 B6
Swaledale Mus★ DL11 38 C6
Swaledale Rd 22 DL9 40 E4
Swalegate DL10 209 C8
Swale Gr DL1 3 C3
Swale Hall La DL11 38 B5
Swale La DL10 41 E5
Swale Pasture La DL10 41 E5
Swale View YO7 115 B6
Swallow Cl
Firth Moor DL1 3 F4
Guisborough TS14 8 D6
Swan Cl YO19 192 A7
Swan Farm Ct YO19 192 A7
Swang Rd YO13 75 A6
Swan Hill Rd YO11 213 A6
Swanhills La YO13 98 F3
Swan La YO7 65 F2
Swanland Rd YO62 92 F7
Swanlow Dr 13 YO32 191 C7
Swann St YO23 233 A1
Swan Rd
Harrogate HG1 219 C2
20 South Milford LS25 195 F2
Swan St BD23 173 B4
Swans Way YO8 232 E3
Swan Syke Dr 8 DN6 206 F2
Swarcliffe Rd HG1 220 B4
SWARTHA 174 D1
Swartha La BD20 174 D2
Swarthlands La YO13 75 D7
SWATHGILL 119 B4
Sweeming La LS25 196 C5
Sweetbecks Cl 12 YO11 100 A6
Sweet Bits La HG5 221 C8
Sweet Briar HG3 219 A4
SWETTON 111 F4
SWILLINGTON 194 A1
SWILLINGTON COMMON 194 A3
Swillington La LS26 194 A2
Swillington Prim Sch LS26 194 A1
Swinburn Ct 12 HG4 86 C3
Swinburne Cl HG1 219 E7
Swinburne Rd TS16 5 E6
Swinburn Rd 11 HG4 86 C3
SWINCLIFFE 160 E4
Swincliffe La HG3 160 D5
Swindale La TS12 9 F5
SWINDEN 154 C1
Swindon La HG3 178 E4
Swinegate YO1 233 B2
Swinegate Court E YO1 233 B3
Swineherd La YO62 70 C1
SWINITHWAITE 59 C4
Swinneybeck Bank HG4 85 E5
Swinsty Ct YO30 224 F1
SWINTON
Malton 121 C4
Masham 86 B2
Swinton Cl 8 YO30 224 E2
Swinton Ct HG2 222 B8
Swinton La YO17 121 B3
Swinton Rd
Masham HG4 86 C3
Swinton HG4 86 B2
Swinton Terr HG4 86 C3
Swires La BD20 173 C3
Swire Way DL10 20 F7
Swordfish Way LS25 196 B4
Sycamore Ave
4 Catton YO7 89 A1
19 Filey YO14 101 B4
1 Hut Green DN14 203 A2
Kippax LS25 194 C1
Knottingley WF11 201 E1
Malton YO17 215 D5
Richmond DL10 209 A8
York YO32 225 D4
Sycamore Bsns Pk HG4 114 D3
Sycamore Cl
Bishop Monkton HG3 140 A5
Clint HG3 160 F8
1 Haxby YO32 225 D7
3 Hurworth-on-Tees DL2 3 E1
Selby YO8 232 A4
Skelton YO30 224 C5
Slingsby YO62 120 B5
Spennithorne DL8 60 F4
Sycamore Ct
2 Catterick DL10 41 D5
Hellifield BD23 154 B3
2 Pontefract WF8 201 C1
Thornton in Craven BD23 172 A3
Sycamore Dr
11 Addingham LS29 175 A4
9 Bedale DL8 63 A2
Harrogate HG2 220 C3
Norton-le-Clay YO7 115 B1
THIRSK YO7 89 E3
Sycamore Gr
Sherburn YO17 124 E7
Steeton with Eastburn BD20 187 F7
Sycamore La DL7 63 D4
Sycamore Mews YO8 232 D2
Sycamore Pk YO12 212 B7
Sycamore Pl
New Earswick YO32 225 D4
York YO30 233 A3
Sycamore Rd
Barlby with Osgodby YO8 198 B5
Ripon HG4 214 B2
Sycamores The
Barwick in Elmet LS15 194 B8
42 Earby BB18 172 A1
Sycamore Terr YO30 233 A3
Sycamore View 17 YO26 165 F1
Sycamore Way 16 BB18 171 D1
Sydall's Way 1 DL10 41 E4
Sydney Avenue E DL6 210 E4
Sydney St 5 YO12 212 F7
Sykehead La YO62 93 D6
Sykes Cl YO19 193 A7
Sykes Gr HG1 219 C5
Sykes La YO61 143 B3

T

Tabard Hamlet 5 DN14 202 F2
Tabard Rd 6 DN14 202 F2
Tabards The 7 DN14 202 F2
TADCASTER 189 D6
Tadcaster East Prim Sch 6 LS24 189 F6
Tadcaster Gram Sch LS24 189 B5
Tadcaster L Ctr LS24 189 E6
Tadcaster Rd
Copmanthorpe YO23 230 C4
York YO24 227 F1
Tadcaster Rd Dringhouses YO23 230 E5
Tadcaster Swimming Pool LS24 189 E6
Talbenny Gr 32 TS17 5 F4
Talbot Ct YO22 208 E5
Talbot St WF6 200 A1
Talisker Wlk YO14 127 C8
Talisman Cl 9 TS16 5 D5
Tally Hill YO61 144 A4
Talybont Gr 19 TS17 5 F4
TAME BRIDGE 26 A7
Tameside TS9 26 C8
Tamworth Rd 9 YO30 225 A1
Tanfield Dr 1 LS29 176 C1
Tanfield La HG4 114 A8
TANG 160 D4
TANG HALL 228 F5
Tang Hall La YO31 229 A5
Tang Hall Prim Sch YO31 228 F5
Tang Rd HG3 160 D4
Tanner Row YO1 233 A2
Tanner's Moat YO1 233 A2
Tanner St YO1 233 B2
Tannery Ct 10 HG5 221 B5
Tannery La
Embsay BD23 217 D8
Northallerton DL7 210 D5
Tannery The 10 YO10 228 E3
Tanpit La
Easingwold YO61 143 C8
Walden Stubbs DN6 206 E3
Tansy Cl 2 HG3 161 B3
Tansy Rd 3 HG3 161 B3
TANTON 7 C1
Tanton Cl TS9 7 A1
Tanton Rd TS9 7 B1
Tarbard Ave 14 HG4 113 D2
Tarbert Cres 2 YO24 230 B7
Tarell Ct 45 TS17 5 F4
Tarn Ct LS29 218 C3
Tarn Moor Cres BD23 216 E6
Tarns La BD23 134 C1
Tarr Steps TS17 6 A3
Tasmania Sq TS7 7 C6
Tate Cl YO8 197 D6
Tatefield Pl 1 LS25 194 D1
Tate Hill YO22 208 E7
Tate Rd DL10 209 C8
Tatham Fells CE Prim Sch LA2 128 F3
Tatton Cl YO30 225 A1
Taurus Ct YO23 233 A1
Taylor Gr LS26 200 C6
Taylor Hill YO18 71 F7
Taylor La LS15 194 A7
Taylorsons Terr 2 YO22 208 E6
Taylor St 8 BB18 171 D1
Taylor Way YO11 99 F5
Teachers Cl YO24 230 F6
Teal Cl
Castleford WF10 200 E3
2 Filey YO14 101 A3
Teal Dr YO24 230 C8
Teal La 6 YO18 95 F7
Teal Rd DL1 3 E5
Teapottery The★ DL8 60 E5
Teasel Gr 31 HG3 161 B3
Tebay Cl
2 Eastbourne DL1 3 D4
Middlesbrough TS7 7 D8
Tedder Ave TS17 6 B6
Tedder Rd YO24 227 B1
Tedworth Cl TS14 8 F5
Tees Bank Ave TS18 5 E6
Tees Cottage Pumping Sta★ DL2 2 F4
Teesdale Ave DL3 3 A4
Teesdale Rd DL9 40 E4
Teesdale Terr 27 DL9 40 E4
Teesgate TS17 6 C8
Tees Grange Ave DL3 3 A5
Tees-Side Airport Sta DL2 4 F4
Teesside High Sch TS16 5 E5
Teesside Ind Est TS17 6 C5
Tees View
Gainford DL2 1 D7
Hurworth DL2 3 C1
Hurworth-on-Tees DL2 22 C8
Teeswater Dr 12 DL2 3 A7
Teesway DL2 4 A1
Telford Cl WF10 200 D4
Telford Terr 1 YO24 228 B2
Temperance Sq BD23 154 B3
Templar Cl DN14 202 F1
Templar Gdns LS22 180 C4
Templar Way YO8 232 C2
Temple Ave YO10 229 B4
Temple Bank DL8 59 A3
Temple Ct DL10 209 B6
Temple Garth YO23 230 C1
TEMPLE HIRST 203 E4
Temple La
Burton cum Walden DL8 82 D3
Copmanthorpe YO23 230 C1
Templemead YO31 228 E8
Temple Rd YO23 230 F4
Temple Sq DL10 209 B6
Temple St WF10 200 E4
Tems Side 3 BD24 131 D2
Tems St 2 BD24 131 D2
Tennant St YO8 232 B6
Tennent Rd YO24 227 B2
Tennis Court La YO61 143 A3
Tennyson Ave
1 Campsall DN6 206 E1
Harrogate HG1 219 E7
Scarborough YO12 212 F7
York YO30 228 C7
Tennyson Cl WF8 201 D2
Tennyson Way 3 WF8 201 B1
Tenter Fields YO7 88 D1
Tentergate Ave 4 HG5 221 A7
Tentergate Cl 3 HG5 221 A7
Tentergate Gdns 2 HG5 221 A7
Tentergate La HG5 221 A7
Tentergate Rd 5 HG5 221 A7
Tenter Hill LS23 188 D5
Tenters Cl WF11 201 E3
Ten Thorn La YO26 227 A4
Tern Pk 6 LS22 180 A1
TERRINGTON 119 F1
Terrington Bank YO60 119 C2
Terrington CE Prim Sch YO60 119 E1
Terrington Cl YO32 167 B8
Terrington Hall Sch YO60 119 F1
Terrington South Bank YO60 119 D1
Terrington View YO60 145 C5
Terror Twr★ YO11 213 B6
Terry Ave YO1 233 B1
Terry Dicken Ind Est TS9 26 D6
Terry St YO23 228 C1
Tetherings La YO13 98 F5
Tewit Well Ave HG2 222 D8
Tewit Well Rd HG2 222 E7
Thackadale La YO17 121 A1
Thackeray Gr TS5 6 E8
Thacking La LA6 103 D4
Thames Ave
Guisborough TS14 8 E6
Thornaby TS17 6 B7
Thanet Rd YO24 227 D1
Thanets Ct 9 BD23 216 F3
Thatch Cl
Selby YO8 232 C4
22 South Milford LS25 195 F2
Thatchers Croft YO23 230 C3
Thatch La TS17 6 B5
THEAKSTON 87 E8
Theakston Hargill DL8 87 E8
Theakston La DL10 209 C5
The Atlernative Sch BB18 171 D1
The Beeches 18 HG4 86 C3
The Cherry Orchard YO26 164 A5
The Conifers YO41 185 A3
The Crescent 1 YO19 191 D8
The Freeston Acad WF6 200 A1
The Grove Acad HG1 219 E4
The Island WF11 202 A3
The Ladle TS7 7 B7
The Link 8 DN14 204 C3
The Meadows
Hunmanby YO14 127 C8
Wilberfoss YO41 185 F5
The Mount 25 WF6 200 A1
The New Selby War Memorial Hospl YO8 232 B4
The Old Woodyard 26 YO41 168 D2
The Paddock
7 Carlton DN14 204 C3
Skipton BD23 217 A4
The Paddocks YO17 122 F5
The Raylor Centre YO10 228 E4
Theresa Cl 6 YO31 225 F1
The Rydal Acad DL1 3 E4
The Sacred Heart Catholic Prim Sch LS29 218 D4
The Sidings
9 Nawton YO62 93 D7
Whitley DN14 202 F1
The Skipton Acad BD23 216 D4
The Spinney DL7 63 F3
The Square
North Stainley with Sleningford HG4 113 C8
York YO24 230 E6
The Vale Prim Acad WF11 201 E2
The Village Prim Sch TS17 6 B7
The Vines 11 YO32 191 C7
The Waterside DL2 4 D4
The Whinfields 7 HG3 138 A1
The Willows YO7 115 F7
The York Hospl YO30 233 B4
Thickrash Brow LA2 129 A7
Thiefgate La DL8 86 E3
Thiefhole La DL7 65 B3
Thief La
Barlow YO8 232 F1
York YO10 228 F3
THIMBLEBY 45 A2
Third Ave
10 Wetherby LS22 180 C3
York YO31 228 F5
Thirkleby Walk 1 YO10 229 D3
Thirkleby Way YO10 229 C4
THIRLBY 90 E7
Thirlby Way 8 TS14 8 F7
Thirlmere Cl 3 YO7 89 C4
Thirlmere Dr YO31 229 A6
Thirlway Dr HG4 214 B6
THIRN 86 B8
THIRSK 211 C2
Thirsk Bank
Angram Grange YO7 117 B8
Thornton-le-Moor DL7 65 B3
Thirsk Bsns Pk YO7 211 B2
Thirsk Com Prim Sch YO7 211 C4
Thirsk Ind Pk YO7 211 D2
Thirsk Mus★ YO7 211 B3
Thirsk Racecourse★ YO7 211 A3
Thirsk Rd
Eaglescliffe TS15 5 E2
Easingwold YO61 117 B1
Kirkby TS9 26 C6
Romanby DL6 210 F1
Thirsk Sch YO7 211 B1
Thirsk Sta YO7 89 D4
Thirsk Swimming Pool YO7 211 C2
Thirty Acre La HG5 163 A6
Thirwall Dr TS17 6 A4
Thistlebar Rd YO51 141 D2
Thistle Cl
Northallerton DL7 210 D1
Selby YO8 232 C2
Thistle Hill HG5 221 B3
Thistle Rise TS8 6 F6
THIXENDALE 170 E7
THOLTHORPE 142 D5
Thomas Gill Rd 7 HG3 137 F1
Thomas Hinderwell Prim Acad YO12 212 D2
Thomason Foss (Waterfall)★ YO22 31 C1
Thomas St
21 Cross Hills BD20 187 E8
6 Selby YO8 232 D6
2 York YO10 228 E3
Thompson Cl
9 Barlby YO8 198 B4
29 Scalby YO12 75 D5
Thompson Dr 2 YO32 167 B8
Thompson Pl 6 YO26 227 E5
Thompson Street E DL1 3 D7
Thompson Street W DL3 3 C7
THORALBY 58 E1
Thoresby La DL8 59 B5
Thoresby Rd YO24 227 B1
THORGANBY 193 B4
THORGILL 49 C3
Thorington Gdns TS17 6 B4
THORLBY 216 B6
THORMANBY 116 F5
Thornaby Acad TS17 6 B7
THORNABY-ON-TEES 6 A7
Thornaby Rd TS17 6 B7
Thornaby Swimming Pool TS17 6 A8
Thornbeck YO19 184 E6
THORNBOROUGH 87 C2
Thornborough Cres 4 DL8 60 D5
Thornbrough Rd DL6 210 E3
Thornburgh Rd
Crossgates YO11 99 F5
6 Eastfield YO11 99 F6
Thorncroft 8 YO19 184 F7
Thorndale St BD23 154 B3
Thornden Bldgs YO8 232 D5
Thorndikes La HG5 141 A2
Thorne Cl 13 WF6 200 B1
Thorner CE Prim Sch LS14 188 A3
Thorner Gr BD20 174 C2
Thorner La LS23 188 B5
Thorner Rd LS23 188 B4
Thornfield Ave
Dishforth YO7 115 A4
5 York YO31 228 F8
Thornfield Bsns Pk DL7 210 B6
Thornfield Dr 7 YO31 225 E2
Thornfield Gr TS5 6 E8
Thornfield Rd DL8 87 C3
Thornhill
6 Eastfield YO11 100 A6
Northallerton DL6 210 E3
14 Richmond DL10 209 C6
Thornhill Rd WF10 200 F3
Thornhills 19 YO32 166 F5
Thornlands 9 YO61 117 D1
Thornley Ave DL7 210 D3
Thorn Nook YO31 228 F8
THORNS 35 E7
Thorns La YO51 140 F4
THORNTHWAITE 159 D6
Thornthwaite Brow HG3 159 E5
THORNTON 6 E4
Thornton Cl
15 Easingwold YO61 143 D8
Stainton & Thornton TS8 6 D4
Thornton Dale CE Prim Sch YO18 96 C5
Thornton Hts BD23 172 A3
THORNTON-IN-CRAVEN 172 A3
Thornton in Craven Com Prim Sch BD23 172 A3
THORNTON IN LONSDALE 103 C4
Thornton La
Dent LA10 78 A4
Marishes YO17 96 B1
Thornton in Lonsdale LA6 103 C4
Thornton-on-the-Hill YO61 117 D4
THORNTON-LE-BEANS 65 B5
THORNTON-LE-CLAY 146 A4
THORNTON-LE-DALE 96 D5
THORNTON-LE-MOOR 65 B3
THORNTON-LE-STREET 65 D1
Thornton Moor Cl YO30 224 F2
Thornton Rd
Coulby Newham TS8 6 D4
Pickering YO18 96 A6
Thornton Road Ind Est YO18 96 A5
THORNTON RUST 58 B4
Thornton St
14 Burley in Warfedale LS29 176 C1
Darlington DL3 3 C5
8 Skipton BD23 216 D3
THORNTON STEWARD 61 D1
Thornton Vale TS8 6 E4
THORNTON WATLASS 86 D8
Thornton Watlass CE Prim Sch HG4 86 D8
Thorn Tree Ave 6 YO14 101 B4
Thorntree Gdns DL2 4 C4
Thorntree Gr YO30 225 B2
Thorntree La DN14 207 C6
Thorntree Rd
Northallerton DL6 210 F6

Thorntree Rd *continued*
Thornaby TS17 6 B7
Thorntree Villas 16 DL2 4 C4
Thornview Rd BD23 154 B3
Thorn Wath La YO62 48 E4
Thornwood Ave TS17 6 A5
Thornwood Covert 1
YO24 227 C1
Thorny Hill La YO51 141 E2
Thorny La YO42 169 F2
THORP ARCH 188 F8
Thorp Arch Pk LS23 180 F1
Thorp Arch Trad Est
LS23 189 A8
THORPE 156 F8
Thorpe Bank 6 YO22 33 C3
THORPE BASSETT 123 A4
Thorpe Bassett La YO17 122 E1
Thorpe Chase HG4 214 E3
Thorpe Green Bank 1
YO22 33 C3
Thorpe Green La YO26 164 B7
Thorpe La
Ampleforth YO62 118 B8
Cawood YO8 197 B8
Cracoe BD23 156 C7
Fylingdales YO22 33 C4
Thorpe BD23 156 D8
Thorpe Prebend House - Heritage Ctr* HG4 214 C5
Thorpe Rd HG4 86 C2
Thorpe St YO23 228 B2
THORPE UNDERWOOD 164 C6
THORPE WILLOUGHBY 197 C2
Thorpe Willoughby Com Prim Sch YO8 197 B2
Thorp Perrow Arboretum & Falconry Ctr* DL8 87 A8
Threapland BD23 156 C7
Three Lakes Ind Est YO8 232 D2
Three Lakes Ret Pk YO8 232 D3
Three Lane Ends Com Prim Sch WF10 200 D4
Three Tuns Wynd 7 TS9 26 C7
THRESHFIELD 134 D2
Threshfield Sch BD23 134 D2
THRINTOFT 64 A8
Thrintoft La DL7 64 A7
Thrintoft Moor La DL7 64 A8
Thrope La HG3 110 C4
Throstle Nest Cl LS21 176 E1
Throstle Nest Dr HG2 222 D6
THROXENBY 212 A7
Throxenby Gr 3 YO12 212 B7
Throxenby La YO12 212 B7
THRUSCROSS 159 A5
Thruscross La HG3 159 B5
Thrussendale Rd YO17 169 E8
Thunderhead Ridge
WF10 200 F3
Thurland Castle* LA6 102 B3
Thurston Rd DL6 210 C7
THWAITE 35 F5
Thwaite Holme La DL8 57 F5
Thwaite La LA2 128 E5
Thwaites Ave LS29 218 C4
Thwaites La
Markington with Wallerthwaite HG3 139 D5
Nether Silton YO7 66 C7
Thirkleby High & Low with Osgodby YO7 90 E1
Thweng Way TS14 8 E5
THWING 126 B1
Thwing Rd YO25 126 E2
Tibby Butts 26 YO13 75 D5
Tibgarth LS22 180 A2
Tickergate La DL7 63 A8
Tidkin La TS14 8 E6
Tile Cl BD23 217 B3
Tillman Cl 6 BD24 131 D2
Tillotson's Ct BD20 173 D1
Tilmire Cl 2 YO10 231 F8
TIMBLE 176 D7
Timble Gr HG1 219 B5
Timmys La DL2 3 F1
Tindall St YO12 212 F5
Tinker La YO23 182 D6
Tinkers' La HG3 139 A1
Tinkingfield La LS22 181 A5
Tinkler La
Milby YO51 141 C6
Winsley HG3 160 E8
Tinkler's La WF11 202 D6
Tinley Garth YO62 70 B1
Tinley Gdns 14 YO62 70 B1
Tintagel Ct WF6 200 A2
Tiplady Cl 18 YO61 143 C8
Tippaty La WF11 202 A4
Tirril Way TS7 7 C5
Tithe Barn Fold LS15 194 B8
Tithe Barn Rd 2 WF11 202 A2
Tithe Barn Way DN14 202 F3
Tithe Cl YO24 227 B1
Tithe Way HG4 114 F1
Tivoli Pl LS29 218 C3
Toadham La DN14 207 C5
Toby Ct YO32 167 A7
TOCKWITH 181 D7
Tockwith CE Prim Sch
YO26 181 C7
Tockwith La YO26 181 D6
Tockwith Rd
Long Marston YO26 181 F6
Tockwith LS22 180 F7
Toc La YO18 97 C5
Todd La DL7 63 B8
Todds Ct 8 YO7 211 C3
Tod Holes La BD23 153 B4
Todley Hall Rd BD22 187 F3
Todmanhaw La BD23 153 E3
Tofta Rd YO13 54 A5
Toft Gn YO1 233 A2
Tofting La YO17 148 B5
Toft Ings La YO61 143 B8
Toft La DL8 63 D2
Tofts Cl TS15 24 B8
Tofts Fort The* DL11 1 E2
Tofts La
Danby YO21 29 B5
Follifoot HG3 223 F4
Humberton YO61 141 F8
Pickering YO18 95 F3
Tholthorpe YO61 142 D6
Welbury DL6 24 B1
Tofts Rd YO17 95 F3
Toll Bar Cl 3 YO8 196 E1
Toll Bar Rd WF10 200 C4
Toll Bar Way LS24 189 F7
Tollergate YO11 213 A7
TOLLERTON 143 A3
Tollerton La YO30 165 B7
Tollerton Rd YO61 143 D4
TOLLESBY 7 A6
Tollesby Bridge TS8 7 A6
Tollesby La TS7 7 B6
Tollesby Rd TS5 6 F8
Toll Hill Ct WF11 201 A3
Toll Hill Dr WF11 201 A3
Tomahawk Trail WF10 200 F3
Tom Cat La
Bilton-in-Ainsty with Bickerton LS22 181 A5
Birdsall YO17 148 B4
Tom Dando Cl WF6 200 C1
Tomgill Bank DL8 58 E2
Tom Hall Ct 12 DL8 63 A2
Tom La
Cowling BD22 186 E7
Dunsforths YO26 141 F3
Hillam LS25 202 B7
Tomlinson Way LS25 195 E4
Tom Smith's Cross YO62 92 B4
Topcliff Ct YO8 232 B7
TOPCLIFFE 115 B7
Topcliffe CE Prim Sch
YO7 115 C7
Topcliffe Rd
Sowerby YO7 89 E3
Thirsk YO7 211 B1
Thornaby TS17 6 C7
Top Fold WF11 201 D6
Top House Ct WF8 206 B3
Top House Farm Mews 2
WF11 201 D6
Top La
Colne BB8 186 B2
Copmanthorpe YO23 230 B3
Norwood LS21 177 A6
Top Stone Cl LS25 201 F6
Toremill Cl YO32 225 D4
Torrance Dr DL1 3 F8
Torridon Pl YO24 230 B7
Torrs Rd HG1 220 A3
TOSSIDE 152 F3
Tostig Ave YO26 227 C5
Tostig Cl 14 YO41 168 D2
Totten La YO62 120 D7
TOULSTON 189 B7
Toulston La LS23 188 F5
Tout Hill YO60 146 E5
Tower Cres LS24 189 D6
Tower Croft 7 YO61 117 D1
Tower Ct YO30 225 A2
Tower Grange DL3 3 B7
Tower Pl YO1 233 B1
Tower Rd
Darlington DL3 3 B6
Ripon HG4 214 C6
Towers Paddock WF10 201 A4
Tower St
Harrogate HG1 219 D1
10 Richmond DL10 209 C6
York YO1 233 B1
Tower Street Castle W 4
DL10 209 C6
Tower View DN14 204 C2
Townclose View LS25 200 C8
Town End YO7 211 B2
Town End Ave DN14 204 C3
Town End Cl
6 Carlton DN14 204 C3
16 Glusburn BD20 187 E7
2 Kirklevington TS15 24 F8
9 Pickering YO18 96 A6
Townend Ct 3 YO26 164 A8
Town End Gdns 8 YO32 166 D5
Townend Pl 5 BD20 187 E7
Townend Rd YO42 193 D1
Townend St YO31 233 B4
Town Farm Cl 15 YO62 70 B1
Town Green Dr TS9 26 E5
TOWN HEAD 174 C1
Townhead 2 BD24 131 E2
Town Head Ave 1 BD24 131 E2
Townhead Croft BD24 131 E3
Town Head Fold 12 LS29 174 F4
Townhead La LA2 130 E8
Townhead Way BD24 131 E2
Town Head Way 14 BD24 131 D2
Town Hill LS23 188 E5
Town St
Bishop Thornton HG3 138 F1
Town St *continued*
Brandsby-cum-Stearsby YO61 118 D3
Malton YO17 215 E6
Nidd HG3 161 E7
Scampston YO17 123 A6
Settrington YO17 122 C1
Townville Infant Sch
WF10 201 B4
Tow Scar Rd LA6 103 C5
TOWTHORPE
Duggleby 149 D1
York 167 B5
Towthorpe Moor La
YO32 167 C5
Towthorpe Rd YO32 166 F5
TOWTON 189 E2
Towton Ave 9 YO24 227 F2
Tow Top La BD20 173 A1
Trafalgar Ct 10 HG1 219 D1
Trafalgar Rd
11 Harrogate HG1 219 D1
Ilkley LS29 218 B4
Scarborough YO12 212 F7
Trafalgar Sq
Meagill LS21 159 E4
Scarborough YO12 212 F7
Trafalgar St YO23 228 B1
Trafalgar Street W YO12 212 F6
Trafalgar Terr YO12 212 F7
Trafford Ct 19 DL1 3 F6
Trafford Rd 4 DN6 206 E2
Train La 14 YO18 95 F7
Tranby Ave YO10 229 D4
Tranmere Ct 2 BD23 153 F5
Tranmire Cl YO7 211 D4
Tranmore La
Eggborough DN14 203 B3
HutGreen DN14 203 A2
Trans Wlk LS24 190 B1
Tranter Rd TS4 6 F8
Trapping Hill HG3 110 C4
Trattles Hill YO13 54 D2
Travellers Garth YO17 121 C1
TRAWDEN 186 B1
Trawden Forest Prim Sch 4
BB8 186 A1
Trawden Rd BB8 186 A3
Treasurer's House* YO1 233 B3
Trecastell 25 TS17 5 F4
Treesdale Rd 1 HG2 219 C1
Trefoil Cl TS14 8 D6
Trefoil Dr 4 HG3 161 B3
Trefoil Wood TS7 7 B7
Trencar La YO61 91 A2
Trenchard Ave TS17 6 B6
Trenchard Rd YO26 227 B6
Trenchard St 8 YO7 89 B1
Trenfield Ct YO24 227 F3
Trenholme Cl 7 TS17 6 D6
Trenholme La TS15 25 B3
Trent Ave
Garforth LS25 194 D3
Pontefract WF6 200 A2
4 York YO32 225 F6
Trentholme Dr 2 YO24 228 A2
Trent Way YO24 230 D7
Trevine Gdns TS17 5 F4
Trevino Ct TS16 5 E5
Trevithick Cl 7 TS16 5 D5
Trevithick Rd WF10 200 E6
Trevor Gr 8 YO24 227 F2
Triangle The TS14 8 D6
Tribune Way YO30 225 B2
Trimdon Ave TS5 6 D6
Trinity Catholic Coll TS4 6 F7
Trinity Church Sq 9
DL10 209 C6
Trinity Cl 1 YO11 212 F3
Trinity Gdns
Northallerton DL6 210 F3
2 Scarborough YO11 212 F3
Trinity La
Ripon HG4 214 B5
York YO1 233 A2
Trinity Mdws YO32 167 D3
Trinity Mews DL3 3 C5
Trinity Pk HG4 214 B6
Trinity Rd
Darlington DL3 3 C5
Harrogate HG2 219 D1
Scarborough YO11 212 F3
Trinket La LA2 128 B6
Trip Garth LS22 180 A1
Trip La
Collingham LS22 180 A1
Sicklinghall LS22 179 F1
Triplins La HG4 113 B6
Tristram Ave DL3 3 C7
Troon Cl 2 YO26 227 B5
Trousdale Hill YO60 147 A7
Troutbeck 7 YO24 230 C7
Troutbeck Cl 11 YO18 95 F6
Troutsdale Ave YO30 224 E2
Trumfleet La DN6 207 D1
Trundles La 7 WF11 202 A2
Truro Cres 8 HG3 161 B3
Truro Dr 19 WF6 200 A2
Truro Rd 7 HG3 161 B3
Truro Wlk 23 WF6 200 A2
Trust Fold LS25 201 E6
Tubwell Rd DL1 3 C5
Tucker Cl DL6 210 E5
Tudor Cl 10 YO8 197 B1
Tudor Ct 7 DL10 41 C7
Tudor Rd
Richmond DL10 209 D7
York YO24 227 C2
Tudor Way YO32 167 C8
Tufton Pl BD23 216 F3
Tuke Ave YO10 229 B4
Tumbledown Cl 5 DL9 40 E3
Tune St YO8 198 B4
TUNSTALL
Catterick 41 B2
Cowan Bridge 102 B4
Tunstall Rd
Catterick DL10 41 D4
Harrogate HG2 220 B3
Turbary La
Hopgrove YO32 226 E6
Huntington YO32 226 D6
Turbary Rd LA6 103 B7
Turfy Hill DL8 56 C4
Turker Cl DL6 210 E5
Turker La DL6 210 F6
Turkey La
Baldersby YO7 88 D1
Catton YO7 114 F8
Turkhan Cl YO7 211 A2
Turkish Baths & Health Spa
HG2 219 C2
Turks Head Ct YO1 233 C3
Turnberry Ave TS16 5 E4
Turnberry Dr
Hunmanby YO14 127 C8
York YO26 227 B4
Turnberry Way TS8 7 C5
Turner Cl DL9 209 C2
Turner Cres 6 LS21 177 A1
Turner La 4 LS29 174 E4
Turner's Croft YO10 229 A1
Turners Sq 9 YO8 232 C5
Turner St 13 BB18 171 E1
Turnham La YO8 198 C2
Turnhead Cres YO8 198 B5
Turnhead Ct YO8 198 B6
Turnmire Rd 1 YO24 230 E8
Turnpike La LS22 181 B5
Turnpike Rd LS24 189 F7
Turnshaw Rd BD22 187 F1
Turpin Ct YO1 233 C1
Turpin La LS25 196 A2
Turton Rd TS15 5 D2
Turver's La WF11 202 C2
Tuscany Way WF6 200 A3
Tuthill 13 YO11 213 B6
Tutin Rd DL7 63 C5
Tweed Ave TS17 6 B7
Tweed St 5 LA2 129 A8
Twelve Acre Bank DL9 40 E1
Twine Wlk 7 LA6 102 F3
Twin Pike Way 14 YO32 166 D5
Twizzie Gill View 6 TS13 11 A8
Two Laws Rd BB8 187 B1
Tyler Cl WF6 200 C1
Tyne Cres DL1 3 D3
Tyn Garth YO19 191 D8
Typhoon Cl DL10 41 F6
Tyseley Gr 4 BB18 172 A1
Tyson Pl HG2 220 B2

U

UCKERBY 21 E1
UGGLEBARNBY 32 C6
UGTHORPE 11 F2
Uldale Cl 5 HG5 221 D5
Uldale Dr TS16 5 E4
Ulla Gn LS24 190 B1
ULLESKELF 190 C2
Ulleskelf Sta LS24 190 B2
Ullswater YO24 230 D7
Ullswater Ave TS5 6 E8
Ullswater Dr LS22 180 B3
Ullswater Rise 5 LS22 180 B3
Ulnaby La DL2 2 C7
ULSHAW 61 A2
Ulswater Ave 5 DL1 3 D4
Under Cliffe 17 YO18 95 F7
Undercliffe Rise LS29 218 E2
Undercroft 7 YO19 184 F7
Underlands La HG4 114 C7
Underwit Rd YO8 204 C4
Union House BD23 217 A3
Union La YO8 232 C4
Union Rd 24 YO21 208 D6
Union St
28 Filey YO14 101 B3
Harrogate HG1 219 D3
2 Knaresborough HG5 221 A5
12 Scarborough YO11 213 A6
Union Terr
5 Skipton BD23 216 F3
York YO31 233 B4
Unity Cl HG1 219 D5
Unity Gr HG1 219 D5
Unity St
14 Barnoldswick BB18 171 E1
1 Earby BB18 186 A7
University of Hull (Scarborough Campus) YO12 213 B1
University of York (King's Manor) YO30 233 A3
University of York (Main Campus) YO10 229 A1
University Rd YO10 228 F2
Univesity of Hull @ Scarborough YO11 213 B1
Upgang La YO21 208 B7
Upgarth Cl 2 TS13 12 A7
Uplands BD23 217 B5
Uplands Ave 8 YO13 99 B8
Uplands Rd DL3 3 B5
Uplands The YO12 212 A7
Upper Carr La YO18 96 A4
Uppercommon La DN14 202 F3
Uppercroft 4 YO32 225 C8
UPPER DUNSFORTH 142 A2
Upper Dunsforth Carrs Nature Reserve* YO26 142 A1
Uppergate LA6 103 D4
Upper Green La TS18 6 A7
Upper Hanover St 6
YO26 227 F5
UPPER HELMSLEY 168 B3
Upper Newborough St 1
YO30 228 C7
UPPER POPPLETON 165 F1
Upper Price St YO23 233 A1
Upper Sackville St 5
BD23 217 A3
Upper St Paul's Terr
YO24 228 A4
Upper Union St BD23 216 F3
Upper Wensleydale Bus Pk
DL8 56 D5
Upper Wharfedale Folk Mus* BD23 134 E2
Upper Wharfedale Sch
BD23 134 D2
Uppleby YO61 117 D1
UPSALL 66 B2
Upsall Dr DL3 3 C4
Upsall La
South Kilvington YO7 211 C7
Thornbrough YO7 90 A8
Upsall YO7 66 B1
Upsall Rd YO7 66 B1
Upwell Rd DL7 210 D4
URE BANK 214 D7
Ure Bank HG4 214 D7
Ure Bank Maltings HG4 214 D8
Ure Bank Terr HG4 214 C7
Ure Bank Top HG4 214 D7
Uredale Glass* HG4 86 C3
URLAY NOOK 5 B5
Urlay Nook Rd TS16 5 C5
URRA 47 A8
Usher La YO32 166 F6
Usk Ct 21 TS17 5 F4

V

Vale Ave WF11 201 E2
Vale Cres
Bishop Wilton YO42 169 F2
Knottingley WF11 201 E2
Vale Crest WF11 201 E2
Vale Ct HG5 221 A6
Vale Gdns LS29 218 D4
Vale The
10 Collingham LS22 188 A8
Middlesbrough TS5 6 F8
Skelton YO30 224 B5
Vale View HG4 114 B2
Valient Way TS17 6 B6
Valley Bride Rd 16 YO11 213 F5
Valley Bridge Par YO11 213 A5
Valley Dr
Barnoldswick BB18 171 E2
Eaglescliffe TS15 5 E3
Great Preston LS26 200 C8
Harrogate HG2 219 C1
Ilkley LS29 218 D4
Valley Gdn TS16 5 D4
Valley Gdns* HG2 219 C2
Valley Mill Ct BB8 186 C3
Valley Mount
Harrogate HG2 219 C2
Kippax LS25 194 D1
Valley Rd
Barnoldswick BB18 171 E1
3 Darley HG3 160 A6
32 Earby BB18 172 A1
Harrogate HG2 219 C2
Ilkley LS29 218 D5
Kippax LS25 194 C2
Northallerton DL6 210 F3
Scarborough YO12 212 E4
Whitby YO21 208 A8
Valley Ridge LS25 194 C2
Valley Street N DL1 3 D5
Valley View
3 Ampleforth YO62 92 C1
Clint HG3 160 F8
Danby YO21 29 C6
3 Glusburn BD20 187 E8
Wheldrake YO19 192 F7
Valuation La 1 YO51 141 B5
Vanbrugh Dr YO10 229 C3
Vanbrugh Way YO10 229 A2
Vane Ct TS21 4 F7
Vane Terr DL3 3 C5
Vangarde Way YO32 226 A1
Van Mildert Way TS18 5 F8
Vasey Cl 5 DL8 63 B2
Vaughan Rd 10 DN6 206 E1
Vavasour Ct YO23 230 B2
Vaynor Dr 17 TS17 5 F4
Venables Rd TS14 8 E7
Verity Wlk HG2 222 D7
Vernon Cl YO23 231 A3
Vernon Ct TS8 6 E5
Vernon Gr 4 YO12 212 D8
Vernon Pl 3 YO11 213 A5
Vernon Rd
Harrogate HG2 222 E7
2 Scarborough YO11 213 A5
Trawden Forest BB8 186 B3
York YO30 224 E2

Vesper Dr YO24 227 B3
Vesper Wlk YO32 225 F6
Vicarage Cl
2 Bubwith YO8 199 D7
12 Hunmanby YO14 126 F8
23 Hunmanby YO14 126 F8
Seamer YO12 99 D6
Vicarage Farm Cl YO17 124 D8
Vicarage Gdns 1 YO10 229 C4
Vicarage La
Bishop Wilton YO42 169 F2
Bramham LS23 188 E5
10 Knaresborough HG5 221 A6
Naburn YO19 191 E8
Sherburn YO17 124 D8
Vicarage Rd
Barnoldswick BB18 171 E2
16 Catterick Garrison DL9 40 E4
Darlington DL1 3 D5
3 Kelbrook & Sough BB18 186 A7
Vicar Hill La YO7 116 D8
Vicars Cl YO23 230 B2
Vicars Croft DL6 210 E5
VICAR'S GREEN 39 F7
Vicar's La YO61 144 C6
Vicars Terr WF10 200 D6
Vickers Cl TS18 5 F7
Vickers Rd 2 DL9 40 E4
Vickers St 1 WF10 200 E4
Victoria Arc LS29 218 A4
Victoria Ave
10 Filey YO14 101 B3
Harrogate HG1 219 D2
Ilkley LS29 175 C2
Knaresborough HG5 221 B8
Ripon HG4 214 D5
Thirsk YO7 211 B2
Victoria Cave★ BD24 131 F4
Victoria Cl
Great Preston WF10 200 E6
Ilkley LS29 218 A4
26 Sherburn in Elmet LS25 195 F4
Victoria Ct
25 Sherburn in Elmet LS25 195 F4
15 York YO26 227 F5
Victoria Dr 9 LS29 175 C2
Victoria Emb DL1 3 C4
Victoria Farm Cl YO23 182 C6
Victoria Gdns 17 LS29 175 C2
Victoria Gr
5 Ilkley LS29 175 C2
Ripon HG4 214 C5
Victoria Mews 45 BB18 172 A1
Victoria Par 13 YO11 212 F5
Victoria Park Ave 2 YO12 212 F7
Victoria Park Mount YO12 212 E7
Victoria Pk 1 YO12 212 F7
Victoria Pl 3 YO21 208 D6
Victoria Rd
1 Barnoldswick BB18 171 E1
28 Burley in Warfedale LS29 176 C1
Cowling BD22 187 B6
Darlington DL1 3 C5
Earby BB18 172 A1
Glusburn BD20 187 E7
Harrogate HG2 219 C1
10 Ilkley LS29 175 C2
1 Malton YO17 215 B4
Richmond DL10 209 B7
Scarborough YO11 212 F5
Thornaby TS17 6 B8
Victoria Sh Ctr HG1 219 D2
Victoria Sq
Skipton BD23 216 F4
21 Whitby YO21 208 D6
Victoria St
24 Earby BB18 172 A1
43 Glusburn BD20 187 E7
Great Preston WF10 200 D6
Pontefract WF8 201 B2
Scarborough YO12 212 F6
Settle BD24 131 E2
10 Skipton BD23 216 F4
1 York YO23 233 B1
Victoria Terr
1 Harrogate HG1 220 C4
Northallerton DL7 210 D4
3 Skipton BD23 216 F4
Victoria Way 2 YO32 228 F8
Victoria Works Ind Est BD20 187 F8
Victor St YO1 233 B1
Victory Rd LS29 218 B4
Viewley Hill Academy TS8 6 F5
Viewley Hill Ave TS8 6 F5
Viking Cl 20 YO41 168 D2
Viking Dr 5 YO19 197 F8
Viking Rd
Stamford Bridge YO41 168 D2
York YO26 227 C5
Vikings Ct 6 DL6 43 F3
Villa Cl YO8 198 F1
Villa Ct YO26 227 B7
Villa Fields 4 DN14 204 C1
Village Farm Cl 9 DN14 202 D4
Village Farm Ct 7 DN14 202 D4
Village Fold DL7 42 B1
Village Garth 1 YO32 166 E5
Village Paddock TS18 5 E8
Village Rd TS15 24 B8
Village St YO30 224 E3
Village The
Boston Spa LS23 180 F1
Haxby YO32 166 E5
Village The *continued*
Skelton YO30 224 B5
Stockton on the Forest YO32 167 D2
Strensall YO32 167 B7
York YO10 229 C4
Village Wy DL7 42 B1
Villa Gr 2 YO31 228 E6
Villiers Ct 8 YO62 92 F6
Vimy Rd DL9 40 E3
Vincent St 9 YO12 213 A7
Vincent Way YO24 230 C8
Vine Cl TS14 8 F6
Vine Farm Cl YO26 164 A4
Vine Gdns YO8 199 D7
Vine Gr YO17 215 E4
Vine St
Darlington DL3 3 B6
Norton YO17 215 E4
6 Scarborough YO12 212 F6
York YO23 228 C2
Vinstra Cl DL10 209 D8
Virginia Gdns TS5 6 E6
Vivars Way YO8 232 D5
Vivers Pl 1 YO62 70 C1
Vivis La YO18 95 F6
Volta St YO8 232 E4
Vulcan Way TS17 6 B6
Vyner St
Ripon HG4 214 D4
York YO31 228 C7

W

Waddington St 37 BB18 172 A1
Wade House La YO8 204 F4
Waggoners Dr 3 YO23 230 B3
Wain Cl
15 Eastfield YO11 100 B7
South Milford LS25 195 E2
Waincroft 8 YO32 167 A6
Wainds Field 30 YO62 70 B1
Waindyke Way WF6 200 B1
Wainers Cl 5 YO23 230 B3
Wainfleet Rd HG1 219 D6
Wain Gap LS25 195 F2
Waingates La YO51 140 F4
Wainman's Cl BD22 187 B6
Wain's Gr YO24 230 D7
Wain's La YO12 99 D2
Wain's Rd YO24 230 D8
Wainstones Cl TS9 7 F1
Wainstones Dr TS9 7 F1
Waite La YO13 53 F1
WAITHWITH BANKS 40 B5
Waithwith Rd DL9 209 B1
Waitlands La DL11 20 A7
Wakefield Pathways Sch WF10 201 B4
Wakefield Rd
Garforth LS25 194 B3
10 Normanton South WF6 200 A1
Swillington LS26 194 A2
WAKE HILL 111 F1
Wakeman Rd HG4 214 C3
Walburn Head DL11 39 D3
WALDEN STUBBS 206 F3
Walden Stubbs Rd DN6 206 E2
Wales St DL3 3 C7
Walker Cl BD20 187 D7
Walker Dr YO24 230 C8
Walker La
Menwith with Darley HG3 160 A6
Wheldrake YO19 192 F7
Walkers Fold HG5 221 B5
Walker's La BD20 174 B4
Walkers Row TS14 8 F7
Walker St YO21 208 D6
Walker Terr HG3 223 F4
WALKERVILLE 41 A4
Walkerville Ave 22 DL9 41 A5
Walkerville Ind Est DL9 41 B5
Walkington La YO30 165 B8
Walled Gdn The★ YO17 123 A6
Wallgates La YO17 215 D4
Walmer Carr
Haxby YO32 166 D5
Wigginton YO32 166 D5
Walmgate YO1 233 C2
WALMGATE STRAY 228 F1
Walmsley Gdns YO12 212 C5
Walney Rd YO31 229 A5
Walnut Ave 45 DL9 41 A5
Walnut Cl
39 Haxby YO32 166 E5
Saxton with Scarthingwell LS24 195 D8
39 Wigginton YO32 166 E5
York YO10 229 A1
Walnut Gn YO17 215 E3
Walnut Gr
Harrogate HG1 219 E6
Sherburn YO17 124 D8
Walpole St YO31 228 D7
WALSHFORD 180 D8
Waltham Cl YO32 167 B8
WALTON 181 A2
Walton Ave
Gargrave BD23 155 C1
Gargrave BD23 172 C8
Middlesbrough TS5 6 E8
Pannal HG3 222 F2
Walton Chase LS23 180 F2
Walton Cl YO61 144 A4
Walton Gdns LS23 180 F2
Walton Head La HG3 178 F4
Walton Pk HG3 222 E2
Walton Pl
Pannal HG3 222 E2
York YO26 227 B3
Walton Rd
Gargrave BD23 172 C8
Walton LS23 181 A2
Wetherby LS22 180 E2
Walton St
5 Cowling BD22 187 B6
Skipton BD23 216 F1
Walworth Ave HG2 220 B3
Walworth Street N 4 YO26 227 F5
Walworth Street S 9 YO26 227 F5
Wandale La YO17 95 A2
Wandales Cl YO17 215 F3
Wandales Ct YO13 75 D8
Wandales Dr YO13 75 D8
Wandales La YO60 146 B6
Wandales Rd YO13 75 D8
Wandell Balk YO61 144 B6
Wandels La YO21 29 B6
Wandesford Gr DL9 209 F1
Wandhill 31 YO32 166 E5
Wand Hill TS12 9 E8
Wandhill Gdns TS12 9 E8
Wandhill La YO7 66 D1
Wand La DN14 203 C3
Wandle The YO26 227 A2
Wansbeck 3 YO24 230 B7
Wapping La YO62 94 C7
Warbler Cl 11 TS17 6 A5
Wardale Ave TS5 6 E6
Ward Ct YO23 233 B1
War Dike La YO13 54 B6
Wardrop Rd DL9 209 C1
Ward St BD23 217 A4
Wareham Rd YO11 99 F6
Warehill La YO61 143 C2
War Field La LS22 180 F6
WARLABY 64 D6
Warlbeck 23 LS29 175 C2
Warley Wise La BB8 186 D6
Warren Ave WF11 201 E2
Warren Cl DL1 3 F4
Warrener La DL10 20 C6
Warren House Rd WF10 200 E6
Warren La
Bramham cum Oglethorpe LS24 189 A5
Brearton HG3 162 A8
Kirkby Malzeard HG4 112 D4
Warren Pl HG1 219 D5
WARSILL 138 C4
WARTHERMARSKE 86 A1
WARTHILL 167 F2
Warthill CE VC Prim Sch YO19 167 F2
Warth La LA6 103 C3
Warwick Cl
Sheriff Hutton YO60 145 D5
Waithwith Banks DL9 40 C4
Warwick Cres HG2 222 E8
Warwick Dr 2 BB18 172 A1
Warwick Pl 2 YO62 92 F7
Warwick St YO31 228 D7
Wasdale Cl 2 YO30 224 E1
Washbeck Cl YO12 212 E4
Wash Beck La YO62 93 F6
Washbrook Dr DL3 3 C8
Washburn Cl 13 YO14 101 A3
Washburn Cotts LS21 159 F1
Washburn Courts HG3 159 F1
Washburn Dr 4 BD20 187 E8
WASHFOLD 18 D1
Washfold La DL8 60 B6
Washford Cl TS17 6 A3
Washington Ave DL2 4 D4
Washington Cl HG4 214 E2
WASS 91 F2
Wass Bank Rd YO61 91 F2
Wass Way TS16 5 D5
Waste La YO62 48 F2
Watchet Rd 11 DL9 40 E4
Watchgate TS7 7 D5
Water Avens Way TS18 6 A7
Water Bag Bank 8 HG5 221 A6
Waterdale Pk YO31 225 E1
Water End YO26 227 E5
Waterfall Fold 1 WF8 201 C2
Waterfalls Wlk★ LA6 103 D6
WATER FRYSTON 201 C5
Water Gap YO18 97 B5
Water Garth DN14 202 F4
Watergate
Mickletown LS26 200 A5
7 Pontefract WF8 201 B1
Watergate Rd HG3 139 A4
Water Hill La YO8 232 D6
Waterhouse La 29 YO11 213 A6
Water Houses BD24 132 E6
Waterings 19 YO32 166 D5
Water La
Camblesforth YO8 204 D5
8 Clifton YO30 225 A1
Dalton YO7 115 E7
Dunnington YO19 184 F7
Eggborough DN14 203 A2
Exelby, Leeming & Newton DL7 63 D4
Hemingbrough YO8 198 F1
Huttons Ambo YO60 147 C6
Kirby Grindalythe YO17 149 B6
Kirby Underdale YO41 170 A5
Kirk Smeaton WF8 206 C3
Knaresborough HG5 221 C8
Water La *continued*
Loftus TS13 10 E8
North Stainley with Sleningford HG4 113 C6
7 Pontefract WF8 201 C1
Selby YO8 232 C6
Sherburn YO17 124 D7
South Stainley with Cayton HG3 139 D2
Thorpe Bassett YO17 123 A3
Welburn YO60 146 E7
Whitby YO21 208 B3
York YO30 228 A7
Waterline Ind Est YO23 191 B7
Waterloo
Grosmont YO22 31 C4
12 Richmond DL10 209 C6
Waterloo Cl WF10 200 C3
Waterloo Rd BB18 186 A7
Waterloo St
Harrogate HG1 219 E4
2 Richmond DL10 209 C6
Waterman Ct 3 YO24 227 B1
Watermill Cl HG4 113 C7
Watermill Croft HG4 113 C7
Watermill La HG4 113 C7
Water St Com Prim Sch 16 BD23 216 F4
Waters End DL2 1 D7
Watershed Mill Bsns Ctr BD24 131 D3
Watershed Mill Visitor Ctr★ BD24 131 D3
Waterside
3 Boroughbridge YO51 141 B6
Hemingbrough YO8 198 F1
Knaresborough HG5 221 A5
4 Ripon HG4 214 C4
Skipton BD23 216 F2
7 Thirsk YO7 211 C3
Waterside Gdns YO31 228 D8
Waterside Mdws LS25 194 F8
Water Skellgate HG4 214 C5
Waters La DL10 20 E3
Water Slack La YO26 164 C4
Watersmeet Cl 5 TS17 6 A3
Watersole La LS22 180 D2
Water St
Earby BB18 172 A1
Gargrave BD23 155 D1
Malton YO17 215 C4
Skipton BD23 216 F4
Waterstead Cres 1 YO21 208 D5
Waterstead La YO21 208 C5
Water Way Garth DN14 207 F6
Watery La
Airton BD23 155 A5
Giggleswick BD24 131 C1
Snape with Thorp DL8 86 F7
WATH
Hovingham 119 F6
Pateley Bridge 137 A6
Ripon 114 A7
Wathcote Cl DL10 209 F8
Wathcote Pl DL10 209 F8
Wathgill Camp DL11 39 C3
Wath La
Catton YO41 185 C8
Copgrove HG3 140 D1
High & Low Bishopside HG3 137 B6
Humberton YO61 141 E8
Ulleskelf LS24 190 B2
Wath Rd HG3 137 B5
Watlass La DL8 86 E8
Watlass Moor La HG4 86 D7
Watling Cl DL11 19 E6
Watling Rd WF10 201 C5
Watson Cl 9 YO14 127 A8
Watson's Houses 7 BD23 216 F4
Watson's La
Newton Kyme cum Toulston LS24 189 B7
Norwood HG3 177 B8
Reighton YO14 127 D6
Watson St
4 Normanton South WF6 200 A1
York YO24 228 A3
Watson Terr 2 YO24 228 A3
Wattlers Cl YO23 230 C3
Wattlesyke LS22 188 C8
Wattle Syke LS22 180 B1
Wavell Com Inf Sch DL9 209 D1
Wavell Rd DL9 209 D1
Wavell St YO8 232 A6
Waveney Gr YO30 228 B8
Waver Ct LS24 195 F7
Waver La DL6 43 F8
Waverley Cl DN14 204 C2
Waverley Cres HG2 222 E8
Waverley St YO31 233 C3
Waydale Cl YO62 70 A2
Wayfaring Cl YO17 215 F2
Waynefleet Gr 3 YO10 229 A3
Wayne Tarbard Cl 12 HG4 113 D2
Wayside Ave HG2 220 B1
Wayside Cl 4 HG2 220 B1
Wayside Cres HG2 220 A1
Wayside Gr HG2 220 A1
Wayside Mews 12 BD20 174 C1
Wayside Terr LS17 178 B2
Wayside The DL2 3 E1
Waytail Slack TS13 10 D7
Weaponness Dr YO11 213 A2
Weaponness La
Eastfield YO11 99 F8
Scarborough YO11 212 F1
Weaponness Pk YO11 213 A2
Weaponness Valley Cl 5 YO11 212 F3
Weaponness Valley Rd YO11 212 E3
Weardale TS14 8 D5
Weardale Rd 20 DL9 40 E4
Weary Bank TS15 25 B8
Weaver Cl TS17 6 B5
Weavers Cl YO23 230 C3
Weavers Ct
3 Stokesley TS9 26 C7
Trawden BB8 186 A1
Weavers Gn DL7 210 C3
Weavers Pk
9 Copmanthorpe YO23 230 B3
York YO23 230 B3
WEAVERTHORPE 124 E1
Weaverthorpe CE Prim Sch YO17 124 E2
Webster Pl 1 WF6 200 A1
Weddall Cl YO24 227 F1
Wedderburn Ave HG2 220 C2
Wedderburn Cl HG2 220 C3
Wedderburn Dr HG2 220 B2
Wedderburn Lodge 2 HG2 220 B1
Wedderburn Rd HG2 220 B2
Weedling Gate LS24 189 D4
Weeland Ct 16 WF11 202 A2
Weeland Rd DN14 202 E3
WEETON 178 C1
Weeton La LS17 178 D1
Weeton Sta LS17 178 B2
Weets View BB18 171 E2
Weighbridge Cl 33 YO62 70 B1
Welbeck Ave DL1 3 E7
Welborn Cl YO10 229 A4
Welborn Ct YO11 99 F2
Welbourn Dr 12 YO12 99 D6
WELBURN
Pickering 94 A7
Westow 146 D7
Welburn Com Prim Sch YO60 146 D6
Welburn Gr TS7 7 D7
Welburn Hall Sch YO62 94 A7
Welburn La YO60 147 A8
WELBURY 24 B1
Welbury Cl 2 BB18 172 B1
Welfare Ave LS15 194 C8
Welford Rd 36 YO14 101 B3
Welham Hill YO17 147 E7
Welham Rd YO17 215 D3
WELL 87 A4
Welland Dr LS25 194 D3
Welland Rise YO26 227 D5
Well Bank
Cleasby DL2 2 F4
Well DL8 87 A4
Wellbrook Cl TS17 6 B4
Well Cl
Addingham LS29 174 F5
Great & Little Preston LS25 200 C8
3 Whitby YO21 208 D7
Well Cl Terr 4 YO21 208 D7
Wellesley Cl YO30 225 A2
Wellesleys Mews DL10 209 B7
Wellfield Ct HG2 222 B6
Wellfield La 13 LS29 176 C1
Wellhouse St 5 BB18 171 E1
Wellington Ct 9 HG2 219 C2
Wellington Gdns 11 HG4 214 C4
Wellingtonia Dr 5 DN6 206 E1
Wellington Mews 9 HG4 214 C5
Wellington Pl DL10 209 B7
Wellington Rd
Ilkley LS29 218 B4
2 Whitby YO21 208 D6
Wellington Row YO1 233 A2
Wellington Sq 6 HG2 219 C2
Wellington St
1 Knaresborough HG5 221 B5
10 Ripon HG4 214 C5
12 Skipton BD23 217 A3
York YO10 228 E3
Wellington Terr YO21 208 D7
Wellington Way 4 DL10 41 C7
Well La
Kippax LS25 194 D1
Redmire DL8 59 C5
Seamer TS9 6 F2
Snape with Thorp DL8 87 A6
South Milford LS25 195 F2
Yearsley YO61 118 C5
Wells Cl YO8 232 A5
Wells Ct YO62 196 F2
Wells Gn DL10 21 D7
Wells La
Barton DL10 21 D7
Kellington DN14 202 E3
Malton YO17 215 C4
Wells Mews 7 LS29 218 B3
Wellspring Cl TS17 6 D7
Wells Prom LS29 218 B4
Wells Rd LS29 218 B3
Wells Wlk 13 YO18 95 F7
Wells Wlk The LS29 218 B4
Welton Ave YO26 227 D5
Welton Ct YO21 208 C7

Welwyn Dr YO10 231 E8
Wemyss Rd
Ripon HG4 113 D2
11 Ripon HG4 113 D2
Wendel Ave LS15 194 B8
Wend The BD23 173 A4
Wendy Ave HG4 214 B3
Wenham Rd YO24 230 C8
Wenlock Dr YO19 192 B6
Wenlock Terr YO10 228 D1
Wenning Ave LA2 129 A7
Wenning Bank LA2 130 A6
WENNINGTON 102 B1
Wennington Hall Sch LA2 102 B1
Wennington Rd LA2 128 A6
Wennington Sta LA2 128 B8
WENSLEY 60 A4
WENSLEYDALE 57 A5
Wensleydale Ave
7 Leyburn DL8 60 D5
2 Skipton BD23 217 B4
Wensleydale Creamery* DL8 56 C4
Wensleydale Dr YO10 229 D4
Wensleydale Gdns 3 TS17 6 C7
Wensleydale Pottery* DL8 56 D4
Wensleydale Rd 21 DL9 40 E4
Wensleydale Rly* DL8 60 B5
Wensleydale Sch The DL8 60 D5
Wensley Gr HG2 222 D7
Wensley Rd
Harrogate HG2 222 D7
14 Leyburn DL8 60 D5
Northallerton DL7 210 B2
Wentcliffe Dr BB18 172 A1
Wentcliffe Rd 5 WF11 201 D3
Wentdale 1 WF8 206 C3
Wentworth Ave YO61 116 F5
Wentworth Cl
Camblesforth YO8 204 D4
Harrogate HG2 220 D4
3 Kellington DN14 203 A2
Wentworth Cres
Harrogate HG2 220 D3
2 Whitby YO21 208 B5
Wentworth Dr HG2 220 D4
Wentworth Gate LS22 180 A3
Wentworth Rd YO24 228 B2
Wentworth St YO17 215 B5
Wentworth Way
Eaglescliffe TS16 5 E4
5 Hunmanby YO14 126 F8
York YO10 228 F2
Werkdyke The YO1 233 C3
Werner Ct 4 WF10 200 F3
WESCOE HILL 178 B1
Wescoe Hill La LS17 178 B1
Wesley Cl 1 LA2 129 A8
Wesley Pl
7 Silsden BD20 174 C1
York YO1 233 C2
Wesley Rd YO22 33 C4
Wesley Way 10 LA2 129 A8
Wesson Cl 6 DL9 40 E4
Westacres 5 DL2 4 C4
West Acres 2 WF11 201 E4
West Acres Cl 7 YO13 99 A7
WEST APPLETON 41 C1
West Auckland Rd DL3 3 A7
West Ave
Boston Spa LS23 180 E1
Burton Fleming YO25 126 E3
5 Easingwold YO61 143 D8
Filey YO14 101 B3
19 Scalby YO13 75 D5
WEST AYTON 99 A7
West Bank
Scarborough YO12 212 E4
York YO24 227 E3
West Bank Rd BD23 216 E4
WEST BARNBY 12 C3
West Barnby La YO21 12 B3
Westbeck Gdns TS5 6 F8
West Beck Way TS8 7 B6
Westborough 1 YO11 213 A5
Westbourne Ave
Garforth LS25 194 B3
Harrogate HG2 222 D8
Whitby YO21 208 A6
Westbourne Cl YO21 208 A6
Westbourne Cres LS25 194 B3
Westbourne Gdns YO8 232 C4
Westbourne Gr
8 Pickering YO18 95 F7
3 Ripon HG4 214 C5
11 Scarborough YO11 213 A4
Selby YO8 232 C4
Whitby YO21 208 A6
Westbourne Pk YO12 212 E4
Westbourne Rd
Scarborough YO11 212 F3
Selby YO8 232 C4
Whitby YO21 208 A6
Westbourne Terr
Selby YO8 232 C4
Thirsk YO7 211 A2
West Brow YO13 98 C5
WEST BURTON 58 F1
West Burton CE Prim Sch DL8 58 F1
Westbury St TS17 6 B8
West Cam Rd BD23 79 E6
West Cl
Carthorpe DL8 87 E6
Middleton Tyas DL10 21 C4
Normanton WF6 200 A1
Swinton YO17 121 B4
WEST CLIFF 208 B7
West Cliff Ave 5 YO21 208 B7
West Cliffe Cnr 9 HG2 219 C1
Westcliffe Gr HG2 219 B1
West Cliffe Mews 5 HG2 219 C1
Westcliffe Mount HG2 219 B1
Westcliffe Terr HG2 219 B1
West Cliff Prim Sch YO21 208 C7
West Close Rd 13 BB18 171 D2
West Craven Dr BB18 172 A2
West Craven High Sch BB18 171 E1
West Craven Sports Ctr BB18 171 E1
West Croft
19 Addingham LS29 174 F4
6 Glusburn BD20 187 E6
Westcroft La YO8 196 E1
West Ct
Muston YO14 100 F2
8 Riccall YO19 197 F8
West Dale LS23 180 E1
Westdene HG2 222 B7
West Dene BD20 174 B2
West Dike Rd YO18 71 F5
West Edge Rd WF8 206 A3
West End
Boston Spa LS23 180 E1
Guisborough TS14 8 E6
Hurworth-on-Tees DL2 3 E1
Hutton Rudby TS15 25 C5
Kirkbymoorside YO62 70 B1
Muston YO14 100 F2
Osmotherley DL6 45 B4
Pollington DN14 207 F6
Rawcliffe DN14 205 A2
Sheriff Hutton YO60 145 C5
Stokesley TS9 26 C7
Strensall YO32 167 A7
West End App LS24 190 B3
West End Ave
Appleton Roebuck YO23 190 F5
Harrogate HG2 222 D8
Richmond DL10 209 A7
West End Cl
North Duffield YO8 199 A8
9 Strensall YO32 167 B7
West End Ct 5 YO11 100 B6
West End Gdns
Egglescliffe TS16 5 D4
Pollington DN14 207 F6
Westend La DN14 207 B6
West End Rd DN6 206 E2
West End View 4 YO11 100 B6
West End Way TS18 5 F8
WESTERDALE 28 E4
Westerdale 4 YO18 95 F6
Westerdale Ct 2 YO30 228 A6
Westerley Cres BD20 174 B1
Western Ave WF8 201 C1
Western Ct 15 WF8 201 C1
Western Gales Way 33 WF6 200 B1
Western Prim Sch HG2 219 C1
Western Rd BD23 217 B3
Westerns La HG3 139 C4
Western Terr YO32 225 D3
Western Way 1 YO18 95 F7
WESTFIELD 232 C4
WEST FIELD 227 A2
Westfield YO8 232 B4
Westfield Ave
Castleford WF10 200 E2
3 Eggborough DN14 202 F2
Rawcliffe DN14 205 A1
6 Scalby YO12 75 E5
Selby YO8 232 B4
Westfield Cl
2 Eggborough DN14 202 F2
21 Haxby YO32 166 E5
Rawcliffe DN14 205 A1
South Milford LS25 195 E2
Westfield Cres 12 LS24 189 E6
Westfield Ct
Copmanthorpe YO23 230 A2
1 South Milford LS25 195 F2
Westfield Dr
Hurworth-on-Tees DL2 3 E1
York YO10 231 D8
Westfield Gdns LS25 194 C1
Westfield Gn YO26 181 C7
Westfield Gr
Allerton Bywater WF10 200 D7
4 Eggborough DN14 202 F2
12 Haxby YO32 166 D5
Westfield La
Exelby, Leeming & Newton DL8 63 C2
Kippax LS25 194 C1
Ledsham LS25 195 C1
Lockton YO18 72 E4
Normanby YO62 94 F4
Norton WF8 206 C2
South Milford LS25 195 F2
Thirsk YO7 211 A3
Thoralby DL8 58 D1
Thorganby YO19 193 A5
Thornton-le-Dale YO18 96 C5
Wigginton YO32 166 D5
West Field La
Arkendale HG5 163 A8
West Field La *continued*
East Witton Town DL8 60 F1
Upper Poppleton YO26 165 E1
Westfield Mews 32 YO62 70 B1
Westfield Pl
19 Haxby YO32 166 E5
York YO24 227 A1
Westfield Prim Com Sch YO24 227 B2
Westfield Rd
1 Eggborough DN14 202 F2
20 Haxby YO32 166 E5
3 North Duffield YO8 199 A7
Rawcliffe DN14 205 A1
Selby YO8 232 B4
2 Stokesley TS9 26 C7
Tockwith YO26 181 C7
West Field Rd 2 BB18 171 D2
Westfields
Castleford WF10 200 E3
Richmond DL10 209 A7
Scorton DL10 41 E7
West Fields YO62 70 B1
Westfields Ct DL10 209 B7
Westfield Sq 8 LS24 189 E6
Westfield Terr
2 Great Preston WF10 200 D7
17 Tadcaster LS24 189 E6
9 Thornton Dale YO18 96 D5
Westfield Way YO17 215 F4
Westfold YO17 215 E6
WEST GARFORTH 194 B3
Westgarth
Collingham LS22 180 A2
Northallerton DL7 210 D4
West Garth
Cayton YO11 100 B6
Sherburn YO17 124 D8
Ulleskelf LS24 190 B3
West Garth Gdns 23 YO11 100 B6
Westgate
22 Barnoldswick BB18 171 D1
Egglescliffe TS15 5 D3
Guisborough TS14 8 F6
Malton YO17 215 E6
Pickering YO18 95 E7
Rillington YO17 122 F5
Ripon HG4 214 C5
Tadcaster LS24 189 E6
Thirsk YO7 211 B2
West Gate
Thornton-le-Dale YO18 96 C5
Wetherby LS22 180 B3
Wykeham YO13 98 D6
Westgate Carr Rd YO18 95 D5
Westgate La
Malton YO17 215 D6
Thornton in Lonsdale LA6 103 C5
Westgate Rd 3 DL3 3 B7
West Gn 15 TS9 26 C7
West Gr
Bishop Thornton HG3 139 A2
Swinton YO17 121 B4
West Grove Rd HG1 219 D4
WEST HADDLESEY 203 A5
West Hall La LS29 175 A5
WEST HARLSEY 44 D5
WEST HESLERTON 123 F7
West Heslerton CE Prim Sch YO17 123 F6
Westholme 10 TS15 25 C5
Westholme Bank DL8 58 F2
Westholme Cres 2 HG4 86 C3
Westholme Ct 3 HG4 86 C3
Westholme Dr YO30 224 E1
Westholme Rd 1 HG4 86 C3
WESTHOUSE 103 C4
West Ing La BD23 171 A5
West Ings Cl 4 WF11 202 A3
West Ings Cres 5 WF11 202 A3
West Ings Ct 1 WF11 202 A3
West Ings La 2 WF11 202 A3
West Ings Mews 6 WF11 202 A3
West Ings Way 3 WF11 202 A3
WEST KNAPTON 123 B6
West La
Appleton Wiske DL6 24 A3
Askwith LS21 176 C3
Azerley HG4 112 F3
Bewerley HG3 136 E4
Boston Spa LS23 180 E1
Burniston YO13 54 C1
Burn YO8 203 C6
Burton Fleming YO25 126 E3
Caldwell DL11 1 B4
Cononley BD20 173 C2
Dalton-on-Tees DL2 22 D6
Danby YO21 29 C8
East Layton DL11 20 A8
Embsay BD23 217 D8
Hampsthwaite HG3 161 A4
Hornby DL6 23 F4
Littlethorpe HG4 214 A2
2 Low Bradley BD20 173 E3
Melsonby DL10 20 E7
Mickleby TS13 12 A4
Nether Silton YO7 66 B7
North Deighton LS22 179 F6
Snainton YO13 97 F5
Stillington YO61 143 F7
Sutton BD20 187 E6
Sykehouse DN14 207 F2
Whixley YO26 163 F5
West La Hill LA2 129 A6
Westland Cl 3 BD20 187 F7
Westlands
Bilton-in-Ainsty with Bickerton YO26 181 D5
6 Kirklevington TS15 24 E8
Pickering YO18 96 A7
Stokesley TS9 26 B7
Westlands Acad TS17 6 C6
Westlands Ave 1 YO21 208 C7
Westlands Gr YO31 228 F7
Westlands La YO7 211 A4
Westlands Rd DL3 3 B6
Westlands Way TS18 5 F8
WEST LAYTON 20 A8
West Lea Ave HG2 222 B7
WEST LILLING 145 C4
West Lodge Gdns YO17 215 A4
West Lund 17 YO62 70 B1
West Lund La YO62 94 B8
WEST LUTTON 150 B8
WEST MARTON 171 F5
West Mead WF10 201 A4
Westminster Bsns Ctr YO26 227 C8
Westminster Cl HG3 222 C3
Westminster Cres HG3 222 D2
Westminster Dr HG3 222 D3
Westminster Gate HG3 222 C3
Westminster Gr HG3 222 D3
Westminster Pl YO26 224 B1
Westminster Rd
Pannal HG3 222 C3
York YO30 228 A6
Westminster Rise HG3 222 D2
West Moor La
Finghall DL8 61 E4
Heslington YO10 184 A4
West Moor Rd
Darlington DL2 3 E3
Raskelf YO61 116 E2
Westmoreland St
Darlington DL3 3 C7
1 Harrogate HG1 219 E3
19 Skipton BD23 217 A3
West Mount LS24 189 E5
Westmount Cl HG4 214 B6
WEST NESS 94 B1
West Nooks 25 YO32 166 F5
West Oaks Sen Specialist Sch & Coll 4 LS23 188 E8
WESTON 176 E2
Weston Cres 7 LS21 176 F1
Weston Dr LS21 176 E1
Weston La LS21 176 F1
Weston Moor Rd LS21 176 E4
Weston Park View LS21 176 E1
Weston Rd LS29 218 B4
Weston Ridge LS21 176 F1
Westover Rd YO12 212 F4
WESTOW 147 B4
West Par LS29 218 C4
West Parade Rd 11 YO12 212 F5
West Park Acad DL2 3 A7
West Park Ave YO12 212 C8
West Park Cres YO12 212 C7
West Park Hospl DL3 3 A7
West Park Rd 13 YO13 75 D5
West Pasture
Kirkbymoorside YO62 70 B1
7 Pickering YO18 95 F6
West Pier YO11 213 B6
Westpit La YO32 167 A7
West Pk
Harrogate HG1 219 D1
Selby YO8 232 A4
Westpoint Rd DL1 3 F6
West Rd
Carleton BD23 173 A4
12 Filey YO14 101 B3
Melsonby DL10 20 F7
Westridge Cres 1 DL9 40 F5
WEST ROUNTON 24 D2
West Row DL2 4 C7
West Sandgate Terr 19 YO11 213 B6
WEST SCRAFTON 83 F6
Westside Cl YO17 215 B4
Westside Rd
Bransdale YO62 48 B5
Fadmoor YO62 69 E7
West Side Rd YO13 53 A1
West Sq 7 YO11 212 F5
West St
Castleford WF10 200 E4
Eaglescliffe TS15 5 D4
Gargrave BD23 155 D1
Gayles DL11 19 E6
Harrogate HG1 219 C5
Ilkley LS29 218 B4
Muston YO14 100 F2
Normanton South WF6 200 A1
Scarborough YO11 213 A4
Swinton YO17 121 B4
WEST STONESDALE 15 E1
WEST TANFIELD 87 A1
West Terr
Richmond DL10 209 B7
Scarborough YO11 212 F4
15 Whitby YO21 208 D7
West Thorpe YO24 230 D8
West Vale 37 YO14 101 B3
West View
Carleton BD23 173 B4
Darlington DL3 3 A5
Draughton BD23 174 B7
Ilkley LS29 218 B3
Kippax LS25 194 D1
Micklefield LS25 195 A3
North Deighton LS22 180 A6
West View *continued*
Ripon HG4 214 D2
Sherburn in Elmet LS25 195 E3
West View Ave 25 LS29 176 C1
Westview Cl
3 Low Bradley BD20 173 E3
York YO26 227 B7
West View Rd 26 LS29 176 C1
West View Terr
Eaglescliffe TS16 5 D4
16 Knaresborough HG5 221 A6
West Villa YO61 144 A4
Westville Ave LS29 218 A4
Westville Cl 6 LS29 218 A4
Westville House Prep Sch LS29 218 D7
Westville Oval HG1 219 C6
Westville Rd LS29 218 A4
Westway
Eastfield YO11 99 F7
Harrogate HG2 222 B8
West Way YO61 118 A1
WEST WITTON 59 E3
Westwood
Carleton BD23 173 B4
Scarborough YO11 212 F5
Westwood Cl 2 YO11 212 F4
Westwood Dr LS29 218 A2
Westwood Gdns 3 YO11 212 F4
Westwood La
Ampleforth YO62 92 A2
West Tanfield HG4 86 E1
West Wood La YO23 182 E4
Westwood Mews
Carleton BD23 173 B4
12 Dunnington YO19 184 F7
Westwood Rd
25 Castleford WF10 200 D3
Ripon HG4 214 A2
Scarborough YO11 212 F4
Westwood Terr YO23 228 B1
Westwood Way LS23 188 E8
Wetherall Rd YO8 204 F5
WETHERBY 180 D4
Wetherby Bsns Ctr LS22 180 B3
Wetherby Bsns Pk LS22 180 C3
Wetherby High Sch LS22 180 C3
Wetherby La LS22 180 D7
Wetherby L Ctr LS22 180 C2
Wetherby Racecourse* LS22 180 E3
Wetherby Rd
8 Boroughbridge YO51 141 B4
Bramham cum Oglethorpe LS23 188 E6
Harrogate HG2 220 B1
Kirk Deighton LS22 180 B5
Knaresborough HG5 221 D4
Sicklinghall LS22 179 E3
Tadcaster LS24 189 D6
Walton LS23 180 F2
Wetherby LS22 180 B2
York YO26 227 B3
Wethercote La YO7 67 C1
Wet Ings La 15 BD20 187 E6
Wetlands La DL11 18 G7
Weydale Ave YO12 212 E8
Weymouth Ave TS8 7 A7
Weymouth Rd 1 HG1 219 E4
Whaddon Chase TS14 8 F6
Whaites La YO7 115 C5
Whales La DN14 202 E3
Wham La BD24 130 F1
WHARFE 131 A8
Wharfedale YO14 101 A3
Wharfedale Ave HG2 222 A7
Wharfedale Cl 1 BD23 217 B4
Wharfedale Cres
Harrogate HG2 222 B7
Tadcaster LS24 189 E6
Wharfedale Dr
Ilkley LS29 218 C4
Normanton WF6 200 A3
Wharfedale Hospl LS21 176 F1
Wharfedale Montessori Sch BD23 157 F2
Wharfedale Nurseries LS23 188 E8
Wharfedale Pl HG2 222 A7
Wharfedale View 6 LS29 174 F4
Wharfe Dr YO24 230 D8
Wharfe Gr 8 LS22 180 B3
Wharfe La
Grassington BD23 134 D3
Kearby with Netherby LS22 179 B1
Wharfe Pk 2 LS29 175 A4
Wharfeside Ave BD23 134 D3
Wharfeside La LS29 218 C5
Wharfe View
Grassington BD23 134 D3
Kirkby Overblow HG3 179 A4
Wharfe View Rd LS29 218 B4
Wharncliffe Pl 14 YO14 101 A3
Wharnscliffe Dr YO30 224 F2
WHARRAM LE STREET 149 A4
Wharram Quarry Nature Reserve* YO17 148 F4
Wharton Ave YO30 228 B7
Wharton Rd 8 YO41 168 D2
Whartons Prim Sch The LS21 177 A2
Whartons The LS21 177 A1
WHASHTON 20 A5
WHASHTON GREEN 20 A5
Whashton Rd
Aske DL10 20 C1
Richmond DL10 209 C8

WHAW 17 B3
Wheatcroft 6 YO32 167 A6
Wheatcroft Ave YO11 213 B1
Wheatdale Rd LS24 190 B2
Wheatear La TS17 6 A5
Wheatfield La YO32 225 C8
Wheatfields Wlk YO19 192 A1
Wheatlands
Great Ayton TS9 8 A2
Ilkley LS29 218 C4
Wheatlands Ave 8 BD20 187 E8
Wheatlands Cl 6 TS14 8 F6
Wheatlands Dr 4 TS13 11 A8
Wheatlands Garth 20 BD20 187 E8
Wheatlands Gr
Harrogate HG2 222 E8
York YO26 227 C6
Wheatlands La
7 Glusburn BD20 187 E8
Roecliffe YO51 140 E4
Wheatlands Rd HG2 222 E7
Wheatlands Road E HG2 222 E8
Wheatlands Way HG2 222 F8
Wheatley Ave
Ilkley LS29 218 E3
Normanton South WF6 200 A1
Wheatley Cl 3 LS29 218 E4
Wheatley Croft 6 YO23 190 F5
Wheatley Dr YO32 225 C8
Wheatley Gdns 2 LS29 218 E3
Wheatley Gr LS29 218 E3
Wheatley La 3 LS29 218 E3
Wheatley Rd LS29 218 C3
Wheatley Rise LS29 218 E3
Wheeldale Cres TS17 6 B7
Wheeldale Dr YO32 226 E2
Wheeldale Rd YO22 51 A4
Wheelgate YO17 215 C4
Wheelhouse Sq YO12 212 F6
Wheelhouse The 4 YO30 224 B5
Wheels La DN14 204 F3
Wheelwright Cl
Copmanthorpe YO23 230 B2
Sutton upon Derwent YO41 185 C1
Wheel Wright Cl YO23 230 B3
Wheelwrights Courts BD23 154 B3
WHELDALE 201 B5
Wheldale La WF10 201 B5
Wheldon Infant Sch WF10 200 F4
Wheldon Rd WF10 201 A5
WHELDRAKE 193 A7
Wheldrake Cl 1 TS14 8 F7
Wheldrake Ings Nature Reserve* YO19 193 C7
Wheldrake La
Deighton YO19 184 B1
Escrick YO19 192 B5
Wheldrake with Thorganby CE VA Prim Sch YO19 193 A8
WHENBY 145 B8
Whenby Gr YO31 225 F1
Whenby La YO60 145 C6
Whernside TS7 7 C5
Whernside Ave YO31 229 A5
Whernside Rd 13 LA6 103 D3
Whessoe Rd DL3 3 C8
Whin Bank YO12 212 D5
Whinbeck Ave WF6 200 B1
Whinbush La 1 HG3 138 A1
Whinbush Way DL1 3 F8
Whinchat Tail TS14 8 D6
Whin Cl
3 Strensall YO32 167 B6
York YO24 230 F7
Whincup Ave HG5 221 B6
Whincup Cl 6 HG5 221 B6
Whincup Gr 7 HG5 221 B6
WHINFIELD 3 F8
Whinfield 34 LS29 175 C2
Whinfield Bglws 5 HG3 138 A1
Whinfield Ct BD23 216 F3
Whinfield Prim Sch DL1 3 F7
Whinfield Rd DL1 3 E7
Whin Garth YO24 230 F6
Whin Gn YO22 32 A6
Whingroves TS17 6 C8
Whin Hill YO17 147 E1
Whin La
South Milford LS25 195 D2
Warlaby DL7 64 C5
Whinmoor Hill YO7 66 C2
Whinney Banks Prim Sch TS5 6 D8
Whinney La HG3 222 A5
Whinney Mire La LA2 103 E1
Whinny Bank YO61 117 C8
Whinny Gill Rd BD23 217 B3
Whinny Hagg La YO8 197 A2
Whinny Hill DL9 40 E3
Whinny La YO60 168 A7
Whinnythwaite La YO26 181 C8
Whin Rd YO24 230 F6
Whins La
Spofforth with Stockeld HG3 179 E4
Thorp Arch LS23 180 F1
Whins The YO12 212 A7
Whinstone Prim Sch TS17 6 A5
Whinstone View 13 TS9 8 A2
Whinwath La DL8 87 F4
Whipley Bank HG3 161 A8
Whipley La HG3 161 A7
Whip-ma-whop-ma-gate YO1 233 C2
Whipperdale Bank
Leyburn DL8 60 A8
Redmire DL8 38 F1
Whistler Cl YO23 230 C3
Whistler Dr
Castleford WF10 200 F2
Pickering YO18 96 A6
Whiston Dr 18 YO14 101 B3
WHITBY 208 C6
Whitby Archives & Heritage Ctr* 25 YO21 208 D6
Whitby Ave
Guisborough TS14 8 F6
York YO31 229 A7
Whitby Benedictine Abbey (rems of)* YO22 208 E7
Whitby Bsns Pk YO22 32 F8
Whitby Dr YO31 229 A7
Whitby Gate YO18 96 D6
Whitby Hospl YO21 208 D6
Whitby Jet Heritage Ctr* YO22 208 E7
Whitby L Ctr YO21 208 C7
Whitby Mus & Pannett Art Gall* YO21 208 C6
Whitby Pavilion Complex YO21 208 C8
Whitby Rd
Guisborough TS14 9 A7
Pickering YO18 96 B8
Staithes TS13 13 K2
Whitby Sta YO21 208 D6
Whitby Way DL3 3 A7
Whitby Wizard (Hands-on-Science)* YO21 208 C8
Whitcliffe Ave HG4 214 B4
Whitcliffe Cres HG4 214 B3
Whitcliffe Dr HG4 214 B3
Whitcliffe Gr HG4 214 B3
Whitcliffe Grange DL10 209 A7
Whitcliffe La
Littlethorpe HG4 139 D8
Ripon HG4 214 A2
Whitcliffe Pl DL10 209 A7
Whitcliffe Terr DL10 209 A7
Whitebridge Dr DL1 3 D8
White Bridge Rd YO21 208 B8
White Canons Ct 4 DL10 209 E8
White Canons Wlk 3 DL10 209 E8
Whitecarr La YO18 95 A5
Whitecliffe Cres LS26 194 A1
Whitecliffe Dr 1 LS26 194 A1
Whitecliffe Rise LS26 194 A1
Whitecote La LS25 195 D2
White Cross Court Rehabilitation Hospl YO31 228 D7
Whitecross Gdns YO31 228 D7
Whitecross Hill DL8 87 F3
White Cross Rd YO31 228 D7
White Cross Way YO41 169 A2
Whitefield Bglws DN14 206 F8
Whitefield La DN14 202 E1
Whitefields Dr DL10 209 E7
Whitefields Gate 1 DL10 209 E8
Whitefields Wlk 2 DL10 209 E8
White Friars Cl DL10 209 F8
Whitefriars Ct 9 BD24 131 D2
White Friars Gdns 6 DL10 209 E8
White Friars Wlk 5 DL10 209 E8
White Gate
Heslerton YO17 123 E6
Sherburn YO17 124 C6
Whitegate Cl 7 TS13 13 K2
White Gate Hill YO11 100 B2
Whitegate La HG4 114 F1
Whitehall Landing YO22 208 E5
White Hart Cres 4 DL1 3 F6
Whitehead Hill 18 YO11 213 B6
White Hill La BD20 172 E1
Whitehill Rd BD22 187 E3
White Hills Croft BD23 216 E6
White Hills La BD23 216 E6
Whitehorn Rd WF10 200 F2
White Horse Cl 6 YO32 225 F5
White Horse Fold WF10 200 F7
White Horse La 9 YO12 99 D6
White Horse Mews 3 HG3 179 E5
White Horse of Kilburn* YO61 91 B4
Whitehouse Ave LS26 200 B8
Whitehouse Cres LS26 200 B8
White House Croft TS21 5 A7
White House Dale YO24 227 F1
Whitehouse Dr LS26 200 B8
White House Dr YO24 227 F1
White House Garth YO8 199 D7
White House Gdns 4 YO24 228 A2
White House Gr 1 YO41 185 B2
Whitehouse La
Great & Little Preston LS26 200 B8
Swillington LS26 194 B2
White House Rise YO24 227 F1
White House Wynd DL6 24 D2
White La BD22 187 F1
Whitelands YO32 225 F8
White Lands DL10 209 E7
Whitelass Cl YO7 211 B4
White Lee Ave BB8 186 B1
White Ley Rd WF8 206 C1
White Leys Cl BB18 171 F1
White Leys Rd YO21 208 A7
Whiteley Yd 18 HG5 221 A6
White Lilac Cl DL10 209 E7
White Lodge YO8 232 B4
Whitemoor Busines Pk YO8 198 E6
Whitemoor La YO8 198 C6
Whiteoak Ave YO61 143 C8
White Pastures DL10 209 E7
Whitepits La LA2 129 A5
White Point Ave 1 YO21 208 B7
White Point Ct YO21 208 B8
White Point Rd YO21 208 B8
White Rose Ave 3 YO32 225 D3
White Rose Candles* DL8 60 B4
White Rose Cl
Huby YO61 144 A5
8 Linton-on-Ouse YO30 164 F7
Nether Poppleton YO26 224 C1
White Rose Cres DL10 209 E7
Whiterose Dr YO41 168 D2
White Rose Gr 5 YO32 225 D3
White Rose Way
Nether Poppleton YO26 227 C8
Thirsk YO7 211 D4
Whiterow Rd DL8 82 F7
White Scar Cave* LA6 104 A4
White Sprunt Hill YO17 125 A1
White St YO8 232 B6
Whitestone Ct YO7 211 D3
Whitestone Dr YO31 225 E2
Whitethorn Cl YO31 225 E2
Whitewall YO17 215 D1
WHITEWALL CORNER 215 C1
Whitewall Corner Hill YO17 147 E8
White Wall La HG3 160 D4
White Way YO13 54 C1
Whiteway Head HG5 221 A4
White Way Heads YO18 51 F4
Whitewood Ctr WF10 200 D3
Whitfield Ave YO18 96 A6
Whitkirk Pl 17 YO14 101 B3
WHITLEY 207 A7
Whitley Bridge Sta DN14 202 F1
Whitley Cl YO30 225 A1
Whitley & Eggborough Com Prim Sch DN14 202 F1
Whitley Farm Cl DN14 207 A8
Whitley Pl WF10 200 E6
Whitley Rd
Elvington YO41 185 A3
Norton-le-Clay YO7 115 B1
Thornaby TS17 6 B6
WHITLEY THORPE 206 F7
Whitley Thorpe La DN14 206 F7
Whit Moor Rd HG3 158 F5
Whitsundale Cl 4 HG5 221 D5
WHITTINGTON 102 A7
Whittle St 6 YO7 89 B1
Whitton Croft Rd 9 LS29 218 B4
Whitton Pl YO10 229 C4
WHITWELL 42 B6
Whitwell Dr HG4 114 B8
WHITWELL-ON-THE-HILL 146 E4
Whitwell Rd YO60 146 E5
WHITWOOD 200 C3
Whitwood Comm La WF10 200 C3
Whitwood La WF10 200 C3
Whitworth Way BB18 171 E2
WHIXLEY 164 A5
Whixley Field La YO26 164 B4
Whixley La LS22 163 E2
WHORLTON 25 E1
Whorlton Castle (rems of)* DL6 25 E1
Whorlton La DL6 45 E8
Whyett Bank YO21 28 F6
Wickets The
8 Hutton Rudby TS15 25 C5
Middlesbrough TS7 7 B6
Widdale Rd HG5 221 D5
Widdowfield St DL3 3 C6
Wide Howe La YO7 114 E8
Wide La YO14 127 E5
Widespan Works YO17 124 E7
Widgeon Cl 4 YO14 101 A4
WIGANTHORPE 119 E3
Wigby Cl HG3 140 A2
WIGGINTON 166 D5
Wigginton Prim Sch YO32 166 D5
Wigginton Rd YO31 233 B4
Wigginton Terr YO31 228 C8
WIGGLESWORTH 153 C4
WIGHILL 181 D1
Wighill Garth LS24 189 E6
Wighill La LS24 181 F3
Wighill St 25 BD20 187 E7
Wilberforce Ave YO30 228 B7
WILBERFOSS 185 F5
Wilberfoss CE VC Prim Sch YO41 185 E6
Wilcock La BD20 173 F2
Wildair Cl 2 DL2 3 A7
Wild Rd DL1 4 A4
Wilfreds Gr 8 YO8 198 B4
Wilken Cres TS14 8 F7
Wilkinson Ct HG4 214 B6
Wilkinsons Cl 13 YO13 99 A7
Wilkinsons Ct 22 YO61 143 C8
Wilkinson St TS12 9 E7
Wilkinson Way
6 Otley LS21 176 F1
3 Strensall YO32 167 A7
Willance Gr DL10 209 A7
Willans Gr YO26 227 E4
Willaston Cres HG2 220 A2
Willaston Rd 1 HG1 220 A3
WILLERBY 99 C2
Willerby Carr La YO12 99 C3
Willgutter La BD22 187 F1
William Ave WF10 200 C7
William Crossthwaite TS17 6 B4
William Ct YO10 233 C1
William Jacques Dr YO8 198 E2
William Plows Ave YO10 228 E2
William Rd YO8 198 B4
William's Hill Ring & Bailey* DL8 60 E2
Williamson Cl 14 HG4 214 C5
Williamson Dr 13 HG4 214 C5
Williamson Gdns HG4 214 B4
William St 16 BB18 172 A1
Willins Cl 13 TS15 25 C5
Willis St YO10 228 E3
Willitoft Rd DN14 199 F6
Willoughby Way YO24 230 B8
Willow Ave LS23 188 E7
Willowbank TS8 7 A5
Willow Bank
14 Brayton YO8 197 D1
York YO32 225 E4
Willow Bank Dr 1 WF8 201 C1
Willow Beck Rd DL7 210 D6
Willowbridge Cl 8 WF10 200 D3
Willowbridge La WF10 200 C3
Willow Bridge La YO7 115 F8
Willowbridge Rd WF8 206 C2
Willowbridge Way WF10 200 C3
Willow Brook Cl YO17 215 F4
Willow Chase The TS21 4 F7
Willow Cl
20 Burley in Warfedale LS29 176 C1
2 Filey YO14 101 B4
9 Leeming DL7 63 F3
5 North Featherstone WF7 200 E1
Willow Cres
Clifford LS23 188 E7
Richmond DL10 209 D8
Willow Croft YO26 182 F8
Willow Ct
Kexby YO41 168 C2
2 North Featherstone WF7 200 E1
16 Pickering YO18 95 F6
Selby YO8 232 D2
Willowdene La WF8 201 B2
Willow Dr
6 Bedale DL8 63 B3
Eston & South Bank TS6 7 E8
1 North Duffield YO8 199 A7
Rainton YO7 114 F6
Willowgarth TS9 25 C5
Willow Garth
Ferrensby HG5 162 F7
Scalby YO12 212 A7
10 Thornton Dale YO18 96 D5
Willow Garth Ave BD20 187 E8
Willow Garth La DN6 207 A1
Willowgate 24 YO18 95 F7
Willow Gdns
Leeming Bar DL7 63 C5
Selby YO8 232 E2
Willow Glade
5 Boston Spa LS23 188 E7
York YO32 225 F3
Willow Gn YO8 232 E2
Willow Gr
3 Boston Spa LS23 188 E7
Dalton YO7 115 F7
Earswick YO32 226 A7
Harrogate HG1 219 E5
Kippax LS25 194 C2
York YO31 228 F7
Willow Green Acad WF11 201 D3
Willow La
Boston Spa LS23 188 E7
Ferrybridge WF11 201 C4
North Featherstone WF7 200 E1
Sleights YO22 32 B6
Willow Lane E 4 WF7 200 E1
Willow Park Rd YO41 185 F5
Willow Rd
9 Campsall DN6 206 E1
Darlington DL3 3 B6
10 Knottingley WF11 202 A3
Northallerton DL7 210 D2
Willow Rise
5 Kirkbymoorside YO62 70 B1
Tadcaster LS24 189 D5
Thorpe Willoughby YO8 197 B1
Willows Ave TS8 6 C4
Willows The
7 Acaster Malbis YO32 191 C7
1 Hambleton YO8 196 E1
Middlesbrough TS7 7 C6
8 Strensall YO32 167 B7
Willow Tree Com Prim Sch HG2 220 B2
Willow Tree Gdns 9 LS29 176 C1
Willow View
1 Catterick DL10 41 D5
Cliffe YO8 198 E3
Willow Way
16 Glusburn BD20 187 E6
16 Sutton-in-Craven BD20 187 E6
Willow Wlk 1 HG4 214 B2
Willy Howe* YO25 126 C3
Willymath Cl YO13 75 D7
Wilmot Rd LS29 218 C4
WILSILL 137 E3
Wilson's La 5 YO13 99 A7
Wilson St
Castleford WF10 200 E4
Guisborough TS14 8 F6
Lockwood TS12 9 F7
16 Pontefract WF8 201 B1
Sutton BD20 187 F7
Wilsthorpe Gr 1 YO10 231 F8
Wilstrop Farm Rd YO23 230 A2
WILTON 97 A5
Wilton Carr La YO18 97 A3
Wilton Ings La YO18 97 A4
Wilton La TS14 8 F7
Wilton Rd LS29 218 A3
Wilton Rise YO24 227 F3
Wimbledon Cl 2 DL1 3 F6
Wimpole Cl 6 YO30 225 A1
Winchester Ave 3 YO26 227 E4
Winchester Gr 1 YO26 227 E4
Winchester Way DL1 3 F6
Windermere YO24 230 D7
Windermere Dr WF11 201 F1
Windgate Hill La YO8 197 B6
Windle La BD20 173 D1
Windleston Dr TS3 7 B8
Windmill Dr 17 YO14 101 A3
Windmill Gdns YO8 232 B7
Windmill Gr LS24 189 D5
Windmill La
Norton DN6 206 D1
York YO10 229 B2
Windmill Mdw 13 DN6 206 E2
Windmill Mdws YO41 185 E6
Windmill Rd LS23 188 E6
Windmill Rise
Aberford LS25 194 F7
Tadcaster LS24 189 D5
York YO26 227 E3
Windmill Way 23 YO32 166 F5
Windrose Cl WF6 200 A2
Windross Sq 11 YO61 143 C8
Windsor Ave
Richmond DL10 209 D8
Skipton BD23 217 A4
Windsor Cl 17 WF6 200 B1
Windsor Cres
Middlesbrough TS7 7 D6
7 Whitby YO21 208 D6
Windsor Dr
7 Airmyn DN14 205 F3
2 Haxby YO32 166 D5
3 Knottingley WF11 201 D3
Lockwood TS12 9 F7
Windsor Garth YO24 227 D1
Windsor La HG5 221 B5
Windsor Pl BB18 171 E2
Windsor Rd
24 Catterick Garrison DL9 40 E4
4 Harrogate HG2 220 A1
Ripon HG4 214 C3
Thornaby TS17 6 B7
Windsor St 1 YO23 228 B1
Windsor Terr YO21 208 D6
Windy Hill LA2 129 B8
WINEWALL 186 B2
Winewall La BB8 186 B2
Winewall Rd 11 BB8 186 A3
WINKSLEY 112 F2
Winksley Banks Rd HG4 112 E2
Winksley Gr HG3 219 A4
Winn La YO7 115 C6
Winnow La LS23 188 D8
Winscar Gr 9 YO30 224 E3
WINSLEY 160 D8
Winston Ave BD20 187 F8
Winston Ct
Northallerton DL6 210 E6
Norton YO17 215 E3
WINTERBURN 155 D5
Winterburn La BD23 155 D5
Winter Gap La BD20 186 D8
Winter Gn 21 HG3 161 B3
Winterscale Ct YO1 228 D2
Winterscale St YO10 228 D2
Winthropp Cl YO17 215 C5
WINTON 44 C3
Winton Rd DL6 210 E6
WINTRINGHAM 123 C4
Wise House La YO17 215 F7
Wisker La
Earswick YO32 226 C6
Earswick YO32 226 C7
Wisp Hill 12 BD23 134 E3
WISTOW 197 D6
Wistowgate YO8 197 B8
Wistow Parochial CE VC Prim Sch YO8 197 D6
Wistow Rd YO8 232 A8
Witch La YO16 127 B2
Witcombe Cl 5 TS17 5 F5
Witham Dr YO32 226 A6
Witherick La HG4 114 B7
Withington Rd 6 YO62 92 F7
Witton Cres DL3 3 A7
Witton Steeps DL8 59 E2
WKM Ind Pk DL1 3 D7
Wobeck La HG4 114 B7
Woburn Cl YO33 167 B8
Woburn Way WF6 200 B1
Woldcroft YO41 185 C2
Wold La YO12 99 D1
WOLD NEWTON 126 A3

Wold Newton Foundation Sch YO25 126 A4
Wold Newton Rd YO25 126 E3
Wold Rd YO17 149 E8
Wold St YO17 215 D3
Wolds Way Lavender★ YO17 123 B5
Wold View YO14 100 F2
Wold View Gr 5 YO12 99 E6
Woldview Rd YO41 185 F5
Wolfe Ave YO31 228 F5
Wolsey Ave YO8 197 B8
Wolsey Cl 11 LS25 195 F4
Wolsey Croft LS25 195 F4
Wolsey Dr YO23 231 A3
Wolsey Gdns 12 LS25 195 F4
Wolsey Grange 7 YO8 197 B8
Wolsingham Dr TS5 6 E7
Wolsley St YO10 228 E3
Wolviston Ave YO10 229 C3
WOMBLETON 93 F7
WOMERSLEY 206 C6
Womersley CE Sch DN6 206 C6
Womersley Park Gdns DN6 206 D5
Womersley Rd WF11 202 A2
Wood Acre Cl BD23 134 C3
WOODALE 83 A2
Woodale Cl 14 TS14 8 F7
Woodall Ave YO12 212 F7
Woodall Ct 9 YO8 197 D6
Wood Aven Cl 35 HG3 161 B3
Woodbank Rd TS7 7 D7
Woodbine Cl 12 TS9 8 A2
Woodbine Terr 9 HG1 219 D3
Woodbridge Ave LS25 194 E5
Woodburn Dr 3 DL8 60 D5
Wood Cl
Bradleys Both BD20 173 D3
Skipton BD23 216 E5
7 Strensall YO32 167 A7
14 Thorpe Willoughby YO8 197 B1
Woodcock Cl
Eston & South Bank TS6 7 F8
9 Haxby YO32 166 F5
Pannal HG3 222 D3
Woodcock Dr 8 DL9 40 F2
Woodcrest Rd DL3 3 B4
Woodend WF10 200 C7
Woodend Creative Ctr★ 13 YO11 213 A5
Woodend Cres WF10 200 C7
Wood End La DL8 59 D5
Wooden Hill La DL7 210 B2
Woodfield Ave HG1 219 E4
Woodfield Cl HG1 219 E4
Woodfield Dr
Harrogate HG1 219 E4
6 Low Bradley BD20 173 E3
Woodfield Gdns 5 HG1 219 E4
Woodfield Gr HG1 219 E4
Woodfield Pl 6 HG1 219 E4
Woodfield Prim Sch HG1 219 F5
Woodfield Rd HG1 219 F7
Woodfield Sq HG1 219 E4
Woodfield View HG1 219 E4
Woodfield Wlk HG1 219 E4
Woodford Pl 1 YO24 227 D1
Woodgate YO12 212 D5
Wood Gate YO13 74 A1
Woodgate La LS17 178 B2
Wood Gn WF10 200 C3
WOODHALL
Selby 199 B2
Thoralby 58 B5
Woodhall Dr HG1 219 F6
Woodhall Gr
Harrogate HG1 219 F6
Mickletown LS26 200 B6
4 Stockton-on-Tees TS18 5 D8
Woodhall La
Hemingbrough YO8 199 B3
Womersley DN6 206 D6
Woodhead Field La YO62 70 A4
Wood Hill Cl YO51 141 D1
Woodhill View 3 LS22 180 C3
WOODHOUSE 200 A1
Woodhouse Fields Rd YO7 89 C6
Woodhouse Gr 4 YO31 229 A5
Woodhouse La BD23 157 B7
Woodhouse Rd
Guisborough TS14 8 E6
Thorganby YO19 193 A3
Wood La
Acaster Selby YO23 191 B2
Austwick LA2 131 A8
Birkin WF11 202 D6
Gainford DL2 1 D8
10 Grassington BD23 134 E2
Great Preston LS26 200 C7
Howsham YO60 146 F1
Low Coniscliffe & Merrybent DL2 2 E4
Newland YO8 205 A3
Spennithorne DL8 61 A3
Thorp Arch LS23 180 F2
13 Thorpe Willoughby YO8 197 B1
Threshfield BD23 134 B3
Whitwood WF10 200 C3
Woodland Ave YO12 212 D6
Woodland Chase YO30 225 B1
Woodland Cl YO12 212 D6
Woodland Cres 8 LS26 194 A1
Woodland Croft LS23 181 A2
Woodland Ct LS23 180 F2
Woodland Dr
Leeming DL7 63 F3
Walton LS23 180 F2
Woodland Gr YO12 212 C6
Woodland Mews LS23 181 A2
Woodland Pl
New Earswick YO32 225 E4
Scarborough YO12 212 C6
Woodland Ravine YO12 212 D6
Woodland Rd DL3 3 B6
Woodland Rise YO12 212 D6
WOODLANDS 220 C1
Woodlands
Escrick YO19 192 B5
Ilkley LS29 218 D4
Woodlands Acad YO12 212 B5
Woodlands Ave
Harrogate HG2 220 B1
Haxby YO32 225 C8
Norton YO17 215 E2
Rillington YO17 122 F5
Tadcaster LS24 189 D5
Woodlands Cl
15 Barlby with Osgodby YO8 198 B4
Goldsborough HG5 163 A3
Harrogate HG2 220 C2
15 Ilkley LS29 175 C2
Sherburn in Elmet LS25 195 F2
Woodlands Com Junior Sch HG2 220 B2
Woodlands Cres HG2 220 C2
Woodlands Croft LS25 200 D8
Woodlands Ct
13 Barlby with Osgodby YO8 198 B4
3 Harrogate HG2 220 B1
Woodlands Dr
14 Barlby with Osgodby YO8 198 B4
Egglescliffe TS15 5 E3
Garforth LS25 194 D3
Harrogate HG2 220 C1
Middlesbrough TS6 7 F8
Middlesbrough TS6 7 F8
Scarborough YO12 212 B5
Skipton BD23 216 E5
Woodlands Gn
8 Harrogate HG2 220 B1
Middleton St George DL2 4 C5
Woodlands Gr
Harrogate HG2 220 C2
8 Ilkley LS29 175 C2
Kippax LS25 200 E8
Rillington YO17 122 F5
York YO31 229 A7
Woodlands La
Hillam LS25 202 B7
14 South Milford LS25 195 F2
Woodlands Pk YO18 96 A7
Woodlands Rd
Harrogate HG2 220 C2
Rillington YO17 122 F5
Woodlands Rise
1 Harrogate HG2 220 C2
14 Ilkley LS29 175 C2
Norton DN6 206 E1
Woodland St 3 BD22 187 B6
Woodlands The TS7 7 D5
Woodlands View
11 Barlby with Osgodby YO8 198 B4
Kippax LS25 200 E8
3 Tadcaster LS24 189 D5
2 Thornton Dale YO18 96 D5
Woodlands Way
Hurworth DL2 3 D1
7 Hurworth-on-Tees DL2 22 D8
Woodlands Wlk
Harrogate HG2 220 C2
Scarborough YO12 212 D6
Skipton BD23 216 E5
Stokesley TS9 26 C8
Woodland Terr DL3 3 B5
Woodland View 5 YO7 89 A1
Woodland Way
8 Airmyn DN14 205 E4
Longnewton TS21 4 F7
York YO32 225 F4
Woodlea TS8 7 A5
Wood Lea 1 WF11 201 E4
Woodlea Ave YO26 227 C4
Woodlea Bank YO26 227 D4
Woodlea Cres YO26 227 D4
Woodlea Gr YO26 227 D5
Woodleigh Ave LS25 194 C4
Woodleigh Cl 2 YO32 167 A6
Woodley Gr TS7 7 D7
Woodman La LA6 102 B6
Woodman Terr BD23 216 F4
Woodmanwray La HG3 159 C8
Woodpark Ave HG5 221 A7
Wood Park Cl HG2 220 B1
Woodpark Dr HG5 221 A7
Woodpecker Rd 12 LS29 176 C1
WOOD ROW 200 A6
Wood Row LS26 200 A6
Woodrow Ave TS7 7 B6
Woodrow Cres LS26 200 A6
Woodroyd Gdns LS29 218 F3
Woodruff Cl 27 HG3 161 B3
Woodrush TS8 7 B4
Wood's Cl YO13 75 C8
Woods Ct HG2 222 C6
Wood's Gr YO13 75 C8
Woodside
Castleford WF10 201 B4
Harrogate HG1 219 E2
Hutton Rudby TS15 25 C6
5 Leyburn DL8 60 D5
Woodside Ave YO31 229 A6
Woodside Cl 3 YO61 117 D1
Woodside Gr
Allerton Bywater WF10 200 C7
3 Stockton-on-Tees TS18 5 E8
Woodside La BD20 173 C2
Woodside Rd
5 Boston Spa LS23 188 D8
Ganton YO12 125 A8
Silsden BD20 174 B1
Woodside St WF10 200 C7
Woods La YO26 142 B2
Woodsmill Quay YO1 233 B2
Woods Pl LS29 218 C4
Woodspring Way YO14 127 B8
Wood St
Castleford WF10 200 E4
Norton YO17 215 D3
York YO31 228 E6
Woodstock Cl DL6 210 B6
Woodstock Way YO7 211 D3
WOODTHORPE 230 C7
Woodthorpe Prim Sch YO24 230 C7
Woodturners Cl 47 BD20 187 E7
Woodvale TS8 7 B5
Woodvale Rd DL3 3 B4
Wood View
Airmyn DN14 205 E3
Embsay BD23 217 C7
Harrogate HG1 219 C3
Wood View Ave WF10 200 D4
Woodview Cl DN14 207 A7
Woodville DN14 204 C1
Woodville Ave
Middlesbrough TS4 6 F8
3 Scalby YO12 212 D8
Woodville Terr YO8 232 E3
Wood Way YO32 226 A4
Woolcotts Cl 1 TS17 6 A3
Wooldale Dr YO14 101 B4
Wooler St YO12 212 E5
Woolmoor Cl YO7 211 D4
Woolnough Ave YO10 229 B3
Woolpots La YO61 117 B4
Woolsington Dr DL2 4 C4
Worcester Dr YO31 229 B5
Wordsworth App 2 WF8 201 B1
Wordsworth Ave 4 DN6 206 E1
Wordsworth Cl YO13 75 C5
Wordsworth Cres
Harrogate HG2 222 C8
York YO24 230 D7
Wordsworth Dr WF11 201 D3
Workhouse Mus★ HG4 214 C6
World of James Herriot★ YO7 211 B3
Worsall Rd TS15 5 D2
Worsall Toll Bar TS15 24 B7
Worsendale Rd YO42 169 F2
Worsley Cl TS16 5 E7
Worsley Cres TS7 7 B5
Worsley Ct YO17 215 A3
WORTON 57 F5
Woundales La
Knayton with Brawith YO7 65 F4
Upsall YO7 66 A2
Wrangham Dr 1 YO14 127 A8
WRAY 128 A6
Wray's Ave YO31 225 E1
WRAYTON 102 B3
Wray with Botton Endowed Prim Sch LA2 128 A6
Wrea Head Cl 2 YO13 75 D5
Wreaks La HG4 111 E6
Wreaks Rd
Birstwith HG3 160 E6
Harrogate HG1 220 B3
Wrea La 1 YO12 212 F6
WRELTON 71 C1
Wrelton Cliff Rd YO18 95 B8
Wrelton Hall Gdns YO18 71 C1
Wrenbeck Ave 1 LS21 177 A1
Wrenbeck Cl 2 LS21 177 A1
Wrenbeck Dr LS21 177 A1
Wren Croft 5 WF8 201 B2
Wren Hall La YO8 204 E6
Wren La 2 YO8 232 D5
WRESSLE 199 D2
Wressle Sta YO8 199 D2
Wrexham Rd LS29 176 B1
Wreyfield Dr YO12 212 C7
Wrights La WF11 206 B8
Wright St 30 BD20 187 E7
Wycar 1 DL8 63 A2
Wycherley Cl TS7 7 D7
Wycliffe Ave
Northallerton DL7 210 C2
York YO10 229 B3
Wycliffe Rd DL7 22 E1
WYCOLLER 186 C2
Wycoller Ctry Pk★ BB8 186 D2
Wycoller Rd BB8 186 B3
Wycoller View BB8 186 C3
Wydale La YO13 98 B6
Wydale Rd YO10 229 D4
Wydale Rise YO13 98 A5
WYDRA 160 A1
Wydra La HG3 159 F1
WYKEHAM
Malton 122 B6
Seamer 98 E6
Wykeham Abbey★ YO13 98 E5
Wykeham Ave TS14 8 E5
Wykeham Carr Rd YO13 98 E3
Wykeham CE Prim Sch YO13 98 E6
Wykeham Dale YO62 93 B8
Wykeham La YO13 98 E7
Wykeham Rd YO26 182 F7
Wykeham St YO12 212 E5
Wykeham Way TS8 7 A6
Wyke La TS7 7 D4
Wylam Ave DL1 3 D7
Wynam La YO41 185 C1
Wynbrook Ct YO13 75 C5
Wynd Cl 12 TS15 25 C5
Wynd The
3 Bedale DL8 63 A3
Burnt Yates HG3 160 F8
Hawes DL8 56 D4
Hutton Rudby TS15 25 D5
Skeeby DL10 20 F1
Wytherstone Gdns★ YO62 69 B1
Wyvil Cres LS29 218 E4
Wyville Gr DL8 61 E7
Wyvil Rd LS29 218 E5

X

Xscape★ WF10 200 F2

Y

YAFFORTH 43 C1
Yafforth Rd DL7 210 B6
Yall Flat La YO21 29 B6
Yan Brow YO62 70 C3
Yarborough Cl DL10 41 B2
Yarburgh Gr 2 YO26 227 E5
Yarburgh Way YO10 229 C3
Yarde Ave DL10 41 E4
Yarker Bank La DL8 60 C6
Yarlside La BD23 171 B4
YARM 5 D3
Yarm Back La TS18 5 D8
Yarm La TS9 7 D1
Yarm Prim Sch TS15 5 E2
Yarm Rd
Darlington DL1 3 E5
Egglescliffe TS16 5 E5
Hilton TS15 6 C2
Middleton St George DL2 4 C4
Yarm Road Ind Est DL1 3 F5
Yarm Sch TS16 5 E3
Yarm Sta TS15 5 E2
Yarrow Dr HG3 161 B3
Yatts Rd YO18 96 A8
Yeadon Wlk 12 DL2 4 C4
Yealand Ave BD24 131 D3
Yearby Cl TS5 6 D7
YEARSLEY 118 C5
Yearsley Cres YO31 228 D7
Yearsley Gr YO31 225 E1
Yearsley Grove Prim Sch YO31 225 F1
Yearsley Moor Bank YO62 118 B7
Yearsley Swimming Pool YO31 228 D8
Yederick Rd YO13 98 B8
YEDINGHAM 97 D2
Yedingham Priory (site of)★ YO17 97 D2
Yedmandale Rd
2 East Ayton/West Ayton YO13 99 A7
Hutton Buscel YO13 98 F7
Yeomans Mount 11 HG3 137 B4
Yewbank Cl 3 LS29 218 A4
Yewbank Terr LS29 218 A4
Yewcroft LS29 218 A4
Yewdale Rd HG2 220 A1
Yew Tree Cl
Acaster Malbis YO23 191 C8
Harrogate HG2 222 C4
8 Low Bradley BD20 173 E3
Rufforth YO23 182 C6
Selby YO8 232 C6
13 Sleights YO22 32 A6
Yewtree Dr 1 LA2 128 F8
Yew Tree Gdns HG2 222 B5
Yew Tree La HG2 222 C5
Yew Tree Mews YO19 229 C5
Yew Tree Pk DN14 207 A7
Yew Tree Wlk HG2 222 B6
Yew Wlk The TS21 4 F7
Yiewsley Dr DL3 3 A5
YMCA & L Ctr YO11 213 A7
YMR Exhibition★ YO24 233 A2
Yoadwath Bank YO62 70 C3
YOCKENTHWAITE 81 A1
Yoredale Ave
Darlington DL3 3 B6
16 Leyburn DL8 60 D5
Yoredale Dr 4 DL3 3 B6
YORK 233 B3
York Barbican Ctr YO10 233 C1
York Brewery★ YO1 233 A2
York Bridge Rd YO61 143 B2
York Castle Mus★ YO1 233 C1
York Cl 2 HG5 221 C5
York Coll YO24 230 E6
Yorkdale Ct 4 YO8 196 F1
Yorkdale Dr 3 YO8 196 F1
York Designer Outlet YO19 231 D4
York Dungeon The★ YO1 233 B2
York Eco Bsns Ctr YO30 225 A3
Yorkersgate YO17 215 B4
York Garth 1 HG5 221 C5
York High Sch YO24 227 C2
York Ind Est LS22 180 C3
York La
Flaxton YO60 167 E8
Knaresborough HG5 221 B5
York Maze★ YO19 184 F4
York Minster★ YO1 233 B3
York Pl
Harrogate HG1 219 E1
Knaresborough HG5 221 B5
Scarborough YO11 213 A5
York Racecourse (The Knavesmire)★ YO24 228 A1
York Rd
Bagby YO7 211 D2
Barlby YO8 198 B5
Bilbrough YO23 182 B2
Bilton-in-Ainsty with Bickerton LS22 181 A4
Boroughbridge YO51 141 B5
37 Burley in Warfedale LS29 176 C1
Cliffe YO8 198 E3
5 Colburn DL9 40 F4
Cottam YO25 151 B2
Dunnington YO19 184 D6
Easingwold YO61 143 C7
Flaxby HG5 163 B5
Green Hammerton YO26 164 B3
Harrogate HG1 219 C2
Haxby YO32 225 D7
Kilham YO25 151 F3
Kirk Hammerton YO26 164 C3
Knaresborough HG5 221 D5
Leavening YO17 147 E2
Long Marston YO26 182 A6
Malton YO17 215 A3
Middlesbrough TS7 7 D6
Naburn YO19 191 D8
North Duffield YO8 199 A8
Riccall YO19 192 A1
Sledmere YO25 150 E1
Sowerby YO7 211 E1
Stillingfleet YO19 191 D4
Strensall YO32 167 A6
Sutton-on-the-Forest YO61 166 C8
Tadcaster LS24 189 F6
Wetherby LS22 180 C3
York YO26 227 C3
York Rise BD23 154 B3
York Road Ind Pk YO17 121 C1
York St John University (Lord Major's Walk Main Campus) YO31 233 B3
York Science Park YO10 229 B2
Yorkshire Air Mus★ YO41 184 F3
Yorkshire Coast Coll (Main Campus) YO12 212 B6
Yorkshire Coast Coll (Scarborough Bsns Sch) 20 YO11 212 F5
Yorkshire Coast Coll (Westwood Campus) YO11 212 F5
Yorkshire Dales Falconry & Wildlife Conservation Ctr★ LA2 131 A5
Yorkshire Dales Mining Mus★ BB18 172 A2
Yorkshire Dales National Park Ctr★ BD24 131 D3
Yorkshire Garden World★ YO8 203 A5
Yorkshire Lavender★ YO60 119 E1
Yorkshire Mus★ YO30 233 A3
Yorkshire Mus of Farming★ YO19 229 F5
York St
Barnoldswick BB18 171 D1
Castleford WF10 200 E4
Crathorne TS15 24 E6
5 Dunnington YO19 184 E7
12 Glusburn BD20 187 E8
1 Selby YO8 232 C5
York Sta YO24 233 A2
York Steiner Sch YO10 228 D1
York Theatre Royal★ YO1 233 B3
York View DL10 209 E8
York Villas WF6 200 A1
YOULTHORPE 169 C2
YOULTON 142 E2
Young Bank La YO62 70 C2
Young's Ct LS25 194 F7
Young's Dr 3 HG3 161 B2
Youngs Way 10 DL10 41 E4
Ypres Rd DL9 209 D1
Yule La YO26 164 C3

Z

Zetland Dr DL10 209 F8
Zetland St DL6 210 D4